THE CAMBRIDGE HISTORY OF IRAN
IN SEVEN VOLUMES

Volume 2

THE CAMBRIDGE HISTORY OF IRAN

Volume 2

THE MEDIAN AND ACHAEMENIAN PERIODS

edited by
ILYA GERSHEVITCH

CAMBRIDGE
UNIVERSITY PRESS

CAMBRIDGE
UNIVERSITY PRESS

University Printing House, Cambridge CB2 8BS, United Kingdom

One Liberty Plaza, 20th Floor, New York, NY 10006, USA

477 Williamstown Road, Port Melbourne, VIC 3207, Australia

314-321, 3rd Floor, Plot 3, Splendor Forum, Jasola District Centre, New Delhi - 110025, India

79 Anson Road, #06-04/06, Singapore 079906

Cambridge University Press is part of the University of Cambridge.

It furthers the University's mission by disseminating knowledge in the pursuit of education, learning and research at the highest international levels of excellence.

www.cambridge.org
Information on this title: www.cambridge.org/9780521200912

© Cambridge University Press 1985

This publication is in copyright. Subject to statutory exception and to the provisions of relevant collective licensing agreements, no reproduction of any part may take place without the written permission of Cambridge University Press.

First published 1985
Fifth printing 2007

A catalogue record for this publication is available from the British Library

ISBN 978-0-521-20091-2 Hardback

Cambridge University Press has no responsibility for the persistence or accuracy of URLs for external or third-party internet websites referred to in this publication, and does not guarantee that any content on such websites is, or will remain, accurate or appropriate.

BOARD OF EDITORS

SIR HAROLD BAILEY (*Chairman*)
Emeritus Professor of Sanskrit
University of Cambridge

BASIL GRAY (*Vice-Chairman*)
Formerly Keeper of the Oriental Antiquities
British Museum

P. W. AVERY
Lecturer in Persian
University of Cambridge

C. E. BOSWORTH
Professor of Arabic Studies
University of Manchester

ILYA GERSHEVITCH
Emeritus Reader in Iranian Studies
University of Cambridge

MAHMOUD SANA'I
Emeritus Professor of Psychology
University of Tehran

H. S. G. DARKE (*Editorial Secretary*)
Formerly Lecturer in Persian
University of Cambridge

CONTENTS

List of plates   page x

List of text figures   xiv

List of maps   xvi

1   ELAM   1
    by I. M. DIAKONOFF, *Senior Research Worker, Oriental Institute of the Academy of Sciences, Leningrad*

2   ANSHAN IN THE MEDIAN AND ACHAEMENIAN PERIODS   25
    by J. HANSMAN

3   MEDIA   36
    by I. M. DIAKONOFF

4   THE SCYTHS   149
    by the late T. SULIMIRSKI

5   THE RISE OF THE ACHAEMENIDS AND ESTABLISHMENT OF THEIR EMPIRE   200
    by J. M. COOK, *Emeritus Professor of Ancient History and Classical Archaeology, University of Bristol*

6   PERSIA AND THE GREEKS   292
    by A. R. BURN

7   CYRUS THE GREAT (558–529 B.C.)   392
    by the late MAX MALLOWAN

8   ALEXANDER IN IRAN   420
    by E. BADIAN, *John Moors Cabot Professor of History, Harvard University*

9   THE PERSIAN OCCUPATION OF EGYPT   502
    by E. BRESCIANI, *Professor of Egyptology, University of Pisa*

CONTENTS

10 THE BABYLONIAN EVIDENCE OF ACHAEMENIAN RULE IN MESOPOTAMIA 529
by the late A. L. OPPENHEIM

11 THE EVIDENCE OF THE PERSEPOLIS TABLETS 588
by the late R. T. HALLOCK

12 ACHAEMENID COINS, WEIGHTS AND MEASURES 610
by A. D. H. BIVAR, *School of Oriental and African Studies, University of London*

13 THE OLD EASTERN IRANIAN WORLD VIEW ACCORDING TO THE AVESTA 640
by M. SCHWARTZ, *Professor of Near Eastern Studies, University of California, Berkeley*

14 THE RELIGION OF ACHAEMENIAN IRAN 664
by M. SCHWARTZ

15 ARAMAIC IN THE ACHAEMENIAN EMPIRE 698
by J. C. GREENFIELD, *Professor of Ancient Semitic Languages, Hebrew University, Jerusalem*

16 OLD IRANIAN CALENDARS 714
by the late WILLY HARTNER

17 CLASSIC ACHAEMENIAN ARCHITECTURE AND SCULPTURE 793
by EDITH PORADA, *Arthur Lehman Professor Emeritus of Art History and Archaeology, Columbia University, New York*

18 THE BEHISTUN RELIEF 828
by ANN FARKAS, *Professor of Anthropology and Archaeology, Brooklyn College of the City University of New York*

19 TEPE NŪSH-I JĀN: THE MEDIAN SETTLEMENT 832
by DAVID STRONACH, *Professor of Near Eastern Archaeology, University of California, Berkeley*

20 PASARGADAE 838
by DAVID STRONACH

21 METALWORK AND GLYPTIC 856
by P. R. S. MOOREY, *Keeper of the Department of Antiquities, Ashmolean Museum, Oxford*

CONTENTS

Appendix I PLANT NAMES 870
by H. W. BAILEY, *Emeritus Professor of Sanskrit, University of Cambridge*

Appendix II THE ACHAEMENID DYNASTY 874

Bibliography 875

Index 931

PLATES

Between pages 814 and 815

1. (*a*) The ascent ("Klimax") from the plain of Elam to Persis.
   (*b*) The road into Persis. The "Valley of the Oaks" west of Shīrāz.
   (*c*) The Caspian Gates, looking east.
2. (*a*) The Kūh-Dāman, looking east to Kapisa (Paropamisadai).
   (*b*) The citadel-mound of Bampūr (Pura in Gedrosia).
   (*c*) Hyrcania under the Alburz, east of modern Behshahr.
3. (*a*) The mound of Agbatana (Hamadān) and Mt Alvand.
   (*b*) One of the high valleys of the Zagros in Media, near Burūjird.
   (*c*) The Euphrates entering the plain of Carchemish.
   (1–3 Photographs, J. M. Cook).
4. Darius III, as portrayed in the Alexander mosaic of Pompeii (Photograph courtesy of the National Archaeological Museum, Naples).
5. Pasargadae, the tomb of Cyrus (Photograph, Olive Kitson, Pasargadae expedition).
6. (*a*) Pasargadae, the Winged Figure (Photograph, Olive Kitson, Pasargadae expedition).
   (*b*) Winged genius from the palace of Sargon II of Assyria, Khorsabad (From E. Strommenger and M. Hirmer, *The Art of Mesopotamia* (London, Thames and Hudson, 1964).
7. Pasargadae, the great stone platform of the Tell-i Takht (Photograph, Olive Kitson, Pasargadae expedition).
8. Painted wooden naos, showing the scroll of Darius I, from Hermopoli.
9. An Aramaic letter from Hermopoli, addressed to Ṇnyḥm at Aswan (From E. Bresciani and M. Kamil, *Le lettere aramaiche da Hermopoli* IV, pl. IV, recto and verso).
10. Label from a mummy written on both sides, from south Saqqara (Photograph, Cairo Museum. From Aimé-Giron, *Textes araméens*, no. 105, pl. XIV).
11. Statue of Psamteksaneit, from Memphis (Photograph, Cairo Museum).
12. Coins and ingots (1–2, 4–8 Photographs, A. D. H. Bivar 3, 9 Reproduced by courtesy of the Trustees of the British Museum).

LIST OF PLATES

13 Persepolis, the terrace and its structures. Model by Friedrich Krefter (Photographs F. Krefter).
14 Persepolis, the southern part of the west face of the terrace (Photograph by courtesy of the Oriental Institute, University of Chicago. Schmidt, *Persepolis I*, pl. 2C).
15 Persepolis, (*a*) the eastern stairway of the Apadana.
   (*b*) The Gate of All Lands (Photographs by courtesy of the Oriental Institute, University of Chicago. Schmidt, *Persepolis I*, pls 17A, 12B).
16 Persepolis, the Parapet reconstructed along the Terrace edge (Photograph, A. B. Tilia).
17 (*a*) Surkh Kotal, merlon (From D. Schlumberger, "Descendants non-méditerranéens de l'art grec", *Syria* XXXVII (1960), pl. VI.1).
   (*b*) Pasargadae, lower part of the figure of the king (Photograph, H. Luschey).
18 Susa, glazed brick relief of guardsman (Le Musée du Louvre, Paris. From Porada, *Ancient Iran*, p. 153, pl. 42).
19 Naqsh-i Rustam, general view (Photograph, J. M. Cook).
20 Naqsh-i Rustam, façade of tomb of Darius I.
21 Naqsh-i Rustam, head of Gobryas from façade of tomb of Darius I (20–21 Photographs by courtesy of the Oriental Institute, University of Chicago. Schmidt, *Persepolis III*, pls 19, 20, 23).
22 Persepolis, Palace of Darius.
   (*a*) Royal hero fighting with a lion.
   (*b*) King walking into his chambers with two attendants.
23 Persepolis, southern Audience Relief, found in the Treasury (Archaeological Museum, Tehran).
   (22–23 Photographs by courtesy of the Oriental Institute, University of Chicago. Schmidt *Persepolis I*, pls 146A, 141B, 121).
24 Persepolis, eastern Audience Relief.
   (*a*) Figure of the king.
   (*b*) Detail of (*a*).
   (*c*) Heads of two attendants.
   Photographs, (*a*) as pls 22–3, pl. 123, (*b*) (*c*) H. Luschey).
25 Susa. Statue of Darius (Archaeological Museum, Tehran).
26 Susa. Statue of Darius.
   (*a*) Detail.
   (*b*) socle.

LIST OF PLATES

(25–6 Photographs courtesy of J. Perrot, reproduced with the permission of DAFI, the National Organization for the Restoration of Historic Monuments of Iran and the Fondation Patek Philippe of Geneva.)

27 Persepolis. Lion and bull motif.
28 Persepolis. The delegations on the Eastern Stairway façade.
29 Persepolis. Archers and "Susian" guards.
30 Persepolis.
    (*a*) Delegation of the Lydians and Babylonians.
    (*b*) Nobles on the Eastern Stairway of the Apadana.
31 Persepolis. Audience scene of Artaxerxes I.
32 Persepolis. Throne relief of Artaxerxes I (Photograph by courtesy of the Oriental Institute, University of Chicago. Schmidt, *Persepolis I*, pl. 99).
33 Persepolis. "Persian" and "Median" dignitaries.
34 Behistun, general view of relief.
35 Behistun, detail of Darius.

(27–31, 33–5 Photographs, H. Luschey)

36 (*a*) A pair of ibex-headed gold bracelets from the Pasargadae treasure (Photograph, Pasargadae expedition).
    (*b*) A silver spoon with a swan's-head handle (Photograph, Les publications d'art et d'archéologie, 27, Rue St-André-des-arts, Paris, 6).
37 The entrance façade of the Zindān-i Sulaimān (Photograph, Pasargadae expedition).
38 (*a*) The partly excavated mound of Tepe Nūsh-i Jān.
    (*b*) A scale model showing the four main Median buildings at Tepe Nūsh-i Jān.
39 (*a*) The stepped walls of the sanctuary of the Central Temple.
    (*b*) The excavated fire altar.
40 (*a*) The west end of Room 23.
    (*b*) A Neo-Assyrian stone stamp-seal.
41 (*a*) The unfinished rock-cut tunnel.
    (*b*) The narrow walls of the squatter occupation.

(38–41 Photographs, Helga Schippmann and Ruth Stronach.)

42 Decorated sheet gold cover for the sheath of an iron short-sword; from the Oxus Treasure (Dalton, no. 22).
43 (*a*) Gold collar or spiral bracelet from the Oxus Treasure (Dalton, no. 118).
    (*b*) Gold bracelet from the Oxus Treasure (Dalton, no. 116).

LIST OF PLATES

44 (*a*) Gold chariot model from the Oxus Treasure (Dalton, no. 7).
    (*b*) Sheet gold jug from the Oxus Treasure (Dalton, no. 17).

45 (*a*) Silver handle from a vessel cast in the shape of a leaping wild goat; from the Oxus Treasure (Dalton, no. 10).
    (*b*) Cast silver bowl.

(42–5 Photographs courtesy of the Trustees of the British Museum).

46 Silver bowls said to be from Tell el-Maskhuta in Egypt (Photographs courtesy of the Brooklyn Museum, New York).

47 (*a*) Inlaid and gilded wooden shrine door showing Darius I with the Egyptian deities Anubis and Isis.
    (*b*) Cylinder seal of a high official, showing Darius I engaged in a lion hunt.

48 Modern impressions from cylinder seals.

(47–8 Photographs courtesy of the Trustees of the British Museum).

TEXT FIGURES

Chapter 4   *page*

Fig. 1   Scythian stone stelae of the 6th century B.C. (From Illinska, "Skilfski sokiri", p. 41, fig. 8).   160

Figs 2–4   Decorated gold articles from Vettersfelde (Museum für Vor- und Frühgeschichte, Berlin. Drawings after Furtwängler. For colour illustrations see Jettmar, *Art of the Steppes*, pls 6, 7, 8).   162–3

Figs 5–7   Bronze parts of horse harness from Maly Kurgan (From Yessen, "La steppe de Mil et Karabagh", pp. 27–9, figs 10–12).   164–5

Fig. 8   Bone cheek-pieces and bronze buckles from Scythian bridles found at Karmir Blur (After Piotrovskii, *Karmir Blur* 1).   166

Fig. 9   An undecorated Scythian bone cheek-piece from Młyniec in northern Poland (From Sulimirski, "La culture Lusacienne et les Scythes", p. 80, fig. 2).   166

Fig. 10   Carved bone cheek-pieces from early Scythian burials at Aksyutintsy (From Minns, *Scythians and Greeks*, p. 189, fig. 81, after Bobrinskii, *Smiela* III, pl. VII).   167

Chapter 16   *page*

Figs 1–22   "Calendrical" animals and symbols (Details of sources are given in the footnotes).   726–36

Diagram 1   The celestial sphere at 4000 B.C.   721

Diagram 2   The horizon of Persepolis, shewing the culmination of Leo.   723

Diagram 3   The Persepolis horizon at the spring equinox.   724

Diagram 4   The Persepolis horizon one week after the spring equinox, at the time of Darius.   739

Chapter 17   *page*

Fig. 1   Plan of Persepolis terrace by Richard C. Haines (From Schmidt, *Persepolis I*, pocket at end).   794–5

Fig. 2   The West Front of the Apadana, reconstructed by

LIST OF FIGURES

Friedrich Krefter (From Krefter, *Persepolis Rekonstruktionen*, Beilage 20).	796
Fig. 3 The West Porch of the Apadana, reconstructed by Friedrich Krefter (From Krefter, *Persepolis Rekonstruktionen*, Beilage 28).	797
Fig. 4 The columns of the Apadana, reconstructed by Friedrich Krefter (From Herzfeld, *Iran in the Ancient East*, pl. LVIII).	799
Fig. 5 The Temple of Haldi at Ardini-Musasir (From P. E. Botta *et al.*, *Monument de Ninève* II (Paris, 1849), pl. 141).	805
Fig. 6 Plan of the buildings on the Tell of the Apadana at Susa by J. Perrot and D. Ladiray.	807
Fig. 7 The Gate of Darius at Susa, reconstructed by J. Perrot and D. Ladiray (From Perrot and Ladiray *et al.*, "Recherches dans le secteur est du tépé de l'Apadana", *CDAFI* IV (1974), p. 201, fig. 17).	810

Chapter 19   *page*
Fig. 1 Tepe Nūsh-i Jān. Plan of the site.   833

MAPS

		page
1	Ancient sites in Fars.	35
2	Approximate distribution of settlements of ethnic groups at the beginning of the 1st millennium B.C.	39
3	Media in the 9th–7th centuries B.C.	98–9
4	The Near East at the end of the 6th century B.C.	111
5	The Median Empire in the 6th century B.C.	120
6	Map of ancient Scythia as conceived by Herodotus, reconstructed by E. H. Minns (From Minns, *Scythians and Greeks*, map V).	151
7	Map showing the diffusion of Scythian burials and those of Scythian type of the 6th century B.C., found within the confines of ancient Scythia and neighbouring countries.	176–7
	Key to map 7	178
8	Map showing the diffusion of Scythian finds of the period *c*. 500–400 B.C. in Europe.	192
9	The Persian presence in western Asia Minor.	275
10	Trouble spots of the western empire.	277
11	The Achaemenian empire.	282–3
12	The western provinces of the Achaemenian empire.	297
13	The Aegean basin, to illustrate the Greek wars of Darius and Xerxes.	304–5
14	Western Asia Minor in the late Achaemenian period.	363
15	The Nile Delta.	373
16	Map showing the extent of the Achaemenian empire under Cyrus the Great and Darius (After the Nonesuch Herodotus, by courtesy of the Nonesuch Press and T. L. Poulton).	400–1
17	Alexander's route.	474–5

PUBLISHERS' NOTE

The Publishers wish to acknowledge the major contribution to the completion of this volume made by Mr Hubert Darke, who willingly undertook a wide range of editorial responsibilities to assist in its publication.

Thanks are also due to Mr Peter Khoroche for assistance with proofs; and to Mr Colin Ronan for help in the preparation of the astronomical diagrams in chapter 16. The index is by Mrs Hilda Pearson.

The Publishers and the Editorial Board of the *Cambridge History of Iran* are grateful for a generous subvention towards editorial and production costs of this volume provided by the Foundation for Iranian Studies, Washington, D.C.

Acknowledgements are due to all who have provided and given permission to reproduce photographs and line drawings.

CHAPTER 1

ELAM

1. *The Emergence of the Elamite City-States*

The earliest part of present-day Iran to reach the level of urban and class civilization was the region which later was called Khūzistān and which in ancient history is usually designated by its Biblical name of Elam (Hebr. '*Ēlām*). It lies outside what geographically is the Iranian Plateau properly speaking, and is a plain surrounded from three sides by mountains and crossed by rivers flowing from the highlands into the Persian Gulf – the Karkhah (or Saimarreh, the Assyrian Uqnû, the Greek Choaspēs) and the Kārūn (the Assyrian Ulāi, the Eulaeus of the Greeks),[1] as well as by the river Āb-i Diz (Copratēs) running parallel to the Karkhah but halfway down the plain flowing into the Kārūn. Through the ages the courses of the Karkhah, the Kārūn and its affluents, and the Āb-i Diz, as they ran across the lowlands of Elam, changed many times, and many canals, later silted up, have at various times been led from them into the parched country around, or between the rivers as their connection. The part of the alluvial plain nearer to the sea was in ancient times covered by shallow freshwater lakes and salt or brackish lagoons, overgrown with reeds and gradually turning into marshland, and the coastline lay farther north than now. The winter on the plain of Elam is mild, the temperature but seldom falling below zero Centigrade, and the summer very hot indeed, the heat sometimes reaching 60° C. The precipitation is scarce, but the valley can be irrigated by the water of the rivers.

Thus, the climate and the general ecological conditions of Elam were very similar to those of neighbouring Sumer in the lower valley of the Euphrates (now in Iraq); the historical development of both countries was also typologically similar and more or less simultaneous. But the two countries were separated by a stretch of marshes and desert difficult to pass, and so the usual road connecting Elam with Sumer led either along the foot-hills towards the north-west, or in the same direction upwards into the mountains along the valley of the Karkhah and then

---

[1] The ancient Eulaeus (Ulāi was apparently the modern Ša'ur plus the lower part of the Karun. [Differently John Hansman, "Charax and the Karkheh", *IA* VII (1967), 21–58.]

1

over a mountain-pass towards present-day al-Badra at the same foothills; thence to the valley of the Tigris (more often than not via the Diyala valley near modern Baghdad), and from there to the Sumerian settlements along the lower Euphrates.

No important culture could develop in Elam until the first men who had descended to the plain from the highlands established communities in sufficient numbers and with techniques adequate to turn the waters of the rivers to their use and to develop an agricultural civilization based upon river irrigation. The first settlers are attested in a side valley (the site of Ali Kosh, early 7th millennium B.C.). They were goat-herds acquainted with some primitive agricultural processes; they were apparently related to the first herdsmen-agriculturists of the more northern regions of the Zagros mountains, but a change of burial customs in the 6th millennium B.C. may testify to the coming of a new population. The men of this later period (as also those at the sites of Jowi and of Ja^{c}farābād) have in their material culture and burial customs much in common with the nearly contemporary inhabitants of Sumer; they already practised artificial irrigation and it is not improbable that these might have been the tribes who later sent out a part of their population to colonize the lower Euphrates valley – the colonists later becoming Sumerians. When, however, in the second half of the 4th millennium a considerable chalcolithic community of a semi-urban type emerged on the site of Susa by a river-bed or an artificial canal between the Karkhah and the Āb-i Diz (now the Sha^{c}ūr), it was probably already inhabited by yet another ethnic group – probably the same people as dwelled on that site later, in historical times, from the 3rd to the 1st millennium B.C. – the Elamites proper, whose language was entirely unrelated to that of the Sumerians.

The ethnic composition of the population of the whole of Iran during the early millennia of history can only be a matter of conjecture; most probably the tribes of the Iranian highlands (in the broadest meaning of that term) belonged to the North-East Caucasian linguistic family in the north-west of the plateau, and to the Proto-Dravidian in the south-east; there might well have also been peoples or tribes speaking archaic languages unconnected with any extant linguistic family, as was the case with Sumerian in the Near East in early antiquity, or with the typologically somewhat similar although unrelated Burušaski language still spoken in the mountains of the borderland between Pakistan and Afghanistan; other tribes may have spoken languages akin to Kassite (an idiom spoken at least since the 2nd millennium B.C. in present-day Luristān, not used for writing and very deficiently attested), or to Elamite. As mentioned above, this latter language was spoken in Elam (and probably in other parts of central and southern Iran) at least from the 3rd or even 4th millennium B.C. until the 1st millennium B.C., but possibly also later, throughout the 1st millennium A.D.[1] There are some grounds for believing that the Elamites, at least in the lowlands, were dark-skinned,[2] and their language seems to have been related to Proto-Dravidian, the ancestor of the Dravidian languages now spoken in southern India and in some parts of Baluchistān.[3]

We may be sure that no tribes of the Iranian Plateau in the very ancient period under discussion spoke Indo-European languages. Proto-Indo-European was spoken in the 4th and early 3rd millennium only by certain late neolithic, half-agricultural, half cattle-breeding tribes in the south-eastern part of Europe. The Indo-Iranian (so-called Aryan) languages, which had branched off from the earlier Proto-Indo-European, prevailed in northern India and on the Iranian Plateau only at a much later date.

Up to the time when the first wave of Indo-European languages reached Iran, the inhabitants of that country spoke languages of which we scarcely know anything. One of these, perhaps the most widespread, was Elamite. It had probably arrived at some earlier period from the east, superseding perhaps Sumerian on the plain of the Karkhah and the Kārūn; but we need not view the migration in question as ousting or destroying the earlier settlers; a merger is more likely to have taken place.

[1] On this, see below, p. 24.

[2] Some of the Elamite (?) warriors are represented as dark-skinned on the Achaemenian glazed tile reliefs of the 5th century B.C., and a rather dark-skinned anthropological type can be encountered in southern Khūzistān to the present day. See Hinz, *Das Reich Elam*, pp. 18ff.

[3] The degree of possible affinity is not easy to define. The pronominal systems of Elamite and Proto-Dravidian are nearly identical; some of the most ancient features of the Dravidian verbal system and declensional system also connect Dravidian with Elamite. Unfortunately, we know very few Elamite words referring to the basic notions of human life and its surroundings, so that comparison with the Proto-Dravidian vocabulary is not very revealing; some of the similarities may be fortuitous. In any case, Elamite is not a Dravidian language. If the modern Dravidian languages (Tamil, Telugu, Malayalam, Gond, Brahui, etc.) were Romance languages, and Proto-Dravidian were Latin, then Elamite would occupy in relation to them the position of some very ancient language belonging to another branch of Indo-European, e.g. Slavic. The relationship between Slavic and Latin (let alone French, Italian etc.), though close enough, is not immediately apparent without penetrating philological analysis. This comparison is, however, not quite adequate, because a longer period of time must have separated Elamite and Proto-Dravidian from their supposed common ancestor than the period separating Latin and Slavic from Proto-Indo-European.

ELAM

The Elamite culture was originally one of the "painted ware" cultures, typical of the early chalcolithic periods in all the more developed parts of the ancient world. The "painted ware" is a characteristic product of the aesthetic creative need of early chalcolithic man, already trying to generalize his emotional impressions (which at that stage are blended with magical and mythical concepts) of the laws governing the external world in a systematic rhythmical pattern derived from human, animal, or vegetable life. But this creative work was part of everybody's productive activity, not yet a monopoly of professional artists. This is why the main objects of art were painted pottery and, probably, woven fabrics, i.e. objects of everyday use, or at least objects with which the dead were supplied for *their* everyday use in the Land of Beyond.

Susa is famous in archaeology for some of the best samples of "painted ware" in a local variant, with geometrically stylized designs of water birds, hunting dogs, ears of corn and palm leaves – a hand-made pottery found in the burials of the so-called "Susa A" period (*c.* 3,500 B.C.). But it is only later, in the "Susa C" period (after 3,000 B.C.), roughly corresponding to the Sumerian Late Proto-Literate period, that certain finds seem to indicate the attainment of a level of "urban revolution" in Elam. This means that more could be produced by labour than was strictly necessary for the sustenance of the labourer; not only could the constant danger of starvation be kept from the door of the hut, but society could allow itself a division of labour into agriculturists and different kinds of handicraftsmen, and the luxury of freeing some of its members from drudgery in order to concentrate on priestly, military, judicial and administrative tasks. By the "Susa D" period (first half and middle of the 3rd millennium B.C.) a class civilization had emerged. This is shown indirectly by the appearance of numerous clay tablets inscribed in a local hieroglyphic script and apparently representing temple archives, administrative and economic; the finds also include cylinder seals,[1] probably serving as symbols or as magical protection of movable property. They are engraved with representations of whole rows of weavers or potters, as well as of mythological figures, half animal and half men. Unfortunately Susa was not always excavated scientifically, and therefore yields much less information than could otherwise have been expected. Moreover the earliest texts in Elamite hieroglyphics have not been deciphered.

[1] Button seals, which probably had a similar function, appear half a millennium earlier.

EMERGENCE OF CITY-STATES

Therefore the only data we have on the history and language of the first Elamite states of the 3rd millennium B.C. must be gleaned from the documents and inscriptions of neighbouring Sumer and Akkad, written in cuneiform, and from the proper names of the Elamite rulers whom they mention.

Apparently there existed several rather primitive city-states, each centred around its own water-supply and therefore occupying either the irrigation-area of one main canal dug by its citizens or, higher up in the hills, one river valley, or a given part of it. From the earliest time the most important community seems to have been Susa – *Sušen* (?), *Sušen*, or *Sušun* in the local language. As already mentioned, Susa was situated in the plain (but relatively near to the hills) between the Karkhah and the Āb-i Diz, and was supplied with water from a canal connecting the two rivers. Most of the city-states of Elam are so far known by name only; a number of hypotheses as to their localization have been put forward, some of them rather vague, others connecting the ancient city-names with actual archaeological sites; but none have as yet been proved. It is possible that Awan, War(a)hše,[1] and Huhunuri lay to the north and north-west of Susa, nearer to Mesopotamia (Awan, in particular, seems to have been closely connected with Dēr, present-day al-Badra on the road from Khūzistān to Baghdad), while Simaški lay probably to the north-east; according to W. Hinz, Huhunuri is modern Mālamīr (Iseh) to the east of Susa.

It is possible that Elam in the narrow sense (Elamite *Haltamti*, *Hatamti*, Sumerian *Adamdun*, Akkadian *Elamtu[m]*, also spelled ideographically NIM^{KI} or NIM.MA, "the high country") was originally a city-state separate from Susa, situated perhaps higher up in the hills, although later the term was used for the country as a whole, including more especially the lowlands.

A very important centre was *Anshan* in the eastern mountains.[2] From the earliest times there almost certainly was an intimate connection between the Elamite lowlands, eminently suitable for irrigational agriculture, and the Elamite hill-lands suited for sheep- and cattle-breeding and in earlier times fairly rich in woods. The hill-lands could also serve as a refuge area for the inhabitants of the lowlands during

---

[1] Written, at different periods, *Barahše*, *Parahši*, *Marhaši*, etc.
[2] Written *An-za-an*^{KI} or *An-ša-an*^{KI}, and probably pronounced *Anžan*. But in modern works the spelling *Anshan* has become usual. [The site of Anshan was discovered after Dr Diakonoff wrote the present chapter, by John Hansman whose account of that city-state is printed below, as chapter 2.]

times of disastrous inundation or excessive heat and drought. In no period was there in Elam such an opposition to hill-people as there was in the neighbouring land of Sumer, although at present it is very difficult to say how far to the north-west, north and east the area of Elamite civilization extended at different stages of its development.

On the other hand some administrative temple (?) records written in Elamite hieroglyphics from the beginning of the 3rd millennium B.C. have been found at Tepe Sialk near Kāshān in the centre of Iran and at other points in the highlands; similar documents, written at Tepe Yahya where they were found, probably date from the same period; and Elamite cuneiform inscriptions of the 13th century B.C. are available from the region of Bandar Bushire on the Persian Gulf. The discovery of the urban settlement of Tepe Yahya, dating from the 4th and 3rd millennia B.C., is due to C. C. Lamberg-Karlovsky. The site is situated 156 miles south of Kirmān and 80 miles east of the Kirmān–Bandar ᶜAbbās road, half-way between Elam and the cities of the Indus civilization. It is contemporary with Susa if not older, and may well have been the legendary Aratta of the Sumerian epics, separated from Elam by "seven mountain ranges".[1] According to these epics Aratta was a strong and influential city-state enjoying a civilization similar to the Sumerian and connected with it by trade relations, but distinct from the Proto-Indus civilization which apparently was known in Sumer under the name of *Meluḫḫa* (the reading is conventional; the cuneiform signs in question are more likely to be read *Melaḫa*). But we are at the mercy of guesswork; the Elamite city-states (or colonies, or whatever they may have been) which lay to the north and east of Elam proper are not mentioned, or at least cannot be identified, in the Sumerian, Akkadian, and Elamite official inscriptions. Therefore, in attempting to trace the history of Elam through the scanty sources made available by chance finds, we shall have to speak mostly of Susa and its immediate neighbours.

Both warlike and commercial contacts between Sumer and Elam are attested in written sources from the first half of the 3rd millennium B.C. According to the legendary history of Sumer as recorded in the so-called "Sumerian King List", a composition dating from the 21st century B.C. but including some older traditions, the first invasion of Elam by

---

[1] [A different location of Aratta has meanwhile been suggested by John Hansman, "Elamites, Achaemenians and Anshan", *Iran* x (1972), 118, n.92.]

Sumerians is ascribed to the reign of En-Menbaragesi, or the *en* Mebaragesi.[1] This was a historical personage, also known from a short inscription of his own, a king of the First Dynasty of Kiš in the northern part of Sumer flourishing in the 27th century B.C.

Subsequently wars between the Sumerian and the Elamite city-states, waged for the sake of plunder, became frequent. A dynasty from the Elamite city of Awan is recognized as a legitimate Sumerian dynasty by the "King List" which dates it to the period corresponding apparently to the 25th century B.C. according to present reckoning; at some time soon after 2500 B.C. Eanatum, a ruler of Lagaš in south-eastern Sumer, made a raid into Elam; no doubt, many other raids on both sides remain unknown to us. Temple records from Lagaš in the 24th century speak of a raid into Sumerian territory by a small detachment of Elamites, and later of temple merchants from Lagaš going to Elam.

About 1900 B.C. or so, the Elamites imitated the Sumerians by composing their own "King List", based on some of their local traditions; a fragment listing the kings of a Dynasty of Awan (probably the Second of that city) and those of the Dynasty of Simaški has survived. Both dynasties include twelve names each, but not all the names of the kings of Awan can be read with certainty. The kings of the "List" were apparently rulers of all Elam, the (Second?) Dynasty of Awan reigning from the 24th (?) to the 22nd (?) century B.C. The last king of that dynasty is PUZUR-Inšušinak (or, according to W. Hinz, Kutik-Inšušinak), also known from his own inscriptions. Of course the correctness of the Elamite historical tradition as written down several centuries after the events is open to doubt.

From contemporary Akkadian and Sumerian records it appears that simultaneously with kings originating from Awan and Simaški (but extending their hegemony over all Elam and probably in actual fact reigning in Susa) there also existed "kings" (Akkad. *šarrum*), "governors" (Akkad. *šakkanakkum*), "priest-princes" (Akkad. *išši'akkum*) and "judges" of the individual city-states, e.g. of Huhunuri, of Elam (= Adamdun), of Zahara etc.; there were also some city-states that had both a "king" and a "governor" (Warahše), or a "king" and a "priest-prince" at the same time (Elam) – beside the "king" of Awan, who exercised some sort of authority over the whole country. The royal

---

[1] An *en* was a priest-prince in early Sumerian city-states; in the later tradition the title *en* often formed part of personal names.

title apparently did not descend from father to son,[1] and the "kings" were perhaps elected from among the lesser dignitaries; these probably belonged as a rule to the nearest kin of former kings.

After the creation in Mesopotamia of the first centralized despotic monarchy by the Dynasty of Akkad, Elam became the target of a number of Akkadian campaigns aimed at subjecting the country. Already Sargon of Akkad (*c.* 2300 B.C.) captured five Elamite princes, among them Luh-Hiššan, son of Hišep-rašer; later he fought with the next all-Elamite king Hišep-rašer II (Hišep-ratep of the Elamite "King List"). It seems that Sargon took possession – at least temporarily – of Elam (= Adamdun) and Warahše, Susa and Awan. A war against Awan, Warahše, Elam and Zahara was waged also by Sargon's son Rimuš. Under the next Akkadian king, Man-ištušu, Elam remained under Akkadian hegemony, and Ešpum, the priest-prince of Elam (= Adamdun) and apparently also of Susa, consecrated a statue of the Akkadian king to the Elamite goddess Narunte in the latter city. One of the next Elamite kings – or a coalition of Elamite princes – concluded a treaty with King Narām-Su'en of Akkad, the earliest written document of diplomatic contents in world history. It is written in Old Elamite in the Eastern Semitic (Akkadian) cuneiform script. Unfortunately, it has come down to us in a poor state of preservation; besides, our state of knowledge of Elamite is still such that a coherent translation of the document is not possible. However, one clause is clear, namely the statement of the Elamite party: "The enemy of Narām-Su'en will be mine enemy, the friend of Narām-Su'en will be my friend!" A list of deities invoked to punish him who would break the treaty gives an insight into the Elamite pantheon of the 3rd millennium B.C.

This was a period of strong cultural influence of Mesopotamia on Elam. It can be observed in art – the "Akkadian Realistic" school prevailing in Elam from then on for many centuries – and in religion. It was probably from this time that Mesopotamian deities began to be included in the Elamite pantheon. We encounter in Elam, at different periods of its history, mostly indigenous Elamite gods: Humpan the Great God[2] and his son Hutran, the mother-goddesses Pinenkir,

[1] Thus Luh-hiššan of Awan was son of one Hišep-rašer I and not of his own predecessor Kukku-sime-temti, and PUZÚR-Inšušinak was son of one Šimpi-išhuk, and not of the preceding king Hita. Cf. the later system of promotion to kingship in 2nd millennium Elam.

[2] It was perhaps Humpan who was associated with, and perhaps even worshipped under the form of, the Great human-headed Serpent. However, it is possible that also Inšušinak and other deities assumed for Elamite believers the same aspect, thus perhaps being remote precursors of the King-Serpent Aži Dahāka of ancient Iranian lore.

EMERGENCE OF CITY-STATES

Kiririša and Parti and the warlike Narunte, the Sun-god Nanhunte (Nahhunte), Inšušinak the city-god of Susa[1] and others, but also some Mesopotamian deities: the two female participants in the judgement over the newly dead, Išme-karāb and Lā-gamāl (Elamite: Išnikarap and Lakamar),[2] Ištar, the goddess of love and strife, Nanna the Sumerian Moon-god, and several others.

The ancient Elamite hieroglyphic writing had apparently been introduced as a developed system in the early 3rd millennium B.C., i.e. at a time when in Sumer the local hieroglyphic system was already being replaced by its offspring, the cuneiform writing; this means probably that the Elamite hieroglyphic system was not the direct descendant of its Sumerian counterpart. But it is most probable that the inventors of the Elamite script were influenced by the idea of using a semiotic system consisting of ideographic or syllabo-logographic signs – an idea developed probably somewhat earlier in Sumer.

In the 23rd and 22nd centuries B.C. the local Elamite hieroglyphic writing seems already to have become too primitive for the demands of a now more developed and sophisticated class civilization. There were three ways of reforming the writing in accordance with the new demands: one could modify the native hieroglyphics, e.g. by developing a system in which more stress was laid on the syllabic values of the signs: the number of signs could thus be limited, and their forms simplified; one could apply the ready-made Sumerian or Akkadian cuneiform system to the Elamite language; or one could simply import Sumerian and Akkadian cuneiform along with the corresponding literary languages.

Actually all three ways were tried. Some of PUZÚR-Inšušinak's inscriptions – if we are to accept Hinz's decipherment – are written in a simplified syllabic variant of Elamite hieroglyphics; the treaty with Narām-Su'en is written in the Elamite language but in the Akkadian script; however, it was the third way which proved to be the most viable. Already PUZÚR-Inšušinak ordered to make inscriptions in

---

[1] The structure of this name suggests that it might have originally been Sumerian, and meant "lord of Šušen (Susa)"; perhaps the worship of this Susan god goes back to the times before the Elamite-speaking tribes settled on the plain of the Karkhah and the Kārūn. Inšušinak was also the supreme judge of the dead, the goddesses Išnikarap and Lakamar acting as counsels for defence and prosecution respectively. The Akkadian *Enunaki* were, apparently, a kind of jury over which Inšušinak presided.

[2] In Akkadian, the names mean "She has heard the supplication", and "No mercy". Curiously enough, there are few signs of a worship of these goddesses in Mesopotamia, and the image of the Nether World seems there to have been quite different from the Elamite.

ELAM

Akkadian, and for several centuries very few texts were written in Elamite in Susa – or, at least, very few have come down to us. The reason was probably that many more well qualified Akkadian scribes were available than Elamite ones, the more so as Susa became in time very much Akkadianized, and Semitic personal names prevailed there for centuries over Elamite ones; even prayers to Elamite gods were written in Akkadian, although the country as a whole retained its Elamite linguistic and cultural character.

2. The Old Elamite Kingdom

However, the political hegemony established in Elam by the Akkadian kings between 2300 and 2200 B.C. did not last long. After 2200 B.C. there began an invasion of the Qutium tribes from north-western Iran into Mesopotamia, and a king of Elam seized the opportunity to create his own empire. Whether this was PUZÚR-Inšušinak I (or, according to Hinz, Kutik-Inšušinak) whom we have already mentioned, or whether it was already one of his predecessors of the Dynasty of Awan, is unknown. In his Akkadian inscription PUZÚR-Inšušinak imitates Narām-Su'en's title of "King of the Four Quarters of the Earth", and states that he conquered about sixty different places or regions, among them Huhunuri and Qutium, and that the king of Simaški had embraced his knees.

But it was precisely the kings of Simaški who after some time seem to have gained hegemony over the country.[1] They must have risen to power soon after (?) the time when Gudea, the priest-prince of Lagaš in Sumer (c. 2130 B.C.), boasted that Elamite workers were being called up to help in the construction of the chief temple of that city; at least some of the Simaškite kings of Elam were contemporaries of the kings of the Third Dynasty of Ur in Southern Mesopotamia, or the "Kingdom of Sumer and Akkad" as it was called officially (c. 2111-2003 B.C.). The kingdom of Ur was a strongly unified despotic monarchy which had reduced a considerable percentage of the Mesopotamian population to virtual slavery, and which in Elam pursued a high-handed policy of intervention. Already the second and mightiest king of Ur, Šulgi (2093-2046 B.C.), could undertake the construction of some temples in

[1] The Elamite "King List" must be partly erroneous, because king Kirnamme, appearing in the list as the first king of the dynasty of Simaški, is mentioned in a Sumerian administrative document only a few years before Enpi-luhhan who is the fifth on the list; there are also other discrepancies between the list and the data of the documents.

THE OLD ELAMITE KINGDOM

Susa, and married one of his daughters to the priest-prince of Warahše and another to the priest-prince of Anshan; however, the latter city later rebelled against him and was sacked. Under the last king of Ur, Ibbī-Su'en, most of the Elamite city-states rose in rebellion. There followed a big campaign against Elam, during which the cities of Susa, Elam (= Adamdun), and Awan were captured, and Enpi-luhhan, the fifth king of Elam of the Dynasty of Simaški according to the "King List", was taken prisoner. However, very soon afterwards the Elamites, using the opportunity created by the invasion of Amorite (Western Semitic) shepherd tribes into Mesopotamia across the country from the Euphrates to the Tigris and thence along the route south of Jebel Ḥamrīn via al-Badra and then again over the Tigris to the west, followed them with a raid in the same direction from the passes over al-Badra. Ur, the Sumero-Akkadian capital, was destroyed, the statues of its deities were carried away, and Ibbī-Su'en himself led into captivity to Anshan. In fact, the leadership in Elam, after the fall of Enpi-luhhan, seems to have passed to the rulers of Anshan, although the Simaškite kings were probably still for a time recognized as nominal overlords. This situation lasted for about one century; no very strong central power seems to have existed in Elam. Thus, King Išbi-Erra of Issin (the successor-state of Ur in Mesopotamia), after a victory over Elam, married his daughter to one Humpan-šimti, *sukkal* of Susa (a new title on which more will be said below), who may have been the son of Hutran-temti of Simaški; it is possible that Susa was practically independent both of Simaški and of Anshan. But about 1900 B.C. a new dynasty arose in Elam, probably of Anshanite origin. Its founder was one Eparti who succeeded Intattu II of Simaški as overlord of Elam. Two more Simaškite kings seem to have reigned nominally in Eparti's time, and it was only Eparti's son who assumed an entirely new imperial title; but there is little doubt that in fact already Eparti ruled over the whole country.

During the reign of the Dynasty of Eparti a curious form of polity is attested in Elam. The system probably goes back to much earlier times; already under the (Second) Dynasty of Awan we know of a simultaneous existence in Elam of a whole hierarchy of rulers with different titles, but it cannot be proved that this hierarchical system was the same as in the 2nd millennium B.C.; and in any case, the change in the titulature of the rulers between the 3rd and the 2nd millennia B.C. seems to indicate that the system itself had somewhat changed.

ELAM

As attested during the first half of the 2nd millennium B.C., the system was as follows:

The overlord of the country bore (in Sumerian) the title *sukkal-maḫ*, which literally means something like "grand vizier" or "supreme messenger" but was apparently used in the approximate sense of "emperor". In order not to introduce anachronistic notions, we shall render this title as "overlord"; it corresponded probably to the earlier title of "king" when applied to a ruler of the whole country, standing above mere "kings" of city-states. Eparti himself still bore only the title "King of Anshan and Susa", while his Simaškite predecessor was "Priest-Prince of Susa and King of Simaški and Elam". It was Eparti's son Šilhaha who first assumed the new title: "Sukkal-maḫ, King of Anshan and Susa".[1]

Alongside the title of sukkal-maḫ, or "overlord", there also existed (in descending order of importance) the titles of simple sukkal of Elam (and of Simaški), a "king of Susa", and a "shepherd of the people of Susa", also called "shepherd of Inšušinak" (the local god of Susa). Sometimes two or even three of these titles were borne by one person at the same time, but at least two of these titles (usually those of sukkal-maḫ and "king") were borne by two different persons, the second being subordinate to the first. They were always related to each other. As often as not, the "king" was the son of the "overlord", but one must not infer from this that the title "king" was that of the heir-apparent: it was usually the overlord's uterine younger brother and not the "king" who inherited his title after the death of the sukkal-maḫ. During the lifetime of the "overlord" his younger brother would usually be sukkal of Elam; only as next in order after the brothers of the "overlord" could his son, the "king" of Susa, be promoted to the dignity of a sukkal, while he could not as a rule become sukkal-maḫ so long as any of his imperial uncles were alive. At least in some cases he would stay "king" to the end of his days, while the sukkal-maḫs were changing, as it were, over his head.

Seeing, however, that the number of an overlord's brothers could be considerable, while we have no evidence of more than two (?) brothers succeeding each other on the throne of the sukkal-maḫ, we may conclude that the promotion depended on some sort of election procedure among the deceased overlord's relatives. It seems that not

---

[1] Šilhaha – but not his successors – bore also the title of "father" (*adda*, or *atta*), i.e. probably "protector" of the Amorite shepherd tribes (?).

THE OLD ELAMITE KINGDOM

every male relative was eligible but only a *ruhušak*, an Elamite term designating a son or direct descendant of the sister of an "overlord" called "the reverend mother" (Elamite *amma haštuk*) who probably was the high priestess of Elam and the wife of her brother the "overlord"; thus, to aspire to the throne, the candidate must have been of imperial blood both from his father and his mother; the latter was even the more important: a sukkal-maḫ, or sukkal, or king, while mentioning that he was son or descendant of an overlord's sister, sometimes omitted to mention the name of his own father; and when he did mention him, it sometimes appears that he had no royal or higher title.

Two points must be stressed here: first, that the "king of Susa" was a very real and active governor of that city, not a mere shadowy figure, just as the "overlord" was no mere ritualistic puppet but an active figure in the political life of Elam; second, that the whole hierarchical system of promotion of rulers had nothing to do with supposed survivals of a matriarchate developed by the native pre-Indo-European population; the Elamite family was definitely of a patriarchal type, and the system described above of inheritance of the crown, limited to princely families only, was designed to keep the imperial heritage strictly within one single patriarchal family and exclude its passing outside through marriage. Similar devices, resulting in brother-and-sister marriages, are known from Ancient Egypt, Asia Minor, and Achaemenian Iran. They survived as common practice in later Zoroastrian communities, where next-of-kin marriages were favoured, especially in noble families.

A number of Elamite "overlords", sukkals, and "kings" reigning between *c.* 1900 and 1600 B.C. are known to us by name, and there are several synchronisms with kings of Babylonia and Assyria.[1] However, the order of their reigns is a matter of some dispute,[2] and few political events of importance in the history of Elam are known during the reign

---

[1] Attahušu, "king" of Susa under the "overlord" Šilhaha = Sumuabum of Babylon, *c.* 1895–90; Širuktuh, "overlord" = Šamšī-Adad I of Assyria, second half of 19th century B.C.; Siwe-palar-huhpak, "overlord" (?) and "king of Anshan" = Hammurapi, after 1790; Kutučuluš, sukkal of Susa (not yet "overlord") = Hammurapi, after 1790; Kuter-Nahhunte = Samsuiluna, son of Hammurapi (after 1752)?; Kuk-Našur III (or, as "overlord", Kuk-Našur I) = Ammiṣaduqa of Babylon, about 1630 B.C.

[2] The order according to Hinz (1964) is Eparti, Šilhaha, Širuktuh I, Simut-wartaš, Siwe-palar-huhpak, Kutučuluš I, Kuter-Nahhunte I, Lila-ir-taš, Temti-agun I, Tan-Uli, Temti-halki, Kuk-Našur, Kuter-Šilhaha, Temti-raptaš, Kutučuluš II (III), Tata, Atta-merra-halki, Pala-hiššan, Kuk-Kirweš, Kuk-Nahhunte, Kuter-Nahhunte II; the order according to Yusifov (1968) is Eparti, Šilhaha, Pala-hiššan, Kuk-kirwaš, Kuk-Nahhunte, Širuktuh, Simut-wartaš, Siwe-palar-huhpak, Kutučuluš I, Kuter-Nahhunte, Lila-ir-taš, Temti-agun I, Tata, Atta-mer-halki, Temti-agun II, Tan-Uli, Temti-halki, Kuter-Šilhaha, Kuk-Našur, Temti-raptaš, Kutučuluš II.

of the Dynasty of Eparti. The inscriptions only mention the construction of temples, and similar pious deeds, by rulers of different rank. But there were other events, for instance the seizure of power in the southern Mesopotamian kingdom of Larsam (1834 B.C.) by the half-Elamite, half-Semitic dynasty of one Kutur-mapuk, *adda* of the Amorite tribe of Yamūtba͑l on the north-western outskirts of Elam. One of the later kings of Elam of the Dynasty of Eparti became dependent on Hammurapi of Babylon (1792–1750); but already the contemporary of Hammurapi's son, Samsuiluna, the Elamite king Kuter-Nahhunte seems to have overrun southern Babylonia.

Much more is known about the social situation in Susa of the period. The population was strongly Akkadianized; Akkadian and Amorite personal names are at least as frequent as Elamite ones if not more frequent, and all the documents, and most inscriptions, are written in a local Akkadian dialect. The main social unit among the free citizens of Susa was the family commune, or "brotherhood" (Akkad. *aḫḫūtu*) embracing several couples with their children, the men being mostly, but not always, closely related to each other. The conditions existing inside such family communes resemble those envisaged by the Old Babylonian and the Hurrian customary family law; no phenomena analogous to the inheritance of the imperial title through the female line of kinship are to be observed. After the death of the father the family property was equally divided among all children but the widow was not an heir; the *paterfamilias* could allot her some property for her personal use during her lifetime, or cede to her the right to manage the family property during the minority of her sons. The grown-up sons could manage the family property together, one of them becoming the head of the family commune (this, apparently, was not necessarily the eldest; the paterfamilias or his widow could choose his successor at discretion). Alternatively the brothers could divide, and start their own family households, or enter severally into "brotherhood" with other related or even unrelated persons. The labour force of the family commune consisted mainly of its members and of men taken into the "brotherhood" by some kind of charity; there seems also to have been a limited number of slave-women, as well as slaves, probably mostly born of the slave-women in the house.

A number of family communes would be set up as a territorial community. There are some indirect indications of the possible existence of popular assemblies of communities, but if they existed, they had little

THE OLD ELAMITE KINGDOM

importance. More important was the authority of the temples; among other things, they regulated the legal life of the community by written or traditional "rules" or "ways of walking [before the god]" (Akkad. *kubussû*).

The private business life in Susa was much the same as in contemporary Babylonia. There exist a number of documents referring to the "purchase" of immoveables, but – just as in other countries of the Ancient Near East – a "sale" of immoveables was probably not an irrevocable act. There are also a number of documents of loan (often from the temple), but debtor-slavery, the plague of most Near-Eastern countries of that epoch, does not seem to have developed to an appreciable extent.

Alongside of private immoveable property of communal family households there existed crown land. Most of it was allotted in small parcels to royal servants in payment of their service; sometimes parts of royal land were presented to higher officials as gifts of the king or "overlord"; such land might be exempted from taxes, and its owner with his dependents from the labour service incumbent on the citizens. In one document Kuk-Našur, sukkal of Susa, legalized the purchase by a royal servant of high standing, of the holdings which had been allotted to royal shepherds, warriors, Amorite policemen (?), messengers etc. for their service. It seems that the royal estate was rapidly disintegrating into separate private estates on what was only technically royal land.

The royal lands, as well as those granted to dignitaries, were apparently worked not by slaves but mostly by men who, while retaining their legal status of freemen (in the same way as younger family members were freemen although under the absolute authority of the head of the family) were devoid of property, had no means of production of their own, and were kept to their labour tasks by forces at the disposal of the body of royal officers.

There also existed temple lands, but we know little about them. Temples partook in commercial and money-lending operations. The temple lands were worked by "temple boys" (Elamite *puhu siyannir*), who despite this designation could be of any age.

In the 18th century B.C. the Elamites seem to have acted in alliance with Kassite mountaineers, who overran central Mesopotamia; in the 16th century Elam, like Babylonia, seems in its turn to have been devastated by Kassites. A big find of Elamite cuneiform documents from about that period at the site of Haft Tepe south of Susa was announced recently, but it will take some time before they are published, It was probably at this time or somewhat later that speakers of Indo-Iranian dialects for the first time reached the outskirts of what in earlier periods had been Elamite territory; at some undefined later period they settled on the borders of Elam.

3. *The Middle Elamite Kingdom*

From Babylonian sources we learn that Elam and Susa were conquered by the Kassite Babylonian king Kurigalzu in the second part of the 14th century. But soon after Kurigalzu's raid the Elamite kingdom was restored and even enlarged, apparently under Pahir-hiššan, son of Ike-halki. Pahir-hiššan's nephew and second successor, Humpan-nummena I, held under his sway, among other places, Liyan near modern Bandar Būshahr (Bushire).

The title of sukkal-mah seems now to have fallen into disuse; Pahir-hiššan and his successors bore only the titles of "kings of Anshan and Susa" and "kings of Elam", but the ancient custom of inheritance of the throne both through the female kinship line and through the male apparently continued. The royal inscriptions – unfortunately preserved not from all the Elamite kings of this "Middle Period" – are written in Elamite, in a local cuneiform script which differs considerably from its Old Babylonian prototype.

One of the descendants of Ike-halki, king Un-taš-napir-riša (or Un-taš-Humpan) who reigned in the middle of the 13th century B.C., seems to have been a powerful monarch; he attempted to preserve his name for posterity by a number of pious inscriptions and buildings. He was the founder of a new royal city, Dūr-Untaš (now Tchogha-Zambil) where a big temple-tower (ziggurat) of the Babylonian type with several adjoining buildings was discovered in a fairly good state of preservation by the French expedition headed by R. Ghirshman. The architecture demonstrates the complete absorption of Mesopotamian cultural traditions in Elam. It is interesting to note that the Elamite sculpture of the 2nd millennium B.C., also continuing the Akkadian art traditions of Mesopotamia, preserved their realistic trends better than the Babylonian itself. One of the best examples is the (now headless) statue of Un-taš-napir-riša's queen Napir-asu.

The last of the dynasty of Ike-halki was perhaps Kiten-Hutran who reigned in the last third of the 13th century B.C. The power of Elam

THE MIDDLE ELAMITE KINGDOM

was still on the rise; this king even raided Babylonia twice, although he gained no lasting results: Babylonia remained under the supreme hegemony of the Assyrian king Tukultī-Ninurta I who raised his own appointees to the throne of Babylon. But Elam itself suffered no injury from the Assyrians.

The period of the 13th and 12th centuries B.C. is again illuminated for us by native inscriptions and archaeological remains. We do not know whether the kings of this period belonged to the descendants of Ike-halki, or whether the successor of Kiten-Hutran, King Hallutuš-Inšušinak I, belonged to another house.

His son Šutruk-Nahhunte I has left a number of inscriptions, not only in Susa, but also in far-off Liyan (Bushire). Among other things, these inscriptions mention a number of military campaigns, apparently in all directions from Susa, although most of the place-names so far defy identification. About 1160 Šutruk-Nahhunte led a campaign against Mesopotamia, capturing Babylon itself, as well as several important cities of northern Babylonia. A tribute amounting to 120 talents of gold and 480 talents of silver was laid upon the conquered country, and many statues, steles and other objects were brought home to Susa as memorials of the victorious campaign (among others the famous stele with the Laws of Hammurapi). But this was not the end of the war with Babylonia; the eldest son of Šutruk-Nahhunte I, Kuter-Nahhunte III, to whom his father had entrusted the rule of Mesopotamia, inherited the hostilities. In 1157 he succeeded in taking prisoner the last Babylonian king of Kassite origin, Ellil-nādin-aḫḫē, but could not conquer the land, either in his father's lifetime or during his own reign, which presumably was short (c. 1155–1150?); in Issin there arose a new Babylonian kingdom; border raids seem to have continued between Babylonia and Elam for more than one generation.

According to ancient custom, the next Elamite king to ascend the throne was Šilhak-Inšušinak I, the brother of Kuter-Nahhunte III. Seeing that the inheritance of the royal title followed the female line, and perhaps not being himself the son of the queen of Hallutuš-Inšušinak,[1] Šilhak-Inšušinak married his own brother's widow. The uncertainty of his rights to the throne made him include in his inscriptions a huge genealogy of Elamite kings, his presumed ancestors, up to the Dynasty of Simaški. Kuter-Nahhunte's own eldest son,

---

[1] In one of his inscriptions he calls himself "the beloved man of (the lady) Peyak"; this lady may or may not have been the queen of Hallutuš-Inšušinak —more probably she was not.

Hutelutuš-Inšušinak, was meanwhile the regent in Susa. A Babylonian legend makes him the murderer of his father (and thus a conspirator bringing his uncle to the throne?). As W. Hinz rightly points out, this tradition can hardly be correct.

Šilhak-Inšušinak I (c. 1150–1120 B.C.) was one of the greatest warriors in Elamite history; he conquered a vast territory reaching from northern Babylonia and the borders of Assyria deep into the highlands of Iran in the direction of modern Kirmānshāh and even further. The place-names mentioned in his inscription do not suggest, however, that he intruded into territory inhabited already by Iranian-speaking tribes.

Hutelutuš-Inšušinak (c. 1120–1110?), who calls himself son of Kuter-Nahhunte *and* of Šilhak-Inšušinak (he was, in any case, the son of Nahhunte-Utu, the wife of both) and drops the title "king of Anshan" (perhaps because this eastern province was already lost – to Iranians??), suffered a defeat from Nebuchadrezzar I of Babylon about 1110; after that a new dark age begins in the history of Elam. It seems that Hutelutuš-Inšušinak had no sons, nor was he succeeded by a brother.

4. *The Neo-Elamite Kingdom*

It is not necessarily to be inferred that there was then a complete decline of the kingdom of Elam. The finds of inscriptions and documents are always largely due to chance. Probably the Elamite state revived not long after it was defeated by Nebuchadrezzar I: neither his successors nor, apparently, he himself had sufficient strength to keep Elam in their power. Admittedly further misfortunes must have befallen Elam between the 11th and the 9th century B.C. In the 9th to 7th centuries B.C. the eastern valleys of what formerly was Elamite territory – modern Fārs including the ancient land of Anshan seem to have been in the possession of the Persians, and no one can say how much earlier they may have settled there. But the Elamite kingdom itself survived, although no native written sources from the period in question are known – nor, for that matter, any Babylonian or Assyrian source. This is because both these Mesopotamian kingdoms, for different reasons, suffered a decline precisely in this period. Their kings could not campaign far from their own frontiers, and thus no countries except the nearest neighbours of Assyria and Babylonia are mentioned in their inscriptions.

When we next hear of Elam – in the annals of the Assyrian king

THE NEO-ELAMITE KINGDOM

Šamšī-Adad V under the year 821 B.C. – the news is of a civil war waged inside a still existing big state, reaching "from Bīt-Bunaki to Parsuaš", i.e. apparently from a region south of Kirmānshāh to Fārs. Parsuaš is here, as we shall attempt to show below, probably already a small kingdom inhabited by Iranian-speaking Persians. However, this is but a casual entry in the Assyrian annals; no other sources on Elam have come down to us from either the ninth or the greater part of the 8th century. Only beginning with the second part of the 8th century B.C. we have a very laconic but trustworthy source on the political history of Elam in the "Babylonian Chronicle", a sort of annals kept in Babylonia from the year 745 B.C. down to Hellenistic times.[1] Apart from this "Chronicle", there exist some Neo-Elamite inscriptions of the late 8th and the 7th centuries B.C., a few documents in Elamite from the same period (mostly concerning loans and not very informative), and an archive of the shops of the royal craftsmen, dating from the very end of the existence of independent Elam, viz. the 6th century B.C. Elamite affairs are also often mentioned in Assyrian royal annals and state letters from the last part of the 8th century to the second third of the 7th century. Thus one may attempt to write a political history of the "Neo-Elamite" period, although allowance must be made for many gaps in our knowledge.

The ancestor of the dynasty of Elamite kings reigning from the middle of the 8th to the middle of the 7th century was one Humpan-tahrah; his date and exact relationship to the following rulers are unknown. Under the year 742 the "Babylonian Chronicle" states that king "Umbanigaš (= Elamite Humpan-nikaš)[2] ascended the throne in Elam". This king was an ally of the famous Chaldaean chieftain and pretender to the Babylonian throne, Merodach-baladan, during the latter's struggle against Assyria; in an attempt to break the Assyrian might, Merodach-baladan tried to create a coalition of its enemies, and Elam was one of the mainstays of the alliance. Moreover, it appears that it was a constant policy of the Neo-Elamite kings to counteract the power of Assyria by gaining control over Babylonia – the richest

---

[1] In the following we will subsume under the general term of "Babylonian Chronicle" all the different texts of this genre which have come down to us, treating them as a single interconnected series.

[2] The Elamite names are also here and below given in their Middle Elamite form. But actually the Elamites of the late period "dropped their *h*'s", did not pronounce final vowels and, to judge by Assyrian and Babylonian transcriptions, tended to pronounce stops between vowels and after sonants as voiced. [This is why the god (whose name forms part of many Elamite proper names) referred to in the present chapter as "Humpan" is widely called "Humban" in modern literature.]

country of the Near East and its undisputed religious and cultural centre – either by overrunning it with their own forces, or by entering into alliance with Babylonian kings or rebellious Chaldaean chiefs. Sometimes they met with considerable success. Thus, in 720 Humpan-nikaš did in fact inflict a serious defeat on the great Assyrian warrior king Sargon II at Dēr (now al-Badra) on the road from Elam to the Tigris.

The policy of the Neo-Elamite kingdom in Iran is little known, and its eastern frontiers have not been ascertained. It seems that at least in the early 7th century (and probably a considerable time before that) a string of (semi-?) independent little states existed along the north-eastern and eastern border of Elam, some of them certainly with Iranian or mixed dynasties: Ellipi (Elymais), Paširu, Anshan, Parsūaš, Hudimeri etc.

The first Neo-Elamite king whose inscriptions have come down to us, was Šutur-Nahhunte, or Šutruk-Nahhunte II, son of the sister (and probably wife) of Humpan-nikaš by another man (presumably his brother), Intattu; Šutruk-Nahhunte II reigned from 717 to 699 B.C.; at first he used the traditional title "King of Anshan and Susa", but we happen to know that a generation later Anshan was in actual fact an autonomous kingdom, probably with an Iranian population; whether or not it was the secession of Anshan which caused Šutruk-Nahhunte to drop the Anshanite title in his later inscriptions, we have no means of ascertaining. He claims to be an "expander (?) of his country", enjoying the spiritual help of a number of former kings who presumably were his ancestors: Hutelutuš-Inšušinak, his cousin (?) and successor Šilhina-hamru-Lakamar, and one Humpan-nimmena (II?) who apparently belonged to the same royal family; Šutruk-Nahhunte claims to be his "son" (i.e. direct descendant). Unfortunately, the inscriptions of Šutruk-Nahhunte II are still difficult to understand in the present state of our knowledge of the Elamite language; it seems, however, that he conquered a considerable stretch of territory to the north-west of Elam proper – one of the inscriptions mentions Karintaš (modern Karind) and Arman (near Sar-i Pul?). We do not know the date of these conquests and the duration of the Elamite occupation there; apparently it was but an episode in the protracted hostilities between Elam and Assyria during the times of the kings Sargon II and Sennacherib, of which a more detailed account will be given in chapter III.

In 699 Šutruk-Nahhunte was deposed by his younger brother

THE NEO-ELAMITE KINGDOM

Hallušu-Inšušinak. Merodach-baladan had by that time suffered another defeat from Sennacherib and had settled with his adherents in the marshes by the Elamite coast, in Nagītu, while Sennacherib's first-born son Aššur-nādin-šumī ruled in Babylon. To end the danger created by Merodach-baladan once and for all, Sennacherib organized a fleet manned by Phoenicians, as well as by Cypriote Greeks; the fleet sailed down the Euphrates and devastated the Elamite coast (694 B.C.). But the Assyrian king left his rear unprotected, and Hallušu-Inšušinak fell into Babylonia along the usual road and took Sennacherib's son as prisoner to Elam, where he probably was put to death. However, already in the following year the allied Elamite and Babylonian troops were defeated by the Assyrian in central Babylonia. Hallušu-Inšušinak retreated to Susa but was not let in by the citizens, who killed him and put his son Kuter-Nahhunte (IV?) on the throne. An Assyrian winter campaign against Elam under its new king did not meet with success, but Kuter-Nahhunte perished in 692 during a mutiny in Elam.

The next Elamite king was Humpan-nimmena (III?), a younger brother of the late king. The Babylonians pinned their hopes on him, knowing that the Assyrian king was bent on destroying their city as a nest of sedition and in punishment for the fate of his son. Humpan-nimmena marched to Babylonia in 691 in alliance with the Aramaic nomads of the steppes between that land and Elam, but (more important) also with a number of vassal states situated on the eastern borders of Elam: Ellipi, Paširu, Anshan, and Parsūaš. Parsūaš in this context being almost certainly Fārs, a computation of generations suggests that the king ruling there at the time may have been Achaemenes, the ancestor of the later Great Kings.[1] The allied army met with the Assyrians at Ḫalulê on the Tigris; the annals of Sennacherib draw a vivid picture of what they treat as if it were the greatest victory of all times, while the "Babylonian Chronicle" states laconically: "Assyria was routed." Apparently the battle was indecisive; both parties retreated to their respective countries. The decisive victory of the Assyrians came later: when in 689 Sennacherib renewed his campaign against Babel, Humpan-nimmena was suddenly crippled with paralysis; the Elamite troops did not come to assistance, and the ancient capital of Babylonia was razed to the ground, only to be rebuilt eleven years later by Sennacherib's son.

Not much is known of the next Elamite king Humpan-hal-taš I

---

[1] [Hansman, "Elamites, Achaemenians and Anshan", 109, argues that the king was Teïspes.]

(688–681), except that he died suddenly. In the following period the order of the kings in Elam is not quite clear, and the land was possibly in a state of civil war.[1] It was king Humpan-hal-taš II who was accepted as king of Elam by the Assyrians and Babylonians; after a period of friendly relations with Assyria, he made a raid in 675 against Assyrian-occupied Sippar in Babylonia.

After 675 we again encounter two kings in Susa. Instead of peacefully dividing their power as in ancient times, they appear as rivals. At first it was apparently Urtaki, son of Humpan-hal-taš II who was overlord; for ten years he had good relations with Assyria, but in 665 he too attempted a raid into Babylonia, without much success. Soon afterwards Urtaki died, or was put to death by his co-regent and rival Temti-Humpan-Inšušinak II. The sons and other relatives of Urtaki and of Humpan-hal-taš II fled to Aššurbānapli of Assyria.

The middle of the 7th century B.C. was disastrous for Elam. It was a critical period in the history of the Near East: a major attempt was made to put an end to the tyranny of Assyria; this time it was an Assyrian who stood at the head of the anti-Assyrian alliance: Šamaš-šumukīn, the vassal king of Babylon and brother to Aššurbānapli, the king of Assyria.

King Temti-Humpan-Inšušinak of Elam (663–653), better known by his Assyrian name Teumman, allied himself, like most of the still independent monarchs of the Near East, with the rebel brother of the Assyrian king. But before Babylon's fate was to be sealed, Aššurbānapli invaded Elam (653) and, after a rout of the Elamites on the bank of the Ulāi, sacked Susa. The Elamite warriors capitulated, and Teumman was beheaded before the ranks of his own army. Humpan-nikaš II, son of Urtaki, was made king of Elam with his brother Atta-hameti-Inšušinak (Attamet) as viceroy or "king" of Susa; a separate kingdom was created for his second brother Tammarit in the city of Hetali. As soon as the Assyrian troops were out of Elam, Humpan-nikaš joined the pro-Babylonian alliance (which by now included countries from Media to Judah), only to be deposed by Tammarit, who, however, followed the same policy. Tammarit made, it seems, an effort to reunite the country, but in vain: this was only a signal for a general civil war, and by 648, when Aššurbānapli made his second Elamite campaign, there were already at least two kings in Elam, beside Tammarit: Humpan-hal-taš

[1] According to W. Hinz, it was at this period that one Šilhak-Inšušinak II reigned at Susa, while the "Babylonian Chronicle" tells us that Humpan-hal-taš II ascended the throne.

THE NEO-ELAMITE KINGDOM

III, son of Atta-hameti-Inšušinak ruled in Dūr-Untaš and Madaktu, and Humpan-ahpi in Pupila.[1]

There were several campaigns of Aššurbānapli against Elam (probably in 653/2, 648, 646/5, 642 and 639). It was during one of these that Cyrus I (Akkad. *Kuraš*), grandfather of Cyrus the Great of Persia, sent propitiatory gifts to the Assyrian king and gave him his son, Arukku, as hostage. The king of the neighbouring (?) country of Ḫudimeri did the same. In 646/5 Susa suffered the worst sack of its history; Humpan-hal-taš III tried to hide in the mountains but was delivered to the Assyrians, with a number of other Elamite nobles, by the inhabitants of Ellipi (Elymais) near modern Kirmānshāh (644).

It looked as if Elam as a state were completely destroyed, but several kinglets still held out in the mountain strongholds, then descended into the lowlands as soon as the Assyrians went away; and at last the Assyrians went for good. After the death of Aššurbānapli a civil war broke out in Assyria, and from the middle of the twenties of the 7th century B.C. most of Babylonia was in the vigorous hands of the general Nabopalassar, founder of the Neo-Babylonian empire. This new Babylonian king returned the statues of the Elamite gods captured by Aššurbānapli to Susa, in order to gain the favour of the Elamites; at about the same time one of the Elamite pretenders seems to have achieved the unification of the devastated kingdom. Later, under the next Babylonian king, Nebuchadnezzar II, war broke out between Babylonia and Elam (596/5), leading to the capture of Susa by the Babylonians; but, as can be gleaned from Jeremiah 49, the attention of the Babylonian king was riveted on other more important political matters elsewhere, and it seems that Elam again regained its independence (Jeremiah 49. 39).

The social and economic conditions in the Neo-Elamite period are unknown, except for scanty information from the archives of the royal workshops at Susa, probably dating from the 6th century B.C., and testifying to independent relations of Elam with Syria, Media (?) and Babylonia. In contrast with texts written in Elamite under the Achaemenian rule, which are full of Old Persian words, the documents of these archives contain as yet hardly any Iranisms.

The circumstances that brought about the final destruction of the kingdom of Elam are obscure. Elam probably recognized the

[1] W. Hinz places Hetali near Behbehan, Madaktu in the valley of the Saimarreh, and Pupila nearer to the Persian Gulf.

supremacy of Cyaxares, king of Media, and became one of Media's semi-independent border provinces. It must have been incorporated into the Persian Empire as a satrapy under Cyrus at about the same time as Babylonia (538 B.C.). Nevertheless during the turmoil between the death of Cambyses and the final victory of Darius I no less than three pretenders to the local throne rose in Elam (522–519 B.C.).

The influence of the Elamite culture on the Old Persian was considerable; Elamite reliefs influenced the sculpture of the time of Darius I; Elamite was still the language of administration in Fārs in as late as the 5th century B.C. All the more curious is the fact that the Elamite cuneiform script seems to have had no influence at all on the so-called "Old Persian" cuneiform writing.

As to the Elamite nation and language, their end, too, is unknown. Susa became one of the royal residences in the Achaemenian Persian Empire; renamed Seleucia on the Eulaeus in the Hellenistic period, it was granted the constitution of a *polis* and used Greek as the official and even as the unofficial language as late as the Parthian period; but the countryside must have remained Elamite for a very long time. Arabic authors of the 10th century A.D. mention a language spoken in Khūzistān which was different from Persian, Arabic and Hebrew. Whether it was a peripheral Iranian dialect like Kurdish or Lūrī, or an Aramaic dialect like the Mandaic of Southern Iraq, or really a remnant of ancient Elamite, remains uncertain.

CHAPTER 2

ANSHAN IN THE ELAMITE AND ACHAEMENIAN PERIODS

For over 1,500 years the land of Anshan occupied a prominent place in the political history of south-western Iran. Anshan is first attested in Akkadian and Sumerian texts of the late 3rd millennium B.C. During the 2nd and early 1st millenniums Elamite rulers traditionally took the title king of Anzan (Anshan) and Shushan (Susa). In the middle 1st millennium B.C. Anshan became the homeland of the Achaemenian Persians.

Different writers have sought to locate the city and region of Anshan in various parts of south Iran. In 1970 a large archaeological site in western Fars called Malyān, was proposed as being that of the lost city.[1] This identification had been suggested from a consideration of historical and archaeological evidence and seemed to be supported by the finding that an early Islamic town called Āsh was once located in the vicinity of Malyān.[2] In two of the dialects spoken in this part of Fars Āsh is a possible development of the ancient toponym Anshan.[3] Fragments of inscriptions in Elamite cuneiform recovered during archaeological work carried out at Malyān in 1971 and 1972 bore parts of the dedication of a temple which is described as being in Anshan,[4] thereby confirming the suggested identification of the site.

In treating the early history of Anshan we shall also note textual references to the Elamite province of Awan and consider the possibility that this toponym and Anshan may have been used at different periods for the same area.

The Sumerian King List states that the Kingdom of Ur (c. 2600 B.C.) was smitten with arms and its kingship taken to the Elamite land of Awan.[5] A king of Kish is reported, in turn, to have invaded Awan and

---

[1] The proposed identification was first made by the present writer in discussions with colleagues in 1970 and later published; see J. Hansman, *Iran* x (1972), 101–24.
[2] *Ibid.*, 120–2.
[3] I. Gershevitch, *Iran* x (1972), 124–5.
[4] E. Reiner, "The location of Anšan", *RA* LXVII (1973), 57–62.
[5] T. Jacobsen (ed.), *The Sumerian King List* (Chicago, 1938), 83–5.

to have taken its kingship to Kish.[1] Somewhat later, around 2500 B.C., the first Elamite dynasty of which we have record, was founded in Awan by a certain Peli.[2]

The dynasty of Peli seems to have flourished for several generations until Sargon of Agade (2334–2279 B.C.) invaded Elam and sacked a number of districts of that region, including Awan and Susa.[3] Rimush, son and successor of Sargon, continued to war in the territories of Awan, Susa and Elam.[4] Manishtusu, successor to Rimush in Agade, speaks of resubjugating Anshan after the ruler of that region revolted from the empire created by Sargon.[5] But whereas Sargon's own texts do not mention Anshan, Manishtusu makes no reference to Sargon's Awan. Naram-Sin (2229–2255 B.C.), a later ruler in Agade, concluded a treaty of alliance with Khita the ninth king of Awan.[6] The dynasty of Peli eventually ends with the fall of Khita's successor Kutil-Inshushinak in about 2220 B.C. At approximately this same period Gudea, a ruler of Lagash, claims to have conquered the city of Anshan in Elam.[7] The possible association of these two events suggests that Anshan may have been the chief city of the district of Awan.[8] The sudden disappearance of Awan could then be explained in a perfectly reasonable historical context. Indeed the sources show that both Awan and Anshan are closely associated with Elam and the Elamites in the earliest historical phase, some time contemporaneously but never in the same text. It would appear that the Kings of Awan of the old Elamite period became the Kings of Anshan and Susa of later dynasties. The political divisions of Awan, Susa, Elam and Simashki, which were contemporary with the dynasty of Awan, would then continue in the districts of Anshan, Susa, Elam and Simashki of the succeeding dynasties. The available evidence suggests that Awan may attest an alternate, perhaps an early Elamite name for the region called Anshan by later Sumerians and Elamites.

---

[1] *Ibid.*, 95–7.
[2] V. Scheil, *RA* XXVIII (1931), 1–3.
[3] G. Barton, *The Royal Inscriptions of Sumer and Akkad* (New Haven, 1929), 114.
[4] *Ibid.*, 124.
[5] *Ibid.*, 128–30.
[6] F. W. König, *Corpus Inscriptionum Elamicarum* I, *Die altelamischen Texte* (Hanover, 1923), no. 3. On the identification of Khita in this text see G. Cameron, *History of Early Iran* (Chicago, 1936), 34.
[7] Barton, *op. cit.*, 184.
[8] Gudea is sometimes placed in the last quarter of the 23rd century B.C. However recent comparisons of dynastic lists show that Gudea would have reigned closer to 2220 B.C. See Hansman, *Iran* X (1972), 101, note 11; also *CAH* I, pt. 1 (3rd edn., 1970), 219.

ELAMITE–ACHAEMENIAN ANSHAN

After the fall of Awan a new Elamite dynasty rose in the district of Simashki which is probably to be located in the region of modern Isfahan.[1] At this period the Sumerians appear to have maintained some measure of political control at Susa in south-west Iran and in Anshan in the east. Shulgi (2095–2048 B.C.), a ruler of the third dynasty of Ur, married one of his daughters to the *ishshak* or governor of Anshan.[2] But Shulgi also claims to have laid waste to Anshan.[3] A temporary peace was apparently established when Shu-Sin, son and successor of Shulgi, like his father gave a daughter in marriage to a governor of Anshan.[4] This state of relations, however, was not to last. In about 2021 B.C., a few years after Ibbi-Sin, a son of Shu-Sin, succeeded to the throne of Ur, the King of Simashki had occupied the land of Awan (Anshan) and Susa in Elam. By 2017 B.C. Ibbi-Sin regained much of this territory;[5] but his success proved only temporary for we learn that within a few years the Elamites had waged a successful military campaign against Ur. Following his defeat, the last King of Ur, Ibbi-Sin, was carried off to Anshan together with a statue of the Sumerian moon-god, Nanna. A generation later Gimil-ilishu, second King of Isin brought back Nanna,[6] the God of Ur, from Anshan.[7] Finally we learn that Gungunum fifth King of Larsa boasts of military victories in Anshan (*c.* 1928 B.C.).[8]

It is evident from the texts that Anshan/Awan had been an important Elamite political centre during the last half of the 3rd millennium B.C. The archaeological remains at Malyān, identified as Anshan, would seem to bear out this assessment. The site is surrounded by a rectangular wall of mud brick, now much eroded, which measures approximately 1 km by 0.8 km. The cultural deposit within the enclosure rises to a height of from 4 to 6 metres.[9] Surface surveys of the pottery remains collected at Malyān indicate that perhaps one third of the ancient settlement there (between 30 and 50 hectares) was occupied from the late 4th millennium B.C. to the later part of the 3rd millennium B.C.[10] The distribution of

---

[1] On the location of Simashki see E. Herzfeld, *The Persian Empire* (Wiesbaden, 1968), 179–80.
[2] F. Thureau-Dangin, *Die sumerischen und akkadischen Königsinschriften* (Leipzig, 1907), 230.
[3] *Ibid.*, 231–7.
[4] C. Virolleaud, *ZA* XIX (1905–6), 384.
[5] L. Legrain, *Business Documents of the Third Dynasty of Ur, Ur Excavation Texts* III (London, 1928), no. 1421.
[6] A. Falkenstein, *Die Welt des Orients* I (1947–52), 379, 383.
[7] Gadd and Legrain, *Royal Inscriptions: Ur Excavation Texts* I (London, 1928), no. 100.
[8] L. Matous, *AfO* XX (1952), 304ff.
[9] W. Sumner, *Iran* XII (1974), 158.
[10] The pottery defining this sequence of occupation is termed Banesh ware. On the extent and the dating of this ware at Malyān see *ibid.*, 160, 167.

later pottery suggests that the major occupation of the site (approximately 130 hectares) occurred during the later centuries of the 3rd millennium and continued into the early centuries of the 2nd millennium B.C.[1] This is the period when Anshan is given prominent notice in the cuneiform texts.

The text of Gungunum (c. 1928 B.C.) referred to above, contains the last mention of Anshan, district or city, to be found in Mesopotamian sources for over 1,300 years. Political strife at home had apparently weakened the control which successive Mesopotamian states maintained from time to time over the affairs of south Iran and a new line of Elamite kings was eventually able to re-establish local rule in their own country. Epart, the founder of this new dynasty (c. 1890 B.C.), was also the first known Elamite leader to call himself King of Anshan and Susa.[2] References to Anshan during the remaining centuries of the 2nd millennium B.C. are attested only in inscriptions and texts of the successive Elamite dynasties of this period.

Shilhakha (c. 1870–1840 B.C.), the heir of Epart in Elam, styled himself, in addition to king, *sukkal-maḫ* or grand regent, a Sumerian appellation. During this period the title *sukkal* or regent of Elam and Simashki and sukkal of Susa are also commonly used.[3] The sons of the ruling sukkal-maḫ normally filled the offices of the two sukkal, though inscriptions show that the sukkal-maḫ on occasion would hold all three titles. However, throughout the approximately 300-year rule of the Eparti kings, there is no record of a sukkal of Anshan. This could mean that Anshan consisted at that time of a district subject entirely to the jurisdiction of the sukkal-maḫ. It has been suggested, on the other hand, that the sukkal-maḫ and the sukkal of Susa were both resident in the city of Susa. A relationship of this sort in the same town could have caused political tension.[4] Indeed, any decree of the Elamite king which might apply to the political district of Susa required ratification by the sukkal of Susa. Yet the case for Susa as the Elamite capital of this period would seem to be the most plausible. Anshan is hardly mentioned in Elamite texts during the whole of the Eparti dynasty except as used in the conventional title of the sukkal-maḫ. A political decline of the older capital is perhaps implied. This finding would appear to be supported

---

[1] Kaftari ware which succeeded the Banesh assemblage at Malyān is tentatively dated between 2000 and 1700 B.C. See *ibid.*, 160, 173.

[2] V. Scheil, *RA* XXVI (1929), 1.

[3] On the term sukkal-maḫ see Cameron, 71–2.

[4] W. Hinz, *The Lost World of Elam* (London, 1972), 5.

by the indications of the archaeological survey carried out at Malyān, the site of the city of Anshan. These show that with the disappearance of the Kaftari sequence of pottery there during the early second millennium B.C., the distribution of the succeeding Qaleh ware on the site is greatly reduced from that of the Kaftari.[1] This suggests that the city of Anshan at Malyān was very severely depopulated during the first third of the 2nd millennium B.C.

Susa, on the other hand, which appears not to have expanded significantly during the ascendancy of earlier Elamite dynasties into a major political centre, was certainly to do so with the rise of Epart and his successors in Elam. Numerous inscriptions found at Susa attest to the building activities undertaken there by different sukkal-maḫ and by various of the sukkal of Susa. The extensive excavations made by Ghirshman in the 'ville royale' at Susa have shown that much of this very large quarter of the ancient city was first built upon in the earlier 2nd millennium B.C.[2] This evidence would seem to support the possibility that the main political centre of Elam may have been moved from its traditional location at Anshan to Susa within the period associated with the expansion at the latter site.

Whereas in southern Mesopotamia the kingdom of Babylonia fell to Kassite and allied invaders from the north in about 1593 B.C., cuneiform texts continue to mention Elamite rulers until the final quarter of the 16th century B.C. It is not known whether these later governments in south-west Iran were subject to the Kassite alliance or, indeed, whether it was the Kassites who eventually put an end to the house of Epart. Whatever the cause, after about 1520 B.C. we have no further record of the Elamites for over 200 years.

During the last half of the 14th century B.C. an apparently independent Elamite dynasty reappears suddenly on the historical scene. The earliest known ruler of this new line to adopt the old title King of Anshan and Susa was Attar-kittah (1310–1300 B.C.).[3]

No inscriptions or other texts are known from the dynastic predecessors of Attar-kittah and no foundation or rebuilding dedications of this king or of his immediate successor Humban-numena (1300–1275 B.C.) were found at Susa. Only at Liyān located near the centre of the Bushire peninsula, an island-like extension of the coastal plain of

---

[1] Sumner, *op. cit.*, 160, suggests that present understanding of the pottery at Malyān indicates a considerable decrease in population there during the last half of the second millennium B.C.
[2] R. Ghirshman, *Arts Asiatiques* XV (1967), 4–12.
[3] R. Labat, "Elam *c.* 1600–1200 B.C.", *CAH* I, pt. 1 (3rd edn., 1970), 384.

modern Fars, have inscribed bricks of Humban-numena been recovered. The Liyān texts commemorate the construction by this king of a religious sanctuary at that site.[1]

Inscriptions of Untash-napirisha (1275–1240 B.C.), son and successor of Humban-numena, are found at Susa in Khuzistan and also at the religious centre of Dur-Untash (now Choga-Zambil) located 30 km to the south-east of Susa. Dur Untash bears the name of Untash-napirisha and was probably his chief place of residence. But the absence of any significant inscriptions of the father of Untash-napirisha at Susa or elsewhere in Khuzistan prompted Labat to suggest that the capital of Humban-numena may have been situated in the province of Anshan.[2] If this were so, however, the finding of only sparse archaeological remains of the corresponding period of occupation at Malyān suggests that the main seat of government was not then located at the city of Anshan. On the other hand, beaker-shaped jars have been found at Malyān which are closely similar to vessels dating from the last quarter of the second millennium B.C. excavated at Susa. Inscribed bricks of the Susian Elamite king Hutelutush-Inshushinak (1120–1110 B.C.) have also been recovered at Malyān.[3] The evidence suggests that Susa and Anshan were culturally and politically linked at this period, but that the latter settlement during the late second millennium was little more than an outpost of the eastern Elamite territories of the kings resident at Susa. The reign of Hutelutush-Inshushinak ended with a devastating invasion of Elamite territories (c. 1110 B.C.) by Nebuchadrezzer I of Babylon.[4] This event marked the effective end of Elam as an independent ruling power for nearly three hundred years.

Not until 821 B.C. do we hear again of the Elamites, who are then found allied with the Chaldeans against the Assyrian king Shamshi-Adad V.[5] Although Elam did not maintain a political unity during these intervening centuries of obscurity, local chieftains must have preserved a semblance of control in areas where their authority had been traditionally exercised. Cameron suggests that local rule would probably have remained strongest in the remote eastern districts of Elamite territories, sc. the region of modern Fars.[6] Even so and despite their

[1] König, *Corpus Inscriptionum Elamicarum*, no. 40.
[2] Labat, *op. cit.*, 8.
[3] See p. 25, n. 4.
[4] R. Thompson, *Reports of the Astrologers of Nineveh and Babylon* (London, 1900), no. 200, rev. 5.
[5] D. Luckenbill, *Ancient Records of Assyria and Babylonia* I (Chicago, 1926), no. 726.
[6] Cameron, 156.

isolation from the aggressive Mesopotamians, the inhabitants of Fars were eventually to suffer new pressures from Iranian migrants moving down from the north. Whether or not the coming of the Iranians caused the divided provinces of Elam to support the rise of a new centralized authority in south-west Iran is a question which cannot be answered on present evidence. Whatever the reason, by c. 742 B.C. Humban-nikash I had become king of an apparently reconstituted Elamite federation.[1]

Humban-nikash was succeeded by a nephew, Shutruk-Nahhunte II (717–699 B.C.), who took the old title Great King of Anshan and Susa.[2] Shutruk-Nahhunte entered into an alliance with the Chaldeans against both Sargon II and Sennacherib of Assyria; his military efforts, however, were not successful and he was eventually replaced in Anshan and Susa by a younger brother, Halludush-Inshushinak (699–693 B.C.). The new Elamite leader invaded Babylonia and temporarily held parts of it from the Assyrians, but Sennacherib quickly retook most of these territories. Halludush-Inshushinak, meanwhile, was deposed in Elam and replaced by his son Kudur-Nahhunte (693–692 B.C.). The short rule of Kudur-Nahhunte is of interest to our study in that from his reign onwards, no Elamite head of state is known to have assumed the ancient royal title King of Anshan and Susa.[3] Such an omission would suggest a loss to the Elamites of at least the area of Anshan either by Kudur-Nahhunte or by his immediate predecessor.

Following the reconquest of Babylonia, Sennacherib invaded the Elamite territories which lay to the north of Susa. As a result of this campaign, the weakened Kudur-Nahhunte was forced to flee and seek refuge in the mountains of Hidalu.

Humban-numena (692–687 B.C.) who succeeded Kudur-Nahhunte in Elam, renewed the old political alliance with Babylonia and sought military assistance from a number of neighbouring districts, including the lands of Anshan and Parsuash.[4] It is to be noted that in these late references Anshan is treated as a separate territory and not subject to centralized Elamite authority. What happened in Anshan at this time is bound up with the political and territorial relationship of that place with Parsua, Parsuash and Parsamash/Parsuwash, and of those same regions with the Assyrian empire. To understand these associations better, we

[1] Luckenbill, *Ancient Records* II, no. 84.
[2] V. Scheil, *Mémoires de la Délégation en Perse* V (1904), no. 84.
[3] See Cameron, 158–65.
[4] Luckenbill, *Ancient Records* II, no. 252.

must establish the location of Parsua and that of the similarly-named Parsuash.

Assyrian texts of the 9th century B.C. give the earliest reference to the land of Parsua. According to the latest studies this district, which was invaded successively by Shalmaneser III, Adad-Nirari III and Tiglath-pleser III, is to be located in the vicinity of Kirmānshāh in western Iran.[1] Inscriptions of Sargon II (721–705 B.C.) identify the same area as Parsuash and show it to have become by that reign an established province of the Assyrian empire. It was presumably the people of a rebellious Parsuash who, under that name, were identified as allies of Humban-numena against the armies of Sennacherib. At some time subsequent to the formation of this alliance a major clash with the Assyrians took place at Halule in Mesopotamia. Sennacherib claims a considerable victory over the joint Babylonian/Elamite forces at the battle (c. 691 B.C.); Babylonian texts record a more inconclusive result.[2]

Following the reign of Humban-numena in Elam, rival claimants to the central kingship seem concurrently to have controlled various parts of the old domains. Periodic attempts were made to reform the pan-Elamite alliance, notably by Tempt-Humban-Inshushinak (663–653 B.C.) of Susa. However, his efforts met with only a passing success. Tempt-Humban was eventually defeated by an army of Ashurbanipal and several districts in Elam which had been overrun were thereafter placed in the control of local chiefs whose support the Assyrians claimed.[3] These supposed loyalties did not last, for a year later, Humban-nikash III, vassal governor in Madaktu, supported a new uprising in Babylonia against the Assyrians. The rebel Elamite suffered an inglorious rout by enemy troops at Der and fled to the mountainous district of Hidalu[4] to seek aid from that region and from the people of neighbouring Parsumash.[5] A revolt in part of Elam at this time, however, caused the fall of Humban-nikash. He was replaced by Tammarit (651–649 B.C.) who continued local resistance against Assyria. Tammarit urged Hidalu and the adjoining district of Parsamash (Parsumash) to send troops in support of his campaign. The people of Parsamash apparently did not respond at once and the delay seems to have proven costly to the allies. By 649 B.C. most of the Elamite lands

[1] For the most recent study on the location of Parsua, see L. Levine, *Iran* XII (1974), 106–13.
[2] See Cameron for sources and discussion.
[3] A. Piepkorn, *Historical Prism Inscriptions of Ashurbanipal* (Chicago, 1933), 70ff.
[4] On the location of Hidalu see Hansman, *Iran* X (1972), 108, note 54.
[5] L. Waterman, *Royal Correspondence of the Assyrian Empire* II (Ann Arbor, Mich., 1930), 410–12.

up to the borders of Parsamash had been overrun by forces loyal to Ashurbanipal.[1]

Although the Elamites seem to have regained a measure of local autonomy in succeeding years, as recounted in Chapter 1, p. 23 later Assyrian and Achaemenian advances finally put an end to independent Elam.

A king of Parsuwash named Kurash is mentioned in an Assyrian text relating to the destruction of Elam by Ashurbanipal.[2] This Kurash, recognized as Cyrus I, offered submission to Ashurbanipal and sent his son to Nineveh as a testimony of good faith. It is with this reference that the House of Achaemenes first enters the historical record.

Cyrus I is given the title "Great King of Anshan" in a text of his grandson Cyrus II (the Great).[3] It would appear that the first Cyrus was political chief in Parsuwash and ruler of the former Elamite province of Anshan, which we have associated with the district of Fars. The two lands would seem to be identical. Parsuwash apparently is an Assyrian rendering of the name from which Old Persian Pārsa derives, the ancestral form of present-day Fars and referring to the same district, the Persis of the Greeks. Anshan remained the traditional name in south Mesopotamia for the northern area of Fars down to the New-Babylonian period. But when did the Achaemenians accede to kingship in Fars?

A comparison of the relevant texts shows that the Achaemenians were governing in Anshan/Parsuwash at least a generation before Ashurbanipal commenced his decisive invasion of Elam. As we have seen, the earlier alliance of Anshan and Elam against Sennacherib (691 B.C.) occurred during the reign of the Elamite king Humban-numena, this being shortly after the rulers of Elam abandoned the old title King of Anshan. Cyrus I (of Parsuwash) recognized the supremacy of Ashurbanipal near the time, or shortly after Assyrian troops had overrun the district of Elam (c. 646 B.C.). As Cyrus II gives both his grandfather Cyrus I and his great grandfather Teispes the title "King of Anshan",[4] the first Cyrus must have already been ruler in Anshan at the time of his contacts with Assyria. Thus according to the relative chronology of these events, we have a period of some 45 years between the first alliance of Anshan/Parsuwash with Elam and the submission of Cyrus I. This length of time could fall well within the limits of the

---

[1] Ibid., 300–03.
[2] E. Weidner, AfO VII (1931), 4.
[3] J. Pritchard, Ancient Near Eastern Texts (Princeton, N.J., 1953), 316.
[4] Loc. cit.

possible reigns of two successive Achaemenian kings. Although Achaemenes (Old Persian Hakhāmanish) is usually recognized as eponymous founder of the Achaemenian royal house, it is his son Teispes (OP Chishpish) who is first called "Great King in Anshan". Thus it would appear more probable that Teispes, rather than his father Achaemenes, established Achaemenian rule in Anshan/Parsuwash/ Parsa/Fars and became the ally of Elam against Sennacherib.[1] It is not likely, on the other hand, that the land of Parsuash, allied with the lands of Anshan and Elam in this campaign (see above pp. 31–2) was Parsa. Had Parsuash and Anshan been under the same local rule, the two would hardly have made separate alliances with the Elamite king (see above, p. 31). Therefore while Parsuash, Parsuwash and Parsumash may be different spellings of one and the same name, there appear to have been several different geographical areas identified by it. The first, Parsuash, is a Persian land which is to be located in the region of Kirmānshāh. The second, Parsuwash/Parsumash, identifies the Achaemenian territories which are to be located in south Iran.

Whereas the Chronicle of Nabonidus, the last king of Babylon (556–539 B.C.), refers in one passage to Cyrus II as King of Anshan, in a later entry Cyrus is identified as king in Parsu[2] (an Akkadian rendering of Old Persian Pārsa). Thus as we have seen in the case of earlier references to Anshan and to Parsuwash, Anshan was also considered at this later period a part of the province now called Fars.

An archaeological survey of the surface pottery at the site of Malyān has produced only a handful of Achaemenian sherds[3] and we may conclude from this that the Achaemenians did not maintain a significant settlement there. However, as suggested above, the name Anshan may have survived in the reduced form Āsh, in the region of Malyān, until the early Islamic period.[4] The replacement of Anshan as name of the province would have occurred much earlier, when the Achaemenian Persians transferred the ethnic name of their nation, Pārsa, to their new homeland.

Anshan is mentioned in §40 of the Behistun inscription of Darius I, but its location is not specified. Classical texts refer only to Persis.

---

[1] It is of course possible that Achaemenes ruled a part of Anshan without having the title "king". On the genealogy of the Achaemenian line see R. Kent, *Old Persian Grammar* (New Haven, 1953), 158–9.
[2] S. Smith, *Babylonian Historical Texts* (London, 1924), 100ff.
[3] Sumner, *Iran* XII (1974), 158.
[4] See p. 25, n. 3.

ELAMITE–ACHAEMENIAN ANSHAN

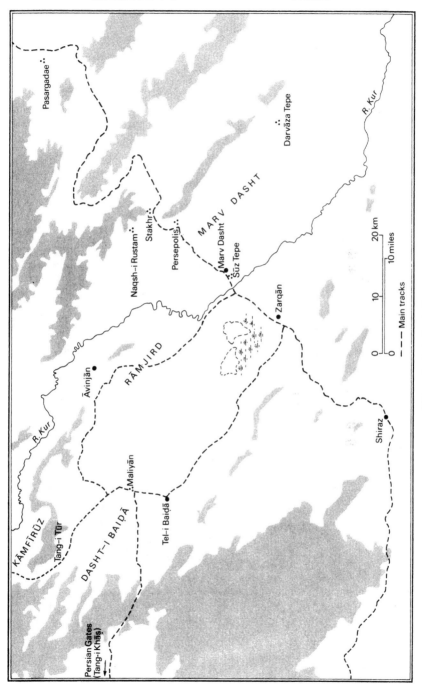

Map 1. Ancient sites in Fars.

CHAPTER 3

MEDIA

I. THE MEDES AND THE NEIGHBOURING COUNTRIES

1. *The earliest recorded information on the population of the Iranian highlands*

During the epoch which forms the subject of this chapter the name Media (Iranian *Māda*), as covering the entire historical region which later bore that name, did not yet exist. However, for the sake of simplicity, we shall with some anachronistic licence speak of "Media" in the broad meaning of this geographical term, understanding by it the territory limited in the west by the Zagros mountain ranges, in the north by the river Araxes and the Alburz mountain range, in the east by the salt desert Dasht-i Kavīr, and in the south by a line passing along the watershed which separates the valleys of the rivers flowing towards the centre of the highland, from those of the rivers Saimarreh-Karkhah, Āb-i Diz, Kārūn and the basin of Lake Nairīz.

Of the other tribes inhabiting the Iranian highlands outside Elam at the dawn of history, written sources in Sumerian, Akkadian, and Elamite mention the Qutī, the Lullubī, and the Kassites, as well as the Hurrians whose original home lay outside Iran but who partly encroached on some regions of present-day Kurdistan up to Lake Urmīya.

The Qutī, under the name of Gu-ti-um^{KI}, or more correctly Qù-ti-um^{KI}, appear in the historical arena at the end of the 23rd century B.C. during the reign of Narām-Su'en, king of Akkade, who at that time held under his sway the whole of Mesopotamia up to the foot-hills of the Zagros, the Armenian Taurus and the Taurus in Asia Minor; Elam, too, was subject to him. To judge from a later Akkadian tradition Narām-Su'en had to fight the Qutī and possibly fell in a battle against them. Apparently at that time the leader of the Qutī, Enridawazir, penetrated deep into Southern Mesopotamia and seized the sacred town of Nippur, where an inscription was composed for him by Sumerian scribes.

Although the Akkadians were undoubtedly far superior in development to the Qutī, the Old Akkadian army was still rather primitive both in equipment (a copper helmet, a hatchet of the same metal, a javelin and a bow) and in organization; this could have allowed the mountaineers to defeat it, probably by overwhelming numbers. Narām-Su'en's son, Šarkališarrī, succeeded in restoring the situation in his favour and in capturing the Qutī leader, Sarlagab. However, after Šarkališarrī's death internecine strife broke out in Southern Mesopotamia in which the Qutī leader, Elulumeš, also took part; as a result Akkade became a state of merely local importance, while the hegemony in Southern Mesopotamia passed into the hands of the Qutī.

The "Sumerian King List" compiled from various sources soon after the fall from power of the Qutī, and intended to show the existence from time immemorial of despotic state rule, includes the Qutī in order to create the appearance of an uninterrupted succession of legitimate dynasties in Southern Mesopotamia. But the enumeration of the Qutī rulers is somewhat peculiar: it allots exceptional brevity to each of the reigns, and in the beginning states in a note that "the Qutī tribe had no king".[1] If, as seems to be the case, this note corresponds to reality, how are we to explain that nevertheless short-lived reigns are attributed to Qutī "kings"? Certainly not by a state of perpetual feud, as this would be incompatible with the retention by the Qutī for ninety-one years, of their dominion over the most developed state of the time. As shown by W. K. Šilejko, their power in Southern Mesopotamia was firmly established; even so powerful a ruler as Gudea of Lagaš apparently paid them tribute. It is possible that the Qutī rulers were not kings but tribal chieftains elected for a term. Their power in Southern Mesopotamia was destroyed in (*c.*) 2109 B.C. by Utuḫegal, ruler of the Sumerian city of Uruk.

The precise location of the original home of the Qutī cannot be established; suggestions that it should be sought in the region of present-day Kirkuk or in the Judi-dagh mountains are not supported by sufficient evidence. Apparently the inhabitants of Southern Mesopotamia gave the name Qutī to the population of the Zagros mountains which belonged to the area of the "painted ware" culture. Their language, judging by their names, differed from that of the neighbouring Hurrians. Although the tribute levied from Southern Mesopotamia must have enriched the Qutī, or at least their tribal chiefs, this does not

---

[1] This is the meaning of the original text of the note in the present author's opinion.

seem to have led to noticeable alterations in their social structure. For later times our information on the Qutī, and in general on the tribes of the Zagros, remains scanty. The campaigns of the kings of "Sumer and Akkad" (the so-called Third Dynasty of Ur) against various strongholds on the western slopes of the Zagros are often mentioned, sometimes together with the names of their rulers (Hurrian and others). There also exist lists of women and children driven as slaves from the mountains into the Sumerian camps where they soon perished. Their names seem to be Qutī.

The Hurrian strongholds in the nearer foot-hills (Simurrum, now Altın-köprü, Urbillum, now Erbil, Kimaš), and those in the more remote regions of the Zagros (Ḫumurti, Ḫarši, Ganḫar, or Karaḫar) seem to have been centres of extremely primitive city-states; the importance of the part that could still have been played by extended family links, with extended families inhabiting characteristic dwelling-towers, and by voluntary, not administrative, unions can be judged even from much later documents (2nd millennium B.C.) from Arrapḫa (Kirkuk), a town situated in the hill-country at no great distance from the plain; the primitivity of the social conditions in these states appears also from documents of the 2nd millennium found in Šuššarā (Tell-Shemshara), and from a Babylonian charter exempting the population from a small contribution of beer, that has come down to us from a fortress in the heart of the Zagros as late as the early 1st millennium B.C. The Lullubī mountaineers were the objects of slave-hunting by the inhabitants of the Hurrian towns of the 2nd millennium B.C.; less frequently it was the Lullubī who carried off Hurrians into slavery. In the mountain regions, in tombs of the 2nd millennium B.C. (e.g. on the site of Geoy-Tepe) burials of slaves together with their masters have been discovered. They testify both to the existence of slavery and to its negligible economic importance, as in a more advanced society slave manpower would not be expended in human sacrifice.

In the foot-hills of the Zagros, along with the city-states larger, though ephemeral, tribal and even state federations were sometimes formed. The most powerful of these was probably that of the Qutī mentioned above. We also know of the state (?) of Lullubum, at the head of which was a certain Sidurru (?) in the days of Narām-Su'en, who defeated it. Another "king" of Lullubum, Anubānini, of Akkadian origin, had an inscription carved in Akkadian on a rock in Sar-i Pul-i Zohāb (the ancient Padir). We do not know whether a certain

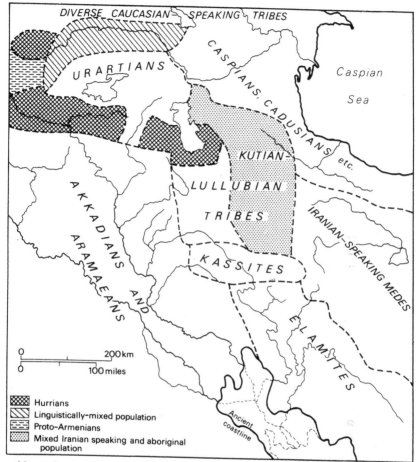

Map 2. Approximate distribution of settlements of ethnic groups at the beginning of the 1st millennium B.C.

Līšir-pir'ini, son of Ikkib-Šaḫmad (?), was a Lullubian or some other king;[1] he too left an inscription, in the mountains of Shēhān above the valley of the Diyālā (Āb-i Sirvān) river.

In the 18th century B.C. (anno 1741) incursions begin into Mesopotamia of another tribe – the Kassites (Akkadian *Kaššī*) – who apparently lived in present-day Luristan where the Kassites, or "Cossaei", survived till the days of Alexander. Southern Mesopotamia came fully under the domination of the Kassites only in the 16th century under the Kassite king Agum II the Merciful Sword (*Agum kak rēme*). In his

[1] Formerly this name was mistakenly read as "Tardunni, son of Ikki", or "Ḫubbani-pir'ini".

inscription Agum calls himself "the illustrious descendant of the god Šuqamuna..., king of the Kassites and the Akkadians, king of the vast land of Babylon, who has populated Ašnunak (Tell Asmar in the valley of the Diyālā river) with numerous people, king of Padān and Almān (mountains to the east of the Diyālā valley and to the north-west of Elam), king of the Qutī – the barbarous men". The new Kassite kingdom in Babylon received the name of "Kār-Duniaš" after one of the Kassite gods. The Kassites of Southern Mesopotamia became entirely Babylonized in culture, although for centuries the Kassite warriors formed here a special privileged stratum; later, apparently as a result of the activity of the Assyrian and Elamite kings, Kassite Babylonia was cut off from the Kassite habitats in the mountains.

An analysis of Kassite glosses in Akkadian texts, as well as of Kassite names of men and gods, has disproved the view that the Kassites were Indo-Europeans, or at least worshipped some of the Indo-European gods. The names of the god Duniaš, of the goddess of the Earth Miriaš, of the Sun-god Šuriaš, and of the storm-god Ubriaš (also Burariaš), of the goddess of the mountains Šimalia etc. have no Indo-European etymologies, contrary to what used to be thought. The first four names, for example, contain the Kassite word *iaš* "earth". Neither has the assumption so far been confirmed of a close parentage of the Kassite language on the one hand with Elamite, and on the other with the language of the Caspii by the Caspian sea. Of the latter in fact nothing has survived except the name of the tribe itself, and even of it we cannot be sure that it was a self-appellation. There are, however, grounds for affirming that the Kassites introduced horse-breeding and the light chariot into Babylonia on a considerable scale.

In the second half of the 2nd millennium B.C. expeditions were led into the heart of the Zagros by the Assyrian kings Adadnērarī I, Shalmaneser I, Tukultī-Ninurta I, Tiglathpileser I and others (14th to 11th centuries B.C.), as well as by the Elamite kings Šutruk-Nahhunte I, Šilhak-Inšušinak I and others (12th century). In their inscriptions some names of localities and inhabited places have survived (in the Assyrian inscriptions they seem to be mainly Qutī, and Kassite (?); Akkadian etc. in the Elamite), but their localization is very difficult and uncertain. Only a few of the inhabited places mentioned by Šilhak-Inšušinak occur also in Assyrian inscriptions of the 1st millennium B.C. A comparison of Elamite and Assyrian texts suggests that these strongholds and settlements must be sought mainly along the road from present-day Khūzistān to Khurramābād – Kirmānshāh – Tuz-Khurmatli and further along the Tigris. It is of interest that some of them were specialized centres for craftsmen. How long Elamite influence in the other parts of the Iranian highlands lasted (cf. Ch. 1) – whether, for instance, only till the middle or the end of the 3rd millennium B.C., or till the end of the 2nd, or even till the beginning of the 1st – is not at all clear.

2. *Iranian-speaking tribes in Iran*

Not later than at some time in the first half of the 2nd millennium B.C. tribes speaking Indo-Iranian reached the Iranian plateau. As mentioned above (p. 3), Indo-Iranian is a branch of the Proto-Indo-European dialects, spoken in the 4th and early 3rd millennia B.C. in eastern-central Europe.

To the problem of the spread of Indo-European from Europe to Iran and India archaeology, and physical anthropology in its historical aspect, contribute decisively, though in a negative sense. The ethnical movements in those early times were not, it seems, migrations of conquering hordes completely displacing, let alone annihilating, the autochthonous population. No tribe of that epoch can have been numerous, least of all any that was on the move. None had means of moving swiftly over vast areas. Therefore new tribes only oozed into countries suitably thinly populated, though not so thinly that the natives were not usually more numerous than the immigrants. Merger came about only gradually, by way of intermarriage, adoption, and sometimes the temporary establishment of social relations in which one tribe was the dominant, the other the dependent. We must bear in mind that before the emergence of class society there could exist *some* ideological difference between the dominant and the dependent group, but hardly much difference in their ways of supporting life, the produce of labour being insufficient to feed two at the expense of one. There were therefore never strong bars to merger. The proof that the ethnical movements had the character described above, is the fact that early migrations can in most cases be established neither by changes in material culture detectable to archaeologists (the culture of natives, being the most suitable for local conditions, is usually taken over by the immigrants), nor by changes in physical type. The population of most areas at any given point between Europe and India has not changed appreciably in the last five to seven thousand years, apart from features which are either late or minor. Thus an early language in migration can be compared not so much to the displacement of the mass of a stream as it runs from its source to the sea, but rather to the surging of waves and the appearance of ripples on the surface of standing waters. It is only the *wave* of the language which changed as it passed from one population to another, not the populations themselves, except for the minor increase in size which the immigration of bearers of new languages caused. But whatever the importance of the change in languages for the subsequent cultural history – the language being a most important vehicle for conveying ideas – it is the autochthones of the Iranian Plateau, and not the Proto-Indo-European tribes of Europe, which are, in the main, the ancestors, in the physical sense of the word, of the present-day Iranians.

What apparently happened was that the neolithic cattle-breeders and agriculturists of central-southeastern Europe who spoke Proto-Indo-European, reached in the early 3rd millennium B.C. by reason of their relatively efficient economy, a level of prosperity at which the survival of children began, if only by little, to exceed the mortality rate; the population grew and expanded in various directions. There is an empirical rule that languages of pastoral populations, usually more or less uniform over vast areas, oust the more isolated languages not understandable outside each of the tiny communities of its speakers, be they forest-dwellers, early settled agriculturists, or mere food-collectors. So the ring-wave of Indo-European began in the middle of the 3rd millennium B.C. to roll out from the centre to the peripheral areas, reaching finally the Atlantic in the west and the Bay of Bengal in the east, the Polar Sea in the north and the Mediterranean in the south.

It is pretty certain that the pastoral tribes with subsidiary agriculture who created the archaeological Srubnaya (Kurgan) and Andronovo cultures of the steppes of Eastern Europe, Kazakhstan and Soviet Central Asia in the 2nd millennium B.C. were the direct precursors of the Scythians and the Sacae, i.e. of the "Eastern" Iranians. But this means that the division of the tribes speaking Indo-Iranian (Aryan), into Indo-Aryans and Iranians, must have antedated the creation of these two archaeological cultures. It also means that the ancestors of the speakers of Indo-Aryan and "Western" Iranian idioms (Median, Persian and Parthian) must have reached the south-western part of Central Asia and Eastern Iran already earlier, by the end of the 3rd or the beginning of the 2nd millennium B.C. During the 2nd millennium a considerable part of the population of the Iranian Plateau must already have spoken Indo-Iranian languages, perhaps even Old Iranian languages.

The ethnical composition of the population of western Media towards the beginning of the 1st millennium B.C. may be thought of as follows:

There still were vast areas inhabited by a population speaking pre-Iranian languages. The whole expanse to the south of Lake Urmīya, and also perhaps small areas scattered in the direction of Lake Van, were probably still inhabited by a population termed Qutī-Lullubī by the Assyrians and Babylonians, the so-called Lullubī mainly in a wide band to the west, the Qutī in the more north-easterly regions. Assyrian sources identify the country Lullume with the country Zamūa (Mazamūa). This last term, in its widest use, was applied to the territories from the hilly lowlands south of Lake Urmīya ("Inner Zamūa") to the head-waters of the Diyālā (Āb-i Sirvan). Within the borders of Zamūa in the broadest sense, it would seem, from a comparison of the itineraries of the Assyrian and Urartian military expeditions in the 9th to the 8th centuries, that among other provinces also the province of Parsūa was situated. However, the actual existence of a distinct Lullubian language is doubtful, as in any case the term *lulu-* represented throughout the Near East, and still does in some places, a common noun.[1]

As late as during the reign of Sargon II (722–705 B.C.) Assyrian sources recorded a Qutī population in the western part of historical Media, approximately from the west of the mountain massif of Shahberdi–Kafelan-kuh (to the west of the valley of the Safīd-rūd, or Qyzyl-üzen) to the mountain range of Alvand.[2] In the regions bordering

---

[1] Akkad. *lullu, lullû* "mountaineer, barbarian, savage"; Urart. *lulu-* "enemy, alien"; Hurrian, Hittite *lullaḫḫe, lūlaḫḫi* "foreign, foreigner"; Greek *Leleges* "local hostile population in relation to new settlers in Asia Minor" – from Carian *lauleki*, from an older *lūlaḫḫi*. Among the present-day Chechens and Ingushes in the mountains of the Great Caucasus *lūlaχo, loalaeχo* means "neighbour". The form *Lullub(um), Lullume* may have been adopted by Akkadian through the intermediary of Elamite, cf. the Elamite markers of the plural, *-b/p-*, and of abstract and collective nouns, *-me*.

[2] Here one should distinguish the term *Qutī* or "*Gu-ti-um*^{KI}", often designating autochthonous non-Akkadian and non-Iranian mountain tribes, from the use of the archaic form *Gu-ti-um*^{KI} in Akkadian texts. Down to later times belonged to the system of archaic geographical terms of the high-flown style and designated the north-eastern and eastern highlands as a whole, and later Media in particular. Such terms go back to the works of Babylonian soothsayers and are to be explained by the practice of applying ancient omina concerning former nations and kingdoms to political situations arising in respect of more modern peoples and states. Therefore *Gutium* – originally "land of the Qutī" – began to designate any political power in the mountainous region

on Lake Urmīya in the west and north, and perhaps also south, there is some evidence of the presence of a Hurrian ethnical element, "Matiēnian" according to Herodotus. Assyrian sources of the 7th century mention also a certain "Meḫrānian" language in the western part of the historical province of Media, but what kind of language this was is at present hard to determine. More to the south, in the mountains of Luristan, lived Kassites and Iasubigallians.[1]

All these were ethnic elements known in this region since the 3rd or 2nd millennium B.C.; they were not related to the new Indo-European element, more exactly, the Iranian.

The question as to when and in what circumstances this element appeared in Iran has not been solved. There seems to be no hope of a direct and precise answer based on archaeological data: the immigration of the relevant tribes into the Iranian highlands must have had the character of a slow and gradual movement which did not bring about any sudden change in material culture.[2] Possible tentative correlation of very early Indo-European tribes with certain archaeological cultures will be dealt with in due course. As for written sources, down to the second quarter of the 1st millennium B.C. we have at our disposal only the laconic military records from Southern Mesopotamia, Elam, Assyria and Urartu which mention individual place-names and names of rulers, rarely of tribes. Even these belong almost exclusively to the western strip of the historical region of Media. Toponyms and personal names are very unsatisfactorily rendered in cuneiform writing. Etymological

in the north or the north-east of Babylonia; *Ummān-Manda*, originally the designation of some northern tribe, began to be applied in turn to the Cimmerians and to the Medes; *Subartu*, originally the "land of the pre-Hurrian population on the upper reaches of the Euphrates and the Tigris", then the "Land of the Hurrians", began to designate "Assyria"; *Amurru* changed from "the province of the tribe of the Amorites" to "Syria", *Magan* from "a land on the Persian Gulf" to "Egypt"; *Meluḫḫa* (or, better, *Melaḫ[ḫ]a*) from "India" to "Ethiopia", etc.

[1] Here was the centre of an extremely original handicraft of metalworkers: with "Luristan bronzes" are reckoned daggers and battle-axes of Babylonian origin, or imitating Babylonian artifacts. They probably belong to the times when Kassite warriors took service under the kings of Babylon and Elam in the 13th to 11th centuries. The same applies to a number of fancifully-worked harness ornaments and ritual vessels with images of deities and monsters, which belong already to the beginning of the 1st millennium B.C. and are sometimes ascribed to Indo-European immigrant tribes of horsemen.

[2] This is a common phenomenon in the history of antiquity. It is likewise impossible to determine on the basis of archaeological data the moment of the Semitization of Mesopotamia, or the time when in Asia Minor the "Hittite" Indo-European-speaking tribes came to prevail over the autochthonous. It should be noted that archaeologists are often too prone to attribute sharp changes observed in pottery and other material to ethnic migrations without sufficiently taking into account that such changes may be due to advances in technique as well as to changes in the structure of an ethnically homogeneous society. The emergence of a new fashion in the details of shape and ornament of vessels is not necessarily linked with ethnical change.

comparisons for determining their linguistic appurtenance can only be doubtful and tend to beg the question as the languages of the autochthones, with the exception to some extent of Hurrian, are known to us only from these very same names. It is for Indo-European languages alone that thousands of roots and word-bases are known that go far back to the times of Indo-Iranian unity, or to the even earlier times of Proto-Indo-European. But as the meanings of the proper names are not known, one can seldom be certain that any similarity with an Indo-European root is not merely accidental. Accordingly the appurtenance of a given name to one language-group or another too often lies beyond proof.

To-day it is held that during the second half of the 2nd millennium B.C. Indo-Aryan dialects prevailed in the northern part of the Indian sub-continent over the more ancient, presumably Proto-Dravidian dialects of the Harappa culture. From the middle of the 2nd millennium B.C. an unknown Indo-Iranian dialect (usually supposed to be Indo-Aryan, though proof of its non-Kafir and non-Iranian character is feeble) is attested by personal names of kings of Mitanni (a Hurrian kingdom in Northern Mesopotamia) and by names of some of the petty kings of city-states in Syria and Palestine. The petty kings in question were possibly of Mitannian origin. In addition, a long list of deities called upon to safeguard a state treaty between the Hittite kingdom and a king of Mitanni, includes among many others the names of four Indo-Iranian deities in Hurrianized form. Moreover, a manual for the training of chariot horses, which was composed after the fall of Mitanni in the 14th century B.C. by Hurrian horse-breeders for the benefit of Hittites who had previously used a different method of horse-training, contains several horse-breeding terms of Indo-Iranian provenance, recognizable despite the disguise successively imposed on them by Hurrian and Hittite transmission. However, Annelies Kammenhuber has convincingly shown that, contrary to previous belief, all this hardly justifies the assumption that live Indo-Iranian speech had spread into those regions.

It seems more likely that the names and terms in question were brought into Northern Mesopotamia from the north-east by a Mitannian (Matianian) dynasty shortly before 1550 B.C. as a result of earlier Matianian–Indo-Iranian contacts somewhere in the mountainous regions of north-western Iran, near Lake Urmīya. Matiāni, or Matiēni, probably the same as Hurrian Mitanni (*Maittanne*, or *Mī(t)tanne*), was the name borne by the Hurrian tribes precisely on this territory; it is here that a Matianian Hurrian dynasty could have formed relationships with Indo-Iranians. Alternatively an Indo-Iranian dynasty, later Hurrianized, may have taken over one of the Hurrian tribes which subsequently seized power in equally Hurrian Northern Mesopotamia.

Another formerly widespread opinion now disproved, is that the Indo-Iranians (or particularly the Indo-Aryans) arrived in the Near East and in India from the steppes of Eastern Europe through the Caucasus or through Central Asia as conquerors possessing a new technique of movement on light horse-drawn chariots and the tactics of horse-chariot battle still unknown to the peoples of the countries which they invaded. It has now been established that in the Near East the horse was domesticated already in the 3rd millennium B.C., when it was probably used for cross-breeding with donkeys. Not only in mountain regions but also in Mesopotamia horses were harnessed to war-chariots already in the 21st to 18th centuries B.C., although they were regarded as less aristocratic than donkeys or mules. In the steppe regions of Eastern Europe, Central Asia and Southern Siberia, by contrast, though bones of horses are found in settlements and tombs from as early as the 3rd millennium B.C. or even earlier,[1] fully reliable information on saddle horses goes back to *c.* the 13th century (the Alakul stage of the Andronovo culture). They belong to the period of transition of the local population to a semi-nomadic existence. But mass cavalry came to be formed in the steppes of present-day Ukraine, in the Volga region and in Central Asia only with the transition to a completely nomadic existence about the 12th–9th centuries B.C., followed by the long-range warlike raids of Cimmerians, Scythians and Sacae-Massagetae. But neither then, nor earlier, did the steppe-dwellers seem to have known the light, spoke-wheel war-chariot. The Pit Graves Culture and the Cis-Caucasian culture have heavy carts on massive wheels,[2] four or seldom two of them, probably harnessed mainly to oxen; in the majority of the regions of the Andronovo Culture (from which the Saka culture originated) even such carts are so far unknown.

The peoples of the Near East did not have to wait for the Aryans

[1] Cf. however the object found by R. A. Munčayev among remains of the Maikop culture in Northern Caucasus dating from the end of the 3rd millennium B.C. which he takes for part of a bridle bit.

[2] As pointed out to me by Miss E. E. Kuz'mina, the heavy wheel, the heavy cart, and the yoke were certainly known to all archaeologically traceable tribes of Eastern Europe that can claim Indo-European descent, these objects being probably invented locally and not imported from the Near East.

to form an army on horses and wheels. This was first formed in south-western Asia, and the reason why it preceded the more effective cavalry troops must have been the long-standing tradition of using war chariots drawn by donkeys; the East European steppe dwellers did not possess such traditions. The Indo-Europeans, when migrating, must have been obliged to move mainly on foot, accompanied by heavy ox-drawn carts, and only in later centuries also by a number of mounted scouts and herdsmen.

The centre of ancient horse-breeding, not only in the 2nd millennium, but as is now clear, at least down to the third quarter of the 1st millennium B.C., were the mountain pastures in the highlands of Iran, Armenia and Asia Minor, especially those of Armenia and Media. In the plains horse-breeding was for a long time not very successful. It is evidently in these highlands that the peoples of the oldest civilizations in the Near East, and after them the Indo-Iranian newcomers, came to know mass horse-breeding and chariot tactics. Existing data, however, show that the Indo-Iranians became particularly accomplished in these pursuits, and this may have contributed to their success in the military field. But the Indo-Iranians were far from being alone in the creation of an army mounted on chariots. In Asia Minor such armies were known to the Proto-Hattic population and to the Hittites already from the 18th, and possibly the 20th century B.C., and it was probably from Asia Minor that the Achaeans borrowed the light chariot.

Everything points to the Indo-Iranian (Aryan) tribes having moved southwards in successive waves. The first in time was the Kafir move; the Kafir languages still exist in the mountainous regions of north-eastern Afghanistan and north-western Pakistan. If the "Mitannian Aryans" were indeed Indo-Aryans or Kafirs, some peripheral streams must have separated from the main current and reached Western Iran, where they left their imprint in the form of Indo-Iranian names and glosses in documents belonging to the Hurrians of Mitanni or communities connected with them. If this was the case, they must have been followed into Iran by the so-called "Western" Iranian tribes, ancestors of the Persians, the Medes and the Parthians. However, the possibility cannot be excluded that the "Mitannian Aryans" themselves were those "Western" Iranian tribes, at a stage prior to their developing the linguistic particularities which in due course were to distinguish them from their Indo-Aryan neighbours. The "Western" Iranian-speaking tribes must have been followed by the "Eastern" Iranian-speaking tribes, of whom only some penetrated to the Iranian highlands in the broad sense, mainly in present-day Afghanistan and neighbouring regions. They included Bactrians and various small tribes, ancestors of the present-day Pushtu-Afghans and Munjani, to be followed much later by a group of Sakas. The majority of the "Eastern" Iranian tribes – Scythians, Alani, Massagetae, Sakas, Chorasmians, Sogdians – remained on the territory of south-eastern Europe and in Central Asia. Here "Eastern" Iranian languages are spoken to-day by the Ossetes (descendants of Scythians and Alani) in the mountains of the Great Caucasus, by the small group of Yaghnobis in Tajikistan (descendants of Sogdians) and by the people of the Pamir (descendants of Sakas). In their majority, however, the descendants of the Bactrians, Sogdians, Chorasmians, Sakas, Massagetae, Alani and Scythians adopted in time "Western" Iranian (Persian) and various Turkic languages, partly also Finno-Ugrian and Slavonic, and amalgamated with the corresponding tribes and peoples.

A very important but likewise as yet unsolved problem is that of the routes by which the Aryan-speaking tribes penetrated into the Iranian highlands which are guarded on all sides by mountain ranges. One must take into account that the tribes who from the 3rd millennium B.C. to the beginning of the 1st migrated along these routes, cannot be regarded as hunters or gatherers, seeing that by the 3rd millennium B.C. this economic stage had undoubtedly long been left behind by all Indo-European-speaking peoples.[1] Nor can one regard the migrating tribes as exclusively agricultural, for tillers of the land do not voluntarily abandon their land except in extreme necessity, and they avoid moving across territories unsuitable for agriculture. These tribes evidently consisted of cattle-breeders, most likely practising subsidiary agriculture, but the cattle-breeders were not horsemen, at least where tribes of the end of the 3rd to the beginning of the 2nd millennium B.C. are

[1] Judging from linguistic data, already the tribes of the Proto-Indo-European linguistic unity were familiar with agriculture and with domestic cattle, sheep, swine, dogs etc. According to E. Benveniste, the prototype of Avestan *pasu-*, Latin *pecu-*, originally meant not merely "cattle" as was previously thought, but "movable property, including cattle and people". However, this connotation more probably belongs to a somewhat later period, cf. the Avestan phrase *pasu vīra* expressing the same notion with two distinct words. There is no need to regard "people" (*vīra*) in this phrase as referring only or specifically to slaves: the reference could be to the subordinate members of the patriarchal *familia* (who were used all over the ancient East for instance as hostages for debt, cf. *Vīdēvdāt* IV, before it became common for the *patres familias* to pledge plots of land, thus bringing down ruin on the family); the presence upon them of patriarchal slaves is possible for the 2nd millennium B.C. and later, but hardly in the neolithic and early chalcolithic period.

concerned. The light spoke-wheel chariot seems to have become first known to the Indo-Iranians only in their new home, Iran; and even on their further way to India it must at best have been used only by the tribal aristocracy, while the main mass of the tribe had to continue on foot accompanied by carts. In such circumstances it is from the northern steppes to the south, that we must seek correspondingly possible routes for their migration.

To sum up: the Indo-European dialects of the Proto-Indo-Iranians must have spread from the original home of the Proto-Indo-Europeans in eastern-central Europe more by a process of osmosis than by mass replacement of whole populations. The natural surroundings were much the same all the way along the steppes of Eastern Europe, Kazakhstan and parts of Central Asia. Not so the way to Iran and India: there an imposing barrier of mountain ranges had to be crossed. The first tribes speaking Indo-Iranian in Iran may not at first have been numerous, but their appearance on the plateau must have been the result of a real migration, probably a slow migration. The tribes moving southwards were most likely unmounted herdsmen practising subsidiary agriculture, and linguistic data suggest that they were cowherds rather than goatherds or shepherds. It was only in the second half of the 2nd millennium that the horse came to be used as a mount among the Indo-Iranians, by herdsmen and perhaps by scouts. It is probably only after they had penetrated into Iran, in particular on their way to Hindustan, that the tribal aristocracy began to use war-chariots. But the main tribal mass, at first all of it, later the majority, moved along on foot with its cattle, probably accompanied by heavy carts. Pastoral tribes possessing neither the saddle-horse as a general means of progression, nor the camel, and therefore unable to undertake regular seasonal migrations that would allow the pastures to recover, in time exhaust the steppe within the region they inhabit and are thus continually compelled to resettle in new places.[1] It is evident that such migrations had to proceed over a territory where the natural conditions were similar to those of the original habitat of the tribes concerned, providing them with free passage and food for cattle and human masses moving on foot, as well as with the possibility to grow corn.

The existing routes from the steppes of Europe and Central Asia to

[1] This was the reason for the migration of the Semito-Hamitic tribes from their original home, the Sahara (a desert created partly through irrational grazing of sheep), and later of the Semitic tribes from Arabia, and of Turco-Mongolian tribes from the steppes in the heart of Asia. It was apparently the same with the Indo-Iranian tribes coming from the steppes of Central Asia.

the south can be divided into several types: (1) mountainous regions covered with subtropical forests and practically impassable for moving tribes of cattle-breeders; (2) mountainous regions cut by narrow gorges and high passes, and therefore accessible to mobile groups of horsemen living on war booty, and at a stretch to sheep-herding tribes, but very difficult for slowly moving half-agricultural, half-pastoral tribes with herds of cattle; (3) hilly regions with steppe vegetation quite suitable for the passage of herdsmen, both mounted and on foot, with herds not only of sheep and goats but also of cattle, and for chariots.

For subsidiary agriculture not less than 200 mm of yearly precipitation is necessary.

To the first type of routes belong:

(a) The Black Sea coast of the Caucasus, in ancient times densely grown with subtropical forest down to the narrow strip of a coast-line littered with large boulders. There was no through-way here either for the Indo-Iranians or, before them, for the Indo-European Hittites;[1] the local population remained here autochthonous down to the 19th–20th century A.D., from the earliest times. No linguistic or archaeological traces of movements of large tribal masses are to be found here.

(b) The south coast of the Caspian is also covered with subtropical forest, and besides, except for the narrow gorge of the river Safīd-rūd and the valleys of the rivers Sumbar, Atrek and Gorgān flowing from east to west, it is cut off from the Iranian highlands proper by mountains of difficult access. According to the information of Graeco-Roman authors, this was the region where, except for the valleys of the three above-mentioned rivers inhabited by Iranian-speaking Amardi and Hyrcanians, the "Caspii" and the "Anariaci" lived, tribes which had hardly anything in common with the Iranian-speaking population of the neighbouring regions;[2] and although to-day the local inhabitants speak

---

[1] I personally checked the impracticability of the passage of herds through the subtropical forests of the Black Sea coast by passing round the forests beyond the modern highways and along the coast-line avoiding the summer resorts. Those who support the opinion that this route was possible argue that it was taken in the opposite direction by Mithridates VI Eupator in 66 B.C. during his retreat with a handful of warriors after the defeat suffered at the hands of the Romans. But this does not take into account that by then the Black Sea coast of the Caucasus was already settled and covered with a net of Greek colonies, nor the telling fact that Mithridates, unable to make the entire journey by land, in some places took to ships along the coast. To imagine that the Cimmerians or the ancestors of the Hittites possessed a fleet is clearly unrealistic.

[2] Among the information of the Graeco-Roman authors the most reliable seem to be two lists of tribes of the southern Caspian regions transmitted by Strabo from Eratosthenēs (XI. 8. 8; cf. Pliny, *Nat. Hist.*, VI. 15) and by Pliny, *Nat. Hist.*, VI. 18ff. From west to east: (1) Utii, Caspii,

Iranian dialects, these are mainly survivals, at a guess for instance of Median which has long since disappeared from the territory of Media proper. This region where at all times remnants of ancient races were preserved, was no route for the penetration of new ethnic masses.

To the second type belong:

(c) The Daryal and the other high passes of Great Caucasus (Klukhor, Mamison-Alagir). Here in the 8th century B.C. the first detachments of Iranian-speaking (less probably Thracian-speaking) Cimmerian horsemen penetrated into Armenia and Asia Minor. They were later followed by Alan horsemen and others. But for a mass movement to the south of considerable ethnic groups with a train of carts and with women and children, these passes were hardly suitable, not only because of the natural conditions but also because crowds slowly moving across them would have been too easy a prey to annihilation by the mountain-dwellers.

(d) The Caspian coast of the Caucasus. This is a rather wide hilly strip mainly with steppe vegetation, certainly passable for moving tribes of all kinds.

(e) The passes from Central Asia over the Kopet-dagh mountains which separate present-day Turkmenia from Iran. These are easier, but here there is a much more convenient route up the Atrek to Nīshāpūr and Mashhad, and another up the Tejen/Harī-rūd towards Herāt and Sīstān.

(f) The passes over the Paropamisus and the Hindukush, as well as over the Pāmirs. Even the most difficult of these, as later history shows, are negotiable by mobile mounted groups. It can be taken for proven that during their invasion of India in the 1st century A.D. the Sakas used the Pāmir passes. What has not yet been checked is the extent to which

Albani, Cadusii, Anariacae, Amardi, Hyrcanii, or (2) Caspii, Tapyri, Anariacae, Staurae, Hyrcanii. Of these the Utii and Albani can be reliably localized on the territory of present-day Soviet Azarbaijan, the Cadusii in the valley of the Akharchay and Qara-su, possibly also in the Talysh. "Caspii" is probably a general designation for these tribes. The Amardi are localized from the delta of the Safīd-rūd (ancient Amardus) to the delta of the Kharaz near the town of Āmul (from ancient *Amrda*); they are probably identical with the Tapyri who gave their name to Tabaristan. The Anariacae (i.e. "non-Arya"), as can be seen from the quoted lists, are located sometimes in the west and sometimes in the east of the southern Caspian region; this term, too, was a general one for the group of tribes of present-day Gīlān and Māzandarān. The Staurae cannot be identified, their name may be a scribal error in the manuscripts (?). Not one of these tribes, apart from the Hyrcanii, figures in ancient Oriental sources, but it is nevertheless to them that the remarkable artifacts must belong of the end of the 2nd and the beginning of the 1st millennium B.C., discovered in Talysh, Gīlān and Māzandarān (Mārlīk, Amlash etc.).

an advance of early cowherds, alone or with wheeled detachments, would have been possible over Bamyan and Khyber, but to me their crossing over these passes seems improbable.[1]

Thus the two routes which stand the greatest chance of having served as gateways for the transmigration of the Indo-Iranians into Iran and India are the following:

(a) The Caspian coast of the Caucasus. This route was taken by the Scythian horsemen at the beginning of the 7th century B.C. and subsequently by various Turkic nomads. However, further on the route leads either to the wooded zone of the southern Caspian region, or to the massifs of high mountains of Bogrovdagh, Sabelan, Bozqush and Sahend, negotiable by horsemen but hardly suitable for mass ethnic migrations. It is noteworthy that neither the Assyrians nor the Urartians, who made deep incursions into the Iranian uplands, ever crossed these mountain masses with infantry and chariots. Therefore, although the route along the Caspian shore is often regarded as the gateway of immigration of all, or of some Indo-Iranians from Europe (a theory warmly supported, for instance, by E. A. Grantovsky, W. Brandenstein and others) to us it seems the less likely of the two, at least in terms of having served as the main road of migration.

(b) The route up the valleys of the Atrek and the Tejen-rūd. This was undoubtedly used by the Sakas who settled in Seistan in the 1st century B.C.

In estimating the probability as between the Caspian coast and the Atrek-Tejen route two considerations must be borne in mind. Firstly, maps of the vegetation-zones and annual atmospheric precipitations in Asia show that it is only along the Tejen-rūd–Harī-rūd valleys and further, slantwise, across the valleys of the rivers flowing towards Lake Hamun, that we find a stretch of steppes unbroken by high mountains and well watered (over 250 mm of annual precipitation), linking an ecologically similar zone in Central Asia with the inner parts of the Iranian plateau on the one hand, and with the valley of the Indus on the other. The general direction of the itineraries must have been Herāt–Mashhad–Nīshāpūr in the first case, and in the second Herāt–

---

[1] Professor Morgenstierne, who travelled much in these parts, told me he was of the same opinion. Besides, if the early chariots in any way resembled those found well-preserved in the burials of Lčašen in Transcaucasia by Lake Sevan (14th to 13th century B.C.) one would wonder less whether they were up to mountain passes, than whether they could cover much ground even on plains without falling to pieces. Admittedly what we have here are burial chariots.

Sabzavār–Farrah–Qandahār and further, most likely towards the valley of the Pishīn, Quetta and Kelat.

Secondly, if we compare the toponyms and personal names established for the western part of the Iranian highlands by cuneiform inscriptions of the 9th and 7th centuries B.C., with the toponyms and personal names, and in general with the vocabulary, of the oldest parts of the sacred book of the Zoroastrians, the Avesta, we find that even taking the most optimistic view on the number of possible Iranian etymologies of names in the Western area, there is no escaping the conclusion that what obtained there during the first part of the 1st millennium B.C. was a mixture of languages. In the Avesta, by contrast, no traces of an alien, non-Iranian, lexicological substratum have been detected. This points to the superimposition of the Avestan language on a substratum which already was Indo-Iranian, consequently to a much longer occupation of the area where the Avesta was composed, by speakers of Indo-Iranian languages.[1] Although this area has not so far been exactly determined, the majority of students will probably agree that it must be located somewhere within a strip of which the central line joins Urganch with Charjuy, and continues further on to Marv, Herāt and Lake Hamun.

Here therefore most likely lay the main gateway through which first the Indo-Aryan, next the "Western"-Iranian, and finally the "Eastern"-Iranian tribes penetrated south, south-east and south-west, though secondary gateways of migration should not be entirely excluded; these could have been the Caspian shore and the passes to the east of Herāt. Of course these transmigrations must not be seen as victorious expeditions of conquerors. Most probably they consisted of separate movements from stage to stage by small groups of pastoral agriculturalists over the spring grass in the course of a number of generations. The transmigrations may have been assisted by old contacts, archaeologically attested precisely here, between the settlements along the foot-hills of southern Central Asia and the towns of northern Iran on the one hand, and the Indus Valley on the other; the immigrants would not have been moving into completely unknown country, but into country with which they were familiar at least from hearsay.

Direct identification of archaeological cultures with ethnolinguistic

---

[1] A similar picture is apparently presented by a comparison of the Avestan language with Sanskrit which, according to M. Mayrhofer's data, contains up to 15% of substratum (Dravidian) vocabulary.

communities are often extremely risky and unreliable. Still, we saw above that in the southern part of the USSR the culture of Iranian-speaking Scythians beginning in the 7th century B.C., was preceded by the genetically clearly related Srubnaya (Kurgan) pastoral and agricultural culture of the late bronze epoch, from about the 14th to the 8th century B.C. Proceeding gradually to the east, into regions where contemporaneous with the Scythians of the coastal regions of the Black Sea, lived linguistically related Sauromatae, Massagetae and Sacae, we meet on the territory of present-day Kazakhstan and Southern Siberia a number of local variants of the Andronovo culture of the 2nd millennium B.C., very close to the Srubnaya. It is therefore probable, although not exactly provable, that both the Srubnaya and the Andronovo cultures were created entirely or to a large extent by "Eastern" Iranian-speaking tribes, pre-Scythian and pre-Sakas.

Further south, on the territory of present-day Qaraqalpaqia, Uzbekistan and Northern Tajikistan, two related pastoral-agricultural cultures can be observed which some students regard as local forms of the Srubnaya-Andronovo cultures: the Tazabaghyab culture in the west, and the Qairaq-qum culture in the east. These pastoral-agricultural cultures of the steppe bordered in the south of present-day Turkmenia (ancient Parthia, Margiana) on the agricultural settlements of a semi-"urban" type, the Namazghah VI culture of *c*. the 17th to the 11th century B.C. Namazghah VI continues in Parthia the preceding local cultures which had definite connections both with the sites of Northern Iran and with the Harappa culture of the Indus valley.[1] In its turn Namazghah VI yields links with Khorasanian sites (Hisar III C)[2] and partly with the post-Harappan culture Jhukar in Pakistan. After a chronological gap, so far insufficiently filled by archaeological data, the Namazghah VI culture is succeeded (at least in Margiana and east up to the right bank of the Oxus, cf. the site Küčüktepe near Tirmidh) by the Yaz I culture and its continuation, Yaz II and Yaz III, created at a time when the population was already Iranian-speaking.[3]

[1] Namazghah V, end of the 3rd to beginning of the 2nd millennium B.C., is synchronic with the culture of the sites of Hisar III A–B, Shahtepe II etc. in Iran; Namazghah IV belongs to the second half of the 3rd millennium B.C.; Namazghah IV, V and VI correspond to Anau III of the old terminology.

[2] It should be noted that both the "city" of Namazghah V and that of Hisar III C were apparently destroyed by enemies in the first quarter of the 2nd millennium B.C., after which the settlement Namazghah VI rose again on a diminished area of the site.

[3] The north-eastern part of the Margiana oasis (Auchin-depe, Tahirbay), now outside the irrigated zone, was according to V. M. Masson settled for the first time during the Namazghah VI period by immigrants from the region which subsequently became northern Parthia. The

THE MEDES AND THEIR NEIGHBOURS

All this suggests that the Namazghah VI culture (and possibly the entire Anau III = Namazghah IV, V and VI) was created by Indo-Iranians or with their participation. Here could have been the centre from which, since the threshold of the 2nd millennium the penetration of the Indo-Iranians radiated both westwards to the region of contacts with the Hurrians, and eastwards into India. As parts of the Aryan population of the south of Central Asia gradually migrated to the south-west and south-east, probably already from the beginning or, at the latest, the middle of the 2nd millennium B.C., their place in the sedentary oases at the foot-hills of the Kopet-dagh and on the lower reaches of the Tejen and the Murghab, as well as in Bactria, must have been taken by infiltrating Iranian-speaking cattle-breeding tribes of the Andronovo and Qayraq-qum culture,[1] very close to them if by then not almost identical in language. As they penetrated into the Iranian highlands these tribes, already having domesticated the horse, familiarized themselves with the art of making light chariots, brought, as S. Piggott has shown, in very similar models into early Indo-Aryan India and into Asia Minor – though not through Mitanni as it now appears – at the break of the 2nd millennium B.C., and presumably from Asia Minor into Mycenaean Greece. This does not exclude the possibility of individual groups of Indo-Iranians, cut adrift from their main ethnic mass at an early date, having penetrated into Iran by the Caspian coast route. However, a direct identification of one or the other archaeological culture with any particular group of tribes would be inadvisable. It would be difficult and perhaps impossible to identify within the boundaries of Iran itself any culture as brought in from outside and thereby define its bearers as newly arrived tribesmen whose language was Indo-Iranian or Iranian.[2]

centres of the Yaz I culture were situated further west (Aravali-depe) or somewhat more to the south (Yaz-depe). For all its originality the Yaz I culture has certain links with "Necropolis B" in Tepe-Sialk (early Median? 8th century B.C.) as well as with the first, or Median stratum of the "Achaemenian" village in Susa of the 7th to 6th century B.C. The chronological limits of the Yaz II culture, which has a number of traits similar to the archaeological objects of Nadi Ali II (Surkh-dagh) in Afghan Sīstān (8th to 7th century B.C.?), are still uncertain, but it seems probable that the culture belongs to the period of 650 to 500 B.C., while Yaz III belongs to the years 500 to 300 B.C. In Achaemenian times, or somewhat earlier, the centre of Margiana was transferred further to the south, to the site of Giaur-qala (Old Marv; platform with citadel; city walls 12 m high).

[1] It must however be stressed that the typical artifacts of these cultures are not met with on the Iranian plateau. The immigrants must in any case have assimilated the local material culture.

[2] One may note, though, the theory of Cuyler Young who connects the Iranian-speaking tribes with grey pottery. It appears for the first time in Namazghah IV (end of the 3rd millennium B.C.) and also in Namazghah VI (2nd millennium B.C.; there is none in Namazghah V) and then spreads

MEDIA

As we have seen, certain Indo-Iranians came into contact with the Near Eastern Hurrians not later than in the first half of the 2nd millennium B.C., perhaps in its first quarter. If they were Indo-Aryans, the appearance in the west of the Iranian highlands of "Western" Iranian-speaking tribes should probably be dated to a later period, although it need not have been much later. Admittedly among the toponyms recorded in the description of the campaigns of the Elamite king Šilhak-Inšušinak (c. 1150–1120 B.C.), there is still none which to any reliable extent can be explained from Iranian, despite this king having marched into the region of present-day Kirmānshāh, and perhaps even further north. But in the rest of the Iranian plateau the ethnical situation is unknown. Even in the Assyrian inscriptions of the 9th to 8th centuries B.C., relating to the campaigns in the *western* part of the historical region of Media, the number of non-Iranian place names exceeds the Iranian,[1] and the number of non-Iranian personal names of rulers falls short by only a few of the Iranian.[2] Thus down to the 8th century B.C. the Iranian-speaking element in these regions had clearly not fully prevailed, although our former assertion that Iranisms were wholly absent down to the end of the 8th century west of a line from Tabriz to Hamadan needs revision.

In eastern Media the penetration of the Iranian linguistic elements must have occurred earlier and been more massive. From the end of

to the west reaching the region of Lake Urmīya (Rezayeh), according to Cuyler Young towards the very end of the 2nd or the beginning of the 1st millennium B.C. However, O. White Muscarella, who excavated Dinkha-tepe in this same region, believes that the newcomers who brought in grey ceramics, appeared here not later than in the 13th century B.C., and perhaps earlier. Here, too, in a tomb of the 11th to 9th century B.C. the oldest known burial in Iran was found of man with a horse.

[1] Let us take, for instance, the strongholds mentioned in an Assyrian inscription under the year 828–827 in the provinces of Mana and Parsūa: Buštu, Pelaria (?), or Perria (?), Šattiuaria, Kinihamānu, Šalahamānu. Of these only Šattiuaria could be an Iranian place-name (*Šitivarya), but as a somewhat later Urartian text calls apparently the same stronghold Šatiraraya, even this Iranian etymology is doubtful. Here is another example of names of strongholds and villages of the region in the mountains of the central Zagros in the second half of the eighth century: Bīt-Ištar, Kingikangi, Kindigiasu, Kingialkasiš, Kubušhatidiš, Upušu, Ahsipuna, Girgira, Kihbahzati. It is hard to regard any of these names as Iranian.

[2] Let us again take two examples: one is a list of rulers in the mountainous regions of the Zagros and west of them of the year 820, the other refers to Media as a whole in the year 714 B.C.: (1) Sirašme, Amahar, Zarišu (twice), Sanašu, Ardarā, Šumā, Tatāi, Bisirain (?), *Parušta, *Ašpaštatauk, Amamaš, Tarsihu (?), *Mamaniš, Zanzar, Sirašu, Gišta, *Adadāna, Ursi, *Bāra, *Arūa, Kirnakuš, Zabānu, *Irtizati, *Barzuta, Šūa, *Satiriāi, *Artasirār(u); (2) Taltā, *Uksatar, Durisi, *Satarešu, Anzi, *Pāiukku, Uzī, *Uakirtu, *Makirtu, Kitakki, *Masdāiukku, Uzitar, *Pāukku, *(?)Humbē, *(?)Uzumanda, *Bagpar⟨ar⟩na, *Darī, *Ušrā, Šarrūti, *Masdakku (twice), Akkussu, Birtati (Birdadi), *Zardukku, *Satarpān(u), Karakku. An asterisk denotes names which in the writer's opinion are possibly (but in most cases not necessarily) Iranian.

the 8th century B.C. to the beginning of the 7th, while the toponymy of western Media was still in the main non-Iranian, in eastern Media, where the Assyrians had penetrated by then, recording descriptions of their expeditions, there were few place-names that cannot easily be interpreted from Iranian. It is usually accepted that the inhabitants of the fortress on the site of Tepe-Sialk (Necropolis B), where at one time an Elamite population had existed, were already Iranian-speaking by the 8th century B.C. In any case, towards the end of the 6th century B.C., or the beginning of the 5th, there was in eastern Media no vestige of any pre-Iranian population, as we have seen is true (judging from sources probably going back at least to the 7th century) with regard to the country where the Avesta was composed. Nor have any pre-Iranian remnants been discovered in the later languages either in eastern Media, or still further east. Curiously enough, within the Median tribal union proper only one out of the six tribes was called "the tribe of the Arya" (Arizanti in Herodotus, Iranian *Arya-zantu) although "Arya" was the general name by which all Indo-Iranians without exception, from Scythia to India, called themselves, and Herodotus reports that the Medes, too, as a whole called themselves Arya (I. 101; VII. 62). Could it not be presumed that, in spite of *all* Median tribes speaking Iranian, only one traced its origin to the immigrant Arya, while the rest were regarded as being autochthonous even though from time immemorial they had lost their original language and had amalgamated with the Arya? The very name of the Medes, Māda, has so far received no sufficiently transparent Indo-European etymology. All this probably points to an early, slow, and long process of gradual Iranization of the local autochthonous population of the Iranian highlands, especially in their eastern area.

3. *Tribes and city-states. The advance of Assyria and Urartu*

In the western part of the plateau, as shown by archaeological finds,[1] there existed at the turn of the 2nd millennium B.C. typical city-states probably still mainly belonging to the pre-Iranian population. Thus a city, situated on the Hasanlu hill and apparently destroyed by an Urartian incursion at the end of the 9th century B.C., had a citadel with massive fortifications which surrounded the ruler's palace and the

---

[1] E.g. excavations by Dyson in present-day Hasanlu in the Sulduz valley near the south-western corner of Lake Urmīya, on the territory of the so-called "Land of the Mannaeans".

dwellings of the aristocracy; the streets were paved; the outer town spread at the foot of the citadel, 17 m lower, with crowded dwelling houses and a burial place near by. Here, besides agriculture, vine-growing and cattle-breeding, the working of metal and other handicrafts were highly developed.

Further to the east, in the region of the Medes proper, the importance of cattle-breeding, and especially of horse-breeding, surpassed that of agriculture, while the standard of social development seems to have been somewhat lower than that of the regions gravitating towards the Zagros and the roads to Mesopotamia; certainly nomadic and semi-nomadic tribes were to be found here. However, the fortress situated on the site of Tepe-Sialk near present-day Kāshān and having, as is generally believed, an Iranian-speaking population, was on the whole of the same type as those situated further to the west. Similar fortresses or "cities" with citadels and tower-dwellings, situated both in the Zagros mountains and on the outskirts of Media proper, are represented on the reliefs of the Assyrian king Sargon II (end of the 8th century B.C.).

We have already mentioned that on the western slopes of the Zagros primitive "city-states" with centres in the form of mountain strongholds, had apparently existed already in the 2nd, and even in the 3rd millennium B.C. One might have thought that the rise of the inhabitants of that region to the standard of the "urban revolution", and with it to civilization, was due to the influence of neighbouring Mesopotamia, were it not for the evidence provided by the cultures of the eastern part of the Iranian highlands and of southern Central Asia, to the effect that there too, and at the same time, settlements existed of the "urban" or at least semi-"urban" type. However, recorded information on the eastern parts of the Iranian plateau comes to us much later than on the western regions.

If one takes into consideration not merely the foot-hills of the Zagros, or the regions bordering on Mesopotamia and Elam, the first recorded information about the western regions of Iran is to be found in the Assyrian accounts of military campaigns. They were carried out as early as in the 19th to the 12th centuries B.C., but the names of localities and tribes (all non-Iranian) mentioned in the inscriptions cannot be definitely located, and no specific data on them are given. A new series of Assyrian campaigns into the Iranian highlands began in the 10th century B.C.

The first target area of the incursions of the armies of the highly developed Mesopotamian civilization into more backward regions was Zamūa (or "Lullume", the land of the Lullubī) from Lake Urmīya to the upper reaches of the Diyālā river (Āb-i Sīrvān). Already Adadnērarī II made an incursion at the very end of the 10th century which impinged on the land of Zamūa as well as on "the land Meḫri". Expeditions against this territory continued also under the succeeding Assyrian kings, but it was under Aššurnāṣirapli that they became most alarming.

His first campaign (883 B.C.) did not affect Zamūa much; after passing along the valley of the Lesser Zāb (Kirruri) the Assyrian king marched on swiftly to the north-west. The inhabitants of the neighbouring mountain districts not only hastened to send him a tribute consisting of horses, mules, cattle, wine and artifacts of bronze and precious metals, but were also laid under various contributions in favour of the Assyrians. The people of Zamūa apparently regarded this campaign as preliminary to the conquest of their country and began to prepare for defence under the leadership of a tribal chief (*nasīku*) bearing the Akkadian name of Nūr-Adad. He succeeded in rallying to himself the whole of Zamūa, and his forces began to build a wall obstructing the Bābītu pass. It seems, however, that Aššurnāṣirapli did not let Nūr-Adad complete the work. In 881 B.C. he broke through the defile with overwhelming forces and penetrated into the centre of Zamūa, the present-day Shahrazūr valley. Nūr-Adad had recourse to the time-honoured tactics of sending the people and the cattle for safety into the mountains. After the devastation of three Zamūan city-states, the Zamūan kings ceased their resistance. Aššurnāṣirapli left them in their kingdoms which he however included in the Assyrian province he created, laying upon its population a heavy tribute in horses, gold and silver. Beside this he introduced here the usual Assyrian taxes in kind (*šibšu* and *tibnu*) and labour service (*kudurru*). It is only this particular part of the Zamūa (in the broad sense of the term) which was conquered by Aššurnāṣirapli; and only it figures later under the name of the province of Zamūa or Mazamūa. The northern part of the country, towards Lake Urmīya, was subsequently called Inner Zamūa.

In 880 two south Zamūan petty kings, Ameka and Araštūa,[1] did not pay the tribute promised to Assyria, thus provoking a punitive expedition. Aššurnāṣirapli, wishing to forestall the military preparations of the Zamūans, set out with only his cavalry and charioteers without waiting for the infantry and sappers to join him, and began the

[1] Iranian *Rša-tavah ?? (E. A. Grantovsky).

devastation not only of the city-state ruled by Araštūa but also of the neighbouring ones up to the Ḥašmar pass (present-day Avromān?). With the exception of one stronghold which got off with a tribute, all the other fortresses and villages were razed to the ground, the adults being led into captivity, the children cast into the flames, the leaders of the resistance subjected to various barbarous executions. Devastation was also carried out in certain "kingdoms" which had had nothing to do with the events. But Ameka and his people succeeded in finding safety in the mountains. The yearly tribute imposed upon Zamūa was now increased; and to the former kinds of tribute were added woollen textiles (coloured, probably woven), bronze vessels, wine, cows, sheep etc. The Zamūans were compelled by way of labour contribution to take part in the king's constructions in the town of Calah in Assyria, and later some of them were deported and settled in this town. Placatory gifts were also sent in from quite distant regions to the north and to the south of Zamūa.

Aššurnāṣirapli rebuilt the fortress of Atlila (now Tepe Bakrawa in the upper reaches of the Diyālā) which had in the remote past belonged to the Kassite kings, making it the centre for the collection of the taxes paid in kind by the newly created province and a store place for fodder and provender for further expeditions to the east. Soon the petty kings originally left in Zamūa under the supervision of an Assyrian functionary, were replaced by an Assyrian administration. The "governor of Mazamūa" is first mentioned in 828, though by this time this province did not include the southern and eastern parts of the Zamūa country (even in a narrow sense) which had evidently succeeded in regaining their independence. Natural hatred of the Assyrians must have been stronger than fear.

Aššurnāṣirapli's campaigns, described in detail in his annals, give a clear idea on the one hand of the character of the military actions undertaken by the Assyrians, and on the other of the standard of development of the economy, of the society and of the state in the western part of the future Media at the beginning of the 1st millennium B.C.

Until then the Assyrians had not crossed the peripheral ranges of the Zagros into the interior regions, but after creating for themselves a military base in Zamūa they began to make deep incursions in the direction of Lake Urmīya, the Median regions and the Caspian Sea. To retain their independence the inhabitants of these countries were obliged to oppose to the Assyrians a more united state or tribal formation. But such a consolidation did not come into being all at once. Thus in Inner Zamūa the most important state was at first ruled by a certain Nigdiara or Meqtiara, but this Nigdiara had numerous rivals. In 855 the Assyrian forces of King Shalmaneser III defeated Nigdiara in a battle on a lake. Both sides used boats woven of willow branches, each operating, as it were, with a fleet of boats. The lake, evidently a large one, was probably Lake Urmīya, although Lake Zeribār has been alternatively suggested.

In 843 Shalmaneser III, after a march across the Land of the Mannaeans (south of Lake Urmīya, probably a part of Inner Zamūa?), Allabria, Parsūa (to the east of Zamūa), Abdadana and Bīt-Ḫamban (the region of the south-eastern affluents on the upper reaches of the Diyālā), crushed sedition in Namar (the valley of the Diyālā, approximately in the region of the present-day towns of Khanaqīn–Baᶜquba) and established there a *ianzi* from Bīt-Ḫamban; *ianzi* is apparently a Qutī or Kassite word meaning a petty king or chieftain, although the annals use it as a personal name. In 834 this *ianzi* refused obedience to Assyria which led to the first expedition of Shalmaneser into Media.

The Assyrian forces descended into Namar from the north-east (?) over the pass Ḫašmar (Ḫašimur). After destroying the strongholds of Namar and seizing the property that had been taken to safety into the mountains – a feat swiftly achieved which left time for further operations during the same campaign – the Assyrians moved into the heart of Media for plunder. The *ianzi* must have fled there, thus supplying the pretext for the incursion.

During the first stage of the expedition the Assyrian army received gifts from twenty-seven "kings" of Parsūa. It should be noted that the term *Parsūa* (only seldom written *Parsūaš*) is always used in cuneiform writing with the determinative[1] of "country", never with that of "tribe": "the tribe Parsūa" is an historical myth.[2] The Akkadian

---

[1] A determinative is in cuneiform writing a sign, not pronounced in itself but defining the category or the type of objects or phenomena to which the word or name supplied with the determinative belongs.

[2] It would be permissible to suppose that in addition to the name *Parsava of the country there also existed a term *pārsava designating persons. But its meaning would only be "borderer", or "inhabitant of the country *Parsava". The latter term does not occur as a tribal name, still less as the name of a tribe in a state of migration. Note that the Akkadian form *Parsūa* is not from *Parsva, a form which in time might have turned into *Parspa or *Parsa. The homonymous southern province *Parsuaš, Parsumaš* is also attested in the spelling *Parsamaš*, which completely excludes that the Iranian form underlying it was *Parsva.

spelling *Parsūa* represents Iranian *Parsava, which presumably meant "border, borderland".[1] This province should not be confused with Akkadian *Parsūaš*, *Parsumaš* (a term borrowed indirectly from Old Iranian through the intermediary of Elamite *Parsawaš), a province situated on the distant borders of Elam, although both names have a similar meaning and etymology. Indeed, this term enjoyed wide diffusion at different epochs in the borderlands of the Iranian plateau: cf. the Parsii of the classical authors somewhere in the region between Lake Urmīya and the south-western coast of the Caspian (Strabo XI. 7.1) as well as in the mountains of present-day Afghanistan (Ptolemy, *Geogr.*, VI. 18. 3; 20. 3) and there, too, the Parsyētae; the mountain Parsica on the border between Kirmān and Makrān (*ibid.*, VI. 8. 1; 21. 4–5); and finally Paštō (from ancient *parsavā) and *paštun* (from *parsavan), designations of the Afghan language, but originally of the people and of the land they inhabited. There are therefore no grounds for supposing that the district in the Zagros which the annals of Shalmaneser III, and later Assyrian sources down to the 7th century[2] call Parsūa was the native land of the Persians.

By contrast the other district Parsūaš or Parsamaš, on the distant borders of Elam, must evidently be identified with the Persis of the ancient Greeks and the Pārsa of the Old Iranian sources, i.e. with present-day Fārs. This latter country Parsūaš is mentioned in Assyrian texts (sometimes with the determinative of "people") almost at the same time as the Parsūa in the Zagros mountains, i.e. from the end of the 9th century B.C. A frequent suggestion, going back to Marquart and Hüsing, is that either the name Parsūa(š) itself was transferred from the north to the south, from the shore of Lake Urmīya to Fārs, or that a supposed tribe "Parsūa(š)" moved along the same route, leaving behind it at every place of its temporary sojourn, like a visiting card, its tribal name which subsequently came to designate a locality. However, these suggestions are quite unacceptable, both because Parsūa (at least in the Zagros mountains) is not at all a tribal name,[3] and because there never

[1] According to E. Grantovsky, the meaning of the term is "side", "rib", and as ethnonym, "those with strong ribs".

[2] The capital of the Assyrian province Parsūa was Nikur; "Parsūa" or "Nikur", as an Assyrian province, is still mentioned in letters and lists of provinces under King Aššurbānapli (669–635 B.C.); moreover, until the seventh century it was surrounded by Assyrian provinces from all sides; yet in *southern* Parsūaš an independent Persian kingdom had by then already existed for a long time.

[3] It is on the contrary more likely that it was the designation of a region as a "borderland", which would cause its inhabitants to be called "borderers"; such is in more modern times the origin of the ethnic appellation, for instance, of the "Ukrainians".

existed a Parsua(š) on the shores of Lake Urmīya while Parsua in central Zagros, and Parsuaš to the east of Elam are almost simultaneously attested, and also because the first Parsua had a sedentary and not a nomadic population (which is obvious from the nature of the tribute received here by the Assyrians), and finally because it is rather unusual for a passing tribe to leave behind on its way its name as a place-name.

Here we must not fail to define the precise location of both the land Parsua in central Zagros and the southern land Parsuaš. The first is easily determined on the basis of a study of the campaigns of the Assyrian and Urartian kings. Parsua bordered in the south-east on Abdadana and Bīt-Ḫamban; in the south-west on Namar, a district on the middle course of the Diyālā; in the west and north-west on the Assyrian province of Zamūa. In the north certain passes, evidently over the ranges Sultan-Ahmad and Kurpah, separated Parsua from the Land of the Mannaeans: the stronghold Buštu or Bustus was reckoned at times to the first, and at times to the latter.[1] Finally, in the east the Assyrian forces moved from Parsua directly into Median districts. All this permits to locate Parsua quite definitely in the region between Avromān and Senna-Senendej.

As for the southern country Parsuaš (Parsamaš), there are only three indications for its more precise localization: firstly, the fact that it marked the border of Elamite territory at a point opposite (cf. below, p. 68) to its border with Bīt-Bunaki, probably the same as Barnaku; the latter country was situated somewhere on the north-western borders of present-day Luristan (cf. below, p. 102); secondly, in an enumeration of the allies and neighbours of Elam, probably listed from the south-east to the north-west, it heads the list, which ends with Ellipi near Kirmānshāh; and thirdly, it is named as bringing propitiatory gifts (on the occasion of the Assyrian conquest of Elam) along with Ḫudimeri, a principality which, judging by the context of a letter from the Assyrian royal archives (No. 521: *Ḫu-di!-mi-ri*), should be sought near the Persian Gulf, probably no nearer than Bushire. The location of Parsuaš (Parsamaš) in the region of Shīrāz and the valleys of the Kur and the Pulvar is quite likely.

Assyrian and Urartian sources of the 9th century B.C. to the beginning

---

[1] This excludes the frequently encountered localization of Parsua near the south-western corner of Lake Urmīya, based on V. F. Minorsky's ingenious but hardly provable suggestion that the term Parsua is identical with the name of the present-day mountain village Qala-yi Pasva in this region. If *Pasva* continues ancient *Parsava* one should have to think about yet another case of the use of this toponymic term, widespread as we have seen, on the borders of the Iranian plateau.

of the 8th mention on the territory of Inner and Outer Zamūa and Parsūa numerous names of localities, mountains and rivers, but among them there is none which could be etymologized from the Old Iranian language with any degree of certainty, and those few which lend themselves to such etymologies may do so by purely fortuitous coincidence. Of the personal names of rulers mentioned here at that time, some are easily open to an Iranian interpretation, but none is *obviously* Iranian. Nevertheless, the designation of part of the former lands of Zamūa by the Iranian term *Parsūa* ("Borderland" if our interpretation is correct) suggests that towards the middle of the 9th century B.C. the area of the Old Iranian language had spread close to the ranges of the Zagros, if not already into its valleys. It is evident that the same situation must have obtained at the prolongation of these ranges which traversed Fārs; there is however some reason to believe that the Old Iranian language had reached the limits of Elam earlier still, perhaps by several centuries.[1]

In any case, the armies of Shalmaneser III entering Parsūa found themselves on the very limits of the area of Old Iranian. Then, after crossing over the mountains in the direction of the Urmīya lowlands, the Assyrians emerged into the province of Messi on the headwaters of the Jagatu river, and from there, without descending its valley, crossed over the mountains to the east and entered the territory of the Median tribal union which is mentioned for the first time in this connection by Assyrian sources under the name of Amādāi. The army then passed through the districts of Araziaš and Ḫarḫar in the upper part of the basin of the Safīd-rūd. Here four fortresses were taken bearing non-Iranian names similar to place-names in Zamūa and Parsūa. The Assyrians succeeded in capturing a number of prisoners, but the greater part of the people and the cattle were in safety in the mountains. In the valley the Assyrians felt themselves for some time masters of the place, and in Ḫarḫar they even had time to carve on a rock the image

---

[1] This may be thought to follow from the Elamite usage of adding to many Iranian words and proper names with a stem in *-a* the ending *-š* where at the oldest reconstructable Iranian stage the ending must have been *$*$-h*. Of the latter, Elamite *-š* was perhaps an imprecise rendering, though admittedly it is curious that it was rendered at all, as towards the 9th century B.C. this very ancient ending of Old Iranian words can hardly have been any longer pronounced. However, if there were Elamite–Iranian contacts at an earlier date, say the middle or second half of the second millennium B.C., it is quite probable that typical Iranian change of $*s > h$ might not yet have occurred. But it must be said that we do not know exactly how Elamite *š* was pronounced; all we know is that it differed from both *s* and the aspirate *h*.

of their king. They then departed, taking with them the captive *ianzi* of Namar without attempting to establish themselves in Media.

In the course of his next campaign in 828 Shalmaneser was already very old, and the Assyrian forces were commanded by the general Daiiān-Aššur. This time the expedition was directed against the city-states of the Urmīya lowlands; here, under the name of Manaš, we find mentioned the subsequently important Land of the Mannaeans, though still not as a unified state but only as one of the small states of this region. In its capital, the stronghold Izirta or Zirtu, ruled a certain Udaki. After pillaging several city-states of this region (besides Manaš there are mentioned Ḫarruna, Šurdira etc.), or receiving tribute from them, the Assyrians moved on into Parsua where they continued their successful activities. A similar expedition was made by Daiiān-Aššur in the next year, 827, along the route: Greater Zāb – western shore of Lake Urmīya – Inner Zamūa – Namar – Assyrian province of Zamūa. Among the rulers who brought propitiatory gifts or a tribute was the ruler of Andia on the lower course of the Safīd-rūd. This province, as appears from another Assyrian source, stretched as far as the Caspian Sea. Probably the rock-tomb Marlik (to the north-west of the delta of the Safīd-rūd) in which, as also in a neighbouring cemetery, very remarkable metal artifacts of the 11th to 10th (?) centuries B.C. have been discovered, somewhat similar to those of Hasanlu and of Ziwiyeh in the Land of the Mannaeans, was the burial place of one of the rulers of Andia.

As for the Urmīya lowlands, although at the time they did not yet form a political entity, they were commonly designated by the general name of "Land of the Mannaeans", and this term began to supplant the former appellation of "Inner Zamūa". No less than fifty separate city-states existed on this territory, of which the states of Udaki and Nigdiara (and later of his son Šarṣina) could lay claim to hegemony.

In the year 827 civil war broke out in Assyria. Not until 823 did the new king Šamšī-Adad V succeed in restoring the unity of power in all the parts of the kingdom. In this connection his inscription gives an account of the frontiers of Assyria from which it is clear that at the time the kingdom did not include either the whole of the Land of the Mannaeans, or Parsua. Apparently it is precisely at this time that the kingdom of Urartu (*Urʾarṭu*), centred about Lake Van, a rival of Assyria, began its advance to the south, and the Urartian king Išpuini occupied the territory between Lakes Van and Urmīya. For this reason in 821 the Assyrian general Mutarriṣ-Aššur was sent into the Urmīya region both to counteract the advance of Išpuini and to reinforce the local leader Šarṣina. An Assyrian inscription says that Mutarriṣ-Aššur reached the Western Sea ("the Sea of the Sunset") by which the Caspian seems to be meant (and not for instance Lake Van or Lake Urmīya): the concept of the Caspian and the Black seas as parts of the Mediterranean which in Assyrian sources is usually called the Western Sea (as distinct from the Eastern, i.e. the Persian Gulf and the Indian Ocean) was still current as late as in the 4th century B.C.

After consolidating their position in the Urmīya region the Assyrians undertook in 820 an important campaign against the Medes (Akkad. *Mădāi*). The Assyrians crossed the Kullar mountains (the main range of the Zagros) and entered into Messi on the upper reaches of the Jagatu river. Here Šamšī-Adad V succeeded in capturing a large quantity of cattle and sheep, asses and a number of two-humped Bactrian camels which were in those days a novelty in that region. Many villages and settlements were burnt down, and the Messians suffered great losses. Here, too, propitiatory gifts were received from the tribes of the region – the Sunbians, the Mannaeans and the Teurlians – as well as from Šarṣina, the petty kings of Parsūa, and others. Thereupon the Assyrians made their way into the Gizilbunda mountains which separated Inner Zamūa (or the Land of the Mannaeans) from the land of the Medes. These are the present-day mountains from Shāhberdi to Kafelān-kūh, and the watershed between the rivers Jagatu and Safīd-rūd in general.

After the Assyrians had seized the first mountain stronghold in Gizilbunda, two local chiefs brought in droves of harness horses as a propitiatory gift, but the third, Pirišati, to whom the Assyrian text ascribes the title of "King of Gizilbunda", decided to offer resistance. The inhabitants of Gizilbunda gathered in his stronghold Uraš, but the archaic fortress, like all these mountain strongholds intended for wars among neighbours, proved no match to the high siege technique of the Assyrians. Uraš and the small neighbouring strongholds were taken, and if we are to believe the Assyrian account, 6,000 warriors fell in the battle while 1,200 others, together with Pirišati himself, were captured. Another leader, Engur, made submission to Šamšī-Adad, and in his stronghold Ṣibar[1] (otherwise Ṣubarā, apparently in the valley of the

---

[1] In old works this name is wrongly given the reading Ṣimašpatti and identified with the Elamite city of Simaški.

Zenjān-chāy river?) the Assyrian king set up a stele with his inscription and image.

Having crossed Gizilbunda the Assyrians were now in the land of the Medes. One gets the impression that while among their western neighbours discord and the short-sighted and grasping policy of individual rival princelings predominated, the Medes were united in a single tribal union headed by a common military leader. This was Ḥanaṣiruka whose residence was in the stronghold Sagbitu. Ḥanaṣiruka attempted to withdraw and to seek safety in the snow mountains of the Alburz, but Šamšī-Adad forced the Medes to give battle and inflicted heavy losses on them: according to the same Assyrian account they succeeded in ravaging 1,200 (!) inhabited places (probably counting isolated homesteads in the mountains) including Sagbitu: 140 horsemen were taken prisoner. Yet the resistance of the local tribes was not broken. On their way back the Assyrians, after recrossing the mountains apparently between present-day Qazvīn and Hamadān, found their way barred by Munṣuarta, ruler of Araziaš, a district which should probably be sought between present-day Hamadān and the headwaters of the Safīd-rūd. However, this force also suffered heavy losses. According to the inscription 1,070 were killed, many people were carried off into slavery and much cattle was taken under the guise of "tribute".

Never before had the Median tribes suffered such defeat. Over the entire territory from Lake Urmīya to the Salt Desert confusion and despair seem to have reigned. More than a score of rulers of various small and even tiny districts of Media and Parsūa brought gifts to the Assyrian king before his return to Assyria over the Kullar pass. Among them some ten bore Iranian names, but of the names of districts only a few can be explained from Iranian.

For Assyria this campaign was of threefold importance: it forestalled possible anti-Assyrian alliances and coalitions in the Mannaean and Median territories, and especially an alliance of local city-states and tribes with Urartu; it secured benefit from plunder and seizure of slaves and cattle; and it furthered the preparation of a campaign against Babylonia, whose armies had in the meantime occupied a considerable part of the valley of the Diyālā. Accordingly next came the war between Assyria and Babylonia. At the same time, during the campaign of 815/814, according to one of Šamšī-Adad's texts he devastated the whole of Elam "from Bīt-Bunaki to Parsamaš". As Bīt-Bunaki seems to have been situated on the north-western frontier of Elam (see above,

p. 63), Parsamaš would be on the south-eastern, and can be identified with Persis. It is clear that Parsua in central Zagros could not have been meant as it never had anything to do with Elam.

In 810 Šamšī-Adad died leaving the throne to the youthful Adadnērarī III. The actual ruler is thought to have been the dowager queen Sammurāmat who figures in history under the name of Semiramis. From the year 805 Adadnērarī began to rule independently, but even then Sammurāmat continued to play an important rôle. The rule of a woman made a great impression on all the neighbouring peoples accustomed to a patriarchal order of things, and legends about "Semiramis" or "Šamiram" enjoyed for a long time widespread fame, surviving in some places into the 20th century.

During the rule of Semiramis and Adadnērarī III eight campaigns were undertaken against the Mannaeans and the Medes (809–788 B.C.). The Assyrians apparently sought not only to disrupt a possible aggression of Urartu, but also to conquer Media. Unfortunately all we know about these campaigns comes from their brief mention in the list of Assyrian annual eponyms on whom the dating was based, and from one solemn inscription of 802. Annals and detailed war records of Adadnērarī have not come down to us. Already in 802 the Assyrians claimed domination over Ellipi (near Kirmānshāh), Ḫarḫar and Araziaš (in the region between Hamadan and the upper reaches of the Safīd-rūd), in Messi (the upper Jagatu valley), the land of the Medes (evidently the triangle Hamadān–Zanjān–Qazvīn), "the whole" of Gizilbunda, the Land of the Mannaeans, Parsua, Allabria (on the headwaters of the Lesser Zab), Abdadana (to the south-east of Parsua), and all the way up to Andia and the Caspian Sea. There exist no later inscriptions of Adadnērarī but it is known that between 802 and 788 the army of Adadnērarī undertook six more campaigns into the "Land of the Medes", i.e. further east. According to the information of Ctesias (an author whose data must be used with circumspection) Semiramis is said to have reached Bactria. We can conclude with certainty on the strength of a letter from the royal Assyrian archives (No. 1,240) that Assyrian agents made their way to the lazurite mines of Badakhshān (probably later, at the end of the 8th or the beginning of the 7th century?), but it seems improbable that in addition their armies could have reached so far east, as Ctesias claims. In any case, down to the seventies of the 7th century B.C. not a single Assyrian military formation penetrated so deep into the heart of Iran as Adadnērarī had done.

Adadnērarī's reign coincided with the beginning of the advance of the Urartian king Minua to the south-east. Between the years 807 and 786 the Assyrian generals led seven campaigns against him, two of which took them into the country of the Mannaeans. Adadnērarī's successor, Shalmaneser IV, also fought Urartu from 781 to 778, apparently without success.

Urartu had become a serious menace to Assyria. Already between the years 820 and 810 the Urartian kings Išpuïni and Minua occupied Muṣaṣir (on the headwaters of the Greater Zab) immediately threatening the centre of Assyria, and made an expedition into the Land of the Mannaeans (Urart. *Mana*). Minua's new expedition into the Land of the Mannaeans (probably in 802/801 B.C.) established Urartian domination in the hilly lowlands to the south of Lake Urmīya. Here the Urartian king built or reconstructed the stronghold Mešta (Messi, now Tashtepe near Miyanduab?).[1] In the conditions obtaining in the ancient East the building of a stronghold usually pointed to the conversion of that territory into a province, but in the 9th to the 8th century there existed in Assyria and Urartu the practice of appointing a chief of provincial administration even when the local authorities were allowed to continue to govern. The kingdom Mana (Land of the Mannaeans) did not cease to exist even under Urartian domination, which continued also during the beginning of the rule of the next Urartian king, Argišti I, from 780/779 (or according to G. A. Melikišvili, from 784 B.C.?).

Already Minua had in the 790s come out onto the western flank of Assyria, on the upper Euphrates (Qara-su). As for Argišti, he attempted to pass round her eastern flank. According to his annals he waged war as far as to the south of Mana, and there clashed three times with Assyrian troops in the fifth, sixth and eighth years of his rule, i.e. in 775, 774 and 772, in the country of 'Arsita and near the towns of Buštu and Baruata – in Assyrian Ḫarši, Bustus and Bīt-Barrūa. Ḫarši and Bustus were situated in the mountains on the road from Mana into Parsua, and Bīt-Barrūa lay between Bīt-Ḫambān and Ellipi, i.e. somewhere on the road from the headwaters of the Diyālā to Kirmānshāh.

The Urartian king penetrated not only into Parsua (Urart. *Paršua*) but also into a province which his annalists call *Babilū*. E. A. Grantovsky identifies it with Silḫazi, "a stronghold of the Babylonians" in Assyrian

---

[1] The statement sometimes met with that Mešta belonged to the land of Parsua is based on an erroneous interpretation of an Urartian text. Neither has Mešta anything to do with the country of Messi.

sources, which he places somewhere to the north-east of the Diyālā valley. But Babilū may alternatively be identified with that valley itself, corresponding to the province Namar of the Assyrians, which had an entirely Babylonian population and at that time was apparently a dependency of Babylon. In fact the war against "Urartu and Namar" is mentioned in an Assyrian source under the year 774. However this may be, Mana was clearly at that time still retained by the Urartians, because when waging war in Parsūa and on the far side of it, their operational base must have been on Mannaean territory.

Somewhat later, however, Mana seceded from Urartu, Apparently it is precisely the struggle against Urartu which enabled Mana to achieve consolidation into a single kingdom covering the entire Urmīya basin, including the southern and eastern, perhaps also the western, shores of the lake. Between the years 773 and 768 (?) Argišti I led five expeditions against Mana which were repeated in the early fifties of the 8th century by his successor Sarduri II; but according to Melikišvili, Mana itself now and again took the offensive against Urartu, for instance in 771. Nevertheless, the expeditions of the Urartian kings brought about a new subjugation of Mana. In the year 771 (?) the eastern shore of the lake (the land *Uyišti*, Assyr. *Uišdiš*) was occupied, and by about the year 750 (?) Sarduri II had gained such a firm hold on Mana that he could again undertake an expedition against Babilū.

The advance of the Urartians so far to the south along the ranges of the Zagros brought about Assyria's loss of all influence east of the Zagros, and the restoration of the independence of the Medes. However, such considerable Urartian successes were made possible only by the fact that Assyria was at the time passing through a period of internecine wars and of general political decay. Her powers were restored as a result of the reforms of Tiglathpileser III (745–728 B.C.). Preparing, it seems, for a struggle against Urartu, Tiglathpileser undertook already in 744 an important expedition over the Zagros, most likely, to judge from certain indirect data, with the consent and co-operation of Mana, which by that time had become a natural ally of the Assyrians against Urartu.

4. Period of the second Assyrian advance.
The Land of the Mannaeans, Ellipi. The Medes. Persis

We shall be returning later to this campaign, noting meanwhile that in the year 743 the reorganized Assyrian army inflicted a crushing defeat on Urartu and its allies on the upper Euphrates. Somewhat later Tiglathpileser even led an expedition into the very heart of Urartu where he unsuccessfully besieged its capital Ṭušpā. This put an end to Urartian claims to dominate Mana, and there began for that kingdom a period of prosperity when in power and importance it could almost compete with the two rival great powers. The defeat of Sarduri II immediately set the Land of the Mannaeans at the head of all the provinces of present-day Iranian Azarbaijan. The king who at the time ruled in Mana (probably Iranzu who died *c.* 718–717, or his predecessor) proved sufficiently energetic to take advantage of the situation. As a result, in the thirties and twenties of the 8th century B.C. Mana, including its dependencies, stretched over the entire southern basin of Lake Urmīya and the eastern shore of the lake up to present-day Tabrīz, perhaps also over the western shore, as well as, apparently, over a considerable part of the basin of the river Safīd-rūd except for its lower reaches. The northern frontier of the area of Mannaean hegemony was formed, to judge from inference, by the watershed between the lake and the Araxes. In the north-west the influence of Mana may even at times have spread as far as the Qotur pass to the west of present day Khoy.

The Iranian element in the Land of the Mannaeans was not yet very strong, but it is not clear which ethnic element predominated in that country. It is often suggested that it was the Hurrian (Matiēnian); indeed still in Hellenistic–Parthian times Lake Urmīya was called Lake Matiēnē or Mantiānē. In favour of the Hurrian origin of the Mannaeans etymologies of some Mannaean and neighbouring names have been adduced,[1] but they are not very reliable, and the majority of names of members of the Mannaean royal dynasty do not look Hurrian. The Assyrians seem to have reckoned the Land of the Mannaeans to "Inner" Zamūa, and identified Zamūa with Lullume, i.e. the land of the Lullubī, but as said above, it is not clear whether the Lullubī represented a particular ethnos. It is possible that the Mannaeans formed a part of the Qutī, about whose language the suggestion has been made, though so far with hardly any arguments to support it, that it was related to the north-eastern Caucasian languages (Nakh-Daghestānī).

We possess some data on the social and political organization of the Mannaean kingdom. The population of Mana, as also of the

---

[1] Erisinni, Metatti, Telusina – cf. the Hurrian elements *šena*, *šenne*, *-atti* in personal names. However, *-ukku* in Dāiukku (in the Land of the Mannaeans), Arukku (in Persis) probably represents Iranian *-auka*, and not a Hurrian *-ukki*.

neighbouring provinces, consisted mainly of cattle-breeders. Sheep, cattle, donkeys and a certain number of two-humped camels were raised; horse-breeding was very important in Messi and in the region of present-day Tabrīz. However in no other part of the future Median state did agriculture play such an important rôle, side by side with cattle-breeding, as in Mana where wheat, barley and vines were cultivated. The Bible (Ezekiel 27. 17) mentions a valuable kind of wheat *minnīth*, which one might translate as "Mannaean".[1] The Phoenician town Tyre traded in this wheat together with horses from the upper Euphrates, ivory and ebony, Syrian artifacts, Damascus wine etc. Although the Biblical text indicates that minnīth wheat was bought by the Phoenicians in Judea and Israel, there, too, it was most likely imported. As shown by N. B. Jankowska, a permanent caravan route existed leading along the valleys of the Diyālā and the Adhēm into Mesopotamia down to the middle course of the Euphrates, and from there to Damascus and across Transjordan into Israel and Judea. In Mana, as in general in Zamūa, handicrafts were also highly developed; recent finds in Hasanlu, Ziwiyeh etc. have revealed to us the artistic metal-work of Mannaean craftsmen.

The Mannaean kingdom that arose from the unification of several small city-states retained a very loose structure. It was divided into separate "lands" (Akkad. *nagû, nagi'u*). Of these we know Subi (Tabrīz valley), Uišdiš (eastern shore of Lake Urmīya), Surikaš, Messi (headwaters of the Jagatu river), Arsianši, Erešteiana and others. Apparently it was at the head of such provinces that the "governors" (*šaknu*) stood,[2] mentioned by Assyrian sources, who behaved with great independence and may have been descendants of former rulers of autonomous city-states. Characteristic figures both in the Mannaean administration and to a still greater degree in the neighbouring Median lands, were the "lords of townships" (Akkad. *bēl āli*) – heads of family or territorial communities. This title is probably a translation of some Iranian term.[3]

The division into provinces apparently reproduced not only the districts of the former city-states but also the division into tribes. Mannaean society preserved to a large extent a tribal structure. It is

---

[1] But a village Minnīth also existed in Transjordan.

[2] In the administrative system of Assyria proper since the times of Tiglathpileser III "governors" (*šaknu*) had been replaced by "chiefs of provinces" (*bēl peḫāte*) with somewhat diminished rights, and apparently recruited exclusively from eunuchs.

[3] The term was not used by the Assyrians outside the limits of the Iranian highlands.

noteworthy that, while the Urartian texts call this kingdom "the Mana, its land" (*Mana.nə ebānə.iə*), Assyrian sources call it "Land of the Mannaeans" (*Māt Mannāi*) although in the earlier Assyrian texts the kingdom (city-state?) of Mana in the narrow meaning of the term is called also *Manaš* or *Munna*. Side by side with the properly Mannaean tribe Assyrian annals mention also other tribes which had come to be included in the Mana state: the Teurlians, the Messians, the Dalians, the Sunbians, the Kumurdians. The city-state Kumurdi is apparently the same as is mentioned under the name of Ḫumurti (along with Ḫarši and others) in Sumerian texts of the end of the 3rd millennium B.C. as a Hurrian or Qutī stronghold.

In the Land of the Mannaeans, unlike in other eastern kingdoms of the time, the people still took an active part in public life. If in other kingdoms we often hear of palace *coups d'état*, harem intrigues, rebellions of individual magnates or generals, and only seldom, at the occurrence of some foreign invasion, of an armed rising of the people against the invaders, here we additionally learn of the revolt of the people against their own unpopular king.

The Mannaean king seems to have ruled not as an autocrat, but with power limited by a council of elders. One Assyrian text states that the Mannaean king was accompanied by "his great ones, elders, councillors, kinsmen, governors and chiefs in charge of his country". In a diplomatic request to the Assyrian king the Mannaean king addresses himself not personally but together with "his great ones, councillors of his country", evidently a kind of βουλή or senate. "The great ones" of the Land of the Mannaeans, who apparently sat in the council of elders, consisted of the king's kinsmen and of governors who of course also belonged to the local hereditary aristocracy and/or were royal kinsmen. The Mannaean kingdom can therefore be characterized as an archaic oligarchy, a state ruled by a king together with a council of elders from the hereditary aristocracy in the presence of persistent public activity of democratic strata who on occasion rose to struggle against the oligarchy.[1]

The society of Mana was clearly already divided into socio-economic classes. The presence in it of slaves may be presumed. Slavery, as we well know, was much developed in neighbouring Urartu which, to judge from its handicrafts and in general its material culture, must have

---

[1] An analogous state structure was to be found in the city-states of early Sumer, in Hurrian city-states, in the Hittite Old Kingdom etc.

differed but little from Mana in its standard of social and economic development. But it was a type of slavery that can hardly have exceeded the limits of the patriarchal and domestic type of slave-ownership.

Another kingdom of some importance, formed not later than at the end of the 9th century on the territory of the future Median kingdom, was Ellipi. This name recorded by Assyrian sources was apparently known to them through the intermediary of Elamite (-*pi*/*e* is the Elamite plural ending). It is not impossible that the land or kingdom of Elymais of the Hellenistic period, which is most often identified with Elam, continued in fact the traditions precisely of Ellipi: territorially Elymais was distinct from Elam proper (Susiana) and linguistically it is difficult to derive its name from that of Elam; but if one assumes that an identical ethnicon here carried the Elamite suffix -(*u*)*me* instead of -*pi*, the reconstruction of an unattested but entirely regular form *E*ll-ume* becomes possible, to which one would trace the name Elymais (cf. *Lullu-b/p-* and *Lullume*).

Ellipi seems to have been situated in the valley of the river Saimarrah, around present-day Kirmānshāh. Assyrian sources mention it from the times of Shalmaneser III and feature it as the most powerful entity between the Land of the Mannaeans and Elam. At the end of the 8th century, until the beginning of the 7th, the country was ruled by a semi-Iranian or Iranized dynasty. Unfortunately we know very little about this kingdom. It had probably inherited the achievements of the culture of the "Luristan bronzes".

The resurgence of Assyria under Tiglathpileser III at the expense of Urartu gave the Land of the Mannaeans the opportunity to increase its power. It was otherwise with Ellipi which, if it managed to continue to exist, most likely did so only by relying on the power of its neighbour, Elam. But it was for the Median tribes, which had no defence against Assyria, that the hardest times now began, marked by almost incessant Assyrian incursions.

Assyrian sources record scores of separate rulers ("lords of townships") on the territory of Media, none of them particularly outstanding. There are, as we shall see, grounds for believing that they did not rule autocratically but to a certain extent depended on collective organs of community self-government.

Herodotus (I. 101) recounts that the Medes were divided into six tribes: Bousae, Parētaceni, Strouchates, Arizanti, Boudii and Magi, but it has proved impossible to identify most of them in Akkadian sources.

It may be thought that the Arizanti correspond to the nomads called "Aribi of the East"[1] (tentatively from an Elam. *ari-pe* "the Arya"), and the Parētaceni to the inhabitants of the country Partakka, Paritaka, Paritakānu, mentioned in Assyrian sources of the beginning of the 7th century B.C.[2] Where these tribes lived is also not clear. The Parētaceni lived evidently near present-day Isfahan; the Arizanti (if they are identical with the "Aribi of the East"") led a nomadic life in the Median desert to the south-east of present-day Kāshān (?). With the Iranian tribes on the territory of Media also the Sagartii should apparently be reckoned (a tribe mentioned in various parts of Iran but possibly living also in the Zekertu country of the Assyrian sources, i.e. between present-day Marāgha and Miyāna), as well as the Mardi or Amardi, nomads also recorded in later sources in the valley of the Safīd-rūd (Amardus) as well as in other very different parts of Iran and Central Asia (this was possibly not a real tribal name but a general pejorative appellation for hostile nomads and mountaineers). But the basic territory of Media, to which alone the Assyrians apply the term *Mădāi*, was the triangle between the present-day towns of Zanjān, Hamadān and Qazvīn or Tehran.

The social order of the Medes must have differed little from that of the Eastern Iranians as described in the Avesta although some changes will naturally have been occasioned by their closeness to neighbours of a different origin and language and possessing a much older and greatly superior civilization.

The division into tribes appears to have gradually lost its former important social rôle with the Medes, for otherwise the Assyrian sources would have given it more attention. But presumably the tribal union of the Medes was not merely nominal. It is to this union that the Medes must have owed at times the possibility of collective action with a choice of capable leaders, which probably explains why in Assyrian inscriptions the epithet invariably given to the Medes in addition to "the distant ones" is "the strong ones". But such unity could manifest itself only occasionally. In the majority of cases the Medes, in spite of their "strength", were divided, and reacted to Assyrian incursions in the time-honoured way: they either sent placatory gifts or else retreated into

---

[1] This expression in the Assyrian dialect of the Akkadian language could be interpreted as "Arabs of the East".

[2] Graeco-Roman literature later than Herodotus knows a *country* Paraetacēnē, corresponding to the Isfahan plain. It is sometimes reckoned not to Media but to Persis.

the mountains with their cattle, abandoning to the enemy deserted dwellings in their small strongholds and villages, which even in times of peace would not be particularly prosperous.

With the conquered territories Tiglathpileser III and his successors dealt differently from his predecessors. While formerly the greater part of the population was massacred and only part of the able-bodied males were carried off into slavery, naked and with yokes round their necks, this was now recognized as unprofitable. Henceforth the inhabitants, in so far as their territory could be incorporated into Assyria, were either left where they were and heavily taxed, or else, more frequently, transferred some time after the conquest in an organized manner, with some of their belongings, with their children etc., into Assyria or the regions previously devastated by Assyrian expeditions, and then replaced with inhabitants of other lands conquered by the Assyrians at the other end of the kingdom. These displaced populations were often settled in frontier villages and strongholds in threatened areas of strategic importance, where self-preservation compelled them to rely on Assyrian support; for this reason they, too, were allowed to bear arms. All these measures ensured a more rational exploitation of conquered territories and a more regular flow of revenue from them. They also led to the disconnection of various ethnic groups, desirable because it would hamper relations among the conquered and in particular attempts to organize rebellions against the Assyrian conquerors.

In 744 the Assyrian armies, after marching up the valley of the Diyālā, entered the territory of Parsūa and the neighbouring region. Here, as at the time of the Elamite campaigns of the 12th century, still lived a basically autochthonous non-Iranian population organized in several tiny city-states which the annals call "Houses", apparently giving them dynastic names (Bīt-Zatti, Bīt-Kapsi and many others). Some of the rulers were captured by the Assyrians, others succeeded in finding safety with their people in the mountains. Many prominent captives were impaled. Part of the territory was annexed to Assyria under the name of the province of Parsūa.

There were, however, some new traits to be observed in the action taken by the Assyrians in conquered territory. Thus in Bīt-Zatti, one of the districts which went to form the new province, Tiglathpileser freed some of the captives after having their thumbs chopped off, which incapacitated them for military service but left them able to work in the fields as objects of exploitation in the new Assyrian province.

Even when a territory was not directly incorporated in the Assyrian possessions, Tiglathpileser endeavoured to organize a regular exploitation of the population by means of a definite annual tribute. So it was, for instance, in Bīt-Kapsi whose king Battānu voluntarily imposed upon his subjects the duty of paying taxes and of making contributions in service, in return for having his stronghold Karkarihundir spared by Tiglathpileser.

Unfortunately the annals of Tiglathpileser III have come down to us in disconnected fragments, and it is often difficult to restore the sequence of events. It is not clear whether it was during this expedition or one of the subsequent ones that Tiglathpileser moved beyond the limits of Parsūa into Media. The strongholds Araziaš, Kišessu (Kišisa) and others are also mentioned. The final point of the expedition seems to have been the stronghold Zakrūti, a Median one as the text stresses, evidently because the fortresses previously enumerated were not Median. In the villages of Rāmatēa (from Old Iranian *Rāmatavya), ruler of Araziaš, stores of lazurite were seized besides horses and cattle. On the way back various other city-states were destroyed and yet another province formed, that of Bīt-Ḫamban, in the basin of the left affluents of the upper Diyālā. After this expedition Tiglathpileser demanded that the mountain "lords of townships" of the entire "Land of the strong Medes" should pay him a yearly tribute in the form of nine tons of lazurite and nineteen tons of bronze artifacts, an order which testifies more to the greed of one of the most capable rulers of Assyria than to his understanding of economics and geography. It is very doubtful that he ever succeeded in receiving this tribute.[1]

The purpose of Tiglathpileser III's expedition into Media was certainly not to render secure the peaceful frontiers of Assyria from raids by mountain dwellers as, for instance, P. Rost would have it. Nothing is known about such raids; besides the Assyrians never justified their incursions by alleging that a weaker enemy posed a threat. But Tiglathpileser's reform of the Assyrian army was based on its being kept permanently active and sustaining itself by plunder. This made the expansion of the limits of Assyria a necessity. Furthermore, this reform presupposed a constant re-population of agricultural districts of Assyria proper, and of the devastated conquered regions, by inhabitants of other

---

[1] Lazurite (lapis-lazuli) is not mined in western Media, and was most probably brought there in transit by caravan for trade with Assyria. It is clear that the uncompensated seizure of lazurite must have discouraged all attempts to continue to trade in it along the caravan road.

conquered lands, and of the latter lands in their turn by inhabitants of newly conquered territories, and so forth. This required a continuous succession of contingents of human element to become available for resettling. In addition the reformed standing army of the Assyrians was in great need of horses, for chariots and especially for the cavalry to which an ever growing importance was attributed, and it was only in mountain pastures, particularly in Media, that horse-breeding was successfully practised during this period. Finally, an expedition against the eastern tribes could have been aimed at securing the flank for the forthcoming struggle against Urartu. In fact the expedition of 744 preceded that of 743 against Sarduri II of Urartu and a prolonged war with his Syrian allies, just as the second expedition against the Medes in 737 preceded the campaigns of 736–735 into the mountains of Urartu. It is noteworthy that in his expeditions against Media Tiglathpileser carefully by-passed the zone of the hegemony of the Land of the Mannaeans which naturally maintained an anti-Urartu position.

The result of Tiglathpileser's first expedition (or of his first two expeditions) against Media and the neighbouring regions was the creation of two new provinces of the Assyrian realm, Parsūa and Bīt-Ḫamban, which remained part of it until its fall. No information exists on a possible "migration of the people of Pārsava" from here to Fārs.

Already in 744 the Assyrians carried off from Parsūa a number of artisans, and under the year 736 the annals of Tiglathpileser mention the transfer of the "Qutī", evidently from the recently conquered provinces, into Syria and northern Phoenicia. The displaced people are mentioned by their tribal names or by the names of their original homes. Among them are named the Budians who could be the tribe Boudii of Herodotus, or more likely the inhabitants of the township Budu on the frontier of Babylonia and Elam, conquered by Tiglathpileser in 745. Probably at the same time Syrians were transferred into the mountains of the Zagros.

In the course of time, as a result of this policy of resettlement, the population of the province Parsūa became strongly Assyrianized and Aramaeanized. Even much later, according to Ptolemy (VI. 2. 6), this and the neighbouring territory were called "Syromedia" (the Greeks often called the Assyrians "Syrians"). As a matter of fact individual Akkadian names occur even earlier among the rulers of these, as well as of more easterly provinces. However, in the text of Tiglathpileser's annals devoted to this expedition the majority of names are neither Iranian nor Semitic.

In 737 Tiglathpileser III made another expedition against Media. It was partly directed against the same districts as in 744, including those which had already been incorporated in the complex of Assyrian provinces. The Assyrian army reached the stronghold Ṣibur (Ṣibar, Ṣubarā), in the valley of the river Zenjān-chāy, which had once been occupied by Šamšī-Adad V in the year 820, and captured it. In Tiglathpileser's annals this region is already reckoned to Media, although in the 9th century it apparently belonged to the eastern part of Gizilbunda. The further account of the expedition is very badly preserved, but it is clear that the Assyrians traversed a number of districts bearing Iranian names, among them Nišāi (Niššā, probably the Nisaean Plain of the Graeco-Roman authors, near Qazvīn (?), famous for its horse-breeding) and a certain "Land of Gold", and reached the mountain Rūa (to the east of present-day Tehran?) and the Salt Desert (Dasht-i Kavīr). On their way back the Assyrians occupied among others Silḫazi, "a stronghold of the Babylonians". In this "Babylonian stronghold" was the local centre of the worship of the Babylonian god Marduk to whom Tiglathpileser offered sacrifice. He also had a stele set up with his inscription. From here the Assyrians returned home apparently through the valley of the Diyālā. In spite of the contrary assertion of one of Tiglathpileser's texts (altogether the least reliable one), on the whole his inscriptions make it clear that this incursion involved no annexation of Median provinces by Assyria.

In the western parts of the country Assyrian texts for the most part call the "lands" not by their own names but by dynastic designations (in combination with the word *Bīt-* "house").[1] This often hampers their identification and localization. One or two of these "houses" are already attested in Elamite inscriptions of the 12th century. But for the eastern parts of Media such designations do not occur, probably because there were no permanent ruling dynasties, the power being in the hands of an organization of clans or tribes, perhaps with elected chiefs. Precisely in these regions the Assyrian sources often call the local rulers "lords of townships".

After 737 during Tiglathpileser's lifetime one more expedition was

---

[1] Cf. also *Bīt-Ištar* "House of (the goddess) Ištar".

undertaken into Media by the general Aššurdanninanni, but the Assyrian texts give no details apart from his having seized "five thousand horses, and men and cattle without number".

Towards 720 the political situation in the country was the following. The region to the north of Lake Urmīya was apparently occupied by Urartu. Almost the entire remaining territory around the lake up to the watershed between the basins of the Lesser Zāb, Diyālā and the Safīd-rūd was directly or indirectly dominated by Iranzu, king of the Land of the Mannaeans, but on the periphery of this kingdom there were possessions of semi-independent rulers even though the texts call them *šaknu*, i.e. "governors" of the Mannaean kingdom. These were the provinces Uišdiš (Urart. *Uyišti*, approximately in the region of present-day Marāgha), Zekertu (in the region of present-day Miyāna and further north), Andia (in the lower part of the valley of the Safīd-rūd), and one more: the name of the district belonging to the Mannaean "governor" Dāiukku (Old Iranian *Dahyauka*, possibly the Deioces of Herodotus) we do not know.[1] In addition, on the frontier of Assyria, and semi-independent of her, were the small kingdoms Allabria and Karalla on the headwaters of the Lesser Zāb and its affluents.

Further south and south-east there still remained independent units apparently included in the general concept of *Mădāi* ("Medes") in its broadest sense, although the union of Median tribes itself, mentioned by Herodotus, if it really existed, did not manifest itself in any way. These units may have been completely independent, or else they depended on the Land of the Mannaeans or on Assyria. Ellipi alone was a comparatively important independent kingdom.

The rise in power of Mana under Iranzu, which transformed it into a first-class state, seems to have been resented by the semi-independent neighbouring regions whose rulers hoped to gain complete independence by exploiting the dissensions among their powerful neighbours. And as the determining factor in international dissensions was the rivalry between Urartu, Mana, Assyria and Elam, the political events consisted mainly of individual betrayals, the siding of petty rulers and governors first with one great power then with another, punitive expeditions, Urartian and Assyrian plots and counterplots, and so on. The Land of the Mannaeans, as the least powerful of the four great

[1] It is probable (as E. A. Grantovsky believes) that Dāiukku's province was Messi. The "House (i.e. dynasty or province) of Deioces" mentioned in some publications does not exist in Assyrian records, the notion of it being due to a misreading of a passage in the annals of the Assyrian King Sargon II.

kingdoms, leaned mostly towards Assyria. The texts of King Sargon II even assert that it was a vassal-state of Assyria, justifying by this his frequent interventions in the affairs of Mana. However, this assertion is belied by the facts showing that, except on a few occasions when the Mannaeans suffered reverses, the Assyrians treated them as junior partners and allies.

For the first time, and apparently at Iranzu's own request, the Assyrians intervened in the affairs of the Land of the Mannaeans in 719. Two strongholds, Šuandaḫul and Durdukka (also called Zurzukka, Zirdiakka, Sirdakka), supported by the infantry and cavalry of Metatti of Zekertu, had seceded from Iranzu. Moreover three strongholds (their location, perhaps outside Mana, is uncertain) namely Sukka, Bala and Abitigna, concluded an agreement with Rusā I, king of Urartu. The strongholds were taken and dealt with according to the time-honoured ancient eastern custom applied in military alliances: the inhabitants and movable property were carried off into Assyria, while the walls and the territory were handed over to Iranzu.

Iranzu died before 716: in that year the throne was already occupied by his son, Azā. A rebellion was led against him by Metatti, governor of Zekertu, Telusina, governor of Andia, Bagdattu (Iran. *Bagadāta*), the governor of Uišdiš, and an unnamed governor of Messi, possibly Dāiukku. The rebels seem to have accused Azā especially of having allied himself with the Assyrians. He was seized and killed, and his body cast out on Mount Uauš (Urart. *Uuši* [wosə], now Sahend). Sargon immediately intervened and succeeded in capturing Bagdattu, whom he ordered to be flayed alive, whereafter his body was displayed for the Mannaeans to contemplate. Ullusunu, another of Iranzu's sons, was set on the throne. But Ullusunu, surrounded by sympathizers of the anti-Assyrian party, was compelled immediately to secede from Assyria, and attempted to conclude an alliance with Urartu. He ceded to Rusā I, king of Urartu, some strongholds apparently situated on territory bordering on Assyria, and drew into an anti-Assyrian movement the rulers of neighbouring valleys: Ittī, ruler of Allabria, and Aššurlē', ruler of Karalla. Sargon, without returning to Assyria, captured the Mannaean capital Izirta and the very important central strongholds – Izzibia (or Zibia, to-day Ziwiyeh) and Armait. Ullusunu surrendered at discretion, but as he apparently belonged to the pro-Assyrian party and had acted only under pressure of his entourage, he was given back his kingdom. Ittī was exiled into Assyrian dominions with his family, and Aššurlē' was flayed alive. Two border regions were detached from the Land of the Mannaeans and incorporated in the Assyrian province Parsūa.

This done, Sargon continued his campaign further south into districts only loosely controlled or not controlled at all by the Mannaeans. The first to fall was the important stronghold Kišessu which probably dominated the approaches to Parsūa from the direction of the headwaters of the Safīd-rūd. Its ruler, bearing the Akkadian name of Bēlšarruṣur, was taken prisoner. The fortress itself was re-named in Assyrian style and transformed into the centre of the new Assyrian province Kišessu. A stele with the image of Sargon was set up there and a garrison installed. This new province now incorporated various districts apparently situated further downstream in the valleys of the Safīd-rūd and its affluents. The majority of the names of these districts, and of their ruling dynasties, seem to be non-Iranian.

Some strongholds, as for instance those on the slopes of the Alvand and to the west of this mountain, now found themselves cut off both from the Land of the Mannaeans and from the heart of Media. The inhabitants of the most important local stronghold Ḫarḫar expelled their "lord of the township", Kibaba (or Kibabiše) and petitioned Taltā, king of Ellipi, to become his subjects. However, after Kišessu Sargon occupied also Ḫarḫar and turned it, too, into the centre of a new Assyrian province. Soon the inhabitants of Ḫarḫar were transferred from here, and others, apparently Israelites, part of the "ten tribes" conquered by Assyria in 721, were brought in their place. It is precisely Ḫarḫar and perhaps Kišessu which are those "cities of the Medes" mentioned in the Bible (II Kings, 17.6). There have come down to us quite a few letters of a certain Mannu-kī-Ninua, appointed governor of Ḫarḫar, with reports to Sargon on the situation in the province. Other districts, too, were joined to Ḫarḫar province, among them the districts of the Upper and Lower rivers (Qara-su, flowing out of the Alvand mountains?), the House of Rāmatēa (Araziaš), Šaparda or Saparda, and others. Although these districts were not usually considered part of Media proper (*Mădāi*), the personal names of the rulers and the place-names go to show the prevalence here of a strong Iranian-speaking element.

Subsequently Assyrian armies penetrated more than once deep into Median territory, but to all intents and purposes the frontier of the provinces properly belonging to Assyria does not seem to have been moved even in later times beyond the limits established by Sargon, and even within these limits it was no easy task for the Assyrians to retain their hold on these mountain regions.

The frontiers of the zone occupied by the Assyrians can be determined as follows: the valleys of the upper stretches of the Diyālā and of the Lesser Zāb, and the Shahrazūr valley were entirely occupied; in the north the frontier followed the mountains Gizilbunda (Shāhberdi–Kafelān-kūh), and extended further towards the region of present-day Zanjān and Qazvīn. From there a rather unstable frontier ran towards the mountain mass of the Alvand and along the watershed between the Diyālā and the Saimarra from east to west, including the affluents of Diyālā. On this territory, from the western slopes of the Zagros to the east, five Assyrian provinces were originally situated: Zamūa, Parsūa, Bīt-Ḥamban, Kišessu and Ḥarḥar. Subsequently (apparently from the beginning of the 7th century?) the last two provinces were somewhat expanded, and then divided into five parts: Kišessu, Ḥarḥar, Mădāi, Šaparda and Bīt-Kāri (or Kār-Kaššī). These five provinces covered the basin of the Safīd-rūd (above Miyāna), of the Zenjān-chāy, of the Abhar and of the Qara-su, as well as the slopes of the Alvand. At that time, too, the province of Arrapḫe with its centre in present-day Kirkuk was enlarged at the expense of "Syromedia" (Parsūa and Bīt-Ḥamban).

In 715 some part of the territory between Mana and the Assyrian provinces seems to have still been in the hands of Dāiukku (Deioces?), who ruled it as technically a provincial governor of the kingdom of the Mannaeans. But this kingdom had entered into an alliance with Assyria. Deioces seems to have felt that his independence was at stake. This was also pointed out to him by messengers sent by the king of Urartu, Rusā I, who in the meantime had begun from the north a punitive action against Ullusunu of the Mannaeans. Deioces supported him from the south, and to prove his loyalty sent him his son as his representative and hostage. But the undertaking of Rusā and Deioces had no success. Sargon seized and directly annexed twenty-two strongholds which a year earlier Ullusunu had ceded to Rusā. This done, he moved against Deioces, captured him and exiled him together with his family (other of course than the son who was with Rusā) to Hamath in Syria. Continuing his advance down the Safīd-rūd Sargon entered Andia, the dominion of Telusina, Rusā's ally since at least 719. From here 4,200 prisoners were carried off as well as a large quantity of cattle. While returning through the Land of the Mannaeans Sargon gave orders to erect his image in Izirta.

MEDIA

Meanwhile a serious revolt broke out in the newly established province of Ḫarḫar; it spread also into the neighbouring provinces, among them into Bīt-Ḫamban and into Namar in the Diyālā valley. Sargon crushed the revolt, and the most important local strongholds were occupied by reinforced garrisons. Particularly well he fortified the stronghold Ḫarḫar, "for the conquest of Media", as the annals put it. Yet the Assyrian king did not succeed in subjugating the territory he had seized here in the way he had subjugated other provinces: the local chieftains remained in their possessions within the limits of the provinces, and merely undertook to pay a tribute to Assyria; this seems to have been the practice in these parts, established already under Mannaean domination. It is possible that local contingents were incorporated in the Assyrian army as special detachments. The rulers of the Medes, *Mădāi*, that is, of the population of the territory of the Median tribal union which the annals of Sargon II distinguish from the Qutī or Gutium who lived further to the west, paid tributes to Sargon all over the country right up to Mount Bigni (Damāvand). But subsequent events show that the Assyrians were able to hold firmly only such regions as were immediately controlled by fortresses with Assyrian garrisons and where the inhabitants had been expatriated and replaced with others brought in from other countries, mainly from Syria and Palestine. To collect regular tribute from remote localities was possible only by means of armed expeditions.

The year 714, the one following upon the crushing of the revolt in the province of Ḫarḫar, was marked by Sargon II's expedition against Urartu, described in detail in a military account which has come down to us. At the beginning of his campaign Sargon entered Mannaean territory where he was met by King Ullusunu and his council; then a military demonstration was staged across the land of Bēlapliddin of Allabria, an Assyrian protégé and apparently a spy, after which the Assyrian army withdrew to its own territory in the province of Parsūa. Here the tribute of the "lords of townships" from previously conquered territories in Media and those immediately bordering on them, was brought to Sargon. The text names twenty-six rulers of whom the majority bear clearly Iranian names. The list is headed by Taltā, king of Ellipi, whose name is non-Iranian. The tribute consisted of horses, mules, cattle and two-humped camels. Two non-Iranian rulers sent in their tribute somewhat later from the mountains of Gizilbunda. All hoped to ward off the next Assyrian incursion into their countries.

But Sargon had no intention of attacking the Median regions just then. From Parsūa, having crossed the mountains, he returned to the Land of the Mannaeans where, as previously agreed, Ullusunu was waiting for him in the stronghold Zirdiakka, having laid in supplies of food and assembled horses and cattle for the Assyrian army. At a conference with Ullusunu Sargon, allegedly upon the request of the Mannaean king, promised to start on an expedition aimed at recovering for the Land of the Mannaeans the territory it had lost on the eastern shore of Lake Urmīya. At a feast in honour of the Mannaeans, in sign of recognition of Mana as an allied state Ullusunu was seated, though lower than Sargon, higher than his father Iranzu had been in his time.

In spite of his promise to make war on Rusā, or perhaps in order to mislead the enemy, Sargon marched along the southern and south-eastern borders of the Land of the Mannaeans against Zekertu and Andia, which had not yet been reduced after the revolt against Azā in 716. Metatti, the ruler of Zekertu, adopted the old tactics: abandoning his residence, the stronghold of Parda (to the west of Miyāna?) he took refuge on the Uašdirikka mountain (Bozqush-dagh?) and from there hastily threw in his forces with Rusā who in the meantime, having heard of Sargon's supposed intention to penetrate into the Caspian regions, had hastened from the north-west in order to cut him off from the rear and crush him.

Meanwhile Sargon, having overcome the defence of Metatti on the pass over Uašdirikka and destroyed several Zekertu fortresses, suddenly swerved to the west into the Mannaean province Uišdiš (the region of present-day Marāgha), occupied by the Urartians. In Uišdiš he received the report of his agent Bēliddin (= Bēlapliddin of Allabria?) about the approach of the armies of Rusā and Metatti which apparently confirmed his surmises. In a battle on the mountain Uauš (Sāhend) the Assyrians inflicted a crushing defeat on the Urartu-Zekertu forces and threw them back on Urartu territory. By forced marches Sargon moved northwards along the eastern shore of Lake Urmīya. The population, warned by fires lit on mountain tops, abandoned everywhere its fortresses and villages. The first to be occupied was the stronghold Uškāia (now Uski) on the western slope of the Sāhend which guarded the approaches to the formerly Mannaean province Subi situated further to the north and famed for its horse-breeding, and also to the province of Zaranda.

The expulsion of the Urartians from these parts presented the Land of the Mannaeans with an opportunity for extending its possessions in the north. But the Assyrians had no intention to enrich their ally with undevastated, populous regions. Everywhere on their path they razed the thick adobe walls of the fortresses, burnt down villages, destroyed fields and gardens and took away the stores of provender. After Uškāia came the turn of Aniaštania where the Urartian army reserve of mounts was kept, and next, in the land of the Dālians, that of the double stronghold Tarui-Tarmakisa (or Tarwi-Tarwakisa (?), now Tabrīz), which was likewise a base of Urartian cavalry. Then the town of Ulḫu, to the north of Lake Urmīya, was destroyed with the fortress Sardurihurda which guarded it, and so on. The Assyrian army, pursuing the retreating Urartians, marched to the west across the Qotur pass; Sargon handed over to Ullusunu the twenty-two strongholds which the latter had ceded to the Urartian king shortly before, as well as two other fortresses, probably Uškāia and Parda or Aniaštania. But it is probable that the Mannaeans took advantage of the situation and attempted to seize also some of the northern regions near Lake Urmīya evacuated by the Urartians which the Assyrians had no means of holding as they did not border on Assyria.[1] If in 714 the Mannaean king still paid the Assyrians his tribute twice within the year, soon the Land of the Mannaeans gained enough power to shake itself free and try to pass over to the offensive against Assyria. But although economically it seems to have been the most developed of all the regions which later came to form part of Media, it did not become a first-class great power, probably owing to its archaic oligarchic social structure and state organization.

In 713 Sargon II did indeed undertake that expedition into the heart of Media the preparation for which in 714 must have served to camouflage the attack on Urartu. The pretext was the revolt in Karalla (in one of the valleys on the headwaters of the Lesser Zāb) where the inhabitants, probably driven to despair by taxes and levies, had expelled the Assyrian agent. Another reason for the expedition was the precarious situation of Taltā, king of Ellipi, whose pro-Assyrian sympathies provoked the discontent of the Ellipi aristocracy that tended towards Elam. After easily crushing the revolt in Karalla, Sargon marched across the borderlands of the Median provinces into Ellipi where he established the order he desired. From there he moved into the inner regions of independent Media. His text enumerates a number of districts, mostly with clearly Iranian names – "remote regions [near] the confines of [the

[1] Later the Urartians recovered many districts between Lake Urmīya and the Araxēs.

land] Aribi of the East, as well as regions of the strong Medes who... wandered in mountains and deserts like thieves". Here evidently the nomadic Iranian tribes are meant, among them possibly, as we saw, the Arizanti. In the list of rulers of the districts devastated by the Assyrians during this expedition only some three names are definitely non-Iranian. Altogether from Sargon's texts we know some fifty Median chieftains, most of them independent.

The last expedition into Media under Sargon II was apparently undertaken in 706 B.C.[1] Taltā, king of Ellipi, devoted to the Assyrians, had died by that time, and the protégé of the Assyrians, Aspabāra, was opposed by his half-brother Nib'ē who had the support of Šutruk-Nahhunte II, king of Elam. Sargon sent against Ellipi the armies of seven "chiefs of provinces". The situation which arose is described in letters from two of them which have come down to us. Sargon intended to annex Ellipi to Assyria but in the end agreed to hand over the country to Aspabāra. The Assyrians besieged the stronghold Mar'ubištu held by Nib'ē with 4,500 Elamite archers, and captured it. Notwithstanding the formal preservation of Ellipi's independence this kingdom lost all importance. It was still further weakened in 702 by the expedition of Sargon II's son Sennacherib. This expedition was part of a prolonged war between Sennacherib and Elam and had partly the character of an outflanking demonstration, and partly must have aimed at preventing the penetration of Elamite influence into Media. The primary object of the expedition were the mountain tribes of the Kassites and the neighbouring Iasubigallians in present-day Luristan, to the south of Ellipi. This region was incorporated in Assyria. In two strongholds some Kassites were settled who had previously fled into the mountains, in a third some of the captives of the Assyrians, apparently Babylonians. From here Sennacherib invaded Ellipi because this time Aspabāra had joined the pro-Elamite coalition. Here the Assyrians seized the fortresses Mar'ubištu and Akkuddu and a considerable booty consisting of men, horses, mules, asses, camels and cattle. At the same time the province Bīt-Barrūa (Baruata of the Urartian inscriptions) was detached from Ellipi, settled with captives driven in from other places and annexed to the Assyrian province of Ḫarḫar. This shows that Bīt-Barrūa, once annexed under Tiglathpileser III, had since managed to secede, probably

---

[1] Yet another expedition may have taken place in 705, in the course of which Sargon was killed. In any case this must be so if the "Kulummians", mentioned in this connection by an Assyrian source, were the inhabitants of the stronghold Kuluman or Kilman in the Ḫarḫar province.

during the rising of 715, and to join Ellipi. The centre of this province was Elenzaš, perhaps the same as Erenziaš of Tiglathpileser's annals. This city seems later to be mentioned by Ptolemy under the name of Alinza.

After the defeat of 702 Ellipi nevertheless ventured to take the field once again against Assyria. In 691 it took part in an important coalition formed by the king of Elam, Humpan-nimmena, and the king of Babylon, Mušēzib-Marduk. It was also joined by various Chaldaean and Aramaic tribes, as well as by the lands of Parsūaš, Anzan (Anshan, Ančan), Paširu and Ellipi. Here Parsūaš cannot be the Assyrian province Parsūa which at that time was surrounded on all four sides by Assyrian possessions, but is evidently Fārs. There is no reason to believe that Parsūaš-Persis was a tribal territory, and not a small state like Ellipi and Anshan. As mentioned above, a calculation of generations shows that Achaemenēs, the founder of the dynasty which subsequently ruled in the Persian kingdom, must have lived not long before the war of 691, and may even have taken part in it. However, the name of the country Parsūaš, as we have seen, is attested in the same area already in the 9th century B.C., and there are therefore no grounds for assuming, as is often done, that Achaemenēs was some king or chieftain of a nomad army invading Fārs. It is much more probable that, long before Achaemenēs, a small state had existed in Parsūaš-Persis but was ruled by some other dynasty. As to Anshan, it was one of the most ancient city-states of Elam. Of the kingdom of Paširu, probably situated somewhere between Ellipi and Anshan (Tepe Malyān), nothing more is known.

The army of the anti-Assyrian coalition clashed with the Assyrians at Ḫalulē on the Tigris. The battle was bloody but undecisive. However, the allies were unable to carry on with the war because of Humpan-nimmena's illness and the internecine strife which it caused in Elam. Meanwhile Sennacherib succeeded in capturing and destroying Babylon. Thus this attempt of the conquered peoples to shake off the Assyrian yoke was as fruitless as the previous ones had been. The beginning of the 7th century B.C. was the time when the consolidation of Assyria's position in Media reached its peak.

THE MEDES AND THEIR NEIGHBOURS

5. *Cimmerians and Scythians.*
The revolt of the Medes and the rise of the Median kingdom

The later popular tradition of the Medes, handed down to us by Herodotus,[1] preserved the memory of a period of independence that followed the period of Assyrian devastations, but preceded the formation of an all-Median state. Herodotus says (1. 95–97): "The Assyrians ruled over Upper Asia[2] during five hundred and twenty years; and the Medes were the first to fall away from them. And fighting the Assyrians for their liberty they showed themselves valiant men and put their bondage from them. And after them other peoples also did the same as the Medes had done... There was a subtle man among the Medes whose name was Deioces, and he was the son of Phraortes. This Deioces desiring to be tyrant did as follows. [At that time] the Medes dwelt in villages. And whereas Deioces had a good reputation in his own, he, although he knew that the unjust is always hostile to the just, began to observe justice still better and more zealously, while in the rest of Media lawlessness obtained. The Medes of his village seeing his behaviour, elected him judge... In so far as robbery and violence in the villages had become worse than before, the Medes assembled in one and the same place, exchanged speeches about what was going on... persuaded one another to submit to royal dominion." It has often been pointed out that we have here a complicated and prolonged process compressed in naïve form within the field of activity and the lifetime of one single person, but nevertheless a true picture of a society on the eve of the institution of the state: independent townships (the term *kōmē* evidently denotes here not a village in the modern sense, but a township lacking political organization), economic stratification, the free for all struggle of each against everyone, the plundering of property, public servants as yet elected but aiming at royal power, a popular assembly etc. Moreover Herodotus' description makes sense both typologically and

---

[1] It is assumed that the information of Herodotus on the history of Iran, apart from possible personal observations, came from the accounts of Zopyrus, a Persian emigrant belonging to one of the great houses of Persia, and also from someone or other of the descendants of the Median magnate Harpagus who played a fatal rôle in the years of the fall of the Median kingdom and subsequently became Persian satrap of Sardis. His descendants had apparently settled in Asia Minor, more precisely in Lycia, not far from Herodotus' native city Halicarnassus. The historian also utilized the writings of Hecataeus of Miletus, who seems to have had access to some official Persian documents of the satrapy of Sardis.

[2] Herodotus calls "Upper Asia" the area east of the river Halys (now Qızıl-Irmaq) in Asia Minor. In general a journey into the interior of the Persian kingdom was called a journey "upwards"; by contrast, the western provinces of the kingdom were called the "Lower Country".

chronologically: it not only conforms to a certain type of social condition, but also fits into a definite period of Median history.

It is difficult to say by what calculations the precise number of 520 years for the Assyrian domination was reached. To go by the general context, as well as by chapter 102 of the same book, this period should be calculated from the fall of the Assyrian kingdom and not from the moment of secession of the Medes. It is in fact to the 12th century (612 + 520 = 1132) that one of the most important periods of Assyrian expansion under Tiglathpileser I belongs. If computed from the date of the actual foundation of the Median kingdom (about 673 B.C.), the period of 520 years brings us up to the reign of a still more famous Assyrian warrior-king, Tukulti-Nimurta I, the Nimrod of the Bible. But the time of Assyria's prolonged domination of the whole of "Upper Asia" which could still have been remembered as part of their history by Medes in the days of Herodotus, should probably be identified with the Assyrian domination from 834 to 788 B.C. After it there actually began in Media a period of independent existence of small fortified townships which, as the fact itself of their fortification shows, were clearly hostile to one another. Their fortress walls were not intended for defence against the Assyrians, since at their approach usually no attempt was made to defend them. It is true that contrary to the legend which reached Herodotus, between this period and the formation of an all-Median kingdom in the 70s of the 7th century B.C. there lay a second period of Assyrian invasions and domination (744 or 737–674 B.C.). But in the memory of later Medes both periods of Assyrian aggression had merged into one, which became linked to the name of the legendary Semiramis. Indeed, according to Herodotus (I. 185), Semiramis lived some time between 770 and 700 by our chronology, and Deioces, the founder of the Median kingdom, according to his calculations and as transposed into our chronology, began to rule in 727 (or 699) B.C.

But Herodotus was mistaken in ascribing to Deioces the founding of the Median kingdom. The historical Deioces (who admittedly may have been only a namesake of the Herodotean Deioces) was a functionary subordinated to the Land of the Mannaeans, although like many others fairly independent. In 715 he was exiled by Sargon II to Syria together with his family (cf. above, p. 83). His connection with the later Median dynasty, though possible, is not attested by any authentic sources. It is not known, either, where exactly he ruled, although this was more probably somewhere in the valley of the river Jagatu than

THE MEDES AND THEIR NEIGHBOURS

in the region which the Assyrians called "*Mădāi*" in the narrow sense, the valley of the Safīd-rūd.

The information of Median tradition on the social organization of Media in the days of Deioces and before him as preserved by Herodotus, can be completed on general lines from the Assyrian annals. We have already cited the meagre evidence we possess on early Median society. What was new in the period to be discussed below, the beginning of the 7th century, was only the increased power of the "lords of townships"; now one "lord of a township" seems to have exercised hegemony over an entire district (*nagû, nagi'u*); even in provinces conquered by Assyria we usually find, side by side with the Assyrian "chief of the province" (*bēl pāḫete*), also a local "lord of the township" (*bēl āli*). If the earlier "lord of the township" is best compared with the Avestan *vīspaiti-* "lord of a kinship group and its village", he now came to correspond most closely to the Avestan *dainhupaiti-* "lord of the district (or land)". For the rest, in Media of the 7th century B.C. some intertribal connections survived within the limits of the Median tribal confederation as a whole, and according to a very credible report of Herodotus (I. 97), it was possible to hold tribal popular gatherings (cf. *hanjamana-* in the Avesta).

As said above, at the end of the 8th or the beginning of the 7th century B.C. Assyrian power was hard put to it to keep the mountaineers of the Iranian plateau in subjection. Meanwhile, at about the same time a new political factor emerged which disturbed the customary balance of power between the four kingdoms Assyria, Urartu, the Land of the Mannaeans and Elam on the one hand, and the self-governing mountain strongholds and tribes on the other. This factor was the nomadic horsemen who during the second half of the 8th century and the first half of the 7th century B.C. penetrated into the Near East from beyond the Caucasus, out of the steppes of the present-day European part of the Soviet Union.

The ancient Oriental evidence on these nomads throws sufficient light on isolated situations but gives no clear idea of the course of their movements as a whole. Archaeological data are of little help because even north of the Black Sea Scythian material can be identified only from the middle of the 7th century B.C., so that the culture which was brought into Asia in the 8th century and the beginning of the 7th by the tribes mentioned cannot be the one which in the archaeology of the steppe expanse of Eastern Europe is conventionally called "Scythian" and itself bears unmistakable traits of Near Eastern influence. Both the Cimmerians and the Scythians of Assyrian and other Asiatic sources belong archaeologically to pre-Scythian cultures. As for Asia, the so-called "Scythian" material in its turn becomes clear as such only when it can be compared with the Scythian material of Europe, in other words, only in strata of the 7th to the 5th centuries B.C. By that time, however, one has to take into account the interaction of Scythian material culture in the Near East with the cultures both of linguistically related peoples (e.g. the Medes, the Bactrians), and of such unrelated peoples as the Scythians came into close contact with in Transcaucasia, on the periphery of the Iranian and Armenian highlands, and in Asia Minor. We are therefore not always justified in regarding the corresponding material as indisputably Scythian.

Thus, for instance, the so-called "Scythian" arrow-heads, well studied and providing a reliable basis for a precise archaeological dating of burial mounds and strata of ruined cities, are also found as weapons of besieging armies under the walls of strongholds where the presence of Scythians is unattested while the presence of Cimmerians (in Asia Minor during the first decades of the 7th century), of Medes (at Carchemish towards the end of the 7th century), and of Persians (in Babylon in the 6th century) has been established.[1] This fully corresponds to the indication of Herodotus (I. 73) that Medes took instruction from Scyths in archery (Scythian arrows and probably all archery equipment were technically and ballistically superior to those earlier used in the Near East); it also goes to show how difficult it is to distinguish archaeologically the Scythians from the Cimmerians, and sometimes from the Medes. These circumstances make it imperative to have recourse to Graeco-Roman narrative sources which, although considerably removed in time from the events they describe, are nevertheless important, containing as they do comprehensive points of view on the course of the migrations of the tribes of horsemen out of Europe. These points of view go back to an old, and most likely reliable, tradition.

In the opinion of the Greeks of the 8th century B.C. the neighbours of the Thracians living on the western shore of the Black Sea were horse-breeding tribes. In the *Odyssey* (XI. 14) in the form in which it has come down to us, the "Cimmerians" are mentioned in an unknown remote northern land.

[1] There are some Neo-Babylonian texts, kindly brought to my notice by M. A. Dandamayev, which testify to the use of Scythian arrows also in the Babylonian army in the 6th century B.C.

THE MEDES AND THEIR NEIGHBOURS

Apparently the Cimmerians were not known in the northern coastal regions of the Black Sea either to Hesiod (c. 800 B.C.), or to Aristeas of Proconnesus (7th century?). Still less were any Cimmerians to be found there in the 5th century B.C., or at the end of the 6th. Herodotus (I. 103; IV. 11ff.) knows a tradition according to which the Cimmerians had at one time lived near the so-called Cimmerian Bosporus (the Kerch Strait), but were ousted by the Scythians and, pursued by them, had gone to the Near East. However, besides recounting this legend Herodotus quotes another that contradicts it but, as can be established, quite correctly tells that the Scythians followed a route entirely different from that taken by the Cimmerians: the latter, according to Herodotus, moved along the Black Sea coast, while the Scythians moved along the Caspian. The eastern coast of the Black Sea being, as we have seen, impracticable for horsemen, the Cimmerians must have passed not along the seashore but over the western passes of Great Caucasus—Klukhor and Alagir, perhaps also the Daryal.

We possess no factual data to show that the Cimmerians at any time represented the basic mass of the population of the steppes north of the Black Sea. Greek names of local mountains, straits and places formed from the name of the Cimmerians prove nothing: they could have been given by the Greeks, as part of the legends common among them about an ancient people that had perished. It was the Greeks, for instance, who gave the name "Cimmerian Bosporus" to the Strait of Kerch which the local inhabitants, as V. I. Abaev has shown, called "Fish-path" in Scythian, *Panti-kapa*, which is why the city built there, now Kerch, was given by the Greeks the name of Panticapaeum. The legend about a valiant lost people, so widespread in folklore, could have existed also among the Scythians, and been fastened to the name of the Cimmerians. It does not follow that Scythian tribes and Scythian culture were *everywhere* preceded by Cimmerian tribes speaking a language different from and by a Cimmerian culture alien to, the Scythian. Archaeological data show that there was no gap between the Scythian culture and the cultures that preceded it in the Ukraine, on the Don, in the steppes north of Caucasus and in the Volga region. Nor have we any factual grounds for believing that "Cimmerian" was the self-given name of the entire pre-Scythian population. The term is probably a rendering of an Iranian (?) word. *gamīra-* or *gmīra-*, meaning "mobile unit".

It is only from the itinerary which brought the Cimmerians into the

Near East that one can infer that a group bearing this name originally lived in the North Caucasian steppes and perhaps also on the other side of the Sea of Azov. According to their archaeological culture in the 8th century B.C. this group must of course have been pre-Scythian. But so was, from the archaeological point of view, the group whom in the 7th century the inhabitants of the Mediterranean region and of Western Asia called "Scythians". The three Cimmerian personal names which have come down to us[1] may be either Asianic, bearing witness to the amalgamation of the Cimmerians with the local population of Asia Minor after the invasion, or else, just as possibly, Iranian. The ancient Babylonians applied the term "Cimmerians" (*Gimirri, Gimirrāi*) also to Scythians and Sakas. All this points to the probability that "Cimmerians" and "Scythians" were the original names of two distinct groups which entered the Near East from south-eastern Europe and belonged to one and the same cattle-breeding pre-Scythian culture borne by speakers of languages quite likely "Scythian", that is, "Eastern" Iranian. It is not impossible that some of the Cimmerians might have been Thracian.

It is true that the information on the Cimmerians which we find in Strabo (I. 2. 9; 3. 21; III. 2. 12; XI. 2. 5; XIII. 4. 8; XIV. 1. 40), a late author who wrote some 800 years after the events but conscientiously utilized many ancient sources, seems to present a somewhat different picture. Strabo apparently thought that the Cimmerians had come from the north-west, across the Thracian Bosphorus, penetrating from there into Aeolis, Ionia, Paphlagonia and "even" Phrygia. But he evidently did not clearly distinguish between the different tribes that made incursions into Asia Minor in the 8th to 7th centuries B.C. Thus he refers to the Treres, unquestionably Thracians (cf. Thucydides II. 96. 4) who invaded Asia Minor from the west, as a "Cimmerian people". In another connection he says: "...the Cimmerians who are also called Treres, or some of those minor peoples..." (I. 3. 21). He calls Madyes sometimes a Scythian chieftain (which is correct, see Herodotus, I. 103), and sometimes a Cimmerian one. There are more such inconsistencies.

[1] In Assyrian sources: Teušpā, Dugdammī, Sandakšatru (this last name can be also read Sandakkurru), in Greek sources: Lygdamis (= Dugdammī). Strabo gives the name of Cobus to the chieftain of the Thracian Treres, allies of the Cimmerians. All Cimmerian personal names have at different times been etymologized from Old Iranian, but the etymologies cannot be said to be certain. The name Lygdamis is often considered Asianic. The identification cherished by some, of Teušpā with one of the early kings of the Achaemenid dynasty, Teispes (Iran. *Čišpiš*) is linguistically untenable.

It looks as if Strabo assumed two invasions, one from the north-west, the other from the east. Actually there seem to have been three: one from the north-west (of Treres, not of Cimmerians) and two from the east (of Cimmerians and Scythians). Hence the confusion in Strabo.

The earliest information on the Cimmerians in ancient Oriental sources is contained in the reports of Assyrian spies from Urartu, belonging, as was shown by B. B. Piotrovsky, to the years 722–715 B.C. At that time the Cimmerians inflicted a serious defeat on Rusā I, king of Urartu; their country (Gamirra) was separated from Urartu by a district (*nagi'u*), Guriania (Urart. *Quriani*), located on the north-western limits of the spread of Urartian influence, i.e. in present-day Georgia. This supports the assumption that the Cimmerians came over Klukhor, Mamison-Alagir or Daryal. In 679/8 the Cimmerians invaded Assyria, but their "king" Teušpā was defeated by the Assyrian King Esarhaddon at Ḫubušna (Greek *Cybistra*) in Asia Minor. In the same year we meet with a regiment of Cimmerian mercenaries in Assyria. In about 679/8 the Cimmerians in alliance with Rusā I, king of Urartu, and apparently not without co-operation on the part of the Assyrians, destroyed the Phrygian Empire. Thereafter they became complete masters of Asia Minor, sacking unhindered its towns and seizing its inhabitants down to the middle of the 40s of the 7th century, when they were crushed by the Scythians, while the supremacy in Asia Minor passed to Lydia.

It is not quite clear whether the Cimmerians advanced also east of Georgia, in particular into present-day Azarbaijan and Iran. The information is not reliable. A letter (No. 112) has come down to us of a certain Arad-Sīn to the "Herald of the Land", "chief of the province" in the valley of the Greater Zāb. It seems to belong to the time of the Cimmerian–Urartian war between the years 720 and 715. It reports that the chieftain of the Cimmerians had penetrated into Urartian territory across the land of a country or tribe the name of which has not been entirely preserved, perhaps "the [Land of the Manna]eans". Later, in the 70s of the 7th century, the Cimmerians are mentioned as possible allies of the Medes in some questions posed by King Esarhaddon to the oracle in connection with his campaigns in Media. But as the questions are written in the Babylonian dialect and the Babylonians, at least in later times, used the term "Cimmerians" very loosely, and one may doubt that the Assyrian authorities were able or cared to distinguish clearly between the various invading groups, it is possible that the group of the Scythians was meant here. The notions of "Cimmerians" (*Gōmēr*) and "Scythians" (*Ashkenaz*, resulting from an old scribal error, the miswriting '*ŠKNZ* for *ŠKWZ*, i.e. *'*Aškūz*) are closely linked also in ancient Jewish traditions. The Biblical "List of Peoples" (Genesis 10. 2–3)[1] includes Ashkenaz, along with Rīphath (of equally uncertain location) and Tōgarmah (present-day Malatya and the valley of the upper Euphrates) under the notion "Gōmēr", as his "sons". Therefore, although possibly the Cimmerians did penetrate into the Iranian highlands,[2] this is not at all certain. Things are quite different with regard to the Scythians.

Soon after the Cimmerian invasion the Scythians invaded the Near East. This is reported by Herodotus who mistook the event for a direct result of the migration of the Cimmerian horsemen from Europe (I. 103; V. 1–4; 11–14). While the Greeks call the Scythians *Skythai*, Assyro-Babylonian sources refer to them as *Ašguzāi*, *Asguzāi*, *Iškuzāi*. These transcriptions show that their native name was *$Skuδa-t$-, later possibly *$Skula-t$-(whence in Greek also *Scoloti*?). Their name was at that time not yet a general designation of northern groups, but referred to one definite group only.

According to Herodotus' account uncontradicted by archaeological data the Scythians, after the Massagetae pushed them out of the trans-Volgan steppes to the west,[3] penetrated into the territory of the Cimmerians and finally appeared in the Near East by moving along the Caspian shore – "having on their right side the Caucasian mountain" (I. 104; IV. 12).[4] Having described how the Scythians made their way

[1] Text of the 6th century B.C. included in the "Priestly Code", a product of the 5th century.

[2] It is hardly correct to call "proto-Cimmerian" the horsemen depicted on a seal of the late 8th century from Necropolis B of Tepe-Sialk, and in general the creators of the culture of a number of sites in Iran at that time, although they are so referred to in some works on art and archaeology.

[3] At this point (IV. 11) Herodotus calls the Volga Araxēs; various large rivers were designated by this name: the Volga, the Jaxartēs, the Araxēs of Transcaucasia, the Araxēs in Atropatene and even the Tigris (?). Later Greek authors more correctly call the Volga Rhā, which name corresponds to its Avestan name *Raŋhā* and was therefore in use much earlier than the time of Herodotus. In Scythian its form must have been *$Rahā$.

[4] The late E. I. Krupnov held the opinion, shared by B. B. Piotrovsky, that the Cimmerians penetrated into the Near East along the shore of the Black Sea, while the Scythians came by four routes: the same as the Cimmerians, over the Mamison and Daryal passes, and along the Caspian shore. But the route along the Black Sea shore is definitely impossible for horsemen. It is true that tombs with "Scythian" arms and implements have been discovered in Abkhazia, i.e. near the Black Sea (Kulanurkhva near Gudauti; Sukhumi), in Georgia (Dvani, Samthavro), in present-day Armenia and in the Azarbaijan republic (Mingechaur). But it seems to us that the "Scythian" objects from Georgia must either belong to the epoch of the general Scythian hegemony spreading from Asia Minor to Iran (652–625), or actually to the proto-Scythian tribe of the Cimmerians. The Cimmerians would not necessarily have reached Abkhazia along the sea

round the Caucasus range Herodotus adds (I. 104): "at this place (i.e. somewhere in present-day Azarbaijan (?), the Great Caucasus having been left behind) the Medes gave battle to the Scythians but were defeated; they lost their rule over Asia, and the Scythians took possession of it". But Herodotus as usual telescopes events; he identifies the time of the clash of Medes and Scythians with the end of the rule of the Median king Phraortes, i.e. with the year 653/2 in our chronology, whereas the Assyrian sources mention the Scythians already in the 70s of the 7th century B.C. It may be assumed that they penetrated into Transcaucasia somewhat earlier, even a generation earlier, i.e. about the year 700. One cannot however accept the view of Sulimirski who, on the basis of representations of unidentified horsemen on reliefs from Nimrud which he ascribes to the time of Aššurnaṣirapli (?), dates the first raid of the Scythians into Asia in the early 9th century.[1]

At the beginning of the 70s of the 7th century the Scythians led by Išpakāi (Old Iranian *Spakāya*[2] or *Aspaka*?) marched, in alliance with the Land of the Mannaeans, against Assyria. According to the laconic assertion of Esarhaddon's inscriptions, the allies were defeated. Subsequent mention of Scythians in Babylonian and Assyrian texts is already in connection with events in Media from the middle 70s of the 7th century which brought about the creation of the Median kingdom.

If the ancient Oriental sources know a land of the Cimmerians, apparently in present-day Georgia,[3] they also know a Scythian kingdom. Students of the problem often localize it in the Land of the Mannaeans

---

shore, as a more likely route would have been across the Klukhor pass and along the valley of the river Kodori. The tombs in question are dated from the 8th to the 5th centuries B.C. in the west of Transcaucasia, and from the 6th to the 4th centuries in the east. It is important to note that no archaeological finds in Asia can be linked to any reliable extent with Cimmerians as *distinct* from Scythians. It is true, as Piotrovsky points out, that the implements from the "Scythian" tombs in Georgia differ greatly, for instance, from those in Mingechaur. But it could not be otherwise: Herodotus (IV. 1) makes it clear, and the conditions of crossing mountain passes require, that the mounted nomads who invaded Asia consisted only of males. They therefore seized women from different local peoples. Each group of women naturally did housework according to the customs, and with household utensils characteristic of their respective original homes.

[1] The very detailed annals of Aššurnaṣirapli contain no information on clashes with nomads. But his palace was later inhabited by Tiglathpileser III (745–729), and on stylistic grounds Sulimirski's horsemen should be dated to the second half of the 8th century B.C.

[2] V. A. Livshits points out that this name might be the ethnonym of the Sakas; on how the term "Saka" was applied see below.

[3] After their period of supremacy in Asia Minor and the defeat suffered at the hands of the Scythians, the Cimmerians settled down in the north-east of Asia Minor. This is why medieval Armenian sources call this region *Gamirkʻ*; it is not the country *Gamirra* of the cuneiform inscriptions.

MEDIA

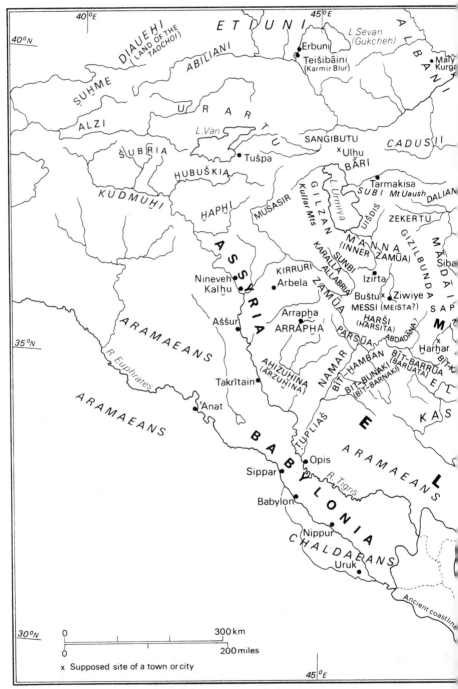

Map 3. Media in the 9th–7th centuries B.C.

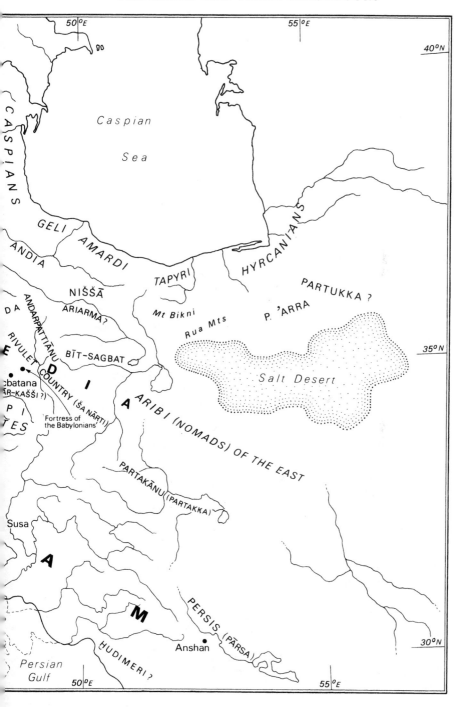

on the strength of the frequent joint mention of Mannaeans and Scythians in inscriptions, and in questions put to an Assyrian oracle. It is indeed in the Land of the Mannaeans (in Ziwiyeh, ancient Izzibia, Zibia, or Uzbia) that a treasure was found which is regarded by some as the tomb of a Scythian chief of the end of the 7th (?) century B.C., although the treasure includes numerous precious artifacts dating from the 8th to the 7th century. However, the Bible names "the kingdom of Ashkenaz" (i.e. *'Aškûz*) side by side with the Land of the Mannaeans (*Minnī*) and Urartu (*'Ararat*). It follows that, as the Mannaean kingdom beyond doubt survived until the end of the 7th century, the Scythian kingdom was not situated near Lake Urmīya. The Scythians must have merely passed through the Land of the Mannaeans, as plunderers or as allies. It is nevertheless right to seek the region which the Scythians of Asia inhabited after they passed along the Caspian shore, on territory which under the Achaemenians formed part of the satrapy of Media. The list of peoples living in the various satrapies of the Persian kingdom as quoted by Herodotus, mentions within the satrapy of Media (III. 92), in addition to the Medes themselves, also the Paricanii and the Orthocorybantii. "Paricanii" seems to be a general designation of various pre-Iranian (?) inhabitants of Iran (cf. Herodotus III. 92, 94; VII. 68, 86), perhaps terminologically connected with the legendary creatures called *paⁱrika-* in the Avesta (from which "peri"); here it perhaps denotes the non-Iranian population of Media, i.e. the Mannaeans and the Qutī. As for the term "Orthocorybantii", this is a translation of Iranian *tigraχauda-* "wearers of pointed caps", a nickname of certain Scytho-Saka tribes in the inscriptions of Darius I and his son Xerxes. The specific use of the term by Darius and Xerxes does not alter the fact that *all* Scytho-Saka tribes, including apparently the Cimmerians, wore originally more or less tall, pointed caps. It seems permissible, therefore, to identify the Orthocorybantes of Herodotus with the Sacesinae of Arrian, the inhabitants of Strabo's Sacasēnē.[1] This region is known to the medieval Armenian authors under the name of Šakašen, and is localized to the south of the middle course of the river Kura, more or less in the region of present-day Kirovabad (Ganja), i.e. near those parts where according to Herodotus the war between the Scythians and the Medes was waged. It should be noted that Herodotus' satrapy of Media stretched in the north beyond the Araxes, for

---

[1] Iran. *Saka.šayana* "the land inhabited by the Sakas"; the Persians called "Saka" all the northern nomads, just as the Greeks called them "Scythians", and the Babylonians "Cimmerians".

according to him (I. 104; IV. 37) the Medes were separated from Colchis only by the Saspires, apparently Georgian-speaking tribes. Settlements of Medes beyond the Araxēs are also known to the medieval historian Moses Xorenaci (5th century A.D.), although his explanation of their origin is fantastic.

The situation in the Median highlands at the end of the 8th century B.C., i.e. before the appearance of the northern nomads, is graphically described in letters from Assyrian governors of the provinces of Ḫarḫar, Kišessu and others, to Sargon II (letters Nos 126–9, 645, 714, 1,045 from the royal archives of Kuyunjik). The re-building and the re-peopling of the strongholds and their districts conquered by the Assyrians was going on simultaneously with spying activities against the independent parts of Media, and intrigues were fostered among the neighbouring independent, semi-independent and dependent chiefs. The same state of affairs seems to have obtained under Sennacherib. Unfortunately the inscriptions of the next Assyrian king Esarhaddon (680–669) are very laconic, and as the events in Media during his reign took an unfavourable turn for Assyria, their mention in his inscriptions is both brief and obscure. What we know of them comes mainly from a very fragmentary series of questions put by Esarhaddon to the oracle of the god Šamaš. It has been established that this series contains no mention of any event before 676 or after 652. The text of some of Esarhaddon's inscriptions, dated in 676–673, mentions events in the Land of the Mannaeans and in Media, but does not yet speak of the expedition against Šubria in the mountains of the Armenian Taurus. We know from the "Babylonian Chronicle"[1] that this expedition was carried out in the year 673. It is therefore clear that Esarhaddon's last Median war began not earlier than in 676, and probably ended in 673.[2] The course of events can be reconstructed as follows.

Esarhaddon's inscriptions mention vaguely, not later than 676, an expedition into the eastern mountains: "I trampled down the country Barnaku, the perfidious enemy, the inhabitants of Tīlašurri, whose name is "city of Pitānu" in the mouths of the Meḥrānians". The country of Barnaku is not mentioned again in the sources unless it can be identified with (Bīt-)Bunaki, a district on the north-western border of Elam (cf.

[1] The so-called "Esarhaddon Chronicle".
[2] Earlier students of the period dated the Median series of questions from 679, the year of the conflict of the Assyrians with Teušpā, chief of the Cimmerians, in Asia Minor, relying on the mistaken identification of the Median province Saparda or Šaparda with Lydia in Asia Minor (Lyd. Sfart, Old Pers. Sparda, Greek Sardis, the capital of Lydia).

above, p. 63). Tīlašurri is first mentioned already by Tiglathpileser III together with Silḫazi, "a stronghold of the Babylonians". It should be sought not far from Hamadan, or to the west of this town, if one takes "Pitānu" for ancient Padān. The Assyrians do not seem to have penetrated deep into Media.

Next, also not later than the year 676, came the expedition against the Mannaeans about which Assyrian inscriptions speak off-handedly, in a rapid patter, a sure sign of the absence of real success: "I dispersed the people of the Land of the Mannaeans, the unsubdued Qutī, I put down by arms the forces of Išpakāi, the Scythian, an ally who did not save them."

The questions put to the oracle show that the initiative of the military operations lay with the Mannaeans. The Assyrian king asks the god whether the Mannaeans would succeed in seizing the Assyrian fortresses Šarruiqbi and Dūr-Ellil. In this the Mannaeans seem to have succeeded, for at least one of these fortresses was recovered by the Assyrians only a generation later.

In the majority of questions the Mannaeans appear without allies, but later it turns out that the "Cimmerians" had joined them. From a letter of a certain Bēlušēzib, a Babylonian soothsayer in the service of the Assyrians (No. 1,257), it is clear that some negotiations took place with the "Cimmerians", who had promised not to interfere in Assyro-Mannaean relations. The author, however, recommends not to trust them and gives advice about spying both on the Mannaeans and the Cimmerians. A certain "Bēlḫabû the Mannaean" is mentioned, who may have been the Mannaean king of the time, although his name is Akkadian (?). In another question the "Cimmerians" are mentioned in a somewhat obscure context, in connection with the name of the Mannaean king Aḫsēri (d. 659/58).

Further on it is no longer the Cimmerians who are on Mannaean territory, but the Scythians, unless this be merely a more precise term for the same tribe. The question to the oracle dated from May–June 676 (?) or 675 (?), refers to the danger of the Scythians "who are in the Land of the Mannaeans" attacking the frontiers of Assyria, apparently across the kingdom of Ḫubuškia on one of the affluents of the upper Tigris, to the south of Lake Van. To judge from another question concerning the same matter, the Mannaeans themselves seem to have taken part in the attack; consequently they had greatly extended their sway to the west at the expense of Assyria. According to

Esarhaddon's inscription the Scythian Išpakāi was defeated (and may have been killed) during the Mannaean war, and the Assyrians may have taken advantage of this to enter immediately into negotiations with his successor (?),[1] Protothyes (Akkad. *Partatūa*, from Old Iran. *Partatava). The Assyrian source calls him "king of the *land* of Iškuza", i.e. of the Scythian kingdom (in Azarbaijan).

Protothyes asked for the hand of Esarhaddon's daughter, and the question put to the oracle is about the expediency of a favourable reply. J. Aro has shown that this question may belong to the earliest in the series. Curiously enough part of the phenomena specified in the text as observed by the priests in the liver of the sacrificial animal for the purpose of answering this question belongs, according to the Assyrian manual for soothsayers, to unfavourable omina. The other part of the omina was considered favourable. The Assyrian priests apparently sanctioned the unprecedented marriage of a daughter of an Assyrian king to a nomad chief, seeing that subsequent events are best interpreted on the assumption that both Protothyes and his son Madyes became and remained loyal allies of Assyria during almost half a century. This does not exclude that the Assyrians may at times have suspected the intentions also of the Scythians, and there could have been frontier skirmishes; this is reflected in later questions put to the oracle.

Meanwhile, not later than in the same year 676, the situation in the Median provinces of Assyria was such that the collection of tribute was considered a hazardous undertaking, on the chances of whose success the king had to consult the oracle.[2] The collected tribute did not always reach its destination (cf. the letter of Esarhaddon No. 242). Three Median rulers, driven from their provinces by rebels, turned to Assyria for help. Esarhaddon's inscriptions state that his armies carried out an expedition into "the land of the remote Medes", on the edge of the Salt Desert near the "lazurite" mountain Bigni (i.e. the Demāvand), into the province Patuš'arra (Old Iran. **Patišhvāra-*) to the west of the later province *Xvār* or Choarēnē. During this expedition two "lords of townships", Šiṭirparna (Old Iran. *Čiθrafarnah*) and Eparna were seized together with their people and cattle.

The help of the Assyrians was requested by the chieftains Uppis, ruler

[1] Prōtothyes was according to Herodotus (1. 103) the father of Madyes who was active in the 50s to 40s of the 7th century. He is unlikely to have been Išpakāi's predecessor.

[2] Questions put to the oracle mention among others the town Karzitali, apparently near Ṣibur in the valley of the Zenjān-chāy, and Andarpatiānu, situated to the east of Saparda, not far from present-day Qazvīn.

MEDIA

of Partakka (Paritakka, Paritakānu, Paraetacēnē near present-day Isfahan), Zanasāna (Old Iran. *Zanaxšāna?*), ruler of Partukku[1] (= Parthia?), and Rāmatēa, or Rāmatāia (Old Iran. *Rāmatavya*), ruler of Urakazaba(r)na (location unknown but according to indirect data this district lay at some distance from the other two). Some opponents were attempting to drive these rulers out of their provinces, and they sent propitiatory gifts of horses and lazurite to the Assyrian king. Assyrian "chiefs of provinces" sent to their assistance subdued the rebellious villages and imposed upon the three rulers an increased annual tribute. This tribute was collected by the Assyrians in the form of horses, but it was here that the difficulties arose: the questions put to the oracle show that already during the expedition against Patuš'arra the Assyrians had feared an attack from the rear by Saparda and other "conquered" Median provinces; but in the less remote Median provinces, too, in Bīt-Kāri (the same as Kār-Kaššī?), in Mădāi, in the self-same Saparda, the collection of tribute by the Assyrians in the autumn of 675 or 674 (?) and in the spring of 674 or 673 (?) was fraught with danger; towards the end of the year there also came Scythian attacks on Assyrian detachments. The Scythians could appear here only across Mannaean territory. As G. G. Cameron believed, the increased tribute in horses from Media must have been imposed to supplement the remount of the Assyrian army in view of the inevitable cessation of the delivery of horses from the Land of the Mannaeans which had been their usual source of supply.

Judging from the questions put to the oracle, the Scythians, apparently towards the beginning of the year 674 (?) or 673 (?), were to be found not on the Tigris, as during the Mannaean war, but in Media. They could ally themselves with the already rebellious Medes, the more so as these were also supported by the Mannaeans, and some information exists which probably shows that, in addition to the nomads and the Mannaeans, Elam, too, was prepared to support the Medes. However, as mentioned before, the Scythians led by Protothyes may have been siding with the Assyrians, and the later questions to the oracle mention almost exclusively the Cimmerians and not the Scythians as allies of the rebels. Of course this might have been just another Scythian

---

[1] The Assyrians liked to juxtapose in their lists of conquered provinces rhyming or alliterated names; it is therefore probable that *Partukku* is either a diminutive or simply a distorted form (for the sake of setting it beside the name *Partakka*) of *Partūa (from Old Iran. *Parθava*) "Parthia". It need not have coincided topographically with the later Parthia.

detachment, called "Cimmerians" to distinguish them from the men of Protothyes.

But whatever may have been the position taken up by the Scythians, revolt broke out in Media towards the Assyrian New Year, i.e. in March–April 674 (?) or 673 (?). In the beginning it covered three provinces (Kār Kaššī, i.e. probably Bīt-Kāri,[1] Mădāi and Saparda). It was correspondingly led by three "lords of townships": Kaštariti (Old Iran. *Xšaθrita), Mamitiaršu (*Vahmyataršī?) and Dusanni. Its moving spirit was Kaštariti, or as we shall henceforth call him, Xšaθrita. The Median districts situated to the east of these three provinces were evidently also lost to the Assyrians and probably joined the rebels. It is likely that Kšaθrita had been formally elected leader of the Median union, although the Assyrians naturally give him no other title above the one that was his before the rebellion: "lord of a township".

Esarhaddon's inscriptions make no mention of the war against Xšaθrita, which makes it certain that Assyria suffered defeat. In some of the inscriptions there is vague mention of an embassy from the "Qutī". The rest we know from questions put to the oracle. In this series it is the Mannaeans (probably King Aḥsēri) and, as has been said, the "Cimmerians" who are usually named as allies of the rebels. In this connection it is difficult to believe that the term "Cimmerians" refers to the basic group of these, who had just then seized the supremacy in Asia Minor. It is here more likely a general designation of nomadic groups that had perhaps detached themselves from the basic Cimmerian, or maybe Scythian, mass. If the question about Protothyes is really of an earlier date than those connected with Xšaθrita, the designation "Cimmerians" may have served to distinguish these nomads from those of the Scythian kingdom in Azarbaijan, friendly to Assyria. Yet they may nevertheless also have been Scythians, because the questions are written in the Babylonian dialect in which, admittedly at a considerably later time,[2] the term "Cimmerian" is used in the broad sense described above.

The simultaneous action of the three chiefs who controlled at least the central part of the valley of the Safīd-rūd and the region of

[1] The alternation in this group of texts of the enumeration of the three provinces (Bīt-Kāri, Mădāi and Saparda) with the names of the three leaders of the revolt (Kaštariti of Kār-Kaššī, Mamitiaršu of Mădāi and Dusanni of Saparda) suggests the identity of Kār-Kaššī ("Colony of the Kassites") with Bīt-Kāri (cf. Akkad. *kār-* "colony").

[2] Cf. the confusion in the use of the term *Qutī* in the Assyrian sources: while the inscriptions of Sargon II distinguish them from the Medes, those of Esarhaddon and Aššurbānapli use *Qutī* for *Mădāi*!

present-day Hamadān, and their alliance with the Mannaeans and the "Cimmerians", allowed the rebels to operate on several fronts at once. The revolt spread like wildfire and soon extended beyond the limits of the three original provinces. Already in April–May 674 (?) or 673 (?) we find XšaΘrita's armies in the neighbouring province of Kišessu besieging the stronghold of the same name.[1] The "Cimmerians", the inhabitants of the province Mădāi (i.e. the people of Mamitiaršu) and the Mannaeans are named as his allies. The Assyrians evacuated their men down the Diyālā valley (letter No. 459). In the same month the Assyrian king asks the oracle about the fate of one more stronghold besieged by XšaΘrita, and of yet another besieged by Dusanni. Several days later a question is put about the fate of the fortress Ṣubar(ā) or Ṣibar in the valley of the river Zenjān-chāy (?). If until now the time limit given for the fulfilment of the augury for each question is one month, for XšaΘrita's siege of the fortress Ušiši (?) the limit is only one week. The Assyrians do not seem to have expected a longer siege.

Curiously enough the Medes no longer confined themselves to cavalry raids, but for the first time dared to lay siege to Assyrian fortresses, evidently not without success. This encourages the assumption that the rebel military leader, or leaders, had received Assyrian, Urartian, or perhaps Elamite training. We shall see below that XšaΘrita was probably the person whom Herodotus calls Phraortes, son of Deioces. May he not have been a son of that Dāiukku-Deioces who we have seen was sent to the Urartian court (cf. above, p. 83), or another member of his family, brought up in the Assyrian possessions to which Sargon II had exiled Deioces? The Assyrians perhaps returned him to his country with the intent of exploiting the prestige of his family in Media, relying on the influence Assyrian upbringing had had on him: indeed, if XšaΘrita was a son of Deioces, he would have been a small boy at the time of the exile forty years previously. But of course all this is mere guesswork. In any case an army that dared to besiege the Assyrian administrative centre Kišessu was quite different from the one which abandoned its strongholds and sought refuge in the mountains at the approach of Shalmaneser's or Sargon's warriors. What certainly also counted was the experience the Medes had gained in the course of more than one century of wars with Assyria. Moreover the mention

---

[1] J. Aro surmises that this question to the oracle (Knutdzon, 1) could have been put even earlier. But it is unlikely to have referred to a time preceding the Assyrian expedition against Patuš'arra and Partukka and the expeditions to collect tribute in the Median districts.

in each question side by side with the armies of the three Median leaders and the Mannaeans, of their nomadic allies may not be fortuitous: the specific tactics of their archer-horsemen would allow them to disperse Assyrian columns on distant approaches to the besieged fortresses, and thus avoid the necessity of meeting in the open field the heavy Assyrian infantry, still the best in the world.

To the end of April or the beginning of May belongs Esarhaddon's question to the oracle about the planned Assyrian counter-offensive. The Assyrians intended to cross over "the pass of Saparda" (^{URU}Sa-par!-du) and occupy as a military base the fortress Kilman or Kuluman (cf. also letters Nos 129 and 1,046) in the south of the province of Ḫarḫar (Saparda originally also formed part of this province). Meanwhile, at about this time danger loomed already over Ṣiṣṣirtu, "the stronghold of the men of Ḫarḫar, which is situated on the frontier of Elam". The Assyrian general Ša-Nabû-šū was sent to its relief. This fortress is known to us as having been wrested from Ellipi by Sennacherib; it was situated in Bīt-Barrūa, i.e. apparently somewhere in the valleys of the upper affluents of the Diyālā. Thus the revolt had spread to five or six provinces of "Assyrian" Media (Saparda, Mădāi, Bīt-Kāri, Kišessu, Ḫarḫar, and perhaps also Bīt-Ḫamban),[1] and Xšaθrita was already threatening the passes leading into Mesopotamia. Unrest seems to have spread even to Parsūa, since it is to this time that a letter may belong (No. 165) from the governor of Parsūa, Nabûrīmanni, to the Assyrian king, in which he reports a raid by the Mannaeans who had intercepted the tribute that was being taken to Nikur, the capital of Parsūa.[2] At the same time in Assyria itself there seems to have been an increase of cases when men refused forced labour service and fled into the mountains. At the end of the year 673 Esarhaddon found himself compelled to undertake an expedition into Šubria in the wooded mountains of the Armenian Taurus to recapture some of the fugitives. Some must have fled also to Media where they were out of reach of their Assyrian pursuers.

In March of the new year 673 (?) or 672 (?) the Assyrians attempted to enter into negotiations with Xšaθrita. More than one messenger was sent to the leader of the rebels, which shows that matters were not going

---

[1] A question to the oracle has come down to us dated from June of an unknown year and connected with the threat to the province Bīt-Ḫamban from enemies among whom are named the Scythians proper. J. Aro is inclined to date it from a later period.

[2] This Assyrian province remained of course in the same region and was not moving in the direction of Fārs. But the letter perhaps dates from the time of the next Assyrian king?

smoothly.[1] The Assyrians tried to set the allies against one another, and to this end sent messengers separately to each of the leaders.[2] Meanwhile Xšaθrita, anxious to obtain diplomatic insurance for his actions, was seeking to establish relations with the Chaldaean chieftain Nabûšumiškun, an old enemy of Assyria.

Until recently it was assumed that the Assyrians succeeded in putting an end to the danger to which the revolt in Media exposed them by rallying to their side the Scythian chieftain Protothyes by means of a diplomatic marriage. Yet, as already mentioned, Protothyes may have abandoned the game already before Xšaθrita's revolt. However this may be, towards 672 military operations in Media came to an end, though the assertion frequently made that Xšaθrita perished in 673 and the revolt suffered utter defeat, is not supported by any of the sources. The Assyrians nevertheless managed to retain possession of the provinces Bīt-ḫamban, Ḫarḫar and Kišessu, to say nothing of Zamūa, Parsūa and the more westerly regions. What is more, when in 672 Esarhaddon brought the inhabitants of his kingdom to swear allegiance to his son Aššurbānapli whose rights to the throne were doubtful, several Median chiefs were among those who swore allegiance. Texts of the oath imposed on them, which is inaccurately described as a "vassal treaty", have come down to us: a separate document was made out for each of the "lords of townships" who took the oath. Curiously enough, only Assyrian gods were appealed to as witnesses to the oath, and seals were impressed on the documents only by the Assyrian side. Such documents have survived for the following persons: Rāmatāia, "lord of the township" of Urakazabana, Tuni of Ellipi, Burdadi (Burtati) "lord of the township" of Karzitali, Ḫatarna "lord of the township" of Sigris, Ḫumbareš "lord of the township" of Naḫšimarta, a certain ruler of Izāia, and Larkutla "lord of the township" of Zamūa. Of these districts Sigris, and possibly Karzitali, belonged to the province of Ḫarḫar. Urakazaba(r)na seems to have been one of the rather remote Iranian provinces and most likely lay to the east of Ellipi. All the others, with the exception of Zamūa, are unknown. It is noteworthy that in Zamūa, too, a province long conquered, a native "lord of a township" – a Qutī

---

[1] J. von Prášek's statement that negotiations with Kaštariti allegedly took place near the town of Amol is based on a misunderstanding.

[2] E.g. to Mamitiaršu. In this connection, among possible enemies who might attack Assyrian messengers, the Scythians are again mentioned. If really the alliance with Protothyes was by then in force, the Assyrians may have feared that their negotiations with the Medes could be regarded by the Scythians as an unfriendly act.

THE MEDES AND THEIR NEIGHBOURS

or a "Lullubian" to judge from his name – existed side by side with the Assyrian provincial governor,[1] just as had been the case not long before in the former Assyrian provinces of Bīt-Kāri, Mădāi and Saparda.

We do not know whether, as D. J. Wiseman, the editor of the texts, believes, a written text of the oath of allegiance was composed for other rulers dependent on Assyria besides those of Media. Most likely not; among the large quantity of fragments of such texts which have been discovered not one relates to any other country. We know that the number of those taking the oath in the Assyrian empire was too large for all the oaths being set out in writing. Written documents were evidently composed only for semi-independent rulers. It is curious that among the "treacherous" actions for which the text of the oath threatens the culprit with malediction, there is the following: "if you convoke a (popular) assembly, swear to one another and confer the royal power on one from your [own] midst". Apparently such cases did occur in Media. In fact, according to Herodotus (1. 97–8), this was how the first Median king was elected.[2] Herodotus speaks of Deioces; but as we know, in actual fact the fate of Deioces (if Dāiukku of the Assyrian sources is the same man) was different, and we must suppose that the elected king in question was the next Median king, whom Herodotus calls Phraortes. In general, Herodotus advances the events linked with Median kings by one reign. The founder of the Median kingdom, who united all six Median tribes and built the new capital of Media, could only have been Deioces' successor, and this successor, Phraortes according to Herodotus, could not have been the conqueror of the Persians (1. 102) and of the rest of Iran because there were still independent kingdoms in Fārs in the 40s of the 6th century, and even in the historical province of Media itself there still existed during the 7th century, besides the Median kingdom, that of the Mannaeans, as well as several autonomous city-states.

[1] An Assyrian "chief of the province" of Lullume (Zamūa) is mentioned in the texts under the year 712 B.C.

[2] It is significant that the new capital built, according to Herodotus, by this king (and actually not once mentioned among the hundreds of strongholds and villages of Media named in the Assyrian sources) bore the name of *Agbatana*, or Ecbatana, in Babylonian *Agmatān(u)*, in the Bible Achmetha (*Akmәthâ*), in Old Iranian *Hangmatāna*, which apparently means "meeting place", or "place of assembly", now Hamadān.

MEDIA

II. THE MEDIAN EMPIRE

1. *The Median kingdom before Cyaxarēs*

The rise of the Median kingdom in *c.* 673–672 seems to be beyond all doubt: it is already mentioned, side by side with Urartu, Ḫubuškia and the Land of the Mannaeans in a letter from the royal archives (No. 434) which can be dated from between the years 672 and 669, and later in an enumeration of independent and dependent kingdoms, as well as of Assyrian and Babylonian provinces dating from between the years 669 and 652. Here Media is named at the end of the list, among the independent states, i.e. after Ashkelon, Edom, Moab, Ammon and Ethiopia, and before the Land of the Mannaeans and the Chaldaean Sea-land none of which were at the time dependent on Assyria. The Assyrians, if one leaves out of account a raid which in 660–659 may have affected the outskirts of the Median kingdom, no longer invaded Media, which explains the temporary silence of cuneiform inscriptions on the history of that country. In the absence, too, of authentic Median sources we have to seek information from Greek authors. Of their writings on the history of Media those of Herodotus have been preserved in full, and those of Ctesias only in excerpts and digests which often make his unreliable account seem even fantastic. The names of the Median kings given by Ctesias are indeed Median, but they must belong to contemporaries he knew from his stay at the Persian court at the end of the 5th century B.C., for they are certainly not the names of rulers of the Median kingdom. In general it is often a hopeless task to try to extract something rational from his narrative. His chronology, as was already proved by Volney at the beginning of the 19th century, is nothing but the inverted and doubled chronological system of Herodotus. Ctesias himself admits that his aim was to refute Herodotus. Herodotus' information, by contrast, is reliable within the limits of what this conscientious author succeeded in rescuing from oblivion, but one must bear in mind that he wrote his history of Asia only from oral tradition two or three hundred years after the events.

In utilizing Herodotus' information one should first of all link up his chronological data with the general chronology of the history of the Near East in the 7th to the 6th centuries B.C. and identify the kings he mentions with personages known to us from oriental sources. As a matter of fact there is obviously some confusion in his chronological canvas.

THE MEDIAN EMPIRE

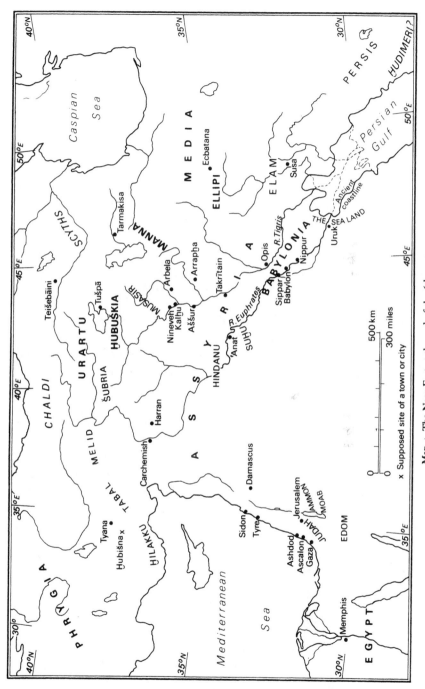

Map 4. The Near East at the end of the 6th century B.C.

MEDIA

According to Herodotus, the first Median king Deioces, son of Phraortes, ruled fifty-three years, the second,[1] Phraortes, twenty-two years; then the Scythians ruled for twenty-eight years, after which Cyaxares reigned for forty years including the years of Scythian domination (this last qualification is absent from some manuscripts of Herodotus); finally Astyages ruled for thirty-five years. The year of the fall of Astyages (550/49) is known from the "Babylonian Chronicle",[2] and we know from Herodotus that Cyaxares made peace with Lydia shortly before his death and soon after the eclipse which, according to astronomical data, took place on 28 May 585. If as is usually done, one relies exclusively on these two chronological landmarks, the following dates emerge for the reigns of the kings of Media according to Herodotus:

Deioces	699–647
Phraortes	646–625
Scythians	624–597
Cyaxares	624–585 (independently of the Scythians: 596–585)
Astyages	584–549

However, this chronological table is incompatible with the undisputed chronological data of Oriental sources. Thus we know that Dāiukku (if Dāiukku and Deioces of Herodotus are one and the same person) ruled till 715 in some district of Mana, Nineveh was destroyed by Cyaxares in 612, and Aššur in 614. Cyaxares is perhaps mentioned even earlier as an enemy of Assyria – the text of the "Babylonian Chronicle"[3] is damaged in the passage in question; but the assumption that he could have waged war on, and destroyed the greatest power in the world while he himself was under the rule of the Scythians, is both highly implausible and in conflict with the information of the selfsame Herodotus that Nineveh was destroyed by Cyaxares *after* his deliverance from Scythian rule (1. 106). Therefore, notwithstanding the fact that the note of Herodotus about the inclusion of the twenty-eight years of

---

[1] A. H. Sayce has voiced the opinion that between Deioces and Phraortes one should insert "Cyaxares I", relying on Diodorus (II. 32. 2). Among the numerous Median "lords of townships" of the end of the 8th century there is actually one bearing this name (Akkad. *Uksatar, Uaksatar*, cf. the later *Umakištar*, Old Iran. *Huxšaθra, Huvaxšθra*). But Diodorus was simply mistaken: he himself says that he is giving a rendering of Herodotus, while in Herodotus there is no Cyaxares I, nor can one insert one into the text of Herodotus without completely reshuffling it. Besides, the chronological system of Ctesias is an inversion of the system of Herodotus as we know it in its reliance on there having been four, and not five, Median kings.

[2] The so-called "Smith's Chronicle on the Fall of Babylon"; see Grayson *Assyrian and Babylonian Chronicles*.

[3] The so-called "Gadd's Chronicle on the Fall of Nineveh", Grayson, Nos 2–4.

THE MEDIAN EMPIRE

Scythian domination in the forty years of the rule of Cyaxares is supported by the most authoritative textual tradition, going back to papyri of the 2nd century A.D., it must be dismissed as resting on an error of either Herodotus himself or some early glossator.[1] If corresponding corrections are introduced, the chronological table will be as follows:

Deioces   727–675
(his exile to Assyria from the year 715 could have been considered illegal by the Median tradition, and the years of exile added to the years of his actual rule; alternatively the ruler may have been a person entirely different from the Dāiukku of the Assyrian sources)
Phraortes 674–653
Scythians 652–625
Cyaxares   624–585
Astyages   584–549

which meets all requirements of independent sources. It should be noted that in this calculation the beginning of the reign of Phraortes coincides with the outbreak of the revolt of Kaštariti-Xšaθrita, Mamitiaršu and Dusanni.

The name of the Median king "Phraortes", mentioned by Herodotus, is a Greek rendering of Iranian *Fravarti-. In the Bīsutūn inscription of King Darius I a Median impostor of this name gives himself out as "Xšaθrita of the house of Cyaxares". Had the founder of the dynasty to which Cyaxares belonged borne the name (or nickname) Phraortes = Fravarti-, the impostor would have had no need to change his name as it would have been a name traditional in the royal family. Evidently the line of Median kings included no Phraortes but did include a Xšaθrita, after whom the Median imposter called himself just as the Persian impostor took the name Bardiya and the Babylonian impostor the name Nebuchadnezzar, both names of men who earlier had been kings. Apparently the names "Phraortes" and "Xšaθrita" were so closely linked in the memory of Herodotus' informant that he confused them, substituting in his story the former for the latter. The

---

[1] This is not the only error in the chronological calculations of Herodotus concerning Median history. Thus he states that the kings of Media reigned altogether "one hundred and twenty-eight years, excluding the time when the Scythians ruled" (I. 130). Many suggestions have been put forward on how to emend the text so as to reconcile the total with the sum of the reigns, but none of them can be considered convincing. Most likely the error lay in the inadvertent omission of the twenty-two years of the "rule" of "Phraortes" (53 + 40 + 35 = 128).

objection raised to this solution, e.g. by R. Labat, is that Herodotus makes "Phraortes" meet his death in the war with Assyria while the Assyrian sources supposedly know nothing of such a war between Assyria and Media. But we shall see on p. 116 below, that Assyrian sources do contain an indication, and precisely under the year 653/2, that such a war took place.

As we have seen, Media was an independent kingdom from the end of the 70s of the 7th century. We may conclude that in the course of the Assyro-Median war of 674(?)–672 Xšaθrita (Kaštariti) became the elected head of this new kingdom, elected just in the way Herodotus describes (1. 97–8), which is hinted at also in the text of the oath of allegiance to the prince royal Aššurbānapli exacted from the Median "lords of townships", namely by a popular assembly. Whether the kingdom of Media really embraced from the very beginning all the Median tribes as Herodotus believed, is not clear. Neither is it clear how far to the south and east the kingdom extended. The texts of the oath of allegiance show that originally not even the whole of Media proper, to say nothing of Persis, was included in the new kingdom.

The stronghold on which Xšaθrita based himself during the revolt was called Kār-Kaššī, which probably meant "colony of the Kassites". West of it, where to-day we have the area of the Kurdish language, the territories began where quite likely non-Iranian languages as yet predominated over the Iranian, and districts whose local population had been deported and replaced with Semites ("Syromedia"). But it was natural for Iranian, as the means of intertribal communication, to become the established language of the new kingdom and of the new city, specially built as capital, Ecbatana. There are grounds for believing that already in the 7th century a special Iranian script was invented, based on the principles of Aramaic, Akkadian and Urartian writing, namely the script which it is usual to call "Old Persian" and whose invention is often ascribed, wrongly in the present author's opinion, to Darius I of Persia. For earlier times documentary proof exists, from the end of the 3rd millennium B.C. to the beginning of the 1st, of the use of Babylonian, Assyrian and Urartian cuneiform writing in the region of the Zagros. Babylonian writing was used also by the local petty princes, as shown by a grant of immunity from a small tax in beer issued in Babylonian language in a city-state of the 9th (?) century B.C. At that early period the native languages of Media do not seem to have been recorded in a writing of their own. However, reading and writing must have existed among the Mannaeans, even though we cannot tell which language and script they used. A silver artifact of local origin from the "treasure" of Ziwiyeh bears signs resembling the hieroglyphics which in Urartu were used side by side with cuneiform writing; but whether they belong to a writing system is not at all clear.

Xšaθrita's brilliant success in creating a single and independent Median kingdom was probably due to wide support given to the movement which he led. As we have seen, according to both Herodotus and the Assyrian sources, Media consisted in the 8th century of a multitude of small pre-state and early-state formations. But towards the end of the 7th century, in spite of the hard times which the young kingdom had had to endure in mid-century, we see the country united in a powerful state except at its periphery, where self-governing units continued in semi-dependence until their final incorporation later. Therefore, between 672 and the beginning of the last Assyro-Median war, that is, not later than 615, the tiny "kingdoms" and independent strongholds which previously had determined the forms of polity on Median territory, were reduced and absorbed. This means that the heads of the Median aristocracy, from being independent rulers, had become court grandees, dependent on the king who had once been their equal (Herodotus I. 99). This development, of great importance for the understanding of the subsequent history of Media, goes to show that its kings found enough support in Median society apart from the aristocracy, evidently in the armed populace whom the Bīsutūn inscription calls *kāra*. This term, as can be gathered from an analysis of its wider context, was used for "people" in general, inclusive of both the armed free peasants and the aristocracy.

While the consolidation of the Median kingdom was thus proceeding, Assyria clashed again with the Land of the Mannaeans, having decided, as is evident from a question put to the oracle (Knudtzon 150) to recover what she had lost in the preceding war. The Assyrian troops of King Aššurbānapli under the command of the general Nabûšarruṣur crossed the Zagros in 660–659. The Mannaean King Aḥsēri attempted to attack and destroy them at night in their camp, but he did not succeed. The Assyrians occupied eight fortresses, from Bustu on the frontier between Parsūa and the Land of the Mannaeans to the Mannaean capital Izirta inclusive, among them Izbia (Izzibia, Zibia, present-day Ziwiyeh), Urmeiate (Armait) and Ištattu. On their way back the Assyrians seized those frontier strongholds which under Esarhaddon had passed into the possession of the Mannaeans. Here they took stores of military equipment and also horses. The Mannaeans may have intended to use these strongholds as bases for further offensives against Assyria.

Probably during the same expedition the Assyrian troops intruded also on Median territory, that is, either the Median kingdom itself, or some rebel region of an Assyrian province where Medes were settled. The text of "Cylinder B" of Aššurbānapli states: "In those same days Birizhadri, the Median "lord of a township", (as well as) Sar'ati and Parihia, sons of Gāgu "lord of a township" (in the country) Sahu, who had thrown off the yoke of my dominion – I conquered seventy-five of their fortified townships, captured their captives, (and) themselves I seized alive in my hands (and) brought them to Nineveh". The country Sahu is not mentioned anywhere else,[1] and the Assyrians themselves do not seem to have attached much importance to this episode as it is not mentioned in any other of the quite extensive versions of Aššurbānapli's annals.

Ahsēri, king of the Mannaeans, aroused discontent in his country. This led to an uprising of "the people of the land", as the Assyrians, like the ancient Jews, called the mass of the peasant population. Ahsēri was killed by the rebels, and with him almost all the members of his house. His surviving son, Ualli, immediately sent his heir Erisinni to the Assyrian king with a request for help, and with him as propitiatory gift his daughter for Aššurbānapli's harem. Aššurbānapli imposed a tribute on the Land of the Mannaeans, but his texts do not show that he gave any military assistance to Ualli. Nevertheless the Land of the Mannaeans remained Assyria's ally until the fall of the latter. It is therefore probable that Ualli did receive some aid from Aššurbānapli, not directly but at the latter's request from his kinsman, Madyēs, king of the Scythians. In any case the weakening of the Land of the Mannaeans made possible the clash between the Scythian kingdom and Media, though whether it occurred to the south of the Mannaean territory or, as one might infer from Herodotus (1. 104), to the north of it, is not clear.

Until recently it was thought that, apart from the episode with the "Land of Sahu", Aššurbānapli's annals make no further mention of Media. Yet such mention does exist. About 653 a political crisis

---

[1] The identifications sometimes offered of Gāgu with Gyges king of Lydia (Assyr. *Guggu*), and of Sahu with the Sakas, are worthless both from the linguistic and from the historico-geographical point of view.

THE MEDIAN EMPIRE

broke out in Assyria, as a result of hostilities between Aššurbānapli and his half-brother and vassal Šamaššumukin, king of Babylon, together with the latter's allies. Among these the annals of the Assyrian king name firstly the "Akkadians, Chaldaeans, Aramaeans", i.e. direct subjects of Babylon; and after them Humpan-nikaš, king of Elam, the main and most active ally of the Babylonians. Additionally listed among the allies of Babylon are the kings of three regions designated by the traditional terms of highflown style (of the same type as "Gaul" for "France"): Amurru (Syria–Phoenicia–Palestine), Melaḫḫa (at that time, Africa) and Qutium (the eastern mountain region). Which Syro-Phoenician and Egypto-Ethiopian kings took part in the coalition was established long ago by M. Streck, but for some reason nobody paid attention to Qutium. Yet in the situation as it then existed Media alone can have been understood under Qutium.

The war against Šamaššumukin and his allies and their final destruction in 648 are described in great detail in the annals, though Qutium is no longer mentioned, probably because the blow to Media was again inflicted not by the Assyrians themselves, but by the Scythians. This is what Herodotus has to say (I. 102–4): "Phraortes...made war on the Assyrians, namely those Assyrians who possessed Nineveh[1] and had formerly ruled over all; but at that time they were forsaken by their confederates who had rebelled albeit they themselves flourished exceedingly. Then as he warred against these men Phraortes himself was destroyed, having reigned two and twenty years,[2] and the greater part of his army was also destroyed. And when Phraortes had died, there succeeded unto him Cyaxares, the son of Phraortes the son of Deioces...And gathering together all that he ruled over he warred against Nineveh, because he wished to revenge his father and desired to destroy that city. But after he had vanquished the Assyrians in a conflict and was besieging Nineveh, there came upon him a great host of Scythians, led by the king of the Scythians, Madyes, the son of Prōtothyes..." (here Herodotus relates how in pursuing the Cimmerians the Scythians made their way round the Caucasus)..."Then the Medes joined battle with the Scythians, and being worsted in the battle were put down from their rule; and the Scythians spread themselves all over Asia". But Herodotus must be mistaken in believing that the Scythians clashed with the Medes only after "Phraortes" had fallen in the battle against the

[1] As distinct from the Babylonians whom Herodotus also calls Assyrians.
[2] (674–653!)

MEDIA

Assyrians, for otherwise his death, as well as the defeat of the Medes at the walls of Nineveh, would surely have found a mention in Aššurbānapli's annals. Still, it is evident that even according to Herodotus the death of "Phraortes" and the invasion of Media by the Scythians were close in time.

The loss of such a military leader as Xšaθrita-"Phraortes" would naturally have had grave consequences for the Medes: the Scythians established their hegemony not only over the whole of Asia Minor and of Transcaucasia, but soon afterwards probably also over Urartu and the Land of the Mannaeans.

It is possible that already in about 654 Assyria was drawn into a war against the Cimmerian Dugdammī (Lygdamis); and the Urartians were in alliance with the Cimmerians.[1] However, although in a hymn by Aššurbānapli to the god Marduk there is mention of the defeat of Dugdammī and of his son Sandakšatru, the leaders of the "Ummān-Manda" (a pompous term which in 7th century Assyria was applied to the Cimmerians, and in Babylonia apparently to the Medes), his annals contain no account of the war against them. Yet from Greek sources (Strabo 1. 3. 21) we know that the Cimmerians suffered a defeat at the hands of Madyēs, king of the Scythians.[2] But the victory of the Scythians over the Cimmerians was not immediate; even after they had established their hegemony in Media there was a period when the Cimmerians got the upper hand: in one of Aššurbānapli's inscriptions, tentatively dated in 641–640 B.C., Dugdammī is called not merely "king of Ummān-Manda" but king of "Saka and Qutium", i.e. of the Scythians (?) and of Media dependent on them (?). Nevertheless the classical authors unanimously assert that the Scythians finally prevailed.

Like Urartu and the Land of the Mannaeans, the Median kingdom continued to exist even under Scythian hegemony. The Scythians seem to have merely plundered the countries conquered by them and levied contributions, being incapable of creating a firm state order of their own. According to Herodotus (1. 73) the Medes sent their boys to the Scythians to learn from them the technique of archery (which is corroborated by archaeological data) and even their language. This last need not refer to the Medes proper who already spoke an Iranian dialect

---

[1] Or depended on them? In the same year 654 Rusā II, king of Urartu, for some apparently weighty reason recognized the Assyrian king as his "father", although until then the Assyrians themselves had regarded Urartu as a power equal to Assyria.

[2] In Strabo mistakenly: defeat of the "Treres" by "Madyēs, king of the Cimmerians"; but cf. Herodotus 1. 103.

sufficiently close to the Scythian, but to the various inhabitants of Media, still numerous at that time, that spoke non-Iranian languages, perhaps the "Paricanii" of Herodotus. Even much later Graeco-Roman authors mention on the periphery of the historical region of Media, in addition to the inhabitants of Syromedia, also "Matiēni" (Hurrians), Caspians etc., populations whose territory formed no part of what originally had been Media proper.

According to Herodotus the king of Media Cyaxares finally succeeded in wiping out the Scythian chieftains at a feast and liberating himself from Scythian domination, so that the "Medes recovered the power and what they had formerly possessed" (1. 106).

Thus, having shaken off the ephemeral yoke of the Scythian kings, the Median kingdom reverted to its previous position (625 B.C.?). Herodotus states that the Scythians returned to their homeland, which this time he imagines not beyond the "Araxes", i.e. the Volga, but to the north of the Black Sea where from the end of the 7th century the material culture actually shows a distinct Near Eastern influence (cf. IV. 2–4, 11). But it seems that not all of them went: Jeremiah (51.27) mentions a Scythian kingdom, evidently in Azarbaijan, as late as in 593; this is corroborated by Herodotus who mentions the Scythians in the Near East in connection with the war between Media and Lydia, the beginning of which is dated from 590.

However, even before this war Cyaxares succeeded in settling the final account with the principal enemy of all the peoples of the Near East – Assyria.

2. *The Assyrian and the Lydian war. The Median Empire*

Towards the end of the period when Scythian hegemony still prevailed in the mountain regions, an anti-Assyrian revolt broke out in Babylon against the new Assyrian king Sīnšariškun (Saracus). From the year 626 the revolt was led by the Chaldaean Nabopalassar; as happened so many times in the history of Babylon, he began to scrape together a coalition against Assyria aiming at her destruction. Until then the principal ally of the Babylonians used to be Elam, whose strategic and inner political situation did little to promote the success of the coalition. As for Media, whose adhesion Šamaššumukin had also sought, she had then been, before Cyaxares' time, as yet too weak a country to be of much use as an ally.

MEDIA

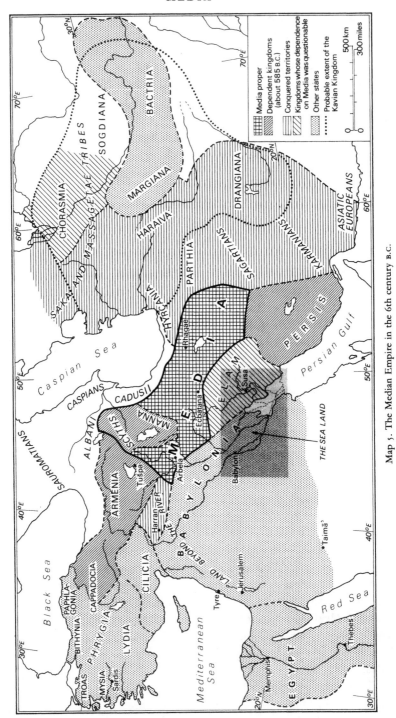

Map 5. The Median Empire in the 6th century B.C.

THE MEDIAN EMPIRE

The orations of the prophet Nahum devoted to the last war of Assyria clearly show whom the peoples of the Near East regarded as their main enemy: the Assyrian nobility (*nōzēr*), including the priests, the military, the officers of the administration (*ṭaphsar*) and the merchants (*rōchēl*). This small clique of men, who had amassed what for those times was great wealth paid for by the peoples' blood, was recklessly exploiting for its own benefit the rest of the Near Eastern population. The entire Orient lived in the hope to see the destruction of Assyria, "the dwelling of the lions", and the fall of Nineveh, "the bloody city". Meanwhile in Assyria itself a struggle was going on between the parties of the military and of the priests. Its army consisted mainly of warriors recruited from among the conquered nations, who fought willingly so long as there were always new countries to plunder, but whose fighting capacity was easily apt to give way in the face of an army equal in organization and armament. This was what sooner or later would make Assyria's destruction inevitable. Yet her prolonged successes had led the ruling class to underestimate the external dangers, while internal disorders within the country increased. Beside Nabopalassar, in 623 (?) another general of Saracus, this time an Assyrian, Sīnšumīlīšir, seems to have staged a rebellion. It had become difficult for Saracus to keep in subjection the peripheral provinces, which groups of Scythians seem to have been invading already earlier than this. Even Josiah, king of Judah, which had miraculously escaped Assyrian conquest, dared now to annex to his small kingdom the Assyrian provinces on the territory of northern Palestine. In 621 Nabopalassar gained complete possession of Babylonia; Elam, not fully conquered by Assyria during the expeditions of the 40s and 30s of the 7th century, seems to have been his ally. It is not clear whether an alliance between Babylonia and Media was already in existence.

In any case Cyaxares, after throwing off Scythian hegemony, was prepared to take part in the war against Assyria, a war of great import. Herodotus (I. 103) says: "He, as they say... was the first to divide the people of Asia into companies, and first established a battle order: spearmen, archers and horsemen to be separate; until then they had all been mixed together in disorder." As often happens with Herodotus, his very failure to understand the essence of the matter proves the genuineness of information which he could never have deliberately invented. It is evident that formerly the Medes went to war as a tribal militia, divided into kinship groups in which each warrior was armed with whatever weapon he wielded best. Cyaxares, however, taking example from his neighbours, the Urartians (Sarduri II's reform of about 760–750), and the Assyrians (Tiglathpileser III's reform after 745) introduced the system of a regular army fully equipped by the state and divided into strictly determined strategic and tactical units according to kinds of weapons. Already Xšaθrita had had a siege force. By now the Median army ceded nothing to the armies of the great powers in matters of organization.

In the following years the war between Assyria and Babylonia was carried on with varying success. In 616[1] Nabopalassar marched up the Euphrates with the intention of conquering the Aramaean tribes dependent on Assyria. From them he learned that higher up the river the Assyrian army and its allied Mannaean contingents had taken up their positions. In the battle that ensued at Qablīn the Mannaeans and several Assyrian generals were taken prisoner. Soon after, however, having at last received reinforcements from Pharaoh Necho II, the Assyrian army passed again to the offensive. In February–March 615 a new battle was fought, this time to the east of the Tigris, near present-day Kirkuk. The Babylonians captured the baggage train of the Assyrians and drove their detachments into the Lesser Zāb, extending their dominion considerably to the north. Meanwhile the rout of the Mannaean army at Qablīn must have laid open the frontiers of the Land of the Mannaeans itself which, probably in the same year 615 (but not later than in 611), fell under the control of Media. This created for Assyria a formidable menace on its flank, and soon the leading rôle in this war passed to Cyaxares.

In April–May 615 Nabopalassar appeared at the walls of Aššur (present-day Qal'at Šerqat). He could not capture the city, but he succeeded in holding the Assyrian stronghold Takrītain (present-day Tekrit). At this moment the entry of Media into the struggle formed the turning-point of the war. In November 615 the Medes, having crossed the Zagros, occupied (?) Arrapḫa (present-day Kirkuk). In July–August of the next year, 614, the Median armies performed a brilliant manoeuvre: marching from Arrapḫa to Nineveh they apparently invested the city. When the Assyrian king hastened to the relief

[1] The account that follows is based not only on C. J. Gadd's publication of the pertinent Babylonian chronicle, reproduced in this part without emendations by D. J. Wiseman, but also on the collation made by the author of the present chapter in the British Museum in the summer of 1954. See Diakonoff, "Armenia and Asia Minor about 600 B.C." (bibliography).

(?) of his capital the Medes, having made their way up the gorges of the Tigris above Nineveh, took by storm the town of Tarbīṣ (Sherif-khan), after which they crossed the river and marched down the right bank of the Tigris to Aššur, thus cutting off from all outside help the remaining genuine Assyrian towns, Nineveh and Calah, as well as the main force of Saracus. The expedition culminated in the successful storming of the sacred and oldest city of the Assyrians – Aššur, the defences of which, ruined as they are, remain imposing even to-day. A massacre was perpetrated in the city, temples were destroyed and innumerable treasures seized which the Assyrians had accumulated by plunder throughout the centuries in all the countries of the Near East. These treasures were now to lay the foundations of what later became the fabulous wealth of the Median aristocracy. As for Nabopalassar, he preferred to mark time until after the sack of Aššur, perhaps not wishing to take part in the desecration of the temples of deities which were revered also in Babylonia; both he himself and his descendants were heavily under the influence of the Babylonian priesthood. This did not prevent him, however, from making his appearance on the ruins of Aššur, and here, in the Median camp, Nabopalassar and Cyaxares "concluded peace and friendship with one another", which was probably on that very occasion consolidated by the diplomatic marriage of Nabopalassar's son Nebuchadnezzar to the Median princess. Even in such circumstances Saracus did not lose heart. In 613 he succeeded in fostering an anti-Babylonian revolt of the Aramaeans on the Euphrates. The "Chronicle" says nothing about the activities of the Medes.

In 612 the Medes and the Babylonians acted in harmony. The two armies joined forces apparently in the valley of the Diyālā river, crossed the river Radān (Adhēm) where it flows into the Tigris,[1] and came up to the walls of Nineveh. Between June and August three battles were fought. Finally, in August the allies succeeded in breaking into the city; as can be inferred from the poetic but rather unintelligible text of the Book of Nahum, and from Greek tradition, the storming was successful because the river Ḫuṣur was diverted to the walls of the city, where it undermined both them and the city gate. Street fighting began. Tradition has it that the Assyrian king, like his uncle Šamaššumukin

---

[1] At this place Cyaxares (Akkad. *Umakištar*, to be probably read *Uwakhištbar*) is for the first time called "king of Ummān-Manda". This disposes of the suggestion that "Ummān-Manda" in this text refers to Scythians and not to Medes.

earlier, threw himself into the flames of his burning palace. The inhabitants were dealt with in the same way as in days bygone the Assyrians used to deal with their conquered: "Art thou better than Thebes of Amon..." says Nahum (3. 8–10). "Yet was she[1] carried away, she went into captivity, her children were also dashed in pieces at the corners of all the streets, and they cast lots for her honourable men, and all her great men were bound into chains..." But the Assyrian people was not annihilated; it merely merged with the mass of Near Eastern Aramaeans, for as a result of the numerous deportations carried out by the Assyrian kings, Aramaic had long become the *lingua franca* of the ordinary people all over the Assyrian empire.

But a kinsman of Saracus, Aššuruballiṭ II, managed to fight his way out of Nineveh with the core of the Assyrian army, and take refuge in the northern Mesopotamian town of Ḥarrān. Here, rallying to himself the remnants of the Assyrian forces, he succeeded in holding out until the Egyptian armies of Pharaoh Necho II came up. In 610, at the approach of the Babylonian and Median armies the Assyrians and Egyptians left Ḥarrān and retreated beyond the Euphrates to Carchemish. Ḥarrān was taken and sacked, this time by the Babylonians; it was not until later, apparently, during the partition of the Assyrian possessions, that this town fell to the lot of the Mede who held it for fifty-four years. However, in 609 Necho and Aššuruballiṭ went over to the offensive and even attempted to besiege the Babylonians in Ḥarrān.

In that same year the Medes (?) undertook an expedition against the capital of Urartu. The kingdom, even if it was not destroyed, became probably at this stage subject to Media, as the Land of the Mannaeans had been for some time. In 608 the Babylonians, possibly together with the Medes, invaded a certain "Land of the House of Ḥanunia, a province of Urartu" (present-day Hınıs?). This may have been part of a kingdom formed somewhat earlier in the valley of the Upper Euphrates with its centre in Melitene (Malaṭiya), the Biblical "House of Tōgarmah", apparently the first short-lived Armenian kingdom. From 607 the military operations of the Babylonians were directed by Prince Nebuchadnezzar. In 605, some time before Nabopalassar's death in the same year, he succeeded in inflicting a crushing defeat on the Assyro-Egyptian armies at Carchemish and at Hamath in Syria, which then passed into the power of Babylon. Median contingents may have taken part in the battle of Carchemish, but contrary to the information

---

[1] The city of Thebes.

of Flavius Josephus, they do not seem to have penetrated deep into Syria and Palestine. Their operations in alliance with the Babylonians came to an end.

The Assyrian empire was partitioned between Media and Babylonia along a frontier which apparently passed from the Euphrates above Carchemish to the south of Ḥarrān and further approximately along the mountain chain Jabal Sinjar, across the Tigris to the south of Aššur, along the mountain chain Ḥamrīn, across the valley of the Diyālā and to the north-western mountain borders of Elam.[1] Assyria proper (the triangle Nineveh–Arbela–Aššur) seems to have been incorporated into Media proper, and part of the Iranian nomads moved into this region.[2]

Soon relations between the former allies, Babylonia and Media, began to deteriorate. In any case, in the 90s of the 6th century it was expected in Palestine that conflict would soon break out, as can be seen from the speeches of Jeremiah, dating from 593 (Jer. 25.25; 50.41–3; 51.27–8). His discourses make clear among other things that Urartu, the Land of the Mannaeans and the Scythian kingdom were under the domination of Media, and that in general there existed "kings of Media" in the plural, alongside with satraps (*paḫōth*, cf. Assyrian *peḫāte*) and governors (*sāgān*, cf. Assyr. *šaknu*). Herodotus gives this characterization of the structure of the Median kingdom (I. 134): "...one people ruled another, but the Medes ruled over all and especially over those that dwelt nearest them, and these ruled over their neighbours, and they again over theirs".

Yet the expected invasion of Babylonian possessions by the Medes did not take place. According to Herodotus (I. 73) a conflict occurred between the Medes and a separate group of Scythians. This seems to refer to the destruction of the illusory independence of the Scythian kingdom which had survived in what is to-day Azarbaijan. The independence of the Land of the Mannaeans and of Urartu must have been put to an end at the same time. In any case, when in 590 Cyaxares went to war to the west of these kingdoms, in Asia Minor, he could hardly have tolerated their independence at his rear.

According to B. B. Piotrovesky this was the time when Teišebaini

[1] In later times Cyrus was able to cross northern Mesopotamia without infringing on Babylonian territory.

[2] Proceeding from the custom of Darius I of executing a rebel in the centre of his province, one can infer that the tribe of the Sagartians had occupied Assyrian Arbela, now Erbil, for it is here according to the Bīsutūn inscription that the Sagartian rebel *Čiθrantaxma* was put to death. Cf. also Xenophon, *Anabasis* III. 4. 7–10.

(now Karmir-blur, near present-day Erevan), on the northern border of Urartu, was taken and destroyed. It is not clear whether Scyths or Medes took it, but the storming troops utilized "Scythian" (or Scytho-Median) arrows; yet there seem to have been Scyths also inside the stronghold. As a result of the conflict with Cyaxares, the Scythians moved out of Transcaucasia on to Lydian territory, as Lydia had been their ally since the times of the war against the Cimmerians. Media's demand to deliver the refugees met with a refusal from the Lydian king Alyattēs, and this was the cause of the war between Lydia and Media which lasted five years (590/589–585). Herodotus gives no details about it, but some data can be gleaned from Ezekiel 38–9. This author mistakenly calls Alyattes by the name of Gōg (Greek *Gyges*), the founder of the Lydian dynasty, giving him the title of "chief prince of Meshech and Tubal", i.e. of Phrygia and Tabal, two of the most important kingdoms of Asia Minor in the 8th to 7th centuries B.C.; they must have become dependants of Lydia after the destruction of the Cimmerian and later of the Scythian hordes. Ezekiel names as allies of "Gōg" Asiatic Thrace (*TRS*, so to be read instead of *PRS* of the manuscript tradition!), Nubia (? – *KWŠ*)[1] and Pontus (? – *PWṬ*), as well as Gōmēr, i.e. "Cimmerians" by which the Scythians should probably be understood, and the "House of Tōgarmah", i.e. the Armenian dynasty of Melitene. The influence of Lydia therefore reached as far as the Upper Euphrates. Ezekiel was already expecting the invasion of Syria and Palestine by Lydians. But Cyaxares succeeded in pushing Alyattēs' armies back to the west. Nevertheless the Medes, fatigued by prolonged wars, were unable to achieve a decisive victory, and when on 28 May 585, during their battle against the Lydians an eclipse occurred, both sides agreed to take this for an omen requiring them to conclude peace. According to Herodotus the kings of Babylon and of Cilicia acted as mediators. The frontier between Lydia and the Median spheres was established along the river Halys (Qızıl-Irmaq). The treaty was strengthened by the ritual of blood-fraternization and the marriage between Astyages, son of Cyaxares, and a daughter of Alyattes. Having thus extended the Median empire to its utmost limits, Cyaxares died.

We have traced the destinies of the Median empire in the West. But

---

[1] Probably to be emended to *KWB* 'Cobus'; this is the name of the first chief of the Treres, here used for the Treres in general (like Gōg for Lydia, 'Elīšā "Elissa-Dido" for Carthage); cf. Ezekiel 30.5; 27.7 *et al.*

THE MEDIAN EMPIRE

all Greek authors unanimously agree on the fact that the Median kings also spread their sway over many provinces east of Media. Thus, according to Herodotus, when subsequently Cyrus took possession of Media he was confronted in the east with the task of conquering the Massagetae (nomads of Central Asia), and also the people of Bactria, i.e. the southern part of the upper valley of the Oxus (to the south of what now is the Āmū-daryā–Wakhsh),[1] in present-day Afghanistan and Tajikistan. But this means that the regions situated further west, Hyrcania (the valleys of the Gurgān and the Atrek), Parthia (Khurāsān and the foot-hills of the Kopet-dagh in Turkmenia), Haria[2] (the valley of the Tejen–Harī-rūd) must have already belonged to the Medes. Drangiana (present-day Sīstān) must also have belonged to the Medes, while Margiana, i.e. the valley of the Murghab, was reckoned to Bactria at least under the first Achaemenids. That Parthia was a possession of the Median empire is stated by Ctesias and Trogus Pompeius, and the former says the same about the "Barcanii", i.e. probably Hyrcania. This is corroborated by Darius I in the Bīsutūn inscription: during the revolts of 522 Parthia and Hyrcania joined the Median impostor Pseudo-Xšaθrita, but Margiana raised its own leader, while Sattagydia and Arachosia (that is, the southern slopes of the Paropamisos-Hindukush) went over to the Persian impostor. According to Ctesias Bactria and the Sacae were in semi-allied, semi-dependent relations with Media.[3]

[1] Some scholars place the northern frontier of Bactria along the mountain ranges of Baysun-tau and Hissar, to the north of the Amu-darya.

[2] In all MSS of Herodotus and of other Greek authors this country is called *Aria* ("Ἄρια, 'Ἀρεία); however this is a very old error arising from contamination with Old Iranian *Arya* ("the Aryans"); the name should be read *Haria* ("Ἀρεία, from Old Iranian *Haraiva-); to avoid further confusion we shall adopt this spelling here and below.

[3] To determine the frontiers of the Median empire the author of the present chapter has suggested, tentatively of course, to utilize the list of satrapies quoted by Herodotus (III. 90ff.). This list is undoubtedly based on some official data, as it would have been impossible to compose such an enumeration of countries and peoples by hearsay. The order of enumeration follows no distinct geographical, economic or political organizational principle, but might it not be founded on historical ones? I have suggested that the satrapies I to XII are those created by Cyrus II and Cambyses II, satrapies XIII to XIX (?) those created by the Median kings, and satrapy XX an addition belonging to the times of Darius I, but probably included in the list by Herodotus himself. The remainder of the list may go back to Hecataeus, an author of the end of the 6th century (cf. Herodotus v. 36), although some scholars date the entire enumeration to the second half of the 5th century B.C. Of course such a division of satrapies into "Persian" and "Median" affects only the place of each in the list, and not its frontiers which could undergo alterations. For instance, Cappadocia, conquered already by Cyaxares, is joined in the list to Phrygia, first conquered by Cyrus, as satrapy III. In the same way, satrapy XVI, probably for some temporary reasons, is unduly enlarged, at the expense even of historically not interconnected regions. Still satrapies Ionia (I), Lydia (II), Phrygia (III), the semi-independent Cilicia (IV), Parapotamia (V), Babylonia (IX), Media

But independently of how deep the Median armies penetrated to the east, the essential fact is that there they were bound to come into contact with another civilization.

General considerations that seemed to be corroborated by Assyrian sources, have until recently led to the belief that the further east of Mesopotamia Iranians lived, the lower was their social development. Some scattered data, such as could be gathered from the so-called "Astrabad treasure", or from the excavations very carelessly carried out by Pumpelly in Anau in Turkmenia, gave no more than a hint at the possibility of rather highly developed cultures having existed in the east. To-day, when Soviet Central Asia counts among the regions of the Near and Middle East most thoroughly studied in archaeological detail, the results obtained permit the reconstruction of a far more informative picture. It now appears that in the foot-hills of the Kopet-dagh (Akhal-Etek, the historical province of Northern Parthia), agriculture based on the damming of mountain streams began not later than in the 6th millennium B.C., almost at the same time as in the most developed regions of the Near East. Like there, this gave the local inhabitants the advantage over their neighbours in the speed of social advance towards class stratification and the so-called "urban revolution". Here already at the end of the 3rd and during the whole of the 2nd millennium B.C. fortified settlements existed of a semi-"urban" type, settlements comparable, according to V. M. Masson, to the contemporary Hurrian cities in the foothills of the Zagros, or the Sumerian of the period of Ubayd, Uruk and Jemdet Nasr. Such are Anau III, Namazghah IV–V (and Namazghah VI, a settlement replacing the city of the Namazghah V culture, which was probably destroyed), Altyn-depe and others. Similar settlements existed in Khurāsān (Tureng-tepe, Tepe-Ḥisār II and others), in Afghanistan (Mundigak IV) and Tajikistan (Sapali-tepe).

(X), Bactria (XII), are known to have been conquered by Cyrus, while Armenia of Melitene (XIII), Parthia (XVI), Urartu (XVIII) are known to have already belonged to Media. If this inference is correct, then Drangiana (XIV) also belonged to Media, as well as Makrān (XVII), the Sacae and the Caspii (XV), i.e. probably the maritime Dahistān to the north of Hyrcania, precisely from where the Sacae must still have supplied marines under Xerxes (Herodotus VII. 184); and of satrapy XVI (besides Parthia) Haria (but hardly Chorasmia and Sogdiana?) probably also belonged to Media; the semi-independent tribes of the Pontus (XIX) could be ranged here, too. In the Bīsutūn inscription the grouping of satrapies also seems to be partly historical: first comes the group of "Cyrus'" and "Cambyses'" satrapies (Elam, Babylonia, Parapotamia, Egypt, the isles of the Aegean, Lydia, Ionia), then the group of "Median" satrapies (Media, Armenia, Cappadocia, Parthia, Drangiana, Haria; here, too, – or with the next group? – belongs Chorasmia), then the group of "Bactrian" satrapies (Bactria, Sogdiana, Sattagydia and Arachosia, Makrān). The only divergence is in respect of Makrān, the dependence of which from any kingdom must have been slight.

THE MEDIAN EMPIRE

Further south, at Tepe-Yaḥyā in Kirmān, a literate civilization flourished as early as the first centuries of the 3rd millennium B.C. During the 2nd millennium, in southern Turkmenia – where the language at that time was probably Indo-Iranian, later Iranian – the technique of building irrigation canals developed which, according to V. M. Masson, allowed the Namazghanians to colonize the eastern part of the delta of the Murghāb; unfortunately the valley of the river Tejen/Harī-rūd, in view of its frontier situation between three modern states, has been but little explored. It is likely, however, that the Namazghanians also occupied the delta of the Tejen, the more so as its distance from Namazghah-tepe is only 40–50 km.[1] Towards that time, too, on the lower reaches of the Āmū-daryā in Chorasmia the Suyarghan agriculturists begin to predominate over the herdsmen-agriculturists of Tazabaghyab.

After the year 1000 B.C. a highly developed agricultural culture with a gradual passing from bronze to iron is known in Hyrcania (and not only in the valleys of the Gorgān and the Atrek, but also in the Dahistān lowlands, now barren), in the north of Parthia (Anau IV), and in its north-west (the stronghold Yelken-depe), probably in Haria, too, very definitely in Margiana (culture Yaz I, c. 900–650 B.C., quite distinct from Namazghah VI, a culture that seems to have disappeared without leaving many traces in those areas; Yaz I is followed by Yaz II, c. 650–500 B.C.), and in Drangiana (Nadi-Ali II, 8th to 7th centuries B.C.).[2] The density of the population grows considerably, as can be well observed

---

[1] For the sake of comparison we may note that from Namazghah-tepe to Tahirbay in the delta of the Murghab the distance is 240 km, to Anau 110 km, and to Tepe-Hisar about 450 km as the crow flies.

[2] There are also "urban" settlements of the 7th (?) to 5th centuries B.C. in Chorasmia and Transoxiana (in Chorasmia, the stronghold Küzeli-ghyr, 7th (?) to 5th century; in the valley of the Zerafshan, Afrasyab I; in the central part of the valley of the Oxus on the northern side of the river, Küchük-tepe, 10th (??) to 7th centuries, Qobadian I, 7th (?) to 5th centuries). However, early Afrasyab was probably not a real urban settlement (there seems to have been only partial occupation of the land inside the walls), and the other fortresses arose, according to E. V. Zeimal and B. Y. Marshak, only during the Yaz II period, i.e. in the 6th or, at the earliest, in the late 7th century, possibly as garrisoned towns. The problem is *sub judice*. The same authors point out that there is no direct connection between the archaeological cultures of Tazabaghyab and Qairaq-qum, and the material culture of the later "urban" centres of Chorasmia and Sogdiana; they therefore suppose that the Chorasmians lived originally in Haria, and the Sogdians on the right bank of the Oxus down to the 6th century and migrated northwards under Cyrus or the Median kings. This has a certain bearing on the problem of the XVIth satrapy of Herodotus. However, a wholesale migration of an agricultural population from Haria to Chorasmia across uncultivated country does not seem very plausible; it seems more probable that the Chorasmians lived in their own country before the military colonists came, and took over the culture imported by them.

on the material of the Yaz I culture in Margiana.[1] According to V. M. Masson, Yaz I is a large settlement of the city type, apparently with a citadel on a platform and constructions possibly representing a palace. The settlement Nadi-Ali II is similar.

These archaeological data give substance to the scattered and vague information of the Greek authors suggesting that in south-western Central Asia and in the east of the Iranian plateau there existed in the 7th to 6th centuries, and perhaps earlier, two political formations, large for the times, which it would be plausible to regard as federations of tribes and city-states, or as states in embryo. What argues against such a definition is that no written documents have been found here; but in history the existence of early state organizations possessing no writing would not be unparalleled, for instance in Africa, and one cannot exclude that some primitive form of writing may have existed, sufficient for economic needs and recorded on perishable material.

One of these federations was Bactria, whose people Herodotus I, 153) regards as equal in power to Lydia, Babylonia, Egypt and the tribal union of the Sacae. Ctesias, and a number of other Greek authors whose information however stems merely from Ctesias, even assert that Bactria vied in importance with Assyria itself. The historians of Alexander's campaigns note the multitude and the power of the Bactrian city-fortresses. The time and the limits of the Bactrian federation are determined, according to Michael M. Diakonoff and V. M. Masson, by the spread of the characteristic "cylindrical jar" pottery (Chorasmia, Sogdiana, Bactria, Margiana, partly Parthia: the period of the sites of Küzeli-ghyr–Afrasyab I–Qobadian I–Yaz II–Yelken-depe; it is significant that at this period the citadel of Yaz-depe was abandoned and the population of this town dwindled, perhaps in connection with a Bactrian conquest?). In as much as a legendary Iranian tradition saw in Kavi Vīštāspa, patron of Zarathushtra, the king of Balkh, some 19th-century scholars thought that the culture of the Avesta, the sacred books of the Zoroastrians, belonged to Bactria. This view is finally disproved by recently discovered inscriptions in Bactria of the 2nd century A.D., which show that the Bactrian language was quite distinct

[1] The density of the population falls sharply during the period Yaz III (at that time Yaz-depe loses its walls, while Aravali-depe, the stronghold second in size within the oasis of Margiana, is destroyed altogether); this is probably connected with the massacre perpetrated in Margiana by Dadrši, the general of Darius I who subdued the revolt of Frāda (55,243 killed and 6,572 prisoners according to the Bīsutūn inscription, many more than in any of the other rebellious satrapies).

from Avestan. The data contained in the preserved parts of the Avesta itself, also in no way support the localization of Kavi Vīštāspa's kingdom in Bactria.

The other Eastern Iranian and Central-Asian political federation was recognized in the sources by J. Markwart. Herodotus (III. 117), states: "There is in Asia a plain enclosed on all sides by mountains, and these mountains have five clefts. This plain once pertained to the Chorasmians, and it borders on the said Chorasmians, the Hyrcanians, the Parthians, the Sarangians (= Drangians) and the Thamanaei... In these mountains rises a great river called Acēs. It divides into five streams and formerly watered the land of the said nations." He further speaks of the damming of the Acēs which turned the plain into a lake. The most rational interpretation of this information would be to identify the Acēs with the Tejen–Harī-rūd. The valley of this river borders on Parthia (which in ancient times usually included Hyrcania) and Drangiana. It is to be assumed that the Chorasmians to whom this valley "belonged" are mentioned here as conquerors. In Achaemenian times, too, the provinces that formerly depended on "Greater Chorasmia", were sometimes administered as one; again according to Herodotus, satrapy XVI (perhaps as that of which in the first year of Darius I his father Hystaspēs was satrap) combined the Parthians, the Chorasmians, the Sogdians and the Harians, although its centre, apparently, was at that time Parthia.

Other, quite different identifications of the river Acēs have been suggested. Some archaeologists doubt even the existence of a "Greater Chorasmia". However the Avestan tradition does support the notion that at some time in the first half of the 1st millennium B.C. a large federation existed more or less in the area about which Herodotus speaks. As for the location of the country where Zarathushtra was active and where the Avesta was composed, the only guide-lines available are the internal evidence of the Avestan texts themselves, and linguistic data. None of the later Iranian languages – neither the "Western" (Middle Persian, Middle Parthian), nor the "Eastern" (Scytho-Alanic, Saka, Sogdian, Bactrian, or even Chorasmian) – descend directly from the language of the Avesta. Evidently in later times other Iranian dialects spread over the country of the Avesta and obliterated its language. It is, however, consonant with the dialectological position of Avestan to seek its homeland somewhere near the oldest line of contact between the "Western" and the "Eastern" Iranian tribes, in a region connected with Chorasmia. This is why the most convincing location of the kingdom of Zarathushtra's patron, Kavi Vīštāspa, is the one proposed by Henning, in the southern part of Markwart's "Greater Chorasmia", i.e. in Haria-Margiana or in Drangiana. I do not suppose, however, that Vīštāspa's kingdom was identical with "Greater Chorasmia". More likely it stood on territory which later had been overrun by nomads from Chorasmia and Bactria who perhaps were responsible for the creation of the extensive federations or "empires" mentioned above, analogous to the Scythian "empire" of 652–625. A wave of Sakas also passed here in the beginning of our era and settled in Drangiana (Sakastāna, Sīstān), and when later, but not later than in the 6th to 7th centuries A.D., the Persian language spread all over eastern Iran and beyond, no trace of Avestan was given a chance to survive here.

The first Median kings, in creating their empire, had perforce to come into contact with these Eastern Iranian and Central Asiatic civilizations, although it needs stressing that the extant Avestan texts betray not the slightest awareness of the existence of Media or Medes, let alone of Persians. The Medes did not conquer either Bactria or Chorasmia, but certain regions formerly included in the Chorasmian and Bactrian federations, or influenced by them, became probably parts of the Median Empire. This it seems safe to presume, not later than in the first half of the 6th century B.C., in respect of at least Hyrcania and Parthia. Ctesias recounts a legend about the war between the Medes and the Saka queen Zarina which led to the conquest by them of the country of the Sakas and of Parthia; if this legend has an historical basis, one could see here not so much the land of the Amyrgian Sacae beyond the Jaxartes, as the Caspian Dahistān (Herodotus' satrapy XV). Thus in the north-east the Median kingdom embraced part of the territories of the former Chorasmian federation (?), and if it did not include Chorasmia itself, the two states were at least conterminous, as may also have been the case with Margiana which by that time probably belonged to Bactria.

So much for the eastern frontiers of the Median empire which, as we have seen, in the west reached the river Halys and in the north-west, in Transcaucasia, apparently the river Kur. The southern frontier of the Median kingdom we have already traced to the borders of Elam. It now only remains to examine the frontier between Media and Persis.

According to Herodotus (I. 102), Persis (Fārs) was subjugated by Media already under Phraortes, i.e. Xšaθrita. This was not so: at the end of the 40s of the 7th century Cyrus I, king of "Parsumaš", i.e. of Persis, grandson of the founder of the dynasty Achaemenēs in Herodotus' genealogy, sent propitiatory gifts to king Aššurbānapli on the occasion of the conquest of Elam, at the same time sending his son Arukku[1] as hostage to Assyria. Gifts were sent on the same occasion by Pizlume, a petty king of the country or city of Ḫudimeri, which judging from the letter No. 521 of the Assyrian archives, was also situated east of Elam.[2] However, none of the Greek sources states that the father of Cyrus II the Great, Cambysēs I, son of Cyrus I, was actually an independent king in Persis. It is therefore probable that Persis became a kingdom dependent on Media some time between the 640s and the 560s, most likely under Cyaxares. Other kingdoms, though we know nothing of the fate of e.g. Ḫudimeri and Paširu, certainly also existed on the territory of Fārs under the hegemony of Media.

Darius I states in his inscription that between Achaemenes and himself eight of his kinsmen had been kings, which means that among them was Ariaramnes, brother of Cyrus I and great-grandfather of Darius, as well as his son Arsames, grandfather of Darius, who still flourished both under Cyrus II and Darius himself. Although we have no contemporary inscriptions of either Ariaramnes or Arsames, inscriptions were composed in their names in the 4th century B.C., in which the title they are given is "king". Cyrus I, like his son and grandson, ruled in two kingdoms: Parsumaš, of which he is called king in the text of Aššurbānapli, and Anshan. In the Babylonian sources, with their general tendency to archaic terminology, Cyrus I, Cambyses I and Cyrus II figure under the title of kings of Anshan, the ancient Elamite province well known in the history of Mesopotamia since the 3rd millennium B.C. But this title does not merely reflect the weakness of Babylonian scribes for highflown ancient terms, for Anshan, as a kingdom different from both Elam and Parsumaš, actually took part in 691 in the battle at Ḫalulē. Where the grandfather and great-grandfather of Darius I reigned is not clear; all that is clear is that Cyrus II was not at first the ruler of the whole of Fārs; Herodotus explicitly says (1. 125) that he originally united only three out of ten Persian tribes.[3]

[1] Akkadian transcription of the Iranian diminutive in -*auka* from some name beginning with *Arva-* or *Arya-*.

[2] It lay by the sea, for this was where the leader of the Chaldaean Sea-Land fled from Mesopotamia, apparently by-passing the dry-land regions of Elam.

[3] It is true that four of these were nomadic, and part of them lived not in Fārs but in Kirmān. The names of all four nomadic tribes (Dai, Mardi, Dropici, Sagartii) occur not only in Greek authors but partly also in the Avesta; distributed over very different parts of Iran and Central Asia the tribes cannot very well be regarded as specifically Persian.

There can thus be no doubt that in Persis, too, as in Media until the second quarter of the 7th century, there existed not one but several small state formations; presumably the most important aristocratic houses both in Media and in Persis were descended from independent petty kings. Participation in the victorious campaigns of the kings of Media, and later of Persis, and in their enormous booty, must have reconciled them to the loss of independence. Nevertheless they must have been a constant source of opposition to the kings.

As for Elam, it suffered terrible devastation by the Assyrians in the 40s and 30s of the 6th century, but they did not entirely conquer the country: there remained certain strongholds and regions held by men who aspired to the throne of Elam. In the 20s of the 6th century Elam seems to have supported Nabopalassar against the Assyrians. Jeremiah (25. 25) still mentions independent "kings of Elam" under the year 604. In 596/5 the Babylonian king Nebuchadnezzar II invaded Elam but the Babylonians retained possession of the Elamite capital Susa only for a short time: there have come down to us from the middle of the 6th century (?) the archives of the administration of the Elamite royal workshops; they show Elam entertaining relations with Babylonia and Syria without, apparently, forming part of any kingdom greater than itself. As we have no reliable information on the conquest of Elam by Cyrus II of Persia, it is probable that Elam, like Persis, the Land of the Mannaeans, Urartu and others, had become one of the self-governing peripheral kingdoms dependent on Media, and was transformed into a satrapy only under the Persians.[1]

The nucleus of the empire of Cyaxares and of Astyages was Media proper, which, as can be assumed from the indirect data already mentioned, now included administratively not only the original kingdom of Xšaθrita, but also "Syromedia" and the regions of the Zagros, as well as Assyria proper and, perhaps, even part of northern Azerbaijan beyond the Araxes.

3. *Society, culture and religion of Media*

In order to hold out, let alone achieve victory, in the struggle with such a state as Assyria, any Near Eastern kingdom of the first half of the 1st millennium B.C. had to possess a social, economic, political and military

---

[1] Let us note here that the "Achaemenian" Iranian village excavated by R. Ghirshman in Susa partly (stratum I) belongs to pre-Achaemenian times, and may be a vestige of the Median occupation of Elam.

THE MEDIAN EMPIRE

structure not inferior to the Assyrian. Thus Media was compelled to cover in the shortest time possible the entire range of development which it had taken Assyria a millennium and a half to achieve. Our information on the organization of the Median state is more than scanty, but we can nevertheless confidently assume that its characteristic features were the following:

Later on within the Achaemenian empire the economic centre of gravity was formed by the western satrapies with very old stratified urban civilizations: Elam, Babylonia, Syria-Mesopotamia, Dascyleium, Lydia, Ionia, were the most highly developed and remunerative parts of the state. A similar rôle must have been played in the Median kingdom by "Syromedia", Assyria, Northern Mesopotamia, the Land of the Mannaeans, Urartu, and the valley of the upper Euphrates. All the other provinces of the Median kingdom must have been in a critical state of general reconstruction: in the beginning of the 7th century small political units still predominated, something like very primitive city-states with persisting tribal and intertribal links and inherited semi-democratic social customs. The most powerful personage bore no higher title than "lord of the township", and was obliged to reckon with organs of self-government of the type of a council of elders and a popular assembly which may even have elected him or confirmed him in his rank, while the standard of wealth, apart from windfalls contributed by lazurite trade in transit, was still estimated by the number of *pasu-vīra*, i.e. domestic animals, mainly horses, and men bound together by their common subjection to the authority of a single patriarch. Though aristocratic households naturally possessed objects in gold, silver and copper, their quantity was not such as to form a separate item in the tribute which Assyria collected here.

But with the conquest of Aššur and Nineveh, the Medians literally overnight acquired unheard-of riches, which naturally were concentrated among the few – the aristocracy and the military leaders. There can hardly be any doubt that the composition of Median society was very similar to the one we know in Achaemenian Iran from the Bīsutūn inscription, the archives of Persepolis and the Greek authors: under the Achaemenids, as we have seen, all free men were called *kāra* "army"; certain contexts show that this term included the aristocracy, but in general it had a much wider meaning, that of all freemen.[1] At the same

---

[1] The assertion still frequently met with that the *kāra* was *das Aufgebot der freien, also* (!) *adeligen Männer* ("a militia of the free, therefore (!) of men of the nobility") is a *non sequitur*.

time a distinction was made between the kāra directly serving the king, and the kāra living at home and probably taking the field only in cases of pressing necessity.

Although the immensely rich aristocracy which occupied all the most important posts in the state was in actual fact sharply distinct from the mass of free warriors – agriculturists and herdsmen – the sources reveal as yet no data to show that the Median or Old Persian society, like the Avestan and Indian, and the later Sasanian Persian, was also formally divided into special estates of "priests", "warriors" (or "charioteers"), and "farmers and cattle-breeders" with distinct religious and social rights and functions. Nevertheless, the swift enrichment of the aristocracy was bound to be linked with the oppression of the peasants and rank-and-file warriors, and with their impoverishment.

Nicolaus of Damascus, who borrowed this information probably from Ctesias, tells of a custom which existed among the Medes for a freeborn pauper to give himself into the patriarchal power of some person of consequence, becoming as it were a slave within the *familia*, although he could, if he so wished and had the economic possibility, leave his patron. This custom existed also in ancient India. The patriarchal family extended to include slaves, appears to have been a feature also of Avestan society. Its existence in Sasanian Persia has been demonstrated by Anahit Perikhanian, and in Chorasmia by V. A. Livshits. Herodotus (1. 109) designated this type of family by the usual Greek term *oikia*. It is noteworthy that according to Herodotus the relations within it were of the simplest: the son of a noble Mede could play with the son of a slave on equal terms. Although the subject-matter of Herodotus' story at this point is legendary, insofar as the legend is a genuine Medio-Persian one, the manners and customs it suggests may very well be authentic.

On the other hand there is no doubt that Media, on the threshold between the 7th and the 6th century, overflowed with captive slaves. The Median slaves were probably designated by the term *māniya-*, an equivalent of the Old Persian *gṛda-*, a term which has been preserved only as a loan word in other languages; the term māniya- is used in the Iranian text of the Bīsutūn inscription. In Achaemenian Persia there seem to have been three categories of slaves: (1) captives, transferred to new places, settled on the land and forming whole villages of people technically or actually in a state of slavery; this category came into being already in Assyria (*šaknūte*); (2) slaves, mainly from among the captives, forming gangs employed in construction and agricultural work for the households of the king and the aristocracy; (3) slaves in personal service drawn into the familia (*nāfa-*). There exists no information on a division of slaves into such categories in Media, but most likely it was there that it took shape.

Special mention must be made of eunuchs. In Achaemenian Persia this category of royal servants seems to have been formed out of the tribute in boys levied from a number of satrapies. But it existed already before the Achaemenids: in Urartu at the court of Rusā II out of 5,507 retainers 3,892 were eunuchs. The situation was similar in Assyria, where from the time of Tiglathpileser III exclusively eunuchs seem to have been appointed "chiefs of provinces". If Ctesias is to be believed, it was the same at the Median court. In contrast to other men risen from the ranks of captives or slaves, eunuchs could attain very important positions.

The kings of Media adopted the Assyro-Urartian system of governing through "chiefs of provincial administration" (Akkad. *bēl peḫāte*, Aram. *paḥāthā*, Hebrew plural *paḥōth*). Their provinces must originally have been small, as in Assyria, but later, still under the Median kings, larger satrapies were introduced, covering the territory of an entire people or even of several peoples. The governor of such a large province was called in the languages of all the peoples dependent on Media, and later on Persia, by the Median term χšaθrapā(n) (Aram. *'aḥašdarpānā*, also used in Akkadian; Greek *xatrapēs, exatrapēs, sadrapās, satrapēs*, Lycian *kssadrapa*).[1] However, like the governors of the smaller provinces (subdivisions of satrapies, e.g. Judea under the Achaemenids), he was even later also referred to by the term *paḥāthā* of Assyrian origin.

The ancient organs of self-government – councils of elders, popular assemblies – do not seem to have been preserved in the Median kingdom. Herodotus (III. 80ff.) tells of a last attempt to revive them, already after the fall of Media.

Passing on to the culture of Media we shall look at it first in everyday life. Unfortunately we still hardly know any important ruins of unquestionably Median times, with the exception of stratum I of the "Achaemenian village" in Susa and the excavations at Nūsh-i Jān (see Ch. 19). If the oldest rock-tombs in so-called "Syromedia", imitating the dwellings of the living, really belong to Median times, this could

---

[1] The Persian form of this term (Old Persian *xšaçapāvan*, Elam. *šakšapawana*) was used only in Persis and Elam.

help to form an opinion on the oldest type of the Median house, different from the Mannaean which is known, for instance, from the town dwellings in Hasanlu. This was a one-storey adobe building, usually with a flat roof; it may have had attached a penthouse on wooden posts, and a small inner court. The exterior aspect of Median strongholds has been preserved for us by Assyrian representations: the fortress was often surrounded by several adobe walls on a stone foundation, each rising above the next. According to the description by Greek authors the capital of Media, Ecbatana, was surrounded by seven walls of different colours. In the centre of a fortified settlement there could have been a citadel on a rock, or on an artificial platform.

The population of the western provinces of Media had become strongly Babylonized in its way of life, as is evident, inter alia, from the clothing. But on the eastern side of the Zagros the attire in common use was the one we know already from the Lullubī in the 3rd millennium B.C. A pelt worn over a short tunic was fastened on the left shoulder and sometimes tucked under the belt: the skin of a panther for noblemen, a sheepskin for the others. The hair was tied with a red ribbon, the beard trimmed. Assyrian eighth century reliefs do not reproduce the characteristic cap of the inhabitants of Media in the 5th to 4th centuries – tall, made of sheepskin or felt with a corrugated look; but that it existed in those days is proved by its reproduction on a relief of Anubānini as early as the last quarter of the 3rd millennium B.C. In the Zagros, caps similar to the Phrygian were also worn. The footwear was shoes with curved toes.

The Greeks no longer saw this attire on the Medians and ascribed it solely to the "Caspii", while calling "Median" a different one: a wide shirt (*sarapis*, Elam. *saharpe*) with long wide sleeves and wide pleated *shalvar*-trousers, actually the skirts of a long robe passed between the legs and tucked into the belt, and a short coat of a cloth woven or embroidered in many-coloured wools. The autochthonous population of western and central Media did not use this kind of clothing before the emergence of the Median kingdom; it slightly resembles the Scythian and was probably originally worn by the horsemen of the eastern steppes of Iran: a seal depicting a horseman in *shalvar*-trousers has come down to us from "Necropolis B" in Tepe-Sialk of the 8th (?) century B.C. On the reliefs of the rock tombs of "Qyzqapan" and "Dukkān-i Dāvūd", regarded as belonging to Median times, long robes are still worn only by Magian priests (clad in accordance with later

Zoroastrian regulations!); the warrior on the "Qyzqapan" relief is still clothed in a belted tunic, different from the Median warriors and courtiers on the reliefs of the end of the 6th or beginning of the 5th century;[1] in the 6th century this later attire was adopted also by the Persians, and after them by other Iranians. In the 4th century it is attested also in northern Azerbaijan (Mingechaur).

We still know very little about the art and material culture of the times of the Median kingdom, and have much difficulty in distinguishing Median objects from the Mannaean, late Lullubī-Qutī and Kassite, as well as from the Scythian on the one hand, and the Achaemenian on the other. As said above, writing must have existed in Media but no examples of it have yet been discovered, except for a small fragment with only part of a cuneiform sign found at Nūsh-i Jān.

The most interesting and controversial cultural and historical problem turning on Media is that of its religion or religions.

On the beliefs pre-existing the rise of the Median kingdom one can form an opinion from the information contained in Assyrian texts, in artistic representations and in personal names. Assyrian texts mention several times Mannaean and other deities and speak of the abduction of these "gods", i.e. of their idols. The old religions of the Qutī, Lullubī, Hurrians and Kassites seem to have continued without any special alterations. Kassite, and even purely Babylonian cults penetrated deep into Media. One of the "lands" of south-western Media was called by the Assyrians "Bīt-Ištar", while in Silḫazi, also on the outskirts of Media there existed the cult of the Babylonian god Marduk, just as it existed, for instance, in Transcaucasia after its conquest by Urartu – in the city of Irbuni, present-day Arinberd in Erevan. In the western part of the historical region of Media certain rulers, even before the Assyrian conquest, bore Akkadian names, some of them theophoric. Of the outer appearance of local deities we may judge partly from "Luristan" bronzes, partly from images on metal artifacts from Mārlīk, Hasanlu and Ziwiyeh, and on bronze *situlae*, variously determined as Luristanian or Mannaean, but possibly originating from Ellipi or the

---

[1] If the "Qyzqapan" tomb is a royal one (which is very likely) this warrior is none other than Cyaxares: the tomb is situated on the territory of "Syromedia", and Cyaxares was the first Median king to conquer it. The next Median king Astyagēs, deposed by Cyrus, would hardly have been buried in such a tomb. However, some scholars incline to a post-Achaemenian dating of these tombs. Note the altar of fire represented on the "Qyzqapan" tomb and compare the absence of personal names testifying to fire-worship in 8th century Media. Burial in a rock does not contradict the (late?) Zoroastrian prohibition to defile fertile earth, fire and water with corpses, a prohibition connected with the worship of these elements.

neighbouring mixed Median region. Particularly characteristic are images of monster-demons, half men, half beasts, winged sphinxes and griffins, so common in Hurrian and partly in Syrian mythology. We shall find them later symbolizing the "dēvas" on the reliefs of Achaemenid kings.

Archaeological evidence for the religion of the Iranian-speaking Medes of the first centuries of the 1st millennium B.C. comes so far only from the burials of "Necropolis B" in Tepe-Sialk, ascribed with some probability to the Medes; these are the usual ancient burials in pits, certainly not Zoroastrian. More information is yielded by the names of Medes in Assyrian records. Clearly distinguishable elements of these names are *masdă-* (i.e. *mazdah-*) "wise" (the epithet of the supreme deity), *auar-, aur*, evidently the Iranian *ahur(a-)* "benevolent deity, spirit",[1] and *bag(a-)* "god". Completely absent are the younger Avestan word for "deity", *yazata-*, and the appellations of the abstract deified virtues of the Avesta (Vohu Manah etc.); but likewise absent are the names of common Indo-Iranian deities re-adopted by the Younger Avesta (Mira, Anāhitā, Vərəθraγna etc.), and in general all proper names of deities;[2] there are no theophoric personal names or traces of fire-worship. It is true that the number of clearly Iranian names of Medes that have come down to us does not exceed a few dozen, so that these conclusions *ex silentio* cannot be taken as very reliable. On the other hand, it would be impossible to take the same number of late Achaemenian or Parthian names without coming across some dedicated, for instance, to Mithra or to Fire. On the other hand there often occur as elements of old Median names such concepts as "truth, righteousness, the magic power of faith" (**Rta-*, in Akkadian rendering *Arta-, Irti-*), "authority, the magic power of authority" (**Xšaθra-*, in Akkadian rendering *Satar-, Kaštar-, -kištar*), "glory, divine radiant essence, the magic power of the king" (**Farnah-* or **Hvarnah-*, in Akkadian rendering *Parna-, -barna, -parn-*).

At all events, before the beginning of the 7th century B.C. the Medes

[1] Like some other ancient peoples, the Indo-Iranians distinguished, as it were, two "tribes" or two "phratries" of supernatural beings, called *asura-* and *dēva-* by the Indo-Aryans, *ahura-* and *daēva-* by the Iranians. In the course of time one of the "phratries" could have acquired the essentiality of benevolent deities and the other that of evil ones, or else both could have been preserved as groups of deities similar in character.

[2] An exception is possibly presented by *Rāman-*, unless the element *Rāma-* in the name *Rāmatavya* be a common noun. Contrary to the opinion of Scheftelowitz, *Rāman-* has no connection with the imaginary Akkadian deity **Rammān* (an outdated reading of the ideogram for the name of the god of storm – Adad, or Addu).

THE MEDIAN EMPIRE

do not seem to have been followers of Zarathushtra's teachings. Some sort of change in religious beliefs, however, happened in Media no less than in other Iranian countries during the 8th or 7th century B.C.[1]

According to Herodotus, already at the court of the Median king Astyages (584–549) there were Magi acting as official soothsayers and priests. In the 6th and early 5th centuries B.C. the Magi were regarded, according to the evidence both of Herodotus (I. 101) and the Bīsutūn inscription (§§ 11, 52, etc.), not as a caste or profession but as a tribe from which religious teachers, priests and soothsayers were recruited. Their teachings were not yet altogether absorbed in Persia even by the time of Herodotus (I. 140). All who have studied the subject, at least from the times of Plato's disciples down to modern times, unanimously regarded the Magi as Zoroastrian priests. It is only relatively recently that it has been suggested that originally the Magi represented pre-Zoroastrian beliefs. The author of this chapter seems to be one of the few scholars who still think they were Zoroastrians, and that Astyages and perhaps even Cyaxares had already embraced a religion derived from the teachings of Zarathushtra (though certainly not identical with his doctrine; indeed they even distorted it). Unfortunately Herodotus, as he many times tells the reader in his history, thought it impious to refer to more than the outward manifestations of religious beliefs; thus, even if he knew of Zarathushtra's teachings or of their interpretation by the Magi, he was not likely to tell what he knew. The little he does tell of the religion in which the Magi officiated for the Achaemenian

---

[1] The burial rites are particularly interesting: the custom of burning the bodies of the dead was discovered by A. M. Mandelštam in tombs of the 14th to 13th centuries B.C. in northern Bactria (the Tulkhar cemetery between the mouths of the rivers Kafir-nigan and Surkhan-darya, to the north of the Amu-darya) and in Western Turkmenia. Later this was replaced by ordinary interment ("pits with pente douce", end of the 2nd to the beginning of the 1st millennium B.C.). At a later period at Tulkhar (the dating is rather vague – the 10th to 8th centuries, or possibly the 7th) a stone coffer was set at the bottom of a pit, and in it the dismembered body was laid (without any accompanying inventory) and covered with reeds; here we see the attempt to preserve the element of the earth from the polluting contact with the corpse. The same can be observed in Parthia and Margiana: in Parthia of the Namazghah VI period a fire was still lit in the grave, although the body was not burnt but laid on its side in a crouching position. For the periods of the cultures Yaz I and II, i.e. beginning with c. the 9th century B.C., no burials whatsoever are so far known, apart from nomad burials, in Parthia and Margiana. The Persians of the Achaemenian period already revered the elements of fire, water (Herodotus I. 138; III. 16) and fertile earth as sacred (which the Medians of the early 1st millennium B.C. apparently still did not); a burial of a corpse covered with wax (Herodotus I. 140), or in a metal coffin, or in a rock tomb did not defile the element earth; more difficult was the burial of fallen warriors on the field of battle. The Persians sought in such cases to prevent the contact of corpses with fertile earth by covering them with branches and leaves (ibid., VIII. 24) – another compromise with the strict rules forbidding defilement of the elements.

Iranians, reminds one of the "Yasna of the Seven Chapters", an archaic but post-Zarathushtrian prosaic part of the Avesta, still written in Zarathushtra's own Gāthic dialect. It certainly does not remind one of the *Yašts* and the rest of the Younger Avesta, because of the absence from it of personified and anthropomorphic deities such as are characteristic of the latter; to our knowledge these deities were re-introduced into the religion of the Magi only in the middle of the 5th century B.C., under Artaxerxes I, simultaneously with the introduction of a new, so-called "Zoroastrian" calendar. The problem is controversial, the opinion opposite to that of the present author being supported by some of the greatest modern authorities, e.g. W. B. Henning. This being no place for polemics, the reader should consult the chapter of this volume devoted to Old Iranian religion.

4. *The fall of the Median empire*

The last Median king was Astyages (Old Iranian *Ršti-vēga, Bab. *Ištumēgu*, to be read [Ištuwēg]). The events of the first years of his reign are completely unknown; the sources relate only the circumstances of his fall. The information of the Babylonian texts is extremely laconic, while our main Greek sources – Herodotus and Ctesias – recount here traditions of clearly legendary origin from which it is hard to extract any historical core. Our preference must as usual go to Herodotus, if only because his history of Media, at least in its most important features, is corroborated by independent sources, while Ctesias, even though he operates with names which may really have existed in Media, builds up a fantastic, completely imaginary dynasty; his main aim is to set upside down every fact given by Herodotus. Still, by way of exception Ctesias recognizes the identity of his last Median king Aspandas with Herodotus' Astyages or Astyīgas. What the third Greek author, Xenophon, relates in his *Cyropaedia* is pure romance. In it both history and geography have nothing in common with the true events and places, apart from cases when some fact was borrowed from Herodotus or from Ctesias. There were other Greek authors who wrote about Median and Persian history, for instance Dinon, but we hardly know anything about their works.

Of the early events of the reign of Astyages ("Aspandas" in Ctesias, "Cyaxares" in Xenophon) Ctesias relates his expedition into the land of the Cadusii (in the mountains to the south of the river Araxes in

Azerbaijan), while Xenophon speaks of an expedition into Armenia to put an end to the war between the Armenii and the Georgian-speaking tribe of Chaldaei (or Chalybes, to-day Lazi, or Čani: not to be confused with the Urartians whose supreme god was Ḫaldi, nor with the Semitic-speaking Chaldaeans or Babylonia). How far this information is historical is difficult to say; some of the details are obviously legendary.

Herodotus (1.123) says that "Astyages was cruel to the Medes" but it is immediately apparent that in fact he meant to the Median aristocracy, to "the first among the Medes", the descendants of kings and "lords of townships". He describes Astyages as taking counsel with the Magi, and in our opinion the two statements agree quite well: if the Magi were Zoroastrians, their orientation at such an early period would be sure to preserve still something of the original anti-aristocratic tendency of Zarathushtra's teachings.[1] Of course the king must have had some kind of social support besides the Magi; it probably still came, as in the days of Cyaxares, from the mass of the warrior peasants; at least, as subsequent events show, the men "of houses no less noble" than the king, "brought up with him" and "not ceding to him in valour" (Herodotus, 1.99), whom Astyages apparently made no effort to enrich by continued conquests, were opposed to him.

Herodotus' story alleging that Astyages served at a feast to the magnate Harpagus the flesh of his son (1.119) is a widespread folklore motif (it figures also in Herodotus 1.73, in connection with the hostility between Scythians and Medes) and has, of course, a purely mythical character. The same is true of the story about Astyages, under the influence of a prophetic dream, ordering Harpagus to kill Cyrus, the son of his daughter Mandanē, and the child, who was to have been thrown to the wild beasts, being miraculously saved by a slave cowherd

---

[1] Ctesias does not mention the Magi but states that Astyages, who had no sons, had given his daughter Amytis in marriage to one Spitamas. This is a name by no means uncommon in Iranian languages, but one that was also the family name of Zarathushtra who must have lived in the 7th to early 6th century at the latest. That Astyages had no sons is also mentioned by Herodotus (1.109). The history of the fall of the Median kingdom and the rise of the Persian, judging from a number of data, was much discussed in Persia as a politically important event in the days when Ctesias lived there, so that together with his fabrications and fantasies Ctesias may have brought to his reader the echoes of more or less genuine traditions. Therefore, if in this case we may for once believe Ctesias, it is not impossible that the son-in-law and presumed heir of Astyages was named after Zarathushtra and perhaps even believed to have been his kinsman and descendant. If this were so, there may here be another trait of the suggested tension between the old aristocracy (i.e. men necessarily connected with ancient cults and places of worship) against the royal power and the Magi. All this, however, is guesswork, and building upon Ctesias is always dangerous.

and returned to his rightful princely position (1. 107ff.). Such stories are common about famous kings, conquerors and founders of dynasties. Herodotus himself contradicts them when he says that after Cyrus II of Persia rebelled against Astyages the latter appointed Harpagus commander-in-chief of the Median army. This seems to be a piece of historical reality, as there is reason to believe that some of the informants of Herodotus may have been descendants of Harpagus. But if Astyages really acted in this fashion, it was certainly not because "god had clouded his mind" (1. 127) but because no cannibalistic feast had taken place and Harpagus, as the foremost representative of the Median aristocracy and kinsman of the king (1. 109) could well be appointed commander-in-chief. Similarly there is nothing astonishing in the fact that Harpagus, standing as he did at the head of the plot of the Median aristocracy against Astyages' unwelcome heir designate, the husband of his daughter, should have put forward as a more acceptable candidate to the throne the son of the king's other daughter, a Persian prince. In Ctesias Cyrus is the son of the Mardus Atradates (probably a variant of Herodotus' shepherd Mitradates who had saved the infant Cyrus in the mountains and had adopted him). But the version about the allegedly lowly extraction of Cyrus is completely disproved by texts contemporary with the events which affirm that both the father of Cyrus II, Cambyses I, and his grandfather, Cyrus I, had been kings in Persis.

Ctesias ascribes the role of Cyrus' instigator to rebellion to the groom Oebares, the slave of a Median magnate. This is apparently the same personage as Oebares, the groom of Darius I in Herodotus (III. 85). Many quite unreliable legends have been woven round this name, but the name itself is genuine: this is evidently Ugbar(u),[1] later satrap of Media (Akkad. *pehāt Gutium*), who on the behest of Cyrus had occupied Babylon in 538, and soon after died. This unexpected and rare case of corroboration by an independent source (the "Babylonian Chronicle") of a report by Ctesias makes it possible to treat this account of his with more confidence than usual, though still with some caution.

According to Ctesias, what happened after this was the following. Cyrus returned to Ecbatana from his expedition against the Cadusii and obtained leave from Astyages ostensibly to visit his father (this is also reported by Herodotus 1. 120ff.) but actually to take up the leadership of the rebellion as Oebares had been urging him to do. Meanwhile the

---

[1] This Ugbar(u) should be distinguished from Gūbar(u), the Gōbryēs of Herodotus, also mentioned in the "Babylonian Chronicle".

plot was accidentally discovered. Astyages took immediate steps and moved personally against the rebels.

The story is somewhat differently told by Herodotus. According to him the rebellion of the Persians was preceded by a plot of the Median aristocracy organized by Harpagus as a result of the mortal offence suffered by him at the hands of Astyages. Harpagus secretly sent to Cyrus who was in Persis a letter in which he urged him to raise a revolt promising him the fullhearted support of eminent Medes. On hearing about the warlike preparations of Cyrus, Astyages summoned him to his presence. Cyrus replied by a declaration of war. Harpagus, who was put at the head of the Median army, passed over to Cyrus with other Median magnates during the decisive battle.

From the two accounts one can deduce that Cyrus was at one time at the court of Astyages but that when the rebellion started he was in Persia. According to both versions Cyrus was not yet king of Persia at the time, but this is not true: Cyrus died in 529 after reigning 28 years (according to Herodotus) or even 30 years (according to Ctesias and Dinon). He had therefore reigned in his native country long before the rebellion which, according to Babylonian sources, began in 553. It is however possible that, as was quite common for sons of petty vassal kings, he was during his father's lifetime indeed at the imperial court.

Herodotus clearly compresses the events when he speaks only about the two last battles, fatal to the Median kingdom, one in which Harpagus commanded the Medes, the other when the command was taken over personally by Astyages. As it stands, the information of Herodotus is correct, because the account of the Median army going over to Cyrus finds a confirmation in the "Babylonian Chronicle" which places this event in 550–49, i.e. towards the end of the war. But the story of Herodotus must be supplemented with the report of Ctesias, due account being taken of doubts as to its veracity, about the initial period of the war.

According to Ctesias, at his first encounter with Cyrus' army at Hyrba Astyages defeated it. Atradates was killed in the fighting. During his pursuit of the Persians Astyages inflicted another defeat on them before the defile leading to the capital of Persis, Pasargadae. Here a wandering folklore motif is introduced about women who shamed the retreating Persians by suggesting that they retreat straight into their mothers' wombs. The battle at the walls of Pasargadae was the turning point, and soon peoples subjected to the Medes, among them the Hyrcanii, and later the Parthians, began to go over to the Persians. What happened thereafter is not clear from the excerpts that have come down to us. The war, as stated above, was a prolonged one and success varied. What gave the victory to Cyrus must have been the treason of the Median aristocracy which may also have been the cause of the defection from Media of borderland peoples. Curiously enough, after a quarter of a century of Persian rule the same Hyrcanii and Parthians joined the pseudo-Deiocid Fravarti who had raised a revolt against the Persians.

Herodotus (I. 128) gives an account of the last measures taken by Astyages. He executed the Magi with whom until then he had entertained the best of relations, allegedly for their advice to let Cyrus leave his court. Possibly some of the Magian priests had established connections with the rebels and the Persians: we see them later in high esteem at the court of Cyrus II and of his son Cambyses. Finally Astyages armed the whole population remaining in Ecbatana and marched out to the last battle in which he was defeated and captured by the Persians.

According to Babylonian data the king of Babylonia, Nabonidus succeeded already in 553 in taking without opposition the town of Ḥarrān in Mesopotamia which had been for fifty-four years in the possession of the Medes: they seem to have drawn their troops away from the frontier in connection with Cyrus' revolt which, along with his defeat of Astyages, is mentioned in an inscription of Nabonidus.

Another Babylonian text on the war between Astyages and Cyrus (the "Chronicle") reads as follows: "...(as to) Ištuwēg(u), his army rebelled against him and he was taken by (their) hands; [(they) ga]ve (him) to Cyrus. Cyrus entered Ecbatana, his royal city; silver, gold, riches, (movable) property [and captives from] Ecbatana they captured, and he took (all this) to Ančan (Anshan)..."

The accounts of Herodotus and Ctesias, and of the Babylonian sources, can be pieced together to give a sufficiently coherent picture of the stages of the development of the events: (1) the internal plot of the Median aristocracy organized by Harpagus, and on the other hand the incitement to rebellion of border tribes probably by Oebares and others; (2) the setting forth of Cyrus at the head of the army of his kingdom which included three Persian tribes (Pasargadae, Maraphii and Maspii); the defeat of the Persians and their retreat (year 553); (3) the prolonged war with alternating success; (4) the betrayal of Harpagus and of the Median aristocracy in the decisive battle, the passing over

THE MEDIAN EMPIRE

to the Persians of the Hyrcanians and Parthians, Astyages' attempt to stem the advance of the enemy, his flight to Ecbatana and the fall of the Median capital. According to Ctesias Astyages succeeded at first in finding safety in the citadel but was compelled to surrender under Cyrus' threat to send to torture his daughter Amytis, her husband Spitamās and their sons.

The different parts of the Median empire, from the frontiers of Bactria to the frontiers of Lydia, submitted to Cyrus without opposition. According to Ctesias the Bactrians and the Sacae who were allied to Media, entered into relations with Cyrus which, at least at first, were friendly.

Since the victory of Cyrus was achieved with the aid of the Median aristocracy it had to be given the appearance of a compromise. Therefore, though Ecbatana was sacked and some of the Medians were turned into slaves, Cyrus possibly did not abolish the kingdom of Media. At least neighbouring peoples seem to have regarded the events which had led Cyrus to power over a great empire as internecine strife common in ancient Oriental kingdoms, and continued to call the Achaemenian empire Media, and the Persians themselves, Medes. Media seems to have retained her privileged position till the rebellion of Fravarti in 522. Darius I in the record of the events of the beginning of his reign still sets off Persia and Media *together* against "other [i.e. conquered] lands", or in Akkadian, "lands of another tongue". However, as in other similar cases (e.g. in Babylonia) Cyrus, though he left to Media the name of a kingdom, nevertheless appointed a satrap (Oebares) there, and apparently laid a tribute on the country.

In order to strengthen the legality of his right to the throne Cyrus, according to Iranian custom and if we are to believe Ctesias, married Amytis, Astyages' daughter-*epicleros*, as the bearer of hereditary rights, having naturally first put to death her husband Spitamās. The determination to gain the sympathy of certain circles of the conquered lands, especially of the aristocracy, was constantly a part of the policy of Cyrus, as after him of Cambyses II. For this reason those members of the formerly reigning houses who had survived the immediate struggle for power, were usually spared. Such was the fate of Arsames in Persis, of Croesus in Lydia, of Nabonidus in Babylonia, of Psammetichus III in Egypt. This custom is probably to be explained by the fact that the Median and Persian empires had come about as a result of the amalgamation and federation of small, formerly independent kingdoms.

Astyages, too, escaped immediate death. According to Ctesias he was sent into honourable exile as satrap of the "Barcanii" (Hyrcanians? But the usual name-form "Hyrcanii" also appears in excerpts from Ctesias). Soon, however, under pretext of being taken to visit his daughter, he was left in the desert by the eunuch Petesacas on Oebares' instigation, there to starve to death.

Many noble Medes entered the service of Cyrus. Thus Harpagus became one of his outstanding military leaders, and third of the Persian satraps of Lydia after the death of Mazares, also a Mede. Ctesias reports that the sons of Amytis and Spitamās, Spitacus and Megabernes, were also satraps of Cyrus in Hyrcania and in the land of the Derbici, and Amytis' brother Parmises (an illegitimate son of Astyages, or the son of Amytis' mother from a first marriage?) was a Persian general. In view of the general tendency of hostility towards Cyrus in Ctesias' account, this report cannot be simply disregarded as incredible. There were Median military leaders under Darius I, too. Down to the times of Xerxēs (very seldom later) a few Median magnates occur occupying important posts in Achaemenian administration. But on the whole even the aristocracy of Media gained little from the change of power: already from the time of Darius I all the most important posts were held by Persian aristocrats, mainly members of the houses of Darius' companions in arms in the *coup d'état* which he brought about in 522. Median noble houses either merged with the Persian, or were pushed into the background if they were not destroyed during the rebellion of Fravarti and Čiθra^{n}taxma (who gave themselves out, the one at the end of the year 522, the other in 521, to be descendants of Cyaxares) and during the tumultuous events of the beginning of Xerxes' reign (486–484 B.C.).

CHAPTER 4

THE SCYTHS

I. THE COUNTRY AND ITS PEOPLES

The country

During the first half of the first millennium B.C., c. 3,000 to 2,500 years ago, the southern part of Eastern Europe was occupied mainly by peoples of Iranian stock; nowadays their only traces are the archaeological remains and topographic names of Iranian derivation scattered over that area. The main Iranian-speaking peoples of the region at that period were the Scyths and the Sarmatians (Sauromatians in Greek spelling), our knowledge of whom derives partly from the works of ancient writers, and also, to a great extent, from the study of archaeological remains.

The most important work relating to the ancient Scyths is the *Histories* of Herodotus. His descriptions, in the light of the results of archaeological research, are on the whole correct. However, the eastern part of Scythia seems to have been little known to him. He often generalizes from exceptional occurrences and seems to have telescoped some events which took place in about the same region but at different periods. These, and some other inconsistencies and gaps in his reports will here be corrected and supplemented by taking into account the evidence offered by the results of archaeological and linguistic research.

The vague notion of the peoples of Scythia entertained by Herodotus and his erroneous idea of the size and shape of the country, have often been commented upon. Several scholars endeavoured to draw the map of Scythia according to the data given by him (map 6) but "the different results to which they come prove that in this it is hopeless to seek more than the establishment of a few facts".[1]

Sixty years after this conclusion was drawn, the position has improved to some extent thanks to a large number of excavations and much research undertaken in the meantime. Nevertheless, one still cannot identify with certainty the peoples mentioned by Herodotus with

[1] Minns, *Scythians*, p. 26.

the archaeological cultures established in the area, or place the countries and peoples mentioned by him on the actual map of the North Pontic region.

Map 7 shows the diffusion of archaeological remains of the 6th century B.C., at a time preceding Herodotus. An attempt has also been made to identify them with the peoples quoted by Herodotus. The physiographic division of ancient Scythia into two main zones is shown, the treeless steppe in the south occupied mostly by pastoral nomad tribes, and the fertile black-earth region in the forest-steppe zone north of the steppe, which was always the abode of an agricultural population.

The Scythian period fell at the time of the wet sub-Atlantic climate, which was more damp than the present climate of the Ukraine.[1] The northern border of the steppe then lay further south than at present. The place-names, and the bones of animals excavated in kitchen refuse of prehistoric settlements of that period, indicate that beavers lived then in the valleys of the lower Dnieper and lower Southern Bug, whereas at present the southernmost existing colony of these animals is on the Teterev, north of Kiev. Bones of elk were found in a series of prehistoric settlements in the south of the Ukraine and even in the débris of the ancient Greek city Olbia. At present, the southernmost region in which these animals live is the forests of the Pripet marshes, some 500 km north of Olbia. Thus the Scyths must have enjoyed very favourable climatic conditions in their country. The steppe, with its luxuriance of grass, permitted the nomads to keep large herds of horses and cattle, and the then well-watered region on the lower Dnieper was afforested (the country of Hylea). Good conditions for agricultural activities seem to have prevailed along the whole strip of land along the sea coast, and also in the other parts of the country.

The people

Although the ancient Persians called all Scyths "Saca" (Her. VII. 64) the population of ancient Scythia was far from being homogeneous, nor were the Scyths themselves a homogeneous people. The country called after them was ruled by their principal tribe, the "Royal Scyths" (Her. IV. 20), who were of Iranian stock and called themselves "Skolotoi" (IV. 6); they were nomads who lived in the steppe east of

---

[1] T. Sulimirski, *Climate and Population* (Toruń, 1935); *idem*, "The Climate of the Ukraine During the Neolithic and the Bronze Age", *Archeologia* XII (Warsaw, 1961), pp. 1–18.

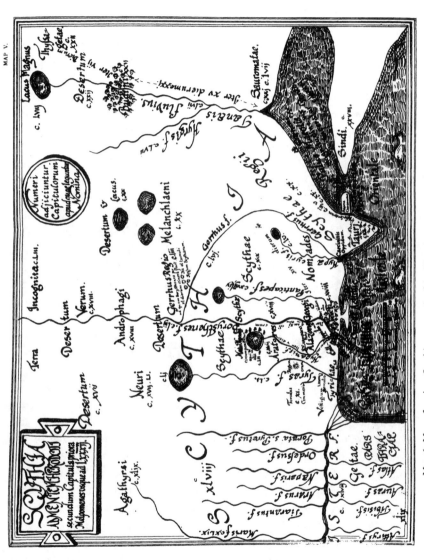

Map 6. Map of ancient Scythia as conceived by Herodotus, reconstructed by E. H. Minns.

the Dnieper up to the Don, and in the Crimean steppe. Another tribe, likewise steppe dwellers, were the "Nomadic Scyths", whose country extended west of the Dnieper bend to the Ingul, a tributary of the lower Southern Bug. Their western neighbours were the Alazones or Alizōnes, who were in possession of the steppe up to the Dniester. Some of them were pastoral nomads, but Herodotus writes that some "sow and feed on wheat, onions, garlic, lentils and millet", although "in other respects they follow the customs of the Scyths". The first part of their name, *Ala* or *Ali*, would be a regular development within Scythian phonology of the ethnic term *Arya* (in the sense of "Iranian"), but some scholars are of the opinion that the Alazones were of mixed blood, Iranian and Thracian.[1]

The linguistic study of the Ukrainian toponymy and of the toponyms and personal names that appear in ancient inscriptions in the débris of the Greek North Pontic colonies, suggests that besides the Greeks in the colonies and the Iranian speaking tribes, people of Thracian stock lived in Scythia, although they are not mentioned by Herodotus.[2] These were presumably descendants of the population native to the country in the Bronze Age, whereas the Iranians were newcomers, the earliest of whom probably arrived in Scythia in the second half of the second millennium B.C. The native Thracians were a settled agricultural population subdued and ruled by the Scythian upper class, to whom they must have paid tribute. It is perhaps their largest group who are meant by the "Scythian Husbandmen" (ἀροτῆρες), "who do not sow wheat for food, but for sale" (Her. IV. 17); these lived in the fertile black-earth region of the Ukraine west of the Dnieper.

Another important group were the Callipidae, the "Greek Scythians", who occupied the wide strip of land along the sea coast west of the estuary of the Southern Bug, extending up to the region of Odessa, or perhaps even beyond it up to the estuary of the Dniester. Finally, the "Scythian agriculturalists" (γεωργοί) were the third agricultural people of ancient Scythia mentioned by Herodotus (IV. 18), and were originally like the other two mentioned above, of Thracian stock; they lived in the valley of the lower Dnieper. Moreover, several ancient settlements of the Scythian period have been recorded along the coast of the Sea of Azov, between Lake Molochnoye in the west and Mariupol (Zhdanov) in the east. Several have been investigated;[3] they belong to

[1] M. S. Sinitsyn, *MASP* II (1959), pp. 24ff.; IV (1962), pp. 61ff.
[2] See bibliography.
[3] O. A. Krivtsova-Grakova, MIA 46 (1955), pp. 151ff., map p. 164.

THE COUNTRY AND ITS PEOPLES

the "Obitochny" type, and are regarded as a further development of a similar group belonging to the Late Bronze Age in the same area. The identity of their inhabitants remains unknown; they were not mentioned by Herodotus.

Scythian tribes who lived within the confines of ancient Scythia were not the only Iranians in the North Pontic region. One may regard as Iranian, or at least of mixed Iranian and native stock, the Melanchlaeni and the Androphagi, whose countries lay outside Scythia, although they bordered on it. These countries extended over the Ukrainian forest-steppe zone east of the middle Dnieper, north of the country of the "Royal Scyths". The eastern neighbours of the "Royal Scyths", the Sauromatians, were also Iranian; their country extended over the steppe east of the Don and the Volga.

The toponymy and hydronymy of the North Pontic area indicates that modern Byelorussia, north of ancient Scythia, was inhabited by Baltic-speaking peoples whose only modern descendants are the Lithuanians and Letts of the Baltic coast.[1] During the Scythian Age, the Neuri were one of these peoples. East of them in the forest zone of Eastern Europe up to the Urals, and probably beyond, there lived a great variety of Finno-Ugrian tribes, among them the Budini mentioned by Herodotus. In the south, on the eastern coast of the Sea of Azov, lived the Maeotians, and the Crimean (Taurian) Mountains were in the possession of the Taurians. Each of these groups was divided into several tribes, whose archaeological cultures differ somewhat from each other.

Scythian way of life

The genuine steppe Scyths were nomads who had no permanent homes; they lived on waggons in which women and children spent their lives. The men, from early childhood, spent most of their time on horseback; their main occupation was fighting: everyone was trained from youth in warlike exercises and in the use of the bow. Scythian customs were for the most part inseparable from nomadic life, as were those of Sauromatians (Sarmatians) and other steppe peoples. Their economy was based on nomad pastoralism; horse, cattle and sheep were reared; hunting was not for the provision of meat; it was practised chiefly for sport and pastime. Scythian princes, and in the Late Scythian

[1] See Sulimirski, "Ancient Southern Neighbours".

period (the 4th–3rd centuries B.C.) also the better-off rank-and-file, drank wine readily, as indicated by the large number of Greek wine amphorae found in their tombs. Scythian women apparently enjoyed no emancipation, unlike the Sarmatian women who went hunting with men, rode on horseback, shot with the bow, and threw javelins.

The Scythian customs described by Herodotus are partly crude. "They studiously avoid the use of foreign customs", says Herodotus, "and least of all Greek customs, and impose punishment on those who introduce foreign customs." (IV. 76, 80)

The genuine Scyths of the steppe were ruled by their tribal kings who had absolute power over them, and who in turn owed allegiance to the king of the Royal tribe. Royal power was believed to have been ordained by the gods. This notion may have been introduced by Scyths who came from Western Asia. It is a notion well illustrated by the toreutic of the Late Scythian period and the cult-symbols depicted on it, whose spread over the country was wide.

The rule of the Scyths in the western part of their empire, west of the Dnieper, was neither very powerful nor very oppressive during the Early Scythian period,[1] and brought about little change in the previously existing social and economic order of the subjugated peoples. The conquerors were on the whole content with the tribute paid by the agricultural population of the country. Conditions were different in the Late Scythian period, as a result of fundamental changes which had taken place by the end of the 5th century B.C.

Dress and ornaments

Scythian dress was not very different from that characteristic of other nomad peoples of the Eurasian steppes. In this respect almost nothing can be added to the splendid study by E. H. Minns, and to his analysis of Scythian figures that appear on Scythian and Greek toreutic and on fine Greek pottery. They wore belts, trousers and, in the early period, pointed caps; bareheaded Scythian men often appear on toreutic of the later period. The Scyths are usually represented with long hair and sizeable beards.

Of women's dress we have only a vague idea; on the toreutic, exclusively of the late period, only upper class women are represented, usually wearing over the dress a cloak with hanging sleeves, and a

[1] Rostovtzev, *Iranians and Greeks*, p. 94.

THE COUNTRY AND ITS PEOPLES

kerchief to cover the head. Some had a great mantle adorned with small gold plaques, triangular or rounded; poorer people wore bronze plaques instead.

Both men's and women's personal ornaments were mostly made of solid gold, but bronze ornaments were also in use. Men wore only one earring. The simple bracelets were of silver or bronze wire, and those of gold, like the neck rings and torques, had the terminals adorned with animal figures or heads. Necklaces consisted of beads of gold and of a great variety of semi-precious stones, all imported from other countries. In better-furnished female burials a bronze mirror was often found, mostly of ordinary Greek type. Some mirrors, especially in early graves, represent fine samples of Ionian craftsmanship. Quite common, and widely diffused in the early periods, were Olbian bronze mirrors with handles adorned with figures of stag, panther, ram, etc.

Weapons[1]

The characteristic Scythian weapon was the short bow of the composite type, convenient to use on horseback, carried in a bowcase always combined with quiver. The latter was usually made of leather or bark and often adorned with a decorated gold or bronze plaque, in the later period often of Greek workmanship. A quiver contained up to 300 arrows made of reed or wood; they had a bronze or rarely an iron point of the "Scythian type", socketed, three-edged. These arrowheads – not a Scythian invention – were an adaptation made by Transcaucasian craftsmen of the very effective, heavy points in common use in Western Asia and Transcaucasia, to suit the light arrows used by the Scythian mounted bowmen. Of Transcaucasian origin also were the "typical Scythian" iron daggers of the ἀκινάκης type with a richly decorated haft, and iron battle-axes (shaft-hole axes), both of which were a development of Transcaucasian, mainly Georgian, Bronze Age weapons. Other weapons used by the Scyths were lances and darts, iron heads of which were found in better equipped graves, and lassoes and slings.

Shields, which are seldom depicted, were rather small in size, made of hide or wicker, often strengthened by iron strips. In princely burials they were often adorned with a central decorative plaque, examples of which are the famous stag figures from the barrows of Kelermes and

[1] See bibliography.

Kostromskaya. Almost all Scythian warriors had protective armour made of leather or hide, but in graves of the Scythian aristocracy scale armour was common; it was found in about 200 burials. This was a West Asiatic invention; once introduced by the West Asiatic Scyths, it became a common feature of Scythian culture in the North Pontic area. Scales were mainly of iron, but also of bronze or bone. Armour was quite often replaced with battle-belts made of wide strips of iron sheet or hide or leather, with scales sewn onto them. About 20 bronze greaves of Greek origin, exclusively of the 4th century B.C., were found in Scythia and the countries around. They were found, as were bronze helmets (about 50 in all), mainly in princely burials of the Early Scythian period and chiefly in the northwest Caucasus. The earliest ones, of the 6th and early 5th centuries B.C., were mostly of Caucasian origin; in the 5th century helmets of the Attic type appeared. Occasionally horses were also protected with scale armour, mainly over the chest.

The Scyths had no saddles and no stirrups, which seem to have been invented by the Sarmatians at a later date; they rode on cloth. Fighting horsemen depicted on ancient toreutic were often sitting with both legs on one side of the horse.

Handicrafts and trade

The Scyths, or rather the native Thracians of ancient Scythia, were skilled in various handicrafts, such as pottery, woodwork, and weaving, and also in bronze metallurgy. The latter was based on raw material imported mainly from Transylvania. It provided the Scyths with simple tools and ornaments, and with some types of weapons.

To the masterpieces of the local Scythian bronze industry belong the large bronze cauldrons, semispheric with a truncated cone forming its foot or stand.[1] Some were decorated in cast and usually provided with two, or four, handles projecting upwards from the rim; they were often given the shape of an animal. In cauldrons found in tombs there are usually horse and mutton bones, remains of food given for the journey beyond. Socketed bronze finials were also characteristic of the industry, mounted upon a pole and crowned with figurines of various animals.

Nothing is known of the organization of the production of Scythian industry in the Early Scythian period. Its centre presumably lay in the area of the "Scythian Husbandmen", within the country of the Tiasmin

[1] A. P. Mantsevich, in: *Issledovaniya po Arkheologii SSSR* (Leningrad, 1961), pp. 145-50.

group of Scythian culture; a similar centre had existed at Belsk on the other side of the Dnieper, outside Scythia in the country of the Vorskla group of Scythian culture, which is attributable to the Melanchlaeni. During the Late Scythian period, the post-Herodotus era, the most important industrial centre of Scythia and its neighbouring countries was the large earthwork of Kamyanka, on the southern bank of the lower Dnieper opposite modern Nikopol. Here were manufactured a wide variety of tools and ornaments, and also weapons, including swords. Iron was made by smelting local bog iron ores in this centre; traces of its exploitation have been found.

The wide commercial connections of ancient Scythia are well attested by archaeological evidence. By the end of the 7th and in the 6th century Greek pottery began to be imported from the Aegean islands.[1] Later, chiefly in the 5th century, Corinthian and Athenian pottery appeared, and in the Late Scythian period, the 4th and 3rd centuries B.C., Bosporan (mainly Panticapaean) pottery predominated in Scythian burials. During the Early Scythian period Olbia was the main supplier of all sorts of luxuries, personal ornaments, gold and silver vases, glyptic, wine, oil, etc., and also of weapons both offensive and defensive, which were either produced in Olbian workshops or imported from the Greek mainland. In the Late Scythian period Olbian commerce was restricted to a small part of Scythia in the west, the Scythian market having been mostly taken over by Panticapaeum and other Bosporan cities. At that period also several small local forges provided the Scyths with weapons and simple personal ornaments. The very fine richly decorated vases, rhytons and other examples of toreutic, decorative plaques for quivers, etc., were undoubtedly made by Greek Bosporan workshops; many of these are admirable examples of "Scythian" art.

In the Early Scythian period an important commercial route passed across Scythia; from Olbia it ran along the Ingul (the "Borysthenes" of Herodotus), crossed the Dnieper and, turning eastwards, reached the country of the Geloni; thereafter, across Don and Volga, it passed over the Urals and penetrated deep into Asia (see map 7, p. 176–8); it linked Olbia with the gold-bearing countries. Herodotus says (IV. 24) that the Scyths who went to these remote countries transacted business through seven interpreters in seven languages. Gold seems to have been the commodity sought by the enterprising traders.

The development of such an extensive trade with distant countries

[1] See bibliography.

implies that the traders felt safe from robbery. Such favourable conditions were evidently the outcome of the conquest by the Scyths of a large part of the North Pontic area, and their establishment there of the "Pax Scythica". The swift growth, since the middle of the 6th century B.C., of Greek cities along the Black Sea coast, illustrates the unfolding possibilities. The trade on which the prosperity of the colonies was based, could have flourished only under the protection and with the co-operation of the rulers of the Scythian hinterland; this trade was also the source of the wealth of the Scythian rulers and aristocracy, and is well documented by the inventories of their tombs. At the same time the North Pontic Greeks, the main suppliers of luxuries and works of art, had a considerable influence on the formation of Scythian taste and Scythian art. Most works of art found in tombs of the Late Scythian period are far from representing genuine Scythian art; they are works of Greek artisans, and the sole aim of their Scythian motifs and scenes from Scythian life was to satisfy Scythian customers.

Beliefs and burial customs

The data relating to Scythian beliefs and religion that can be drawn from the remarks by Herodotus and from the representations on Scythian toreutic, pottery and objects of art in general, have been much discussed.[1] It is thought that Scythian beliefs, names of deities, etc., exhibit some similarity to, and analogies with those of other contemporary peoples. The names of the main male deities were sometimes of Thracian origin, evidently taken over by the Scyths from their subject peoples;[2] parallels can be found chiefly in Thracia and among Thracian peoples of ancient Anatolia. No such close analogies can be found in other countries for Scythian female deities. But the nature of these, their association with special cults, and the forms of their worship and symbols, also connect them with Thraco-Anatolian culture. In the Late Scythian period the Scyths living in the vicinity of the Bosporan Kingdom adopted several Greek symbols and representations of Greek deities.

Some of the peculiarities of worship, symbols, etc., mentioned above reflect the engagement of the population in agricultural activities and settled life. They do not mirror a nomadic society. Purely nomadic

[1] See bibliography.
[2] Elnitskii, bibliography.

and Iranian was the Scythian worship of the war-god, Ares, in the form of a sword cult (Her. IV. 62); this worship still continued among their descendants, the Alans, in the 4th century A.D. The genuine Scythian nomads sacrificed to their gods all sorts of animals, and chiefly among them horses (Her. IV. 60); the manner of their offering seems to have been proper to nomads. Wizards were numerous among the Scyths; their usual method of foretelling the future is described by Herodotus (IV. 67). A widespread custom was that of intoxicating oneself with vapours of hemp (IV. 75); the vapours took the place of bathing, for the Scyths never washed their bodies with water.

The cruel Scythian royal funeral mentioned by Herodotus (IV. 71–3) with its hecatombs of horses and human offerings, fits in well with the northwest Caucasian royal burials of the Early Scythian period. But this description does not apply to the richly equipped princely burials of Scythia proper, not even those of the Late Scythian period.

Sepulchral structures and burial rites in various parts of Scythia differed somewhat from each other, and in the process of time underwent changes, chiefly owing to the influx of new ethnic elements. The differences in the equipment of tombs reflect the social divisions within almost all Scythian groups. Burials were mostly supine inhumation; cremation was practised chiefly among the "Scythian Husbandmen".

Typical of the Early Scythian period were burials in rectangular shafts covered with a mound of earth. In the Late Scythian period "niche" or "catacomb" graves became common, shafts with an underground burial chamber dug out in one of the sides, presumably introduced into Scythia by the end of the 5th century B.C. by newcomers from the steppe of the lower Volga. In the regions of the "Scythian agriculturalists" there appear so-called "flat" graves, with no exterior marks.

Many graves under mounds, especially the richly furnished princely burials, had special timber constructions sunk in a large shaft, or built on the ground. During the later period some had an elaborate sepulchral construction built on the Crimean Greek model; these are found chiefly in the southern part of the country.

Of particular interest are large stone slabs or stelae, often over 2 m high, which were given the shape of a crude human figure (fig. 1).[1] Their surface is usually covered with a carving in relief representing an armed

---

[1] N. G. Elagina, *SA* 1959.2, pp. 187–96; A. A. Formozov, *Ocherki po Pervobytnomu Isskustvu* (Moscow, 1969), pp. 183ff (MIA 165).

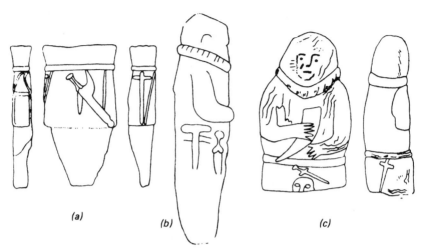

Fig. 1. Scythian stone stelae of the 6th century B.C. (*a*) from the region of Zhdanov, (*b*) from Dobrudja and (*c*) from the region of Kherson.

man. Special care was given to the essential details of his dress, and in particular to his sword and other weapons. The details give an idea of Scythian dress and show the manner in which weapons were carried, allowing the date of the stelae to be fixed.

The stelae were originally erected on the tops of grave mounds of outstanding chiefs or princes. Their erection in the Ukraine is attested already for the third millennium B.C.; this ancient local custom survived to the Late Bronze Age and was then evidently taken over by the Scyths. The sword represented on stelae was presumably intended to underline the might of the buried war-lord, counting as his main royal attribute.

Scythian art

Much has been written on "Scythian" art,[1] which is usually wrongly regarded as synonymous with the art of almost all nomad peoples of the Eurasian steppes. Only a few points will here be raised in this connection.

It should first be emphasized that each branch of "Scythian" art (in its broadest sense) sprang up and then developed independently. Their basic similarity comes from two main factors, which were at the root of the formation of all the branches. One of these, the most important,

[1] See bibliography.

was Oriental culture and art. It had affected the Scyths, exclusively their upper class, during their occupation of Media (see above, pp. 96–7). Oriental culture and art, adopted by Achaemenian Persian, spread through the medium of the Achaemenian culture into what is now Soviet Central Asia and into countries further to the north in Asia.

Another factor was the "static" naturalistic art of the forest dwellers of Eastern Europe and Siberia which affected especially the art of the peoples of the Scythian forest-steppe zone. Decisive for the development of Scythian art in Europe also was the Greek contribution, and likewise Thracian influence.

Moreover, when discussing Scythian art the circumstance must be taken into account that at the time of crossing the Volga, the ancestors of the Scyths did not know any "Scythian" art, nor possessed any "typical Scythian" weapons or other articles. Their ancestors, the peoples of the Srub and Andronovo cultures, applied exclusively geometric patterns to the decoration of their pottery and of their bone cheek-pieces.[1]

"Scythian" culture and art were born in the second half of the 7th century B.C. in Western Asia to serve the aristocracy of the Scythian branch that had subdued a large part of Western Iran and countries far to the west of it. The articles from the royal burial of Ziwiyeh, discussed further below, mark the beginning of Scythian art in the second part of the 7th century B.C. The continuing aristocratic character of Scythian art in the 6th century is attested by the furniture of princely burials in the northwest Caucasus, and in the areas further to the north, by the Melgunov barrow in the Ukraine, and the Witaszkowo (Vetterfelde) find in Poland on the Oder (figs. 2, 3, 4).[2] On the other hand, the preference for geometric patterns in decoration, inherited from their Srub and Andronovo ancestors, was still vivid among the Scythian aristocracy of the late 7th century B.C. outside Western Asia: this has been well demonstrated by articles from the barrow Maly Kurgan in southeastern Azarbaijan (figs. 5, 6, 7).[3] Articles from the Urartian fortress Karmir-Blur, destroyed by the Scyths around 600 B.C., imply that the rank-and-file Scyths had at that time still not adopted the "Scythian animal style"; the genuine Scythian bone cheek-pieces found

---

[1] K. F. Smirnov, *SA* 1961.1, pp. 46–72.
[2] Artamonov, *Treasures*, pls 1–61; M. Ebert, "Vettersfelde", in Ebert (ed.), *Reallexikon der Vorgeschichte* XIV (Berlin, 1929), pp. 156–60.
[3] A. A. Iessen, MIA 125 (1965), pp. 22–30; A. I. Terenozhkin, *SA* 1971.4, pp. 71–84.

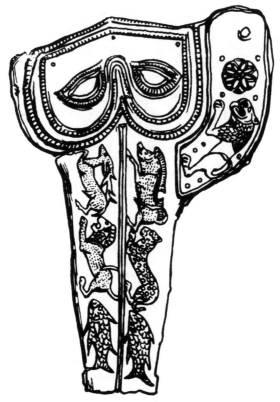

Fig. 2. Gold sheath covering the upper part of the *akinakes* (ἀκινάκης) scabbard from the find of Witaszkowo (Vettersfelde), the westernmost Scythian "princely" burial in Europe.

there and the bronze buckles, are plain, functional and undecorated; they show no attempt to give their terminals the shape of animal heads (figs. 8, 9), unlike the artifacts of nomads belonging to groups of Scythian culture (fig. 10). The early plain undecorated bone cheek-pieces have also been found in the Ukraine (the earthwork of Trakhtemirov) and in Poland (Młyniec, fig. 9). The two carved bone griffin heads found at Karmir-Blur were presumably acquired from the local Urartians.[1]

[1] See bibliography.

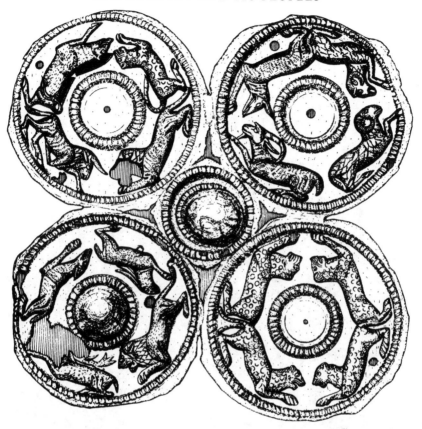

Fig. 3. Ornamental gold disc, perhaps part of a horse's harness. Greek workmanship, with Oriental motifs. Vettersfelde. About 500 B.C. Length 17 cm.

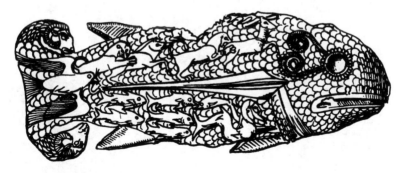

Fig. 4. Gold fish, thought to be a shield ornament or the frontlet from a horse's harness. Vettersfelde. About 500 B.C. Length 41 cm.

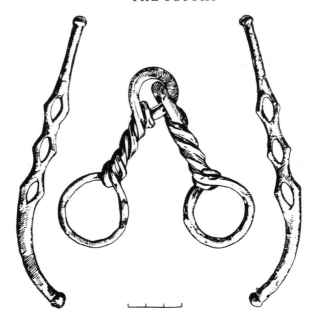

Fig. 5. Bronze bridle-bits and curb-chains with rings (ψάλια) from Maly Kurgan.

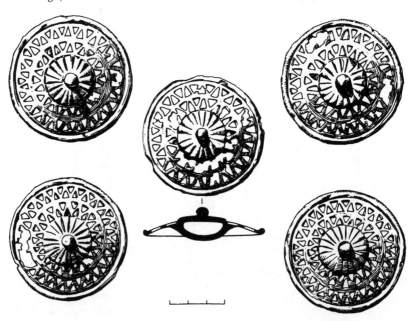

Fig. 6. Bronze cheek-pieces (phalerae, φάλαρα) from Maly Kurgan.

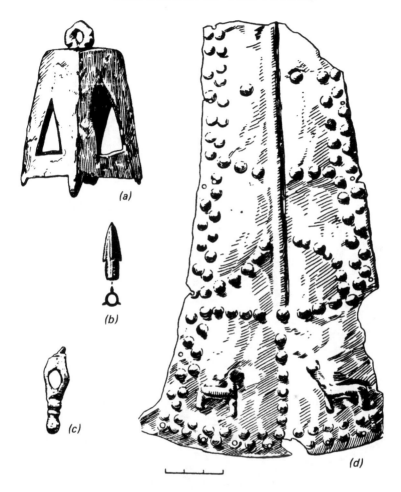

Fig. 7. Bronze objects (a) bell, (b) arrow head, (c) buckle, (d) frontlet (chamfron), from Maly Kurgan.

II. THE ORIGIN OF THE SCYTHS

Three legends

Herodotus (IV. 5–13) quotes three accounts of the origin of the Scyths. According to the first, the first man born in Scythia was Targitaus who had three sons, Lipoxais, Apoxais, and the youngest, Colaxais. Only the last was able to take the golden plough, yoke, axe and bowl which fell from heaven, wherefore his brothers made him sole king. From

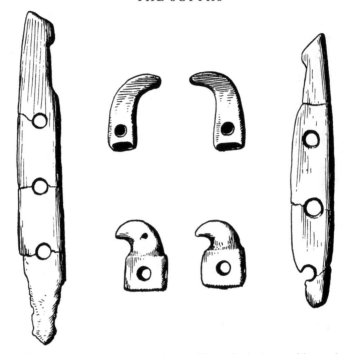

Fig. 8. The earliest so far discovered undecorated bone cheek-pieces and bronze buckles from Scythian bridles found at Karmir Blur.

Fig. 9. An undecorated Scythian bone cheek-piece from Młyniec in northern Poland. 6th century B.C.

Lipoxais sprung the Scyths called Auchatae; from Apoxais the Scyths called Catiaroi and Traspies; and from Colaxais the Paralatae, the "Royal Scyths" or Scolotoi.

The above names, except for the name "Scolotoi" and a mention of the "Royal race", appear only once in Herodotus' work. However, some of these names are met with elsewhere in ancient onomastics, ethnonymy and toponymy of the Pontic and Caspian regions.[1] Thus the

[1] Elnitskii, *SA* 1970.2 (bibliography).

Fig. 10. Carved bone cheek-pieces from early Scythian burials at Aksyutintsy (the Sula group of the Scythian culture).

Auchatae and Catiaroi appear in Pliny's list of North Caucasian tribes, and again in his list of Transcaspian tribes; the latter reference presumably relates to the seats they formerly held, at a time preceding their move to the Caucasus and the Ukraine.

Since at least the name "Paralatae" is clearly Iranian, the idea that the legend stems from the Late Bronze Age, and was connected with early Iranians belonging to the Srub culture is plausible. Being pressed by their eastern neighbours, they were forced to move from the steppe on the lower Volga, and entered the North Pontic steppe around the 13th century B.C. According to archaeological evidence, they must have reached the Carpathians in the west, and the Caucasus in the south. It follows that some Iranian tribes seem to have lived in the Ukraine before the arrival of the genuine Scyths. If the date given by the legend itself of the appearance of the mythical king Targitaus is taken into account, the arrival of the Iranians in the North Pontic area must have taken place soon after the middle of the second millennium B.C. This date would fit the invasion of the country by the people of Srub culture.

The plough and yoke mentioned in the legend look like symbols of an agricultural people, possibly of the "Scythian Husbandmen" who were most likely original Thracians subdued by invading Iranian Scyths. On the other hand, however, all four golden objects which fell from the sky, are mentioned in the allocution of the Transcaspian Sakas to Alexander the Great.[1] Thus the legend may nevertheless belong to an ancient Iranian tradition.[2]

The second account, given to Herodotus by "the Greeks who inhabit Pontus", says that Hercules once "came to the country now called Scythia", where he met a monster, half serpent, half woman, who bore him three sons. At his departure he gave her the bow and the belt which had a golden cup at the extremity of the clasp, and recommended to her, when the boys reached manhood, to test their ability to bend his bow and put on his girdle. When they grew up, only Scythes, the youngest of the three, passed the test; the other two, Agathyrsis and Gelones, were expelled by their mother. From Scythes sprang the Scythian kings. His brothers bear the names of two peoples one would like to identify with groups of Scythian culture situated close to ancient Scythia, one to the west, the other to the east, outside the confines of Scythia and independent of the Royal tribe.

The third legend

The third version, which Herodotus considers the most probable, relates to the crossing by the Scyths of the Araxes-Volga and the Don. This event may plausibly be connected with the data furnished by archaeology. According to these data, there were at least two, or perhaps three, westward expansions of the Srub culture from beyond the Volga, the bearers of which were presumably Iranians. Only the last

---

[1] *Op. cit.*
[2] In Avestan tradition the beginning of Yima's millennium was marked by divine intervention comparable to the dropping from the sky, in the Scythian legend, of the four golden objects: the god Ahura Mazdāh presents Yima with two golden objects, a *suwrā* (meaning unknown) and an *aštrā* "whip". By applying the two implements to the earth Yima greatly extends the area of it inhabitable by domestic animals and men (*Vendidad* II. 10, 14, 18). Since the whip plays a part in nomadic existence, the suwrā perhaps relates to agriculture. Both forms of life will have been practised, each by different Iranians, in Yima's millennium. The noun suwrā looks like belonging to the Iranian verbal base, attested for instance in Persian *suftan*, meaning "to pierce". The action to which Yima subjects the earth by means of the suwrā, is expressed by the equally unclear Avestan past tense *aiwišvat̰*, which the Pahlavi commentator translated *suft* "he pierced (the earth with the golden suwrā)". Hence the meaning of suwrā was reasonably conjectured by F. Justi in 1864, and afresh by J. Scheftelowitz in 1923, to be "plough" or "ploughshare". By 1895, however, Justi had switched to J. Darmesteter's "ring" (1892), which also H. Lommel (1927) and Christensen (1934) accepted. C. Bartholomae (1904) preferred "arrow", H. W. Bailey (1971) "goad", J. Duchesne-Guillemin followed by G. Gnoli (both in 1980) "(musical) horn". Of all these guesses the first would seem the most down-to-earth, and may even be thought, since at least in divine provision of implements to an early king the Avestan account resembles the Scythian, to derive support from the latter. Ed.

THE ORIGIN OF THE SCYTHS

of these migrations, which is believed to have taken place in the 10th or 9th century B.C. may be connected with the migration of the "Royal Scyths".

Archaeological evidence indicates that a branch of the Srub people crossed the Caucasus along the Caspian coast, in accordance with the account given by Herodotus, and settled down in the steppe of modern Azarbaijan, the ancient country of Sakasene which derived its name from them. Constant contact with the Urartians and with the Transcaucasian tribes, whose culture was much more advanced, resulted in the Scythian newcomers beginning to adopt gradually many elements of their neighbours' higher culture, and above all acquiring their more effective weapons. Thus the original Srub culture of the newcomers, which had a considerable admixture of Andronovo Siberian elements, began to change into the new "Scythian culture", which developed a distinctive character.

The Northwest Caucasian Scythian group

We have already said that in the 7th century B.C. the Scythians invaded Iran and subdued Media and other West Asiatic countries, where they had ample opportunity to acquaint themselves with Oriental culture and art, of which the Scythian upper class in particular got a taste. Eventually, however, in around 600 B.C., the Scyths were overthrown by the Medes and "expelled from Asia". In "returning home", they must have passed through the northwest Caucasus where their larger groups seem to have remained and imposed their rule over the native Maeotians. This is suggested by over a score of sumptuously furnished Scythian barrow-graves in the steppe stretching from the river Kuban southward to the mountains and also over the area around, including the Taman peninsula.

Scythian antiquities from Western Asia and those from the Caucasus mentioned above, seem to support a succession of events as related by Herodotus. The fact is that the "Scythian" antiquities found in the countries south of the Caucasus date from the 7th century B.C., whereas the earliest "Scythian" remains from the countries north of the Caucasus date from the 6th century B.C.[1] A most important fact is that the earliest "Scythian" antiquities north of the Caucasus show definite

---

[1] K. Schefold, *Eurasia Septentrionalis Antiqua* XII (Helsinki, 1938); Artamonov, *Treasures*, pp. 22ff; E. D. Phillips, *World Archaeology* IV.2 (1972), pp. 129–38.

features of Western Asiatic origin. They differ from later Scythian discoveries in the same territory in which the Oriental articles were found to have been replaced by those made locally and by masterpieces of Greek origin.

One of the earliest Scythian burials in the northwest Caucasus was barrow grave 1 of Kelermes dated in about 675–550 B.C. The equipment of the princely warrior buried there consisted exclusively of Oriental, mainly Median, partly Urartian, articles. In the male burial of barrow 2, of a little later date, objects were found adorned with deer figures in the "Scythian style", but in the female grave already a Greek Ionian silver gilt mirror of the 7th–6th century type formed part of the grave goods.

A special feature of the northwest Caucasian princely barrow graves were hecatombs of horses: 16 or 24 horse skeletons were found in some of them, but in this respect the Ulski barrow exceeded them all. It was of the early period, measured 15 m in height, and contained skeletons of over 400 horses. The layout of its sepulchral construction and of its contents corresponds almost exactly with the description by Herodotus (IV. 71, 72) of the funeral of a Scythian king; one year after the funeral 50 Scythian youths were killed and their bodies impaled and mounted on bodies of slaughtered horses around the top of the mound. The funeral must have been famous among all Scyths for its cruel extravagance, and its fame undoubtedly reached Olbia where it impressed Herodotus during his stay in that city in the mid-5th century B.C.

The description by Herodotus is usually regarded as depicting a customary type of "Royal Scythian" funeral. The archaeological evidence, however, suggests that this was a unique example of a particularly cruel procedure not adopted anywhere else in the Scythian world. The importance of the description lies in the king, and also the immolated youths, being Scyths, as Herodotus states, although the northwest Caucasus was not a part of his Scythia, and was not even mentioned by him.

The very rich equipment of the northwest Caucasian Scythian barrow graves, of which the earliest included Western Asiatic, Oriental articles, with their hecatombs of horses and immolated servants buried with their chief, are without precedent in the Eurasian steppe country. No such burials have been found in any barrow grave of the Srub or Andronovo cultures, both ancestral to the Scythian and Sarmatian, nor in any of the pre-Scythian period in the Ukraine. They were also unknown to the

THE ORIGIN OF THE SCYTHS

Saka tribes and to the so-called "Early Nomads", ancestral to the Sarmatian Alans in the steppe east of the Urals.

We have therefore to look elsewhere for the prototypes of this kind of Early Scythian royal burial in the northwest Caucasus. The sole Scythian predecessor of such tombs, known so far, is the so-called "treasure" from Ziwiyeh in Iran, which came from a tomb of a "great Scythian king".[1]

Oriental heritage

The grave from Ziwiyeh was ruined by its casual discoverers and its equipment was badly damaged and dispersed. The circumstances in which the articles were found suggest that the king was buried in a sarcophagus.[2] Immolated and buried with the king were his queen, possibly some female servants, and also a number of armed guards together with at least eleven horses and a chariot. The king's equipment consisted of a ceremonial golden sword and scabbard, decorated with ivory, gold and silver, breast plate, pectorals, a silver shield; three iron daggers, seven long iron lance-heads, and bronze disc-shaped umbos of shields probably constituted the armament of guards. Several "Scythian" arrow-heads indicate that bows were also present. The large number of precious personal ornaments belonged mostly to the endowment of the queen. In addition there were several gold and bronze vases, pottery, horse-gear, a decorated silver chamfron, ivory carvings, etc.

The find, its character, significance and its date have been discussed by several authorities. Its articles, which do not form a homogeneous collection, were most probably made over several decades in the second half of the 7th century B.C. They were deposited in the grave by the end of the 7th century or around 600 B.C. Opinions differ as to the origin of both the equipment and the identity of the buried prince, and as to whether he was a Mede, a Mannaian, or a Scyth. The striking similarity of the funeral ritual and of some pieces of equipment to those of the Scythian princely burials in the northwest Caucasus of the immediately following period, favour the hypothesis that the Ziwiyeh prince was of Scythian nationality, despite the very mixed provenience of his equipment. The dating of the sarcophagus will depend on the date

[1] See bibliography.
[2] Ghirshman, *Persia*, p. 100.

emerging from the study of the engravings on the rim of the "bath-sarcophagus" found in a slip of the eroded part of the Ziwiyeh hill, halfway down the slope. The rim, c. 5 cm wide, is covered with engraved scenes, representing rows of Median, Urartian and Mannaian tribute-bearers being marshalled into the presence of an official of exalted rank, an Assyrian prince or viceroy.[1] These scenes must have been engraved at a time when these three nations were subject to the Scyths, or Assyrians, some time between 652 and 625 B.C. The personality portrayed on the rim must be the Scythian King Bartatua, and most probably he was buried in this sarcophagus. Bartatua, through his marriage to the Assyrian princess, daughter of King Esarhaddon, became a member of the Assyrian royal family, and had to take an oath of allegiance to the king, thus becoming an Assyrian liegelord.[2] So it was natural to depict Bartatua on the rim of his coffin in Assyrian robe as an Assyrian viceroy. The date of his death, 645 B.C., fits in well into that postulated by the engravings on the rim.

It would be wrong, however, to suppose that at Ziwiyeh a Scythian king would have been buried "in strict accordance with Scythian tradition". For the Ziwiyeh tomb is the earliest, the first Scythian burial of this type known so far. Ziwiyeh could only have set an example, to be followed by Scythian rulers of subsequent periods; it is there that the tradition would have begun.

The Scyths buried in the northwest Caucasian barrows of the 6th and 5th centuries B.C., were clearly descendants of members of the Scythian ruling class expelled by the Medes from Western Asia not later than c. 590 B.C. This is shown by Urartian and other Western Asiatic elements of their culture and art. They must also have brought to the new country the idea of cruel and bloody funerals of rulers, behind which may have stood a notion of the divine origin of royal power. This idea was alien to the Scyths, but had deep roots in the countries of Western Asia (Ur) and in Transcaucasia (Trialeti).

Early in the 4th century B.C. the northwest Caucasian Scyths were forced to move again and abandon their country, this time under pressure from the advancing Sarmatian Siraces. They seem to have moved into the Ukraine and settled in the steppe on the lower Dnieper; there richly endowed princely burials under mounds of the 4th and 3rd centuries B.C. have been excavated, whose contents and burial rites agree

[1] Wilkinson, "More details on Ziwiye".
[2] D. J. Wiseman, "The Vassal Treaties of Esarhaddon", *Iraq* xx (1958), p. 6.

with the ancient Ziwiyeh tradition as elaborated in northwest Caucasus, except for their being much less bloody.

The cruel funeral customs, however, were not the sole Oriental heritage which the Scyths had brought from Western Asia into Europe. Of much greater importance and durability was the so-called Scythian art, that is the art of the Scythian upper class. In its earliest stage it was a blend of various Western Asiatic elements in which the genuine Scythian elements played but a subordinate role. In Ziwiyeh the beginning of this process can be observed: all the Western Asiatic components, altered only slightly from their original form, are there discernible. Later Greek elements were added to this amalgam, and stronger blending took place in the Caucasus and the Ukraine, where in new surroundings and under the influence of Greek art and the art of the peoples of the East European forest zone, further changes and developments took place. Subsequently this blended Scythian art spread into Romania, and ultimately some elements of the ancient Oriental heritage, Western Asiatic or Iranian, reached even Western Europe and affected Celtic art.[1]

III. HERODOTUS' SCYTHIA

Seizure of the country

The earliest "genuine Scythian" or "Royal Scythian" remains north of the Black Sea date from the 6th century B.C., which tallies well with the data of the expulsion of the Scyths from Western Asia. The Oriental features of the earliest remains attest the eastern origin of their users.

In North Pontic lands the conquering "Royal Scyths" had met their kindred folk. These were bearers of the "late Srub" culture, and were descendants of the "Early Scyths" who, unlike the forefathers of the "Royal Scyths", after crossing the Volga probably in the 9th or 8th century B.C., pressed westwards across the Don up to the Dnieper and beyond. They mingled with the natives, who presumably were of Thracian stock, and later formed the substratum of the Nomadic Scyths and the Alazones.

The conquest by the "Royal Scyths" of a large part of the North Pontic lands and their consolidated rule over a large territory, was of

---

[1] P. Jacobstahl, *Early Celtic Art* (Oxford, 1944), pp. 156ff; T. G. E. Powell in *The European Community in Later Prehistory* (London, 1971), pp. 183ff; N. K. Sanders, *Antiquity* XLV (1971), pp. 103ff.

utmost importance for the evolution which took place within the whole country. It fostered the development of wide trade connections with distant countries. During the 7th century B.C., the "pre-Scythian period", only a few small Greek emporia were in existence there. It is only by the middle of the 6th century B.C., after the "Royal Scythian" conquest, that permanent Greek colonies were founded and rapidly expanded.

The study of Scythian antiquities within the whole North Pontic area can be very instructive. Differences in the type and age of these seem to indicate the different dates of the initial stage of the various groups which it is possible to distinguish. This in turn may be indicative of different periods at which the peoples of these regions submitted to the rule of the "Royal Scyths". The task of the "Royal Scyths" in subduing these people was made easier by the conquerors' superiority over their adversaries in armament (e.g. iron weapons) and by the experience they had gained in wars with the superior Western Asiatic armies.

A question arises, however, as to which country in the North Pontic area was conquered first by the invading Western Asiatic Scyths, and as to which was the centre of their power in the new area.

The steppe

A passage of Herodotus (IV. 3) seems to suggest that the Scyths, in retreating northwards from Western Asia, passed through the Crimea before entering the Ukraine. But no Scythian burials of the 6th century B.C. have been found in the Crimea or in the adjoining part of the Ukraine, except for two famous graves on both sides of the Straits of Kerch (Temir Gora near Kerch and Tsukur barrow on the Taman Peninsula), both of which belong rather to the northwest Caucasian group of Scythian culture. The other three well-known Scythian princely burials (Simferopol and Kulakovski in the central part, Karamerkit barrow near Ak-Mechet on the western coast), presumably attributable to the "Royal Scyths", were all of the 5th century B.C., and cannot, therefore, be taken into account when discussing the route of the Scyths from Western Asia to the Ukraine.

On the other hand, the diffusion in the Ukraine of Scythian barrow graves of the 6th century B.C. (map 7) suggests that the Western Asiatic Scyths entered the country by advancing straight northwards from the Caucasus. They do not seem, however, to have conquered the country in one sweep. At first, they probably seized the eastern section of the steppe west of the Don; seven 6th-century "upper-class" Scythian barrow graves seem to mark its extent. They are distributed at nearly even distances along the western bank of the Don from Taganrog to the junction of the Medveditsa with the Don. The eighth barrow grave of this group, at Alekseyevka-Krivorozhe on the Kalivta deserves special mention. The important items of its equipment were a silver terminal in the shape of a bull-head, probably part of an Assyrian stool of the 7th century B.C.; an electron wreath, adornment of a bronze helmet perhaps of Transylvanian provenience;[1] and an Ionian zoomorphic vase of the 6th century B.C. originating from Samos. This seems to have been the burial of a Scythian newcomer from Western Asia, or at least of a descendant of such a one.

No later Scythian burials were found in that region, which by about 500 B.C. was seized by the advancing Sauromatians. By the end of the 5th century the whole steppe right up to the Dnieper was already in their possession.

Further west, the only larger group of Early Scythian burials attributable to the "Royal Scyths", are some 20, mainly secondary graves in Bronze Age moulds recorded on the northern border of the steppe in the region of Kramatorsk. They were mostly burials of rank-and-file Scyths of the 5th century, but a few were of the 6th century B.C. A few more burials attributable to the "Royal Scyths", all exclusively of the 5th century B.C., have been recorded in other parts of the steppe further west, at some distance from each other. They seem to indicate that this part of the steppe was conquered by the "Royal Scyths" not earlier than about 500 B.C. This is corroborated by two barrow graves of the "pre-Scythian type" in this area, south of the Dnieper bend (Tsymbalka, Mala Lepetykha), both of the early 6th century B.C.

Less than 40 Early Scythian burials recorded within the whole steppe country are attributable to the "Royal Scyths", thus disproving the remark by Herodotus (IV. 20) that the royal tribe was the most numerous among the Scyths. We may conjecture, therefore, that either Herodotus meant another region peopled by the Royal tribe, or the rank-and-file "Royal Scyths" then still retained their ancient Srub culture; the latter alternative is suggested by the discovery in the Srub

---

[1] A. P. Mantsevich, *SA* 1958.2, pp. 196–202; *Archaeologiai Ertesitö* LXXXVIII (Budapest, 1961), pp. 77–81.

THE SCYTHS

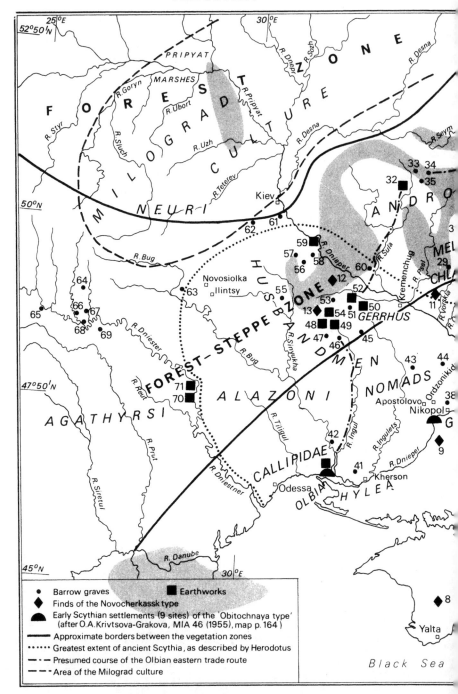

HERODOTUS' SCYTHIA

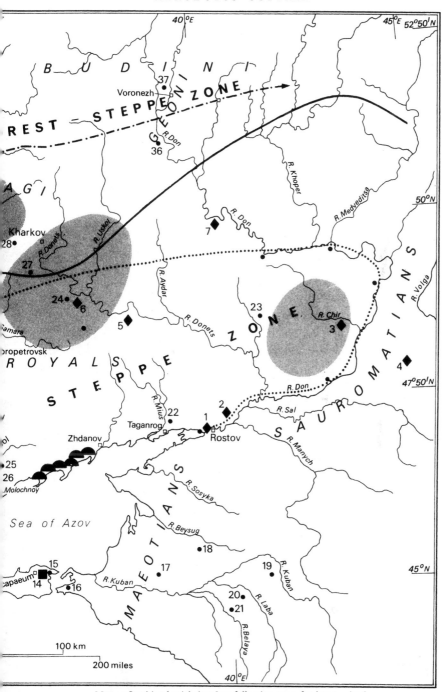

Map 7. Scythian burial sites [see following page for key to sites].

177

THE SCYTHS

Map showing the diffusion of Scythian burials and of those of the Scythian type of the 6th century B.C., found within the confines of ancient Scythia and its neighbouring countries. Only selected barrow graves and earthworks are spotted on the map, and the more important ones have been numbered. Also finds of the "pre-Scythian" Novocherkask type have been spotted and numbered; they belong mainly to the end of the 7th, some to the early 6th century B.C.

Finds of the Novocherkask type
1 Rostov
2 Novocherkask
3 Chernyshevskaya
4 Aksay
5 Kamyshevakha
6 Chornohorivka
7 Staraya Tolucheva
8 Simferopol
9 Mala Lepetykha (Shirokyi Kurhan)
10 Velika Bilozerka (Tsymbalka)
11 Butenki
12 Zalivki
13 Nosachevo

Crimean and northwest Caucasian sites
14 Panticapaeum (Kerch)
15 Temir Gora
16 Tsukur barrow on the Taman Peninsula
17 Staromyshastovskaya
18 Novokurskaya
19 Voronezhskaya
20 Kelermes
21 Ulski

"Royal Scythian" barrow graves
22 Zolotaya Kosa near Taganrog
23 Alekseyevka-Krivorozhe on the Kalitva
24 Shpakovka
25 Akkermen
26 Konstantynivka

Forest-steppe zone east of the Dnieper
 Donets group:
27 Bolshaya Gomolsha
28 Khutor Pokrovskii
 Vorskla group:
29 Machukhy
30 Lukhachivka
31 Belsk earthwork
 Sula group:
32 Basivka
33 Aksiutyntsi (Starsha Mohyla)
34 Budky
35 Volkovtsy (Shumeyko)

Voronezh group (very end of the 6th century B.C. and later periods)
36 Mastiugino
37 Chastye Kurgany

Steppe west of the Dnieper (Nomad Scyths)
38 Kut
39 Tomakovka
40 Kichkas
41 Rozhnivka
42 Ternivka
43 Annovka
44 Boltyshka

The Tiasmin and Kiev (Kanev) groups "Scythian Husbandmen"
45 Litoi-Melgunov barrow
 Tiasmin group:
46 Martonosha
47 Zhurovka
48 Makiivka – earthwork and barrow grave cemetery
49 Pastyske earthwork
50 Matronin earthwork
51 Zhabotin
52 Hulay-Horod earthwork
53 Smiela
54 Sharpivka earthwork
55 Ryzhanivka
 Kiev-Kanev group:
56 Siniavka
57 Beresnyagi
58 Grishchintsy
59 Trakhtemirov earthwork
60 Mala Ofirna
61 Khlevakha
62 Bobritsa

Podolian sites
63 Nemirov earthwork
 West-Podolian group:
64 Nowosiółka Grzymałowska
65 Bratyszów
66 Dupliska
67 Sapohów
68 Krągłe
69 Lenkivtsy

Bessarabian sites
70 Sakharna earthwork
71 Soloncheni earthwork

graves in the steppe of the Donets, of "Scythian" arrow-heads, parts of horse harness, and similar articles.[1]

It seems that some splinter groups of the Scythians who arrived in the region of Donets–Kramatorsk, were responsible for the formation in the forest-steppe zone – already outside Scythia proper – of the Vorskla and Sula–Donets groups of Scythian culture, which were independent of the "Royal Scyths". These groups will be discussed further below.

Circumstances during the Early Scythian period in the steppe west of the Dnieper were similar to those east of that river. Only a few odd graves of Scythian commoners of that time, attributable to the Nomadic Scyths[2] were found between the Dnieper and the Ingul, although several barrow-grave cemeteries in this area were excavated completely. At Kut, west of Nikopol, 315 burials were found in its 32 mounds, and 190 burials in 53 barrows near Nikopol; a large portion of these were Scythian, but exclusively of the Late Scythian period (4th and 3rd centuries B.C.). Investigations also revealed that there was no break in the settlement of the country; the Late Scythian remains immediately followed those of the Srub culture.

A few richly furnished princely burials in barrows have been recorded in that area. From one of these comes a fine Greek painted vase of the early 6th century (Boltyshka, 70 km west of Dnepropetrovsk), and in two others (Annovka; Rozhnivka near Kherson) were found Ionian bronze mirrors of around 500 B.C.; they imply connections between the local Scythian, or possibly pre-Scythian, aristocracy and the Greek colonies. Of about the same date was the important, definitely Scythian, secondary burial in a mound at Tomakovka near Nikopol; its iron dagger and scabbard were covered with gold sheets decorated in the Oriental style.

Several other richly furnished, famous princely burials in this region were either of the very end of the 5th, or, more often, of the 4th and 3rd centuries B.C.; they all belonged to the post-Herodotean age, the Late Scythian period.

No burials of the Scythian type of the Early Scythian period have been found further west, in the steppe area attributed to the Alazones. Lack of such burials suggests that the local "pre-Scythian" Sabatynivka culture must have survived there until about 450–400 B.C., the time of the appearance there of remains of the Late Scythian type.

[1] A. I. Terenozhkin, *KSIIMK* XLVII (1952), pp. 6ff.
[2] Terenozhkin, *Arkh. Ukrain.* II, p. 42.

THE SCYTHS

Scythian Husbandmen

Our knowledge of the Early Scythian culture of the 6th and 5th centuries B.C., comes from the study of the northwest Caucasian group which, however, lay outside Scythia proper, and from the study of the Tiasmin group of the Scythian culture, and its derivative the Kiev group. The two latter extended over a strip of land in the forest-steppe zone, c. 75 km wide, along the western side of the middle Dnieper over a distance of c. 150–200 km from Kremenchug up to Kiev.

The country, the most fertile black-earth region, was relatively densely populated during the Scythian Age, as suggested by the number of settlements and earthworks, and by the size of the cemeteries, which often consisted of up to 300 mounds. Cemeteries usually lay close to the settlements to which they evidently belonged, and served as burial ground for several generations. The study of the grave goods reveals continuity of settlement during the entire Scythian Age.

Graves were of two distinct categories. Those modestly equipped in shafts were burials of common people; those in large burial chambers dug in the ground or with a more or less elaborate timber sepulchral construction, and endowed with Greek pottery, weapons, and personal ornaments often decorated in the Scythian animal style, were obviously graves of the upper class. The disparity, and the fact that the richly furnished graves were for the most part ransacked in antiquity soon after the funeral, imply considerable social differences within this population. The looters were evidently of a social stratum different from that of the buried person, and probably were members of the native population of Thracian origin subdued by the Scyths; some scholars unjustly claim that they were Slavs.[1]

The strongholds of the Tiasmin group suggest that its warlike people was organized in small territorial units, the strength of which can be judged from the size of their cemeteries. Many strongholds had a large industrial quarter and played the role of industrial centres, comprising an area of 16 to 24 hectares; the largest one (Matronin) covers 52 hectares.

The many imported goods, Greek pottery and personal ornaments, weapons, etc., found in graves and settlements of the group, were probably purchased in exchange for agricultural products of the

---

[1] E.g. A. I. Terenozhkin, *SA* xxiv (1955), pp. 7–28; I have commented on such theories in "Ancient Southern Neighbours".

country; and these may have been taken as tribute from the subjugated population. But an important source of income for the Scythian rulers seems to have been the position of the country on the vital commercial route mentioned in the first Section, which connected Olbia with the hinterland and, via the country of the Geloni, with the Urals and other distant countries in Asia. Olbian-made goods were found at several points along this route up to the Urals. On the other hand, approximately along the same track, a number of articles characteristic of the region on the middle Volga and of west Siberia have been excavated.

During the Early Scythian period the Tiasmin group was presumably an important economic, military and political centre of Scythia, perhaps the core of the considerable power of the "Royal Scyths". By the end of the 5th century B.C. tribal migrations resulted in a shift of central power in Scythia to the south, into the region of the Dnieper bend; it would seem that the Tiasmin group, although still powerful, had lost by then its leading position.

The country of Gerrhus

A hitherto unsolved problem, connected with the "Royal Scyths", is the identification of the mysterious country of the Gerrhi in which the Scythian kings were buried at the time of Herodotus (IV. 71). The country has usually been placed in the southern part of the area enclosed by the bend of the Dnieper. The drawback of this view is the fact – almost never taken into account by its propounders – that the sumptuously furnished Scythian royal tombs excavated in that area were all of the Late Scythian period. No Early Scythian royal burials have been found there, that might have come to the notice of Herodotus during his stay in Olbia in the mid-5th century B.C. The only exception is the secondary burial from Tomakovka previously mentioned.

The country of Gerrhus must, therefore, be located in some other region of ancient Scythia. According to the description by Herodotus (IV. 19, 53) its site should be sought further north. In fact, on the maps by both Niederle[1] and Minns (map 6), attempting a reconstruction of the map of Scythia as conceived by Herodotus, the country of Gerrhus is placed near the region where the Dnieper bend begins and in the vicinity of the sources of the Ingulets and the Ingul (wrongly identified by Herodotus as lower Dnieper). Furthermore, exactly in that area, on

[1] L. Niederle, *Slovanské starožitnosti* I (Prague, 1925), pp. 286ff.

the border of the steppe and forest-steppe zones, several richly furnished Early Scythian barrow-graves have been discovered, in particular the famous Litoi-Melgunov and the Martonosha burials, and those which form part of the Tiasmin group of Scythian culture, e.g. Zashchyta, Zhabotin XV, Zhurovka 407. The latter have been attributed to the "Scythian Husbandmen"; the question thus arises as to the reciprocal relations between the Gerrhi and the "Scythian Husbandmen".

It should be noted that the Scythian tribal names mentioned by Herodotus relate only to tribes that lived in the vicinity of Olbia. The names of tribes in remote regions are only descriptive, e.g. "Scythian Husbandmen", or "Androphagi" (Man-Eaters). This reflects a limited knowledge by Herodotus of such tribes. It seems likely that Gerrhi was simply the name of one of the tribes of the "Scythian Husbandmen", or perhaps of a people who preceded the Scyths in that area, whose name had been handed down by their neighbours.

The Litoi-Melgunov barrow-grave mentioned above is probably the earliest Scythian burial so far known in ancient Scythia. It was excavated in the 18th century. Its grave goods have been described and published repeatedly, and its date has been established at approximately 575–500 B.C. The articles exhibit a predominantly Oriental aspect. The style and technique of most of the articles is Western Asiatic with hardly any Greek influence. Median and Urartian elements are recognizable in the weapons, which must have been made before the end of the 7th century B.C., shortly before the departure of the Scyths from Western Asia. Several North Caucasian and Transcaucasian imported articles (unless they were brought by Scythian newcomers) of the late 7th or early 6th century B.C. have also been found in a number of early burials of the Tiasmin group of Scythian culture. They support the notion that at least some of the people buried in these graves were members of the Royal tribe, who initiated the formation of the group.

Other agricultural tribes of ancient Scythia

Two other agricultural peoples of Scythia, mentioned by Herodotus, were the Callipidae and the "Scythian Agriculturalists"($\gamma\epsilon\omega\rho\gamma o\iota$); both lived within the steppe country of Scythia.

The Callipidae, the "Greek-Scythians" on the Black Sea coast, were most likely a people of Thracian stock under Scythian overlordship. Those who lived in settlements close to Olbia were to some extent hellenized, or at least their culture had absorbed many Greek elements. They must have been influenced in varying degrees by their Scythian rulers, and many of them may have been Iranianized.

Well over a score of settlements and at least two earthworks have been recorded in that area and investigated. Cemeteries were "flat" and rather small. Some consisted of mounds in which several graves were of the Scythian type, probably burials of local Scythian chiefs, e.g. Adzigol (at present Solonchaki) or Marizin (at present Ostrovka).[1] Their sepulchral construction and grave goods, of the Early Scythian period, were similar to those of the Scythian Tiasmin group and imply close links between the two regions. Scythian rulers of both the Callipidae and the natives of the Tiasmin group,[2] seem to have originally belonged to one and the same group of Scythian conquerors.

Several settlements around Olbia bore a purely Greek rural character, and articles found there were also Greek. They imply that in that region two different populations with a different culture lived side by side in different villages. They did not mingle with each other.

The other agricultural people, the "Scythian Agriculturalists", probably lived in the valley of the lower Dnieper, including the bend of the river. Two settlements of the Early Scythian period known so far in that area (Khortitsa, Nizhni Rogachik) are probably attributable to this people as are possibly some late settlements of the Sabatynivka culture in this region.[3]

IV. PEOPLES AROUND SCYTHIA

The west

During the Scythian Age several peoples lived in the North Pontic area beside the Scyths, some of whom, according to Herodotus, were dressed like Scyths and followed Scythian customs. Archaeological evidence also suggests that the "Scythian" culture was shared by a number of non-Scythian peoples who lived around ancient Scythia but were not subject to the "Royal Scyths".

"Scythian" remains have been found in various regions west of Scythia, in West Podolia, central Transylvania, Hungary, Slovakia, etc.; they mostly form distinct groups of Scythian culture, but also appear

[1] Ebert, *Südrussland*.
[2] M. S. Sinitsyn, *MASP* II (1959), pp. 13ff.
[3] O. A. Krivtsova-Grakowa, MIA 46 (1965), pp. 151ff., map p. 164.

scattered in parts of Romania and Bessarabia. They probably represent various tribes of the Agathyrsi who, according to most authorities, were of Thracian stock, although their ruling class seems to have been of Scythian origin, as suggested by the Iranian name of their king, Spargapeithes, and by various remarks of Herodotus (IV. 25, 49, 78, 100); moreover, the name of the people appears in one of the legends about the origin of the Scyths.[1] These groups, formed mostly around the mid-6th century B.C., exhibit a specific character due to the local Thracian elements absorbed by the Scythian invaders.

The West Podolian group of Scythian culture shows a close relationship with the Tiasmin group, identifiable, as we saw, with "Scythian Husbandmen". It is noteworthy that many settlements of the Bessarabian group, situated along the valley of the middle Dniester,[2] were destroyed by the end of the 6th century B.C.; this seems to have been the outcome of the Scythian war against the Persians who invaded the country at about that time.

The northern neighbours of the Agathyrsi were the Neuri, whose territory also bordered on the "Scythian Husbandmen", at its south eastern end. An examination of all the remarks of Herodotus relating to the Neuri (IV. 17, 100, 125), suggests that most probably the Milograd culture of Byelorussia,[3] which reached southward nearly to the upper Southern Bug, is attributable to them.

The study of the toponymy and hydronymy of that area, including the basin of the middle Dnieper, the Desna and the Pripet,[4] reveals that in the pre-Slavonic era this territory was held by Baltic-speaking tribes. Accordingly, the people of the Milograd culture, the presumed Neuri, may be regarded as a Baltic-speaking people,[5] although some scholars unconvincingly regard them as proto-Slavonic. The remark by Herodotus (IV. 105) that the Neuri "observe Scythian customs" seems to refer to the Neuri in the southernmost part of their country, bordering on the "Scythian Husbandmen": the Milograd culture in that border region includes many Scythian elements.

[1] I. H. Crişan, *Dacia* IX (1965), pp. 133ff.
[2] A. I. Meliukova, MIA 64 (1958), pp. 5-8.
[3] O. N. Melnikovskaya, *Plemena Iuzhnoy Byelorussii v rannom zheleznom veke* (Moscow, 1967).
[4] See p. 152, n. 3 and p. 153, n. 1.
[5] As above; in addition: Melnikovskaya, *op. cit.*; M. Gimbutas, *The Balts* (London, 1963).

Peoples east of the Dnieper

East of the "Scythian Husbandmen", and of the Neuri, lived the Androphagi, "Man-Eaters", and the Melanchlaeni, "Black-Cloaks", as well as the Budini and the Geloni, of whom neither were subject to the Scyths. Their countries clearly lay east of the middle Dnieper, but in that area they have been very differently placed by scholars.

Hundreds of barrow-graves and over 150 settlements of the Scythian Age have been recorded in the Ukrainian forest-steppe zone east of the middle Dnieper. They all bear a decisively "Scythian" character and form three groups which differ somewhat from each other. The largest one, the Sula group, consists of finds from the valley of the Sula, and of some smaller rivers. The next, the Vorskla group embraces remains from the valley of the river of that name, a part of which much resembles those of the Tiasmin group of Scythian culture on the other side of the Dnieper. Further east, on the upper Donets and its tributaries within the forest-steppe zone extending east of the Dnieper, was the area of the Donets group. All these groups were formed in the 6th century B.C., and two periods have been distinguished in their development, on grounds similar to those applying to other groups of Scythian culture.

The major part of the area belonged to the Sula group. Some of its barrow-grave cemeteries comprise up to 450 mounds, several of them up to 20 m high, with well-endowed princely burials (e.g. Starsha Mohyla, Shumeyko). As in the case of the Tiasmin group, the equipment consisted of weapons, including battleaxes of the North-Caucasian type, scale armour, the so-called finials crowned with an animal or other figure, and horse gear. The cheek-pieces were mostly of bone and had an elk, horse or ram head carved on their terminals in the "Scythian" animal style (fig. 10). Human and horse offerings were rarely found; instead of horses several sets of horse gear were often deposited, up to 18 in a single grave. Greek pottery of the 6th century B.C. was found only occasionally.

Several earthworks have been recorded, built mostly in the 6th century and abandoned at the end of the 4th century B.C. The largest was that at Basivka on the upper Sula, nearly 2 km long and 600 m wide.

The Sula people may safely be identified with the Androphagi, the "Man-Eaters", who "wear Scythian dress; they speak a peculiar language; and of all these nations they are the only people that eat human flesh" (Her. IV. 106).

The "peculiar language" may have been an early Iranian (Srub?) dialect that differed from the speech of the "Royal Scyths". For not only the Sula, but also the Vorskla and Donets groups, extended over the area of Iranian toponymy and hydronymy. The last sentence of the above quotation is the most important for the identification of the country of the Androphagi on the strength of archaeological remains. Human bones were found in the kitchen refuse mixed with cut and broken animal bones in at least seven earthworks investigated within the area of the Sula group and its neighbours.[1] No traces of cannibalism have been found, however, in the remains of other cultures of the region, neither within the area of Baltic toponymy and hydronymy, nor in the country further to the east, of Finno-Ugrian toponymy.

The unbroken human bones found in the earthworks above suggest that the cannibalism of the Androphagi was ritual, similar to that reported about the Sacian Massagetae and the Issedones (Her. I. 216; IV. 26), east of the Urals. Similar practices have also been ascertained among the Sauromatians, in their barrow-graves in the Southern Urals near Orsk, and on the lower Volga.[2] It is of interest to note that traces of similar cannibalism have been found in barrow-grave XV at Smiela, one of the earliest of the Tiasmin group of Scythian culture.[3]

It seems that the customs and beliefs connected with cannibalism were quite common among the early Iranians in the Kazakhstan steppe, who were descended from the people of the Andronovo culture of the Bronze Age. They might have been brought into the North Pontic area by those Iranians who had some Andronovo ancestry.

The unfavourable opinion expressed by Herodotus of the lawlessness and injustice of the Androphagi (IV.106) probably reflects the strained relations of Olbian Greek traders with that people, across whose territory passed the important Olbian trade route linking the city with the Urals and possibly with other gold-bearing countries further to the east.

Closely related most probably to the Sula people were the bearers of the culture of the Donets group. The relevant group of archaeological remains may be attributed to the Melanchlaeni, whose country according to Herodotus (IV. 20, 107) lay north of the "Royal Scyths". The country

[1] B. A. Shramko, *Drevnosti Severskogo Dontsa* (Kharkov, 1962), pp. 233f; V. A. Illinska, *AK* XXIII (1970), pp. 29, 35.
[2] Smirnov, *Savromaty*, p. 208; Sulimirski, *Sarmatians*, pp. 58, 66.
[3] Bobrinski, *Smiela* I, p. 38.

extended over the basin of the upper Donets within the forest-steppe zone; the steppe zone, abode of the "Royal Scyths", bordered on it to the south. Herodotus says about the Melanchlaeni that they were "a distinct race, and not Scythian" and that they "all wear black garments, from which they take their name; they follow Scythian usages". The substratum of both the Sula and the Donets groups contained a strong Srub component, but there were some differences between them.

By the end of the 4th century B.C., the bulk of the Melanchlaeni seem to have migrated southwards, settling subsequently in the vicinity of Olbia. This is suggested by the inscription in Olbia of the 3rd century B.C. in honour of Protogenes, in which a people is mentioned, called the "Savdarati", living then in the vicinity of the city. This name lends itself to an Iranian interpretation as meaning "those who wear black garments"; it seems very likely that these were identical with the "black-cloaked" Melanchlaeni, who arrived there from the north. A black-coated tribe still living in the vicinity of Olbia was mentioned in the 1st century B.C.

The settlements of the third group of the area, the Vorskla group, were mostly "open"; the few recorded earthworks lay in its northern periphery. The largest of these was the earthwork at Belsk which, in fact, consisted of three earthworks forming a single defensive system encircled by common ramparts, enclosing an area of 4,400 hectares. The site represents a considerable trade and industrial centre built in the mid-6th century B.C.; it was in existence until the end of the 4th century B.C. Of importance is the fact, revealed by excavation of the site by B. A. Shramko,[1] that two of the earthworks were built simultaneously at a date earlier than the third. The structure and the archaeological material from the two earlier earthworks were not alike and evidently must have belonged to different peoples. Shramko conclusively argues that this must have been the wooden city of Gelonus, mentioned by Herodotus (IV. 123), which the Persian army of Darius set on fire during its pursuit of the Scyths. The city was inhabited by two distinct peoples, the Budini and the Geloni, who lived there side by side but separately, evidently in the two earlier earthworks.

The difference between the inhabitants of the two early earthworks is well reflected in their archaeological remains. The "eastern" earth-

---

[1] B. A. Shramko, "Vostochnoe ukreplenie Belskovo gorodishcha", in *Skifskie Drevnosti* (Kiev, 1973), 82–112; *idem*, "Krepnost' skifskoy epokhi u s. Belsk-Gorod Gelon", in *Skifskiy Mir* (Kiev, 1975), 94–132.

work was the industrial, commercial and political centre; potsherds of the "Chornoles culture" from the other side of the Dnieper imply that this must have been the city inhabited by the Geloni, who according to Herodotus were a small enterprising, originally Grecian group, which "being expelled from the trading ports settled among the Budini". Much poorer were the inhabitants of the "western" earthworks – evidently the indigenous Budini. The two peoples, briefly described by Herodotus (IV. 108, 109), did not use the same language, nor the same mode of living. The Budini, blue-eyed and red-haired, were the indigenous nomads and hunters, and were "the only people of these parts who eat vermin". Their country, according to Herodotus, was thickly covered with trees of all kinds. They hunted otters, beavers and other animals, with whose skins they bordered their cloaks. On the other hand, the Geloni "are tillers of the soil, feed upon corn, cultivate gardens, and are not at all like the Budini in shape or complexion".

According to Herodotus (IV. 22) "to the north", which by his orientation should mean to the east, of the territory of the Budini "there is a desert of seven days' journey across, and beyond the desert, if one turns somewhat to the east, dwell the Thyssagetae, a numerous and distinct race", who live by hunting. The "desert" mentioned by Herodotus was very likely the strip of land, up to 200 km wide, between the sources of the Donets and its tributaries and the Don, almost entirely devoid of settlements. It extended partly over the forest-steppe zone, but mostly over the steppe. At its narrowed end towards the east, measuring about 75 km in width, extended the region of the Voronezh group of Scythian culture. East of it, east of the Don already, lay the very large territory of Ugro-Finnish toponymy, the country of the Thyssagetae (Her. IV. 22).[1] In the light of actual archaeological finds in the country belonging to the Scythian period and of the extent of the Ugro-Finnish toponymy and hydronymy, the Thyssagetae cannot be regarded as an Ugro-Finnish population. It seems that they were identical with the Androphagi and were descended from the Bondarykha culture people.

In the region of Voronezh, an isolated group of the Scythian culture, the "Voronezh group", has been distinguished. It consisted of a number of settlements and barrow-grave cemeteries, the earliest of which were of the 6th or early 5th century B.C. The group was in

[1] I. I. Lapushkin, MIA 104 (1961), map 2 on p. 20; P. A. Liberow, in *Problemy Skifskoy Arkheologii* (MIA 177, 1971), pp. 103–15, maps figs 1, 3, 4.

existence until the 3rd century B.C. Its graves were mostly well furnished, some with Greek imported goods, but a large number of burials were ransacked in antiquity. Remains typical of the group did not much differ from those of the Sula and Donets groups, but the outfit of graves suggests a greater affluence among the people. The Chastye Kurgany ("Frequent Barrows") near Voronezh, and those at Mastiugino, are its best known barrow-grave cemeteries.

The Voronezh group seems to have lain on the Olbian trade route of the Early Scythian period, that ran far to the east. Connections with Olbia are indicated by Greek vases of the 5th century B.C. and by other imported Greek and Olbian manufactured articles. Later, in the 4th and 3rd centuries B.C., Bosporan imported articles replaced those from Olbia. Many articles were decorated in the "Scythian" animal style, of a variety, however, that shows many Sauromatian features. Sauromatian impact on the Voronezh group has been noticed also in other fields.

The Geloni probably had a strong admixture either of genuine Scyths, or of Early Iranians. This is suggested by both their "Scythian" culture and the fact that their name appears, jointly with that of the Agathyrsi, in the second legend on the origin of the Scyths.

The Sauromatians

The eastern neighbours of the "Royal Scyths", the Sauromatians (Sarmatians) were a nomad steppe people of Iranian stock, kin to the Scyths, who "used the Scythian language speaking it corruptly" (Her. IV. 117), evidently speaking a different dialect. Their culture was in many respects similar to the northwest Caucasian Scythian culture, under the influence of which it seems chiefly to have developed. The impact of Achaemenian civilization, which extended there via Soviet Central Asia, can also be discerned, but mainly during the 5th century B.C., in the north-eastern region of the Sauromatian territory.

The Sauromatian culture, formed in the 6th century, lasted to the end of the 5th century B.C. It extended over the steppe of the South Urals country and of the lower Don and lower Volga, reaching southwards nearly to the eastern foothills of the Caucasus. Its remains consist almost exclusively of graves, which were mostly secondary burials in already existing mounds.

The equipment of the graves presents the Sauromatians as well-armed mounted warriors, although many fought on foot. Horses were seldom sacrificed and appear mainly in richly furnished princely burials in the region of Orenburg. Also human offerings were rare, and restricted to princely burials. Distinctively Sauromatian was the relatively large number of graves of armed women, which may be considered a survival of the ancient pre-Sauromatian social order based on a matriarchate, clear hints of which are found in Herodotus (IV. 110–17) and Strabo (*Geography* XI.6.1.). According to Hippocrates, Sauromatian women were not only warriors but priestesses. This is confirmed by pedestalled stone "altars", or flat stone dishes with a raised rim, found in a series of well-equipped female burials. The priestesses seem to have held a high position in Sauromatian society.

Sauromatian armament differed only slightly from that of the Scyths. By the end of the 5th century B.C. articles and weapons of Central Asian types, mostly modelled on Achaemenian prototypes, began to appear first in the South Urals, and then also on the lower Volga. This was due to the influx of the Sarmatian Alanic nomads from the Kazakhstan and Central Asian steppes who overran the Sauromatian country. The bulk of the Sauromatians yielded to the invaders and retreated southwards into the northwest Caucasus, and westwards into the Ukraine, where they brought about great changes in Scythian culture and initiated the Late Scythian Period.

The Darius Expedition

An important event in the early history of Scythia was the invasion, in about 512 or 514, of the Persian army under King Darius.[1] Many controversial opinions have been expressed about the aims of Darius, and also about the extent and consequences of his invasion. Many authorities suppose that Darius' sole intention was to prevent the Scyths from interfering in the Persian war against Greece, and to protect the Persian army from a flank attack. Others think that his idea was to extend his rule over all countries around the Black Sea.

Herodotus says that the Persian army traversed the whole Scythian steppe, crossed the Don (Tanais) and entered the country of the Sauromatians; the Budini, Geloni, Melanchlaeni, Neuri and Agathyrsi were also affected. Ostensibly Darius covered a distance of no less than 2,300 km at the rate of at least 40 km a day. Such a performance does not seem credible. Either the enterprise lasted much longer, or the

[1] V. D. Blavatskii, *KSIIMK* XXXIV (1950), pp. 19–28.

distance covered was much shorter. Some scholars believe that Darius went no further than the border of the Neuri, others think that he only reached the Dniester, because the crossing by a whole army of that river, and then of the Dnieper, would have involved bridges and dangerous operations in the face of an active foe.

It seems, however, that the account of Herodotus should be given some credit. He visited Olbia about 70 or 80 years after the event, a period not long enough for the general outlines of the Persian Expedition to pass entirely out of the memory of the Olbiopolitae. Crossing the fords of the Dniester and of other Ukrainian rivers in their middle course would not involve any major difficulties. But as yet, no tangible traces of his invasion have been found, except perhaps for the destruction of settlements in the valley of the Dniester which, as mentioned previously, occurred at the end of the 6th century.

The western drive of the Scyths (map 8)

The very important role that the Scyths played in the history of eastern Europe has commonly been recognized. This is not the case with their role in the history of Central and Western Europe, or rather with their interference in this history.

The large group of Scythian antiquities in Central Europe, and in particular in Bessarabia, Transylvania, Hungary and Slovakia, have been dealt with by many scholars.[1] Most of them agree that the Scyths must have invaded Transylvania and the Hungarian Plain at the turn of the 6th and 5th centuries B.C., and that soon all contact ceased between those Scyths and their kin in the Pontic lands. On the other hand, Scythian antiquities of Bessarabia and Bulgaria suggest that a new influx of Scythian elements took place around 400 B.C.

Scythian antiquities were also found in many countries beyond the Hungarian Plain. Destroyed earthworks in the lands of the Lusatian culture, with Scythian arrowheads sticking in their outer defensive walls, and traces of other hostile Scythian activities, have been found all over its territory. The shock inflicted was the cause of the downfall of the Lusatian culture. The advance of the Scyths may be followed, via Southern Germany, as far as France.[2] The Scyths appear as the forerunners of the Huns and Avars of the Migration period, or of the

[1] See bibliography.
[2] See bibliography.

THE SCYTHS

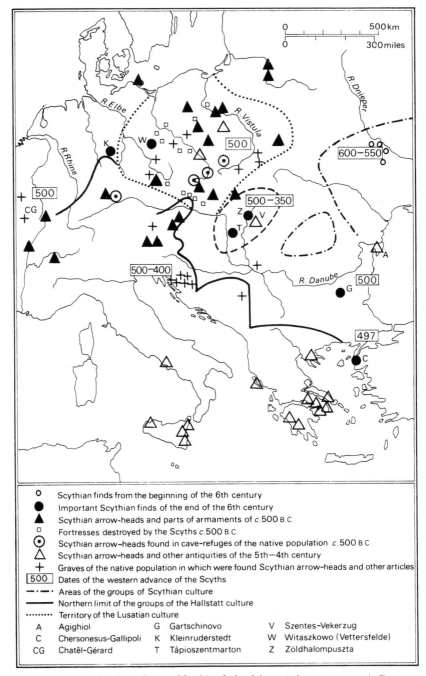

○ Scythian finds from the beginning of the 6th century
● Important Scythian finds of the end of the 6th century
▲ Scythian arrow-heads and parts of armaments of c.500 B.C.
□ Fortresses destroyed by the Scyths c.500 B.C.
⊙ Scythian arrow-heads found in cave-refuges of the native population c.500 B.C.
△ Scythian arrow-heads and other antiquities of the 5th–4th century
+ Graves of the native population in which were found Scythian arrow-heads and other articles
500 Dates of the western advance of the Scyths
—·—· Areas of the groups of Scythian culture
——— Northern limit of the groups of the Hallstatt culture
······· Territory of the Lusatian culture

A	Agighiol	G	Gartschinovo	V	Szentes-Vekerzug
C	Chersonesus-Gallipoli	K	Kleinruderstedt	W	Witaszkowo (Vettersfelde)
CG	Chatêl-Gérard	T	Tápioszentmarton	Z	Zöldhalompuszta

Map 8. Map showing the diffusion of Scythian finds of the period c. 500–400 B.C. in Europe.

Tartars of the Middle Ages. Their impression on the contemporary inhabitants of Europe must have been similar to that made by the Tartars nearly 17 centuries later. It is reflected in Etruscan bronze figurines of Scythian archers shooting from the saddle, and Scythian influence may be traced in Celtic Art.[1]

V. FURTHER DEVELOPMENT AND DECLINE

The Late Scythian period

The turn of the 5th and 4th centuries B.C. witnessed considerable changes in the archaeological material of Scythia and in most other countries of the North Pontic area.[2] These changes mark the beginning of the Late Scythian period which lasted roughly for two centuries, until about 200 B.C. The only written references existing for this period are one by Pseudo-Scylax who *c.* 338 B.C. noted the presence of Sarmatians ("the Syrmatai") in the steppe west of the Don in the former area of the "Royal Scyths", and one by Pseudo-Hippocrates, according to whom the Sarmatians (the Sauromatians) had already crossed the Don and entered Scythia by the end of the 5th or the beginning of the 4th century B.C.

The Late Scythian culture differed considerably from the preceding Early Scythian; and on no account can it be regarded as derived from the latter by way of normal evolution. It exhibits several eastern elements, hitherto unknown in the country, some of which may be traced back to the Sauromatian culture of the Volga steppe of the preceding period, while some were evidently of northwest Caucasian Scythian derivation. The Late Scythian culture was undoubtedly a hybrid, to the formation of which several factors contributed.

The appearance in the steppe of burials of rank-and-file Scyths, which were almost entirely absent in the preceding period, ranks among the new occurrences. Graves of the "catacomb" type became characteristic, shafts with a deep niche or subterranean chamber, dug out in the wider side of the shaft, not previously met with in Scythia. No cremations were recorded in the steppe. The furniture of graves became more uniform over the whole country, so that the differences between the local groups of the culture considerably diminished.

The usual equipment of male graves of the common Scyths

---

[1] See p. 173, n. 21.
[2] M. I. Viazmitina, *SA* 1969.4, pp. 62–77; B. N. Grakov, *ASE* VI (1964), pp. 118–27.

consisted, as previously, of weapons, local pottery, and of heaped animal bones (horse, cow or sheep) with an iron knife sticking in them. In female burials bronze mirrors and personal ornaments were common, and a few beads, rarely made-up into necklaces. No human or horse offerings are recorded. Instead of a horse, parts of its harness were deposited in graves. Straps were often decorated with animal figures in the Scythian style; in better-furnished burials plaques were sometimes of gold. They seem to have been the work of Greek goldsmiths, like the more exquisite personal ornaments; the simple ones were presumably products of indigenous workshops.

Princely burials

A feature characteristic of the Late Scythian period is the large number of sumptuously equipped graves in barrows of the Scythian ruling class. In their basic plan they mostly correspond to those of the common Scyths of the area; the disparity between the two types of burials consists primarily in their equipment, its quality and kind. Human and horse sacrifices were common.

The grandiose barrow graves, well over 20 of which have been recorded, are concentrated mainly on both sides of the southern part of the Dnieper bend, extending westwards to the river Ingulets, and south-eastwards to the river Molochna (Melitopol). Most were ransacked in antiquity. They have all been described, their contents published, discussed and dated by many authorities. Recently a few more were excavated, some unscathed, but the very fine articles found there, although of great value and interest, do not alter the hitherto established picture of the culture of the Scythian ruling class.

Only a few points relating to the "royal" graves may be raised here. Thus in the famous Chertomlyk barrow-grave of about 400 B.C. were buried the king, his wife, several serfs and a groom; its undoubtedly sumptuous equipment was for the most part looted in antiquity. "Some articles found in the grave point to eastern connections of the royal family. Furthermore, about 250 decorated horse bridles, saddles, finials, etc., found in the mound, seem to have meant a symbolic immolation of this number of horses; this calls to mind the 300 horses immolated at the funeral of the northwest Caucasian Scythian king buried in the Ulski barrow. The results of a similar study of the cranial material from the barrow grave excavated near Alexandropol are also striking.[1]

[1] B. V. Firshteyn, *Voprosy Antropologii* XXII (Moscow, 1966), p. 56.

Its "royal" skull represents a type characteristic of the Sauromatians of the steppe on the lower Volga, whereas those of serfs from the same grave are typical of the North Pontic steppe Scyths. Eastern elements are also noticeable in the equipment of several princely graves; significant are the large cast-bronze cauldrons of Siberian type.

A few genuine Sauromatian graves of the 4th century B.C. have been recorded on the lower Dnieper (Hrushivka, Ushkalka); buried in these were members of a group presumably retreating westwards from their original country on the lower Volga. The same probably applies to a few burials of armed women, a feature characteristic of Sauromatian culture.[1] Bronze arrowheads in a quiver, or a dagger, and once even scale armour (Akkermen on the Molochna) were found there alongside the equipment proper to female burials.

All these occurrences imply that a wave of the Sauromatians must have entered the country and, in mingling with the Scyths, contributed many elements to the resulting new culture. The same seems to have taken place in other parts of the North Pontic area. Thus articles of eastern type and origin appeared then among the remains of the Sula–Donets group. In Kiev bronze daggers were found typical of the Tagarskaya culture of Siberia; they were of the 6th–5th centuries in their original country, but most of them reached Scythia around 400 B.C., or later. Mongoloid racial elements are attested in several graves of the Late Scythian period of the Tiasmin group: they were never recorded there in graves of the preceding period.[2] A skeleton of a camel, an animal of Kazakhstanian or Central Asian provenience, was excavated in the princely burial at Novosiolka near Lipovets; single camel bones were found in the earthwork of Kamyanka.

By the end of the 5th century B.C., the northwest Caucasian Scythian group ceased to exist, its country having been seized by the advancing Sarmatian Siraces; only a small part of their country, the westernmost, and the Taman Peninsula still remained in the possession of the Scyths, or rather the Sindians. The Scyths of the lost area seem to have retreated northwards and entered the steppe country of ancient Scythia. Their arrival there in the Late Scythian period is suggested by horse harness, decorative plaques etc., found in Ukrainian graves, particularly the princely burials, which have the closest analogies in

---

[1] O. D. Ganina, *Zapiski Odesskovo Arkheolog. Obshchestva* I (Odessa, 1960), pp. 96–104; A. I. Terenozhkin, *SA* 1966.2, pp. 33–49; idem, *Arkh. Ukrain.* II, pp. 56f; Smirnov, *Savromaty*, pp. 200ff; idem, in *Problemy Skifskoy Arkheologii* (MIA 177, 1971), pp. 191–6.

[2] Bobrinski, *Smiela* II, p. 20.

the northwest Caucasus; and by human and horse offerings. The king, buried around 350 B.C. in the recently excavated barrow "Gaimanova Mohyla" at Balky south of Zaporozhe, was probably one of the fugitives, or their immediate descendant.[1] In the dromes and the large subterranean chamber ("catacomb" with niches) of the barrow, ten persons were buried including the king, his family, armed guards and female servants. Only one horse skeleton was discovered, but parts of many horse bridles stood for several of these. The grave was looted but in its unscathed cache several gold and wooden vessels covered with gold sheet were found. The rich decoration of these consisted of Western Asiatic motifs. This occurrence, jointly with human and horse offerings, point to northwest Caucasian Scythian connections.

In another recently excavated barrow, "Tovsta Mohyla" near Ordzhonikidze west of Nikopol,[2] six horses and several persons were buried; and in the "Rozkopana Mohyla" near Apostolove, skulls of 17 horses were found, and a large bronze cauldron believed to have been cast in Olbia at the end of the 5th century B.C.

Another significant fact is that, unlike in the preceding period, no Olbian products appear in burials of the Scythian upper class in the steppe. The fine toreutic, plaques, ornaments, etc., were mostly products of Bosporan goldsmiths. Sometimes identical articles were found in co-eval burials in distant parts of the country, e.g. gold covers of the gorythi in the "royal" burials at Chertomlyk, Melitopol, Ilintsy and Elizavetovskaya on the Don.[3] Their decoration was only slightly adapted to the taste of the princes. Greek influence is reflected in the stone construction and plan of several royal graves under mounds. They appear not only in the Crimea (Kul-Oba) but also in the Ukrainian steppe, although mainly south of the Dnieper. Very few objects decorated in the genuine Scythian animal style were found in the royal graves of this group.

[1] V. I. Bidzilya, *AK* 1872.1, pp. 44–56; Terenozhkin, *Arkh. Ukrain.* II, pp. 68f.

[2] B. M. Mozolevski, *AK* 1972.5, pp. 72–82; *SA* 1973.3, pp. 268–308; R. Roll, *Praehistorische Zeitschrift* XLVII.1 (Berlin, 1972), pp. 47–77; Terenozhkin, *Arkh. Ukrain.* II, pp. 69f.

[3] A. I. Terenozhkin, *KSIAK* V (1955), pp. 23–32, fig. 11; V. P. Shilov, in *Arkheologicheskie Raskopki na Donu* (Rostov-on-Don, 1962), pp. 52–69, fig. 5.

FURTHER DEVELOPMENT AND DECLINE

The earthwork of Kamyanka[1]

Scores of Late Scythian settlements, of the 4th and 3rd century B.C., have been recorded in the valley of the Dnieper and its tributaries, from the region of the rapids down to Kherson. But the most important of these was the huge earthwork of Kamyanka on the southern bank of the Dnieper opposite Nikopol. It enclosed an area of 1,200 hectares and consisted of two main parts. The larger of these was a major industrial and metallurgical centre. Iron worked there was smelted from local bog ores, and tools, simple ornaments, and weapons were manufactured there for the needs of the agricultural population of the Dnieper valley and of other areas.

No traces of industrial activities were found in the other, smaller section, the "Acropolis", which was the administrative centre, and very likely the seat of the rulers of the Late Scythian people. Many imported articles, Greek pottery, etc., found there imply close connections with the Bosporan cities during the 4th and 3rd centuries B.C. By the end of the 3rd century B.C. the site had to be abandoned under the pressure of the invading Sarmatian Roxolani.

King Ateas

Around 400 B.C. Scythia was flooded with eastern newcomers. The question thus arises as to the fate of the rulers of the country, the "Royal Scyths".

The very limited archaeological evidence, and some very slight hints in the written records, suggest that the "Royal Scyths", at least their rulers, retreated westwards before the invaders, jointly with their faithful tribes. The former country of the Alazones might possibly have still remained in their power, but they seem to have tried to enlarge their possessions further south and to establish themselves in Dobrudja. The presence of the Scyths in the Dobrudja in the 4th century B.C. is attested by a number of Scythian articles found there. The Scyths may even have reached Bulgaria: several authorities have pointed out that Bulgarian royal barrow-graves of the 4th century B.C. of the Berezovo-Panaguriste type[2] were dependent upon Greek and Scythian cultures.

---

[1] Grakov, *Kamenskoe Gorodische na Dnepre* (MIA 36, 1954); *idem, Skify*, pp. 61ff.
[2] Rostovtzef, *Skythien*, pp. 539ff; N. Zaharia, M. Petrescu-Dîmboviţa and E. Zaharia, *Aşezări din Moldova* (Bucharest, 1970), pp. 50ff, 640.

In the Dobrudja, the retreating Scyths had to fight with the native Dacians. By the middle of the 4th century B.C., Ateas, "King of the Scyths", was engaged in war with the "King of the Istrians" (Rex Istrianorum), a Dacian people in southern Dobrudja; the king died soon afterwards. Thereafter Ateas started a campaign against the Macedonians, which ended disastrously in 339 B.C. Ateas, then about 90 years of age, was killed, his army crushed, and the Scythian camp with about 20,000 women and children and herds was captured. Scythian families were ultimately settled probably in the south of the Dobrudja; presumably on this account the country was called "Scythia Minor" by the Romans.

The position of Ateas in Scythian history is equivocal. Some scholars[1] think that he originally ruled a Scythian tribe on the Don and, after defeating the "Royal Scyths", became the master of the whole country, and that he tried then to expand his kingdom south of the Danube. However, more credible is the idea that he was the chief of a Scythian tribe who retreated before the advancing Sauromatians and other eastern invaders, and ultimately struggled to establish himself in the Dobrudja.

Archaeological evidence seems to support the latter view. A very important relict of that time in northern Dobrudja was the huge, sumptuously endowed barrow-grave at Agighiol.[2] Its dromos, burial chamber, and human and horse offerings, correspond almost exactly to several Late Scythian burials in the south of Scythia (Ogiz, Solokha, Kul-Oba, etc.) which as previously mentioned, show links with the Scythian burials of the Early Scythian period of the northwest Caucasus; their elaborate stone tombal constructions remind one of those of the Bosporan Kingdom. The precious masterpieces and articles, weapons, vases, toreutic, found in the Agighiol grave, were decorated in a specific style called the "Thraco-Scythian" style, a modified version of the North Pontic Scythian animal style which still carried on some traditions of its Oriental origin. The articles were evidently made by highly skilled Thracian, or rather Greek goldsmiths

[1] Grakov, *KSIIMK* XXXIV (1950), pp. 7–18; *idem, Kamenskoe Gorodische na Dnepre*, p. 20; A. W. Pickard-Cambridge in *CAH* VI, p. 256; D. M. Pippidi in *Griechische und einheimische Völker der Schwarzmeergebietes* (Berlin, 1961), pp. 81–105; Pippidi and Berciu, *Din istoria Dobrogei* I, p. 130; Venednikov, *Bulgaria's Treasures*; Meliukova, *SA* XXII (1955), pp. 240ff; P. Nicorescu, *Dacia* II (1925), pp. 22–8; D. B. Shelov, in *Problemy Skifskoy Arkheologii* (MIA 177, 1971), pp. 54–63.

[2] Berciu, *Romania before Burebista*; *idem, Arta tracogetica*, pp. 33–76, 94ff; *Idem, 50 Bericht der Römisch-Germanischen Kommission für 1969* (Frankfurt am Main, 1971), pp. 209–65; Pippidi and Berciu, vol. I, pp. 110ff.

FURTHER DEVELOPMENT AND DECLINE

from Histria. Similar masterpieces of the same period found in several sites in Romania and in Bulgaria, illustrate the impact on Thracian art of the Scythian decorative art, the roots of which go back to Iran.

The king buried in the Agighiol barrow seems to have been a Scythian ruler of northern Dobrudja of the turn of the 5th century, entombed early in the 4th century B.C. At that time Ateas, then about 40 years old, might have succeeded to the chieftaincy of the Scythian branch which settled in northern Dobrudja. The buried prince might have been his predecessor, or even his father.

The twilight

At the turn of the 5th century B.C., the ancient centre of Scythian power shifted to the south, to the region of the Dnieper bend, where the large earthwork of Kamyanka with its "Acropolis" became the main industrial centre and probably the seat of the rulers of Scythia of the Late Scythian period.

But around 200 B.C. a new onslaught, that of the Sarmatian Roxolani, overwhelmed the Late Scyths. They had to abandon their Kamyanka centre and move south into the Crimea.

From then on the Crimea became the Scythian refuge for several centuries. The Crimean Scythian kingdom was set up there, called also the "Tauro-Scythian" kingdom. The city of Scythian Neapolis built in the vicinity of modern Simferopol, came to be the political centre and the seat of the kings of the country. There, the Scyths who progressively mixed with the Taurians and the infiltrating Sarmatians, survived until the 3rd century A.D., when the country was seized by the invading Goths and other Teutonic tribes, and the Scythian kingdom and its capital city were destroyed.

This was the end of Scythian history in Europe.

CHAPTER 5

THE RISE OF THE ACHAEMENIDS AND ESTABLISHMENT OF THEIR EMPIRE

At the beginning of his *History*, for which he was gathering the material in the middle of the 5th century, the Greek writer Herodotus tells us what Persian men of learning had to say about the first confrontations of Europe and Asia, and for a moment in his whimsical way he conjures up an illusion of a living tradition of Persian historical scholarship. But as we read on we discover that it is to the Greek legends that their critical acumen is being applied; the Persians have no contribution to make from their own side; and in the event we find that there is no evidence of a native Persian literature in Achaemenian times, still less of a library of texts such as Ashurbanipal had built up at Nineveh. Stories of course grew up round their historical figures, for songs with a narrative content formed an important part of Persian education; and we can gauge the inventiveness of this oral tradition from the fact that Herodotus claims to have known four different versions of the tale of Cyrus the Great's origins and many different ones of his end. But it was not until Sasanian times that anything purporting to be a national history came into being, and even that by our standards was legendary.

The one ancient Persian document we possess which gives a narrative of historical events, the "res gestae" of Darius I inscribed about 520 B.C. on the cliff face at Behistun, is unfortunately confined to a period of a year or two, and it seems to be directed as much towards self-justification as to historical truth. Beyond this, if we address ourselves to the question of the extent and articulation of the Persian empire, we find that some thirty subject peoples are named in the inscribed monuments of the Achaemenids, and the bare list is enlivened by graphic presentation of them in reliefs on walls and tomb fronts at Persepolis; but even this information is neither so complete nor so circumstantial as that which Herodotus gives us, and the monuments tell us nothing about the organization of the empire, or the conditions of Achaemenid rule. At the other end of the scale we have a wealth of contemporary documents, the tablets that have come to light at

Persepolis and in Babylonia, and papyri in Egypt. These are valuable additions to our knowledge of the places and communities concerned, and they cast a welcome light on the administrative system in Persis itself. But they tend to be the small change of history, and economic and social rather than political; so they cannot fill the place of a literary tradition. In addition some historical light is shed on the campaign of 539 B.C. by the Babylonian Cyrus chronicle and on Zionist activities by a few books of the Old Testament.

The Persians were fortunate in having the one really literate people of their world as their biographers. It is to the Greek writers alone that we owe such fundamental information as that Asia Minor was conquered by Cyrus, that Persia was for considerable periods of time a naval power, that the organization of the tribute and the introduction of an imperial coinage were due to Darius I, that under him and his son Persian arms were carried into Europe, that a younger Cyrus invaded Babylonia in a bid for the throne, that the unity of the empire was shattered by revolts of the satraps under Artaxerxes II and restored by Artaxerxes III, and that the regime was eventually overthrown by an expeditionary force led by a Macedonian king. But it is not only the broad outlines of history that our Greek sources provide. It is from them that modern scholars have been able to reconstitute that intelligible historical pattern which the more localized detail of contemporary documents and archaeological discoveries now serves to illuminate, to supplement, and on rare occasions to correct.

I. THE PRINCIPAL SOURCES FOR EARLY ACHAEMENID HISTORY

1. HERODOTUS was born some time around 485 B.C. in the Persian empire, at Halicarnassus on the west coast of Asia Minor. His great work was a systematically planned history of the rise and repulse of the Persian power, in which he incorporated discursive accounts of the nations, great or small, which in succession the Persians conquered or at least encountered in their relentless advance before 480 B.C. He travelled in some parts of the empire including Egypt, the Levant coast, and as far east as Babylon; and he seems to have observed the burial practice of the Magi, though probably not in Iran.[1] He presumably

---

[1] Scholars of two and three generations ago were inclined to question Herodotus' good faith and earnestly contested his claims to have travelled abroad. Such doubts are not now often entertained; but in any case his historical statements are not dependent on eye-witness.

spoke some Persian; but he was evidently no philologist, and when we find that he believed that Mithra was a goddess and the word "arta" meant "great", we may have misgivings about his ability to sustain a conversation in Persian on an intellectual level. In spite of this, however, he acquired detailed information from Median and Persian sources which can be shown to be correct at a number of points; so we may accept the fact of his prosecuting enquiries without prying more closely into the linguistic mechanism of it.

Much of his information relating to Persian affairs of course came from Greek sources. He had inside knowledge of two councils of war that Xerxes held in Greece in 480 B.C.; and while we cannot treat the speeches that he retails as though they were verbatim transcripts, we can hazard a guess that he had a genuine source of information. For Artemisia, who had been present at both the councils and treated with signal honour, was the despot of his own native city, and in his pages we can detect the echo of the returning heroine's tale of personal success and the disparaging rumours circulated by the political opposition (to which the historian's family belonged). Herodotus also lived on the island of Samos in his youth and had information from there; some detailed knowledge could have been acquired by hearsay from the dependants of Syloson, who is said to have been to the Persian court and obtained support from Darius I for his restoration to the island. A lengthy story set at the Persian court concerns the escape of Darius' Greek doctor Democedes (see below, p. 299); this has been impugned on the ground that Herodotus could not have known what passed between the King and his wife Atossa in bed, but in fact the King's doctor must have known enough of harem routine to understand where the conversation would naturally take place and Herodotus probably heard the whole story from Democedes' descendants in southern Italy. Herodotus knows in detail of Xerxes' activities in the Troad and at the Hellespont, as well as of the sneezing fit that put an end to Hippias' hopes at Marathon; this information could well have been acquired at the Pisistratid refuge at Sigeum, and there are other items of information from the Persian side which were evidently gathered at the exiled Spartan king Demaratus' fief on the Caicus in western Asia Minor.

Herodotus' good faith and reliance on sources rather than invention is illustrated by his account of Xerxes' march westward. The detailed narrative only begins at the point where Xerxes is approaching the metropolis of the Eastern Greek world at Sardis. Before that Herodotus

SOURCES FOR EARLY HISTORY

knows nothing of the march, and he frankly admits that he cannot say who won the prizes at the general inspection of the assembled army in Cappadocia because he had found nobody who could inform him.

From the Persian side the information is often detailed and precise, as for instance that concerning the noble families, and not least the six wives and twelve sons of Darius. More particularly, there are two long and circumstantial bodies of narrative fitted into Herodotus' history of the Medes and the Persians. The first carries us from the foundation of Agbatana and the Median kingdom under Deioces at the end of the 8th century through the capture of Nineveh to the origins of Cyrus the Great and his rebellion against Astyages; and though detached from it in Herodotus' systematic arrangement, the war between the Medes and the Lydians under Alyattes is evidently part of the same continuous story. There are recurring elements of folklore in this narrative; but it has an impressive continuity, and several details receive confirmation from cuneiform tablets, while the tale of Deioces appears to have been given a Zoroastrian flavour. It seems clear that Herodotus had a Median source here; and in fact the prominence given to the renegade Mede Harpagus in the Cyrus story, both here and in the account of the capture of Sardis and reduction of Ionia and Lycia, has led some scholars to assume that Herodotus may have been acquainted with his family in Asia Minor.

The second of the stories referred to begins with King Cambyses in Egypt and the secret murder of his brother Smerdis (the Bardiya of the Behistun inscription), which was carried out at Cambyses' command by his principal adviser Prexaspes. It continues with the seizure of the throne by the two Magi and the fatal accident and confession of Cambyses, and leads on to the conspiracy of the Seven which resulted in the assassination of the usurpers. Herodotus here gives a remarkably detailed and consistent account which contrasts sharply with his ignorance of Darius' immediately ensuing struggles to retain power; and the inside information about the fight in the royal apartments and the secret deliberations of the Seven is so precise that the story can only be imagined as having been transmitted through one of the Seven. In one matter of detail the accuracy of this account can be checked; for in the Behistun text Darius also names his six fellow conspirators, and he would hardly have falsified a matter of such public knowledge. In Herodotus' account the names of five of these paladins agree with Darius (Otanes, Intaphernes, Gobryas, Megabyzus, Hydarnes), though one father's name is different. But the sixth is erroneous (Aspathines instead of what has been read as Ardumaniš). Now Aspathines (Aspačana) is later found as the bow-bearer of Darius (Naqsh-i Rustam); and a son of Aspathines called Prexaspes is named by Herodotus as one of Xerxes' admirals in 480 B.C., while the father's name on the seal of Aspathines, who is found authorising payments at Persepolis to some hundreds of workmen and "cultivators" in Xerxes' third year (483 B.C.)[1] is read by Cameron as Parrakašpi (i.e., perhaps Prexaspes). It is an easy conjecture that Aspathines was the son of the Prexaspes who in Herodotus' account was brought to confess to the killing of the true Smerdis and then leapt to his death from a tower; and this Aspathines could thus have been a key witness to the seven conspirators' claim that the Smerdis whom they killed was a pretender. Aspathines will no doubt have been very closely associated with the Seven after the coup d'état. The error by which he figures among the Seven in Herodotus cannot be one of misreading; rather, it looks like a lapse of memory on the part of a person who knew of the events from the inside. This is not to say that the whole story is true; but basically it should be what the Seven Families claimed to be the truth. On internal grounds the story seems most likely to have worked its way down to Herodotus through either Otanes, who was active on the Greek fringe in the West and closely associated with Syloson in Samos, or (as Wells suggested) the family of Megabyzus, with whose descendant Zopyrus Herodotus could have been acquainted when he fled to Athens; these in fact are the two whom Herodotus portrays as playing speaking parts along with Darius in the conspiracy.[2]

At one point Herodotus' information goes beyond the oral. This is in his survey of the administrative divisions of the Persian empire (below, p. 268). The names of the twenty satrapies that he attributes to Darius' re-organization would not perhaps have been difficult to obtain by casual enquiry. But Herodotus distributes some seventy names of peoples and communities among them and adds precise figures

[1] In the Treasury tablets. Aspathines' name also appears in the Fortification tablets from ten years earlier. Cf. p. 590.
[2] A sidelight is shed on Herodotus' Persian stories by K. Reinhardt in his essay "Herodots Persergeschichten" (in his *Von Werken und Formen* (Godesberg, 1948) 163–224, and elsewhere). Reinhardt does not concern himself with the historicity of these stories. But he finds that the long narratives referred to above (in contrast to those stories which have western connections or relate to Xerxes' Greek expedition) belong to a developed novelistic tradition, and that their social and conceptual milieu is that of the Persian court-aristocracy; the stories composing them had been skilfully worked up orally before coming to Greek ears.

SOURCES FOR EARLY HISTORY

of the tribute and gifts due from each satrapy. So, unless with Altheim and Ölsner we charge him with deliberate forgery, this list presupposes some sort of document to which an informant of his had had accesss. Herodotus refers his list to the time of Darius. It is possible, as scholars used to argue, that he took it without acknowledgement from an earlier Greek writer, and this might perhaps affect our estimate of his conscience as a historian; but the information contained in it would not be any the less reliable if it did in fact date nearer to the time alleged. More probably, however, Herodotus is using information from a list that was current in his own time and adjusting it according to his knowledge of changes since Darius' reign (to which the strict chronological arrangement of his Persian narrative compelled him to assign it).

In sum, Herodotus provides us with a wealth of information. Much of it has been obtained by hearsay, and his longer narratives present some detail which borders on the mythical. But there does seem to be a firm substratum of genuine historical knowledge, much of which has been obtained from Persian and Median sources.

2. CTESIAS was an Asclepiad of Cnidus who was taken prisoner and became the Persian King's doctor, a post that he occupied for a number of years (17 on his own admission, and ending in 397 or at the latest 393 B.C.). He is supposed to have attended Artaxerxes II when he was wounded by his brother at the Battle of Cunaxa (401 B.C.). On his own showing he is a priceless firsthand authority. For he claimed that at the Persian court he had studied royal historical *diphtherai* (parchments, though in literary Ionic the word could mean books generally), and it is almost certainly from his writings that the later universal historian Diodorus was able to cite episodes of oriental history that were supposedly recorded in the Persian royal archives (*anagraphai*). Unfortunately, when we discover that what was recorded in the Persian *anagraphai* relates to the prowess of Memnon son of Tithonus and his death in a Thessalian ambush at Troy, and that Ctesias' familiarity with the Persian records did not prevent him from interpreting Darius' Behistun text as a description of Semiramis' ascent of the cliff (pl. 34) on a mountain of army pack-saddles, we have no choice left but to reject his entire claim to documentation. He also once speaks of having information from the mouth of the Queen Mother Parysatis; but all this amounts to is that she was the mother of thirteen children.

Ctesias had perused Herodotus before writing the 23 books of his *Persica* and was patently concerned to give him the lie. The Hellenistic and Roman writers recognized his single book of *Indica* as largely miraculous; but in other matters concerning the Orient they tended rather to class Ctesias along with Herodotus and his less important contemporary Hellanicus, seeing them all as historians whose fault was a penchant towards story-telling and dramatization; and the Patriarch Photius, who rediscovered the text of Ctesias in the 9th century, believed that he had unearthed a treasure. It is principally to Photius that we owe our knowledge of Ctesias' Persian history; but what we possess is only excerpts, and so in the study of the ancient sources the "argumentum a silentio" cannot be used with Ctesias in the same way as with Herodotus and Xenophon, whose text is fully preserved.

We can now check Ctesias at many points against Assyrian or Babylonian texts and the Old Persian inscriptions; and we find that – apart from the tittle-tattle about personages of the court which we have little means of checking – the specific information that he gives is usually quite false. Presumably he had not thought seriously of collecting material for an oriental history when he was at the Persian court but was tempted by his success as a raconteur on his return home to put his memorials into writing; certainly he could not have foreseen so complete an exposure of his fictions as has befallen him in the last hundred years. Modern scholars have varied greatly in the use they make of him for early Achaemenid history, but they tend to give him the benefit of the doubt when he is not in conflict with other authorities. For the times nearest to his own even the more sceptical moderns, following Canon Rawlinson, have generally maintained that being released from the temptation to contradict Herodotus and Thucydides he becomes a less disreputable authority. Yet even here we may note that Darius II, who reigned from 424/3 to 405/4 B.C. and so must have been known to Ctesias, is credited by him with a reign of 35 years. It is possible that Ctesias' world of eunuch chamberlains and femmes fatales, of poisoning, exquisite tortures, and vicious harem intrigue gives some reflection of the corruption of the royal court. But he is no Procopius. On balance it seems most prudent to disregard him as a serious historical source, though the narrative of events will be the poorer for doing so; and this obliges us to jettison much of the historical information transmitted by later writers who used him as an authority.[1]

---

[1] If his work had survived in the way that Ctesias' does, we should probably need to speak in similar terms about Dinon, who continued the account of the Persian court to 343 B.C. and, like Ctesias, was utilized by Plutarch in his life of Artaxerxes II.

SOURCES FOR EARLY HISTORY

3. One other Greek work could be of paramount importance if there were reason to believe that its author had made a point of collecting and transmitting genuine historical information. This is XENOPHON's *Cyropaedia* (*Institutio Cyri*), which presents a Life of Cyrus the Great in no less than eight books. It is of course true that Xenophon had first-hand knowledge of the Persian empire; for he was in the Greek mercenary force (the "Ten Thousand") which accompanied Cyrus the Younger across Asia Minor and down the Euphrates to his death on the battlefield by Babylon (401 B.C.), and then returned up the left bank of the Tigris and across Armenia to the Black Sea; and he followed this with some years of service in the Spartan expeditionary corps ranging about western Asia Minor. The *Cyropaedia* contains much of interest on Persian institutions that is attributed to the time of Cyrus the Great, with frequent mention of customs and arrangements that are said to have survived to the author's own day. But the patches of local colour are largely camouflage; Xenophon's true aim is to present his own imaginative conception of a benevolent despotism, and in war and peace Cyrus and his nobles are made to conduct themselves in the manner of moralizing aristocratic Greeks. It is consequently not easy to distinguish anything that might be authentic. A similar idealism may be discerned in the three or four pages of Xenophon's *Oeconomicus* (section IV), in which the King's solicitude for his subjects and attention to the civil and military spheres of government is set up as an example.

As regards the history of Cyrus' reign the narrative of events in the *Cyropaedia* shows a certain indebtedness to Herodotus but is in general composed, as Cicero remarked, not "ad historiae fidem" but "ad effigiem justi imperii". Thus Cyrus is depicted not as a rebel but as loyal throughout to Astyages and his fictitious son and successor Cyaxares; his wars against Lydia and Babylon are telescoped into one single operation against an aggressive coalition; he is spoken of as the conqueror of Egypt, and he is allowed to die at peace in the fullness of years. Only when he introduces an "Assyrian" (i.e. Babylonian) noble called Gobryas who defects to Cyrus before the campaign against his master does Xenophon produce information which fits with the Cyrus chronicle and is not to be found in Herodotus.

In the *Cyropaedia* Xenophon does not even seem to have the historical novelist's aversion to palpable anachronism; for instance, his list of Cyrus' western satrapies is quite false for the early years of the empire, and he has wealth hoarded in "darics" though the royal Persian gold coinage only began under Darius close on twenty years after Cyrus' death and was almost certainly named after him. In contrast with his historical works, which give a factual account of events in which he himself took part, Xenophon's *Cyropaedia* is a counterpart to Plato's Republic and a forerunner of the later Greek genre of utopian romances. It is his misfortune that this most creative of his works has in modern times been disregarded as a contribution to political thinking and overestimated as history.

The historians of Alexander the Great belong to Chapter 11. Their works are known to us only through later writers. But like Xenophon in his genuinely historical writings, they do provide first-hand information about the Persian empire; and in particular it is to them that we owe our knowledge of the eastern Iranian lands as they first come into the light of recorded history.

4. DARIUS I's trilingual inscription carved on the cliff face (pl. 34) at Behistun (the ancient Bagastāna, "place of the gods") has a main text of about 3,600 words in the Old Persian (or as Darius calls it, "Aryan") version. This, with the present Elamite version, constitutes a re-editing about 518 B.C. of his original text (of which the Babylonian version was a translation). A block found at Babylon also gives parts of the Babylonian text, while a copy (of which fragments have been discovered in the Jewish troops' barracks at Elephantine on the Nile) was in Aramaic and written in large handsome lettering on papyrus. The main text of the inscription at Behistun describes the King's activity in the first year of his reign, when he was involved in a series of campaigns against pretenders and rebels; and it is followed by a short postscript in Old Persian which records the mopping-up operations of the two following years. But at the beginning, after the preamble in which he proclaims his title to the kingship, Darius briefly relates the events which led to the killing of Gaumāta and his own accession; and it is on this part of the "res gestae", combined with his statement of his own ancestry, that he reposes his claim to have been the legitimate heir to the throne. In the preamble he also gives his first list of lands, 23 in all, that were subject to him and presumably had been subject to his predecessors.

We have no control over the main narrative, that of the events that followed his accession. In the early part, however, the document is patently unsatisfactory. Darius traces his ancestry back to Čišpiš

CONQUESTS IN ASIA AND EGYPT

(Teispes) and Hakhāmaniš (Achaemenes). He does not say that Aršāma and Ariyāramna (his grandfather and great-grandfather) were kings, but by claiming that eight of his family had been kings before him he leaves it to be necessarily inferred. At the same time he takes care to stress that he alone stood up against the usurper and that it was on him that Ahuramazda bestowed the kingdom. And finally he insists overmuch on "The Lie", which first seduced the people from Cambyses and then his subjects from himself. His royal proclamation seems to betray a lively anticipation of disbelief on the part of its hearers.

There is no other Old Persian text comparable to this in scope or historical importance.

II. THE CONQUESTS IN ASIA AND EGYPT

Of the origins of Cyrus (Kūruš) the Great, the founder of the Achaemenid empire, many stories were told; but from the documentary evidence it now seems certain that he came of a royal line. He was king of what the Babylonians in their anachronistic style called Anšan (a region that had long previously been up-country from Susa) and proclaimed himself son of Cambyses, grandson of Cyrus, descendant of Teispes (Čišpiš), and an Achaemenid (Hakhāmanišiya). Since the Achaemenids belonged to the Pasargadae clan of the Persians according to Herodotus and Cyrus was evidently king of the Persians, it is natural to suppose that his ancestral rule was in Pārsa (Persis) itself.

Scholars have, however, noted an objection to this. Darius I, who became the King after the death of Cyrus' sons, claimed in the Behistun inscription that his own ancestry was Hystaspes (Vištāspa) – Arsames (Aršāma) – Ariaramnes (Ariyāramna) – Teispes (Čišpiš) – Achaemenes (Hakhāmaniš); by implication he claims that from Arsames backwards all were kings, and support for this is found in two gold tablets from Agbatana in the Old Persian script purporting to be prayers inscribed by Arsames and Ariaramnes, in which both are styled "Great King, King of Kings, King in Pārsa". On this evidence it has been assumed that after Teispes there were for a generation and more two Achaemenid reigning houses, the one (that of Cyrus) in Anšan (see chapter 2, and map 1), the other (Darius' ancestors) to the northeast. Herodotus knows Darius' lineage as given by him, though he does not know of it as a royal line parallel to that of Cyrus; but we must note that the two gold tablets have been recognized as antiquarian fabrications of a later date (probably of the fourth century B.C.), so that we do not seem to have any record of Darius' claim to royal ancestry which does not depend on his own personal statement of it.

There are two objections to Darius' claim. First, in the Behistun inscription there is no mention of a legitimate king being still alive; yet many years later, in his Palace inscription at Susa, Darius related that at the time of his own accession (522 B.C.) both his father Hystaspes and his grandfather Arsames were living.[1] Secondly, Herodotus tells the story of Darius' accession in a version that must ultimately derive from one of the six fellow conspirators who set Darius on the throne (above, p. 203), and the narrative makes it abundantly clear that Darius was not at that time regarded as being in any way more royal than the others. In any case the two gold tablets seem to betray an imposture, for there could hardly have been room for a "Great King, King of Kings" in the corner of land that Ariaramnes and Arsames supposedly occupied. It seems therefore simplest to assume that Darius falsified the record; that in fact there was only one genuine Achaemenid royal house – that of Cyrus – and that Cyrus' ancestors ruled in Pārsa.[2]

According to Herodotus the Persians were conquered by the Median king Phraortes (perhaps the historical Khšathrita, who seems to have united the Median tribes when the Assyrians' back was turned). But a Cyrus of Parsuwash (evidently an ancestor of Cyrus the Great) is found joining with Elam in resistance to Assyria about 640 B.C. and afterwards making amends by sending his son Arukku to Ashurbanipal's court. He or his successor was no doubt brought into subjection by the Medes under Cyaxares (Uvakhštara), the formidable conqueror of Nineveh (612 B.C.).[3]

Cyrus was evidently a vassal of the Median king Astyages, son of Cyaxares, when he succeeded to the throne about 559 B.C.; but Astyages was growing old and had no son, and Cyrus did not lack ambition. If we may believe Herodotus, only three of the six settled clans of Persians paraded under his banner when he first took the field. But he evidently

[1] This statement of Darius' is one of fact that would be within the memory of many people at the court, and is not likely to be false. The now current chronological table of the Achaemenids, which brings this Arsames to the throne in 615 B.C., illustrates the difficulty of reconciling the data with Darius' statement of his genealogy.

[2] Since these paragraphs were written an American mission has discovered Elamite inscribed bricks and tablets identifying the site of the prehistoric city of Anšan at Maliyān, 30 miles north of Shīrāz. It is therefore certain now that Anšan was in the heart of Pārsa, and the theory of two collateral reigning houses in Pārsa becomes untenable.

[3] For a short up-to-date conspectus of Median history see D. Stronach, *Iran* VII (1969), 2ff.

CONQUESTS IN ASIA AND EGYPT

won over some of the Median nobles to his side; and he proceeded to conquer Astyages in a war of which Nicholas of Damascus gives a lengthy account that goes back to Ctesias. Astyages, as we learn from the Babylonian chronicle, was betrayed by his own troops when he marched into the rebel's territory, and Cyrus the Persian supplanted him as ruler of the empire in the Median capital of Agbatana;[1] this entry relates to the year 550/549 B.C., though a dream-text of the Babylonian king places it earlier.

To the Eastern Mediterranean world it may have appeared nothing more than a change of dynasty; for in the eyes of Jews, Greeks, Egyptians, and Arabs the ruling power long after continued to be the "Mede". And Nabuna'id of Babylon seems at first to have welcomed the attack on a dangerous neighbour and joined in on his own account at Harran. But in Asia Minor the advent of Cyrus was viewed with concern. A generation or two previously the Lydian king Alyattes had fought an indecisive war with Cyaxares, which is said to have ended in an alliance by marriage and the fixing of their common boundary on the River Halys. The overthrow of Astyages was not welcomed by Alyattes' son Croesus; and according to Herodotus he sought to form an alliance with Babylon and Egypt and prepared for war against the Persian upstart. To Cyrus, Lydia with its formidable cavalry was a greater menace than Babylon, whose king, Nabuna'id, had withdrawn from the capital and was concerned with occupying a string of oases in Western Arabia; and he prepared to strike the decisive blow there. We are told that it was Croesus who crossed the Halys first, but that Cyrus for his part was in contact with Croesus' Greek subjects, trying to raise them in revolt behind his back. The Babylonian chronicle notes that Cyrus crossed the Tigris below Arbela in the spring of 547 and proceeded to conquer the land of Lu(?)-; and many scholars take this to refer to Lydia.[2] From Herodotus we learn that after a drawn battle east of the Halys Croesus returned to Sardis and, not expecting to be

---

[1] The "Median" narrative in Herodotus (above, p. 200) makes Cyrus a grandson of Astyages; but it also makes him a descendant of the Lydian king Alyattes, thus legitimizing his rule over both conquered nations. There was also a comparable story which made Cambyses the son of an Egyptian princess, and in later Persian legend Alexander the Great was made a brother of Darius III.

[2] The reading of the syllable at the break as "lu" seems to be no more than a possibility and if it is not the correct reading we may imagine that what Cyrus was engaged on in 547 was a campaign in the eastern marches of Anatolia to prepare the way for his offensive against Croesus, which would then have followed in 546 or soon after. But the chronicle does at least show that in 547 Cyrus was beginning to move towards Asia Minor.

THE RISE OF THE ACHAEMENIDS

followed, dismissed his levies for the winter; but Cyrus came after him, defeated him in the Lydian plain, and stormed the citadel in fourteen days. Having thus added Anatolia to his empire Cyrus returned to Agbatana, leaving his generals to deal with the insurrection that followed and crush the opposition of the Greek cities and native peoples of the coast. No concerted resistance was encountered there; but in the fragmented terrain of south-western Asia Minor Cyrus' Median aide, Harpagus, had many citadels to capture before the Pax Persica could be established. For the conquest of Asia Minor see below pp. 292ff.

Half a dozen years passed before Cyrus finally descended on Babylon. In the meantime he had made overtures to the priesthood of the capital, which had been alienated by the insouciance and provincial attachments of Nabuna'id. The defection of Ugbaru, the governor of the territory east of the Tigris, had been secured; and after dominating the countryside for some months Cyrus effected his entry into Babylon at the end of October 539. There he was received as the righteous prince chosen by the god Marduk to restore the old religion flouted by Nabuna'id. With Babylon went not only the great plain of the Euphrates and Tigris from the Persian Gulf to the Armenian foothills, but also the subject peoples of the Babylonian empire west of the Euphrates (Abarnahara) from the river crossing at Thapsacus to the Egyptian approaches at Gaza. The chronicle tells us that the kings from sea to sea, even those of the West who dwelt in tents, came with heavy tribute to Babylon and kissed the conqueror's feet. The whole of Western Asia as far as the Arabian desert was now under Persian suzerainty.[1]

It was with his Persian army that Cyrus achieved his conquests, and he is not known to have displayed any interest in the sea, which quite possibly he never sailed on. In his last years he turned to the East. Unfortunately we know too little of the situation there. The Medes had certainly possessed an empire. Herodotus speaks of them as having gone conquering all Asia, people by people, a generation or so before they destroyed the Assyrian empire (612 B.C.); the word that we know as "satrap" was Median, the Persian name of the region Bactria (Bākhtriš) is not Persian in form, but could well be Median, and Greek tradition

---

[1] Following Grote, some scholars have pointed to a statement in Herodotus (III. 34) that Cambyses added "Egypt and the sea" to his father's dominions and have maintained that the Phoenicians cannot have been subject to Cyrus; but this presses the text unduly, the more so since the context is one in which the King is depicted as inviting his courtiers' flattery. We also now know that Abarnahara (the lands west of the Euphrates) was in the Persian satrapy of Babylon in 536/535 B.C.

CONQUESTS IN ASIA AND EGYPT

does not represent Cyrus as achieving new conquests of substance in Eastern Iran. So it could be that the Median empire had already reached the Hindu Kush and crossed the Oxus into Sogdiana. But the evidence is not so positive as we could wish. Indeed Herodotus once speaks of the Bactrians and the Sakai, along with the then unconquered realms of Babylon and Egypt, as being an obstacle to Cyrus and the cause of his not wishing to dally in Sardis after the defeat of Croesus.[1]

The later Greek tales of Cyrus' disastrous Indian expedition, concluding with his death or his return with only seven survivors, command no respect; and we are left to make what we can of Herodotus' account of Cyrus' end. This shows him as mounting a great expedition against the Sakā nation of Massagetae in what is now Turkestan, as crossing the Araxes (in this context not the Oxus but the Jaxartes) on a bridge of boats, and falling in a hard-fought battle against the warrior queen Tomyris. That Cyrus was active on this frontier is confirmed by the survival of a city of Cyrus (Kyroupolis or Kyreschata) near the Jaxartes until the time of Alexander the Great.

We know little about Cyrus, but we can say that few conquerors have won such unqualified admiration. To the Babylonians he was the elect of Marduk, to the Jews the Lord's Anointed. The Medes do not seem to have felt that he was an alien master. Xenophon in the *Cyropaedia* built his ideal of monarchy round Cyrus; and the two conquering heroes that Alexander is said to have emulated were Cyrus and Semiramis. Herodotus tells us that the Persians spoke of him as a father, for he was kind and contrived everything that was good for them. He shows him as quick to anger, but that could be a generous fault. It is only when he comes to Cyrus' last campaign of world conquest that a harsher note creeps in: elated by unbroken success and seeming to himself more than human, Cyrus ends up by justifying Tomyris' phrase when she calls him "insatiate of blood". But Herodotus knew that no mortal may expect good fortune to the last; and this characterisation in the spirit of Attic tragedy is not one that he is likely to have heard on Persian lips.

[1] I. 153: "for Babylon was an obstruction to him, and the Bactrian nation and the Sakai and Egyptians, and he wanted to invade them". This certainly implies that Herodotus thought of Bactria as still remaining to be annexed to the empire, and perhaps due to be invaded after Babylon. But in I. 201 he says "when this nation too [Babylon] had been conquered, Cyrus set his heart on making the Massagetae his subjects", which seems to imply the opposite. We may infer that Herodotus did not have accurate knowledge.

THE RISE OF THE ACHAEMENIDS

Cyrus was killed in the high summer of 530 B.C. He left two sons. The elder, named Cambyses (Kambūjiya) after Cyrus' own father, had been designated as successor by his installation as regent of Babylon; the younger was Bardiya, known to Herodotus as Smerdis. Cambyses may have had to begin by restoring the situation on the north-east frontier after his father's death. But if so, he did not spend long on it, for only four years elapsed before he started his attack on Egypt, and in autumn 528 he had been resident at Uruk in southern Mesopotamia. The Phoenician city princes, who had accepted Cyrus' rule after the capture of Babylon, will have provided the bulk of the fleet that was needed to accompany the invasion; at the same time their Cypriot counterparts were induced to make a voluntary submission to Cambyses, and contingents were summoned from the Greeks of the west coast of Asia Minor. A supply base was formed at the south end of the Palestinian coast; and the problem of providing water for the army as it crossed the desert of Sinai was solved in the same way as by Esarhaddon 150 years earlier, an agreement being reached with the bedouin to supply camel trains of skins. A commander of the Greek mercenaries in the Delta transferred his allegiance and provided military intelligence; and Cambyses may have been in touch with disaffected Egyptian priests, of whom one, Udjahorresne of Sais, was in command of the fleet. It also happened that the resourceful old Pharaoh Amasis died while the expedition was on its way. After a hard-fought battle at Pelusium the Egyptians withdrew to Memphis; and instead of wearing down the invader by making him fight for every dyke, they allowed themselves to be blockaded in the fortress. Before midsummer of 525 B.C. Cambyses had established himself as King of Upper and Lower Egypt. Using the same arts of conciliation as his father had done at Babylon, he posed as the lawful successor to the throne and – at the outset at least – respected the native religious traditions. Libya and the Greek cities to the west offered gifts to him in token of submission; and then, leading a Persian army up the Nile into Nubia, he made part of Aethiopia subject to him at what Greek tradition represented as a heavy cost in manpower. An inscription of an Aethiopian king Nastasen records the defeat of Kmbswdn or Hmbswtn somewhere north of Meroe; and this used to be taken as a reference to Cambyses' expedition. But there is apparently good reason to believe that Nastasen should be dated in the 4th century; and Cambyses' losses are said by Herodotus to have been due to lack of food, and not to enemy action.

CONQUESTS IN ASIA AND EGYPT

Before he could return to Babylon, Cambyses received news that his throne had been usurped in the name of his brother Bardiya. Soon afterwards, early in 522 B.C., he died according to Herodotus as the result of a wound accidentally self-inflicted as he was returning from Egypt to quell the insurrection. The word describing the manner of his death on the Behistun inscription (uvāmaršiyuš, "by own (or self) death") was perhaps chosen by Darius to emphasize that he was not murdered.[1] His reputation in antiquity was a bad one; indeed he was said to have gone mad after his Aethiopian expedition. This judgement mainly depends on Egyptian (and in the story of his sister's death, Greco-Egyptian) sources, in which – since he had offended the priesthood by curtailing their revenues – we can expect some defamation of his character, and indeed detect at least one malicious fabrication (the killing of the divine Apis bull).[2] But we hear ill of him from the Persian side; for we have not only Darius' questionable assertion that Cambyses killed his own brother, but an act of quite wilful killing that links up with Herodotus' story of the Seven (Prexaspes' son the cupbearer), and we are told that the Persians remembered Cambyses as a "tyrant" in contrast to Cyrus the "father". In the few years of his reign he had carried the empire into Africa and given it the use of the sea. But he left no son to succeed him.

For the events of the year 522 we have two sources – column I of Darius' inscription at Behistun and Herodotus' long narrative in Book III.[3] There are discrepancies between the two sufficient to show that Herodotus did not have firsthand knowledge of Darius' text. But being

---

[1] See G. Lazard, *Bulletin de la Société de Linguistique de Paris* LXXI (1976), 175–8.

[2] Herodotus (III. 27–9) relates that after his return from the Aethiopian expedition Cambyses wounded the Apis bull in the thigh, and the bull died and was secretely buried by the priests. In fact the Memphis Serapeum stelae show that a bull (born in the 27th year of Amasis) died soon after Cambyses' invasion of Egypt; but it was buried in a handsome sarcophagus which was the gift of Cambyses himself. The tradition that Cambyses destroyed Egyptian temples was, however, current a century and more later when the Jews of Elephantine spoke of their own temple of Yahwe having been spared. Scholars have attempted to find a reference to such acts in Udjahorresne's mention, in his naophoric statue inscription, of great troubles that followed the Persian conquest of Egypt; but on this see G. Posener, *La première domination perse en Égypte* (Cairo, 1936), 168ff. The inscription certainly shows Cambyses as the benefactor of the Temple of Neith at Sais, which he took the trouble to visit. For Cambyses in Egypt and the Apis see K. M. T. Atkinson, "The legitimacy of Cambyses and Darius as Kings of Egypt", *JAOS* LXXVI (1956), 167–77.

[3] In Ctesias and Justin (Trogus) there are conflicting versions of these events. But apart from a resemblance between the name Cometes in Justin and Gaumāta at Behistun there is no correspondence with anything that we can establish as factual; and in any case Justin gives the name Cometes to the other Magus (i.e. to Herodotus' Patizeithes, not Smerdis-Gaumāta).

an embroidered version of what must have been related by one of Darius' six fellow conspirators, the story in Herodotus has the same central justification as Darius', that it was not the true Bardiya that the Seven killed but a pretender. Darius' account is brief and explicit: Cambyses had secretly killed Bardiya before he went to Egypt; while he was there the pretender, a Magus named Gaumāta, rose in revolt, and the Persians, Medes, and other peoples of the empire, who were unaware of Bardiya's death, were seduced from their loyalty to Cambyses, so that "The Lie" prevailed. Cambyses meanwhile died, and no one dared to stand up against Gaumāta until Darius himself arrived at the end of the summer (522 B.C.). Darius then, with six other Persians, killed Gaumāta and his followers at a place called Sikayauvatiš in Media. Herodotus' narrative is much fuller, with circumstantial details of the secret killing of Smerdis (Bardiya) by the King's chief counsellor Prexaspes, Cambyses' accident and death, the formation of the conspiracy of the Seven, the struggle with the Magi in the palace, the deliberations of the Seven after the event, and the trick by which Darius obtained the kingship. There are several curious points that emerge from this narrative. One that we have already remarked is that Darius was not held to have any better claim to the throne than others of the Seven. Another is that the pretender was said not only to be the living image of the true Smerdis but to have even had the same name; and finally the circumstances in which Prexaspes is made to admit to the killing of the true Smerdis and then immediately pass beyond the reach of questioning are not such as to inspire great confidence in the minds of a generation so addicted to detective fiction as ours or so suspicious of official accounts of political coups. It is also perplexing that in Darius' account of the events, which ought to stand on its own merits, we are asked to believe that the heir to the throne could have been dead for three years and more without people having any suspicion of it. In consequence the majority of writers in the last thirty years have followed Olmstead (and before him Beloch) in the view that Darius has falsified the facts and that he usurped the throne from the true Bardiya.[1]

Whether he was Bardiya or not, the ruler whom the Seven killed had taken up his residence in Media, gained the confidence of the Magi, won the support of Median and other provincial nobles as well as Persians, and earned the goodwill of the subject peoples by a three-year remission of military levies and (like Shāh 'Abbās in a like situation) of taxes. It

[1] Cf. Burn, *Persia and the Greeks*, 90ff.

CONSOLIDATION OF THE EMPIRE UNDER DARIUS

is sometimes said that his aim was to break the power of the Iranian feudal aristocracy, and that the Seven were concerned to re-establish the supremacy of this class. But Herodotus certainly understood that what was at stake was Persian predominance; and it seems more likely that the action of the Seven was a counter-revolution on the part of the high nobility of Pārsa.[1] As we shall see later, the victory of Darius was followed by a contraction of the circle from which the imperial élite was drawn. It was also followed by a resumption of wars of conquest.

III. THE CONSOLIDATION OF THE EMPIRE UNDER DARIUS

Darius (Dārayavauš) the First was a son (the eldest according to Herodotus) of a leading Persian Hystaspes (Vištāspa), who seems to have held an important position as a governor (satrap in Persis itself, Herodotus says, but on the evidence of the Behistun inscription he was in charge in Parthia in 522 B.C.). It is difficult to accept Ammianus Marcellinus' implication that this Hystaspes was the same person as Zarathustra (Zoroaster)'s patron kavi Vištāspa in Bactria; Darius' father was an Achaemenid and could hardly have been a hereditary ruler in Eastern Iran. Herodotus tells us that Darius was a spearman (*doryphoros*) of Cambyses in Egypt. Many scholars have assumed that this means the King's spear-bearer (arštibara) and that Darius was therefore the holder of high office in attendance on the King; the historian goes on to add "and of no consequence at the time", so in fact he is using the word in its normal Greek sense of "guardsman". But Herodotus may have misunderstood. After the killing of Bardiya-Gaumāta in September 522 B.C. Darius obtained the kingship. This was evidently achieved with the assent of his fellow conspirators; indeed in the Behistun inscription he names them as his supporters and calls on his successors to protect their families. Of his own assumption of the kingship he says only "By the favour of Ahuramazda I am King; Ahuramazda bestowed the kingship on me". In Herodotus' account the Seven turned out for an early morning ride on the understanding that the one whose horse neighed first after sunrise should become King, and Darius' groom arranged that his master's horse should encounter a mare for which it had a particular liking. The story of course sounds "ben trovato"; but

---

[1] For an emphatic statement of Darius' feelings and aims at this stage see H. S. Nyberg, "Das Reich der Achämeniden", in Fritz Kern, *Historia Mundi* III (Berne, 1954), 75ff; more recently Dandamayev, *Persien unter den ersten Achämeniden*, 164.

the notion of such a compact is not necessarily to be disregarded, because, as von Osten has pointed out, with no obvious successor to the throne a portent could have been needed to make the divine will manifest.

The rule of Bardiya-Gaumāta had been accepted by the peoples of the empire, but the news of the new coup d'état was a signal for insurrection in all the central lands; for Herodotus tells us that the Magus was mourned by everyone in Asia except the Persians (III. 67).[1] Within a few days a "Nebuchadnezzar" was crowned king of Babylon and another man set himself up as king in Elam. These seem to have been genuine revolts of the subject peoples aimed at throwing off the Persian yoke. Darius acted quickly. The trouble in Elam came to an end, and in December he forced the crossing of the Tigris, fought a couple of battles, and seized Babylon. His army was small, he says; but presumably it was the seasoned Persian and Median troops that had returned from Egypt. In the meantime, however, more dangerous risings occurred. Some of them may have been secessionist movements, like that under Frāda the Margian in Margiana and the further revolts in Babylon and Elam. But in Iran itself the situation was different. There Darius was faced with rival claimants to the imperial throne, one setting himself up as Bardiya – by denying that it was him they had killed the Seven had left the door open for pretenders – and two descendants of the great Cyaxares who had built up the Median empire. The Median movement under Fravartiš was perhaps the most serious; it extended eastward to Parthia and may have embraced revolting Armenians also. Darius detached one of the Seven, Hydarnes (Vidarna), to check the enemy at the Zagros passes; and he sent off other commanders whom he could trust to contain the insurgents in Armenia, and later to Persis. He himself prepared a great spring drive northward into Media, which was in due course carried through to Rhagae and round into Armenia. By midsummer of 521, less than ten months after the coup d'état, the worst of the fighting was over save in the north-east, and the hopes of a revived Median empire were at an end. Exemplary punishment was meted out to the rival kings ("Kings of the Lie"). The losses of the insurgents in some of the battles are recorded in the Babylonian and Aramaic versions of the Behistun text. In four battles on the Armenian fronts 12,000 or so were killed or taken prisoner, a similar number in

---

[1] Herodotus knew that "things flared up" after the accession of Darius, but the Behistun inscription is our sole authority for what actually happened.

CONSOLIDATION OF THE EMPIRE UNDER DARIUS

Parthia where Darius' father was in command, and on the southern front in Arachosia and Persis (where the pretended Bardiya and his followers fought a far-ranging campaign) perhaps about the same. In Media the fighting seems to have been heavier, the dead being innumerable and the prisoners reckoned at 18,000 (or 108,000) in the battle at Kunduruš (presumably on the way up to Agbatana). Most surprising, however, are the figures for the battle fought by the satrap of Bactria, a Persian called Dādaršiš, against the rebels under Frāda in Margiana: barely 7,000 prisoners but 55,243 dead. If these numbers are to be accepted, we may wonder whether the Sakā of the steppes had not been brought in in a do-or-die effort to put an end to Persian rule in Upper Asia. It is noteworthy that Darius' first campaign after his accession wars were over was against the Pointed-hood Sakā, whose captured leader Skunkha is depicted at the end of the line of "Kings of the Lie" in the relief at Behistun (see plate 34).

The Persian satraps in the far western provinces of Asia Minor and Egypt were not involved in the clashes of rivals, though Oroites in Sardis took the opportunity to avenge an insult on the satrap of the Hellespontine region and bring practically the whole of peninsular Asia Minor under his control.[1] When victory was complete Darius was faced with the problem of disciplining the satraps who had not supported him. A full-scale expedition against them might have provoked widespread revolts, and diplomatic action was therefore to be preferred. To Sardis he dispatched one of his nobles, who tested the allegiance of the Persian guard there and found a means to have Oroites killed (below, p. 298). Aryandes seems for the time being to have been too strong to be attacked; for though Egypt is listed among the lands which rebelled while Darius was in Babylon (Behistun inscription), there is no word of fighting there, and Aryandes was not removed. It is of course possible that it was Egyptian patriots, and not the satrap, who rejected Darius' rule; but it was on the charge of rebellion that Darius had Aryandes put to death ten years or so later, and Herodotus expressly remarks that he was not rebelling at the time. The issue is complicated by Herodotus' statement that Aryandes caused offence by issuing his own silver coinage, for which no satisfactory explanation can be given. Aryandes had in the meantime subjected Libya to Persian rule.

Darius' wars of accession were followed by wars of conquest. The

---

[1] According to Herodotus (III. 127) Oroites then held both the Phrygian satrapy and the Lydian and Ionian one.

first to be attacked – evidently in 519 B.C. – were the Pointed-hood Sakā, who (as we have suggested) may have taken part in the great insurrection in Margiana in the winter of the previous year. They evidently lived in the steppes of modern Turkestan east of the Caspian. The enemy resisted, and Darius records making a sea or open-water crossing in order to bring them to battle. It has long been clear that this cannot refer to Darius' Scythian expedition beyond the Black Sea, for that took place some years later; and the majority of recent scholars have assumed that what Darius did was to ferry troops across the corner of the Caspian; but there can be no certainty because the Egyptian text of Darius' Suez inscriptions refers to "Sakā of the Marsh". Darius ended by capturing the big chief Skunkha and replacing him with a nominee of his own.

The Greek Polyaenus of the 2nd century after Christ, author of a miscellany of stratagems selected on merit rather than authenticity, makes Darius undertake an expedition to Egypt to quell a revolt, and many scholars have accepted this as historical and dated it in 518 B.C. at the end of his wars of accession. Fitting, as the stratagem requires, with the known date for the death of an Apis bull, this could be correct, though the Suez canal project, which has been claimed as resulting from it, could have suggested itself to Darius when he passed that way in the army of Cambyses.

The eastern lands called Gandāra and Thataguš (Herodotus' Sattagydians) had been incorporated in the empire either by Cyrus or by one of his Median predecessors; and though the position of Thataguš is not known there can be little doubt that the empire already reached to the confines of the Indus. The Behistun inscription, however, names Thataguš among the lands which had revolted in 522/521 B.C., and there is no mention there of any steps taken to recover it. It may be that the revolt faded out. But the necessary action may equally well have been deferred until a full-scale expedition could be mounted. In the next official list of subject lands, at Persepolis (DPe), a new name Hi(n)duš is added, and it is clear that by this time (apparently before Darius invaded Europe) the expedition had occurred of which Herodotus succinctly remarks that Darius "conquered the Indians". The new land perhaps comprised the Indus valley in Sind, bounded on the east by the desert which closely accompanies the ancient course of the river there. According to Herodotus the expedition was preceded by a voyage of reconnaissance under the guidance of Scylax of Caryanda in Caria,

CONSOLIDATION OF THE EMPIRE UNDER DARIUS

who sailed down the Indus to its mouth and coasted round in thirty months to Suez.[1] Apropos of this, Herodotus remarks that large parts of Asia were discovered by Darius.

We have now reached a date perhaps about 514 B.C. on our reckoning. Darius' arduous and on the whole unrewarding ventures in Europe lie ahead and will be taken up in the next chapter. In Asia the empire had reached its limits. It had for the most part been easily won and, so far as we can tell, as easily absorbed. We know little of the steps that Cyrus took to organize it; and though he evidently set up his own satraps in preference to vassal kings on the Assyrian pattern, it seems likely enough that he made little change in the methods of administration that had prevailed under Median, Babylonian, and Lydian rule. His genial and forthright personality may have been the best guarantee of salutary government. Darius, on the other hand, had a talent for administration; and what he left to his successors after a 36-year reign was certainly a centralized, though not by any means integrated empire. Its general structure will be described in the later sections of this chapter; the remainder of the present one will be concerned only with those traits and policies in government that seem to reflect the peculiar genius of Darius himself.

A chance remark of Plato's in his notorious seventh letter has conferred on Darius the posthumous distinction of being the great law-giver of ancient Persia and thereby the conserver of its empire. This goes beyond the facts. Darius certainly did not originate a body of law for the Persians or for the Persian empire. But he did recognize the importance of codified law and was much concerned to have the regulations or patents that existed in the socially advanced provinces of the empire written down and transcribed for the use of officials there. This is most evident in Egypt, where a rescript of 518 B.C. to the satrap enjoined the formation of a commission to collect the law as it had stood in Pharaoh Amasis' 44th year (i.e. at the end of his reign) and translate it into the scripts of everyday use. In Ionia, however, where each lived by its own laws, Darius' brother Artaphernes is found encouraging the Greek cities to regulate their differences with one another by treaties.

At some date probably after 514 B.C. Darius introduced a royal Persian coinage in fine gold (known to the Greeks as darics) and silver

---

[1] IV. 44. Herodotus by his wording implies that Scylax was in charge: we should expect the supreme command to be vested in a high-ranking Persian.

(sigloi), both with the type of the mural-crowned King as archer (see pl. 12). It will have been used, as were the later satrapal coinages, to cover military expenditure. But Darius no doubt had more in mind than this; indeed, since in his re-organization of the satrapies he is credited with the fixing of the tribute due from each of them in silver, it is at first sight probable that the revenues were intended to be paid in the new coin. In effect, if this was his aim, it miscarried. So long as the empire lasted, it seems that only a small proportion of the gold and silver that went to swell the imperial treasuries was put back into circulation; there was a chronic shortage of cash in Babylonia in Achaemenid times, and the royal coinage hardly circulated at all in the eastern half of the empire. Indeed, it has recently been claimed that the royal silver coinage was only minted in western Asia Minor for use in the part of the empire that was accustomed to Greek coins, while bar-ingots and cut silver held their own elsewhere.

Darius carried out some works that may have been partly aimed at encouraging trade but more obviously served strategical purposes. The voyage of discovery from the Indus to Suez (that of Scylax of Caryanda) was eventually followed by the opening of a Suez waterway which owed its inspiration to the works of earlier Pharaohs and was proclaimed in the usual phrase "Never was the like done before". It led from the Nile by Bubastis to the Arabian gulf at Suez. The excavated canal was wide enough for two ships to pass, and the stelae that commemorated its completion speak of two dozen or more vessels setting out with tribute for Persia. There seems to be no doubt that Darius was particularly interested in the use of the sea; for we also know that not later than about 513 B.C. he sent a small flotilla with the doctor Democedes as guide to reconnoitre the Greek and south Italian coasts, he had a fleet accompany him to the Danube mouth on his Scythian expedition, and in 490 B.C. a complete sea-borne expedition with horse transports was launched against Eretria and Athens and returned safely after the defeat at Marathon. As we have seen, Darius may possibly have taken the opportunity to build a fleet on the Caspian during his early campaign against the Pointed-hood Saka. No doubt, like Alexander the Great and in more recent times Nādir Shāh (both of whom also set to work to build a fleet on the Caspian), Darius kept ships on the Persian Gulf (scholars in fact now incline to the belief that he transplanted Ionians and Carians to the head of the gulf to serve his naval aims); Herodotus speaks of him "using" the Indian Ocean after Scylax's voyage of reconnaissance; the islands of the Persian Gulf were occupied

CONSOLIDATION OF THE EMPIRE UNDER DARIUS

as penal settlements; and of course the Susa palace inscription shows building materials being transported on the river system of Mesopotamia. In the event little came of all this. The Persians were not a maritime people (Herodotus pleasantly notes this when he makes Xerxes' cautious uncle Artabanus remark "They say that winds stir up the sea"); when the Greeks reached the Indian Ocean nearly two centuries later they found the torrid coasts devoid of harbours and shipping, and by that time it was believed that Darius' canal had never been completed.

The most striking characteristic of Darius as a ruler was the personal attention that he gave to imperial affairs. He seems to have had something in the nature of a staff of specialists on provincial affairs whom he could retain as advisers or send out to act as his agents. Udjahorresne, the priest of Neith at Sais, collaborator of Cambyses, and King's chief doctor, was Darius' principal adviser on Egyptian matters, and perhaps also his counterweight against the power of the satrap; Histiaeus of Miletus was his expert on Aegean affairs and was dispatched to the spot at the climax of the Ionian revolt; Zerubbabel of the old royal house of David may have been sent from the Persian court to be governor of Judaea; an exiled Spartan king, Demaratus, was welcomed at the court, and a Mede, Datis, seems to have received a high commission on account of his connections with the free Greeks beyond the imperial frontier. The letter of Darius to his governor Gadatas, recorded in a later inscription at Magnesia on the Maeander, shows the King administering a rebuke because the privileges of the local priesthood had been curtailed,[1] and at the same time expressing approval of attempts to introduce new fruit trees from Syria. In Egypt we find the temple college at Sais, where theology and medicine were taught, being restored by Udjahorresne at the King's command, several temples being constructed, and Darius likewise concerning himself with the qualifications for appointments to the higher priestly offices. No less characteristic was his personal interest in manoeuvres aimed against the free Greeks of Europe and the islands, of which several examples are recorded. It is no surprise to find Herodotus observing that when Darius was firmly seated on the throne "everything was filled with power [*dynamis*]". In fact, Darius thought big and he made things hum.

In attempting to complete our estimate of the character of Darius'

---

[1] To judge by the results, the policy of winning support for Persian rule through concessions to the responsible priesthoods proved less successful among the Greeks than it had done in Babylonia and Egypt.

rule we have a little more help from Herodotus. The word *aplestos* ("insatiable", and so lacking in self-control) is used in two contexts only by the historian – one of Cyrus when Queen Tomyris is made to call him "insatiable of blood", the other of Darius when he is dubbed "insatiable of money" in the cautionary tale of Nitocris' tomb above the gate of Babylon. We may also suspect that a quality which the Persians recognized in Darius was mendacity; for Herodotus knew that they set great store by speaking the truth, but in his account of the deliberations of the Seven he put into Darius' mouth a lengthy, casuistical defence of lying to achieve one's ends. But the most illuminating phrase is that in which Herodotus says the Persians accounted Cyrus a father, Cambyses a tyrant, and Darius a "shopkeeper" (*kapelos*, i.e. retailer of wares as opposed to *emporos* = merchant). Apologists of Darius have seen it as a testimonial of good management, and this quality could hardly be denied to him. But an Aryan nobility which eschewed buying and selling would not have intended the word as a compliment; the implication is that Darius was not the mirror of Aryan chivalry. Monuments and inscriptions also provide evidence of Darius increasing the distance that separated him from his subjects,[1] and he seems to have shown little respect for the dignity of his satraps. His conception of rule was expressed in his own phrase: "what was said to them by me both night and day that was done".

Thirty years ago Schaeder argued that the effect of Darius' reforms and policies was to transform an Aryan kingship into an oriental monarchy, and he sought the seeds of decay there rather than in the corruption of the court under his successors. This view was vigorously opposed by Junge in his full-length biography of Darius. But, for all his learning, Junge can be seen to have overlooked the evidence in Herodotus. More recently Toynbee has thought to find a serious change for the worse in the necessity that circumstances imposed on Darius of abandoning Cyrus' policy of rule by consent in favour of repressive partitioning. It would at least be fair to say that while it may have been suited to his own capacities, Darius' style of government was not one that adapted itself well to the rule of less determined and industrious

---

[1] The Gadatas letter shows him addressing his governor as his "slave" (*doulos*). Some scholars have assumed that Gadatas must have been a royal slave set in a high position in his master's service. But in the Behistun inscription a like term (bandaka) is applied by Darius to his generals and satraps, including some of the Seven; and Herodotus confirms the usage by making Xerxes speak of Pelops as "the slave of my forefathers". Cf. Xen., *Anab.* II. 5, 38, where Cyrus the Younger is spoken of as the slave of his brother, the King. So too, according to Chardin, the courtiers of the Safavids called themselves slaves.

men. Nevertheless the fact remains that the empire which he moulded continued in the hands of the Achaemenid house for a hundred and fifty years after his death.

IV. THE PERSIAN COURT

In his *Persae* of 472 B.C. Aeschylus makes the chorus address Darius' widow Atossa as consort of a god and mother of a god; and the Alexander historian Aristobulus is reported as saying that every month a horse was sacrificed at Cyrus' tomb by the Magi who guarded it. Consequently, it is sometimes claimed that the Achaemenids were worshipped as divine. This is false. Except in Egypt, where like other rulers they began by conforming to the native traditions, there is no question of the Achaemenids having been gods either after death or during their lifetimes. On the other hand, the inscriptions of Darius and his successors represent the King as receiving his kingdom from the great god Ahuramazda as a sovereign imperium. All men under the King's rule were his slaves. He had power of life and death. All property was at his disposal.[1] He was the fountainhead of justice, and it was axiomatic that he could do no wrong.

The pinnacle of power was a lonely perch. The King was required to live mainly in seclusion, to dine in an inner room separated by a curtain from his table companions, to meet his subjects in circumstances that prohibited frank discourse, to allow no one to rival him in the display of physical prowess, to reward or requite on a scale commensurate with his exalted station, never to revoke an order or go back on a promise. A strong ruler like Darius I might break through the shackles of absolute power, the more so if the system was largely of his own making. But his successors seem too readily to have let themselves become prisoners of court protocol, rigid canons of behaviour, and a mentality conditioned by the obligations of a royal code of honour, by the obsequiousness of those around them, and finally by the encroachment of corruption and treachery. Herodotus evidently understood much of this; and it enabled him to give a by no means unsympathetic

---

[1] In practice of course private ownership of land and property was normally respected. What the Kings personally owned was what they themselves inherited, what had belonged personally to rulers whom they conquered, and what fell to them by confiscation. King's land in the satrapies was often granted in feu to relatives, nobles, and deserving supporters and warriors (with obligations of military service proportionate to their standing); but much was managed for the King by agents or royal factors, and revenues accrued to the crown from, for instance, fisheries, canals, and water supply.

presentation of Xerxes. In particular, when he first brings him onto the stage at the beginning of Book VII he represents him as declaring himself in honour bound to engage in some great enterprise that would render his glory equal to that of his forefathers; and he later shows him as falling a prey to counsellors who say only what they think the King would wish to hear.

The Persian King had no equal in the world and so could not marry outside his own circle. We know of six wives of Darius I. But five of them were taken after he came to the throne; and they were alliances of policy, one being to a daughter of one of the Seven, and three to the princesses in whose veins flowed the last of the blood of Cyrus. Herodotus tells us that the one Darius loved best was the previously unmarried Artystone, and it was to her that he is found making gifts of 2,000 quarts of wine and a hundred sheep in "Fortification" tablets of spring 503 B.C. (at the time of the New Year festival) at Persepolis.[1] But we learn that the wife who exerted most power was Atossa, the mother of Xerxes. Junge speaks of her as the "Königin des Reichs", thus making us think of the "Queen of Queens" under the Sasanids and of more recent titles like the "Glory of the Empire" (the mother of the heir apparent) under the Qājārs. There is in fact no certain evidence of any such official title; but we do find that the mother of the heir apparent or (if alive) of the King held a dominant position in the royal household and was treated with such respect that in later times she might even impose her will against the King's. Indeed, the impression that we obtain is that the successors of Darius, or at least of Xerxes, became monogamous; and we should be chary of assuming that the position accorded to women generally in Persian family life and society was a low one. For his private enjoyment the King kept a harem, to which girls were sent up on approval from the provinces (though not, so far as we know, in accordance with specifications of ideal beauty such as one Sasanian king circulated to his satraps). The concubines were reckoned at around 360 – a figure that is niggardly by Sasanian and Safavid standards. Heracleides of Cyme spoke of them as sleeping by day so that at night they could watch over the King with music and song by lamplight. Those in a condition to travel accompanied the King

[1] Artystone bore Darius two sons who appear as army commanders in 480 B.C. Darius is also said by Herodotus to have had a statue of beaten gold made of her (VII. 69). The Persepolis tablets show that she owned a village estate with a tapestry factory and also a palace (at Kuganaka) in Persis; and no doubt she had a detachment of troops assigned to her. In 498 B.C. she entertained Darius in Persis (as the seal shows, at his expense).

on safari, being transported in closed carriages so that they should not be visible to ordinary human eyes. Service was provided by eunuchs; and as under the Qājārs there was no admittance to the harem save for the doctors (mostly foreign) in attendance at the court.

In general, the succession to the throne was by primogeniture.[1] But the principle was breached by Darius I when he designated his eldest son out of Cyrus' lineage as his successor on the pretext of his being the first born to him as King; and Cyrus the Younger may thus have had a precedent when he contested the throne with his elder brother in 401 B.C. The succession in fact was not often peaceful, nor was the tenure of the throne always secure. If we are to believe the Greek writers, four – and if we count Bardiya, five – of the thirteen Kings seem to have been murdered, and at least half a dozen of them to have reached the throne through intrigues of their own or of others. On the other hand, only the ruthless Artaxerxes III (Ochus) behaved like the Parthians and Ottomans and put all possible rivals to death; and there is no evidence of the Achaemenids adopting what, referring to Shāh 'Abbās's predecessors, Sir Anthony Sherley at the end of the 16th century called the less inhumane practice of blinding them. The stability of the throne was achieved through the longevity of those Kings who weathered the storm of their accession; in the first two centuries of the monarchy four of the Kings between them reigned for a total of a hundred and fifty years.

The royal princes received a healthy upbringing along with the sons of the chief nobles. But it is not clear what training they gained for the exercise of the royal power. Cyrus and Darius I each designated his own successor, and had him accepted as king of Babylon, though like the viceroyship of Tabrīz in late Qājār times this may have been a sinecure. It could be that some of the heirs to the Achaemenid throne were confined within an orbit of court ceremonial and sporting activities that gave them little experience of administration and affairs; but the evidence is not really of a kind to throw light on the matter. Like the Sasanids, the Achaemenid Kings did not give their daughters in marriage abroad, for they recognized no equals among the princes of the earth. Princesses of the royal blood were, however, often married to Persian nobles, who were not always happy to receive them; and this

---

[1] This statement is based on practice rather than on any ascertained principle. We do not know whether in theory the Persian host had the power of approving or acclaiming; but under the empire this would have been unworkable.

may sometimes have been used as an instrument of royal policy, as when Pharnabazus was brought from a career of honourable service in the West to become the King's son-in-law.

By his six known wives Darius I had at least twelve sons whom he might "make princes in all lands", and eight of them appear in high commands under Xerxes in the expedition of 481–480, while another two fell at Thermopylae. But Darius was a usurper and the founder of a dynasty, whereas his successors did not lack for kinsmen. Artaxerxes I, on the authority admittedly of Ctesias, had only one "legitimate" son. But on the other hand he had seventeen sons by his concubines, and Artaxerxes II is said to have had 115 sons (with three "legitimate"). The offspring of the concubines did not normally rank in the succession; but the accumulated progeny of the harem might well have constituted a serious social problem, as under the Qājārs when what Curzon calls a "plague of royal drones" infested the land with their palaces and harems, occupying the lucrative appointments in the provinces. There is little trace of any such "Shāhzades" in our sources. But in Curtius Rufus' description of Darius III's order of march (III. 3. 9–25), which affords some interesting contrasts to that of Xerxes as described by Herodotus, the King is escorted by the 200 noblest of his *propinqui* and preceded by an elegant regiment of 15,000 *cognati* (it is perhaps not inappropriate to recall that 15,000 is also the number that we find given in the 4th-century Greek writers for the regular complement of diners at the King's table, though one may wonder where they were accommodated).[1] So we may perhaps surmise that, to the great benefit of the empire, the generations of royal progeny were retained to swell the ranks of pensioners at the court, where they would act as escort to the King and scour the countryside when he went hunting. Reliefs of Persepolis enable us to imagine them thronging the palace balustrades as they ascended in their costume to the banquet (see pl. 33).

Many Greeks at different times went up to the court, and not a few lived there for years. The King's person, the ceremonial, and the spectacle of unimaginable wealth and luxury excited their curiosity. If the Persians considered the Greeks parsimonious, unable to lay beds fit to sleep in and finishing their meals before the serious work of eating had begun, the Greeks on their side found matter for moralizing and

---

[1] Heracleides of Cyme tells us that the soldiery was fed in the courtyard. It is of course possible that the number of diners is exaggerated; it is considerably greater than that for which the kitchens of the Ottoman imperial palace in Istanbul could cater.

ridicule in the life of the Persian court. But admiration and envy were never far away. There was quite a body of literature in Greek on such matters, and later writers like Athenaeus excerpted enough from it to give us an impression of life at the court. The detail may often be exaggerated; and certainly when it comes to scandals such as Ctesias retails, we may question whether the sources of information were much more reliable than those which inform the disclosures in contemporary French newspapers about the private life of royalty in countries where the institution of monarchy flourishes. In this chapter we may ignore the scandals. But a brief survey of the court is necessary to an understanding of the Achaemenid regime. It is true that we know very little of the Persian court before the reign of Darius I; and a moralizing tradition as old as Herodotus has delighted in contrasting the luxury of the court as the Greeks knew it with the supposed frugality of Cyrus the Great's time. But we lack the evidence to support this notion of pristine simplicity. So far as we can judge, there may have been some change in moral standards during Achaemenid times, but in their outward forms Persian customs and institutions seem to have remained immutable.

The King's person was decked in such colourful splendour as to conjure up the image of a peacock. If we may simply follow Xenophon, he wore a long purple robe, full-sleeved and embroidered with designs in gold, on top of a striped tunic and crimson trousers – this almost sounds like a winter dress. The head-gear that distinguished the King from all others was a tall flat-topped cap (*kidaris*), probably of felt, with a scented blue and white ribbon. In his hand he held a golden sceptre, and out of doors a parasol was supported over his head. The throne was high, provided with a footstool and a purple canopy resting on columns. Choice unguents and cosmetics were liberally applied to the King's person, and jewellery hung from his neck, ears, and wrists. Plutarch speaks of 12,000 talents of silver (about £3 million gold) as the value of what Artaxerxes II stood up in. Reliefs at Persepolis give us some impression of the King's stature and poise; and those in which Xerxes (if it is he) is shown as the crown prince standing behind his father's throne (see pl. 23) fit so well with the majestic appearance that as King he presented in his battle array before Thermopylae[1] that Junge

---

[1] Herodotus VII. 187: "among so many myriads of his men there was not one who for beauty and stature was more victory-worthy than Xerxes himself to hold this sway". Herodotus, however, may have had in mind the comparison with Homer's Agamemnon, just as Aeschylus in his *Agamemnon* may have had Xerxes in his mind's eye.

declared him justly reckoned the handsomest man in Asia. This would apply equally if the King on the Treasury reliefs were Xerxes himself.[1]

The Greeks believed that the Persian court style was derived from the Medes. This is confirmed by the Median words and forms in the titulature and structure of government, and it explains the transmission of artistic motifs (and in the Cyrus cylinder literary usage) that seem to be Assyrian rather than Babylonian. Scholars have recently tended to stress the assumed connection between Cyrus' Anšan and Elam, and therefore look to Susa as a principal source;[2] and we can certainly say that Elamite was used for royal rescripts and palace documents at Persepolis (below, p. 235). Under the command of the chiliarch (*hazārapatiš*) a corps of pages with wands served as ushers. Persons admitted to the royal presence made obeisance (the *proskynesis* which was so unacceptable to Greek notions of equality); hands were buried in the sleeves, and servants in close attendance were muffled so that their breath should not touch the King. Reliefs show menials of the court bearing parasol and fly-whisk, napkin and scent bottle; flowers are carried, and censers are near at hand (see pl. 31). When the King crossed the palace courts Lydian carpets were laid down, which no one else might tread on. When he went to his chariot a golden stool was set for him to mount. The King would not go on foot outside the palace, and indeed we are told that any Persian noble would mount on horseback to cover even the shortest distance – a habit that has died hard.

For the King and his 15,000 fellow diners a great assortment of livestock was served at table, including camels and ostriches. Satraps and governors were likewise expected to entertain according to their rank; as governor in Jerusalem, Nehemiah fed 150 notables, and 150 appears later to have been a regular figure for the followers of Iranian nobles (and curiously, in Josephus, of that Jesus whose kingdom was not of this world). We might surmise that 1,500 would have been a suitable figure at satrapal courts. We can gain an impression of the furnishings from the descriptions of the field mess-kits of Persian nobles

---

[1] Since this was written it has been shown that the Treasury reliefs were originally intended for the Apadana stairs, where they would have faced the approaching delegations of the subject peoples. Consequently the dating to Darius' reign is no longer certain, and the King on the reliefs could possibly be Xerxes. For the reliefs cf. Farkas, *Achaemenid Sculpture*, 38ff, 117–19; A. B. Tilia, "Recent discoveries at Persepolis", *AJA* LXXXI (1977), 69.

[2] Especially for court costumes and accoutrements (see Hinz, *Altiranische Funde und Forschungen*, 68ff.). H. von Gall has most recently sought to recognize three different types among the men-at-arms in the Persian robe on the reliefs and identify them with Herodotus' three principal Persian clans or tribes (*AMI* v (1972), 261ff.).

THE PERSIAN COURT

like that of Mardonius which was captured by the Greeks at Plataea (Herodotus IX. 70. 80–3), with costly fabrics, gold and silver vessels, beds and tables, even a bronze manger for the horses. In the field there was a complement of ferrashes, bakers, pastry-cooks, perfumers, chaplet-weavers, drink-mixers and wine attendants, at home also a host of porters, chamberlains, and domestics, who may have been largely eunuchs, and of course scribes, store-keepers, and guards. The Persians are said to have had a passion for gold cups (three or four tons of golden and gem-encrusted cups were captured in Darius III's treasure after Issus), while according to Ctesias those who were in disgrace were punished by being served off terracotta. Like Nebuchadnezzar and Assyrian kings before him, the Persian King had his own special Helbon wine from the vineyards on the slopes above Damascus; he also had bread from wheat of Assos in the Troad, salt from the oasis of Ammon, and scented thorn oil from Karmania. A portable ointment chest of Darius III acquired fame, having been captured by Alexander the Great; among the royal unguents we hear of a skin cream of gum-ladanum boiled in lion's fat, to which were added saffron and palm wine. The King had water sent up to him from rivers under his sway like the Nile and (we are told) Danube. But when he travelled he was too fastidious to drink the local water, and a train of mule carts carried boiled "golden water" from the river of Susa (Choaspes) in silver urns for his personal consumption. Wine was drunk to excess by the noble Persians, but their conduct at banquets did not become disorderly.

The King dined to music and singing. The Persians danced for exercise, and the King danced the shield dance (*persikon*) annually in a state of intoxication on the festival of Mithra. As in other oriental courts, novelties were eagerly sought after, and the inventors of new dishes or amusements were given prizes.[1] There is some uncertain ground for the belief that wood carving was a favourite hobby of the Kings (Shāh 'Abbās too found recreation in such manual skills). Hunting was much affected by the Persians; like the Assyrian rulers, the King and his satraps maintained paradises (parks) with game of various kinds which could be driven into nets for the killing, and landscape gardening was not beneath the dignity of a royal prince. According to Xenophon, Cyrus the Younger was reported as telling Lysander that he hâd himself

---

[1] The King's habit of awarding prizes is frequently referred to and evidently caused some amusement to the Greeks; the name of the place Gaugamela, where Alexander defeated Darius III, was explained on the ground of the pasturage there having been given as a prize to the camel that performed best in Darius I's commissariat on the Scythian expedition.

planted trees in his park at Sardis and that he would never dine without having sweated from some exercise of military training, gardening, or the like.

Conflicting opinions are held on the subject of the religion of the Achaemenids. The Old Persian inscriptions show that Darius I and his successors acknowledged the special protection of a single all-powerful god Ahuramazda, who is generally recognized as the symbolic figure in an Assyrian mode which is seen hovering overhead on their reliefs and receiving the King's adoration at a fire altar (see pls 31, 32).[1] In the Elamite text of the Behistun inscription Ahuramazda is called the "god of the Aryans", and the revelation of his supremacy by Zoroaster was presumably known to Darius. On the monuments the god – if such it is – is depicted in the likeness of a winged bust of the King, and one is tempted to say that the Achaemenid rulers appropriated him as their house god. It is probable that other Iranian gods were also worshipped, and that under Xerxes the sacred haoma drink had a place in court ritual. But for four generations none are named in surviving royal inscriptions; and it is not until the reign of Artaxerxes II that Anahita and Mithra, the deities most widely worshipped by the Persians in the empire, take their place alongside Ahuramazda. Religious ceremonies seem normally to have been conducted by Magi, who attended the King and were the interpreters of portents.

The Achaemenid reliefs show high-ranking Persians in attendance on the King; the chiliarch (hazārapatiš), the King's bow-and-quiver-bearer (who at Naqsh-i Rustam also carries the royal battle-axe), and the King's spear-bearer. The King's charioteer was another noble. It would seem that the most important of the court officials was the hazārapatiš (= commander of a thousand). The title is known to us in Greek sources, and it involved not only the command of the palace guard but the regulation of royal audiences. Junge, to whom we owe the most detailed study of the office, recognized the hazārapatiš in the sceptred usher depicted in military costume facing the King on Achaemenid audience reliefs (see pl. 23). On the evidence of the Greek writers this seems probable enough. Junge went on to contend that the treasury came under the hazārapatiš' jurisdiction; and indeed he assigned him control of finance and the chancery, not to mention the presidency of the King's council, thus making him in effect a grand vizier. These claims

[1] For details of offerings to Ahuramazda and other deities as attested in tablets of Darius I's reign at Persepolis see W. Hinz, *Orientalia* XXXIX (1970), 427–30.

seem to have been overpitched; certainly the connection with the treasury now falls to the ground. But this is not to deny the importance of the office, which is likely to have increased under weak Kings and was indispensable enough to be taken over by the Macedonians and continued in use in Sasanian times. If Prexaspes, who appears in Herodotus as Cambyses' right-hand man, was hazārapatiš, it was hardly less important in early Achaemenid times.

The Greek noun *epitropos* (or the corresponding verb) is applied several times by Herodotus to persons placed in a position of special trust by the King. Scholars have noted that the name that he gives to the Magus whom Cambyses left as *epitropos* of his household when he went to Egypt, Patizeithes, could be a Persian title, and have related it to a word, pitiakhš or the like, used to denote an official of the Sasanian court with a role corresponding perhaps to King's deputy or vice-regent at home or in the field. The difficulty in assuming that such an office existed under the Achaemenids is that Herodotus is clearly referring to a temporary arrangement for supervision in the King's absence and certainly had no thought of a regular office in the Persian contexts where he used the word *epitropos*. There are similar objections to Benveniste's view that there was an official position of Second to the King in the Achaemenid power structure. Most recently Lewis[1] has subjected these posts at the Persian court to a more critical appraisal.

Better established is the official known as the "King's Eye". This curious title is frequently mentioned by the Greeks, to whose sense of the ridiculous it evidently appealed. Occurring as it does in Aeschylus and Aristophanes, as well as Herodotus, the existence of this specific title in the 5th century B.C. can hardly be denied. The King's Eye had his place beside the King, on whose behalf he saw and reported. Xenophon in his *Cyropaedia* insists that the King had a plurality of "eyes" and "ears", in the sense of informers; and elsewhere he speaks of men of trust sent by the King to inspect peoples at a distance. But we cannot tell whether he is speaking from firsthand knowledge. Herodotus would date the use of a network of royal spies and listeners back to the foundation of the Median kingdom (I. 100). Various other titles of officials have been more or less conjecturally restored from Akkadian documents by Eilers and Benveniste; but as yet they do not add to our understanding of the system of government.

That the King will have been in a position to summon a council to

[1] Lewis, *Sparta and Persia*, 15–20. On epitropos as a rendering of OP framānadāra "Befehlshaber", see I. Gershevitch, *AMI* suppl. x (1983), 51–6.

advise him goes without saying. To speak of a "council of ministers", however, goes beyond the evidence. The phrase might be used of the Sasanians. But we know of nothing to suggest that that sort of specialization of functions existed in Achaemenid times; and the newly propounded notion of a federal diet of representatives of the subject peoples is not to be entertained, though we might imagine that when visiting a satrapy the King would hold a durbar like that summoned by Alexander in Bactria. Herodotus represents Xerxes as calling the noblest Persians into conference to approve the project of invading Greece (VII. 8) and also holding councils of war in the field, Cambyses as summoning the noblest Persians in his train to hear his last instructions (III. 65), and Darius as calling the noblest Persians together to depute one of them to proceed against Oroites (III. 127). But he knows of no regular council of state; and elsewhere, as in the book of Nehemiah, the Kings are represented as making policy decisions single-handed. Curiously, Ezra's firman represents him as undertaking his mission to establish the law in Jerusalem with the authority of the King and his seven counsellors (VII. 14), and the Book of Esther – a post-Achaemenid *hieros logos* – knows of "seven Princes of Persia and Media which saw the King's face, and which sat the first in the kingdom" (I. 14). The mention in Esther could be taken for a literary allusion to the seven paladins with their direct access to the King. It caused an earlier generation of scholars to assume that the heads of the seven families formed a council of state. But we must note that they would only have been six apart from the King, and five after Darius destroyed Intaphernes and his house; and the number of those available at any one time would have been further depleted through service as generals or governors in different parts of the empire. The notion of a Council of Seven has been generally discounted since its rejection by Meyer. But there is in fact one small piece of supporting evidence that has gone unnoticed: Xenophon relates that in the course of his march against Artaxerxes II, when he had already assumed the tall head-dress worn only by the King, Cyrus the Younger had occasion to court-martial a high Persian noble for treachery and summoned for the purpose a council consisting of the seven noblest of his Persians (*Anab*. VI. 4). We know from Herodotus that the King had a panel of royal judges at the court, who were appointed for life to judge cases and could be called upon to interpret the Persian law. It may be that they formed a council of seven, which served as a model for Cyrus and could have been called upon to approve the law that Ezra was to introduce. But this can only be a conjecture; it must not blind us to the fact that the King's word, however uttered, was binding, and his pledge inviolable; the machinations of local governors were frustrated when Cyrus' decree on the building of the Jerusalem temple was discovered at Agbatana, and as we shall later see the King's promise to irrigators of waste land, granting them the enjoyment of it for five generations, seems to have remained irrevocable to the end of Achaemenid times.

The workings of the Persepolis treasury between 509 and 458 B.C. are to some extent known from two finds of tablets in Elamite published by Cameron and Hallock (see Ch. 14). These are payment orders or record of issues in kind submitted to the treasurer of the royal household there and almost wholly concerned with wages (in kind and in silver), rations, and other expenses or deliveries. They provide much valuable information about the treasury and administrative services in Persis. But despite the tantalizing references to known people and places, little light is shed on either political or imperial matters. The Kings certainly had scribes at hand in the field to note down military statistics and deeds worthy to be rewarded; but we cannot uncritically accept Ctesias' claim to have read historical parchments (above, p. 205) or the bland mention in the Book of Esther of "memorials of the days" and the "book of the Kings of the Persians and Medes". Darius had a new cuneiform script invented for writing Persian (or, as he calls it, "Aryan");[1] though much less economical of space than Babylonian it was regularly used along with Elamite and Babylonian for the Achaemenid monumental inscriptions. The vehicle of imperial communications was, however, Aramaic, for whose use there is abundant evidence not only in the western half of the empire but at Persepolis and – to judge by post-Achaemenid usage – in the eastern satrapies also. Imperial correspondence was carried by royal couriers along the main roads of empire; the Fortification tablets at Persepolis hint at arrangements for their maintenance en route (with regular victualling stations between Persepolis and Susa), and sealings, presumably from documents, have come to light at satrapal centres such as Daskyleion and

---

[1] This is the most widely held view in what has become a controversial issue; it seems to have the support of the Elamite text of the Behistun inscription, and also of a reputed letter of Themistocles which is carefully researched if it is not genuine. It involves the assumption that the titles of Cyrus the Great in Old Persian at Murgab were inscribed a decade or more after his death; but we now have positive evidence that this was the case. Some scholars, including Hallock, prefer to have the script introduced by Cyrus the Great, some even by the Medes.

Memphis, as well as some lesser seats of administration. From the fact that the series of Treasury Tablets of Persepolis does not go down beyond the early years of Artaxerxes I's reign Cameron surmised that cuneiform ceased to be used there for accounting purposes and therefore that Aramaic was by that time completely established. The use of Aramaic will have meant a predominance of Semites, like Ezra, the Babylonian scribes of the Persepolis pay-roll, and the clerks of Samaria and Elephantine, in the personnel of chanceries and imperial bureaux.

The Greeks had a keen interest in education; and Herodotus, Xenophon, Plato, and Strabo give us accounts of Persian practice which are not in complete agreement with one another but have a good deal in common. We hear only of education for the sons of the upper class, who were brought up at the King's court or, in the provinces, at the courts of satraps. It is said to have lasted from the age of five, when boys were weaned from the harem, to twenty or upwards. Purely intellectual development had little part, and there was no place for reading and writing – Darius I, like Shāh 'Abbās, did not read. Emphasis was laid on speaking the truth and on learning the examples afforded by the legends; and older children might listen to the judgements of the royal justices. What were principally inculcated were the physical skills and virtues: riding, shooting the bow, and spear-throwing, together with hunting and tracking. The life in the open was hardy, and there was training in leadership for those who would most require it. The emphasis on military training accords with Darius I's own words about himself in the inscription on his tomb: "Trained am I both with hands and with feet; as a horseman I am a good horseman; as a bowman I am a good bowman, both afoot and on horseback; as a spearman I am a good spearman, both afoot and on horseback."[1] The other virtues on which Darius prides himself in the same place – his passion for justice, his self-control and understanding – are qualities that he ascribes to the favour of Ahuramazda and not to the Persian educational system. But that educational system did produce great gentlemen like Cyrus the Younger and Pharnabazus, who evoked the admiration of aristocratically orientated Greeks.

It is not clear where Cyrus the Great had his capital before he founded

[1] Kent, *Old Persian*, p. 140. These words were transmitted in a free translation by the Alexander historian Onesicritus, and lent themselves to good-humoured parody by later Greeks (as in Athenaeus x. 434 d, where we read that Darius I had inscribed on his tomb "I could drink much wine and I could carry it well" – a boast elsewhere attributed to the younger Cyrus).

THE PERSIAN COURT

Pasargadae on the battlefield where he defeated Astyages (see pls 5–7). There are some indications (in Herodotus I. 153, Ezra VI. 2, and Babylonian tablets) that the old Median capital of Agbatana was still a royal residence under Cyrus; the city seems to have been a customary summer residence of later Achaemenids. Babylon is said to have had the task of providing sustenance for the court for four months in the year and was probably the winter capital of the earlier Achaemenids; with numerous Persians settling there as judges, officials, and already before Darius I as property-owners, it must have ranked as the most important imperial city; a new palace was built there for the crown prince in the early 490s. From the time of Darius I, if not of Cambyses, the tombs of the Kings were up in Persis by the later Stakhr (see pl. 19); and before 511 B.C. Darius built a great fortified terrace four miles to the south, at which he and some of his successors constructed palaces. This latter is what is known as Persepolis. It is sometimes asserted that the Kings went there for the New Year festival at the vernal equinox and that the reliefs of the Apadana are realistic representations of a procession that actually took place there, with delegations of all the subject peoples coming with their gifts. It is however difficult to believe that (excluding Ctesias) the Greek writers before Alexander's time could have remained ignorant of Persepolis if delegations from Sardis, Yaunā, and Cyrenaica had been in the habit of travelling there annually. It seems likely that few of the Kings stayed there for any length of time, though Darius I evidently liked to visit the place and take the opportunity to call in on his favourite wife in passing.

More important of course was Susa, the old Elamite capital, which in Herodotus figures as the capital of Persis already under Cambyses. There Darius I seems to have had his administrative centre and built himself a palace in the course of his reign. On a hot open shelf little higher than the Tigris plain, this must have superseded Babylon as the winter capital. The Fortification tablets, of the middle years of Darius' reign, show travel to Susa as dropping to a minimum in the summer months. Two other metropolitan palaces of the Achaemenids are mentioned, both on the confines of Persis. The one was at Gabae, whose situation should be to the north of Persepolis, though on the evidence of Eumenes and Antigonus' campaign of 317–316 B.C. hardly as far north as Iṣfahān (the ancient Aspadana). The other, inland from Taoke on the Persian Gulf and so in the vicinity of the modern Burāzjān at the inner edge of the coastal shelf, was assumed by Junge to be a foundation of Darius I overlooking the "dockyard" he was presumed to have built. This palace seems to have been discovered accidentally in 1971; to judge by what has come to light it may date back to Cyrus.

Greek writers speak of the Kings as dividing their time between their main palaces, and it is the generally accepted view that they moved seasonally between three or four capitals. But the distances are great. It requires no deep study to reveal that the court would have spent a quarter of the year on the road; and it is difficult to see how chancery business could have been conducted in so bureaucratic a state without any permanent base, for we are not here dealing with a simple feudal monarchy like Plantagenet England. In fact we find that from Aeschylus (in 472 B.C.) onward Greek writers place the residence of the Persian Kings at Susa; and Herodotus speaks two dozen times of Susa when he is referring to the location of the Persian court. It is quite clear that in some cases he names Susa when what he means is the King's seat. If it were a matter of the Greeks only, we might think in terms of a literary convention. But the writers of the Old Testament, and above all Nehemiah, no less insistently place the court at "Shushan the palace". So we must assume that though a King might take a vacation elsewhere (especially at Agbatana in summer), Susa had become the normal recognized centre of government.

V. PERSIS

The land called Pārsa by the Persians and Persis by the Greeks was in general the mountain country rising over the north-east side of the Persian Gulf and enclosing the high basin in which Persepolis and Shīrāz are situated. The name survives as Fārs. Herodotus names ten clans or tribes which occupied this Persian homeland.[1] Only three of them, he says, were mobilized by Cyrus when he took the field against Astyages: the Maraphioi, the Maspioi, and – noblest of all – the Pasargadae, of which the Achaemenids were a sept. The last-named presumably occupied the region in which the palaces of Pasargadae and Persepolis were built. These three tribes were cultivators of the soil, and so also were three others – the Panthialaioi (perhaps at Sīrjān), the Derousiaioi,

---

[1] I. 125. Xenophon in the *Cyropaedia* (I. 2, 5) speaks of twelve Persian tribes but does not name them. Strabo speaks of five (XV. 727); but they do not seem to be tribes or clans in the same sense (his Patischoreis must be the Old Persian Pātišuvariš).

and the Germanioi whose name is known to us continuously from Darius I's inscription Susa f (Karmāna providing sissoo-wood for the palace) down to the existing name Kirmān. This would imply that Pārsa stretched futher to the east than the modern Fārs, though in Alexander the Great's time Karmania was a separate satrapy and extended south of Persis along the lower Persian Gulf west of Hurmuz. Herodotus ends his list with four nomadic tribes: the Daoi, Mardoi, Dropikoi, and Sagartioi. Of these the Dropikoi are unknown, and so also these Daoi though their name is doubtless the familar Dahā. The Mardoi that he speaks of were in the west of Persis next to the non-Persian Uxii. The name Sagartian is known from inscriptions of Darius and presents a problem that will be considered later (p. 284).

The name Pārsa seems to have belonged to the people before it belonged to the land, and from the geographical context (in Kurdistān) in which the name Parsūa occurs in the Assyrian records it has been conjectured that the Persians were immigrants who had not been settled in Persis for many generations before Cyrus the Great. The continuity of the titulature on the Babylonian Cyrus cylinder would perhaps suggest that the settlement dates back as far as his great-grandfather Čišpiš (Teispes). The remoter ancestor Hakhāmaniš (Achaemenes) was said to have been nurtured by an eagle (whence no doubt the royal standard of a gold eagle with wings displayed); whether or not he is too mythical a figure to be assigned a role in the historical establishment of the Persians, we can at least say that he is the backstop of the line. It is impossible to determine whether the various tribal groups that were recognized as Persian constituted a single block that had entered Persis together, or whether (as some scholars would believe) there was also a wave of immigration from north-eastern Iran. The archaeological evidence does not seem to be of a kind to throw light on this.

Persepolis, Pasargadae, and the palace inland from Taoke have already been mentioned. In fact a number of place names of Pārsa occur in the Behistun inscription and well over 100 in the Persepolis tablets. Persepolis itself was built as a fortified compound, and the treasury there may have been the principal store for the precious metals (as it certainly was in 331 B.C.). Hinz reckons that in 504 B.C. it had a guard of 200 men. Palace building was proceeding apace, and in 467/466 about 1,350 workers were employed there (mostly women and girls!). Royal building was also proceeding at Badrakataš; this is assumed to be the name of Pasargadae. A place Nupištaš ("inscribed (mount)") in the tablets has been proposed by Gershevitch and Hinz independently as corresponding to Naqsh-i Rustam, where the tombs of Darius I and three successors were carved in the cliff (see pl. 19). The name would no doubt have derived from the Elamite relief which preceded the Achaemenid tombs there. Work is reported as in process in tablets of about 497 and 493, and in 490, when Egyptian stone-workers were active there; there seem also to have been a treasury and temple there, and a paradise which yields pears and grapes. Some other place names recorded in Pārsa may be identified, mainly through resemblance to medieval and modern names, and with varying degrees of probability: Shīrāz (Tirazziš) and Nairīz (Narezzaš) in central Fārs, to the south-east Furg (Parga) and Tārum (Taravā), Rakkan (perhaps Arrajān near Behbahān, halfway to Susa), and possibly also Hunar, which Hinz places south of Mālamīr-Izeh. On the ground, tombs of Persian types have been found in the west, both north of Fahliyān and south of Kāzarūn; and archaeological survey has been revealing clusters of minor sites up the Kur basin and to west and south of Persepolis.

Hallock's study of the Persepolis Fortification tablets has induced a systematic investigation of the administrative system that was centred on Persepolis (see below, pp. 588ff.), and Hinz has given a detailed analysis of it in the years between 509 and 458 B.C.[1] It appears that in Pārsa Darius had a well graded hierarchy of officials. Very occasionally nobles of the highest rank appear in the tablets as present there, like Gobryas and Aspathines, the King's spear- and bow-bearer respectively. But the other persons named belonged to the Persepolis establishment, whose jurisdiction seems to have extended down into the border-country of Elam. The controller of the administration at Persepolis was evidently a high-ranking official, perhaps equivalent to a satrap, and maintaining a guard of 300 men. The first incumbent known was Pharnaces, son of Arsames, who held the office for at least a dozen years until 497 B.C. and may have been Darius' uncle; and the last named in the period covered by the tablets was Artasyras, who was appointed under Xerxes and continued in office after Artaxerxes I came to the throne. This high official had general charge of the treasury, the household, and the administrative service, though not apparently of the military establishment. Under him the head of the treasury in Persepolis had jurisdiction over the regional treasuries at a large number of places in Pārsa; these were not merely repositories, but also factories where

[1] See especially "Achämenidische Hofverwaltung", *ZA* LXI (1971), 260–311.

robes, furniture, tapestries, objects in precious metals, and probably leatherwork were produced, and the employees in each were numbered in scores and even hundreds. When silver was being transported in quantity a small detachment of troops accompanied it. There were five supply departments with stations in various places in Pārsa: they covered grain, livestock (sheep-raising being particularly important), wine and beer (the latter apparently preferred in the Elamite land), fruit (mainly dried, as dates, figs, and raisins), and poultry large and small. The officials in charge seem to have had deputies who did the hard work; and there was scope for transference between different branches of the service and even promotion. In the chancery the secretaries were largely Iranians who had a staff of scribes writing in Elamite and Aramaic. Persis, as Herodotus tells us, did not pay tribute; but Hinz finds some evidence of taxes paid in kind (livestock, wine, and fruit). Since this paragraph and the preceding one were written systematic study of the tablets has resulted in more detailed understanding both of the administration and of the relative positions of stations on and adjacent to the main route to Susa.[1]

In conjunction with archaeology, modern animal-bone, soil and vegetation studies in the field may be expected to provide increasingly precise information about the condition and use of the land in antiquity. But for the present we cannot dispense with the firsthand description by Greeks who actually traversed the country in the years immediately following the collapse of the Achaemenid empire.[2] These not only expand but correct the Herodotean commonplace that the homeland of the luxury-loving master race was rough, with little soil and neither

---

[1] Hinz, *Darius und die Perser, passim*; Dandamayev, "Forced labour", pp. 74–8; Lewis, *Sparta and Persia, passim*; idem, "Datis the Mede", *JHS* c (1980), 194–5; Hallock, "The use of seals"; idem, "Selected Fortification Tablets", *CDAFI* VIII (1978), 109–16; Briant, "L'élevage ovin"; all these add to our understanding, and in Hallock's case to the source material also. From a topographical point of view main road stations seem to have become more firmly fixed, but acceptable identifications (e.g. Tamukkan = Taoke, Nupištaš = Naqsh-i Rustam, and perhaps Badrakataš = Pasargadae) have become more questionable; the much frequented centre Matezziš (Uvādaičaya) is now located by Persepolis though this is hardly a possible position for the presumably identical Humadešu of Babylonian tablets. Recent gains are the discovery of Gobryas travelling in Persis in 498 B.C. with the King's daughter (Artozostre) who was married to his son Mardonius in Darius' expert on Greek affairs, Datis the Mede, travelling to Persepolis to report to the King in January 494 B.C. when the Ionian revolt was reaching its final stage; on this latter occasion Darius seems, as Lewis has ascertained, to have spent a large part of the year at Persepolis.

[2] Apart from Ctesias, who probably visited Persepolis as well as Agbatana in the King's train, no Greek writer shows first-hand knowledge of Pārsa in Achaemenid times; to judge by the Persepolis tablets, the arrangements for the authorization and maintenance of parties journeying on the imperial highway east of Susa were such as to make unofficial travel difficult, if not impossible.

vines nor figs. The fullest account is preserved in Arrian's *Indica*, where the context is that of Nearchus' voyage of reconnaissance from the Indus mouths to the head of the Persian Gulf in 325–324 B.C., and the description proceeds from the coast into the interior of Persis; but the only journey up-country that Nearchus is known to have made was further east when he went up from Hurmuz into Karmania to report to Alexander, and in fact Arrian seems to be using another source here. Three stages or climates are described. The first, on the gulf, was torrid; the ground was sandy and unfruitful, lacking any trees save for palms. The second, to the north of this, was an intermediate zone, with the seasons well tempered. The land was grassy, with damp meadows and vineyards; all fruits grew except the olive. There were gardens (paradises) of all kinds, and clear streams and lakes. Water birds and horses flourished, and the grazing for stock was good. In many places there were woods with game. Further north was the third stage, which was wintry and snow-bound. Strabo likewise (xv. 727, 729) speaks of the three stages, with camel-rearers on the inland fringes, and also of a fertile vale in the east of Persis adjacent to Karmania with the rivers of the Persepolis plain flowing through it (probably what is now the lake of Nairīz).

We may compare with this the account given in Diodorus (xix. 21) from Hieronymus of Cardia, who accompanied Eumenes on his campaigns in the years following Alexander's death. Eumenes had confronted Antigonus' army on the line of the River Kārūn (Pasitigris) south of Susa. After the intense midsummer heat had compelled his adversary to withdraw, Eumenes presently set out for Persepolis. The first part of the journey was across a hot plain which offered no sustenance. But after the "staircase" (*klimax*) was reached, the terrain was higher with a healthier air, and yielded fruits all the year round. There were many valleys, which were shady and planted with paradises of all sorts, glens with natural forest of every kind of tree, and sources of water gushing out. The inhabitants supplied the army's needs. They were the most warlike of all the Persians, being archers and slingers. Presumably, as Pliny's phrase *arduo montis ascensu per gradus* would imply, the *klimax* was a kotal with rock-cut steps, perhaps where the road takes to the mountains after reaching the Mārūn (see pl. 1*a*). Curtius Rufus (v. 4) also speaks of the long ridge of the Zagros being opaque and shady, of ravines by the Persian Gates which were so densely wooded as to be almost impassable, and of plane trees and poplars in the river valleys of Persis.

PERSIS

The south of Fārs, with its parallel rocky ranges which wall in several narrow cultivated valleys inland from the coast (now, as partly in antiquity, attached for administrative purposes not to Fārs but to the Karmanian litoral) and enclose a number of isolated pockets of good land further up-country, was probably not known to the Greek writers. But the sheltered western fold belt, with an oak-cover which is now relatively sparse, appears clearly in the descriptions of the intermediate zone. The road from Susa to Pārsa will have followed these long fold valleys as far as the royal lodge at Jinjān (by Fahliyān) on the Sorun (Zuhreh) river. But from there it presumably struck up into the mountains on the left, because if it had continued along the fold line like the modern road (see pl. 1b) the important centre at Shīrāz (Tirazziš) would have been named among the supply stations for travellers in the Fortification tablets. At the end of the empire, however, when the tribesmen were no longer under effective control, the longer southerly route may have been preferred.[1] Strabo's description of the three climatic stages seems to proceed from the inner end of the Persian Gulf eastwards to the high mountain barrier, so that the Persepolis basin is not assigned to a climatic stage but lies beyond all three. It was however fertile; and we may imagine that a richer vegetation diversified these plains which now merge imperceptibly into the waste and clothed the hill slopes that bound them.

In his derivative history of Alexander, Curtius Rufus was interested above all in the platitudes and rhetorical contrasts of the classroom; and in reading him we must be prepared for exaggeration. But we cannot ignore him, because it is he who has transmitted to us the story of a thirty-day campaign that Alexander undertook supposedly early in 330 B.C. before the spring thaw allowed him to move northward against Darius (v. 6). Braving storms and extreme cold, Alexander first set off into the interior. Dismounting, he traversed roads frozen with perennial snow or ice and trackless woods, the only inhabitants being pastoral people who lived in scattered huts; later he was able to take possession of many villages. Then he invaded the Mardi, a people more warlike than the other Persians, and different in their way of life. Their homes were caves dug in the mountains, and they lived off their flocks and the flesh of wild animals. The women were as fierce as the men, their dress above the knee, their hair unkempt, and their heads bound

---

[1] Sir Aurel Stein's "Persian Gates" defile (Tang-i Khas) up the valley from Fahliyān has served as the direct route into central Persis in various epochs. The southerly route, generally used in modern times, went round by Kāzarūn; but it has recently been superseded by a modern motor road which enters the mountains sooner through the spectacular gate of Tang Bu'l-ḥayāt.

with a bandeau which served also for a sling. The contrast with the passage in Diodorus betrays a difference of attitude on the part of the original narrators: Eumenes' companions were enjoying themselves, Alexander's were not. But it also serves to underline the very real contrast between summer and winter conditions; and it is thus easier for us to understand the hardiness that was an essential part of the Persian character.

VI. THE EXTENT OF THE EMPIRE

The names of peoples who composed the Achaemenid empire are listed in Old Persian texts and in Herodotus.

The oldest of the Persian lists is that in the preamble of the Behistun inscription (about 520 B.C.). The word with which Darius introduces it is *dahyāva*, which is taken to mean districts or lands; and it is mainly lands that are named in this first list (e.g. Pārsa = Persis). But on the façade of his tomb at Naqsh-i Rustam and on those of his successors the names appear as ethnics (e.g. *iyam Pārsa* = "this is the Persian"), and there each name refers to an individual figure in the relief of dais-bearers, so that the dahyāva are seen to correspond to peoples of distinctive dress and physical appearance. Darius' original list is as follows: Pārsa (Persis); Ūvja (Elam, Herodotus' "Kissian land"); Bābairuš (Babylon); Athurā (i.e. "Assyrians");[1] Arabāya (Arabia); Mudrāya (Egypt); *tayaiy drayahyā* ("who are at/in the sea"); Sparda (Sardis); Yaunā ("Ionians" = Greeks); Māda (Media); Armina (Armenia); Katpatuka (Cappadocia);[2] Parthava (Parthia); Zranka (Drangiana, no doubt the people called "Sarangai" in Herodotus); Haraiva (Areia); Uvārazmīy (Chorasmia); Bākhtriš (Bactria); Sugda (Sogdiana); Gandāra (Paruparaēsan(n)a in the Babylonian and Elamite);[3] Sakā (Sakai, Scyths);[4] Thataguš (land of Herodotus'

---

[1] Herodotus (VII. 63) speaks of the "Assyrioi" in Xerxes' army who were so called "by the barbarians"; but he seems in general to include the Babylonians in the term.

[2] Herodotus himself calls the Cappadocians by the name "Syrioi" but says (VII. 72) that the Persians call them "Kappadokai". The proposal to identify Katpatuka with Cataonia, and not Cappadocia, is therefore misconceived.

[3] Gandāra has recently been identified with Kandahar. The origin of the name Kandahar is quite uncertain; for we have no means of choosing between the three derivations that have been proposed (Alexandria, Gondopharron, and, by a conjectural migration of the name, Gandāra). But it is clear that Kandahar cannot have been in the dahyāuš of Gandāra because its situation on the Argandāb (Arachotos) river places it securely in Arachosia, which is a separate dahyāuš (Harauvatiš) (see below, p. 249).

[4] Sakā, and Yaunā are plurals in Old Persian, the inhabitants denoting the country.

THE EXTENT OF THE EMPIRE

Sattagydai); Harauvatiš (Arachosia); Maka. In all, twenty-three dahyāva: excluding Pārsa twenty-two.

There are changes in later lists, both in the order of citation (Māda and Ūvja being next to Pārsa, and the eastern lands generally coming higher up), and by the addition of new names which bring the total up to 30 or 31.[1] Hi(n)duš (Sind) appears for the first time, and Asagarta (Herodotus' Sagartioi) for the only time, in Darius Persepolis e; Putāyā (Libyans?), Kušiyā (Aethiopians), Karkā (Carians), and Skudra (Thrace?) make their first appearance in Darius Naqsh-i Rustam, Dahā (nomads of the north) and Ākaufačiyā (a mountain folk) in Xerxes Persepolis h. The lists show subdivisions of the Sakā and Yaunā entries: S.haumavargā (the "Amyrgian Sakai" of Herodotus, apparently = "haoma-drinkers"), S.tigrakhaudā ("pointed-hood wearers"), and (at Naqsh-i Rustam) S.paradraya (= "beyond the sea" and apparently in a western context, so evidently the Scythians of Europe whose territory Darius had raided but not occupied): the Yaunā (Greeks) in Darius Persepolis e have three locations, on the mainland, by (or in) the sea, and beyond the sea (apparently repeated in Susa e and Xerxes Persepolis h), while in Darius Naqsh-i Rustam they are divided into Yaunā unspecified and Yaunā takabarā (apparently "(shield-shaped) sun-hat wearers", so probably of northern Greece). The dais-bearer reliefs of the later royal tombs seem to follow the model set by Darius without consideration of any changes the empire might have undergone; but in Xerxes' list (Persepolis h), if not already in Darius Susa e, one entry (Sakā beyond the sea) has justly been omitted. Apart from this the changes in the lists of Darius and Xerxes seem to reflect new acquisitions, whether major ones like Hinduš or minor ones like Karkā.

The standard unit of provincial administration was the satrapy. Herodotus enumerates twenty territorial divisions of the empire, which he calls *archai* or *nomoi*, at the same time remarking that the Persians call them satrapies; Persis itself is excluded as not being subject. These satrapies, he says, were established by Darius at the beginning of his reign. Unfortunately, they do not correspond to Darius' dahyāva either in number or in identity, and attempts like Olmstead's and Kent's to explain the differences as a matter of administrative changes over the years have not been successful. Equally unconvincing are imaginative

---

[1] R. G. Kent, "Old Persian Texts", *JNES* II (1943), 302–6. For the significance of the word *"dahyāva"* see now G. G. Cameron, "The Persian satrapies and related matters", *JNES* XXXII (1973), 47–50, with the comments of Gershevitch, *TPS* 1979, 160ff.

THE RISE OF THE ACHAEMENIDS

hypotheses like Junge's and Toynbee's contention that the twenty nomoi were not, as Herodotus supposed, administrative divisions but represent a quite separate subdivision of the empire into fiscal districts.[1] It thus appears that one of two things must be the case: either Herodotus' information is quite erroneous, or Darius' dahyāva are not satrapies. There is a strong presumption that it is the latter which is true. Of the twenty nomoi ten receive attestation as satrapies outside the pages of Herodotus; of the thirty dahyāva only seven or eight can be attested as corresponding to satrapies, and it is difficult to make out a case that Athurā, Arabāya, Karkā, Kuš, and the three distinct groupings of both Yaunā and Sakā could have been separate satrapies under Persian rule. On the other hand, if we take the dahyāva in the lists of Darius to represent major ethnic groups (with a few lesser ones in cases where new conquests are being publicized) we obtain a broad sample of peoples in the empire which corresponds well to Herodotus' more detailed list of about 57 peoples who took part in Xerxes' expedition of 481–480 against the free Greeks.

Herodotus gives two lists. The one just mentioned (VII. 61–95) comprises the peoples in Xerxes' army in 481–480. Scholars often speak of it as though it must depend on a Persian parade-state document; but military intelligence is not a modern invention, and it would be astonishing if a people as alert as the Greeks, of whom many were arrayed on Xerxes' side or watched his army go past, had failed to identify the different enemy contingents and note their equipment. Similarly, the view that Herodotus is there drawing names from Hecataeus' gazetteer of before 480 B.C. seems unnecessarily far-fetched. This list should contain firm information that Herodotus found ready to hand. The other (III. 90–97) is the list of nomoi or satrapies (above, p. 245), in which the different peoples contained in each are recorded. There are 50–53 names of peoples which can be regarded as common to both lists. About 18 peoples seem to occur only in the satrapy list, whereas there are only two or three names in the army list which do not admit of any rapprochement with the other. The satrapy list, which most concerns us, is here given in Herodotus' numbering, which will hardly have constituted an official order of precedence:

1. Ionians, Magnesians in Asia, Aeolians, Carians, Lycians, Milyeis, Pamphylians: assessment for tribute 400 talents of silver.

[1] The apparently decisive point in the argument, that Herodotus (1. 72) says that the lands east of the Halys were in the Median *arche*, is in fact fallacious; what Herodotus is referring to is not the Persian satrapy of Media but the old Median empire.

2. Mysians, Lydians, Lasonioi, Kabalioi, Hytenneis: 500 talents of silver.

3. Hellespontioi, Phrygians, Thracians in Asia, Paphlagonians, Mariandynoi, Syrioi (= Cappadocians): 300 talents of silver.

4. Cilicians: 360 horses, 500 talents of silver (140 spent locally on cavalry).

5. Phoenicia, Syria called Palestine, Cyprus: 350 talents of silver.

6. Egypt, with Libya, Cyrene, Barca: 700 talents of silver, Moeris fishery dues (in silver), corn for garrison troops.

7. Sattagydians, Gandarians, Dadikai, Aparytai: 170 talents of silver.

8. Susa and the territory of the Kissioi: 300 talents of silver.

9. Babylon and the rest of Assyria: 1,000 talents of silver, 500 eunuch boys.

10. Agbatana and the rest of Media, Parikanioi, Orthokorybantioi: 450 talents of silver.

11. Caspians, Pausikai, Pantimathoi, Dareitai: 200 talents of silver.

12. Bactrians as far as Aiglai: 360 talents of silver.

13. Paktyike, Armenians and their neighbours as far as the Euxine: 400 talents of silver.

14. Sagartians, Sarangai, Thamanaioi, Outioi, Mykoi, islands of the 'Red Sea': 600 talents of silver.

15. Sakai, Caspians: 250 talents of silver.

16. Parthians, Chorasmians, Sogdians, Areioi: 300 talents of silver.

17. Parikanioi, Aethiopians of Asia: 400 talents of silver.

18. Matienoi, Saspeires, Alarodioi: 200 talents of silver.

19. Moschoi, Tibarenoi, Makrones, Mossynoikoi, Mares: 300 talents of silver.

20. Indians: 360 talents of gold dust, valued at 4,680 Euboic talents of silver.

Total: 14,560 Euboic talents of silver.[1]

Gifts were brought by the Aethiopians bordering on Egypt (gold, ebony, boys, ivory), the Colchians and their neighbours as far as the Caucasus (boys and girls), the Arabians (incense).

Ethnically, the most homogeneous bloc within the empire was the Iranians of the upper satrapies. Trousered and heavily turbaned, these Aryans lived in the valleys and basins of the multiple mountain crust that encloses the central deserts of what is now Iran or that

---

[1] The assessment for silver (nomoi 1–19) was in Babylonian talents, which were heavier than the Euboic: hence the discrepancy in the addition.

THE RISE OF THE ACHAEMENIDS

radiate from the snow-capped massif of central Afghanistan. North of Persis was Paraitakene, the border country of the Greater Media which stretched to Rhagae and the Caspian Gates (see pl. 1c). Beyond this the route led eastward through the bare inhospitable land called Parthia (Parthava) across which, we are told, the Kings had to journey in haste for lack of sustenance; Isidorus' "Parthian Stations" shows that then, as now, villages were few there, and the Greeks noted that the inhabitants became less civilized to the east of the Gates (Strabo XI. 518); the centre of this satrapy may have been at Shahr-i Qūmis (the later Hecatompylus) near Dāmghān. Beyond this were the dahyāuš of Haraiva (Areia) with fertile land up the valley of its river (the modern Harī Rūd) and its capital at Artakoana, and the oasis of Marguš down the river of Marv.

East of Persis the road led to Karmania (originally perhaps included in Pārsa), whose principal centre was further south than the modern city of Kirmān, probably in the direction of Harmozia (Hurmuz).[1] With some broad valleys, which were well cultivated until the later middle ages, the land produced vines and all fruits except the olive; it had also a variety of mines, and it provided a special sort of timber (sissoo) for Darius I's palace at Susa. Its ancient inhabitants, we are told, lived and fought like the Persians, though they used asses rather than horses.[2] Further east beyond the sand desert was the dahyāuš of Zranka, later known to the Greeks as Drangiana (and presumably the Sarangai of Herodotus' 14th nomos); the region received its name Sakastana (Sīstān) after it was occupied by Sakai in Parthian times. Fed by the Helmand (Haētumant = "with dams" in the Avesta, Greek Etumandros), the low-lying, wind-blasted basin supports sedentary cattle-breeders and raises good crops of wheat under the pale skies. Sīstān, with the lower Helmand valley as far up as Beste (Bust)[3] is capable

[1] The present city of Kirmān only received the name in medieval times. The centre in Karmania where Alexander the Great halted was five good days' journey inland from Harmozia; it may have been in the fertile Jīruft valley, where Abbott's and Sykes' enormous Islamic site of Shahr-i Dakyanus at Sabzvārān could go back to ancient times.

[2] Xenophon in his *Cyropaedia* speaks of Cyrus the Great's Persians as not having been accustomed to ride horses until he formed his army. This sounds like an invention to give greater credit to Cyrus. But there may be something in it; for the famous Nesaean horses of the Achaemenids were bred in Media on a great plain six days' journey from Agbatana; and it is the donkey, with its great endurance on desert marches, that provides transport for the sedentary population of Fārs as well as Karmania. The Bashakird country east of Hurmuz has been particularly noted for its donkeys.

[3] This place, which Pliny speaks of as in Arachosia, is marked by the great mound on which the Ghaznavid citadel was built (Qal'a-yi Bust); it yields coins of the Greco-Bactrian rulers and their successors, and an Achaemenid stone weight has recently been reported from there. This

of great fertility; and it must have had a larger cultivated area in antiquity than it now has. The Drangae were said to live like the Persians in all respects save for a shortage of wine. In Sīstān the river has from time to time dictated the position of the capital city, and it is not clear what the pattern was in Achaemenid times; but remains of what may have been a satrapal centre have recently been uncovered by an Italian mission at Dahan-i Ghulāmān on the edge of the creeping sandhills west of the Helmand.

To the east of this was Arachosia (Harauvatiš, which is a dahyāuš in the royal inscriptions but does not appear in Herodotus' satrapy list). It is curious that in his Susa building inscription Darius I speaks of Harauvatiš as one of the places from which the ivory came. Many centuries later the Ghaznavids kept elephants at Bust in the valley where the Argandāb river (Harahvaitī, Greek Arachotos) joins the Helmand, but there is no reason to think that the Achaemenids did so. Strabo (XI. 516) in fact makes the territory of the Arachosians descend to the Indus, but in Alexander's time there were people called Indians between the two. According to the Elamite text of the Behistun inscription (§47 Weissbach) the seat of the satrap of Arachosia in 521 B.C. was Aršada, perhaps at the key position of Kandahar, where there is a huge fertile oasis on the main route to India and third-century inscriptions of Aśoka have come to light.[1] The wind-swept, treeless Hindu Kush (Greek Paropanisos or Paropamisos) in the region of the Kabul River and its northern tributaries cannot have been in Arachosia; it seems rather to have been part of Gandara (Paruparaēsana in the Babylonian and Elamite versions at Behistun, Greek Paropamisadai),[2] perhaps with Kapisa in the Kūh-dāman plain as its principal centre

stretch of the Helmand probably belonged to the Ariaspae who befriended Cyrus the Great and were given the name (Euergetae = Benefactors) on that account; they would have been in a position to earn his gratitude if he had arrived exhausted after a desert crossing. They were, according to G. Gnoli, *Zoroaster's Time and Homeland* (Naples, 1980), pp. 44ff, 227, one of the peoples among whom Zoroaster personally spread his teaching.

[1] Pliny speaks of Arachosia as having a town and river of the same name. From the road mileages which he cites from Alexander the Great's pacers the town of the Arachosians would seem to have been at Kalat-i Ghilzai, whose great mound 90 miles north-east of Kandahar still awaits exploration; and the situation at over 5000 ft. would have been much less sultry in the summer months. But Kandahar must have been the main inhabited centre of the country, and a report of soundings there in 1974 speaks of Achaemenid and earlier levels underlying the existing fortification trace.

[2] [The Babylonian name of Gandara suggests that that country lay south of the Hindu Kush; see Gershevitch, *The Avestan Hymn to Mithra* (Cambridge, 1959), 174f., where of the three peoples next mentioned in the text above Thataguš and the Aparytai are sought west of Gandara, and the Dadikai are regarded, following Marquart, as possible ancestors of the present day Dardic tribes. Ed.]

(see pl. 2*a*). The Gandarian does not, however, wear the wintry garb of the upper Iranians on the Achaemenian tomb-reliefs, but seems more akin to the light-clad Sattagydian (Thataguiya) and Indian (Hinduya) and Gandara presumably extended down-river to Charsadda (Peukela) and the Indus. From its placing in Herodotus' 7th nomos, whose total tribute is said to be only 170 talents of silver, and the fact that it was in the empire before Darius I came to the throne, we may infer that Thataguš did not, as some scholars believe, lie beyond the Indus, and the light clothing seems to place it south rather than north or west of Gandara; but we can hardly imagine that the Persians would have attempted to control the tribes of the ragged south-eastern edge of the Iranian plateau where the rivers cut their way through the barren Sulaiman range. Aparytai could conceivably be the same name as the modern Afridi in the Khyber region. The remaining people in the 7th nomos, the Dadikai, have recently been identified with the present-day Tājīks; but Tājīk is a word that had its origin long after Achaemenid times on the borders of Mesopotamia, where it was first applied to the bedouin. Hinduš may have been some distance down the Indus from the confluence of the Kabul River.

From Herodotus we learn that the 20th nomos (Indians) had a great population and paid a tribute in gold dust whose value was enormous.[1] It was conquered by Darius I and no doubt corresponds to his dahyāuš of Hinduš. At the same time Herodotus speaks of many peoples of India who were not included in the Persian empire; and later Greek writers, including Megasthenes who went on embassies to the Mauryan court a couple of decades after Alexander the Great, seem to have believed that the Persians never conquered "India" (i.e. the lands east of the Indus). From the Alexander historians it seems clear that Achaemenid rule did not extend east of the river under Darius III, and we cannot be sure whether it ever did. To the Greeks Arianē, the greater Iran, ended at the Indus (below, p. 290).

To the south of the Iranian plateau the shore of the Indian Ocean from the Straits of Hurmuz (Harmozia) to the vicinity of the Indus delta is torrid almost beyond endurance, much of it barely even fit for palms. It was along this coast of what is now Balūchistān that Alexander's naval

[1] The problems created by this apparent wealth in gold in the 20th nomos cannot be discussed here. Tarn (106ff.) considered Herodotus' information erroneous, and we may question whether all the gold was provided by the one Indian satrapy – the tribute in silver payable by the 7th nomos is surprisingly light.

THE EXTENT OF THE EMPIRE

mission under Nearchus encountered Stone Age communities and fish-eaters (the Ichthyophagi) living in almost total seclusion. The coast is backed by the rocky mountain ranges of Makrān; and beyond them is a great area east of Karmania in which water and food are barely procurable save in a few relatively favoured localities. This is what was called Gedrosia, with a satrapal seat at Pura (almost certainly the modern Bampūr with its huge mound which shows ancient occupation) (see pl. 2b). A sparse population of no very settled abode may eke out a meagre living in the wilderness by a combination of herding and occasional agriculture. But no power could take out of this country more than it is prepared to put in; and to an army such as Alexander led through it in imitation (as he believed) of Semiramis and Cyrus the region east of the Bampur river is a desert.[1] In Herodotus' satrapy list the floating 17th nomos, whose only known connection is with the Indians, could take in Gedrosia, and the 14th nomos includes the western part of the coast south of Persis together with the interior as far as Drangiana. There is no name among Darius' dahyāva which can possibly be assigned to this unproductive belt except Maka; and most scholars therefore attempt to fill the gap by identifying Maka with the Mykoi of the 14th nomos (and with the modern name Makrān). But the land of the ancient Makai in 'Umān is an equally acceptable candidate for Maka;[2] so it is not certain that the barren belt of southern Iran has a place in the Persian dahyāva lists. This unpatrollable region, which no army could easily traverse without heavy loss, was probably of as little interest to the Achaemenids as it seems later to have been to the Arabs of the eastern caliphate. Philostratus, who composed a biography of Apollonius of Tyana for Julia Domna in which he brought the sage back from India by this route, could not improve on the Alexander historians; nor was any accurate knowledge of the region to be had until the last century.

[1] From the researches of Sir Aurel Stein and others it seems clear that human occupation was more widespread in the third millennium B.C. than it is now. The factor here is probably not so much climatic change as denudation due to cultivation and grazing which has robbed the ground of its ability to retain water; and there is no evidence that conditions in Achaemenid times differed greatly from those which prevail now.

[2] In the Fortification tablets (of Darius I's middle years) at Persepolis there is mention of two satrapal seats or centres – Makkaš (PF 679 and 680) and Puruš (PF 681). Puruš is presumably Pura in Gedrosia. As regards Makkaš we may note that in PF 679 a wine ration for the satrap seems to have been issued at Tamukkan (or Tawukkan), which Hallock identified with the port of Taoke on the Persian Gulf (below, p. 596). This new evidence makes the equation Makrān (Gedrosia) = Maka more difficult to sustain.

THE RISE OF THE ACHAEMENIDS

On the north side of the Paropamisos lay Bactria. Its green valley bottoms led down to fertile basins in steppe land reaching to the sand dunes of the Oxus; and to it may well have been attached the valleys that join that river from the north in Tājīkistān, where groups of village sites of Achaemenid date have recently been discovered. The capital was Zariaspa (Bactra, presumably at Balkh). Bactria was an extensive satrapy; and in fact it seems to have been the key province of eastern Iran both in Achaemenid times and later. Beyond the Oxus was Sogdiana, a land where nobles of heroic temper fought a running fight against Alexander the Great or defied him in well provisioned fastnesses. Its chief centre was Maracanda (Samarkand); but, as with Bactria, irrigation could produce great fertility in the vicinity of the rivers, and settlements were evidently fairly numerous, especially in the rich Polytimetus (Zarafshān) valley. Down the Oxus is the great outlying oasis of Khwārazm (Chorasmia) or Khiva, which may once have been included in the empire of the Achaemenids.[1] These oases north of the Iranian plateau, such as Khwārazm, Marv, and Bukhārā, were later to blossom as leading centres of Islamic civilization; but – unless material evidence from Russian excavations can eventually substantiate a different estimate – upper Asia generally would seem not to have been culturally advanced when Achaemenid sway was established there.[2] Beyond Khiva the Oxus strains to its end in the shallows of the Aral Sea; but there does not seem to be sufficient reason to doubt that in antiquity, as in later medieval times, an arm flowed west to the Caspian and so provided a corridor linking Chorasmia to Hyrcania (Vrkāna, the modern Gurgān). Apart from the Sakai, Darius' dahyāva on this flank of the empire are readily identifiable. Herodotus' nomoi, on the other hand, are at their most intractable here. He puts the Parthians, Chorasmians, Sogdians, and Areioi all together in a single satrapy (the 16th) paying only 300 talents, and this has rightly caused disquiet to modern scholars. Though Areia and Parthia were separate satrapies at the end of the empire, there is no insuperable difficulty in their being

[1] The combined testimony of Hecataeus and Herodotus would by itself lead to the assumption that in earlier Achaemenid times the Chorasmians were living south of the steppe (in Khurāsān). Recent Russian discoveries have been brought into relation with this; and the theory that the Chorasmians only moved down to the Oxus when Achaemenid control had begun to slacken has much to commend it now. But the archaeological evidence here is not easy to appraise. In antiquity there seems to have been a much greater area of habitation than now, extending north-eastward to the Jaxartes along a network of watercourses in what is now desert and marshland. Cf. Frumkin, 82ff.

[2] Some recent assessments of the cultural condition of the upper satrapies may be found in Deshaves (ed.), *Le Plateau iranien*.

united at this time, perhaps along with Hyrcania, not listed by Herodotus, which was united to Parthia later; but the extension of the satrapy eastward to the Farghāna Gate might seem to set a strain on our credulity. The people called Caspians would most naturally be placed where Strabo places the memory of them, on the west side of their sea; but they are named in two separate nomoi (the 11th and 15th). In the 15th, if the text is correct,[1] they form a satrapy with Sakai. The other names in the 11th nomos cannot be identified; the Pausikai could perhaps be the same as the Apasiakai of Polybius and Strabo between the Oxus and the Jaxartes; the Pantimathoi and Dareitai have been placed by the Caspian Gates, but without compelling reason.[2]

The gently undulating deserts of salty flats and shifting sand billows that stretch for hundreds of miles to either side of the lower Oxus are devoid of running water and have only rare brackish wells. The lesser rivers lack the energy to traverse this waste; and so agriculture is confined to relatively short riverain strips like those of the Zarafshān (Polytimetus) and to the basins where their streams go to ground. The extent of this oasis-cultivation depends on the use of artificial irrigation (Russian explorations seem to indicate that in Marv and Khwārazm, as well as up the Oxus opposite Bactria, irrigation systems had been established by the middle of the first millennium B.C., and a date far back in the prehistoric has been claimed for canals in the terminal basin of the Harī Rūd at Tājand). But outside the oases the only way of life that has been possible up to our own times amid formidable extremes of summer and winter climate is the nomadic one; and the archaeological evidence from Central Asia seems to show that that way of life was especially dominant in the Iron Age before the Achaemenids set their frontier there.

The Persians gave the single name Sakā both to the nomads whom they encountered between the Hunger steppe and the Caspian, and equally to those north of the Danube and Black Sea against whom Darius later campaigned; and the Greeks and Assyrians called all those who were known to them by the name Skuthai (Iškuzai). Sakā and Skuthai evidently constituted a generic name for the nomads on

[1] Leuze preferred to emend Herodotus' text slightly so as to have "Caspian Sakai" instead of "Sakai and Caspians"; other scholars have tried to find a home for these Caspians further east (in Kashmir for instance).

[2] Tomaschek proposed to interpret Apasiakai as Āpa-sakā = 'water-Sakai', and Tolstov has more recently assigned this name to the Iron Age culture that he discovered in the waste south-east of the Aral which once formed the delta lands of the Jaxartes (above, p. 252, n. 1). Dareitai suggests the Parthian Dara on the south edge of Turkestan east of the Caspian.

the northern frontiers.¹ Some specific names are recorded, notably Massagetae for a great nation of these nomads against whom Cyrus campaigned on the Jaxartes (above, p. 127), and Dahā (Daai in Greek) for an apparently intrusive people who first appear in Xerxes' list of dahyāva.²

In Darius' first list of dahyāva at Behistun, which enumerates peoples already in the empire at the commencement of his reign, there is a single entry Sakā. But soon after this he engaged in his campaign against the tribesmen of Skunkha (above, pp. 219–20), who seem to be spoken of as wearing pointed hoods; and the annexe at the right end of the relief shows the captive chief with a very high pointed headpiece (see pl. 34). After this we find two dahyāva of Sakā with descriptive names (the tigrakhaudā = "with pointed hood", and the haumavargā); and a third ("those beyond the sea") is added later, evidently after Darius' incursion into the western Scythia north of the Danube. The first two must be placed in Central Asia east of the Caspian. This does not necessarily mean that in this great area there were two (and no more than two) distinct groupings of Sakā; we may note that all the Sakā on the Persepolis reliefs wear pointed hoods (or, to be correct, caps), and Herodotus remarks that the Sakai in Xerxes' army wore pointed caps but he calls them "Amyrgian" (i.e. haumavargā). But if Darius' campaign against Skunkha followed on the insurrection in Margiana (above, pp. 218–19) and it was Sakā of the Caspian-Aral region who then received the special title "tigrakhaudā", there is a presumption that the title "haumavargā" should be applied to the "Sakā beyond Sogdiana" whom Darius cites (Persepolis h and Hamadān) as forming the opposite limit of his empire to Kush (the Aethiopians). The dahyāuš of the haumavargā should therefore be placed further east than that of the tigrakhaudā. Some scholars have looked to the Pamirs, or (with Canon Rawlinson) Sinkiang. But in that case these Saka should have been spoken of as beyond Bactria rather than (as Darius says) Sogdiana; so the frontier on the Jaxartes seems the most appropriate location; this agrees with Gershevitch's suggestion that the word "haumavargā",³

---

¹ The name Gimirri (= Cimmerians) which the Babylonian scribes used in place of Sakā is obviously an archaism.

² In later times the Daai formed a large group of nomadic tribes on the east side of the Caspian.

³ In the 5th century B.C. the Greek writer Hellanicus spoke of a plain of the Sakai called Amyrgion. An eponymous Saka king (Amorges or Homarges) appears in Ctesias. Haoma (soma) was the Indo-Iranian sacred intoxicant, obtained by pounding the fibres of a plant that cannot now be identified.

which he interprets etymologically as meaning "consuming haoma", was a nickname of the people called Tūra in the Avesta.[1]

It is questionable whether the Sakā known to the Persians were racially so homogeneous as is commonly supposed. No doubt there were major Indo-European-speaking elements. But the graphic representations of Saka cavalrymen who were stationed at Memphis in Egypt show Mongol features; and Nöldeke's interpretation of the name Carthasis for the Saka king's brother in an Alexander historian[2] as the Turkish *kardaşı* ("—, brother of him") is perhaps still worth bearing in mind. Darius I represents his three divisions of the Sakā as subject peoples. We know this is not true of the European Scythians; and though Herodotus does include some Sakai in his 15th nomos, others seem later to have been serving as mercenaries rather than subjects when the Greeks came face to face with them. We may therefore doubt whether these nomads as a whole were subjected to regular Persian rule. The Persians certainly seem to have been successful in maintaining peaceful relations on this long frontier. But though their manufactured carpets travelled far afield, their knowledge of the world beyond their borders may have been slight; for it was from Greco-Scythian sources on the Black Sea that Herodotus acquired such knowledge as he possessed of the tribes of Central Asia, and Alexander the Great seems to have been unable to obtain correct information about the waterways there.

Adjoining the south-east corner of the Caspian Sea was the low-lying piedmont of Hyrcania (Vrkāna in the Behistun inscription), whose capital was at Zadrakarta when Alexander went that way. With forested mountainsides leading down to yellow fields and thick copses, with numerous muddy streams, thatched houses, and well-fed horses, the countryside now has a rustic charm (see pl. 2c). But during antiquity, as into recent times, it was underdeveloped because of the destructiveness of the nomads of the steppe. The Hyrcanians are not named in the lists of dahyāva; but they are found as garrison troops in the provinces, and in his *Cyropaedia* Xenophon speaks of them as being given positions of trust in Cyrus the Great's empire. The greater part

---

[1] See Gershevitch, "An Iranianist's view of the Soma controversy", in P. Gignoux and A. Tafazzoli (eds), *Mémorial Jean de Menasce* (Louvain, 1974), 54–6.

[2] Curtius Rufus VII. 7, 1. The skulls from supposedly Saka burials of Achaemenid date by the Ili river in Central Asia are said to show an admixture of Mongoloid features; the description of Scyths in the Hippocratic Corpus also reveals Mongol traits. Relics of a Saka cap 20 ins. high have come to light recently in a burial.

of the humid coast at the south end of the Caspian, with the high deciduous-forested mountains that back it, belonged to a numerous and warlike people, the Kadousioi, against whom Artaxerxes II is said to have carried out an unprofitable campaign that he inherited from his father and left to his son to complete half a century later. Being then far away from the seats of Persian rule, they were probably not often under effective control, and it is significant that there seems to have been no continuous road along the south shore of the Caspian when Alexander the Great tried to force his way along it at the east end. Protection against the steppe nomads counted for more there than Persian control.

The bare elevated highland of Armenia, a country where living beings went to ground in the long winter until the melting snows gave way to corn lands and green hill pastures, had been incorporated in the Median empire presumably not long after the fall of Nineveh; and it is connoted by a single entry (Armina) in the Achaemenid dahyāva lists. But Herodotus divides it between two nomoi; and in the winter of 401 B.C., when they cut a devious route across it, the Ten Thousand encountered the levies of two different satraps in turn there. Some scholars prefer to envisage a single satrapy and have therefore argued that one of the two satraps must have been subordinate to the other; but it is difficult to imagine that either Orontes, the King's son-in-law, or Tiribazus, the King's most trusted friend, would have been appointed in a junior capacity. The one nomos (the 13th, which would correspond to Tiribazus' satrapy) probably encompassed the territory occupied by an Indo-European-speaking people called Haik, who must have been asserting their identity in what we might call the greater western part of Armenia in the decline of the kingdom of Urartu (Ararat), while the other (the 18th) included a remnant of the older Haldian population that presumably remained in the region of Tušpa (Van) and the later Urartian fortress-capitals in the Araxes valley beyond the present Mt Ararat (Alarodioi, a name identified with Urartu by Sir Henry Rawlinson),[1] together with parts of Greater Media (Matiene around Lake Urmīya and the tangled belt of crags and deep gorges above the

[1] The name also survived (Uraštu) in the vocabulary of Babylonian scribes in place of Armina in the Babylonian texts of the Old Persian inscriptions. The name Haldian occurs as "Chaldaean" in Xenophon, applying to a warlike people not then controlled by the Persians (and supposedly at enmity with the Armenians before Cyrus' time). The high civilization of Urartu had no successor under the Armenians, who seem to have left nothing substantial for the archaeologists to find.

THE EXTENT OF THE EMPIRE

Tigris valley, with the Saspeires further north). In 401 B.C. the Kardouchoi in the mountains east of the confluence of the Eastern and Western Tigris were no longer subject to the Persians, and the King's writ did not run in the north where the "neighbouring peoples as far as the Euxine (Black Sea)" that Herodotus speaks of – the Taochoi, Chalybes, and Phasianoi of Xenophon – seem to have been quite independent. The region name Paktyikē that Herodotus gives is unintelligible in the context of the 13th nomos, and we may perhaps suppose that an error has crept in there. There is an inscription of Xerxes on the Rock of Van, but the only known relics of palatial buildings of Achaemenid times in the region of the 18th nomos seem to be at Arinberd by Erivan and perhaps Armavir. In the 13th nomos a similar establishment may possibly have existed at Altıntepe near Erzincan.[1] In Matiene an early Achaemenian stratum has been reported in the recent excavation at the stronghold of Haftavan Tepe near the north-west corner of Lake Urmīya.

North of Armenia the empire extended to the barrier of the Caucasus in Herodotus' time. The Arab geographers called the Caucasus the "mountain of languages"; Strabo talks of seventy different tongues being spoken there (the figure of 300 given by Pliny from Timosthenes is hardly to be credited), and a good fifty are reported even at the present day. This mountain-girt refuge between the Black Sea and the Caspian would seem to have been a museum of forgotten races for the best part of three thousand years. On the west was an organized nation, the Colchians, who lived in humid jungle and forest under gloomy skies; according to Herodotus they paid no tribute to the Persians but did send gifts. To the east in the region of Mtskheta (by Tiflis) and the Kur there may possibly have been a satrapy (the 15th or the 11th nomos); there are certainly links with ancient Iran, but it is not clear how much goes back to Achaemenid times.

Media is the country of the Zagros, whose ranges rise in succession with increasing steepness from the Tigris to wall in and constrict the Iranian plateau, reaching 11–12,000 ft. above Behistun and Agbatana

---

[1] The arrangement of the two satrapies here proposed depends on the assumption that the Saspeires are to be placed in the region of Persian Azerbaijan and the Araxes valley, and that they cannot be identified with the Hesperitai of Xenophon and the modern kaza name Ispir between Erzurum and Trebizond. The independent Kardouchoi, who seem to have broken away from Orontes' satrapy (the 18th nomos), are thought to have been the ancestors of the Kurds, or at least the original nucleus to which Iranian-speaking peoples in what is now Kurdistān have been attached since Sasanian times.

(see pl. 3*a*) and greater heights further to the south-east. It is a land of many fertile valleys, mostly at altitudes of 4,000–6,000 ft. and suitable for cultivation in settled times (see pl. 3*b*).[1] But on the north Media always included the plateau as far as the Alburz (Ariobarzanes in Orosius, 5th century) mountains and the Caspian Gates (see pl. 1*c*), and its eastern region of Paraitakene extended to the central deserts and marched with Persis well south of the modern Iṣfahān. The Median dominion in Asia, which preceded that of the Achaemenids, was made possible by the centralization of authority in the capital city of Hagmatāna (= "the moot", Greek Agbatana or Ekbatana) in the high basin behind Mt Alvand (Orontes) (see pl. 3*a*). Until we have some definite archaeological evidence to set against Herodotus, we cannot positively discredit the tradition that Deioces, the founder of the dynasty, selected the site for a city and built a kremlin there about the end of the eighth century. This is Herodotus' 10th nomos, consisting of Agbatana and the rest of Media together with the Parikanioi and the Orthokorybantioi. Modern attempts to extend the limits of the satrapy to Turkestan by identifying these Parikanioi with the people of Hyrcania (Vrkāna) or even Farghāna, and by interpreting the name Orthokorybantioi in Herodotus as a distortion of a Greek word meaning "upright-topped", which would be equivalent to (Sakā) tigrakhaudā, seem to be insufficiently thought out; in fact a Median region of Barikānu in the Zagros is mentioned in the annals of the Assyrian king Sargon II.

In the windless plain south of the Median homelands was the old city of Susa (Šušan), long the capital of a substantial kingdom but devastated by Ashurbanipal and apparently under Babylonian control from the time of Nebuchadnezzar. Its territory, which is separated from Mesopotamia by a belt of marshes, was known by three different names: (i) in the native tongue Ha(l)tamti, more widely known as Elam, (ii) the land of the Kissioi (Herodotus' 8th nomos), which is thought to be related to the Babylonian and Assyrian name Kaššu, and (iii) Ū(v)ja in the Old Persian dahyāva lists (Arabic Hūz, modern Khūzistān). The territory evidently reached up into the Zagros; and we find two of these names, if not indeed all three, applied to peoples that the Greeks later

---

[1] Luristān has been intensively surveyed by archaeologists in recent years; but unfortunately the dating of the Iron Age cultures there is still uncertain, and it is not clear how far we are justified in believing that settlement was lacking in Achaemenid times. For a lowering of the pottery dates which would affect this issue see D. Stronach, "Achaemenid Village I at Susa and the Persian migration to Fars", *Iraq* XXXVI (1974), 239–48.

THE EXTENT OF THE EMPIRE

encountered and described as divided into cultivators in the lower ground and predatory nomads in the mountains: (i) Elymaioi and (ii) Kossaioi, which between them covered the greater part of Luristān and the Bakhtiari country, and perhaps also (iii) the Uxii (Ouxioi) who opposed Alexander's passage when he entered the mountains south-east of Susa. Some scholars have believed that the original kingdom of Anšan that Cyrus the Great inherited was centred on Susa, or at least adjacent to it,[1] and have maintained that Persian landlords were already established in Elam before the Achaemenid empire came into being. Junge even claimed that the delegates of the Elamites (Ūvja) depicted on the Persepolis reliefs have a recognisably Indo-European physiognomy; but this is not to be distinguished within the conventions of the art. What is understandable is that, straddling the exits of the main rivers of the central Zagros, Susa was well situated to dominate the winter grounds of the mountain tribes and so to maintain its influence over them; and certainly there was contact between Susa and Persis with messengers and products of handicrafts coming and going before the time of Cyrus.

Before leaving Media and Elam we may note one point of archaeological interest that has been overlooked. The palaces at Susa and Agbatana were royal residences; and they could hardly have housed a satrap with his court and harem in addition to the King's court. Satrapal residences are therefore to be sought at or near both of these centres. At Susa the newly discovered "Palace of the Shaour" is too royal and too central to be a satrap's court. At Agbatana the regional palace where Antigonus wintered in 316 B.C. was at a village in the countryside (Diodorus XIX. 44), perhaps (as Isidorus would lead us to believe) in the sheltered plain of Asadābād at the foot of the declivity of Mt Alvand.

The great plain of the two rivers, Tigris and Euphrates, stretches 700 miles from the foot of the Armenian mountains to the Persian Gulf. About halfway down, at less than fifty metres above sea level, the dry undulating steppe gives way to the alluvial deposit of the rivers, and only a little higher up than this is the limit at which dates ripen. Thus Upper and Lower Mesopotamia are quite different in character. The lower, alluvial part of the plain, which we may call Babylonia, could be irrigated by a system of canals from the Euphrates; in antiquity it produced fabulous crops of barley, while the palm trees provided

[1] This is now untenable (above, p. 210, n. 2).

THE RISE OF THE ACHAEMENIDS

abundant food and served a great variety of other needs. The upper Mesopotamian plain is largely steppe or desert. But the Assyrian homeland on the middle Tigris, together with the shelves and deep mountain valleys east of the river, yields winter cereals and temperate fruits. At an elevation of 400–500 metres the mountain foot at the north end of the Mesopotamian plain likewise affords fertile patches where streams emerge; but the flat ground below it is too dry to be inhabited in comfort all the year round save in the stream valleys, and so it has tended to lie open to the nomadic peoples of the Syrian desert.

West of the Euphrates was the complex of lands that had for centuries been known under the name Abarnahara ("Across the River").[1] From the point of view of settled habitation this amounted to a zone rarely reaching as much as a hundred miles inland from the Levant shore, with the former neo-Hittite principalities in the north coalescing with the Aramaeans of Syria, Sidon and the other prosperous Phoenician cities along the middle stretch of coast, and Palestine trailing off into desert on the south. The fertility of the coast was repeated in the long trough of the Orontes valley and Hollow Syria that separated the Lebanon from Antilebanon and Hermon; but to the east of the mountain barrier only a few favoured regions – around Aleppo and Homs (Emesa) in the north, the intensely fertile oasis of Damascus under Antilebanon, and in a small degree the plateau of Amman east of the Jordan – receive the water needed for cultivation. In the economy of Syria a large part seems to have been played by sheep raising, which was well situated to provide wool for the Phoenician purple-dyers. The great triangle between these settled lands and the Euphrates was the Syrian desert, difficult for travellers to cross save where a line of hills links up with the basin of Palmyra to provide the necessary string of water points between the Euphrates and Damascus. The main axis of communications ran from the Syrian Gates on the Cilician frontier or the boat bridge on the Euphrates at Thapsacus (somewhere below Carchemish) (see pl. 3c) by Emesa to Damascus, then south of Lake Tiberias to the pass of Megiddo and down the coast to Gaza and the "brook of Egypt". The residence of the satrap which Xenophon saw in 401 B.C. was in the north near Aleppo, close to the entries to the province.

The neo-Babylonian kingdom seems to have embraced upper Mesopotamia after the fall of Nineveh, and "Across the River" was added

---

[1] The name does not occur in the texts in Old Persian; Abarnahara is the form read in Aramaic (Babylonian Ebirnari).

THE EXTENT OF THE EMPIRE

to it under Nebuchadnezzar. So when Cyrus captured Babylon in 539 B.C. the Persians acquired another empire. Babylonian documents show that at first the whole was administered as one combined satrapy of Babylon and Abarnahara. But at some date later than the sixth year, and probably after the middle of Darius I's reign it was split into two; and in Herodotus we find one nomos (the 9th) comprising "Babylon and the rest of Assyria", and a second (the 5th) which contains all Phoenicia from the Orontes mouth, the Syria called "Palestine", and the island of Cyprus. The Babylon satrapy paid a huge tribute (1000 talents of silver, in addition to other great impositions). Herodotus believed that it included upper Mesopotamia to the borders of Armenia (I. 194); and in his closely argued book on the satrapies of Syria and Mesopotamia Leuze has abundantly demonstrated that this must normally have been the case. Dillemann has recently argued that the "Royal Road" which Herodotus describes as leading from Sardis to Susa (v. 52) must have diverged southward from the Western Tigris at Amida (Diyarbakır) and traversed the piedmont of upper Mesopotamia to Nisibis and the Tigris, and he therefore maintains against Leuze that this piedmont must have been in the satrapy of Armenia, through which Herodotus makes the road run in the relevant sector. As far as concerns the royal road, his argument seems persuasive. But it is now clear from the new Harran stelae of Nabuna'id that Harran itself and adjacent neo-Hittite lands belonged to Babylon at the time of Cyrus' attack in 539 B.C., and Nisibis had at least fallen into the hands of the Babylonians in 612 B.C. Presumably therefore this edge of the plain will have been included in the Babylon satrapy, except perhaps at its extreme east end if Cyrus was able to cross it in 547 B.C. without violating Babylonian territory (above, p. 212).

The Old Persian dahyāva lists name Babylon, but not Abarnahara, which could not be considered a distinct people. They do, however, include a name Athurā, which corresponds to the old name Ashur (Assyria). This name was known to later Greeks, who recognized a region of Atouria, apparently in the Assyrian homeland around Nineveh. The name Athurā has caused great difficulty in the minds of scholars who believe the dahyāva to be satrapies. Despite the documentary evidence, some have followed Meyer in regarding it as the official name of the Babylonian satrapy (Herodotus' 9th nomos). But the discovery of copies of Darius' building text Susa f revealed that people of Athurā (explained as Ebirnari, i.e. Abarnahara, in the Babylonian version) brought timber from Mt Lebanon to Babylon, and a historically ill-conceived identification of Athurā with the satrapy of Abarnahara became prevalent. From Cameron's re-reading of the Behistun inscription in 1948 it is now certain that a name cited in connection with Darius' Armenian campaign and as being a district in Athurā is in fact Izalā, the mountain that lies behind Nisibis; and so there can no longer be any doubt that Athurā had a foot in high Mesopotamia. Since Abarnahara cannot have included Izalā, it is now certain that Athurā cannot have been an administrative unit in the Persian empire. What precisely the word meant to the Achaemenids is less clear; we may suggest that the ethnic Athuriyā comprised Assyrians/Syrians of the former Assyrian kingdom, which the Medes would have known as distinct from Babylonia. Athurā appears in the original list of dahyāva of the time of Darius' accession when Abarnahara was not yet a separate satrapy.

One other dahyāuš is named in south-west Asia. This is Arabāya, whose representatives are depicted leading an Arabian camel in the Persepolis Apadana reliefs.[1] The Persians must have been in contact with nomadic or semi-nomadic Arabs at many points on the fringes of the Syrian desert; and Cambyses had made an alliance with the bedouin before he invaded Egypt (above, p. 214). It could be of these latter that Herodotus reported that they are not tributary, though they (or other Arabs) made a regular annual gift of frankincense. But from the new Harran stelae we now know that only half a dozen years before Cyrus' conquest of Babylon Nabuna'id had conquered and perhaps colonised a group of six oases in Western Arabia which extended some 200 miles between Tema and Medina; grave stelae of the ensuing period in Aramaic have been coming to light at Tema, Dedan and the Suez canal zone and yielding inscriptions from which it can be inferred that Persian authority was recognised a hundred years later. It therefore seems probable that Arabs of this region were among the tent-dwelling sheikhs who made their submission to Cyrus after the capture of Babylon (above, p. 212) and that the dahyāuš of Arabāya, though of comparatively little consequence, did consist of more than just shadows on the desert fringe. Southern Arabia, however, was not under Achaemenid rule, and Minaean merchants came to control Dedan in the 4th century.

[1] It has been suggested (e.g. by Sidney Smith) that the dahyāuš of Arabāya is the same as the satrapy of Abarnahara. But the reliefs seem to show Arabs with the peculiar haircut that Herodotus describes (III. 8); and it is the dahyāuš of Athurā that figures as Ebirnari in the Babylonian version of Susa f (see above).

THE EXTENT OF THE EMPIRE

With only brief interruptions, Egypt (Mudrāya) was governed by the Achaemenids for 120 years after its conquest by Cambyses in 525 B.C. Persian rule in the satrapy is the subject of Chapter 12. With Egypt went the Libyans and the Greeks of Cyrenaica, whom Aryandes had incorporated in the empire. These are now generally identified as the Put of the Persian lists, with the Aethiopians as Kush. The Aethiopians according to Herodotus were not tributary but brought biennial gifts of boys, gold, and ebony, and elephant tusks such as are shown (along with a giraffe-like animal) on the Apadana reliefs at Persepolis; but like the Arabs with their camel column, the Aethiopians did provide one of the most colourful, as well as warlike, contingents in the army with which Xerxes invaded Greece. From the fact that the Persian frontier defence was based at the first cataract we may conclude that Herodotus was right in making these gift-bearers the blacks who bordered on Egypt and not the 'long-lived' Aethiopians of Meroe against whom Cambyses' campaign had been directed.

In Hellenistic and Roman times Cilicia was a region on the eastern half of the south coast of Asia Minor, consisting of the "Rough" where the Taurus bulges out to make a mountainous riviera and (on the east) the "Plain" where it withdraws into the interior. But it had once been bigger than this. A ruler of Cilicia appears in history not long after the collapse of Assyria when Syennesis – a name or title applied to the kings of Cilicia – acted as a mediator to end the Lydo-Median war on the Halys; and the dynasty seems to have been in possession of a considerable realm.[1] The kingdom was narrow in a north–south direction, being entered from the Anatolian plateau by the pass through the Taurus called the "Cilician Gates". But between the Pisidian border on the west and the Euphrates in Melitene where the corner of the kingdom was intersected by the Achaemenid "Royal Road" the Cilicia of Syennesis stretched over 400 miles; and it included the Amanus on the Syrian border and presumably Kummuh (Commagene) in the bend of the Euphrates.

[1] The evolution of this kingdom cannot be satisfactorily explained. The Cilician plain must more or less correspond to the Que (Huwē) of Assyrian and Babylonian texts, which was invaded and traversed by a succession of kings down to Nabuna'id in 555 B.C. It would be tempting to suggest that the original Cilician kingdom of Syennesis lay further north-east between the Halys and the Euphrates, and that the plain was a later acquisition. But Ḥilakku, which appears as an invaded mountain land alongside Que in the texts and must have given its name to the Cilician kingdom (Hilik in Aramaic), seems also to have lain in the west of the region not far from Tarsus; and the Greeks associated the name Cilicians (Kilikes) with a people who had moved by sea from the Aegean.

THE RISE OF THE ACHAEMENIDS

As an independent ruler on friendly terms with the Medes and no doubt welcoming protection from Babylonian aggression, Syennesis was not conquered; and after Cyrus' victories in the West converted it into an enclave, Cilicia seems to have entered the Persian empire as a client kingdom. To some extent its territorial integrity may have been respected; the route to Anatolia followed by the royal post road was not the direct line of communication that leads through the Cilician plain but a northerly one traversing only fifty miles of Cilician territory; and guard posts were maintained on both sides of the frontier crossings. But according to Herodotus Cilicia ranked as a nomos (the 4th); tribute was paid of which a part was spent on a cavalry garrison in the country; Syennesis led a fleet of a hundred ships in Xerxes' invasion of Greece, and Darius I used Cilicia as a base of operations a couple of times and also requisitioned ships there.

The client status of Cilicia evidently depended on unhesitating co-operation with the Persians. Retiring into his eyrie above Tarsus the Syennesis of 401 B.C. endeavoured to steer a course of ostensible loyalty to each of the two brothers when Cyrus the Younger passed through to contest the throne with Artaxerxes II. But it seems likely that he was afterwards punished for not waging war against the loser; for in the early 4th century the "part of Cilicia next to Cappadocia" is found incorporated in a new satrapy (Cappadocia), and coins show that from 380 B.C. Persian military commanders minted in Tarsus and other Cilician cities, while after the middle of the century Hilik was governed by a regular Persian satrap (Mazdai = Mazaeus).[1]

Until the 4th century the bulk of peninsular Asia Minor was divided between two satrapies. The one (Herodotus' 2nd nomos) was centred on the old Lydian capital of Sardis, which gave its name to the dahyāuš of Sparda; like Bactria in the East, this seems to have played a key role. It included Mysians on the north-west and some minor peoples on the south-east towards the Taurus. The other nomos (Herodotus' 3rd) had its centre at Daskyleion south of the Sea of Marmara and was ruled by five generations of a family known to us best in the Pharnabazus of Xenophon's *Hellenica*. The satrapy was already established before the time of Darius I, and the governor's seat at Daskyleion yields Greco-Persian reliefs and Achaemenian sealings. Until the early 4th century the satrapy extended across the bare Phrygian

---

[1] Silver staters of the later 5th century show Nergal (the local Baal of Tarsus) on the reverse and in some cases Syennesis on horseback on the obverse.

THE EXTENT OF THE EMPIRE

plateau to Tyana and the approaches of the Cilician Gates and apparently took in what was then Cappadocia (the Katpatuka of the Persian lists, Herodotus' "Syrians"). It thus comprised practically the whole of the central Anatolian plateau – an expanse superficially similar to the Iranian plateau, but with the great difference that big rivers have cut through the mountain rim and so drain their basins instead of forming salt wastes. To judge by the survival of Iranian names and cults in later times, there must have been many fiefs granted to Persians in the east part between the Halys and the upper Euphrates, and none more attractive than that at the modern Bünyan with its orchards and waterfalls. In the north of Asia Minor, where steep mountain ridges run parallel with the coast, Paphlagonia and, to the east of it, a string of barbarous tribes which Herodotus places in the 19th nomos were nominally subject to the King; they provided contingents for Xerxes' great expedition, but they had been independent for a generation and more when the Ten Thousand descended on them in 400 B.C., and the Paphlagonians were ruled by kings of their own. Here, as along the south coast of the Caspian, the Persians do not seem to have constructed a road, and without control of sea communications they could not effectively dominate the inhabitants until in the 4th century their satraps became implicated in Greek inter-state politics on their own account.

Though yielding a tribute of 500 talents of silver, the Lydian nomos was not so large in extent; but it had good river plains, and many Persians seem to have held fiefs there and in the temperate valleys of mid-western Anatolia. The entry Yauna (Greeks, or rather their land) in the preamble of the Behistun inscription must refer to the Greeks of western Asia Minor who had been conquered by Cyrus. Herodotus speaks of a nomos (his 1st), consisting of Ionians and other Greeks of the west coast and (continuing round the south coast eastward) the native peoples of Caria, Lycia, and Pamphylia. This of course purports to refer to the time of Darius before the Ionians and others were liberated from the Persians in 479 B.C. It is nevertheless surprising, because on the occasions on which they are referred to in a Persian context by 5th-century Greek writers these peoples appear to have been subject to the satrap in Sardis, and Darius himself more than once speaks of Sparda as the limit of his empire opposite Hinduš, which he would hardly have done if the jurisdiction of his Sardis satrap had not extended to the sea. So on the evidence it seems more likely that Herodotus had no precise information about the satrapal organization here prior to the preparations for the great invasion of Greece and was making an erroneous assumption. A dahyāuš of the Karkā, which first appears in Darius' tomb inscription (Naqsh-i Rustam), has been variously identified; the old conjectures Colchians (who brought gifts) and Carthaginians (who might have sent tokens of submission) ceased to be satisfactory when the discovery of Darius' Susa building text (f) revealed Karkā, along with Yaunā, as ferrying timber from Babylon to Susa. Though philologically awkward, the identification with Carians (Kares) is now confirmed and so enables us to date the inscription on Darius' tomb later than the commencement of the Ionian revolt in 499 B.C.,[1] and the Susa inscription should be later than the collapse of the revolt (494 B.C.). There was of course no satrapy of Caria until 395 B.C., when Hyssaldomos and his son Hecatomnos set up the fortunes of a dynasty which reached its peak under Mausolus.

In Europe the Persian dominion was short-lived. Though named in Darius' later lists the Scythians north of the Danube and Black Sea were never subjected; for this is a matter in which the Ionians could not have been ignorant of the facts.[2] After the Scythian expedition Darius left Megabazus behind as general in Europe; a garrison position was established at Doriskos by the mouth of the Hebrus, and a Persian army seems to have penetrated beyond the Strymon into Macedonia. Several of the Greek islands were also captured at different times. Whether a satrapy was established on the north coast of the Aegean and tribute was regularly exacted is uncertain; but from the freedom with which Greeks who refused to recognize Darius' suzerainty were able to move about in the vicinity of the Bosporus, the Hellespont, and even Doriskos itself, we might infer that southern Thrace was not in any real sense occupied before the preparations for an invasion of Greece commenced. And after 479 B.C. only a couple of Persian garrisons remained to be cut out.

[1] Cameron's contention that it is earlier than 499 (*JNES* II (1943), 312 n. 31) is theoretically possible but historically very improbable. From mentions of individuals with this ethnic in Bablyonian documents of the early years of Darius I, W. Eilers was able to make a strong case for the identification of Karkā (Akk. Karsa) with Carians ("Das Volk der karkā in den Achämenideninschriften", *OLZ* xxxvIII (1935), cols 201–13). Herzfeld preferred to regard the Karkā as exiled Carians of a supposed "naval base" in the Persian Gulf, and this seems now to be the prevailing opinion on the Susa palace inscription (Darius Susa f), to which may now be added the tablets DSz and DSaa, discovered in 1970.

[2] It may be that Darius' expedition did not come so near to disaster as Herodotus believed; but with their colonies among the Scythians, the Ionians had much more accurate information about the aftermath of the expedition than Darius could ever have obtained. See below, pp. 301–3.

ADMINISTRATION OF THE SATRAPIES

It is difficult to keep track of the various Yaunā in Darius' dahyāva lists, the more so because in Persepolis e we find "Yaunā by (or in) the sea" in the list of subjects but nothing to suggest that the Scythian expedition had yet occurred. At Naqsh-i Rustam, dating later than the Scythian expedition, there is a dahyāuš called Yaunā takabarā = "bearing shields" (glossed in the Babylonian text "on their heads", so referring to sun-hats) which must relate to Greeks of either part or the whole of the land between Thessaly and the Black Sea; unfortunately the evidence does not suffice to show whether or not the Persians regarded the Macedonians at that time as Greeks.

There remains the dahyāuš of Skudra, whose representatives on the Apadana reliefs of Persepolis (if correctly recognized) are cloaked and seem to be hooded like Sakai but not trousered. From their position in the lists they would seem to be people of Thrace between the Danube and the Marmara. Persian occupation of the interior of what is now Bulgaria does not seem to be attested by archaeological discoveries. For the name Skudra no explanation has yet proved acceptable; but the resemblance to Skythai-Iškuzai might not be fortuitous. A problem is created by the appearance of what Hallock takes to be Skudrian workers in the Fortification tablets of Persepolis between the 18th and 24th years of Darius I's reign. The mentions of these people (Iškudra) are numerous and the groups very large (one containing no less than 520 workers); and the associated words or names do not suggest that a dahyāuš is in question. Possibly we are dealing with a people who had been deported, like the Paeonians whom Herodotus speaks of as having been settled in Phrygia (v. 12–23, 98); but the name in the tablets at Persepolis could be that of some local community or group.

VII. THE ADMINISTRATION OF THE SATRAPIES

As the King's governors in the provinces, the satraps ("protectors of the realm") were viceroys. Their jurisdiction embraced the spheres of civil and military action; they seem to have been responsible for the payment of the annual tribute, the raising of military levies, and for justice and security; their courts are also said to have been frequented by the Persian notables in the satrapies and to have served as cadet schools for the education of their children.

The above view of the duties of a satrap is based on the known evidence of their actions or the King's expectations of them. But it is not a universally accepted view; and the arguments must therefore be considered. Xenophon in his *Cyropaedia* speaks of Cyrus the Great sending out the first satraps to be civil governors on the understanding that the existing garrison commanders in the provinces were to remain responsible directly to himself (VIII. 6); and in the same passage he speaks of a King's controller-general who visits the provinces every year with an army and corrects abuses or derelictions of duty. But in another idealizing passage, in his *Oeconomicus* (IV. 4), where this notion of control of the provinces by separation of the civil and military arms is developed at greater length, he underlines the unreality of what he has been saying by an unexpected concluding remark: "but where a satrap is appointed the charge of both arms is combined in him". This last statment seems to be the truth. The Behistun inscription shows Darius using the existing satraps as military commanders in regions beyond his reach, and after that we constantly find satraps having armed forces at their disposal and taking the field when necessary in their provinces. This was regular practice not only after the mid 5th century when the western satraps began to interest themselves in recruiting Greek mercenaries for their own service, but for instance under Darius I in 521 B.C. and also when Artaphernes, the satrap of Sardis, took the field as a commander of operations in his satrapy. There is, as we shall see, no other level in the provincial administration at which Xenophon's theory of dual control could apply; and the picture he presents is on his own showing fictitious. We may therefore reject the notion of divided control in the provincial government.[1]

Another theory, competing with Xenophon's rather than harmonizing with it, that has become prevalent in recent years, is that of "toparchies", which was put forward by scholars versed in Iranian institutions and built into an imposing structure from the Greek side. The assumption behind it is that the main military divisions of the empire were not the satrapies as we know them from Herodotus but a smaller number of larger areas each forming a single command. Christensen originally thought in terms of the four "toparchs" among

---

[1] Since Herodotus (III. 128) speaks of a royal secretary as being attached to every satrap (*hyparch*), modern scholars have inclined to the belief that these officials were responsible directly to the King and have seen this as a further restriction on the satraps' powers. But the secretary in Herodotus' story (the Sardis satrapy in 521 B.C.) simply read out the King's messages as they were handed to him; and the other Persian cited by some scholars as a royal secretary, Hieramenes, sounds more like a trusty emissary sent by the King in 411 B.C. and adviser at court five years later.

ADMINISTRATION OF THE SATRAPIES

whom the Sasanian empire was quartered; he sought to project the arrangement backwards through Parthian to Achaemenid times, apparently with the same ruling families. This involved a self-evident contradiction, that the Achaemenid empire, which comprised Egypt and Asia west of the Euphrates, could not be fitted into the Sasanian fourfold division; and Ehtécham proposed to increase the number of the original Achaemenid toparchies to a maximum of seven; but the effect of this was to convert a speculative hypothesis into a specific contention which is impossible if tested against the known facts.

From the Greek side the evidence is at first sight more substantial, and the notion of four army commands in the fourth century in fact goes back to E. Meyer. Xenophon speaks more than once of locations (*syllogoi*) for the marshalling or inspection of army groups, and in his *Anabasis* (1. 9, 7) he says that Cyrus the Younger was given command of all those whose marshalling point was Kastollou Pedion, and that he was designated 'karanos' – a word that may be related to Old Persian *kāra* = army: from this the conclusion is drawn that Cyrus' military command, which certainly exceeded the territorial limits of a single satrapy, was one of a small number of great "Armeebereichen" which formed the major divisions of the empire – if not indeed, as Junge and Toynbee would have it, the true "satrapies" of Darius. Xenophon might carry more authority here if the two syllogoi which he actually names were not both in the west of Asia Minor – hardly a likely location for the normal marshalling point of a group of satrapies; and here, as elsewhere, he seems to be converting an isolated phenomenon that he has only half understood into a general rule.[1] In fact, Cyrus the Younger's command as we know it in Xenophon was not at all in accordance with rule; it was what as aspirant to the throne he made out of a unique situation. The rest of the evidence that has been brought into play lends no positive support to the theory of "Armeebereichen". The concentrations of great military forces that we meet in the sources were not associated with standing territorial commands but with campaigns in which armies were assembled. For instance, when Pharnabazus was in command in Syria in the early 4th century it was not that he had been promoted to the post of "toparch of Western Asia", but that the King had appointed him commander-in-chief of the expedition to recover Egypt; and similarly in 401 B.C., when Xenophon

---

[1] Local musters were held as for instance (on the evidence of tablets) at Uruk in 421 B.C. and perhaps at Ur.

found the general Abrocomas and not the satrap Belesys in control in the north of Syria, we can assume that Abrocomas had been appointed as the King's commander-in-chief in the West with a view to preventing Cyrus from invading Babylonia – or possibly, as Rehdantz and Judeich, and more recently Olmstead, have supposed, to prepare for an expedition against the newly revolted Egypt. There can be no doubt that the standard territorial divisions of the empire were the satrapies as, following the Greek writers, we understand the term.

This is not to say that the satrapies were immutable. In the 4th century, if not earlier, there was some breaking up of satrapies, with the formation of new ones (as Caria after the death of Tissaphernes in 395 B.C., and Cappadocia in the dismemberment of Cilicia sometime after 401 B.C.; in the East probably a separate satrapy of Karmania (including southern Fārs), and a dismemberment of Herodotus' composite 7th and 16th nomoi, if we believe in them). We also once find two satrapies under the rule of a single satrap, though perhaps not before the last years of the empire (Abarnahara joined to the reduced Cilicia under Mazaeus after the reconquest of Phoenicia in 345 B.C.). But in general the satrapies were stable units. What did constitute a danger to the empire was the hereditary principle by which in some of the satrapies, as Abarnahara, Matiene, Daskyleion, and finally Caria, sons seem to have succeeded their fathers as though by right, with the result that some of them became semi-independent principalities. This enabled the hereditary Persian dynasties of eastern Anatolia to perpetuate their rule after Alexander and resulted in the kingdoms of Pontus, Cappadocia and Armenia; but it may already have been a cause of serious disunity in the empire before Artaxerxes III. It is in fact necessary to bear in mind that the first half of the 4th century witnessed a very great change in the character of Persian rule in Asia Minor. With the loosening of the links between the satraps and the central authority went a new understanding between the Persian grandees and the Greeks or natives with whom they were in contact. When even the King did not know for certain which of his satraps were loyal and which in revolt, it ceased to be a simple matter of Persians versus subjects (or Persians versus Greeks); and our picture of Persian rule in the West would be seriously distorted if we allowed the evidence of this period to be brought into play along with that for the 6th and 5th centuries.

For Darius I's "reform" of the satrapal system Leuze's lengthy discussion remains the locus classicus.[1] According to Herodotus (III.

---

[1] *Die Satrapieneinteilung*, especially pp. 13ff. and 43ff. in the separate page numbering.

89), after his accession Darius proceeded to establish the twenty satrapies, fixing for the first time the amount of tribute due from each, and fixing it in each case in silver (or gold). It is difficult to accept without qualification his statement that under Cyrus and Cambyses nothing had been fixed about tribute and the subject peoples simply brought gifts; for at several different points in his work Herodotus speaks of the fixing of tribute before Darius' time. But there must have been some fiscal innovation, since it was for this above all that Darius is said to have received the soubriquet "shopkeeper"; and it is in the statement that the tribute was fixed in gold and silver that the principal reform must be sought. The procession reliefs of the Persepolis Apadana have frequently been adduced as evidence that the subject peoples did nevertheless continue to bring their tribute in kind; but there are serious objections to this interpretation of the scene.[1] What the reform of Darius did was to guarantee the receipt of fixed revenues by the King; there is no certainty that it entirely guaranteed the subject peoples against extortion at the hands of Persian officials or grandees on the spot but it meant that there was no occasion for the latter to seek favour or preferment by exacting a greater tribute for despatch to the treasury. As regards the date, it is hardly possible to envisage the reform of the satrapal system as emerging complete in the opening years of Darius' reign; for the necessary step of detaching Abarnahara (the 5th nomos) from Babylon was not taken before his sixth year at the earliest (above p. 212), and if the land measurement was an essential part of his assessment for taxation, Ionia was not finally incorporated in the system until late in his reign (Herodotus VI. 42).

On the infrastructure of rule in the satrapies our information is patchy. In Egypt the "nomes" continued in being; and some at least of the governors of these territorial divisions of the country were Persians holding office under the satrap. In Abarnahara, on the other hand, there

---

[1] Some of the objects carried by subject peoples in the reliefs (as the Indians' pots of gold and the Aethiopians' elephant tusks) do correspond to tribute and statutory gifts mentioned by Herodotus. But this sort of literal interpretation of the scenes on Achaemenid reliefs creates more difficulties than it solves; and we may note that the scholars who insist upon it are nevertheless prudent enough to apply the term "throne-bearers" to the subject people on the reliefs who are depicted lifting the entire canopied dais which supports the royal party. In fact, the objects shown on the Persepolis Apadana reliefs seem to correspond quite well with the presents brought to the Persian kings in more modern times by envoys of governors and other rulers: in Chardin (the 1670s) we read of horses, cloth, and jewels, of hunting dogs from a place in Armenia, and of an ostrich and young lion from Basra; a giraffe also was noted by J. Barbaro in 1471 (from an Indian prince), and likewise an Indian buffalo by Pietro della Valle.

was a variety of governors, none of whom was normally a Persian. The cities of Cyprus, as well as Phoenicia, were governed by their own kings. The Greek cities of Asia Minor had a considerable degree of local autonomy, at first under bosses (tyrants) supported by the Persians, and after 494 B.C. under oligarchic regimes on the occasions when they found themselves subject to Persian rule. It is commonly said that in the Persian empire the great "Statthalterschaften" (the satrapies) were divided into "Unterstatthalterschaften", and these into smaller "Bezirke".[1] At first sight the resulting pyramid of power seems to apply well, as Leuze applied it, to the situation in Abarnahara at the beginning of Darius' reign. But it only needed the establishment of the separate satrapy there to make it appear totally different: after that only a Persian satrap, perhaps generally resident at the north corner near Aleppo, stood between the King and the native governors in Samaria, Jerusalem, and Amman, the Qedarite Sheikhdom and the authorities in Philistine Ashdod, perhaps priestly rulers as at Bambyce-Hierapolis, and Phoenician and Cypriot city princes. In general these native governors and princes will have had their chanceries which maintained contact with the satrap. There does not seem to be evidence of any other link in the chain of command. It is true that in Ionia towards 400 B.C. we find men, some of them Persians, named in our Greek sources as governors (*hyparchs*) of Tissaphernes and Cyrus the Younger in cities of the Aegean coast, and an impression is thereby created of a regular establishment of "Unterstatthalter" in the Sardis satrapy. But this was a time of war, with the Sardis satrapy as the seat of command; and in fact there seems to be no doubt that these were men of the satrap's entourage who were sent to act as his lieutenants in places where operations or negotiations were taking place. A similar example is provided by the Persian naval commander Sandoces, a former King's judge, whom Herodotus (VII. 194) names as being hyparch at Cyme on the coast of the Aeolis in 480 B.C.; this might have greater significance if we did not learn also from Herodotus (VIII. 130) that Cyme was serving as the main fleet base of the Persian armada in the autumn of that year. Phrygia on the Anatolian plateau may possibly have become a subordinate hyparchy in the course of time; but the normal organization of rule in the Asia Minor satrapies did not have the neatly graded structure that Leuze's hierarchies would imply.[2]

[1] As formulated by Leuze (his p. 40).
[2] One great difficulty in this study is that in the Greek writers the words "satrap", "hyparch", and "archon" are used almost as synonyms and do not in themselves permit the distinction of

ADMINISTRATION OF THE SATRAPIES

There were standing garrisons at many places in the empire: at satrapal centres like Memphis and Sardis, in frontier zones as at the first cataract, the southern border of Palestine, and the entry points of the Delta, or at the crossings into Cilicia, and no doubt at other nodal or dominant points.[1] These garrisons seem commonly to have been composed of imperial troops and not of local levies; so it is possible that in theory Xenophon is right in portraying the garrison commanders as directly responsible to the King. Canon Rawlinson took the mention in Herodotus (III. 91) of 120,000 measures of wheat due from the Egyptians for the maintenance of the Persians (or, to be accurate, of the Persians and their auxiliaries) in the White Fort at Memphis as indicating that there was a standing garrison of that number of Persians at Memphis, and this has even been used as a base for estimating the population of Persia. But it is not within the bounds of credibility; and in fact Herodotus' phrase, if taken in conjunction with a passage in Demosthenes, yields a figure of 16,000 men, not necessarily composed mainly of Persians.[2] From what little evidence there is, it does not seem to be the case, as has been supposed, that the principal activity of the male Persians consisted in garrisoning the empire; as regards numbers, it would seem clear that the Sardis garrison, assumed to be the most important one in the West, was no more than a guard on the citadel in 499 B.C. when the Ionians captured and burnt the city, and that it did not constitute an operational field force. Reinforcements were available in 499, and they arrived in time to engage the Ionian commando before it left Ephesus; but they were contingents brought by "the Persians who held nomoi within [i.e. west of] the River Halys".[3]

With the burning of Sardis in mind we may turn to the question of

grades. Similarly, a single word is applied to governors at all levels both in Babylonian documents and in the relevant books of the Old Testament.

[1] For graves attributed to imperial garrison troops in the vicinity of Aleppo and the extreme south of Abarnahara see Culican, *Medes and Persians*, 146ff., P. R. S. Moorey, "Iranian troops at Deve Hüyük in Syria in the earlier fifth century B.C.", *Levant* VII (1975), 108–17; for a sanctuary of Arabs in the vicinity of Darius' Suez canal see I. Rabinowitz, "Aramaic Inscriptions from a Shrine in Egypt", *JNES* XV (1956), 5–9.

[2] We have evidence, for instance, for Chorasmian, Caspian, Saka, Babylonian, Syrian, Cilician, and Jewish troops in Egypt. For the garrisons there see E. Bresciani, "La satrapia d'Egitto", *Studi classici ed orientali* VII (1958), 147–53.

[3] Herodotus v. 102. The word *nomos* is the one that Herodotus applies, along with *arche* (command, empire) and the Persian word satrapy, to Darius' provinces. But it cannot have the same precise meaning here. The normal range of meaning covers "assigned abode" as well as "administrative division"; in this context it could as well mean "estate or fief assigned by the King" as "sphere of command". In 521 B.C. the satrap of Sardis had a guard of 1,000 Persian spearmen (Hdt. III. 127). The account of the Ionian expedition against Sardis given above comes from Herodotus; Burn points out that according to Plutarch the Persian forces were depleted at the time because of an offensive against Miletus (below, p. 309).

the Persian military presence in western Asia Minor. The evidence from the Greek sources is scrappy, but we know of a number of cases of fiefs being granted and of Persians having taken over good land. It is generally in rich plain land that we discover Persian landowners, in the Maeander valley, in the Colophonian plain, the Hermus plain (Buruncuk), and the Caicus plain. Between these last two plains is the rough mountain country of Southern Aeolis, where we are told that the King's writ did not run in the 460s when Themistocles went into hiding in one of the Greek cities there; and when the Persians took over the Maeander plain after the fall of Miletus (494 B.C.) the mountain country of the Milesians to the south was handed over to intransigent herdsmen of the Halicarnassus peninsula. We also know that to the north, in the region of Mt Ida, there were cities that had not been subjected by the Persians until well on in Darius I's reign; and the impression that we receive is that the Persians occupied the good land without troubling themselves unduly over the control of the unproductive hill country, which was not suitable for fiefs.

In the fertile regions we find Persian landowners maintaining their own household brigades (our information comes mainly from Xenophon and so dates to the years around 400 B.C.). Details are not often given; but we are told that Spithridates had a force of 200 cavalry, and we hear of Hyrcanian and Bactrian cavalry and Assyrian infantry in the west. The nearest troops were brought quickly into action when Greek raiding parties appeared, just as those from a wider area had rallied to the defence of Sardis a hundred years earlier. This pattern is different from that of the satraps with their substantial corps of Greek mercenaries. It is a matter of mobile squadrons. The landowners who maintained these brigades were presumably the same Persian grandees who are said to have frequented the satrapal courts.

In the extreme west, on the troublesome Greek fringe, the situation was more of a compromise. In the Daskyleion region around 400 B.C. we find the Persian noble Spithridates established with his 200 cavalry somewhere to the east or the south; but a Greek was given a big fief in the hinterland of Cyzicus, and on the west in the less secure valley of the Scamander the maintenance of order was entrusted to a Greek or native despot, Zenis, who held the inland Greek cities with garrisons of Greek mercenaries. Down the coast we find the families of Greek refugees such as Demaratus, Gongylus of Eretria, and Themistocles holding fiefs alongside the Persian landowners. In Lycia, where fertile

ADMINISTRATION OF THE SATRAPIES

Map 9. The Persian presence in western Asia Minor.

valleys lie at the foot of the mountains, Persian control was evidently patchy; but among the names of magnates in western Lycia around the beginning of the 4th century we encounter Iranian ones like Harpagos, Otanes, Mitrobates, Arsames, and Artembares the Mede. These people seem to have been despots (a deputy of the Sardis satrap Autophradates is also mentioned), and unfortunately we cannot be certain that we are dealing with long-established landowning families. But it is presumably grandees such as we have mentioned who constituted the permanent infrastructure of Persian rule in western Asia Minor both in 499 B.C. and a hundred years later.

Our evidence for this Persian presence in peninsular Asia Minor will some day build up into a well-dotted map, of which Map 9, though hastily drawn up without adequate research, may nevertheless rank as a distant precursor. The evidence comes in the first instance from the literary sources; but unfortunately these do not multiply. To this we may add Persian names in inscriptions, to some extent contemporary ones like the Lycian, but in a greater degree Greek inscriptions of Hellenistic times which bear witness to the survival of Persian proper names, as well as the cults of the Persian deities in regions like Lydia and Lesser Armenia. No less important are the archaeological evidences of buildings and tomb architecture of Persian types, reliefs (and at Elmalı even tomb paintings) in Greco-Persian style reproducing the favourite despotic themes, of sealings at places where written contact was maintained with the Persian authorities, silver vessels, jewellery, and other objects of Iranian types, and (with their provenience far too rarely recorded) Greco-Persian and Achaemenian seals. The evidence is as yet too thin on the ground for firm patterns to emerge. But in general the fiefs on which Persians were established seem to have been in plains and in fruitful valleys such as those where the Phrygian hill country descends towards the river plains of the west coast.

These pleasant places could be beautiful with lodges, woods, animal parks, gardens and orchards, and no doubt in places with fountains of running water. The mountain country, on the other hand, offered little attraction, and the Persian presence seems generally to have been lacking there. We have seen that in the west of Asia Minor the King's writ did not run in the mountain regions. Further back, the whole of the mountainous Pontic region was virtually independent during much of the 5th and 4th centuries. We read of punitive expeditions being mounted, or at least contemplated, by Cyrus the Younger or Pharnabazus against Bithynians, Mysians, and Pisidians; and in the east of the Anatolian plateau the Cataonians and Lycaonians were accustomed to prey upon the neighbouring settled lands. In his description of the "Royal Road", which ran for ninety days' journey from Sardis to Susa with its royal posting stations, guards, and hostelries, Herodotus (v. 52f.) speaks of the King's highway as traversing inhabited and safe country throughout its entire length. This has caused modern scholars to assume that in the mid 5th century complete peace and security prevailed in the western empire. But it would seem that Herodotus' words must be taken more literally. Presumably the road worked its way through country settled with Persian fiefs and was kept secure from interference. But there would be no guarantee for the traveller who turned off into the hills. The lifeline of Persian communications with

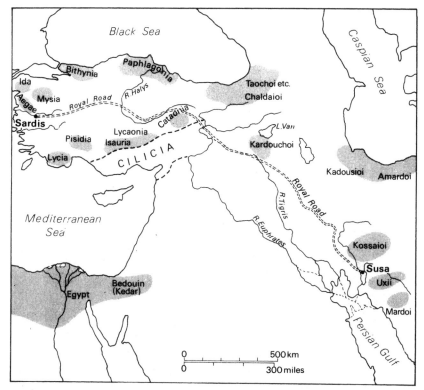

Map 10. Trouble spots of the western empire.

the West, like that of the Seleucids with Bactria and the East, must be thought of as a pacified and patrollable corridor. Map 10, which shows the course of the "Royal Road", also marks the trouble-spots – the regions which we know that at different times the Achaemenids failed to keep under regular control; it prompts the reflection that quite apart from the revolts and rebellions with which the later Achaemenids were faced, one of the inherent weaknesses of Persian rule was the lack of security within the provinces.[1]

[1] For the Percepolis road see above p. 243. In the years around 400 B.C. Cyrus the Younger was blinding highwaymen who infested roads in Asia Minor and Ezra had qualms about travelling to Palestine without an armed guard.

THE RISE OF THE ACHAEMENIDS

VIII. THE QUALITY OF ACHAEMENID RULE

The organization of the empire and the machinery of government have been considered, and it now remains to attempt some sort of appraisal of the prevailing conditions and the acceptability of Achaemenid imperial rule. This is – or was at the beginning of the 1970s – still a relatively uncharted field, for oriental empires have not usually been studied in this way; and in the circumstances we cannot hope to reach more than a very tentative assessment, whose value is likely to consist as much in the identification of problems as in the solutions offered.

First we may consider the question to what extent the subject peoples were admitted into the ranks of those who governed. Despite Herodotus' clear statement that the Medes were enslaved by the Persians (I. 129f.) and the evident lack of Medes as well as other provincials in important positions of which we have record, a view has become accepted that the Medes and Persians merged into a single ruling people. This requires serious consideration.

Herodotus (VII. 61) describes the Persian military costume (*skeuē*), and he goes on to say that it is in origin Median, not Persian, but the Persians adopted it from the Medes. He elsewhere, in a non-military context (I. 135),[1] speaks of the Persians adopting the Median dress (*esthēs*), which they found more congenial than their own. It is clear that he regards the Persians as dressed in the Median style whether at court or in the field. Scholars like Canon Rawlinson recognized that it is not possible to distinguish Medes from Persians in terms of the normal costumes worn on Achaemenian reliefs. By convention, however, a habit has been formed of distinguishing one dress prevalent on reliefs – the flowing court habit and straight-sided cap worn for instance by the King (cf. pl. 24a) – as Persian, and the other prevalent costume – the cavalryman's trouser-suit and round felt cap worn by the King's principal officials (cf. pl. 23) – as Median; and scholars now take it for granted that those who wear the one are Persians and those who wear the other are Medes.[2] An impression is thus created that the principal officials of the court were largely Medes, and that Medes alternated with Persians in

---

[1] This is clear from the fact that he immediately adds that for warfare they adopted the Egyptian breastplate.

[2] A further refinement that some scholars affect is the distinction of Elamites, as well as Medes, among the guardsmen depicted on Achaemenid reliefs; the criteria used for this (a braided hair-style and a dagger-type) are of course artistic variations which need not have any special significance.

THE QUALITY OF ACHAEMENID RULE

the corps of ushers, among the great body of courtiers, and – despite the quite explicit statements of Herodotus and Heracleides of Cyme to the contrary – in the ranks of the Immortals. If this view is correct, there could be no doubt that Medes did have their place with Persians in the high échelons of Achaemenid rule.

The difficulties in this current view are considerable. We are obliged to assume that while the holders of the office of hazārapatiš or chiliarch known to us in reputable literary sources were Persians, the holders of the office at the times represented by the audience reliefs of Darius I[1] and Artaxerxes I happened to be Medes. Aspathines, the bow-bearer of Darius I, has come to be spoken of as "Aspathines the Mede" because on the King's tomb front he is depicted wearing the 'Median' costume; but we have seen reason to believe that Aspathines came of a very high-ranking Persian family (that of Prexaspes, above p. 204). If we seek for a test, we must turn to the stairway reliefs of Darius' Apadana at Persepolis, where there is little doubt about the identification of the Median delegation at the head of the procession. There all members of the Median delegation wear the familiar trouser-suit. But only the leader wears the round felt cap; the eight Medes who follow him wear a hood rising over the brow to a triple peak. It thus appears that there is a distinct head-dress by which Medes can be recognized, but it is extremely rarely worn by the "Median" courtiers, officials, and Immortals of the reliefs. For the question of Medes in high positions we are therefore thrown back on the literary evidence, and above all on Herodotus.

Under Cyrus the Great and his son there is no doubt that Medes and indeed others of the subject peoples were promoted to positions of responsibility. Harpagos and Mazares, the first generals of Cyrus, were both Medes. In 522/521 B.C. Darius presumably had no choice but to use commanders already in post; of seven whom he despatched against the revolting subjects five (as he tells us) were Persians, one was a Mede, and one an Armenian. After this the Mede Datis was Darius' special agent for Greek affairs and was in joint command at Marathon (490 B.C.); and his two sons were accepted into the aristocracy of empire and held posts as cavalry officers in 480 B.C. But that is all. Every satrap of Darius known to us was a Persian. We have no detailed knowledge of Persian military activities under Darius save in the West; but every one of the fifteen or so high-ranking officers that we know to have been

---

[1] Or Xerxes. See above, p. 230, n. 1.

despatched there by him was a Persian. The evidence for 480 B.C. is the same. Of forty top-ranking officers all seem to have been Persians.

Here we see the further development of a practice that was already noticeable under Darius; approximately half of this body of commanders in 480 B.C. came from the immediate kin, by blood or by marriage, of the King himself. Achaemenid rule was becoming a family concern. And it was not only at the King's court that this narrowing of the circle of the élite took place. As we descend beyond the reign of Xerxes we find the satraps also tending to use their own relatives for important commissions. The notion that the Persians associated the subject peoples with them in their rule stands revealed as a chimera. It would be unreasonable to expect anything else from a proud imperial people in that age. But the fact must be stated, without any implied criticism, that there was no sharing of the perquisites of empire, little encouragement of talent or training of suitable candidates for high office, no conception of an integrated empire. The ranks of the administrative hierarchy were of course filled with native officials; for they possessed the knowledge and skills that were needed. But the governing class was Persian. Only in the 4th century do we find natives of the provinces assuming the higher control; and that resulted from their own ability to outface their rulers in an international epoch when the central authority had decayed and even Persian satraps were glad to ally themselves with strong men. In 522 B.C. there is no doubt what the Seven were fighting for; it was absolute and undivided imperium for the Persian nobles.

The Persian fief-holders have been discussed in the last section. To what extent the empire suffered from the curse of absentee landlords is not clear. Some of course must have been so, like Arsames, the satrap of Egypt, who seems to have had substantial estates not only in his satrapy but in Abarnahara and Babylonia and as far north as Arbela, and the queen-mother Parysatis, whose possessions included a group of villages (her "girdle") near the Tigris, or Warohi, who lived in Babylon and had an estate in Egypt; and 5th-century Babylonian tablets show Persians who had landholdings managed for them by agents. But Babylonia and Egypt may have been exceptional. It is in fact Xenophon who speaks of the fief-holders in the provinces as being normally absentee; and in western Asia Minor – the region that he knew at first hand – the evidence in favour of his contention is by no means satisfactory. The eastern half of the empire is inscrutable. We cannot judge the situation in the upper satrapies when we do not know whether the great landowners who dominated Bactria and Sogdiana were the old native nobility or (as in the West) immigrant Persian grandees (Altheim, Bickerman and Soviet scholars have assumed the one, and Junge and Frye the other).

As regards the growth of a feudal system under Achaemenid rule, the evidence is slight and difficult to interpret. G. Widengren in his recent study[1] devotes several pages to this topic, but only succeeds in isolating two or three minor facets of the matter. The general assumption that the classes (nobility, priesthood, clerks, workers) found in Sasanian times must go back to the Achaemenids carries no conviction; a clerical caste could hardly have come into being so soon, and the Magi seem rather to have been a clergy in the service of Persian (and, more generally, Iranian) masters.[2] Almost certainly the Achaemenid empire was more of a "Beamtenstaat" and less of a "Feudalstaat" than the Parthian and Sasanian states. In the Iranian social structure we have no evidence of a legal concept of slavery other than that by which, to commence at the highest level, all men were slaves of the King; but there seem to have been imported workers, at Persepolis and elsewhere, whose condition (whether permanently or not) was effectively that of slaves.[3] At the same time the development of a market economy in 482–480 in preparation for Xerxes' expedition (Herodotus VII. 23) and apparently of a monetary economy after that time in the Persepolis Treasury tablets implies that corvée workers were not quite slaves. Similarly, temple craftsmen at Uruk in Cyrus' time could bargain about their terms of employment.

One of the chronic problems of Asiatic empires is the control of nomadic tribes. The Achaemenid empire did not lack for them. According to Herodotus four of the ten clans of which the Persians were composed were nomadic.[4] One of these tribes – the Mardoi – is marked on map 11, with the Uxii and other non-Persian nomadic folk

---

[1] *Der Feudalismus im alten Iran* (Cologne, 1969), 102–8.

[2] The problems associated with the Magi cannot be discussed here. But we may say that they seem not to have been disseminators of a religion so much as officiants who performed ceremonies as needed. Herodotus recognized the Magi as a Median clan (I. 101), and there seems to be no good reason for regarding them as non-Aryan.

[3] For a sober statement of our knowledge of the social structure see Frye, *Heritage*, 51–5, and idem, "The institutions", in Walser, *Beiträge*, 83–93, and on slavery M. A. Dandamayev, in *ibid.*, 33–45.

[4] The Greek word of course means simply pastoral people as opposed to cultivators.

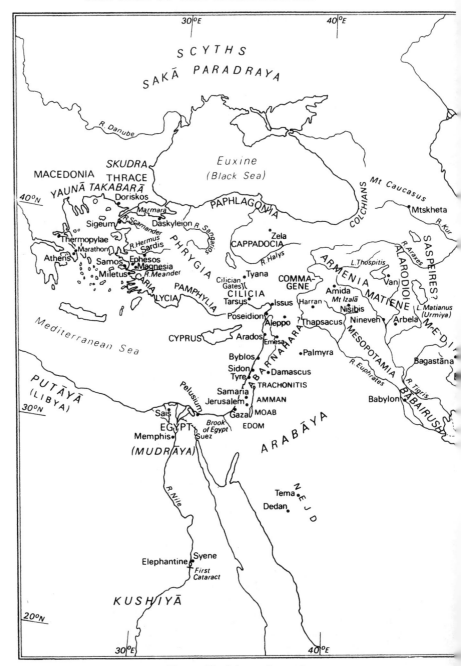

Map 11. The Achaemenian empire.

THE QUALITY OF ACHAEMENID RULE

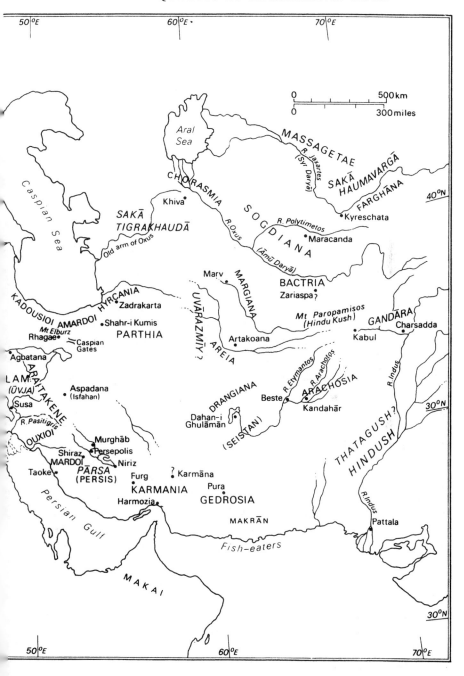

stretching north-west along the Zagros. It seems generally to have been supposed that the nomads of ancient Iran were tribes of the plateau who ranged freely over steppe and desert; and the lassoo-throwing Persian clan of Sagartians (Asagartiyā), whose cavalry accompanied Xerxes to Greece, has been cited in evidence of such movement because Herodotus (III. 93) places them in his 14th nomos south or east of Persis whereas it was in Media north of Persis that Darius defeated them in 521 B.C. (Behistun inscription).[1] This is a case where comparison with modern practice could after all be illuminating. At the present day the principal nomad confederation of Persis is the Qashgais. In summer they are to be found as far north as the high Zagros south of Iṣfahān, that is to say in Median Paraitakene; but in the autumn they descend through central Persis to the lower lands near the Persian Gulf. If the ancient Sagartians worked to a similar pattern, they would have spent the summer months in Media, where Darius' general fought them in the high summer of 521, but in winter, when they would be approachable by the fiscal authorities, their habitat would have been in the lower lands of the 14th nomos; and despite all this they could have been, as Herodotus makes them out to be (I. 125), a Persian tribe. With regard to the Sagartians we can of course only conjecture. But with the Mardians and the non-Persian tribes of the Uxii, Elymaioi, and Kossaioi of the Zagros we can infer from the Greek writers that these nomads were semi-nomadic or transhumant, moving high up the mountains in summer and descending to the low ground in winter without transgressing the limits of their own territory. As far as concerns internal security the problem was one of seasonal nomadism.

In Iranian monarchies nomads have been kept under control in periods of firm centralized rule. They are encouraged to co-operate by the opportunity of gainful employment in the armed forces, provided always that the government ensures that agreements are honoured and the promised maintenance, equipment, and payments are regularly supplied. At the end of Achaemenid times we find the Zagros nomads out of control. The Uxii even demanded payment from the King in return for allowing him to travel between Susa and Persis (they incautiously made the same demand of Alexander in 331 B.C., but he was accustomed to conquering tribesmen, not conciliating them, and so they disappear from history). In earlier Achaemenid times, however,

[1] The most recent tendency among scholars is to place the Sagartians in the region of the Karmanian desert; but that is no country for horsemen.

we hear nothing of these nomads save as auxiliaries in the armed forces, and there is no evidence of patrol posts or defensive measures to contain them; indeed the Fortification tablets of Persepolis, of Darius I's reign, seem to envisage unhampered movement of small parties of people between Persis and Susa, and the recently discovered Achaemenian pavilion or residence at Jinjān near Fahliyān looks like an entirely peaceful establishment on flat ground near the river. In Ctesias also, at the end of the 5th century, there is still no hint of interference with the route to Persis. On the evidence, slight as it is, it seems fair to assume that until a late period the Achaemenids were on good terms with the mountain tribes of the Zagros. What we may perhaps reasonably infer, when we take into account the apparent slightness of traces of permanent habitation of this date in the mountain regions, is that the Achaemenids were not greatly interested, as other rulers have been, in promoting sedentary agricultural settlement in the Zagros, and that the tribesmen of the mountains were left in undisputed possession both of the potentially fertile high folds and of the winter camping grounds in the warm lands. Under these circumstances there should have been little cause for friction.[1]

One measure that is often adopted in the interests of internal security in Asiatic empires is deportation, the aim being to transfer troublesome communities to strange surroundings where they inevitably become less refractory. We know of a number of examples of deportation by the Achaemenids. It was generally a punishment inflicted on communities that had revolted, though in one instance (the Paeonians) Darius I is said to have acted with the intention of improving the human stock inside his realm, while the Branchidae were removed to Bactria for their own safety. In the nature of the evidence we know only of those cases which were of interest to the Greek writers and so recorded by them, that is to say, of Greek and other western communities which were deported eastward (Milesians and Carians, Eretrians, Barcaeans of Cyrenaica, Jews, and Sidonians); and of course there will have been more instances of deportation which have left no record (unless we place the work-gangs of the Persepolis tablets in this category). But what we

[1] For a concise attempt at a reconstruction of the history of nomadism in Iran see *CHI* 1 (1968) 410ff. (X. de Planhol). H. Bobek, whose theoretical reconstruction of ecological conditions in post-glacial Iran (*Geogr. Jahresb.* xxv (1953–4) 30ff.) fits excellently with what the Greek writers tell us about Persis (above, p. 241), seems to assume that in the first millennium the centre and the inner parts of the mountain crust of Iran were in the grip of militant "Vollnomadentum"; this cannot, however, be reconciled with the settlement pattern as it appears in the Greek descriptions (especially Diodorus xix. 19–44, dating 317–316 B.C.).

do know of was on a relatively small scale; and it seems unlikely that the Achaemenids used deportation systematically as an instrument of imperial policy in the way that the Assyrians did or that Stalinist Russia has more recently done. Still less likely is Narain's contention that the hellenization of the eastern satrapies (as seen in Greek script and coinages) dates back to Greeks already settled there before the time of Alexander the Great.

The Arab problem seems to have been successfully handled. Admittedly, the revolt of Egypt caused confusion in the adjacent parts of Asia, of which Nabataeans may have taken advantage; and before 333 B.C. Arabs had established themselves in the Lebanon and were ready to prey upon the settled lands when the opportunity arose. But no disturbances are heard of before this late period of Achaemenid rule. In the 5th century Geshem of Qedar and his son seem to have been good march wardens. Persian authority was respected in Dedan; the camel-leading bedouin seem regularly to have brought their gifts, and their natural desire to harry the settled fringe lands in their seasonal movements or to annex them must have been curbed by the satraps of Babylon and Abarnahara. Here again, as on the north-eastern frontier where the dangerous tribesmen of the *limes* were evidently encouraged to participate in its defence, peace (as Toynbee remarked) seems to have been maintained with remarkably little exertion of force. As regards the other frontiers, the Caucasus seems to have presented no serious problem during Achaemenid times; and strong garrisons at the first cataract neutralized any threat from Aethiopians. The more thorny problems of the western frontiers belong to another chapter. The recently claimed recognition of a chain of fortified sites of Achaemenid stamp along the Levant coast requires closer investigation before credence can be given to it. In general, after the failure of the great expeditions against the Greeks, Persian military undertakings in the West came to labour under an increasingly cautious and cumbrous organization which allowed little scope for bold leadership, and the Persians' most effective weapon was the gold which they used to divide their enemies or to secure for themselves the services of Greek commanders and mercenaries.

Babylonia has provided much written material for the study of economic history in the period of Persian rule. But we can hardly ascribe an economic policy to the Achaemenids. Darius I may have had some idea of the benefits of commerce, as well as of navigation. But none of his successors show signs of having been conscious of the common market potential of their realm. So long as the revenues of empire continued to accumulate in the royal treasury, the King need feel no concern about the economic well-being of the realm; and in the hoarding of wealth the world has rarely seen anything comparable. Ehtécham's complaint in the peroration of his book that the greatest crime of the Balkan (i.e. Macedonian) hordes consisted in wantonly dissipating the carefully husbanded treasures of the Achaemenids seems to be a reversal of any reasoned judgement. Babylonia seems to have gone into a decline after Xerxes' reign. After a rapid rise in commodity prices shortage of money (silver) was cramping the economy; and the alienation of the land must have resulted in increasingly widespread impoverishment. The impression is given that it was only by a cultivation of the date palm as intensive as that of the potato in early 19th-century Ireland that the population continued to subsist.[1]

The Achaemenids were Persians. They had a love of natural beauty and a desire to live in pleasant surroundings; Darius I even wanted others to benefit, for the Gadatas letter shows him commending a governor for transplanting fruit trees from Abarnahara to Ionia. They liked their setting to be an "oasis", with parks and gardens and running water, with animals for the hunt, game, and fish. Whether they could think beyond the oasis to a larger whole, whether it is true that (to quote Ghirshman) "throughout the country public works were undertaken to increase productive capacity" is by no means so certain. It is true that under Darius I and Xerxes there were gangs of workmen and labourers in Persis paid for by the treasury there, and Persian nobles may have profited by the opportunity of providing a labour force; but we hardly know what works were going on apart from palace-building and tomb-cutting, and the evidence from literary sources is disconcertingly slight.

In Iran the greatest of all problems is water. Artificial irrigation by channels was practised in neolithic times on the fringes (Khūzistān and Turkestan) and in the southern uplands at least. These methods were no doubt used under the Achaemenids, but they cannot as yet be placed

---

[1] There is much detailed information in Olmstead, Chs 5, 14 and 21, though it was written before the publication of Cardascia, *Les archives des Murašû*. Recent essays on Achaemenid Babylonia are Meuleau's Ch. 17 in Bengtson, *Medes and Persians*, M. A. Dandamayev, "Achaemenid Babylonia", in I. M. Diakonoff (ed.), *Ancient Mesopotamia* (Moscow, 1969), 296–311 and in Walser, *Beiträge* 15–58, and R. Zadok, "The Nippur region during the Archaemenian period", *Israel Oriental Studies* VIII (Tel Aviv, 1978), 266–332.

THE RISE OF THE ACHAEMENIDS

in a time-scale calibrated in centuries. What is currently attributed to the Achaemenids is the introduction of two altogether grander and more effective methods of irrigation – the dam and the long underground aqueduct (*qanāt* or *kārēz*). Of the first there may be a notable example in Herodotus (III. 117). There was, he tells us, a mountain-ringed plain with a great river which ran off through openings in five directions. It had belonged to the Chorasmians but passed into the possession of the Persian Kings (this statement has given rise to a modern notion that a Great Chorasmian State existed in Khurāsān-Sīstān until the time of Cyrus!). One of the Kings blocked the openings, so that the water ceased to flow out to the people who depended on it. In the meantime he had sluice gates constructed; and when they protested, the gates were opened and turn by turn the inhabitants received their water again; but they now had to pay a fancy price for it. As it stands, the story is barely intelligible; and the circumstantial detail has a fairy-tale quality. But presumably an attempt at water control is being described, and it is attributed to a Persian King. Some modern scholars take the story as proof that great works of land improvement were carried out by the Achaemenids. But it is impossible to tell what it is that we have here and whether it constitutes the rule or the one exception to the rule which was worth relating; and in any case the story is presented as an example not of land improvement (there is no hint of that intention) but of fiscal rapacity. Apart from this, there are traces of dams on the river near Persepolis and perhaps Pasargadae which could be of Achaemenid date. But we are not yet in a position to say how the Achaemenids' achievement in water conservation compared, for instance, with that of Shāh 'Abbās: certainly the Persepolis tablets give no hint of anything on the scale of his attempt to divert the upper waters of the Kārūn to Iṣfahān.[1]

The question of qanāts is more easily resolved. There certainly were qanāts in existence in Iran in Achaemenid times. Polybius in his description of the eastern campaign of Antiochus the Great in 206 B.C. (x. 28) accurately describes the qanāts (*hyponomoi*) of the north edge of the desert under the Alburz (his Taurus); he speaks of them as numerous and as being so long that in Antiochus' day those who used the water no longer had any idea where it came from! Ctesias (about 400 B.C.) also refers to an aqueduct or qanāt that brought water to Agbatana in Media from Mt Orontes (Alvand); its great age is indicated

---
[1] Herbert speaks of 40,000–100,000 men being employed on this project.

THE QUALITY OF ACHAEMENID RULE

by the fact that the work was already attributed to the mythical queen Semiramis.[1] Qanāts, then, were almost certainly older than the Achaemenids. But the Achaemenids recognized the value of this method of irrigation, for in this matter they were prepared to make a remarkable financial concession: Polybius tells us that they had allowed anyone who brought water to barren land to reap the benefits of it for five generations (i.e. before it passed to the crown). Because of that, he says, the inhabitants of the Alburz undertook the construction themselves. The reason why qanāt-building has been so infrequently undertaken is that the expense is great and no private person could afford such an outlay when the benefit from it went to the crown. The Achaemenids are here shown as forbearing and far-sighted, unique perhaps in this among Iranian monarchs before our own times.

No empire easily escapes the charge of oppressiveness. Herodotus tells us, and the documents tend to confirm, that Babylonia and Egypt both suffered grievously after their revolts at the end of Darius' reign; and in the west the Greeks with their insistence on freedom were intolerant of the Persian yoke. But this does not mean that the subject peoples as a whole resented it; accustomed to alien masters, many of them may have found the Persian rule relatively easy-going. It does no service to the Achaemenids to represent them, as some recent writers have done, as a great civilizing force in the ancient world, or as an imperial people whose political thought rose superior to that of the Greeks and "transcended the narrow limits of the polis". They did not build cities, though the peace they brought may have encouraged others to do so.[2] There was no ancient Persian literature or cultural development, no Persian scholarship or science; the doctors at the Achaemenid courts were Egyptian specialists and Greek general practitioners. The Achaemenids' monumental architecture from the time of Cyrus the Great was firmly rooted in Greek and Lydian (and to some extent Egyptian) practice. Their imperial art was a composite with an imposing present

---

[1] The canal at Tušpa (Van), attributed to Semiramis both in antiquity and at the present day (Turkish "Şamransu"), dates back to Urartian rule about 800 B.C. Qanāts seem to have made their appearance not long after this in Urartu and Assyria. There is a fair case for believing that Darius I had qanāts made in the Khargeh oasis.

[2] As in the Indus valley, where Wheeler has pointed out that the revival of cities like Charsadda dates to Achaemenid times. On the other hand, there is remarkably little trace of settled life in that era in eastern Anatolia and Armenia; and in Iran it was the Seleucids, and especially the Sasanians, who concerned themselves with city-building, with Greco-Bactrians and Kushans active in the upper satrapies.

but no past or future; and where it breaks through the ceremonial to present the individual and informal it could be that we are justified in sensing the originality of an Ionian master. But their rule was one which induced racial and cultural fusion.[1] They respected the institutions and religious beliefs of their subjects.[2] They were rarely bloodthirsty, and often they were magnanimous;[3] and until corruption became prevalent they seem to have had the gift of commanding loyalty, for our sources give no hint of treachery or defection in the motley army of Xerxes and Mardonius in 480–479 B.C. In particular, we may surmise that there was a strong sense of Iranian unity lending solidarity to the eastern half of the empire. It is only in the generations after Alexander, in Eudemus and in Eratosthenes (ap. Strabo), that we find mention of the concept of a greater nation of Iran (Arianē) stretching from the Zagros to the Indus; but the sense of unity must have been there, for Herodotus tells us that the Medes were formerly called Arioi,[4] and Darius I (followed by Xerxes) in his inscriptions proclaims himself an Iranian (Ariya) by race – he speaks of himself in ascending order as an Achaemenid, a Persian, and an Iranian (Naqsh-i Rustam). Certainly the Seleucids were never able to obtain the support of cavalry from the upper satrapies in the way that the Achaemenids had done.

The impression that we get of the Persians in the Greek writers is in some ways a deceptive one. Too much emphasis is laid on what is

[1] We may here quote Bickerman in *La Persia e il mondo greco-romano*, 103: "In Persian Babylonia we see men of all nationalities living peacefully together – from Egyptians, Jews and Moabites to Afghans and Indians – under the rule of the Achaemenids. A contract of marriage between a Persian and an Egyptian woman is written in cuneiform script. Arameans, Babylonians, Egyptians are witnesses." Dandamayev reckons non-Babylonians as forming about a third of the names that occur in records of the great estate-management firm of Murashu in Nippur and including Persians, Medes, Sakai, Areians and other Iranians; he also mentions as resident in Babylonia West Semites (especially Aramaeans), Elamites, Lydians, Greeks, Phrygians, Carians, Arabs, Egyptians, Indians etc. (Walser, *Beiträge*, 57).

[2] Exceptions can be found, notably in the behaviour of Xerxes and Artaxerxes III towards the gods of subject nations (Babylon and Egypt) who had revolted. But in addition to their generally favourable attitude towards the responsible priesthoods in the satrapies, the Kings showed a remarkable propensity to flatter Jewish religious sentiments at least, even to the detriment of good-neighbourly relations; and Darius I, Artaxerxes I, and Darius II are on record as concerning themselves personally with religious concessions in different places.

[3] Any remark of this sort is of course relative. There were barbaric punishments and tortures. Some of the Achaemenids showed themselves cruel, especially if Ctesias is to be believed; and Artaxerxes III (Ochus) was undoubtedly ruthless. Darius I consigned the "Kings of the Lie" to atrocious deaths; but, whether justly or not, this could rank as exemplary condign punishment. In general, the Achaemenids do not seem to have been in the habit of shedding the blood of enemies and subject peoples unnecessarily, and they were honourable in their treatment of hostages.

[4] This word is quite distinct from the name Areioi which designates the inhabitants of the dahyāuš of Areia (Old Persian Haraiva); etymologically there is no connection between the two names, and so there can be no question here of a metropolis of the Aryans.

pejorative – the familiar clichés of the Persian Wars in which the weaknesses of the imperial people were exposed, and the commonplaces of a later era when decadence and corruption were plain to see. If we read Herodotus carefully, we find in him not only tolerance but a genuine respect for the Persian nobles who figure in his pages: for their courage, their loyalty, their feeling for beauty, and on occasion generosity. Aristocratically-minded Greeks like Xenophon found still more to admire. Cyrus the Younger, who fell at Cunaxa, was Xenophon's great hero, and in his *Cyropaedia* the Cyrus whom he had known can never have been far from his thoughts; by contrast of course Tissaphernes, the satrap of Sardis and adversary of Cyrus, in whose eyes loyalty to the King ranked higher than honouring his agreements with others, appears as a treacherous scheming Oriental. But nothing in Xenophon creates a stronger impression than the chivalrous exchange in which another great Persian noble, Pharnabazus, was involved with the Spartan king Agesilaus when the two adversaries met to parley in a field near Daskyleion. The story is told in another chapter (below, p. 362); but it is relevant to refer to the effect that the Persian's reply to the invitation to join forces had on Agesilaus and Xenophon. To Greeks brought up on Homer honour could not shine brighter than this.

It was this almost Homeric sense of honour that made the most favourable impression on Greeks and may equally have won the admiration of the subject peoples. Alexander the Great, who himself traced his descent from Achilles, affected to despise the Persians, and as far as Persepolis he continued overtly in this frame of mind; but he had in fact learned to appreciate them, and thereafter he sought to make them partners with his own followers in empire. This was not a matter of an imaginative ideal, of the brotherhood of mankind, but a hard-headed appraisal of those qualities which are required in a ruling race. Once again, it is from the Greek writers, and from them alone, that we can come to an understanding of the ancient Persians, and see what were the qualities that made them an imperial people.

CHAPTER 6

PERSIA AND THE GREEKS

I. THE GREEKS AND THE IMPERIAL EXPANSION (TO 500 B.C.)

1. *The First Conquest of Ionia*

Before Cyrus marched against Croesus, he had made overtures to the Asian Greeks, of whom the Ionians were the most important; a very reasonable effort to stir up trouble in the enemy's rear, or at least to induce Croesus' recently conquered subjects, with their armoured infantry, not to march. It is a warning, such as Eduard Meyer emphasised, against conceiving the oriental monarchies as "much too primitive" in their geographical knowledge. Cyrus controlled Assyria and the same secretaries as had served the Medes in their dealings with Lydia; and his agents could travel on Greek ships trading with Trebizond or Phoenicia. When Ionian delegates waited upon him at Sardis, he may well have told them that the terms would now be stiffer. But Cyrus knew enough to renew Croesus' treaty with powerful Miletos.

When envoys from Sparta landed at Phokaia, the most powerful of the remaining Ionian states, their name was perhaps new to him, though Croesus had made alliance with them too. (He had not received any actual aid either. Sparta, dominating a never completely conquered Peloponnese, never in her history sent her unmatched but unreplaceable main citizen forces over sea.) But when Cyrus asked "the Greeks who were beside him" (so he was already using Greeks) "who were the Spartans, and *how many?*" it was no mere sarcasm. He asked those who knew for a report. However, the envoys' warning that Sparta "would not regard with indifference any interference with the Greeks" fell flat. Herodotus indeed opines that their envoys were sent chiefly as an intelligence mission, to have a look at Cyrus' forces. For the rest, their bluff had been called.

Cyrus is said to have added: "I never yet feared men who have a place demarcated in their city, in which to meet and deceive each other on

GREEKS AND IMPERIAL EXPANSION

oath! If my health holds, they shall have troubles of their own to think about." If he really said that, it is ironic that he should have said it to Spartans, who had deliberately turned their backs upon commercial civilisation and the market. But the story sums up at once, at the outset, the tragic incompatibility and failure of understanding between Persia, the highest manifestation of oriental imperialism, and the still developing *bourgeois* culture of the Greek cities.

Cyrus returned up country, never to visit Sardis again. He was preoccupied, says Herodotus, "with Babylon and Bactria and the eastern nomads and Egypt; against these he intended to march in person, while sending another general against Ionia". He left a Persian garrison at Sardis, with Paktyas, a Lydian, in charge of taxation and finance. Native officials were to serve him well in Babylonia, and his son in Egypt; but Paktyas, who had presumably spoken him fair when present, promptly revolted, hiring mercenaries and calling the coastal Greeks to his aid, and besieged Sardis. All the harsher was the sequel. The revolt was quickly crushed by reinforcements sent back by Cyrus, and Paktyas fled to Kyme (mother-city of the Kyme or Cumae on the Bay of Naples), where the people, not daring to keep him, put him over to the neighbouring island of Lesbos. Here he should have been safe, since Persia had still no sea-power; but Mazares the Mede, commanding the force that had relieved Sardis, had orders to bring him back alive at all costs, and in negotiations with Mytilene soon reached the stage of "How much?". This stage took longer, and meanwhile the men of Kyme rescued their suppliant and transferred him to Chios; but the Chians did sell him, for a piece of coast opposite to Mytilene, leaving the Mytilenaeans deeply regretful at having missed their chance. Paktyas' fate is unrecorded, but was probably horrible.

Mazares next harried the plain of the Maeander down to the Milesian border, and sold the people of Priene as slaves. He then died, and northern Ionia fell to his successor, another Mede: Harpagus, who figures in the saga of the Rise of Cyrus (p. 203). The men of Phokaia both strove and bargained hard. Harpagus reduced his demands to a minimum: would the Phokaians demolish but one bastion and "dedicate" one house (as a royal residency?) – and, it goes without saying, pay tribute – he would call off his army; i.e., the city would not be occupied, but must admit that it *could* be. The Phokaians asked for a twenty-four-hour armistice "to consider the terms"; and Harpagus, though he said he guessed what they meant to do, let them have it. Then, we are told, the whole population went on shipboard and sailed away; but before they had gone far "more than half of them" lost heart and returned; a shrunken Phokaia thus survived. A Phokaian sculptor, Telephanes, later worked at Persepolis.

The die-hard Phokaians, after pawky Chios had refused to sell them the inshore "Wine Islands" for fear of their trade competition, sailed to Corsica, where they already had a colony; but their piracy made them such a plague to their non-Greek neighbours that Carthage, then rising as a military protector of the western Phoenicians, combined with the Etruscans to force them out. This is typical of the situation that was soon to make the eastern Phoenicians too into Persia's loyal vassals.

The men of Teos also sailed away, to their colony of Abdēra in Thrace; they saved their liberty only for a generation. Most of the Ionians simply defended their walls. This was second nature to Greeks; but against the eastern tactics of the siege-mound supported by archery, the surrender of each in turn was only a matter of time.

In the south there was another sign of things to come. The Dorians of Knidos tried to cut through their rocky isthmus; but the work was arduous, and they seemed to suffer an excessive number of eye-injuries from splinters. They consulted the Delphic Oracle, and the reply was "Stop digging; Zeus would have made it an island, had he wished". So the famous oracle, which had already "hedged" with celebrated ambiguity when Croesus asked whether he should attack Cyrus, embarked on its consistent policy of advising Greeks to accept the King's peace. Its priests were well-informed men, and had much to lose; and the Branchidai, the family that ran the oracle at Didyma, near Miletos, were already committed to peace. The Persians for their part consistently treated Apollo with respect; and certainly Apollo served them well.

The Karians, native neighbours of Miletos and sharing Ionia's basic material culture, also surrendered easily. Only the mountain Lykians of Xanthos, in the far south, fought to the death. Their city was reconstituted by incomers together with eighty families which "happened to be absent" (at summer hill-stations?); and both Karia and Lykia, under local dynasts who learned both from Persia and from the arts of Greece, became an interesting zone of interpenetration of the two cultures.

Nothing had yet happened to change Cyrus' estimate of the Greeks (or Ionians, as Asians have continued to call all Greeks ever since) as a "nation of shopkeepers". The Ionians had consulted together, but had fought separately. Their heavy armour reduced their mobility; and behind their walls a Persian field-army could deal with cities one at a time. They had not taken the advice of their wise man, Thales of Miletos, who advised them to turn their League into a federal state; or of Bias of Priene, who advised that all Ionia should sail to colonise Sardinia; and the Paktyas affair had shown them venal. The Phoenicians knew them as formidable pirates; but it did not seem necessary to take them very seriously.

Herodotus, like Cyrus, now turns away to deal with Babylon, Egypt, and the eastern frontier where Cyrus fell in battle with nomads who still used bronze weapons, about 529. But when we next hear of western Asia Minor, the pattern of Persian government is already established. Two satraps, at Sardis and at Daskyleion south of the Marmara, were responsible respectively for the south-west and the north-west, called by the Greeks Hellespontine Phrygia and by Darius the satrapy of "the Men on the Sea". At times there were also lesser satraps in Ionia, Karia and parts of the north-west, and at times a supreme commander (*karanos*) of the Men on the Sea, whose authority might overlap or, by royal command, override that of the two chief satraps. Not every district in the area could be patrolled, and in the Troad we even hear of Greek cities engaging in local war; the satraps apparently did not interfere so long as they paid their tribute.

To collect the tribute, the Persians took the natural course of identifying a suitable "boss" in each Greek city, and making him governor. Some of the cities, it transpired, had such bosses already; their friends sometimes called them "kings", but their enemies used a foreign word, "tyrants". Most cities managed their own affairs through town-meetings, electing weak executives; but Persia wanted one strong enough to collect the tribute promptly and to be personally responsible. This inevitably meant an armed guard, and control of arms generally; and what then happened to local representative institutions did not interest the satrap.

The word *tyrannos* may not always have been pejorative. Greek drama uses it of any king, and some *tyrannoi* had risen as popular leaders against closed aristocracies; but it became part of Greek popular philosophy that few men, given such power, would control their greed or lust. Persia's tyrants became intensely unpopular, and in the end, after fifty years and after learning its lesson at heavy cost – Persia had the good sense to change the system (p. 312). Yet, even then, in the great revolt, far more "tyrants" were let go than were actually lynched. They were men, not monsters, and they and their fellow-citizens shared some secrets against Persia. Also, in the early days, the state of affairs across the Samos Channel, where within a few years the pirate-king Polykrates was holding islands to ransom, was no very attractive advertisement for liberty. For the time, there was peace.

2. *The Empire, Egypt and the Mediterranean (c. 525–515)*

Cyrus' son Cambyses, continuing his father's agenda, in 525 assailed Egypt, and as a prelude to this – a great matter, for which his courtiers praised him – he "won the sea". The city-kings of Phoenicia did him homage, as did Syennesis (a dynastic name or title), king of the Cilicians, also no mean seamen. Ionia was his already. The old Pharaoh Amasis had done what he could to prepare defence, increasing his Greco-Karian mercenary forces, establishing suzerainty over the several Greek and one Phoenician city-kings of Cyprus, and making alliance with Polykrates; but when Cambyses moved, they deserted in a body. (Herodotus indeed says that Amasis first broke off the alliance with Polykrates; but in a context of fable.) Polykrates' squadron, indeed, did not join the invasion; but only because the captains, said to have been chosen from among those notables whom Polykrates considered expendable, turned back from Karpathos and attacked him, unsuccessfully. The other eastern Aegean islands sent their squadrons, and it was a ship of Mytilene, which had old trade-connexions with Egypt, that, after Cambyses had broken through the frontier defences, carried to Memphis his herald to demand surrender – only for all its crew to be massacred by the Egyptians in an explosion of impotent rage.

On land indeed there was a sharp struggle before the Persians broke through; the first battle in which Greeks in great force met Persians in the field; and the Persian combination of archers and cavalry won a complete victory. Unfortunately we have no tactical account of it. Egypt was conquered, and its fall was followed by the submission of the Greek colonies in Cyrenaica.

The satraps of the north-west at this time were Oroites at Sardis and Mitrobates at Daskyleion, who made a dangerous enemy by taunting Oroites with his inability to suppress Polykrates. About 523 however

GREEKS AND IMPERIAL EXPANSION

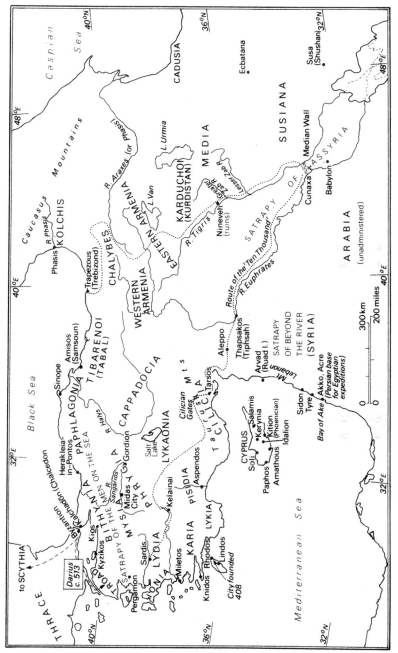

Map 12. The western provinces of the Achaemenian empire.

Oroites achieved this coup. Pretending to be in trouble with his king and in fear of assassination, he wrote to Polykrates asking to be taken off; and by making much of the amount of treasure he would be bringing, he induced the Samian to come in person to see to it. He was then seized on the beach, taken up country and tortured to death. His power however did not at once collapse. His minister Maiandrios, left in charge at Samos, did think of restoring the republic; but, says Herodotus, "having desired to be the most just of men, he was not able". He found some prominent citizens so hostile to him, and so incautious in saying so, that he gave up the idea, continued to pay Polykrates' mercenaries, and went on as before.

However, at least Maiandrios was not Polykrates. Oroites was proud of his coup, and amid the brief anarchy that followed the death of Cambyses in 522 and Darius' assassination of Smerdis (or, as official history insisted, the Pseudo-Smerdis), with his peace-policy and his Magian friends, the satrap's ambitions soared. He killed Mitrobates and took over the northern satrapy; conserving his forces, he sent no help to Darius against the Medes and Armenians; and even when Darius and the regular army, against all expectation, had crushed all other rebellions within two years, Oroites, with his own Persian guards and holding nearly half of Asia Minor, still hoped that the upstart king, so far away, would be unable to interfere with him. He continued to withhold his tribute; and when Darius sent a courier to him, merely returned a respectful answer in public, and arranged for the despatch-rider to disappear mysteriously on the return journey.

Satrap revolt in Asia Minor was indeed to be a recurrent phenomenon; and Darius did not commit his weary army at once to a new civil war. But Oroites had underestimated both the strength of Persian loyalty to the King as such, and Darius' capacity for evoking heroic service. A nobleman named Bagaios, selected from among numerous volunteers, carried the next "bag"; and while, in general audience, Oroites' secretary read out messages on routine topics, Bagaios watched the reactions of the guards to the King's name and style. Seeing them respectful, he produced an order addressed to them directly: "Persians! King Darius orders you no longer to bear the spear for Oroites!" They grounded their arms, and Bagaios followed with "King Darius orders the Persians who are in Sardis to kill Oroites". The nearest drew their daggers and obeyed.

So the King's writ ran again from the Punjab to the Aegean; and,

GREEKS AND IMPERIAL EXPANSION

probably while still engaged on his great overhaul of the administration, Darius took steps to gain first-hand intelligence on what lay beyond, not choosing, evidently, to depend entirely upon the Phoenicians, who, however loyal, were notoriously secretive. Herodotus heard details of one mission (not necessarily the only one), handed down from the reminiscences of a Greek who accompanied it: Dēmokēdēs, a physician of the Pythagorean school of Krotōn in south Italy. He had been in the suite of Polykrates, who had enticed him with an increased salary from the service of the Peisistratid brothers, dynasts of Athens, who had themselves enticed him from that of the island republic of Aigina; had been captured and forwarded to Susa among the other belongings of Polykrates; had languished awhile as a captive, but then had gained recognition – rather to his alarm, since he feared that he might now never be let go. He had, he said, rendered valuable service both to the King and to Queen Atossa, daughter of Cyrus and now Darius' main link with legitimacy. (Indeed, Herodotus says that he personally, through the queen, was responsible for turning Darius' attention to the west and for getting the mission sent. This is typical both of Greek oral tradition in all ages, and of Herodotus' limitations.)

The mission comprised fifteen Persian officers, carried on two warships from Sidon, accompanied by a large freighter. Demokedes (he admitted) was kept under surveillance, though he added that the King had exacted from him a promise to return, which he had no intention of keeping. Sailing over to Greece, they "explored the coasts and made notes" (or "had them written down"; maps of a kind were not unknown in Babylonia). No one apparently raised any objection, until when they put in, still quite openly, at Taranto, Demokedes, having reached Italy, succeeded in passing the inflammatory word "Spies!". Aristophilidas, the constitutional king of Taranto (a colony of royalist Sparta), thereupon ordered the detention of the ships, though he released them before long; and Demokedes escaped. The Persians followed him to Kroton and demanded his extradition as "a runaway slave of the King"; but they met with mob resistance, and retired, protesting loudly that Kroton would find this a dangerous way to behave.

On their way back, they were wrecked by a storm in the Straits of Otranto and captured by the Iapygian natives. They were released through the mediation of Gillos, an exile from Taranto, who asked in return that the King should use his good offices to get him restored;

he thought this might be effected through the mediation of the King's Greek subjects at Knidos, which had close trade-relations with Taranto. The *démarche* was duly made, but failed. The era of intelligence missions, diplomatic relations and protests over a defecting scientist had thus fully arrived; but the western Greeks, quite justifiably, did not feel the danger to be immediate.

Nearer Persia, it was different. About 517 an expedition under Otanes, one of the Seven Conspirators, at last captured Samos, under the pretext of restoring the rightful heir, Syloson, a brother of Polykrates, driven out by him. Maiandrios, whose heart had never been wholly in the perilous game of tyranny, offered no resistance, and his brother Lykarētos, compromised at Samos by having executed a number of political detainees when Maiandrios was dangerously ill, entered the Persian service; he was later governor of Lemnos. But a second brother, who had been kept under restraint as mentally unstable, egged on the mercenaries not to surrender without a struggle. He attacked the Persians unawares, killing several officers and provoking a massacre, so that "room to spare" in Samos became a proverb. However, Syloson was reinstated over a still quite numerous population, and transmitted his power to his son Aiakes after him.

Maiandrios went to Sparta; according to Herodotus, to solicit aid for his restoration, which is hardly consistent with his realism or his recent conduct; more probably, invited to consult. Sparta did nothing so rash as to provoke Persia; but she did (according to a fragment of Diodoros, on Sea-Powers) send out an expedition which dominated the central Aegean for two years, and was followed by a consolidation of the Cyclades, led by an aristocratic republic of Naxos. Naxos had been under a populist tyrant who had been friendly to Peisistratos of Athens and to Polykrates, and was overthrown by Sparta. It was becoming the policy of conservative Sparta to suppress revolutionary "tyrannies"; but another consideration may have been to prevent a "power vacuum" in the Cyclades which, with piracy and disturbances, might provoke Persian intervention. In the event, the breakdown of Naxos' "empire" after ten years did have just that effect (p. 307).

3. *The Persians enter Europe*

Darius, with his hands now free, was indeed planning operations in Europe, but more in the Iranian style: massive land operations, using the Asian Greek navies only for transport and supply; especially for the construction of boat-bridges over the Bosporus and then over the Danube, the most practical method of getting many thousands of men and animals across. He would invade Scythia, modern south Russia, the European nomad-land. Why?

Rationalist scholars have been anxious to impute to a supposedly great man only rational motives: to reconnoitre, to find out whether nomad-land was, as it had been a century earlier, in a state of eruption. (Herodotus puts revenge for this among his chief motives.) But if we compare the last campaigns of Cyrus and Cambyses, and the first of Xerxes, we may conclude that he was simply extending his power as far as he could; a proceeding which many in the ancient world considered to be compulsive for human nature,[1] and which would accord with Darius' announced conviction of his divine mission. He would attempt Europe (having no idea of its extent); and if he mastered the continent, the Mediterranean lands would follow.

The army crossed the Bosporus probably in 513. Herodotus saw in the great temple at Samos a painting dedicated by the Samian Mandrokles, chief engineer of the bridge of boats; it showed Darius enthroned, watching the crossing. Darius also set up two inscriptions (as on the completion of his Suez canal) with inscriptions in Greek and cuneiform; but of them Herodotus saw only one stone "covered with Assyrian writing"; for before his time the Byzantines had demolished them, "taken them into the city, and used them for building the altar of Artemis". (Pieces may conceivably still exist, buried somewhere among later foundations.) The tribes of eastern Thrace, where northern invaders dominated an indigenous peasantry, were subdued, mostly without resistance. The east-Greek fleets had meanwhile gone ahead to the Danube, to organise their ships into another bridge above the Delta; and Darius entered Scythia.

He was probably not doing so without previous collection of information; for Ktesias, an unreliable writer but here perhaps correct, describes a (presumably earlier) sea-borne reconnaissance, conducted by Ariaramnes, Satrap of Cappadocia, with a light squadron of thirty fifty-oared galleys. Ariaramnes took prisoners, including a brother of the Scythian king, who was in disgrace (perhaps *residence forcée* in the supposed security of the Crimea). From him, as well as from Greek colonies such as Olbia (near modern Odessa) Darius could learn the

[1] Cf. the Athenian imperialist speaker in Thucydides v. 105. 2.

situation: a royal horde, immigrant from Asia six or seven generations earlier, taking tribute both from other nomad tribes and, nearer the coast, from peasants who had existed there since neolithic times. There were even some Scythians who, while themselves keeping to the nomad diet of meat and milk, grew corn on the famous "black earth", having found that the Milesians of Olbia would give for it wine and silver and other desirable trade-goods.

Darius spent something over two months north of the Danube; not nearly long enough for the campaign described by Herodotus. If there were really, as he says, the remains of seven forts planted by Darius, east of the Don mouth, they must have been planted by some other, probably sea-borne, expedition. One of his tales is that Darius originally planned to march home via the Caucasus, and was only dissuaded by Koës, the admiral from Mytilene, from abandoning his ships and bridge and taking the crews with him as infantry. That Darius made Koës "tyrant" of Mytilene for his services on this campaign was a "public" fact; but that his distinguished service included saving his crews from what Greeks considered the awful fate of being marched far away from the sea is a story that he might well have invented for himself, in search of popularity.

Back at the bridge, no doubt the Ionians grew restive. Two months passed. Darius, beset by the nomads, could send no message; and instead, Scythians appeared and urged them to go home; they, the Scythians, would then deal with the King. But the city-dynasts, headed by Histiaios of Miletos, held them to their posts, Histiaios pointing out to his colleagues that liberation from Persia would mean liberation of the cities from *them*. Miltiades, the Athenian dynast of the Chersonese (Gallipoli Peninsula), claimed later to have advocated accepting the Scythian proposal; but Herodotus, who tells this story as fact, later remarks that he had to flee from his principality, not because of the wrath of Darius (to whom such a proposal in council would certainly have been reported by someone), but because of a Scythian counter-raid![1] Darius knew his men.

East of the Caspian, Darius had actually captured the nomad king Skunkha, perhaps by some form of pincer-movement; but in south Russia it is clear that he failed. It is clear not only from stories that he regained the bridge only by abandoning his camp and his sick and wounded (which *could* be Greek fictions), but from the public facts of

[1] iv. 137; cf. vi. 40.

what followed. He returned to Asia by ship from the Chersonese (Miltiades' country!), *leaving the Bosporus cities out of control*. Something had encouraged revolt; and that Darius did not immediately suppress it suggests that he did not have the troops. He had left his army in Europe; Greek writers, who regularly number royal armies in hundreds of thousands, say only a corps, or one-tenth of it; but if only one-tenth, where were the nine?

The troops left in Europe, while Darius displayed himself safe and sound at Sardis, were under Megabazos, the most sagacious and most highly valued of the King's marshals. Eastern Thrace having been subdued already, Megabazos turned west. Samian Perinthos on the Marmara resisted and was taken by storm. The horse-riding Paionians were drawn, by a demonstration in force, to resist Megabazos' debouchement into their plain by the coast route, neatly outflanked by a column sent over mountain trails, and forced to surrender. Envoys were sent to Macedonia, and its king Amyntas submitted. His daughter married Megabazos' son Boubares, and both he and his son Alexander remained loyal until after the repulse of Xerxes. That Alexander murdered the envoys for insolence to Macedonian ladies, and gave his sister in marriage as part of a bribe to hush it up, must be counted another propagandist fable; Herodotus' Athenian informants were anxious to whitewash Alexander "the Philhellene" for the sake of Macedonia's timber and minerals, and insist throughout that, though he actually served with distinction in Xerxes' invasion, he was really in the Resistance. Megabazos however had not time to conquer the mountain tribes, nor even the west-Thracian lake-dwellers, of whom Herodotus' account is of much interest.[1] Nor had he forces to leave in occupation; so, following an ancient oriental policy, to weaken possible trouble-makers outside the occupied zone, he rounded up the Paiones and brought them back to Asia. Darius settled them in Phrygia. At the same time Histiaios of Miletos, who had asked and received a vast land-grant on the Strymon as reward for his services and was preparing to found a city there, was on Megabazos' advice summoned to court "for important consultations" and kept in honorific captivity.

Darius took Megabazos and Histiaios back with him to Susa. He left his half-brother Artaphernes as viceroy at Sardis with, as "commander of the Men on the Sea", another Otanes, reckoned a safe man; he was son of a judge who had been executed for corruption by Cambyses, and

[1] v. 16.

PERSIA AND THE GREEKS

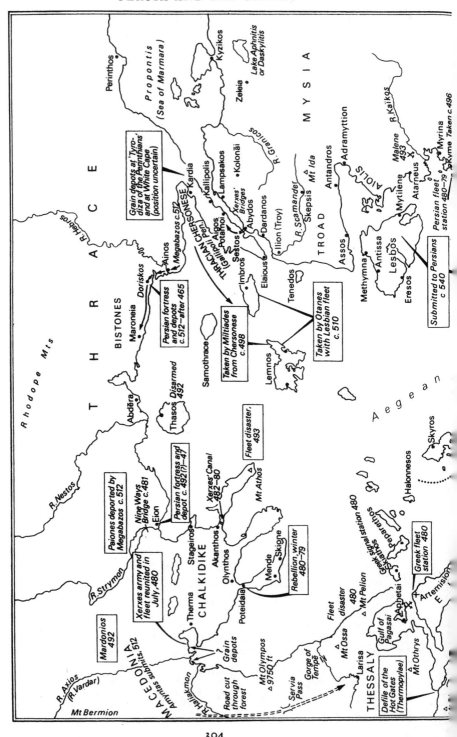

GREEKS AND IMPERIAL EXPANSION

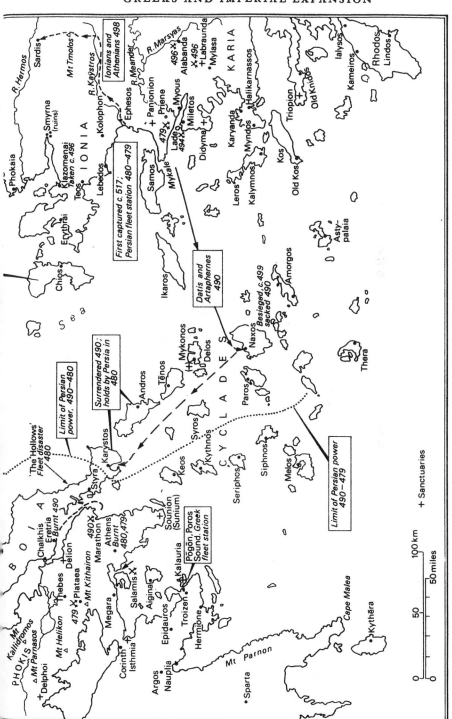

Map 13. The Aegean basin, to illustrate the Greek wars of Darius and Xerxes.

this, it was thought, should have made him all the safer. Otanes, with the field-army now available, then at last took Byzantion and Chalcedon, and mopped up some resistance in the Troad. Then, with Koës' fleet from Lesbos, he occupied the still non-Greek islands of Lemnos and Imbros and, crossing to eastern Thrace again, punished peoples who had harassed or deserted from Darius' army on the retreat from Scythia. Persian prestige was thus fully restored, and Herodotus reports a "let-up" (*anesis*) for a few years in the troubles of the region. But in Ionia, discontent was growing.

There was still, it seems, no military occupation beyond the sea; but Artaphernes was soon made aware of the disadvantages of a frontier running through the middle of the Greek world. A poet of Megara, the mother-city of stiff-necked Byzantion and Chalcedon, gives our first European reference to the menace of "the Medes"[1] (as Greeks continued loosely to call imperial Persia; cf. the modern continental use of 'England'). Athens, Megara's neighbour, with a large territory by Greek standards (some 2,500 square km.), a teeming population and a booming economy since the reforms of Solon *c.* 592, was also interested in the grain trade. Peisistratos, the beneficent despot (d. 528), and his sons had holdings on both sides of the Dardanelles: Sigeion, near Troy, reft from a resentful Lesbos and held by a Peisistratid cadet, and the Gallipoli Peninsula, indirectly controlled through the family of Miltiades, a powerful clan, whose chiefs usually got on well with the Peisistratids so long as they were at a distance. In 510 Sparta, prompted by the Delphic Oracle through the influence of another great Athenian noble, Kleisthenes the Alkmeonid, expelled Peisistratos' son Hippias; and Hippias retired to Sigeion, where his kindred must already have been paying tribute to Persia. Athens then moved towards democracy, led by Kleisthenes himself, who found the other aristocrats "ganging up" against him; to the consternation of Sparta, which tried in vain to put the city back, first into the hands of the nobles and then of Hippias himself. Beset by enemies on all sides, the Athenians in 507 appealed for protection to Artaphernes; though Kleisthenes at least must have known what such protection would mean. Artaphernes made it quite clear. They could have it, if they gave to the King the symbolic earth and water, symbolising the surrender of their land. In desperation, the ambassadors promised it. By the time they got back, in face of Athenian resolution the danger had passed, and they were repudiated; but the mischief was done.

[1] Theognis, 757ff., 773ff.

Hippias at Sigeion gave his daughter in marriage to the son of Hippoklos, tyrant of Lampsakos, an opulent Ionian colony further up the straits. This meant dropping Miltiades, his old ally, whose principality had fought wars with Lampsakos, and thus making a determined, personal enemy of him; but Miltiades was in exile (probably with his father-in-law Oloros, a king in Thrace). Hippoklos on the other hand was in high favour with Persia; he was another of the dynasts who had saved the bridge on the Danube. With his help Hippias laid his case before Artaphernes, and was favourably received. The Athenians sent a renewed embassy, pleading that they were doing no harm and only wished to be left in peace; but this time the answer was even more explicit. If they wanted the King's peace they could have it – under Hippias. Athens refused; "and with that, they made up their minds that a state of war existed with Persia".[1]

II: THE GREAT WARS (499–449 B.C.)

1. *The Ionian Revolt*

However, Artaphernes was not provided with troops with a view to new conquests, nor authorised to attempt them without reference to his royal brother. No doubt he received a stream of applicants; even the exiled Miltiades may have been one, for he is later said to have had a grudge against a man of Paros for "reporting against him to Hydarnes". (Hydarnes, presumably the son of Darius' friend of that name, thus appears serving in the west before the great wars as well as after.) There is no saying how long the peace or "cold war" might have lasted had not Artaphernes received another application, which seemed more promising, in that the applicants offered material help in their own cause.

About 505, Naxos seems to have lost its special position in the Aegean to Eretria, a city with broad lands in southern Euboia; an event probably not unconnected with the overthrow of the Knights of Chalkis, Eretria's rival, by revolutionary Athens. Soon after this, Naxos' own oligarchs were overthrown, and appealed for help, initially to Miletos; to Aristagoras, son-in-law and deputy of Histiaios, who was still kept at court. Aristagoras, scenting aggrandisement for himself, introduced them to Artaphernes, stressing the strategic importance of Naxos and offering funds to pay for an expedition. This was an attractive enough proposition for Artaphernes to refer to Darius; and

[1] Hdt. v. 96; cf. 73.

next spring an expedition sailed from Miletos, it was given out as a cover-plan, for the north. In Kaukasa Bay on the west of Chios it halted, ready to swoop upon Naxos on the wings of the summer north wind.

But the surprise failed. As to how, Herodotus' story is incredible on the main point, but illuminating on the difficulties which Persia could face in dealing with Greek allies.

Megabates, a cousin of the King, the admiral appointed by Artaphernes, inspecting the ships at Kaukasa, found one with no guard set, and inflicted a severe "field punishment" upon the captain, tying him up to a rowing bench with his head sticking out through the porthole. Aristagoras, who knew the captain, asked for his release, was rebuffed, and went and untied him himself. This led to a violent quarrel as to who was really in command. What is incredible is Herodotus' story that Megabates, an Achaemenid officer, then betrayed the cover-plan to the Naxians, to spite Aristagoras! – though no doubt Aristagoras in frustration might have imagined it. The fleet reached Naxos, only to find it ready for a siege. The Naxians, seeing it preparing in a quarter to which, as they must have known, their exiles had repaired, had probably doubted the cover-story from the first.

Megabates evidently had not the men for an expensive storming operation; so the siege dragged on for four months, and by that time Aristagoras' economic resources were exhausted. Rather than confront Artaphernes with an expensive failure, he determined on desperate measures; prompted thereto, moreover, by a famous message from Histiaios (tattooed on the scalp of a slave, who was then concealed until his hair had grown again), begging him to stir up some trouble so that Histiaios might be sent home to settle it.

Once more, then, an Ionian and Karian fleet came home having seen Persian forces baffled; and this time its Greek leader was prepared to exploit popular discontent. He proclaimed liberation; and the crews mutinied with one accord, arrested their tyrants and dispersed to raise their cities in rebellion. Koës of Mytilene was stoned to death; but most of the fallen rulers were released – and rejoined the Persians. Aristagoras at Miletos resigned his power, and was elected general; and delegates at the Panionian sanctuary organised a Commonwealth of the Ionians, with an executive which directed joint operations.

The six-year war that followed was well conducted on both sides. Artaphernes, though it would be months before he could be heavily reinforced, refused to be thrown on the defensive, and sent all available troops against Miletos. But meanwhile (winter, 499/498) Aristagoras was seeking aid from Old Greece. He failed at Sparta, which once more had a war with Argos impending; but Athens sent a force in twenty ships (4,000 men if the soldiers rowed the galleys, as was sometimes done). Eretria added five, and also, it is said, sent her main fleet to the Levant, where (with allies?) they "defeated the Cypriotes off Pamphylia",[1] a prelude to revolt in Cyprus too. In Ionia the "war cabinet" planned a bold counter-stroke. They directed the reinforcements not to Miletos but to Ephesos, where they were joined by Ionian contingents, even one from Miletos under a brother of Aristagoras, who himself remained in the city. "In great force" they struck inland, with guides from Ephesos, and crossing Mount Tmolos came down on Sardis; the deepest Greek penetration in Asia for many a year.

The moral effect was great; but the cost was heavy. Artaphernes himself held Sardis citadel. The grass huts and thatched roofs of the lower town went up in one wind-borne conflagration, embracing the great temple of Kubaba; an inevitable accident, which only made the Lydians hostile. With enemies on all sides, including the army drawn off from Miletos, the Greeks could not stay. They regained the coast, but there they were overtaken; and their re-embarkation was a shambles. The Eretrians lost their general; Ephesos was in hostile hands when next we hear of it; and the effect of the expedition's return at Athens was that the peace-party, led by a brother-in-law of Hippias (Hipparchos, Archon in 496), won control in the Assembly.

Meanwhile however the revolt spread. The Greeks of Cyprus besieged Phoenician Kition. An Ionian fleet sailed to the Marmara and "brought under their control Byzantion and the other cities". The phrase does not suggest that, after being left to fall alone in their own revolt, they joined the new one with enthusiasm. Miltiades returned to the Chersonese and took Lemnos and Imbros, recolonising them with farmers from crowded Attica, a step that won him great favour there. By the end of 498 the revolt had reached its high-water mark; but the empire had mobilised, and though it is not true that the Ionians made no effort to co-ordinate their operations, the position of the cities, strung out along hundreds of miles of coast, made nonsense of a defensive war.

In 497 the Persians fell upon Cyprus. An Ionian fleet sailed to its aid, and defeated Phoenician and Cilician squadrons; but they failed, as Greek fleets were to fail repeatedly, to prevent the enemy from running

---

[1] Lysanias of Mallos and other writers, according to Plutarch, *On the Meanness of Herodotus*, §24.

troops across from Cilicia on the north wind. A Cypriote army under city-kings, still using the archaic chariot, was beaten in the central plain; some contingents deserted or showed little fight. The Ionian fleet, with its land base gone, withdrew (for a large fleet could not get inside the small city harbours); and though some Cypriotes stubbornly defended their walls, in a year all was over.

Then it was Ionia's turn. The south coast of the Marmara and the Troad fell quickly. Hippias at Sigeion no doubt welcomed the invaders; he reappears later, still in favour. In the south there was furious fighting; the Karians and Milesians gave battle in the field, and after two bloody defeats even ambushed and destroyed a Persian army, attempting a night march. (Among Karian leaders we hear of a prince Pixodar, son of Mausōlos; the *pair* of names suggests ancestors of the later Karian dynasty.) In the centre Artaphernes in person, with Otanes, broke through to the sea, taking the major cities of Kyme and Klazomenai. The area still in revolt was being carved up.

All this took two years; but in 494 the Persians closed once more upon Miletos, while bringing up the Levantine navies to blockade it by sea. The Ionian congress decided that on land only passive defence was now possible; but a victory at sea might yet save at least the islands. The geographer and sage Hekataios of Miletos had advised his own people too to withdraw to Leros island for the duration of the crisis; a far stronger position than that of the Athenians later at Salamis; but his advice was not followed.

As a result, the Greek fleet off Miletos had to use an appallingly cramped base on the inshore islet of Ladē. Much even of their drinking water must have had to be brought by sea. Their strength in ships was still formidable: Chios 100, Lesbos 70, Samos 60, Miletos 80; five other surviving cities (with their own walls to guard) only 43; but the total of 353 was probably greater than that which actually fought at Salamis. The imperial fleet is given as 600 strong, a conventional figure and no doubt exaggerated. They did not behave as if they were vastly superior; instead, the Persians resorted to political warfare, prompting the exiled tyrants to get into touch each with his own people, suggesting that terrible reprisals might be avoided by being the first to surrender.

As the hot summer wore on and sickness increased, the Ionians began to crack. They ceased to exercise in formation daily, mutinied against their Phokaian admiral, "put up shelters on the island and sat in the shade" – and began to listen to the whispered propaganda. Aiakes of

Samos, a city usually hostile to her present major allies, had particular success with his people; and so at last, when the Phoenicians offered battle and the Greeks accepted it, nearly the whole Samian fleet, on the seaward flank, fled for home. The Lesbians, next in line and outflanked, broke away in turn; and though Chios and Miletos fought bravely, there could be only one end to it.

There remained only the "mopping up". Disheartened Miletos was taken by storm. Aristagoras had already perished in western Thrace, after sailing off in the middle of the war to resume Histiaios' colonising enterprise – perhaps as a source of food for the beleaguered cities. Histiaios, sent down at last, found himself suspect on both sides and, after adventures which have been interpreted both as mere piracy and as a gallant attempt to keep the revolt alive in the north, was captured south of the Troad, on a large-scale foray after food for Lesbos, crowded with troops and refugees. The Persians engaged him in front and then, when the infantry was locked in battle, caught him in flank with cavalry: our earliest account of Persian battle-tactics. Artaphernes, fearing that Histiaios might, even now, re-establish his personal ascendancy with the King, averted this danger by sending Darius his head only; Darius is said to have been much upset.

Miletos suffered the full reprisal programme: men slaughtered, boys made eunuchs, maidens carried off "for the King". It is said to have been "depopulated" and recolonised, with Persians in the strategic centre and Karians further out; but this, like most reports of annihilation, appears to have been exaggerated; at least, there were Milesians still there in 479 who were no loyal Persian subjects.

There were similar gruesome reprisals, with burning of temples "in revenge for Sardis", elsewhere too; but when "pacification" was over, Persia's permanent settlement was constructive. Artaphernes "sent for messengers from the cities" (*angeloi*: men to carry his orders; he was not negotiating), "and compelled the Ionians to make treaties providing for the judicial settlement of disputes, instead of border-raiding". That Greeks, despite having a common language, had never organised a common peace among themselves, was to Persians a subject of surprised contempt.[1] The satrap also "measured their territories in *parasangs* (a Persian term for thirty Greek furlongs), and on this basis assessed the tribute for each city, which they have paid ever since and still do, in my time". (Since Herodotus wrote after the Athenian "liberation" of

[1] Hdt. vi. 42; vii. 9.

Ionia, this statement is startling.) "Then, in the spring [492?] Darius superseded the other generals, and there came down to the sea Mardonios the son of Gobryas [Darius' old friend], with a large army and fleet [relieving the troops too]; a young man, recently married to the King's daughter Artazostra." Arriving by sea ahead of his men, who marched overland, he carried out a still more startling reform: "he suppressed all the tyrants of the Ionians, and established democracies". (So much, says Herodotus, for those who deny that the Persian conspirators ever considered a republic for themselves.)[1]

"All the tyrants" does seem to be an exaggeration; e.g., Strattis, tyrant of Chios in 479, bears the same name as the tyrant of Chios in 513, and might be either the same man or a grandson. Perhaps he was restored later. However, the great revolt, disaster though it was, had led to some redress of grievances. Herodotus, or his oral sources, did treat it as disaster only; but there is transparent reason for this. His native Halikarnassos took no part in it; his second home, Samos, betrayed it at the last; Athens, which he admired in his maturity, justified her imperialism by a claim to have liberated Ionians who could not liberate themselves. It is insufficiently emphasised in many books that this was far the longest and fiercest war for freedom ever fought against the empire by Greeks.

2. *The Second Invasion of Europe*

Mardonios pressed on to where his fresh army and fleet awaited him, at the crossing into Europe. Events had shown Darius that occupation only as far as the coast of Asia was not satisfactory; and since the burning of Sardis, Athens and Eretria were on the agenda. The mutual accusations of rivals for power suggested that Athens was politically vulnerable; and Eretria was to prove even more so. Herodotus' story, that the King ordered his chancery to bring forward the matter of Athens regularly, might, shorn of its coffee-house details, be perfectly true. However, Mardonios held to the view that the way to get at the Greek peninsula was from the continent.

The first step was to secure the coast of Thrace; but Mardonios' fortunes were chequered. The mountain Brygoi (European Phrygians?) fell upon his camp by night, wounding Mardonios himself, though he "went on with the campaign till he had subdued them"; and his fleet,

[1] Hdt. vi. 42f.; cf. iii. 80.

too large all to take refuge in the small bays, was "piled up" by one of the fierce Aegean north-easterly gales while trying to round Mount Athos. There was much loss of life from drowning (the Iranian marines could not swim), the attacks of sharks, and exposure. Yet the flag had been shown sufficiently for the Greek islanders of rich and powerful Thasos, when ordered to disarm in 491, to comply without resistance.

Thasos had daughter colonies and exploited gold-mines on the adjacent coast. The Strymon area keeps reappearing in Herodotus' narrative. Histiaios, Megabazos, Aristagoras, Histiaios again (he tried to secure Thasos during his last adventures) and now other Persians, all were impressed with its economic potential. It had gold, resources of timber for ship-building and oars, such as were beginning to run short near the coasts of the south Aegean, and cultivable land for a much denser population than it yet had. Athens, Sparta, even Thebes, in the days of their power all campaigned there; and when the many-sided struggle was at last won by Macedonia, the correctness of Histiaios' and Megabazos' foresight was dramatically proved.

For the present, the north-west had been made safe. Macedonia was still 'tribal' and thinly populated, and there was a Persian governor at Doriskos, west of the Evros (Hebros). But with Mardonios withdrawn, wounded in body and perhaps a little in reputation, other commanders were permitted to try a new strategy: a direct advance through the Cyclades, with a force including cavalry in specialised horse-transports; presumably "landing-craft", with doors that could be let down to form a ramp.

The new commanders were Artaphernes, son of the old satrap, and Datis the Mede, who led a picked corps from Iran and embarked it in Cilicia. Datis is an interesting though little-known character. He too had already served in the west. A later Greek inscription refers to him besieging Lindos, then the chief city of Rhodes, perhaps during the Ionian revolt; and he spoke fluent if occasionally comic Greek.[1] He was a man well fitted to operate Persia's not merely military but also political and religious strategy towards the King's destined subjects.

This strategy and policy was by now well established. The Persians treated important prisoners with humanity, aiming at integrating them into the empire. Herodotus notes that in his own time in Egypt even

---

[1] The Hellenistic *Lindos Temple-Chronicle* (ed. Blinkenberg in *Kleine Texte* series, pp. 26f., 34–8); discussion in Burn, *Persia and the Greeks*, p. 218; on Datis' Greek, Aristophanes' *Peace*, 292ff.; cf. A. Raubitschek, 'Das Datis Lied', in *Charites* (ed. Schauenburg, Bonn, 1957).

the sons of determined rebels were restored as governors of their fathers' subjects.¹ Even Greek gods might be favoured, and especially the oracular god Apollo. His sanctuary at Didyma had indeed been sacked; but that was because wicked men, the presiding clan of the Branchidai, had misused it to levy war against the King. Elsewhere Apollo was treated with conspicuous favour. A Greek inscription from the inland Ionian city of Magnesia – recopied in Roman times from an Ionic original, but convincingly reproducing the style of Darius' Persian inscriptions, which late Greek forgers could hardly have known – shows the King commending a governor for his enlightened (and good Zoroastrian) agricultural policy, but also making it clear that appeals from the governor to the King might be favourably received:²
King of Kings Darius to his servant Gadatas. This:

> I hear that you are not in all things obeying my orders; for in that you are cultivating my land, introducing food-plants from Trans-Euphrates [i.e. Syria] into lower Asia, I commend your initiative, and for this credit shall be given you in the house of the King. But in that you are ignoring my policy on behalf of the gods, if you do not change your ways I shall give you cause to know that I am angered; for you have levied tribute upon the sacred gardeners of Apollo and ordered them to dig unhallowed ground, not understanding the mind of my forefathers towards the god who spoke all truth to the Persians and...³ [*Here the stone is broken off.*]

Causing temple gardeners to dig unhallowed ground, thus contributing to their own maintenance, was in fact no more than Cambyses had required of some priests in Egypt. The unfortunate Gadatas (not otherwise known), thus publicly rebuked, was merely behindhand in his knowledge of the official "line"; placating Apollo now had high priority, as was to be shown in 490 by Datis at Delos.

Examples of upper-class integration appear at the same time. Boubares, son of the invaluable Megabazos, named *his* son after his royal father-in-law, Amyntas; Herodotus mentions him as well known. The King made him lord of Alabanda in Phrygia. More striking still is the treatment of Metiochos, Miltiades' eldest son (not by Oloros' daughter but by an Athenian lady; that she was related to the Peisistratids is a guess). He was captured in command of one of his father's five ships, when Miltiades fled from the Chersonese on the collapse of the revolt; "but Darius did him no harm, but gave him a house and estate and

---
[1] iii. 15.
[2] For another such appeal, cf. *Ezra*, chaps 4–6.
[3] Meiggs and Lewis, *Greek Historical Inscriptions*, No. 12.

a Persian wife, by whom he had children who live as Persians". Darius apparently did not even try to use him as a hostage – or if so, his father treated him as expendable. Meanwhile Miltiades reached Athens with his other ships.

When in 491 Darius sent heralds (as it were emissaries under flag of truce) to demand the symbolic earth and water from every known Greek state, there were signs that this "peace offensive" was paying. Many states gave it, including the rich, eastward-trading island of Aigina in the Saronic Gulf, with the best navy remaining in independent Greece – some sixty triremes. But there were two great failures. The Spartans, proud as medieval knights and fierce as Vikings, threw their herald into their pit of execution; and the Athenians, in a suspiciously neat parallel story, claimed to have thrown theirs into a well.[1] Having thus put themselves beyond the pale of civilised negotiation, they prepared for war; and Kleomenes, the original and autocratic (his envious half-brothers said "mad") King of Sparta, acting as overlord of Sparta's allies, took hostages from Aigina and delivered them to Aigina's bitter enemy, Athens. Kleomenes had in 508/507 tried to stop Athens' move towards democracy, and met with a humiliating failure; but in face of the Persian menace, he had the breadth of vision to see that Spartans and democrats must make common cause.

In Athens the Persians still hoped to find collaborators. Hippias, though now eighty years old, was to accompany the expedition; and his brother-in-law Hipparchos (p. 309), still had influence. Miltiades indeed, his determined enemy, had perhaps still more; but this in turn was a blow to the Alkmeonidai, Kleisthenes' family (he himself was probably dead). Hippias, to whose house they had been by turns allies and enemies for two generations, had hopes of them too. Miltiades' enemies (certainly the Alkmeonid faction, who afterwards ruined him) had already prosecuted him on his arrival in 493, for "tyranny" over Athenians in the Chersonese; and when we note that the Archon for that year was Themistokles, a democrat and determined on fighting, it appears that the minor gentry, prepared to rally round Miltiades against Peisistratids and Alkmeonids, and Themistoklean democrats were making common cause. Themistokles was himself a man of the Kleisthenean revolution; for though his father was of the ancient Lykomid family, his mother was a non-Athenian concubine. He owed his citizenship to the law by which Kleisthenes, "taking the commons

[1] In Hdt. (out of order) vii. 133.

into his party" as his enemies said, had made citizens at one stroke of all free residents in Attica.

So there were four significant parties, and the Persians had the alliance of one and hopes of another. Where their calculations broke down was over the fact that their opponents were rather more like modern parties, based on broad class support; that of families who could not hope to dominate the city through a family faction (though Miltiades himself may have hoped to), and so needed an ordered republic, and under pressure could combine to defend it. The Peisistratid and Alkmeonid parties, on the other hand, *were* family factions; and though both had some popular support, won by real services, it was dwindling as a new generation, Themistokles' generation, grew up. The Persians' great failures in Greece were failures, above all, to deal with the new Athenian popular state.

In 490 the new-style, amphibious expedition, reinforced with Ionian contingents, set out to take in the central Aegean and, specifically, to punish the cities that had injured the King's majesty: Naxos, Eretria, Athens. The Naxians, knowing what had been done to Miletos, quailed at the sight of a much larger expedition than before, and fled to their island's extensive wooded interior. The Persians burned the city and temples and raided inland, taking some prisoners. The Delians fled to Tenos, where there was room to hide; but Datis, after enquiries, got them back, protesting his reverence for the holy priests of Apollo, and pleased them with a huge offering of frankincense. From other islands, which had given their earth and water, he collected small contingents, *e.g.* one ship from Paros, a fairly large Cyclad; hostages as much as reinforcements. Karystos in southern Euboia, with its fine citadel, closed its gates, but submitted in time to escape destruction; and with it and Andros secured, the Persians held both sides of the Andros Channel, and important positions within the sight of Attica. Meanwhile, if not earlier, Datis in person actually seems to have visited Athens, to urge submission before it was too late; Aristophanes[1] knew of a song with jokes about his bad Greek. But Athens remained stubborn; and moreover, there was no sign of help from Athens' old enemy, Aigina.[2]

All this had taken time, and it was now late summer; but Datis and

[1] See p. 313, n. 1.
[2] Herodotus expressly says that Aigina was *already* again at war with Athens, having seized some important Athenians at sea as counter-hostages for those taken by Kleomenes; but his story (vi. 49–51, 61–75, 85–94) both involves squeezing an intolerably long sequence of events into twelve months, and does not account for Aigina's quiescence in 490.

Hippias were still hopeful. Meanwhile, the Persians moved on to their penultimate objective, Eretria. Their forces, though judged adequate, were clearly not sufficient to tackle both cities simultaneously. They landed their horses well south of Eretria, moved up and opened a full-scale assault. For six days there was furious fighting at the walls; and then a gate was opened by dissidents within. The Persians sacked the city, rounded up the people according to Darius' orders (he settled them in Elam), and after a few more days for this operation crossed to the plain of Marathon, recommended by Hippias as "good cavalry country".

Then there was a hitch. Hippias was disappointed to find no flow of supporters coming in, even from his father's old "section" in the hill country; and the Athenian army, marching out on the advice of Miltiades, blocked the road to Athens at the south end of the plain. Athens had already sent news of the fall of Eretria by runner to Sparta, with an appeal for help (it was impracticable to do so earlier, before it was known where the sea-borne enemy would strike); but the Spartans were keeping a festival, and could not move with hope of divine favour before the full moon, still six days ahead. (Some have considered such superstition incredible; forgetting that *Athens*, 77 years later, lost a war because a general, with the approval of his troops, postponed an urgently necessary move on account of an eclipse.)

So for five days the armies faced each other; the Athenians waiting for the Spartans, the Persians for a move by their collaborators; but still nothing happened. Then, just in time to forestall the arrival of the Spartans (Hippias probably knew very well what they would do), Datis did provoke a battle. He closed up upon the Athenian position, and he probably embarked, by night and further north, a force including the bulk of his cavalry, for a dash to the beaches near Athens behind the enemy's back.

(This interpretation rests upon a Byzantine encyclopaedia's explanation of an old proverb, "Cavalry apart: used of those who split a formation" – with reference to Datis at Marathon; but also upon the fact that the Athenians after the battle made their famous "Marathon" march home *to forestall a sea-borne move*, while the Persian ships remaining at Marathon did not "dash for Athens", but first picked up the Eretrian prisoners, dumped on small islands off Euboia.)

Everything now happened quickly. Some Ionians are said to have revealed the Persian move; and at dawn the war-archon Kallimachos, again on the advice of Miltiades, launched his heavy infantry to the assault, thinning out his centre to equal the length of the enemy line; swept away the half-hearted Ionians on both flanks; checked the pursuit and united his two flank brigades (a remarkable feat of discipline, and surely premeditated); and turned upon the native Iranian troops, who had meanwhile broken through his centre. These broke away to a flank (trying to reach their original camp and sheltered anchorage at the north end of the plain?); but many were killed when they were driven into a large marsh, which fills the north-central part of the plain but for a strip of hard ground near the shore. The Athenians buried 6,400 bodies in rough trenches (many bones have been found, along the edge of the marsh); and this figure may be considered reliable, since, under a vow made by the war-archon (he himself was killed), every slain enemy had to be paid for by the sacrifice of a kid.[1]

Then, when the surviving Persians "were already in their ships", someone was seen to be "showing a shield to them"; presumably flashing it, heliograph-wise, from somewhere well away up Pentelikos. Everyone at once thought "Traitors!" and many said "The Alkmeonidai!"; but there was no evidence, and no one was brought to trial. It is quite likely that some persons in touch with Hippias – they too knowing that the Spartans were coming, and it was now or never – may have signalled "Ready!", even though not as ready as they wished. The thought speeded the march of tired men going "as fast as their feet could carry them"; and when the first Persian squadron reached Phaleron Bay, they were already in position. Datis did no more, but returned to Asia, having suffered grievous losses, but having notably advanced the frontiers of the empire. On the way, finding that a gilded image of Apollo had been looted by some of his Phoenicians from a temple on the coast, well to the north of Marathon, he confiscated it and left it at Delos with orders for its return.

The leading Spartan brigade, having marched 150 miles in three days, arrived soon after, having indeed missed the battle, but through their known intentions having contributed not a little to the result.

3. *The Invasion of Xerxes*

If the burning of Sardis could not be ignored, much less could the bloody repulse at Marathon; yet the great effort to take in Greece was

[1] Xenophon, *Anabasis* iii. 12.

delayed for ten years. We know little about the empire's other preoccupations. Also Darius died in 486; and Xerxes, eldest of his four sons by Atossa (p. 299), though long since designated crown prince, may have had to guard against the rivalry of his elder brothers, sons of Gobryas' daughter. There were no fratricides yet, as there were at later demises of the crown; but Artobazanes, Darius' eldest son, was not employed in high command, though his two full brothers were. Then there were revolts in Egypt (recovered, 485) and Babylon (482); but meanwhile the long-term preparations against Greece had already begun.

There was little chance of the Greek question being shelved indefinitely. Mardonios, Xerxes' brother-in-law, was eager to be satrap there; and exiled Greeks were as ready to resort to Persia and offer their valuable services as their descendants were, to Rome: the Peisistratids; the Aleuadai of Larissa, expelled by other Thessalian barons who feared their claims to kingship, even a king of Sparta, Dāmarātos, of the rival house to Kleomenes and long his opponent. Kleomenes had got rid of him by casting doubts on his paternity. Kleomenes was now dead in disgrace; he was put under restraint as mad, by his half-brothers Leonidas and Kleombrotos, and found dead one morning shockingly mutilated; it was officially given out as suicide. But the kings Leonidas and Leotychides (in Doric, Latychidas; the cousin who had succeeded Damaratos) showed no sign of wanting Damaratos back.

The long-term preparations included huge food-dumps along the Thracian coast. The low isthmus north of Athos, once Mardonios' undoing, was cut by a canal; in charge, with a colleague, was Boubares, son of Megabazos and brother-in-law to Alexander, now king of Macedon. The milder and more sheltered peninsulas to the west were left to be rounded. The Strymon was bridged; and so were, most spectacular of all, the Dardanelles, by two bridges of old warships, lashed together, anchored, especially upstream against the fierce current, which carried away the bridges at the first attempt, and all secured to two immense cables for each bridge, reaching right across the strait, ordered years before from Egypt and Phoenicia. Rope-making was highly developed in those lands; a piece actually found in an Egyptian quarry was 15 cm. thick, and attached to a block weighing 68 tons. As to what could be produced for an imperial military operation, the weight of the rope itself was the chief limiting factor. Cables a mile long and a foot thick, as described by Herodotus, would have weighed nearly ninety tons! Xerxes, "marching his army over the sea and sailing his fleet through the land", became for later rhetoric a proverb for megalomania; but as compared with ferrying a large army and its animals in the boats of the time, the bridge was a practical measure.

As to the size of the army, an upper limit is set by water supplies. General Sir F. Maurice, going over the route in 1919–20 and using the data collected for the British Admiralty handbook, reckoned that in summer they would be strained by a host of some 200,000 men with 70,000 horses, mules and camels; and Herodotus says that they *were* strained: "water ran short, except at the major rivers"[1] – a statement amplified in the childishness of later rhetoric into "they drank rivers dry". Of ancient estimates, the earliest are the most outrageous, beginning with the contemporary inscription, on the war-memorial at Thermopylae, which said three million. Herodotus, who works manfully to get his estimates (including non-combatants) up to an even higher total, adds with his usual candour that he had no official figures. Presumably they were secret. But he does reproduce, evidently from some Persian source, a list of contingents, without figures but with details of armament. Of these, the only troops mentioned in the land battles are Iranians, armed with the bow, spear (shorter than the Greek spear, which was to be serious), dagger and large wicker shields. Few except the Guards, the 10,000 Immortals, had any armour. But also mentioned are all manner of auxiliaries, from Lydians armed in the Greek manner (but not mentioned in the fighting) to primitive Caucasian tribesmen (four contingents, all presumably small) and stone-age warriors from the Sudan, who painted themselves before battle, half red and half white. It has usually been doubted whether the Persians would have reckoned these worth their rations; but it may be remembered that Trajan's Column shows us, beside the Roman legions, some half-naked barbarians, stripped to their trousers and armed only with clubs and stones for throwing (perhaps recently conquered north Britons). It may have been a principle that when the King in person went on a major expedition, "everyone" should go.

Hacking its way through the forest, "making the crooked straight and the rough places plain" in the Persian manner, the army reached Macedonia in perhaps 45 days from the Hellespont. The Thracians gaped at the new road with awe. On the Thermaic Gulf the main body rested, while one-third of the army went ahead, to clear a road west

[1] vii. 21; cf. 43, 58, 108.

of Olympos by the wide and sandy vale of the Haliakmon; for Greece had been reached, and enemy forces were reported holding the Olympos line at the gorge of Tempē.

The nationalist Greeks had not been idle. An alliance had been formed, naturally under the presidency of Sparta, including all the mainland except defeated and disgruntled Argos. But the most important thing that had happened since Marathon was that Themistokles (p. 315), after eliminating all rival leaders in fierce but bloodless party strife, had persuaded the Athenians to devote the profits from a rich "strike" in the state-owned silver mines to increasing the navy. Athens had now 200 robust and up-to-date galleys, though she manned them with difficulty; some of the rowers were hill peasants, who had to be taught the elements. First and last, the allies manned 380 ships, though it had to be admitted that, while theirs were heavier, those of the Phoenicians and other eastern navies were faster and more manoeuvrable.[1]

Themistokles, who, unlike most of his countrymen, had long seen the invasion as inevitable and studied the necessary strategy, was for starting to fight as far forward as possible, exploiting the geography of Greece and the enemy's difficulties; and he persuaded the Peloponnesians, though their instinct was for fighting only at the Isthmus of Corinth. He himself commanded the Athenian contingent among the 10,000 armoured troops (plus auxiliaries) who held Tempe, and could have held that formidable defile indefinitely. Meanwhile a fleet, initially probably 100 Athenian and 100 Peloponnesian ships, took post at the north end of Euboia, at a cape marked by a Temple of Artemis (Artemision). To attack them the invaders would have to approach *en masse* – not in squadrons small enough to use the scattered beaches – along the mountainous coast of Thessaly; too far to row in a day with a battle at the end of it, and exposed to the same gales that had caused the disaster off Athos.

The Greeks also kept a second fleet in the Saronic Gulf, based on Pōgōn (Poros Sound), in case the enemy struck through the Andros Channel, theirs since 490. The Persians did in the end – after the Greeks had reinforced the northern fleet from the south – try to outflank Artemision by that route; but only *from the north*, not direct from Ionia. This proved to be a mistake; but it is an intelligible one. Their fleet was kept under unified control, so that operations might be co-ordinated. They clearly did not have ships enough to squander; nothing like the

[1] Hdt. viii. 10 and 60.

1,200 or 1,000 of Greek estimates. The main strategy was that of a direct land advance, backed by the political warfare that had already paid off so well, with the fleet used for tactical support and (probably; we are not told) to cover the transport of food from the forward dumps. When possible, it was not even ordered to advance until the army had secured the coast ahead, with the water-points essential for thousands of thirsty oarsmen.

The Persians, it appears, knew – they had had years to find out – that the sandy mountains west of Olympos could be made passable for large numbers as soon as a belt of forest was cleared (the Germans in 1941 got tanks over them); and *the southern Greeks did not*. "Mad" Kleomenes, who had visited Thessaly, might have been able to enlighten them; but Kleomenes was dead and damned. More than once in this campaign we are impressed with the fact that the east was technically more advanced than Greece. When, in the operations at Artemision, some Phoenician ships had run on a shoal, the Greeks noted with surprise that they then carried stone out and built a sea-mark on it; and when Persian marines set themselves to save the life of a Greek who had fought till he was "all cut to pieces", they "treated his wounds with myrrh, and bound them up with strips of fine cotton"; thus Herodotus,[1] as if he had never heard of a bandage (Greeks tore up rags as required); while the Sidonian ship apparently carried a medicine chest.

And now political warfare paid off again. Persian agents had been penetrating northern Greece for many years; both heralds (brave men, for though they were supposed to be inviolable, Sparta had shown that they could be murdered), and Greeks, including at least one beautiful courtesan: Thargēlia of Miletos, who had settled at Larissa,[2] and could remind her numerous lovers, including the would-be "king" Antiochos, who had fled to Xerxes, of what had happened to her native city. Thanks to them, all the hill-peoples of northern Greece now followed the example of Macedonia; and with that, the chance of resistance west of Olympos sank to zero. Thessalian barons opposed to the Aleuadai had indeed joined the allies with their cavalry; but the country was obviously deeply divided. King Alexander, that most successful of double agents, visited the camp at Tempe and urged "as a friend" that it would be suicide to stay there; and without waiting for the threat to become immediate, the force marched back to its ships on the Gulf of Pagasai (near modern Volo) and sailed for Corinth. Xerxes, who had

---

[1] vii. 181. [2] Plutarch, *Pericles*, §29.

an eye for natural beauty, was able to visit Tempe at leisure; but his army, even without opposition, avoided the defile and used their new road. Meanwhile, if not before, the Delphic Oracle threw all its weight into the cause of non-resistance, encouraging neutrality (which meant surrender) and pouring gloom and despondency upon Athens and Sparta.

Themistokles, however, reckoned that Artemision might still be held, if the Mount Oita line were defended; especially the coast road near the hot springs of Thermopylae, where Mount Kallidromos, an outlier of Oita, drops to the sea in ferocious cliffs. And held it was, though by a scratch force, smaller than that which had fled from Tempe; for the Spartan Karneia and (480 being an Olympic year) the sacred Games for all Greece were at hand; so superstition reinforced the more or less conscious search for an excuse for not sending armies far away. No large army could be expected before the full moon, probably that of 19-20 August. However Leonidas, the brother who had succeeded Kleomenes, collected 4,000 Peloponnesians, mostly Arcadians, to whom paid service was attractive. The rest were small forces from the towns on his route, and 1,200 Laconians, including his guard of 300 Spartiate nobles; for this forlorn hope, he selected not youths, but men who had sons living, who might carry on their families. The other 900 were probably Helots, armed by the state.[1] With 1,100 Boiotians and the slender local armoured forces of Phokis and Lokris, not many more than 7,000 armoured men held the land front. They held it just long enough to make possible the operations of the 65,000 Greeks at Artemision, which, as the contemporary poet Simonides said, "laid the foundation" for victory in the war.

Themistokles, now with the fleet, not without difficulty kept it where it was; and then the Winds, to whom Apollo had advised his own Delphians to pray, fought for Greece. As the imperial fleet advanced, and anchored overnight off the coast of Thessaly, several rows deep off the insufficient beaches, the dreaded "Hellesponter" blew up at dawn and raged for three days before the Magi "by prayers and incantations, at last stopped it" (or perhaps, adds Herodotus, it just stopped). The damage, including many total losses, may well have exceeded all that was inflicted by Greek arms in two great battles.

Nevertheless it was still a massive armament that, when the storm ceased, reached the Bay of Pagasai. The Greeks, who had sheltered

---

[1] Cf. Hdt. viii. 25.

under the lee of Euboia, got back in time only to catch a few stragglers, though they inflicted more damage in two hit-and-run raids on the anchorages during reorganisation. Meanwhile the army (the 2nd Median and 3rd Sousiana divisions, and then, according to Herodotus, the Immortals themselves) assaulted Thermopylae, but made no progress and suffered heavy losses. They did, however, no doubt contribute to causing Leonidas to keep all his best troops on the coast road, leaving local allies to guard the wooded hills inland.

The third was the decisive day, when the imperial fleet came out in force. The Greeks, still outnumbered, drew up their heavier ships in a defensive half-moon; and a savage boarders' battle went on all day. Both sides, says Herodotus, were glad to regain their anchorages; and Themistokles' reaction appears, from the sequel, to have been a resolve never again, if he could help it, to let the enemy fight with the outside station and the greater room to manoeuvre which it gave. The Greeks, in no state to renew the battle, withdrew in the night, after sending a cutter to warn Leonidas; but Thermopylae too had fallen.

Ephialtes, the man who sold Thermopylae, naturally became the Judas Iscariot of Greek tradition; but one should remember that Greece was not a national state. There was no reason why a Malian hillman should feel loyalty to Athens or Sparta, and he was positively serving "his people" (if he thought of them) by getting the enemy moved on out of their country. Nor is it likely that he was a mere windfall to the Persians. They were experienced mountain fighters, which the Greeks, in the conditions of inter-city warfare, on the whole were not – as Mardonios is said to have explained to Xerxes.[1] They *must* have been probing the hills and looking for guides ever since the arrival of their first cavalry scouts, four days ahead of the main body. They found, indeed, three whose names are recorded, but used one, who knew of a route practicable for a formed body of troops; a route, not for a strategic invasion of Greece over mountain trails, but tactically, to unblock the vital coast road. It ascended between Mount Oita and the Trachinian Cliffs, which rise west of the Asōpós gorge, which descends west of Thermopylae; a long way round, and clear of the Greek flank guards.

Marching all night, through oak forests but under the Olympic full moon, the Guards under Hydarnes turned east on easier ground above the cliffs, crossed the Asōpós above the gorge and, up another steep

[1] Hdt. vii. 9.

but not precipitous slope, reached the top of the mountain behind Thermopylae; a top so unexpectedly grassy and easy that the whole ridge was called Anopaia, the Upper Way, or Kallidromos, the Fair Runway. This was held by the Phokians, who would have been watching practicable ascents *east* of the gorge; but Hydarnes dealt summarily with them. "Shot up" at dawn by enemies arriving from an unexpected angle, they did what armoured Greeks naturally would. They "pulled in" to a rising ground to defend themselves; and the Persians, peppering them with arrows to keep them fixed, went straight on, after the main objective.

Leonidas' vedettes were only in time to tell him that his flank was already turned. There was just time to save some of the troops, if a sacrificed rearguard gave them a long enough start to beat a pursuit by cavalry. Leonidas sent away his Peloponnesian allies. Like a brave man and good brigadier, he stayed himself, with the Three Hundred, the Helots, whose bodies were seen on the field, indistinguishable from Spartans, and the Boiotians, whose cities were now bound to fall. Some of the latter were taken prisoner. He himself fell leading a violent counter-attack, in which two young half-brothers of Xerxes were also killed.

The well-publicised story of Leonidas' sacrifice was fair enough; but the stark fact was that central Greece lay open and that a king of Sparta had been defeated and killed. The moral effect was seen at once: "a few Arcadians – poor men, seeking employment", came in to join Xerxes. Since Arcadia is far, it is probable that they were deserters from the Greek army, now feeling, in regular mercenary fashion, that a live Xerxes was better than a dead Leonidas. Herodotus describes their interrogation, once more implying surprise at the Persians' professionalism: "One Persian conducted it on behalf of them all".[1] (In a Greek army, everybody would have wanted to join in!)

Thereafter, western Arcadians did no more fighting. Phokis was devastated with deliberate frightfulness. Thebes and most of Boiotia, hostile to Athens, submitted quickly, Alexander of Macedon making their peace for them. The Peloponnesians mobilised in force – and, to the disgust of the Athenians, "dug in" at the Isthmus. Athens was evacuated in haste. Some citizens indeed, in accordance with a decree passed earlier, had already sent their women and children to Troizen; but for the rest, there was now time only for a short carry across the

[1] Hdt. viii. 26.

sound to Salamis or, at furthest, to Aigina. A volunteer garrison held the Acropolis; but it too fell to Persian prowess in climbing "impossible" rocks; and Xerxes sent news of victory to his uncle, Artabanos, in charge at Susa.

4. *The Defeat of Xerxes*

But Xerxes had still not won the war. The Greek fleet, the Peloponnesians having helped with the evacuation of Athens, was in the Salamis strait; and beyond it, the Athenian government and land forces still defied the King. Xerxes badly needed to eliminate this resistance before winter accentuated his supply problems.

There were councils on naval strategy. Artemisia, the Karian queen commanding her own squadron from Halikarnassos, is said to have advocated simply blockading Salamis till *their* supply problems forced the Greeks out. Damaratos had already proposed detaching a squadron to occupy Kythera island and threaten Sparta from the rear; but Akhaimenes the King's brother, viceroy and admiral of Egypt, objected that after its storm losses the fleet was no longer strong enough to divide in face of the enemy. Xerxes, supported by most of his commanders, was already bent on forcing the issue, when a secret message from Themistokles (mentioned, without names, by the contemporary Aeschylus) brought him the false information that the Greeks were about to retreat by night. This had the effect of causing him to send the Egyptian fleet, which had done well at Artemision, to block the western strait, and the rest, after a night at sea waiting to cut off a retreat that did not materialise, to enter the eastern strait at dawn. There, as they tried to fan out after passing the narrowest point (narrower then than now) the Greeks swarmed in upon them and, with the advantage of the outside station (in contrast to Artemision), in a day's hard fighting inflicted a heavy defeat. The King's elder half-brother Ariabignes, admiral in chief, was killed, the Phoenicians, leading the advance, largely destroyed; and thereafter the rest of the fleet was considered unreliable. It was withdrawn for the winter to stations guarding Ionia and the Dardanelles; and the Greeks, following cautiously, regained control of the Andros Channel.

Without command of the sea, Xerxes at Athens, though in no personal danger, was intolerably isolated from his empire; and his return to show himself safe and sound at Sardis (not Susa), though represented by the Greeks as a flight, was no more than Darius had done after the Scythian campaign. The war would have to go on for another year; but Mardonios, whose honour was engaged, professed confidence that he could finish it. Xerxes left him in Thessaly, where there was food enough for the winter. Mardonios "streamlined" the army, dismissing the more bizarre auxiliaries; but Xerxes (like Darius) left his general the main force, including all the good Iranian troops, even the Guard division; though Hydarnes (since the guard-commander or *Chiliarch* had a position something like that of a Roman Praetorian Prefect) went back with the King. One Iranian division escorted Xerxes to the Marmara (the Hellespont bridges had been broken by gales), and even that then returned to Greece. It was under Artabazos, son of Pharnakes, perhaps the former finance minister (p. 591); a man destined to fame.

Details from Herodotus show that there was an extensive reshuffle of commands for the campaign of 479, and make it probable that few of the senior generals were eager to take part in it. Of six generals, besides Mardonios, who reappear in the last book of Herodotus, all are in new positions, and four of them are the *last* four in his list of twenty-nine infantry commanders (exclusive of Hydarnes). A table is revealing:

Name	Command in 480 and ref. to Hdt. vii	Position in 479	Fate and ref. to Hdt. ix
Tigranes	2nd Median (62)	GOC Land-forces, Ionia	Killed (104)
Artabazos	9th Parthian (66)	2nd in command to Mardonios	Survived
Artaÿktes	26th Caucasian (78)	GOC Hellespont	Captured and executed (116)
Pharandates	27th Colchian (79)	At Plataia	Presumably killed (76)
Masistios	28th Caucasian (79)	GOC Mardonios' cavalry	Killed (22–5)
Mardontes	29th "Deportees" (80)	Commanded fleet off Ionia	Killed (114)

It transpires that any more senior generals who voluntarily gave these, their juniors, a chance, showed enlightened self-interest.

Mardonios returned to diplomatic warfare; but the results were poor. Argos indeed was ready to help – could the Persians but reach her frontiers; but Athens, Sparta, Corinth and the rest of the eastern Peloponnese hung together, though there was exasperation at Athens when their allies made every effort to retain Athens' navy without fighting to save Athens' land; offering her, instead, economic support for the duration of the war. The allies seem to have hoped that the Persians might be forced out by sea-borne threats to their communications – i.e., mainly by Athenian efforts; though it was Corinth which succeeded in engineering one such operation, a brave revolt in the westernmost Chalkidic peninsula, headed by Poteidaia, a Corinthian colony, which bestrode the isthmus.

Artabazos, returning from the Straits, found this revolt in being, and acted energetically. He stopped it spreading by massacring, on suspicion, the population of Olynthos, Poteidaia's non-Greek mainland neighbour, and handing over its valuable site and lands to Chalkidian Greeks who had not rebelled; and at Poteidaia the Greek commander of troops from Skiōne inside the peninsula, who were taking part in the defence, gave ear to his propaganda and offered to concert a betrayal. Then his luck ran out. His reply to a message from his "contact", Timoxenos of Skiōne, was written on a small piece of papyrus, rolled on to an arrow, with the feathers stuck on *through* it; but his archer missed the (wooden?) turret which Timoxenos had specified as a "post-box", and wounded a defender. The letter was noticed, and the traitor's identity was suspected (it was hushed up for the sake of inter-allied relations). Then an exceptionally low tide, probably seismic, laid bare the sea-bed at the ends of the wall, and Artabazos promptly tried to rush troops past, into the interior of the peninsula; but the sea came back in a tidal wave, and many were drowned. Soon after this, he was called off by Mardonios for the summer campaign.

Athens had refused the Persian's utmost blandishments: the offer of an amnesty for the past, aid to restore her ruined temples, even increased territory (this would have been at the expense of Persia's ally, Thebes!). Athens refused, as she reported to Sparta, on the grounds of "our Hellenic community of blood and language and religion and ways of life";[1] the Persian pressure had actually called into being a pan-Hellenic patriotism, and the brief vision of Greek unity; but when the pressure was relaxed, the vision faded. Baffled, Mardonios reoccupied Athens (midsummer, 479), reported the advance by beacons to Xerxes, and, on the rejection of his last offer, began to demolish it stone by stone. From Salamis again the Athenians reminded Sparta that their endurance had limits; and in view of the fact that without Athens' navy the Isthmus wall would be useless, the scales of debate at Sparta turned at last. Almost overnight Peloponnesian forces, aggregating some 30,000 armoured men, marched against Mardonios.

[1] Hdt. viii. 144.

THE GREAT WARS

Mardonios withdrew to Boiotia, where his cavalry would have room to manoeuvre. They attacked the head of the Greek column as it descended from the pass east of Mt. Kithairon, but were driven off with the loss of their commander – largely by an Athenian specialised archer regiment, something new in Greek armies. For some weeks the armies faced each other across the muddy bed of the Boiotian Asōpós, a slight but not negligible obstacle. They were perhaps not very unequal in numbers; the size of Mardonios' entrenched camp, given as ten furlongs (*c.* 1,800 metres) square, suggests perhaps 75,000 horse and foot; but with the difference in armament – the Greeks having some 38,000 unmatched armoured foot (8,000 from Athens), but no cavalry, and with their light-armed a rabble – either side could lose all by an immediate offensive.

There was depression among the Persian officers. They were isolated in a strange land. Supplies were short, all sea routes were cut, and even land convoys from Thessaly were harassed by Phokian guerillas from Mount Parnassos. Artabazos proposed a slight further withdrawal, to Thebes, which could be made to yield supplies, and a continuance of political warfare from there. As it was, some anti-democratic Athenians are said to have been detected plotting treason; but this too was hushed up.[1] However Mardonios, sanguine or desperate, was bent on forcing a decision; and the Greeks were in difficulties too. Mardonios' cavalry cut in behind their position, on a low ridge fronting the Asōpós, destroying on one night a large food-convoy from the Peloponnese, fouling and blocking springs. At last Pausanias, the young Spartan commander (regent for his cousin, the still younger son of Leonidas), ordered a retreat by night to a line running along the hill-foot of Kithairon, with its eastern flank covered by a rocky gully and its western by the evacuated and ruined city of Plataia. The result, and probably Pausanias' intention, was to provoke a battle.

The movement as planned was complex. The centre, half the army, was to go first, straight back to the hill-foot, which it did, thus covering a pass by which more food-convoys were waiting to come down. The Spartans, with some eastern Arcadians, on the right (11,500 armoured men), waited till nearly dawn before withdrawing, and then left one battalion, probably deliberately, as bait; it joined the main body just before being overtaken. The Athenians (8,000), who had been on the left, were ordered to move across, after the centre had gone, and close up on the Spartans; Pausanias wanted, and did not get, the support

[1] Plutarch, *Aristeides* 13.

of their archers; and they too waited, the men anxious and puzzled and circulating various improbable rumours, some of which reached Herodotus. They were still on the move at dawn.

Mardonios, seeing the Greeks in disarray (the whole centre was out of sight), at once launched his army in pursuit. His starting-line, owing to the course of the Asōpós, was curved, with his wings (Persians facing the Spartans, and Boiotians the Athenians, their old enemies) ahead of the centre (other, mostly Iranian, troops under Artabazos). The wings also faced the two best crossing-places, used by cart-tracks from Thebes to Athens and to Plataia. Naturally they got ahead; and the Boiotians, hot on the track of their old enemies, came across the front of Artabazos' corps. Since movements intended to draw an enemy out of formation were not alien to Spartan tactics, and since Pausanias gained great renown for this battle, it is likely that this result was planned; though Herodotus' Athenian informants told the story in such a manner as to reflect minimum credit upon the allies, who by his time had become Athens' enemies.

One thing alone went wrong: the Athenians failed to complete their movement. The Boiotians, who had some cavalry, brought them to bay between the two former centres; and the former Greek centre, instead of being able to come in on a flank in one mass, had to divide and advance to cover their allies' flanks. But the decisive struggle was what both commanders had wanted, a stand-up fight between Persians and Spartans. The latter had to stand, or kneel behind their shields, exposed to archery to which they could make no reply; though, thanks to their armour, they are said to have had only 92 men killed. But the Persians edged closer, "bunched" as more came up from the rear and pushed forward; and when they were too massed to get away, Pausanias at last gave the order to charge. The Persians fought with desperate courage, "grasping at the pikes and trying to break them";[1] but Mardonios' headlong advance had committed them to the wrong kind of battle. He himself, conspicuous in the press on a white horse, was felled by a stone. The Thousand, the élite regiment of the Immortals, fell around him. At last the Persians broke; and the Boiotians then got out in good order, covered by their cavalry. Artabazos, who could have seen it all from the ridge once occupied by the Greeks, declined to compound disaster by committing his miscellaneous corps against the ordered Greek line. He pulled it out too, and made for the north, leaving the remaining

[1] Hdt. ix. 62.

Persians to be slaughtered in an attempt to defend their camp. He has been much criticised by modern writers for abandoning comrades; but Xerxes, who was no easy master, reckoned that he had done well.

Thus ended the great invasion; an effort never to be repeated, though the Greeks long expected that it would be. All was decided, says Thucydides, by two battles at sea and two on land; but his most acute comments on it are those which he puts into the mouth of the military expert Hermokrates of Syracuse. "Few great expeditions far from home," says he, "have ever succeeded; for *they cannot bring superior numbers*, when those threatened unite; and if they are defeated through lack of supplies in a foreign land, still they give enhanced reputation to those whom they attacked, even if their disasters were largely their own fault; just as these Athenians, when the Persians failed at many points, contrary to reasonable expectation, have gained renown because Athens was their objective."[1]

Why did the Persians never try again? There were no doubt many reasons: weakness at the top, with horrible court and harem melodramas – Herodotus takes his leave of Xerxes with one such; and probably the fact that the Persian nobles, installed in rich satrapies, and many of their household cavalry too, felt no need for further aggrandisement. In the short run, the mere losses may account for much. Xerxes lost the first of his six marshals, the first of his four admirals – and another, not previously named, at Mykale; five (at least) of the thirty divisional commanders; three of his ten brothers who served. The losses of the rank and file are not likely to have been lighter; and the loss of the flower of Persia's regular soldiers and Phoenicia's sailors could not quickly be made good. The great expedition had been an enormous effort. That it reached Athens at all was an achievement. It was not defeated by geography alone; Athens, Sparta and the north-east Peloponnese saved their way of life by hard fighting under sagacious leaders. Nevertheless, the supply problem had counted for much. Both Xerxes in 480 and Mardonios in 479 met with their great disasters *because they were in a hurry*.

[1] Thuc. i. 23, 1; 33, 5–6.

PERSIA AND THE GREEKS

5. *The Empire on the Defensive*

In the same summer, a reduced Greek fleet, since the main effort was being made on land, reoccupied Delos, a symbolic gesture, but was slow to advance further, despite conspiratorial overtures from Chios and Samos. When at last it did, the Persians, finding no heart for battle in their own sailors, evacuated Samos, beached their ships south of Mykale and protected them with a palisade; but the Greeks, though they cannot have had at the outside more than 4,000 armoured marines, landed further along the coast and stormed it, routing the Persian covering force (clearly nothing like Herodotus' alleged 60,000 men!) and killing its commander, Tigranes. Many fugitives were killed by Milesian levies, whom the Persians had withdrawn to lines of communication as suspect, and who now showed the suspicion to be well justified. The ships were burned, and revolt spread fast in Ionia, though some cities still held by, or were held for, Persia for years. Class struggles within them tended to polarise, with some oligarchies or dynasts holding to the empire against stirrings of democracy.

The new revolt in Ionia embarrassed the Spartans, who did not think it could be defended, and had no wish for a commitment overseas. They therefore proposed to evacuate Ionia and settle its people on the lands of those northern Greeks who had surrendered to Xerxes; a quite impracticable suggestion which was soon dropped. But Athens, which claimed to be the mother-city of the Ionian states, was more sanguine; and the Spartans were willing to let Athens try. For a start, while the Peloponnesians went home after Mykale, the Athenians, with allies from Lesbos, Chios and Samos, sailed for the Dardanelles and, after a blockade lasting through the winter, took Sestos, the bridgehead city, and in it, a significant capture, the huge master-cables that had held the bridges.

Greek objectives were now to deny forward positions to the enemy, should Xerxes try again; to reopen trade-routes, and, in Homeric style, revenge. Kimon, son of Miltiades, Athens' rising general, maintained that through spoils and ransoms the war could be made to pay. In 478 the victors of Plataia, Pausanias and the Athenian Aristeides, appeared at sea. They liberated Cyprus – though the city-kings returned to Persian allegiance within ten years, when the Phoenician navy was rebuilt. With the Levant cleared, they then sailed to Byzantion, which held a Persian garrison, took it after another siege, and freed the Black

Sea grain-route. But at Byzantion, Pausanias made himself unpopular by tyrannical behaviour, including making free with the daughters of citizens. He even adopted (like Alexander the Great) the Iranian jacket and trousers instead of the primitive Greek costume; and he got in touch with Megabates, the satrap at Daskyleion, first no doubt over ransoming prisoners, but presently proposing to marry the satrap's daughter as part of a peace settlement. He was recalled to Sparta, and fined for his offences against individuals, though on a charge of high treason he was acquitted. The liberated allies refused to obey his less distinguished successor, and invited Athens – that is, Aristeides the Just, a refreshing contrast – to take over the command; and Aristeides organized them into a permanent confederacy, with oaths sworn "for ever", and with a treasury and meeting-place at holy Delos. Sparta, once more, acquiesced.

Meanwhile the young Kimon cleared Persians out of the rest of the Gallipoli Peninsula, and laid siege (477–476 ?) to Eïōn on the Strymon, protecting the bridge at Nine Ways. The Persians proved as tough behind walls as in the field. Those at Sestos had held out till they had boiled the straps of their hammock-beds for soup. Boges, governor of Eïōn, likewise held out through a winter, hoping that its continental severity would break the blockade; but the Athenians were tough too. When there was no food left, Boges scattered all gold and silver that he could find into the river, slew his women and children on a pyre of the Residency furniture, set fire to it and the building, and slew himself. Xerxes honoured him posthumously, through the children he had left in Persia. Maskames, at Doriskos, the great supply-base, was as stubborn and more successful; he lived to enjoy his honours. Herodotus, whose main narrative ends at the fall of Sestos, adds that, while other posts fell, "no one ever captured him, though many tried".[1] Perhaps his garrison finally withdrew by command of the King.

Pausanias was not yet finished. He reappeared at Byzantion, where he must have had some faction-support, unofficially but still with personal prestige, and held it for some years, while negotiating with Persia in good earnest. He is said to have asked for a daughter of the King in marriage; and Xerxes took him seriously enough to send his best expert on Greek affairs to take over at Daskyleion: Artabazos, whose family kept that satrapy as long as the empire stood. The Athenians at last expelled Pausanias from Byzantion by force; but he

---

[1] vii. 105f.

moved only to a castle at Kolōnai in the Troad, where they could not get at him. What he was really up to, as well as the chronology, remains uncertain; but finally Sparta had had enough of him too, and summoned him home on pain of being declared a public enemy. At home in Sparta, his lust for power at last betrayed him. He was convicted of "intriguing with the Helots", i.e. wishing to revolutionise Sparta's archaic constitution; and like Kleomenes before him, he perished miserably.

His papers were alleged to incriminate Themistokles, who, in a conservative post-war reaction at Athens, had already been politically exiled, and was living at Argos. Summoned to stand trial, he declined to do so and, after an adventurous escape, reached Asia and threw himself upon the mercy of the King. Xerxes was delighted; but his murder (465) seems to have supervened very shortly, and it was his son Artaxerxes I, who succeeded after the first of many bloody rounds of palace revolutions in Persia, with whom Themistokles may have had a personal interview. The King made him governor of Magnesia-on-the-Maeander, an inland Ionian town, "for his bread", with the addition of Myous (near Miletos) and Lampsakos, "for wine and meat"[1] (evidence that Myous and Lampsakos were not yet, as they were later, in league with Athens). At Magnesia he died, perhaps about 460.

Meanwhile the proposed Athenian "war of revenge" had been much interrupted by troubles in Greece. Athens launched, in fact, just three major eastern expeditions in the twenty years 469 to 449, sandwiched between revolts by League members, who began to regret their oaths sworn for ever, and wars with Corinth, Aigina and, after 459, Sparta herself.

In or about 466, Kimon won Phasēlis in Lykia – it is noteworthy that this Rhodian colony stood a siege before agreeing to come over – and in a great victory at the mouth of the River Eurymedon destroyed the rebuilt Phoenician and Cilician war-fleets and their Cypriote allies; but then came a revolt and two-year siege of Thasos, a breach (not yet war) with Sparta, and the political exile of Kimon, at the time of a radical democratisation of the Athenian constitution.

During these events the new radical leaders Ephialtes (soon assassinated) and the young Pericles conducted sweeps in the Levant with modest forces, profiting by Kimon's victory. The democrats (contrary to what some anti-democratic later Greek writers say) were no less keen on the *revanche* than Kimon; and indeed, the Athenian economy had

[1] Thuc. i. 138, 5.

become geared to war, supported largely by the contributions, in lieu of ships, paid by most of the League states. When their hands were free in 460, just before the outbreak of open war with Corinth and Aigina, a League fleet of 200 ships sailed to liberate Cyprus once more; and then lower Egypt revolted under the Libyan Inaros son of Psammetichos, and the fleet sailed to its aid.

The Egyptian war was the sternest struggle ever fought between the empire and the Delian League. The Egyptians defeated and killed the satrap Akhaimenes; the Greek fleet controlled the Nile, and joined in the siege of the White Fort, the citadel of Memphis, held by "the surviving Persians and Medes and the Egyptians who had not joined the rebellion".[1] But this was the limit of their success. A war with "many vicissitudes"[2] went on for years; and the empire ponderously mobilised. Artabazos commanded the fleet, Megabyxos, youngest of the chief marshals of 480, and now Satrap of Syria, the land forces. (There is no reason to doubt that this is the veteran Artabazos; he is mentioned *before* Megabyxos when they appear together, both here and in Cyprus later, and in the final peace negotiations.)[3] In 456 Megabyxos broke into Egypt and relieved the White Fort. For eighteen months the allies stood on the defensive in the Delta, evidently able to keep Artabazos out of the waterways, while both sides waited in vain upon events in Greece. At the outset, King Artaxerxes had sent Megabazos (perhaps an admiral named in 480, son of Megabates) to Sparta, with gold for Athens' enemies; but as they seemed to be making no effective use of it, he brought some of it back again. Athens in 457–455 actually won her most spectacular victories, crushing Aigina and temporarily winning control of Boiotia; but with or without Persian gold, these wars diverted her energies, and reinforcements for Egypt were too few and too late. In 454 Megabyxos, by a typically Persian huge engineering operation, drained a channel of the Nile that guarded the Athenian position on the island of Prosopitis, stranded their ships and took the position by storm. All the ships were lost, and 6,000 Greeks are said to have surrendered with Inaros; only a minority of the men escaped by a desert march to Cyrene. Further, a belated relief squadron of 50 ships sailed unsuspecting into the delta and was captured too. Whether or not the expedition had been kept at 200-ship strength (Athenian and allied), it was a huge disaster, and marks the end of Athens' career of

[1] Thuc. i. 104. [2] Thuc. i. 109.
[3] Diodorus xi. 74. 6; 75. 1; 77. 4; xii. 3. 2; 4. 5.

victory; though the Persians, still unable to subdue all the difficult delta country with its warlike inhabitants, did not exploit their success further afield.

Megabyxos went home with his prisoners. He "found the King much embittered against Inaros for the death of his brother Akhaimenes", and had to plead hard, saying that he had obtained the surrender of Byblos ["Papyrus"; otherwise unknown as a place-name in Egypt], their last strong position, only by pledging his word that their lives should be spared. At last Artaxerxes promised this, and Megabyxos handed them over. But the Queen-mother Amestris, one of those tigress-mothers whose uninhibited instincts repeatedly bedevilled the attempts of kings to act wisely, wore down her surviving son at last. Five years later, it is said, she got him to hand over Inaros and had him impaled; "and she beheaded fifty Greeks, which was all she managed to get". Megabyxos, his honour outraged, got the other Greeks away to Syria, and there defied the King.[1] He defeated two expeditions sent against him; was reconciled; is said to have lived at court, got into trouble again at a hunt for shooting before the King at a lion, which he thought was endangering the King, and been exiled; but at last to have died, restored to favour, aged 76.

There are difficulties about this story, which we have only on the authority of Ktesias; that historian nowhere shows better that he was concerned only to be "popular"; for example, no battle takes place without a "Homeric" duel between the generals. For (a) "five years" takes us to 449, when the war with Athens ended (and the prisoners were released?); and (b) Megabyxos was then still in favour (below, p. 337). His prolonged revolt must be after 449. But possibly Ktesias is wrong only in putting together the execution of the fifty Greeks (at once, 454/453?) and that of Inaros, later, at which he revolted?[2]

In Greece the war languished. In 451 Athens and Sparta concluded a five-year armistice; and in 450 old Kimon, back from exile, sailed yet again with 200 ships for Cyprus. Athens was to show herself still formidable; but Kimon's last expedition, like Drake's, proved an unsuccessful attempt to repeat what had been done before. Phoenician Kition held out; the besiegers ran short of food (which shows that the Greek Cypriotes were showing no enthusiasm for Athens); and the dispatch of sixty ships to support the resistance in the Delta did not

[1] Ktesias epitome, 66ff.
[2] Cf. David M. Lewis, *Sparta and Persia* (Leiden, 1977), 51, n. 5 (Ed.).

THE GREAT WARS

prevent Artabazos and Megabyxos from transferring troops to Cilicia. There an Athenian general, Anaxikrates, was killed, presumably in a "spoiling" raid. Then the Persians, as in 497, succeeded in running troops across on the north wind; and Kimon, dying of a sickness, gave his last order, to break away. Off the Cypriote Salamis (Famagusta) the Athenians claimed victory both by land and sea; but a safe retreat was all that they gained by it.

Both sides at last saw the war as unprofitable; and Artabazos and Megabyxos were authorised to negotiate. For Athens, the plenipotentiary was Kallias the Rich, Kimon's brother-in-law. Athens withdrew permanently from Cyprus and Egypt, and Persia undertook not to send warships into the Aegean; boundaries are mentioned by later writers at the Chelidonian Islands (off the cape still called Gelidönü) in Lykia, and at the Blue Rocks east of the Bosporus. There seems to have been an exchange of prisoners; and in Asia Minor, a demilitarised zone. Athens ceased to keep garrisons there, as an inscription, regulating the affairs of Erythrai, shows her doing earlier; the cities, when next we hear of them, are without walls[1] (though this *might* mean only that they had outgrown them); and Persia agreed not to send troops within a certain distance, variously reported, of the coast. The cities were thus *de facto* independent of Persia, and Athens continued to levy Delian League contributions from them; but it does not appear that the Great King abandoned *de jure* his claim to tax Ionia too! For the present, the satraps were merely unable to collect; but in 412, when Athens had fallen on evil days, Darius II at once reminded them of their duty (p. 343).

Athens was not proud of this compromise end to the great war. Indeed, it was an embarrassment, since thereafter her right to collect League "defence" contributions was disputable. She did not advertise it; and a (perhaps embellished) version of it which she did set up on stone long after – as propaganda, in contrast to the much worse terms accepted by Sparta in 387 (p. 368) – was denounced as a forgery by the historian Theopompos. There is even a hint that, at the time, Kallias got into trouble. However, it does seem that on these terms hostilities came to an end. Ionia had peace; though both here and in Cyprus archaeology seems to indicate a much lower standard of prosperity and artistic achievement in the fifth and fourth centuries than in the sixth and the third.

[1] Thuc. iii. 32. 2 (427 B.C.); cf. viii. 31. 35. 41. 50. 62 etc. (after 413).

PERSIA AND THE GREEKS

III. PERSIA REGAINS GROUND (449–387 B.C.)

1. *The Satraps and Greece (449–413)*

Even during the great wars, but much more as the dust of conflict settled, Greeks and Persians were getting to know each other as human beings; and with the development of Turkish archaeology, the study of works of art should, as Professor J. M. Cook has well said,[1] shed increasing light on "the meeting of Greek and Persian in Anatolia". In literature too, a number of anecdotes and reported dialogues reveal to us the Persians, or at least a few of their grandees, more intimately than purely official and military history. Most of these come from the 4th century, as will appear below, and especially from that engaging eye-witness, Xenophon; but the earliest and one of the best is told by Herodotus.

Perhaps about 469, two Spartan aristocrats, when Sparta attributed her post-war troubles to the wrath of Talthybios, patron-hero of heralds, volunteered to surrender themselves to Xerxes, in expiation of the murder of the Persian heralds in 481–480. On their way they were entertained by Hydarnes, who had commanded the Guards at Thermopylae. Hydarnes' descendants appear later as quasi-hereditary satraps of Armenia. He himself, however, is here described as "general of the Men of the Coast" (cf. p. 303), a position sometimes in abeyance but, when it existed, apparently outranking ordinary satrapies. Persia was then still at war with Athens. Long an admirer of Spartan courage, he is said to have said: "You can see here that the King knows how to honour brave men. If you Spartans would surrender yourselves to him, each of you might be a ruler in Greece by the King's gift." But they answered: "Hydarnes, you are at a disadvantage in offering us advice... for you know what it is to be a subject; but freedom you have not tried, so as to know if it is sweet or otherwise. If you had tried it, you would advise us to fight for it not only with spears but with axes too!"[2] So they went on their way; but Xerxes said that he would show himself better than the Spartans, and let them go free.

Satrapies were not strictly hereditary. They were in the King's gift; and not only might a satrap be dismissed or executed; he might also be called to still higher service, as we shall see happening in Artabazos'

---

[1] In the Hellenic Society's *Archaeological Reports* for 1970–1 (p. 60).
[2] Hdt. vii. 135.

family. But the early satraps had already become great local grandees and land-holders, even if legally the land-*owner* was the King. It was difficult even for the King to dislodge such a family, as several satrap-revolts were to show; and, with their local knowledge, when a satrapy fell vacant, a son or kinsman of the late incumbent, if personally suitable, was the obvious man to appoint. It was on this basis that the Pharnakids, Artabazos' family, ruled at Daskyleion[1] for so long. Daskyleion was not a large city, but as a fortress with good natural communications it conveniently housed their treasury and secretariat. The Pharnakids themselves preferred, in the Persian manner, to live a country life in their vast park or *paradise*, as the Persians called it, on the lake near by, well wooded, well watered, full of game and fish, as Xenophon describes it. Near the south-east corner of the lake (modern Manyas Gölü), near Ergili, have been found at various dates a number of pieces of provincial Achaemenian relief sculpture. Some are pretty certainly grave-monuments – the sculpture being cut actually on re-used Greek *stelai* with the common ornament of a palmette at the top; Greeks, it is well known, had colonised inland in the Rhyndakos valley in earlier days. Others, a number of slabs no doubt meant to join together to form a frieze-like composition, come from a more ambitious structure. It may have been a built tomb, of a type well known in Lykia and (later) Cilicia, or, as some have thought, the inside of the enclosure-wall of a Persian place of worship.[2] Some show a processional scene, including ladies riding, accompanied by horsemen and grooms on foot, and a loaded cart, with two horses and two high wheels, whose cover *might* conceal the sarcophagus of the deceased; another is part of a scene of sacrifice, with musicians seated on top of a wall or high plinth, the heads of sacrificial animals shown at their feet. Whatever its nature, this was an expensive monument, probably set up by members of the satrap's family; while the *stelai* might commemorate either these or other well-to-do members of this opulent colonial community.

The courts of these western satraps probably provide the answer to a question that has puzzled many readers of Herodotus: who were those Persian *literati*, *logioi*, whom he repeatedly cites, *e.g.* as trying to make a synthesis of Greek and Persian history out of Greek (and perhaps

---

[1] The only Daskyleion *located* by ancient literary evidence was on the coast E. of Kyzikos, and paid a small tribute (500 drachmas, irregularly) to Athens; but it is generally agreed that the satrapal seat must have been at another place, near the Lake Daskylitis of Strabo's *Geography*.

[2] The latest discussions, by P. Bernard and J. M. Dentzer, both in the *Revue archéologique* for 1969 (pp. 77ff. and 195ff.) argue for a funerary character for this too.

Persian) mythology? At such a court Herodotus, himself born a Persian subject, could have met Persians *and their secretaries*, whose business it was to be familiar with Greek affairs. He could enlighten them, and from them he could have got his own knowledge, detailed and interesting though liable to error, of Persian manners and religion – without learning Persian (as he clearly did not) or visiting Persia, which he nowhere claims to have done. In the west, no doubt, settled that Ostanes, said to have been in Greece with Xerxes, whom later writers cite as their earliest authority for the name of Zoroaster.[1] Herodotus may have met him, though he does not name the prophet, and rather seldom names his sources. His account of Artabazos, which emphasises his failures – despite which he alone of Persian generals emerged from the war with an enhanced reputation – hardly comes from Pharnakid circles, but it might well have come from the rival court of Sardis. Thus too Herodotus may have obtained his detailed list of Xerxes' officers and contingents; though another possible source is Zopyros, the son of Megabyxos, whom he names as defecting to Athens after his father's death.

The name Megabyxos ("Servant of God") actually passed into Greek, as a title for a priest of Artemis of the Ephesians, no doubt identified in that orientalising city with the Iranian Anahita. It is well known how Xenophon, about 395, deposited some money with a Megabyxos for an offering to the goddess, which the priest was to arrange if "anything happened to him" in the coming campaigns in Greece; and how, having survived the war, he received it back from the priest, who visited Greece for the Olympic Games; and the same name for a priest of Ephesian Artemis appears, after the Persian Empire had fallen, in an inscription from the neighbouring city of Priene.[2] But religious syncretism affected what M. Louis Robert has called "the Iranian *diaspora* in Asia Minor" too; even to an extent which worried a Satrap of Sardis, probably in the fourth century, apparently lest it might amount to infidelity to the religion of Iran.

A Greek inscription, in ornate script of the Roman period (c. A.D. 180–200?), discovered by the American excavators of Sardis in 1974, purports to give the gist (not the whole text, as in the Gadatas Letter) of some already ancient documents, which were perhaps themselves preserved in the same temple. The text may be translated:

[1] Pliny, *Nat. Hist.* xxx. i. 8; cf. Diogenes Laertius' Introduction §2.
[2] Xen., *Anabasis* v. iii. 6f.; *Inschr. von Priene* no. 231; cf. the name, Megabyxos son of Megabyxos, *ib.* no. 4; perhaps the priesthood was hereditary.

In the thirty-ninth year of the reign of King Artaxerxes, Droaphernes the son of Barakes, Governor of Lydia, [dedicated] the statue to Law-giving Zeus. [Leaf-stop.] He orders the priests who enter the Sanctuary as his [the god's] servants, and garland the God, to take no part in the mysteries of Sabazios, [that is] of those who carry the burnt offerings, nor of Aggdistis nor of Ma. And they order Dorates the priest to abstain from these mysteries.

In the last sentence, it is not made clear who "they" are; but apparently three documents are summarised, as it were by a museum-label. The 39th year of Artaxerxes might be 426/425, the last year of Artaxerxes I; but in view of the lengths to which the development (or corruption) of Mazdaism at Sardis has gone, we should probably understand Artaxerxes II, of whom more below; the date will then be 359/358. Droaphernes the Governor (*hyparchos*; a word which, like "*satrapes*" is used by the Greeks for officers of various ranks), clearly Satrap of Lydia, bears a name new to modern scholarship, but of good Iranian coinage: "Strong Glory", cf. Greek Kleosthenes, Kleisthenes. What is striking, and marks a departure from popular Mazdaism as described by Herodotus, is that "Zeus the Lawgiver", who must be Ahura Mazda, now has a temple, and even a statue, dedicated by the Governor himself. One is irresistibly reminded of biblical accounts of the "backslidings" of the Children of Israel, under the influence of their neighbours in conquered Canaan. The new statue is perhaps the governor's own innovation; "idolatry" was creeping in. According to Clement of Alexandria, citing Berōsos of Babylon, Artaxerxes III even set up statues of Aphrodite (Ishtar?) in his own capitals.[1] But while the Satrap, evidently a man of some religious convictions (for a cult-statue was costly), may go thus far, perhaps shocking his more conservative fellow-Iranians, he is, for that very reason, all the more determined to show himself orthodox in what he thought really mattered. The gods whose esoteric worship is banned for priests of Ahura Mazda are all native to Asia Minor: Sabazios, sometimes identified by the Greeks with Dionysos the wine-god; Aggdistis, (usually spelt Agdistis), whose cult also spread to some Greek ports, a Phrygian name for the Mother-Goddess, associated with the legend of Attis and served by eunuch priests; Ma, an armed war-goddess, with a sanctuary at Komana in Cappadocia; all, clearly, deities attractive to those who liked their religion highly flavoured.

We return to the history of the fifth century.

[1] Clem., *Protreptikos* v. 65; cited by L. Robert in the commentary on his model first publication of this inscription, in *CRAI* 1975, with plate of the text.

PERSIA AND THE GREEKS

At Sardis the next known satrap is Pissouthnes, son of Hystaspes; the latter name, that of Darius I's father, *may* well have been borne by a son of Artaphernes (I or II); but we do not know. Pissouthnes backed Samos in revolt against Athens in 440, but failed to get a Phoenician fleet sent to its relief; King Artaxerxes was presumably unwilling to disturb the recent peace. But relations were still tense, and the satraps, unable in practice to collect the tribute which the peace of 449 *probably* promised them, were ready to assist Athens' enemies if they could; supporting a *party* in a Greek city might be claimed not to break the treaty.[1] In 431 war between Athens and the Peloponnesian League broke out again; and the Peloponnesians at once planned to seek Persian aid. Ambassadors in 430 tried to make their way overland "to the Hellespont, to reach Pharnakes the son of Pharnabazos, who was going to conduct them to the King";[2] but they were captured in Thrace by a chief whom Athens had courted, and sent to Athens, where they were summarily put to death. Some later envoys got through; but the King found their proposals vague and inconsistent.[3] Pharnakes, whose father's name as well as his own recurs in the Pharnakid family, is the first known successor of Artabazos; no doubt either his nephew or (quite possibly) his grandson. Pissouthnes, also in 430, assisted Kolophon in Ionia, which was a few miles inland, to break loose from Athens; an anti-democratic party admitted his Arcadian mercenaries and native troops into the city. In 425 Athens intercepted an Artaphernes, on a mission to Sparta to clarify terms. However, when Artaxerxes died, Darius II, "the Bastard", King 423–401 after the bloody episodes of Xerxes II and Sogdianos and no doubt feeling insecure, renewed the treaty with Athens.[4] But Athens, it is not known how long after (probably after the short-lived peace of 421 with Sparta), made what turned out to be a major blunder. No doubt misinformed on the weakness of Darius' position, she supported her sometime enemy Pissouthnes in rebellion, and an Athenian named Lykon is said to have commanded the satrap's Greek mercenaries.

But against Pissouthnes was sent a commander destined to fame: Tissaphernes, able and devious, perhaps the son (it has been presumed from a Lykian inscription)[5] of a Hydarnes; and if so, descended from

---

[1] Cf. Lewis, *Sparta and Persia*, p. 61 and n. 79.
[2] Thuc. ii. 67.   [3] Thuc. iv. 50.
[4] Andokides, *On the Peace* §29. (Thucydides omits this non-military event.)
[5] *Tituli Asiae Minoris* I no. 44. The names are juxtaposed, but the actual Lykian word for "son" does not appear; and the epitome of Ktesias (§53; Jacoby 688 F 15), though it shortly afterwards

the two famous Hydarnes, father and son, of Darius I and Xerxes' reigns. He bribed Lykon, and perhaps Athens too, since there is mention of "territory and cities" (places in revolt from Athens?) as the price of betrayal. Abandoned by his Greeks, Pissouthnes surrendered on a promise that his life would be spared. It was, by Tissaphernes; but Darius had him thrown into a furnace.

The date of this is probably well after 420; for Pissouthnes' natural son, Amorges, was still in arms in Karia in 412.

2. *The Satraps and the Peloponnesian War, 412–408*

A new epoch opened after Athens lost an army and fleet before Syracuse in Sicily. Every malcontent in her empire was stirred by the hope of freedom; and Persia by that of upsetting the humiliating peace of 449. Tissaphernes, recently "needled" by the King on the subject of the tribute of Ionia, sent envoys to Sparta; and so did Pharnabazos, who had just succeeded his father Pharnakes at Daskyleion; a character as impetuous, sincere and forthright as Tissaphernes was devious, and the satrap under whom scattered Greek references give us our clearest picture of conditions in his region. The two men were mutually jealous, and their satrapies, which met at the south of the Troad, were evidently not clearly demarcated; for we hear that Pharnakes had given the Delians (expelled by Athens in 422 in an effort to "purify" that holy place) a refuge at Adramyttion, and that later Arsakes, a deputy of Tissaphernes, called them out on military service, and treacherously massacred them.[1] Tissaphernes, backed by secret overtures from Chios, the last league city to keep its own navy, secured the despatch of the first Peloponnesian and soon also Syracusan ships; and most of Ionia, including Chios and Miletos, came over to them, followed within a year by Dorian Rhodes and Knidos. Persian money for the fleet and the denial of money to Athens were vital considerations; and for the sake

---

deals at length with the disaster to the house of Hydarnes, the Conspiracy of Teritouchmes (below, p. 349, n. 1.), nowhere hints that Tissaphernes was Teritouchmes' brother as assumed by Tarn (*CAH* VI, p. 3). Unfortunately the Lycian text still cannot be translated. The language is now known to be related to Hittite and Luvian, and the writing is a form of the Greek alphabet; but too little is yet known of the vocabulary, despite the French discovery of a trilingual text (Lycian, Greek and Aramaic) of the charter of a religious foundation at Xanthos, to make possible the translation of texts on military and political matters; cf. E. Laroche, *CRAI* 1975, pp. 124ff. The name Hydarnes (Old Persian *Vidarna*; Elamite *Mi-tur-na*, *Mi-tar-na* in the Persepolis tablets) appears, in fact, to have been not uncommon.

[1] Thuc. v. 1; viii. 108.

of this the Spartan admiral Chalkideus concluded at Miletos the first Greco-Persian treaty of which we have contemporary record:

Terms of alliance concluded with the King and Tissaphernes by the Spartans and their allies:

"All territory and cities which the King holds and the fathers of the King held shall belong to the King; and from these cities all money or other aid which used to go to Athens, the King and the Spartans and their allies shall unite to prevent it going, whether money or anything else.

"The King and the Spartans and their allies shall jointly prosecute the war with Athens; and they shall make no separate peace. Any persons who revolt from the King shall be at war with the Spartans and their allies" [and vice versa].[1]

The last clause had in mind, particularly, Amorges, whom the allies captured by an unexpected attack from the sea, and handed over to Tissaphernes. The Spartans were worried, however, by the terms of this treaty, and drafted a fuller text, to which Tissaphernes agreed:

"Agreement of the Spartans and their allies with King Darius and the sons of the King and Tissaphernes: there shall be peace and friendship on the following terms:

"Against any territory or cities which belong to King Darius or belonged to his father or his forefathers, the Spartans and their allies shall not proceed in war or with hostile intent; nor shall they levy tribute from these cities; nor shall King Darius nor his subjects proceed against the Spartans or their allies in war or with hostile intent. Any claims which the Spartans or their allies may make upon the King, or the King upon the Spartans or their allies, shall be settled by negotiation. The war with the Athenians and their allies shall be prosecuted jointly, and any peace shall be concluded jointly; and for any forces operating in the King's territory or by request of the King anywhere, the King shall bear the expenses. If any of the cities which have made [this] agreement with the King commit hostilities against the King's territory, the others shall oppose them and defend the King with all their power; and if anyone in the King's territory or of the King's subjects commit hostility against the Spartans or their allies, the King shall prevent it and defend them with all his power."[2]

This text got rid of the implied obligation in the earlier one, for the allies to turn over to Persia any Asian Greek city which joined them; but the Spartans at home were still indignant at the recognition of Persian claims to territory which had belonged to the King *or his ancestors*. This, as was pointed out, could include the Cyclades and the northern Greek mainland. They refused to ratify, and sent out, early in 411, eleven commissioners, headed by Lichas, an elder statesman, with authority to supervise and if they saw fit supersede Chalkideus'

[1] Thuc. viii. 18.   [2] ib. 37.

successor, Astyochos; he was being accused by the Spartan commander at Chios of doing nothing to relieve it from the mounting pressure of an Athenian counter-offensive. Arriving at Knidos, where he found the fleet refitting and Tissaphernes present, Lichas, after a swift study of the situation, denounced both treaties and demanded that the allies should "either make a better one, or at least not observe this, even for the sake of economic support". At this, Tissaphernes not unnaturally left in a rage,[1] and turned to a new adviser, who knew the inside of Greek politics as no other man.

Alkibiades, long the uncrowned king of Athenian youth, politician and general (a very bad one in his early days), facing ruin in 415 for sacrilege – in a witch-hunt stirred up by another sacrilege, of which, ironically, he was probably innocent – had deserted, and served Sparta against his own city all too well; but he was by now in trouble with Sparta too, accused *inter alia* of having seduced King Agis' wife. He fled from the allied camp, and is said to have initiated Tissaphernes' new policy, which was to continue paying the Peloponnesians, but only on half the hoped-for scale, and always late; and above all, not to bring up to their aid the Phoenician fleet which he had advised the King to mobilise, and which actually advanced to Aspendos, on the Eurymedon, nearly 150 strong. Since the strengths of both belligerents off Asia were around 100, such a fleet could have ended the naval war quickly; but Alkibiades argued that to crush Athens would merely unite the Greeks behind Sparta, which was still flying the banner of liberation, and therefore would find it morally difficult to do a deal with Persia; whereas Athens, now considerably chastened, might be prepared to trade the mainland cities in order to keep the islands. Meanwhile, best of all was to keep the war in being and wear down both sides.

Alkibiades was already hoping, if he could pose as the benefactor who had won over Persia from support of Athens' enemies, to get invited home again. In this, in the end, he succeeded, after an amazing series of intrigues, double-crossing his Athenian enemies, who were no mean intriguers themselves; but he did not manage to bring Persian support for Athens as a bride-gift. Athenian envoys did visit Tissaphernes in the hope of negotiating a separate peace; but Alkibiades, aware that he did not have the satrap in his pocket, as he had pretended, forced a breakdown in the talks by so stepping-up his demands – nominally as interpreter for Tissaphernes, who evidently did not understand Greek –

[1] *ib.* 43. 3.

that the Athenians at last walked out. The demand on which negotiations broke down was that Athens, having already agreed to cede Ionia, should "allow the King to build [war] ships and sail them on the coast of his dominions" without limit of numbers; a matter of interest, supporting the view that Persia really had agreed to a treaty excluding her fleets from the Aegean.[1]

The Peloponnesians meanwhile supported their fleet for a while by levying contributions from Rhodes, which an aristocratic *coup d'état* had brought over to them; but these resources would not last long, and even Lichas realised, swallowing his pride, that they could not do without Persian support. Tissaphernes for his part still wanted their fleet kept in being; and so yet a third and fuller treaty was agreed, this time also with Pharnabazos and his brothers, with whom Pharnabazos evidently shared power:

> In the thirteenth year of King Darius, and in the Ephorship of Alexippidas at Sparta, this Treaty was agreed in the Plain of the Maeander by the Spartans and their allies with Tissaphernes, Hieramenes and the sons of Pharnakes [...]
>
> The King's land in Asia shall belong to the King; and concerning his own land, the King may take such measures as he pleases.
>
> The Spartans and their allies shall take no hostile action against the King's land, nor the King against theirs [...]
>
> Tissaphernes shall provide maintenance for the fleet now present, until the King's ships arrive; thereafter, the Spartans and their allies may maintain their own ships if they choose; and if they ask for maintenance from Tissaphernes, he shall provide it as a loan for repayment without interest at the end of the war...

The usual clauses follow, about joint prosecution of hostilities and no separate peace; but Tissaphernes had probably already decided that the King's ships should never come.

Hieramenes, the other official named in such exalted company, was probably a royal secretary; he appears again in history, reporting to the king against a satrap[2] (p. 352).

Simple and patriotic soldiers had perhaps been placated by the phrase "the King's land", omitting "cities"; but there was little likelihood of Persia excluding cities. Tissaphernes had already introduced garrisons into Miletos, when it was attacked by the Athenians, and Knidos; and now the Spartans had promised not to interfere with them! Disgusted, the Milesians took the law into their own hands. While Astyochos was

---

[1] Wade-Gery, "The Peace of Kallias", in his *Essays*, p. 220; Thuc. viii. 56.
[2] Thuc. viii. 58; Xen., *Hellenica* ii. 1. 9.

confronting riots among his unpaid sailors, they attacked the Persians' fort within their city, and drove them out; and Knidos did the same. Lichas felt constrained to protest. "He said that the Milesians should positively accept subjection to Tissaphernes to a reasonable extent" [ominously vague phrase!] "and act to please him, until victory was won. The Milesians were furious... and when he later fell sick and died, they refused to have him buried in the place which the Spartans on the spot desired."[1] Sparta was "hooked" on that Asia Minor problem, which she was never to solve.

Mindaros, the new Spartan admiral for 411/410, thus arrived to find a general atmosphere of frustration. He waited awhile, still hoping that the Phoenician ships would come. Tissaphernes, taking along the now compliant Lichas, had gone to Aspendos "to bring them" – only to return with the singularly unconvincing excuse that he had not brought them because the 147 galleys mustered were still "not the full number that the King had ordered". Alkibiades, who from the Athenian base at Samos had gone with a small squadron to reconnoitre off Aspendos, was able to claim credit for having personally deprived the Peloponnesians of effective Persian aid. However, the Spartans decided to have done with Tissaphernes, and sailed for the north, where Pharnabazos, eager to "liberate" the towns on his own coast, not only made promises, but really tried to keep them.

The tempo of the war quickened. The Spartan move, threatening the vital Black Sea corn-route, was strategically sound, and at once, for a start, drew off the Athenians' main forces from hard-pressed Chios. But their new navy, rebuilt and retrained since 413, was now an efficient force. With 76 ships against 86 they defeated Mindaros, after a severe and chequered fleet action in the Dardanelles, and in late autumn, after both sides had been reinforced, again and more decisively, chasing his fleet to the beaches of Abydos. In vain did Pharnabazos dash to the rescue, "riding his charger into the sea and urging on his horse and foot"[2] to defend the beached ships. The Athenians towed off thirty of them; a crippling blow, and prelude to yet a third, in which Mindaros was killed and all his last sixty ships captured or burnt on shore, near Kyzikos in the spring of 410.

Pharnabazos then proved a friend in need. He distributed clothing and ration-money for two months to the stranded men, who must have numbered over 10,000 (his magnificent portrait-coins probably

---

[1] Thuc. viii. 84. 5.   [2] Xen., *Hellenica* i. 1. 6.

commemorate this); and, marching them across to Antandros, south of the Troad, he gave them facilities to rebuild their fleet with timber from Mount Ida. (He must also have presumably provided tools.) He had an ulterior motive too; the Greeks of Antandros had already called in a Peloponnesian garrison to defend them from *Tissaphernes'* officer Arsakes (cf. p. 343). Pharnabazos was incidentally securing this border town against his fellow-satrap! Tissaphernes had been in the neighbourhood lately, having come north to try to restore diplomatic relations with his late allies and in fear that Pharnabazos might "steal the show".[1] He had also received a reprimand, or at least a directive not to forget that Athens was the enemy. This transpired when Alkibiades, in the winter after the battle of Abydos, went to visit him in state, with gifts, as a friend. Tissaphernes arrested him saying that these were his orders. He escaped however, after a few weeks, and contributed much by his planning and his fiery oratory to the crowning victory off Kyzikos.

Masters of the sea for two years, the Athenians recovered cities in the north that had revolted, among them Thasos, Kyzikos, Lampsakos, Chalkedon and, after a long siege, Byzantion. An expedition against Ionia made little progress, and was defeated before Ephesos by Tissaphernes and the allies; but Pharnabazos, after failing to break the blockade of Chalkedon, actually agreed to an armistice: Chalkedon was to pay Athens an indemnity and its arrears of tribute, but not suffer occupation; and Pharnabazos would facilitate the passage of an Athenian embassy to the King. It was time; for a Spartan and allied embassy had already gone. Pharnabazos and the ambassadors wintered at Gordion in Phrygia (408/407); but when, with the spring, they were able to resume their journey, they met another caravan coming down. With it were the Spartans, triumphant, having obtained all their points; and the young prince Cyrus, appointed supreme commander in Asia Minor, with instructions to support Sparta, was following close behind.

The Athenians waited, and saw Cyrus; but he refused to hear them, much less let them pass. He ordered Pharnabazos to hand them over to him or, if he preferred, to detain them so that Athens might not be forewarned of the change of policy. Pharnabazos carried out his instructions, and with cruel suavity kept assuring them, now that he would at last take them up to the King, and now that he would send them home "with nothing to complain of". It was not till 405 that,

[1] Thuc. viii. 109.

pleading with Cyrus that he had sworn solemn oaths to look after these men, he got permission to release them. He committed them to the care of one Ariobarzanes, probably one of his brothers, who brought them to the coast at Kios (later Nikomedeia, Ismid). This small Milesian colony, long a member of Athens' League, became, about this time, the fief and residence of Ariobarzanes' family, a branch of the Pharnakids destined to a long history.

3. *Cyrus the Younger (407–401), and the "Ten Thousand"*

The royal insistence that Athens was the enemy, and rejection of the subtler Tissaphernes–Alkibiades policy, looks like a product of advice from a civil service that kept its memory in tidy archives, already over a century old; the "man on the spot" abroad often finds metropolitan policy in such conditions hard to shift. But the appointment of Prince Cyrus, very young – he is *said* to have been born after his father's accession, so only sixteen! – was no doubt due to the influence of his mother, Parysatis, Darius II's strong-minded and ruthless half-sister and wife.[1]

Cyrus, though so young, was a character in the great Achaemenid mould. In the court "cadet school" a king's son would learn to command almost from childhood; but he is said to have been distinguished also for readiness to learn from men of experience. A daring horseman and hunter, his body scarred by the claws of a bear that he had killed in close fight, he was also a keen gardener and, in the best

---

[1] Since the alleged discovery that Tissaphernes' father was named Hydarnes (above, p. 342, n. 5), it has been customary also to link the appointment with a horror-story narrated by the romancer and court-physician Ktesias (*Epitome*, 53–56, from book xviii, and *ap.* Plutarch, *Artaxerxes* 1f.): a noble named Teritouchmes, son of Hydarnes, in love with his half-sister Roxana, a great archer and horsewoman, planned to murder Parysatis' daughter Amestris, the royal bride forced upon him on succeeding to his father's satrapy. The plot was betrayed, and Parysatis procured the destruction both of Teritouchmes and of all his brothers and sisters except one, Stateira, wife of the crown-prince Arsakes (later Artaxerxes II), who pleaded for her with his father; and Parysatis poisoned her too, years later. Modern writers (in English, Tarn in *CAH* vi, 3f., Olmstead, *Persian Empire*, 364) have assumed that Tissaphernes must have been a brother of Teritouchmes (mis-spelt Teriteuchmes by Olmstead's executors), spared for his diplomatic services (Olmstead) or because he was out of reach (Tarn). But no source on Tissaphernes mentions this sensational story of his relations with the court; nor does Ktesias mention Tissaphernes as a survivor of the massacre, though he has much to say of him. Moreover, Tissaphernes still had a brother at the time of Cyrus' rebellion (Xen. *Anabasis* ii. 5. 35)! The whole modern story seems to be a figment based on the assumption that two contemporary nobles called Hydarnes must be the same man, though the sources do not suggest it. It is better jettisoned. See also Lewis, *Sparta and Persia*, 84 and nn. 13, 14. Parysatis' later hatred of Tissaphernes, which is well attested, is sufficiently motivated by his having foiled the attempt of her favourite son, Cyrus, to seize the throne from his elder brother.

Zoroastrian manner, considered it no less honorable to sweat, before he dined, at planting fruit trees than at hunting or fencing. His young officers and friends were like him, capable not only of leading a charge but, in all their Persian finery, of heaving on the wheels of baggage-wagons stuck in a *wadi*. A strict keeper of his word, he also enjoyed using his opportunities to practise the code of "Thou shalt repay with interest both service and trespass". Lavish in largesse of all the good things that the empire provided for its princes, he was ruthless to subjects who tried by short cuts to get any of that social surplus back; for that, of course, was robbery. Xenophon, who as a young gentleman-mercenary adored Cyrus from the middle distance, remarks that along the roads in his provinces one was constantly seeing beggars who had been blinded or had their hands or feet cut off for crimes; and that, as a result, travel was safe, even for one carrying valuables. Cyrus also smote the Mysian and Pisidian hillmen, north and south of the Royal Road, who often resorted to raiding. For Athens, he was the hand of fate.

Lysander, the Spartan admiral for 407–406, was a man indifferent to riches but thirsty for power. He and Cyrus took to each other at once. Cyrus had brought 500 talents, or three million drachmas' worth of bullion, from the royal treasury, earmarked for subsidies for Sparta; at the current rate of half a drachma per day per man, enough for 150 ships' crews for over six months; and Cyrus promised to add to it from his own resources, "even if he had to coin his own gold and silver throne". Lysander persuaded him to make the daily rate two-thirds of a drachma; and within a year a trickle of desertions of non-Athenian oarsmen from the Athenians, who could hardly pay the old rate, even forced the Athenian admiral Konon to lay up some ships. With such backing, Lysander could afford to take no risks. Time was on his side.

In 407 he achieved only a partial victory off Ephesos; but that was enough to ruin Alkibiades, the one Athenian who was his match. Alkibiades had left his fleet at Samos, to confer with Thrasyboulos, his colleague in northern Ionia, and collect desperately needed money. He left in charge not another general, but the pilot of his flagship, a man of his own; probably for political reasons, for he had jealous enemies, who resented being outshone by him and put it about that his power was a menace to the democracy. This worthy disobeyed orders to avoid battle, and lost fifteen ships. Alkibiades on his return offered battle himself, but now Lysander refused it. He knew what he was doing.

Alkibiades' enemies got him suspended and recalled to face investigation for leaving an unfit person in charge; and rather than do so, Alkibiades retired to an informal barony which he had set up in the Gallipoli Peninsula.

At the end of his year, both Lysander and Cyrus deplored the Spartan law, which removed an admiral as soon as he had gained experience, and forbade reappointment. Lysander thoughtfully made things difficult for his successor, Kallikratidas, by turning in to Cyrus the balance of all money in hand, so that Kallikratidas had to go and ask for it; and Cyrus co-operated. Kallikratidas was informed that Cyrus could not see him, because he was drinking. Kallikratidas said "I will wait"; and the Persian chamberlains laughed at him. After waiting for two days, and realising that Cyrus was making a fool of him, he departed, cursing the conditions that forced Greeks to dance attendance on orientals, and swearing, if he got home alive, to do all he could to reconcile Sparta with Athens.

He did not get home alive. After collecting money and more ships from Rhodes, Chios and Miletos, after winning a great victory and shutting up Konon the Athenian in Mytilene, he was defeated and killed by a great relieving armada raised in a last and splendid effort by Athens.

In 405 Lysander was back, the law having been circumvented by making him Secretary (Adjutant-General and nominal second-in-command) to a puppet High Admiral. Cyrus welcomed him, and raised money for him, though now with some difficulty, the great special grant being exhausted; and when, soon afterwards, Cyrus was summoned to the bedside of his father, who had fallen sick on a campaign against the Cadusian mountaineers, south of the Caspian, he actually committed to Lysander control of the local revenues. With 170 galleys, Lysander sailed once more for the Dardanelles, drawing the Athenians after him with 180; and there, after refusing battle until the Athenian generals grew over-confident and let their men (after a morning demonstration in force) forage inland for food, he caught their whole fleet by surprise on the beaches of Aigospotamoi. Konon alone escaped with nine ships and, sending one home with the news of disaster, fled himself to Cyprus. There he took service with Euagoras, a scion of the old royal house of Salamis, who had recaptured that city from a Phoenician usurper and, without open rebellion against Persia, had traded in naval supplies for Athens during the last seven years.

While Athens went down in defeat and revolution (though the

democracy was soon restored), Cyrus was at the deathbed of his father. He had taken Tissaphernes with him; but Tissaphernes, after Arsakes had been enthroned as Artaxerxes II, warned the King to beware of his brother. Darius had already been similarly warned by the secretary Hieramenes, after Cyrus had put to death two of his own kinsmen for failing to salute him with royal honours. Cyrus' life may have been in danger; but Parysatis' influence saved her favourite son, and got him returned to his command. There Cyrus prepared in earnest for an attempt to seize the empire. He subsidised Greek captains in several quarters, to collect fighting men unemployed after the war; the most prominent was Klearchos, lately Sparta's commandant at Byzantion, a rough man with a rasping voice. He had disobeyed an order to come home and, on the pretext of protection against the Thracians, stayed on as an independent "boss". He was now an exile. Tissaphernes, still satrap of Ionia and Karia, where he had his "paradise", broke with Cyrus; but the Greeks preferred Cyrus, who soon won all the cities except Miletos. There Tissaphernes supported the faction in power; and Cyrus refused to buy surrender by dropping his friends, the exiles. He continued to remit the tribute, and no doubt represented Tissaphernes as a rebel, until Tissaphernes broke away with 500 horsemen and fled to the King.

Others tried to warn the King too. Alkibiades, in flight from the Spartans, found refuge with Pharnabazos; but when he set out for Susa he was murdered by night in a Phrygian village. Most people suspected agents of Pharnabazos, wishing to be first with the news himself, *or* prompted by Lysander, prompted by King Agis whom Alkibiades had cuckolded, or by Lysander's puppet government in Athens; but others said that he was killed by the brothers of a Phrygian girl whom he had seduced.[1] Every newsmonger had his own story. However, Artaxerxes was still quite unready when Cyrus set out on his famous March Up-Country in 401. With him were 14,000 Greeks under Klearchos and others, and large Asian contingents under the Persian Ariaios, a suave homosexual with high powers of survival.

For as long as he could, Cyrus used the "cover" story that he was marching against the Pisidians – partly in order not to alarm his Greeks when they were still near home and might desert; but he had already called upon Sparta to reciprocate his recent services. A Spartan and allied fleet sailed to Cilicia and thus outflanked the Taurus line; but the

---

[1] Ephoros in Diodorus xiv. 11 (the first story); *aliter* Plut., *Alk.* 38f.

PERSIA REGAINS GROUND

reigning Syennesis had already sent his family "on a visit" to Cyrus; Artaxerxes afterwards deposed his dynasty, for failing to resist. Cyrus duly had trouble with his Greeks when the truth had to be told to them; but by offers of increased pay he got them to proceed. The decisive battle was fought at Kunaxa on the Euphrates, only sixty miles from Babylon. People had begun to ask whether the King would flee without fighting at all. "Not if he is my father's son," said Cyrus.

The Greeks were on Cyrus' right, near the river. The King's much larger army far overlapped Ariaios on the other wing. High in its centre rose the imperial standard, a spread eagle of gold. Cyrus intended to win by a direct charge at Artaxerxes himself, with 600 armoured cavalry, and ordered Klearchos to incline left in support; but Klearchos, stereotyped in his Spartan drill, gave a vague answer and refused to draw his right, unshielded flank away from the river. The result was that Cyrus, though he broke into the ranks of the Guard and wounded his brother, was overwhelmed by numbers and killed; and the Greeks, though the Asian infantry opposite them fled without even meeting their charge, had lost their cause. Klearchos had not even saved his right flank; for Tissaphernes with a cavalry brigade simultaneously rode, almost bloodlessly, through the light-armed Greeks who were supposed to be covering it. Fortunately for the Greeks, the horsemen were out of control and swept on to plunder their baggage instead of turning to take them in rear. However, Tissaphernes' spectacular if not very damaging success brought him great prestige, the hand of a royal princess, and the succession to Cyrus' command in Asia Minor.[1]

The sequel showed how little most Greeks and Persians even now understood each other's societies. The Greeks, having turned and charged back again through another Asian corps, which fled before they got near them, felt that all they needed was a candidate for the throne. Finding that Cyrus was dead, they offered it to Ariaios; but he laughed at them, saying that he was not of nearly high enough nobility to be tolerated. However, having reassembled the bulk of Cyrus' army, he then successfully negotiated his surrender (did he claim to have betrayed Cyrus?), and reappears later, satrap of inland Phrygia. The Greeks rejected a demand for the surrender of their arms; but they offered to join the King in a body, and to serve, for instance, against Egypt, which

---

[1] Against some scholars, I continue to follow the account of Xenophon (*Anabasis* I. viii); that of Diodorus (xiv. 22ff.), based on Ephoros (*ib.* 22. 2), whom Polybios, a soldier, found very bad as a military historian (Pol. xii. 25 F 1), reads like a romance.

had lately revolted. Finally Tissaphernes, now the King's right-hand man, half-promised to escort them to Asia Minor, and did in fact escort them for some weeks up the Tigris, where food was plentiful. But suspicions developed, and he thought they would be at his mercy, to employ or massacre, without their leaders. He therefore invited them to a conference, attended by Klearchos, four other generals and twenty colonels, and arrested and executed them. He then expected the common soldiers to collapse; but they, after a night of dismay, next morning held an assembly (called by Xenophon, the educated Athenian volunteer, as he tells us), elected new generals, headed by a Spartan, Cheirisophos, and marched north for the hills, where they could shake off cavalry harassment.

Thus began the famous March of the "Ten Thousand" (13,000 at the start). Tissaphernes left them when they reached the mountains of Kurdestan. The Kurds would look after them there. The last royal army to invade Kurdestan had been totally destroyed. But while he returned to the west, to take over Cyrus' command and with it the Greek Question, the Ten Thousand fought their way through, though the Kurds "did them more damage than all they had suffered in their engagements with the King and Tissaphernes".[1] After that they had to fight successively the troops of Orontes, the new Satrap of Armenia (son of Artasuras the Bactrian, the King's Eye or intelligence chief, and the King's son-in-law) and his western neighbour Tiribazos. They brushed them off with less trouble. They got lost in the mountains, went further than they need have, were overtaken by winter, suffered from frostbite and snow-blindness and lost many men from exhaustion and exposure; and then they met other warlike tribes, including the iron-working Chalybes. Yet two-thirds of them emerged, still formidable, as well as many women, children and sick, on the Black Sea in spring of the year 400. They served for a while under Seuthes, a king in Thrace, whom they found an unsatisfactory paymaster, and in 399 the last 6000 (many having gone home) found employment with Thibron of Sparta, who had been sent with a small force to aid the Greeks of Asia.

On the state of the empire, what emerges from Xenophon's fine story, along with many anthropological details that supplement Herodotus, is the fact that all the hill tribes, many of which appear in Herodotus' list of contingents marching under Xerxes, were now out of control.

[1] Xen., *Anab.* IV. iii. 2.

Orontes and Tiribazos presumably ruled and policed with their cavalry the richer, valley lands, keeping the hillmen at bay with *ad hoc* punitive expeditions, as did even Cyrus (cf. p. 351) and Pharnabazos further west. This, and still more the weakness of the empire's hordes of conscript infantry, was not lost upon the Greeks. Throughout the fourth century, men such as the publicist Isokrates of Athens, and speakers cited by Xenophon, pointed out that, would the Greeks but unite, the empire would be an easy prey. The cure for social unrest, the land that everyone wanted, was there for the taking. (Aristagoras had said as much, when appealing to Sparta in 499.) But Greeks would not unite. Old feuds, immediate jealousies, Greek *philotimon* (the sensitive pride that Homer studied in the *Iliad*) were still too strong; and Persia's gold and diplomacy continued to keep them divided for two generations.

4. *Sparta and the Satraps, 399–394*

Thibron's mission was in answer to an appeal from the Ionians, terrified of Tissaphernes, especially after having sided with Cyrus against him. But Pharnabazos was encroaching on Greek cities too; and when Thibron was superseded for bad discipline, letting his men plunder Greeks, his successor Derkylidas turned north. Tissaphernes was delighted to grant an armistice; and Derkylidas, who knew about the jealousy between the satraps, also had a personal grudge against Pharnabazos. During the war, when he was commandant at Abydos, Pharnabazos had reported him to Lysander, probably for rudeness; and Lysander had sentenced him to "pack-drill", standing for several hours with his shield; a bitter disgrace for a Spartiate.

It is needless to go into full details of the inconclusive campaigns waged by Spartan generals in Asia; but some of these details, especially those reported by Xenophon, an eye-witness with more of Herodotus than of Thucydides about him, shed a light upon local conditions and individual characters, rare in Achaemenian history. We hear, for example, of the families of Greek renegades, still holding the fiefs granted by Xerxes. Themistokles' family had returned to Athens; but descendants of Dāmarātos of Sparta were still governors of Teuthrania and Halisarna in the north-west of Tissaphernes' satrapy. The incumbents whom Xenophon knew, two brothers, were named Eurysthenes and Prokles, after the legendary twin founders of Sparta; Prokles served under Ariaios in Cyrus' expedition. Next to them, the family of Gongylos of Eretria, a henchman and go-between of Pausanias, held Gambrion and Old Gambrion, inland near Pergamon, and Gryneia and Myrina on the coast; the latter pair had for a time paid tribute to Athens.

North of them, in Pharnabazos' part of Aiolis, we hear of, actually, a woman satrap. (The title of satrap was borne by district as well as provincial governors.) Xenophon tells us:

> The satrap here had been Zēnis of Dardanos [a Greek city on the Dardanelles]. When he fell sick and died, Pharnabazos was preparing to give the satrapy to someone else; but Zenis' widow Mania, also from Dardanos, assembled a caravan and set out with presents, not only for Pharnabazos himself but for the women of his harem and his most influential servants.

She persuaded him to give her a trial;

> and having got the district, she paid up her tribute just as punctually as her husband. Also, when she visited Pharnabazos she always brought him presents, and when he visited her district she gave him the best and most elegant entertainment of all his governors. She kept safe for him the cities she had taken over, and captured some on the coast which he had not held before, attacking their fortifications with Greek mercenaries, while she looked on from a carriage; and any man whom she approved, she rewarded richly, so that she made that force a very fine one. She also used to go with Pharnabazos on his campaigns, when he attacked the Mysians or Pisidians for raiding the King's land, so that Pharnabazos in return esteemed her highly, and asked her advice on some occasions.[1]

When Derkylidas arrived, this remarkable woman had just been murdered by her son-in-law, Meidias, who in turn sent gifts to Pharnabazos and asked to keep the governorship. "But Pharnabazos told him to keep them until he came and took them, and him; for he said he would rather die than fail to avenge Mania. However, at that point Derkylidas appeared."[2] He received the surrender of nine cities in eight days, (for the people and soldiers had no love for Meidias) and turned Meidias loose to live as a private citizen if he could. We are not told what happened to him. Derkylidas then asked Pharnabazos whether he wanted peace or war. Pharnabazos, seeing him strongly established, with all Greek Aiolis behind him, agreed to an armistice for eight months; and Derkylidas wintered in Bithynia, at the expense of its Thracian inhabitants. "Pharnabazos had no objection to that either; he had often had to fight the Bithynians."[3]

Pharnabazos was not being merely feckless. The fact was that the

---

[1] Xen., *Hell.* III. i. 10–13. [2] Xen., *Hell.* III. i 15f.
[3] Xen., *Hell.* III ii. 2.

imperial government had seen quite clearly that the key to reconquering Ionia was command of the sea. Work was on foot to build up the navy again to 300 galleys; and Pharnabazos, stealing a march on Tissaphernes, is said at this time to have commended to the King the Athenian admiral, Konon, whom he will have known since the time of his armistice with the Athenians in 408, and who was still in Cyprus, with Euagoras. The King made a grant of 500 talents, to build a hundred galleys in the Cypriote ports.[1] But this would take time. Meanwhile Sparta too was growing restive. The satraps might make armistice after armistice, but the threat to Ionian independence was still there. To put pressure upon Tissaphernes, Sparta urged Derkylidas, back at Ephesos in 397, to invade Karia and threaten his "paradise".

Reinforcing his Peloponnesians and "Cyrus' brigade" (as it was still called) with Ionians and islanders, Derkylidas marched; but meanwhile Pharnabazos, as in duty bound, had joined his superior. Together they withdrew into Karia, garrisoned the fortified places, and then, slipping past Derkylidas' slow-moving footmen, returned to threaten Ionia, drawing him after them. Near the Maeander, Derkylidas suddenly found his way barred by a formidable army: "Karians with their white shields, all the Persians who were in the area, the two satraps' own Greek troops [!] and a powerful cavalry, Tissaphernes' horse on the right and Pharnabazos' on the left." Derkylidas got his force into line, with his own cavalry on the flanks, "such as it was" (comments the veteran Xenophon) "and offered sacrifice.... Some of his Ionians began to sneak off, leaving their arms in the corn, which was standing high in the plain; and even those who stood their ground so far were obviously not going to. Pharnabazos, it was reported, was for giving battle; but Tissaphernes remembered Cyrus' brigade and how he had fought them before; and supposing that all Greeks were like that...he offered a parley."[2]

The result, next day, was an actual peace conference; but it was at once deadlocked. "Derkylidas' terms were that the King recognise the independence of the Ionian cities; those of Tissaphernes and Pharnabazos, the withdrawal of Greek forces from the country, and of Spartan governors from the cities; and with that, they concluded an armistice",[3] until both sides could consult their governments.

[1] Diod. xiv. 39.
[2] Xen., *Hell*. iii. ii. 15–18. Scholars inclined to prefer Diodorus on these campaigns to Xenophon should read him on this affair (xiv. 39. 4ff.).
[3] Xen., *Hell*. iii. ii. 19f.

News of the naval build-up in Phoenicia reached Sparta about the same time, brought by a Syracusan merchant who had just been there, and caused a "flap";[1] but Lysander, still very influential, took a low view of Phoenician fighting capacity. Prompted by him, King Agēsilaos offered, before a congress of the Peloponnesian League, to counter by increasing the pressure in Asia, for which he asked only modest forces: a staff of thirty Spartans, 2,000 liberated helot armoured men and 6,000 Peloponnesians; only about twice the force originally sent under Thibron.

Agēsilaos had lately succeeded his brother Agis, through the influence of Lysander, who suggested that the late king's putative heir was really a son of Alkibiades. He was over fifty, and lame since infancy; but his handicap made him only the more eager to distinguish himself in war, as indeed he did. Lysander was sent as his chief of staff; but in Ionia, Agesilaos made it so publicly clear, who was master, that Lysander found his position humiliating and asked for a command elsewhere. Agesilaos sent him to the Marmara.

Meanwhile Tissaphernes sent to ask what he wanted in Asia. He replied: the complete independence of the Greek cities. Tissaphernes offered to renew the armistice till he could again submit this to the King, suggesting that the demand might be granted; but this was shortly seen to be a mere device to gain time. He wrote for troops; and indeed, reinforcements arrived so soon (in a matter of weeks) that he had probably asked for them already.

In the north, Lysander had had a windfall. Spithridates, a Persian baron in Pharnabazos' country, found that the satrap wanted his daughter – but not in regular marriage, since Pharnabazos was hoping to marry a daughter of the King. Affronted, Spithridates defected, with his family and his feudal retinue of two hundred horse. Lysander harboured them in the Kyzikos peninsula, and sent Spithridates to Agesilaos, who interrogated him about Phrygia. But he was interrupted by an ultimatum from Tissaphernes, who had now got his reinforcements: Leave Asia, or fight.

Tissaphernes expected another attack on his Karian home, especially as it would suit the Greeks, not being cavalry country; and Agesilaos made overt preparations in that direction. Tissaphernes garrisoned his forts, and prepared to attack the Greeks with his cavalry in the plains on the way. But Agesilaos then marched north, unopposed and

---

[1] 'Flap' is literal translation; Xen., *Hell.* III. iv. 2.

sweeping up plunder, almost to Daskyleion. Only there did he run into Pharnabazos' cavalry, and there was a minor skirmish, which Xenophon describes for its tactical interest. The two cavalry forces, about equal in strength, met over a ridge, face to face, with not 150 yards between them; and both halted. "The Greeks were in line, like infantry, four deep; the Persians in column, not more than twelve abreast, but in great depth. Then the Persians charged; and all the Greeks who hit their man broke their spears; but the Persians, who had javelins of cornel wood, quickly killed twelve men and two horses; and the Greek horse gave way."[1] On the advance of the Greek infantry, the Persians in turn retired; but they lost only one man killed, and Agesilaos realised that without better cavalry he could not give battle on level ground. During the winter he provided it, by requiring cavalry service of the wealthiest Ionians, according to old Greek custom, but accepting paid substitutes if well horsed and armed; this soon produced a good semi-professional force.

Next spring (395) he announced that he was now going to strike into the heart of Lydia. Tissaphernes, duly informed by his spies, naturally scented deception again, and was sure that now he would really attack Karia; but this time it was "double bluff"; Agesilaos did exactly what he had said, and marched for Sardis. It was three days before the Persian cavalry overtook him, and killed a number of camp-followers who were out plundering. On the fourth day he sent his baggage-train ahead, to camp beyond the Paktōlos, the river of Sardis, while the troops followed. The Persian cavalry hung on their rear and began to ride round them. But Agesilaos had left the commander of his mobile forces behind, in ambush. When the Persians, whose infantry was still far behind, had passed the place, Agesilaos turned, formed line and attacked. Caught between the two forces, about 600 of the Persian horse were killed or driven into the river. Far more got away; but it was a very complete rout, and was followed by the capture of their camp, camel train (a marvel, when displayed in Greece) and much spoil, including Tissaphernes' lordly camp equipment.

During the battle, Tissaphernes was in Sardis. He must have ridden hard to get there before the Greeks; and the city was not taken. He was, of course, accused of abandoning his men; but what happened next happened so quickly that it must have been planned already. Tissaphernes' recent record was indeed far from impressive. He had

[1] Xen., *Hell.* III. iv. 13f.

been out-generalled, had fought no battle, and had forwarded Greek demands that might be considered insulting. His enemies at court, including the implacable Parysatis, had their chance. It was decided that his head must fall; and Tithraustes the Guard Commander, the second man in the empire, was sent to get it.

To arrest him among his own troops (clearly still loyal) was reckoned no light matter; and Tithraustes went about his business with cold circumspection. He brought two letters under the royal seal: one to Tissaphernes, appointing him supreme commander (by land and sea?); the other to Ariaios, in inland Phrygia, bidding him arrest Tissaphernes. Ariaios invited him to Kolossai "for important consultations" (presumably with Tithraustes); and confident in his new appointment, and escorted by his own horsemen, he left his satrapy. Even then, Ariaios waited till he got him alone and unarmed. When he unslung his sword and undressed to bathe (while his men were probably at dinner), Ariaios' men walked in on him; and gagged, bound and in a covered cart, "sewn up", the old deceiver made his last journey to Sardis.[1] Such were Achaemenian methods for "liquidating" a grandee.

Tithraustes at Sardis then sent to Agesilaos, offering, on the King's authority, precise terms: the cities would be left autonomous if they paid their old tribute, and if Agesilaos left Asia. Would he not do so, now that Tithraustes himself had killed the Greeks' great enemy? Agesilaos in his turn replied that he must consult his government. Meanwhile, he continued to live on the country. Tithraustes, anxious to get him away from Sardis, asked cynically, could he not at least make war somewhere else? (This, in effect, meant in Pharnabazos' country.) Agesilaos demanded a subsidy if he was to withdraw without further devastation; and Tithraustes got rid of him at the cost of thirty talents out of Tissaphernes' property.

The next problem was that of the fleet. Already in 396 Konon had won his first major success, when Rhodes came over to him; but his sailors (Greek, especially Cypriote, not Phoenician) were now in a state of near mutiny over arrears of pay. These cost 220 talents, found from the same source; and Tithraustes sent a Rhodian named Timokrates to Greece with another fifty, to grease the palms of some of Sparta's numerous enemies. The balance, out of an alleged thousand talents

[1] Diod. xiv. 80; Polyain. *Stratagems* vii. 16; accused of "betraying his troops", Xen. *Hell.* iii. iv. 25. The papyrus *Hellenica Oxyrhynchia*, though fragmentary at this point, shows that a detailed near-contemporary account existed. That T. was really sacrificed to a change of policy (H. Schaefer in Pauly, Suppl. vii, *s.v.*, relying on Nepos, *Conon* 3. 4) seems not to be sufficiently supported.

found in the late satrap's treasury (the round figure suggests a mere guess) was left as a war-fund in the hands of Ariaios, promoted temporarily to Sardis, and one Pasiphernes, when Tithraustes returned to court.

Persian hopes of a naval offensive were still hanging fire; but now Konon (in winter, 395–394?), by way of Phoenicia and the Euphrates, visited the King. He obtained a personal audience, and secured both more money and the confirmation of his position as admiral, with Pharnabazos, the man of his choice, as his nominal superior. More decisive action was now possible.

The Spartan government had realised that the danger at sea was growing; for Agesilaos on his way north received, at Kyme, a commission to take over the command at sea too, and appoint his own admiral. He exhorted the islanders and maritime states to set about building more ships, and 120 are said actually to have been built,[1] though nothing like this number ever went into action. He appointed as admiral his wife's brother Peisandros, a brave man but lacking in naval experience.

His autumn campaign in Phrygia was therefore without a morrow, though he won superficially brilliant successes; and Xenophon's account of it includes the last and some of the best of his first-hand pictures of the Persians in action. He harried the lands of Pharnabazos, who was still in his satrapy, and on the advice of Spithridates (p. 358) he got in touch with the king of Paphlagonia, east along the coast, who joined him with 1,000 cavalry and 2,000 light infantry; just what he most needed. Agesilaos cherished hopes of breaking up the empire by detaching its subjects; and he arranged the marriage of Spithridates' beautiful daughter to the young King. Returning westward, he ravaged Pharnabazos' park at Daskyleion, of which Xenophon has given such an enthusiastic description. There he wintered, while the satrap was reduced to waging guerilla war; but in this he could still hit back. Scythe-armed chariots (their drivers presumably protected by some form of cab) were an arm which had totally failed to break up the Greek formation at Kunaxa; as later under Alexander, the Greeks opened ranks and let them through; but Pharnabazos showed that they could be useful, at least with the help of surprise. "While the troops, made bold and careless by impunity, were scattered foraging over the plain, Pharnabazos appeared with two scythed chariots and some four

[1] Xen., *Hell.* III. iv. 28.

hundred horse. The Greeks ran together, some 700 of them; but he, without hesitation, with the chariots leading and himself following with his cavalry, gave the order to charge. The chariots broke the dense Greek formation, and the cavalry quickly cut down about a hundred of them; the rest escaped to Agesilaos, who was near by with his armoured men."[1]

Soon after this, Spithridates discovered where the satrap was lurking in a large village; and Hērippidas, the Spartan chief of staff, captured it in a night raid, driving Pharnabazos in flight and capturing his baggage with many of his valuables. But the sequel was disastrous. Hērippidas next day surrounded his allies, who had got most of the plunder, with Greek troops, and took it off them on the pretext of disposing of it officially; whereat the Paphlagonians and Spithridates on the next night deserted in a body. Spithridates rode off to take service with Ariaios at Sardis, feeling that he, "having himself been in armed rebellion against the King" would understand their position.[2] This, says Xenophon, was the most serious blow suffered by Agesilaos during the whole campaign.

A Greek of Kyzikos, who had long known the satrap, soon afterwards approached Agesilaos with a suggestion that the two might meet; and a place and time were arranged. Agesilaos and his thirty Spartans arrived first, and

lay down on the grass to wait. Then Pharnabazos arrived, magnificently dressed. His servants began putting down rugs for him, such as the Persians sit on for comfort; but when he saw Agesilaos' simple arrangements, he disdained such luxury and sat down on the ground too, just as he was. They exchanged salutations, and clasped hands; and then Pharnabazos, the older man, spoke first:

"Agesilaos and you Spartans present! I was your friend and ally during your war with Athens. I provided money to make your navy strong; and on land I fought beside you, riding my horse into the sea in pursuit of your enemies. I never let you down, like Tissaphernes, and you have never had a deed or word of mine to complain of. And now, in return for these services, I have been reduced by you to such a plight that I cannot get a dinner in my own country except by picking up your leavings, like the wild animals. And all the beautiful houses and parks, full of trees and game, that my father left me and in which I delighted, I now see cut down and burned. Now, if I do not understand what is right in the eyes of gods and men, will you please explain to me what sort of conduct this is, from men who have any sense of gratitude?"

[1] Xen., *Hell.* IV. i. 17ff.   [2] Xen., *Hell.* IV. i. 27.

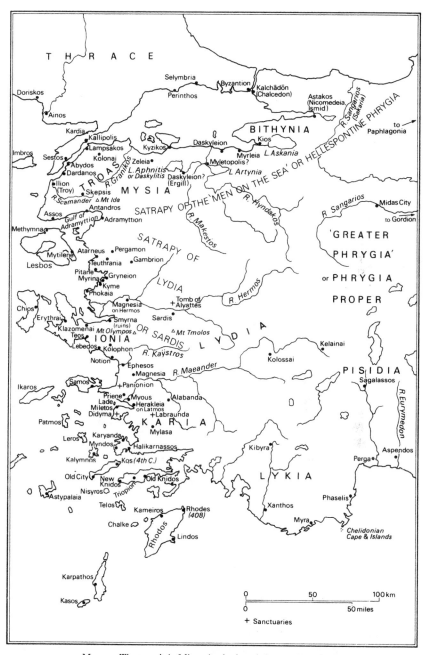

Map 14. Western Asia Minor in the late Achaemenian period.

Pharnabazos diplomatically omits the *casus belli*. However:

All the Thirty felt thoroughly ashamed, and had nothing to say, until after a long pause Agesilaos spoke. He said that even among Greeks, men who were personal friends might have to injure each other if their states were at war; and he then proceeded directly to invite Pharnabazos to change sides, "liberate" himself from the King, and join in "making his former fellow-slaves into his own subjects".

(Still we notice that Greek obsession with the semantic fallacy that even satraps were slaves.)

"Shall I tell you frankly what I shall do?" said Pharnabazos.

"That would be decent."

"Well, if the King sends another general and puts me under him, I will gladly become your friend and ally; but if he gives the command to me...such, it seems, is the love of honour...you can take it from me that I will fight you with all my strength."

When he heard that, Agesilaos grasped his hand and said "You splendid man, I wish you may become our friend! But as things are...in future, even if there is war between us, we will keep off you and your land as long as we can manage to operate elsewhere."

With that, Pharnabazos mounted and rode away; but his son by Parapita, still in the bloom of youth, lingered behind, and suddenly ran up and said "Agesilaos, I make you my friend!" "I accept that," said he. "Remember, then," said the boy; and with that he gave Agesilaos his throwing-spear, a very fine one. Agesilaos accepted it, and took some fine horse-brasses that were round the neck of his secretary's horse, and gave them in return. The boy vaulted into his saddle and rode after his father; and when later, after Pharnabazos had left his satrapy, his brother deprived Parapita's son of his inheritance and drove him into exile, Agesilaos looked after him...[1]

Agesilaos then withdrew to the south of the Troad, and in spring, 394, "was preparing to march as far up-country as he could go, reckoning that every nation he could put behind him would be lost to the King".[2] But that was not to be. Meanwhile, Persia's gold had ignited all the smouldering discontents against Spartan arrogance in Greece. Thebes, Athens, Argos and Corinth were in arms together; Lysander had been killed in a mismanaged invasion of Boiotia; and Sparta sent for the expeditionary force to come home.

Leaving some garrisons in Asia, Agesilaos set out by Xerxes' route, complaining that he had been driven from Asia by "ten thousand golden archers", meaning those on the reverse of Timokrates' darics. In summer he was about to fight his way through Boiotia when he heard, and concealed from his troops, even more disastrous news. Pharnabazos

[1] Xen., *Hell.* IV. i. 29–40. [2] Xen., *Hell.* IV. i. 41.

and Konon were at sea in the Aegean, and Peisandros, giving battle off Knidos with inferior numbers, had been defeated and killed.

5. Sea-power, and the King's Peace

Sparta won bloody victories in Greece that summer; but no city fell away from the allies. In Asia, 100 years after the battle of Lade and 85 after Mykale, once more a victorious imperial fleet ranged the coast. Pharnabazos and Konon proclaimed liberation from Spartan military governors, and left the cities to their own devices. Persia's tribute could be exacted later. Only Miletos, still held by Sparta's friends, resisted pressure. As in 479, the only serious resistance was at the narrows of the Dardanelles, where the veteran Derkylidas held Abydos and Sestos against blockade. In spring 393, the allies left him there and sailed through the Cyclades, meeting no opposition. They raided the coast of Lakonia itself, and occupied Kythera (Sparta's old Achilles heel, cf. p. 326), letting the people depart to the mainland, and leaving a garrison under an Athenian governor. Pharnabazos then sailed to Corinth, where he addressed a session of the allied war council, presented them with a welcome sum of money and urged them to prosecute the war vigorously and show themselves loyal to the King(!). No other Persian ever achieved such a position in Greek affairs.

Pharnabazos then returned home; but he left most of his fleet with Konon, who promised that he could support it from Greek sources without more money from Asia, and proposed to employ it in restoring Athens' Long Walls down to the sea, breached by Sparta in 404. With help from the allies (Thebes, for instance, sent 500 masons) this was soon done, and there was wild enthusiasm; Konon was honoured with a statue, as no Athenian ever had been while living, and exemption from taxes; and soon Athens was rebuilding a navy, re-establishing her old citizen colonies on Lemnos and Skyros, making alliances and supporting democracies from Byzantion to Rhodes. Konon held advanced ideas on sea-power, and tried, through emissaries, to foster an alliance between the two island kings, his friend Euagoras in Cyprus and Dionysios of Syracuse, who had risen to power by exploiting the crisis of a war with Persia's old ally, Carthage. Nothing came of this, however; and in Persia, Konon's sensational revival of Athenian power was less favourably viewed.

Artaxerxes was not content to leave Sardis in the hands of the ambiguous Ariaios. He appointed a new high commander, Tiribazos (probably the satrap whom the Ten Thousand had encountered in western Armenia). He was at once approached (392) by a Spartan ambassador, Antalkidas, offering peace on the old terms, that the cities in Asia should belong to the King and the islands be independent. (This would block the reconstitution of an Athenian league.) Tiribazos was inclined to listen, and when a counter-embassy arrived, headed by Konon, Tiribazos put him under arrest for abuse of his command; but he could not change alliances on his own initiative, and went up country to consult the King. He did, however, give Antalkidas a subsidy, to assist the reconstruction of a Spartan navy as a counterpoise to the Athenian; thus reverting once more to the balance-of-power policy. It was the end of Konon's career; he escaped once more to Euagoras and died in Cyprus.

New names now appear in all the western commands; at Sardis Autophradates – a name that reappears in the next generation, suggesting the establishment of a new satrapal 'dynasty'. From the Hellespont Pharnabazos, whose policy was being set aside but whose distinguished services cried out for recognition, was recalled to Susa, to marry, like Orontes and Tissaphernes, a daughter of the King. He was not returned to his satrapy, but does reappear, years later, in high command elsewhere (p. 371). His successor was named Ariobarzanes, a name which also recurs fifty years later, among Pharnabazos' descendants; and he was "an old friend"[1] of Antalkidas. This makes it reasonable to suppose that he was identical with the officer who conducted the Athenian ambassadors to Kios in 405 (p. 348–9), and the father of a Mithradates, called "of Kios", who later betrayed him. He could have known Antalkidas in those days; and he is "the brother", i.e. probably of Pharnabazos himself, who drove Pharnabazos' son by his first wife into exile when Pharnabazos was away at court.[2]

In Karia, Tissaphernes had been succeeded by a native prince-satrap, Hekatomnos of Mylasa, who also founded a dynasty that lasted until Alexander's time; but to Ionia, while Tiribazos was at court, Artaxerxes sent a soldier, Strouthas. Once more, the central government was a whole stage behind the man on (or rather from) the spot; Strouthas was vehemently anti-Spartan, remembering Agesilaos' devastations, and

---

[1] Xen., *Hell.* v. i. 28.
[2] Beloch, *Griech. Gesch.* III². xii. p. 146. (All this gives Ariobarzanes a public career of about fifty years; but this is quite possible in this notably vigorous and long-lived family.)

pro-Athenian. Sparta, with the war in Greece still dragging on, was constrained to reinforce the cities in Ionia that still held by her. Thibron, a convivial character, was sent out again; but Strouthas, after watching him carefully and noting his carelessness, drew him and his men out one afternoon, roused from their siestas, in disorderly pursuit of a raiding party, and then "appeared himself with a numerous cavalry, in ordered formations",[1] and routed them with great slaughter. Thibron was killed. His more self-disciplined successor Diphridas was left with no adequate field-army; but by luck and cunning he captured Strouthas' daughter and her husband Tigranes while making a journey, and was able to extort a huge ransom, which he used for paying his troops. Here, then, the war languished.

It was, as Xenophon remarks,[2] a time of extraordinary cross-purposes on both sides; for simultaneously, Athens was supporting her old ally Euagoras in rebellion against Persia. In 390 she sent ten ships to his aid; but a Spartan squadron, which was trying to recover Rhodes, intercepted and captured them.

Euagoras, since he seized power in Salamis about 411, had been recognised by the empire, and on occasion had proved very useful. But he was now extending his power over other cities, and non-Greek Amathous and Kition complained to Sousa. Artaxerxes ordered Autophradates and Hekatomnos to suppress him; but Hekatomnos' heart, at least, was not in the enterprise. He could see that, while Cyprus was independent, so, at least relatively, was he; and a little later he is reported even to have been secretly financing the Cypriote. Athens in 388 also sent further aid: 800 specialist light infantry under her young, rising general, Chabrias. Not surprisingly, this Persian attack made no progress.

Behind Euagoras stood the power of rebel Egypt. This needs to be stressed, since our Greek sources, while they have much to say of Egypto-Persian wars, mention them as a rule only incidentally to Greek participation. If we had Persian documents we should no doubt find that for the King the recovery of the Nile valley stood highest on his agenda, with the Greeks, for all their high nuisance-value, important chiefly as obstacles to achieving this, or as tools to be used. For Egypt, rich but militarily weak, the assistance of Greek arms was essential. Thus

---

[1] Xen., *Hell.* IV. viii. 19. For 'Strouses' (probably = Strouthas) as satrap of Ionia, cf. Tod, *Gk. Hist. Inscrs.*, no. 113, confirming an Ionian arbitration of a boundary-dispute.
[2] Xen., *Hell.* IV. viii. 24.

Hakoris (in Greek Achoris or Akoris; c. 394–381), the most important Pharaoh of Dynasty XXIX, anticipating the Ptolemies and following the example of Amasis, made Cyprus the outwork of his defences and also sought for allies among the Pisidians. For Artaxerxes the reduction of Cyprus was desirable not only in itself but with a view to the greater objective; and first, Cyprus must be isolated.

Meanwhile Sparta had grown confirmed in her willingness to sacrifice the Asian Greeks for the sake of a free hand at home, and already in 389 had sent out Antalkidas, with his Persian contacts, as high admiral, "in order to please Tiribazos".[1] Handing over his fleet to other officers at Ephesos, he followed Tiribazos to Sousa; and in spring, 388, they reappeared at Sardis together. Athens, which had rejected the terms of autonomy for all islands four years before, was to be offered a concession: her old citizen colonies were to be excepted, by name. Combining a threat with this offer, Antalkidas proceeded to Abydos, where Sparta still had warships, captured a small Athenian squadron and, reinforced by twenty ships from the west sent by Dionysios and more from the Greek cities controlled by Persia, closed Athens' grain-route through the Bosporus with a fleet over eighty strong.

That was decisive. All the belligerents were under great strain; and in 387 all sent plenipotentiaries to Sardis to hear the King's terms. Tiribazos exhibited the royal seal, and his secretary read:

> King Artaxerxes deems it right that the cities in Asia be his, and of the islands, Klazomenai [an Ionian city based on an inshore islet] and Cyprus. The other Greek cities, both small and great, shall be independent, except that Lemnos, Imbros and Skyros shall, as of old, belong to Athens. And whichever side does not accept this peace, against them I will make war together with those who accept it, by land and by sea, both with ships and with money.[2]

This was the famous King's Peace, or Peace of Antalkidas. Demobilisation and withdrawal of foreign garrisons were complete by 386, and Sparta happily accepted the rôle of breaker-up of rival power-blocks in the name of "independence". But Persia was the real winner.

IV. REBELS AND MERCENARIES (386–334 B.C.)

1. *Reconquest of Cyprus; Failure in Egypt*

Thereafter, the King's Peace and his influence were repeatedly invoked in Greek inter-state politics. The chief factor limiting Persian inter-

[1] Xen., *Hell.* v. i. 6. [2] Xen., *Hell.* v. i. 31.

vention was the empire's preoccupation with rebellions elsewhere; especially with Egypt, which at the fifth attempt, after sixty years of independence (Dynasties XXVIII to XXX) and never having lost sight of the objective, the empire at last reoccupied in 343. It was an age of continual employment of Greek troops under the most famous captains of the time, in Persian or Egyptian pay.

Immediately after the Greek peace, all the commanders in the west of the empire received marching orders: Autophradates and Ariobarzanes to deal with those peoples of Asia Minor, whose normal unruliness had been encouraged by Agesilaos; Tiribazos, commanding by sea, and Orontes of Armenia, by land, to attack Cyprus; the highest dignitaries of all, Tithraustes and Pharnabazos, with Abrokomas of Syria, to mount the invasion of Egypt, from which Abrokomas had been called off in 401 by Cyrus' rebellion. Egypt was attacked, c. 385–383, but with total lack of success. Chabrias, ordered away from Cyprus by Athens under the terms of the peace, on his own initiative accepted an invitation to Egypt, where he trained Egyptian trireme-crews on rowing-machines on land, and where place-names – "Chabrias' Village" in the Delta, perhaps where this activity took place, and a Palisade of Chabrias, thrown out towards the Serbonian Bog on the Sinai coast – long commemorated his presence. The campaigns ended with Achoris in control of at least part of Palestine, while his ally Euagoras held several posts on the mainland, even including Tyre.

But presently (exact dates are not available) Tiribazos' and Orontes' expedition, largely Greek, and sailing from Kyme and Phokaia, the ports nearest Sardis, came down from the west. It secured the Cilician coast and, as of old, ran troops across to Cyprus. In naval command under Tiribazos was Glous or Glōs, son of Tamōs, an Egyptian, who had served under Tissaphernes in Ionia, then commanded Cyrus' fleet, and finally fled to Egypt and been murdered for the sake of the money which he brought with him. Kition was taken and its Phoenician prince restored. Euagoras with the help of "pirates" (Pisidians?) attacked the expedition's food-convoys, provoking a nearly-fatal mutiny; but Glōs then organized a successful convoy-system. Euagoras was constrained to risk a fleet action with (it is said) 200 ships, including 50 from Egypt, against 300; his surprise attack, off Kition, won some success, but Glōs kept his head and finally numbers told. Salamis was now under siege; but Euagoras was still able to run the blockade with ten ships to seek aid from Egypt (nothing came of it), and to return. Realising that he must negotiate, he asked to keep only his ancestral kingdom of Salamis, paying tribute "not as a slave, but as one king to another".

Tiribazos was for granting these terms, and forwarded them to the King; but Orontes, jealous of him, accused him of betrayal, and Tiribazos was arrested. Glōs, fearing the fate of Konon, then fled to Egypt. Orontes however, left alone in command, found that he could do no better, and finally had to agree to the same terms; terms, on which Euagoras reigned as vassal-king of Salamis until he was murdered in 374, and his son Nikokles succeeded him.

The sequel to this, at court, was a great state trial; the Royal Judges were ordered to inquire into the mutual complaints of Orontes and Tiribazos. Tiribazos was rehabilitated, and Orontes disgraced; some Greek reported a rueful remark of his, comparing the swiftly varied positions and powers of the King's Friends (an official rank) to those of digits in arithmetic.[1] He *may* have been relegated to a minor governorship in Asia Minor, since he is later described as "satrap of Mysia"; not a regular satrapy, but a tract of hill-country, recently out of control. There for twenty years he nursed his resentment. History had not heard the last of him.

Tiribazos remained high in honour. Like some other senior ex-satraps, he was retained at court, while his deputy, Autophradates, took over Lydia permanently. The last great service of Tiribazos was his extricating the King from a very nasty situation in an attack on the ever-troublesome Cadusians. (These, we notice, being on the borders of metropolitan territory in Media, regularly receive the attention of the King in person.) Artaxerxes was no great fighting man, and his expedition became bogged down in the defiles of the Elburz mountains, with supply-routes cut and in real danger of destruction; but Tiribazos, experienced in diplomacy, negotiated separately with the two chief and rival Cadusian kings, who were encamped separately (perhaps on opposite sides of the beleaguered royal army), led each to suspect that the other was betraying him, and so persuaded both to make peace. Artaxerxes is said to have got out of the mountains only on foot; but he was glad to get out at all.

Mysia had presumably been reduced by Autophradates and Ariobarzanes. Under the former served the son of a Karian guardsman, who had gained promotion to governorship of "the part of Cilicia next to Cappadocia", i.e. the wild northern side of the Taurus. There the ex-

---

[1] Plutarch, *Sayings* (*Moralia*, 174b); context, Diodorus xv. 10f.

guardsman, Kamisares, married the daughter of his northern neighbour, the king of Paphlagonia, and had a son, Datames. Datames in turn had served under the King against the Cadusians, and been rewarded with the succession to his father's minor satrapy. Distinguished again in repelling an attack which had burst into Autophradates' camp, he was next sent to call to order his cousin, Thys, king of Paphlagonia, son of or identical with Otys, Agesilaos' sometime ally.[1] He tried to do this peaceably, by a family visit; but Thys, probably suspecting his kinsman of designs on the kingdom, would have murdered him, had not Datames' mother, who was with him, got wind of the plot. So war it had to be, and Datames, though ill supported by Ariobarzanes (also not anxious to remove a "buffer"?), captured Thys, and occupied Paphlagonia. Anxious to make sure of the credit, he conducted the shaggy barbarian to court himself and introduced him, in royal dress but on the end of a chain, like a bear-leader; causing such a sensation that the King, before receiving him, sent Pharnabazos out to ascertain whether the report was true.

Pharnabazos was about to prepare, with Tithraustes, another attack on Egypt, and the King posted Datames to their general staff (our source actually says, to an equal share in the command);[2] but he, whose successes were all won by speed and daring, must have found the experience frustrating. Tithraustes disappears from the scene; perhaps, in old age, he retired to estates in central Asia Minor, where there is mention, as late as 356, of "Tithraustes' country". Pharnabazos began with a diplomatic success. He protested to Athens about Chabrias' presence in Egypt as "alienating the King's goodwill towards the people"; and Athens in a fright sent him a peremptory message of recall. (He was home in time to be elected a general at Athens for 379.) At the same time Pharnabazos requested and received the loan of Athens' most famous commander, Iphikrates, a specialist in the latest tactics and a hero of the Greek wars. But for the formidable task before him, Pharnabazos was determined this time to leave nothing to chance. If he was really older than Agesilaos (cf. p. 362), who was born *c.* 443, he was now in his middle sixties; no longer the dashing cavalier of thirty years before.

It was not altogether nonsense. To attack Egypt behind her desert

[1] The barbarian name (Gk. acc. Thyn, cf. Otyn) may have had some unfamiliar aspirated dental at the beginning. ("Thyus", uniformly in Olmstead, *Persian Empire*, 401, 409, 554, seems to be a mere editorial error.)
[2] Nepos, *Datames*, 3.

and water defences, a massive combined operation was to be launched; and the empire, as it grew older, seems to have become even more dependent upon elaborate supply services than in the time of Xerxes. The contemporary Greek historian Theopompos, in fact, echoes Herodotus' account of Xerxes' expedition in writing about this one: "What city or what people of Asia did not..." (contribute); with the difference that Herodotus had written: "What people of Asia did not Xerxes *bring with him*?"[1] There had been a shift from masses of men to masses of material, and Theopompos goes on to detail it: the luxurious camp equipment (clearly only for officers, but he omits to say that); huge stores of arms, both Greek and oriental, huge numbers of beasts of burden, huge quantities of food and...bales of paper. The army's increasing "tail" required an increased military bureaucracy. The dumps of salt meat alone "looked from a distance like a range of dunes"[2] along the beaches of the invasion-base on the Bay of Ake (Akko, Acre).

All the same, Pharnabazos' preparations were painfully slow. They took even longer than Xerxes' against Greece. Iphikrates, noting that the supreme commander was still quick of wit, ventured to comment on the contrast. Pharnabazos said: "That is because my words are my own, but my actions are the King's".[3] Nothing of any importance was done without reference to the court. Meanwhile Artaxerxes, reckoning that war in Greece, which had started again, was bad for the supply of mercenaries, is said in 375 to have induced the states, in conference at Sparta, to renew the peace on the basis of universal autonomy; but Thebes, the rising power, bent on making a reality of her hegemony in Boiotia, stood out.[4]

In spring, 373, Pharnabazos at last launched the invasion with, we are told, 200,000 oriental troops (no doubt an exaggeration, but a fraction of earlier figures), 300 triremes, 200 30-oared galleys (important for shallow waters) and, at the lowest quotation, 12,000 Greeks.[5] The

---

[1] Hdt. vii. 21; Theopompos, SCBO, fr. 283 (Jacoby 115 F 263).
[2] Cf. de Joinville, ii, on St Louis' grain-dumps in Cyprus, for his Egyptian expedition.
[3] Diod. xv. 41. 2.
[4] Diod. xv. 38. Diodorus' account of the conference is suspiciously like that of the equally abortive conference of 371, given in xv. 50 and also by the contemporary Xenophon (*Hell*. vi. iii), who does not mention this earlier one. Diodorus is notorious for loose chronology and duplication of events. However, Xenophon omits many important events, and most recent authorities accept this story; e.g. Bengtson, *The Greeks and the Persians*, p. 226; J. Buckler, "Dating the Peace of 375/4 B.C.", *GRBS* XII (1971), 353–61.
[5] 12,000, Nepos, *Iphicrates* 2, 4; 20,000 Diod. xv. 1, who gives the other figures.

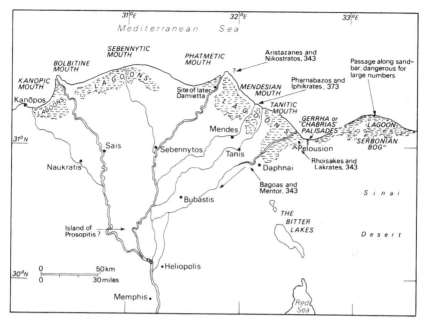

Map 15. The Nile Delta.

Egyptians were ready, behind a network of inundations and embankments that rendered their main position on the Pelusian mouth of the Nile almost unapproachable either by land or water, while all the other main mouths were blocked by pontoon bridges overlooked by forts. Pharnabazos in person, with Iphikrates, therefore, after demonstrating before the main position, fetched a compass out of sight of land with a strong squadron, and put a first wave of 3,000 men ashore on the beaches off the central or Mendesian mouth. The Egyptians from the fort, about equal in numbers, counter-attacked with horse and foot; but Persian reinforcements then took them in flank. The resistance was broken, many were taken prisoner, and Iphikrates' men rushed the fort along with the fugitives.

With the channel thus opened, Iphikrates urged an immediate dash for Memphis with the troops available, before the enemy could re-deploy; but Pharnabazos insisted on waiting for his main forces. Iphikrates in vain offered to sail with the Greeks alone; only to find the Persian officers looking sourly at him and muttering "Wants it all for himself, does he?" By the time Pharnabazos' reinforcements were ashore, Memphis and Mendes were held in force, and the Persians found themselves confined to their beach-head, locally outnumbered and thrown on the defensive. Weeks passed, with no improvement in the military situation and amid worsening staff-relations; and with the coming of high summer and the Nile flood it became evident that the whole campaign, so brilliantly opened, was a failure. The beach-head was evacuated, and the whole armament returned to Palestine.

At Ake Iphikrates, fearing to be made a scapegoat – he too remembered Konon – secured a ship and escaped by night. Pharnabazos sent ambassadors after him to Athens, making grave charges. The Athenians politely promised to examine them; but the sequel was that, like Chabrias after *his* return, he was elected a general, to render signal services at sea in 372.

It was the end of Pharnabazos' military career – he was now over seventy – and Datames was ordered to prepare for another attempt. Trouble however arose in his own country; a Taurus chief was again raiding the Royal Road. Artaxerxes ordered Datames to deal with him, but shortly afterwards decided that in taking his best general away from the main front he had got his priorities wrong, and sent a counter-order. Datames however, never a man to waste time, had already left Ake, not by the long land route to raise an army in Asia Minor, but by sea. Crossing the Taurus from Cilicia with a small force, he found his enemy unprepared and, without a blow struck, intimidated him into surrender. He is said to have been back at Ake before the King knew he had gone.

At court there was jealousy among the grandees against the non-Iranian Datames. Datames however had friends there too, and the treasurer Pandantes wrote to warn him that a clique had formed, bent on his destruction.

His slightest mishap would be interpreted as misconduct. Datames thought that in that case he had certainly better not attempt Egypt. He resigned and, leaving his Greek condottiere Mandrokles in acting command, withdrew to his satrapy. There he completed his occupation of Paphlagonia (was he not descended from its former kings?) and even mastered the Greek colonies of Sinope and Amisos (Sinub and Samsun), entrepôts of the Black Sea trade. At the former he struck his coins. He also cultivated friendly relations with Ariobarzanes, who, having driven a son of Pharnabazos from his patrimony (we do not know just when) – whereas Pharnabazos himself had shared his privileges with other sons of Pharnakes (p. 346) – could be sure that he too had enemies at court.

2. *The breakdown of the King's Peace, and the Satrap Rebellions*

The ambiguous positions and behaviour of Datames and Ariobarzanes were to be a hinge of fate. On it turned the loss of the Persian ascendancy in Greece, which Greek divisions had enabled Artaxerxes and his diplomatic advisers to build up.

In 371 that ascendancy was demonstrated in a peace-conference at Sparta. Athens, which since 378 had reconstituted a naval league – with built-in safeguards to secure the autonomy principle – was uneasy at the growing power of Thebes, and also at the news that Antalkidas was returning once more from Persia with the now familiar peace-terms and, it was suspected, money for Persia's friends. Much better, said Athens' spokesmen, make peace at once. Sparta, which in 381 had put herself in the wrong by seizing the citadel of Thebes in time of peace with the support of a faction, and since its liberation (379) had shown reluctance to squander Spartan man-power in pitched battles, was willing; but Thebes (just as in 375, if that is historical), stood out, claiming that Boiotia was one state and that occupying Plataia (for instance) and expelling its people was a matter of "internal affairs". So Thebes was isolated, and it was expected that, since with powerful allies she had been unable to overthrow Sparta, she would now be crushed.

The whole situation changed overnight when King Kleombrotos (for Agesilaos had lately been dangerously ill) was defeated and killed, along with 400 Spartan "peers" (more than half those present, and a third of all that there were, between eighteen and sixty), at Leuktra in Boiotia that same summer. Heroes of the battle were Epameinondas, Thebes' intellectual tactician, and Pelopidas, her dashing fighting man.

Sparta was permanently weakened, though she still kept some prestige and some allies; but this need not have been to Persia's disadvantage. The reaction at Athens to the "joyful" news of victory over the old enemy, officially sent from Thebes, was one of undisguised gloom, followed by the calling of a new conference at Athens itself, of "all peace-loving states", in an effort to save, explicitly, "the peace which the King sent down", i.e. the autonomy principle.[1] The peace was not saved. In the following years the Thebans, dominating mainland Greece and joined by Argives and Arcadians, invaded Sparta's own territory and liberated Messenia in the south-west, whose peasants had for centuries been Sparta's serfs. But Athens, now more afraid of

[1] Xen., *Hell.* VI. v. 1f.

Thebes than of Sparta, made alliance with the latter, and in 370 sent
Iphikrates with her main army to the Peloponnese, to restore a miserable
balance of armed power.

Naturally both sides looked to Persia. In 368 Ariobarzanes sent
Philiskos, a condottiere from Abydos, to Greece with money; and
Philiskos called yet another peace-conference, at Delphoi, where he tried
to mediate on the basis of the *status quo ante bellum*. Athens voted both
Philiskos and Ariobarzanes Athenian citizenship; but Thebes, naturally,
refused to hand back the Messenians to Sparta. Philiskos then began
to hire a mercenary army in Sparta's interest. Sparta also sent an
ambassador to the King; and Thebes in turn sent Pelopidas, accompanied by delegates from her allies, Argos, Elis, Arcadia (now trying to
form a federal state), and shortly afterwards two from Athens. Artaxerxes
in person presided over a session representing both sides in Greece; and
the two Athenian delegates split.

Pelopidas scored a personal diplomatic triumph. A man of great
personal magnetism, he was also able to remind the King that Thebes
had been Persia's ally even in Xerxes' time; and the King, having found
both Athens and Sparta sufficiently slippery, was prepared to give
Thebes a trial. He agreed to Pelopidas' interpretation of the autonomy-principle, which recognised Messene as a state, and added that Athens
should demobilise its navy. (Pelopidas was prepared to see how long
Athens' new League would last without the presence of Athenian
cruisers.) Leon of Athens "said, in the King's hearing, 'My God,
Athenians, it is time, apparently, for you to seek some other friend than
the King!' The secretary reported what he had said, and then came out
with an addition to the text [a standard diplomatic saving-clause of the
time]: 'And if the Athenians have any more equitable proposal to make,
they shall come to the King and explain it.'"[1]

The Arcadian delegate also returned disgruntled, the King having
found for Elis in the matter of some border communities. (This was to
be a serious matter for Thebes.) Athens actually put to death her other
ambassador, for treason; he was said to have consorted too much with
Pelopidas, and to have done very well out of it. The Thebans called
a congress at Thebes, to hear the terms read by a royal secretary, and
then called upon "those who wished to be friends with the King and
with them" – a disguised threat – to swear to observe them. But there
was an immediate outcry. Delegates said that they had come only to
hear the terms. Any oaths must be taken at their cities. Lykomedes of

[1] Xen., *Hell.* VII. i. 37.

Arcadia added that anyhow the congress ought not to be meeting at Thebes, but at the seat of war (in the Peloponnese); and when the Thebans complained that he was "splitting the alliance", the Arcadian delegation walked out. The Thebans still comforted themselves with the thought that no city, when approached separately, would rebuff both Thebes and the King; but that happened too. The Corinthians said bluntly that they "'were not interested'",[1] setting an example that was widely followed. The rôle of Keepers of the King's Peace was proving difficult.

So war continued, with Sparta still hoping to recover Messenia, and Arcadia split between federalists, backed by Thebes, and old-fashioned separatists; and the Persian empire, meanwhile, was paralysed by revolts, backed, naturally, by Athens and Sparta. The confused events on both sides of the Aegean gain something in clarity if viewed together.

Datames had no reason to wish for war with the King; but his hand was forced when his son Sysinas deserted him (we are not told why) and denounced him as a rebel. The test of this was simple; it was whether he would obey a summons to court to give an account of his stewardship. We are not told whether it was applied; but in or about 367, Autophradates of Sardis was ordered to suppress him. Meanwhile a metropolitan army advanced from the east, and the Pisidians, who naturally if unreasonably hated Datames, gave it the Cilician Gates through the Taurus before Datames could stop it. It was probably under Artabazos the son of Pharnabazos, mentioned in one source as commander of the expedition; Autophradates, who had orders to restore him to his father's satrapy, no doubt as the senior officer took command when the armies joined hands. A list of Autophradates' Asia Minor contingents (in addition to the metropolitan troops, put at 120,000!) adds up to 51,000 – but including only 3,000 Greeks; such were the effects of war in Arcadia, the great source of mercenaries. Datames was outnumbered; but so skilfully did he use the ground, which he knew well, in his Paphlagonian mountains, that the King agreed to accept his nominal submission (Datames suspected that this meant no more than an armistice), thus releasing the expedition to proceed to Phrygia.[2]

---

[1] Xen., *Hell.* VII. i. 40.
[2] Nepos, *Datames* 8; Artabazos as commander, Diod. xv. 91, 2ff. (introducing a story told by Nepos earlier, in §6). Beloch (*Gr. Gesch.* III², ii, pp. 254–7) would make Artabazos' a separate and later expedition.

In Phrygia Autophradates had more success. He besieged Ariobarzanes in Assos, on the gulf of Adramyttion, while Mausōlos the son of Hekatomnos (prince-satrap of Karia since 377) blockaded it by sea. But Ariobarzanes' Greek friends came to the rescue. Athens sent out a fleet under Timotheos the son of Konon, but with orders to help him "without breaking the peace with the King". (Ariobarzanes must have told them a misleading story.) When Timotheos found that Ariobarzanes was definitely at war with royal forces, he temporised, filling in his time by besieging Samos, which had been "occupied by a garrison under Kyprothemis, installed by the royal governor Tigranes... He besieged, rescued and liberated it; and to this day [says Demosthenes some fifteen years later] you have had no war [with Persia] on those grounds".[1] To garrison Samos, indeed, was for a Persian a breach of the autonomy principle in the King's own Peace of 387. This will be why there were no repercussions. (Tigranes, very likely that son-in-law of Strouthas, satrap of Ionia, who had been held to ransom by Diphridas in 390 (p. 367), would probably have claimed that *he* was liberating Samos from a faction.) But soon after, Athens introduced Athenian settlers, probably planting them on the lands of the opposite faction. This in turn was a clear breach of Athens' own treaty with her allies, of 378, and did have repercussions; it aroused all the allies' fears of Athenian "neo-imperialism".

However, with Samos secured (spring, 365), Timotheos sailed north, to join Agesilaos, who had already reached the Troad. He too avoided fighting; but by diplomacy, we are told,[2] he induced the besiegers of Assos to withdraw. No doubt the presence of Timotheos' fleet materially assisted. Ariobarzanes paid Sparta well for his rescue. Timotheos relieved Sestos, which Ariobarzanes had been holding and which Kotys, king of eastern Thrace, had besieged when he appeared to be doomed, and kept it as Athens' reward for *her* services.

The show of force by Athens and Sparta together evidently deeply impressed the satraps. Mausolos went home, and Autophradates put Artabazos under arrest! That is to say, they joined the revolt. But they held back during 364–363, when Boiotia – which had long possessed a few warships, and now controlled the adjacent coast of Lokris and had the alliance of the Euboian cities – suddenly sent out a powerful fleet under Epameinondas himself; and Rhodes, Chios and Byzantion, all now deeply suspicious of Athens, came over to him.

[1] *On the Liberty of the Rhodians*, §§9f.   [2] Xen., *Agesilaos* ii. 25.

REBELS AND MERCENARIES

This foray, which appears as an odd and isolated event in purely Greek histories, is a natural sequel to Persia's alliance with Thebes. Epameinondas in a great policy-speech, had urged his people that they must take to the sea, like Athens long before, if they were to achieve supremacy in Greece. But fleets were expensive, as Athens, with a far greater economic potential than Thebes, knew well. The money for building a planned hundred ships, which must have been laid down in 366–365, presumably came from the King, whose declared policy was to support his friends in Greece "with ships and money" (p. 368). A Theban inscription of about this time also shows the Boiotian League honouring a Carthaginian, whose name may have been Hannibal, son of Hasdrubal; he may, it has been conjectured, have been a naval architect – especially as Syracuse was allied to Corinth and Sparta. The alliances of 480 had reappeared in some detail. In 364 Epameinondas sailed, and won over Byzantion from Athens.

However, he fought no fleet action; clearly he had nothing like the hundred ships of the paper programme. Timotheos is recorded in a dateless anecdote to have relieved Kyzikos; we are not told from whom, but it may well have been from Epameinondas' fleet; and if so, Athenian naval intervention in force, which we should expect, against any threat to the Black Sea corn-trade, accounts for Epameinondas' failure to do more. After his return home the Boiotian navy, doubtless for economic reasons, never played a strategic part again. Meanwhile Arcadia was so divided that, while Epameinondas was winning allies in the Aegean, some Arcadians, even old federalists, made overtures to Athens. In 362 Epameinondas was sent there with a great allied army once more; and there, before Mantineia, once more he broke a Spartan battle-line – and was killed in the loose fighting that followed.

The battle of Mantineia was indecisive; but the death of Epameinondas, the only internationally famous Theban – for Pelopidas had fallen two years earlier – was a fact to carry weight even east of the Aegean. Thebes thereafter floundered, as if she had suffered brain-damage; as indeed she had. Athens and Sparta, allied, looked more powerful than they were; and the satraps of Asia Minor hesitated no longer. They made alliance with Sparta, and with Tachos the son of Nectanebos of Egypt. They found a figurehead in old Orontes "of Mysia" (p. 370), who struck coins in Greek mints of Asia, including Lampsakos and Klazomenai; not only silver and bronze but also gold, to strike which may have been an explicit act of treason; and for commander in the front line they had

Datames, who believed that the court meant to destroy him anyhow, and whom geography had placed in that position.

After Mantineia, too, old Agesilaos felt that he could be spared from the home front, to accept an invitation from Tachos to command the Egyptian army. He would strike another blow at the Persian enemy; and the reward, payable to the Spartan treasury, would be huge. Chabrias of Athens, who found the life of a general abroad more congenial than that of a citizen, was already there. In 361, with Chabrias commanding the fleet and Agesilaos the Greek mercenaries, the Pharaoh invaded Palestine. Orontes seems to have gone to north Syria, and Datames, according to an undated story, probably now, crossed the upper Euphrates.

Artaxerxes was saved by individual self-seeking among his opponents. His agents got into touch with Orontes, offering him his old position back as reward for treachery; and Orontes deserted, delivering his war-chest and many troops. Datames withdrew; and simultaneously in Egypt Tachos' nephew, Nectanebos II, seized the kingdom behind Tachos' back. Chabrias would have fought for Tachos; but Agesilaos, discontented at Tachos' having kept the command in his own not very competent hands, decided that Nectanebos would be the better ally. He withdrew to Egypt and helped Nectanebos to defeat a popular rising (no doubt provoked by certain novel war-taxes, devised by Chabrias) in favour of a third candidate. Having collected his money (230 talents) he then started for home, but died in Cyrenaica (winter, 361/360; aged c. 83).

Tachos threw himself on the mercy of the crown-prince Ōchos, commanding in Syria for the aged King. Ōchos was not a charitable man, but he saved Tachos, hoping to win Egypt by restoring him as a puppet; a Persian way with surrendered rebel kings already familiar to Herodotus.[1] Chabrias went home. Meanwhile Rheomithres, the envoy of the rebel satraps to Tachos, had been sent back by Tachos to Asia Minor with ships and money; but hearing on the way how things were going, he arrested the officers who came to meet him on arrival, and took them and the money to Ochos as a peace-offering. He had left his wife and children as hostages in Egypt; a matter which excited unfavorable comment. Autophradates and Mausōlos, who had temporised throughout, then sued for peace, made their excuses, and kept their satrapies, though Mausolos at least was temporarily deposed in favour

[1] Xen., *Agesilaos* iii. 15.

of Pixodar, his youngest brother; and Artabazos, released, was in possession of his within 360.¹

Ariobarzanes and Datames dared not surrender; but treachery eliminated them too. The former's son, Mithradates of Kios, turned against his aged father. He obtained through royal agents a promise of forgiveness, even for future acts of war committed in order to gain the confidence of Datames, and at last, for all his wariness, succeeded in assassinating him; and he betrayed his father, who was sent up-country and put to death; another celebrated crime.² Datames' son Sysinas (p. 377), if his name in Aramaic is rightly read on a coin of Sinope, succeeded to his satrapy; but the Kios branch of the house of Pharnakes, in the person of Mithradates, may now or soon after have begun its long control of the south-east coast of the Black Sea, or Pontus.³

Meanwhile Ochos, an energetic man, had advanced on Egypt, with Tachos in nominal command of his forces; but Nectanebos' position proved to be already firm, and the defences organised long since by Chabrias were still formidable. Operations were called off by the end of 359, when Ochos was called to the deathbed of his father; he succeeded him in 358 as Artaxerxes III.

Artabazos is commonly supposed to have been Pharnabazos' son by his royal bride, Apame, married *c.* 388; but the only ancient evidence for this is a vague statement that he was "of royal descent", in the story that Alexander the Great left an illegitimate son by Artabazos' daughter Barsine; a story perhaps invented after Alexander's death, when some of his generals wanted a pretender to the throne whom they could control.⁴ On the other hand, a writer given to rhetoric, but with good sources and (here) no axe to grind, says that he was 95 when he resigned from Alexander's service on grounds of age in 328!⁵ It certainly seems

---

¹ *Date from Demosthenes* XXIII. 155ff. (before the death of King Kotys of Thrace in 359. Pixodar is unexpectedly found as satrap of Karia and Lykia in 358 in the Aramaic text of the Xanthos trilingual inscription; cf. A. Dupont-Sommer in *CRAI*, 1975, esp. p. 140.

² Xen., *Cyrus* VIII. viii. 4 (mentioned with Rheomitres); Aristotle, *Politics* v. 1312a.

³ Diodorus (XV. 90. 3) confuses the ill-fated Ariobarzanes with a later namesake who died in 337/336 (far too late for the mention by Xenophon) and whose father and son were both named Mithradates. Cf. Meyer, *Gesch. des Königreichs Pontus* (1879), pp. 31ff.; Geyer, *s.v.* Mithridates (5, 6, 7) in Pauly-Wissowa, *Real-Encyklopädie*; C. L. Sherman, note on Diod. *loc. cit.* (*LCL* vol. VII, pp. 202f.). A coin of Sysinas, cf. J.P. Six in *NC* 1894, p. 304.

⁴ Plut., *Alex.* 21; cf. J. R. Hamilton's edition (1969), *ad loc.*; Tarn's *Alexander*, II, pp. 330ff., and article in *JHS* XLI. Berve, *Das Alexanderreich, s.v.* Artabazus (II, no. 152) continues however to believe the story; and Professor P. A. Brunt, *Rivista di Filologia* CIII (1975), pp. 22ff., argues that it is at least not absurd.

⁵ Q. Curtius VI. 5. 3 (cf. Arrian IV. 17). Did C.'s source say that he *lived to be* 95?

likely that a member of his family and a man of his individual vigour was then considerably over sixty.

He was married to the sister of two Rhodian *condottieri*, Mentor and Memnon, the former of whom became, after 344, one of the most important men in the empire. In 360 they were still young and obscure, and delighted with such a brilliant family alliance. It was a highly successful marriage. Artabazos had eleven sons and ten daughters, all (it is said, but need not be true) by the same mother. But this match, too, seems much less likely for a king's grandson, brought up at court, than for a Persian who had knocked about in the Greek world; and we know that Pharnabazos had a son who had done so – that son of Parapita, not yet adolescent in 395, who was driven from home after 388 and fled to Sparta (p. 364). Pharnabazos, who was ambitious, presumably did not want his grown-up son about the court during the early years of his marriage to the princess Apame. Our sources are far too incomplete for a certain identification; but certainly this great figure of the last years of the empire was a Persian with uniquely strong Greek connexions, and with a large family of gallant and half-Greek sons.

In contrast to his father's earlier and his own later loyalty to the throne, Artabazos, established in his father's satrapy, was very soon in rebellion himself, along with none other than that old betrayer, Orontes. Orontes had bargained for the high command in Asia Minor as *karanos*, but received only Armenia again, while he apparently held on to Mysia. Artabazos' motive was probably Artaxerxes' demand for the disbandment of his private army. Athens in 356 suffered the defection of her chief naval allies, Rhodes, Kos, Chios and Byzantion (the same that had briefly defected to Epameinondas, p. 378); they were now encouraged by Mausolos. The veteran Chabrias fell attacking the harbour of Chios; and in 355 Athens' general Chares let himself be diverted to helping Artabazos, to get pay for his mercenaries. He won successes, and even raided "Tithraustes' country" (whatever that means), somewhere far inland. In his dispatches, he recalled the memory of Marathon; and public opinion showed a dangerously chauvinistic tendency to rise to the echo of the brave days of old. Both the veteran pamphleteer Isokrates and the young orator Demosthenes, in his maiden political speech, though no friends of Persia, were constrained to argue for a more realistic attitude;[1] and when the King threatened war, Chares was recalled, and Athens recognised the independence of

---

[1] Isocrates, *On the Peace*; Dem. xiv (*On the Navy Boards*).

the insurgents (354). Rhodes and Kos were soon supporting 'protective' garrisons from Mausolos.

Artabazos meanwhile appealed to Thebes; and Thebes, though she had her own troubles (failing to coerce Phokis, her own neighbour, whose people could draw on the Delphic treasury to hire mercenaries), sent her best general with 5,000 men: Pammenes, a pupil of Epameinondas, and the citizen who had once been entrusted with an important hostage, the prince Philip of Macedonia. He too won successes; but Artabazos became suspicious that he intended treachery (no doubt he was being approached by royal agents); and when he in turn withdrew, Artabazos fled, with his family and Memnon, now his son-in-law, to Philip, ruler of Macedonia since 359. Mentor, Memnon's elder brother, took service in Egypt.

Orontes, with extraordinary tenacity, held out, not only in Mysia but in Lydia. We hear (but without dates) of his holding hill-positions in Mount Tmōlos, near Sardis; of operations round Kyme and Ephesos; of his moving the population of Pergamon back from lower ground into their ancient citadel; of his making native troops look like Greeks, and thus outwitting and defeating Autophradates (whether this is the old satrap or the younger one, who commanded the fleet against Alexander in 333–332). Like Ariobarzanes, he exchanged ambassadors with Athens and was awarded Athenian citizenship; his services included the supply of grain for forces under the generals Phokion, Chares and Charidemos. This we learn from an inscription which, if correctly restored, mentions as already *past* the Archonship of Kallimachos (349–348);[1] over fifty years after Orontes' first encounter with the Greeks under Xenophon. Finally, it seems, he even succeeded again

---

[1] *IG* II², i, 207 (Kirchner); H. Bengtson, *Staatsverträge* II, no. 324; discussions, H. W. Parke, *Proc. Royal Irish Acad.* XLIII (1935), M. J. Osborne, *ABSA* LXVI (1971). The first part of the text, with the name of Orontes and that (already defaced) of the archon, was copied by the Greek scholar Pittakis on the Acropolis shortly before the Greek War of Independence, and published after it. Pittakis' original copy appears to have read *ENIKAMMAXOYAPXONTO*... which he emended when publishing to *ΕΠΙΝΙΚΟΜΑΧΟΥΑΡΧΟΝΤΟ[Σ]*. Nikomachos was archon 341–40, which seems impossibly late. Pittakis' stone disappeared during the fighting of 1821–29; Rangabé, who republished the text with additional fragments (still extant), supposed to be of the same text and giving the names of the Athenian generals, proposed *ΕΠΙ ΚΑΛΛΙΜΑΧΟΥ*, which suits the generals' names, and could when mutilated have looked like *ENIKAMMAXOY*. Kirchner, with due reference to the uncertainty, retains this. Osborne (*op. cit.* p. 302) points out that other archons are not precluded, and tentatively suggests *epi Kallimedous* (360–59). This would relieve us of supposing that Orontes lived long after 354; and the undated stories of his stratagems (Polyainos vii. 14. 2ff.) could be of the Satraps' Revolt, before Autophradates joined it. But *epi Kallimedous* looks a good deal less like a text which, when defaced, might have been copied as *ENIKAMMAXOY*.

in making his peace; a historical inscription from Pergamos adds that he "made over the city to Artaxerxes" before he died;[1] not an attractive character, but another striking example of Persian vigour in old age. His family long continued to hold Armenia. An Orontes, probably his grandson, commanded the troops of that satrapy against Alexander at Gaugamela and, having been by-passed by Alexander and beaten off an attack by his successors, was still there in 317. The last Orontes of Armenia, still proudly claiming descent (it was probably in a female line) from Hydarnes,[2] ruled under the Seleukid Antiochos III. Only after Antiochos' defeat by Rome did Armenian princes replace the Hydarnids; and in Cappadocia and Commagene kings of the Ariobarzanid (and so, Pharnakid) dynasty emphasised their descent from the Achaemenids (through the old Orontes' royal bride) even in the last century B.C.[3]

4. *The Reconquest of Egypt*

Artaxerxes rewarded Thebes for recalling Pammenes with a subsidy of 300 talents. (If Thebes could only finish off Phokis, it would be good for the supply of mercenaries; and in view of Athens' relations with Orontes, it was time to encourage Thebes again.)

Asia Minor was now at peace, though some coastal dynasts probably paid tribute much as they pleased. One such was Klearchos of Herakleia (Eregli; 363-351), a tyrant who claimed divinity (anticipating Alexander and some of his successors) and in other matters modelled himself on Dionysios I. More important was Mausolos of Karia, who made Halikarnassos his capital, moving into it the people of eight old Karian towns, and conducted his own foreign policy. Like the Ptolemies and earlier Pharaohs, he married his sister. He died in 353, to be buried in the great Mausoleum, whose sculptures are among the finest surviving remains of fourth-century Greek art. His sister-wife Artemisia[4] (a name no doubt chosen in deliberate reference to history) continued to reign as queen until her own death two years later, while her brother Idrieus, who outlived her, bore the title of satrap and struck the coins. But it is said to have been Artemisia herself whose stratagems captured

---

[1] Dittenberger, *Orient. Graec. Inscrs. Selectae*, 264.
[2] Strabo's *Geography* XI, p. 531. (But the Pergamene inscription calls O. son of Artasuras "a Bactrian".)
[3] Dittenberger, *op. cit.* nos. 391-2 (from the Nimrud Dagh).
[4] Artemesia (Olmstead, consistently) is an editorial error.

REBELS AND MERCENARIES

Herakleia-on-Latmos and recaptured Rhodes, when the islanders had thought that under a woman's rule they could themselves seize Halikarnassos!

Of all this, Artaxerxes took little notice; though royal officers are mentioned, reminding Mausolos of his duties in the matter of tribute. The King was still bent on the main objective, the reconquest of Egypt.

His next attempt was made about 353; but it failed again. We have no narrative of this, but it is mentioned by Demosthenes,[1] *c.* 352, as having just happened. This blow to Persian prestige was followed by new revolts in Phoenicia, led by Tennes (Tabnit), king of Sidon, who was reinforced by 4,000 mercenaries from Egypt under Mentor, and in Cyprus. Here Nikokles, son and successor of Euagoras I, had been murdered and succeeded by his brother, Euagoras II, who reigned for four years. He was now expelled by Pnytagoras (perhaps a cousin – he bears a family name), who headed a federation of nine Cypriote city-kings. Artaxerxes ordered Idrieus of Karia to suppress the revolt, and with forty warships and 8,000 mercenaries under Phokion of Athens he soon intimidated most of the cities. Athens was now more afraid of Philip of Macedonia, who was in alliance with Thebes against Phokis, than of the Great King. But Pnytagoras held out strongly in Salamis and, after Euagoras II had been denounced to the King for some double-dealing, was allowed to make peace; he reigned in Salamis till the time of Alexander.

Concurrently with these events, which certainly went on long after the year 351-350 into which Diodorus crowds them,[2] Artaxerxes himself closed on Phoenicia. He intended to make an example of Sidon, whose people had destroyed supplies accumulated for the Egyptian campaign, killed Persian officers and devastated the local royal park. King Tennes is reported, in panic, to have betrayed his people; but since Artaxerxes put him to death after his surrender, the story may be untrue. What is certain is that Mentor the Rhodian, said to have been his accomplice, let the Persians into the town at the point which he was guarding; and he, with his mercenaries, was taken into Persian service – and so lived to tell the tale. There was massacre, plunder and burning; though, since Sidon in Alexander's time was again an important city with its own fleet, stories of its destruction are clearly exaggerated. The year was probably about 345.

[1] *On the Liberty of the Rhodians*, §11; cf. Isokr., *Philip*, 101.
[2] xv, 40–4.

Simultaneously Artaxerxes had not merely collected mercenaries, but officially approached the principal Greek states, with requests for troops for the great Egyptian campaign. Athens and Sparta declared their friendly neutrality. In fact Diophantos of Athens, a friend of Isokrates, and two Spartiates, Lamios and Philophron, were at the time commanding mercenaries for Nectanebos. But cities of the opposite camp officially sent troops. Thebes, now at peace – for Philip, in 346, had crushed Phokis and forced peace upon Athens – sent 1,000 armoured infantry under Lākrates; Argos, unscarred by recent wars, sent 3,000, and from thence the King hand-picked a general: a "mad" hero, Nikostratos, said to have used Herakles' array of lion-skin and club as his battle-dress. Asian Greece sent 6,000; Mentor still had his 4,000 mercenaries; and these were not all.

Artaxerxes approached the Delta defences with three corps in line, each with a Greek commanding its armoured spearhead as second-in-command to a Persian, and a fourth kept under his own hand. Lākrates, leading his Thebans, under Rhosakes, satrap of Lydia and Ionia and a descendant of one of the Seven Houses, fiercely and frontally assaulted Pelousion, where Philophron of Sparta commanded the defenders. The Persians diverted the water from its moat, filled up ditches, battered the walls, only to find breaches sealed off by new barricades behind. It was a long-drawn and costly holding operation. On the left Bagoas the eunuch, the King's chief confidant and guard-commander, with Mentor and his mercenaries, "felt" the river defences up to Bubastis. On the right Aristazanes, the Master of Ceremonies and "next to Bagoas in the King's confidence",[1] with 5,000 picked soldiers and eighty triremes, repeated Pharnabazos' manoeuvre of an attack by sea; and here Nikostratos of Argos, with Egyptian guides whose families the Persians had seized, found a channel by which he made the first penetration of the defences. Local reserves under one Kleinios of Kos counter-attacked, but he was defeated and killed; and Nectanebos, commanding in person, finding his river-line turned, sped back to secure the defences of Memphis. Inevitably his Greeks blamed his generalship for their defeat. So far he had kept his head; but his "strategic movement to the rear" left the garrison of Pelousion isolated; and, offered by Lākrates safe-conduct to Greece with

[1] The Gk. title is *Eisangeleus*; Diod. XVI. 47. 2. See O. Szemerényi in (*Monumentum H. S. Nyberg* II, (1975), 354–92 (Acta Iranica 5), pointing out that this official must be the Persian *hazārapatiš* (so glossed by Hesychius s.v. *azarapateis* (plural)), and not, as has long been commonly supposed, the Guard-Commander (Gk. *Chiliarchos*).

what property they could carry, if they surrendered at once, they did so. Lākrates kept his word, even to setting his own troops upon some of the Asiatics, who tried to rob the surrendered men; and Artaxerxes, when complaint was made, upheld his action.

This was virtually the end. Mentor, with the inland column, now offered the same terms to all who surrendered quickly or deserted, while threatening with the fate of Sidon any city that had to be stormed. There was a stream of deserters, and soon the Greeks and Egyptians in the chief garrisons were competing for the credit of surrendering first. At Bubastis, the Egyptians opened negotiations with Bagoas, and the Greeks with Mentor, each behind the back of the others; which did not prevent the Greeks from being much incensed when they got wind of the Egyptian negotiations. Mentor then scented the opportunity for a characteristic coup. He prompted the Greek garrison to let Bagoas enter the city, and then to close the gates behind him and attack the Egyptians. Bagoas was a prisoner of the Greeks and trembling for his life, when Mentor appeared and saved him. Such at least was the story; and it was a fact that for the rest of the reign these two comrades-in-arms acted in unison. Bagoas, as Guard-Commander, was the second man in the empire; and Mentor, with his support, became, in a manner unprecedented for a Greek, the first man, at least in military affairs, in the western provinces. He also enjoyed great prestige in Greece for his part in "saving the Greeks in Egyptian service when Egypt was conquered by the Persians". This is recorded in an Athenian decree of Alexander's time, honouring a younger Memnon (son of Mentor's son Thymondas, who commanded Darius' mercenaries at Issos (p. 429). The decree also remembers the services to Athens of the young man's "ancestors" Pharnabazos and Artabazos (accurately, only if Thymondas had married his cousin, which is quite likely).[1]

5. *No cause for alarm (341–334)*

With Mentor controlling the main supply of mercenaries, the empire was secure against further satrap-revolts in Asia Minor; and with Bagoas' support, Mentor was secure against court intrigues such as had toppled the last non-Iranian high commander, Datames. There remained some clearing up to be done in north-west Asia Minor, and Mentor dealt with it, capturing by treachery Hermeias, the eunuch-dynast of Atarneus,

[1] *IG* II², no. 356, under archon Hegemon, 327–6.

who held much of the Troad. Hermeias was the friend of Aristotle, who stayed at his court for three years after the death of Plato in 348, and married his adopted daughter. He was now seized at a conference, tortured for information, and impaled. He had (of course) been in touch with Philip of Macedonia; but Philip at this time was in treaty-relations with Persia. Mentor then secured all Hermeias' towns and forts, in characteristic style, by sending men armed with letters under Hermeias' seal.

The more easily because of the peace with Philip, he was also able to bring back from Macedonia his brother and brother-in-law, Memnon and Artabazos, and to make their peace with the King. Artabazos' family had grown during his long exile. Two of his daughters were young enough to be married to Alexander's officers, Eumenes and Nearchos, in 324; but as this was part of Alexander's so-called "marriage of east and west", they may, like the daughters of Darius and of Artaxerxes, whom Alexander himself married, have been then not in their first youth. Artabazos was not however returned to his satrapy. (He next appears in the company of Darius III in flight before Alexander, when he and three of his sons were that unhappy monarch's last faithful Persian noblemen.) His sons, on the other hand, were promoted by Mentor, and several of them figure in the tale of resistance to Alexander. Pharnabazos, probably the eldest, commanded the fleet (along with an Autophradates) in 333–332; was captured, escaped, and lived to fight under Eumenes after Alexander's death. Ariobarzanes commanded troops at Gaugamēla, defended the Persian Gates in a Persian Thermopylae, and survived to surrender with his father; and Kōphēn, the last of that party, was promoted into the Royal Horse-Guard squadron in 324. But it was their cousins, of the house of Mithradates of Kios, who had the greater destiny, founding, in the person of another Mithradates, son of another Ariobarzanes, that dynasty of Pontos, which was to fall only to Rome. Here, then, so far as Achaemenid Persia's dealings with Greece are concerned, we take our leave of this great family.

Mentor died soon after achieving this restoration, and Memnon took over command of his mercenaries. He captured Lampsakos, which since Artabazos' revolt had been independent and in alliance with Athens; but he was often short of money, and the surviving stories of him before Alexander's invasion are chiefly of tricks and shifts to raise it, to pay his troops. He was no *karanos*, but only a commander of troops not under the local satraps; an arrangement (as Darius I, who invented it, very well knew) likely to cause friction; and he had not Mentor's prestige. The satraps, Arsites at Daskyleion (whether he was a Pharnakid we are not told) and the brothers Spithridates and Rhosakes (Rhoesakes) in Lydia, may have preferred to keep him short; and in a crisis, unfortunately for Persia, it was they who determined strategy.

Philip was certainly growing very powerful. He controlled, since 346, a majority of votes on the Delphic Amphiktyonic Council, an archaic and sacred League of Neighbours which, even after centuries of abuse of religious sanctions for political ends, still had some prestige; and Greek anti-Persian propaganda was now turning to him. Isokrates, who nearly forty years before had urged Athens and Sparta to unite and sweep through Asia in the steps of the Ten Thousand, had lately addressed a pamphlet to him in the same vein. But his fleet was not fit to look that of Athens in the face, though it could annoy Athens with hit-and-run raids; and this annoyance, re-emerging in 343–342 with his capture of the north-Aegean islands of Halonnesos and Peparethos, combined with fear of Philip's land forces to turn Athens back to co-operation with Persia.

The sequel showed what Athens and Persia in combination could do. With Athens holding, since 353, the Gallipoli Peninsula, except Kardia, which was under Philip's protection, border incidents, in which Athens' general Diopeithes was largely to blame, led to a breach of the peace; and in 340 Philip attacked Athens' ally, Perinthos on the Marmara. He breached and stormed the land wall; but the besieged fought on in the narrow barricaded streets and tall houses, which rose tier above tier up the landward slope of their rocky peninsula. The Macedonians attacked in relays, hoping to wear them out; but reinforcements arrived from Byzantion, and the satraps, with approval from Susa, sent in mercenaries, food, arrows and sling-bullets, in a steady stream. Philip tried a swoop on Byzantion, hoping to find it weakly held; but his surprise failed; Rhodes, Kos and Chios, Byzantion's allies, sent help; an Athenian squadron under Chares arrived to convoy the grain-fleet, which Philip had hoped to hold up at the Bosporus; and then came the main Athenian fleet, 120 ships under Phōkion. Philip gave up, and plunged into the interior, where he had severe battles with recently conquered tribes, and was himself wounded. It was the most conspicuous failure in his career.

For two years the affairs of Greece and Persia fell apart; and in 338, with no crisis looming, Bagoas poisoned Artaxerxes III and set up, he hoped, a less formidable master in his son Arses. (As usual, we hear nothing of the growing tension that must have gone before the murder.) But this was the year in which Philip, taking advantage of a Greek quarrel, which the Amphiktyonic Council invited him to settle, decisively defeated Athens and Thebes, allied too late. He then called a conference at Corinth, where the League of the Hellenes had had its headquarters in face of Xerxes. The league against Persia was revived, and Philip was unanimously elected its general. Sparta alone, still refusing to sit with Messene, sulkily stood out; and without the Athenian navy, the Persian empire found itself facing invasion.

A peremptory demand for reparation for the aid given to Perinthos, inevitably rejected, provided a *casus belli*; and in 337 advance-guards landed both in Ionia and the Troad, proclaiming liberation. In the north Kyzikos, in the south Ephesos joined them. So did Pixodar of Karia, last of the sons of Hekatomnos, who had dethroned Ada, the sister-widow of Idrieus; he offered a daughter in marriage to one of Philip's sons. But in 336 the great danger seemed to have passed, when Philip was assassinated. The Great King boasted, whether truly or not, of having inspired the deed; and several Macedonians who found themselves in danger of arrest fled to Asia.

The Great King was no longer Arses. Bagoas had found his attitude unsatisfactory, poisoned him in turn, and slew his children. Ochos had left none of his own brothers alive; and the nearest heir was now a second-cousin, a great-grandson of Darius II. As Darius III he ascended the throne; a decent man, caught in a storm too great for him. However, at the moment there seemed to be no abnormal cause for worry, at least after he had forced Bagoas to drink his own medicine. Philip's son Alexander was only twenty, and was at once confronted by rebellion on every side; and the imperial forces in Asia Minor, without special reinforcement, went over to the offensive.

Orontobates, a Persian officer, took over Karia without resistance; Pixodar (perhaps now, and hastily) gave *him* his daughter in marriage, and opportunely died. The anti-democratic faction at Ephesos let in troops under the younger Autophradates. In the north, Memnon crossed Mount Ida with 5,000 mercenaries and appeared suddenly before Kyzikos, pretending to be the Macedonian officer Kallas. This typical stratagem failed; but returning across Ida, he forced Parmenion,

Alexander's chief marshal, to abandon the siege of Pitane in Aiolis. Meanwhile, a Persian army defeated Kallas and drove him back to a toe-hold near Troy. And so matters stood when the "boy" Alexander, having packed three tough campaigns in Europe into a single year, landed in the Troad in the spring of 334.

CHAPTER 7

CYRUS THE GREAT (558–529 B.C.)[1]

THE FOUR-WINGED GUARDIAN FIGURE

From a lonely pillar at Pasargadae the phantom of Cyrus, clad in an Elamite robe, flits across the ruins of the long-deserted city and beckons us to consider the remains of one of the world's greatest imperial dynasties: by a strange freak of archaeology we have a fleeting glimpse of a royal image arrested for eternity in stone. Many will be familiar with this great winged figure (pl. 6*a*) naming the king, the sole survivor of four which once stood on opposite sides of two doorways in the hypostyle building known as Portal R at Pasargadae.[2] The top of this monument, now vanished, was once inscribed in three languages, Old Persian, Elamite and Babylonian, and posterity must be grateful to Ker Porter[3] who, just before 1820, copied the inscription, and likewise to Flandin and Coste who left another record of it twenty years later.

The inscription itself makes a simple statement: "I (am) Cyrus the king an Achaemenian", an authentic and contemporary record of the style used by the early forerunners of the dynasty, before the reign of Darius, when titles became pompous and elaborate.

The crown worn by the king is in remarkable contrast to the simplicity of the inscription, and was perhaps intended to signify imperial majesty: a strange Persian version of a concept of the divine Pharaoh. The splendid splayed horns are those of the *Ovis longipes*

---

[1] This chapter is an amended version of an article written by the same author in *Iran*, x (1972), pp. 1–17. The chronology follows the scheme proposed by Sidney Smith in his Schweich Lectures 1940; see p. 404, n. 5.

[2] I owe this suggestion to David Stronach whose forthcoming book *Pasargadae*, on the excavations which he directed on behalf of the British Institute of Persian Studies at Pasargadae, will demonstrate the probability that four such figures, not more, existed and were, in the symmetrical fashion of Achaemenian art, placed in pairs. [Ed. Note: Actually, in *Pasargadae* (1978) 55 n. 82, Stronach modified somewhat this suggestion.] Plan of the building showing emplacement of the doorways may be conveniently examined in Carl Nylander's *Ionians in Pasargadae*, 104, fig. 34a entitled Palace "R". The doorways presumed to have been decorated with the winged figures were on the north east and south west long sides of the building.

[3] Ker Porter, *Travels in Georgia, Persia etc.* II (London, 1822), pl. 13; C. Texier, *Description de l'Arménie, la Perse et la Mésopotamie* II (Paris, 1852), pl. 84. For an illustration of Ker Porter's original water-colour sketch, now in the British Museum, see R. D. Barnett, "Sir Robert Ker Porter, Regency Artist and Traveller", *Iran* x (1972), 21f. and Pl. IV.

palaeoaegyptiacus, a variety of ram apparently common during the Middle Kingdom in Egypt, but rare thereafter.[1] It is clear that this unique crown must have come to Pasargadae from some unknown source on the coast of Phoenicia, and that it carried with it the prestige and authority of some quasi-Egyptian god which had thus travelled far beyond the Nile, in a form appropriate to Ba'al. A convincing explanation of this strange transference has recently been made by Dr R. D. Barnett: he sees in it an expression of the oecumenical attitude of the Achaemenian kings who, from the time of Cyrus onwards, adopted a liberal policy of tolerance and conciliation towards the various religions embraced within their empire.[2] I find this interpretation of the winged Cyrus the more attractive because in the nearby "Palace of Audience"[3] to which Portal R gave access there were the remains of other carvings, including a god or priest clad in a fish cloak, clearly Assyrian in origin, and derived from the protective magical figures which had once adorned the portals of Nimrud and Nineveh (pl. 6*b*). On another portal the foot of a raptorial bird reminds us not only of the legs of a divine guardian on a doorway of Sennacherib's Palace at Nineveh, but also of the claws of the dragons on the Ishtar gate at Babylon.[4] Here indeed at Pasargadae, in these quasi-Phoenician, Assyrian and Babylonian images, we have a forerunner of the Gate of All Nations which later on Xerxes was to erect at Persepolis.

[1] See F. L. Griffiths, *Beni Hassan* II, 15 and pl. 3. 35 and *AAA* IX (1922), pl. XXXVII. 1; F. E. Zeuner, *A History of Domesticated Animals*, pp. 154, 178. This type of sheep, long extinct in Egypt, is said to be represented by the modern Abyssinian, maned sheep.

[2] R. D. Barnett, "'Anath, Ba'al and Pasargadae" *Mélanges de l'Université Saint-Joseph* XLV, fasc. 25 (Beirut, 1969), 407–22 and figs. 5, 6.

[3] Now generally referred to as Palace "S", plan in Nylander, *loc. cit.* above.

[4] The Pasargadae reliefs depicting a pair of human feet followed by the clawed feet of a mythical beast are illustrated in E. Herzfeld and F. Sarre, *Iranische Felsreliefs* (Berlin, 1910), fig. 84. Brick reliefs on the Processional Street at Babylon in E. Koldewey, *The Excavations at Babylon*, translated by A. S. Johns (London, 1914), figs. 32, 33 – leg of a *sirrush* and raptorial bird on p. 48. C. J. Gadd, *The Stones of Assyria*, pl. 17, divine guardians of Sennacherib at Nineveh. See also E. Strommenger, *The Art of Mesopotamia* (1962), pl. 226, which illustrates a four-winged Assyrian figure facing right, carrying bucket and cone, and wearing a royal helmet with divine horns. This protective genius set up in the Palace of Sargon at Khorsabad, probably in 706 B.C., is iconographically in line with that of Cyrus and separated from it by not more than one hundred and sixty years. See also note 8, and T. Kawami, "A possible source for the sculpture of the Audience Hall, Pasargadae", in *Iran* x (1972) 146f.; among many antecedents there mentioned we may note in particular the relief of Sargon and Sennacherib and especially the prophylactic images flanking the doorways of Palaces and temples. Other illustrations of bull figures and fish-cloaked guardians may be seen in Carl Nylander, *Ionians in Pasargadae* (Uppsala, 1970) figs. 42a–b, 43, pp. 123, 124. Fish cloak carved on jamb of the south east doorway of the "Audience Hall" or Palace S, illustrated in *Iran* x (1972), pls II a and b (after page 163), well compared with the relief in Sennacherib's Palace at Nineveh illustrating fish man and bucket, *loc. cit.* pls. IIIa, b. Similar iconography on a cylinder seal No. 773 in the Pierpont Morgan Library, illustrated in *Iran*, x, pl. III c.

CYRUS THE GREAT

Let us return to our rather sinister winged figure (pl. 6a) which may have been remembered by Herodotus who tells us that Cyrus saw in his sleep the eldest of the sons of Hystaspes (Darius) with wings upon his shoulders, shadowing with the one wing Asia, and Europe with the other.[1] Herodotus therefore, as I surmise, may have known of the close connection between this type of winged figure and the image of Iranian majesty, which he associated with a dream prognosticating the king's death before his last, fatal campaign across the Oxus.[2]

The building in which originally four of these magnificent figures stood must have served as a processional way and portal of access to the larger hypostyle palaces, P and S, which were in the vicinity, and we can imagine the intention, namely that the king should pass on his way to the state apartments and ceremonial halls under the cover of his guardian angel. This image at Pasargadae reminds me of a magical winged guardian which at Nimrud (Calakh), the ancient military capital of Assyria, three centuries earlier had been set up in the N.W. palace of Ashurnasirpal and watched over the king as he passed along the corridors from his private apartments to the throne-room and of another, about one hundred and fifty years older, erected by Sargon II in his Palace at Khorsabad.[3]

Authorities concerned with the history of Assyrian and Iranian art have been careful to point out that these winged prophylactic genii are not portraits of the king himself, even though the Pasargadae image has a superscription identifying the figure with Cyrus. But it is worth remembering that the corresponding Assyrian winged genii often carry inscriptions naming the king, and recounting his prowess and military exploits. It is clear to me, and perhaps I am heretical in expressing this opinion, that such figures were directly associated with the magical and charismatic powers ordinarily attributed to a king in the Orient, and that these winged phantoms corresponded with a concept, as so often best expressed by Shakespeare, "There's such divinity doth hedge a king".[4]

[1] Herodotus I. 209.
[2] Herodotus I. 210: "Thus Cyrus spoke in the belief that he was plotted against by Darius; but he missed the true meaning of the dream, which was sent by the deity to forewarn him, that he was due to die then and there, and that his kingdom was to fall at last to Darius."
[3] Mallowan, *Nimrud and its Remains*, I, 103, for the reference to the winged figures along the passage ways. *Op. cit.* 120 and Folding Map III for position and description of passage P. The Assyrian relief was on the wall of the corridor between P and N. See also p. 393, n. 4. The later figure in Sargon's palace at Khorsabad is even more closely related to the winged one at Pasargadae (pl. 6a).
[4] The quotation is taken from the mouth of Claudius in *Hamlet* and in full runs, "There's such divinity doth hedge a king, that treason can but peep to what it would": singularly apposite to

THE FOUR-WINGED GUARDIAN

Much has been written about the simple formula of the trilingual inscription which once ran across the top of the image of Cyrus at Pasargadae, and it has been well demonstrated by R. Ghirshman that this is an authentic and contemporary record of the style used by the early forerunners of the Achaemenians; it was from the reign of Darius onwards that titles became pompous and elaborate.[1] The simple style of Cyrus was undoubtedly a reflection of Elamite royal custom and recalls the curt inscription at Choga Zanbil, 13th century B.C., which simply names the founder as "I Untash-Gal". None of the inscriptions at Pasargadae describe the monarch as "King of Kings". Nor do they refer to his paternity, only to the name of the clan, Achaemenian, as with Zoroaster who was never known by the name of his father, but as "the Spitamid". In this way these Pasargadae legends of which there were probably not less than twenty-four,[2] on the Palace portals, probably in three languages, are a remarkable contrast to the one hundred and ten or more royal[3] inscriptions of the later members of the dynasty, scattered throughout Persepolis and elsewhere. Inconsistencies in the style of these titles which simply mention the king, sometimes the great king, and variations in orthography belong to a time when the royal house was groping to establish itself with the aid of formulae that later would become set.

Many and elaborate dissertations have been written about whether or not the Old Persian writing on these monuments was actually inscribed during the lifetime of Cyrus or after his death. The reason for this apparently strange hesitation is a passage written by his second successor, Darius, in paragraph 70 on the great rock of Behistun which has generally been taken to mean that Darius himself claimed to have been the first to write in the Old Persian language,[4] that is, that he had invented the alphabetic cuneiform used to express his native language. Hitherto court writing had perforce used Elamite, Babylonian or Aramaic. Not all scholars accept this interpretation of the Behistun inscription and many think, and probably rightly, that Darius was not denying the existence of prior inscriptions by Cyrus in Old Persian; on the contrary he was merely claiming that he was the first to make his proclamations through the medium of Aramaic as well as other languages.

the dream of Cyrus which foretold the transference of his dynasty to a collateral branch of the family, an event which occurred after the death of his son Cambyses.

[1] R. H. Ghirshman, *JNES* XXIV (1965), 246.
[2] Nylander, "Who Wrote the Inscriptions at Pasargadae?", 156.
[3] Nylander, *op. cit.*, 158.   [4] Ghirshman, *op. cit.*, has well exposed this fallacy.

Nylander, after some hesitation, favoured the thesis that the Old Persian legends were added later, over the Elamite and Babylonian.[1] But more recently Hallock applying methods appropriate to a computer has brilliantly and briefly demonstrated the probability – it cannot amount to certainty – that the simplicity of the signs and their restricted number are to be ascribed to Cyrus himself, whose scribe was in an experimental stage of writing, and that Darius added to and elaborated the system.[2]

Archaeology comes to the support of epigraphy in elucidating the problem, for as a result of the excavations conducted by David Stronach on behalf of the British Institute of Persian Studies it has now been possible to establish the fact that while Pasargadae ceased to be the main imperial capital after the death of Cyrus, it was continuously inhabited down to Seleucid times, and moreover, from the use of the toothed or claw chisel, an instrument unknown to Cyrus' masons, it may be deduced that work was continued and completed in some of the palaces and other buildings during the reign of Darius, who added more inscriptions naming Cyrus after that monarch had died.

We know from Behistun[3] that Darius did nothing to recall the past achievements of Cyrus, neither did he name him among the eight rulers of his family whom he claimed as predecessors. Indeed the name of Cyrus is only mentioned inevitably, in a single context which tells us that the usurper Smerdis claimed to have been his son. No doubt Darius was jealous of the achievements of a major branch of the clan to which he was alien. It is interesting that this bitterness between the two separate branches of the royal house persisted over the centuries, for Ctesias the Greek physician who served for many years at the court of Artaxerxes II, 405–359 B.C., claimed that Cyrus the Great was not an Achaemenian by birth but a commoner who had ingratiated himself with Cambyses and rebelled against him.[4] We may however safely discount this statement for we know that Ctesias was an unreliable historian fed on tittle-tattle and harem gossip, and his story was merely

---

[1] On the Cyrus inscription there are two lines of Old Persian at the top, then below one line of Elamite, and finally at the bottom one line of Babylonian.

[2] R. T. Hallock, "On the Old Persian Signs", *JNES* XXIX (1970), 52–5. Hallock counted the frequency of occurrence of 2, 3, 4 and 5 wedge signs and their distribution in the various inscriptions. The apparent early occurrence of the low-frequency values *ku* (attached to the two wedge sign) and *ru* (attached to a 3 wedge sign), both employed in the writing of the name Kuruš, strongly suggests that CMa or some lost Cyrus inscription served as basic text. This is not incontrovertible evidence, nor does any such evidence exist.

[3] R. G. Kent, *Old Persian Grammar and Texts*, p. 159.

[4] Ctesias, *Persica* in Photius, *Bibliothèque* I (Paris, 1959), p. 106.

aimed at discrediting the line of Cyrus and justifying the seizure of the throne by Darius. It seems likely that the occasion for this falsification of history would have been the recording of the unsuccessful revolt of Cyrus the Younger, killed at the battle of Cunaxa, whereupon Ctesias entered the service of Artaxerxes II who may well have been gratified at being exhibited as a true scion of a branch of the Achaemenian line, which needed support for its legitimacy. The tendentious pseudo-history of Ctesias as reported by Nikolaos of Damascus thus strengthens the general credibility of Herodotus, and of Xenophon, who record the legitimate claim to the throne of Cyrus the Great as the son of Cambyses I, and therefore grandson of Cyrus I.[1]

We have seen that on the great trilingual inscription carved to the order of Darius in 520 B.C. on the precipitous rock at Behistun there is but a bare mention of the name of Cyrus. But paradoxically there is in that same inscription a wonderful testimony to the extent of Cyrus' power, for in the sixth paragraph we have a record of the twenty-three provinces which Darius the king proclaimed as having come to him by the favour of Ahuramazda – and he might well have added by the legacy of Cyrus. This we must deduce, for the inscription was completed in the third year of Darius' reign, and the first two years were wholly occupied in repressing rebellions by pretenders to the throne – the false Smerdis among others who tried to establish that he was the son of Cyrus and brother to Cambyses II. Now we know that Cambyses' reign must have been largely occupied with his conquest of Egypt, that he was troubled by internal rebellions – an unbalanced, perhaps insane monarch[2] who in his comparatively short reign of seven or eight years could not have acquired the vast empire bequeathed to Darius. We may therefore have every confidence in the later Greek and Roman historians who have left us a record of Cyrus' domains.

Thus we may accept the list of Darius' provinces on Behistun as a more or less accurate presentation of what Cyrus had first achieved for the Achaemenian empire. The Old Persian version records these countries as follows: Persia, Elam, Babylonia, Assyria, Arabia, Egypt, those who are beside the sea, Sardis, Ionia, Media, Armenia, Cappadocia, Parthia, Drangiana, Aria, Chorasmia, Bactria, Sogdiana,

---

[1] Whose reign first appeared in history through the discovery at Nineveh by R. Campbell Thompson of this earlier Cyrus in the annals of Ashur-bani-pal who exacted tribute from him, see *AAA* xx (1933), 95. Parentage in Herodotus I. 46, Xenophon, *Cyrop.* I. II. I.

[2] Herodotus III. 30. He was an overbearing monarch; allegedly killed the Apis Bull and committed suicide when his throne was in danger.

Gandhara, Scythia, Sattagydia, Arachosia, Maka: in all twenty-three provinces. We may therefore deduce that territorially Cyrus had been the first to acquire for a subsequently united Iran recognition of subject peoples who under the satrapal system were to be incorporated within a well defined jurisdiction for purposes of administration and taxation. As George Cameron and long previously Eduard Meyer have pointed out, even the lists of Darius were not concerned with administration, but were primarily lists of peoples.[1] Cyrus and indeed Darius thus represent an embryonic stage in the development of the Achaemenian empire when preparations were being made for its later juridical organisation. But already under Cyrus it is clear that the newly established monarchy included tracts of land which extended from the Greek cities on the western seaboard of Asia Minor, Palestine, Syria and Babylonia into the Caucasus and Transcaspian provinces, into the distant territory of Bactria and the vast tract of land between the Oxus and the Jaxartes rivers. There is little doubt that he had set himself the task of conquering Egypt, but death intervened and this target was left to his son Cambyses who fulfilled the grand design.

It is instructive to compare the list on the rock at Behistun with the more detailed list in Herodotus[2] which applies to the state of the empire controlled by Darius at the end of his thirty-six-year reign when he had substantially added to the legacy at his disposal at the beginning of it. Here we have the empire for administrative purposes divided into twenty provinces, each a separate satrapy paying a specified tribute: the notable and distinctive additions were of course Egypt and India, or rather the Indians who paid "a tribute exceeding that of every other people, to wit, three hundred and sixty talents of gold dust" which was reckoned at thirteen times the worth of silver or 4,680 talents. This would have been the most precious jewel of all for Cyrus' crown, but although in encompassing Bactria, Sogdiana and Gandhara he may well have gazed at the Pamirs and the Hindu Kush, he could not quite achieve that more distant goal.[3] But it is known from historical and

---

[1] See the acutely reasoned article by George G. Cameron, "The Persian Satrapies and Related Matters" in *JNES* xxxii (1973), 47ff. As regards Darius, Cameron plausibly argues, p. 50, that in the OP "the Great King or his scribes were giving in their lists less the names of provinces or satrapies [than] the names of peoples whom they deemed worthy of recognition". But the intention surely was to arrive at a system under which the peoples named would be incorporated within the empire for purposes of jurisdiction and taxation. [On the king's list being in fact a list of countries, see I. Gershevitch, *TPS*, 1979, 160f.]

[2] Herodotus III. 90–4.

[3] Arrian, *Indica* 9, 10.

topographical evidence that he established a powerful frontier fortress named Cyropolis (Kurkath),[1] which was identified as his foundation by Alexander the Great, and later by the Arabs, on the river Jaxartes. In this city he established for the first time an Achaemenian frontier post on the very boundaries of Central Asia – a bulwark against the hordes of migrant tribes who were perpetually threatening Iran from as far afield as Outer Mongolia.

We may however safely accept the testimony of Alexander's historian Arrian who says "but no one else ever invaded India, not even Cyrus, son of Cambyses, though he made an expedition against the Scythians and in all other ways was the most energetic of the kings of Asia". But he had the thrill of discovering new and unknown peoples, of incorporating them in the comity of Iranian nations, of exacting gifts in his honour and doubtless of laying down and initiating the lines on which his enormously stretched civil service was to operate under the Persian system of satrapies. Herodotus tells us:[2] "During all the reign of Cyrus, there were no fixed tributes, but the nations severally brought gifts to the king. On account of this and other such like doings, the Persians say that Darius was a huckster, Cambyses a master, and Cyrus a father; for Darius looked to making a gain in everything; Cambyses was harsh and reckless; while Cyrus was gentle and provided them with all manner of goods."

From Darius' tribute list we are able to compare the amounts paid in silver talents by each province and we may note that the ninth province of Darius, Babylonia and Assyria, which contributed a thousand talents was by far the richest prize: the acquisition of these Mesopotamian territories occurred in the last decade of Cyrus' reign, 539 B.C. It is also noticeable that as soon as Sardis and Lydia fell into his lap, probably about 545 B.C., or possibly a year or two later,[3] together with the wealthy Greek cities of Ionia, he must have been enriched by a great accretion of gold and silver indispensable to the financing of his campaigns.

---

[1] See E. Benveniste, "La Ville de Cyreschata", *JA* CCXXXIV Années 1943–5 (1947), pp. 163–6 for a summary of the evidence and references to the classical authorities. Alexander, according to Strabo XI. 4, and Quintus Curtius VII. 6. 20, had desired to spare the city out of respect for the memory of its founder, Cyrus. The position of this site has been marked on Map 16.

[2] Herodotus III. 89.

[3] H. T. Wade-Gery in *JHS* LXXI (1951), p. 219, note 38, deduces from Herodotus that Sardis did not fall before 544 B.C. – battle of Pallene 546, fall of Sardis perceptibly later; he therefore prefers Herodotus' evidence to the conjecture based on the Nabonidus Chronicle that Cyrus defeated Croesus in 547 B.C. See also p. 404, n. 5.

CYRUS THE GREAT

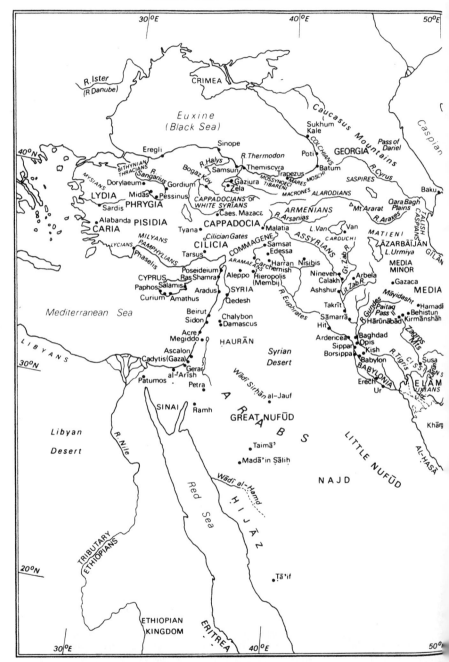

Map 16. Map showing the extent of the Achaemenian empire under Cyrus the Great and Darius.

THE FOUR-WINGED GUARDIAN

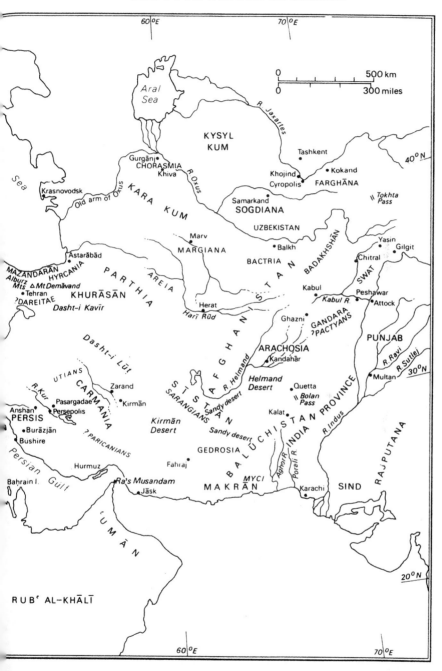

Much money must also have been added to the Persian treasury through Cyrus' incorporation of the provinces that stretched along and behind the southern Iranian seaboard, particularly the hinterland which contained the lines of caravan routes to India – Parsa, Drangiana, Arachosia and the territory called Maka, probably the ancient Makkan which at this period presumably referred to territory on either side of the Persian Gulf and may have included Oman. We have only to turn to Darius' tribute lists to appreciate the outstanding value of these satrapies. And here archaeology comes to the aid of history, for Strabo[1] tells us that there were other palaces besides Persepolis and Pasargadae and he mentions one "on the coast near Taokē as it is called". We may ask if this is not to be identified with a remarkable discovery appropriately made in Cyrus' twenty-fifth centennial year by an archaeological expedition under the direction of 'Alī Akbar Safarāz: two lines of beautifully and simply carved column bases found in the course of excavating a palace of Cyrus the Great, some 30 kilometres from the Persian Gulf off the highway connecting Bushire and Burāzjān, in an area which had previously turned up Achaemenian artifacts.[2] This, we may be certain, is a herald of other discoveries to come, and in the course of time, remains attributable to Cyrus himself will surely be found in more than one outpost of his empire.

In assessing the accretion of wealth that came to Iran from the time of Cyrus onwards we should not forget the great influx of men and animals as well as timber and other commodities – gold from Sardis and Bactria, which together with Sogdiana supplied lapis lazuli and carnelian: in the time of Darius, Cilicia, according to Herodotus, contributed 360 white horses and Babylonia 400 boy eunuchs.

ANCIENT TRAVEL

These considerations lead us to broach another topic, namely ancient travel. How long did it take for the armies, embassies, officials and traders to cross from one end of the empire to another? We know that relays of post horses supplied at regular stations spread out at a day's interval over the royal roads and the Royal Mail were elaborately organized, as indeed they had to be if so vast an empire was not to fall

---

[1] Strabo xv. 3.
[2] "Palace of Cyrus Unearthed", A. T. Zand in *Tehran Journal*, June 1, 1971, with illustration of three column bases.

apart.¹ How long did it take Cyrus to march across to Sardis in the campaign which resulted in the capture of that city? According to Herodotus² the distance from Susa to Sardis over the approved route worked out at about 1,700 miles and was accomplished in 90 days; at the rate of about 19 miles a day – an exhausting rate of travel – it is likely that the preliminary subjugation of Western Asia Minor and the intervening territory must have taken Cyrus at least a year. In the opposite direction we have remarkable evidence of envoys travelling from Iran to Afghanistan, a distance which I would reckon at approximately 1,200 miles over one of three possible routes. On one of the Persepolis Fortress tablets published by R. T. Hallock³ we have a record of a guide named Zišanduš and his five boys who escort a lone woman, perhaps a princess, all the way from Susa to supposedly (Kandaraš) Kandahar. This is one of the set of texts of the 5th century B.C. which give evidence of distinguished couriers who escorted Indians, Cappadocians, Egyptians, men of Sardis and others. "Nothing mortal travels so fast as these messengers" says Herodotus in another context – speaking about the Royal Mail – "and these men will not be hindered from accomplishing at their best speed the distance which they have to go, either by snow, or rain, or heat, or by the darkness of night."⁴ These distinguished couriers who escorted special parties were the ancestors of those who conduct Swan's Tours and the like – they had to know every inch of the road and to be *persona grata* in the potentially hostile or friendly territories through which they passed. Perhaps the most distinguished of all these messengers was the angel Raphael who in disguise and for wages offered Tobit to escort his son all the way from Nineveh through Ecbatana (Hamadān) to Rhages (near Tehran). "Do you know the way to Media?" Tobias asked. "Yes," he said "I have often been there. I am familiar with all the routes and know them well."⁵ Journeys of this kind had of course to be provided for by the house of Tobit, Jewish bankers, who during the late Assyrian empire under Sennacherib and Ezarhaddon had wisely dispersed their

---

¹ Herodotus VIII. 98 and note in the Nonesuch Herodotus on the Persian posts. See also Esther 8. 10, Ahasuerus (Xerxes) 485–464 B.C. sent letters all over the empire by means of swift horses that were bred from the royal stud.

² Herodotus V. 53 and note in the Nonesuch Herodotus.

³ R. T. Hallock, *Persepolis Fortification Tablets* (Chicago, 1969), PF 1440 and 1550. The ration documents, written in Elamite, date from the thirteenth through the twenty-eighth year of Darius I, 509–494 B.C.

⁴ Herodotus VIII. 98. The mounted couriers of the express service to whom Herodotus refers are named as *pirradaziš* in the Elamite texts.

⁵ Tobit 5. 6–8. Long distance couriers in the reign of Artaxerxes, see Esther 8. 9–12.

CYRUS THE GREAT

interests both in Assyria and in Media, in anticipation of a clash between the two.

CURRICULUM VITAE

A consideration of the vast distances that had to be covered by the armies of Cyrus for the acquisition of the empire must lead us to reflect, if only briefly, on the order and sequence of his campaigns. We know that he was about 40 years old when he came to the throne and about 70 when he died on campaign in Transoxiana. He must have been a very tough old man: so far as we know, his *curriculum vitae* runs approximately as follows: born 598 B.C., son of Cambyses I[1] and of Mandane daughter of Astyages king of the Medes;[2] married, probably not later than 578 B.C. to Cassandane[3] his best loved wife who bore him a son and heir, Cambyses II; when she died he ordered all his subjects to go into mourning; married secondly to Amytis; ascended to the throne 558 B.C.; conquest of Medes, capture of their king Astyages, and of the Median capital Ecbatana (Hamadān) 550 B.C.; submission of Hyrcania and Parthia[4] 549 B.C.; submission of Lydia, capture of Sardis and of king Croesus about 545 B.C.; capture of Babylon and king Nabonidus 539 B.C.; death beyond the Oxus fighting the Massagetae 529 B.C.[5]

[1] Herodotus I. 107 Astyages feared the vision too much to give his daughter to any Mede worthy to mate with his family, but wedded her to a Persian, a man whom he had known to be well born and of a quiet temper: for Astyages held Cambyses to be much lower than a Mede of middle estate.

[2] List of Median and Persian tribes in Herodotus I. 125. The Persians had long been ill content that the Medes should rule them, I. 132. The Medes had ruled all Asia for 128 years (except for 28 years of Scythian sway) I. 130. Note the remark in Herodotus I. 120 that the Medes and the Persians were of different stock and that the Medes lived in mountainous country, with access to the plains I. 110: "The foothills of the mountains where this cowherd pastured his kine are to the north of Agbatana, towards the Euxine sea: for the rest of Media is everywhere on level plain, but here, on the side of the Saspires [Azerbaijan] the land is very high and mountainous and covered with woods."

[3] Herodotus II. 1 for Cassandane wife of Cyrus. See also Herodotus I. 107, 108 for Mandane mother of Cyrus, who was married by Astyages to a Persian of good family "but much inferior to a Mede of even middle condition"; but his father was none the less king of Anshan, at that time no doubt a petty vassal state of Media. Ctesias, *Persica, loc. cit.* differs from Herodotus but is unreliable.

[4] Herodotus I. 130, 153, 177, and notes in Nonesuch Herodotus on the sequence of these campaigns.

[5] I accept the general chronology proposed by Sidney Smith, Schweich Lectures, *op. cit.*, p. 29. "According to Dinon, Cyrus the Great was 40 years old when he came to the throne, and reigned 30 years. Dinon is not reliable, and the figures are suspicious, but they fit the probabilities. Cyrus died in 529; his reign may well have begun in 558, and he may have been born in 598 for his grandfather was already king of Parsumash in 640." Smith also recalls, *op. cit.* 123 note 35, that Herodotus gives 29 years for the length of Cyrus' reign against Ctesias and Justin 30 and that the difference may be due to the months of the Babylonian year, "beginning of Kingship".

The date of the fall of Sardis however is still uncertain. It seems improbable that it can be Lydia that is mentioned in a corrupt passage in the Nabonidus Chronicle which states that in *Iyyar* (that

CHRONOLOGY OF CONQUESTS

The situation which confronted Cyrus at the beginning of his reign has been admirably and succinctly expounded by Sidney Smith in his Schweich Lectures of 1940 as follows: "The Assyrians by hard fighting had kept open the passes into Media, Armenia and Cappadocia for three centuries. After the fall of Nineveh (in 612 B.C.) the eastern and northern passes were held by the Medes, the north-western were only open by favour of the Cilicians and Lydians, and subject to a treaty. The traffic from the Phoenician ports was interfered with by pirates from the Lydian coast, and by Greeks, the allies of the Egyptians." Further, Nabonidus, the last king of Babylon, "had attempted to secure that trade from the Persian Gulf was not diverted westwards; it was desirable to control the increasingly prosperous trade of Southern Arabia and the Red Sea".[1] Cyrus, in his ambitious attempt to assume empire in western Asia was governed by such considerations. The cycle of trade had to penetrate these political and geographical barriers, and we may watch him in pursuit of these objectives during the thirty years of his reign. The first decade, or most of it, was occupied in consolidating his position under the king of the Medes, whose daughter, Mandane, was his mother, that is to say, Astyages was his grandfather on the maternal side. These years must have been devoted by Cyrus to increasing his authority over the confederation of Persian tribes and to the intrigues which led to the capture of Ecbatana. Thereafter he inherited a not inconsiderable Median empire about which we know little except in so far as scattered references in the later Greek

is May) of the 9th year of Nabonidus Cyrus marched to the land of Lu(?) ... – the reading of the cuneiform signs is uncertain – and fought its king, for there would, here, in any case be a discrepancy between the Chronicle and the account in Herodotus I. 77 as regards the timing of the capture of Sardis, which tells us that Croesus had decided to summon his allies in the Spring in the 5th month after his indecisive encounter with Cyrus. He was taken by surprise, for Cyrus proceeded immediately to the attack which must have happened in November and not in May, the month mentioned in the Nabonidus Chronicle for Cyrus' march. See p. 399, n. 3, p. 412, n. 4. I am indebted to Professor O. R. Gurney for informing me that H. T. Wade-Gery had written to him, calling attention to these discrepancies; Wade-Gery has referred very briefly to the fact that the date of the capture of Sardis is lost, in *JHS* LXXI (1951), p. 215 note 15, but on p. 229 note 38, on the basis of Herodotus' evidence in connection with Greek historical events, proposes 544 B.C. as a more likely date. We may safely conclude that Sardis did not fall in 547 nor in 546, the date given by Eusebius, for there is no mention of Cyrus in the Nabonidus Chronicle for that year, but the city could have fallen at any time between 545 and the attack on Babylon in 540. A date as near to 545 as possible on grounds of historical probability is acceptable, for Cyrus must have required some years to consolidate his conquests in Asia Minor before proceeding to attack Babylonia, his most valuable prize. For dates proposed by the Greek Chronologers see How and Wells, *A Commentary on Herodotus* I. 98. Note also that Apollodoros *apud* Diog. Laert. I, 37f. gives a date which may be fixed at 546/5, see F. Jacoby, *Apollodors Chronik* (Berlin, 1902).

[1] Sidney Smith, *op. cit.*, p. 39.

histories[1] bear witness to its extensive ramifications in the east. The year after the defeat of Astyages, Hyrcania and Parthia in Transcaspia acknowledged a new master, readily enough perhaps, and this allegiance secured Cyrus' eastern flanks and enabled him to conduct the first of his great imperial campaigns – against Sardis; but probably that had entailed a distant march to the Caspian in order to establish his authority there.

It seems unlikely that he would have attempted the campaigns further east against Bactria and the Sacae or Sogdiana at so early a stage in his career. The take-over of Parthia and Hyrcania, formerly Median dependencies, provided him with a bulwark of security before embarking on his distant marches into Asia Minor where, according to Herodotus, "Cyrus in person subjected the upper regions, conquering every nation, and not suffering one to escape".[2] He also adds: "of these conquests I shall pass by the greater portion, and give an account of those only which gave him most trouble, and are the worthiest of mention" – proof that much information was available for which he could not find room in his histories – an assurance that we need not wholly discard the amplified accounts in the later Greek histories of Cyrus' activities here and elsewhere.[3]

The second decade must have been largely spent in the conquest and consolidation not only of the whole of Iran, but also of those distant flanks which were to put him in touch with the countries controlled by the great cities now named Marv and Samarkand. How many campaigns were involved we do not know, though as more excavations are to be conducted on these eastern confines, I do not doubt that we shall gradually come into possession of many wonderful clues.

We must however accept the fact previously mentioned that Cyrus never reached India, a design no doubt frustrated by his death in the field some hundreds of miles distant from its frontier. Arrian's testimony in this respect is certainly sound.[4]

How many campaigns in the field did Cyrus conduct in the course of this second decade 545–539 B.C. that is between the capture of Sardis

---

[1] We may accept the historicity of some Median control in the east – at least as far as Hyrcania and Parthia, but Arrian was not a wholly reliable historian, for he believed that the Indians living between the Indus and the Kabul rivers had been subject to the Assyrians. *Indica* 9, 10, also 1. 3.

[2] Herodotus I. 177.

[3] Herodotus I. 96: "I know besides three ways in which the story of Cyrus is told, all differing from my own narrative."

[4] *Indica* 9, 10. Pliny, *H.N.* VI. 92 recorded that Kapisa (modern Kafshan) perhaps not much more than 250 miles from the upper Indus river was destroyed by Cyrus. The place is thought by A. D. H. Bivar to have been north of Kabul. See his chapter in *Central Asia*, ed. Gavin Hambly (London, 1969), p. 20.

and of Babylon? It is difficult to believe that he would have been away from home during all that time, for continued absence from the seat of government for so long would have constituted a danger to his dynasty. We know that his great imperial predecessors the Assyrians had conducted annual campaigns, but such marches to and fro rarely exceeded some five or six hundred miles, whereas Cyrus had to undertake the moving of armies up to five times that distance. It is reasonable to think that in the course of this second decade, approximately, he must have returned to his bases in Elam and Media at least three times,[1] however confident he may have been in his satraps and allowing for the fact that his kingdom was sustained by the continuous acquisition of wealth that surged to the homeland on the tides of victory.

We have unfortunately no knowledge of the order in which he conducted his campaigns during this period, but perhaps we may be justified in postulating that Alexander, whose historians must have had intelligence about Cyrus' military logistics, trod on much the same tracks, and for this reason I would suggest that although at the outset he must have marched due eastwards below the Caspian, at least one march was conducted by him down from the direction of Bactria through the Helmand basin, Arachosia, Gedrosia, Kirmān and Makrān. Again we may consult Arrian, as I think, with some confidence; Nearchos reported that an attempt to reach India through South Baluchistan resulted in the loss of the greater part of Cyrus' army.[2]

However that may be, Berosus follows Herodotus in asserting that Cyrus possessed all the rest of Asia at the time when he first attacked Babylon in 540 B.C.;[3] as is confirmed by the famous inscribed cylinder in which Cyrus says "The kings of the Westland dwelling in tents, all those brought heavy tribute to me in Babylon and kissed my feet."[4]

---

[1] Xenophon, *Cyrop.* VIII. 1–3 states that before his death, Cyrus, now a very old man, returned for the seventh time in his reign to Persia. This statement may well be a true record of the facts – long absences punctuated by visits to the seat of government at home, about three times during each of the last two decades when he was acquiring his empire.

[2] *Anabasis* VI. 24. *Indica* 9. "Cyrus son of Cambyses had got through with only seven survivors, for Cyrus did come into these parts intending to invade the country of India; but before he could do so he lost the greater part of his army by the barrenness and difficulty of the route."

[3] He entered the city on 3rd Marcheswan, 539 B.C. (corrected date). Sidney Smith, "A Persian Verse Account of Nabonidus", *Babylonian Historical Texts* (1924), p. 28. It should be noted that Sidney Smith, Schweich Lectures, *op. cit.* p. 119 note 18, drew attention to the fact that all the years given in his *Babylonian Historical Texts* are one too late – an error in the use of the Canon of Ptolemy. Corrected dating has been used here.

[4] See in general the note in Nonesuch Herodotus I. 177 and Dougherty, *Nabonidus and Belshazzar* (1929), p. 161.

This climax of his military career was, according to Xenophon,[1] immediately preceded by the reduction of Arabia where Nabonidus for ten years exiled to the oasis of Taimā' had perhaps been attempting to establish control over the caravan routes and trade on the Persian Gulf. At all events the year 539 B.C. marks the triumphant beginning of Cyrus' third and last decade.

Precisely what Cyrus achieved militarily during the last, third, decade of his reign we do not know, although the consensus of Greek historians is that he died somewhere at the north-eastern end of the empire, between Oxus and Jaxartes, according to Herodotus slain in battle by Tomyris, queen of the Massagetae – perhaps a Scythian tribe. It is logical to assume that this was a period of consolidation, as is attested by the fact that he appointed his son and designated successor Cambyses as religious ruler of Babylon, while, according to Ctesias, before his death he designated Cambyses' younger brother as ruler over the eastern provinces.[2] We may, therefore, be certain that Cyrus conducted at least one great march on his eastern frontier during that last stage of his life.

CAPTURE OF BABYLON

Whatever he may have achieved militarily between 539 and 529 B.C. it is clear that the moment of his greatest triumph was in 539 B.C. when according to the Nabonidus Chronicle "In the month of Araḥsamna, the third day, Cyrus entered Babylon. Green twigs, doubtless reeds or rushes to smooth the path of his chariot, were spread in front of him. The state of 'peace' was imposed on all the city. Cyrus sent greetings to all Babylon."[3]

The event marked a critical shift in the balance of power held by the contending forces of Western Asia. The peoples of Iran had for three quarters of a century been allied to Babylon, ever since the Medes made a combined attack on Nineveh in 612 and overthrew the empire of Assyria. Even as late as about 550 B.C. Cyrus had an understanding with Nabonidus that enabled this Babylonian monarch to invest Harran which had suffered Median occupation, and rebuild the temple of the Moon God. But when once Lydia had been overthrown the balance of power was upset and the interests of Babylonia and Iran were in conflict.

---

[1] *Cyropaedia* VII. 4.
[2] Herodotus I. 208. Nonesuch note and Ctesias, *Persica*, p. 109.
[3] Nabonidus Chronicle III. 12–22, and see Xenophon, *Cyropaedia* VII. 5. 20–6.

THE CYRUS CYLINDER

The capture of Babylon, richest of all the Persian satrapies, inevitably brought in its train hegemony over the rich cities of Syria and Palestine, as well as the Phoenician coast which had formerly fallen within the Babylonian orbit, if not entirely under its control. There followed the return of the Jewish exiles from Babylon, and the charter granted by Cyrus which we shall consider briefly later. Maurice Dunand has recently well demonstrated that the tolerance and liberal help granted on this occasion for the return of the Jews to Zion was the corner stone of a policy which was designed to take over the remnants of the old Babylonian empire in Phoenicia and Palestine. There is much archaeological evidence that the rebuilding of the temple of Jerusalem was followed by the repair and foundation of a chain of fortified sites which ran down from the Gulf of Issus at about the latitude of modern Alexandretta to the marches of Palestine where the Jews were doubtless expected to co-operate in sustaining a defensive bulwark against Egypt. The prophet who is usually referred to as Deutero-Isaiah leaves us in no doubt about his loyalty. "Thus says the Lord to his anointed Cyrus, whose right hand I have grasped, to subdue nations before him and ungird the loins of kings..." (Isaiah 45.1). The interests of Jewry and Iran thus went hand in hand and although we do not yet know to what extent Cyrus himself took a hand in engineering these defences, his impetus must be discerned behind the great quadrangular blocks of dressed masonry which the Achaemenians encouraged on the margins of river beds and rocky hill sides, as well as in the temples and fortresses at Sidon, Byblos, Banyas, Amrith-Marathus, Jerusalem, Lachish and other sites on the way to Egypt.[1]

CUNEIFORM RECORDS: THE CYRUS CYLINDER

Nothing could be more interesting historically than the examination of Cyrus' campaigns in Babylonia and of his final peaceful entry into the capital. For our reconstruction of these events we depend not only on Greek sources, principally Herodotus, who wrote less than a century later, and Xenophon, but on the contemporary cuneiform records themselves – both the laconic and incisive Nabonidus Chronicle relating

---

[1] Maurice Dunand, "La Défense du Front Méditerranéen de l'empire Achéménide" in *The Role of the Phoenicians in the Interactions of Mediterranean Civilizations*, ed. by William Ward, Beirut American University Centennial Publication (1968). The full list of sites is therein mentioned: doubtless Phoenician masons were often used in their construction, but plans and siting have in many cases an Achaemenian impress.

to these last days and the vivid records of Cyrus himself, first the famous Cyrus cylinder which he must have deposited in Babylon and then a highly coloured and prejudiced verse account. These two latter documents are masterpieces of political propaganda and although not the first of their kind in the ancient world are skilled instruments of tendentious history: and in addition there are the official proclamations, inscriptions on bricks and the ordinary day to day business records from which we may strike a balance and arrive at a proper appreciation of the situation.

It is significant that in many of the documents which relate to Cyrus' activities in Babylonia the titulary describes him as king of Anshan which, at this period and in this context, may well have denoted the extensive tract of territory south east of Elam where Pasargadae and later, Persepolis, were situated.[1] The Cyrus cylinder in an appropriate Babylonian form, and in contrast to the simple titulary of the Pasargadae inscription says: "I am Cyrus, king of the world, great king, legitimate king, king of Sumer and Akkad, king of the four quarters (of the world), son of Cambyses, great king, king of Anshan, descendant of Teispes, great king, king of Anshan, of a family (which) always (exercised) kingship; whose rule Bel and Nabu love, whom they want as king to please their hearts."[2] In this way Cyrus characteristically and with diplomatic astuteness assimilated the acceptable style of titulary to which Babylonia, heir of Sumerian kingship, had by long tradition been accustomed.

We cannot doubt that as with all great conquerors the elements of

---

[1] Sidney Smith, Schweich Lectures, *op. cit.*, p. 28 and map No. 1 opposite, "both Parsumash and Anzan designate the province round Pasargadae" and pp. 120–3. In *PBA* LV (1969), "Elamite Problems", p. 256, the present writer took the view that Anshan was "approximately coterminous with the present-day territory of the Bakhtiari", a theory which perhaps finds support in the Sumerian Epic entitled *Enmerkar and the Lord of Aratta*, translation by S. N. Kramer (U. of Pa., 1952) introduction page 1 and lines 70–82, 106–10, 165–7, where Anshan appears clearly to have been associated with mountainous territory in the reign of Enmerkar, third millennium B.C., E.D.II period. Dr Georgina Herrmann has also kindly recalled for me a passage translated by S. N. Kramer in *The Sumerians* (1963), p. 273 with reference to the Epic entitled *Lugalbanda and Enmerkar*. Lugalbanda a henchman of the latter volunteered to seek help for his master by making a dangerous journey to the city of Aratta. "He takes up his weapons, crosses the seven mountains that reach from one end of Anshan to the other" – or, as the poet puts it, from the "shoulder" of Anshan to the "head" of Anshan – and finally arrives with joyful step at his destination. The identification of frontiers, never firmly fixed in antiquity, is however always difficult and boundaries frequently changed in the course of time, so that we need not accept evidence which holds good for the third millennium as applicable to later periods. John Hansman's view coincides more nearly with that quoted from Sidney Smith *supra*, see *Iran* X (1972), "Elamites, Achaemenians and Anshan", 111f.

[2] Pritchard, p. 316, has mention of Anshan in the fourth line.

luck and good timing enabled Cyrus to triumph over Babylonia, which proved to be the richest of all his satrapies. Nabonidus, the last king of Babylon, who ascended the throne in 556 B.C., was tainted by his northern ancestry; he was the son of the great high priestess of the temple of the moon god Sin, named E-Ḫul-Ḫul in Harran and reigned for seventeen troubled years. He soon fell foul of the priesthood by introducing an alien theology and an unacceptable image of the moon in eclipse that amounted to heretical practice. So uneasy did relations with the priests become that he went into self-imposed exile in the oasis of Taimā' in N.W. Arabia, a ten year Odyssey, leaving behind him as regent his son Belshazzar who, according to the Old Testament,[1] witnessed the final writing on the wall of the palace at Babylon, on the eve of its downfall. During the many years of his exile the New Year festival at Babylon which required the personal presence of the king could not be celebrated, and the people of that city and of the surrounding country did not forgive him for this disgrace.

Thus when Cyrus began to undertake his campaign in 540 B.C. Babylonian affairs were at a low ebb and there was little loyalty to the ruler of the country. Gobryas (Gubaru), governor of Gutium,[2] who had been the principal general of Nebuchadrezzar, defected to the side of Cyrus, who within a year was able to make a peaceful entry into Babylon having first, according to Herodotus, used a cunning stratagem, namely the diversion of a main canal in order to overcome a formidable obstruction to entry.

The Cyrus cylinder tells us of the restoration of the derelict city and of its sanctuaries, of a return of the gods to their ancient enclosures both in Babylon and elsewhere[3] and of the re-institution of the New Year festival, for Marduk in his mercy had granted forgiveness on account of the probity and right conduct of the new prince, Cyrus, who respected the ways of the gods of the country. Not only did Cyrus burn the false images of his predecessor, but he instituted within the city a new slum clearance scheme and: "brought relief to their dilapidated housing (thus) putting an end to their (main) complaints".

It seems most probable that Cyrus' entry had been assisted by the

[1] Daniel 5. 5; wrongly therein described as the king.
[2] Sidney Smith, Schweich Lectures, *op. cit.*, p. 47 considers that Gubaru is to be identified with the Gobryas in Xenophon's account and is not to be confused with the Persian Gubaru who was appointed by Cyrus satrap of Babylon immediately after his own entry. The latter was probably the Gobryas mentioned by Herodotus, one of Darius' trusty officers.
[3] J. Jordan, "Ausgrabungen in Uruk-Warka 1928/9", *APAW* 1929. 7 (1930), 48 (= *U.V.B.* 1). He is known to have contributed to the restoration of E-anna in Uruk (Erech).

large community of Jews which had been deported by Nebuchadrezzar II from Judah under Jehoiakin[1] sixty years before; these exiles believed that in spite of their captive prosperity they would receive more liberal treatment at Persian hands. In this they were right and, as we learn from the book of Ezra, Cyrus gave a charter to the Jews for the restoration of the temple in Jerusalem and the return of the utensils sequestered by Nebuchadrezzar.[2] It is interesting that no images or statuary came into question for these would have been anathema in the Jewish Temple. However that may be, part of the community under Sheshbazzar (probably a Jew) and Zerubbabel returned to Zion and joined the small remnant that still held Israel together.[3] The remainder were loath to leave the commercial prosperity which they must obviously have acquired under Babylonian rule, however intolerant in religious matters their Babylonian masters may have been.

CYRUS' TOLERATION: FOREIGN POLICY

Religious toleration was a remarkable feature of Persian rule and there is no question that Cyrus himself was a liberal-minded promoter of this humane and intelligent policy. Many other examples of Cyrus' help in restoring Babylonian and alien shrines could be quoted, for this was part of a well thought-out policy. At Ur of the Chaldees, for example, a great centre for the worship of the Moon god Nanna, Cyrus installed a new gate in the great Temenos wall which had first been built by Nebuchadrezzar as a sacred enclosure for the principal temples in that city. Within the lining of the gatebox socket, Cyrus' bricks proclaimed his might and liberality and he himself restored one of the temples.[4] At the neighbouring city of Uruk, one of the principal urban centres of S. Babylonia, a command was given to four of the king's officers for

[1] II Kings 24. 10.   [2] Ezra 6. 1–5.

[3] Ezra 2 gives a register of those who returned but there is a discrepancy between the figures given there and those recorded in Nehemiah and Esdras. None the less, between 30,000 and 40,000 Jews took advantage of the offer. A much smaller contingent of 1,500 persons returned later from Babylonia under Ezra in the seventh year of Artaxerxes (458 B.C.).

[4] Cyrus adopted the pompous style of titulary used by royalty in Babylon. Burnt bricks of Erech (Uruk) are inscribed "Cyrus builder of Esagila and Ezida, son of Cambyses, Great King am I". In this manner he honoured Marduk and Nabu under a titulary used previously by Nebuchadrezzar. See George Smith, *TSBA* II (1873), opp. p. 148, Weissbach, *Die Keilinschriften der Achämeniden* (1911) pp. 8–9. In the same city, Uruk, he also contributed to the upkeep of E-anna. Similarly at Ur bricks were inscribed "Cyrus King of all, King of Anshan, son of Cambyses, King of Anshan. The great gods have delivered all the lands into my hand; the land I have made to swell in a peaceful habitation." *UET* I (1928), No. 194.; *UE* IX (1962), 7–8; *Antiqs. Journal* III, No. 4 (Oct. 1923), p. 315, pl. XXV.

CYRUS' TOLERATION

the provision of bowmen to guard the shepherds: "in accordance with the yearly arrangement in the barracks which are upon the great river", that is on the Euphrates. This edict delivered in the very first year of his occupation, shows that Cyrus was determined to keep order in the administration of Babylonia immediately after occupation, and that his Civil Affairs Officers had in readiness a properly prepared and well thought out plan for taking over the administration of a newly conquered country.[1] From these official proclamations, as well as from many other documents, we know that business went on as usual, for the selling of date groves, the acquisition of land, the renting of ships, the transactions of goldsmiths and the like. Eight out of the twelve Achaemenian business documents found at Ur were written in his reign.[2]

One remarkable characteristic which many historians have attributed to Cyrus is his clemency to fallen rulers, in the true fashion of medieval chivalry. We may consider the treatment of three of his chief opponents: Croesus, Astyages and Nabonidus. It is Herodotus' story that Cyrus condemned Croesus to be burnt on a pyre and there follows the legend of the miraculous intervention of Apollo to save him, when the flames could not have been extinguished by human hands. But historians have rightly objected that the pollution of fire by human sacrifice would have been anathema and contrary to Persian religious practice. Bacchylides[3] who lived nearer to the time of Croesus – he was born about forty years after the fall of Sardis – preserved the truth: that Croesus attempted suicide. We may infer that Cyrus saved him from the flames – a more probable story, and one that accords with Greek tradition, namely that Cyrus used conquered princes to advise him in the administration of their former domains. There is no need to invoke a mutilated passage in the Nabonidus Chronicle which some scholars have interpreted as meaning that Cyrus marched against the country Ly...possibly Lydia[4]

---

[1] R. P. Dougherty, *Archives from Erech, Neo-Babylonian to Persian Periods* (1933), p. 34, No. 102. The document was dated "1st year of Cyrus, king of countries".

[2] Dougherty, *op. cit.*, Nos. 92, 101, 109.

[3] Bacchylides, ed. by R. C. Jebb, *Epinikion III*, lines 28f., dated 468 B.C. Commentary on this episode, see A. R. Burn, *Persia and the Greeks*, p. 42 and note 9. There was good oriental precedent for the burning of a defeated prince: best known is the case of the Assyrian Shamash-shum-ukin, in Greek legend known as Sardanapalus who, when defeated by his brother Ashur-bani-pal, perished in the flames of his own palace: see Mallowan, *Nimrud and its Remains* I, 246; the record of that event was preserved on a fragment of a prism found in "the library", room N.T.12 of the building known as Ezida, in Calah. Other examples of self-immolation on a funeral pyre are: Boges, Herodotus VII. 107; Hamilcar, Herodotus VII. 167; Zimri, I Kings 16, 18.

[4] Pritchard, p. 306. Sidney Smith, *Babylonian Historical Texts*, p. 112, line 16. See also p. 404f., n. 5.

and killed its king, for it is now recognized that the Akkadian word *iduk* can mean fought, not necessarily killed.[1] Moreover the sign read as Ly is almost illegible. Even if the sign may be read Ly... another interpretation is possible: that the country was Ly(cia) conquered by Cyrus before its neighbour Caria which capitulated without striking a blow because the Carians had seen the fearful fate that had befallen its neighbours. Incidentally Lycia is mentioned in Hittite records and once in an Akkadian text from the ancient Syrian city of Ugarit.[2] It may be however that the Nabonidus Chronicle in this passage refers to some other country, neither Lydia nor Lycia, and in any case this text as it stands cannot be taken as evidence that Cyrus killed Croesus: we may still accept the testimony of the Greek historians who reckoned that his life was saved.

As regards Astyages there is no question that Cyrus treated him honourably after the fall of the Median Empire and the investment of Ecbatana. Indeed Cyrus was his grandson, and grandsons do not kill their own grandfathers. The case of Nabonidus the last king of Babylon was different, even though Abydenus according to Eusebius and Josephus alleged that the captive king was honourably exiled to Carmania. The virulence of Cyrus' propaganda against Nabonidus however and the deadly hostility of the Babylonian priesthood allowed of no generous solution: Cyrus was nothing if not a diplomatist and knew that here mercy would have been dangerous. Xenophon knew better and has left us a dramatic picture of the king dagger in hand awaiting death at the hands of two of Cyrus' nobles Gadatas and Gobryas, probably in the great Throne-Room of his palace at Babylon.[3] Sidney Smith has commented aptly: "The stories of the invariably merciful treatment of conquered kings by Cyrus are propaganda material in the legends, and also testimony to a new conscience in international affairs, for no conqueror would previously have desired such a reputation."[4]

The Gadatas mentioned as one of the assassins of Nabonidus may

---

[1] H. Tadmor, "Historical Implications of the Correct Rendering of Akkadian *dâku*", *JNES* XVII (1958), 129.

[2] J. Garstang and O. R. Gurney, *The Geography of the Late Hittite Empire*, see index under Lycia and Lukka Lands, particularly p. 82 for various references and discussion of topographical problems in the Hittite records. See also *Ugaritica* v, 87, letter from the king of Ugarit to the king of Alashia mentioning *mât lukkaa*, line 23, and note 5 on pp. 88–9 on geographical identifications at this period.

[3] Xenophon, *Cyropaedia* VII. v. 29, 30.

[4] Sidney Smith, Schweich Lectures, *op. cit.*, p. 36.

RELIGION

possibly have been the officer named as satrap in Ionia under Darius,[1] who gave him a sharp reprimand for not having respected the privileges accorded to the priests of Apollo in a sanctuary near Magnesia. The only predecessor who can have rewarded the priests of Apollo in this district was Cyrus for whom "a favourable oracle was worth more than a battle".[2] This instance of intelligent diplomacy towards foreign priesthoods is one that is wholly in accord with what we know of Cyrus' policy when laying down the foundations of the Achaemenian empire.

INTRODUCTION OF COINAGE

Cyrus' conquest of Lydia resulted in yet another important innovation in so far as Persia was concerned, namely the introduction of coinage into his realm – an innovation usually attributed to Darius. Herodotus[3] recorded that it was Croesus who introduced the first coinage of gold and silver side by side, and the very scarce heavy lion and bull coinage is attributable to him.[4] But there are, as Sir Edward Robinson has informed me, two known Croesid "lion and bull" issues the second of which has been discovered in various hoards, all later than Croesus, and lighter than the old standard – conforming more closely in weight with the first darics and silver sigloi. It is therefore tempting to infer that it was Cyrus, not Darius, who first introduced current coins into his empire, a medium of payment which became indispensable as skilled foreign labour was increasingly attracted to employment in the capital cities of Iran. Perhaps therefore we may be justified in crediting Cyrus with the far-seeing ability to adopt a monetary innovation which was destined to revolutionize the older methods of fiscal procedure, as well as commerce, in Western Asia.

RELIGION

In Babylonia as in Judah and elsewhere we have seen ample evidence of Cyrus' toleration in religious matters and there is no trace of national

---

[1] The objection to this assumption is that if the Gadatas of Darius is to be identified with the satrap of Cyrus he would have been a young man for office under the latter and an old man under the former. The identification is possible but not probable.

[2] Sidney Smith, *op. cit.*, p. 41.

[3] Herodotus I. 94 – the new issues of Croesus superseded the older Lydian electrum currency.

[4] Barclay V. Head, *Historia Nummorum* (Oxford, 1911), p. 646.

fanaticism. What then were the beliefs of Cyrus himself and of the Iranian State? It is clear from many sources that polytheism was practised in Iran, and no doubt the fire cult played a prominent part in religious ceremonial. At Nūsh-i Jān, an ancient Median site of the eighth century B.C., not far from Hamadān, David Stronach has recently unearthed a fire tower in which the sacred fire was extinguished, most probably if we are to follow the later testimony of Diodorus[1] on the death of the king, and in Achaemenian times there are many representations as well as actual monuments of fire altars. It may also be recalled that about one generation before Cyrus, north-eastern Iran had come under the influence of the great religious teacher and prophet, Zoroaster, whose main scene of activity and preaching was Khwārazm (Chorasmia) in territory which today includes Marv and Herat. It was perhaps in or about 586 B.C. that Zoroaster at the age of 42 made a notable convert in king Vištāspa, apparently the last of his royal line.[2] Perhaps Cyrus who about fifty years later incorporated that king's territory within his empire may have come under the influence of Zoroaster's teaching – he may even have been a Zoroastrian himself, although there is no evidence yet for saying that Zoroastrianism became a state religion before the time of Darius and his successors. But it seems probable that the noble teachings of this prophet who, for the first time in history, preached the doctrine of free will, would have found a kindred spirit in the liberal-minded Cyrus. In this powerful new religion it was man who held the balance between good and evil; the eternal combat between good and evil, strikingly represented in Iranian religion through the contrast between the powers of light and darkness. The doctrine harmonizes well with the part played by fire in the older polytheism of Iran. One may sense that Cyrus' new concept of mercy and justice may have emanated from such beliefs.

[1] Diodorus Siculus XVII. 114. 4.
[2] W. B. Henning, *Zoroaster*, Ratanbai Katrak Lectures 1949, (1951) makes a good case for three possible dates of Zoroaster; 630–553, 628–551, 618–541, remarkably supported by a Syrian writer, Theodor bar Kōnai, 628 years and seven months before Christ: the latter probably arrived at this date by using the book which Theodore of Mopsuestia had written against the Magian religion. More recently Mary Boyce, "On the calendar of Zoroastrian Feasts", *BSOAS* XXXIII (1970), p. 538, has argued for a date of 665–588 B.C. on the assumption that it was his death that was thus calculated in the Sasanian calendar – to which must be added 77 years for the known length of his life. Cogent arguments are used in accordance with more recent Zoroastrian practice which involves a religious duty to keep the days of remembrances for the dead of his own family, hence to record the years from the death of an ancestor. But in my opinion, Henning's lower dates are more appropriate to the historical setting, which seems to require a date for Zoroaster not more than a generation before Cyrus – perhaps less. The debate is likely to continue.

PORTRAIT OF CYRUS

Great military achievements speak for themselves, but when we seek to receive a glimpse of his character and qualities we inevitably turn to Xenophon's *Cyropaedia*, which is an artist's portrait of the Ideal Ruler and the best form of Government. This is a picture of Cyrus the Great seen through the form of Cyrus the Younger, the hero slain on the field of battle – so greatly admired by the mercenary Greek who served him. In this work, as Gilbert Murray has aptly said "Truth is subordinate to edification." Let us recognize immediately that Xenophon does violence to the historical facts. "Media was subdued by force and treachery in the lifetime of Astyages, not voluntarily ceded to Cyrus by Cyaxares as the dowry of his daughter" – "the beautiful account of the peaceful passing of Cyrus is wholly out of accord with the well-established record of his violent death in the battle against the Massagetae (529 B.C.)".[1] It was his son Cambyses, and not Cyrus who conquered Egypt. But this picture of a great hero could not have been painted had there not been a credible memory of such a Cyrus – Cyrus the Great, addressed in the Old Testament as the "Lord's anointed". "The Lord, the God of heaven" has given him "all the Kingdoms of the earth" – equally lauded by Ezra, and by Isaiah,[2] who says of Cyrus, "He is my shepherd, and he shall fulfil all my purpose."

We should therefore recognize that although the account which Xenophon has left us of Cyrus' campaign in Asia Minor is not strictly historical, it gives us an insight into both the Achaemenians' military mind and diplomatic practices: Cyrus II, the Great, the model prince, may have initiated many of these. Thus we read of his extraordinary generalship, his lightning Napoleonic thrusts and the way in which after a preliminary skirmish at Pteria in Cappadocia he made an immediate unexpected attack on Croesus and thereby worsted him.[3] Most interesting, in addition to the accounts of ruses and stratagems for capturing fortresses, are his exceptionally intelligent handling of his soldiers, his understanding of their psychology and his ability to make them fear, respect and love him: the mark of a true general. We also have a remarkable account of the training of Persian soldiers through lion hunting, a picture which corresponds very well with what we see on

---

[1] W. Miller, *Introduction to Xenophon's Cyropaedia* (Loeb edition, 1914), pp. ix, x. Death of Cyrus in *Cyrop.* VIII. 7, a contrast to the historical account in Herodotus I. 214.
[2] II Chronicles 36. 23; Ezra I. 1–2; Isaiah 44. 28; 45. 1.
[3] Herodotus I. 76. 77.

the Assyrian reliefs, and there can be no doubt that this formed part of the specific military training for young officers in the Persian army: a practice which no doubt they had received from their imperial Assyrian predecessors.[1]

Xenophon is singularly ignorant about the northern peoples concerned, confuses Syrians, Cappadocians and Arabs and seems to be unaware of the role played by Babylonia and Assyria. But he has one extraordinarily interesting passage concerning the north Syrian frontier which, if properly followed, would help solve one of the intractable Palestinian problems today. Cyrus realized that some of the northern frontier forts were an insoluble bone of contention between the frontiers of Asia Minor and Syria. He persuaded the warring parties concerned to disarm and to let him hold the key forts in his supra-national hands, while flocks on both sides could cross the frontier unmolested and likewise farmers could have freedom of movement. This today would be the answer to the Golan Heights and many other similar problems.[2]

It was entirely owing to the imaginative insight of Cyrus that through his military and administrative skill Iran was for the first time brought into a close political relationship with the rich trading cities of the East Greek world and in touch with her merchants and bankers, many of whom were ready to accept Persian suzerainty rather than the cut-throat and spiteful competition of rival Greek cities, and for that reason Miletus, with its powerful fleet, a rival to Sardis and Ephesus, welcomed Persian intervention and did nothing to support Greek resistance.

CHOICE OF PASARGADAE AS CAPITAL

We conclude, as we began, with a brief reference to the site of Pasargadae itself of which the ancient name is now known, for it occurs in the Persepolis Fortress Texts as Elamite Batrakataš, and Bašrakada.[3] Ilya Gershevitch has made the attractive suggestion that the capital was called after the Pasargadae tribe and that the name of the latter was descriptive, meaning "wielders of strong clubs".[4] Why did Cyrus

---

[1] Xenophon, *op. cit.* I. ii. 9–11; VIII. i. 38; I. iv. 16–24.
[2] Xenophon, *Cyropaedia* III. 21.
[3] P.F. 908 mentioned below p. 595. Ancient name of Pasargadae, see Hallock, *Persepolis Fortification Tablets*, p. 676 under Batrakataš.
[4] Interpretation of the name given by Ilya Gershevitch "Iranian Nouns and Names in Elamite Garb", in *TPS* 1969, 168.

choose this place for the building of his new capital city? How much of the architecture and sculpture bears the authentic impress of his work? The answer to the first question must in my opinion rest on a clue provided by Herodotus;[1] the relevant passage runs as follows: "Now the Persian nation is made up of many tribes. Those which Cyrus assembled and persuaded to revolt from the Medes were the principal ones on which all the others are dependent. These are the Pasargadae, the Maraphians, and the Maspians, of which the Pasargadae are the noblest. The Achaemenidae, from whom spring all the Perseid kings, form one of their clans." It seems a legitimate inference that Cyrus was a member of the "noblest tribe" which frequented this district and, like Sargon II of Assyria when he came to the throne, built his capital in the heart of his true homeland. Moreover, the omens for that foundation were no doubt deemed to be good, for later Greek historians[2] certify that it was here that Cyrus won the decisive victory over Astyages the Mede that resulted in the submission of the Median peoples and the transfer of power and the seat of authority to the Persians. Some scholars, but not all, would derive his name from the river Kur, the principal waterway of this district.[3]

Finally, in answer to the second question which seeks to know what at Pasargadae are the authentic marks of Cyrus, we are indebted to David Stronach who, aided by Carl Nylander, has rendered a notable archaeological service in demonstrating the technological differences between the art and architecture of Cyrus and that of his successors. This evidence may be examined in detail in various journals[4] as well as in the lavishly illustrated volume on the excavations at Pasargadae.

[1] Herodotus I. 125.

[2] Polyaenus VII. 6. 7; Strabo XV. 3. 8. The final victories were gained in Persian territory at the frontier pass of Pasargadae. See also Nicolaus of Damascus in Jacoby, *FGrHist* IIa, p. 367, and note in Nonesuch Herodotus, I. 128. 1.

[3] Strabo XV. 3. 6. This appears to have been the ancient name of the river Polvar.

[4] See especially David Stronach in *Iran* I–III (1963–6), and Nylander, "Who wrote the inscriptions at Pasargadae?" and *Ionians in Pasargadae*.

CHAPTER 8

ALEXANDER IN IRAN[1]

The pervasive source problem that makes a proper history of relations between Greeks and Persians almost impossible – the absence of any historiographical record and paucity of evidence on the Persian side – must inevitably bedevil any attempt to write the history of Alexander's conquest of Iran, where these relations culminate in temporary fusion. It is clear from earlier periods that even the best evidence on the Greek side, quite apart from its bias and its focus of interest, is factually unreliable where it can be checked. Thus Herodotus gives us a Persian satrapy list differing from the great list of Darius at Behistun, and no modern ingenuity has plausibly reconciled them; to take a small point of fact: Herodotus (III.70.3) makes Hystaspes, the father of Darius, satrap of Persis (a post that may in fact not have existed at the time) when the Persian record shows he was satrap of Parthia and Hyrcania.[2] In the case of Alexander the situation is far more unsatisfactory. The historical record as we have it is not only a Greek record, but is so much centred in Alexander's person that even the history of Greece under his rule is difficult to disentangle, despite the existence of at least some independent primary evidence and our familiarity with the general background. In the case of Iran, evidence on the last generation of Achaemenian rule (not to mention Alexander's) is so far almost non-existent; the background must be largely filled in by extrapolation from an earlier age, and it is in part the Alexander sources that provide us with occasional glimpses of the later Achaemenian empire. Not only do these sources give us little that does not concern Alexander's personal actions, but they are vague about, and uninterested in, institutional and topographical details,[3] and difficult to interpret because of multiple

[1] The following abbreviations are used for the main sources: A. = Arrian, *Anabasis*; A.*Ind.* = Arrian, *Indica*; C. = Q. Curtius Rufus, *History of Alexander the Great*; D. = Diodorus Siculus, *Library of History*, Book XVII; J. = Justin, *Epitome of Trogus*; P. = Plutarch, *Life of Alexander*. Where sources give identical information, not all are usually cited. Numbers in square brackets refer to sections of the bibliography.

[2] See M. A. Dandamayev in G. Walser (ed.), *Beiträge zur Achämenidengeschichte* (Wiesbaden, 1972), 19f., 23 (*Historia*, Einzelschriften 18).

[3] In particular, accounts of Alexander's route are so vague that much of the time only a general

layers of distortion due to bias and mere romance; we should be only too grateful for a Herodotus. Yet Alexander's conquest is a turning-point in the history of Iran, and although a full treatment of Alexander would be out of place here, an attempt will be made to select what is most relevant within the context of that history.[1]

The King's Peace of 387–6 marked the triumph of Persian diplomacy in Greece. By subsidizing and exploiting Greek disunity, Artaxerxes Mnemon had achieved what Darius and Xerxes had failed to achieve by force of arms – a position of virtual hegemony over Greece, which made Susa the capital of the Aegaean world, much as Rome was to be two centuries later. The hegemony lasted for about twenty years. In 366 the king decided it was in his interest to support the rising power of Thebes, and sent down an edict taking her side against Sparta and Athens. But the outbreak of the Satraps' Revolt and the inability of Thebes to act as the king's executive agent in Greece combined to destroy respect for his power. While a new king, Artaxerxes III Ochus, slowly asserted the central authority and arrested the process of disintegration in the empire, the new Macedonian power gradually filled the vacuum created by the end of the Persian hegemony, and began to extend its intrigues into Asia Minor. Philip II, at least from the time of his victory over Phocis, Athens and their allies in 346, prepared to proclaim himself the champion of a united Greece against the barbarian.

Philip's negotiations with a philosopher-tyrant in north-western Asia Minor, Hermias, a friend and relative of Aristotle, seem to have been revealed to the king by some pardoned exiles – just when, with the conquest of Egypt after sixty years of successful rebellion, he had restored the empire to greater power and unity than it had known since the days of Xerxes – and his reaction was immediate. Hermias was executed; and when Philip tried to gain a foothold on the Dardanelles, Persian troops helped to defeat him, and at the same time the king established diplomatic contact with anti-Macedonian forces in Greece.

It was at this point that court intrigues impenetrable to us assured the destruction of the Persian empire. While Philip was just preparing for the final battle against a coalition of Athens and Thebes, Ochus was

direction can be discerned: it is only archaeology that has at times made precision possible. In eastern Iran and Afghanistan (less familiar to Greek writers) practically nothing detailed can be said over large and important stretches of the itinerary; the chronology of the fighting in that area is in equally bad shape.

[1] Unfortunately students of Alexander and Iranologists have traditionally worked without the close co-operation that would be desirable. The reader unfamiliar with Alexander historiography, ancient and modern, and its problems, will find the works cited in the bibliography useful.

assassinated by a minister named Bagoas, early in 338. For three crucial years there seems to have been chaos at the centre of the empire, as Bagoas put Arses on the throne; eliminated the new king's brother and finally Arses himself; then – probably frightened at the developing threat to the empire – found in Achaemenid of a cadet line named (in our Greek sources) Codoman, who had a distinguished record as a soldier, and made him king as Darius III (late 336). Finally, while plotting to remove him again when he turned out too strong-minded, he was himself assassinated by the new king, who at last firmly grasped the reins, probably not before some time in 335.[1]

During these years Macedonia had also passed through a time of troubles. But it had begun a few months later than in the empire and finished a little earlier; and the difference in chronology (slight but important) was exaggerated by the difference in size. In Macedonia, power could quickly make itself felt; while in the empire, though weakness and relaxation of control only too quickly encouraged disintegration, reasserting control had always been at best a painfully slow process. This must be borne in mind as we examine the first stages of the conflict.

In autumn 338 Philip won the battle of Chaeronea against Thebes and Athens. With no one left who could hope to resist him, he settled matters throughout Greece and in the next year united the Greeks (except for Sparta) in a common peace and alliance, leaving him (as commander-in-chief) in effective control. The League declared war on Persia, and in spring 336 Parmenio, Philip's most experienced commander, invaded Asia Minor and, with the Persian defences disorganized, gained control of several of the Greek cities. Meanwhile, however, a harem intrigue led to disaster. Philip had married a noble Macedonian's daughter and divorced and exiled Olympias, mother of the recognized crown prince, Alexander. Alexander fled the country, and though he was allowed to return, he was caught intriguing with a Carian dynast, his personal friends were exiled, and his future looked grim. Parmenio and his family followed their king, and Parmenio's daughter married the new queen's uncle, who accompanied the invasion force in Asia. That turned out to be a mistake. At the wedding of his

[1] The evidence for the chronology is most clearly set out and discussed in K. J. Beloch, *Griechische Geschichte* III.2 (Berlin–Leipzig, 1923), 126–31; see also the chronological appendix at the end of this chapter. The Greek name of Darius III is puzzling; in the Akkadian sources his personal name is Artašata/Artašata; see A. Sachs, *AJAH* II (1977), 143), presumably attempting to render a compound of Arta-.

daughter, in autumn 336, Philip was assassinated – clearly at the instigation of a faction hoping to rule through Alexander, who was at once presented to the army and, not quite twenty years old, was hailed as king. When Olympias returned, Philip's widow and daughter and some possible rivals were executed, and Alexander was firmly on the throne. Parmenio recognized the situation and sacrificed his new son-in-law, and in return secured recognition for, and extension of, the powerful position he had won for himself and his family under Philip.[1]

The new king overawed the Hellenic League into recognizing him and renewed Philip's treaty with them. When Thebes (encouraged by Athens) rebelled again, while Alexander was fighting barbarians to the north and west of Macedonia, he appeared before the city within a few days, stormed it and – after a *pro forma* decision by his Greek allies – razed it to the ground, selling the surviving inhabitants into slavery. Athens, with the strongest navy in Greece and impregnable walls, was pardoned. Both Alexander and the Greeks now knew where they stood. In Asia, eminent Macedonians and Greeks were soon found loyally fighting for Darius. But Alexander was free to resume his father's mission of leading a Hellenic crusade against the barbarian. In fact, if he ever thought about it (which, in his dreams of Homeric glory, he probably did not), he had little option: his treasury was bankrupt, and he could choose only between filling it by means of further conquest and giving up most of what Philip had won.

Early in 334, Alexander mustered his army and crossed from Sestos to Abydos – the only city in Asia still under Macedonian control. For the troubles in Macedonia had necessitated the withdrawal of most of the troops there, and the Persians, ably led by the Rhodian condottiere Memnon – related by marriage to Artabazus, son of the great Pharnabazus who had married a daughter of Artaxerxes Mnemon – had retaken the whole seaboard except for the beachhead at Abydos and had strongly garrisoned it. The strength of Alexander's army is variously given and cannot be accurately determined; but it was probably about 32,000 infantry and 5,000 cavalry, less than a third of them Macedonians. Strong forces had to stay with Antipater, whom Alexander had left behind as viceroy of Europe, and financial stringency prevented massive

[1] For the Hellenic League see H. H. Schmitt (ed.), *Die Staatsverträge des Altertums* III (Munich, 1969), no. 403; for Alexander's renewal(?), 404. On Philip's death and Alexander's accession, see Badian, "The death of Philip II" [V]. (Older literature is in Seibert, 72 [I].) The events surrounding Philip's death have produced a spate of articles in the last few years, not worth listing in the context of this volume.

hiring of mercenaries. Bypassing the Greek cities on his route (for they were now either garrisoned by enemy forces or held by hostile régimes), Alexander made straight for Zelea, the main Persian base in the area.

Something must now be said of this army, which was to begin a new age in the history of both Europe and Asia. Its backbone was the Macedonian phalanx and the cavalry: these were the forces that Philip had trained to an unprecedented standard of fitness, courage and discipline. The phalanx consisted of six tribal regiments of 1,500 men each, and 3,000 "hypaspists" (a Macedonian term for "foot guards", it seems), divided into three regiments of 1,000 each. These troops are usually described as hoplites, but it is now believed by some scholars that only their greaves and helmets were in fact like those of Greek heavy-armed infantry. Philip had made changes, in the light of experience. His soldiers may have worn no corselets, which made them more mobile than true hoplites; if it also made them more vulnerable, that did not matter – they were not trained chiefly for defence. Their shields were smaller than the hoplites' and had no hand-grip (also a disadvantage for defence), leaving both hands free to wield the *sarissa* – a formidable pike up to eighteen feet long and weighing 12 to $14\frac{1}{2}$ lb. For close combat, they also had a short sword. Superior mobility, superior training and the sarissa made protection less necessary: in fact, though the figures for losses given in our sources are quite untrustworthy, it does seem that infantry losses were usually light. Of course, we must remember that in antiquity victory kept losses down; it was the defeated who were killed in large numbers, after the battle was over. The hypaspists were an élite corps, often used on their own, especially on forced marches where only light-armed men could keep up with them. Their superb training was the key to Alexander's at times almost unbelievable speed of movement. The Macedonian cavalry were the "Companions" – it is not known precisely how or where recruited, but clearly aristocratic and perhaps mainly from the Macedonian heartlands. They were divided into eight squadrons (one of them Alexander's personal horse guards), and originally seem to have numbered 1,800; later they were reinforced and reorganized. Their arms are not well attested, but probably consisted of body-armour, a helmet, a lance and sarissa, and a sword; a shield is mentioned in some sources and should probably be accepted. They stood on the right wing and, under Alexander's personal command, would deliver the decisive charge. On the left wing Alexander placed the Thessalian cavalry – the only completely loyal Greek force, in numbers and fighting quality equal to the

Companions. They were normally commanded by Parmenio and had the more difficult task of defence, usually against superior enemy forces. In addition there were contingents of light-armed and of specialists (slingers, archers, engineers).[1]

The army was accompanied by a unique assortment of civilians. There were, of course, the usual traders and camp-followers; there were the usual priests, physicians and surveyors – these more than ever essential on a campaign into unfamiliar countries – and the usual intelligence officers, skilled at languages and at interrogation. The success of these last two classes is shown by the astonishing ease and assurance with which the army moved through what had been totally unknown territory. What was unusual was the array of intellectuals who accompanied the expedition, most of them probably through Alexander's association with Aristotle, who had been his tutor in Macedonia for three years. How many came along from the start and how many joined later we cannot tell. One who was there from the start was Callisthenes, Aristotle's nephew and an eminent historian. He came as the official chronicler – to confer fame on Alexander, as he is said to have tactlessly put it. His chief purpose was to stress Alexander's success and his divine mission, thus making him more acceptable to his Greek allies. There were many other writers – poets as well as prose historians – and artists whose purpose was essentially similar, though Alexander's standards were high and he discouraged hack work. There were also philosophers and scientists, interested in the new worlds the army was expected to reach. By the time the army reached Iran, it was accompanied by an array of talent unsurpassed (perhaps) even in Bonaparte's Egyptian campaign.[2]

Before Zelea, Alexander found the Army of Asia Minor awaiting him in defensive positions along the right bank of the small river Granicus (Koçabas). The details of the battle are more uncertain than usual, as we have two irreconcilable accounts. According to Arrian Alexander

---

[1] D. 17 gives a detailed army list, but there are textual errors in it and it may not be wholly reliable. The other sources (both quoted and surviving) give varying totals. See P. A. Brunt's tabulation in his LCL edition of Arrian, vol. 1 (1977), pp. lxixff.; it is followed by a brief, but useful, discussion of the army as a whole. On the infantry, see R. D. Milns, *Historia* xx (1971), 186ff.; on the cavalry, Brunt [VIII]. On the armament, see G. T. Griffith, *Proceedings of the Cambridge Philological Society* IV (1956–7), 3ff.; and (especially for the sarissa and its use) Markle [VIII]; Markle suggests that the hypaspists were ordinary hoplites and that only the tribal regiments regularly carried the sarissa and (consequently) lighter armour and shields; and that, in the time of Alexander, all Macedonians (including cavalry) were trained to use either weapon, as the situation required. For a brief general discussion see R. D. Milns in *Alexandre le Grand*, 87ff. [III].

[2] On these men see the prosopography in F. Pfister, *Historia* x (1961), 30ff., with the entries under their names in Berve.

rejected Parmenio's advice to wait until morning and attacked across the river at once, in the afternoon; according to Diodorus the battle did take place on the following morning, on the other side of the river, after an uncontested crossing. Arrian's account is (as usual) to be followed, with allowances made for propagandist distortion: thus the steep banks on the Persian side are shown by the account of the battle (1.15.1) to have been interrupted by stretches rising more gently; and the 20,000 Greek mercenaries on the Persian side can be shown to be a gross falsification (there cannot have been more than a few thousand, plus light-armed and ill-trained native levies). The river was easily fordable and the bank in parts easy to climb; and Alexander must at once have seen that the Persian cavalry, massed near the bank to stop him, were inadequately armed. Since the equipment of Persian (or perhaps rather West Iranian) cavalry is variously reported, and no representations appear to be known, the description of Xenophon, who had known them well two generations earlier, should probably be accepted: in addition to their swords they carried two lances suitable both for throwing and for thrusting, of which one was normally thrown, the other retained for hand-to-hand combat. The missiles could be caught by the Macedonians' shields, and the Companions' cornel-wood thrusting-spear was both longer and stronger than the Persian lance, as indeed Arrian makes clear (1.15.5). It did not need an Alexander to assess this, if he was not aware of it before, nor to see that, if he attacked at once, the Persians – men and horses – would be fighting with the afternoon sun in their eyes, while a wait till morning would transfer this handicap to his own forces. Of course, fighting was fierce, especially as the satraps, in the best Persian tradition, challenged Alexander in person. But it was soon over, the Persians routed, and four governors, the commander of the mercenaries and three members of the king's family lay dead. Of the Greek mercenaries, those taken alive were sent to forced labour in Macedonia, as traitors to the Hellenic League – and (of course) to discourage the others.[1]

It is clear that the king and his advisers had underestimated Alexander, no doubt misled by the evidence of political division in Macedonia and by the ease with which the seashore had been recaptured

[1] The battle: A. 1.13 (cf. P. 16); D. 19–21. Diodorus' fanciful account is useless, although attempts are occasionally made to defend it (see below). For topography see Janke [VI]; his description is, however, vague on some crucial points and the photographs are useless. See now the different accounts in Badian, "Granicus" [VII], 271–93, and Bosworth [II.2], 114–27, who misunderstands A. and defends D. For Persian cavalry equipment see Xen., *Cyropaedia* I. 2.9; IV.3.9; VI.2.16; cf. *Hellenica* III.4.14.

in 335. With the Army of Asia Minor wiped out, he had to adopt a new strategy. Darius I and Xerxes had also lost battles, but, on a long view, the empire had usually won wars: Marathon and Salamis had been avenged a century later, without even a battle, and Egypt had been reduced after sixty years. The Achaemenids were masters at waiting and trying again. Darius III had been chosen as a warrior king, and his new plan showed real grandeur. It was a two-fold strategy, with little room left for error. Memnon was appointed commander-in-chief in Asia Minor, with permission to carry out his plan, which he had unsuccessfully urged upon the satraps before the battle: to avoid meeting the enemy in the field and try to carry the war to Europe, where hostility to Alexander in Greece and Macedonia might be exploited. The history of the past two years showed that such a scheme was feasible. As Memnon had conceived it, it was to go with a scorched-earth policy in Asia Minor, drawing the enemy into fruitless advance. But this seems to have been rejected by Darius, as it had been by the satraps: the king's subjects were not expendable. Thus the major fortresses (Miletus and Halicarnassus) were prepared for defence, and the land was handed over to Alexander intact. But the main plan was approved, and while it was being carried out, the king began to collect an army that could meet and destroy the invader if he did not withdraw.

Alexander, meanwhile, occupied Zelea, which was "pardoned", and Sardis, where the Lydians were "given their freedom", i.e. Macedonian administrators took the place of the Persians. Similarly, the satrapy of Dascylium was taken over. At Ephesus, finally, Alexander took the long-delayed decision about the Greek cities. The Greeks clearly showed no hatred for their overlords: there is no record of any attack on garrisons or any harm done to the king's representatives. But they felt strongly about the collaborating oligarchies and tyrannies supported by the Persians: indeed, at once in Ephesus and later in other cities Alexander intervened to save these men from summary vengeance. While at Ephesus, Alexander received envoys from two neighbouring cities (which had presumably overthrown their régimes), asking him to take them over. He at once sent Parmenio to do so, and at the same time sent another general to free the Aeolian and Ionian cities and to establish democracies; to restore their own laws to them and to remit all tribute. (The policy was later extended to the Dorians.)[1]

[1] A. 1.18ff. On the Greek cities in Asia see Badian, "Alexander the Great and the cities of Asia" [IX]; and now Bosworth's notes on Arrian's account. The cities were nominally "free" and perhaps joined to the Hellenic League, but in fact controlled by representatives of Alexander and bound by his orders.

Miletus was taken after stiff resistance. But it was here that Alexander took a decision that seemed to play into Memnon's hands: he dismissed the fleet he had collected from his Greek allies (except for a few Athenian ships) before it had even made contact with the enemy. Parmenio – as usual, the account makes him the giver of mere common-sense advice, rejected by Alexander's genius – thought this an error; but Alexander explained that he could not risk losing a naval battle, since this might lead to revolts in Greece. In our source he refers only to the Greek allies' inexperience as a reason for possible defeat; but he must have been aware of that when he first collected the fleet. The fact must be that he was now aware of the unreliability of the Greek sailors; perhaps there had even been rumours of treason. The dismissal of the fleet turned his campaign into a gamble, which he clearly would not have undertaken without very grave reason. It is the most striking commentary on the true nature of the Hellenic Crusade.[1]

The consequences were to become clear before long. Meanwhile, however, Alexander advanced into Caria, ostensibly to assist its queen, Ada (sister of Mausolus), against a pretender supported by Persian forces. It is characteristic of his pragmatic approach, and his readiness to appear as the liberator of oppressed barbarians as well as of oppressed Greeks, that he recognized her as queen, while she in return adopted him as her son and, of course, accepted Macedonian garrisons, especially since Alexander could not wholly take Halicarnassus. On her death, a few years later, he legitimately succeeded to the throne and sent a governor to Caria; he had lost nothing by waiting. Alexander now occupied Lycia and Pamphylia without serious resistance, then turned into Phrygia (which he entrusted to Antigonus, later one of the greatest of the Successors), and at Gordium, early in 333, cut the famous knot, in a gesture that promised him the rule of Asia.[2]

While Alexander was advancing into undefended territory, Memnon was preparing his counterstroke. By early 333, several of the islands and one or two mainland cities had been recaptured, in a campaign hardly noticed by our sources, yet sufficient (as a modern scholar has put it) to "form a not inadequate content for a book of Thucydides or

[1] The recurring theme of Parmenio's inferior advice, rejected by Alexander, is probably due to Callisthenes, who is cited for hostility to Parmenio in the account of Gaugamela. It is found most succinctly in the anecdote concerning the rejection of a peace offer (D. 54.4 and similarly elsewhere): "If I were Alexander", says Parmenio, "I should accept the offer and make peace." Alexander replies: "So should I, if I were Parmenio."

[2] On this see Bosworth [II.2], 184–8; Atkinson [II.2], 86–90. Aristobulus reports that the knot was untied, in a manner more characteristic of the scholar who narrated the action than of the Macedonian king said to have performed it.

Xenophon".[1] But now Alexander had his greatest stroke of luck, in a career not devoid of them: Memnon died, and the fleet was taken over by a less imaginative Persian noble. Even so, it finally crossed to Siphnos (not far from the Peloponnesian coast) and there the commander met Agis, the Spartan king who hoped to lead the rising in Europe. Memnon's plan was apparently to be carried out. But the delay proved fatal, for the negotiations were interrupted by the news that Alexander had crushed the royal army at Issus. The Persian fleet now gradually disintegrated and Alexander, enrolling a fleet of his own, soon had unchallenged command of the sea. He had justified his gamble by winning.

It seems that, with the death of Memnon, the king had in fact lost confidence in the European plan. He knew that he had no first-class commanders left in the western areas; above all, he had no more distinguished Greeks, who might succeed in making a scheme to liberate Greece from the Macedonian yoke proof against the "antibarbarian" slogans of Macedonian agents and sympathizers, which had for a long time hindered co-operation against Philip II. Memnon, who had had good Athenian connections, was irreplaceable. Having reached this conclusion, the king seems to have reduced the scale and importance of Memnon's plan. The mercenaries who had served under Memnon were ordered back to Babylon, and an envoy sent by Agis to co-ordinate action was kept waiting, perhaps even at Damascus, and given no answer. This must have contributed to making the execution of the plan less effective. The king was now staking the whole future on a battle with Alexander's army.[2] One result of the new policy was that that battle had to be joined quickly. Had Memnon reached Europe, the king could have afforded to wait and watch. With the European plan no more than a diversion, Alexander had to be stopped by the king's army, if the king's name was to be reasserted. Quite consistently, no attempt was made to sacrifice small forces in defending the passes into Cilicia and Syria: Alexander was allowed to pass through without resistance, while the king waited at Sochi, on the Syrian plain.

The preliminaries to the battle were mismanaged: in the end it came

[1] A. R. Burn, *JHS* LXII (1952), 83; Bosworth's *Commentary* should now be consulted throughout.

[2] A. II.2.1; 15.2; C. III.2.1; 3.1. There is no justification for disbelieving the account of Memnon's intentions or his ability to have carried them out; naturally, the offshore islands had to be firmly in his hands first, and that took longer than no doubt expected. On Memnon and Athens, cf. M. N. Tod, *A Selection of Greek Historical Inscriptions* II (Oxford, 1948), no. 199 (cf. *Supplementum Epigraphicum Graecum* XXI.286 on the date), with E. Badian, "Agis III", *Hermes* XCV (1967), 179.

about almost by accident, not as either of the contestants had planned it. As so often, we cannot say precisely what happened, since the sources are confused and unreliable. Despite the "official" version, suggesting (inevitably) that Alexander eagerly marched against Darius, it is clear from his movements that he in fact marched quickly down the Syrian coast, after he had heard that Darius was waiting inland, on the plain beyond the mountain range. This suggests that he was hoping to carry out his plan of "defeating the Persian fleet on land" by seizing the coast of Syria and Phoenicia, thus bringing about the disintegration of the Aegean fleet, which he still regarded as the major danger.

Darius, meanwhile, some time in November 333, had left his favourable position at Sochi and marched north into Cilicia, in search of the enemy whom he hoped to annihilate. Arrian (II.6) clearly tells us what had happened: Darius suffered, as Persian kings always did, from being surrounded by sycophancy and largely cut off from reality. Advised by a Macedonian exile to stay where the broad plain would allow him to take advantage of his superiority in cavalry, he listened instead to the optimistic voices of those who claimed Alexander was afraid to meet him and should be challenged and crushed in Cilicia. As a result, when he crossed the mountains to reach the coast near Issus, he was not surprised to find that Alexander had left his sick and wounded there and moved south: it seemed to confirm the optimistic assessment. He immediately set off in pursuit. Alexander meanwhile had heard that the king was in his rear, and at once hurried back. Not that he would worry about his lines of communication being cut – an event that modern scholars take far more seriously than ancient generals (like Alexander, Hannibal or Caesar) on major invasions did. But with his unfailing grasp of tactics, already demonstrated on the Granicus, he could at once see that on the small coastal plain Darius had *de facto* given up the advantage of numbers (particularly in cavalry), so that the superior discipline and toughness of his own army gave him an opportunity he could not miss. So, once more, Alexander faced a Persian army across a river, this time with a chance of defeating the king in person.

Once more the details of the battle are almost irrecoverable, owing to incompetence and distortion in our sources:[1] enemy numbers and

---

[1] See Polybius' criticism (XII.17ff.) of Callisthenes' account, with F. W. Walbank's notes (too hostile to Polybius) in *A Historical Commentary on Polybius* II (Oxford, 1967), 364ff. The plain where the battle took place is either that of the Payas or that of the Deliçay. The former is said to be about 4 km in width, the latter up to about 9 km. Since there may have been hydrographical

armament are vastly exaggerated; the movements of detachments are often described too vaguely to make sense; and into an account ludicrously biased against Darius, Callisthenes has injected further bias at Parmenio's expense. But in outline we can see what happened: Alexander, with the Companions, some light-armed and part of the phalanx successfully crossed the river and routed the Iranian infantry on the Persian left. In the centre of the line, however, a strong force of Greek mercenaries prevented the rest of the phalanx from crossing, thus opening a gap in the Macedonian line; while on the other wing the Thessalians under Parmenio managed – with difficulty, but without serious danger, it seems – to hold the assault of the greatly superior Persian cavalry, which was prevented by the narrowness of the front from taking full advantage of its numbers and breaking through on Parmenio's left flank that firmly rested on the sea. Finally the part of the phalanx that had crossed the river with Alexander succeeded in taking the mercenaries in the flank, whereupon the battle was quickly ended.

Persian losses, particularly among the mercenaries and the cavalry, were heavy, and 8,000 mercenaries who escaped decided to make their way to Egypt or Greece rather than rejoin the king. Darius' own chariot and arms were captured, when the king abandoned them in headlong flight.[1] What was worse: the royal household, including Darius' principal wife and his mother Sisygambis, was captured, giving Alexander valuable hostages – and the chance of treating them with a royal graciousness which made it far more difficult to depict him as a mere destructive barbarian. The king's honour was shattered, and there was little he could do to rebuild this basis of his rule. More concrete advantages for Alexander soon followed. First, the royal treasury at Damascus, stocked up for the war, was captured and for the moment

changes since antiquity, the issue may never be settled, unless perhaps excavation becomes possible. See Atkinson [II.2], 458–61, 470–6, preferring the Deliçay for the site. Engels' arguments for the Payas (131–4) are invalidated by errors. For a different view see Bosworth, 203f.

[1] On the course of the battle, C.'s account differs from A.'s in detail, but the general structure corresponds. It was the failure of the Persian cavalry (the main hope of the king's supporters in Greece: see Aeschines III.164) that was decisive. A story of a single combat between the two kings was put about quite early: it is found in the memoirs of the court chamberlain Chares. The better sources show that it is false, but it prevailed in romantic fiction. It is thought to be illustrated in the so-called "Alexander Mosaic"; see Seibert [I], 55–8 for bibliography; add, now, especially the careful study of B. Andreae, *Das Alexandermosaik aus Pompeji* (Recklinghausen, 1977). That work, whatever the battle to which it refers, was commissioned by Alexander's enemy Cassander, some time after Alexander's death (see Pliny, *Nat. Hist.* xxxv. 110), and its hero is obviously Darius (pl. 4). Modern Alexander mystique has led many scholars into total misinterpretation.

relieved him of financial worry. Next, as we have already noted, the European counter-offensive had to be finally abandoned: the Persian fleet (consisting as it did largely of Levantine ships) began to disband and Alexander's new fleet gained control of the sea practically by default, as Alexander moved south into Phoenicia and occupied most of the sailors' home cities.

It was probably this very calculation that decided him not to pursue Darius into Mesopotamia (which he could have occupied without resistance) and perhaps take the royal capitals. Though always eager to seize a sudden chance, in strategy as in politics, Alexander tempered his opportunism with a firm grasp of what mattered. It is this that chiefly distinguishes him from mere royal adventurers like Demetrius the Besieger or Pyrrhus, who could probably never have conquered the Achaemenian empire. On this occasion he had (as we saw) even been prepared to leave Darius' undefeated army in Syria, in order to complete his plan of occupying the Levantine coast. With Darius' army shattered, that strategic necessity remained unchanged – the only change was that the aim could now be pursued without danger or worry. Indeed, the Phoenician cities surrendered without resistance, and their rulers were confirmed in power – until he came to Tyre. That city, while offering submission, refused to admit him to perform the royal sacrifice to "Heracles" (Melkart), as he demanded. Alexander could not leave this defiance unpunished and had to settle down to besiege the island fortress. Tyre's resistance is interesting chiefly in showing that, despite all that had happened, the downfall of the Achaemenids was even then by no means regarded as inevitable. By admitting Alexander, the city could obviously have had as good terms as Sidon and her other neighbours. And though Tyre was traditionally more loyal to the king than Sidon, yet loyalty would, in the circumstances, hardly have gone to the lengths of suicide. Presumably it was still conceivable, to loyal but reasonable subjects, that if one could hold out long enough, the royal army would return to the lands beyond the river. In fact, the siege dragged on, even when Alexander's new naval superiority established a tight blockade, until Alexander built a causeway to the island and, after several unsuccessful attempts, took the city by storm, late in 332.[1]

[1] The siege of Tyre is a showpiece of colourful description in our sources, especially in Curtius. It has had a great deal of influence on the literature of sieges. C. IV.1.10f. and D. 40.3 mention a Carthaginian promise of support for Tyre. The story is made less plausible by C.'s later statement that a Syracusan invasion prevented its fulfilment. The invasion is fictitious. On the siege, see Atkinson [II.2], 293–319.

The inhabitants were sold into slavery. Alexander had made his point. There was no more resistance until he reached Gaza, where the commander seems to have vainly hoped for help from Egypt. But none came, and the fortress was stormed. For the satrap of Egypt, surrounded by a population whose upper class was actively hostile after the Persian reconquest only a decade earlier and the punitive measures that followed, decided not to attempt resistance. The rich country that so many invaders had found impregnable was surrendered to Alexander without his having to strike a blow. The world of the Near East had recognized a new master.

Alexander did not stay to organize Egypt, but at once went to the Western Desert, to consult the oracle of Ammon at Siwah, long known and respected in Greece. What he heard there cannot be known. Callisthenes – who did not go into the sanctum with him, but who certainly produced the account Alexander wanted him to – fitted the incident into his general interpretation of Alexander: the god (he wrote) had greeted Alexander as his son. Other writers embroidered the story. Oracles brought from Asia Minor soon "confirmed" that he was the son of Zeus. It may be that Alexander had in fact gone to Siwah in order to obtain this important pronouncement, and there need be no doubt that he did get it – it was not much to ask. But there was more than a banal political announcement: it was to become clear later that Alexander retained a unique faith in Ammon, beyond all the gods he ecumenically worshipped, right down to the moment when he asked that his body be taken to Siwah for burial. It is not too much to say that, if we could ever know what Ammon told his son, some of the puzzles concerning Alexander's motives and actions might be solved. But it is doubtful whether anyone other than the participants ever knew.

It was only on his return from Siwah that Alexander organized his new province (taking care to subdivide power and authority to such an extent that he did not even appoint a satrap); perhaps he now had himself crowned Pharaoh in Memphis and (probably according to Ammon's instructions) completed the foundation of Alexandria[1] – for what purpose is not entirely clear: it did not, at any rate, become a great

---

[1] On this, see Appendix, p. 497; for a different account, see P. M. Fraser, *Ptolemaic Alexandria* (Oxford, 1972) I.1 and II.2–3 (n. 6); Fraser mistakenly cites Arrian as his authority for his own statement that Alexander was crowned Pharaoh before his visit to Ammon. No ancient Alexander source, except for a portion of the *Romance* written in Egypt, mentions any such coronation (which would have been a colourful ceremony). It is quite likely that he was never crowned, even though (of course) Egyptian documents depict him as legitimate ruler.

trading centre or a capital until a generation after Alexander's death. In the spring of 331 he left Egypt, and after a stop at Tyre, where he surveyed and completed arrangements for the large empire he had won, moved across the Eastern Desert to cross the Euphrates at Thapsacus. He had given Darius nearly two years to collect another army from the central and eastern provinces.

Darius, after Issus, had first tried to negotiate. The details are variously reported in our sources, but it is clear that he offered Alexander large sums of money, the cession of part of the empire (first Asia Minor, then everything west of the Euphrates) and the hand of his daughter. Alexander rejected all offers, proudly announcing that the empire was already his and Darius could only hope to be his vassal.[1] Darius had no option but to renew the struggle. Much had been lost – in manpower, resources, above all in prestige – yet at least he now had enough time to collect his forces; he still had the wealthiest and most loyal provinces at his disposal, and those which provided far the best cavalry. What is more: he could make sure that next time he would fight on ground of his own choice. Darius fully intended to profit by his experience.[2] He did not contest Alexander's crossing, for he expected him to advance through the summer heat on Babylon, where he had assembled his own forces for a battle on the Mesopotamian plain. But Alexander refused to play into the enemy's hands. Issus had taught him (partly by accident) how to avoid it. Ignoring Darius' challenge, he moved north and east, towards Nisibis, where the heat was less unbearable. Before Darius had realized what was happening, he had crossed the Tigris and was moving downstream on its left bank, towards Arbela. About 1 October, 331, battle was joined near the village of Gaugamela, about 70 miles from the city of Arbela (Arbil), after which the battle was later normally named. Alexander, not entirely familiar with the country, had not been able to pick his terrain: the king had found the wide plain he wanted, north of the Maqlub ridge, and had further levelled it. On the other hand, Alexander, moving to attack Darius, had the advantage of picking his time; and he was to show that, in the hands of a commander of genius, this could be used no less

[1] On the confused accounts of these negotiations, see Hamilton, 76ff.; G. Wirth, *Chiron* I (1971), 146ff. The letters quoted by Arrian cannot be shown (any more than most other "documents" or speeches in Greek historians) to be close to authenticity, and the details of the negotiations cannot therefore be known.

[2] It seems that cavalry was greatly increased in numbers and given improved arms: see C. IV. 9.3f., with Atkinson's notes, 376f.

decisively than advantage of terrain and could be used to counterbalance the latter.[1]

In fact he took care to rest his army, first after the Tigris crossing, then again for four days within a few miles of the enemy; finally, when within sight of the enemy, on a ridge a few miles away, he decided not to attack at once, as Darius expected, but to spend the day in thorough observation of the enemy and the terrain and the night in sleep, since the ridge secured him against surprise attack. Darius, on the other hand, had to face the disadvantage of the terrain he had chosen: unprotected in the middle of a flat expanse, he kept his men on alert in case of a night attack. This was unfortunate, and in Arrian's judgement (III.11.2) the fatigue and tension it produced led to the loss of the battle. But in view of the difficulty of calling his large and variegated forces to arms quickly, and with a mobile and highly disciplined enemy watching from three or four miles away in a safe position, it is hard to see how it could have been avoided. Alexander merely gave him a choice of ills. Parmenio is said to have advised a night attack; this is not to be lightly rejected as absurd. There can be little doubt that, had the king been seen to lower his guard, it would have been launched, throwing the Persians into fatal confusion.

As it was, the battle came by day and found the Persians tired and demoralized. Darius' aim, as we have seen, had been to build up overwhelming superiority in cavalry, now better armed than most of them had been at Issus. Bessus (satrap of Bactria) and Mazaeus (satrap of Syria) commanded the greater part of the cavalry from the central and eastern provinces, on the left and right wing respectively. Darius himself had the remainder with him in the centre, and also some archers and what good infantry – the "pomegranate-bearers" and the remaining 2,000 Greek mercenaries – he had been able to muster. Behind, a mass of light-armed native levies were perhaps chiefly meant to provide an

---

[1] For the site, see Schachermeyr, *Alexander der Grosse* [IV], 270 with notes. The most detailed discussion in English is by E. W. Marsden, *The Campaign of Gaugamela* (Liverpool, 1964) – topographically sound, but vitiated by unawareness of the source problems. C. and D. are disfigured by errors and at times seem to reproduce stock battle models. Arrian is basically sound, but vague on positions and movements, fanciful in his figures, and uninterested in the fighting in which Alexander and the forces under his direct orders were not concerned. Precise reconstruction is impossible, as in other ancient battles. (On this see the classic article by N. Whatley, *JHS* LXXXIV (1964), 119ff.) The existence of the Persian battle order which Aristobulus (*apud* A.) claims to have seen cannot be accepted with much confidence: though we are given somewhat more details on the Persian battle-line than on some other occasions, there are (significantly) no figures. Atkinson, 486–8, discusses the various accounts and modern interpretations of Alexander's march to Gaugamela and dates the battle 28 September.

illusion of strength and to improve morale. In front, there were the famous 200 scythe-chariots, mainly for the same purpose, and 15 elephants. The chariots had been totally unsuccessful in the battle of Cunaxa,[1] and it could hardly be expected that they would do better against Alexander. But they looked formidable, and it was perhaps hoped that they would frighten the enemy's horses. The elephants can certainly have had no other purpose. It is characteristic of the nature of our information that we never even hear what happened to them.

Alexander posted his forces basically as at Issus: himself with the Companions on the right, Parmenio with the Thessalians on the left, the Macedonian infantry in the centre. It was the customary and successful order, and no great amount of staff planning was needed. What was wanted was protection against encirclement, and this was obtained by mixed flank guards and a strong second line of infantry, with orders to turn about if it became necessary – the whole formation could be converted into a defensive rectangle if encircled. The battle, too, went essentially as at Issus. Alexander's only hope was to create a weakness in the vastly superior enemy line, which his more rested and more disciplined forces could exploit, with himself (as usual) in the lead. Moving gradually over to the right, he threatened to move off the terrain Darius had chosen and prepared and thus forced Darius to attack him. The scythed chariots again proved useless, and the Persian attempt to envelop Alexander's right wing produced a weakness between the forces concerned in this and the centre. Alexander charged, with the Companions and most of the phalanx, deliberately causing a break in his own line, since Parmenio on the left was hopelessly pinned down by greatly superior numbers. His calculation proved correct: although some enemy forces broke through the gap, Parmenio's long experience of defensive fighting sufficed to prevent panic and keep the enemy right occupied, while Alexander rolled up the Persian centre, forcing Darius himself to take to flight. This decided the battle, and though there was still some fierce fighting (rather obscure in our sources), the outcome could not be in doubt. The Persian army was routed and the central provinces lay open to the invader.

Our tradition (probably based on Callisthenes) reports a message from Parmenio, asking Alexander to come to his aid when Alexander was just pursuing Darius. It is possible that Alexander was really so

[1] On Cunaxa see Xenophon, *Anabasis* 1.8, 10, 20; this time the chariots were posted against cavalry.

engrossed in the attempt to capture the king that he forgot about the remainder of the battle – a kind of mistake frequently made by dashing commanders in antiquity, most notably by Demetrius at Ipsus (301 B.C.), where it cost his father Antigonus the battle and his life – and that the story of the appeal was meant to put the best possible interpretation on it, with Parmenio (as so often) taking the blame. But it may also be that the appeal is mere invention – an attempt to exculpate Alexander for the failure to capture Darius, which might be felt to make the victory incomplete.

Whatever the truth, the king, with a small force, managed to escape to Ecbatana, where Alexander, for the moment, could not follow him. However, he seems now to have proclaimed himself king of Persia in Darius' place, and a new stage in the war thus began: it remained to be seen whether victory would persuade a sufficient number of Darius' subjects to recognize the arrogant claim.

The first test came at Babylon, which Alexander reached after a fast march, probably still in October. It was held by Mazaeus, the loyal satrap who had distinguished himself against Parmenio at Gaugamela. Mazaeus surrendered the city without a fight, and the population enthusiastically welcomed the conqueror. It was a good start for the new king. In fact, Babylon marks the political turning-point. Xerxes (and perhaps his immediate successors) had destroyed the great temple of Bel there, and had discontinued the policy of toleration and the ceremonial of Babylonian kingship established by Cyrus; and none of his successors seems to have made any effort to retain the loyalty of the priests and the people. Alexander was clearly welcomed as a liberator, almost as in Egypt; and he took care to honour the priests and arranged for the rebuilding of the temple. Yet Alexander could no longer continue to be the liberator: he was now the king; and his very next stop would be the royal capital of Susa (Shūsh), and after that the heartlands of the empire. He had to gain the allegiance of the Persian nobility – the men who had governed the empire for centuries, and whom (as a class) no one could replace in that task. The transition appears at Babylon, where Alexander appointed Mazaeus satrap. In part, of course, this was a reward for handing over the city and recognizing the new king: recognition by such a man was vital. Mazaeus was now over sixty; he had been a trusted servant of three Persian kings, most recently governor of Mesopotamia and Syria (the province "across the river"), and he had fought for Darius with distinction. Moreover, it is possible that in his very person he marked the transition Alexander wanted to accomplish. He seems to have had Babylonian family connections: one may even conjecture a Babylonian wife. This was perhaps why he had surrendered the strongly fortified city, to save it from destruction. By appointing him, Alexander could have the best of both worlds. That a Greek was appointed to command the forces under him was both wise and acceptable. It in no way diminished his standing, which was underlined by the permission he received to continue coining in silver, as a true satrap of the new king. There is no doubt that in theory Mazaeus – like other Persian satraps appointed later – was in supreme command of his province, military forces and all, whether or not a Greek or Macedonian commanded the European forces under him.[1]

After more than a month at Babylon, Alexander moved to Susa, arriving in over twenty days. There was no need to hurry, for he had sent an officer ahead to take over the royal capital, and the satrap, deserted by his king, had peacefully surrendered it, together with a treasure worth 50,000 talents of silver – more precious metal than the invaders had ever seen before.[2] At Susa he reorganized his Macedonian forces, adding to them reinforcements that had just reached him. But with the reinforcements had come bad news: Agis, the Spartan king, had succeeded in collecting a large army in Greece and obtaining a great deal of support. Alexander, who had known about the rebellion ever

[1] On Mazaeus, see Berve, no. 484, and (for the Babylonian connections) E. Badian, *Greece and Rome* XII (1965), 173ff. (also for the Greek commander, a brother of Alexander's most distinguished soothsayer). The coins of Mazaeus seem certain, even though no other satrapal coinage is known under Alexander in the East. Perhaps the practice was discouraged, and made unnecessary by royal coinage. The appointment of the commander and also of a Greek or Macedonian tax-collector and garrison commander (some similar appointments are reported elsewhere) shows Alexander's care to put loyal men even in subordinate posts. We do not know whether the Achaemenids also appointed tax-collectors for the satrapies, as they certainly (originally) appointed scribes and garrison commanders. (See R. N. Frye, in Walser (ed.), *Beiträge*, 90f.) The appointment of a *strategos* continues this aspect of Achaemenian policy, though (of course) we cannot exclude extension by imitation. These subordinate officials, under Alexander as under the Achaemenids, were under the satrap's orders, but not removable by him: it can easily be shown (see Badian, *loc. cit.*, and cf. below) that satraps commanded the forces of their provinces.

[2] In A. III.16.6 Alexander only received news of the surrender of Susa after leaving Babylon, even though he had sent an officer there straight after the battle of Gaugamela. This is obviously impossible, even if the 34 days of feasting at Babylon (C. v.1.39) are an exaggeration. That the son of the satrap of Susa met Alexander on the road from Babylon is credible; it was probably Arrian himself who took this to be the first news of the surrender of Susa. On the amount of treasure captured the sources vary. The figure here given is Arrian's. Philip II was said to have drawn 1,000 talents of gold from his mines near Philippi (Diodorus XVI.8.6), and that gave him wealth unknown in Greece. The Athenian empire, at the height of its glory, had had a reserve of 9,000 talents of silver (Thucydides II.13.3).

since the spring, now sent 3,000 talents back, for use by Antipater if needed; and he also sent, or at least promised to send, back to Athens the statues of the Athenian tyrannicides Harmodius and Aristogeiton, which Xerxes had removed to Susa in 480 and which he had just recaptured. The attitude of Athens was likely to be the key to the fate of the rebellion, and Athens was known to be divided on whether to risk open support.[1]

We do not know how long Alexander stayed in Susa, but he can hardly have left before the middle of December, by which time the weather might be quite pleasant. He now had to choose between two courses: to move into Persis and seize its treasures and palaces, or to make for Ecbatana (Hamadān), to prevent Darius from reorganizing his forces. Strategically, the latter course was almost mandatory: the capture of the king must take precedence over further conquest of territory and treasure. Yet Alexander chose the other alternative – we do not quite know why. Perhaps he had found out that it was inadvisable for an invading army to attack Ecbatana in mid-winter; though he was to show often enough that snow and ice did not frighten him, and this reason does not seem wholly adequate. Perhaps the capture of the religious centre of the empire was regarded as essential for prestige and propaganda. In any case, he decided to march on Persepolis.

The route he took cannot be clearly discerned. Our sources, both immediate and original, were Greeks, and they had never seen a map of Iran. Even those who took part in the march would not thereby become able to give a geographically satisfactory account of it. In particular, they would not necessarily come to know much about the country they were traversing, beyond what they could themselves observe. The way in which Alexander succeeded in moving with assurance and apparent ease through countries totally unknown to him and his companions is perhaps his most remarkable achievement. It was done by brilliant intelligence work, using prisoners and local guides, as we can see in many detailed instances; and we are lucky enough to know something about the man in charge of the interrogation of prisoners. He was Laomedon,[2] who, with his brother Erigyius, had left

---

[1] On Agis' rebellion and its interaction with events in Asia see Badian, "Agis III", 170ff. (as corrected below). Accounts vary as to the fate of the statues of the tyrannicides: see Bosworth, 317.

[2] On Laomedon, see Berve, no. 464, with references to discussions on the "Alexander sarcophagus" (see Seibert [1], 59–61), on which he is said to be represented; after Alexander's

his native Lesbos and settled at Amphipolis under Philip II. The two brothers became close friends of the crown prince and were banished when he fell into disgrace. When he became king, they reaped their reward: Erigyius, after a series of important commands, finally killed Satibarzanes in single combat (see below) and, at the time of his early death, had already risen higher than any other Greek; while Laomedon, who, according to Arrian (III.6.6), was "bilingual", was put in charge of the enemy prisoners. Arrian describes this as one of the highest posts, parallel to that of commander of the allied cavalry (Erigyius) and chancellor of the royal exchequer (Harpalus). We must deduce an organized intelligence section, which Laomedon headed. Its work did not attract the attention of authors in search of colour and action, and we cannot observe him at his work. But we know that he remained close to Alexander, even though the literary sources hardly mention him.

It was in this way that knowledge of the country was gained. Naturally, it was patchy and *ad hoc* knowledge; and though Alexander did later send out men to explore and survey the new lands, there is no real evidence that the results of their studies reached those who accompanied the expedition and wrote about it. Nor were their successors, who might have used the increasing knowledge of eastern lands, interested in working it into their accounts – no historian like Polybius ever wrote on Alexander's expedition. Hence our accounts of Alexander's movements are so vague as to be almost unusable. Where ancient cities have been identified (and comparatively few have), this gives us some fixed points. It still does not enable us to join them. East of Susa, the Achaemenian road system is almost unknown, and argument from mediaeval and modern caravan routes always leaves a large margin of error; nor can we be certain that Alexander always followed the royal road: in the case of his march to Persepolis, we know he did not, at least for part of the way. It is as well to make this clear at the start, and to give a general warning that identification of routes (and often even of sites), where attempted, should not be regarded as more than conjectural.

However, it is certain that Alexander went south from Susa, probably crossing the Kārūn near Ahvāz, where there was a permanent Bridge of Boats. We are told that he crossed the "Pasitigris" on the fourth day

death, he received the key province of Syria-Phoenicia. Some useful information on Alexander's intelligence will be found in D. W. Engels, *CQ* n.s. xxx (1980), 327–40 (oddly enough, missing Laomedon and not mentioning the most important source for Greek intelligence, Xenophon's *Anabasis*). See also Borza, "Alexander's Communications" [VIII], with references.

and (it is implied) about 600 *stadia* from its mouth. By modern road, the distance from Shūsh to Ahvāz is about 70 miles, the distance from Ahvāz to Ābādān about 75 miles: the figures fit perfectly.[1] On the left bank lived a large group of tribes called Uxii, spread over the eastern plain into the foothills of the Zagros. The hill tribes (as often in Iranian history) had never been properly subject to the central government: their ruler had been linked to the royal family by marriage and seems to have received danegeld from the king – diplomacy was no doubt more successful than war. Alexander refused to pay, and by his usual co-ordination of speed and intelligence inflicted a defeat on them, after which he was happy to pardon them at the request of Darius' mother Sisygambis and put them under the satrap of Susa. He was glad to show conspicuous courtesy to the Queen Mother, and he could in any case hardly have conquered and occupied the whole of that vast area. How lasting the conquest was we do not know: Alexander left no garrisons and we cannot be certain that he imposed a tribute. It is unlikely that "in twenty-four hours Alexander settled a problem which for two centuries the Persians had feared to tackle". Shortly after Alexander's death we find the Uxii casually described as "independent".[2]

[1] D. 67 = C. v.3. Nearchus *apud* Strabo xv.3.5 mentions the Bridge of Boats, presumably at the point where the Kārūn ceased to be navigable. The figure of 60 *stadia* from this point to Susa in the text is clearly corrupt. If, as seems most likely, it should be read as 600, then it would be the same as in the other accounts and Nearchus may even be their ultimate source. Strabo mistakenly cites Nearchus as putting the Bridge of Boats 150 *stadia* from the mouth of the river. (Cf. A. *Ind.* 42.5–7, unfortunately not telling us how much further upstream the bridge was.) Nearchus' stadion appears to vary in length, but is here to be taken as the usual Greek unit of length, about one eighth of a mile. Though the coastline was not at that time near Ābādān (see *CHI* 1.34f.), the coastal swamps would certainly be regarded by a Greek observer as being part of the sea. The sources report no crossing of the river Diz; hence Alexander must have crossed the Kārūn well south of Susa. Strabo xv. 3.6, speaking of rivers along Alexander's route, mentions the Diz (ancient Copratas) and has been taken to imply that there was a tradition that Alexander had crossed it. But Strabo makes it clear, in fact, that he got the name from a list of rivers and had no direct evidence for Alexander's movements at this point. We must be guided by the Alexander sources, particularly since they make good sense. Alexander presumably crossed on the Bridge of Boats, which he must have heard about at Susa.

[2] The quotation is from J. F. C. Fuller, *The Generalship of Alexander the Great* (London, 1958), 228. Bosworth rightly rejects this view, which has often been accepted. The Uxii may have recovered a good deal of independence even in Alexander's lifetime (they are called an "independent race" in Arrian, *Ind.* 40.1, probably from Nearchus, and in Diod. xix.17.3 (317 B.C.); which must at least mean that they were not under a satrap, even towards the end of Alexander's life). [Their name may be identical with the Old Persian name of Elam, *Hūǧa* (with initial *h* not represented in writing), the ancestral form of present-day *Khūz(estān)* and, as an Arabic plural, its capital *Ahwāz*; cf. Ernst Herzfeld, *Altpersische Inschriften* (Berlin, 1938), 316; see also E. Herzfeld, *The Persian Empire*, ed. G. Walser (Wiesbaden, 1968), 303 and cf. 189. Herzfeld does not cite the Alexander historians. Ed.]

The account in C. v.3 and D. 67 differs from Arrian's in most respects: they relate the capture of a town under an Iranian commander, related by marriage to the king, but have nothing to say

He now divided his forces, sending Parmenio along the royal road through the plain. He himself, with more mobile forces, took what he had learnt was the shortest way through the mountainous area of southern Fārs, perhaps (as Aurel Stein suggested) the caravan route through Fahliyān: all we know is that it was above the royal road and shorter, and that he reached the pass at the "Persian" or "Susian" Gates on the fifth day.[1] There Ariobarzanes inflicted on him the only defeat that our sources allow us to know of in the whole campaign; Alexander lost many men and had to leave them on the field. For once his intelligence had failed. It looks as though the Persian prisoners would not give him the needed information. For it was a Lycian who finally showed him a way round the pass and thus enabled him to dislodge the defenders. Ariobarzanes was now refused admission to Persepolis and either was killed or joined Darius. Alexander entered Persepolis without resistance.[2] Unfortunately we do not know how long the march

about a demand for payment. There are other, relatively minor, differences in the battle itself and more important ones in what follows: A. reports that Alexander imposed a tribute of thousands of animals (including 30,000 sheep!); C. stresses that he was generous enough not to impose one. (That difference is not difficult to resolve: the figure in A. is incredible as an annual tribute and was presumably an immediate contribution, which the army could well do with. It is very doubtful whether he would have succeeded in collecting an annual tribute, and he may have been wise enough not to attempt it – see beginning of note.) Both accounts mention a successful intervention by Sisygambis. Goukowsky, in his note (219) on D.'s account in the Budé edition of D., suggests there were two battles, one in the plain (as in C. and D.), one in the mountain passes (as in A.). Bosworth (321–3) seems to put both in mountain passes and suggests the one in C. and D. was omitted (by A. or already by Ptolemy) because it showed Alexander in difficulties. In fact, C. and D. put their battle at the entrance to the plain of the Uxii, and the conquest of their "cities" (D.) follows the victory. (In C., the commander himself defends a "city", which is besieged and stormed.) Such attempts to distinguish between Uxii of the plain (or highlands) and Uxii of the mountains are unnecessary; and I have, with the majority of scholars, interpreted the accounts as referring to only one battle, with its difficulties played down by A. and exaggerated by the "Vulgate" tradition of C. and D. (This case is best argued in Pauly, s.v. "Uxii".)

[1] See M. A. Stein, *GJ* xcii (1938), 314ff.; *Old Routes*, 18ff. Part of the route he suggested between Behbahan and Persepolis may have found support in new finds at Maliyān, which J. Hansman (Ch. 2 and Map 1) has identified with Anshan. But although the route looks plausible, I cannot agree with him that it is difficult to envisage an alternative site for the "Persian Gates", except on the circular argument of taking the main part of the route as proved. A major new study of the sources and the topography, based on autopsy, is being published by Henry Speck. M. B. Nicol, *East and West* xx (1970), 269ff., has published remains of an Achaemenian road near Ardakān, which may show (contrary to his belief) that Stein was mistaken regarding that part of the route. The old identification of the Gates with a site near Istakhr, which Nicol follows, is impossible. W. Kleiss, *AMI* xiv (1981), 45ff. now reports traces of an Achaemenian road, not coinciding with the old caravan route, between Naqsh-i Rustam and a village in the northern Marvdasht plain.

[2] A. III.17–18; C. and D., *ll. cc.* Stein (*ll. cc.*) is not very clear on the distinction between the royal road and Alexander's route. We do not know precisely where he divided his army, but with his élite force he must have covered at least 70 miles in the four or five days before he reached the Gates from that point. The Gates are at least two days' forced march from Persepolis: the sources are too vague to permit a more accurate statement. (But this suffices to exclude Istakhr:

from Susa had taken. Strabo (xv. 3.1) gives the distance as 4,200 stadia (about 500 miles), which is a gross overestimate even for the royal road. Perhaps 3,200 (about 375 miles) was the intended figure, for there must have been an official figure. In view of the fighting and the (in places) difficult terrain, one should probably allow a month for the march. His arrival at Persepolis should then be put around mid-January 330. This fits in with the fairly accurately transmitted time of his departure, four months later.[1]

Arrian has little to say about Alexander's stay in Persis (Fārs) and gives no chronological indications. The rest of the tradition gives details, which in many respects seem trustworthy. He allowed his army to plunder the city after its surrender (C. v.6, with rhetorical elaboration; D. XVII.71.3) – not an incident easily accommodated by eulogistic tradition, hence all the more credible. It is made more palatable by having Alexander meet, just outside Persepolis, with several hundred (or thousand) Greek prisoners who had been mutilated by the Persians – a story that may or may not be true. In any case, it was necessary to give the army some compensation after the shock at the Persian Gates, the more so as the king himself again seized a large royal treasure. Diodorus (*loc. cit.*) stresses Alexander's distrust for the local population – understandable after his recent experience of their hostility, and no doubt fully shared by his men.

At Persepolis the army stayed four months, interrupted only by a thirty days' campaign by Alexander himself and a small force, to subdue the tribes in the Persian highlands. (Pasargadae with its treasure was also seized, probably soon after Persepolis, but we are not told when.) Just before leaving, Alexander set fire to the palace area, which had been spared when he arrived. It is the most puzzling incident of Alexander's campaign. First: why should he have stayed in Persepolis as much as four months (much longer than at any other stop), giving Darius time

see last note.) A. does not mention the nationality of the "prisoner" who showed Alexander the way – no doubt to disguise the fact that no Persian prisoner could be prevailed upon to do so. In view of the brutality of traditional methods of intelligence, this is remarkable. C. reports (v. 4.34) that Ariobarzanes fell in battle outside Persepolis. If so, he is obviously not identical with the Ariobarzanes who remained loyal to Darius and then was honourably received by Alexander. But C. may have made up a suitably dramatic climax for his story, and we cannot be sure,

[1] See Appendix on Chronology. As has been variously pointed out since, I underestimated the time needed for the march ("Agis III", 186), but others have perhaps been over-lavish. As a useful check against fanciful overestimates, we should remember that the official time, presumably by royal road, from Ahvāz to Persepolis was 24 days (Diod. XIX.21.2). As to distance, Strabo's use of "stadion" may have varied with his sources, but these figures should be in standard Greek stadia.

to mobilize another army? Next: why, having spared the palace area when the town was sacked, should he have deliberately destroyed it before leaving?

In answer to the first question, it has been suggested that the only – and sufficient – reasons for Alexander's long stay were geographical: he had found out that the pass to Ecbatana would be blocked by snow and ice, and there would in any case be no supplies for the army until the grain was far advanced, by late May: hence Alexander left "at the earliest possible moment".[1] There is no mention of any such calculation in the sources, but it is perfectly possible: it would not be sufficiently "heroic" to excite their interest. On the other hand, Alexander was to show in the Hindu Kush that he was not afraid, for himself or for his forces, of snow and ice. And unless it was an exceptionally cold winter, the pass was not likely to be blocked all the time until May. As for supplies, it was impossible for a large army to pass that way; but a large army was not needed. Alexander could have left a fair part of his forces at Persepolis or, better still, in the plain of Isfahan and made the ascent with the relatively small forces he usually took on such expeditions, trusting to surprise Darius.

Arrian gives us an explanation, for what it is worth: it is that Alexander was just getting the information that Darius was at Ecbatana. It is unlikely that it really took him four months to hear this, or that he did not guess it if he had not heard. Though it is possible that, knowing that Darius had gone to Ecbatana after Gaugamela, he did not know whether he had not long since withdrawn to the east: the city itself was not worth a difficult march in winter; it could wait. However, perhaps the most important point to emerge incidentally from that report is that it was apparently known and taken for granted that his communications over the mountains did not function as smoothly, in winter in a newly conquered land, as scholars often imagine.

We must bear this in mind. As for the other question: in Arrian, Parmenio soberly points out to Alexander that the destruction of the palace area would be senseless, since it was now his own property; and it would mark him out as a barbarian in the eyes of Asia. To this Alexander replies that it is an act of vengeance for the destruction wrought in Greece by the barbarians in 480. In our other sources this revenge is still the proclaimed motive, but the conflagration is actually

---

[1] The explanation here quoted is by Engels, pp. 73–8 [VI], in the course of a long discussion of Alexander's stay at Persepolis.

instigated at a drunken rout, by the Athenian courtesan Thais. The latter version, due to Cleitarchus, may well be correct as far as it goes: Alexander's heavy drinking, in the Macedonian tradition, is well attested. But it cannot be the whole explanation. It is noticeable that there is no other instance where a momentary impulse overrode serious considerations of policy; in fact, passion and policy usually coincided. Moreover, the palace area seems to have been stripped of its most valuable contents before it was destroyed, and there is some evidence to show that the fire was then deliberately set, and that destruction was concentrated on the three buildings that Alexander would know had been erected by Xerxes. All this, if wholly or even largely true, would confirm that the burning was an act of policy, no matter in what circumstances it actually came to be carried out.[1]

What, then, could be the purpose of it? For *prima facie* Parmenio's reported comment is just: the act seems nonsensical, indeed dangerous if one considered the future. It has again and again been said that it was meant to show that the Persian empire was destroyed: "a sign to Asia", as Tarn put it, "that E-sagila...was avenged and Achaemenid rule ended".[2] This view, however, is untenable on serious examination. It fails to consider either the nature of the Persian empire or the development of Alexander's policy. Very few of the King's subjects would know or care about E-sagila; and as for Achaemenian rule, Alexander (as we have already noted), far from wanting to proclaim its end, had, at least ever since Babylon, been trying to demonstrate that he had lawfully taken it over. The "official" motive, in fact, must be accepted: of all his subjects, only the Greeks were important enough to account for this sudden reversal of policy. It was a striking return to the policy of the Hellenic crusade.[3] When we recall how even at Susa Alexander had shown anxiety over Agis' war in the Peloponnese, it

---

[1] Sources: A. III.18.11 (cf. Strabo xv.3.6); C. v.7; D. 72; P. 38. Each author adds his touches to embellish the tale. Berve (no. 316) rightly suspends judgement. For the limitation to three buildings, see H. Luschey, *AMI* I (1968), 28ff. For the looting see E. Schmidt, *Persepolis* I (1953), 172, 179 *et al.*; the burning: *ibid.*, ７ *et al.* The thorough looting refutes the Thais story as we have it (i.e., a spontaneous drunken orgy).

[2] Tarn I, 54. Revivals, with slight variations, have been no more plausible. We happen to know that during his stay at Persepolis Alexander regularly sat on the royal throne (P. 37.7 = 56.1), again, no doubt, to advertise his legitimate occupancy. Even then, he obviously had as yet no intention of avenging E-sagila and officially ending the empire.

[3] G. Wirth, *Historia* xx (1971), 625, suggests jettisoning the initial looting of the city and the four months' stay on *a priori* grounds; after which, the problems have been removed and no explanation is needed. But where we have so little evidence, it is better to try to explain specific and reliable-looking evidence than to discard it.

becomes obvious that the long stay at Persepolis when he ought to have been pursuing Darius, and the last, desperate act at the end of it – soon regretted by Alexander, as the sources tell us (A. VI.30.1) – are likely to be the effect of uncertainty and anxiety over what was happening in Greece.

Agis' war was a serious and well-planned move, which at one time threatened to raise most of Greece against Macedonian rule, with the aid of a rebel in Thrace. Until he was sure of its outcome, it was inadvisable to resume the pursuit of Darius, at the risk of losing touch with Greece and Macedonia. Unfortunately our sources, centring their interest on Alexander's person, took little interest in the war in Greece and give us little reliable information about it. It is only from Alexander's reactions, first in Phoenicia in the spring of 331 and later at Susa near the end of the year, that we can at times deduce chronological indications. As for Agis' defeat, we have only one chronological statement. Curtius (VI.1.21, following an unfortunate gap in our text that has destroyed most of his account of the war) puts the end of the war before the battle of Gaugamela – even though his report of it comes only after Darius' death. Justin (XII.1.4ff) shows us Alexander receiving a report on the war, along with two others, precisely at that point. It is therefore almost certain that a common source accounts for the sequence in these authors, even though each individually often introduces chronological errors into his narrative. However, the official accounts recorded after the death of Darius are not actually said to be the first notification. Presumably, news of a major victory would be brought as soon as possible by a courier, while the victorious Antipater prepared his report, to be collected (evidently) at some intermediate station and forwarded to Alexander in a bundle along with other reports of the same kind.

Curtius' apparently precise date (before the battle of Gaugamela), for its part, finds no explicit support anywhere (though Diodorus may also have had it in his source). It has usually been accepted, for want of explicit contradiction. But it is now recognized that it is in fact contradicted by valid contemporary evidence: the orator Aeschines (III. 133) shows that, by midsummer 330, the Spartan hostages taken after the Macedonian victory were just expected to be sent on to Alexander, and that Alexander had not yet decided the fate of Sparta. This suffices to make a date as early as Curtius' (before the end of September 331) impossible; and indeed, this was already indicated by the fact that at Susa, in December 331, Alexander had as yet received no word of it.[1]

The war in Greece, therefore, cannot have been over until some time in the spring of 330; and with communications over the mountain passes poor at the time, as the report that he had just learnt Darius' whereabouts shows, we can believe that Alexander had not yet heard of Agis' death by May. Yet with spring well advanced, he could wait no longer: Darius was at Ecbatana, and it was clear that he still commanded a great deal of loyalty. Alexander, no doubt reluctantly, lit the funeral pyre of the Hellenic crusade, and moved on. By the time he reached Ecbatana, he knew it had been unnecessary: he there ceremonially dismissed the Hellenic League forces in their official capacity. The step is conceivable only if by then he knew that Agis was dead and Greek hostages no longer needed.[2]

When Alexander reached Ecbatana, he found Darius had left some days before, withdrawing to the east and scorching the earth to impede pursuit. Alexander now decided to make Ecbatana his main treasury, leaving his boyhood friend Harpalus there as his imperial treasurer and Parmenio in charge of an army to guard it. The task was by no means dishonourable, but it is clear that Alexander was glad of an opportunity

[1] The relevance of Aeschines' contemporary testimony was for the first time, in recent years, brought into the debate by G. L. Cawkwell, *CQ* XIX (1969), 171. It can no longer be ignored. E. N. Borza, *CP* LXVI (1971), 231ff., successfully refutes some of Cawkwell's other arguments, but has nothing cogent to bring up against this decisive one. (I take the point about the despatches from him.) However, as for the beginning of Agis' war, Alexander's anxiety about the events in the Peloponnese when he was in Phoenicia (A. III.6.3: a recent attempt to explain "Peloponnese" there as meaning Crete shows how far ingenuity will go in denying the facts) and later at Susa (A. III.16.9–10; cf. 7) lets us see, in the only way possible in view of the nature and interests of our sources, how seriously Alexander at all times took this war.

[2] I have suggested ("Agis III", 190) that the news may first have been brought to Alexander by a detachment of Macedonians who reached him on the road to Ecbatana (C. v.7.12) and who had apparently gone first to Ecbatana, then marched down to meet him. As Arrian's comment on the time at which he first heard about Darius' staying at Ecbatana implies, there was, during that winter, no properly working courier service over the mountains controlled by native tribes. Control of the defeated Uxii cannot be taken for granted, and the Cossaeans were not subdued until near the end of Alexander's life. From Susa, neither the road to Persepolis nor the road to Ecbatana could necessarily be safely used by a despatch-rider, even if a strong Macedonian formation might pass unmolested. On Alexander's communications in general (but with no discussion of, or relevance to, these attested special conditions) see Borza [VIII].

Bosworth (*CQ* XXVI (1976), 132–6; repeated *Commentary*, 335f.) has attempted to argue that Alexander did not enter Ecbatana, but by-passed it. In view of Arrian's repeated and explicit references to the stay at Ecbatana and to arrangements made there which are not likely to have been made except in a major city (III.19.5–8), this view is not likely to find much acceptance. If true, it would mean that Ecbatana was the only royal capital and major city on his route which Alexander chose not to enter.

to free himself of the old general's overpowering presence.¹ He then turned east, hoping to overtake Darius, and in eleven days reached Rhagae (Ray – a distance of some 200 miles; the direct road runs partly through difficult country). There he stopped when he heard that Darius was too far ahead to be caught, and made arrangements for the satrapy of Media. It was only when he heard that Darius was a prisoner of his own officers that he resumed his pursuit, now travelling at lightning speed through the heat of July, with a progressively smaller and more mobile force, until he caught up with the enemy, probably somewhere on the road to Hecatompylus. By that time, Darius was dead.²

Curtius (v.8–12) gives a long and circumstantial account of the

---

¹ A. III.19. He also mentions an order to Parmenio to invade Gīlān and Māzandarān. No more is heard of this. Bosworth (337) suggests it was later cancelled; this is quite possible. Alternatively, it was in fact carried out while the king operated further east and (as could well happen, in view of the interests of our sources) we never hear of it.

The story of the treasure is more complex and illustrates the inadequacy of our sources. D. 71.2 reports that it was taken to Susa from Persepolis, except for what Alexander wanted to take with him. (C. mentions only the latter part.) A. reports that the Persepolis treasure was to be taken to Ecbatana and that Harpalus was set up ἐπὶ τῶν χρημάτων to take charge of it. Some years later, we find Harpalus residing at Babylon in regal splendour and D. (108.4) reports that he had been "entrusted with guarding the treasure and revenue in Babylon". That this is probably his own interpretation and need not mark a genuine transfer or perhaps a diminution in his responsibilities is shown by D.'s next statement, that he had been "appointed satrap of an enormous territory". Each has found defenders among modern scholars, but they serve only to discredit him. Presumably Alexander continued the Achaemenian practice of dividing his treasure among the principal central cities, Babylon, Susa and Ecbatana (for Persepolis had been stripped), for safety and convenience. It may simply have been found that Ecbatana was geographically unsuited to being the principal treasury (the question is surely rather why Alexander ever arranged this) and that Babylon became the centre – quite possibly at the suggestion (it would certainly be with the agreement) of Harpalus, who had experienced its legendary luxury (cf. C. v.1.36ff.). A unified central administration would still be needed, and there is no one other than he who can have held that post. We find him, e.g., making expensive purchases of supplies to forward to Alexander (C. IX.3.21). The death of Parmenio might offer a suitable time for the reorganization here postulated.

² The route in general is clear, but A. is hopeless on the details. See Bosworth 338ff.; R. D. Milns, *Historia* xv (1966), 256. A.'s figures, if trustworthy, suggest that the king did not take the shortest route (about 190 miles) to Rhagae. He may have preferred a longer and easier route (perhaps via Qazvīn), especially since there was at that point no intention to pursue Darius. The sources are, as usual, confused about distances from the Caspian Gates, which marked a principal point of reference for ancient geographers. Pliny vi.43f. gives 20 Roman miles from Ecbatana to the Gates and 133 on to Hecatompylus. Strabo, citing different sources in successive chapters, gives 1,960 and 1,260 stadia (there are 8 to the Roman mile) for the latter distance (xi. 8.9; 9.1). There is no way of reconciling the figures. (Engels' tables of measurement, 157–8, unfortunately do not mention the source difficulties: they are based on a selection of emended figures.) This state of affairs has led some scholars to conclude that the "Caspian Gates" was not a single pass, but two or more passes. (See B.'s excellent treatment, 342f.) Hecatompylus may now have been found by J. Hansman (*JRAS* 1968, 111f.; 1970, 29f., with D. Stronach), who presumably followed up an old suggestion by A. F. von Stahl (*GJ* LXIV (1924), 325). The site is near Qūsheh, about 32 km southwest of Dāmghān, on the road to Tehran. There is as yet no positive identification.

conspiracy against him, which, though rhetorically elaborated, may in part rest on the later account of a Greek mercenary leader, who plays a conspicuously honourable part in the story: Cleitarchus certainly collected eyewitness accounts. At any rate, Arrian's brief summary (III. 21) gives the same outline: Bessus, satrap of Bactria and related to the royal house, and Nabarzanes, called "chiliarch" by Arrian and hence perhaps holder of the much-discussed office of *hazārapati*,[1] were the leaders in the plot; Barzaentes, satrap of Drangiana, is named with them. Artabazus and the Greek mercenaries were loyal to Darius and after his arrest left the assassins' service. Curtius makes ambition for the royal title or the hope of gaining Alexander's favour by surrendering Darius the motives, which in the circumstances is absurd: Darius was a fugitive; and when the opportunity came, they made no attempt to surrender him or themselves to Alexander. On the contrary, they kept Darius alive – bound with golden fetters, as was proper – as long as there was any chance of escape. Even at the end, according to Curtius himself, they implored him to flee with them on horseback. It was only when he refused, and they saw they could not prevent his capture, that they killed him and saved themselves.

Clearly, they acted as they did in order to prevent his falling into Alexander's hands alive. Alexander himself, by his superhuman efforts to reach Darius before he could be killed, confirms their judgement of the importance of this. Nor is it difficult to understand. Never yet had the king's person been in the hands of a foreign invader: his capture would give Alexander towering prestige and make the organization of resistance difficult. Moreover, Darius seems to have despaired of the war. Even before Gaugamela, he had offered Alexander half his kingdom and the hand of his daughter. If he were now captured, it could be feared (or hoped) that he would be persuaded by courteous and honourable treatment to acknowledge Alexander as his lord and do homage to him as the new king. That would have made further resistance impossible. As it was, that final danger was at least avoided. Bessus, a relative of Darius, who now assumed the royal insignia and the royal name "Artaxerxes", had a patently better claim to the throne than his Macedonian rival. The struggle could go on.

In fact, as the burning of the royal palaces had been Alexander's sole miscalculation, his failure to capture Darius alive was his sole misfortune down to 325. He gave Darius royal burial. But that hardly mattered.

[1] On this office see Frye, in Walser (ed.), *Beiträge*, 88; Schachermeyr, *Alexander in Babylon*, 31–7.

He was now faced with a long and bitter war in eastern Iran – a foreign invader who, partly by his own deed and partly through bad luck, had lost all real claim to legitimacy.

With the country not nearly conquered, Alexander now tried a significant variation on his policy. So far, ever since Babylon, he had appointed Persian nobles to satrapal posts. Now, a Parthian – Amminapes, who had once been an exile in Macedonia and had later helped to win Egypt for Alexander – was made satrap of Parthia and of Hyrcania (roughly Gurgān–Māzandarān). The availability of this loyal man was a godsend. But it is clear that for the moment, even though he naturally still called himself king, his claims to Persian legitimacy were not considered worth stressing. That battle seemed lost, and a Parthian was the best candidate to win Parthia from Bessus. Alexander had not yet heard that Bessus was calling himself king.

Leaving the pursuit of Bessus and his allies, who had split up to organize resistance in eastern Iran, for later, Alexander again followed his strategy of always securing his rear, by invading Hyrcania and, in a brief campaign, striking terror into the tribes of the northern slope of the Alburz and the southern shore of the Caspian (Mardia and Tapuria) as far as Rasht (though he himself cannot have got much past Āmul) and receiving at least their formal submission. During the campaign, his hopes were restored by the surrender of several Persian satraps. Artabazus, who had been loyal to Darius to the end, naturally made his submission, together with several of his sons; Nabarzanes also surrendered, after negotiations. His case was more precarious, as he had taken part in the rebellion against Darius. But he was pardoned, it was said because of the immense gifts (including above all a beautiful eunuch) he brought with him. No less important, perhaps, was the fact that Alexander could not just then afford to antagonize Persian nobles: he was cautiously exploring the way towards a new understanding with them. Phrataphernes, satrap of Hyrcania and Parthia, was gladly received – though too late to be confirmed in office, since Amminapes already held it – and Autophradates, satrap of Tapuria, was confirmed in his satrapy and had Mardia added to it: he was to protect the western flank of Hyrcania. The Greek mercenaries also surrendered and, after a pose of implacable hostility towards Greek "traitors", Alexander discharged some and enlisted the rest. Some Greek envoys, perhaps captured at Ecbatana, were now also dealt with: those from states not in the League were dismissed, those from Athens (a member) and from Sparta (at the time an open enemy) imprisoned.[1]

After a fortnight's rest at Zadracarta (Sārī?), Alexander quickly marched east, no doubt along the traditional straight road from Shahrūd, and, on entering Areia (the district with Herāt as capital), probably near Mashhad, stopped at Ṭūs and received the submission of its satrap Satibarzanes, who was duly confirmed; Alexander even left a small force there to protect the satrapy against looting by his own forces. It was probably Satibarzanes who informed him that Bessus had now proclaimed himself king and was collecting forces in Bactria and even beyond the imperial borders, in Scythia. Alexander at once left and moved towards Bactria, to meet the new threat. No sooner was he gone than Satibarzanes rebelled, massacred the protective garrison and seized Artacoana. Alexander left most of his army with Craterus, probably – as has been plausibly suggested – at Kalāt-i Nādirī, which seems to be the characteristic mountain described by Curtius, and turned off the road to Bactria towards Artacoana. Unfortunately our sources do not enable us to gather in which direction he marched, so that the site of Artacoana is unknown. It has been customary to place it near (or even at) Herāt, but it may well be much further north: it has recently been suggested that it might even be in Soviet Central Asia. In any case, Satibarzanes, unwilling to face him in person, fled to Bessus. The revolt was easily put down and another Persian appointed satrap. Ignoring Bactria, Alexander, who had been forcibly reminded that his flank was not secure, turned south into Drangiana, towards Sīstān, probably sometime in the summer of 330. It was less than six months since Darius' death.[2]

[1] For the route from Hecatompylus to Areia, see Engels, 83ff. He comments on the excellence of Curtius' basic geographical information, despite that author's rhetorical manner. On Nabarzanes and the eunuch Bagoas, see E. Badian, *CQ* VIII (1958), 144ff. It was in the semi-legendary country of Hyrcania that Cleitarchus (and probably others) located the supposed meeting of Alexander with the Queen of the Amazons (cf. p. 484, n. 2).

[2] Satibarzanes is named in A.'s text (III.21.10) as one of Darius' murderers. As the fact that he met Alexander when the latter entered his province and that he was at once confirmed (A. III.25.1) in it shows, he was clearly innocent. (Compare the actions of Nabarzanes, who, even after being pardoned, was not given a satrapy.) Arrian's own account makes it quite clear that he had never left his province before his submission. Whether the text should be emended (to "Nabarzanes", who is certainly meant) is uncertain: the error may be Arrian's. (Cf. Bosworth, 344f.) The chronology and topography of Alexander's movements from 331, obscure in the sources, are usefully discussed in Brunt's LCL edition of Arrian, vol. I, 487ff. See also chronological Appendix. The suggestions regarding Kalāt-i Nādirī and Artacoana are by Engels (87ff.). See also *ibid*. 153–6 for march rates, based on his figures (see p. 448, n. 2) and his very useful sketch maps (159–75). The evidence and all previous views on the identification of points in and near southern

It was there, at Phrada (usually thought to be Farah), that he struck his first blow against the Macedonian "opposition". At various times before this – after Issus, in Egypt, after Gaugamela, at Ecbatana, after Darius' death – we hear of the unwillingness of some Macedonians to march on into unknown dangers, for no reason but Alexander's personal glory. Dissatisfaction was intensified after Gaugamela, when Alexander decided to claim the Achaemenian throne, gradually adopted a modified form of Persian royal costume, created a Persian court with eunuchs and a harem in addition to his traditional Macedonian one, and (as we have seen) installed Persian nobles as satraps. This, plus increasing luxury and ceremonial, gave the impression that the King of Macedon for whom the army had fought and conquered was turning into an "oriental". The old guard of Macedonian barons made no secret of its opposition, and Philotas, son of Parmenio, commander of the Companion cavalry, was its leader. Ever since Egypt, Alexander had had him under surveillance. But it was only now, with the removal of Parmenio from the court, and after the accidental death of Parmenio's other two sons, that action became possible. At the beginning of his reign, Alexander had had to accept a stranglehold of Parmenio and his followers on the army, as the price of that support without which the young king might not have survived. He had gradually asserted himself and, by success and personal charisma, made the army his own. But now the personal strains were threatening to merge into major policy differences. Even with some of the family dead, Parmenio controlled the supply lines and the treasuries of the empire, Philotas the Macedonian cavalry. Alexander decided to strike when the chance offered. At Phrada, an obscure "conspiracy" against Alexander – almost certainly one of many such, as at every court – was reported to Philotas, who did not think it important enough to warn the king. On this pretext, Alexander organized a *coup d'état*: Philotas was arrested in the middle of the night by trusted friends of Alexander (chief of them Hephaestion, his dearest Companion), then presented before the stunned army as guilty of high

Afghanistan are set out by K. Fischer, *Bonner Jahrbücher* CLXVII (1967), 129–232, an outstanding contribution. (See especially 196–9 on Alexander.) He identifies Kandahar as "Alexandria in Arachosia" (but oddly denies its foundation by Alexander, on no real evidence), chiefly on the strength of the Aśoka texts. Herāt must be on the site of Alexandria in Areia, which claimed an Alexander foundation (Pliny, *Nat. Hist.* VI.93). It is not noted as such by the Alexander sources, and the claim is most probably spurious: we know that early Hellenistic kings gave Alexander's name to some of their foundations, and some of those later forged the obvious pedigree. The canon of Alexander's "cities" ultimately rose to 70. (Herāt may have been founded by Antigonus I.) [On Kandahār add now P. M. Fraser, *Afghan Studies* II (1979), 13.]

treason and (when Alexander demanded it) at once condemned and executed. Some sources speak of torture.

That was only the beginning. As soon as Philotas was dead, a courier was despatched to Ecbatana to arrange for Parmenio's assassination: the old man had too much prestige for Alexander to be able to keep to the legal forms he had used in the case of Philotas. At the same time some other eminent Macedonians – some friends of Philotas, but at least one noble not connected with him – were executed; others were allowed to be acquitted by the army: Alexander could not afford to engage in visibly arbitrary and indiscriminate killing. Another compromise followed: command of the Companions was divided between Hephaestion and a Macedonian of the old guard (but of proved personal loyalty: he had saved Alexander's life in battle), Cleitus.[1]

There may have been another result, though we have no direct evidence. When Phratapherenes had joined Alexander in Hyrcania, a few months before, he had not been given a satrapy, his own or another: this appears clearly from Arrian's careful record of appointments at this stage. Yet shortly after the events at Phrada, Arrian (III.28.2) introduces him as "satrap of Parthia". It is likely that he had been given back his old satrapy of Parthia and Hyrcania, and there seems to be no suitable time for this except for the reorganization following Philotas' death. Amminapes is never heard of again. It is possible that he, once an exile in Macedonia, had connections with the family of Parmenio. Moreover, politically, it seems, Alexander was again aiming at the support of the Persian aristocracy, trying to woo them away from Bessus, the late king's relative.

What Phratapherenes, with two others, was called upon to do was to deal with Satibarzanes, who had raised another revolt in Areia. Erigyius, Alexander's Greek boyhood friend, succeeded in bringing on a full-scale engagement, in which he personally killed the rebel. This was the end of the last outbreak of guerrilla war within the empire. As had at once become clear in Asia Minor, when the satraps opposed Memnon's suggestion of a "scorched-earth" policy, the aristocratic

[1] On the plot against the house of Parmenio, see E. Badian, "The death of Parmenio", *Transactions and Proceedings of the American Philological Association* XCI (1960), 324ff. Alexander probably seized a chance offered by the "conspiracy" (whether it was real or not). He was enthusiastically helped by men at the court who hated Philotas, especially Hephaestion and Craterus. Arrian, following his apologetic sources, describes Philotas as manifestly guilty. Curtius is the most important source: though his rhetoric and distortions due to it must be discounted, he here (as elsewhere) offers us the only glimpses into court intrigues and feuds that our tradition affords. But any attempts to exculpate Alexander are mere paradox or special pleading.

order of the Achaemenian empire did not lend itself to guerrilla war. Persian nobles were expected to lead in battle and to protect the king's subjects, even if they could not raise forces able to face the Macedonians of Alexander. They could not for long wage war by destroying the subjects' property. Resistance now had to be, on the whole, transferred beyond the borders of the empire. But Areia seems to have remained troubled: late in 329, its Persian satrap was arrested and replaced by a Cypriot Greek.

Alexander, meanwhile, was engaged in a terrible winter march through central Afghanistan, fortunately against little resistance. As he marched (we cannot tell with real assurance by what route or precisely when) from "Phrada" to Kandahār, the local and (it seems) even some distant tribes submitted without trouble: whether they could be controlled, only time would show. The Arachosians were placed under the formal command of a satrap and the strange tribe of the Ariaspians (once "benefactors" of Cyrus, as was presumably remembered in Persian as well as in Greek records) and even the distant Gedrosians were apparently put under some sort of control, though the details, owing to the lack of real interest on the part of our sources, are irrecoverable. Then, at a time excruciatingly vague for us, came the crossing of the mountains between Ghazna and the Kabul valley that struck the imagination of romantic historians, with the ice and snow and the strange tribe that survived in them by building houses weirdly adapted to the climatic conditions. There is no doubt that Alexander's intelligence had been imperfect and that conditions were worse than he had expected; perhaps, however, this could be taken as another indication (too precious, for our interpretation of the whole route and chronology of this march, to be ignored) that the crossing was made at the approach of winter, when he simply could not afford to wait, rather than in spring, when he easily could have.

The army emerged into the Kabul valley and, either there or around Begrām, Alexander let them rest for the winter and recover from the effects of the mountain crossing. There, almost certainly near Begrām, he founded "Alexandria of the Hindu Kush" (Paropamisus). A satrapy of Paropamisadae was created, with its capital in the new city, and a Persian (not otherwise known to us) was appointed its governor. Then, at last, Alexander was ready to meet the challenge of Bessus, with his rear and flank – for the moment, at least – clear of enemies and under formal control.¹ He left early in the season, crossing another Hindu Kush pass (probably the Khawak) with some difficulty, and reached Drapsaca (Kunduz), where the army again rested. The army of Bactrians and tribesmen that Bessus had collected simply disintegrated, and Bessus fled beyond the Oxus (Āmū Daryā), to continue resistance from the steppe. Alexander occupied "Aornos" (probably Khulm/Tāshkurgan) and Bactra itself (Balkh) and appointed the loyal old Persian Artabazus satrap. (We do not even hear of a Macedonian commander attached to him.) No sooner had he crossed the Oxus than two of Bessus' senior officers deserted and betrayed their leader, enabling Alexander to capture him. The captured usurper and regicide could be used as an object lesson. After rhetorical examination and public humiliation, he was cruelly mutilated and sent to Bactra to be executed under the personal supervision of Oxyathres, a brother of Darius, whom Alexander had honoured and received among his friends. That (it was announced) was the punishment for regicide. His usurpation does not appear to have

¹ The evidence for Alexander's route becomes even more unsatisfactory for these campaigns and the figures given in our texts of Pliny and Strabo are little help. *A priori* logistical considerations can be used to supplement the sources, and Engels has demonstrated the possibilities and the dangers of this approach. The figures from "Phrada" to Ortospana (Kabul) make little sense. The only firm fact we have is that the army reached the Paropamisadae (i.e., crossed the mountains between Ghazna and the Kabul valley) "about the setting of the Pleiades" (Strabo xv.2.10). It has been much discussed whether this means the heliacal (evening) or the cosmical (morning) setting. The former would at that time have been in early April, the latter in early November. (See E. J. Bickerman, *Chronology of the Ancient World* (London, 1968), 143 for details.) Engels makes out an interesting and plausible *a priori* case for the view (for which, see Fischer, *op. cit.*) that the army spent the winter in the lake area of Sīstān, densely settled in antiquity, where supplies would be ample, and marched to Kandahar from there, taking advantage of the Helmand for shipping supplies; however, the road from Farah to Kandahar is far from devoid of cultivated land (see F. R. Allchin and N. Hammond (eds), *The Archaeology of Afghanistan* (London, 1978), 26), and the lower Helmand valley, with the river given to flooding, would not be easy to use either for shipping or for marching. Brunt (in LCL edition of Arrian, *Anabasis*, 499ff.) argues for the direct route. That implies the autumn setting (330), the other the spring setting (329) of the Pleiades. At both times snow would be expected in the mountains. (This has been denied for November; but accounts of the climate in the area lend no support to such a denial.) Strabo's further report that Alexander "spent the winter" (διεχείμασε) in that area and then left after founding a city must imply that he spent it in the Kabul valley and/or near Begrām. (The city is at or near Begrām.) This seems decisive against Engels. (He does not discuss the point.) Bosworth's suggestion (369) that he waited from May over the *next* winter is unlikely. Where and in what sense the Gedrosians submitted to Alexander (A. III.28.1, not saying what he did with them; D. 81.2, with an improbable "Tiridates" (see Berve, no. 755) appointed their satrap) is not clear. The governor could be Tyriespis (called Terioltes by C.: see Berve, no. 758), who was appointed satrap of Paropamisadae in 327 and about whom we know nothing before. Alexander at other times too is known to have transferred satraps. An obscure Greek or Macedonian called Menon was named satrap of Arachosia – the first break in the chain of Iranian satraps.

been mentioned: perhaps it was better to ignore the fact that he had called himself – and had gained some recognition as – king.

But the two nobles who had betrayed Bessus had not done so out of love for Alexander. Spitamenes and Dataphernes were apparently Sogdians, unwilling to serve under any Persian king against a rival. Instead, with the aid of some Bactrians and Scythians, they now organized a national resistance in their own country, which kept Alexander occupied with difficult operations for two years. Even when, late in 328, the two leaders were betrayed to Alexander by their allies on the steppe, who were tired of unprofitable fighting and were themselves in no danger of effective conquest by him, a new Sogdian noble, Oxyartes, emerged to lead the resistance. He was finally shut up in his supposedly impregnable fortress; it was stormed by Alexander and he was captured with his family. Then came an unexpected development: Alexander asked for the hand of his daughter Roxane in lawful marriage. Early in 327, the marriage was celebrated, in a ritual that probably followed Iranian custom. If it had been love at first sight, and a credit to Alexander's nature and gentlemanly conduct, it was also – as Plutarch (*Alex*. 47.7) justly comments – very good policy. The war that had detained Alexander for so long, and that had always flared up when (as now) it seemed ended, was at last within sight of a real end, and a happy one. With Oxyartes as his ally and sponsor, Alexander had just one more siege to undertake. After its success, he could claim the pacification of Sogdiana and associated "Paraetacene" – a feat that the Achaemenids had never perfectly achieved. It never again gave him any real trouble. On the Syr Daryā Alexander founded one of his major colonies, "Alexandria the Farthest", a mixed settlement of Greek mercenaries and natives, as both a bastion against the steppe and a great city to be.[1]

Some time before this happy outcome, there had been less pleasant incidents. One effect of this first serious experience of guerrilla war, constantly marked by victories without success over a hydra-headed enemy, was to strain men's nerves. Alexander's troubles with his officers

---

[1] Arrian is the main source for these campaigns (which must be summarily treated here). The geography is again uncertain, with the main rivers (Āmū Daryā, Syr Daryā, Vakhsh) at least providing a framework. On Alexandria Eschate, see A. IV.1.3f.; 4.1. See Brunt, *op. cit*., 504ff.; Engels, 95ff.

Engels (97) denies the traditional identification of Aornos and suggests Shahr-i bānū, where Hellenistic pottery has been found. But it is a much less impressive site; and we must remember that practically nothing pre-Hellenistic has been found at Balkh, which he (like all others) admits must be the site of Bactra.

flared up again. This time it came about by accident, at a feast in Maracanda (Samarkand). But drink merely brought into the open what must long have been suppressed. Cleitus, objecting to some remarks of Alexander's that he took to be an insult to Macedonians, insulted Alexander in turn; Alexander reacted with anger and suspicion of conspiracy, and in a drunken fury killed the man who had once saved his life. The incident was manslaughter rather than murder – not to be compared to the plot that destroyed the house of Parmenio. But it showed Alexander the danger of his position. As so often, he turned it to advantage. For three days he sat fasting in his tent, announcing his intention to atone for his deed by this slow form of suicide. Meanwhile, it was made clear to the army that the whole affair had been caused by Dionysus, offended by an accidental omission in his cult. It did not take long for the army to realize what their fate would be if they were left at Samarkand without Alexander. They entreated him to live, and he finally agreed – in return for which the army posthumously convicted Cleitus of treason. Alexander generously permitted the body to be buried.[1]

The incident thus acquired importance through its consequences. As Curtius put it, it was the "end of liberty". Alexander had shown first his barons and then his men that he was master. Henceforth he could expect to have no more trouble. Within a few months, the king who previously had not even felt politically able to marry Darius' daughter, which might have brought him immense profit, was able to marry Roxane. It was probably even before that marriage that he followed up his success by trying to introduce *proskynesis*.

Proskynesis was the term used by Greeks to describe the Persian ceremonial salute of an inferior towards a superior, and in particular of subjects towards a king. It is debated in what precisely it consisted and whether (e.g.) the Persepolis reliefs provide illustrations of it. Presumably it could vary according to circumstances. But the Greeks certainly regarded proskynesis to the king, which had at times been exacted of Greek envoys, as involving prostration, and anyone who has read relevant passages in the Bible can hardly doubt that this is how subjects saluted any oriental king. Moreover, the Greeks regarded it not only as servile and humiliating: it is clear that, for them, the gesture involved worship. (How the Persians regarded it, we cannot be sure;

[1] See P. 50–2, with Hamilton's commentary: C. VIII.1.19–2.12 (with more important information).

but it is surely obvious that, however hedged about with divinity, an Achaemenid king could not himself be a god.) The whole subject of proskynesis, in the standard account as our immediate sources found it, was introduced by a formal debate between Callisthenes and a sycophantic philosopher on whether Alexander ought to be deified. The debate, though it goes back to contemporary or almost contemporary tradition, is not, of course, a genuine document. We therefore cannot be sure that the setting of the proskynesis affair in terms of deification is historical: it may be *ex post facto* interpretation. On the other hand, the fact that an account later written by the court chamberlain, known as an apologist who wrote for the greater glory of Alexander, takes care to deprive Callisthenes of the reputation he had gained for opposing proskynesis and, by implication, deification of the living king suffices to show that the story should not be as lightly ignored as it has been by rationalist modern historians. At the very least, we must accept that Alexander, brought up fully in the Greek tradition, realized that the ceremony would be taken to involve deification by Greeks and (probably) Macedonians, and that he had no objection to this.

For what actually happened, we have only the apologetic story; but perhaps it is basically trustworthy in itself, though divorced from its context and slanted to convey a favourable impression of Alexander and an unfavourable one of Callisthenes. It seems that the arrangements had been prepared by Hephaestion. At a banquet attended by Greeks, Macedonians and some Persians, everyone was to perform ceremonial proskynesis to Alexander and receive a kiss in return, which would make him, officially, a "relative" of the king – a high distinction at the Persian court. Callisthenes omitted the ritual, Alexander did not (or would not) notice, but his attention was drawn to the fact and he refused to bestow his kiss. Callisthenes, in this story, departed with a childish quip. The ceremony, however, seems to have continued. When it came to the Persians' turn, a high Macedonian officer, Leonnatus, burst out laughing at the awkward manner in which a dignitary performed the act. That was the end. It was clear that the Macedonians (who had apparently been left to the last) would not perform it, and equally clear that they could not be compelled. Alexander gave up and never required proskynesis of Greeks and Macedonians.[1]

[1] Proskynesis has been interminably and fancifully discussed. The main sources are A. IV.10–12; C. VIII.5; P. 54–5 (and see Hamilton's commentary). All are based on the same accepted version, which fits into the debate on deification; though Plutarch does not set it out, he takes it for granted (wrongly denied by Hamilton). Chares wrote an apologetic account, in which Callisthenes becomes

Both Callisthenes and Leonnatus paid for their opposition. The king's temporary anger against Leonnatus, attested by Arrian's source (IV. 12.2), can be demonstrated. He had been a trusted friend and had helped Alexander in the coup at Phrada. Even now, though he was not actually punished, he failed to gain promotion as quickly as some of the others who had shared in that action. After he saved the king's life in India, he was fully forgiven and finally awarded a golden crown.

Callisthenes paid with his life. He (it must be recalled) was the man who had joined the expedition in order to proclaim Alexander's achievements to the Greeks and to posterity. Now his Homeric hero (whom he had made the son of Zeus) had turned into an oriental despot claiming divine worship from his slave-subjects. It was a grotesque parody of his ideals. However, in view of his previous enthusiasm, Alexander was all the more offended. There could be no forgiveness. At Bactra, after the end of the campaign, some royal pages – sons of nobles kept at court, in part as hostages – conspired against the king. It was claimed that Callisthenes, who was in charge of their education, had inspired them to do it. The claim, as far as we can see, was false. But Callisthenes was arrested and (probably) at once executed.[1]

As will be clear, the sources will never permit us to give a clear description and evaluation of the proskynesis affair. Certainly, to keep up a split personality on the throne – to be a Homeric king to Greeks and Macedonians and the Chosen of Ahura Mazda to Iranians, with all the differences in personnel and ceremonial that went with these two positions – was technically and psychologically an almost unbearable strain. Each of the facets was made unacceptable by the existence of the other. A traditional Macedonian kingship was not easy to occupy in personal union with a traditional oriental one. And they had, of course, to be unified at the Persian level, which Alexander now thought more

---

a hero by chance and Alexander does his best to be lenient. Of course, opposition from one Greek intellectual would not have been enough to kill the attempt: the expression of Macedonian opinion must be accepted (cf. next note). On the whole subject, see my discussion in "The deification" [X]. On the reliefs, see G. Walser, *Audienz beim persischen Grosskönig* (Zurich, 1965), 12ff., plausibly controverting the view that the reliefs show this act.

[1] For the pages' conspiracy see A. IV.13f.; 22.2; C. VIII.6f.; P. 55 (with Hamilton's notes). Ptolemy (*apud* A.) reported that Callisthenes (whom, of course, he regarded as guilty) was at once executed; Aristobulus (*ibid.*) that he was arrested and taken round under guard with the army, until he finally died of disease. This account probably comes from Chares (*apud* P. 55.9), who added that the intention was to have him tried by the Council of the Hellenic League. That story is patently absurd (if that was intended, he could have been sent off to Europe at once) and makes the whole apologetic version unacceptable. For the innocence of Callisthenes, as far as the pages' conspiracy is concerned, see Hamilton [II.2], 155 (with references).

fitting. As it was, it turned out a humiliating and – after the death of Cleitus – probably an unexpected defeat. He was not master after all. The pages' conspiracy, coming soon after, had – although not a major event in itself – an indirect importance that he was presumably not slow to see: boys would do what their fathers no longer dared to.

Whether Alexander positively wanted deification is a more puzzling question. As we have seen, it is clear that he must have known the implications of his demand for Greeks and Macedonians; i.e., he was willing to *accept* deification. What he had been told about the status of the Persian king, of course, we cannot even guess. In any case, the version that makes his demand an order for deification and Callisthenes the leader of a heroic Greek resistance to this arose (as we have noted) within a short time. Chares already had to contradict it. This fact must also be borne in mind in any attempt at evaluation.

Thus nearly two years of nerve-racking tension beyond the Oxus ended at last, with the murderous finale at Bactra following upon (or perhaps preceding) a wedding in royal style. Meanwhile other administrative arrangements had been made: mostly the replacement of suspect Persian satraps with other Persians.[1] There was one really important change: the aged Artabazus, given Bactria (perhaps) as an honour rather than as a serious responsibility, resigned after a few months for reasons of age. It was probably expected. We are told by Curtius (VIII.1.19; 2.14) that Cleitus was appointed to succeed him, but that his death intervened. Amyntas, a Macedonian, took his place, and the province turned out to be not merely Bactria, but Bactria and Sogdiana – the whole northeastern frontier of the empire, to be defended against rebels within and invaders from the steppe outside. Greek mercenaries were settled at various points and, after a minor rebellion during Alexander's temporary absence had shown the vulnerability of the province, Alexander left 10,000 infantry and 3,500 cavalry

---

[1] Atropates, governor of Media under Darius and loyal to him to the end, now received back his old satrapy, part of which (Āzarbāījān) was later to immortalize his name. Stasanor, successful in the troublesome province of Areia, took over Drangiana. (But it is possible that A. is mistaken and he had received it before.) Autophradates seems to have acted suspiciously in the Caspian provinces, and Phrataphernes was deputed to arrest him and add the provinces to his own (Parthia-Hyrcania), which gave him a vast province and made him a key figure on the northern frontier, as Amyntas was on the north-eastern. (Autophradates was executed after Alexander's return from India: C. x.1.39.) Mazaeus had died, and a man of (to us) unknown origin and background, Stamenes, was sent to replace him. (All A. IV.18; see Berve, nos 180, 719, 814 (cf. 189), 718; but there is no particular reason to think Stamenes (no. 718) a "noble Persian", as Berve does; he may equally well have been a Greek or Macedonian.)

(we are not told who they were, but presumably mostly mercenaries) with Amyntas, when he finally left for India. It was clear that he needed them. When the province is next mentioned, it is in connection with the mercenaries' rebellion: by then, we find another Macedonian in charge. As usual, the sources give us no details of how and when this came about.[1]

In that vast province, only recently pacified, a reliable Macedonian was essential. Another arrangement made about this time shows that Alexander, though he still depended on his Macedonians, was already beginning to look beyond them – perhaps (but we do not know the precise sequence) because of the failure of the proskynesis attempt. In any case, it is our first indication of a new policy. Curtius (VIII.5.1) reports that he now collected 30,000 native boys "from all provinces" (presumably, however, only those in Iran are meant), to use them both as soldiers and as hostages. We learn that they were to be taught the Greek language and the use of Macedonian arms (P. 47.6). They were to make an impressive appearance a few years later.[2]

After completing his arrangements in Bactra, Alexander marched back to Alexandria of the Hindu Kush in ten days (this time, with the country pacified, no doubt taking the shortest route). It was presumably late summer 327, and the passes would be clear. After strengthening the city with new settlers and appointing a new Iranian satrap for the province of Paropamisadae, he divided his forces and began his invasion of India. He had been in touch with various Indian chieftains for some time, and they had promised him support in return for his aid against their rivals.[3]

India had been part of the kingdom of Darius I, certainly as far as Gandhara and Sind (Hinduš). Scylax of Caryanda had sailed down the Indus in his service and, after a magnificent *periplous* – known, as he

---

[1] A. IV.22.3; C. VIII.2.14ff.; cf. Strabo XI.9.4. If Aï Khanum, recently excavated by French archaeologists (see *CHI* III, 1032ff.), is an Alexander foundation (for which there is no good evidence), it would be one of these military colonies that were in certain respects different from cities, though with many civic institutions.

[2] Plutarch, as often, has the story out of chronological order. The time is made clear by Curtius; he reports the incident just before the proskynesis scene, as one of the events that happened just before Alexander's departure. There appears to be no intention of implying chronological sequence, which C. himself perhaps did not know.

[3] A. IV.22.3 says "at the end of spring", but late spring seems impossible in the light of the preceding campaign, plus the fact that Alexander left Begrām only in November (Strabo XV.1.17). The emendation of "spring" to "summer" has been suggested (reading θέρους for ἦρος), and this would save A.'s credit. But it may be another of his slips. For earlier contacts with Indians, see A. IV.30.4; C. VIII.12.5. The new satrap was Tyriespis (cf. p. 455, n. 1 above).

later recorded it, to Hecataeus and Herodotus (IV.44) – had reached the Gulf of Suez. The coast of Makrān had become a trade route after this, and India still appears in the monuments of later Achaemenian Kings: Gandhara is on all the surviving lists; Xerxes mentions Hinduš among his provinces; and the carvings on the tomb of Artaxerxes III, who restored the empire in the 4th century, show an Indian among the subject nations. After this, we have no concrete evidence until the time of Darius III himself, who had an Indian corps in his army. Summoned as reinforcements after Issus (C. IV.9.2), they appear in the battle of Gaugamela (A. III.8.3: the "Indians bordering on the Bactrians" – the only attempt to define their precise origin; 11.5; 14.5 (the dash for the Macedonian baggage-train); also in C. and D.). The definition in Arrian shows that these Indians – clearly contrasted, as subjects, with the Sacae, who are allies – must come from the satrapy of Gandhara. In so far as Herodotus' satrapy list can be taken as corresponding to any administrative reality, this is the seventh province, yielding 170 talents (Hdt. III.91). Alexander, of course, had read Herodotus. But Achaemenian rule over India was by no means dead. It is often stated in modern books that India had been entirely lost during the troubles of the 4th century in the empire. Our Alexander sources show that this is not true. Not only are there the troops from India, but there are further indications which, though not by themselves secure, must be taken in close conjunction with the attested fact of some remnant of Achaemenian control.[1]

[1] For Gandhara and Hinduš see R. G. Kent, *Old Persian*[2] (New Haven, Conn., 1953), DP^c 17–18, DN^a 24–5, XPh 25, A?P 12–13 etc. It seems to be generally assumed (see, as a random specimen, Tarn in *CAH* VI, 19) that Achaemenian control over India had been lost in the 4th century (Tarn adds that he does not know when). Yet the fact that there were Indian subjects of Darius III, "bordering on the Bactrians", shows that at least part of Gandhara was still under *de facto* control. (India is constantly mentioned as a province in Curtius' speeches. That should mean that he found it as such in his sources and regarded it as a matter of course.) Strabo, citing Eratosthenes, tells us (XV.1.10) that at the time of Alexander's invasion the Indus was regarded as the boundary between "Ariana" (held by the Persians) and "India". He adds that later the Indians, after taking it over from the Macedonians, also held much of Ariana. Ariana must therefore be Gandhara, and although we cannot tell how far actual control extended, it was in principle a Persian satrapy, just as it had been in the earlier satrapy lists. (There is no trace of Sind – according to Herodotus the richest province, with a tribute total of 460 talents, whereas Gandhara only yielded 170: see, for what it is worth, Hdt. III.91, 94.) The same boundary is reported, with reference to Alexander, by Arrian, who (V.4.3) makes Alexander "cross into the land of the Indians" when he crosses the Indus, and appends his geographical excursus at this point (cf. *Ind.* 2.1, after Eratosthenes 3.1); though at other times (e.g. IV.21.3) he uses "India" for the country (roughly) beyond the Khyber Pass, as Curtius also does (VIII.10.1, with the excursus at this point). Unwillingness to accept the reported fact leads to strange results, as when Berve (p. 354) makes Sisicottus a prince of the Indo-Bactrian border areas and says he had joined Bessus "for unknown reasons". In fact, he had clearly joined him because he had been summoned by

ALEXANDER IN IRAN

We have seen that Alexander had been in touch with some Indian leaders. It is noteworthy that Sisicottus, clearly from somewhere in the general area of the satrapy of Gandhara, had joined Bessus and then changed to Alexander. Similarly, the embassy from Taxiles to Alexander, when he was fighting Bessus, was presumably concerned to render homage to the rightful king – naturally, to the vassal's advantage. When Alexander entered India, we find him sending a herald to Taxiles and the rulers of the land up to the Indus, bidding them to meet him (A. IV.22.6); they all met him and brought gifts, we are told. In the circumstances, we are entitled to say that he was, here as elsewhere, entering into what he had for some time been claiming as his rightful inheritance. Moreover, the challenge came at precisely the right time. The campaign could purge the army of the horrors (military and civil) of Bactria and Sogdiana.

The Indian campaign took less than two years, covering a remarkable amount of territory unknown to the Greek world in that time, in climatic conditions which even the hardened Macedonians soon found burdensome. In view of the facts just set out, the campaign is certainly relevant to Iranian history: it is, like Alexander's campaign as a whole, a tailpiece to Achaemenian history. But it would take us too far to follow it in detail. A sketch must suffice, concentrating on administrative arrangements.

Alexander divided the army, sending Hephaestion and Perdiccas along the main route with one part, while he took a more difficult northerly route himself – a strategic idea similar to his invasion of Fārs. All the local tribes were subdued, at times by bloody methods, and he reached the Indus and duly found it bridged for him, with gifts from the friendly Taxiles. He was lavishly entertained in Taxila itself (e.g. he received a gift of elephants, though he seems never to have used them in battle) and was briefed on the situation in the area. Taxiles' main enemy, against whom he wanted Alexander's help, was "Porus", the

---

him to do so, as a vassal by his king. It was only when he reached Bactria that he found out that there was a contest over who was really king, and decided to join the obviously stronger side (see p. 461, n. 3 above, *ad fin.*). C. VIII.12.5, though using the terminology of the Roman Empire and its client kings, suggests that Taxiles too had in fact recognized Alexander as his suzerain. If so, even Sind was not entirely beyond the empire's reach. Alexander was later apparently unwilling to admit that any one had preceded him into "India" (beyond the Indus): see p. 473, n. 2 below. But not only had the upper Indus presumably been the boundary between the two Persian provinces in India; the fact that Scylax sailed down the river to its mouth and that Darius used it for trade shows, by comparison with Alexander's experiences (see below), that he must have controlled the other bank as well. For the absence of a satrap in Gandhara, see below.

king of the Paurava, beyond the Hydaspes (Jhelum). It was clear that he would try to prevent Alexander from crossing the river.

It was probably at this point, after receiving the information he needed, that Alexander finally decided on the general shape of his Indian administration after the expected conquest. From Asia Minor to the Hindu Kush he had basically taken over what he had found, with such adaptations (e.g. the "freedom of the Greeks", or Ada in Caria) as policy might suggest. From Babylon to Paropamisadae, he had (with the exception of a few Macedonians in key posts such as Bactria-Sogdiana) mostly appointed Iranian satraps, even (like Phrataphernes) to positions of considerable power and trust. In fact, wherever possible he had reappointed existing satraps. In this and in his subordinate appointments, he had, as we saw, at most extended Achaemenian practice. It therefore seems clear from his actions in India that he found no Achaemenian administration, i.e. no actual satrap over the territory up to the Indus, even though (as we have seen) Achaemenian suzerainty had been recognized. How long there had been no satrap, we cannot tell; but at least in the recent past Achaemenian control had been exercised (not ineffectively, as we saw) through client rulers. What evidence we have surveyed suggests that the satrap of Bactria was the one to whom the Indian rulers had been in some sense attached. Alexander at once decided to leave the general system intact, but to tighten control by appointing a satrap. He may, of course, have been told that this had been the Achaemenian system even within living memory.[1]

West of the Indus, even before the country was fully conquered, the Macedonian Nicanor was appointed. (There were in any case no suitable Iranians here.) He would control all that was not yet organized of Achaemenian Gandhara. Under him, the loyal Sisicottus was before long promoted to a position that set him apart from the other rulers; while they, as far as loyal to Alexander and recognized, continued to rule their tribes. Before Alexander left Taxila, another Macedonian, Philip son of Machatas, was appointed to govern the territory from the Indus to the Hydaspes. Under him, Taxiles in view of his power and his loyalty, had a special position, perhaps even stronger than that created for Sisicottus.[2]

[1] Alexander's route and battles can be followed in Arrian, with relatively few problems. See also any standard work on Alexander. I shall confine references to important and/or difficult (and relevant) points.

[2] Nicanor was made satrap before Alexander even reached the river. But Sisicottus was at first given only a very minor post (A. IV.30.4: garrison commander at the newly taken rock of

ALEXANDER IN IRAN

He succeeded with difficulty in crossing the Hydaspes, defeated Porus in a major battle and took him prisoner. The meeting of those two knights soon became a topic for biographical romance. Alexander was impressed with Porus and decided to trust him, after formally binding him to himself with appropriate gifts. He was fortunate that Porus survived: there would (as far as we know) have been no one else to take his place. Alexander founded two settlements in the area (one named after his horse Bucephalus, which had just died) and received the formal submission of Abisares, ruler of much of Kashmir. Then he advanced to the Acesines (Chenab) and, through the monsoon rains, to the Hydraotes (Ravi). Those resisting were harshly treated, but most of the towns and tribes surrendered without trouble. After a nephew had been forced to submit to Porus, the latter was sent home, ordered to collect troops and instructed to rejoin Alexander with them. Needless to say, Porus had been "reconciled" with Taxiles, i.e. both had been bound over to keep the peace.[1]

Before he reached the Acesines, he heard that Nicanor had been killed in a rebellion. He did not let that distract him, but ordered the governors of the two adjoining provinces, Philip from the east and Tyriespis from Paropamisadae in the west, to restore order; Sisicottus, meanwhile, seems to have been deputed to take charge as satrap.[2]

When Porus returned with the newly collected forces, he was ordered to garrison the newly conquered area, while Alexander advanced to the next river, the Hyphasis (Beas). He was eager to cross it, particularly since the area on the other side was said to be fertile and prosperous. Whether, as late sources assert, he wanted to go on to the legendary

---

Aornos). We do not hear of his promotion; but when we next hear of him, it had certainly taken place (see n. 2 below). For Taxila, about 20 miles from Rawalpindi, see Sir John Marshall's classic excavation report, *Taxila*, 3 vols (Cambridge, 1951). For the appointments, see A. v.8.3 (Philip); A. is again not very helpful, but we hear that Taxiles had all the territory he wanted added to his (v.8.2), and we later find him in a position of major authority (A. vi.27.2; cf. C. x.1.20).

[1] C. viii. 14.14ff. shows the elaboration to the full; cf. P. 60, *fin*. Later authors return to it. For the battle, see Hamilton, 163ff. The famous decadrachms usually called by scholars "Porus decadrachms" in some way seem to commemorate the battle, as do the tetradrachms with bowman and elephant that probably go with them. (See M. J. Price, in *Archaeological Reports for 1973–74* (xx. The Hellenic Society and The British School at Athens, 1974), 68.) For the "reconciliation", see A. v.20.4; C. ix.3.22 (sealed by a marriage). For cruel punishment see A. v.24.5 (exaggerated).

[2] A. v.20.7: a message from the "satrap" Sisicottus, that the "hyparch" had been killed. There is clearly some confusion, as the man killed can only have been Nicanor. But we may take the promotion of Sisicottus for granted; and since Nicanor was not immediately replaced, Sisicottus presumably became acting satrap. It is also of interest to see that a Macedonian and an Iranian satrap are treated on a footing of complete equality for the purpose of an important military operation.

Ganges, or even to the Circumambient Ocean, we cannot tell. He had no doubt started with only the vaguest notion of Indian geography, since neither Greeks nor (probably) even Persians had got as far as he now had. But he is said to have heard (correctly) that he was twelve days from the Ganges, and since this would be a feasible objective, we may believe that he did want to reach it: he must certainly by now have been aware of its importance. But if Nearchus knew (*apud* Strabo xv. 1.12) that it was four months' march across the Indian plain, Alexander too must by then have heard some such estimates; and it is unlikely that he was forming plans as extravagant as that, although, had things gone well, he might possibly have kept marching forward as long as he could, without any definite plan of stopping.[1]

This must have been obvious to his soldiers. They had come to many historic landmarks, from the Halys to the Indus, and they had never been allowed to stop. They must have begun to suspect that Alexander never would stop. It was not the twelve days to the Ganges (even in the monsoon rains) that worried them, let alone the elephants of the Indian tribes in the way: they were now familiar with elephants, and the veterans of Alexander's marches could put up with rain for a limited time. The trouble was simply that there was no end in sight. Sooner or later, what happened now had to happen. At the Beas the men refused to go on. Coenus, one of the senior officers, became their spokesman. Coenus had been a son-in-law of Parmenio, and his brother Cleander second-in-command to Parmenio at Ecbatana. When Philotas was arrested, Coenus was active in securing his conviction; and his brother had supervised Parmenio's assassination and had succeeded him. These men may have been kinsmen of the Treasurer Harpalus – all from the district of Elimiotis in Upper Macedonia. This, then, was the officer who presented the men's case to the king. Alexander had used the army in order to suppress opposition among the nobles: it was the army that had been persuaded to convict Philotas and Cleitus. The new development boded no good.

For the moment, he tried to use the weapon that had succeeded

---

[1] The Ganges: C. IX.2.2; D. 93.2. (The distance is about 200 miles.) The question of Alexander's aims at this point has often been (fruitlessly) discussed; see, e.g., Tarn II, 281f. (showing confusion in the sources) and, on the other side, F. Schachermeyr, "Alexander und die Ganges-Länder", in R. Muth and J. Knobloch (eds), *Natalicium Carolo Jax...oblatum* I, (Innsbruck, 1955), 123–35 (Innsbrucker Beiträge zur Kulturwissenschaft 3); repr. In Griffith [III], 137–49. See, with further bibliography and sensible summing up, Hamilton, 170f.

before. He withdrew to his tent, for three days. But this time it did not help. The men were determined, and as Coenus had made clear, they had the officers' support. Alexander could not divide them. All that remained was to save face. He announced that he would go on nonetheless and ordered the sacrifices for crossing the river to be performed. Fortunately, they turned out unfavourable. Amid universal jubilation, he submitted to the will of the gods (though not of the army) and decided not to go on. Coenus shortly after this died of illness. Whether his death was divine punishment or more sinister, we cannot tell. Certainly, Alexander could not have openly executed the champion of the army; nor could he continue to trust him. As we shall see, later events suggest suspicion; though nothing, of course, could be said, let alone proved.[1]

Turning back did not mean returning. Perhaps the army was in any case too large to march back: ancient armies, for logistical reasons, could not easily return the way they had come. But with the country fully pacified and its rulers friendly, and rivers available for transport, it is hard to believe that this was an important factor. Deprived of his opportunity of continuing eastwards, Alexander decided to march south and reach the Ocean at the mouth of the Indus. He ordered a fleet to be built at the Hydaspes,[2] handed the recently conquered territory over to Porus, and established a new settlement of natives and veterans on the Acesines; he also helped to reestablish the two earlier ones, which were already beginning to disintegrate. Abisares was now confirmed as ruler of Kashmir. When the fleet was ready, he put his boyhood friend Nearchus in charge of it and, after impressive religious ceremonies, he himself, with selected contingents, embarked on it, while the rest of the

[1] For the mutiny see A. v.25–9. (It must be stressed that all the speeches are A.'s own composition: they have sometimes been misused as historical evidence.) Cf. C. IX.2–3.19. For Coenus, whose championship of the men must be true (as a substratum for the speeches written for him by our sources), see Berve, no. 439; for his death, A. VI.2.1 (not precisely dated); C. IX.3.20 (at the Acesines). He had a magnificent funeral.

[2] C. IX.1.3f. and D. 89.4f. relate the building of the fleet straight after the victory over Porus. Curtius, characteristically, shows that he could make no sense of this. He adds: "...ut, cum totam Asiam percucurrisset, finem terrarum mare inuiseret". In view of his attested plans for advancing eastwards, Alexander can hardly have ordered a fleet to take him south to be built at this point. Arrian (v.29.3; VI.1.6) puts preparations for the voyage only at the Acesines and final arrangements only at the Hydaspes. Aristobulus (Strabo XV.1.17) mentions that the army waited for the ships to be built there. If ships were built earlier, they were meant for different purposes: for supplies, of course, and perhaps for exploration, in connection with his momentary idea that he had found the sources of the Nile (see A. VI.1). Engels (109) suggests the logistic consideration as one among others, in making Alexander decide to turn south.

army, under Hephaestion and Craterus, began the march south along the banks. Philip with his satrapal forces was to follow. According to Nearchus (*apud* A. *Ind.* 19.5), the whole force numbered 120,000 men.

On his way south, Alexander attacked two major Indian tribes, called in our sources Oxydracae and Malli. The campaign was difficult and hazardous, and it is clear that the Macedonians had no stomach for it. While personally leading the assault on one of the towns of the Malli, Alexander found little support among his troops and was seriously wounded inside the fortress. Only Peucestas and Leonnatus were there to save his life. For a time it was feared that the king was dying. The shock threw the army into despair: they realized, what they had perhaps recently forgotten over their grievances, that only Alexander's genius stood between them and destruction in a hostile country. When he could walk and ride again, relief erupted in an almost hysterical fashion. It had probably been Alexander's intention, in that fierce and (on strict military grounds) avoidable campaign, both to punish the army for their mutiny (and their resentment shows that they understood it in this way) and to bind them to himself anew by his personal actions. Thanks to the wound, he fully succeeded. With Coenus dead, the orgy of emotion on his recovery could be considered to have purged the memory of the Hyphasis.[1]

At the junction of the Acesines and Indus the army rested and Alexander reviewed the administration of his Indian conquests. Philip was appointed satrap of the whole Indian territory from the Hindu Kush to the Hydaspes–Acesines line down to the point of junction with the Indus, with the Oxydracae and Malli under his supervision. At this point (unfortunately not precisely identifiable) a city was founded, to serve as a bastion and an administrative and commercial centre. Alexander's father-in-law Oxyartes had been asked to meet him here, which shows that the reorganization had been planned ahead. He was sent to take over Paropamisadae (the key satrapy securing the roads from Afghanistan into India) from Tyriespis. Peitho (another Macedonian) was appointed to govern the Indian territory still to be conquered, down to the mouth of the Indus. No change was made in arrangements further

---

[1] A. VI.4–13, with some embroidery; C. IX.3–6, with ample rhetoric. Cleitarchus' statement that Ptolemy helped to save Alexander's life (nothing of the kind is mentioned by Ptolemy himself) is picked out for special condemnation by both A. VI.11.8 and C. IX.5.21 – hence presumably already by an earlier source. The conflict of evidence is important in the debate over priority of original sources.

north, where Porus had been put in charge of "all the Indian territory conquered up to the Hyphasis".[1]

The organization tells us much about Alexander's plans for India, and for the eastern frontier of his empire. It is clear that he now indeed thought in terms of an eastern frontier. Porus was left practically independent, attached to Alexander merely by the bond of homage. There were no Macedonian forces in his kingdom; on the contrary, he had been instructed to put his own garrisons into the newly added territories. The Hydaspes–Acesines line, south of Kashmir, on the other hand, was strongly held by Philip, with Taxiles in charge of the native chieftains, at least in the north, and several fortresses newly built on both sides of the river frontier to defend it. The concept of the frontier is reminiscent of that of the Achaemenian (where we know about it) and the later Roman frontier: a firmly held frontier province with a natural boundary, and client states beyond, in whatever degree of dependence could be maintained without costly effort. And behind the frontier lay a solid block of provinces held by Greeks or Macedonians – Bactria-Sogdiana, Areia-Drangiana, Arachosia – with the key to the whole structure, Paropamisadae, in the hands of the only oriental east of Parthia: Alexander's Sogdian father-in-law Oxyartes. It is clear that the policy of attracting the Persian nobility into Alexander's service was no more pursued with romantic heedlessness than the Hellenic crusade had been. Alexander was no dreamer.

The journey down the Indus was combined with the ruthless subjugation of the inhabitants on both banks, in the east probably as far as the edge of the great desert. The Brahmins, who had already been the centre of resistance among the Malli, inspired constant major revolts in Alexander's rear, and only the planting of numerous garrisons and,

[1] A. VI.2.1 reports that Porus was made "king of the Indian territory so far occupied" before the embarkation on the Hydaspes. This is clearly false as it stands, as there was a satrap between the Indus and the Hydaspes. But Porus may have retained the royal title while technically satrap over the area east of the Hydaspes. This was a practice known under the Achaemenians, and Alexander had come across it in Caria. The son of Abisares, who was allowed to be "satrap" of his kingdom (A. V. 29.4 – the term, as often in A., is probably not technical), does not appear in the satrapy list of Diod. XVIII.3, as Porus and Taxiles (on whom see below) do: presumably he had made himself independent. Strabo quotes a statement in a late source, that Porus was given all the territory between Hydaspes and Hyphasis, containing nine tribes and 5,000 large cities, as a typical exaggeration. It is closely related to Arrian's source, which gave seven tribes and "over 2,000 cities" and extended the territory to the Indus (unless that is A.'s own mistake). Arrian's text states (VI.15.4) that "Oxyartes and Peitho" were appointed to the new territory. As Oxyartes' new appointment has just been mentioned, this must be a textual error. C., in a very confused account (IX.8.9f.), reports that Tyriespis was executed.

at times, a policy of extermination secured the frontier. On his arrival at Pattala, at the head of the Indus delta, about midsummer 325, he found that, even though the ruler had earlier made his submission, both he and all the inhabitants had fled. Alexander had deservedly acquired the reputation of a Chingiz-Khan.

Several days before, he had begun to make his final arrangements for the return to the west, at a point some distance upstream from Pattala. Craterus was given about half the army (including all the veterans to be later discharged) and the elephants, and ordered to march over the Bolan pass through Arachosia and Drangiana, pacify the country (which had never been thoroughly conquered), and meet Alexander in Carmania. He himself intended to march through the Makrān, with the rest of the army, completing the conquest of his empire by incorporating the tribes west of the Indus on the way. The policy of extermination, directed particularly against the Brahmins and their followers, had no doubt been deliberate: the Indian desert provided a natural frontier for the empire in the southeast, but with Alexander about to leave, it was essential that no focus of future guerrilla war should be left within those boundaries. Thus the plans for the eastern frontier that had taken shape at the junction of Acesines and Indus were carried to their logical conclusion. Unlike the northeast, the southeast had offered stubborn guerrilla resistance, and no native ruler had emerged who was willing and able to undertake the function of a client king, a Porus or even a Taxiles. Alexander had adopted the only feasible alternative.

At Pattala he stopped for about two months, ordering the fortification of the city and collecting his supplies for the journey. Ignoring climatic facts (as often), he decided to sail down one of the two main arms of the river against the force of the monsoon. This was accomplished with difficulty, but he reached the Ocean and duly sacrificed to Poseidon in a splendid ceremony. He then explored the other main arm and the immediate coastline, completed local arrangements, and put Nearchus in charge of a large fleet, which was to sail along the coast from the Indus to the Persian Gulf, following the example set, long ago, by Scylax. It was planned that fleet and army should support each other along the difficult coast.[1]

[1] On Nearchus see E. Badian, *YCS* xxiv (1975), 147–70. For his account of his commission see A. *Ind.* 20. On the nature of Nearchus' account (in part written as an apologia and for self-glorification) see Badian, *loc. cit.* For Craterus' instructions, see A. vi.17.3; cf. 27.3. Craterus must have marched via the Mulla and Bolan passes to Kandahar; after that, his route cannot be reconstructed in detail, since his duties might take him well off the shortest route. Our sources are not interested in his march or achievement. For Alexander's treatment of the Indians in this area, see A. vi.16–17; cf. C. ix.8.15 for an example. Strabo (xv.2.4f.) makes Craterus set out

ALEXANDER IN IRAN

Setting out without waiting for the monsoon to abate, Alexander crossed the Arabis (Hab), traditionally the boundary between India and Iran, and, by his usual terror methods, subdued the Oreitae, who refused to surrender. He founded an Alexandria at their main town (near Bela) and appointed Apollophanes satrap of the area, adding (in his usual optimistic anticipation) Gedrosia, which he was about to enter. Leonnatus was left there with a force, for additional security, and Alexander, with the main army, entered the Makrān desert.

The sufferings of his army and, more terrible still, of the non-combatants he had taken along, during that march of nearly two months, are aptly described in our sources. Arrian (not from his main, apologetic, sources) paints a vivid and credible picture of the horror. A modern survey (admittedly only a rough estimate) has put the number of men with Alexander at about 60,000, of whom about 45,000 were lost; and that in addition to the non-combatants, who, where we can check, greatly outnumbered the soldiers.[1] It was a major disaster by any standards, even if we like to scale the figures down – much the worst disaster that Alexander ever suffered. Inevitably, one has to ask how and why it happened. Why did Alexander undertake the expedition, instead of going back by an easier route? What went wrong, to lead to the disaster?

Both in ancient and in modern times, the answers proceed on similar lines. The admirers and apologists have tried to allege perfectly rational motives, and unforeseeable accidents: "to support the fleet [under Nearchus]...by digging wells and forming depots of provisions". Moreover, Alexander was unaware of the nature of the country he was to cross, or of the nature of the monsoon, which stranded him when he could no longer turn back. A highly sympathetic picture can be painted, showing him choosing the least among evils, which were not due to his own error or wilfulness.[2]

---

from the Hydaspes, with orders to conquer Ariana: this, unfortunately, makes Strabo's testimony suspect where he cannot be checked; but there is no alternative to using him in such cases. Pattala and other places in the lower Indus valley cannot be identified, since the course of the Indus at that time is quite unknown.

[1] There has been much discussion about Alexander's route in the Oreitan campaign and in the desert. Sir Aurel Stein's work first showed what could be done, and it has been further developed by recent archaeological investigations. For an excellent and detailed summary of the results (which are more accurate than for many other parts of Alexander's route), see Engels, 115ff., 137–43. For discussion of the desert march (but with the route wrong), see H. Strasburger, *Hermes* LXXX (1952), 456ff. (the numbers too high).

[2] The quotation is from Tarn 1.106, based on the apologetic source in A. VI.23.1. (And cf. next note.) The development is by Engels (110ff., especially 114f.), with implausible reasons for an economic motivation added. He does not properly ask the simple question why Alexander did

But this will not do. That he was unaware of the nature of the Gedrosian desert is denied by an ancient source that ought to know: none other than his friend Nearchus. That he was unaware of the nature of the monsoon, if arguable, would be unforgivable in itself. He had spent two months at Pattala, quite long enough for thorough intelligence: as we have seen, it had functioned better in other situations, equally unfamiliar, even when the army was constantly on the move. That, in all that time, and while constantly engaged on preparations for the journey, he should have failed to find out about a natural phenomenon of predictable regularity, which (in essence) he had already come across in the previous year (cf. Aristobulus *apud* Strabo xv.1.17), is an argument to appeal to faith rather than reason. As for supporting the fleet: not only did it turn out (again, on the whole, foreseeably, in view of the known advantages of moving on water over moving on land) that the fleet needed far less support than the army; but, in actual practice, how could places be found where wells might be dug? How, in a hostile desert, could the wells be protected against nature and enemy tribesmen? How could provisions be laid down by an army that did not know where its own provisions would be coming from, and again, how could depots be protected, for an unknown length of time, by soldiers who themselves would have to survive in a desert? Even purely strategic and political considerations are unsatisfactory: if the area had to be pacified, to round off the empire, Pura could have been taken from the other side; and the desert did not matter: Alexander had not taken extreme steps to "pacify" desert nomads further north. In any case, for this or any other legitimate purpose (e.g. exploration), the force was many times too large, and so, even more, was the number of non-combatants. Rationalizing explanations simply will not work.

It was Nearchus who provided the major part of the answer, while (in fact) going out of his way to glorify Alexander: Alexander knew the dangers of the route, but took it because he had heard that Semiramis and Cyrus, setting out to conquer India, had marched that way and had lost nearly all their forces. He felt challenged to surpass them. How and from whom he heard this, we cannot know: perhaps from friends trying to warn, perhaps from enemies trying to issue that very challenge. But the heroic explanation is entirely credible. Imitation of heroes – Achilles, Heracles, Dionysus – had always been part of

not return along the route assigned to Craterus, perhaps despatching a small and mobile force to achieve any serious objectives he may have had in Makrān.

Alexander's personality. However rational and calculating in his methods, he was a mystic in his ultimate motivation.[1] But this time there may be more to be added. His defeat by his own men had shaken his supernatural standing among men, and (worse still) his own belief in himself and his divine protection. What had happened since – the all but fatal wound that had restored his soldiers' love and loyalty; the conquest of southern India, which, in the purely military sense, was as outstanding an achievement as, from any purely rational strategic point of view, it had been unnecessary – all this had helped him recover. But something more striking was needed: a countervailing triumph to erase the memory. Nature and myth provided the challenge.

Of course, whatever his motives and his trust in his divine protection, Alexander, as usual, took reasonable care. Yet he made mistakes, and he was unlucky. First, to depart while the fleet was detained by winds was inadvisable: soon after he had gone, it was attacked by the natives on whom he had inflicted so much merciless punishment, and that forced Nearchus into a hurried departure. He had arranged for supplies to be sent to the army along the route by adjacent satraps: Apollophanes (Oreitae), Stasanor (Areia-Drangiana), perhaps also Menon (Arachosia). But not only were the distances so large that adequate supplies could not be carried: two of them could not even try. Apollophanes was killed in fighting and Menon died, we do not know when. Stasanor reached him, with numerous camels and other transport animals he had collected, only in Carmania, probably just as he had been ordered to do. No supplies reached him on the march, therefore; and after the guides lost their way, there was no chance of success. When the depleted army finally struggled through to Pura (probably somewhere near Bampur), the challenge had failed, and a search for scapegoats began.[2]

[1] Nearchus is quoted by A. VI.24 (adding that another motive was to support the fleet); Strabo XV.1.5; cf. 2.5. A. VI.24.2 is obviously confused, but fortunately explained by the other references. On imitation of heroes see Edmunds [X].

[2] A. reports Nearchus as recording the "history" he had heard from the Indians, to the effect that in many generations since Heracles (a gap conceals the number) no one – not even Cyrus – had conquered India, but "Alexander had come and conquered by armed force all the countries he entered, and would have conquered the whole world, if his army had been willing." Nearchus himself, of course, knew of the Persian conquest of India, at least by Darius I; as indeed all the Greeks, and particularly those on the expedition, must have. That this known fact is suppressed, and a totally imaginary attempt invented, and that this is coupled with a reference to the Hyphasis mutiny, provides welcome background to what was being talked about at Alexander's court before the Gedrosian expedition. For the care in Alexander's preparation, see Engels, 110ff. For the satraps named see Berve, nos. 105, 719, 515. A. VI.27 makes Stasanor's collection of baggage animals his own idea, as he had "conjectured" that the king would need them. It is unlikely that Alexander himself had not foreseen the need.

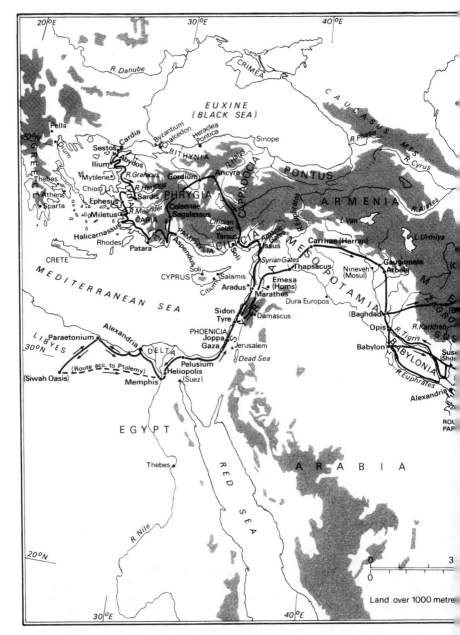

Map 17. Alexander's route.

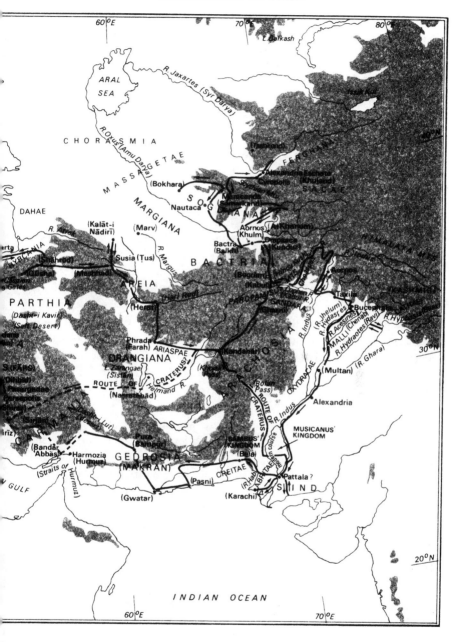

Even there, Alexander was unlucky. The first action he took was to depose Apollophanes. While still at Pura, however, he received a despatch from Leonnatus, announcing that he had defeated a rebellion by the Oreitae, in which Apollophanes had died![1] It was the signal for a reign of terror.

The reign of terror among the satraps and commanders that began at Pura and ended only when Alexander reached Susa was inevitably disguised by the king's propaganda. As a result, it puzzled our immediate sources and has misled most modern historians. The facts are plain, and fairly simple. Of twenty-one satraps in the Asian part of Alexander's kingdom in early 325, four died by early 324 of various causes not connected with Alexander. Of the remaining seventeen, six were deposed, all but one of them (Apollophanes – who, as we saw, was already dead) executed. Four senior army commanders were also summoned to the king's presence and executed. In two more cases (Babylonia and Bactria – both key provinces) a new governor appears about this time, and our sources give us no idea how and precisely when. Since the time is at least close, it seems reasonable to associate these changes with the six others. In another satrapy (Lesser Phrygia) a cousin of Harpalus disappears some time within an even wider chronological margin; modern speculation has put the incident in 327; but again, a connection with Harpalus' own fate is indicated. Thus, to six certain cases (out of seventeen), three possible ones might be added, as well as the four commanders. Of the remainder, one (in Armenia) was *de facto* independent and only nominally subject to Alexander, one (Phrataphernes) sent his two sons to Alexander (where they would serve as hostages), two (Oxyartes and Peithon) had, as we saw, been appointed only late in 326. Five were at one time or another summoned to court – which was obviously quite harmless in some cases (e.g. Peucestas, Alexander's special benefactor), but might in others be a sign of danger only just avoided, for we know that four satraps and four commanders were executed after obeying such a summons. One could not know what to expect.

[1] A. VI.27.1 and *Ind.* 23.5; both should be accepted. For this and what follows see my account in "Harpalus" [IX]. Attempts to exculpate Alexander cannot deny the facts here given: they can merely return to the apologetic sources which, while admitting that Alexander was by now too ready to listen to slander, assert that he wanted to punish corrupt and oppressive governors. Quite apart from the facts given in the text, which make this interpretation highly unlikely, it assumes a singular inability to judge men's characters in Alexander, which would make his successes hard to explain. See A. VI.27.5; VII.4.3; C. X.1; D. 106.2; P. 68 (cf. 42), for discussions of his motives.

The reason given was either disloyalty or exploitation of the governed. As for the former, Apollophanes is a typical case: the charge is not often plausible. There *were* would-be rebels about, especially Persians; but they were, on the whole, not satraps or commanders. One might call them the disappointed. Nor is the interpretation of just punishment of the wicked easy to sustain. Indeed, our sources here regretfully admit that the king's character was deteriorating: that he was too ready to listen to sycophants and to believe the worst; even though in principle, at least, he meant to protect the governed. Modern scholarship has accepted this, on the whole without question; yet it is patently false. One of the few governors entirely unmolested was Cleomenes, a wily Egyptian Greek, who had done Alexander good service, at some profit to himself. Known to be ingeniously extortionate, he in fact received a notorious letter from Alexander forgiving him any crimes he might commit, on account of his timely sycophancy after Hephaestion's death. That was a little later. But Cleomenes, clearly, had never been in the slightest danger.[1]

The reign of terror can be shown to be due to two main causes: failure and fear. The search for a scapegoat for the disaster in the desert accounts for several of the victims. Fear was no less powerful. We have seen how, at the Hyphasis, Alexander was faced with the threat of co-operation between nobles and army against him, and how Coenus had died straight after. His death would in any case arouse suspicion. But suspicion is turned almost to certainty by the fact that, from Pura at the latest, Coenus' brother Cleander and three of his senior associates were summoned from Media to the king's presence; when they arrived, they were executed. This was a step that would be popular among Parmenio's old soldiers, who had never taken to his murderer; just as the execution of a hated satrap might bring a bonus of applause. But the real motive was fear. No sooner were these four generals disposed of, than an order issued from Carmania, disbanding all the mercenary armies which the satraps had – legitimately and even necessarily – enrolled. The disruptive social and political results of this order were soon to appear. But its immediate effect was to sound a warning to Harpalus, the imperial treasurer, closely associated with Cleander and his family. Anticipating the inevitable summons to court, Alexander's

---

[1] Cleomenes: A. VII.23.8, and cf. Berve, no. 431; Hamilton, *CQ* III (1953), 157. For a recent attempt to explain away the reign of terror (chiefly by arguing that the figures here cited do not justify the term) see W. E. Higgins, *Athenaeum* LVIII (1980), 140ff.

old friend fled with as much of the imperial treasure as he could take with him, and with 6,000 mercenaries. He was to cause Alexander a great deal of trouble, and Athens (which, at the height of his power, had given him citizenship) even more, before dying an inglorious death, just too soon to play a part in the Lamian War, which he indirectly helped to bring about.[1]

That story takes us beyond our immediate subject; but the reign of terror that sheds such light on Alexander's character and methods cannot be omitted in any account of Iran, especially since so many Iranian satrapies were profoundly affected by it. Alexander had already begun to substitute his own men – obscure men, not known in senior offices before – for the eminent satraps and commanders, both Iranian and Macedonian, whom he had earlier preferred to trust in high office. The events of 325 increased the trend. Peucestas of Mieza, who saved Alexander's life in India, had not been heard of till just before, when he appears, in a very mixed company, as a trierarch on the Hydaspes. He now received the key satrapy of Persis, where he humoured the natives by learning their language and honouring their customs.

Another great discovery was Sibyrtius, whose very nationality is unknown. He is first heard of when he receives Carmania, after Alexander's arrival at Pura and punishment of the satrap of that province. But he was marked out for higher things. Alexander soon heard of the death of Menon in Arachosia, and (as it happened) the newly appointed governor of Gedrosia at once died, at a moment when Alexander, on his way to Carmania, had just heard that Philip, his governor in northern India, had been killed by rebellious Indian mercenaries. Alexander had to rethink his whole eastern frontier. The result was one of his quick and surprising decisions, like (earlier) the appointment of Porus as satrap. He saw that northern India, on which he had spent so much military effort and administrative thought, could not be securely held after all, without a return in arms, which – in the foreseeable future – was inconceivable. So he decided to cut his losses. Taxiles was appointed "temporary" satrap – and no other appointment was made before Alexander's death, eighteen months later. Porus and Taxiles could safely balance each other. The Greek cities would no doubt be swallowed up, but one had to cut one's losses: India was best written off.[2] Adaptability was Alexander's greatest virtue, and he had

[1] See "Harpalus" [IX] for full documentation and discussion.
[2] See Berve, nos. 634, 703 (misinterpreting A.). A. vi.27.2 mentions the general Eudemus as Taxiles' partner in the satrapy (cf. C. x.1.20, mentioning him as sole satrap). C. (*l. c.*) also reports the death of Abisares, who was succeeded by his son: Alexander had never seriously tried to control

begun to learn the limits of the possible – much as his spirit strove against admitting it.

Southern India, of course, was still held by Peithon. But the backbone of the frontier now shifted further west: to the two great military provinces in the north and centre – Bactria-Sogdiana and Areia-Drangiana – a third was added in the south: Gedrosia-Arachosia was entrusted to Sibyrtius. (Bactria-Sogdiana, probably at the same time, received a new Macedonian governor.) This was henceforth to be the eastern frontier, with Paropamisadae (still under Alexander's father-in-law) now no longer a highway of empire, but in the long run an advanced bastion of defence; while southern India would be held as long as possible, supported from Arachosia and (if he stayed loyal) by Taxiles – but, one must suspect, would be given up if it became necessary. Alexander's new dispositions suggest that he was under no illusion that he could hold it against serious attack. Sibyrtius turned out to be a brilliant appointment; he held his difficult and inhospitable province safe until after Alexander's death and survived the king in it by several years, becoming an important (though never ambitious) figure among the Successors.

The tradition not based on the court sources reports a Dionysiac festival in Carmania, to celebrate the escape from the desert.[1] Curtius links it, with obvious rhetorical glee, with the execution of a governor, also in Carmania. Though the stories obviously lost nothing in the telling, the facts should be accepted, especially in view of Alexander's life-long love-hate relationship with Dionysus.

It was while the king was celebrating games and theatrical contests that Nearchus and the fleet, after a long and difficult voyage, reached the Strait of Hurmuz. Where the meeting took place, we cannot tell, since Nearchus throughout dramatizes the story and demonstrably misreports even known facts. But Alexander's relief at the safety of the expedition should be accepted, and Nearchus was sent on to complete the sea and river journey to Susa.[2] It was by now about December 325.

Kashmir, and was content with homage. In the list of satrapies after Alexander's death in Diod. XVIII.3.2 Taxiles appears as satrap and Eudemus is not named. This should be accepted, especially as it fits in with the arrangements made for Porus and Abisares, all now *de facto* client kings. The satrap Philip appears to have been a brother of Harpalus; so from the purely political point of view his death may have been not unwelcome to Alexander.

[1] D. 106.1; P. 67; above all C. IX.10.24ff. A. refuses to believe it, because it was not in Ptolemy or Aristobulus; but that is a very poor argument; we may compare their omission of the Bacchic details of the destruction of the Persepolis palaces (p. 445, n. 1, with text).

[2] On Nearchus' distortions, fortunately sometimes contradicted by a more reliable source, see *art. cit.* (p. 470, n. 1). The story of the meeting in Carmania is embroidered with dramatic fiction, which makes it impossible to tell even whether the meeting took place inland (as he reports) or on the coast (as in D. 106.4).

Hephaestion was sent along the coast road with the main forces and the baggage train, while the king, with a small picked force, took the more difficult inland route, probably via Sīrjān, to Pasargadae (where he found Cyrus' tomb plundered and ordered Aristobulus to supervise its restoration) and on to Persepolis and Susa. The satrap of Persis was deposed and Peucestas, known for sympathy with Persian ways, substituted. By about February, the fleet and army were reunited at Susa.[1]

At Susa the long war at last officially came to an end. So, after two final executions (the governors of Susiana and Paraetacene), did the reign of terror. Instead, rewards and honours were now distributed, in what was to be a new era. It was officially inaugurated with a great international love-feast: eighty of Alexander's Greek and Macedonian courtiers and senior officers married Iranian noblewomen. Alexander himself attached himself to both lines of the Achaemenian house by taking Darius' eldest daughter Barsine for a second wife and a daughter of Ochus for a third. (The fact that he still had no child may have had something to do with the decision to practise the traditional polygamy of Persian kings.) Hephaestion was honoured by receiving another daughter of Darius, and Craterus received a niece. The faithful Nearchus married the daughter of another Barsine, who had been Alexander's mistress before the marriage to Roxane, and thus became the only Greek to be distinguished by a connection with the Achaemenian house and with Alexander. It was made clear who were now the leading men of the empire.

At the same time Alexander also officially registered the connections of 10,000 Macedonian soldiers with native women as marriages, giving them all wedding presents. He then paid off all the debts incurred by the soldiers, who had probably not received any regular pay for a long time and who, in any case, had no doubt lost most of their savings (which we must, of course, envisage in very concrete form) in the Gedrosian desert.[2]

[1] For Peucestas, see Berve, no. 634. For the route, cf. Engels 117f. (suggesting Sīrjān and Nairīz; but a small picked force could have used a more northerly route than that via Nairīz). We do not know where precisely the army was divided: probably not far from the meeting-place with Nearchus. But A. VI.28.7 is vague. The execution of Orxines, satrap of Persis (A. VI.29: never officially appointed, it is alleged; 30.1–2: guilty of serious crimes), is told differently by C. (X.1.22–38: falsely accused by the eunuch Bagoas). We cannot decide. But if it is true (thus C.) that he claimed descent from Cyrus, he could in any case hardly be allowed to live.

[2] A. VII.4–5 has the fullest account. The number of courtiers concerned and the total paid out to the troops are variously given. The amount of the debts (whether 10,000 or 20,000 talents) shows that they cannot have been due merely to riotous living: the march through Gedrosia must be taken into account. But the troops' suspicion suggests that Alexander was not normally generous to common soldiers.

The purpose behind this unaccustomed generosity was suspect in the eyes of the hard-headed Macedonian troops. They were soon further incensed when Alexander had the 30,000 native youths, who had earlier been collected in order to receive a Greek education and Macedonian arms drill, put through their paces, and pointedly referred to them as the "Successors" (*epigonoi*).[1] It was as though now, with the long campaign finished, Alexander was challenging the troops to repeat their mutiny, at a time when he could do without them.

For the moment nothing further happened. Before leaving Susa, the king sent down a rescript to the Greeks, ordering all the cities to receive back their exiles. This, at one bold stroke, was to solve the serious social problem that had been created when Philip II and Alexander had brought about the expulsion of anti-Macedonian elements from their cities; that had been intensified when those tens of thousands of Greeks who fought for Darius were condemned as traitors; and that had become intolerable and menacing when Alexander had recently deprived most of them of their livelihood by dissolving the mercenary armies. We have a grim picture in our sources, of bands of ex-soldiers roaming about Asia and trying to make for Europe; of more than 20,000 exiles attending the Olympic Games in the summer of 324, when their restoration (which had previously been announced) was officially proclaimed. The problem that the king found insoluble now had to be solved by the Greek cities. Many of them struggled long and hard against it, and ultimately it was another major factor in the outbreak of the Lamian War.[2]

From Susa Alexander sailed down to the sea; then, while Nearchus took the rest of the fleet up the Euphrates to Babylon, he had the Persian defence works, which stopped navigation on the Tigris, removed and sailed up that river to Opis.[3] At Opis he discharged all the Macedonians who were over age or unfit for service and promised to send them home with ample rewards. It was at this point that the discontent that had long been simmering exploded. The soldiers felt that what they had long suspected – especially after the events at Susa – was true: Alexander had sucked them dry and was now discarding them, to replace them with Orientals. Nothing better shows the gulf of bitterness and

---

[1] A. vii.6.1; D. 108.1f.; P. 71.1. See p. 461, n. 2 and text.

[2] See "Harpalus" [IX], 25–31, where it is also stressed that the decree was not confined to the Greek cities in Europe.

[3] A.'s description (vii.7) implies that the Euphrates, the Tigris and the Kārūn had separate mouths (Cf. *Ind.* 41f., from Nearchus); but see Strabo xv.3.4–5, showing variant reports.

suspicion that had opened between the king and his men than the fact that it was the very chance they had so often longed for – the chance to go home and enjoy their rewards – that now drove them into mutiny.

Arrian gives their main grievances, and it is clear that they all stem from Alexander's actions as Great King of Persia.[1] We know very little about Alexander's actual use of Iranians, except for a few eminent personages (such as satraps) and, in a very general sense, auxiliary units. Our sources were not interested, and even *their* sources had not been, except where serious trouble resulted. But it can be conjectured – with no approach to certainty, alas – that, since native Iranian units were used as auxiliary cavalry, their most eminent members, in very small numbers, gained admission to the Macedonian élite, the Companion Cavalry. The process apparently started in Bactria: before Darius' death no Iranian auxiliaries had been used. It was extended (we hear) to Sogdiana, Arachosia, Drangiana, Areia and Parthia, and finally to the "Euacae" – no one knows who they were – among the Persians. How this was organized, we are not told. Presumably the Iranians fought in separate units, inside the ranks of the Companions – who (we must remember) are only twice recorded as receiving Macedonian reinforcements: at Gordium in 333 and at Susa in 331. Instead of dangerously denuding Macedonia of cavalry, Alexander preferred to draw on the proved quality of eastern Iran. This naturally caused resentment. After the Gedrosian disaster, when heavy losses had to be made good and Alexander in any case wanted to accelerate his policy of integration, the process was carried further. The original Companions were organized into four regiments, and a fifth was added, consisting (it seems) almost entirely of Iranians. (Presumably the senior officers were Macedonian.) Iranian manpower was to be used to the full, on honourable terms. Alexander (after all) was the Great King – much as his Macedonians disliked it. At Susa (finally) a further step was taken: eight of the noblest Iranians – Roxane's brother the only known non-Persian among them – were taken into the *agema* (Alexander's personal Horse Guard), under the command of an Achaemenid.[2]

[1] A. VII.6.2f. (Susa); 8.2 (Opis); the two are doublets from different sources: the first corresponds to the whole of our tradition outside A., whose second account is the only one to place the mutiny at Opis. On this see Badian, "Orientals" [VIII]; the grievances listed in part went back to long before the Indian campaign; but Susa was the ultimate provocation. See now A. B. Bosworth "Alexander and the Iranians", *JHS* C (1980), 8f., 15ff.

[2] The others named are the sons of Artabazus, Mazaeus, Phratapherenes (the most distinguished of the Persian satraps who had remained loyal) and two men unknown to us. (This is again characteristic of our tradition.) Their commander Hystaspes, called a Bactrian by A., must have

That and the "Successors", followed by the dismissal of many (perhaps most) of the Macedonians — the answer was mutiny. The soldiers shouted out that they *all* wanted to go home: let the king go on campaigns with his father Ammon — for his belief in that god and his relationship to him had become more marked, hence more offensive to Macedonian sentiment. But this time Alexander was ready for them. As we have seen, he may (even at Susa) have actually provoked their reaction, in order to show them who was master now. The ringleaders were at once executed, and Alexander once more shut himself up in his tent, to wait on events. When two days produced no change of mind among the men, Alexander announced that they were all discharged, and that he was forming Persians into the traditional Macedonian regiments — Companions, Foot Companions, Foot and Horse Guard. At last the men knew they were beaten. Alexander was in no urgent need of them, and could well leave them to make their own way home as best they might, penniless and without official support or protection — if that was what they wanted. The defeat at the Hyphasis was avenged.

They at once decided to beg abjectly for pardon. In an emotional scene, Alexander readily granted it, bestowing the Persian honorific title of "kinsman" on every one of them. He had won, and could afford to be generous, for those who were to stay would still, for a long time to come, be his best soldiers. After a magnificent sacred feast, marking the official reconciliation between Alexander and the Macedonians, and between the Macedonians and the Persians — with the most eminent men of all nations invited, the Macedonians carefully placed around the king, the Persians a little further away, and the rest at a distance, as spectators and witnesses — Alexander proceeded to carry out his original intention. He discharged the veterans and sent them home under Craterus (as we have seen, one of his most trusted officers), who was to take over the command of Europe (including Greece) from Antipater.[1]

What is perhaps most interesting: the wives and children were not allowed to go with the men, so that many of the marriages just celebrated were *de facto* dissolved. Alexander promised to look after the

---

been an Achaemenid descended from the branch that had been satraps of Bactria (see Berve, no. 763). The precise arrangements reported by A. VII.6.3f. are debated; the text is doubtful. See Bosworth, *op. cit.*, 13.

[1] For the mutiny see (above all) A. VII.8-11, with the feast as a tailpiece. Alexander's impassioned speech in that account is, of course, like all such passages, a piece of neo-Attic rhetoric, not a genuine account. On the feast (told with precision, after Ptolemy) see my analysis in *Historia* VII (1958), 428-32 (repr. in Griffith [III], 290-4).

children and bring them up as Macedonians. It now becomes clear why Alexander had encouraged such interracial marriages: he wanted the children. True children of the camp, with no home or national tradition, socially unacceptable in either East or West, they would of necessity provide the king, in a few years' time, with the kind of army that had nowhere to turn but to him, so that he would avoid the problems he had so far encountered. Similarly, one might say, the Susa marriages of his courtiers and commanders would in due course provide him with a band of senior officers in the same position. Alexander was only thirty-one, and could plan for a distant future. By the time he was in his fifties, the plans would have come to fruition.[1]

From Opis he marched to Ecbatana; there he was lavishly entertained by the satrap Atropates, who even produced a hundred fully-armed Amazons from his province.[2] Alexander himself put on games and feasts, with lavish drinking. It was in the course of this that Hephaestion died, apparently of a sudden illness made worse by immoderate drinking. It was a more serious blow than any Alexander had yet suffered.

Hephaestion, though probably not one of his childhood friends, had been the only person really close to him. A wealth of legend and anecdote deals with their relationship, which was not clouded by any known quarrel. Politically, Hephaestion had been one of the leaders in the coup against Philotas and had had his first major promotion as a result. It was he who had worked to introduce proskynesis and had put the blame for his failure on Callisthenes, thus preparing Callisthenes' downfall. He had proved himself as a soldier in Sogdiana and had henceforth held a series of important and (often) independent commands, although never more prominent than his chief rival Craterus. The rivalry between them was known, and the king seems to have encouraged it; though if there is any substance in Plutarch's famous anecdote (*Alex.* 47.9), he did not tolerate open fighting. In fact, despite his attachment to Hephaestion, Alexander (as Plutarch's anecdote also shows) took care not to let him forget that he held his power from the king – and it is clear that Hephaestion never aspired to more than second

[1] D. 110.3 puts the number of children at 10,000 – suspicious since we are also told that 10,000 men married native women and that 10,000 went home; he puts the mutiny at Susa and gives an elaborate itinerary from there to Ecbatana, perhaps in part based on genuine tradition.

[2] A. VII.13 (not from his main sources). Since that was part of extensive festivities, it may have been no more than a conscious charade; it is probably the origin of the numerous tales of Alexander's meeting with Amazons further east.

place. Even this, however, he seems for a long time to have merely shared with Craterus. He was hated by Eumenes, the Greek chancellor, yet Alexander did not let him touch that intriguer, whom Hephaestion no doubt despised. However, Alexander came more and more to rely on Hephaestion, both in his official and in his personal capacity, in the troubled period that followed the Hyphasis mutiny. Craterus, though utterly loyal, was out of sympathy with Alexander's personality and policies. The result, in its personal aspect, was Hephaestion's special distinction in the Susa marriages, which for the first time formally raised him above Craterus. Politically, it seems to have been at Susa that, as commander of the reorganized Companion Cavalry, he received the title of "chiliarch" – the word which, under the Achaemenids, had been the Greek for "*hazārapati*", the commander of the Royal Guard and certainly one of the most distinguished men in the kingdom.[1]

It was soon after Alexander had finally decided in favour of Hephaestion that Craterus was sent back to Macedonia; this would at last put an end to the old rivalry and compensate Craterus for the loss of power at court by giving him the most independent of the major commands and – for an old-style Macedonian – much the most prestigious. It would also have the advantage of giving the king a chance of dealing with Antipater, the last of Philip's great generals still in his service, and a man who would clearly have nothing to do with Alexander's view of his own person and his empire. Olympias had long stoked the suspicion Alexander naturally felt for Antipater, especially since the murder of Philotas and Parmenio. In the end Antipater forced her to leave the country and return to her native Epirus, without any interference by Alexander. In fact, Antipater's position was so strong, after years of semi-independent rule, that nothing could be done about it until Alexander's return to Susa.

Once the chance offered, he acted (as usual) decisively. Antipater's supersession was announced at Opis, and responsibility for the oppressive measures taken in Greece was now attributed to him: it was soon made clear that complaints against him would receive an attentive hearing.[2] To anyone who had lived through the reign of terror, this method was familiar and the outcome predictable. But Antipater was no Asian satrap, totally within the king's power. By various political

[1] Eumenes: Plutarch, *Eumenes* 2; A. VII.12.2. Craterus: P. 47 (*cit.*); Plutarch, *Eumenes* 6; D. 114.2. There is no support in the sources for the belief that Hephaestion held all the actual powers of a Grand Vizier; see especially Schachermeyr, *Alexander in Babylon* [IV].

[2] For this and what follows, see "Harpalus" [IX], 36–40. On Olympias, see Hamilton, 105.

and diplomatic manoeuvres he managed to maintain his position and dissuade Craterus from attempting to displace him; and when Alexander died, in June 323, Craterus was still waiting in Cilicia and Antipater was as firmly as ever in control of Macedonia.

Hephaestion's death, just after Alexander had taken the decision to raise him to the second place in the empire, was both personally and politically an almost unbearable blow. The king's reaction was immoderate: there are many reports of extravagant grief; and if some are touched up for effect, enough is certain. He sent to his father Ammon, asking – unsuccessfully, as it turned out – for permission to have his dead friend raised to divine status; and in anticipation he ordered the construction of a memorial costing 10,000 talents at Babylon, which was probably meant to become his temple. Diodorus (XVII.114.4) reports that he ordered the sacred royal fire to be put out, as if at the death of the king.[1]

After a long period of mourning, Alexander launched a winter campaign against the Cossaeans, a tribe that (like many others) had been left in semi-independence under the Achaemenids, in the mountains between Ecbatana and Susa. The operation could be defended on military and administrative grounds and fits in with his campaigns against other tribes of this kind in western Iran. But this time most of the tribesmen seem to have been massacred: as Plutarch (*Alex.* 72) has it, they were sacrificed to the shades of Hephaestion. As in the case of the Gedrosian desert, it would be unsound to postulate a purely "rational" Alexander and, from this premise, deny the multiple attestation of irrationality, especially at this period of his life.[2]

Early in 323, probably straight after the winter campaign, Alexander left for Babylon. After crossing the Tigris, he was met by a deputation of "Chaldaeans" (Babylonian priests), who in the name of Bel first tried to dissuade him from entering the city, then advised him to enter it only from the east, if he must do so – which, as they knew and he soon found out, was impossible because of the swamps. Otherwise, they warned,

[1] A. VII.14; cf. D. 114f. (claiming that Ammon permitted divine cult – but cf. A. VII.23.6: merely hero cult); P. 72 (hero cult). On the "royal fire" in general and this incident in particular, see Schachermeyr, *op. cit.*, 38f. But it is possible that Diodorus' item is anachronistic fiction by a later source.

[2] Plutarch's explicit statement seems to be confirmed by A. VII. 15.3 (ἐξεῖλεν) and is not refuted by Nearchus (*apud* A. *Ind.* 40.6f.), who states that Alexander tried to settle the nomadic tribes and names the Cossaeans in a list along with others; it is not stated how many Cossaeans survived to be settled, after the forty days' war. The suggestion that the Lion of Hamadān was set up by Alexander as a memorial to Hephaestion (H. Luschey, *AMI* 1 (1968), 115–22) is an attractive conjecture, though it is obviously incapable of strict proof.

he faced imminent death. Other stories about omens and divine warnings were later told and believed. It is likely that, as Diodorus reports, Hephaestion's death and the king's exaggerated reaction to it had created a predisposition to believe that his end too was approaching. Nor would he himself be immune to this. He had (inevitably) seen the relationship between himself and Hephaestion in terms of that between Achilles and Patroclus and had probably encouraged others to look at it in that heroic light. Both in him and in them, this must have added an element of foreboding to Hephaestion's death, in which omens of this kind were readily believed and, being believed, as readily reported.[1]

Alexander, in the circumstances, took the Chaldaeans' warning seriously — perhaps more so than Arrian will admit, when (following Aristobulus: VII.17.5f) he makes him look for a way round to the east for two or three days and then enter the city by the forbidden route. According to Diodorus, Alexander settled down to wait for some time, to avoid challenging the prophecy of doom: it was only after reassurance by his friends and his court philosophers that he entered Babylon. If we accept this, we might add that it was probably they who suggested to him that the Chaldaeans might have reasons of their own for not wanting the king to look too closely at their accounts of the temple-building with which he had entrusted them and which had made little progress. There is reason to believe that this was in fact the course of events. For "on his way back to Babylon" (as Arrian vaguely puts it) we find him giving audience to a large number of foreign embassies — variously reported by Arrian (VII. 15) and Diodorus (XVII.113): far more, and more varied, than one would have expected to meet him somewhere on the road between Ecbatana and Babylon, especially as it was known that he was making for Babylon. In fact, Diodorus puts the reception of the embassies in Babylon, where it makes better sense. Although there is clearly confusion and possibly distortion in our accounts of this episode, it is at least possible that Alexander in fact received the embassies just outside Babylon, when — as Diodorus reports — he had settled down, technically still on the way from Ecbatana, to avoid entering the fatal city.

When at last he did enter it, it had to be made clear that the prophecies were baseless.[2] After seeing some Greek embassies and ordering

---

[1] Omens: A. VII.18f.; P. 73f. and other sources. Achilles: A. I.12.1; VII.14.4. The warning: A. VII.16.5f.; D. 112; P. 73.

[2] Arrian comments on their apparent non-fulfilment (VII.22.1).

preparations for a large-scale Arabian expedition, the king left Babylon again, partly (no doubt) cheered by the non-fulfilment, partly in order to demonstrate that non-fulfilment by his safe departure. He embarked on a short voyage of exploration on the Euphrates and its canals and made improvements in the drainage system. After founding a city on the lower Euphrates, he returned to Babylon to proceed with the final preparations for the Arabian expedition, which was to start almost at once. It was now – ironically, as Arrian notes (VII.23.2) – that Greek embassies came to him, approaching him as though he were a god, perhaps in accordance with a decision to deify him that had been taken – it is not clear whether actually at his request or merely in order to please him – in at least some Greek cities a few months earlier.[1] It was during these months after Hephaestion's death, according to a fairly reliable contemporary witness, that Alexander would dress in the costumes of various deities at banquets.[2] His apparent escape from the threatened fate at Babylon must have increased his confidence in his own divinity.

It was also at Babylon that, by arrangement, he was met by his satrap of Persis, Peucestas, with a Persian levy which (with some neighbouring tribesmen) came to 20,000 men. The Persians, in a sense his chosen people, had apparently been particularly loyal and co-operative under their new governor, who adopted their customs; and the king now proceeded to carry out a tactical reform, clearly planned for some time, which would amalgamate Macedonian and Persian fighting men into composite units of four Macedonians acting as non-commissioned

[1] On the question of the deification, see J. P. V. D. Balsdon, "The 'divinity' of Alexander", *Historia* I (1950), 363f., denying any request and discounting the evidence on deification; E. J. Bickerman, *Athenaeum* XLI (1963), 70ff., denying even any Greek decision to deify him. The older view (as in Tarn, Wilcken and others) of a direct order for deification has been severely shaken by these investigations, but it still finds occasional defenders; e.g. F. Taeger, in *The Sacral Kingship* (Leiden, 1959), 394ff. (Supplements to *Numen* 4). The exact interpretation of A. VII.23.2 is important here. It has recently been argued by E. Fredricksmeyer (*AJAH* IV (1979), 3–5 with notes) that the Greek envoys can be shown to have really been sacred envoys, come to worship Alexander as a god. He concludes: "Some initiative from Alexander...may be considered as certain." I have argued that his interpretation of A. is not the most natural one ("The deification" [X], 54ff.) and that nothing follows as to an order, or even a widespread spontaneous decision, to deify him. However, I have also suggested (*op. cit.*, 65f.) that one of Ammon's promises to him may have been that he would become a god in his lifetime. Bickerman points out that what clearly emerges is the fact that Alexander was known to appreciate deification.

[2] Ephippus (Jacoby [II.3] 126 F5), in connection with a scene at Ecbatana that involves a prominent man known as an enemy of Athens. Ephippus wrote a history of the deaths of Hephaestion and Alexander: the fragments suggest that the intervening period was also covered. He seems to have been in Alexander's and later in Ptolemy's service and, although given to dramatizing his stories, seems to be a fairly reliable witness.

officers and twelve Persians. As he had frequently made clear – not least at Susa and at Opis – these two, with the Macedonians for the moment still superior, were the nations on which his kingdom rested. It is unlikely that the reform was to apply to the whole of his army; he would hardly have sacrificed his best fighting-force to such a gamble. It is best regarded as an experiment. In any case, it was evidently abandoned straight after his death, and no such force seems ever to have fought. Both nations were unhappy about the policy of fusion, but it is clear that Alexander had by now overcome active opposition and could command the acquiescence of both. In this amalgamation of nations, as in his constant founding of cities, he no doubt felt himself acting out his divine role.[1]

It was in the midst of his preparations for his expedition to Arabia – an expedition that, at least in part, was undertaken for the sake of having his divinity recognized by a recalcitrant people (or so it was reported)[2] – that Alexander suddenly fell ill. Immoderate feasting, to which, particularly in this last period of his life, he was in any case given, either caused the disease or accelerated it; and on 10 June 323 Alexander died, after (we are told) the gods had refused to help him. The nature of his fatal illness has inevitably excited speculation: poisoning at the instigation of Antipater was suggested almost at once, in the course of the propaganda war among the Successors, and it still finds defenders. That is perhaps the only version that may confidently be excluded. He certainly died of disease, undiagnosable to us;[3] and he made no

---

[1] In Greek practice, the founder of a city received "heroic" (but not divine) honours. Whatever the true number of Alexander's cities (see p. 451, n. 2 and p. 461, n. 1, with text), the founding of cities on such a scale was completely unparalleled in the Greek world. The "army reform" is accepted by Bosworth, "Alexander and the Iranians", 18ff., as forced on Alexander by shortage of Macedonians; but the projected invasion of Arabia was surely not the time for an unprecedented tactical experiment to be introduced throughout the infantry.

[2] The "irrational" motive, in addition to the more obvious and practical ones, is once more given by a source known to be friendly to Alexander: Aristobulus (*apud* Strabo XVI.1.11; cf. A. VII.20 (not naming the source)), known in antiquity as an apologist (see Jacoby 139 T5, amply confirmed by the fragments).

[3] A. and P. give a full account of his last days, taken from the "royal diary". The nature of that source has been much debated. At one time it used to be regarded as an authentic daily account of the king's actions, and some scholars fancifully extended its existence to earlier periods of his life (where it is never mentioned). It is now generally regarded as very limited in scope (A. E. Samuel, *Historia* XIV (1965), 1ff.) or as forged (L. Pearson, *Historia* III (1954–5), 249ff. (a hellenistic forgery)); A. B. Bosworth, *CQ* XXI (1971), 117–23: forged as a propaganda document straight after Alexander's death. The date of Alexander's death is now known, from Babylonian records, to have been 10 June 323 (Samuel, *op. cit.* 8). The illness has been "diagnosed" as, in particular, malaria (Engels, *CP* LXXIII (1978), 224–8, tracing the history of the "diagnosis" back to 1872), aggravated by heavy drinking; Schachermeyr, *Alexander in Babylon*, 65–71, suggests a leukaemia added to the malaria. But diseases described in ancient authors can never be diagnosed

provision for a successor. When asked who should succeed him, he is said to have answered: "The bravest." However, just before his death, he seems – whether consciously or not – to have passed his signet ring on to Perdiccas, who was the most likely person to receive it: ever since Hephaestion's death, he had – without being able to replace Hephaestion, in Alexander's view – in fact been performing the duties to which the king had originally raised his friend. It was Perdiccas, at any rate, who emerged, in the period of hard bargaining among the assembled marshals at Babylon that followed Alexander's death, as the recognized regent of the empire.

What Alexander's further plans were, apart from the Arabian expedition and one or two projects of exploration already in hand, must have been known to some at the time; but we cannot know. Arrian, recognizing this, refused to guess, and modern historians will be wise to follow him. There is certainly no evidence that he had any serious plans for internal organization and consolidation of his empire. The Arabian expedition shows that, like Caesar centuries later, he preferred to avoid the serious business of governing and looked to war to provide the answers. He had, of course, laid long-range plans for the future, and he seems to have been content to wait for these plans to mature in the course of a generation. Presumably the years until they did would have been spent in further military adventures; even though there is no real support for the later story that he planned the conquest of the western Mediterranean lands. There certainly were draft plans, and at least the senior officers and the Chancellor Eumenes knew about them. But when those tough men hammered out the settlement that was to reconcile their ambitions and antagonisms, it proved essential to make certain that any plans Alexander had left, or might be claimed to have left, should never be used by any one of them as a weapon against the rest. It was therefore agreed that Perdiccas should submit a list of Alexander's supposed last plans to the army and have them officially cancelled by its vote. Part of that list has been preserved for us by Diodorus, probably from the contemporary account of Hieronymus of Cardia, and it is clear that those who presented it stressed the extravagance and

---

from those descriptions with any degree of confidence. For poisoning, see R. D. Milns, *Alexander the Great* (London, 1968), 255–8 (strychnine: certainly wrong, as Engels, *op. cit.*, has shown); Bosworth, *op. cit.* 112–36 (the most elaborate poisoning theory). As Engels has remarked, it is most unlikely that Alexander would not have suspected he was being poisoned; rumours of poisoning by an enemy always arose in antiquity when an eminent man died before his time, and they were certainly readily used in propaganda.

unreasonableness of what was projected. It is also illuminating that the fantastic schemes thus produced were apparently believed to be genuine by the army, and duly voted down. It was in this way that all genuine trace of Alexander's projects was erased, both from the stage of history and from the record open to the historian.[1]

Nor is there any reliable information about how Iran reacted to its conqueror.[2] What is certain is that there was no general or significant dissatisfaction. When Alexander died, there were only two major rebellions to take advantage of the unsettled situation, and both were

[1] For the "last plans", see E. Badian, *HSCP* LXXII (1968), 183ff. (misreported by Seibert [I], 10); for Arrian's view, see VII.1.

[2] [It is only in the 9th–10th century A.D. that one of the most popular Zoroastrian works, written in Pahlavi (i.e. Middle Persian) language, reports in some detail the Zoroastrian view of Alexander as a monster of iniquity, which it is reasonable to think originated across the Sasanian and Arsacid eras in the grim reality of the Macedonian conquest: "The accursed Alexander the Roman who dwelt in Egypt came to Iranshahr with heavy tyranny, war and affliction. He slew the ruler of Iran and destroyed and laid waste the Court and the Empire. The whole Religion, namely the Avesta and its Exegesis, as written in liquid gold on prepared ox-hides... Alexander the Roman who dwelt in Egypt carried off and burnt, the evil-destined adversary, the heretic, the holder of lies, the doer of evil. He slew ever so many teachers, lawyers, herbads and mobads, the supporters of the Religion, the rich and the wise of Iranshahr. The great ones and governors of Iranshahr fell into hatred and strife one with the other. He himself was broken and fled to Hell." Thus the *Ardāy Wīrāz Nāmag* 1.3–11. See also H. W. Bailey, *Zoroastrian Problems* (Oxford, 1943 and 1971), 151f., and W. B. Henning, *JRAS* 1944, 136; Mary Boyce, *A History of Zoroastrianism* II (1982), 290 (*HO* I.VII.1.2.2a) defines "the Accursed" as Alexander's "standing title given him in Zoroastrian tradition". Ed.]

The fact that Alexander here appears as a "Roman who dwelt in Egypt" suffices to show that his person has been fused with those of other invaders, through the long conflicts with Rome and Byzantium and, quite possibly, the Arab Conquest, which, like Alexander's, followed the conquest of Egypt. Whether the whole of the Avesta and its exegesis had in fact been written on ox-hides in liquid gold and, in 331–330, was waiting at Persepolis (?) for Alexander to seize and destroy them is for experts on ancient Iranian religion to decide, if indeed it can be decided. That Alexander killed the Persian King is certainly the opposite of the truth, and the charges of indiscriminate outrages against the Iranian religion are thus discredited; they are in any case improbable, since (as we note in the text) at least some of the public royal ceremonial, in part religious, is known to have been adopted and continued. (Thus the sacred fires were kept burning, to be extinguished only when Hephaestion died – which, of course, was recognized as a bad omen.) The appointment of the "Persianizing" satrap Peucestas and, on the other side, the Macedonian complaints detailed in our narrative attest to the truth of the expected attempt to induce loyalty among the conquered, whom (in the words of the Opis prayer) Alexander wanted to "share in the rule" with his reluctant Macedonians. The myth attested in the passage quoted is about equal to the *Shāh-nāma* in authenticity. It, and the attitude it reports, clearly flourished under the revived nationalism of the Sasanians, who sought to link themselves to the Achaemenids, and had good reason to continue under the Arabs. Whether it was first planted under the Arsacids is uncertain: the fact that many of their kings were conspicuously philhellenic does not necessarily disprove that possibility.

It is interesting to compare the contrary interpretation of Alexander that gained entry into the Jewish tradition and is first found in the famous description of Alexander's homage to the True God in Josephus, *Antiquities* XI.317ff. Based (almost certainly) on Caesar's attitude to the Jews, it was before long variously expanded and distorted in Talmudic tradition. (On all this see the useful discussion by R. Marcus in his Appendix C to volume VI of the LCL edition of Josephus.)

raised by Greeks – the Lamian War in Europe and the revolt by the conscripted Greek settlers in the military cities and colonies of the northeast of the empire. There is no sign of any reaction by any of the peoples of Asia. Some of the nobles, inevitably, had rebelled when Alexander was in India: Baryaxes the Mede was defeated by the loyal governor Atropates; one or two others were captured by Craterus on his return from India. There is no sign of their having much support. What is noticeable is that Persians, on the whole, could not be trusted as governors: as we have seen, Alexander, at Babylon, began by employing them in order to stress his legitimacy as Great King; but after various ups and downs in their mutual relations, he ended by having (apart from his father-in-law) only two Iranian satraps: Atropates (probably a Mede) and Phrataphernes, the only Persian. It is remarkable that, despite all the honour shown to eminent Persians, such as the enrolment of some of the most distinguished in his personal bodyguard, these same men were not entrusted with satrapies. Alexander had no doubt found out what most of his Achaemenid predecessors had also discovered: that there were few Persian (or indeed Iranian) nobles who could be fully trusted to remain loyal, especially in adverse circumstances. Alexander, realistic as usual in his political dealings, trusted the few who had proved their worth, but no others.

It must be added that both the history of the Achaemenian empire and Alexander's own practice must make us cautious about assuming any national resistance at the end of Alexander's life.[1] We have already seen that there were no rebellions after: and we have noted in passing that Alexander ceased to entrust satrapies to the most eminent Macedonians no less than to Persians. His satraps, at the end of his life, are nearly all men of whom little or nothing is heard before their appointment. Alexander preferred to trust only men whom he himself had raised to greatness; and it is very likely that among Iranians the social system and the military organization simply prevented men not of the very highest birth from acquiring sufficient experience of command and from attracting the king's notice. (For we must remember

[1] S. K. Eddy, *The King is Dead* (Lincoln, Nebr., 1961), ch. 2, tries to find a national resistance movement, but admits that Persians of all classes were divided over allegiance to the conqueror; he traces back the extraordinary legend of Alexander's "Persian" birth, in the *Shāh-Nāma*, to "collaborating" Persian circles under Alexander (73f.). In fact, although the Achaemenids obviously were "legitimate" in a sense in which the Macedonians could not be (they could not claim Aryan descent and election by Ahura Mazda), it must be noted that legitimacy had not saved Achaemenian kings from constant rebellion, often led by Persian nobles. Alexander will have kept up the symbols of Achaemenian cult, as he certainly kept up Pharaonic symbols in Egypt.

EPILOGUE: INTERREGNUM

that, in his dealings with them, Alexander would largely follow Persian court ceremonial.) It was probably for reasons like these, and not through any distrust of Persians or Iranians as restive under his rule, that he finally made the choices he did. He was no doubt waiting for the Susa marriages to provide him with the long-term answer.

EPILOGUE: INTERREGNUM

The generation that followed Alexander's death was an interregnum for his empire.[1] As he had left no heir, the royal title was conferred on a son of Philip II who took the name of Philip (III) himself. He was said to be half-witted, and he had certainly been so unlikely a candidate for the kingship that he was the only member of the royal family whom Alexander had left alive. Before long Roxane bore Alexander a posthumous son, who was recognized as joint king by the name of Alexander (IV). A regency was necessary on behalf of both, and Perdiccas, who had received Alexander's signet-ring, could not be prevented from legitimizing his *de facto* power. After much intrigue and some violence, most of the satraps in possession were confirmed, since they could not easily be dislodged. The only exception was Cleomenes, the Greek from Naucratis, who had gained the satrapy of Egypt by assiduous personal courtship of Alexander. In a world of Macedonian barons he did not count. Ptolemy, one of the Bodyguards, was sent to supersede him and before long eliminated him, establishing his own power and, in due course, the longest-lived of the Successor dynasties.

The Iranian satrapies were not much troubled by the conflicts that developed over the next two years. The battles were fought further west. Perdiccas, after an unsuccessful attempt to discipline Ptolemy, who had been joined in resistance to the regent by some of the other western satraps, was assassinated on the borders of Egypt in 320, and Antipater, Alexander's old viceroy of Europe, who had the highest prestige and the fewest enemies, assumed the regency. An old-style Macedonian, he had never set foot in Asia during Alexander's lifetime and was indifferent to it. Some new satraps were appointed in the East, most

---

[1] Most of the information on the period immediately following Alexander's death comes to us from the solid and reliable history of Hieronymus of Cardia, a contemporary. Diodorus' Books XVIII–XX (from Alexander's death to the eve of the battle of Ipsus (301)) are based on his history, but we then lose Diodorus' text. Plutarch's *Life of Eumenes* is also partly based on Hieronymus and adds useful details for the Iranian satrapies. Justin and some fragmentary sources offer very little of use, but some useful fragments of Arrian's *History of the Successors* survive (Jacoby 156).

important of them Seleucus, who was given Babylonia. If there was any fighting or disorder, our sources do not report it.

Antipater's death in 319 removed the last figure of universally acknowledged prestige. He left the regency (which he had no real right to dispose of) to an officer of his own generation, Polyperchon; but his son Cassander, thus disappointed in his ambitions, refused to recognize Polyperchon and fled to Antigonus, Alexander's satrap of Phrygia, who had profited by the war against Perdiccas and was now eager to expand his power. He had been busy fighting Eumenes of Cardia, Alexander's Chancellor, who had remained loyal to Perdiccas and had in consequence been declared a rebel. With the central power disintegrating, Antigonus preferred to let him go and instead proceeded to consolidate his power over Asia Minor by eliminating the satraps who held other parts of it.

But he had underestimated Eumenes. As a Greek, Eumenes could not hope for any prominence except (as already under Alexander) under the royal aegis. He therefore put himself at the disposal of Polyperchon (and Olympias, who was supporting him) and was given the title of royal representative and commander-in-chief over all of Asia. Armed with the royal commission, he managed to attract a large army and, after various exploits further west, made his way into Babylonia, with the intention of rallying Iran to the royal cause. Seleucus opposed him, but Eumenes moved on into Susiana and called on the satraps of Iran to obey the royal warrant and join him against the rebels.

They, on the whole, were so far uncommitted, and there was some hope that they might prefer the authority of the distant kings to the proved ambitions of their immediate neighbours. Led by Peucestas, to whom the tenure of Persis and the memory of Alexander's special favour gave some prestige, they came – from Carmania, Arachosia, Areia-Drangiana, even a representative sent by Oxyartes from Paropamisus, and Eudamus (who, we now hear, had assassinated Porus – we have no details) from India, with 120 elephants. But most of them were unwilling to serve under a Greek, unwilling even to recognize one of their own number as superior: Eumenes had to treat them all as equals, and to establish his own position, he consulted with them in a tent, under the presidency of an empty throne reserved for the spirit of Alexander. About midsummer 317 he managed to inflict a major defeat on Antigonus, who had made his way as far as the Kārūn (somewhere near Susa); but Antigonus now seized Ecbatana, where he was safe from the unbearable heat of the plain and had time to collect another army.

EPILOGUE: INTERREGNUM

Eumenes now marched east to secure Persepolis. There Peucestas, using and displaying his popularity with the Persian nobles, played the generous host and tried to put Eumenes in his place. We hear of a splendid banquet he gave, clearly in imitation of Alexander's banquet at Opis, but with a significant difference: this time the Persian nobles were in the innermost circle, on a footing of full equality with Macedonian generals. Eumenes countered by circulating a forged letter asserting that Cassander had been killed and that the royal army was advancing into Asia to bring him support.

After various negotiations and an indecisive battle somewhere in southern Media, Antigonus, about the end of 317, launched a surprise attack on Eumenes' position in Gabiene (on the road from Persepolis to Ecbatana), through a desert separating the two armies. The surprise failed, and Eumenes managed to collect his greatly superior forces from their separate encampments. The battle was again indecisive, but Antigonus succeeded in capturing Eumenes' baggage-train – largely, it was later said, owing to Peucestas' treason: Peucestas, as master of Persis, clearly hoped to strike a favourable bargain with Antigonus. As a result the Silver Shields (Eumenes' Macedonian veteran élite corps), unwilling to lose all their possessions and their lives' savings, surrendered Eumenes to Antigonus, who had him executed.

Antigonus now ruthlessly secured and exploited his advantage. At first he firmly occupied Media, disposing of various supporters of Eumenes, but also of Peithon, the lawful satrap of Media, who had been his own principal ally and a friend of Seleucus. He gave the satrapy to a Mede, with a Macedonian commander under him, and they soon gained control of the whole of the country. He himself now occupied Persepolis, where Peucestas did not venture to resist him. Indeed, he at once removed Peucestas from the satrapy (though he escaped with his life) and, distrusting the natives as friendly to him, put a Macedonian (or Greek) in charge in his place. Areia-Drangiana, where there was an opportunity to intervene, was also handed to one of Antigonus' men; but the other Iranian satrapies were left as they were, since Antigonus had no time for a major campaign in Iran. With Media and Persis secure, he turned west and occupied Susa, where he appointed a native as satrap (for the first time in generations, it seems), and then moved to Babylon, with the vast treasures seized in western Iran. Seleucus received him with wary courtesy, but when he demanded to see the satrap's accounts, Seleucus – aware of the fate of his ally Peithon and of others – preferred to flee and escaped to Ptolemy, where he found a ready ear for his warnings against Antigonus' dangerous ambitions. Antigonus installed another Macedonian satrap in Babylon and then moved west, making for the Mediterranean, and plundering all the treasures he found on his route. It is clear that he, like the rest of the Macedonian barons (except perhaps for Peucestas), had no real interest in the eastern satrapies. Unlike Alexander, he merely wanted to appropriate their resources and treat them as a strategic and economic base for what really mattered: the struggle for the Aegean area, and especially for Greece and the Macedonian homeland.

Our sources, all of them Greek, share that outlook. Nothing at all is heard of events in the eastern satrapies over the next few years. All attention is concentrated on the struggles further west, where the major barons (Ptolemy, Cassander and Lysimachus) at once formed a coalition against the alarming increase in Antigonus' power and resources. By 316 King Philip and his wife had been eliminated by Olympias, and Olympias herself was now eliminated by Cassander, who gained control of Macedonia and imprisoned Roxane and her son Alexander. Although Antigonus naturally tried to exploit this, it turned out that the royal name no longer commanded the loyalty of the Macedonian army or people: henceforth the barons could practically ignore the "king" in their struggles for their own aggrandisement.

In 312, as an incident in those struggles, a step was taken that was to have quite unforeseen consequences for the history of the eastern satrapies. Seleucus had kept up his contacts in Babylon and felt sure of a welcome there: Antigonus seems never to have been popular with those whom he ruled with a heavy hand. Ptolemy, facing an attack by Antigonus in Syria which he knew he was not strong enough to resist, decided to accede to Seleucus' request to risk an investment of about 1,000 men in a mission to cause trouble for Antigonus behind his lines. But Seleucus succeeded beyond all expectations. He seized Babylonia with the support of his friends there, defeated Antigonus' commanders in Media and Susiana, beat off an attempt by Demetrius (Antigonus' son) to recapture Babylon, and so weakened Antigonus' position that in 311 he agreed to make peace with his enemies in order to have a free hand to deal with Seleucus. Characteristically, they all (including Seleucus' old friend Ptolemy) agreed to this arrangement, and Seleucus had to face the whole of Antigonus' power.

At this point our Greek sources totally fail us. All that we know –

EPILOGUE: INTERREGNUM

and we gather it incidentally – is that Antigonus failed and that Seleucus finally established his power from Mesopotamia to the Hindu Kush, clearly with the co-operation of prominent elements among the natives: he, after all, was the only one of the Susa bridegrooms who had not repudiated his Iranian wife after Alexander's death. Yet he too, as it turned out, was marked by the fatal flaw: his world was centred on the Aegean. In 301 he was in Asia Minor, to take a decisive part in the battle of Ipsus, which ended the power and the life of Antigonus. In 281, after another great victory in Asia Minor, he lost his own life, at the age of over eighty, in an attempt to gain control, at last, of the Macedonian homeland. Alexander's death had ended his plans for a joint Macedonian-Persian empire, administered and principally defended by men of mixed descent. Except for Seleucus, his generals and courtiers seem to have repudiated the Iranian brides he had bestowed on them. His experiment with a mixed Macedonian–Iranian army – both the training of Iranian young men after the Macedonian fashion and the combination of Macedonian and Iranian infantry into mixed units – was also abandoned. Peucestas might have carried it on (though we have no positive information that he did); but Peucestas lacked both the calibre for success in the game in which he involved himself and the sense to see his limitations. After more than two centuries of empire, Persia, and with it most of Iran, sinks back into mere provincial territory, governed by men whose main interest lies in the west and who regard its possession as a means to an end: an outlook that would have shocked Alexander almost as much as Darius.

Nor did the conquest lead, as the Arab conquest was to do, to a revolution in Iranian culture. Alexander had always respected native cultures and particularly favoured that of Achaemenian Persia. Far from aiming at hellenization, he had not even planted colonies or founded cities in Persis and Media, and he had adopted aspects of their culture and favoured those of his subordinates who did likewise. Once it was clear that western Iran was no longer the centre of an empire, the result of this policy was – perhaps paradoxically – provincial stagnation. It was to be many centuries before Persia became an imperial power again, and then she had to find inspiration in a semi-legendary past. In eastern Iran – in part thanks to Alexander's policies there – things turned out different. But that is beyond the scope of this survey.

ALEXANDER IN IRAN

APPENDIX: CHRONOLOGY

The chronology of Alexander's march through Asia can only be approximately recovered. The one fixed astronomical point is given by the eclipse of the moon on 20 September 331: if, as most scholars believe, Gaugamela was fought on the eleventh day (inclusively) after this, it is 1 October. Most of our other chronological evidence is less precise.

(1) There are statements of the rising and setting of constellations, usually given in approximate terms ("*about* the rising...") and without indication as to whether the morning or the evening rising or setting is meant. Fortunately we can normally date sufficiently precisely not to make an error of six months. But in one case (see below), it must be admitted that we cannot.

(2) Next, we have statements in terms of seasons, perhaps with some attempt to subdivide; "At the first appearance of spring" is one of Arrian's favourite chronological indications.

(3) Occasionally (most frequently in Arrian) we get an Athenian dating by archon and month, *very* occasionally even day. The Athenian archons for this period are known and the relationship of Athenian months to the natural calendar is normally approximately (though rarely precisely) known. These, then, should be reliable. Unfortunately, there are possibilities of error. First, the names of archons in Arrian are often corrupt in our texts; this is not serious. More seriously, Arrian obviously has at times made his own calculations, in order to express a date that he may have found (say in Ptolemy) in a Macedonian form in terms of the much better known Athenian calendar. For this, he would take the contemporary equation he knew, which was not likely to give the same result as the original correspondence, since these correspondences were standardized under the Roman Empire. Sometimes we can check. Thus, he puts the battle of Gaugamela in Pyanepsion (III. 15.7), whereas Plutarch (*Alex.* 31.8; *Camillus* 19.5) puts it near the end of Boedromion, the preceding month. Plutarch is generally considered to be right, as he relates it to the eclipse, which (he says) occurred about the beginning of the Mysteries in Athens (which would be the 15th of that month). Of course, there is a possibility that *he* is calculating by contemporary correspondence (as he too can at times be shown to have done), except that he has supplied an Athenian "explanation" for the eclipse date as well. This illustrates as well as anything the difficulties sometimes posed by these apparently precise statements. Once (*Ind.* 21.1) Arrian is two years out (the archon of 323–2 instead of the one of 325–4) when aiming at special precision. (The error is not likely to be due to his source Nearchus, a contemporary of the events writing about his own voyage.)

(4) We can sometimes deduce dates from a fixed point, where a duration is also given. Though this inevitably introduces another uncertainty, durations in terms of days are likely to be precise. Durations in terms of months are demonstrably less so. Thus Aristobulus, a participant in the campaign (though writing much later), allocates ten months to the march down the Hydaspes and other rivers as far as Pattala, while the precise astronomical indications he

APPENDIX: CHRONOLOGY

himself provides for the beginning and end add up to about $8\frac{1}{2}$ months. Significant durations are included in the table below.

(5) At the worst, deductions may be cautiously made from comments on natural phenomena: heat and cold, snow, rain, drought, or the state of the crops. These are normally useful only in supporting a more precise indication (e.g. where there is a conflict of evidence) and are not included in the table below.

It will be seen that even apparent precision in our sources is no guarantee of accuracy. Accuracy to the day is normally impossible, and even approximate indications, within reasonable limits, can only be given relatively rarely.

The standard discussion of the chronology is by Beloch (see p. 422, n. 1), 304–22. However, he makes the pervasive mistake of assuming fixed and regular intercalary cycles (which would yield a calendar easily convertible into Julian dates, where we have enough data) for the Athenian calendar of this period. His exact conversions into Julian dates should therefore be treated as, at best, approximate. The best short reference work on ancient calendars and other problems of chronology is E. J. Bickerman, *The Chronology of the Ancient World* (London, 1968). Dates based on astronomical phenomena given in the table below are based on his lists.

TABLE

Statements resting on deduction (other than duration calculated from a fixed date) are in square brackets. Winter usually stretches into the following year. The annotations [a] and [n] stand for instances where, respectively, Aristobulus and Nearchus are cited as sources for a date. This attestation is better than most others.

334	Early spring (A. 1.11.3)	Invasion of Asia
	Daesius 6 (April–May?) (See Beloch, 314)	Battle of Granicus
	[Early autumn] (cf. A. 1.24.1)	Carian campaign
	Midwinter (334–33) to late winter (A. 1.24.5)	Phaselis to Phrygia
333	[Spring] (deduced from A. 1.24.1; 29.4)	Gordium
	Maimacterion (November?) (A. 11.11.10)	Issus[1]
332	[January??] (also, seventh month before next item: P. 24.5; D. 46.5; C. IV.4.19)	Beginning of siege of Tyre[2]
	Hecatombaeon (July–August?) (A. 11.24.6; cf. P. 25.1–2, making it the beginning of a Macedonian month	Capture of Tyre[2]
	[Near end of year] (D. 48.7: 2 months' siege)	Capture of Gaza
331	April 7	Official foundation of Alexandria[3]
	'Very early spring' (A. III.6.1)	Departure from Memphis[3]
	Hecatombaeon (July–August) (A. III.7.1)	Euphrates crossed at Thapsacus
	September 20–1 (see Beloch, 315) (A. III.7.6; P. 31.8)	Eclipse of moon
	October 1? (P., *l.c.*; Plut. *Camillus* 19.5: Boedromion 26)	Battle of Gaugamela[4]
330	[Mid-January] (deduced from following items)	Arrival at Persepolis
	About April 7 (C. v.6.12)	Beginning of Persis-Mardi campaign
	About May 7 (*ibid.* 19: 30 days later)	Return to Persepolis
	[Mid-May?] (cf. P. 37.6; C., *l.c.* ff)	Departure from Persepolis

ALEXANDER IN IRAN

	Hecatombaeon (late June–July) (A. III.22.2)	Death of Darius[5]
	About November 6 (Strabo XV.2.10)	
	or	Arrival at Paropamisus[6]
329	About April 6 (*ibid.*)	
	Winter (330–29) *or* spring 329 (*ibid.*)	Camp near Begrām (?)[6]
	Midwinter (329–28) (A. IV.7.1)	Winter at Bactra
328	Midwinter (328–27) (A. IV.18.2)	Winter at Nautaca
327	'Very early spring' (A. IV.18.4)	Campaign againt Oxyartes
	[Summer?]	Bactra; pages' conspiracy[7]
	[Late summer?]	Departure from Bactra[7]
	After November 5 (Strabo XV.1.17)[a]	Departure from Begrām for India
326	Early spring (*ibid.*)[a]	Departure from winter camp for Taxila; beginning of monsoon
	Summer solstice?? (But cf. next two items!) (A. V.9.4)	Arrival at Hydaspes[8]
	Mounychion (April–May) (A. V.19–3)	Battle of Hydaspes
	Summer solstice (Strabo XV.1.18)[n]	Arrival at Acesines
	Before September 23 (Strabo XV.1.17)[a]	Return from Hyphasis to Hydaspes; end of monsoon
	Just before November 5 (*ibid.*)[a]	Departure down Hydaspes
325	About July 15 (*ibid.*)[a]	Arrival at Pattala
	Some time before next item (September?) (A. VI.21.3)	Departure of army from Pattala
	About October 9 (Strabo XV.2.5)[n]; Boedromion (September–October) 20 (A. *Ind.* 21.1)[n]	Departure of fleet from Pattala
	22 days after departure from Pattala (C. IX.10.5–6) (see Beloch, 320)	Army reaches borders of Gedrosia
	60 days later (A. VI.24.1; P. 66.7) [December?]	Arrival at Pura after march through desert
324	Winter (A. VI.28.7)	Departure from Carmania
	In 7th month after departure from Pattala (Pliny, *Nat. Hist.* VI.100) [March?]	Arrival at Susa
	Autumn (see next item)	Death of Hephaestion at Ecbatana
	Winter ('a considerable time' after preceding) (A.VII.15.3; cf. *Ind.* 40.6 f; Strabo XI.13.6[n])	Campaign against Cossaei, completed in 40 days (D. 111.6)
323	June 10 (see A. E. Samuel, *Historia* XV (1965), 8)	Death of Alexander in Babylon

---

[1] Beloch (312ff.) thinks Arrian has made another mistake and would put the battle earlier; but see Bosworth, 219.

[2] Hecatombaeon, for the year 332, may be June–July or July–August. But the festival of "Heracles" mentioned by C. IV.2.10 at the beginning of the siege was probably in January (cf. Atkinson, *Commentary*, 296); the siege therefore is likely to have lasted from January to July or August.

[3] The official "birthday" of Alexandria can be calculated to have fallen on that day. Arrian and Plutarch mention the foundation of the city before the visit to Siwah (that would have to be some months earlier); Curtius, Diodorus and Justin, as well as the *Romance* from which the "birthday" is derived, after the visit. Welles argued that the later date should be accepted, Fraser returned to the earlier, but failed to explain satisfactorily how the confusion could have arisen. For a summary of the controversy and discussion, see R. S. Bagnall, *AJAH* IV (1979), 46–9, rightly accepting the transmitted date, and pointing out that Arrian's phrase, "very early spring", for the departure from Memphis, need not be pressed, especially as it is not required by the timetable

APPENDIX: CHRONOLOGY

for his later movements. In view of the attestation of the April date and the division between the groups of sources (but note that Welles was wrong in claiming that Aristobulus gave the April date: see Brunt in his LCL edition of Arrian, vol. 1, p. 457), it is most probable that the site was actually marked out before the visit, but that the formal inauguration had to wait until Ammon's approval had been obtained; after which, Alexander could at once leave Egypt. Thus Atkinson, [II.2], 362 (also hinted at by Bagnall, *op. cit.*). Bosworth, 263 (with reference to an earlier article) does not succeed in reconciling the sources, as he misinterprets Curtius. Curtius does, however, stress the quickness of Alexander's departure after the foundation.

[4] Cf. discussion in the introduction to this table. Whether Arrian's account of Alexander's movements after the eclipse can add up to eleven days is uncertain. Atkinson, 486–8 puts the battle on 28 September, but does not comment on Plutarch's reference to eleven days after the eclipse.

[5] Bosworth, 346 suggests that Arrian is mistaken and that Darius' death should be put in August. His arguments are not compelling, in view of the paucity of concrete evidence on dates and march rates.

[6] See p. 455, n. 1 for discussion of this well-known crux; no firm conclusion is possible, but the April date ignores Strabo's reference to a *winter* spent after (and Strabo may possibly be misreporting here, as occasionally elsewhere); the suggestion that the winter spent near Begrām was the following winter (329–8) is inherently unlikely and, as this table will show, would not lead to an acceptable scheme for Alexander's further movements down to his departure for India.

[7] A. IV.22.3 puts the departure from Bactra in late spring; but since the march to Begram only took 10 days (*ibid.*), it would be hard to explain Alexander's long delay there (see table); on the other hand, Arrian also gives early spring for the beginning of the campaign against Oxyartes, and the time between this and a departure in "late spring" would not be adequate. It is clearly the departure date from Bactra that is wrong, and an assumed departure in summer (perhaps late summer) will give a smooth fit. A textual change has been proposed, introducing "summer" for "spring" into the text of Arrian. It is not a difficult change ($\theta\acute{\epsilon}\rho o \nu s$ for $\mathring{\eta}\rho o s$), but probably unnecessary, as A. makes other mistakes.

[8] Arrian's text may be disturbed at this point.

CHAPTER 9

THE PERSIAN OCCUPATION OF EGYPT

The imperialist expansion of Persia pursued by Cyrus the Great, founder of the Achaemenian Empire, already loomed ominously over Egypt by the end of Amasis' rule. The conquest of Egypt was after all a natural objective of that expansionist policy, the Nile Valley being the most important, if not the only source of economic and political power in Africa. When Cambyses, after succeeding his father Cyrus in 529 B.C., had settled his family affairs and the internal problems of his Asiatic empire, he led his army to the eastern borders of Egypt. Amasis, penultimate Pharaoh of Dynasty XXVI, had tried to protect himself against the Persians by an alliance with Polycrates of Samos, but his ally deserted him the moment that an attack by Cambyses became inevitable. There could be little hope of safety for Egypt when Phanes, the general commanding Amasis' troops on the eastern border, chose to betray his king and go over to the more powerful Cambyses, to whom he disclosed all the most valuable Egyptian military secrets. At his advice Cambyses got the support of Bedouins from the Arabian desert whose camels, laden with waterskins, enabled the Persian army to cross the desert and reach Pelusium.

Amasis died probably early in 525 B.C. It therefore fell to his son, Psammetichus III to put up a last stand against the foreign invaders. The Egyptian defence was routed at Pelusium and what was left of the army retreated to Memphis, but before long Memphis fell and Psammetichus was taken prisoner. In accordance with a Persian policy of making defeated sovereigns vassals of the empire, Cambyses treated Psammetichus leniently at first. But soon afterwards he had him killed for inciting rebellion.

Cambyses stayed in Egypt until 522 B.C. The so-called "first Persian domination", also called, after Manetho, Dynasty XXVII, begins with the year of his victory, 525 B.C., and lasts until 402 B.C.

From the point of view of Persian foreign policy, the conquest of the Nile Valley could be considered the end of expansion to the south-west: to extend their rule beyond the Egyptian province, which

THE PERSIAN OCCUPATION OF EGYPT

was already far-flung and hard to control, would have been judged politically dangerous. Yet, between 525 and 522 B.C. we see Cambyses embark on an "African" policy with expeditions against Carthage, the oases of the Libyan Desert, and Nubia. One must bear in mind that Cambyses, who wished to be regarded as Pharaoh in Egypt, pursued an Egyptian policy as if he were an Egyptian king, and that he was inspired by the natural policy of the Saïte kings when, in the wake of Psammetichus II, he embarked on the Nubian campaign.

All three campaigns failed. His Phoenician allies refused to attack their sister colony, Carthage; the expedition against the Libyan oases ended in disaster when, if we may believe Herodotus, his 50,000 men perished in a sandstorm; the ill-prepared and hasty expedition against Ethiopia, which had aimed at taking Napata, was a failure; and the Nubia which acknowledged Persian rule (Herodotus III. 97–98), paying tribute every two years, was the northern Nubia which had been under Egyptian influence and sovereignty for centuries. Cambyses, who had personally led the Nubian campaign, strengthened the Jewish garrison at Elephantine which had been there since Dynasty XXVI, and built up the Semitic settlement, military and otherwise, at Syene which had also been there before the Persian conquest.[1]

Cambyses' Pharaonic claims are known from the statue of Udjahorresne, a high Egyptian official and court physician who had served under the previous Saïte kings and continued his brilliant career under Cambyses and Darius I. The statue kept in the Vatican Museum whence its title of "Vatican Naophoros"[2] was originally set up in the Temple of Neith at Saïs in the third or fourth year of Darius I. From the statue we learn that Cambyses instructed Udjahorresne to draw up for him the royal titles so as to put himself on a par with the Pharaohs who had preceded him. Above all the conqueror of Egypt wanted to present himself to the Egyptian people as the legitimate descendant of the Saïte dynasty, who had come to claim the throne which the "usurper" Amasis had taken from the rightful Pharaoh, Apries. The legend which made Cambyses the son of a daughter of Apries is noteworthy in this connection.[3] Cambyses, blood descendant of the Saïte Pharaohs had come to Egypt to revenge the betrayal by Amasis of his grandfather

---

[1] Cf. Kraeling, pp. 41–8.
[2] Posener, Text 1; G. Botti-Promanelli, *Le Sculture del Museo Gregoriano greco-egizio* (Città del Vaticano, 1951), p. 33, Tav. 28.
[3] Herodotus III. 1–3; Athenaeus XIII. 560d–f (from Ctesias).

Apries and to claim the kingdom. What Herodotus says (III. 16) about the posthumous persecution of Amasis, whose mummy is supposed to have been burnt by Cambyses, makes sense in the light of this legend. The Greek historian notes that the action of the Great King was contrary to both Persian and Egyptian beliefs: to Persian, because it was inconceivable that a devout Mazdean would contaminate fire; to Egyptian, because the burning of a corpse ruled out survival after death. If in fact Cambyses did burn Amasis' body, he will have done so to effect a drastic "damnatio memoriae" of the usurper; and though we cannot check the truth of Herodotus' story, we do have proof of just such an attack on Amasis' name during the years of Cambyses' invasion, witnessed by a series of Egyptian monuments which show the intentional erasure of Amasis' name from the royal cartouche.[1]

A series of Greek witnesses, beginning with Herodotus,[2] describes Cambyses' behaviour in Egypt as mad, godless and cruel. Besides having burnt Amasis' mummy he is supposed to have mocked and profaned the Egyptian gods, burnt and sacked temples, and killed the sacred bull at Memphis. However, the primary sources, represented by Egyptian monuments contemporaneous with Cambyses enable us to put these testimonies in perspective and in some cases to discount them.[3]

As for the killing of the sacred Apis bull, Herodotus (III. 27–29) says that when Cambyses had returned without success from the Nubian expedition he was incensed at finding the people of Memphis in a festive mood due to the appearance of the new Apis. This is why he mortally wounded the sacred bull which was then buried secretly by the priests. This information is disproved by a stela from the Serapeum – the burial ground of the sacred bulls at Saqqāra – dating from the sixth year of Cambyses,[4] which testifies to the solemn burial in that year of the Apis bull born in the twenty-seventh year of Amasis: the rich sarcophagus[5] which housed the animal's mummified remains has been found in the Serapeum and had been donated by Cambyses himself. Another stela from the Serapeum[6] contradicts Herodotus even more clearly for it says that the Apis born during the rule of Cambyses and successor to the

---

[1] For the burnt mummy of Amasis, cf. H. De Meulenaere, *Herodotos over de 26ste Dynastie* (Leuven, 1951), pp. 124–8. For the erasure of Amasis' name and a bibliography, cf. E. Bresciani, "Una statua della XXVI dinastia con il cosiddetto 'abito persiano'", *SCO* XVI (1967), p. 277 and 279.

[2] Herodotus III. 27–38; Diodorus I. 46; Strabo XVII. 27; Plutarch, *De Iside et Osiride* 44 (368 F).

[3] Cf. Posener, especially pp. 171ff. On the other hand A. Klasens, "Cambyses en Egypte", *Ex Oriente Lux* III (9–10) (1952), pp. 347ff., still thinks that because of its detail Herodotus' account cannot be judged false.

[4] Posener, Text 3.   [5] Posener, Text 4.   [6] Posener, Text 5.

THE PERSIAN OCCUPATION OF EGYPT

bull buried in the sixth year of Cambyses, died a natural death in the fourth year of Darius I.[1] The naophoros statue of Udjahorresne already mentioned throws further light on Cambyses' activity in Egypt. In the hieroglyphic text that covers the statue Udjahorresne admits that with the coming of the 'foreigners' who had taken quarters in the sanctuary of Neith at Saïs, there "was much disorder" in Egypt, but that Cambyses had come to the aid of the sanctuary, driven out the foreign troops and cleared away the remains of their encampment. He had purified the temple of Neith and restored the revenues to the goddess; he had re-established the attendant priests, had made provision for the ceremonies and processions to take place as before, and had personally offered homage to the goddess of Saïs.

The objection that Udjahorresne was a courtier of Darius and that therefore his statement, so far from telling the truth, may be a mere piece of adulation of his Persian masters, does not hold. It is hardly likely that he would have distorted the truth about Cambyses when the events were contemporary and when the statue was on public show in the Temple at Saïs. He does not deny that the occupying troops were brutal and savage,[2] but he does not blame Cambyses who tried to curb their abuses as soon as he heard of them. It is probable that the Persian troops, in the initial violence of a military take-over, behaved more or less everywhere as they did at Saïs. We find another hint of violent sieges, sackings and destruction of Egyptian sanctuaries by Cambyses' army, in an Aramaic papyrus from Elephantine dated 408 B.C.;[3] the text (ll. 13–14) states clearly that with the conquest of Cambyses there were disruptions in temples throughout Egypt: "When Cambyses came into Egypt he found this temple [i.e. the temple of Yahu at Elephantine] built; *they overthrew* all the temples of the Egyptian gods, but no one damaged this temple". So, Cambyses is not personally responsible for the sackings, but they are attributed to the general disturbance following the military invasion.

A Demotic papyrus (Pap. dem. 215 verso, Bibliothèque Nationale, Paris)[4] mentions a decree promulgated by Cambyses in which he

---

[1] The so-called problem of the "coexistence of the Apis bulls", is solved brilliantly by Posener, p. 174.
[2] Cf. for example the Babylonian bill of sale, dating from 525 B.C., of a female Egyptian slave who was part of war spoils, B. Meissner, *ZÄS* XXIX (1891), pp. 123–4.
[3] Cowley, no. 30 (a petition for the reconstruction of the Yahu temple at Elephantine).
[4] Spiegelberg, *Demotische Chronik*, pp. 32–3. There is a Demotic papyrus from Siut (Lycopolos) dating from the 8th year of Cambyses (Spiegelberg, *Demotischen Denkmäler* III, no. 50059) as well as various fragments which contain the date of the 5th and 6th year of Cambyses (no. 50062).

ordered that all Egyptian sanctuaries except three (Memphis, *Pr-Ḥʿpj-n-Wn* (?) and *Wn-ḥm* (?))[1] which were "to be maintained as before") were to suffer a diminution of the revenues "given to the temples of the gods during the time of Pharaoh Amasis". The decree did not prevent worship, even in the temples affected by the restrictions. But wood for the sacred vessels, and wood for burning and flax, had to be gathered from one area of the Delta and another in Upper Egypt; the supply of animals for the rituals was cut by half, and the supply of birds was cut completely. It must be made clear that Cambyses' decree did not prevent the priests from offering birds to the gods, but, to quote the text, "the priests must offer to the gods the geese that they themselves have reared". Although the characters on the papyrus do not give an absolutely clear reading, it seems that the total value of the silver, animals, birds, grain etc., given to the temples during Amasis' time, and which Cambyses now ordered "not to be given to the gods", will have been at least 376,400 deben.

Cambyses' provision, which reduced the enormous financial obligations to the temples that Amasis had considered good policy to undertake, must be considered in its true light as an economy measure, and not one dictated by "impiety" or by hatred of the gods and beliefs of his Egyptian subjects. So much so that he allowed three temples to maintain their traditions and did not prevent worship in the others. It is also possible that by abolishing the revenues granted in Amasis' time, Cambyses meant to strike at the memory of the "usurper". Naturally enough the decree was not of a kind that would foster the Persian conqueror's popularity; it gave rise among the Egyptian priestly caste to implacable hatred, which surely is what lies at the root of the anti-Cambyses tradition.[2] The already-mentioned inscription on the "Vatican Naophoros", states that under the influence of the court physician Udjahorresne, Cambyses had made provision to restore to Neith and the other gods of Saïs the revenues they had earlier enjoyed; but Saïs is definitely not one of the three privileged cities named in the decree (which was copied at a time much later than Cambyses'). Thus

---

[1] *Pr-Ḥʿpj-n-Wn*(?) is possibly Nilopolis or Heliopolis, *Wn-ḥm*(?) is perhaps Hermopolis.

[2] In Egypt Cambyses takes on the mythological mantle of the detested god Seth. Cambyses came from Asia just as Seth returned to Egypt to conquer with his armies the land which the gods had given to Horus as the legitimate heir of Osiris. Cf. E. Drioton, *Pages d'Égyptologie* (Cairo, 1957), pp. 307–27. The tradition that sees in Cambyses the enemy of Egypt goes back as far as the Coptic text of "Cambyses' Conquest of Egypt", in which Cambyses is likened to Nebuchadnezzar. Cf. H. L. Jansen, *Cambyses' invasion*.

THE PERSIAN OCCUPATION OF EGYPT

for Saïs it was not a question of modifying the decree, which as we shall see was abrogated by his successor, but of making a special concession.

While Cambyses resumed the role of Pharaoh in Egypt his downfall was being planned in Persia. It is symptomatic that the rebellion should have stemmed from the court circle in Susa. The Magus Gaumata took advantage of Cambyses' long absence to claim the Persian throne, presenting himself as legitimate successor to Cyrus as if he were Smerdis, the brother of Cambyses whom the latter had had secretly killed before the Egyptian campaign. Cambyses departed at once from Egypt, leaving behind Aryandes as satrap, only to die on the return journey early in 522 B.C.[1]

Darius I (522 B.C.–486 B.C.), son of Hystaspes the governor of Persis, re-established order in the Empire, at once getting rid of the false Smerdis, quelling vigorously by continuous and successful wars the long series of rebellions in Asia, and winning for the Empire the new province of India. He had to intervene in Egypt to crush Aryandes' movement for independence. The date when that rebellion was put down is not certain, but it must have been between 510 – the year when Aryandes led an expedition against Barca – and 492 B.C. by which year Pherendates was already satrap of the Egyptian province.[2]

Darius I displayed tolerance and respect for the Egyptian province, as for the other provinces of the empire, leaving notable traces of his organizing genius and of a policy aimed at attracting the support of the Egyptian priestly class. The Nile Valley, which Darius certainly visited at the beginning of his reign and probably later, held an important place among the provinces, and Herodotus (III. 89ff) puts Egypt sixth in the list of the twenty satrapies. Diodorus' claim (I. 95) that Darius was the sixth and last legislator of Egypt finds clear confirmation in an Egyptian document, the demotic text already mentioned, on the verso of Pap. dem. 215 in the Bibliothèque Nationale. It says that in the third year of his rule Darius instructed his satrap in Egypt to assemble "the wise men among the soldiers, priests and scribes of Egypt", to codify the previous Egyptian legal system up to the forty-fourth year of Amasis. The commission sat for 16 years, until the 19th year of Darius. Between this

[1] Herodotus III. 64–6 relates that he died through an accidental knife-wound and that the wound was exactly on that part of the thigh where Cambyses had struck the Apis bull.

[2] For the rebel satrap Aryandes cf. Herodotus IV. 166–7, 200–3. The satrap Pherendates is mentioned in three Demotic papyri, the Pap. dem. Berlin 13539 and 13540 and the Pap. Loeb 1. Cf. W. Spiegelberg, "Drei demotische Schreiben aus der Korrespondenz des Pherendates des Satrapen Darius' I., mit den Chnum-Priestern von Elephantine", *SPAW*, 1928, pp. 604–22.

year and the twenty-seventh year (legible in the text after a serious lacuna), Spiegelberg, the editor of the text, believed one could assume that the commission was gathered at Susa, with the king. The collection of laws was transcribed onto papyrus "in Aramaic script and in Demotic script". In this way the Great King performed the task of legal codification, gathering together the Egyptian laws that had been binding until the end of Amasis' reign.[1] A clear-cut guide to local Egyptian law was particularly useful for the Egyptian satrapy of the Achaemenian Empire, administered as it was by officials who were as a rule Persians or Babylonians, from the satrap down. That this was the purpose is proved by the fact that Darius I ordered a copy of the juridical corpus to be made also in Aramaic, so that it would be ready to hand for government officials, in the administrative language of the empire.[2]

Between the end of Amasis' rule and the beginning of Darius' there was a period of crisis for the "temple law" which had been in force under Amasis, on account of Cambyses' decree which abrogated in large part the revenues which the Egyptian sanctuaries had formerly enjoyed. The priests on Darius' legal commission probably told the Great King how Cambyses' decree conflicted with the state of law that had existed prior to the Persian conquest. Cambyses' successor restored the old temple laws: clearly he judged that he needed the support of the priests to forge a lasting union between Egypt and his empire. Darius was also lenient to the memory of Amasis, as one gathers from the "Vatican Naophoros" which dates from Darius' reign, where the name of Amasis appears along with those of Apries and the Achaemenid sovereigns, surrounded by the royal cartouche.

The Great King's protection of Egyptian worship and its priesthood was also expressed in the building of a grandiose Temple to Amon-Ra in the Oasis of El-Khārga. Proof of Darius' building activity in Egypt is given by the inscriptions in the caves at Wādī Hammāmāt;[3] and blocks

[1] Cf. Bresciani, "La Satrapia d'Egitto", pp. 153–5. Changes according to Iranian law must be ruled out, and there seems little to support N. J. Reich's opinion in "The codification of the Egyptian Laws by Darius and the origin of the 'Demotic Chronicle'", *Mizraim* I (New York, 1933), pp. 178ff, that the Egyptian laws were adapted to the political system and will of the Great King. E. Seidl's definition of Darius I as simply a "compiler" of already existing laws is exact, *Ägyptische Rechtsgeschichte der Saiten-und Perserzeit* (Glückstadt, 1956), p. 84. As Diodorus I. 95, notes, Cambyses' provision had been not only impious but also illegal under Egyptian law, and the legislative activity of Darius I was meant to remedy precisely that illegal impiety.

[2] Cf. H. H. Schaeder, *Iranische Beiträge* I (Halle, 1930), p. 202.

[3] Posener, Texts 24–34 and p. 17; G. Goyon, *Nouvelles Inscriptions rupestres du Uâdi Hammamât* (Paris, 1957), Text 109, p. 118.

THE PERSIAN OCCUPATION OF EGYPT

bearing his name have been found at El-Kāb in Upper Egypt and at Busiris in the Delta.[1] A great number of stelae from the Serapeum can be dated to between the third and fourteenth year of Darius;[2] A stela from Fayyūm[3] is dedicated to Darius as the god Horus; and we know from the statue of Udjahorresne that Darius gave orders for the restoration of the "house of life" at Saïs.[4]

One of Darius' public works which was important for contact with the Egyptian satrapy was the opening of a navigable canal from the Nile to the Red Sea, thus completing a waterway that had been conceived and partly built by Necho II[5] nearly a century before. It ran from Bubastis through Wādī Tumilat to Lake Timsah, on to the Bitter Lakes and finally to the Red Sea.[6] Four large bilingual stelae, hieroglyphic and cuneiform, the so-called "Canal Stelae" were set up by Darius along its course.[7]

Shortly before Darius' death in 486 B.C. Egypt rose in revolt. Some scholars believe that a slackening of Persian control brought about conditions favourable to rebellion, because the Great King now engaged in a war of revenge on the Greeks who had defied him at Marathon in 490 B.C. It is also possible that it was a rebellion like the one led by Aryandes even if there is no proof that the satrap Pherendates, who was certainly in office in 486, was involved in it. This is the view I take, and it may be thought to be supported by the fact that Xerxes, son of Darius and his successor from 486 to 465–464 B.C. appointed his brother Achaemenes as satrap in Egypt as soon as the revolt was put down (Herodotus VII. 7). Meanwhile, with the defeat at Marathon crying out for revenge, it was Greece that remained Persia's real enemy, and we know that another defeat lay in store for Xerxes in his campaign against the Greeks. Victorious at Salamis, Plataea and

---

[1] The cartouche of Darius I at El-Kāb, Somers Clarke, "El-Kāb and its temples", *JEA* VIII (1922), p. 27; a block from Busiris, now in the British Museum: E. Naville, *The mound of the Jew and the city of Onias* (London, 1890), pp. 27–8, pl. VII. A.

[2] Cf. Bresciani, *op. cit.*, "Appendice Archeologica", pp. 177–8.

[3] *Ibid.*, p. 178.

[4] For the "house of life", a cultural institution connected with the temples, cf. H. Gardiner, "The House of Life", *JEA* XXIV (1938), pp. 157–79. Neith, the Goddess of Saïs, was much acknowledged by the Persian sovereigns of Dynasty XXVII, and Darius I proclaims himself "son of Neith".

[5] Herodotus II. 158; Diodorus I. 33.

[6] G. Posener, "Le canal du Nil à la mer Rouge avant les Ptolémées", *Chronique d'Égypte* XIII (Brussels, 1938), pp. 259–73.

[7] Posener, *La première domination*, pp. 180–1; Kienitz, p. 65. Another, but unacceptable, interpretation of the text of the stelae is given by A. Servin, *Bull. Société Études hist. et géogr. de l'Isthme de Suez* III (Cairo, 1951), pp. 25–96.

THE PERSIAN OCCUPATION OF EGYPT

Mycale, having freed Ionia and taken Sestos on the Hellespont, the Greeks were the natural allies of any subjects of the Great King intent on regaining their own freedom.

Early in the reign of Artaxerxes I, successor to Xerxes from 465–464 to 425 B.C. there was a move towards an insurrection in Egypt in 460 B.C. It was led by the Libyan Inaros, son of Psammetichus (cf. Thucydides I. 104), sprang up in Marea and gained strong support in the Delta, inciting all Egypt to revolt. Inaros sought help from Athens and a fleet of 200 ships bound for Cyprus changed course for Egypt, finally sailing up the Nile towards Memphis. The classical sources are not clear on this point, but it seems likely that they sailed up the western Canopic arm, the one close to Inaros' centre of action and long known to the Greeks for whom the Saïte kings had set aside Naucratis as a river port. The Greeks occupied two thirds of Memphis while the Persians and the Egyptians loyal to Persia defended themselves strongly, occupying the fortified inner city of Memphis, the "white wall" as Thucydides termed it. In a battle at Papremis in the Western Delta[1] between Inaros and the Persian troops fighting against the rebels who had gathered at Memphis, the satrap Achaemenes brother to the king, was killed in action. When Herodotus journeyed through Egypt about 450 B.C. he visited the battlefield at Papremis and studied the remains of the Persians who had been killed there. What he found confirmed his theory why the Egyptians, used to going bareheaded in the sun, had strong cranial domes, while those of the Persians, who wore a helmet, were weak (Herodotus III. 12).

When Megabyzus the satrap of Syria was sent to Egypt he retook Memphis, driving off the Greeks and Egyptians; he then blockaded the Greek fleet at the island of Prosopitis and finally took the island after a siege of 18 months (Thucydides I. 109); the few Greeks who managed to escape fled to Cyrene. A small Athenian flotilla which had sailed up the Mendesic arm of the Nile, unaware of what had happened, was wiped out (Thucydides I. 110). The Greek intervention in support of Egyptian freedom thus ended in disaster. Inaros was handed over to the Persians and crucified (454 B.C.). The revolt had been confined to one part of the Delta, and certain Egyptian monuments confirm that Upper Egypt had remained in Persian control during that period. An inscription from Wādī Hammāmāt naming the Persian official Atiyawrata is dated in the fifth year of Artaxerxes,[2] while from Elephantine

---

[1] For a new siting and etymology of Papremis cf. E. Bresciani, *SCO* XXI (1972), pp. 299–303.
[2] Posener, *Text* 31.

THE PERSIAN OCCUPATION OF EGYPT

two Aramaic papyri are from the sixth year, and one each from the ninth and tenth year of Artaxerxes.[1]

The peace that was restored to Egypt showed no sign of being disturbed for a long time after the reign of Artaxerxes; moreover by the peace treaty of Callias signed in 449 B.C. Athens was obliged to keep out of the political affairs of Cyprus and Egypt. After Achaemenes' death at Papremis and once the intervention by Megabyzus was at an end, the Egyptian satrapy was taken over by the royal prince Arsames, who stayed in office for the entire reign of Darius II (424–404 B.C.). He is known from Greek sources,[2] as well as from the seven Aramaic papyri from Elephantine,[3] and the Aramaic letters written on leather found in a leather bag perhaps at Memphis or possibly at a site in the Western Delta, and published by Driver in 1954.[4]

We know little about Persia's political relations with Egypt during the reign of Darius II. We do know that a decree published in his fifth year (419 B.C.) obliged the Jewish colony at Elephantine to observe the feast of Unleavened Bread from the 15th to the 21st day of the month of Nisan: the decree had been sent to Arsames so that he could let the Jews in Egypt observe this new religious feast which meant no work for seven days. An Aramaic papyrus from Elephantine which preserves Hananiah's letter to the Jewish military garrison[5] tells us of this decree of Darius. It is clear that royal interference in the religious observance of his subjects had the political end of securing Jewish support, yet loyalty to Persian rule cost the Jewish community at Elephantine the temple of Yahu which was destroyed in the agitation against Persian rule that began in the last years of Darius' reign. Between 411 and 408 B.C. while Arsames was at Susa, there were disorders in the Delta[6] and it is possible that the agitator was Amyrtaeus who several years later was to rule an Egypt free of foreign domination.

In this same period while Arsames was away, the Jews of Elephantine saw their temple destroyed by the Egyptians led by priests of the god Khnum and even with the connivance of Persian officials, the civil governor and the commander of the garrison. The rebels also destroyed

---

[1] Cowley, Nos 8 and 9, Nos 10 and 11 respectively.
[2] Polyaenus, *Stratagemata* VII. 28 ('Ἀρσάμης); Ctesias, *Persica*, §35 (Σαρσάμας: ed. Müller, p. 52, ed. Gilmore, p. 162, ed. König, p. 14; ed. Henry, p. 119), §47 ('Ἀρξάνης: ed. Müller, p. 55, ed. Gilmore, p. 168, ed. König, p. 19, ed. Henry, p. 124).
[3] Cowley, Nos 17, 21, 26, 27, 30, 31, 32.
[4] Driver, *Aramaic Documents*.
[5] Cowley, No. 21. Cf. Kraeling, p. 95.
[6] Driver, Letters V, VII, VIII. For Arsames' absence from Egypt when he went to the king at Susa, see also Cowley, No. 30, line 4.

a "warehouse of the king", attacking at the same time the governing officials and the Jewish colony loyal to the Great King.[1] One should see the episode not as an act of religious intolerance, but as politically motivated and perhaps part of the ferment taking place in the Delta. Another Aramaic document from Elephantine[2] confirms this political interpretation: it is a letter sent by the Jewish community to Arsames in which they petition to have the temple rebuilt and reaffirm their loyalty to Persia: "when the Egyptian detachments rebelled we did not leave our posts and no disloyalty was found in us".[3]

In spite of riots and disorders Persia continued to exercise her authority at least as far as the southern borders of Egypt until 402 B.C., and the dating of several Aramaic papyri from Elephantine[4] proves that Artaxerxes II was still acknowledged there as king. From this date Amyrtaeus, founder of Dynasty XXVIII, is recognized as Pharaoh in all Egypt as far as Elephantine, and so begins a sixty-year period in which indigenous dynasties once again rule in Egypt. I shall deal presently with the historical events of this period from Dynasties XXVIII to XXX before Egypt suffered a second, short Persian domination. But first it will be useful to consider the form Persian rule took in Egypt during the century or so in which the Nile Valley was organized as a satrapy; and to note its administrative, economic and financial aspects, as well as its effect on intellectual and religious life.

The satrap (*ḫštrpn* in demotic), representative of the Great King to his subjects in the provinces of the empire, resided in Egypt at Memphis, the country's ancient capital. His chancery, modelled on that of the Great King at Susa, employed numerous officials and scribes, including Egyptian scribes for correspondence in indigenous languages. For, although the official and international language of the Achaemenian Empire was Aramaic, the Egyptian satrap was free to write to natives in demotic even in official communications, and they would reply in demotic. As with Aramaic documents, so also with demotic documents[5] issued from the satrap's chancery, there is always distinction made between the scribe who is a mere amanuensis, and the royal scribe. The

[1] Cowley, Nos 30, 31. The Aramaic papyrus in the Brooklyn Museum proves that the temple of Yahu was rebuilt or at least that the cult of Yahu continued at Elephantine for years after the destruction of the temple. Cf. Kraeling, pp. 102ff.
[2] Cowley, No. 27, cf. also No. 30 (31).
[3] *Op. cit.*, No. 27, lines 1ff.
[4] Kraeling, Nos 10, 11, 12.
[5] Pap. dem. Berlin 13539 and 13540, and Pap. Loeb 1, cf. p. 507, n. 2 and Bresciani, "La satrapia d'Egitto", p. 133.

THE PERSIAN OCCUPATION OF EGYPT

latter is the head of the chancery, responsible for the writs emanating from the chancery itself.

The whole of Egypt kept the same administrative and juridical division into large districts as had been in force prior to Persian domination. There are, however, some indications which seem to suggest that these districts did not invariably retain their former extent, but may have been larger and therefore fewer in number. Each district was run by a governor, called *fratarak* in the Aramaic documents. For the district of Tashetres, "the southern district", which ran from Aswan to Hermonthis where the district of Thebes began (we know the southern district particularly well thanks to Aramaic documents from Elephantine and Syene), the fratarak during the years round 410 B.C. was the Persian Waidrang, who with his son, the military commander, took part in destroying the Yahu temple at Elephantine. His predecessor had been Damandin[1] during which time Waidrang commanded the army. The seat of the fratarak in the "southern district" was Syene, "the market", on the Nile bank opposite the island of Elephantine. Many "provincial scribes" were employed to administer the districts together with other officials, called *azdākarya*[2] in the Aramaic papyri. The smaller administrative units, the cities and towns, had their own governors of lower rank dependent on the fratarak. Hieroglyphic inscriptions discovered in the stone caves at Wādī Hammāmāt give the names of two Persians, the brothers Atiyawahy and Ariyawrata, sons of Artames and Qangiu (possibly an Egyptian woman). Atiyawahy was governor of Coptos in the district of Thebes and as well as that title bore the title of *saris* of Persia. His inscriptions date between 486 and 473 B.C. while those of his younger brother, between 461 and 449 B.C. It is interesting to note that in the more recent inscriptions, those of Ariyawrata, the title "saris of Persia" is translated into Egyptian by two terms used alternately: *r Prs* "provost of Persia", and *ḫrj Prs* "leader of Persia", which shows the increasing influence of Egyptian society on the foreign rulers.[3] This increasing influence of conquered over conquerors is confirmed by other details found in the inscriptions of the two brothers just mentioned (as well as by other features, such as the presence of Egyptians in high office). Ariyawrata takes a purely Egyptian surname, *Dd-ḥr*, Tachos, and makes offerings to the Egyptian

---

[1] Cowley, No. 20.
[2] Cowley, No. 17; the word meant "announcer" in Persian.
[3] Cf. Posener, p. 178; Bresciani, *op. cit.*, pp. 139–40.

gods, a fact we know from the lid of a jar of ointment he gave to Horus of Edfu, which bears a cuneiform inscription containing his name.[1]

An Aramaic papyrus now in Turin[2] mentions Mitrawahishta, a high official of the Persian bureaucracy in Egypt, and contains a letter sent to him which uses after his name the formula "living in health and strength", this being the exact translation of the Egyptian ʿnḫ wḏ꜄ snb, used originally for the Egyptian Pharaohs: here the pharaonic title has been democratised and the monuments that have survived of the Persian kings in Egypt show that for them the formulae "may he live for ever", "may he be granted eternal life", or "may he live like Ra, eternally", were preferred.[3]

Greek sources tell us that Egypt paid Persia an annual tribute of 700 talents (Herodotus III. 91). Moreover Egypt had to maintain the non-Persian mercenaries, as well as the Persian troops garrisoned at Memphis; had to pay 120,000 measures of grain and the revenue from the fish caught at Lake Moeris, which amounted to 230 talents a year (Herodotus III. 91, 149). The Egyptians had to supply the Great King's table with salt and Nile water (Athenaeus II. 67b); while the city of Anthilla belonged to the Queen of Persia and provided money for her needles, shoes (Herodotus II. 98) and girdles (Athenaeus I. 33f). The state treasury was at Memphis, under the protection of the god Ptah, and is mentioned in two Theban papyri and one from Gebelein dating from between the 30th and 35th year of Darius.[4] The expression "the weight of Ptah" applied to a sum of shekels in an Aramaic papyrus from Elephantine[5] is, I think, equivalent to the expression "from the house of Ptah's treasure" used in contemporary demotic papyri to guarantee the legality of *deben* and *kedet* (a tenth of the deben's value) which were the most common currency and weight units used in Egypt. In demotic documents of the Persian period metal is referred to on a weight basis; and in Aramaic documents coinage is measured in *kerashin*, *shekelin* and *hallurin*, while higher values are weighed out in accordance with "the king's weight". It is interesting to find in Aramaic papyri the Greek term *sttry* "stater" about the end of the 5th century.[6]

[1] Cf. *ASAE* XLIII (1943), p. 96.
[2] CIS, Part II, vol. I, no. 144 (p. 148).
[3] Cf. Bresciani, p. 140.
[4] Griffith, *Catalogue* III, No. 57, No. 62; W. Spiegelberg, *Die demot. Papyri Loeb* (Munich, 1931), No. 48.
[5] Bresciani, p. 135; Kraeling, p. 38.
[6] Cowley, Nos 35, 37; Kraeling, No. 12.5 (the stater is called explicitly "the coinage of Yowan" i.e. of Greece).

THE PERSIAN OCCUPATION OF EGYPT

Greek currency had begun to circulate in Egypt from the Saïte period, but the Greek coinage was accepted by the Egyptians according to weight. Shekelin, the Median silver shekels, are not among the coins discovered in Egypt; the shekels circulating in Egypt were Phoenician-Jewish. However, what Herodotus says about the silver money coined by Aryandes, which rivalled Darius' gold daric for pure metal content and which he says was still in circulation at the time of his journey (IV. 166), points to at least a limited circulation of money coined in Egypt. The expression "according to the weight of Ptah" used of shekelin, is found only once, and only in the above-mentioned Aramaic document. One imagines that the shekelin whose weight was guaranteed by the state treasury were different from the shekels mentioned in other documents, i.e. they were Median and not Phoenician-Jewish.

Near the end of Darius' reign the "head of the treasury" of Ptah at Memphis was the Egyptian Ptahhotep, whose naophoros statue in the Brooklyn Museum[1] shows him wearing the so-called "Persian dress", with what is clearly an Achaemenian necklace, perhaps a decoration bestowed on him by the Great King. There is also in the Louvre a stela from the Serapeum of Memphis bearing his name and dating from the 34th year of Darius.[2]

Administering "the treasure", both of money and kind, involved a large number of officials. Each district had its own "treasure" with its "treasurers" and "book-keepers". Aramaic documents from Elephantine tell us that besides the "book-keepers" (or "treasury book-keepers") the treasury employed "treasury scribes" connected with "the king's house", which seems to have been the storehouse for government supplies of cereals and other goods paid in as tribute, and from which were drawn the rations given to mercenaries over and above their wages.[3] A group of officials called *pakhuta*, evidently belonged to the treasury staff: in a letter sent to Elephantine[4] from Migdol in the Western Delta they are mentioned as deciding about payment to certain members of the Jewish military colony at Migdol.[5]

---

[1] J. D. Cooney, "The portrait of an Egyptian Collaborator", *Bulletin of the Brooklyn Museum* xv. 2 (New York, 1953), pp. 1–16.

[2] É. Chassinat, "Textes provenant du Sérapéum de Memphis", *Recueil de travaux relatifs à la philologie et à l'archéologie égyptiennes et assyriennes* xxi (Paris, 1899), pp. 67–9.

[3] For the two forms of government payment, in money (peres) and kind (paθfa), cf. E. Bresciani, "Papiri aramaici di epoca persiana presso il Museo Civico di Padova", *RSO* xxxv (1960), pp. 13–14.

[4] Cf. Bresciani, "Papiri aramaici", p. 1 (and the notes) and Pap. 1 vs. 4.

[5] This is probably the Migdol mentioned by Jeremiah as an important Jewish centre, comparable with Daphnae and Memphis. Cf. Bresciani, "Papiri aramaici", p. 15, note 2.

THE PERSIAN OCCUPATION OF EGYPT

The letters published by Driver show that a special feature of satrapal bureaucracy in Egypt was the administration of goods held by the satrap in his own name. Arsames had properties in Upper and Lower Egypt, but this group of letters refers to a property of his in Lower Egypt, managed by a *peqid*. This official (and from the letters we know the activities of two peqids, Psamtek and his successor Nekhtihur) had at his disposal a company of soldiers to protect the satrap's possessions; he was also in charge of those private funds of the satrap made up of revenues from the property in his care, which he administered with his book-keeping colleagues. From these same letters, which date from between 411 and 408 B.C. we know that another Persian, Warfich and his wife, owned private goods in Egypt; also the Persian prince Warohi owned places in the Delta, as did Artawant whom it seems Arsames left as his representative in Egypt while he was away.[1] The mention of Papremis and its wine in one of the letters, indicates that the satrap's property was in the Western Delta.[2]

The Achaemenian government based a strong military contingent in Egypt for border defence and internal security. Herodotus (II. 30) says that the Persians kept up the border garrisons at Elephantine, Daphnae and Marea as they had been during Dynasty XXVI. Our knowledge of how the army was organized and where the military detachments and colonies were placed in the Nile Valley during the Persian occupation, comes basically from Egyptian documents in Aramaic, the most informative being those from Elephantine and Aswan. These shed much light on the life of the Jewish military settlement which was part of the Persian garrison on the southern border of Egypt. The garrison (*haila* in Aramaic) was divided into companies or detachments, *degelin*, each one going by the name of its commanding officer who, according to the names in the Elephantine papyri, was either Persian or Babylonian; and each *degel* was divided into 100 man units, *mata*. The Jewish haila was quartered on the island of Elephantine, where the Yahu temple also stood, but the non-Jewish military, the Phoenicians, Aramaeans and Egyptians, were at Syene where the *rab haila*, the general, had his quarters. It seems that the military units throughout Upper Egypt as far as Memphis were under the command of the rab haila at Syene. An Aramaic papyrus[3] mentions the "two fortifications" of Syene. The city

---

[1] Driver, *Aramaic Documents*, p. 7 (revised version pp. 14ff.).
[2] Driver, Letter XII. 6.
[3] Cowley, No. 26.

had temples consecrated to the Semitic gods worshipped by the foreigners, and the "Hermopolis letters"[1] speak of the temples of Nabu, Banit, Bethel and Melkat-Shemin, at Syene. We do not know whether these temples which, depending on their particular god were places of worship for Babylonians, Aramaeans, Phoenicians and the Jewish devotees of "the Queen of Heaven", already existed in Egypt before Cambyses' conquest, as did the Yahu temple at Elephantine; but it is possible that they went up after the Achaemenian conquest, as a result of the expansion of the Jewish colony on the country's southern border.[2] The Jewish cemetery at Syene stood close to the Temple of Isis at Aswan.[3] There is a stela from Syene, datable to the seventh year of Artaxerxes, 458 B.C., which mentions the rab haila of Syene, but it has a lacuna where the name would be.[4]

Mercenaries were paid monthly by the Persian government in cash and kind, the payment being made by the "treasury" or "the king's house".

Thebes was also fortified and had Jewish military quarters as did Edfue at Abydos. In central Egypt Aramaic texts have been discovered in the tomb of Sheik el-Fadl near Oxyrhynchos,[5] at El-Ḥība,[6] and at Hermopolis, where a jar containing the so-called Hermopolis letters, some of them addressed to Thebes, others to Syene, was found in the galleries of the sacred Ibises. A naos of painted wood was also found near the jar, with the name of Darius in hieroglyphics within the cartouche. Whether this refers to Darius I or II is not known, though

[1] E. Bresciani and M. Kamil, "Le lettere aramaiche di Hermopoli", *Atti Accademia dei Lincei*, series 8, XII (Rome, 1966), pp. 361–428.

[2] Bresciani-Kamil, *op. cit.*, p. 367. On the basic distinction between "Hebrews" and "Aramaeans" (as against Kraeling, p. 7), cf. the fundamental article on this question, E. Volterra, "'yhwdy' e 'ʾrmy' nei papiri aramaici del V secolo provenienti dall'Egitto", *Rendiconti Accademia dei Lincei*, series 8, XVIII (Rome, 1963), pp. 131–73. Volterra penetratingly underlines the deep difference between Hebrews and Aramaeans that already existed in the Bible, and later in rabbinical literature, where "Aramaean" is equivalent to "heretic". More recently, see B. Porten, *Archives from Elephantine* (Los Angeles, 1963), p. 3ff. For the religious syncretism at Elephantine, cf. A. Dupont-Sommer, *RHR* CXXVIII (1944), pp. 28–39.

[3] Cf. W. Kornfeld, "Aramäische Sarkophage in Assuan", *WZKM* LXI (1967), pp. 9–16.

[4] M. de Vogue, "Inscription araméenne trouvée en Egypte", *CRAI* 1903, pp. 267–76; J. Naveh, *The Development of the aramaic Script* (Jerusalem, 1970), p. 42. There are two statues from Aswan, one of granite the other of sandstone, both now in the Cairo Museum, J.E. 31919 and J.E. 35562 respectively, each engraved with a proper name in Aramaic. Cf. S. Ronzevalle, "Notes sur les statues", *ASAE* XVII (1917), pp. 265–71.

[5] N. Aimé-Giron, "Note sur une Tombe découverte près de Cheikh-Fadl", *Ancient Egypt* 1923, pp. 38–43; Naveh, *op. cit.*, pp. 40–1.

[6] E. Bresciani, "Un papiro aramaico da El Hibeh del Museo Archeologico di Firenze", *Aegyptus* XXXIX (1959), pp. 3–8, cf. J. T. Milik, *Aegyptus* XL (1960), pp. 79–81, with observations acceptable only in part.

it is probably the latter: if it is Darius I the form of his name would suggest a time near the end of his reign.[1]

Memphis, the capital city, and its citadel, the "White Wall", were fortified (Herodotus III. 91); the presence of Semitic soldiers and degelin is well documented, and they were also employed in the government dockyards of Memphis (the "house of ships").[2] Included in the Aramaic material of the Persian period, from the Jewish necropolis at Saqqārah, are funeral stelae (one of them bilingual, hieroglyphic-Aramaic, from the fourth year of Xerxes, 482 B.C.),[3] sarcophagi, papyri and other documents.[4] There were Semites at Fayyum,[5] and Semitic units were based in the Delta at Daphnae and Migdol;[6] and at Tell Maskhuta there was a group of Arabs who worshipped the goddess Ilat (Han-Ilat).[7]

The commanding position of the Egyptian military class is acknowledged by the decree of Darius I mentioned above: in fact they were considered competent, along with the scribes and priests, to gather the Egyptian laws that were to be codified. There is evidence for the presence of Egyptian degelin at Syene;[8] and hieroglyphic documents from the Persian period speak of Egyptian "military chiefs" such as the Ahmosi mentioned in two stelae from Memphis[9] in one of which he claims to have won a place for the sacred Apis bull "in the hearts of the whole nation and of the foreigners from all the foreign lands, who were in Egypt". Even the architect Khnumibra, who practised during the reign of Darius I,[10] is styled "army chief" and "head of the regiment".

Among the soldiers of the Persian occupation in Egypt there were Ionians and Carians based particularly at Memphis; there had already

---

[1] The hieroglyphic script of Darius' name is the one that was current at the end of his reign, cf. Posener, p. 163.
[2] Cf. Aimé-Giron, *Textes araméens*, pp. 12ff.
[3] The stela comes from Saqqāra and is now in the British Museum, No. 7707; cf. CIS, Part II, vol. I, no. 122 (p. 123).
[4] Cf. Bresciani, "La satrapia d'Egitto", Appendice archeologica, pp. 177ff. For the Phoenician inscriptions and papyri cf. *ibid.*, pp. 184 and 188.
[5] Cf. E. Bresciani, "Una statuina fittile con iscrizione aramaica dall'Egitto", *Hommages à André Dupont-Sommer* (Paris, 1971), pp. 5–8, and note (1) on p. 6.
[6] Cf. above, p. 515, and p. 515, notes 4 and 5. For the cult of Baal-ṣapun at Daphnae in the Delta, cf. N. Aimé-Giron, "Adversaria Semitica (III)", *ASAE* XL (1940), pp. 433–60 (a 5th-century B.C. papyrus from Saqqāra).
[7] Rabinowitz, "Aramaic Inscriptions".
[8] Cf. p. 512, notes 2 and 3 above.
[9] Posener, Texts 6, 7.
[10] Posener, Texts 11–23.

been Ionian and Carian mercenaries in the hire of the Egyptian kings of the Saïte dynasty.[1] The Persian army – called Persian only because it was in the service of Persia – was a mixture assembled from various provinces of the Achaemenian Empire. There were in Egypt during the Persian occupation Persians, Babylonians, Phoenicians, Cilicians and Greeks, and not only as soldiers but also in other capacities, especially as traders. The early military settlers of the Persian government established themselves securely in Egypt, and stayed on after the Persian domination had ended. One may recall that the word for "a Mede" (in the sense of "a Persian") in Egyptian and Aramaic is found in Coptic as *matoi*, which no longer has a geographic sense, but means simply "soldier", just as in Syria *romaya*, "Romans", meant "soldiers".[2]

As the supreme authority in Egypt, the satrap also administered justice. Darius showed his respect for local law by assembling an Egyptian juridical corpus which he authorized by the decree several times mentioned above. Our knowledge of how the law was administered derives largely from Aramaic documents, especially those of the Jewish colony at Elephantine. It is clear from the latter – as also from the demotic papyrus Rylands IX from El-Ḥība[3] – that final appeal was to the satrap, who had the last say. In the districts the fratarak presided over a civil tribunal which, since it applied whichever law bound the accused, dispensed Egyptian law for the local inhabitants under his jurisdiction. The Aramaic documents also mention the "judges" and the "king's judges" as well as the "provincial judges" – who may have exercised the same functions as the "king's judges". Also mentioned are *tipati* "sheriffs", and *gauśaka* "the ears" – informers (the "ears of the king" quoted by Xenophon, *Cyropaedia* VIII. 2. 10). The judicial powers of the rab haila were restricted to military matters, and the fratarak could join with the rab haila to pass judgement on crimes involving the military.

We have a good idea of private and contract law in the Jewish colony at Elephantine.[4] The demotic documents of the Persian period are

---

[1] Cf. Austin, "Greece and Egypt". "Ionians" and "Carians" are mentioned in the Aramaic papyri found at Saqqāra in the excavations by W. B. Emery (not yet published). Cf. *Exhibition of Recent Discoveries in Egypt and the Sudan by the Egypt Exploration Society at the British Museum*, 16 October–30 November 1968, p. 22.

[2] E. Bresciani, "Annotazioni demotiche ai Πέρσαι τῆς ἐπιγονῆς", *La parola del passato* XXVII (Naples, 1972), pp. 123–28.

[3] Griffith, *Catalogue* III, pp. 60ff.

[4] Bresciani, "La satrapia d'Egitto", 153ff.; Kraeling, pp. 36–7. A fundamental study of this subject is R. Yaron, *Introduction to the Law of the Aramaic Papyri* (Oxford, 1961).

concerned with private law, which, like the set of legal formulae peculiar to it, presents no break of continuity with the Egyptian law of the immediately preceding period.[1] Later, elements of Egyptian law and legal formulary seem to have entered the practice of the Jewish mercenaries at Elephantine (whose contact, however, with the Egyptian population went back to a period preceding the Persian invasion). Certain juridical elements are common to both Egyptian and neo-Babylonian law,[2] as for example the obligation to show documents proving ownership and transfer rights, or the exact description of land and buildings bought and sold.

I have already spoken about the policies adopted by Cambyses and Darius I towards the temples and priests of Egypt. Egyptian temple life seems to have suffered no particular interruptions or changes during the period after Cambyses' constrictive measures were revoked, and there is evidence that both Xerxes and Artaxerxes made votive offerings to the temples. Towards the end of the reign of Darius II there are signs that the Egyptian priesthood was less than resigned to foreign rule, because we find that the priests of Khnum at Elephantine encouraged an opposition to the Jewish military colony, on grounds which we have seen were political. Within their sanctuaries the priests seemed to continue as usual and to receive temple revenues as before. The only noteworthy change was at Thebes, where the office of "divine worshipper", peculiar to women, an office of great political as well as religious importance, disappeared during Dynasty XXVII. The vast possessions which the "divine worshipper" owned and administered were perhaps absorbed into the "dominion" of Ammon.

The "Instructions of Ankh-sheshonqi",[3] an interesting literary work in the demotic language, seems to have been written during the Persian period. The composition of these "Instructions", which take the form of a series of moral precepts arising within an historical framework, is closely reminiscent of the structure of the Assyrian "Wisdom of Ahiqar", the Aramaic text of which must have circulated among Semites in Egypt, seeing that a copy of it on papyrus dating from the 5th century B.C. was found at Elephantine. A demotic text of the Roman

---

[1] Cf. Seidl, *Aegyptische Rechtsgeschichte*; M. Malinine, *Choix de textes juridiques en hiératique "anormal" et en démotique* (Paris, 1953).
[2] Cf. particularly Yaron, *op. cit.*, pp. 114ff.
[3] Glanville, *Instructions of 'Onchsheshonqy*; E. Bresciani, *Letteratura*, pp. 563ff.

period in which the sage Ahiqar is twice mentioned[1] proves that his proverbs were known in the Egyptian world.

In the fields of artistic work, architecture, sculpture and bas reliefs, the Persians made no drastic break with the Egyptian tradition. Darius I built the temple at El-Khārga in pure Egyptian, Saïtic style, the stelae and the tombs being dated in Dynasty XXVII. Egyptian influence on the artistic as well as religious expression of Semites settled in Egypt can be seen in the stelae and sarcophagi of Semitic provenance, although the Egyptian elements in them have been re-interpreted and altered.[2] As for statue sculpture, a number of statues from Dynasty XXVII show an interesting tendency towards a realism of facial expression, compared with many other statues carved in the conventionally idealistic style of the Saïte dynasty. A number of monuments, statues and reliefs of the Persian period are of male figures wearing distinctive dress – a long gown, fastened at the chest, worn over a jacket with short or long sleeves and a V neck. Up till now scholars have thought that this garb dated a sculptured piece automatically to Dynasty XXVII, hence the name "Persian dress" for this kind of garment.[3] But a statue in the Cairo Museum which I published in 1967[4] with this so-called Persian dress and coming from Saïs in the Delta, bears the date of the 39th year of Amasis, whose name was erased from the cartouche as part of the "damnatio memoriae" carried out during the reign of Cambyses and attested on other monuments. This statue forced me to re-examine the problem of the "Persian dress"; and since we are dealing with a fashion that was already common in Egypt during Dynasty XXVI and was localised at Saïs, one may think of Assyrian influence and suppose that the Asiatic fashion took a new lease of life during the Persian conquest.[5] There is no doubt that the statues of Udjahorresne in the Vatican

---

[1] W. Spiegelberg, "Aḥikar in einem demotischen Text der römischen Kaiserzeit", *OLZ* xxxiii (1930), pp. 962ff; cf. Kraeling, pp. 97–9 for the bibliography and critical opinion of the Ahiqar text.

[2] Cf. the scenes on the stelae in Berlin, the Vatican and the Louvre, and the Aswan sarcophagi quoted p. 517, n. 3; cf. also H. Donner, in P. Derchain (ed.), *Religions en Égypte hellénistique et romaine* (Paris, 1969), pp. 35–44.

[3] B. V. Bothmer, *Egyptian Sculpture of the Late Period*, (The Brooklyn Museum, 1960), pp. 77–9, 83–4, especially pp. 75–6.

[4] E. Bresciani, "Una statua della XXVI dinastia con il cosidetto 'abito persiano'", *SCO* xvi (1967), pp. 273–80, especially pp. 279–80.

[5] Bresciani, *op. cit.*, p. 279 and note (4). The fashion seems to have been restricted originally to Saïs, and one recalls that Psammetichus I, the prince of Saïs, had been brought up in Syria, before throwing off the Syrian yoke and starting Dynasty XXVI.

THE PERSIAN OCCUPATION OF EGYPT

Museum, and of Ptahhotep in the Brooklyn Museum, both mentioned above, date from the Persian period, as do the two statues of Psamteksaneit, one in the Cairo Museum and the other in the Ashmolean Museum in Oxford.[1]

Various objects in the Persian style have been found in Egypt, either imported from Persia or made in Egypt by Persian craftsmen. They include seals, vases with cuneiform or bilingual inscriptions, and lions in serpentine or alabaster.[2] That Persian artists worked in Egypt is happily confirmed by one of the letters sent by the satrap Arsames to his peqid in Egypt,[3] in which the satrap asks that the sculptor Hanzani execute the figure of "a horse with his rider, as he has already made for me, and other sculptures", and that the pieces be brought to him soon to Susa. On the other hand Egyptian monuments have been found in Persia. We know that Egyptian architects and workmen took part in the building of Darius I's palace at Persepolis, and the influence of Egyptian architecture on that of Persia is well known.[4]

Returning to Egyptian events after the first period of Persian rule, we have seen (p. 512) that Amyrtaeus was the first native Pharaoh to rule after the Persians lost control; he held the throne for six years, and there was no other ruler in Dynasty XXVIII (405/404–400/399 B.C.). An Aramaic papyrus from Elephantine[5] dating from the 5th year of the sovereign, shows that for the Jewish military colony the change from Persian domination to local rule took place quietly. Amyrtaeus accepted the garrison "en masse" with its Persian officers commanding the degelin, since an Aramaean at the Elephantine garrison claims in the papyrus that he belongs to the degel of Nabukudurri. Amyrtaeus is named in the "Demotic Chronicle",[6] written at the beginning of the Ptolemaic period, which consists of a series of oracles followed by their explanation, referring to Egyptian political events between Dynasties XXVIII and XXX. He is called "the first lord to come after the foreigners, that is, the Medes", and the fact that he was the only Pharaoh

---

[1] Bresciani, *op. cit.* pp. 279–80, with note (5).

[2] J. D. Cooney, "The Lions of Leontopolis", *Bulletin of the Brooklyn Museum* xv. 2 (1953), p. 17–30; A. Roes, "Achaemenid Influence upon Egyptian and Nomad Art", *Artibus Asiae* xv (1952), pp. 21ff. For the bases, cf. Roes, p. 19.

[3] Driver, Letter IX, 2–3.

[4] Posener, p. 190, note (2). For the influence of Egyptian on Persian architecture, cf. G. Perrot and C. Chipiez, *Histoire de l'art dans l'Antiquité* v (Paris, 1890), p. 513; M. Dieulafoy, *L'art antique de la Perse* v (Paris, c. 1884), p. 198, s.v. Égypte.

[5] Cowley, No. 35.

[6] Spiegelberg, *Demotische Chronik*; cf. Kienitz, p. 136ff.

of his dynasty, and that his son did not succeed him, is explained by saying that "it was ordained that the law should not be fulfilled" – which seems to confirm the deposition (taken prisoner at Memphis?, put to death?) mentioned in an Aramaic papyrus from Elephantine.[1] We know that to forestall a Persian offensive and to pose a threat to areas still under the Great King, Amyrtaeus sought and obtained a useful alliance with the king of the Arabs (Thucydides VIII. 85, 99, 108; cf. Diodorus XIII. 46). But the attention of Persia was distracted from the rebel province of Egypt first by the rebellion of Cyrus, brother to Artaxerxes, and then by the events in Asia Minor, where the Greeks revolted against the Persian yoke.

Nepherites (399/398–395/394 B.C.), a native of Mendes in the Delta, deposed Amyrtaeus in a military takeover, and so began Dynasty XXIX. During his reign the constantly changing interplay of Greco-Persian political affairs brought Sparta into friendly relations with Egypt. In 395 the Pharaoh sent supplies to the Spartan fleet anchored at Rhodes, supplies that fell into the hands of the Persians under the command of the Athenian Conon. Nepherites' successor Achoris (394/393–382/381 B.C.) entered the alliance against Persia which brought the Pisidians and Palestinian Arabs together under the Cypriot Evagoras. Athens also took part, sending Chabrias and Cimon with ten ships, in 387; but the alliance was dissolved at the peace treaty of Antalcides.

Under Achoris, whom the "Demotic Chronicle" calls "benefactor of temples", Egypt became important again in the international political scene. The defences of the coastal area, exposed to the danger of Persian invasion, were strengthened, Greek mercenaries were taken into the fighting force, and Egypt became a sea power. A sign that Achoris also established control over the Libyan oases is the fact that Seteshirdis, ruler of the oasis of Siwa, acknowledged his dominion.[2] Achoris' successor, Nepherites II ruled only a few months and the "Demotic Chronicle" dismissed him with the words "he was not; the gods ordained that he be not."

Nepherites II was deposed by Nectanebo I (381/380–364/363 B.C.) who founded Dynasty XXX. He had been a general under the previous king[3] and came to power in a coup d'état, but it seems that he did belong

---

[1] Kraeling, No. 13.   [2] Cf. Kienitz, p. 198, No. 133, note (1).
[3] For the chronology of Dynasty XXX, cf. Kienitz, pp. 173–5; E. Bickermann, "Notes sur la chronologie de la XXXe dynastie" in P. Jouguet (ed.), *Mélanges Maspero* I (Cairo, 1934), pp.

to the family of Nepherites I. If it is clear that Egyptian affairs fluctuated according to the balance of political and military alliances in the Mediterranean basin for the three previous dynasties, this is particularly true of Dynasty XXX. To quote just one example of this dependence, it is well known that the Greek generals Agesilaus and Chabrias played a vital role in Egyptian defence during the rule of Nectanebo I and Tachos. The peace treaty of Antalcides (386 B.C.) had given Persia a free hand to attack Egypt and we know that Athens recalled Chabrias at Persia's request, and that she sent one of her generals, Iphicrates, to Persia for the campaign against Egypt in 373 B.C. (Diodorus xv. 29.4). A formidable army, supported by a powerful fleet under Pharnabazus, got as far as Pelusium, but the Persian invaders were thrust back by Nectanebo's defences, and then, having launched a new attack at the Mendesian mouth of the Nile, were forced to withdraw because of the Nile floods.

Tachos, son of Nectanebo (363/362–362/361 B.C.) planned to reconquer Syria and Palestine by force, taking advantage of the rebellious movements in those regions against Artaxerxes II. Sparta sent Egypt an army of mercenaries led by Agesilaus, and Chabrias came from Athens to take command of the fleet. An undertaking of this size, involving so many mercenaries, would have been too costly for the royal coffers if Tachos, on Chabrias' advice, had not taken economic measures (Pseudo-Aristotle, *Oeconomicus* II. 2. 25a–b), which affected the priestly class and the entire people: he suspended the revenues which maintained both temples and priests, allowing them only a tenth of their income; he imposed a dwelling tax on every citizen, a grain tax of one obolus for every artabe, and a tithe on vessels and handicraft work. At Chabrias' further instance he obliged all citizens to surrender whatever uncoined precious metal they possessed, promising repayment in kind (Pseudo-Aristotle, *ibid.* 256; cf. Polyaenus III. 11. 5). Tachos and his army were victorious in Palestine; but wanting, against Agesilaus' advice, to lead the Asian campaign in person, he was forced to leave Egypt in charge of a general who rebelled against him and pressed his son Nectanebo, who had accompanied the Pharaoh on the Syrian campaign, to rise against Tachos and seize the crown (Diodorus xv. 92;

77–84. For Nectanebo I's military career before he took the throne, cf. G. Roeder, "Zwei hieroglyphische Inschriften aus Hermopolis", *ASAE* LII (1954), p. 389. Nectanebo I was son of a general by the name of Tachos; cf. H. de Meulenaere, "La famille royale des Nectanébo", *ZÄS* XC (1963), p. 90; Tachos was probably the son of Nepherites I, but he was replaced on the throne by Achoris and then by Nepherites II.

THE PERSIAN OCCUPATION OF EGYPT

Plutarch, *Parallel Lives*, Agesilaus–Pompeius, XXXVII. 3). The authors do not give this general's name, but we know from Egyptian sources that he was called T̯ꜣj-Ḥp-im.w, and that he bore the titles 'chief-of-staff", "father to the king" (Nectanebo II), and "brother to the king" (Tachos); and in all probability his wife was "mother to the king" Wḏꜣ-šw.[1] At this betrayal Tachos sought refuge with the King of Persia, while Chabrias chose to return to Athens.

Nectanebo returned immediately to Egypt where a usurper (from Mendes, hence probably a descendant of the ruling house of Dynasty XXIX), had proclaimed himself king. Nectanebo and Agesilaus, who had remained loyal to him, were besieged in a city in the Delta where Agesilaus managed to break the siege and defeat the enemy (Diodorus XV. 93. 2–4). Nectanebo II (361/360–343 B.C.) weathered successfully two attempted invasions by Persia, the first in 358, when the Persian army was led by prince Artaxerxes; the second in 351, when the army had the same leader, now king Artaxerxes III Ochus.

During the rebellions of Cyprus and Syria between 349 and 346 Nectanebo remained neutral, but in 346 he sent 4,000 mercenaries to the King of Sidon at the request of Mentor of Rhodes (Diodorus XVI. 42. 2). By 343, when Artaxerxes III had retaken Cyprus and Sidon and was free to concentrate all his forces against Egypt, he was able to advance as far as Pelusium. Just as in the time of Cambyses, it was through treachery that the Persians got information of the Egyptian defence line: then it had been Phanes who betrayed Egypt, now it was Mentor of Rhodes. In this way the Persian commander Bagoas took first Pelusium and other cities in the Delta, while Nectanebo remained in Memphis. Once he learned that all Lower Egypt was in Persian hands he fled to Nubia with his possessions (Diodorus XVI. 51. 1–2) probably hoping to return with the support of the Nubian king. But he never returned. Legend was later to make him father of Alexander the Great, claiming that through magic powers[2] he had taken on the appearance

---

[1] Meulenaere, *op. cit.*, p. 91 (Sarcophagus of Wnnefer in the Metropolitan Museum, New York, N. 11. 154, 1, for T̯ꜣj-ḥp-im.w; there is also in the same museum a statue from Memphis, discovered by W. M. F. Petrie, *Memphis I* (London, 1909), p. 13, plates XXXI–XXXII; cf. Meulenaere, *op. cit.*, pp. 90–2). Differing from the opinion of Meulenaere, p. 92, I think that Wḏꜣ-šw is the wife of T̯ꜣj-ḥp-im.w and the mother of Nectanebo II (there is a sarcophagus of Wḏꜣ-šw in the Cairo Museum, Gen. Cat. N. 29317). As for the "wife of the king and mother of the king" Khedeb-Neitiretbinet, whose sarcophagus is in the Kunsthistorisches Museum, Vienna, this is, in my opinion, again differing from Meulenaere, pp. 92–3, the wife of Nectanebo I and therefore mother of Tachos and T̯ꜣj-ḥp-im.w. For Tachos' economic policies, cf. E. Will, "Chabrias et les finances de Tachôs", *Revue des Études anciennes* LXII (Bordeaux, 1960), pp. 254–75.

[2] Pseudo-Callisthenes.

of Zeus Ammon and in that form coupled with Olympia, the mother of Alexander. Egyptian national sentiment found satisfaction in this legend, which made the conqueror of Egypt at the same time the legitimate heir to the throne of the Pharaohs and the man who had driven the Persians from the land of his father Nectanebo.

Egypt was now once more under Persian control. It was a short period of rule, known as the "second domination" or Dynasty XXXI,[1] lasting only until 332 B.C. As was the case with Cambyses, the classical sources heap against Artaxerxes III accusations of odious conduct and violence, with details of even more refined cruelties.[2] He kills and eats with his friends the Apis bull, offering in its stead an ass for worship by the Egyptians. As if that were not enough he kills the Mnevis bull and the goat of Mendes; sacks the temples and destroys the city walls. The "Satrap's Stela" (Ptolemy, satrap of Alexander IV)[3] tells us that Artaxerxes Ochus[4] confiscated a property belonging to the goddess of Buto. The Lille demotic papyrus 27[5] on the other hand depicts Egypt during the time of Artaxerxes as enjoying a normal life, with temple possessions remaining untouched.

Little is known of events in the ten-year period of the "second conquest". According to Diodorus (XVI. 51. 3) Artaxerxes left Pherendates as satrap in Egypt. In 338 Artaxerxes was poisoned by the eunuch Bagoas, who put the king's youngest son, Arses, on the throne; two years later Arses too was killed by Bagoas. There is an Egyptian jar-lid, kept at University College London, which bears Arses' name.[6]

Under Darius III the satraps of Egypt were first Sabaces, who fought and died at Issus,[7] and then Mazaces.[8] Between the end of 338, after the death of Artaxerxes III, and 336 B.C. comes the episode of the Pharaoh Khabbash who ruled independently of Persia for that brief period.[9] The classical sources make no mention of this ruler, but several Egyptian monuments bear his name, including a demotic papyrus from

---

[1] Dynasty XXXI is a later addition and not part of Manetho's original redaction.
[2] Plutarch, *De Iside et Osiride* 11 (355C), 31 (363C); Aelian, *Varia Historia* VI. 8, *Natura animalium* X. 28; Dinon, fragm. 30.
[3] Cf. H. Brugsch, "Ein Decret Ptolemaios' des Sohnes Lagi, des Satrapen", *ZÄS* IX (1871), pp. 1–8; K. Sethe, *Urkunden des Ägyptischen Altertums* II (Leipzig, 1904), pp. 16–18. The "Satrap's Stela" is in the Cairo Museum. Cf. Kienitz, pp. 188–9 and 232.
[4] The text says "Xerxes", but cf. p. 527, n. 2.
[5] H. Sottas, *Les Papyrus démotiques de Lille* (Paris, 1921), N. 27, p. 54.
[6] Cf. W. M. F. Petrie, *Scarabs and cylinders* (London, 1917), pp. 33–40 and Plate LVII.
[7] Arrian, *Anabasis* II. 11. 8; Diodorus XVII. 34. 5.
[8] Arrian, *Anabasis* III. 1. 2.
[9] Cf. Kienitz, pp. 188–9, 232.

Tebendel dating from his first year, an Apis sarcophagus from the Serapeum of Memphis, from his second year, and other small undated monuments.[1] The "Satrap's Stela" mentions how in his second year Khabbash was inspecting defences placed in the Delta to resist Persian attacks, when he came across a tract of land called "The land of Buto" which "the evil (Arta)xerxes" had taken from them. When the priests and leaders of Buto were questioned, they hastened to inform Khabbash that the gods take fearful revenge on such acts of impiety: for it was by an act of divine revenge that (Arta)xerxes and his son died in their palace, according to the news as received in Saïs. To avoid the divine anger Khabbash restored the land to the gods of Buto; the stela reports the decree of Alexander IV ratifying Khabbash's decision. Spiegelberg has shown convincingly[2] that the Xerxes of the stela was Artaxerxes III, killed by Bagoas, and that the Arses killed in the same year, 336 B.C., was his son. Thus, if news of the death of Arses was received in the second year of Khabbash, his rule must have begun in 338 B.C. Khabbash's capital city was probably Memphis and the title that he bore, "the chosen one of Ptah-Tenen" links him with the Memphite deity. The most diverse hypotheses have been advanced for his origin, all of them drawn basically from what seems to be a non-Egyptian name. There are those who have thought him a rebel satrap, an Arab, a Libyan prince, or of Ethiopian origin, finding in the last case an affinity between his name and that of Ethiopian sovereigns.[3] After 336 B.C. all trace of Khabbash disappears. Clearly, when Darius III took the throne, Egypt fell under Persian control and found herself once more under the rule of a Persian satrap.

After Alexander the Great had defeated Darius at Issus in 333 B.C., Persia lost the western part of the Achaemenian Empire. Sabaces, satrap of Egypt at the time, also died at Issus and in that battle there fought on the Persian side the Egyptian noble Somtutefnekhet from Heracleopolis. In the Naples Museum there is a hieroglyphic and autobiographical stela, the "Naples Stela", which tells how he fought beside the Persian king against the Greeks, and how, after the defeat, escaping to foreign lands and then crossing the sea he managed to re-enter Egypt under divine protection.[4]

---

[1] For the list and bibliography of the monuments, cf. Kienitz, p. 232, nn. 1–7.
[2] W. Spiegelberg, *Der Papyrus Libbey* (Strassbourg, 1907), pp. 5–6.
[3] Cf. Kienitz, p. 188, with a bibliography that covers the various hypotheses.
[4] The most recent editor of the "Naples Stela" is P. Tresson, "La Stèle de Naples", *Bulletin de l'Institut Français d'Archéologie Orientale* xxx (Cairo, 1931), pp. 369–91.

THE PERSIAN OCCUPATION OF EGYPT

The episode of the Macedonian Amyntas occurred after the battle of Issus. Having entered the service of the Persians and become a general in Darius' army (Arrian, *Anabasis* II. 6. 5; Plutarch, *Lives*, "Alexander", 20), he fled after Issus first to Tripolis, next to Cyprus, and then to Pelusium. In Egypt he claimed to have been sent by Darius III to replace Sabaces. Amyntas got as far as Memphis, but the genuine new satrap, Mazaces, confronted the Macedonian and his bands, and massacred them (Arrian, *Anabasis* XIII. 2–3; Quintus Curtius Rufus IV. 1. 27–33).

When Alexander appears in Egypt, in 332 B.C., the satrap Mazaces hands over the country without a struggle. The Achaemenian empire is at an end, and Egypt becomes a province of Alexander's empire. The Ptolemies assume the hereditary kingship of Egypt, and in their turn will have to hand over the country to the Romans. Henceforth Egypt will be ruled exclusively by foreigners.

CHAPTER 10

THE BABYLONIAN EVIDENCE OF ACHAEMENIAN RULE IN MESOPOTAMIA*

To present the Babylonian evidence – cuneiform texts[1] and archaeological remains – for the Achaemenian rule over the satrapy *Babairuš* is to write a history of Mesopotamia from 539 B.C. to 331 B.C. This task has not yet been seriously undertaken and seems, at the moment, to be well nigh impossible. There is simply not enough documentation available to erect more than a chronological framework based on dynastic facts, i.e., on the names, genealogies and dates (of accession and death) of the ten kings and, at least, five usurpers who were recognized in cuneiform sources as the legitimate rulers of the country. To write a history of Mesopotamia during these two hundred years would moreover necessitate the complete and critical utilization of contemporary and later classical sources (mainly Herodotus, Ctesias, Xenophon and Strabo) which for a number of reasons are quite abundant, and also those of the Old Testament which are so insufficient and contradictory that their investigation has produced but a bewildering array of hypotheses and interpretations.[2] Much critical

---

* The author wishes to thank his colleagues Edith Porada, Erica Reiner and M. N. van Loon for advice and suggestions. Miss Reiner and Dr van Loon were also kind enough to read the manuscript.

[1] A Mesopotamian source, though not written in cuneiform script, is represented by what is left of the *Babyloniaka* of Berossos. Born under Artaxerxes III (about 350 to 340 B.C.), this Babylonian scholar dedicated his work to Antiochus I. What is extant in quotations and other references has been collected in Schnabel, *Berossos*, also in F. Jacoby, *Die Fragmente der griechischen Historiker* III C 1 (Leiden, 1958), pp. 367–95. Of the historical section supposed to have reached "from Alaros to Alexander" only §52 to §55 of Schnabel's edition refer to the period investigated in this chapter. Not much information has been preserved in these sections. We learn of the defeat of Nabonidus by Cyrus, son of Cambyses, §52; that Cyrus gave Carmania in S.E. Iran to Nabonidus after the fall of Babylon but Darius reduced that province in size, §53; and that Nabonidus capitulated to Cyrus in Borsippa as is known from a quotation from the *Babyloniaka* in Josephus *Contra Apionem* cited in §54. In §56 we read that Artaxerxes II erected a statue of the Iranian goddess Anahita in Babylon. The length of the reigns of Cyrus, Cambyses and Darius (I) are given respectively as nine, eight and thirty-six years.

[2] For the Old Testament material, I have utilized Galling's new edition of earlier articles in *Studien zur Geschichte Israels im persischen Zeitalter*.

acumen and a very diversified philological competence would be needed to sort out the relevant facts from the complex literary traditions and historiographic conventions that dominate the development and the final form of both these sources of information. The same holds true with regard to the political, ideological and religious attitudes that determine the selection of topics, the distribution of emphasis and – above all – the reliability of the Old Persian texts available.

While the scarcity of cuneiform texts bearing directly or indirectly on the political and military events of this period is a known fact, the social and economic developments in Mesopotamia seem, at first sight, better documented inasmuch as there is available a rather large and steadily growing corpus of legal and administrative documents datable to the reigns of nearly every Persian king. Though several museums have already given us some of their documents, they have many more such texts stored unpublished. Therefore a systematic utilization of this material, for which statistic evidence – as to typology, provenience and dates – is as crucial as individual contents, is severely limited.

In view of these difficulties, I have restricted myself in the present chapter to two main purposes: first, a detailed analysis of all available cuneiform texts which bear on the history of the Achaemenian kings in Babylonia (Section 1), pp. 532ff.); and second, a survey, necessarily far more sketchy, of the main features of the economic and social developments which can be discerned during this period (Section 2, pp. 568ff.). The specific problems which hamper investigation in both directions will be presented and discussed in the introductory paragraphs of both Section 1 and Section 2. In Section 3 (pp. 582ff.), the sparse archaeological evidence for the period under discussion will be presented. A short "Conclusion" follows.

There can be little doubt about the importance of Babylonia and Babylonian civilization within the Achaemenian empire.[1] It should be the task of the historian of that period to gauge the extent and intensity of the impact of the older civilization on the new empire in the Ancient Near East, rooted as it was in Iranian soil. The incorporation of Media provided Cyrus with the manpower required for his military aspirations, also in some measure with the administrative technique and machinery for holding an empire together, and not least with the artistic traditions

---

[1] Babylonia continues as an important and rich satrapy beyond the Seleucid period into the reigns of the Parthian, Arsacid and Sasanian rulers. Cf. Klíma, *Manis Zeit*, p. 31.

BABYLONIAN EVIDENCE

needed for the adequate display of the power of the "king of kings".[1] The subsequent conquest of Lydia initiated – apart from the prestige and the immense booty it gave Cyrus – the eventually fateful contact with the West. What Babylonia, after it fell so readily to the conqueror, was able to contribute to the first supernational empire[2] remains difficult to pinpoint except in a few specific and perhaps only superficial respects. One telling revelation of the importance of the satrapy Babylonia[3] is the use of the Akkadian language on a par with the Elamite and the Old Persian (the latter probably intelligible also to the Median subjects). The official dating formulae (see pp. 535ff.) of cuneiform texts recognize the singular role of Babylonia within the empire and mention, from the date of the conquest on, the new overlord's title "king of Babylon(ia)" before that of "king of all countries" (see pp. 536, 558f. and 566f. for details). Note also that immediately after the fall of Babylon, Cyrus' son Cambyses was made co-regent and king of that city.[4] As a satrapy, Babylonia is mentioned in the earlier lists of satrapies after the core provinces (after Persia and Elam in Behistun §6, after Elam and Media in the Persepolis inscription of Darius).[5] Moreover, as royal seat, the castles of Babylon vied in importance with Susa, Persepolis (which became capital only late in the rule of Darius I) and Ecbatana.[6] In fact, Babylon's position seems to have improved under the later Achaemenian

---

[1] For the ideological background of the new empire, I refer here only to the books of four authors, although a much wider literature can and should be listed: Herzfeld, *Zoroaster*; Widengren, *Iranische Geisteswelt*; Frye, *Heritage*; and Duchesne-Guillemin, *La religion de l'Iran*. Note also Bickerman, "The Seleucids and the Achaemenids".

[2] For some of the problems here alluded to see Junge, "Satrapie und *natio*".

[3] For the Akkadian cf. Rössler, *Untersuchungen*, who investigates only the morphology of the language of the Akkadian versions of the trilingual inscriptions of the Achaemenian kings and neglects the vocabulary. The latter would have yielded more interesting results concerning the educational background of the scribes who composed the text. For the Elamite of the Behistun inscription, I refer to Paper, *Phonology and Morphology*; for that of the administrative tablets found in Persepolis, to Cameron, *Persepolis Treasury Tablets*, pp. 17ff.

[4] Only Cilicia seems to have had a special position among the western satrapies of the empire inasmuch as its ruler was allowed to bear the native title *syennesis*. See Olmstead, *History*, pp. 39, 154, 295ff., 373.

[5] Kent, *Old Persian*, pp. 136ff. In the list of satrapies given by Herodotus (for an extensive discussion see Leuze, *Satrapieneinteilung*, pp. 43ff.) Babylonia appears in the eighth place in an arrangement that is clearly geographic and might well have been meant for internal Greek consumption (as Altheim, "Das Alte Iran", p. 175 suggests) rather than as a description of the fiscal system of the Persian empire. For a discussion of the Behistun list and that of Persepolis, see likewise Leuze, *Satrapieneinteilung*, pp. 87ff. and pp. 91ff. respectively. Schmidt, *Persepolis III* studies in detail the changes in the later lists of nations under Darius which placed Babylonia in less prominent positions.

[6] Only in Babylon and in Ecbatana was there a royal archive, a "house of books"; Ezra 5. 6ff.

BABYLONIAN EVIDENCE

rulers (Darius II died there) in spite of the reverses under Xerxes (see pp. 565ff.) and the revival of Nippur (see pp. 578ff.). This is illustrated by the city's fame in the Greek world; Alexander the Great's campaign aimed directly at Babylon and there he established residence. The cause of its lasting importance as a capital was most likely the economic pre-eminence of the satrapy Babylonia, reflected in the size of the tribute allegedly imposed on it by the Persian overlords: 1,000 talents of silver,[1] as against 700 on Egypt, 500 on Lydia, and 350 on the satrapy Eber-nāri. The capital itself remained the winter residence of the Achaemenian kings (for seven months, as against three in Susa and two summer months in Ecbatana).[2] As such it contained, according to custom, part of the immense treasure of gold and silver which the Persian rulers hoarded in their palaces.[3]

I. CUNEIFORM TEXTS

Generally speaking, the cuneiform evidence of Achaemenian rule not only confirms the sequence of Persian rulers as known from Old Persian inscriptions and from Greek writers, but adds important chronological refinements not provided by other sources. Its contexts are usually strictly factual or historiographic.

Among the historiographic texts in cuneiform literature, kinglists take up a special position. These compositions enumerate kings and record the lengths of their rules. At times they add their filiation and other significant information. They are varied in style and structure, and

---

[1] Apart from the tribute payable in silver, Herodotus tells us that 500 boys had to be delivered to the Persian authorities for castration. This is quite atypical both for the general tenor of the tribute list and for the situation of Babylonia proper where human castration was practised neither for specific purposes nor as a punishment. I would suggest that here Herodotus attributes to the time of Darius I a situation which developed only later, in his own time. The importance of the harem of the later Achaemenian kings for court and world politics is well known – Ctesias is our main source in this respect – and one may safely assume that eunuchs were in great demand not only in the royal entourage but also in that of princes, high Persian officials, etc. Boys may have been castrated and sent to court from Babylonia, but hardly as early as Herodotus wants us to believe, and not by way of regular tribute. Herodotus has two more references to fiscal obligations imposed on Babylonia: first, that the satrap Tritantaechmes (see p. 565) was to receive an *artabe*-measure of silver every day from that satrapy and, second, that the dogs of the royal (Persian) hunt had to be maintained by four villages in Babylonia. Both may in some way reflect actual situations: for the flow of silver from Babylonia to the capital see pp. 577f.; for the interest of the Persian rulers in hunting see p. 580, n. 1.

[2] See Xenophon *Cyropaedia* VIII. 6, 22; *Anab*. III. 5. 15.

[3] Note the size of the booty seized in Babylon by Alexander, as calculated by Altheim and Stiehl, *Aramäische Sprache* I, pp. 120ff.

quite often serve not only historiographical but also political purposes. So far only one such document has come to light in which Achaemenian rulers figure, a small fragment of a tablet found at Warka.[1] It forms the central part of a small one-column tablet which seems to have contained originally the names of Babylonian kings (preceded by the number of years of their rule) from about 700 B.C. to the time of the late Seleucid rulers. What is preserved of the text covers the period from the middle of the 7th century to the end of the rule of Seleucus II Callinicus (226 B.C.). For the Achaemenian period we have only the names of the first three rulers (Cyrus, Cambyses and Darius), badly damaged at that; the indications of the lengths of their rules are missing. After a break – the lower part of the tablet is destroyed – there appears a line which poses a problem to be discussed presently. It is followed by the names of Darius and Alexander. It is clear that the third Darius is meant; he ruled from 335 B.C. to 331 B.C., the same length of time as the remark ⌈MU⌉ 5 (i.e. "five years") before his name indicates. The difficult line preceding the one that contains the name Darius runs [...šá M]U šá-nu-ú ᵐNi-din-ᵈE[N], and should be restored as follows: "[royal name] [whose] second name (is): Nidin-ᵈBēl". The predecessor of Darius III was Arses who ruled for two years (338/7–336/5 B.C.), but he is very unlikely to have assumed a Babylonian name.[2] It is therefore quite possible that in this line we have evidence for another Babylonian usurper of Achaemenian rule whose short reign preceded that of Darius III.[3] As yet we know of no cuneiform texts with dates mentioning either Artaxerxes III, Arses or Darius III, i.e., of the period between 358 B.C. and 331 B.C.; thus the above suggestion concerning yet another usurper in Babylonia who assumed the name Nidintu-Bēl in or before 336 B.C. rests on precious, even if sadly mutilated information provided exclusively by the quoted line.

Next in importance to the kinglists, and closely linked to them in origin, purpose and historical value, stands the chronographic tradition

[1] Published by J. van Dijk, "Die Tontafeln aus dem rēš-Heiligtum", in H. J. Lenzen, *UVB* XVIII (1962), pp. 53–61 and Pl. 28a (W 20030, 105).

[2] Let alone a name resembling, though still not identical with (because of the scribe's omission of one sign), the name of the first Babylonian rebel king Nidintu-Bēl, who defied Darius I in the crucial year 522 B.C. My proposed emendation Ni-din-⟨tu/ti⟩-ᵈBēl can be supported by the observation that the name Nidin-Bēl is extremely rare (known to me only: *VAS* III, 102.14, and *AJSL* XVI, pp. 65ff. No. 19.9, and once each: Nidin-Ištar in *BIN* II, 76.19, and Nidi-Marduk *BRM* I. 76:6) while many hundreds of persons of the Neo-Babylonian period are called Nidintu-Bēl, -Anu, -Marduk, etc., very often abbreviated to Nidintu.

[3] For the circumstances of the death of Arses and the beginning of the reign of Darius III, cf. Olmstead, *History*, pp. 489ff.

of Mesopotamia, represented by the cuneiform chronicles. In spite of their diversity of contents and literary patterns, these chronicles are somewhat restricted in subject matter. They provide mainly, in annalistic arrangement, bare facts about the accessions and the deaths of kings and military data, occasionally also reports of events pertaining to the cults of the main sanctuaries. Best covered, and in a way which best meets the expectations of the present-day historian, is the period from the eighth century B.C. to the third. This does not mean that we have either a complete or even an adequate coverage for the whole of that period. Large gaps still remain, but there is always hope that additional fragments will be discovered, as has repeatedly happened in recent decades. In the Achaemenian period the gaps outnumber by far the lines of text extant at present. Our main source of information is the tablet usually called the "Nabonidus Chronicle".[1] Of this text we have little more than 75 of the original 300 to 400 lines, beginning with the first years of Nabonidus and ending with Cambyses. Actually only a few lines are pertinent to the present topic: the passages col. ii 15–18 and iii 12–22 are concerned with the conquest of Babylon, while col. iii 22–28 records an incident involving Cambyses (see pp. 554ff.). The early history of Cyrus is mentioned in lines 1–4 of col. ii (see pp. 538f.). Another chronicle is preserved on a small tablet containing an excerpt with events of the seventh month of the 14th year (345 B.C.) of Artaxerxes III (see p. 560).

Another historiographic source seems to have been restricted to the late, i.e., the Chaldean, Achaemenian and Seleucid periods, and is represented by what A. Sachs has called the "Diary Texts".[2] These are of great importance for the history of astronomy, as they contain day-by-day records of planetary phenomena, lunar data, the rising of Sirius, solstices, equinoxes, etc., to which were added quite regularly records of a wide range of daily occurrences. We find there listed meteorological events, reports on fires ravaging the city, on the death of important persons, and on epidemics; also fluctuations of the prices of staples (barley, dates, sesame as well as essential condiments), and the heights of river levels. The time range of these "diaries", all of

---

[1] Known since 1882, the last edition in autograph is that of Smith, *Babylonian Historical Texts*, pp. 98ff. and Pls. XI–XIV. I acknowledge with thanks that I was able to utilize the collations of this tablet made by A. K. Grayson for his forthcoming edition of all chronicles entitled "Assyrian and Babylonian Chronicles" in *TCS* vi.

[2] "A Classification of the Babylonian Astronomical Tablets of the Seleucid Period," *JCS* II (1948), pp. 271–90.

which come from Babylon, extends from the years of Šamaššumukīn (667–648 B.C.), brother of Assurbanipal, to 91 B.C., so that the period of Achaemenian rule in Mesopotamia is included. However, one will have to wait for the publication of the tablets by A. Sachs before they can be utilized for whatever information they contain on the political, social and economic history of our period. In the present chapter I have been able to make use only of such passages as were accessible to me in texts already published. See below p. 560–1.

There is one more source of direct historical information at our disposal: the Mesopotamian custom of dating nearly all legal and business documents, often also administrative transactions and ledgers, at times even letters and especially letter-orders. This is a great boon to the historians of Mesopotamia, especially on account of the abundance of such material. In the texts originating before the middle of the second millennium B.C. the value of this source lies primarily in what Assyriologists call the "date formula", i.e., the official name given to the year. In later texts, after it became the practice to date according to the years of a named king's reign, the importance of this information is somewhat lessened. However, the indications concerning day, month and year in which the tablet was written remain essential for determining finer chronological points such as the exact date of the death of a ruler or of the accession of his successor to the throne, which in turn can establish the length of possible interregna, etc.[1] For identifying these dates the student of the Achaemenian period has at his disposal the excellent book of Parker and Dubberstein. It is true that, since its appearance, new material has accumulated, and more is bound to come forth from the stores of museums and from the soil of Mesopotamia. Still, the evidence assembled by Parker and Dubberstein as to dates attested, intercalary months, length of reigns of kings, etc., is abundant enough to justify the prediction that only refinements of the results obtained can reasonably be expected from further dated texts of the Achaemenian period. Regarding only one point can additional information be forthcoming from this source. The name of the king is always followed by his titulary, which, in the Achaemenian period, changes at times; from "Cyrus, king of Babylon and of (all) countries" to "Darius (II) (or Artaxerxes II), king of (all) countries" the inclusion or omission of the name of Babylon has been considered to reflect the changing

---

[1] Such unusual formulations of dates as attested in three extant texts for Darius II (see Parker and Dubberstein, *Babylonian Chronology*, p. 18) cannot be explained.

BABYLONIAN EVIDENCE

relationship between the satrapy and the empire. So have the references to the Persian overlord as "king of Pārsa and Māda" in certain dates of Xerxes and Artaxerxes I. Details of such changes will be given below (pp. 557f. and 565f.) in the discussions of the cuneiform material concerning individual Achaemenian kings. New texts may come to reveal further changes in the titulary.

Apart from such direct historical evidence, the student of Mesopotamian history can also rely on the inscriptions often written or stamped on bricks destined for temples, palaces, city walls, etc. In contrast to the preceding period, such evidence is very scarce for the Achaemenian. Only three brick inscriptions are known, two from Uruk and one from Ur, and all carry the name of Cyrus (for details see pp. 553f.). This is quite in harmony with the archaeological evidence of the Achaemenian rule in Mesopotamia, to be discussed later (pp. 582ff.); there remain few traces of their building activities, but enough to suggest that the kings did not consider it necessary to inscribe on all bricks their names, titulary, the nature and destination of the buildings etc., as had been the Mesopotamian custom ever since Ur-Nammu.[1]

A similar situation obtains in the texts referred to as "royal inscriptions", "building inscriptions", "foundation documents" and the like. As these designations indicate, the inscribed objects were deposited in buildings erected by the king, dedicating the buildings to particular gods.[2] In such texts, the praise of the deity addressed, the presentation of the king with all his titles, the information concerning the circumstances of the construction, its purpose, etc., are given in sequences of which the distribution in space and the emphasis varies considerably from period to period, from region to region, quite often also from king to king. The very nature of these documents provides for the reporting of only certain kinds of historical events, and that in a style which is obviously meant to serve politico-religious purposes rather than to inform posterity.[3] Only two such texts from our period are extant, one called the Cylinder of Cyrus,[4] (see below, pp. 545ff.), and another cylinder which most likely was also written for this king[5] (see

---

[1] Note, however, that in Susa bricks had a stamped inscription in Old Persian mentioning Darius I. Cf. Kent, *Old Persian*, p. 110 *sub* DSk and DSl.
[2] For the carriers of such inscriptions cf. Ellis, *Foundation Deposits*, especially pp. 108ff.
[3] For the literary aspect of this genre of cuneiform texts, cf. Oppenheim, *Ancient Mesopotamia*, index *s.v.* Royal inscriptions.
[4] Rawlinson, *Cuneiform Inscriptions* v, no. XXXV; English Translation in Pritchard, p. 315.
[5] *UET* I, p. 307.

p. 552). Just as for any other document of this literary genre, their contents have to be carefully analysed with regard to style and motivation before they can be utilized to reconstruct the historical situation out of which they grew.

In Mesopotamia as elsewhere historical events have left their imprints on literary creations and, conversely, literary creations have been used for political purposes, specifically to influence "history" or, rather, to convey to the reader or listener the "true" meaning of certain events. There are many such texts in Mesopotamian literature and their investigation has hardly begun.[1] A special position among them is held by a poetic composition which bears directly on the fateful downfall of Nabonidus and the appearance of Cyrus on the Mesopotamian scene.[2] Although it is written very much in the same vein and with the same intentions as the Cylinder of Cyrus, it does contain some additional material which shows that the propaganda for Cyrus and his rule in Babylonia was well co-ordinated, with respect to both the praise of the new ruler and the attacks against Nabonidus.

I now turn to the evidence concerning individual rulers and specific problems. Here, selection of topic and form of presentation has to depend on the amount of documentation available at present. Of the Achaemenian kings, I discuss separately only Cyrus (Section A) and Cambyses (Section B) and assemble under the heading "Later Kings" (Section C) what bits of textual or archaeological material I was able to collect on some of these rulers. Of specific historical problems, I have singled out three, not so much for their immediate relevance but because they present topics of interest even though little evidence is at hand: usurper kings, satraps, and the conflict between Xerxes and Babylon (Section D).

(A) Cyrus

I shall make the Nabonidus Chronicle the basis of my presentation of the fall of Babylon to Cyrus. Two further sources, the Cylinder of Cyrus and the poetic text which contrasts so eloquently the reigns of Cyrus

[1] For an outstanding example of such a study cf. H. G. Güterbock, "Die historische Tradition und ihre literarische Gestaltung bei Babyloniern und Hethitern bis 1200", ZA XLII (1934), pp. 1–91 and XLIV (1938), pp. 45–149. For the important Assyrian epical text we have, so far, only Ebeling, *Bruchstücke*.

[2] Smith, *Babylonian Historical Texts*, pp. 83ff. and Pls. v–x; revised and improved translation by B. Landsberger and T. Bauer in "Strophengedicht von den Freveltaten Nabonids und der Befreiung durch Kyrus", ZA XXXVII (1926–7), 88–98; English translation in Pritchard, pp. 312ff.

BABYLONIAN EVIDENCE

and Nabonidus, will be discussed subsequently and utilized mainly to round off the picture obtained from the Chronicle, as well as to incorporate whatever further evidence can be extracted from the patently poetic elaborations and wilful exaggerations of both these texts.

One important reservation must be stated. No attempt has been made to fill the obvious gaps in our information about Achaemenian kings with snippets of information culled from Herodotus, Xenophon or other Greek sources, nor am I trying to weigh separately the evidence of the cuneiform texts, of the Greek writers, and of any other later material to determine their veracity or even their probability. I have refrained from creating a patchwork of accidentally preserved bits of information to reconstruct the "history" of the Achaemenians in Mesopotamia. My presentation is representative solely of the cuneiform records available at the time of writing and is therefore incomplete.

Although the Persian domination of Babylonia[1] clearly begins with the fall of the capital, Babylon, to Cyrus (539 B.C.) and ends with the equally spectacular entrance of the victorious Alexander into the city (330 B.C.), the cuneiform sources happen to contain some information on Cyrus before his appearance on the Mesopotamian scene.[2] The Nabonidus Chronicle reports in col. ii, lines 1 to 4 (sixth year of Nabonidus) as follows:

He (Astyages, king of the Medes) set (his) army in motion and marched out in order to defeat Cyrus, king of Anšan [...]; Astyages' army turned against him and he was ha[nded over] to Cyrus in fetters. Cyrus ⟨marched⟩ to the royal city Ecbatana [and took as booty] gold, silver, precious objects.

[1] For Assyria from the fall of Nineveh to the Medes under Astyages, see Wiseman, *Chronicles*, especially pp. 15f., also Gates, *Studies*, pp. 58ff. Medes as well as Persians (Lydians and Greeks) are mentioned already in texts datable to Nebuchadnezzar II (604–562 B.C.); cf. Weidner, "Jojachin, König von Juda", pp. 923–35, and note the unique reference to a Median campaign in the letter *TCL* IX. 99 (= Ebeling, *Neubabylonische Briefe aus Uruk* and see F. Thureau-Dangin, "La fin de l'empire Assyrien", *RA* XXII (1925), pp. 27–9) written by Nebuchadnezzar as crown prince. For the Persian empire, as the Behistun inscription tells us (§6), *Aθurā* is mentioned after *Babairuš* as a satrapy but its territorial extent remains uncertain; in the Behistun inscription Aθurā is rendered by KUR *Aš-šur* while the Akkadian version of the palace inscription from Susa translates it by *Eber-nāri*. The subsequent history of the region of Assyria on the left bank of the Tigris is still quite obscure. Much of this is due to the confusion between Assyria and Babylonia introduced by Herodotus in the Greek historical and geographical literature. See also Leuze, *Satrapieneinteilung*, pp. 117ff., 129ff., 174ff.

[2] For the cuneiform evidence bearing on the early history of the Persians, cf. R. M. Boehmer, "Zur Lage von Parsua"; idem, "Volkstum und Städte der Mannäer"; Young, "Iranian Migration". Direct information on ᵐ*Ku-ra-aš* LUGAL KUR *Par-su-*(var. adds *u*)-*ma-aš* comes from the late Assurbanipal cylinder found in the Ištar temple at Nineveh (R. Campbell Thompson and M. E. L. Mallowan, *Annals of Archaeology and Anthropology* XX (Liverpool, 1933), pp. 80ff. and pls xcff.), line 115, and on a cylinder of the same king, found in Babylon, and dealing with the same subject matter. Cf. Weidner, "Die älteste Nachricht", especially p. 3, line 7.

CUNEIFORM TEXTS

[Whatever] he had taken as booty from Ecbatana he(?) brought to Anšan. The spoils of the soldiers [...].

The nature and the implications of Cyrus' victory over the Medes (also referred to in 1. 13 of his Cylinder) will be discussed presently, see pp. 545 ff.

Cyrus reappears in the Chronicle (col. ii. 15–18; ninth year of Nabonidus) after a few lines, in a report on his victorious campaign against Lydia(?). He is given there a new title – probably due to his victory over the Medes – and called "king of Persia"; we are told that he crossed the Tigris downstream from Arbela on his march to Ly[dia], defeated (or killed) its king (Croesus), and left his official and a garrison there (first half of 546 B.C.).[1] None of the later conquests of Cyrus (reported in the *Cyropaedia* and in Josephus) are mentioned in the Chronicle.[2]

Here is a translation of lines 12–22 of column iii of the Chronicle:

In the month Tašrītu when Cyrus made an attack against the Babylonian army in Opis on the Tigris the Babylonians retreated. He (Cyrus) obtained booty and killed many. On the 14th day, Sippar was taken without battle. Nabonidus escaped. On the 16th day, Ugbaru, the governor of the province of Gutium, and the army of Cyrus entered Babylon without battle. Afterwards, Nabonidus was seized in Babylon when he (attempted to) withdraw. Until the end of the month the army of Gutium surrounded the gateways of Esagila, no interruption of any (rite) was made in Esagila and the other sanctuaries and not even a delay (in the ritual performances) occurred. On the third day of the month of Araḫsamnu, Cyrus entered Babylon. They filled (the streets?) with (palm) branches in front of him. (The king's) peace was placed upon the city. The proclamation (*šulmu*) of Cyrus was read to all of Babylon. Gubaru, his governor, appointed (minor) governors (there) in Babylon. From the month Kislimu to the month Addaru, the images of Babylonia which Nabonidus had brought down to Babylon returned to their cities (see p. 551, n. 1). On the night of the 11th day of the month Araḫsamnu, Ugbaru died.

As can be seen, the military events are recorded by the annalist with restraint, in fact, with a certain vagueness. In the month Tašrītu, i.e. in October 539, hostilities began with an attack by Cyrus against the Babylonian army stationed at Opis on the Tigris. Since the homeward

---

[1] R. Borger *apud* Galling, *Studien zur Geschichte Israels*, p. 21, n. 4, suggests that in this line the designation of an official had been left out before *šar-ri*. The reading of the geographical name is quite uncertain according to the collations reported in Galling, *op. cit.*, p. 22, though Lydia seems to be meant; (Grayson has ⌈Lu⌉-⌈ud⌉-[du]). Cf. however König, "Naboned und Kuraš", especially p. 180 n. 11.

[2] For the problems here involved cf. Galling, *op. cit.*, pp. 25 ff.

march of the Ten Thousand[1] began with the crossing of the Tigris at Opis – from where they moved into what was then called Media – one must assume that this was the usual and the best place to cross the river. And the usurper Nebuchadnezzar (III) was defeated in the same region by Darius I (see p. 561f.). Obviously the move of Cyrus was not unexpected, and the necessary military precautions were taken by either Nabonidus or one of his generals. However, the text does not make it clear whether Nabonidus was with the army or awaited the outcome of the battle in Sippar.[2] The latter appears more likely because the Chronicle reports that, after Sippar was taken without battle, Nabonidus escaped, using the word *ḫalāqu* which normally refers to the flight of a slave or a prisoner. Still, in spite of the obvious disorganization of the country, the stationing of the army at the invasion road and on the bank of the river, which had patently become, at that time, the border line of the heartland of Babylonia, suggests some sort of military planning. However, after the army stationed near Opis[3] was defeated and its camp plundered (as is suggested by the wording of the Chronicle), all military activities ceased. Nabonidus apparently went to Babylon, but the Chronicle says nothing further about the Babylonian army.

Although the military collapse cannot be overlooked, there is no reasonable hope of tracing its complex causes. There is only one point I should like to make, mainly because it might have some bearing on the later developments in Mesopotamia under Achaemenian rule. The traditional modern interpretation of the troubles that increasingly beset the rule of Nabonidus is based on the writings of his enemies, which clearly served propaganda purposes. They couched their opposition to him in terms of an ideological conflict between the priesthood of Bēl and the worship of Sin, promulgated and energetically fostered by Nabonidus. The king appeared to many of his contemporaries as a mad dreamer[4] and reformer, dangerous to the stability of the country, and

[1] Cf. Xenophon, *Anabasis* II. iv. 25.

[2] Nabonidus' preference for this city was due, according to Galling, *op. cit.*, pp. 6ff., to his home having been in the neighbourhood; his mother died (see Chronicle i. 13) in Dūr-karāši nearby. However, the Chronicle passage found it necessary to describe exactly where this town was situated ("upstream from Sippar on the Tigris") which seems to show that it was not the normal domicile of the king's mother. She might well have stayed there temporarily.

[3] The city of Opis is mentioned in two texts of the second year of Cambyses (*Camb.* 143 (wr. AKŠAK^{ki}) and 145 (wr. *Ú-pi-ia*)) and in one each of the fourth year of Darius I (*Dar.* 149 (AKŠAK^{ki})) and the seventh of Darius II (*PBS* II/1. 140 wr. *Ú-pi-ia*). For the problem of the location of that city, cf. Barnett, "Xenophon and the Wall of Media", especially pp. 19ff.

[4] For the last discussion of this topic, see Meyer, *Das Gebet Nabonids*.

unfit to be the ruler of Babylonia. He presented himself in his own inscriptions as a man having visions and dreams, as one guided by miraculous events, which is quite exceptional in such texts.[1] Thus the picture painted of him in the Cyrus Cylinder and the Poem (see pp. 537f.) is not at all incongruous with that yielded by his heavily autobiographical inscriptions. This impression is deepened, moreover, by the idealistic representation of Cyrus not only in the inscriptions we are studying here, but also in the Old Testament and even in the classical sources.[2] The typological contrast so accentuated in the Poem between the mad king and the king as saviour should be recognized as mainly a propaganda device, created for political reasons. The internal conflict which overshadowed the reign of Nabonidus and eventually brought about his downfall need not have been primarily a religious one – though it was, according to the mood of the period, expressed in religious terms. That the king is presented as a heretic by the priesthood is a novelty in Mesopotamian religious politics. Customarily, in both Sumerian and Akkadian sources, a tension between the king and the priesthood finds expression in the refusal of the latter to provide answers (or, at least, favourable answers) to the demands for omens made by the king. We know this because Sargon of Agade and Nabonidus, too, in the new Ḫarran inscription (col. iii. 1f.) complain expressly about the absence of communications from the gods.

It will therefore not do to see in Nabonidus solely a religious fanatic, bent on promoting the worship of the moon god Sin at the expense of the traditional Marduk cult of Babylon.[3] Though Sin, especially the Sin of Ḫarran, was obviously important to the king, two major points should be borne in mind which support my interpretation. One is that Nabonidus did have an interest in the cities of the Sun god, Sippar and Larsa; the other is that all the rebellions against the king originated in large cities such as Nippur, Borsippa, Larsa, Uruk and Ur, as he himself reports in the Ḫarran inscription.[4] A careful reading of this document

---

[1] See Oppenheim, *Interpretation of Dreams*, pp. 202ff.

[2] Cf. F. H. Weissbach, "Kyros (6)" in Pauly, Supp. IV (1924) pp. 1128–66.

[3] For an extreme formulation of this theory see Lewy, "The Late Assyro-Babylonian Cult of the Moon".

[4] See the works of Gadd, Moran and Röllig in the bibliography. A perceptive analysis of the text shows that Nabonidus while wandering around during his exile was supported by those of his subjects who lived in the open country or, as he says, in distant regions (i. 9ff.). Upon his return to Babylon, Nabonidus rewarded them for their loyalty (col. iii. 15ff.). Nabonidus feels obliged to interpret even this "popular" support as made possible through divine intervention on his behalf; he tells us (col. i. 37ff.) that, miraculously, rain fell twice even in summer to produce the abundance needed to provide him and his followers with food during his entire exile. I intend to come back to this interesting document in a different context.

suggests that there was a considerable degree of popular support for the king outside the cities and that the non-urban segment of the population supported the king even in adversity, as Nabonidus clearly states there. To what extent the conflict between city and open country – between institutionalized and popular religiosity – coincided with cult conflicts like the one between the priesthood of Bēl-Marduk and that of Sin cannot be established. But the assumption of a city versus open-country tension, would help to explain the sudden military collapse of Babylonia: in that country the army was at all times drawn from the non-urban population, and would therefore hardly be willing to defend the hated cities against an invader.

According to the Chronicle, a curious shift in the Persian campaign against Babylon occurs at the very moment when defeat and collapse of resistance became evident. The advance against the capital was – we are told – not led by Cyrus but rather by the governor of the province of Gutium who marched on Babylon with the "army of Cyrus". The Persian king himself is not mentioned until he enters Babylon about ten days after the army. The satrap and, as such commander of the contingent of his province, Gobryas (spelled Ugbaru), marched into the capital on the 16th of Tašrītu; Nabonidus was apprehended soon after when he was about to leave the city.[1] The use of the verb *neḫēsu* with reference to the king suggests that Nabonidus did not flee or stealthily abscond, but simply left the city. If this terminology is intentional (contrast with it the use of *ḫalāqu*, above, p. 540), it could throw light on the entire situation, and especially on the reaction of the defeated king.

The events in Babylon from the entry of the invading army to the arrival of Cyrus are difficult to ascertain; the text shifts again, no doubt deliberately, from the "army of Cyrus" to the "army of Gutium". It seems to me wholly likely that the city was indeed given the treatment traditionally to be expected from a conquering army, especially one that consisted of the semi-barbarian hill people from beyond the Tigris. Three considerations, in my opinion, point to this. First, the already mentioned absence of Cyrus. He seems to have known what to expect when the Guti tribesmen entered the rich and famous city as victors, and therefore kept the Persian army, and above all himself, away from Babylon until he could enter the city as liberator and saviour. Second, the Chronicle says expressly that a contingent of the Gutians surrounded

---

[1] Berossos (see p. 529, n. 1) tells a slightly different story.

the temple complex of Esagila; its task obviously was to keep the sanctuary untouched by the pillaging soldiers. The apparent contradiction that the same Gutians were plundering the city and protecting its sanctuary suggests that a master plan was here being executed. Both the rights of the conquering soldiers[1] and the political interests of Cyrus were to be upheld. As stated explicitly, the cultic life of the sanctuary was not interrupted, nor was the programme of ritual acts which made up the daily routine of the temple. Third, upon the entry of Cyrus, the "king's peace"[2] was placed upon the city. The already mentioned Poem (see p. 551) refers to this fact in identical wording, thus bearing out the importance of this royal act. It can mean only that the king, upon entering Babylon, declared the end of the period of pillage and forbade weapons to continue to be drawn in the city. Small wonder that Cyrus was greeted with enthusiasm by the suffering citizenry and that palm twigs were spread out before his advance, as is often done at the solemn entry of a victor and liberator.[3]

The next public act of Cyrus was to have a proclamation read to the assembled Babylonians or, as the Chronicle literally says, "a greeting was said to all of Babylon". This phrase may mean several things. It could refer to an *ad hoc* address to the assembled crowd spoken in their native tongue by a representative of the conqueror, promising safety from the treatment normally inflicted on a defeated enemy; or it may represent a foreign custom, the official message of a new king to his subjects, outlining his aims and presenting his promises. Such a "king's speech" would fit quite well the social climate germane to Persian kingship,[4] and could not have failed to induce the Babylonians to expect an improvement of their political condition under Cyrus.[5] The following

[1] Though it is certainly coincidental, it is amusing to note that Xenophon (*Cyropaedia* VII. v. 73) puts the following sentence into the mouth of Cyrus after the conquest of Babylon: "For this is a law established for all time among all men that when a city is taken in war, the persons and the property of the inhabitants thereof belong to the captors." (Trans. W. Miller.) Cf. also Kiechle, "Humanität".

[2] For the "king's peace" which is in fact a written royal command for establishing a new order, see Olmstead, *History*, pp. 395 and 408.

[3] The word is listed in *CAD* H p. 102b *sub ḫarinû* but omitted in *AHw*.

[4] This touches on a problem complex that so far has not evoked much interest among the linguists dealing with the Old Persian corpus of royal inscriptions. In style, these "speaking" inscriptions correspond to those written by the Urartian kings (cf. van Loon, *Urartian Art*, p. 9) and to those in hieroglyphic Hittite, but their function in each civilization needs separate investigations. Copies of the Behistun inscription were made available in various parts of the empire (cf. p. 559), which means that they were treated as royal utterances, intended to convey to the subjects the achievements, aspirations and expectations of their king.

[5] One is reminded of the first verse of the Book of Ezra referring to Cyrus: "The Lord stirred up the spirit of Cyrus King of Persia, that he made a proclamation throughout all his kingdom, and put it also in writing". See also Bickerman, "The Edict of Cyrus".

sentence in the text confirms the impression that the "saying of the king's greeting" established the internal administrative organization of Babylonia. Gobryas (spelled Gubaru), the king's governor (of Gutium), appointed a number of local governors then and there in Babylon.

Here, two often discussed problems have to be dealt with. One arises from the two different spellings in the Chronicle ("Gubaru" and "Ugbaru") of the Persian name Gaubaruva, which the Greeks rendered as Gobryas; the other, pointed out first by M. San Nicolò concerns the attestation of one Gubaru as "governor of Babylonia and Eber-nāri" from the fourth year of Cyrus (535/4 B.C.) to the fifth of Cambyses (525/4), and not earlier. San Nicolò's solution relies on Babylonia having had as chief administrator under the Chaldean kings an official called šakin māti.[1] At the time of the events here discussed he was a certain Nabû-aḫḫē-bulliṭ attested in Uruk up to 535 B.C., that is, up to the establishment of the new order[2] presently to be discussed. This would mean that the large satrapy comprising Babylonia and the regions beyond the Euphrates (up to the Phoenician city states)[3] was established by Cyrus only in his fifth year and then entrusted to a satrap called Gubaru. Hence the Ugbaru/Gubaru mentioned in the Chronicle as governor (or satrap) of Gutium, who installed the minor governors of Babylonia and whose death is reported soon after, and the Gubaru appearing later on as satrap of Babylonia and "Transpotamia" were two different persons.

This solution has to contend with only minor difficulties as compared with those facing previous proposals.[4] The difficulties are: the spelling variants within the Chronicle, the fact that the governor of Gutium appoints minor administrators in Babylonia where a šakin māti is still holding the top administrative position as an appointee of Nabonidus, and the fact that Cambyses, the son of Cyrus, is mentioned in date formulae for less than one year (538/7 B.C.) as "king of Babylon" (see

[1] The official called šakin māti occurs only rarely in post-Kassite Babylonia, cf. Brinkman, Post-Kassite Babylonia, notes 1945, 1952 and 1965. In Neo-Babylonian administrative texts coming from Northern Babylonia, this official (mentioned without a personal name) is attested from Kandalau to Nebuchadnezzar II; in the South, i.e., in Uruk, a named šakin māti is somewhat more frequent, cf. San Nicolò, Prosopographie, pp. 62ff. [2] Op. cit., p. 61.

[3] Note the texts from Neirab (see p. 569, n. 3), near Aleppo, which mention the Achaemenian kings in their dates.

[4] The literature on the problems connected with Gobryas is extensive. Cf. Schwenzner, "Gobryas"; also Leuze, Satrapieneinteilung, pp. 25ff., and the references in San Nicolò, Prosopographie, pp. 54ff. Additional evidence for Gobryas published in the meantime is: P. A. Pohl, "Neubabylonische Rechtsurkunden (I)", AnOr VIII. no. 45 (fourth year of Cyrus) and 61 (eighth year).

pp. 557ff.). It is obvious that the Chronicle and the date formulae of the contemporary legal texts do not tell us everything about the administrative situation in Babylonia from the fall of Babylon to the creation of the new satrapy. One gains the impression that this was a period of administrative uncertainty and experiments, the reasons for which we may never learn.

It is worth noting that the Chronicle mentions no co-regency of Cyrus and Cambyses, in contrast to the Cylinder and date formulae (see pp. 557f.). Yet only a few lines later we find Cambyses, called the son of Cyrus, participating in a religious ceremony in a function traditionally reserved for the king of Babylon (see p. 556 for details).

The next lines in the Chronicle record as first achievement of the conqueror the return of the images from Babylon to their respective local shrines. Then the text relates the death of Gobryas (written Ugbaru), also that of the wife of the (Persian) king, and mentions the official mourning which followed that event exactly as was reported earlier in the same Chronicle after the death of the mother of Nabonidus. Clearly, in the eyes of the chronicler, normality had returned to Babylonia.

Most of the events recorded in the Chronicle are also mentioned or alluded to in the Cylinder inscription of Cyrus (see p. 536). Of course, since these texts represent different literary genres the presentation of even identical events is bound to vary at times.

The beginning of the Cylinder is destroyed. After an enumeration of the crimes and misdeeds of Nabonidus (the text here is too damaged to be legible, but mention may be made of the building of a "counter Esagila", for which see p. 552), the Cylinder turns in line 11 to Cyrus. It tells in some detail how it came about that this foreign king was selected by Marduk himself to become the liberator of Babylon. The pious scribe uses the motif of the god's search through "all countries" for a ruler who was "just" as well as "beloved" by him, to be entrusted with the task of leading the god in his festival, the celebrated New Year's rite, in other words, to become the legitimate ruler of Babylonia. While the expression *bibil libbi*, "beloved one", is typically Mesopotamian in its reference to the emotional relationship between god and king, the epithet *išaru* (which recurs in *libbašu išara* in line 14) is quite untypical a definition of requisite royal quality.[1] We seem to have here a

---

[1] Not listed in Seux, *Epithètes royales*.

non-Akkadian use of the word, which in Akkadian normally means "straight" or "correct".[1]

The political situation conceived here on a mytho-political plan is a curious repetition of the one Nabonidus himself conveys in his cylinder in reporting on the restoration of the sanctuaries of Ḫarran and Sippar:[2] "When the third year (after the promise made by Marduk to the king) came,[3] he (Marduk) made Cyrus, king of Anzan, his servant, the younger (of this name)[4] march out against him (Astyages, called in line 27, "the *ummān-manda*")[5] and he (Cyrus) scattered with his few soldiers the ummān-manda's numerous soldiers. He captured Astyages, the king of the ummān-manda, and took him as a prisoner to his (Cyrus') country (col. i. 28–32)." The motif of Marduk's intervention in history by means of a foreign ruler whose activities he is supposed to direct appears thus in a text written in the name of Nabonidus as well as in one which is clearly directed against that same king; this forces us to see in the very concept of such an intervention an intrinsic feature of the political, if not the religious outlook of the period.[6] It seems to reflect a mood of desperation in the country during the rule of Nabonidus.

Such a climate of "messianic" expectation so soon after the flourishing empire of Nebuchadnezzar II, the military successes of Neriglissar, and even those of Nabonidus himself in the West,[7] under apparently constant social and economic conditions, requires an explanation. One may surmise that it arose from specific apprehensions, such as fear of an impending foreign invasion. What else could have caused this longing for release, and even for a restoration of a previous and better state of affairs, to be brought from outside by a foreign ruler? The rapid succession of rulers between the death of Nebuchadnezzar II and the usurpation of the throne by Nabonidus bespeaks a deep-seated malaise quite likely ideological, in fact, religious, in origin. However, since

---

[1] Only in a footnote dare I suggest the possibility that *išaru* might represent an attempt to reproduce the notion of Old Persian *arta* "Truth", or *arštā* "justice".

[2] *VAB* IV. 218ff.

[3] For the chronological problem involved, cf. Galling, pp. 8ff. and 12ff., also Tadmor, "The Inscriptions of Nabunaid", especially pp. 351ff.

[4] For the practice of referring to a second king of the same name in Akkadian either as *ṣeḫru* or *arkû*, see *CAD* sub *ṣeḫru* mng. 1c-2' and *arkû* mng. 1b-1'.

[5] On the designation *ummān-manda* in Old Babylonian omen texts, cf. J. Nougayrol, "Textes hépatoscopiques d'époque ancienne", *RA* XLIV (1950), p. 20.

[6] Note the passage: "(he, i.e. God) that says of Cyrus: He is my shepherd, and shall perform all my pleasure" in Isaiah 44. 28 and "the Lord hath loved him: he will do his pleasure on Babylon, and his arm shall be on the Chaldeans", *ibid.*, 48. 14.

[7] See the Nabonidus Chronicle ii. 9–22; *VAB* IV, p. 220, i 39ff.

Nabonidus and his adversaries exhibit the same expectations, internal political tension may not be the sole underlying reason. At all events it is clear that the religious "establishment" echoes the traditional Mesopotamian concept of the main god activating historical events in order to impose his will on his country, using foreigners and barbarians as his tool. This pattern is well established in Mesopotamia from the intervention of Enlil in the "Curse of Agade" onwards.[1] What is new in this specific context is the idea that this time the invasion will bring not punishment but deliverance; a foreign ruler is to help Marduk to re-establish his divine rule and bring about a new order.

The role of Cyrus in the cited account of Nabonidus is pinpointed by two remarks in the text; first, Cyrus is called an *ardu* of Marduk, i.e., a worshipper of the Babylonian god, and secondly, Cyrus' army is expressly called small. This was either meant to show that it was the power of Marduk which enabled Cyrus to overcome the dangerous Mede, or else was simply a statement of fact. The use of the term *suppuḫu* "to scatter" in characterizing the encounter between the Medes and the Persians, and the report of the "Nabonidus Chronicle" on the meeting of the army of Astyages (see p. 538f.) seem to be in harmony. The apparent ease and the speed of Cyrus' conquest of the country of the ummān-manda (for which our Cylinder uses [in 1. 13] the term Guti)[2] suggest that it was a revolution rather than a defeat by a foreign conqueror which made Cyrus the lord of Iran. This event might well have established his reputation as a military power in Mesopotamia. Possibly his fame was further enhanced by the nature of Cyrus' takeover in Media and his subsequent rule there which our text takes pains to exalt in the following terms: "He always took care of the people by exercising justice."

The stress on the dispensation of justice – a topic quite traditional in Mesopotamian royal inscriptions – as a specific aspect of Persian rule reminds one of the reference to the "laws (*dātu*) of the king" in cuneiform texts from Mesopotamia under Achaemenian rule,[3] not to

---

[1] For the problem of gods and history see Albrektson, *History and the Gods*.

[2] In literary texts of the first millennium (and this includes royal inscriptions and chronicles) the old geographical term Gutium is used to refer specifically to the half barbarian hill people from the piedmont ranges of the Zagros northward to the two lakes (Urmia and Van) whatever their ethnic background or political status was. The relationship between the two terms, Guti and *ummān-manda*, both often used in a generic sense, remains to be investigated.

[3] The references to the *dātu* of the king are to be found only in a few texts of the reign of Darius: *Dar.* 53 (second year) and *VAS* III. 151 (31st year) from the North, and *UET* IV. 101, from the South. A late text, dated 218/7 B.C., is given in J. N. Strassmaier. "Arsaciden-Inschriften", *ZA* III (1888), no. 13, pp. 137–9; in the latter instance, however, reference seems to be made to a specific

speak of the "Laws of the Medes and the Persians" in the Old Testament.[1] Whatever striking new attitude and different emphasis in the role of government are involved here, related as they are to Cyrus as a person rather than as an exponent of an alien people or civilization, the writer of the Cylinder insists that this very justice of Cyrus prompted Marduk to order him (*qabû* is used here) to march against Babylon.

At this point, the author waxes poetic and uses a phraseology of decidely "messianic" overtones. Marduk marched side by side with Cyrus, like a friend, the Persian army being all of a sudden so large as to be beyond counting ("like the water of a river"), proceeding leisurely (*šadāḫu* means "to march in a procession"), their weapons put away. We know, however, from the "Nabonidus Chronicle" that Cyrus did make an attack near Opis and that the entry into Babylon was not made by the Persian army under Cyrus but by a contingent of Gutians under the command of their satrap. Thus we catch the author patently disregarding historical facts well within the memory range of his public, for the sake of applying a pattern: the coming of the saviour king whom nobody opposes, who assumes kingship under divine orders and guidance. This need not imply that there was no genuine joy in Babylon over the collapse of the rule of Nabonidus; a passage in the Chronicle, though still somewhat obscure, could well be so interpreted (see p. 541, n. 4). What matters is that the joyous entry of Cyrus is but part of a sequence of ceremonial acts which lead up to the proclamation of the new king. Part of the preparation of this event is the homage rendered him not only by the city of Babylon and all its inhabitants but by the entire population of Sumer and Akkad, by nobles and officials alike. With happy faces they greeted Cyrus as king, with benedictions (*karābu*) and shouts of joy (*šamāru*) they praised him – as the text expressly says – as the one who had brought them back to life from death and had saved their lives.[2]

---

royal edict concerning deposits (*puqdû*) so that *dātu* here may no longer refer to what *dātu* probably stood for in the Achaemenian texts. The word has become a synonym for the Akkadian *dīnu*. There is moreover an official called *ša muḫḫi dātu* "in charge of the law" (*VAS* VI. 128, 12th year of Darius I), as well as the official called *dātabara* (known from Daniel 1. 2) in the texts of the Murašû archives (see p. 565). In these texts only one person bears this title and he is apparently connected with the satrap of Babylonia.

[1] Cf. Daniel 6. 8, 12 and 15, also Esther 1. 19 for "the law of the Medes and the Persians which altereth not"; for the *dathe dᵉ malkā*, also Esther 1. 8, 13–15; 2. 2 and 12; and for the Akkadian passages note 52. For the problems involved, cf. Olmstead, "Darius as Lawgiver", and Kraeling, *Aramaic Papyri*, p. 30.

[2] The *acclamatio* of the new king here described is quite alien to Mesopotamia. This clearly emerges from the coronation ritual of the Assyrian king (see Müller, *Königsritual*, pp. 14ff.) where

At this point (line 20 of the Cylinder) Cyrus is introduced abruptly and speaks to us in the first person throughout the rest of the inscription. This change is quite extraordinary for a Mesopotamian royal inscription, because the literary pattern of the text category to which the Cylinder belongs does not admit such "mimesis". It is as if an attempt had been made to render an actual event, possibly the *šulmu*, i.e., the address of the king to his new subjects. Cyrus first gives us his titles, which are in traditional Mesopotamian style,[1] and his genealogy. He stresses his royal extraction (*zēru dārû ša šarrūtu*) – exactly as Darius I does in the Behistun inscription – as well as the fact that it is Bēl and Nabû who love him and want him to become king. All this is quite traditional. Then the author of the text shifts his vantage point abruptly: Cyrus tells us in the style of a report on achievements what he has already done for Babylon since he took up residence in the royal palace – how pious he has been toward Marduk, how well his troops have behaved in Babylon, how security is re-established in all the cities of the realm, the ruins rebuilt, etc. For this reason Marduk has blessed Cyrus himself, his son Cambyses, and his army, and "we", i.e., the king and the crown prince, in turn worship the god. This "we" is a strange and quite unprecedented use of the first person plural by a king in a Mesopotamian inscription. It can mean only that Cambyses was there and then installed as co-regent of Cyrus in Babylon (see below pp. 558f.).

Next, all the foreign rulers from the Upper to the Lower Sea are mentioned as bearing tribute and doing obeisance in Babylon by kissing the king's feet. The passage is damaged, but what is left speaks of the kings of the Western Land (Amurru) who live in tents, an old theme not to be taken literally. The extent of the realm, or rather what Cyrus considered Babylonian territory, is not clear at all.[2] In lines 31ff. of the Cylinder the following region is singled out: "from [three or four signs are missing here] as far as Aššur and Susa, Agade, Ešnunna, Zamban, Me-Turnu and Dēr to the borders of Guti-land". All these cities are

---

the enthronement is enacted only before the high officials of the realm who prostrate themselves and kiss the feet of the king while musicians play and sing. In the Old Testament (I Kings 1. 34 and 39; II Kings 11. 12), trumpets, clapping of hands and the shouting of "God save the King..." form the *acclamatio*. In Kantorowicz, *Laudes regiae*, pp. 76ff. and especially p. 77, n. 38, the wide distribution of this ritual pattern is pointed out and its inner-Asiatic background traced. It is therefore possible to see in the scene described in the Chronicle a Medio-Persian custom and to interpret it as the enactment of the *allocatio* and the subsequent *acclamatio* of the new king.

[1] The title is a curious mixture of several patterns: *šar kiššati šarru rabû šarru dannu ša Bābili ša māt Šumeri u Akkadī šar kibrāti erbetti*.

[2] For the problem of Elam (apart from Susa proper) see Galling, p. 46.

characterized as "cities with temples on the other side of the Tigris" (*maḫāza [ša eber]ti Idiglat*), a description which fits well, though Aššur is actually on the right bank of the river, and the location of Agade[1] is still unknown. These cities had been in ruins but Cyrus resettled them and rebuilt their sanctuaries. Though this specific statement is important – it shows the depopulation of the region beyond the Tigris, which previously belonged to Assyria – its purpose in the present context is difficult to ascertain.[2] Possibly the region was to be resettled and added to the satrapy Babylonia. Then follows a report on the return to their native cities in Sumer and Akkad of the images which Nabonidus had gathered to Babylon. The author seems to turn here from a report on Cyrus' achievements to another attack on Nabonidus, who is mentioned for a second time by name in this text.

The unprecedented and perhaps desperate measure of Nabonidus, of concentrating in his capital the images from all the major Babylonian sites, must have had implications which we cannot fully understand today; it certainly antagonized the priesthood of Esagila, quite apart from the psychological effect of such an extreme royal act, on the population of the cities bereft of their divine protection. The return of the images mentioned in the Cylinder and the Poem as ordered by Cyrus – but not presented as a royal act in the Chronicle – underlines the significance of that move of Nabonidus. The vagueness which characterizes the references to these events in the Poem, the Chronicle and the Cyrus Cylinder looks like an attempt to hide what was considered an act of supreme blasphemy in terms of Mesopotamian religiosity. To religious historians it may seem that Nabonidus made a desperate attempt to concentrate in his capital all the divine potency invested in the individual images normally scattered over his realm, in order to protect Babylon. However, such an explanation could be upheld only on the somewhat primitive, pseudo-rationalistic level of modern theories, hardly adequate to do justice to the motivations of so complex a personality as Nabonidus. To win over the city-dwelling population of the newly conquered and deeply disturbed country, Cyrus

---

[1] For the possibility that Agade was actually situated beyond the Tigris, cf. Brinkman, *Political History*, note 874, penultimate section. Note that the city is still mentioned in our period as *A-gada*^{ki} in *CT* IV. 4 41b: 14, and that the personal name A.GA.DÉ^{ki}-*ú-a* "Akkadian" occurs in *Cyr.* 360: 22.

[2] For Achaemenian constructions of irrigation facilities in that region, cf. Adams, *Land Behind Baghdad*, pp. 59ff.

ordered the return of the images to their local shrines.[1] The final prayer for intercession which customarily crowns an inscription of the type discussed here is addressed to all these repatriated gods. It requests that they mediate for him before Bēl and Nabû and even speak a prayer of intercession, given verbatim but badly preserved on the Cylinder, for both Cyrus and Cambyses. From this point on, the Cylinder is very broken and only a few signs can be made out here and there. It appears that the king instituted – as is customary – specific offerings to be given to these gods in their individual shrines, while other traces suggest that building work in Babylon and its temples was listed (see p. 552).[2]

The restoration of the religious status quo ante is confirmed by a very damaged cylinder excavated in Ur. As far as the text is preserved, it contains the usual phraseology of such documents, but the mention of the unnamed king's restoring of images to their shrines points directly to Cyrus.

The strange poem we have repeatedly mentioned (see p. 537) provides further information on these events. When the sixth column sets in, the first statement is: "He (Cyrus) declared *šulmu* for (the inhabitants) of Babylon." This has an exact parallel in the Chronicle; the implications of the royal act involved are discussed above p. 542. When the next topic is introduced we find Cyrus in a new role. We are told of sacrifices made and fumigations offered by him to the gods, and also of deliveries of offerings increased upon his order (see p. 550 for a parallel in the Cylinder). What is startling in the first mentioned passage is that the subject of the two verbs referring to the slaughtering of cattle (*pulluqu*) and of sheep (*ṭubbuḫu*) is clearly the king himself. Such activities are unheard of for a Mesopotamian king, let alone a foreign one, and square ill with the Persian aversion to animal sacrifice. It is clear that the poet's imagination got the better of his judgement, as a text meant to be read in religiously oriented circles would hardly include so unlikely a statement. The reference thereafter to Cyrus prostrating

[1] The transfer of the images is described in the following way: In the twelfth year of Nabonidus we are told that New Year's rites were duly performed, but the gods of Marad and Kish and those of what the text calls "Babylonia above and below the ḪAR (mng. unknown)" entered the city with the exception of those of Borsippa, Cutha, [...] and Sippar (iii 11–2). The return of the "gods of Babylonia" is recorded without detail, *ibid.*, line 21. In the broken lines 2 and 3 of the same column (col. iii) the image of the Ištar of Uruk and, presumably, those of [the god]s of the Sealand are mentioned. This could refer to a transfer of images in the year preceding the move recorded in the earlier passage.

[2] Dr P. R. Berger informs me that he has been able to fill the gap in the Cylinder in his forthcoming edition of all Neo-Babylonian royal inscriptions.

himself before Marduk may likewise not correspond to reality, even though it would not have been objectionable to Babylonians.

A new topic is brought up next, the building activities of Cyrus in Babylon, specifically on its immense walls. This was to complete the original plan of Nebuchadnezzar II, as well as to add new fortifications. In view of the known reluctance of the later Persian rulers to permit the fortification of conquered capitals,[1] one might doubt also this statement. However, there is a parallel in the rebuilding of the walls of Jerusalem. Cyrus may have made such a promise on similar grounds, bent on securing the loyalty of the population of an important province. The verse in which Cyrus carries baskets with clay for the building of the walls represents but an appropriate motif for a traditional royal inscription and need not be taken literally. The scribe simply followed the descriptive pattern of activities expected from a pious Mesopotamian king. Toward the end of the poem the mood of liberation is stressed again. Life under Nabonidus is likened to prison life; the Cylinder used the even more exaggerated simile of death and resurrection.

With characteristic priestly malice, the description of Cyrus' building activities in the temple Esagila ends with a report of the destruction of all that Nabonidus had changed or added to the temple complex. Even his name, appearing on what were probably votive offerings, was erased. Thus the author of the Poem takes up a subject matter touched upon in the Cylinder inscription, in the badly broken introductory lines. There, at the beginning of the enumeration of Nabonidus' sins against the traditional cult, Nabonidus is said to have built a *tamšīl Esagila*, i.e., an "imitation-" or "counter-Esagila", near the real temple. Whatever the factual basis of such an allegation, as a theme it certainly harks back to the charge levelled at Sargon of Agade in the "Weidner Chronicle",[2] namely that he built a "counter-Babylon" in front of his own capital Akkadi and was punished for this sin by the loss of his world dominion. The implications of the sin of which Nabonidus stood accused must therefore have been obvious to any educated reader.

The reaction against Nabonidus was not confined to the priesthood of Esagila, as is shown by the broken cylinder excavated in Ur and mentioned above, p. 536, n. 4. This document discloses Cyrus speaking as if he owed his kingship to Sin, as is only to be expected in an inscrip-

[1] For a characteristic statement see what is said in the letter to Artaxerxes given in Ezra 4. 13ff. "...if this city is builded, and the walls set up again, then will they not pay toll, tribute and custom, and so thou shalt endamage the revenue of the kings."
[2] See Güterbock, *ZA* XLII (1934), 52 and 54: 18.

tion found in the sanctuary of that god: "[when the god = Marduk?) had kindly selected (me, literally: called the name) [to rule the country of Babylonia] and (its) people, Sin, the luminary of heaven and netherworld handed over to me, upon a favourable (astral) sign of his, the four regions of the world and I made the gods return to their shrines (...)". Though Ur is not expressly listed (in the Chronicle) among the sanctuaries whose images had been brought to the capital upon the order of Nabonidus – perhaps an accidental omission – the text's specific mention of the return of the images illustrates its importance for the religious politics of Cyrus.

Ur and Uruk are the only sanctuaries whose ruins have given us bricks with the name of Cyrus. From Ur (see pp. 582f.) comes the longest of these texts.[1] Two four-line inscriptions come from Uruk, where Cyrus is the last king to build in Eanna.[2] The Ur brick is unusually explicit: "Cyrus king of the world (*šar kiššati*), king of Anšan (wr. *Aššan*), son of Cambyses, king of Anšan: the great gods have assigned to me all the countries (of the world) and I have made the land live undisturbed." In the two bricks from Uruk, Cyrus presents himself as follows: "I am Cyrus (*UVB* I, No. 31 adds: king of all countries) who built (*UVB* I, No. 31 has atypically: who loves) Esagila and Ezida, son of Cambyses, the powerful king."

Note that in none of these inscriptions does Cyrus call himself king of Babylonia.

Cyrus is the only Persian king who left an imprint in cuneiform sources beyond the mere acknowledgment of a foreign overlord in official formulae, as was to be the case with all his successors. His image thus left to us agrees to a considerable degree with that derived from biblical and classical sources. Its consistency may be due to a specific political situation obtaining all over the ancient Near East when Cyrus appeared on the scene, or to his own personality and behaviour as conqueror and ruler, reflected in disparate sources. At any rate the uniqueness of Cyrus must be regarded as a basic factor in the developments that accompanied the creation of the Persian empire under his leadership. In any attempt to account for the achievement of Cyrus, one has to take into consideration the extraordinary contrast between his role as liberator hailed by all nations, and the quick collapse under his son Cambyses, of the supra-national political structure he had

---

[1] *UET* I, 58, No. 194 and pl. 48 and W.
[2] *UVB* I [1928/29], 63 and pl. 31, No. 31 and see D. E. Hagen, "Keilschrifturkunden", p. 257.

created. With a vengeance all his subjects turned back to the old dynasties from whose yoke they had only recently been so happy to escape.[1]

(B) *Cambyses*

Of Cambyses we know very little from cuneiform sources apart from his being mentioned in the Cylinder as co-regent with Cyrus, and apart from the incident recorded in lines 24ff. of the third column of the Nabonidus Chronicle which are so badly damaged that the passage has always been disregarded by historians. In view of the extreme scarcity of available evidence, I contend that an effort should be made to utilize these broken lines by discussing the various possibilities of restoring the words lost at points of breakage, in order to obtain a meaningful context. Here is a literal translation of the passage with indications as to the size of the gaps:

(col. iii, line 24b) On the fourth day (of the month of Nisannu), Cambyses, the son of Cy[rus],

(line 25) when he went to (the temple) É.NÍG.PA.KALAM.MA.SUM.MU, the É.PA priest (of) Nabû [gave him, or: refused him] the sceptre [...]

(line 26) [when] he came, because of the Elamite dress(!), the hands of Nabû [he was, or: was not allowed to seize...]

(line 27) [the s]pears and quivers from [two signs missing] x ⌜the son of the king(?)⌝ to the service(?) [two or three signs missing]

(line 28) [three signs missing] the god Nabû to the temple Esagila turned back (in the procession) × × × in front of the god Bēl and the son of B[ēl four signs missing]" (end of col. iii, beginning of col. iv destroyed).

The only correction made in this translation of the text is in line 26, changing the senseless *lu-bu-uš-bi* into *lu-bu-uš-tu₄*(!), as both signs (*bi* and *tu₄*) begin with a similar arrangement of wedges. The breaks usually occur at the end of lines, which makes it difficult to discover the connecting thread in the narrative, especially on account of the terse diction of the text and the use of logograms, i.e., word signs, which may well make the gaps more extensive than the physical space suggests.

My interpretation of the report is based on a small number of restorations with which I propose to fill the gaps. But first let us consider the setting and the timing of the story, because these broken lines certainly contain a story important and interesting enough to have been recorded by the annalist. The place of the incident is a famous

[1] The key to the latter problem lies in the effect on them of the interlude of the False Smerdis, which shook Cyrus' empire to its foundations. See below, pp. 561ff.

Nabû temple in Babylon whose Sumerian name, É.NÍG.PA.KALAM.MA.SUM.MU, is conveniently explained in the East India House inscription of Nebuchadnezzar II (*VAB* IV. 128. iv 18ff.) in the following context: "For Nabû, the sublime vizier, who had given me the righteous sceptre to rule over all inhabited regions (I rebuilt) his temple in Babylon (called) É.NÍG.PA.KALAM.MA.SUM.MA", i.e., "Temple-in-which-is-given-the-sceptre-for-the-entire-country". Nabonidus, likewise, refers to the role and importance of this temple in a stela found in Ḫarran (*VAB* IV. 278. vii 23ff.), with these words: "I entered the temple É.NÍG.PA.KALAM.MA.SUM.MU into the presence of Nabû who grants me a long rule (and who) entrusted into my hands the just sceptre, the legitimate staff which enables (me to) enlarge (my) realm." Therefore it was for the equivalent of a "coronation" ceremony that Cambyses set forth on the fourth of Nisannu, i.e., on 15 March, 538 B.C., to the temple of Nabû, to act for the first time as king in the traditional rituals for the participation of a king of Babylon in the New Year's festival. On that occasion something unusual happened, as the writers of the Babylonian chronicles would not otherwise have described a routine ceremony.

What happened when "Cambyses went to the temple"?

The clue to the nature of the incident is contained in the short phrase which makes sense only with the above proposed emendation: "because of the dress from/of Elam". Since the priest of Nabû, the god of the temple where the sceptre was to be handed over to the king, is the subject of the sentence in which these words occur, one may propose the following reconstruction of the scene: Cambyses arrived at the sanctuary in Elamite dress; the chief priest of the temple considered this attire unfit for the occasion, and refused him the sceptre. The text should then read (lines 24 to 26) with due caution as follows: "On the fourth day (of Nisannu), the É.PA priest of Nabû [refused him, hardly: gave him] the sceptre (NÍG.PA) [and...] when he came to the temple É.NÍG.PA.KALAM.SUM.MU as soon as he came. On account of the Elamite dress [he could not (or: was not allowed to)] lead the image of Nabû (in procession)."

The main difficulty with this reconstruction is the fact that the phrase *kî illiku* "when he arrived/came/went" appears twice. The first time (line 25) Cambyses is clearly the subject and the verb refers to his going to the temple. The second time (line 26), however, the subject is lost in the break at the end of the preceding line. It could be either the priest or the prince. The latter seems at first glance more likely because Cambyses is mentioned in the line before, though a break thereafter might well have contained a now missing verb. Moreover, since the "sceptre" is clearly the direct object of the verb of which the priest is the subject the missing verbal form should be either "he refused him" or, "he handed over to him". The former is more appealing because it gives a point to the story told. The latter would make sense only if Cambyses was given the symbol but not permitted to "lead" Nabû in procession. Of course, the subject needed for the second *kî illiku* might have been neither Cambyses nor the priest, but this is rather far fetched because the incident clearly involves only two protagonists. The translation I propose assumes that Cambyses was also the subject of the second "when he came".

The alternative that the priest did hand over the sceptre to Cambyses in front of the temple in order to fulfil the primary purpose of the ceremony but the prince was refused permission to participate in the procession which was to bring him into closer relation with the image of Nabû, remains open on account of the break in the tablet which makes it impossible to clarify this point.

In the second act of the ritual, so we have to assume, the new king, provided with the royal symbol, was to lead the god who had just bestowed legitimacy upon him in a procession – and eventually to the temple of Bēl. Whatever the physical performance of this act implied – the phrase *qātē ṣabātu*[1] means fundamentally "to lead/help walk (a sick or weak person)" – it represents a unique privilege for the Babylonian king to come into some form of direct contact with the image of the god, be this Marduk on the occasion of the annual New Year's festival, or Nabû on the occasion of the ceremony under discussion. For elucidation on this point one may turn to the sequel of the story, unfortunately even more damaged on the tablet than the preceding lines.

The passage "spears and quivers from [...]" in line 27 invites the restoration: "He (Cambyses), or: they (his servants, or: the priests) [took] from [him] the spears and quivers (with which he was attired in Elamite fashion)." If so, then Cambyses gave in to the demands of the priest, deciding that it was more important to participate in the ritual than to insist on wearing his warlike attire. The subsequent lines, badly broken as they are, support this interpretation: "The ⌈crown prince(?)⌉

---

[1] Cf. for this idiomatic expression *CAD ṣabātu* mng. 8, *qātu* usage b, and Oppenheim, *JAOS* LXI (1941), pp. 269ff.

[went] to the ser[vice(?)...] Nabû made his (processional) round [and went] to Esagila [the prince(?) prayed or prostrated himself(?)] before Bēl and the Son-of-Bēl."

Whatever conviction might be carried by the restorations here proposed, the passage gives us additional information about the ceremonies connected with the New Year's ritual and the king's participation in it. Apparently the king accompanied the god Nabû on his round through several sanctuaries of the city to reach eventually the main temple, the residence of the god Bēl. Here the king had to participate in ceremonies culminating in his adoration of the city's god, Bēl, and his son, Nabû. The ritual mentioned in the Chronicle clearly complements the ceremonial of the New Year's festival as it is described in the later ritual texts (Thureau-Dangin, pp. 127ff.). In both instances the king comes to Esagila in the same procession as brings Nabû for his visit with his father. However, according to the late (Seleucid) texts of Thureau-Dangin, this happens on the fifth day of the New Year's festival, when Nabû arrives by the sacred barge Iddaḫedu. Sacrificial food is then served to him and immediately afterward to the king (Thureau-Dangin, pp. 143, 409ff.), who obviously has accompanied Nabû to Esagila. According to the Nabonidus Chronicle the handing over of the sceptre to the king and his procession to Esagila happens on the fourth day. I would not venture to harmonize these discrepancies; actual practice might have changed or not conformed to the late "scenario", or the Nabû residing in the temple in Babylon and the one coming by boat from Borsippa may have participated in parallel rituals on successive days.

One question remains to be examined. Was Cambyses' behaviour a premeditated attempt to reject the ceremonial of a foreign religion, prompted by the prince's unwillingness to conform to the culture of the defeated, or was it a lapse due to the youth of the prince or the novelty of the situation? The last explanation is improbable notwithstanding the prince's short stay in Babylon (assuming he came with his father). The Babylonian priesthood, having thrown in its lot with the Persians, would not have failed to coach the prince adequately to prevent just such an incident as the one under discussion.

There remains the explanation of a planned affront, one that could be interpreted as springing from a deep-seated religious conviction outweighing political considerations. I am aware that the scholars who have investigated the Persian domination of Egypt no longer accept the numerous stories about Cambyses' mad behaviour in Egypt with respect to alien religious institutions.[1] Yet his appearance at the temple of Nabû in Elamite attire, armed to the teeth with spears and quivers, in order to receive from the god, under due religious ceremonies, the sceptre with which to rule Babylonia, remains strange.[2] Equally irrational, it would seem, was his sudden change of mind, which made Cambyses reverse his attitude, put away his weapons, and participate in the ritual. The Chronicle seems to record this as a triumph of the native religion over the still uncouth conqueror. Still, it may be meaningful that the first appearance of Cambyses on the scene of history was as strange as his exit when he was confronted with the revolt of the usurper Brdya.[3]

The problems connected with the co-regency of Cyrus and Cambyses should be discussed at this point not only because the fact is historically interesting, but also because of a possible connection with the incident just mentioned.

The co-regency is attested in date formulae and in a text which cites an oath sworn by both Cyrus as king of all countries and Cambyses as king of Babylon(ia).[4] The date formulae are of two types: one runs "first year of Cambyses, king of Babylon, son of Cyrus, king of (all) countries" attested in *Camb.* 36, 42, 72, 98, and with reversed order in *Camb.* 16; the other is found in *Camb.* 46 and 81 as "first year of Cambyses, king of Babylon, when his father Cyrus was king of (all) countries". Two important restrictions can be made on the basis of the evidence so far available: Cambyses is mentioned as co-regent only for the first nine months of the first year of Cyrus,[5] and he is recognized as such only in tablets coming from Babylon and its surroundings and from Sippar, but not from Uruk.

It seems that Cambyses resided in Sippar from the fifth year of Cyrus onward, i.e., from the moment when Cyrus appointed Gubaru as satrap of Babylonia and Eber-nāri (see p. 544). This is established by a few texts from Sippar that mention the *sipiru*-official, the *ša rēši* official and the

[1] Cf. Posener, *La première domination*; and Kienitz, *Politische Geschichte*.
[2] It would be interesting to find out what "Elamite attire" meant specifically in this instance in view of the well-known relationship between Elamite and Persian dress. Cf. also Porada, *Ancient Iran*, p 158.
[3] The death of Cambyses is recorded in Herodotus III. 62 and 64 in a much-discussed manner; see Schaeder, "Des eigenen Todes sterben", pp. 24–36; and Galling, p. 48.
[4] This is the text *Camb.* 426, for which see San Nicolò, *Prosopographie*, p. 54.
[5] Pointed out by San Nicolo, *Prosopographie*, pp. 51ff., against Dubberstein, "The Chronology of Cyrus and Cambyses", pp. 417–19.

purkullu (i.e., seal cutter) of the crown prince.[1] Though this might be mere coincidence, it could also indicate that Cambyses, after being replaced by Gubaru, had to move from Babylon to Sippar.

The main historical importance of the incident in the Chronicle lies in the fact that in the New Year's ritual of Babylon Cambyses, though expressly called son of the king, acts as legitimate king of Babylon. Obviously, as the wording of the Cylinder inscription suggests (see p. 549), the "proclamation" of Cyrus must also have served the purpose of installing his son as king of Babylon. The incident itself might offer the explanation of why the co-regency of Cambyses was so short-lived. There were, possibly, other such episodes which prompted Cyrus to discontinue this arrangement. However, he waited until the fourth year of his rule over Babylonia before he appointed Gubaru as satrap, replacing Cambyses.

(C) Later Achaemenian kings

Mesopotamian sources provide very little written evidence for Darius I (521–486 B.C.) – apart from the mention of his name in the Uruk kinglist (see pp. 532f.) and in date formulae. Of more interest is a fragment of the Akkadian version of the *res gestae* of Darius I, the Behistun inscription, found in Babylon on a diorite block of which 26 lines in two columns are still partly legible. They correspond to lines 55 to 72 of the original.[2] The importance of the fragment lies in its very existence and original location. Apparently, the full wording of that inscription of Darius I was made public in the capital of Babylon and in the language of that country.[3] Another example of the same practice can be found in the fragment of an Aramaic translation coming from Elephantine in Egypt.

A badly damaged chronicle fragment in the British Museum[4] contains in line 7 the words "⌜son⌝ of Darius, king of king[s]". The remainder

---

[1] These are the pertinent texts: *Cyr.* 199, 270, 325 and 364 (see Olmstead, *History*, p. 87, n. 4).

[2] Text in Weissbach, *Babylonische Miscellen*, pp. 25ff. and pl. 9 as No. 10. [See now Voigtlander, 63–5. (Ed.)] It contains only a few additions to the Akkadian version as known from Behistun. A second fragment of this or a similar stela has been found in Babylon but it seems that the object (Bab. 41. 446) was lost later on, see Koldewey, *Königsburgen* II, pp. 23ff. Its text corresponds to Behistun §52, 67 and 68. [See now Voigtlander, 63–5. (Ed.)]

[3] This is expressly mentioned in the Behistun inscription (§70): "Afterwards this inscription I sent off everywhere among the provinces" (translation of Kent, *Old Persian*, p. 132). For the Aramaic translation cf. Schaeder, *Iranische Beiträge* I, p. 64; Sachau, *Aramäische Papyrus und Ostraka*.

[4] BM 36304, published by S. Smith in *CT* XXXVII. 22 (old number 80-6-17, 30).

BABYLONIAN EVIDENCE

of the text (17 partly preserved lines on the obverse, 13 on the reverse) is too damaged to offer more than a word or two here and there. Its content is quite in line with the characteristic phraseology of documents in the chronicle style: military events, the festival of Bēl in Borsippa, the behaviour of the Euphrates, etc. The use of the late and literary designation *ummān Ḫanê*, "Hana people", referring here to a foreign people or army to the northwest is, however, noteworthy.[1]

An excerpt from a later chronicle gives us an event of the 14th year of Artaxerxes III (358–338 B.C.). The text is well preserved and runs as follows:[2]

Fourteenth year of Umasu whose (royal) name is Artakšatsu: In the month Tašrītu, the booty which the king had made in Sidon[3] [came] to Babylon and to Susa. In the same month, on the 13th day, a few prisoners of war from among them entered Babylon, on the 16th day beautiful women[4] captives from Sidon which the king had dispatched to Babylon (arrived), on the very day (of their arrival) they went into the royal palace.

The tablet not only illustrates the lasting political importance of the city of Babylon, which is mentioned on the same level as Susa, the other capital of the empire, but it shows also that the chroniclers were still at work in the last third of the Achaemenian rule in Babylonia. Hence, new cuneiform fragments can well be expected to elucidate the periods that are at present still quite obscure.

Artaxerxes III (Ochus) is furthermore mentioned in the datings of astronomical observation texts which are also attested for the preceding periods of Darius II (423–405 B.C.) and Artaxerxes II Mnemon (404–359 B.C.).[5] For a characteristic passage see the subscript: "Observations of Jupiter from the 18th year of ^{m}Ár-šú ša ^{m}Ar-tak-šat-su LUGAL MU-šú SA$_4$-u (Aršu who is called Artaxerxes, the king) to the 13th year of ^{m}Ú-ma-su

---

[1] The Chronicle dealing with the Diadochi (Smith, *Babylonian Historical Texts*, pl. xv and p. 140: 16) mentions likewise the [LÚ] *Ḫa-ni-i* "whom the king Philippus [had placed] between [...] to keep guard". From the latest kinglist published by Sachs and Wiseman, "A Babylonian King List of the Hellenistic Period", we learn that Seleucus I was slain in the country Ḫani (*ina* KUR *Ḫa-ni-i* GA[z] line 8), somewhere in northwestern Asia Minor (see *ibid.*, p. 206).

[2] The text was published first by J. N. Strassmaier in 1893 in *Actes du VIIIe Congrès Internationale des Orientalistes* (2nd Part, Sem. Section B) Beilage, pp. 31ff., No. 28; cf. also Smith, *Babylonian Historical Texts*, pp. 148ff.

[3] For this event which took place in 345 B.C., see Olmstead, *History*, pp. 436ff. in the chapter "Reconquest of Phoenicia".

[4] The logogram SIG stands here clearly for the more complex sign SIG$_5$ as is a frequent practice in late texts, such as A.SIG for A.SIG$_5$ in certain Neo-Assyrian texts and in the Hellenistic kinglist cited above in n. 1 above.

[5] Cf. J. N. Strassmaier in *ZA* VIII (1892), pp. 200ff., also Kugler, *Sternkunde und Sterndienst in Babel* I, pp. 80ff.

ša ᵐ*Ar-tak-šat-su* LUGAL MU-*šú na-bu-ú* (Umasu who is called Artaxerxes, the king), a copy [from Babylon]."[1]

I terminate this enumeration with a reference to small fragments of black marble found in Babylon in 1906.[2] They are in Old Persian and Elamite and only one of them (No. 13) can be assigned with any certainty, to Artaxerxes II. They contribute nothing.

(D) Usurper kings

At least twice, if not more often, the continuity of Achaemenian rule in Babylonia was interrupted by usurpers. We know of them either through the Behistun inscription of Darius I and from datings of legal documents or from the latter alone. For the possibility of one of these native usurpers being mentioned in a kinglist, see the suggestion made above (pp. 533f.) concerning Nidin⟨tu⟩-Bēl.

The first usurper went under the name of Brdya (also called Smerdis and Gaumata), the brother of Cambyses. He is mentioned in dates of cuneiform texts as early as one month after his rebellion; see for evidence the data presented in Parker and Dubberstein, *Babylonian Chronology*, pp. 14ff. Texts dated in his name are attested from the middle of April 522 to 20 September 522.

In October of that year a certain Nidintu-Bēl, son of Aniri', assumed the name Nebuchadnezzar (III) and texts mainly from Babylon, but also from Borsippa and Sippar mention him in their dates up to 8 December.[3] On the 13th of that month he was defeated at the crossing of the Tigris near Babylon and eventually killed by Darius I (see p. 539). The Behistun inscription reports on this usurper in §§ 16, 19 and 20 in a way that suggests that Darius himself participated in the suppression of the rebellion in Babylon.

A year later, while Darius was in Media, rebellion broke out again in Babylon; a certain Araḫa (Old Persian: Arakha, Elamite: Ḥarakka) whom the Behistun inscription, § 49, identifies as an Armenian (the son of Haldita) in his turn assumed the name Nebuchadnezzar (IV). He was recognized as king mainly in Uruk but also in Sippar (two texts), Babylon (two texts), and Borsippa (one text) for less than three months

---

[1] *LBAT* 1394. 4. ii; both Aršu and Umasu recur in *LBAT* 1397. ii. 1 and 17; and in the "Diary Texts" *LBAT* 167, 171, 190. See also pp. 581f.

[2] See *MDOG* xxxii; published in Wetzel, Schmidt and Mallwitz, *Das Babylon der Spätzeit*, pl. 26c and presented by Weissbach, *Babylonische Miscellen*, pp. 48ff., Nos 1 to 7, 10(?), 11 and 12.

[3] See also Cameron, "Darius and Xerxes", pp. 316ff.

until his capture by Persian forces under Vindafarna on 27 November 521 B.C.[1]

After the death of Darius I, Xerxes' (486–465 B.C.) conflict with Babylon was highlighted by the appearance of two usurpers. They are attested in a small group of texts coming from Borsippa (6 tablets) and by one each from Babylon and Dilbat.[2] Their names, both quite typical and apolitical, are given as Bēl-šimanni and Šamaš-erība. Since each ruled less than one year the month names of their dates suggest that Bēl-šimanni may have been the first, but it is possible that they assumed royal status in different years.

From the change in Xerxes' titulary after his fourth year, G. G. Cameron deduces that these uprisings in Babylonia occurred between the second and the fifth years of that king, i.e., 484 and 481 B.C.[3]

Although the rise and fall of usurpers of the throne is well attested for both Assyria and Babylonia, we learn about them only accidentally, mainly when their names appear in kinglists. The frequency of such events in the Babylonian satrapy is worth noting. Of course, rebellions did occur also in Egypt,[4] but there they seem to have been more substantial and serious than in Babylonia, perhaps because of Egypt's geopolitical situation.

If there are any conclusions to be drawn in the face of the extreme paucity of evidence, then it might be suggested that the two usurpers who saw fit to assume the name of the last glorious and militarily powerful king of the Chaldean empire, Nebuchadnezzar, represented a political – or even nationalistic – reaction against Persian rule,[5] while the two other rebellions were sparked off by religious unrest, that is,

---

[1] For details see Poebel, "Chronology of Darius' First Year"; Olmstead, "Darius and his Behistun Inscription"; Hinz, "Dar erste Jahr des Grosskönigs Dareios"; Hallock, "The 'One Year' of Darius I". As an Assyriologist, let me inject a note of caution into the elaborate attempts of modern historians to relate recorded facts to the pronouncements of Darius. The boast of having defeated a number of enemies in the opposite ends of the world within one year is also attested for Esarhaddon (see R. Borger, *Die Inschriften Asarhaddons Königs von Assyrien* [Graz, 1956], p. 48), as well as in the newly discovered stela of Adad-Nirari III (see S. Page, "A Stela of Adad-Nirari III and Nergal-ereš from Tell Al Rimah", *Iraq* xxx [1968], pp. 142: 4), and could well represent a *topos* in this genre of texts. Note a new theory about the extent and importance of the Babylonian rebellion under Araḫa presented by Schedl, "Nabuchodonosor, Arpakšad und Darius". Also see Cameron, "Darius and Xerxes in Babylonia", especially pp. 318ff.; Parker and Dubberstein, *Babylonian Chronology*, p. 16; Böhl, "Prätendenten zur Anfangszeit des Darius".

[2] See Cameron, *Op. cit.*, p. 325, n. 49.

[3] See Cameron, *Op. cit.*, pp. 319ff.

[4] Cf. Kienitz, pp. 67ff.

[5] The suggestion was made by Böhl in *BiOr* xxv (1968), p. 152, that the Nebuchadnezzar who only in the Behistun inscription is called "son of Nabonidus" was actually assuming the name of a son of that unfortunate king.

if the clash between Xerxes and the priesthood of Esagila of which so much is made in Classical sources did evoke a popular reaction.

Satraps

The names of only a few satraps of Babylonia have as yet appeared in cuneiform sources; others are mentioned by Greek historians. The two best known are one Gubaru, who was in office from the fourth year of Cyrus to the fifth year of Cambyses (534–525 B.C.),[1] and Uštani (called Hystanes in Herodotus vii 77), from the first year of Darius I (521 B.C.) on.[2] The title LÚ . EN . NAM DIN . TIR^{ki} (E^{ki}) u (KUR) *Ebernāri*, "governor of Babylon(ia) and (the country) Beyond-the-river", was borne by Gubaru, and he is last mentioned as such on 20 September 525 B.C.[3] Uštani, designated by the same title, is twice attested in dated texts (*Dar.* 27: 3 of the first year of Darius, and *Dar.* 82: 2 of the third year), while in *BRM* I. 101. 4 (undated) the title is written in Akkadian LÚ *pi-qit-tu* E^{ki} *u* URU E-*bir*-ÍD.

It should be mentioned in this context that the satrap of the province called Eber-nāri, which was split off from Uštani's satrapy Babylonia in a reorganization of the satrapies of the empire under Darius, is indirectly attested in a cuneiform text of the 20th year of Darius I, 502 B.C.[4] The presence of an official of the satrap of Eber-nāri in Babylon becomes more meaningful when one links it to another passage of a similar nature dated to the eighth year of Cambyses. In *Camb.* 344:3, a text which as a purely administrative document does not indicate the place where it was written (Babylon or Sippar are most likely), we find mention of the *sipiru*-officials of the satrap of Egypt (*sipiri ša* EN . NAM *ša Mi-ṣir*). The satraps apparently had their representatives at the royal court in order to be informed about the politics of the central administration.

[1] The tablet *YOS* VII. 137 (dated in the last day of the third year of Cambyses), mentions in line 22 a son of the satrap Gubaru called *Na-bu-ú-gu*. For Gubaru before he became satrap, see Schwenzner, "Gobryas", pp. 45f.

[2] For the administrative arrangements during the time from the accession of Cyrus and the installation of Cambyses as king of Babylon to the appointment of Gubaru, see pp. 558–9, where it is shown that the Nabonidus-appointed official called *šakin māti* remained in charge.

[3] *TCL* VIII. 168. For reasons suggesting that the gap between Gubaru and Uštani is but accidental and that Gubaru was in charge until Darius I appointed Uštani, see San Nicolò, *Prosopographie*, pp. 57ff.

[4] *VAS* IV. 152. 25; a witness is identified in this text as a servant (*ardu*) of *Tatt[annu š]a* LÚ . NAM E-*ber nāri*, who appears as Tatnai in Ezra 6. 6 and Herodotus VII. 63; cf. Olmstead, "Tettanai", p. 46.

An entirely new designation of the satrapy of Babylonia is encountered in the archives of the Murašû family, which date approximately between 455 and 405 B.C. and come from Nippur. There we meet another Gubaru[1] who is called LÚ. NAM ša KUR URI^{ki}, i.e. "satrap of the country of Akkadī".[2] The texts date to the third (*PBS* 11/1. 72), fourth (*ibid.* 96) and fifth years (*BE* x. 101 and 118) of the king. However, the same person appears without his title yet obviously as a prominent official in other documents of the archive, whose range of date slightly exceeds that of the tablets just referred to. The earliest of them is *PBS* 11/1. 70 of the third year of Darius II (Kislimu 22nd[?]), January, 420 B.C., and the latest (*PBS* 11/1. 133 of the seventh year (Ululu 21st) of the same king, September, 417 B.C.

There can hardly be any doubt as to the importance of this "new" Gubaru. His place of office is the bāb Gubara ("gate of Gubara")[3] where judges sit and *sipiru*-officials act;[4] he has officials attached to him called *patiprasu*,[5] *sipiru*,[6] and *daššia*,[7] as well as other persons simply called *ardu*.[8]

The existence of two satraps with the name Gubaru is not at all surprising because this Persian name occurs quite frequently.[9] More important seems to be the change in titulary, or rather, the change in the designation of the satrapy in which Nippur was situated and where the satrap apparently resided. One could speculate that an administrative reorganization of the country occurred after the Xerxes incident in Babylon. Since the title of this king as given in the cuneiform legal and administrative texts after the incident no longer mentions Babylon (or Babylonia), the possibility arises that a new name was used to designate a new administrative unit. After all, as early as the Sargonid period, learned Assyrian scribes used to refer to Babylonia as *Māt Akkadī*.[10]

[1] Already noticed by Schwenzner, "Gobryas", p. 247, n. 2, and San Nicolò, *Prosopographie*, p. 64, n. 1.
[2] *PBS* 11/1. 72 lower edge, *ibid.*, 96. 16, and *BE* x. 101. 25, and LÚ. NAM ša KUR (copy LÚ) URI^{ki} in *PBS* 11/1. 96. 16, also, damaged, in *BE* x. 118. 14 and *PBS* 11/1. 105. 13.
[3] *BE* x. 84. 20, 108. 25 and 128. 14; *PBS* 11/1. 23. 9.
[4] *BE* x. 128. 27.
[5] *BE* x. 97. 17, 22; for this official cf. Eilers, *Iranische Beamtennamen*, pp. 10ff., 24, etc.
[6] *PBS* 11/1. 70. 15, 21; 72. 33; 133. 28; *BE* x. 101. 25, 128. 18; for this official cf. Cardascia, *Les archives des Murašû*, p. 15 (with previous literature); also Ebeling, "Die Rüstung", p. 212, and Lewy, "Problems of the Behistun Inscription", pp. 191ff.
[7] *BE* x. 91. 19, 28; for daššia see *CAD* and *AHw*. s.v.; linguistic provenience unknown.
[8] *BE* x. 84. 5 and 9; 85. 15 and 22; 124. 14; *PBS* 11/1. 127. 17; *TuM* 11–111. 190 upper edge.
[9] As indicated by the name index in Olmstead, *History*, p. 545b, s.v. Gobryas.
[10] For this interpretation cf. Landsberger, *Brief des Bischofs*, pp. 38ff., also *ibid.* notes 56, 57. For an earlier occurrence cf. Brinkman, *Political History*, note 1975.

CUNEIFORM TEXTS

Without being actually given the title LÚ.NAM, i.e. satrap, the personage called in the Murašû archives Artaremu must have had that function in Babylonia.[1] We know from Greek sources (cf. Olmstead, *History*, p. 312) of a Menostanes, son of Artarius, who was the king's brother and satrap of Babylon; he appears in the Murašû archives as ᵐ*Ma-nu-uš-ta-nu* LÚ.DUMU.É.LUGAL A *ša* ᵐ*Ar-ta-ri-me*.[2] The extant references to Manuštanu mention only his servants (ardu)[3] and his dealings with the family Murašû. Those for Artaremu, however, list his databara (who has an Akkadian name),[4] his sipiru-official,[5] and his servant (ardu).[6] This array of officials, which is partly the same as that of Gubaru the satrap of *Māt-Akkadī*, shows that Artaremu was actually satrap of that same province and ruled, as the dates of these texts tell us, from 431 to 424 B.C. Clearly Artaremu (attested 431–424 B.C.) preceded Gubaru (420–416 B.C.) in office.

We may conclude this section with an enumeration of the Persian officials to whom the Greek sources refer in one way or another as satraps of Babylon. There is first Zopyrus, allegedly killed during a rebellion in Babylon (see Olmstead, *History*, p. 236). The others are Megapanes (*ibid.* p. 240), Tritantaechmes (see p. 532, n. 1), son of Artabazus (*ibid.* p. 293); and Astaries, brother of Artaxerxes I (*ibid.* p. 312).

The Fate of Babylon

Some time during the first years of the reign of Xerxes (486–465 B.C.) a rebellion occurred in Babylonia. Our only direct evidence is found in the few tablets mentioning two native usurpers, Bēl-šimanni and Šamaš-erība (see p. 562).[7] Several Greek historians, especially Ctesias, provide us with stories about Xerxes entering "the tomb of Belitanes" in Babylon and committing some sacrilege; about a rebellion in which Zopyrus, the satrap, was killed; also about a punitive expedition under Megabyzus, who conquered the city, destroyed its walls and its sanctuaries, especially the famous temple tower, and took away the gold

---

[1] See W. Eilers in *AfO* IX (1934), p. 332b.
[2] *BE* X. 84. 4 (= *TuM* II–III. 202). For the logogram DUMU.É.LUGAL as a designation of the crown prince, see Benveniste, *Titres et Noms Propres*, pp. 23ff.
[3] E.g. *BE* IX. 83. 9; 88. 19ff. and X. 84. 4, 8.
[4] *BE* IX. 82. 32; 84. 11 (= *TuM* II–III. 202. 11); 88. 18; *BE* IX. 107. 16.
[5] *BE* IX. 48. 7 (= *TuM* II–III. 144).
[6] *BE* IX. 72. 11.
[7] Note that Šamaš-erība is even given the title *šar Bābili u mātāti* in a tablet of the Böhl Collection; cf. Böhl, "Prätendenten zur Zeit des Xerxes".

statue of Bēl.¹ The reports about Xerxes "visiting" the main sanctuary of Babylon are now usually combined with the statement in his *Daiva* inscription in which he asserts that where the false gods (*daiva*) had been worshipped before, there he worshipped Ahura Mazda.² The basic tenor of the Greek reports on Xerxes' politics is confirmed by the stern measures following the rebellion in Egypt (485 B.C., after the defeat at Marathon) and the reconquest of that satrapy, especially the measures directed against religious institutions (see Kienitz, pp. 67ff.).

With regard to the Mesopotamian evidence for the above mentioned incidents, four points can be made. First, there are texts bearing in their dates the names of short-lived usurpers. Second, changes in the titulary of the Achaemenian king, revealed by date formulae, seem to coincide with the mentioned events. Third, there is for a time thereafter a scarcity of cuneiform texts from Babylon proper. Last, when cuneiform texts from Babylon reappear after the conquest by Alexander the Great, Esagila was obviously in ruins and beyond repair, as shown by the information that its rubble had to be removed at great expense.

The temporal relationship between the usurper kings and Xerxes' intervention has been examined by G. G. Cameron.³ The changes in the titulary of Xerxes present themselves as follows. During the first months of his first year Xerxes is given the traditional title "king of Babylon, king of all countries". Thereafter the king is called "king of Persia and the Medes" in texts beginning with the fifth month of his first year.⁴ Then, in texts ranging from the eighth month of the first year to the fourth month of the fourth year, there is added to the same title the old "king of Babylon and all the countries".⁵ Beginning with a text

---

[1] The Greek sources (assembled in Olmstead, *History*, pp. 236ff.) about the several rebellions in Babylon and the resulting punitive actions of the Persian overlords diverge considerably both as to factual content and date. For the destruction of Esagila see also Baumgartner, "Herodots Babylonische und Assyrische Nachrichten", especially p. 71, n. 18 and p. 100, n. 152. Secondary elaborations of writers primarily intent on offering "interesting" stories and basic misunderstandings of the mores of the country greatly diminish the value of these reports. Here belong the "tomb of Belitanes", whatever this formulation might actually refer to, and the colossal golden statue – weighing twelve talents (i.e., 800 pounds) – of the god Bēl which was carried off by the Persians and melted down. However, as far as we know, Mesopotamian images were always human-sized if not smaller and hardly made of solid gold. A less sensational and therefore probably correct bit of information is that the satrapy of Babylonia was united with that called "Assyria" and that "Syria" (probably Eber-nāri) was made a new satrapy on that occasion. See, however, p. 564.

[2] For a translation of this text cf. Herzfeld, *Altpersische Inschriften*, No. 14, pp. 27ff.; also Kent, *Old Persian*, pp. 150ff. and Pritchard, pp. 316ff.

[3] Cameron, "Darius and Xerxes", pp. 319ff.   [4] Strassmaier, *VIIIe Congrès*, No. 19.

[5] *VAS* IV, 193; *BE* VIII. 119; *PSBA* IX (1887), p. 238; Evetts, *Appendix*. Nos 3, 4; *BRM* I. 85; Strassmaier, *op. cit.*, No. 20; *TuM* II–III. 98.

dated to the fourth month of the fifth year of Xerxes,[1] he, as well as all subsequent Achaemenian kings ruling in Babylon, is referred to solely as *šar matāti*, "king of all countries". It is obvious that changes occurred there and then which affected the status of Babylon and Babylonia. It is possible that the change in name of the satrapy pointed out above (p. 564) occurred at the same time, even though the evidence comes from some 70 years after the event.

As to the scarcity of cuneiform texts coming from the city of Babylon after Xerxes' fifth year,[2] one can say only that in general a much smaller number of texts is available from the reign of Xerxes than from the period of his predecessor Darius I, and that only one of them (third year)[3] comes from Babylon proper,[4] the others coming from Sippar, Borsippa and Nippur. The evidence is therefore not as clear-cut as one would like. Whether such statistics have historical implications can only be revealed by tablets from museum collections still awaiting publication.

As to the ruins of the Esagila after the Achaemenian period, not only is this accumulation of rubble mentioned twice in the "Chronicle concerning the Diadochi",[5] but we learn from texts of the time of Alexander the Great that a considerable amount of silver owed as tithes by private persons was dedicated out of piety to the "removal of the rubble of Esagila".[6] This illustrates the seriousness of the situation; possibly there was an Achaemenian prohibition against the rebuilding of the sanctuary after its destruction under Xerxes. The religious freedom brought about by the Greek conqueror spurred the pious to dedicate money to this first step in the rebuilding of the sanctuary. That the temple had to rely on private initiative might suggest that Xerxes had severely curtailed if not blocked the sources of income of Esagila, exactly as Cambyses had done and Xerxes himself did to temples in Egypt in 485 B.C.[7]

[1] Evetts, *Appendix*, No. 5.
[2] For an enumeration see Cameron, "Darius and Xerxes", p. 320, n. 33.
[3] Strassmaier, *op. cit.*, No. 24.
[4] For conditions in Babylon after Xerxes see F. Wetzel, "Babylon zur Zeit Herodots", and "Babylon bei den klassischen Schriftstellern ausser Herodot".
[5] Smith, *Texts*, pl. 15 and pp. 140ff., lines 5 and r. 15.
[6] *CT* IV. 39c = *CT* XLIX. 5 and *CT* XLIX. 6.
[7] See Kienitz, pp. 60, 69.

II. ECONOMIC AND SOCIAL CONDITIONS

Except for the relatively few aspects we have discussed – the dating of individual kings' reigns, the titulary referring to the Persian overlords, and the provenience of documents – the value of the cuneiform legal and administrative texts for the investigation of the Mesopotamian evidence for Achaemenian rule is difficult to assess.

It is of course only to be expected that legal documents would undergo changes in form and phraseology and reflect other developments in scribal and court practice brought about by the conquest and by the serious social and economic upheavals of a change-over from political independence to the status of a province – which province, moreover, as a satrapy within the confines of an empire, extended over a much larger area than any Babylon-centred kingdom had ever held or even known of before. In the rather considerable number of administrative texts, predominantly ledgers, receipts, lists, etc. which originated in the temple organizations of the Chaldean empire, the change of political status was presumably reflected to a much lesser extent.

But to investigate thoroughly the problems outlined above on the basis of a well-documented study of these tablets would require years of concentrated research. What I can give here is merely an impressionistic presentation of my interest in many of the documents, an interest whose orientation is chiefly lexical.

I will begin with a succinct survey of the rich text material at our disposal. Whatever is available represents, however, but a fraction of what is stored in the museums of three continents, Europe, America and Asia. Many more tablets than are here listed are still unpublished and will most likely remain so in the foreseeable future. The reason for this pessimistic prediction is that such tablets are individually rather uninteresting, at times quite difficult to understand because of our lack of knowledge of their specific background, and more often than not unrewarding as to results. Their very number deters any but the most tenacious scholars willing to invest much work in an undertaking which decidedly does not promise sensational insights.

Published texts coming from scientific excavations are from only two important sites, Nippur and Ur. The Nippur tablets which belong to our period and were excavated by the first expeditions to that site come

ECONOMIC AND SOCIAL CONDITIONS

mainly from the archives of the Murašû family.¹ They are published in *BE* IX and X; *PBS* II/1; and *TuM* NF II–III; and are kept in the University Museum of the University of Pennsylvania (Philadelphia), and in the Frau Professor Hilprecht Collection of Babylonian Antiquities of the Universität Jena. However, a considerable number of tablets (200 to 300) of the Murašû archives lie still unpublished in the University Museum and in the Archaeological Museum of Istanbul. Other Nippur texts of the period are published in *BE* VIII (72 texts). The tablets found during the Oriental Institute excavations in Nippur have not been published.²

From Ur we have more than 70 tablets which H. H. Figulla published in *UET* IV. Whether this represents all the texts of our period that were excavated in Ur by Sir Leonard Woolley remains uncertain. From excavations at Kish comes a very small group of pertinent documents, in fact only two were published by S. Langdon.³

---

¹ The site where all these tablets were found at Nippur is indicated by Hilprecht, *Explorations*, pp. 408ff. as the area on the west mound, marked "VII" on his map, p. 350. This is about 100 to 200 yards to the NW of the place where the large number of Kassite tablets dealing with the activities of the palace administration were excavated.

² As far as dated texts of this excavation are concerned, about 35 tablets are clearly of the Achaemenian period. It so happens that the "extensive and important-looking house" excavated in TA Level I (cf. McCown and Haines, *Nippur I*, p. 71) was the residence of the *šandabakku* (GÚ.EN.NA) official of Nippur. Three of the nine texts found on the level of that house (see the list, *op. cit.*, p. 76) mention that official (1 N 133, 2 NT 330 and 2 NT 29 – as well as 2 NT 93). The latest of these tablets date in the thirteenth year of Xerxes (473/472 B.C.) and are therefore only some twenty years older than the earliest tablets of the Murašû archives. The latter, however, no longer know of a *šandabakku* official although he can be traced back in Nippur texts to the Old Babylonian period, i.e., for more than a millennium. For this break in the tradition, cf. the explanation proposed pp. 576ff. The administrators of Nippur are now called *paqud ša Nippur* (*BE* IX. 19. 15 and *passim*), also abbreviated to LÙ *pa*, and they seem to have officiated at the city gates (for the pertinent residential quarters). Their relationship to the *šaknu ša Nippur* (*BE* IX. 23. 17 and *passim*) remains uncertain. Much work remains to be done on these texts concerning persons and offices. For a promising beginning for such research cf. Dandamayev, "Bagasarū *ganzabara*".

³ See bibliography. Two groups of texts of the period under discussion come from small excavations. The first is of no importance: Langdon, "Tablets from Barghuthiat". The second happens to be quite informative. A small group of legal texts was found in Syria – in Neirab near Aleppo – and published by Dhorme, "Les tablettes de Neirab". In their date formulae these tablets recognize as the overlord of the city Niribi first Nebuchadnezzar (II), then Neriglissar and then Nabonidus. The last text dated to Nabonidus is of his 16th year, to be exact of 5 January 539 B.C.; the first tablet to acknowledge Persian domination is of the first year of Cambyses (name of the month destroyed), i.e., of 529/528 B.C. In it the king is called "king of Babylon NUN^ki" as e.g. in *Cyr.* 358, and "of (all) countries". The later texts of Cambyses from Neirab and those of Darius I use the title "king of (all) countries". However, none of the Darius texts bears a complete date. The importance of this small find is that it attests to a continuation of the subjugation of Syria, i.e., of Eber-nāri from the time of the Chaldean kings to that of the Achaemenids. The gap of ten years may well be accidental, since the general coverage is rather widely spaced. In *JNES* IV (1945), p. 45, n. 22. A. Goetze suggests that the Neirab text which is dated in the first year of Nebuchadnezzar and written in Babylon refers to the fourth rather than the second king of that name.

BABYLONIAN EVIDENCE

Published tablets of the Achaemenian period coming from official excavations are vastly outnumbered by texts which have come into the various museums from undisclosed sources. The largest group of such material is in the British Museum, and was copied and chronologically arranged by J. N. Strassmaier.[1] His edition contains somewhat more than 1,400 texts, with only a few undated ones. The originals seem to come mainly from Babylon, also from Sippar, with a scattering of texts from all over Babylonia, from Ur to Akkadī. An appendix by B. T. A. Evetts (Leipzig, 1892) offers four tablets of the same provenience dated during the first five years of Xerxes. In the *Actes du VIIIe Congrès International des Orientalistes* J. N. Strassmaier produced seven more Xerxes and nine Artaxerxes I tablets.[2]

Next in number come the texts published by A. Ungnad. They amount to about 430 tablets of our period. Their provenience is varied.[3] This, however, is not so in the case of two volumes containing tablets which come definitely from Uruk (though acquired from dealers) and fall into the period under study.[4] It should be noted in this context that many more Uruk tablets were published in the series issued by the Louvre,[5] the Pierpont Morgan Library,[6] the Nies Babylonian Collection in New Haven,[7] the Berliner Museum,[8] and the University of California, Berkeley,[9] not to speak of those scattered in scholarly periodicals, etc.

Texts of exactly the same type were actually excavated in Uruk by the Deutsche Orient Gesellschaft.[10] They, however, do not belong to the Achaemenian period.

In Part B of the Bibliography are listed all publications, large and

---

[1] See bibliography.

[2] *CT* II (1896) one text; *CT* II (1898) seven texts; *CT* XLIV (1963) ten texts; and 5 R 68 No. 2.

[3] See bibliography. Other tablets from that museum were published by Pohl (see bibliography); 47 of them belong to the Achaemenian period. For a small group of texts (Darius I, Artaxerxes) found in Babylon see Koldewey, *Königsburgen* II, p. 24. A small group (*AnOr* IX. 20–33) comes from excavations in Uruk (1928/29) and belongs to a body of texts published in H. Freydank, *Spätbabylonische Wirtschaftstexte aus Uruk* (Berlin, 1971); the corpus contains 23 tablets of our period.

[4] See bibliography, Tremayne and Dougherty.

[5] *TCL* XIII, with 80 texts.

[6] *BRM* I, 26 texts.

[7] *BIN* I and II, 24 texts.

[8] Expecially *AnOr* VIII and IX, about 50 texts.

[9] *UCP* IX/1, 159 texts.

[10] The texts and fragments excavated at Uruk in 1954–55 (now in Heidelberg and Baghdad) are very similar in content to the Uruk texts already published; they antedate the Achaemenian period. I owe this information to a letter of Dr H. Hunger dated 19 June 1968.

ECONOMIC AND SOCIAL CONDITIONS

small, of legal and administrative documents of our period known to me.

Only through patient, detailed work will it be possible one day to assign to archives or other groupings on a prosopographic basis those numerous published tablets which are broken and lack exact dates or indications as to place of origin. This will be all the more necessary as we are approaching a phase of diminishing returns from excavations. Tablets of the late period have much less of a chance to survive destruction by human activities and especially by climatic conditions than those safely buried in the deeper layers of mounds. Wherever large accumulations of debris from later periods, such as from Seleucid, Parthian, Sasanian and Islamic settlements, protect tablets of the Achaemenian period, large-scale excavations are needed, but regrettably we have reason to entertain less and less hope of such work being undertaken in the foreseeable future.

There is another point to be mentioned in this catalogue of woes. The fact that cuneiform tablets diminish in number rather rapidly after the death of Darius I can be blamed not only on the consequences of the Achaemenian rule after Xerxes, but to a large extent on the increasing use of leather, parchment and even papyrus-like writing materials.[1] The shift from Akkadian (with interspersed Sumerian expressions and legal formulae) to Aramaic as the language used for private legal agreements was neither consistent nor universal throughout the region in which clay and Akkadian had been the traditional vehicles for such transactions. Up to the period of the Arsacid kings (after 250 B.C.) clay tablets with legal and administrative transactions are extant though quite rare, and in certain enclaves, mainly those connected with sanctuaries, particularly in Uruk, the old practices were maintained well into the Seleucid period.

To characterize the social and economic structure of the Achaemenian period in Babylonia in the light of these cuneiform documents – which, as stated before, is feasible at present solely on a rather superficial level – I

---

[1] As new writing materials for non-cuneiform script in the late period in Mesopotamia are attested leather, parchment and a papyrus-like material. The latter is known only from Assyria (cf. B. Landsberger, *OLZ* XVII (1914), col. 265), the former from both Babylonia and Assyria (the imported rolls were called *niaru*, the inscribed ones *magallatu*, cf. Leichty in *Studies Oppenheim*, p. 151, n. 14, also D. J. Wiseman, *Iraq* XVII (1955), p. 12, n. 118). From there we know of documents written on leather (KUŠ *giṭṭû*, KUŠ *šipištu*) and of the "guild" of parchment-makers (*magallata-karranu*, see p. 579, n. 7) in the Nippur of Muraŝû. For the use of leather as writing material by the Persian kings, cf. Driver, *Aramaic Documents*, pp. 1f.

should like to offer a number of propositions. I am fully aware that not only new material but a better understanding of the texts already known is bound to affect these propositions in many and often decisive ways.

(1) I cannot detect a pronounced break or even a definite shift in the structure of Babylonian society and its economic basis that can be related to the Achaemenian domination, at least nothing comparable to the gap between the Neo-Babylonian period, the Chaldean, and that which preceded it. The private legal documents and the administrative tablets (mainly from the temple in Sippar) continue in form and substance until the eclipse of Babylon after the fifth year of Xerxes.[1] The social and economic climate of the Chaldean documents which I tried to characterize in my *Letters from Mesopotamia* (pp. 42ff.) obtains in the main. Suffice it to repeat here a few pertinent key points that stress the contrast with the preceding periods: lower social status for women; slaves no longer adopted to assure childless persons' subsistence in old age, but allowed to work on their own to produce an income for their masters; a trend toward gentility and enlarged role of the family; free use of silver as a means of payment (not only as a standard); large-scale overland trade in the hands of private persons linked with similar organizations in distant lands, even as far as Egypt and the Ionian trade settlements.[2]

Only where social institutions are concerned, can one ascribe innovation to effects of the Persian domination. The contexts in which reference to such changes occurs are stereotyped and not very revealing. Although the evidence is thus indirect and rather slim, it cannot be ignored. My starting point is a stipulation which appears in a number of contracts dating to the Achaemenian and the subsequent Seleucid periods, which record the sale of slaves and slave girls. In these the seller assumes guarantee that the individual sold does not belong to the several categories of persons who legally cannot be the object of such a transaction. In other words, the seller assures the buyer that he is acquiring a *bona fide* slave. By enumerating the designations of the several classes of people who cannot be bought and sold, the stipulations conveniently provide us with a complete picture of the stratification of Mesopotamian society in the Achaemenian and later periods.

It now falls to me to discuss these designations, some of which are obvious while others are difficult to define.

---

[1] On the conservative nature of the legal practices of the period see Petschow, "Die Neubabylonische Zwiegesprächsurkunde", especially p. 104.

[2] Cf. Oppenheim, "Essay on Overland Trade".

ECONOMIC AND SOCIAL CONDITIONS

The stratum of free persons is that of people of *mār-banûtu* status. They cannot be sold or bought and must be able, as we know from contemporary texts, to prove in court their personal status. Equally unequivocal is the position of those males and females (as well as their offspring) who have been given to a temple and are called individually *širku* and *širiktu*, their status, *širkūtu*. Each such person is marked with a divine symbol branded on the back of his hand. Persons who belong to the class called *arad-šarrūtu* and *amat-šarrūtu*, i.e., respectively, slaves or slave girls of the king, are palace property; we know very little about them.

In contrast to these three classes, which are also attested for the preceding, Chaldean period, two more are either new or seldom mentioned before the Achaemenian period. The first of these classes is made up of persons whose various designations are all composed with the word *bītu*, "estate, landed property". They are *bīt sīsê*, literally "horse land"; *bīt narkabti*, "chariot land"; and *bīt kussî*, "throne land". These terms, referring as they do to persons, should be rendered as "(person belonging to an estate called) horse/chariot/throne-land". The other class, the *šušānūtu*, consists of persons called *šušānu*, a foreign word in Akkadian for which many etymologies have been proposed, none in my opinion convincingly.[1]

In order to ascertain the meaning of the terms composed with *bītu*, mention must be made of another expression new in Achaemenian Babylonia: *bīt qašti*, "bow land". Here we are somewhat better informed; the expression refers to fields and gardens held in a kind of feudal tenure by a group of persons (only rarely is one name given, most likely that of the man in charge) called individually *bēl qašti*, "bow (land) owner", or, as a group, *kinattātu*, "colleagues".[2] They are responsible for the annual delivery of certain amounts of staples produced on their holdings. Their obligation is to "serve" the king[3] and, in one instance,

---

[1] Since the word is attested already in pre-Achaemenian Neo-Babylonian texts (especially in early tablets from Uruk where the šušānu are maintained by the temple) it should not be discussed here. Whatever its linguistic background and early history (see lastly M. Mayrhofer, *IIJ* VII (1963–4), pp. 208–11), in the Achaemenian period, outside of the Murašû archives, the *šušānu* are assigned to the king (*VAS* 6. 276; *TCL* 13. 147; *YOS* VII. 106, 111 and 114) and live in separate settlements (*ālu ša* LÚ *šu-ša-an-na* . MEŠ *Cyr.* 158). In the Murašû archives they are assigned to individuals, to institutions (*bīt nakkamdu*), and to collectives of all sorts (see Cardascia, *Archives*, index *s.v.*).

[2] In the tablet *UET* IV. 60, found at Ur, also reservists (*kutallu*) belong to such a unit; cf. also from outside Nippur: *Camb.* 292, *Dar.* 370 and 530.

[3] The phrase used is *ana ṣibūtu ša šarri ana alāku ana Uruk*, "to go to Uruk upon the wish of the king" (in *BE* x, 61, 62). This obligation is replaced in earlier texts by the payment of an amount of money destined for the equipment of a soldier (*kasap rikis qabli*); see *Dar.* 156 (with added *ana*

the verb used in Akkadian is *palāḫu*, which refers in such a context to the fulfillment of a social and moral obligation.[1] Their parallel formulation notwithstanding, the terms composed with *bītu* fall into two groups: the *bīt qašti* held in fief by soldiers (called LÚ.GIŠ.BAN, in Akk. *ša qašti*, i.e., "archer") as some sort of military colons on the one hand; and on the other, persons who are denoted with reference to estates called "horse land", "chariot land", and "throne land".

By their inclusion in the guarantee clause it is obvious that the latter group cannot be the holder of a fief the very name of which points in the direction of élite troops (cavalry, chariotry) or the throne itself. It is much more likely that the persons called *bīt sīsê*, *bīt narkabti* and *bīt kussî* were actually *glebae adscripti*, i.e., persons assigned permanently to the fields and gardens which make up these holdings, and that for this reason they could not be sold individually.[2] There seems therefore to have existed an essential difference between the kinds of fiefs handed out by the Persian government on Mesopotamian soil: archer-held fiefs assigned to groups of soldiers who either worked the land themselves or in some instances, farmed it out;[3] they are abundantly attested in the archives of the Murašû family in Nippur as well as in texts from Uruk; and "horse", "chariot", and "throne" fiefs worked by menials "bound" to the soil for an absentee fief holder, usually a member of the royal family, of the court or of the administration. The latter practice is likewise attested in the Murašû archives, though it should be noted that we know there of only six instances of estates called "horse land", and one each for "chariot land"[4] and "throne land".[5]

It now remains to turn our attention to the *šušānūtu* class and to attempt to ascertain its function and position in the social structure of Achaemenian Babylonia. So far we have enumerated free men and slaves, the personnel of palace and temple as well as the menials of the large estates. Since the exact meaning of the word *šušānu* is unknown and pre-Achaemenian references to it are quite rare (see p. 573, n. 1), I have to concentrate on what evidence can be gathered from texts of

alāku ana pani šarri), also *Cyr.* 331; *Camb.* 17, 276, 291, 322; *Dar.* 46, 112, 141, 164, 220, 234, 253, 308 (paid to Elam = Susa), 481.

[1] Moore, *Neo-Babylonian Documents*, No. 203. The same verb *palāḫu* is used to refer to filial duties.

[2] The position of the menials working on the estates of the Persian high officials is illustrated by the Aramaic letter of Aršam, satrap of Egypt, from which we learn that these menials were branded (see Driver, *Aramaic Documents*, No. 7). There is no indication that this was the case in Babylonia where only the oblates of the sanctuaries were thus marked, though private slaves sometimes had the names of the owners branded on their hands.

[3] E.g. *BRM* I. 85; *BE* VIII. 122, 125, 128; *PBS* II/1. 62.

[4] *PBS* II/1. 209. [5] Strassmaier, *VIIIe Congrès*, No. 31.

ECONOMIC AND SOCIAL CONDITIONS

our period. Two points can be made, based on the Murašû material. First, in *BE* x. 51 and 75 the word is written in Sumerian, ideographically, as KI.ZA.ZA,[1] which means, as a verb, *šukēnu*, "to make a prostration". This late use of a learned Sumerian word is revealing inasmuch as it shows that the scribes connected the designation šušānu with the word *muškēnu* of the Old Babylonian period. The meaning of *muškēnu* is still under discussion but this much can be said: it denotes in certain contexts persons of restricted freedom, socially between free men and slaves. Second, the Murašû tablets never mention individual šušānu, but speak solely of the "overseer of the šušānu", who in a considerable number of instances acts as collector of revenues for the government, as do in Nippur the overseers of other professional and ethnic groups. Hence the šušānu people are basically a distinct association, as are, e.g., the associations of certain craftsmen or of foreigners. What sets them apart, however, is the fact that they alone are mentioned expressly in the guarantee clauses of contracts concerning the sale of slaves. The reason for this discrimination cannot be established; it could have been due to specific (perhaps public?) functions.[2]

It has been suggested[3] that the feudal system was imposed by the Persian conquerors and that the terminology – *bīt qašti*, *bīt sīsê*, *bīt narkabti* and *bīt kussî*[4] – was originally Persian but was translated into Akkadian. I should like to argue a more cautious and especially a more discriminating approach to the problem here involved. To me it seems important to stress the differentiation outlined above between military colons and *glebae adscripti* on large feudal holdings, and to point to their prototypes in early Mesopotamia more than a millennium before the Achaemenian domination.

The sustenance fields assigned to soldiers in the Hammurapi period, and the even earlier large royal and temple holdings with their numerous workmen of the GURUŠ[5] type fulfil the same functions as the

---

[1] The Sumerian KI.ZA.ZA never corresponds in Akkadian to the designation *muškēnu*. Wherever in texts of the Achaemenian period we find the writing KI.ZA.ZA-*ú-tu* it has to be read *šušānūtu* (cf. *BE* x. 51. 16 with 65. 15).

[2] Apart from *šušānû(tu)* there appears another non-Akkadian designation of such persons in the tablets from Achaemenian Nippur. This is *gardu* which corresponds to Elamite *kurtaš* in the tablets from Persepolis. See I. Gershevitch in *Asia Major* II (1951), pp. 139ff. and W. B. Henning *apud* Driver, *Aramaic Documents*, p. 63.

[3] Dandamayev, "Die Lehnsbeziehungen in Babylonien".

[4] The designation *bīt kussî* is also quite old; it occurs in an Old Akkadian tablet where it refers to a royal field, see *CAD* sub *kussû* in *bīt kussî*.

[5] On the social structure of the Akkad period see Gelb, "The Ancient Mesopotamian Ration System", pp. 238ff.

"bow lands" of the archers and the *glebae adscripti*, the royal slaves and the temple oblates of our period.[1] It is true that the early classes of persons with restricted freedom faded out with the rise of the Hammurapi dynasty and remained submerged or unrecorded until the imposition of a new and foreign power structure of a pronounced military character.[2] It seems that whenever agricultural production in Babylonia was managed by a strong administration and was based on irrigation projects of certain surface and productivity dimensions, the necessary labour force had to be and always could be provided by persons of restricted freedom. If this be not the consequence of the characteristic syndrome of water, soil and labour conditions in Babylonia, then a similar political and economic situation in the third and early second millennium as well as in the Achaemenian period should be assumed, even though direct evidence in the early historical and literary documents is lacking. The latter exhibit solely the traditional political and religious phraseology created at the end of the third millennium B.C. It proved a regrettably effective screen of high ideological consistency, hiding from us the important social and political forces which produced the economic situation of that era. These forces are nevertheless reflected in that avalanche of administrative tablets produced in the first half of the second millennium B.C.

There can be little doubt that what I would term a "conditioned reaction" of Mesopotamian society to the political situation triggered by the Persian conquest was utilized by the new overlords for their own military and economic ends. As a matter of fact, their efforts seem to have been quite effective, since we find the same type of large agricultural holdings worked by military colons, called now *katoikoi*, in the documents which tell us of the economic life of the Seleucid and later periods in Mesopotamia.[3]

[1] Not in this category belong the tenant farmers called *ikkaru*, although they might well have been *de facto* as badly off as *glebae adscripti*. Still, they cannot be described as "*ein Stand abhängiger Bauern*" as is done (according to the German resumé) by Dandamayev, "Tempelbauern im späten Babylonien", because they are not *de jure* of restricted liberty. If that had been the case, the term *ikkaru* would have been included in the clauses discussed above.

[2] There are certain difficult problems involved which can only be alluded to here. In the beginning, Persian military power seems to have relied in the main on cavalry, rarely on chariots, using archers as auxiliaries only. Later, horsemen equipped with bows and protected by coats of mail became the mainstay of the offensive might (see p. 585, n. 2). It is difficult to harmonize this development with the designations of the military fiefs established by the Persians in Babylonia which refer mainly to archers, more rarely to chariots and least of all to horses.

[3] See Klíma, *Manis Zeit*, pp. 29ff. and 32ff. Of course, it is well known that similar institutions are attested throughout the entire Hellenistic world. Any conquest situation is bound to produce such a phenomenon – especially where the conqueror (in this instance the Persians) can think of social organization only in "feudal" terms.

ECONOMIC AND SOCIAL CONDITIONS

(2) (See (1) on p. 572.) The Persian influence would hardly be noticeable were it not for the names of certain officials,[1] the expression *dāta* "law (of the king)", *bara* "tax" and *usbarra* "estate",[2] as well as the designation of the measure *ardaba*.[3]

(3) The archives of the family Murašû in Nippur reveal a different economic set-up. Their texts are separated from the mainstream of Chaldean and post-Chaldean Babylonia because they reflect a specific ecological and economic setting which is not in evidence in the pre-Murašû texts from Nippur. It appears that the Achaemenian rulers created, probably after the fateful events in Babylon, what might be called a project of internal colonization in the region of Nippur, which was to become – as I shall try to show presently – the economic capital of the satrapy. The creation of an area of high agricultural productivity around Nippur seems to have had several specific aims: to produce the staples with which the satrapy of Babylonia was to provide the royal household at the rate of one third of its annual needs (the balance being furnished by all of Asia, Herodotus I. 192); to provide the royal family, kings, queens[4] and the top functionaries of the court with extensive and rich holdings;[5] and, last but not least, to exact maximal amounts of silver in tax payments for the mint in Persepolis.[6] In this last respect, the business firm Murašû occupies a key position, its other commercial activities notwithstanding. Here, once more, the Old Testament offers us an insight which cuneiform texts never seem able to achieve; we read in Neh. 5.4 of the complaint of the taxpaying subjects of the

---

[1] See Eilers, *Beamtennamen*, index.

[2] For *bara* cf. Eilers, *OLZ* XXXVII (1934), col. 96; Cardascia, *Archives*, p. 99; for *usbarra* Cardascia, *op. cit.*, p. 130.

[3] For *ardaba* cf. the dictionaries. The Aram. *karša* (weighing ten shekels) occurs only in Old Persian (*karša*) and Elamite (*kuršaum*), but it forms the basis of the calculations in the Neo-Babylonian text, Cameron, *Persepolis Treasury Tablets*, p. 201. See also Schmidt, *Treasury of Persepolis*, p. 62.

[4] The king's holdings (*usbarra*) are not too frequent (*BE* IX. 67, 73, 32^a and x. 31, 32). The queen Amestris (Greek, in cuneiform *Ammaisiri*) had many holdings around Nippur, as Dr M. N. van Loon informs me. For the queen Parusatis, who likewise had estates there, see B. Meissner, *OLZ* VII (1904), cols 384–5; W. Eliers, *ZDMG* XC (1936), p. 177, n. 3, and *idem*, *Beamtennamen*, p. 14, n. 6. In a few instances (*BE* IX. 28: 1, 32: 4, etc.) the designation SAL šá É. GAL (see *CAD sub ekallu* in *ša ekalli*) is used to refer to holdings of the Persian queen. They refer, as Dr van Loon informs me, to Damaspia, wife of Artaxerxes I who was queen from 464 to 424 B.C.

[5] Such holdings are attested, e.g., for Aršama, the satrap of Egypt, as can be seen in Driver, *Aramaic Documents*, Appendix pp. 88–92; note also the village called URU É *ša pani ekalli* "manor of the official in charge of the palace" in *PBS* II/1. 137. 3; and the designation íD. NAM "canal of the satrap" *TuM* II–III. 147. 6 and 13, etc.

[6] An interesting illustration of such transactions is the much earlier (19th and 20th years of Darius I) isolated, Akkadian cuneiform tablet found in the Persepolis Treasury and published by Cameron, *Persepolis Treasury Tablets*, pp. 200ff. as "The Akkadian Text from the Treasury".

Achaemenian kings: "We have borrowed money for the king's tribute, and that upon our land and vineyards." It was clearly the main function of the firm Murašû to provide the landholders in and around Nippur with the silver they had to pay as "the king's tribute".

The tremendous agricultural potential of the region around Nippur is borne out by the Murašû texts; they mention not only large amounts of dates and cereals (especially emmer-wheat) but, more important, quantities of millet, linen and vegetables which are unparalleled in number and variety in the previous periods. Moreover, the fact that two harvests are reported indicates the size and the reliability of the water supply provided by new irrigation installations and, still more important, by new techniques. The use of novel terms such as GIŠ. APIN[1] and *silihtu* "sluice gate" may indicate technical innovations that made better utilization of the available water possible. Since the region around Nippur is nowadays covered by slowly moving sand dunes, no surface survey can be made to find and trace canals or lines of settlements, as has been done for other regions to the south and north of the city.

One has to realize, furthermore, that the economic life of Nippur of the Murašû period was already under the indirect but all-pervading influence of silver coinage which had not yet engulfed Mesopotamia, specifically, the Achaemenian satrapy that was apparently called *Māt Akkadī* (cf. p. 564).[2] It would appear that this exclusion was not accidental but planned. In Babylonia an agricultural "hinterland" had been created in order to support the administration, the army and the court. The archives of the Murašû family furnish us, on account of the family's unique economic position, with a curiously slanted though quite wide overview of the political, military, social and economic structure of that region in and around Nippur. They tell us, not too clearly, about the crucial role of the firm in the workings of the large agricultural holdings (financing, administration and manpower) as well

---

[1] Cardascia, "Faut-il éliminer giš APIN = nartabu?", has drawn attention to the existence of new irrigation machinery in the tablets from Nippur. Though the use of the old Sumerogram GIŠ. APIN does not establish its contemporary reading (see for a parallel instance p. 575, n. 1), the technological reasons offered by Cardascia have to be accepted. Note furthermore in the Murašû texts a new institution of specialized judges ("water judges" BE x. 91. 17). See Eilers, *Beamtennamen*, p. 6, n. 2 and 3.

[2] It is relevant to stress that coins, specifically, Greek coins, were not unknown in Achaemenian Babylonia, as has been shown by Porada, "Greek Coin Impressions from Ur". Even under Seleucid rulers coins (staters) were weighed rather than counted (see Oppenheim, *Ancient Mesopotamia*, p. 87) though sometimes referred to by the representations on them (*passim* in CT XLIX). For the use of Greek coins as bullion in Achaemenian Babylonia see E. S. G. Robinson, "A Silversmith's Hoard from Mesopotamia", *Iraq* XII (1950), pp. 44–51.

ECONOMIC AND SOCIAL CONDITIONS

as about the rich manorial organizations and the swarms of Persian officials who administered the province.[1] We also learn from these tablets that Nippur was a rich city inhabited by so many foreigners[2] that we can assume it to have been the capital of the satrapy, or at least that it must have functioned as such after the downfall of Babylon. In Nippur we find people from India, from Hamath, Malatya, Tabal and Tyre, we find Arabs, Cimmerians, Lydians, Phrygians (*Muškaja*), Urartians, and even Carians (*Ban[a]nešaja*).[3] The latter, incidentally, must have been there as mercenary soldiers; they fought against Alexander the Great at Gaugamela for the last of the Achaemenian kings as part of the Babylonian contingent (Arrian III. 8. 5). Only a capital can harbour such an international population.[4]

Once this new interpretation is put forward, there can be assembled a number of arguments which taken individually do not provide ready proof but as a group support the theory that Nippur was, after the eclipse of Babylon, in effect the capital of the new satrapy *Māt Akkadī*. Only in texts from a capital could one expect references to two or more successive satrap officials. Near Nippur was even a locality called *ḫuššēti ša* LÚ *magušu* "settlement of the Magi",[5] which means that these exponents of Iranian priestcraft were needed for the service of the Persian court and its officials and yet had to live in a separate settlement to avoid contact with the Babylonian *daiva* worshippers.[6] The existence of a "guild" of parchment-makers suggests a demand for this writing material far beyond the needs of a provincial town.[7] The official called "who-is-in-charge-of-the-'birds'-of-the-king" (see *CAD issūru* in *ša ana*

---

[1] In spite of the work done on this important source material its riches are far from being exhausted. The remarks and suggestions which I have been offering here are made solely in connection with specific points to which my attention was drawn in the course of my investigation. A systematic presentation would yield many more and better insights.

[2] Cf. for specific aspects: Weissbach, *Keilinschriften*, p. 144, n. 1; Cardascia, "Le statut de l'étranger"; Dandamayev, "Foreign Slaves". For foreigners in the empire in general: Goossens, "Artistes et artisans". For many specific identifications of foreigners mentioned in the texts of the Murašû archives and earlier tablets, see Eilers, "Kleinasiatisches".

[3] For the Lydians and the Phrygians cf. Eilers, *op. cit.*, pp. 205ff., for the Carians called *Bananešaja* cf. *ibid.*, pp. 225ff.

[4] In spite of the important work done by G. Cardascia in *Les Archives des Murašû*, the social and administrative structure of the city remains largely unknown. It is moreover uncertain whether these rather stereotyped texts will ever be able to shed light on the web of political, i.e., "feudal", bureaucratic and economic interrelations in which the businessmen, officials and citizens of Nippur were engaged.

[5] *BE* IX. 88. 4; *TuM* II–III. 184. 8.

[6] The few other extant passages which refer to magi (*YOS* III. 66. 7 and *BIN* I. 40. 35 from Uruk *VAS* III. 138/9. 2 from Babylon) yield no information.

[7] For this guild cf. Eilers, *Beamtennamen*, p. 49.

muḫḫi iṣṣurī ša šarri) would then not be concerned with poultry for the royal table but rather with the king's falcons, since the Achaemenians' interest in hunting is well known; Arabic legend has it moreover that Old Persian kings invented the art of falconry.[1] Lastly, one might mention the presence of a substantial number of deportees from Judah, who, apparently attracted by the opportunities of the capital,[2] had moved to Nippur from rural settlements or engaged in large-scale agricultural undertakings of the region.

There are nevertheless indications that Babylon continued as a royal residence (a "*Pfalz*"): firstly, the large booty in bullion seized there by Alexander the Great (see p. 532), secondly, the mention of Babylon in Letter XII of the Aršama correspondence,[3] and thirdly, the rental, by the head of the family of Murašû, of a house in Babylon for the time of the presence of the king there (*BE* x. 1 dated to the accession year of Darius II, 423 B.C.).

(4) (See 3. on p. 577.) It is important to separate the two aspects just described of Achaemenian economic structure. In one, previous practices are continued in private contexts and in the bureaucracy of temple organizations.[4] In the other, the royal administration created a new situation by means of projects of internal colonization, as was the case around Nippur.[5] But no doubt there were other urban centres in Babylonia, where similar situations obtained of which we have as yet no direct evidence.[6] So far only the texts excavated at Ur – few as they are – provide data; they seem to reflect both aspects under consideration.[7] The situation in Nippur then, as far as we know about it through the archives of the Murašû family, would be rather

---

[1] Falconry is denoted in Arabic with a Persian word (see *Encyclopedia of Islam*, 2nd. ed. *s.v.* "Bayzara") and is said in Arabic sources to have been invented by a Persian king. At any rate, hunting was a favourite pastime of the Achaemenian rulers and was done not only with falcons but also with dogs, as is indicated in the passage on p. 532, n. 1. Both methods are alien to the Mesopotamian tradition.

[2] Cf. Galling, *Studien*, pp. 52ff.

[3] Driver, *Aramaic Documents*.

[4] The temple archives of Uruk have yielded most of the tablets of the Seleucid period so far. Texts from Babylon are now being published by the British Museum in *CT* XLIX. The provenience of a few other tablets is not known. No systematic study of this important source of information is yet available apart from Krückmann, *Babylonische Rechts-und Verwaltungs-Urkunden*.

[5] The interpretation of the political position of Nippur here proposed should go a long way to explain the sphere of activity of what is still quite often called the "bank" Murašû. See the characterization of these activities in Bogaert, *Origines*, pp. 118ff.

[6] The picture offered by the temple archives of Uruk might well be characteristic for similar institutions in other cities, though it is unlikely that it will be rivalled anywhere in size and importance.

[7] Cf. especially *UET* IV. 41, 42 also 106, 109.

exceptional. This, however, is only to be expected for a project of internal colonization of the size we have to assume on the basis of the transactions recorded. The validity of the interpretation here suggested will have to be tested against new tablets of the period that originated in secular situations.

What has been outlined above concerning certain changes in the native economic and social framework during the Achaemenian period should be supplemented by pointing to the continuity on other levels of the Mesopotamian civilization. To be specific: the literary, scientific as well as the scholarly traditions continued through the era of Persian domination without any observable changes. As usual such a statement requires strict qualification in view of the factor of accidental survival, which may have played a much larger role in our scanty evidence than we think. Also, formal continuity does not preclude even trenchant internal change.

Nevertheless, regarding the literary tradition, the non-economic tablets even of the Seleucid period demonstrate unequivocally the continuation of what I call the "stream of tradition". This is particularly in evidence in the religious and epical writings, in divinatory texts, and in the domain of vocabularies, the *philologia perennis* of Mesopotamia, all attested in Seleucid copies. The existence of individual literary creations of new text types, etc., does not affect the surviving importance of the corpus of traditional material.

A contributing factor in the maintenance of all these traditions was that although the cities outside the capital were provincial in political and administrative respects, they contained in their old and important centres of learning very extensive holdings of tablets embracing the whole learned tradition of Mesopotamian scholarship. Whatever destruction depleted some of these collections, the deep concern of the native scholars for their "books" made up for deterioration, and new copies of old tablets were added from other centres where they had been preserved.[1]

In the domain of scientific texts, the dates of the astronomical observation records given by A. J. Sachs in *LBAT*, pp. xiiff. establish beyond a doubt that such observations went on in Babylon (from where

---

[1] For a well-known example of this, reference may be made to the subscript of the Seleucid ritual (Thureau-Dangin, *Rituels Accadiens*, p. 80) which runs: "According to the tablets which Nabopolassar, king of the Sealand, had taken as booty from Uruk and (which) when Kidin-Anu, native of Uruk,...discovered these tablets in Elam, he wrote down during the rule of King Seleucus (I) and his son King Antiochus (I) and brought into Uruk."

BABYLONIAN EVIDENCE

these tablets come) under Darius I (attested in 493/2 B.C.), Artaxerxes I (in 440/39 B.C.), Darius II (in 418/7 and 417/6 B.C.), Artaxerxes II (from 384 to 360 B.C.), Artaxerxes III (from 353 to 337 B.C.) and Darius III (in 332/1 B.C.).[1] The richness and variety of the pertinent documentation under the Seleucids, even down to 69/68 B.C.[2] bears witness to the growth and vitality of the Babylonian scholars' interest in mathematical astronomy, no matter what the political status of the capital was and in spite of the ruined sanctuaries and – very likely – the desolation of the city itself.

III. ARCHAEOLOGICAL EVIDENCE

The political and military power of Babylonia collapsed before the onrush of the conquering Iranians and was never again restored by its own initiative. It now became the fate of Babylonia to be used as the basis for the more or less ephemeral power structures of Alexander the Great and, to a much larger extent, of the dynasty of Macedonian rulers founded by Seleucus I. In the sphere of economic activities the region maintained for many centuries its importance as an essential link in the network of trade relations connecting the regions around the Mediterranean Sea with India, across the Iranian Plateau and beyond. Overland trade and overseas transportation to the East found their junction in Lower Mesopotamia, specifically in Babylonia, Seleucia, Vologesia, etc., and produced much profit. The intellectual creativity of Mesopotamia continued unabated through the period of Persian domination, particularly in the field of mathematical astronomy and non-judicial astrology.

In the realm of art the encounter of the two civilizations, that of Mesopotamia and that of Persia, produced a different result. The impact of Persian art – whatever its prehistory was – seems to have been sustained by the political power behind it which imposed an unparalleled uniformity on all its manifestations, as evidenced not only in Babylonia proper but wherever Persian domination was extended, i.e., ultimately from Egypt to Van. A growing number of beautiful stone and metal objects of impressive craftsmanship, of known and unknown pro-

[1] This holds true also for horoscopes as Sachs, "Babylonian Horoscopes", especially 54ff., for the time of Darius I (510 B.C.) has shown. For a curious astrological text mentioning the 14th and 15th years of a king named Artaxerxes see Oppenheim, "Divination and Celestial Observation", note 50.
[2] Cf. Neugebauer, *Astronomical Cuneiform Texts* I, p. 7.

venience, confirms this impression. In the realm of monumental art evidence is much less abundant and less spectacular outside Iran proper. Only from Susa do we have a report about royal building activities which in some respects echoes the Akkadian inscriptions recording the work done on palaces and temples. In this trilingual inscription of Darius I[1] gold, precious stones, ivory, rare wood and building stones are brought from the ends of the empire to Susa and many nations contribute artists and workers to erect and to beautify the palace in Susa. The role of the Akkadians is – perhaps not unintentionally (see p. 586) – rather minor; they make the bricks. Practically nothing is preserved in Ur. In the Neo-Babylonian and Persian periods Sir Leonard Woolley can assign to Cyrus but a few ill-defined walls and repair work on a gate in the *temenos* section of the temple.[2] A hinge box made of a group of bricks all bearing the stamp with the name of this king (see p. 553) testifies to work done in this locality. In the sector of the temple called E-nun-maḫ, some post-Neo-Babylonian buildings, fragments of pavements and what Woolley calls "altars and tables of offerings" are assigned to the Persian period though no bricks bearing the name of a king have been found there. Persian buildings on the "*ziggurat*" terrace are dated by means of a clay pot containing almost-destroyed tablets and by Persian coffins.[3] Among these coffins are several made of copper,[4] and the contents of the burials seem to bear out certain pecularities such as glazed polychrome pottery which separate them from early, Neo-Babylonian, graves. All in all, this is an extremely meagre find which is in some contrast with texts of the period that reflect a degree of prosperity not revealed in earlier layers of pre-Neo-Babylonian Ur.

The situation in Babylon is somewhat better. There the German archaeologists excavated before World War I a charming structure called by Koldewey *Perserbau* (also *Kiosk*) to the west of the southern palace complex (*Südburg*) in Babylon. Its predominant features are a column-supported porch looking north, a three-layered flooring with red surface, the dark limestone column bases (and steps) as well as the wall decoration consisting of glazed brick-shaped composition-stone

---

[1] Kent, *Old Persian*, pp. 142–4. [Two new versions of this inscription, referring to a different building and each differently abridged, came to light in 1969–70; see F. Vallat, *Syria* XLVIII (1971), pp. 54–9; idem, *RA* LXIV (1970), pp. 149–60; *StIr* I (1972), pp. 3–13. (Ed.)]
[2] *UE* IX, pp. 2, 4, 7.
[3] *Ibid.*, pp. 55ff., 68–87, 90.
[4] *Ibid.*, p. 56, fig. 1.

and fragments of an inscription (Artaxerxes II).[1] This clearly establishes that entire structure as a transplant from Iran.[2] In fact, Koldewey thought the glazed bricks were actually brought to Babylon from Susa because their composition shows a technique not known in the Mesopotamia of the period. One might even venture the guess that the column bases (of two types: flat and bell-shaped) were likewise of foreign origin. This could also have been the case with quite similar architectural elements found in 1904 in Abu Chulfat near Hatab (now called Khalfat or Tuweirij, 30 km. east of Babylon).[3] I suggest this because imported Persian column bases were found at Sidon.[4] At any rate the export of characteristic architectural elements such as the glazed bricks and, possibly, ornamented column bases, as well as the construction of royal dwellings according to Persian ideas, are a clear symptom of the new empire's attitude toward artistic expressions in the domain of architecture, sculpture and wall decoration. The extent of this tendency is unfortunately impossible to gauge because only very few and broken traces of buildings have been preserved outside of Susa and the sites on the Iranian plateau. For Babylonia proper, reference should be made to the survey of such sites (up to 1953) given by Schmidt.[5]

The impression that buildings erected by the Achaemenian kings, princes and satraps exhibit in style and decoration the uniformity of an "official" art is corroborated by other artistic media such as metalwork, seal cuttings, etc.,[6] originating (or found) in Mesopotamia. In all these instances the creative effort in design and execution is certainly Persian in origin and not Babylonian. This is likewise the case in the Seleucid period – apparently Mesopotamian artistic vitality had become ex-

[1] The authorship of the inscription is not certain. The dating to Artaxerxes II by Koldewey (*Königsburgen* I, p. 121) has been disputed by Schmidt (*Persepolis I*, p. 28) who, following Olmstead, *History*, pp. 162ff., assigned it to Darius I. However, if inscription and glazed brick decoration are contemporary, the latter should support Koldewey in view of very similar work done by Artaxerxes II in Susa.

[2] The three-layered flooring with red surface is now dated later than the Achaemenian period, cf. E. Schmidt in Wetzel *et. al.*, *Das Babylon der Spätzeit*, p. 47. For the inscription cf. Weissbach, *Babylonische Miscellen*, pp. 48ff. The column base fragments and reliefs are not published to my knowledge.

[3] Discussed and published in Wetzel *et al.*, *op. cit.*, p. 2 and pl. 26a and b.

[4] See Clermont-Ganneau, "Paradeisos", p. 106, and the pertinent discussion in Galling, *op. cit.*, pp. 208ff.

[5] *Persepolis I*, pp. 28ff.

[6] On Achaemenian private houses in Uruk cf. the report of H. J. Lenzen in *AfO* XXI (1966), pp. 140ff., and E. Porada, *Archaeology* XX (1967), p. 65; on pottery of that provenience, see Adams, *Land Behind Baghdad*, p. 130.

hausted with the Chaldean period. However, it is not my task here to enumerate and discuss these objects.

Technologically, too, Persian influence seems to have been preponderant, though we know little of it. One could adduce as textual evidence first a Nippur text[1] describing the equipment of the armoured cavalryman to whom the later empire owed many of its victories.[2] Even more remarkable seem to have been the contributions of the Persians in the field of agricultural techniques (see p. 578, n. 1). Finally one could point out that textual references to bridges (apart from the famous bridge over the Euphrates in Babylon) begin only with the tablets of the Achaemenian period.[3] This again is in harmony with the interest of the empire in roads and bridges.[4]

IV. CONCLUSIONS

The encounter between the Achaemenian empire and Babylonia seems to have left a surprisingly insignificant impact on the latter. Much of this impression is patently caused by the inherent sterility of the extant writings and the scarcity of the archaeological evidence. Still, one can hardly use this state of affairs with good conscience as an excuse for shelving the problems here involved until the happy day when more and better evidence will turn up. There is one reason that should prompt us to try, at least, to answer the question posed by the nature and extent

---

[1] *UCP* IX, p. 269; studied by Ebeling, "Rüstung".

[2] For the origin, development, military importance and historic impact of this new and effective strategic weapon (armed cavalry) see Rubin, "Entstehung", with an extensive bibliography. The Babylonian "*Panzerreiter*" from a text from Nippur belongs only to the "forerunners" of the cataphractarii (see also Klíma, *Manis Zeit*, p. 82, and for an inventory of the armour especially p. 99, note 61), and so do those military fief holders who were given a *bīt sīsê* "horse land".

[3] See *CAD* and *AHw*, sub *gišru*. With the exception of two passages from Harper, *Assyrian and Babylonian Letters* referring to bridges beyond the Tigris (no. 100) and in Elam (no. 917), all references come from tablets dating from the Achaemenian period. Note especially the "guild of the bridge-builder" (*rākisu ša gišri*) in a tablet from the Murašû archive (*PBS* II/1. 140), a novel profession in Babylonia. Note that there was a bridge across the Tigris at Opis by 401 B.C., as Xenophon tells us in his description of the homeward march of the Ten Thousand (see p. 540, n. 2). It was obviously built by the Persians and was, as we happen to know from a Nippur text (*PBS* II/1. 140) supervised by the "chief custom (inspector) of Opis" (GAL *miksi ša Upia*). The few references to toll payable at pontoon bridges by passing ships (*TCL* XIII. 216 and *YOS* VI. 171) suggest their importance as a source of income. In this connection I should like to mention that a tax on salt (and the pertinent salt monopoly) is known from all countries which were once part of the Achaemenian empire, cf. Klíma, *Manis Zeit*, p. 33. It is attested in post-Achaemenian Babylonia but not in cuneiform documents of that provenience.

[4] See Mazzarino, "Le Vie di Comunicazione", especially p. 78. Cf. Schiwek, "Der persische Golf". Note that according to Arrian, *Exped.* VII. 17, 19 boats were loading even in Babylon for overseas journeys.

of the encounter which I have tried to outline: this encounter was not a unique and isolated event; two no less fateful confrontations occurred in Babylonia subsequently to the Persian conquest; twice again the slowly disintegrating Mesopotamian civilization was to suffer foreign domination after the defeat of the last Achaemenian king. First came the traumatic impact of the invasion by Alexander the Great, which was followed by the overwhelming surge of the Hellenistic civilization engulfing not only Mesopotamia but all of Western Asia. Then followed a second tide from Iran, which produced the Parthian Arsacid rule enduring for at least as long as the Achaemenian, to be followed by that of the Persian Sasanian dynasty.

Though evidence is still far from adequate, the flowering created by the contacts of Babylonia with Hellenism and the Parthian civilization respectively,[1] stands in unmistakable contrast to the sterility and lack of interaction which seems to characterize the Achaemenian presence in Babylonia. One gains the impression that the Achaemenian rulers aspired to nothing more than the imposition of political and military rule on an alien civilization to which they apparently reacted with a mixture of admiration and contempt. They readily took residence in world-famous Babylon, accepting the amenities and attitudes of a civilization considered superior in certain respects, while any Babylonian aspiration they met with violence and disrespect. The violence is exemplified by the clash between Xerxes and Babylon, the contempt is pointedly expressed in the representation, on the tomb of Darius I, of the thirty nations shown as bearers of his throne, and in the same pictorial motif on the tombs of his successors. E. Schmidt points out in the third volume of his monumental opus *Persepolis* that only the figures of the Babylonian throne bearers are shown unarmed in all instances. This, he thinks, is meant as a deliberate humiliation of proud Babylonia ordered either by Darius himself or by Xerxes, who supervised the execution of most of his father's projects in and around Persepolis. Though this humiliating discrimination may well be a direct consequence of the repeated rebellions against Darius I – as E. Schmidt suggests – it might also be considered symptomatic of the basic conflict between the Achaemenian conquerors and the old capital. If so, the tension must have been engendered by the difference in culture felt by

---

[1] An excellent indication for the return of prosperity to Mesopotamia in the Parthian period is the re-urbanization of the region, which extended from the revived city of Aššur over Hatra, Ctesiphon, Vologesia to Spasinu Charax.

CONCLUSIONS

the conquerors, at least on a certain social and intellectual level. Such an attitude, in turn, would go far to explain why the Parthian domination could achieve integration and fusion with the Babylonian civilization and could create in Mesopotamia its great architecture – temples, palaces, fortresses, etc. Doubtless the Hellenistic intermezzo had produced in Babylonia an acceptance of international contacts in spite of the loss of political independence, thus preparing the old civilization for its second encounter with Iran, which proved much more productive and historically significant than the first one, with the Achaemenian kings.

CHAPTER 11

THE EVIDENCE OF THE PERSEPOLIS TABLETS

The Achaemenid Elamite texts found at Persepolis add a little flesh to the picked-over bones of early Achaemenid history. They inform us about the far-reaching organization of men and materials for economic purposes and give us hints about the difficulties which the organizers faced in setting up the system and in promoting its efficient operation. These texts are in two distinct groups: the fortification texts and the treasury texts.

The fortification texts, which date from the thirteenth to the twenty-eighth year of Darius I (509–494 B.C.), record many kinds of transfers of food products. Most numerous are ration payments, monthly, daily, and special, to named individuals (including huge daily payments to high officials), to travellers, to mothers, to wide-spread work groups, and even to horses, camels, cattle and fowls. The fortification texts are very numerous.[1]

The treasury texts are later in date, coming from the thirtieth year of Darius I to the seventh year of Artaxerxes I (492–458 B.C.). Also they have a different function, namely, the recording of disbursements of silver from the Persepolis treasury. Like the fortification texts they chiefly deal with ration payments. But here silver is paid in lieu of part (rarely all) of the ration. There are only 139 of these texts, and many are incomplete.[2] They have their own interest and provide useful sidelights. Yet in the material as a whole they constitute a special case. The following discussion refers to the treasury texts only when they are specifically mentioned.

[1] Transliterations and translations of 2,087 texts, here referred to as PF 1–2087, are presented in my *Persepolis Fortification Tablets* (University of Chicago Press, 1969). About 900 additional texts, here referred to with the prefix "Fort.", have been studied. Of the texts still unread there may be a thousand or so which contain useful information. Clay tablets in the same find with Aramaic text are being prepared for publication. These are not considered here.

[2] Most of the texts, referred to as PT 1–84, are to be found in G. G. Cameron, *The Persepolis Treasury Tablets* (Chicago, 1948). The same author has published five texts (PT 1957-1–5) in *JNES* XVII (1958), 172–6, and another twenty texts (PT 1963-1–20) in *JNES* XXIV (1965), 170–85 (note the important collations of PT 1–84 on pp. 187–9). For collations and additional commentary see Hallock, *JNES* XIX (1960), 90–100.

THE EVIDENCE OF THE PERSEPOLIS TABLETS

The fortification texts were written at many sites in a region which, it seems, surrounds the Persepolis–Susa axis. As we shall see, many of the geographical names (mostly not known from other sources) can be assigned to three areas: one around Persepolis, another around Susa, and a third which lies between. Few texts seem to have originated at Persepolis or at Susa. Though these cities are often mentioned in various connections, activities at Persepolis and Susa normally lay outside the purview of our materials.

With the treasury texts the case is different. They deal only with Persepolis and the surrounding area. Many, perhaps most, of the texts were presumably written at Persepolis.

The texts mention the names of many officials, who are definable more by the roles they play than by titles. Evidently in a developing situation, in which an effective administrator was a pearl of price, it was found useful to assign functions as need arose, rather than to set up a rigid hierarchy. By all evidence the chief economic official from the sixteenth to the twenty-fifth year of Darius was Pharnaces (Elamite *Parnaka*, OP *Farnaka*), son of Arsames. He is given no title.[1] He twice transmits royal orders: in PF 1795 for 2,000 quarts of wine, in Fort. 6764 for 100 sheep, both for the princess (*dukšiš*) Irtašduna (= Artystone, wife of Darius).[2] Many times Pharnaces, as addresser of letters, issues orders on his own authority, as in PF 1793, where he orders Harrēna the "cattle chief" (*kāsabattiš*) to issue 13½ sheep to Bakatanna and his 134 companions, who are feeding (?) the horses and mules of the king and the princes (*misapušašpe*).

Pharnaces receives an extraordinary daily ration of two sheep (e.g. PF 654) plus 90 quarts of wine (e.g. PF 665) plus 180 quarts of flour: in Fort. 1383 he receives 180 quarts, while his 300 "boys" receive each one quart. Very often Pharnaces authorizes travellers (usually, it seems, going from Persepolis) to receive rations on the road. Thus in PF 1375 Pišiya and his two "boys", en route from Persepolis to Susa, receive flour rations on the basis of a "sealed document" of Pharnaces.

Parallel to Pharnaces in all such occurrences, though on a smaller

[1] PF 787 mentions "Pharnaces the delivery man (*ullira*)". This is a lesser Pharnaces, perhaps the one who, in PT 4:12, receives 200 shekels of silver, along with other "chiefs" (*araššap*, var. of *iršap*) who receive up to 600. The greater Pharnaces is shown to be the son of Arsames by the Aramaic legend on one of his seals (Seal 16 occurring e.g. on PF 1802–10, letters addressed by Pharnaces). ["OP" stands for "Old Persian".]

[2] Fort. 6764 (wrongly designated "Pers. 6754") was published by Cameron, JNES 1 (1942), 214–18. For *dukšiš* = "princess" see E. Benveniste, *Titres et noms propres en iranien ancien* (Paris, 1966), p. 43.

scale, is Ziššawiš, evidently his right-hand man. Travel parties carrying his authorization seem always to originate at Persepolis. As daily ration he receives less than half as much as Pharnaces: 1½ sheep (PF 678) plus 30 quarts of wine (e.g. PF 677) plus 60 quarts of flour (e.g. PF 670). Ziššawiš continued active through the eighteenth year of Xerxes (see PT 33), long outlasting Pharnaces, who retired or died after the twenty-fifth year of Darius.

Pharnaces obviously was an important figure. There is evidence to suggest that he was very important indeed. The letters sent by Pharnaces and Ziššawiš all have a subscript naming the scribe. Most other letters, sent by lesser officials, lack this subscript. But there are two other addressers of letters with subscripts, and both of them bear names known to history. One is Artavardiya (Elamite *Irdumartiya*) in PF 1830 and 1831. The other is Aspačanā (Elamite *Ašbazana*) in PF 1853. Now many an historical name occurs in our texts. But usually it occurs without paternity, in contexts which do not encourage us to suppose that the historical person is involved. Thus we find Mardonius (Elamite *Mardunuya*) supplying six ewes in the twenty-first year (PF 60) and serving as scribe in a Pharnaces letter in the twenty-fourth year (Fort. 8265). Possibly this is evidence of the early grooming of Mardonius, son of Gobryas, who in the thirtieth year (492 B.C.), while still youthful, became a generalissimo (Herod. 6. 43). It seems improbable. It is very probable, on the other hand, that the above Artavardiya is in fact the general who fought Vahyazdāta (DB §§ 41–2), and that the above Aspačanā is the "bow-bearer" pictured on the tomb of Darius (DNd). In our texts Aspačanā makes his appearance in the twenty-eighth year of Darius and lasts till the third year of Xerxes (PT 14).

There are three persons who receive extraordinary daily rations in texts similar to those of Pharnaces and Ziššawiš. In PF 684 Radušnamuya, a woman otherwise unknown, receives 44 quarts of wine per day. In PF 689 and 690 Artavardiya, mentioned above, receives 50 quarts per day (less than Pharnaces, but more than Ziššawiš). In PF 688 Gobryas (Elamite *Kambarma*) receives 100 quarts of beer per day. It seems likely that these persons were entitled to rations, including also sheep and flour, on the same basis as Pharnaces and Ziššawiš. If so, the payments must normally have been recorded on a perishable material or have gone to a different bureau. Gobryas, with his 100 quarts of beer, is favoured over Pharnaces, with his 90 quarts of wine (wine and beer being of equal value). This Gobryas should be the same as the "helper"

THE EVIDENCE OF THE PERSEPOLIS TABLETS

of Darius (DB §68), the queller of an Elamite revolt (DB §71), the father of Mardonius. The elegant stamp seal of Gobryas, depicting a stag attacked by two hunting dogs, is impressed on PF 688.

There are many other persons who, like Pharnaces and Zissawis, authorize rations for travellers. Only two occur more often than they in this capacity: the king (most commonly for parties leaving Susa) and Bakabana (almost always for parties leaving Susa), who may be the Megapanus who commanded the Hyrcanians in the army of Xerxes and later became satrap of Babylon (Herod. 7. 62). Other occurrences of the name Bakabana are not numerous, and some evidently apply to a different person. Of eleven other persons authorizing travel rations two or more times, five or six bear historical names. One is Aspačanā (mentioned above) in PF 1444 and Fort. 1873. Another is Artaphernes, brother of Darius and satrap at Sardis; in the twenty-seventh year a man named Dauma, carrying a sealed document of Artaphernes (Elamite *Irdapirna*), received rations at Hidali for twenty-three men and twelve "boys", en route from Sardis to Persepolis (PF 1404). Bakabaduš occurs ten times (e.g. PF 1351, Arachosia to Susa; PF 1358, Kandahar to Susa); he may be the Megabates, a nephew of Darius, who commanded the fleet in an abortive attack on Naxos (Herod. 5. 32-4). Miturna (PF 1363, 1483, 2055) may be the Hydarnes (OP *Vidarna*), "helper" of Darius (DB §68), who commanded the army in Media (DB §25). Irdabanuš (PF 1287 and 1555, both Bactra to Susa, twenty-second year) may be Artabanus, brother of Darius (Herod. 4. 83). Also Irdapirzana (PF 1463, 2052) is possibly Artabazanes, eldest son of Darius (Herod. 7. 2).[1]

The association of Pharnaces, in his main roles, with so many persons who are or may be of exalted rank enhances the likelihood that he was himself a very important person. It is therefore not at all improbable that his father Arsames (see p. 589, n. 1) was the king of that name, grandfather of Darius, who was still alive when Darius became king (DSf §3b, XPf §3). Quite likely our Pharnaces was the one named as father of Artabazus, who commanded the Parthians and Chorasmians in the army of Xerxes (Herod. 7. 66, also 8. 126-9). No doubt the exact nature of the position that Pharnaces occupied depended to a considerable extent on his own ability and influence. In the treasury texts in the time of Xerxes there are three persons who seem to occupy approximately the same position. As Pharnaces addresses many letters

---

[1] See Benveniste, *Titres et noms propres...*, p. 84.

ordering various lesser officials to issue commodities, so these persons (among others) address letters to the Persepolis treasurer ordering him to issue silver in lieu of commodities. Tarkāwiš addresses ten letters from the second year to the fourth year, eighth month (PT 19). Irdatakma addresses more than forty-six letters, starting in the next month (PT 21) and continuing until the twentieth year, third month (PT 63). In the fourth month of that year Irdašura addresses a letter (PT 68), and he addresses one more covering the tenth to twelfth months (PT 75). At this point we are coming to the end of our material. There is only one later letter, dated in the seventh year of Artaxerxes I, with a different addressor (PT 25).

Just below the level of Pharnaces there are various officials whose roles cannot, for the most part, be clearly defined. One role that can be defined, from the treasury texts, is that of the treasurer. The texts name four treasurers serving consecutively from the thirty-second year of Darius to the seventh year of Artaxerxes I.[1] We shall find the first of the four, named Baratkama, also in the later years of the fortification texts, apparently in a different role. The Persepolis treasurer of course paid out silver. Surprisingly, he had the further responsibility of setting apportionments for various kinds of work groups in and around Persepolis (see below).

Below the level of the treasurer, apparently, stand those officials whose characteristic role is the assignment of work groups and the setting of apportionments. In the assignment of work groups three persons are far more frequent than any others: Iršena in the Susa area, Karkiš and Šuddayauda successively in the Persepolis area. The texts with these persons in this role enable us to place many geographical names in the two areas. Other evidence associates other names with these names, and makes it possible to place all the frequently mentioned geographical names in the Susa area, in the Persepolis area, or in an area between the two. The three persons as assigners of work groups occur most often in texts concerned with regular monthly rations. An example is PF 882, which tells us that thirty-five workers subsisting on rations at Shiraz, assigned by Karkiš (m.*Kar-ki-iš da-man-na*, lit. "Karkiš sending"), received 470 quarts of wine... in the sixth month, sixteenth year, ten men receiving twenty, nineteen men ten, one woman thirty, five women ten. This text is one of a series of ten which gives

---

[1] For four treasurers see Hallock, *JNES* xix, 90–1. PT 1963–19 now seems to indicate that there was an additional treasurer, Bauka, in the thirtieth year of Darius.

remarkable coverage on wine rations for this work group, from the ninth month, fifteenth year, to the tenth month, eighteenth year. Over this period the number of persons in the group declines from thirty-seven to thirty-five, then jumps to forty-seven. One of the texts (PF 877) qualifies the group as "treasurers" (*kapnuškip*).

In the treasury texts it is clear that the assigner was limited in the kinds of workers he assigned. There is for example a group of six or seven "artisans, ornament-makers" which occurs in eight texts with the assigner named.[1] The assigner is Mannanda in the years 16 to 19, Parnadadda in the years 19 and 20. Mannanda and Parnadadda do not occur as assigners for any other groups. Similarly Mirayauda assigns only *razape* ("masons") and *dukape* ("plasterers"?), and no one else assigns them.[2] The treasurer assigns only accountants.[3]

In the fortification texts the evidence is not so clear. The texts with Iršena, Karkiš and Šuddayauda as assigners rarely mention the qualifications of the work groups, presumably because the phrase "assigned by Karkiš", for example, plus the mention of a geographical name, was thought sufficient to identify a group. Among the other scattered assigners is Pharnaces, the chief economic official discussed above. In this capacity his particular concern is with Babylonian scribes, usually described as "(writing) on parchment".[4] His understandable interest in record keeping is documented elsewhere (see below). Incidentally, the reference to scribes who wrote (no doubt in Aramaic) on perishable materials warns us that the surviving records are not complete.

The limitations attached to the assigning function suggest that there was a close relationship between the interests of the assigner and the special qualifications of the groups which he assigned. He may have been responsible for their training. He may have maintained a pool of workers to which the group returned after an assignment was finished. The case of the "artisans, ornament-makers" (see above), who over a period of four years, while working for the Persepolis treasury, were identified by their assigning officer, indicates that the latter exercised a continuing function.

The role of setting apportionments, though parallel in use and

---

[1] PT 30, 33, 34, 35, 43, 62, 70, 1963-1. "Artisans" is expressed by *marrip* or *kurnukaš* (from OP *kṛnuvaka-*), "ornament-makers" (only in PT 30 and 62) by *be(a)šiškurrašpe*.

[2] PT 49a-1, 68, 68a, 1957-3.   [3] PT 48a, 1957-5.

[4] So described (KUŠ.lg *uk-ku*) in PF 1808, 1947: 23-4 and 25-6, and Fort. 8265. Babylonian scribes assigned by Pharnaces occur also in PF 1807 and 1828.

exercised by the same persons (along with many others), is quite distinct from the role of assigning. The three frequent assigners, Karkiš, Šuddayauda and Iršena, occur even more frequently as apportioners, at some of the same sites and at many additional sites. Karkiš and Šuddayauda also as apportioners seem to be confined to the Persepolis area: but Iršena in this role, surprisingly, is not confined to the Susa area. One of the texts is PF 878: eight treasury workers subsisting on rations at Nīrīz, whose apportionments are set by Šuddayauda (m.⌈Šu⌉-ud-da-ya-u-da ša-ra-man-na, lit. "Šuddayauda apportioning"), received 240 quarts of wine...in the first and second months,...year 22, two men receiving 20 (per month), five men 10, one woman 30.

PF 878, it may be noted, is quite similar to PF 882, cited above, with Karkiš as assigner. The texts which name apportioners are in general quite similar to the texts which name assigners, though less stereotyped. They differ particularly in providing a wider range of qualifications, both professional and geographical (Assyrians, Bactrians, Egyptians, Sardians, etc.), for the work groups. Karkiš, Šuddayauda and Iršena all bear the title *kurdabattiš*, "chief of workers".[1] The other persons to whom this title applies all serve as apportioners.[2] The title therefore seems to relate particularly to the apportioning function.

The apportioners evidently provided lists of the names of workers in groups under their general supervision, stipulating how much each worker should receive. Such lists guided the local supply officers in the issuance of rations. Two such lists survive. PF 2038 gives the names of eight males receiving from 18 to 30 quarts (of grain per month), twenty-one females receiving 21 or 24 quarts, and one woman, presumably a supervisor, receiving 60 quarts; seven of the males should be boys and perhaps half of the females girls; the group is at Bardubara, otherwise unknown; the name of the apportioner is unfortunately not mentioned. The other such text, Fort. 471-1, originally named fourteen males and sixty-four females; but it is sadly damaged, with place name and other details lost. The treasury fragment PT 84 may have been a list of this kind. PT 4, though similar, seems to be a record of a single payment.

In contrast to the assigning role, which was sometimes exercised by exalted officials, including even the king (e.g. PF 1946: 73–6), the role

[1] Karkiš, e.g. PF 1161; Šuddayauda, e.g. PF 1792; Iršena, e.g. PF 1368.
[2] The other persons are Mišparma (PF 158), Bakadada (e.g. PF 159), also, with some doubt, Datukka and Zimakka (both Fort. 528). In the treasury texts Bakurada (PT 42, 60) and Napizza (PT 49a-3, 53) bear this title.

of apportioner often was exercised by officials of relatively low rank. Thus Masdayašna, a supply officer for large work groups (e.g. PF 960), is also apportioner for a few horses (e.g. PF 1942: 7–10). Šuddayauda as assigner and apportioner in the Persepolis area disappeared in the year 26. His successor in both roles was Baratkama, later the Persepolis treasurer (see above).[1]

In the treasury texts the treasurer, who is assigner only of accountants (see above), serves as apportioner for groups with many qualifications.[2] The range of his responsibilities, in Persepolis and its environs, is astonishing. But one responsibility he did not normally have, even for the workers whose apportionments he set, was the actual issuance of rations. The treasury texts deal with the very special cases in which he is required, on behalf of those who did have that responsibility, to pay out silver in lieu of rations.

The texts with Karkiš and Šuddayauda assigning work groups, as mentioned above, provide the names of places in the Persepolis area. Nearly all of these texts are associated with two seals, Seal 1 used by both officials and Seal 32 used by Šuddayauda. Seal 1 and Seal 32 occur also with other texts, some of which name Šuddayauda as apportioner, while some do not name either Šuddayauda or Karkiš. These other texts provide additional names of places in the Persepolis area. The most frequent place names are Shiraz, Matezziš and Uranduš. Matezziš (OP *Uvādaičaya*) is known (from DB §43), but its location is not. In PF 1572 a group of Indians travelling from the king to India receive rations at Matezziš; this should indicate that it lies east or north-east of Persepolis. The supply officer in PF 1572, Bakawiš, appears in the same capacity at Pasargadae (Elamite *Batrakataš*, PF 908), indicating that the two places may be near one another. Matezziš, on the evidence of our texts, is the most important site, after Persepolis, in the Persepolis area. Shiraz is mentioned just as often. But the largest work group at Matezziš is much larger than any at Shiraz.[3] Matezziš is, after Persepolis, the most

---

[1] Baratkama occurs twice as assigner (PF 879, Fort. 5904), four times as apportioner (e.g. PF 1120), in the years 27 and 28. Five of the six texts qualify the workers as "treasurer", meaning simply people who work in the treasury; four of the texts (e.g. PF 865) define the men and women (but not the boys and girls) by more exact qualifications, mostly untranslatable, including "treasurers" in a narrower sense.

[2] In PT 39 he is apportioner for 1,348 "treasurers", surely not all treasurers in a narrow sense. He sets apportionments also for stonemasons (e.g. PT 1963-3), carpenters (e.g. PT 32), blacksmiths (e.g. PT 23), sculptors (e.g. PT 1957-1), even for shepherds (e.g. PT 61), among others.

[3] Fort. 1292 (cf. PF. 959–61) shows 712 workers at Matezziš, while PF 1028 shows 490 workers as the maximum at Shiraz.

common destination for travellers from Susa. In all there are twenty-seven place names associated with Seals 1 and 32. Most, including Uranduš (with fourteen occurrences), are otherwise unknown. The other known place names are Persepolis (three times with Seal 1), Pasargadae, Rakkan (OP *Raxā*), Nīrīz, Tukraš (presumably Tukriš) and Tamukkan (presumably Taoce).

The occurrence of certain supply officers with two or more place names should indicate that the places are close together. Thus Matezziš is associated not only with Pasargadae (see above), but also, by Masdayašna, with Persepolis, and, by Datapparna, with Tenukku; Tenukku is associated with Tukraš by Miturna.[1] In like manner Shiraz is associated with Uranduš by Akkaya, Uranduš with Parmizzan, Hiran and Nīrīz by Šiyāna.[2] This set of names, since Shiraz and Nīrīz are a hundred miles apart, defines a rather large sub-area. Perhaps Uranduš is near Shiraz, Parmizzan and Hiran closer to Nīrīz. Nīrīz, in turn, is associated with Tamukkan, Kutkuš and Rutannuzzan by Bakabada.[3] Such evidence has its limitations, since supply officers might be transferred, or there could be two with the same name (see below). But the evidence can be accepted tentatively, in the absence of contradictions.

It remains a question where the texts were written. They may have been written at the various sites by scribes who periodically travelled about, carrying Seal 1 or Seal 32. Or they may possibly have been written at Persepolis on the basis of information conveyed from the various sites.

In the Susa area Iršena as assigner employs Seal 4, which appears also with a number of texts which name Iršena as apportioner. Of the twelve place names associated with Seal 4, only Hidali is certainly known from other sources.[4] As in the Persepolis area, the place names can be divided among sub-areas on the basis of supply officers. Here there is other evidence which makes the divisions sharper and extends the list of names. Ištimanka as supply officer connects Kurra and Kaupirriš, which evidently lie on the boundary between the Susa area and the middle area,

---

[1] For Masdayašna see e.g. PF 987–8 and 782. For Datapparna see PF 880 and 881. For Miturna see PF 939–40 and 1135.
[2] For Akkaya see PF 947–9. For Šiyāna see PF 878 and 896–902.
[3] For Bakabada see PF 962, 984–5 and 990.
[4] Hidali, very frequent in the fortification texts, occurs with Seal 4 only in PF 874. At Hidali travellers between Susa and Persepolis (e.g. PF 1400), Kerman (PF 1398–9) and India (PF 2057) frequently receive rations. PF 2057 indicates that it lies at six days' journey from Dašer, hence, presumably, seven days' or more from Susa.

since both are elsewhere connected with middle area sites (see below).[1] Irtuppiya is supply officer at seven sites, including Hidali and the frequently mentioned Liduma.[2] In this and other roles Irtuppiya is extremely active in the Susa area (see below). Mišparma is supply officer at Zappi, perhaps to be placed with or near the Irtuppiya sites, since Irtuppiya in another role is connected with Zappi.[3] Finally, Pirtiš is supply officer at Tašpak and Hišema, which seem to lie closer to Susa.[4] In other texts Tašpak and Hišema are connected, via Seal 15, with certain other places, notably Šurkutur.[5] Šurkutur, never with Iršena or Seal 4, seems to lie beyond the jurisdiction of Iršena. As supply officer Parru appears not only at Šurkutur and sites in its sub-area, but also at Tašpak.[6]

The middle area is defined primarily by Seals 3 and 30. They yield eighteen place names. Kurra and Kaupirriš, which evidently lie on the border of the Susa area (see above), are connected by Umaya as supply officer with Kemarukkaš and Uzamannaš.[7] The supply officer Turpiš connects Kansan and Kuristiš.[8] Similarly Mazaentiš connects Kuristiš and Kušan.[9] These latter sites may be relatively close to Persepolis, since PF 1593 records the transportation of flour from Kušan to Persepolis.[10] From Maturban commodities were transported both to Persepolis and to Susa.[11] As compared to the other two areas the middle area seems to be small. At only one site in this area is the issuance of rations to travellers recorded. This is Uzikurraš, often mentioned as a stopping place for travellers between Persepolis and Susa.[12] Since work groups here are relatively small, the area may be lightly populated. Notably frequent are ration texts for animals, especially small numbers of horses.[13]

---

[1] For Ištimanka, see e.g. PF 873 and 925.

[2] For Irtuppiya, see e.g. PF 847, 874, 876, 924, 936; Fort. 720 connects him with Tiliman (Tilmun?), Fort. 997 with Parmadan.

[3] For Mišparma, see e.g. PF 929–32. Irtuppiya with Zappi occurs in PF 1790.

[4] For Pirtiš, see e.g. PF 917 and 934.

[5] For Seal 15, see e.g. PF 553 and 578; it occurs also on Fort. 2077 (at Tašpak).

[6] For Parru, see e.g. PF 1088 (at Šurkutur), 1089 (at Tašpak), 1242 (at Atuk).

[7] For Umaya, see e.g. PF 869 (at Kurra), 870 (at Uzamannaš), 1659 (at Kemarukkaš), 1869 (at Kaupirriš).

[8] For Turpiš, see e.g. PF 851 and 1637.

[9] For Mazaentiš, see e.g. PF 966 and 1876.

[10] Cf. however PF 1594, in which cereals supplied by Umaya (presumably at Kurra or a nearby site) are transported to Persepolis.

[11] See PF 41 and 57. For Maturban with Seal 3, see PF 447.

[12] See e.g. PF 1414–20. In PF 1436 the travellers were going from Kerman to Susa (via Persepolis?). That text does not mention Uzikurraš, but names Pirratamka, the supply officer at Uzikurraš. For Pirratamka and Uzikurraš with Seal 3, see e.g. PF 964.

[13] Cf. e.g. PF 1657–9. For fowl rations cf. e.g. PF 1718–21.

THE EVIDENCE OF THE PERSEPOLIS TABLETS

While all the very frequent place names and many of the less frequent place names can be firmly located in one of the three areas, there remains a large number of place names which can be so located only provisionally or not at all. Places provisionally located often are connected with unlocated places. PF 2084 provides a striking example; it lists fourteen places from which quantities of sheep and oil are withdrawn, for Puksika to apportion at Maknan. One of the places, Tikrakkaš (line 2), is provisionally located in the Persepolis area.[1] But another, Kuntarruš (line 5), should be the place in Media mentioned in DB §31 (OP $Kud^u ruš$). There can be no firm decision in which area the fourteen places belong. The evidence suggests, indeed, that they belong in different areas, even outside of the three areas which have been defined.

The fact that a supply officer of the same name occurs at two places is not, by itself, proof that the two are close together. In other roles the same name very probably indicates the same person. But supply officers are extremely numerous. Quite likely there are cases of two persons with the same name in this role. Where there is supporting evidence the same name certainly or probably represents the same person. Otherwise we cannot be sure. Supply officers occur abundantly in nearly all classes of texts, usually following the commodity at the beginning of the text, as in PF 1155: 1–3: 70 *mar-ri-iš* W.GEŠTIN.lg *kur-min* m.*Ú-ša-ya-na*, "70 *marriš* (of) wine supplied by (lit. entrusting of) Ušaya". The addressees in letters are often supply officers. Thus in PF 2067 the same Ušaya, with the title "wine carrier", is ordered by Pharnaces to issue wine to priests at Kemarukkaš. Ušaya supplies several commodities, but chiefly wine, at various sites on the border between the Susa area and the middle area. Some supply officers are limited in their operations. Ammamarda, for instance, supplies only cereals, only at Hišema.[2] Most occur rarely, many only once. Of those that occur frequently, some are more or less confined to this role, while others, notably Irtuppiya (see below) are frequent also in other roles.

In certain texts the seal of the supply officer is impressed on the left edge of the tablet, the seal of the recipient on the reverse and other edges. This is regularly the case with the travel texts (excepting those without seals). Thus texts with Seal 18 on the left edge all name Mirayauda.[3] Seal 10 occurs on many travel texts, only one of which (PF 1309) names

---

[1] Tikrakkaš is associated in PF 2080 with Mandumattiš, which occurs with Seal 1 in PF 905.
[2] See e.g. PF 797 and 1770.
[3] These are mostly travel texts, e.g. PF 1374–7, but there are also some which provide rations for settled groups, e.g. PF 1095–6.

THE EVIDENCE OF THE PERSEPOLIS TABLETS

both the supply officer, Haturdada, and the place at which the ration was received, Kurdušum (in the Susa area). In other travel texts with Seal 10 the presence of the seal no doubt identified both the supply officer and the site. Seal 10 occurs with four texts of other categories, all of which name Haturdada, while three mention Kurdušum. In two of these texts he supplies flour rations.[1] In the other two he receives flour delivered to Kurdušum, doubtless to replenish his stock.[2]

Many texts inform us, generally in vague terms, of commodities received by supply officers. Thus one text tells us of 56,490 quarts of grain provided for provisions (*haduš*) for Šati-Šimut to apportion, entrusted to Ammamarda (see above) and Basaka at Hišema, in the year 21.[3] A similar text (PF 434) tells us of 3,065 quarts of grain entrusted to Ammamarda to be set aside for seed at Hišema, for Šati-Šimut to apportion, in the year 22. The mention of seed indicates that the administration, through Šati-Šimut the apportioner, exercised some control over production. But the texts do not inform us whether the grain was produced by state employees or by private farmers under contract. The function of the supply officer, however, seems clear. He received the grain, held it, and issued it on order. As for Ammamarda, he was not under the exclusive jurisdiction of Šati-Šimut; he was entrusted with grain earmarked also for other apportioners.[4]

There are several large accounting texts which give a complete record of receipts and disbursements at a given time and place. PF 1960, for example, starts out with six detailed entries concerning amounts of grain dispensed at Šimparra in the year 23 for rations of workers and horses, and for other purposes, adding up to 7,530 quarts. It then lists the carry-over from the year 22, the amount provided for provisions (*haduš*), and other receipts, adding up to 18,425 quarts on hand; this total is then balanced by the 7,530 quarts dispensed plus a new carry-over plus an amount paid for carriage plus an amount "withdrawn". The texts name not only the supply officer, Hindukka, but also two associated officials, a *haturmakša* and an *etira*.[5] Such texts, as well as other accounting texts which lack one or another of the elements, give a fuller record of the

---

[1] PF 1081 and Fort. 585.   [2] PF 83 and Fort. 1232.

[3] PF 552. The exact meaning of *haduš* remains unclear. In other contexts (e.g. PF 2086: 6) it refers to the increase of livestock.

[4] The other apportioners are: Zazzap, PF 435 (seed); Uštana, PF 553; Kitete, PF 554; Nariyapikna, PF 555.

[5] The *haturmakša* (of uncertain derivation, presumably OP) is replaced in similar contexts by *ullira*, "delivery man". An example is PF 1968: 12–14, which identifies the supply officer by the title *tumara*, "grain handler". In other contexts, e.g. PF 741, the *haturmakša* plays a religious role.

activities of the supply officer than can be gained from the available small texts recording individual disbursements.

The most versatile of the supply officers is Irtuppiya. He supplies not only cereals, beer and wine, but also certain rare, perhaps exotic, commodities.[1] In this role he appears more or less simultaneously at twelve sites. Though less ubiquitous suppliers may have issued commodities by their own hands, this can hardly have been the case with Irtuppiya. At some of the same sites and at other sites Irtuppiya appears in other roles. Thus he is apportioner as well as supplier at Umpuranuš.[2] He writes letters ordering others to issue commodities.[3] There is mention of his estate (*irmatam*) at Parmadan.[4] His seal, Seal 2, is the third most frequent, after Seals 1 and 3. Irtuppiya, despite his appearance in some rather humble roles, is clearly a man of consequence. His most frequent other role is that of agent. For example, in PF 1071 Irtuppiya receives 2,220 quarts of *tarmu* grain, supplied by Hapuya, and gives it to thirty-four workers of the place Hutpirri.

The role of agent evidently differs from one case to another. The travel texts often specifically state that the agent is one of the recipients, as in PF 1290, where Rumada receives $3\frac{1}{2}$ quarts of flour, $1\frac{1}{2}$ for himself, one each for two "boys" (not really boys, but subordinates). Probably the agent is a recipient also in many travel texts and in certain other texts which do not state the fact. But Irtuppiya in this role is not likely to be a recipient. He cannot be a recipient in PF 1065, where he receives 60 quarts of beer and gives it to one man, a tax handler (*baziš huttira*), for six months. Nor can the agent be a recipient in texts dealing with rations for mothers and animals.[5]

Often there is more than one agent. In PF 1077 Mišbaturma and Uššaba receive flour for twenty-four men (quite likely including the agents) and fourteen "boys". Usually the name of only one of the agents is given, as in PF 1059, where Midasa and his companion(s) (*akkayaše*) receive grain for nine workers conscripted (*rabbap*) at Nīrīz. Midasa and the "companion(s)" seem to be on the same level, and it might be a matter of indifference which of the two (or more) was named. Whether

---

[1] E.g. *razi* (PF 717), *banura* (PF 725) and *madukka* (Fort. 6767), all of unknown meaning, all requisitioned by the king.

[2] He is supplier e.g. in PF 876 (Iršena being apportioner). He is apportioner in PF 1115.

[3] PF 1845–8, also Fort. 1472 and 441–3.

[4] PF 330. In Fort. 1091 fifty-five cattle are sent from the estate of Irtuppiya for the herdsman of King Darius.

[5] Cf. e.g. PF 1202 (mothers) and 1650 (horses).

there was such a thing as a professional agent is unclear. Perhaps the mysterious *titikaš* persons fall into this category. They occur often as agents for special rations at places in the Susa area.[1] Only rarely do the texts give the names of *titikaš* persons.[2] Agents are mentioned most commonly in texts which do not name an apportioner or an assigner. One purpose for mentioning the agent would be to aid in identifying the recipients. There probably are other purposes not yet apparent.

More definitely than the agents, the "chiefs" (Elamite *iršap* or *matištukkašpe*, derived from OP) are always attached to groups. Women are particularly prominent in this role. In PF 875 a woman "chief" receives 30 quarts of wine per month, while two men get 20 each and two men 10. There are many texts in which one woman, without title, receives 30 quarts of wine, while men get 20 or 10 and other women get 10.[3] In such cases the one woman is no doubt a "chief". Where male "chiefs" are mentioned they also receive 30 quarts of wine per month.[4]

The women "chiefs" occur in work groups which include far more women than men. This fact is not apparent in the wine texts, since only a small part of the total group receives wine rations (boys and girls never receive wine). With the wine text PF 875, mentioned above, we may compare the grain text PF 935, which in all probability concerns the same work group: in both the place is Kurra, the apportioner is Iršena, the year is the twenty-second. Whereas in PF 875 one woman and four men receive wine, in PF 935 one woman (untitled) receives 50 quarts of grain and four men (also nine women) receive 40, while twenty-three women and eleven men (along with boys and girls) receive lesser amounts. PF 865: 23 indicates that 50 quarts of grain was a normal monthly ration for a woman "chief".

From other contexts it is apparent that the title "chief" does not in itself convey high status. In the travel text PF 1330 the "chief" Pisukka is presumably one of the ten "boys" who receive the minimum daily ration of one quart of flour; while in Fort. 1000 the "chief" (name illegible) is in charge of a travelling party of 460 "gentlemen" and 100 "boys". The named "chiefs" in PT 4, who receive up to 600 shekels of silver by order of Darius, seem to be of higher rank than any of the

---

[1] Cf. e.g. PF 1088 (at Šurkutur), 1089 (at Tašpak), 1125 (at Dašer).
[2] Bakapukša (OP *Bagabuxša*) the *titikaš* is agent in PF 1953: 22–4 and 25–8. Travel parties of *titikaš* persons occur in PF 1344 (naming Mamakka) and Fort. 1620 (naming Marrezza); they travel from, and carry the sealed documents of, the king and Pharnaces, respectively.
[3] Cf. e.g. PF 882–8.   [4] See PF 1063, 1064 and 1076.

"chiefs" in the fortification texts. That payment is, however, impossible to evaluate. No time period is mentioned. It may be a regular payment in lieu of or in addition to payments in kind. It may be a special bonus. Work groups which, judging by amounts received, include "chiefs", contrast with other groups which receive only standard rations, all men receiving 30 quarts of grain per month and all women 20.[1] Work groups with women receiving 50 quarts always include other women, and often some men, receiving more than the standard amounts. Thus in PF 948 there are twenty-two women and seven men receiving 40 quarts of grain, sixteen men receiving 35, fifty-five women receiving 30, and only three men and twenty-two women receiving the standard amounts. We may presume that such groups included highly qualified personnel. One unusual text, PF 865, provides titles, mostly untranslatable, for all the men and women, even those receiving standard rations; it mentions one man, an *atna* keeper, who receives 60 quarts, more than the woman "chief" receives.[2]

The regular monthly ration texts usually do not provide titles, even for the work group as a whole, and the titles which occur are rarely helpful. For example, the six "goldsmiths" in PF 872 include two men and three women receiving standard rations, and one girl receiving the minimum ration of 5 quarts of grain per month. The term "goldsmiths" means that they are attached to a goldsmith group. None is likely to be a full-fledged goldsmith. On the other hand, the five "Egyptian goldsmiths" receiving each 40 quarts of flour per month in Fort. 1858 may well be genuine goldsmiths.

Certain titles of individuals must be differently interpreted in different contexts. For example, Rumada the *ullira* ("delivery man") who in PF 788 receives the standard ration of 30 quarts of grain per month is just what his title implies. But Zitrina, "*ullira* in the treasury" in PF 1947: 31–2, who receives the extraordinary ration of 90 quarts of flour per month, is no ordinary delivery man; probably he is in charge of delivery services in the treasury.

Of the texts dealing with regular rations for work groups less than one-fifth convey wine or beer. Nearly all the rest convey grain (presumably barley) or, on occasion, flour or *tarmu* grain (perhaps

---

[1] See e.g. PF 848–55, 857–8, 860–3, 867–9, 909–14. In these texts the boys receive from 5 to 25 quarts per month, the girls from 5 to 15.
[2] Similar texts are PF 864 and 866, which in line 7 mentions a scribe (*tuppira*) receiving 40 quarts. The whole groups in PF 864–6 are called "treasurers". The boys and girls have no special titles.

wheat) substituted at the same rate. It follows that most work groups did not receive wine or beer on a regular basis.

The grain ration scale is based on a unit of 5 quarts per month: this is both the minimum ration (given to some boys and girls) and the common factor in all rations.[1] With all texts combined, 83% of the men receive 30 quarts (six units), nearly all the rest 35, 40 or 45 quarts. Of the women, 87% receive 20 or 30 quarts, nearly all of the rest 40 quarts. The same scale can be discerned, as we shall see, in the treasury texts in which silver is paid in lieu of grain rations.

The treasury texts in which silver is paid in lieu of wine and sheep rations are spread thinly over a period of thirty-five years, while those involving grain (nearly half of all texts in which the commodity can be identified) are confined to eight or ten months in the years Xerxes 19–20. All payments of silver for wine or sheep, as far as can be ascertained, are based on the fixed equivalences: 1 shekel = 10 quarts of wine, 3 shekels = 1 sheep, which are often expressly stated (see PT 1: 12–13). The reason for payment in silver presumably was administrative convenience at a time of commodity shortage.

Grain obviously was the basic food, and the grain rations for the most part approximated the minimum dietary requirements. Only under dire circumstances, therefore, could silver be paid in lieu of grain. Such circumstances arose in the ninth month of Xerxes 19, when the administration began paying silver in lieu of half the grain ration. In PT 37: 10–11 and 17–18, $\frac{5}{12}$ shekel ("a third and a twelfth") is paid in lieu of half the minimum ration, that is, $2\frac{1}{2}$ quarts of grain. Thus $\frac{1}{6}$ shekel = 1 quart. This is already five times higher than the normal rate, which should be at or near $\frac{1}{30}$ shekel per quart (see below). But it was still insufficient. During the next two months the rate stood at $\frac{1}{4}$ shekel.[2] Subsequently it declined to $\frac{2}{9}$ shekel, rose again to $\frac{1}{4}$, declined to $\frac{1}{5}$, and, in the fourth month of Xerxes 20, returned to $\frac{1}{6}$ shekel.[3] There is only one grain text outside of the period described. This is PT 1963–20, dated in the fifth and sixth months. It seems likely that the unmentioned year

---

[1] A different scale based on the *bawiš* (= 3 quarts) occurs very rarely. See e.g. PF 1956: 4–10, where three persons (boys or girls) receive 3 quarts and one woman (no doubt a "chief") receives 60 quarts, while most of the rest receive 27 quarts. This scale is used in the two lists of the names of workers, PF 2038 and Fort. 471–1, discussed above.

[2] $\frac{5}{8}$ shekel = $2\frac{1}{2}$ quarts, e.g. PT 39: 27 (tenth month), PT 42: 21–2 (eleventh month).

[3] For the rate $\frac{2}{9}$ see e.g. PT 46: 18–20 (twelfth month) and PT 49: 17–19 (first month). For the rate $\frac{1}{4}$ see e.g. PT 53: 20–2 (second month). For the rate $\frac{1}{5}$ see e.g. PT 66: x+13 (third month). For the rate $\frac{1}{6}$ see e.g. PT 69: 23 (fourth month), where silver is paid for only a third of the ration.

is Xerxes 20.[1] Since there is no indication of fractional payment, silver apparently is paid for the full ration. If so, the rate is $\frac{1}{20}$ shekel = 1 quart, approaching normal.[2]

The period of the grain texts must have required unhappy decisions on the part of the economic officials. They would prefer to carry on as usual and to keep the silver in the treasury. It may be significant that Mawiš, who had been treasurer for at least ten years, was replaced by Ratininda in the first month of Xerxes 20. There must have been distress also among the book-keepers who had to make computations with unfamiliar fractions, and among the scribes, who could express some of the results only very clumsily (thus in PT 46: 19–20, $\frac{5}{9}$ is expressed as "a half and a half of one-ninth"). Not surprisingly, a number of discrepancies resulted.[3]

In the fortification texts there are indications of relatively mild commodity shortages. In PF 1034, for example, a group of 257 workers receives half-rations of barley. In PF 1035 the same group, in the same month and year, receives the other half of its rations in *tarmu* grain. Certain wine texts give half-rations to women. Thus PF 889 gives 15 quarts to one woman, 5 each to sixteen women; while the otherwise nearly identical text PF 888 gives 30 quarts to one woman and 10 each to sixteen; both texts give 20 quarts each to nine men and 10 each to twenty-one. Evidently the male administrators decided that women could tolerate a reduced wine ration better than men. Presumably the women received compensation in some other commodity, or in silver.

The payments in silver recorded by the treasury texts imply the existence of a private commodity market. It would be a mockery to give silver to hungry workers if they had no place to spend it. The private market must have had sources of supply and regular customers. We cannot expect the records of the state economy to shed much light on it. Any official whose rations were more than he could consume might supply the private market. Notably Pharnaces and the other high officials with huge daily rations would want to sell or exchange their surpluses. We have of course no records of such transactions. But the state itself sometimes had surpluses of grain, wine and fruits, and

---

[1] If the year is Xerxes 20, the treasurer addressed in line 1 must be Ratininda, not Mawiš, as restored in the published text.

[2] The rate results from $\frac{1}{4}$ shekel = 5 quarts. Although the minimum ration does not occur in PT 1963–20 we may assume that it is $\frac{1}{4}$ shekel, since that is the common factor in the rations that do occur (if our present understanding of the text is correct).

[3] In PT 46, for example, the allotment for women does not fit the scale, and the total given is incorrect on any terms.

THE EVIDENCE OF THE PERSEPOLIS TABLETS

officials sought to exchange them for livestock. Thus in PF 1978 Battiš the storekeeper (*amparabaraš*) at the "fortress" Udarakka withdrew 8,907 quarts of grain, made a deal for one male mule and one cow, both of prime quality (*pirratammiyaš*), at a cost of 11,000 quarts, and added the necessary 2,093 quarts; whereupon the mule was entrusted to Annamasa the "horse master" (*aššabattiš*), the cow to Bakaparna. We are not told, here or ever, with whom the deal was made. But most likely it was made with a private party rather than with another public agency. The majority of such texts record the failure to make a deal. Evidently it was difficult in times of surplus to exchange the commodities for something of more lasting value. Two officials actually died in the attempt![1]

Besides the regular monthly ration texts there are several other kinds of ration texts. None of these other kinds, except for the special case of the travel texts, is nearly so frequent. Clearly they do not apply to the great bulk of the work force. There are texts which convey small extra amounts, usually equal to one day's ration per month, of wine, flour, beer or grain. All recipients receive the same amount. Thus in PF 1088 fifty-two workers at Šurkutur receive monthly for six months one quart of flour as *sat* plus ⅓ quart as *karmaziš* (meaning unknown). Wine, which as regular ration is confined to a small proportion of the adults, in these texts is distributed much more widely. In PF 1107 there are 527 workers at Parmizzan receiving as *sat* a half quart of wine monthly for six months, while in PF 891, for example, only five persons at Parmizzan receive wine as regular ration: three men each 20 quarts per month, two women each 30. Texts like PF 1088 and 1107 may involve monthly feasts, possibly religious. We may compare such texts as PF 337, in which 800 quarts of grain, 400 for Ahuramazda, 400 for (the god) Mišduši, are utilized for a divine ceremony (*bakadaušiya*), after which "the workers consumed (it)". Animal ration texts commonly employ the verbal form of *sat, sati-*, which may mean "to feed".

There are texts which convey regular rations on a daily basis. Usually the work group is small and the time period short, as in PF 1259, where Zamašba the accountant (*mušin zikkira*) receives 1½ quarts of flour, two "boys" each one, for ten days, on the basis of a "sealed document" of Pharnaces. Larger work groups sometimes occur, as in PF 1262, where 118 "gentlemen" and 173 servants, Median nurserymen(?) (*maršaparrape*), receive flour for twenty-five days. The time period

[1] See PF 1974: 8–9 and 1978: 13–14.

occasionally is longer, as in PF 1241, where Dattanna the auditor(?) (*halnut hašira*) and his three servant "boys" receive flour for twelve months in the year 23.[1] The recipients in these texts are itinerant. Apparently they are almost all adult males, including those called alternatively "boys" and "servants".[2] As in the travel texts they usually receive flour, because it is easier to prepare, rather than grain. The daily rations, like the travel rations, are often said to be authorized by "sealed documents".[3] It was more convenient to handle the rations in this way than to arrange for regular rationing at temporary locations.

There are texts which record single payments to mothers. Those who bear boys receive 10 quarts of wine or beer, or 20 quarts of flour, barley or other cereals; while those who bear girls receive half as much. The fact that these are single payments is shown by PF 1219; this text covers a period of twelve months; the forty women with boys and the forty-two with girls receive each a single payment of 10 quarts of beer or 5 quarts, respectively. The recipients are sometimes called workers, as in PF 1206, where the mother is a "worker subsisting on rations". But they must have had special status; otherwise the texts would be much more numerous. The woman Matmabba, who in Fort. 196–2 receives 20 quarts of flour (presumably as the mother of a boy, though this is not stated), recurs in PF 1790: 8 as one of five women "chiefs" who are signally rewarded by Pharnaces with four sheep per year. Since wine and beer texts greatly outnumber cereal texts there is reason to doubt that all recipients received both. Yet the mothers Lanunu and Parrukuzziš receive grain in PF 1226, wine in Fort. 290–2, a nearly identical text with the same date.

In the travel texts work groups are relatively rare. Featured here are various professional travellers, especially the "elite guide" (*barrišdama*) who shepherds Indians, Cappadocians, Egyptians, Sardians and Skudrians.[4] Prominent also are the mounted couriers of the express

---

[1] In PF 1241 the twelve months are figured as 360 days, though the year 23 had only 355 days. Regularly in the daily ration texts one month = 30 days, even when a particular month had only 29.

[2] The letter PF 1824 dealing with daily rations is an apparent exception. There men and women, a boy and a girl receive daily rations which are exactly one-thirtieth of standard monthly rations. This group, however, is not itinerant. It has just been transferred from one fixed station to another. The boy gets a half quart of grain daily, unlike the "boys" in itinerant groups, who usually get a quart of flour.

[3] The king is a frequent authorizer (e.g. PF 1242). Pharnaces appears several times (e.g. PF 1259, cited above). Bakabana occurs in PF 1238–40, Zissawis in Fort. 445.

[4] See e.g. PF 1363, 1409, 1557, 1572, 1577. Zišanduš and his five "boys" guide a lone woman from Susa to Kandahar; they all receive flour, she receiving 3 quarts per day (PF 1440), but she alone receives wine (PF 1550).

service (*pirradaziš*) so lauded by Herodotus.[1] There is the messenger (*hutlak*), and the "forerunner" (*karabattiš*), who may be an advance agent for large parties.[2] There are a few very large parties. In PF 1532 there are 2,454 "gentlemen" who receive each ⅓ quart of beer; 1,500 "*lin* makers" receive the same in PF 1542, as do 1,150 workers in PF 1527. Two large parties of Egyptians going to Tamukkan receive, exactly or approximately, ⅓ quart of wine in Fort. 1967 (690 "stone removers") and PF 1557 (547 workers). The fact that most of the rations were for a single day shows that the stations were regularly spaced at intervals of about twenty miles. The fact that the tablets commonly bear the seal of the supplier shows that the texts were inscribed at the station. To set up and maintain the stations required an effort which could be justified only by very heavy traffic.

In the texts concerned with rations for animals occur horses of the express service (*pirradaziš*), presumably used by the mounted couriers of the travel texts.[3] Horses, variously qualified, are much the most common animals in these texts. Fowls are surprisingly frequent, chiefly the larger ones, *basbas* ("duck"?) and *ippur* ("goose"?), but also many smaller ones.[4] In the ration texts for animals the numbers are relatively low. Very high numbers of animals occur in certain inventory texts. PF 2007 itemizes 16,843 sheep and goats. Another text itemizes 435 camels.[5]

In addition to the ration texts there are many other kinds of texts, mostly not very explicit, dealing with export, delivery, deposit and various other matters. Exports go to many places, but chiefly to Persepolis, as in PF 6, where 30,000 quarts of grain, supplied by Sunkana, place unmentioned, is taken to Persepolis; the purpose of the text presumably is to credit the supplier. Noteworthy among deliveries are hides of animals, usually sheep and goats, delivered to treasuries at Shiraz (PT 59–61), Pasargadae (PF 62–3), Matezziš (PF 70–1) and other places, perhaps to make parchment for Aramaic scribes; Persepolis is unmentioned, but may be involved in texts with no place name (e.g. PF 67–8).

---

[1] Herod. 8. 98. The couriers travel mostly to and from the king (see e.g. PF 1285 and 1315).
[2] See e.g. PF 1301–3 (*hutlak*), PF 1340–1 (*karabattiš*).
[3] See e.g. PF 2061–2.
[4] See especially PF 1943: 21–30, where the smallest fowl receives only one-fiftieth as much as the large fowls.
[5] Fort. 626–2: 1–7 classifies the camels as male and female adults, four-, three-, two- and one-year-olds, and calves. This unusual text continues with two large herds of cattle and, after a long break, ends with small numbers of asses and *basbas* fowl, "this (being) the total (of) living livestock" (PAP *hi aš ka-da-ka*).

There are numerous deposits, almost all of fruits or *tarmu* grain, "upon" many persons, often at a *partetaš* (derivation uncertain, presumably OP). Thus in PF 145 forty quarts of dates are deposited "upon" Dattukka, to be kept at Barašba in the *partetaš*, for Masdayašna to apportion. What was done with the fruits, which rarely appear in the ration texts, remains uncertain.

The six exchange texts (PF 274–9) and a few other texts (including texts such as PF 1978, cited above) inform us about relative values. Though the evidence is not completely consistent, the commonest equations are 1 sheep = 100 quarts of grain, 1 quart of wine = 3 quarts of grain. In terms of the fixed equivalences of the treasury texts (1 sheep = 3 shekels of silver, 10 quarts of wine = 1 shekel), the above equations make 1 quart of grain = $\frac{3}{100}$ or $\frac{1}{30}$ shekel.

Of some special interest are the requisitions made by the king or by certain members of the royal family, though it seems impossible to determine exactly for what purpose and on what terms the requisitions were made. Most involve common commodities, sometimes in very large amounts, as in PF 701, where 126,100 quarts of flour, supplied by Masdayašna, are dispensed "before" the king (*sunki tibba makka*) at Persepolis. Some involve rare commodities in small amounts, for example one quart of *madukka* in PF 719. Making requisitions, besides the king, are Irtašduna his wife, sometimes alone, as in PF 731, sometimes coupled with Arsames (presumably her son), as in PF 733, and also the woman Irdabama (e.g. PF 735), taken to be a member of the royal family because of her occurrence in such contexts.

Both Irdabama and Irtašduna are otherwise concerned in economic activities. A number of work groups are said to be "of" Irdabama, for example a group of 490 at Shiraz (PF 1028). One might suspect that she was merely a ceremonial sponsor. Irtašduna, however, appears not only in this role, but also as addresser of letters ordering the issuance of wine.[1]

The accounting texts have many forms, some simple, some quite complex. The forms tend to occur for a limited period and then to disappear.[2] Evidently the authorities were groping towards a workable system. Certain forms are too elaborate for the information to be conveyed. In PF 1986: 33–42 a six-column tabulation concerning five

[1] PF 1835–9. For workers of Irtašduna see e.g. PF 1236. Workers of the king occur e.g. in PF 1092.
[2] See e.g. PF 1972–80 and 2078, all covering the years 18 and 19, except PF 1979, for year 20. Some forms have only a single exemplar, e.g. PF 1981, 1989, 2006.

kinds of fruit tells us only that 200 quarts carried over from year 18 survived unchanged through year 19 (the fruits were presumably dried), there being no receipts or expenditures.

There is evidence that the system did not always work smoothly. PF 1940, recording expenditures of grain in the years 14 and 15, and PF 1997, recording receipts and expenditures of wine in the years 15, 16 and 17, were not inscribed until the second month of year 21. In PF 1957 the space for the carry-over in line 26 is left blank, and lines 37–8 state: "Battiš [the supply officer] and his companions say: 'Mirinzana did not give us a sealed document for what was carried forward in the year 21!'"[1]

The most striking evidence of administrative difficulties is provided by Fort. 2858, a letter from Šakšabanuš to Mirinzana. Despite puzzling details, the main purport is clear. A sealed document was sent off to Pharnaces concerning the fact that the accountants had not been delivering the accounts. "The man who carried(?) that tablet fled away. Now do you catch that man and send him off to Media(?). In Media (he will be) brought strictly to account. Furthermore, when you send off a tablet from yourself to Pharnaces, send it off then (with) the name of Pirrutu(?) – he will be carrying the tablet – written on that tablet. Thus Pharnaces has ordered, and I had (it) inscribed(?). Formerly the name of that man was not written." Evidently there was a lack of competent personnel. But in any case it would have been very difficult by the use of clay tablets to achieve an adequate accounting system for such varied and extensive operations. The problem might in the end have been solved by the use of records in Aramaic written on perishable materials. But we may never learn whether this was so.

[1] Cf. PF 2084: 12–13 and 18–21.

CHAPTER 12

ACHAEMENID COINS, WEIGHTS AND MEASURES

It is evident from the research of recent years that the lands constituting the Achaemenid Empire had inherited from earlier centuries two entirely separate currency systems. These systems continued in existence side by side until the last decades of the Empire. On the one hand, the territories south and east of the Taurus operated what can be described as a silver standard. The system, originated no doubt even as early as Sumer, and inherited by the Babylonians, had spread under the Assyrians, and later under the Achaemenids, to embrace Egypt, Syria, Eastern Anatolia, the Iranian Plateau and the Indo-Iranian borderlands. In those regions (though commodities such as gold, lead, corn, meat or wine may have served from time to time as media of payment), the most usual, and ultimate standard of worth was provided by fine silver. As necessary, this was tested for purity in the crucible, then reckoned for weight upon the scales, according to metrological standards already well established. Fundamentally, under this system, currency was silver – irrespective of the shape or form in which it was presented, and of whether or not it was made up in convenient units.[1] There was no requirement for the silver to be offered in the form of coin, though during the 5th century B.C. and later it was often obtainable in that form. In particular, much silver coin arrived by trade and tribute from the states of the Aegean and the Greek world. Naturally such sources contributed an infinite variety of differing denominations and weight-standards, which, when lumped together, could not readily be reckoned by counting, but only on the balance, like the earlier bullion. Indeed, apart from the trading cities of Phoenicia and Southern Anatolia, there is no evidence that in Achaemenid times mint for coinage existed within the greater part of this silver-zone. The system did not require that pieces used in current transactions were necessarily adjusted to regular individual weights. There was no need for the stamp of an authority

[1] Fossey (1937).

responsible for accuracy of weight or fineness. The only matters of consequence were total bulk weights, and the appearance of pure metal.

Under such a currency-system, numismatic and metrological study are not distinct as they are with later coinage. They have rather to be treated together, since taxes could as easily have been increased by raising the weight-standard as by increasing the assessment – so long as it could be arranged to issue the necessary new weights to the fiscal authorities. Thus a subject could have been required to pay two "heavy" minae of metal, instead of having his assessment lifted from two "normal" minae to four.

The traditional, and best established scale of bullion weights throughout the Middle East before the rise of Cyrus the Great is that known as the Babylonian standard. Its system of multiples is sexagesimal, and familiarity with their table (see Table I) is basic for any understanding of the subject. Here names of the denominations are given first in their Akkadian forms, as known from cuneiform documents: *biltu* "talent", *manū* "mina", *šiqlu* "shekel", *zūzu* "half-shekel, drachma". In English, the accompanying classical equivalents are commonly used, this practice being followed in the subsequent discussion. The absolute values quoted in the final column were derived from extant early Babylonian weights by Lehman (-Haupt).[1] There is discussion over the details of the calculation, but figures preferred for the mina by other authorities are no more than a few grams higher.[2]

Local circumstances (together with the sheer difficulty of maintaining, with the technical resources of the day, everywhere a precise and uniform standard) no doubt led to modification of the archetypal norms in certain areas and periods. At Ugarit, for example, there is evidence of certain transactions with a mina containing not 60, but 50 shekels.[3] This innovation is important, for later, during the 5th century B.C., the enormously influential Attic standard operated with a mina consisting of 100 drachmae, each of which was effectively half the Babylonian shekel. This arrangement seems to trace its inspiration, through channels still uncertain, to the same origins as the standard of Ugarit.

More frequently however, as already indicated, it was the absolute value of the unit that underwent change, rather than the system of multiples. It has been claimed, for example, that under the Assyrian

[1] Regling and Lehman-Haupt (1909).
[2] Thureau-Dangin (1921), p. 130 gives a figure of 502 gm.
[3] Thureau-Dangin (1934), p. 141; Lehman (-Haupt) (1889), p. 202.

kingdom, an enhanced "Royal" mina (of 1010 gm., thus almost exactly twice the weight of the original Babylonian mina) was enforced in certain transactions.[1] If that view is correct, the change could be seen as a Draconian increase in tribute, effected not by raising the assessment, but by enhancing the weights.

It also seems certain that during the later Assyrian period (towards 738 B.C.), shekel weights at a standard of 11.4 gm. were in use in Samaria and Judaea.[2] Like the presumed Assyrian "Royal" standard, such an innovation could have arisen from fiscal manipulations. Yet it is interesting too for its relation to the value-ratio between gold and silver. Just as the Achaemenid silver siglos after the reforms of Darius (p. 617 below) was valued at 20 to the gold daric of 8.35 gm., and itself weighed 5.60 gm., so the Judaean shekel at just over double the last figure, may have been adjusted to correspond to a unit of gold representing an Assyrian "Royal" shekel. Thus the Judaean shekel seems to have been significant for early experiments in bimetallism – the enforcement of a fixed ratio between the two metals – which later was established practice under the Achaemenids.

There is, at any rate, considerable evidence that "Bulk Silver" in various forms, constituted the main circulating medium in the Levant, Babylonia and Iran during the Achaemenid period. Some of the metal will have been in the form of rings, similar either to earrings or finger-rings (*unqu*, *ḫullu* and *šewēru*); or in the form of the heavier torques (*rikṣu*). Some of these pieces had been in use from very early periods in Babylonia, but once fabricated, continued to pass from hand to hand for many centuries. Dayton provides the only systematic treatment of this 'Ring-money', but his approach is not entirely satisfying. He is less concerned with the description and typology of the existing pieces than with a very hypothetical attempt to determine the particular species of grain from which its basic unit of mass could have been derived. Here there is danger both of a logical, and of a metrological error. The supposition that the early systems arose through the multiplication of the weight of a particular grain is an assumption as much unproven as was that of Thureau-Dangin, that the entire basis of Babylonian metrology was the unit of length, the cubit; and that the weight-denominations were defined by the weight of water contained in a cube with sides of this length, and various fractions of that weight.[3] Both

---

[1] C. H. W. Johns, *Assyrian deeds and documents* II (Cambridge, 1901), p. 262.
[2] Yadin (1961).
[3] Thureau-Dangin (1921), p. 132; *idem* (1909), pp. 79–111 and especially p. 94.

theories can hardly be valid at the same time, and there is no argument of substance in favour of either. That of Dayton has the further disadvantage of being based on an infinitesimal unit, which is thus especially liable to the play of chance and error. In metrological speculations the subjective element is a particular danger. Work of the 19th-century metrologists from similar faulty premises was therefore justly criticised by Beloch:[1] "Ancient metrology seems on the point of losing all solid ground under its feet, and becoming a meeting-place of wild fancies." It is more legitimate to concentrate attention on the careful description of the material evidence, than to pursue unproven assumptions as to the theoretical bases of ancient metrological systems.

We return, therefore, to considering the remaining forms of "Bulk Silver". Over a zone extending from Eastern Anatolia to Egypt, the flat "Cake Ingots" have been reported, for example at Zincirli, Ras Shamra and other sites. "Bar Ingots" of various sizes were the favoured medium in the zone of Assyrian influence, and in the Median Empire of northern Iran.[2] Smaller varieties of such bars remained in use on the Iranian Plateau under the Achaemenids, and came to influence the development of the Ancient Indian "Bent-Bar" coinage. Thus a carefully shaped bar in the Kabul Museum, weighing exactly 8.35 gm. (and thus representing the standard, as we shall see, of the reformed Babylonian shekel of Darius), is all but certainly an Achaemenid issue. The large, flat "Slab-Ingots" are decidedly rare, but several pieces in the following category may have resulted from their dismemberment. "Cut Silver" (*kaspu šebirtu*,[3] German *Hacksilber*) was produced by the subdivision of large pieces of "Bulk Silver" to provide small change. Raw material might be provided by any of the forms of ingot already mentioned, particularly "Bars" and "Slabs". If these were not to hand, silver tableware could be dismembered, or personal jewellery such as earrings and necklaces.[4] A few pieces of "Cut Silver" are even known bearing fragments of cuneiform inscriptions, for example a specimen at Kabul,[5] and another from Nūsh-i Jān. These were probably derived from inscribed "Slab-Ingots", though whether complete inscriptions could throw further light on the working of the system is still unknown. Finally, as we enter the period of coined silver during the 6th century B.C. and later, the various categories of "Bulk Silver" are increasingly

---

[1] *Griechische Geschichte*, 1, pt. 2, p. 333.   [2] Bivar (1971).
[3] cf. Jean Bottéro, *Textes économiques et administratifs* (*Archives Royales de Mari*) (Paris, 1958), p. 332.
[4] Robinson (1950).   [5] Henning (1956).

found mixed with Greek silver coins, of numerous states, and different metrological standards. Indeed it was such association with Greek coinage which first drew attention to the phenomenon of the so-called "Silversmith's Hoards", and made it possible to fix, at least approximately, the chronology of such finds. Until recent years, the accompanying "Bulk Silver" was usually disregarded, melted down (as in the Tigris Hoard of 1816)[1] or eliminated by the operation of the antiquities-market. "Ring-Money", though frequently found in excavations, has, with the exception of Dayton's treatment, languished almost unnoticed.

Like the other materials, the pieces of coined silver found in such deposits were commonly subdivided with the chisel, or simply dented by that means, to prove the solidity of the metal. Such tests were not for nothing, for noteworthy frauds are related which involved the use of plated specie having copper or lead cores. The tale of Polycrates' bribe to the Spartan force at Samos (Hdt. III. 56) was substantiated by Robinson's discovery of plated "electrum" staters.[2] There was the notorious Athenian issue of plated "tetradrachms". The rough-and-ready precautions of which signs have been widely reported were evidently necessary.

Since the coins typically found in Middle East hoards represented a mixture of different metrological systems, totals, as in the case of scrap silver, could only be determined on the balance. No radical change of the traditional system was therefore involved. Only towards the middle of the 5th century B.C., when the Athenian tetradrachm began to dominate the silver circulation of the eastern Mediterranean, did preference begin to develop for a single denomination. Only then did coin, in the southern Achaemenid territories, come to be regarded as specie for counting, rather than bullion to be reckoned on the scales. Even the siglos, official silver coinage of the satrapal province of Lydia, enjoyed no higher status than the imported Aegean coinages in the Achaemenid lands, appearing only in small numbers mixed with the others in hoards, and like them to be reckoned on the balance.[3] Schlumberger ("L'argent grec", 15), it is true, claims for the gold daric, and its predecessor the Croeseid, a substantial rôle in the Achaemenid territories at large. This case finds a modicum of support in the

[1] Jenkins (1964).
[2] E. S. G. Robinson, "Some electrum and gold Greek coins", *American Numismatic Society Centennial Publication* (New York 1958), p. 592.
[3] Schlumberger, p. 15.

occurrence of Croeseids in the Persepolis foundation-deposit,[1] and in the remote find reported by Roychaudhury at Mari Indus in the Punjab. Yet in the main the wider expanses of Syria, Egypt, Babylonia and the "Upper Satrapies" in Iran were the region of silver currency. The first coinage to assume an international rôle in those parts was the Athenian tetradrachm. In fact, there are reasons to think that the Athenians may have taken pains to adapt their denomination for convenient exchange with their Persian rivals.

The standard of the Athenian tetradrachm at 17.2 gm. may have been called "Euboic" by the Athenians themselves (Hdt. III. 88), but it represented a key unit in relation to the two Achaemenid currency systems. So far as the "silver area" was concerned, it stood marginally in excess of two Babylonian shekels' weight in silver ($8.40 \times 2 = 16.8$ gm.). For the purposes of the Lydian "gold area", it exceeded by a similar margin the metal content of three Achaemenid sigloi. This margin, nearly 2.4%, could have been calculated to cover margins on exchange or re-coinage. The Attic tetradrachm seems admirably contrived for conversion into the units of the Achaemenid 'silver area', where, from the Greek στατήρ it became known as *sttr*, and was valued at exactly two shekels of silver. In Egypt, and possibly other Achaemenid provinces, the circulation of Athenian coinage attained an enormous volume.

It is to be noticed that when coins were struck to the Attic type and standard in Achaemenid territory, the weight was brought even closer to that of two Babylonian shekels at 16.8 gm. The famous Tissaphernes tetradrachm – incidentally the first portrait coin of Greek style – weighed 16.96 gm.[2] It has been suspected that dies for coins with Attic types recovered in Egypt belonged to mints under Persian rather than Athenian control.[3] This is certainly the case of the piece with the Demotic inscription in the name of Artaxerxes III – who controlled that province between 343 and 337 B.C.[4] – and of which the better-preserved example weighs 17.06 gm. Also explicitly of Achaemenid origin are the

---

[1] E. Herzfeld, "Notes on the Achaemenid coinage and some Sasanian mint-names", *Trans. Int. Numismatic Congress 1936* (London 1938), p. 414; Erich E. Schmidt, *Persepolis II*, p. 110.

[2] Robinson (1948), p. 48.

[3] J. Mavrogordato, "Was there a pre-Macedonian mint in Egypt?", *Numismatic Chronicle* 1908, 205; J. H. Jonkees, "Athenian coin-dies from Egypt", *Numismatic Chronicle* 1950, 298–301; Cornelius C. Vermeule, *Some notes on Ancient Dies and Coining Methods* (London, 1954), p. 10.

[4] Otto Mørkholm, "A coin of Artaxerxes III", *Numismatic Chronicle* 1974, 1–4.

issues with names of the satraps Sabaces and Mazaces in Egypt.[1] The mysterious group with the legend *AIΓ* in Greek letters is dated as early as 380–360 B.C., but the distribution of the finds extends from Babylonia to Afghanistan, so their place of origin is quite uncertain.

In view of the close relationship between the Athenian and the Achaemenid currency systems, it was natural that the régime of Alexander the Great chose the Attic standard for their Imperial currency in the East. The small discrepancy of weight that had existed between the Athenian and the Babylonian standards soon almost disappeared.

THE ACHAEMENID GOLD-STANDARD IN WESTERN ANATOLIA

In contrast to the regions east of the Taurus, which had an Assyrian heritage, the ancient states of Western Anatolia, already in the period of Lydian domination, evolved a currency of gold, either mixed or pure. In that region the earliest true coins had been struck in electrum, the natural alloy of silver and gold. (Some authorities use the term "white gold" for the natural alloy, electrum for the artificially compounded metal.)

In Lydia a bimetallic system finally evolved during the reign of Croesus (561–546 B.C.), with separate units in fine gold and silver, between which a fixed exchange-rate was guaranteed by the state. After an initial electrum issue at 13.96 gm., the Lydian ruler introduced separate denominations of either metal, the former around 10.71 gm. and the latter close to 10.56 gm. These are the issues termed "Heavy Croeseids": it is argued that twelve of the silver were equal in value to one of the gold. Since it is known that the ratio of value between gold and silver was 13.3:1, the silver must, in this case have been over-valued – a situation not uncommon with lesser denominations.

The final issue of Croesus was again bimetallic, and brings us close to 546 B.C., when Cyrus of Persia conquered the Lydian Kingdom. Once more, a drop in weight is seen in both metals, so that the final issues are designated "Light Croeseids". The gold stater now weighs about 8.05 gm., the silver, 5.40 gm. If the ratio of value between the two metals was 13.3:1, twenty silver pieces should have passed current for one of gold.

After the taking of Sardis by Cyrus, it seems certain that the issue

[1] E. T. Newell, *Miscellanea Numismatica: Cyrene to India* (New York, 1939), pp. 62, 82 (ANSNNM 82).

of "Light Croeseids" continued uninterrupted. Specimens of the gold were discovered in the Foundation-Deposit of the Apadana at Persepolis, dated by Herzfeld to 516 B.C., and in any case earlier than 511 B.C. Naster distinguished two styles in the engraving of the "Light Croeseids", which are thought to correspond to two phases of production: a "neat style" attributed to the closing years of Croesus, and a "bold style" representing the continuation under Cyrus the Great. Evidently the coinage of Darius – the daric – had not been inaugurated at the moment of the deposit. For otherwise Darius would surely have included it in the foundation-deposit of his palace.

The masterly study of early daric coinage by Sir Edward Robinson[1] shows that the first typically Persian issues at Sardis must have begun about 515 B.C. There were evidently parallel types in gold and silver, those of the latter being as follows: (a) half-length figure of the king; (b) king *shooting* with the bow; (c) king *running* with bow and spear.

In the gold coinage, type (a) is so far unrecorded. Type (b) is known from four specimens, which differ in weight. One weighs 7.87 gm., thus conforming to the standard of the "Light Croeseids" previously discussed. (The deficiency of 0.18 gm. may be ascribed to wear.) The remaining three, at 8.34, 8.32 and 8.31 gm. respectively, conform to the Babylonian shekel standard established by Darius. Since the earliest darics follow the standard of the gold Croeseid, it is evident that the inauguration of the daric coinage anticipated by a short period the metrological reform.

Evidence for the earliest gold is so far limited to this single specimen of an evidently scanty issue. If "type (a)" gold were ever reported, and its weight should turn out to be that of the Croeseid, the argument would be clinched. Yet a similar story is told by the silver denomination known as the siglos. (It is important to remember at this point that the name is a misleading one, for though etymologically the same as "shekel", it was not the silver, but the gold coin which weighed a shekel according to the Babylonian standard).

In circulation, as was the case with the light Croeseids, twenty silver sigloi equalled in value one daric. The ratio between the metals was 13.3:1, so that the siglos corresponding to the gold of Croeseid standard should have weighed 5.35 gm. ($8.05 \times 13.3 = 107.06 \div 20 = 5.35$). Such is in fact the case with the sigloi of types (a) and (b). However, when the weight of the daric rose during issue (b), the corresponding siglos

[1] Robinson (1958).

did not at once rise accordingly. Thus during the financial reforms of Darius, the value of gold weakened against silver to a ratio of 13:1. Indeed, this is exactly the figure reported by Herodotus (III. 95) in describing the tribute assessments of the time. Throughout issue (b) the siglos remained at about 5.35 gm, and the same situation prevailed during the earliest issues of type (c). It was only after the lapse of several years that the old ratio of 13.3:1 re-asserted itself, and the type (c) siglos rose to 5.55 gm. Thus for dating the type (c) sigloi the metrology is critical. Those of the lighter standard represent the inaugural issue. The heavier standard then continued down to the close of the dynasty.

There is no definite evidence for the date of the appearance of type (c), nor yet for the following metrological change in the silver. The earlier of the two events is likely to have taken place either just before, or at the time of the demise of Darius I in 486 B.C. Probably after the accession of Xerxes, the striking of type (c) continued unchanged in gold, and in silver of the heavier standard. Such later changes of type as have been detected in the daric coinage have seldom been related to specific rulers. Attempts to distinguish individual portraits have been shown to be unreliable. Robinson noted one clear innovation of type, the appearance of type (d), which shows the king running to the attack with bow *and dagger*. This development seems to occur towards the end of the 5th century B.C., but has not been attributed to a particular ruler. Before long, type (c) appears to have been restored, and to have been continued, so far as is known at present, during the 4th century B.C.

Mention should be made of two other unusual types. One shows the king youthful and beardless, in the usual posture running with bow and spear. The type is engraved in a specially delicate style, and the royal robe is decorated with rich embroidery.[1] The issue is plausibly attributed to Cyrus the Younger, as pretender at Sardis against Artaxerxes II in 401 B.C. Another unusual siglos type is in the Istanbul cabinet. From Yazilikaya, it shows the king with *upright spear and dagger*. On certain daric issues of the late 5th century B.C., the incuse punch of the reverse contains a decoration; a face of the Greek deity Pan, and a lion's mask have been reported.

Fractions of the daric in gold are decidedly rare. There could only have been issues on limited occasions. There are twelfths in Berlin and London (0.71 gm.; 0.69 gm.). Berlin has even a specimen that is possibly a fifty-fourth.

[1] E. Babelon, *Les Perses Achéménides*, p. xv; Hill (1919), p. 122.

ACHAEMENID GOLD-STANDARD

There is no definite evidence at present that coins of the daric–siglos series were minted by the Achaemenids anywhere other than Sardis, though it was recently suggested that there are indications of the existence of more than one mint.[1] In hoards from western Anatolia, sigloi are reported in enormous preponderance.[2] In Achaemenid lands further afield, their occurrence is sporadic. Probably the fixed rate of the siglos against the daric at Sardis kept the silver coin there at a premium, and induced holders in other provinces to repatriate stocks of sigloi whenever possible. The well-known claim of Herodotus (IV. 36), that Aryandes, satrap of Egypt under Cambyses and Darius, issued silver coins of exceptional purity, thus emulating the pure gold of the daric, deserves passing notice. Yet despite much discussion,[3] there is no numismatic evidence that sigloi were issued, or extensively circulated in Egypt.[4] Though the witness of Herodotus commands respect, this report is probably best taken as apocryphal.

After the capture of the Achaemenid royal treasures by Alexander the Great, huge volumes of darics from the reserves were put into circulation, so that the market value of gold declined. This period saw the minting of double darics, a denomination previously unknown, and several of the issues were distinguished by the presence of Greek monograms.[5] A few singles also bore issue-marks identical with those of the doubles, and are naturally attributable to the same post-Achaemenid times. Some of these pieces were evidently struck at Babylon or Susa, but before the fall of the Empire there is no evidence that darics or sigloi were struck at either of these places, or, as already noted, anywhere other than Sardis.

Apart from the well known daric–siglos series of Sardis, other silver coinages were issued in Anatolia by various satraps during the closing years of the 5th century B.C. and later, mainly no doubt for the payment of Persian and allied forces. The earliest is the famous tetradrachm of Tissaphernes, satrap at Sardis, issued in 411–412 B.C. for payments to

---

[1] C. M. Kraay, "The Asyut Hoard: some comments on chronology", *Numismatic Chronicle* 1977, 194.

[2] Schlumberger, pp. 6–7; Sydney P. Noe, *Two Hoards of Persian Sigloi* (New York, 1956) (ANSNNM 136).

[3] J. G. Milne, "The silver of Aryandes", *Journal of Egyptian Archaeology* XXIV (1938), 245–6. K. Regling, in *Wörterbuch der Münzkunde*, s.v. Aryandikon nomisma.

[4] Of the great Egyptian hoards, only that of Asyut has a substantial number of sigloi, 18 out of a total of 900 pieces, cf. Martin Price and Nancy Waggoner, *Archaic Greek Silver Coinage: the "Asyut" Hoard* (London, 1975), p. 15.

[5] *BM Arabia*, p. cxliii; pp. 176–9.

the Spartan fleet then serving his cause – payments, as we know, stipulated to be made in coinage of the Attic standard (see above, p. 615). During the early 4th century B.C., there were numerous issues of silver by the satraps resident at Tarsus, then a key station for Achaemenid strategy. These bear the names of Pharnabazus, Datames, Tiribazus and Mazaeus, all in the official Aramaic script of the Achaemenid chanceries. Coins with the name of Pharnabazus were also minted at Cyzicus, Greek entrepot on the southern shore of the Sea of Marmara (Propontis), probably in 396 B.C. Besides occasionally commanding in Cilicia, this officer governed Hellespontine Phrygia, the province occupying north-west Asia Minor, with its capital at Dascylium on the Manyas Lake.

Curiously, while the satrapies of Lydia and Trans-Euphratesia (Syria: Aramaic '*br nhr*') issued coinage for much of their period of Persian rule, there is no indication that Hellespontine Phrygia possessed a coinage of its own. Here currency seems mostly to have been supplied by two important Greek cities: Cyzicus (already mentioned), and Lampsacus, its neighbour further down the strait. The coinages of both are typically Greek in form, yet the types often allude to events in Achaemenid territory. That of Cyzicus (unlike the bimetallic issues at Sardis), consisted chiefly of a large denomination in electrum, the alloy – here artificially compounded – of gold and silver. This medium avoided fluctuations resulting from changes in market value between the two metals, which could place strains on the fixed ratios of a bimetallic currency. The types were changed from year to year, and it seems possible that the ratios between the two metals were varied in response to changes in their market values. The obverse of the coinage was thus occupied by a varied series of beautiful, and iconographically unusual subjects; the reverse by a primitive quartered incuse square. The weight-standard stood constant at a little over 16 gm., and the coinage was one that circulated widely in the Black Sea and the Aegean, with minor denominations, especially the sixth, playing a subsidiary role. It will be seen that the economic theory of the Cyzicene electrum presents a fascinating study, and the series has been described as "the most interesting coin-series of any period or country".[1]

Lampsacus, during the 5th century B.C., likewise struck electrum coinage, but to a standard of 15.25 gm. peculiar to that city. During

[1] K. Regling, "Der griechische Goldschatz von Prinkipo", *Zeitschrift für Numismatik* XLI (1931), 3.

STANDARD OF WEIGHTS

the 4th century, there was a change to a coinage of pure gold, obviously related to the daric, since the standard approaches 8.40 gm. Though in practice the daric falls between 8.35 and 8.33 gm., there is little doubt that it was meant to be exchanged with the Lampsacene at par. The slight excess in weight would balance minting costs, or the premium commanded by the coinage of a suzerain power. During the "Satraps' Revolt" of 362 B.C., the portrait of Orontes, leader of the dissident forces, appears on the gold staters of Lampsacus, the city being then, no doubt, subject to his control.

THE STANDARD OF WEIGHTS

As we have seen, the introduction by Darius of his new daric coinage took place soon after 515 B.C., and actually before the enforcement of the new metrological reforms. The archaeological evidence for the date of the new coinage makes it clear that it began during the reign of Darius, and that its name, in Greek *statēr Dareïkos*, could in fact have commemorated its founder, as was the general belief in ancient Greece.[1] The interesting alternative theory, that it merely reflects an Old Persian form **dārīka*, signifying "gold coin",[2] seems over-ingenious in the absence of chronological necessity, and is now no longer pressed, even on philological grounds.[3]

So far as his metrology was concerned, Darius had evidently the double aim of providing a unified system for his empire, and of correcting in the Babylonian system the fraudulent diminutions and arbitrary increases of Assyrian and neo-Babylonian times. We shall see (below, p. 623) that the shekel of this reformed system has been commonly reckoned at 8.40 gm., the key value for the study of Achaemenid metrology. There are indeed indications that before these reforms the Iranians had possessed a different system of their own, based on the decimal rather than the sexagesimal principle. In the reformed table, besides the units that had become familiar in Babylonia, a new and strictly Iranian unit, the *karša* (equivalent to 10 shekels), is added. The complete system of Darius is shown in Table II.

---

[1] Harpocration and Suidas, s.v. δαρεικός, together with the Scholiast on Aristophanes, *Eccleziazusae*, 602: "The darics are gold staters. They are called 'darics' not, *as most imagine, after Darius the father of Xerxes*, but after another even more ancient king (!)." The popular view is vindicated by Schwyzer, p. 9.

[2] A. Meillet, *Grammaire du vieux-perse* (Paris, 1915), p. 67; followed by E. Herzfeld (1938), p. 416.

[3] E. Benveniste, "Persica", *Bull. Soc. Linguistique de Paris* xxx (1929), 59.

The *karša* and shekel regularly figure in the payments of silver mentioned in the Elamite tablets from Persepolis, the latter denomination being designated *pan-su-kaš*. The term was explained by Gershevitch as representing an Old Persian **pančuka* "piece worth five",[1] a denomination which he suggests can be squared with both the quaternate *dānaka* (below) and the indications of a pre-reform Iranian decimal metrology, by supposing that the Babylonian shekel came to be equated not with five *units* of the older system, but with five quarters of the older unit. However, until material evidence for the pre-reform metrology comes to hand, this reconstruction is necessarily subject to some caution.

At all events clearly the foregoing discussion should exclude any possibility that the shekel was represented under Darius by an actual silver coin. The half-shekel, Aramaic *zwz*, was later to become identified with the Attic drachma, and its name in due course provided the ideogram for the drachma in Pahlavi; but a special Old Persian term for "half-shekel" seems unattested. Further down the scale, the evidence of the Persepolis tablets establishes that the *dānaka* was a unit of weight for silver representing the one-eighth part of the shekel, therefore presumably 1.05 gm. This too, conceivably, may have survived from an ancient Iranian system. After this early use of the term had become obsolete, the same word, with its Greek form *danakē*, became in Hellenistic times and later the usual designation for the Attic obol (0.71 gm.). This was originally a small silver piece representing the sixth part of the drachma, whence NP *dāng* has acquired its meaning of "one sixth". Hints in the late Greek lexicographers imply that the *danakē* was already mentioned in Achaemenid times, *c.* 350 B.C., by Heracleides of Cyme, in a lost work, the *Persica*.[2] Yet the explanation offered by Pollux, that this unit was a "Persian coin",[3] must be as much an anachronism for Heracleides' day as is the same authority's strange bookman's notion that *danakē* was the name appropriate for the coin placed in the mouth of the dead in the funeral rite of "Charon's obol". These comments seem to have been preserved by the accident of their having become attached as a gloss to some lines of Callimachus.[4] Though it is now widely realised that the Hellenic ritual of "Charon's obol" was actually practised in Iran during Parthian and even Sasanian times,[5] the coin

[1] Cameron and Gershevitch (1965), pp. 183–4. [2] Hesychius, s.v. δανάκη.
[3] Pollux IX. 82. [4] Ed. Pfeiffer, II, fr. 278.
[5] *JRAS* 1970, 157. The interpretation has since been confirmed by recent discoveries at Hamadan, cf. Mas'ūd Āzarnūsh, "Kāvishā-yi gūristān-i muhavvaṭa-yi Sang-i Šīr" (Excavations of the graveyard of the precinct of the Stone Lion) in F. Bagherzāde (ed.), *Proceedings of the IIIrd*

then used was normally a drachma. It is hard to believe that a reference to the *danakē* in this connexion could be as old as the actual text of Heracleides.

The smallest of the recorded Achaemenid weights is the *ḫalluru*, known thus from its Akkadian, and also from its Aramaic form *ḫlr*. The exact place in the table, and absolute weight, have been subject to controversy. Assyriological authorities reckon that in their earlier period the *ḫalluru* was one-tenth of the shekel.[1] Yet Aramaic papyri quote certain payments reckoned in *karša*, shekels and *ḫlrn*, with figures in the final column as high as 20.[2] Had there been no more than ten *ḫlrn* to the shekel, an increase in the shekels column would have been required, so Hoftijzer concluded that the *ḫlr* represented one-fortieth of the shekel. Such a sub-unit would fit conveniently, since 20 *ḫlrn* would then correspond to the half-shekel or *zwz*; and five *ḫlrn* would be the equivalent of the *dānaka*. Such a solution is plausible, though the evidence is still less than conclusive.

The foregoing discussion of the Achaemenid weight-standard has been based in the main on literary evidence in various languages. Fundamental evidence for the calculation of the talent of the Reformed Babylonian Standard of Darius is the statement of Herodotus (III. 89) that the Babylonian talent under the Achaemenids was equivalent to 70 Euboic minae. It can be assumed that by the "Euboic mina" the historian intends that of the Athenian standard of his own day (generally known as "Euboic"). This value may be taken as 432 gm.,[3] and the Babylonian talent consequently $432 \times 70 = 30240$ gm. Though such a theoretical figure results in a shekel marginally higher than the observed weights of well-preserved darics surviving at the present day, the consequent value of the shekel at 8.40 gm., and the other corresponding figures in Table II, are widely accepted by modern investigators.[4] Emendations of the text of Herodotus to give a higher number of Euboic minae than 70, proposed by certain editors under the influence

Annual Symposium on archaeological research in Iran (Tehran, 1975), p. 55 and figs. 8–9; again at Qandahār, D. MacDowall, *Afghan Studies* 1 (1978), 5; and at Malyan, cf. Jack Martin Balcer, "Excavations at Tal-i Malyan: Part 2, Parthian and Sasanian coins and burials (1976)", *Iran* XVI (1978), 87–90.

[1] CAD Ḫ pp. 47–8.

[2] A. Cowley, *Aramaic papyri of the fifth century B.C.* (Oxford, 1923), pp. 46, 132; E. G. Kraeling, *The Brooklyn Museum Aramaic Papyri* (New Haven, Conn., 1953), p. 205; Charles-F. Jean and J. Hoftijzer, *Dictionnaire des Inscriptions sémitiques de l'ouest*, p. 90.

[3] Herbert A. Cahn, "Etalons monétaires en Asie-Mineure jusqu'au Ve siècle", *Congresso internazionale di numismatica, Roma 11–16 settembre 1961*, II, Atti (Rome, 1965), pp. 19–23.

[4] K. Regling, "Dareikos und Kroiseios".

of different metrological theories,[1] are naturally to be rejected. The same might be said of the claim of the rhetorician Aelian, that the Babylonian talent was equivalent to 72 Attic minae,[2] unless it is assumed that he refers to a reduced Attic mina of a later period; or unless it were supposed that the resultant higher figure for the talent, $432 \times 72 = 31104$ gm., has some relation to the standard of the Abydos lion-weight noticed below.

Such theoretical values for the Achaemenid talent, mina, and shekel need to be compared with the archaeological evidence of surviving weights listed in Table III. These usually fall short of the assumed standard, but most have evidently suffered some wear and tear.[3] Where the inscriptions do not explicitly state the units, the possibility can be entertained that they are objects of special function, for the weighing of particular totals of coin or bullion. From this point of view two of those listed are particularly interesting, the pyramidal weight from Kirman, now in Leningrad, and the lion-weight from Abydos. The first carries no metrological inscription, but only the name and titles of Darius.[4] The observed weight is 2222.425 gm. There are two ways of explaining this figure, which does not conform to the usual standard. The quotient, when it is divided by 400, is 5.56 gm., the weight of the reformed siglos. This might suggest that the Kirman weight was intended for checking stocks of silver equivalent in value to 20 darics in gold, a purely monetary, not a metrological transaction. A different view was suggested by Trousdale, who maintained that the Kirman weight was originally of 30 *karša* ($\simeq$ 2499 gm.), but was reduced to its existing weight through the loss by damage of approximately 3 *karša* ($\frac{1}{2}$ mina), say 249.9 gm. It counts against this view that published photographs[5] show no sign of major damage.

Also remarkable is the weight from Abydos on the Dardanelles, of bronze in the form of a lion, and bearing an Aramaic inscription of which the meaning has been the subject of debate:

'sprn l-qbl stry' zy ksp'

[1] e.g. 78 minae, by C. Hude (ed.), *Herodoti Historiae* (Oxford, 1951): ⟨ὀκτὼ καὶ⟩ ἑβδομήκοντα μνέας. The contrary view was taken by W. W. How and J. Wells, *A Commentary on Herodotus* (Oxford, 1928), p. 281.
[2] *Varia Historia* I. 22.
[3] Kent, *Old Persian Grammar*, pp. 114 and 157 with earlier references; his "Weight a" is no. 1 in our table; his "Weight c" is No. 2; his "Weight d" is no. 3. Unlike Schmidt, Kent did not discuss the Babylonian and Elamite texts.
[4] Kent, p. 157 "Weight b" is No. 4 in Table III, below.
[5] A. V. William Jackson, "Textual notes on the Old Persian Inscriptions", *JAOS* xxvii (1906), 190–4; idem, *Persia past and present* (New York, 1909), pp. 181–4.

UNITS OF LENGTH AND DISTANCE

The difficult word *stry'* may be a loan-word from the Greek στατήρ, a term widely used in the east for the Athenian tetradrachm; or a Semitic participle meaning "melters", "assayers", or the like. Yet whether the meaning of the text is "Correct for the assayers of the silver", or, as seems more probable, "Correct for (the weighing of) staters of silver", doubts concerning the translation of the Aramaic are of little consequence when it comes to determining the function of the weight. Recent re-weighing[1] gives the result of 31.808 gm. Though we should expect the equivalent of a Babylonian talent (30.240 gm.) there appears to be an excess of nearly 5%. This margin could be intended to cover costs of refining and recoinage on foreign, presumably Attic, silver. Thus both the Kirman pyramid and the Abydos lion-weight are at present most easily explained as pieces designed for special functions.

The Babylonian system, as reformed by Darius the Great, remained the essential basis of the Achaemenid standards of weight and coinage. They possibly preserved some traces of an earlier Old Iranian weight system of which otherwise little is known. Standards of length, distance, and volume were likewise adjusted to the Babylonian scheme, though Iranian terms are attested for several units, and traces of an underlying decimal plan can occasionally be detected. This metrological system, current throughout the vast area of the Persian Empire, also exercised great influence on the metrologies of the Greek states, and notably Athens, and later left lasting traces in the history of the Hellenistic Kingdoms and the Classical World.

UNITS OF LENGTH AND DISTANCE

"Almost nothing is known, so far, about the metrological system(s) in use in Achaemenid Iran."[2] Nylander's proposition refers specifically to units of length in the context of Pasargadae, but may seem at first sight over-pessimistic. Further investigation none the less reveals a complex scene. From the courses of the plinth and cella wall of the Tomb of Cyrus, Nylander could deduce a foot of approximately 345 mm., and a cubit (ell) of 515 mm. This result closely approaches the foot of 347–8 mm. derived by Roaf at Persepolis (below, p. 627). In all the contemporary systems, the ratio between foot and cubit was 2:3.

Already this is an interesting co-incidence with the values on the

---

[1] Mitchell (1973).
[2] Carl Nylander, *Ionians in Pasargadae*, p. 96.

metrological relief at Oxford,[1] often treated by scholars in a purely Greek context. The sculpture is a male torso, the span of its outstretched arms being 2070 mm., which is understood as a fathom (Gk. ὀργυία) of six feet, each precisely 345 mm.; or four cubits, by the editor's measurement, of 517.5 mm. The marble of this piece of sculpture has been considered of Samian origin. Though its units have been compared with those of ancient Egypt, Samos before the Persian Wars had been under Achaemenid rule, and the standards of Cyrus might have been enforced there. Nylander, on the other hand, saw evidence for the adoption of a Lydian standard both at Pasargadae and in Ionia.

Superimposed on the metrological relief is the outline of a foot, presumed from its measurement to represent the Attic foot of 296 mm. The addition must refer to the imposition of Attic measures at Samos at the time of the Athenian currency reform.[2] It is useful to note this figure also, since it provides a check on other Achaemenid measures of length to be encountered shortly.

So far as the Babylonian measures of length are concerned, the system of multiples is complex,[3] and not all the units can be related to the Achaemenid evidence. There is agreement as to the currency of a foot of 330 mm., and a corresponding cubit of 495 mm. Lehman (-Haupt) was ready to entertain the existence of a larger "Royal" Cubit, which seems to be specified by Herodotus (I. 178), and which the German scholar was even prepared to calculate at a mean of 551.23 mm., giving a consequent foot of 367 mm.[4] Thureau-Dangin, on the other hand, maintained a total scepticism as to the reality of such a "Royal" measure. Yet he did develop an interesting line of reasoning when he observed that the standard Babylonian (and indeed Achaemenian) building-brick has a side of one foot according to the current measure, while that of the floor-blocks is one cubit. The purpose of this arrangement was to allow builders to fix the dimensions of a project by counting the bricks, and without the necessity for measuring-rods. Discrepancies tended to arise in practice, if the shrinkage of the bricks on drying did not exactly equal the thickness of the mortar between the courses.

Arguments from the dimensions of the bricks in Achaemenid palaces were further developed by Hesse, who used statistical procedures to

[1] Michaelis (1883).
[2] E. S. G. Robinson, "The Athenian Currency-decree and the Coinages of the Allies", *Hesperia* (Supplement VIII) (1949), 338, n. 10.
[3] Thureau-Dangin (1921), p. 127.
[4] Lehman (-Haupt) (1889), p. 198.

UNITS OF LENGTH AND DISTANCE

determine the mean of the measurements observed. He thereby demonstrated that the values at the Apadana of Darius in Susa were higher than those of the Palace of the Shaur. Bricks at the latter varied from 330 mm. to as little as 323.6 mm. At the former site he takes the mean at 359.4 mm. The cubit of the first standard would amount to 538 mm., and of the second to 495 mm; but to these values must be added an allowance for shrinkage, since it would be the moulds, not the clay itself, that were exactly measured. These calculations were designed to show a diachronic change, but approximate to Lehman (-Haupt)'s estimate for the "Royal" and "Common" Babylonian foot.

As a check on the admittedly variable dimensions of the bricks and floor-blocks, Hesse compared the stone foundation-tablets found in various palaces. The Elamite tablet of Darius the Great at Susa had a mean side of 336 mm., and so approximates to the "Common" Babylonian foot. When the same test is applied to larger documents such as the Harem foundation-tablet, or the Daiva-inscription of Xerxes, dimensions vary from 515 mm. to 543 mm., but with a marked peak at 523 mm. These figures could again be compared with the cubit of Cyrus, but are too inconsistent to establish a rigorous standard. Earlier writers too had frequently reported the foot of 330 mm., for example at Naqsh-i Rustam, but the contexts are not closely datable. Hesse concluded sceptically that there were more unknowns amongst the Achaemenid measures of length than there were firmly established relationships between them.[1]

Recent calculations by Roaf[2] from the distances between survey-marks in the palace of Xerxes, and from the dimensions of the palace of Darius at Persepolis, have indicated that the significant units for the builders were a foot of 347.6 mm., and its quarter, a "palm" of 87 mm. These values are extremely close to those obtained by Nylander at Pasargadae, and significantly more precise than those which had previously been proposed by F. Krefter.[3] Since all these values apply, at latest, to the period of the foundation of the Persepolis platform, and are therefore presumably earlier than the date of the metrological reforms of Darius, they do not exclude the possibility that the Babylonian units of length, and in particular the foot of 330 mm., may have been brought into use for official purposes, in the same way as

[1] Hesse (1972), p. 239.
[2] Roaf (1978), p. 68.
[3] *Persepolis Rekonstruktionen* (Berlin, 1971), pp. 29–32.

the Babylonian shekel, at least in certain periods and districts, if not in the Achaemenid homeland of Fārs.

Links are most easily found between the ancient Persian units of length and those of distance by the intermediary of Greek units, for we have seen how Greek and Persian measures may share a common ancestry. A general feature of the Greek systems is that 600 feet, or 100 fathoms, were equivalent to one stade. The precise value of the foot, and therefore of the stade, varied according to the local standard. When we take the Attic foot of 296 mm., there results a stade of 177.6 m. Moreover, Herodotus (II. 6) clearly attests that the parasang, best-known Persian measure of distance – of which the memory even survives in the *farsakh* of modern parlance – was equivalent to 30 stades. On this basis, the parasang should have amounted to 5.33 km., or 3.3 English miles. The widespread tradition that the parasang represented the distance that infantry could march in the hour makes such figures plausible. One could, of course, derive a longer stade, and thus a longer parasang, from one of the longer eastern feet already discussed, and in this way seek a direct link between the parasang and the Babylonian system. Yet that approach is shown to be mistaken, since empirical tests in the field by Hansman,[1] reckoning ten stades to the English mile (1.609 km.), and three miles to the parasang (4.827 km.), have given excellent results in practice. Whatever the basis of calculation, theoretical values for the stade and the parasang must be sought which do not greatly exceed Hansman's estimates. It is, in fact, precisely the Attic foot which gives a key for such an evaluation.

Herodotus (II. 6) notes a further unit of distance, in Greek *schoinē* ("rope"), which he defines as 60 stadia, or two parasangs. This seems closely comparable with the Babylonian *bēru*. Thureau-Dangin[2] reckoned the *bēru* at 3600 *qanū* "reeds" of 2.97 m., consequently 10.69 km. Half of this measure, 5.34 km., is evidently suitable for the parasang, which therefore corresponds to 1800 Babylonian "reeds". It is the "reed" which provides the needed common denominator between the Babylonian and Attic systems, and illustrates the basis of Herodotus' calculation: that measure is made up of six "common" Babylonian cubits of 495 mm., but is also obviously equal to ten Attic feet. (The discrepancy between Michaelis' measurement of the Attic foot at 296 mm., and the figure of 297 mm. resulting from this calculation is

[1] John Hansman, "The Problems of Qūmis", *JRAS* 1968, 118.
[2] Thureau-Dangin (1921), p. 133.

UNITS OF LENGTH AND DISTANCE

naturally insignificant.) Consequently the parasang can be expressed as 10,800 "common" Babylonian cubits, or 18,000 Attic feet, both figures exactly (Table V, below). The calculation not only vindicates the precision of Herodotus' information on Persian measures. It shows the ingenuity of the Attic metrologists, who, vigorously asserting their "independence" of the Achaemenid system, nevertheless strove to maintain a system of direct equivalences necessary for commercial exchanges with so important a state. At the same time, our workings tend to confirm that the Achaemenid parasang represents the half-*bēru*; thus, as one might expect, an exact unit of the Babylonian system. In this it resembles other standards originating from the reforms of Darius.

The discovery *in situ* of marked distance-stones would have the greatest value for confirming the reliability of such theoretical arguments. Assyrian distance-stones have actually been reported, which might provide the precedent.[1] It is, indeed, denied that παρασάγγης "parasang" is etymologically connected with Old Persian *aθanga* "stone".[2] Though the alternative derivation from *frasāŋha* "indicator"[3] does not explicitly specify a marker of stone that might survive, yet it by no means excludes one. So far, however, no distance-stone of Achaemenid date is known from which modern measurements could be taken, and until such a discovery is reported, the possibility of any existing must seem doubtful.

An even longer measure of distance probably used by the Achaemenids is reflected in the newly-discovered Aramaic inscription of the Indian emperor Aśoka at Lāmghān in Afghanistan.[4] The distance from that spot to Tadmor (Palmyra) in Syria is quoted at 200 *qštn* "bows", according to the editor's explanation. He estimates the actual distance to Palmyra at 3,800 km., thus making the unit 19 km. Such a distance is comparable with the *stathmoi* "royal stations" listed by Herodotus (V. 52–3); though the strict average of his stages, reckoning the parasang at 5.33 km., works out to 23.3 km. That figure, however, is artificially raised by the evident omission of several stages in Cilicia. A more normal distance for the stage (excluding the doubtful section) is thus between 21 and 19 km. The lower figure agrees with Dupont-

---

[1] A. T. Olmstead, *History of Assyria* (New York, 1923), pp. 271, 334 and 556.
[2] Rudiger Schmitt, "Medisches und Persisches Sprachgut bei Herodotus", *ZDMG* CLXXVII (1967), 138.
[3] See further on the etymology of *frasang* Gershevitch, "Amber", p. 213.
[4] A. Dupont-Sommer, "Une nouvelle inscription araméenne d'Aśoka trouvée dans la vallée de Lamghan (Afghanistan)", *CRAI* 1970, 165–6.

Sommer's estimate of the kilometrage. Though a theoretical full march might have been of four parasangs (21.32 km.), or even five, the rest-house would necessarily have been placed short of the maximum distance, to avoid mishaps; and in difficult country extra allowance would need to be made.

It may be informative to compare with the historically attested evidence for Achaemenid measures of length, the purely Iranian units of length and distance mentioned in the Avesta. Henning[1] concluded that the notices in two late works, the *Vendidad* and the *Nirangistan*, reflected Hellenistic influences, and conformed closely to the Attic-Roman system. There was little evidence for absolute values, but the following Iranian terms are recorded: Av. *paδa* (Pahl. *pay*) "foot", Av. *frārāθni* (Pahl. *frārāst*) "cubit", Av. *gāya, gāman* (Pahl. *gām*) "pace", Av. *vībāzu* (Pahl. *jud-nāy*) "fathom" and Pahl. *nāy* "reed" – units several of which have already figured in our story. In earlier texts, such as the Yashts, a different system is reflected. This involves the *hāθra* and its double, the *tačar* or *čaratu-*. Efforts by the Pahlavī glossarists to define the first are somewhat puzzling, since it is explained as the parasang, as an hour's journey, or, conflictingly, as a quarter-parasang, and even as 1000 paces (the Roman mile). Herzfeld explained the *tačar* as related to the term for "horse-race". His observation that the great Abbāsid race-track at Sāmarra measures 10.5 km. (thus a double-parasang), fits well on the first interpretation of the *hāθra*.[2] On this hypothesis, the *tačara* will coincide with the Babylonian *bēru*. Such dimensions for a racecourse could reflect traditions from Achaemenid times; though it would be hard, unless a possible shade of meaning is "grandstand", "pavilion" (associated with a racecourse), to find a semantic link with the palace of Darius at Persepolis, also called *Tačara* in inscriptions. Herzfeld sought, inconclusively, to accommodate the second definition of the term "quarter-parasang", postulating a racetrack 700 yards (741.5 m.) in length, 1,440 yards (1,512.4 m.) in circuit. Neither figure appears particularly well established or significant, and uncertainty remains whether the *hāθra* as a quarter-parasang represents a recollection of archaic standards prior to the time of Darius, or an anachronistic allusion in the Pahlavi glosses to the Roman mile, or other intrusive standards of later periods.

[1] W. B. Henning, "An astronomical chapter of the Bundahishn", *JRAS* (1942), 235.
[2] Ernst Herzfeld, *The Persian Empire* (Wiesbaden, 1968), p. 21.

MEASURES OF CAPACITY, DRY AND FLUID

It is convenient to deal first with the theoretical evidence for the Achaemenid measures of capacity. By combining details from different periods, a clear picture can be obtained, which may then be verified from archaeological data. So far as the dry measure is concerned, the upshot is clear enough. That concerning the fluid measures is more debatable.

A large measure, the *irtiba*, occurring frequently in the Elamite tablets from Persepolis,[1] evidently represents an Old Persian term. It appears in Aramaic as *'rdb*, and in Greek as *artabē*. Herodotus (I. 192) describes the *artabē* (> "bushel") as fractionally larger than the Attic *medimnus*. He reckons the excess as 3 *choenices* (i.e. 3/48ths or 6.25%). Later writers, who reflect Hellenistic adjustments, treat the *artabē* as identical with the *medimnus*.[2] The *choenix* was familiar to Greek audiences, since it constituted the soldier's basic daily ration of flour.

It is beyond the present purpose to investigate critically the value of the *medimnus*. Good results can be obtained with published figures, for example those of Segrè, who variously estimated it at 52.40,[3] or at 51.80 litres.[4] The higher estimate is preferable, and on that basis the *artabē* is 55.67 litres. The evaluation of the *medimnus* at 51.84 litres, given in a standard work of reference, is almost as satisfactory.[5] Table VI, below, is based on the highest figures, and these find close independent confirmation. To issue silver in such a measure, as done by the Achaemenid king for the satrap of Babylon,[6] was a proverbially grandiose gesture. Aristophanes (*Acharnians*, 108) caricatures a Persian state visitor to Athens, calling him "Pseud-Artabas" (a pun at once on the historically notorious Pseudo-Smerdis, and the resemblance between the well-known measure, and familiar Persian names such as Artabazus and Artabanus). The greedy Athenian politicians were expecting their Persian visitor to bribe them with gold pieces, not only by the "bushel", but by the *achanē*. This was an even larger Persian measure, reportedly 45 *medimni*, and probably corresponding to a wagon-load, though there is no means of confirming the exact value. They were soon "undeceived" when he retorted in Greek with an earthy rejoinder.

Further units of the system can next be inferred from parallel

---

[1] Hallock, p. 72, n. 6. [2] Hesychius, s.v.
[3] Angelo Segrè, *Metrologia e circolazione monetaria degli antichi*, Bologna 1928, p. 105, n. 2; idem, "Babylonian, Assyrian and Persian measures", *JAOS* LXIV (1944), 76.
[4] *Metrologia*, p. 131. [5] *OCD*, p. 659.
[6] Hdt. I. 192.

evidence of the Sasanian period. The *Shāpūr KZ* inscription mentions the *grīv*, made up of ten *hōfan*.[1] Since the corresponding Greek version renders *grīv* by *modius* (the Roman term for one-sixth of the *medimnus*), it is reasonable to reckon the *grīv* as one-sixth of the *artabē*. We shall see below, however, that the Elamite tablets from Persepolis edited by Hallock indicate that there were no more than three *grīwa* to the *artabē*, at least in Persis during the earlier Achaemenid period. This evidence is not easy to reconcile with the statement of Herodotus. Though the Attic measures are well established for the end of the 5th century (cf. Suzanne Young, "An Athenian clepsydra", *Hesperia* VIII (1939), 279–80), conceivably the Herodotean figure could have been based on a lower *medimnus* standard. Yet it is hard to imagine one lower than the *artabē* found by Hallock (below). Otherwise, we should have to suppose that a lower standard had prevailed in some Achaemenid regions, or periods, than that with which the Father of History was acquainted.

As to the *grīv*, Achaemenid evidence for this unit, OP **grīwa*, comes from Persepolis, where the Aramaic spelling *grw* is scratched on an Elamite tablet.[2] Elamite *kurrima* was there recognised by Gershevitch as rendering the same term. In other Aramaic documents, the abbreviation *g.* was identified by Maricq as also representing the **grīwa*.[3] Hallock concluded that in the Elamite texts, the logogram BAR actually indicates the **grīwa*. Yet assuming that this is correct, his inference[4] from documents such as PF 1,995–6 that 3 BAR were equal to the *artabē* (*irtaba*), gives rise to a paradox. Since, as we shall see, the QA and the *hōfan* are firmly established, this *artabē* would amount to 27.90 litres. Other authorities, working from somewhat higher units, prefer a figure of 29.1 litres.[5] Yet either of these reckonings amounts to little more than half the value Herodotus implies

Several Achaemenid Aramaic texts mention the *hōfan* (in its earlier spelling *hpn*, cf. Akkadian *upnu*), clearly described as the quantity of meal forming the daily ration of a soldier.[6] The calculations in Table VI produce the result of 0.93 litre for the *hōfan*, a figure agreeing closely with the soldier's ration at Athens at 1.09 litres.

[1] P. Gignoux, *Glossaire*, p. 53, s.v.
[2] Hallock, p. 72–3 and p. 644.
[3] A. Maricq, *Classica et Orientalia* (Paris, 1965), p. 61, n. 7 (= *Syria* XXXV (1958), 318); A. Cowley, *Aramaic Papyri of the Fifth Century B.C.* (Oxford, 1923), pp. 2 and 24.
[4] Hallock, p. 532–8.
[5] V. A. Livshits, "New Parthian documents from South Turkmenistan", *AAntASH* XXV (1977), 174
[6] G. R. Driver, *Aramaic Documents of the Sixth Century B.C.* (Oxford, 1965), p. 28 and 60.

MEASURES OF CAPACITY, DRY AND FLUID

In view of the manifestly sexagesimal basis of the preceding system, it is natural to seek confirmation of the result from the Babylonian measures of volume. For the Babylonians, the daily ration of meal for a slave was represented by the logogram QA. Earlier attempts by Assyriologists to establish the value of the QA gave undependable results. The new investigation by Schmidt, based on an actual vessel from Persepolis, confirms a result between 0.92 and 0.945 litre. It is therefore clear that the QA is indeed synonymous with the *hōfan*, and our theoretical evaluation is confirmed. The Elamite document PF 1,574 agrees that 10 QA are equivalent to the *kurrima* (**grīwa*).[1]

Less clear than the units of dry measure is the separate system of terms applied in Achaemenid times to liquid measures. Most prominent is the *maris*, which frequently occurs in Greek texts, particularly in Polyaenus' superb account of the commisariat of Cyrus (see Appendix A, below). The same term is represented in Elamite by the *marriš* of the Persepolis tablets,[2] and even in Greek script on a Persepolis fortification tablet.[3] The term is no less familiar as the *mry*, the measure of wine repeatedly detailed in the Nisa ostraca, with its sub-unit, abbreviated *k.*, to which we shall return.

Values quoted for the *maris* by various Greek authors display a lamentable state of confusion. According to Polyaenus it was equal to 10 Attic *choes* (or 32.27 litres); according to Aristotle,[4] it was equivalent to six Attic *cotylae* (or 1.64 litres). Gershevitch, no doubt rightly, rejected the classical evidence as hopelessly corrupt. From the Persepolis fortification tablets, Hallock deduced that the *marriš* is a measure of liquid identical with the **grīwa* (= 9.28 litres), and likewise composed of 10 QA. As a liquid measure, its subdivision is the *kapithē* or *kapezis*, defined by Xenophon as equal to two Attic *choenices*:[5] but by Polyaenus, more convincingly, as (approximately) equivalent to one *choenix*. The second calculation would make the *kapithē* identical with the QA or *hōfan*, and like it the tenth part of the next highest unit. The only difference then between the table of dry measures, and that for liquids, would consist in the use of a different set of terms.

In the Nisa ostraca the abbreviation *k.* presumably indicates the *kapithē*, but in currently available texts never more than three such units

---

[1] Hallock, p. 439.
[2] I. Gershevitch, review of George C. Cameron, *Persepolis Treasury Tablets*, in *Asia Major* II (1951), 143.
[3] Hallock, p. 2.   [4] *Historia Animalium* VIII. 9. 1 (= Pollux x. 184).
[5] *Anabasis* I. 5, 6.

are specified, which might support Xenophon's version, that there were no more than five *kapithai* to the *maris*. Polyaenus, who spells the term *kapezis*, accurately renders Parthian **kapič*,[1] also in Sogdian as *kpc* and *kpc'kk*.[2]

The only difficulty, therefore, in Hallock's explanation, based on Elamite tablets, of the Achaemenid system of fluid measures as identical with the system of dry measures, is that a *maris* of 9.3 litres makes the quantities of wine involved in various transactions appear surprisingly large. No other solution seems possible, however, on present evidence. It is true that his material indicates the existence of another unit of dry weight, the *bawiš*, one-tenth of the *artabē*, and therefore equal to 5.57 litres. If its liquid equivalent were the *maris*, that would have consisted of six *kapithai*, making three *kapithai* the half. In Sasanian times, the *Shāpūr KZ* inscription mentions another fluid measure, the *pās*. This too seems likely to have been a survival from the Achaemenids, but its metric value is so far undetermined.

Despite certain complexities, it is therefore comforting to find that the basic unit of the Achaemenid system of measures, whether known as the *hōfan*, QA or even as *kapič*, was closely equivalent to the modern litre. Because of the sexagesimal basis of Babylonian mathematics, its largest measure, the *artabē*, should have been just short of 60 litres. Though this inference appears correct for later periods, the Persepolis tablets indicate an *artabē* of only 30 QA. Throughout this discussion of Achaemenid metrology, close parallels are noted with the systems of ancient Athens, and on the other hand with those of Babylonia. While some classical scholars have been concerned to deny that metrological standards in Greece – for all its "Orientalising period" – derived eventually from the East, that thesis, maintained by Lehman (-Haupt) and others, seems sufficiently convincing. On the one hand, classical values tend to resemble the "common" Babylonian standards, which had suffered some decline. On the other, the Achaemenid units generally conformed to the somewhat higher values established by Darius. In commerce and in financial administration, as in the field of law, the restorer of the Achaemenid dynasty often saw himself as the heir to the great Babylonian kings – the renewer of time-honoured fundamentals, on which economic life, and with it the possibility of civilisation itself, had been built up.

[1] Diakonoff and Livshits, *Dokumenti iz Nisy*, p. 14.
[2] *Sogdijskie documenty s Gory Mugh* II, 60 and 128 n. 11. (see *CHI* III, bibliography, p. 1392).

GLOSSARY OF TECHNICAL TERMS

achanē (Gk.) "chest, wagon-load" (about 2,505 litres)
ammatu (Akk.) "cubit"
arašan- (OP) "cubit"
artabē (Gk.) "bushel" (according to Hdt 55.67 litres; or, at Persepolis, 30 BAR or 27.90 litres.)
BAR (Elamite etc.) logogram for **griwa* (?)
bawiš (El.) "one-tenth of the *artabē*" (5.57 litres)
bēru (Akk.) "two marches, double-parasang" (10.69 km.)
čaratu- (Av.) "double-parasang" – cf. *tačar*
choenix (Gk.) "ration", "quart" (1.09 litres)
dānaka (OP), *danakē* (Gk.) "groat" – originally a weight-unit for bulk silver, later the name of a coin, the obol.
daric – Achaemenid gold coin, weighing marginally less than the Babylonian shekel (i.e. 8.35 gm.)
foot (Attic) (296 mm.)
   (Babylonian) (330 mm.)
   (Persepolitan etc.) (347.6 mm.)
frārāθni (Av.), *frārāst* (Pahl.) "cubit"
gāya, gāman (Av.), *gām* (Pahl.) "pace"
grīv (MP), **grīwa* (OP) 'peck' (9.30 litres)
ḫalluru (Akk.), *ḫlr* (Aram.) "grain", or $\frac{1}{40}$ shekel (0.21 gm.)
hāθra (Av) "parasang", or "quarter-parasang"
hōfan (OP, MP), *hpn* (Aram.) "ration", "quart" (0.93 litre)
ḫullu (Akk.) – a type of ring – currency
irtaba (El.) – Elamite spelling of *artabē*
jud-nāy (Pahl.) "fathom"
kapezis, kapithē (Gk.), **kapič* (Parth.), *kpc* (Sogd.) "litre" – probably the fluid equivalent of the *hōfan*
karša (OP), "unit of weight", "ten shekels" (84 gm.)
kaspu šebirtu (Akk.) "cut silver, German *Hacksilber*"
kurrima (El.) – Elamite spelling of **grīwa*
maris (Gk.), *marriš* (El.) (9.30 litres)
medimnus (Gk., Lat.) "bushel" (52.40 litres)
mina – unit of weight (504 gm.)
nāy (Pahl.) "reed"
**pančuka* "piece of five", "shekel"
parasang "(hour's) march" (5.33 km.)

pās (MP) – an uncertain fluid measure
QA – Elamite, etc. logogram for *hōfan, upnu*
qanū (Akk.) "reed" (2.97 m.)
qšt "bow", "stage" (about 19 km.)
rikṣu (Akk.) "torque" – a type of large ring-currency
šewēru (Akk.) – a type of ring-currency
shekel – standard unit of weight in any system; under Darius equal to 8.40 gm.
siglos – Achaemenid silver coin valued at 20 to the daric; etymologically, but not semantically, identical with shekel
stade – "hundred-fathom distance" (177.6 m.)
stathmos (Gk.) "stage" – see *qšt*
tačar (Av.) "double-parasang" or "double-*hāθra*"
talent – "manload" (in the Babylonian standard, 30,240 gm.)
unqu (Akk.) – a type of ring-currency
upnu (Akk.) "ration", "quart" – the Akkadian form of Iranian *hōfan*
vībāzu (Av.) "fathom"
zūzu (Akk.), *zwz* (Aram.) "half-shekel", "drachma" – originally a unit of weight, esp. for bulk silver; later applied to a coin (4.2 gm.)

TABLE I *Basic Babylonian weight-standard according to Lehmann (-Haupt)*

1 *biltu* ("talent") = 60 *manū* ("minae")	=	29,472 gm.
1 *manū* = 60 *šiqlu* ("shekels")	=	491.2 gm.
1 *šiqlu* = 2 *zūzu* ("drachmae")	=	8.18 gm.

TABLE II *Babylonian standard after the reform of Darius the Great (theoretical values)*

1 talent	= 60 minae	=	30,240 gm.
1 mina	= 6 *karša*	=	504 gm.
1 *karša*	= 10 shekels	=	84 gm.
1 shekel	= 2 *zwz* (drachmae)	=	8.40 gm.
	= 8 *dānaka*	=	8.40 gm.
1 *zwz*	= 4 *dānaka*	=	4.20 gm.
1 *dānaka*	= 5 *halluru*	=	1.05 gm.
1 *halluru*		=	0.21 gm.

APPENDIX

TABLE III *Evidence of surviving Achaemenid weights*

	Provenience	Inscription	Observed weight	Damage	Implied shekel
1	BM 91117	"2 karša"	166.724 gm.	Unnoticeable	8.33 gm.
2	Persepolis PT3 283	"20 mina" "120 karša"	9,950 gm.	Chipped	8.29 gm.
3	Persepolis PT4 736	"10 mina" "60 karša"	4,930 gm.	"Badly chipped"	8.22 gm.
4	Leningrad (from Kirman)	Darius titles only	2,222.425 gm.	Not visible in photo	See text
5	Abydos lion (BM E. 32625)	See text, presumably a talent	31,808 gm.	"Some loss by corrosion"	See text

TABLE IV *Units of length: the foot and the cubit*
(equivalents in millimetres)

		Foot	Cubit ($= 1\frac{1}{2}$ foot)
1	The foot of Cyrus, according to Nylander	345	517
2	"Samian" cubit, according to Michaelis	—	517+
3	Persepolitan foot, according to Roaf	347+	521+
4	"Royal" Babylonian standard, theoretical, according to Lehmann (-Haupt)	367	551
5	Apadana at Susa, according to Hesse	359+	538
6	Susa, Palace of the Shaur	330−	≃ 491
7	"Common" Babylonian standard, theoretical reckoning	330	495
8	Attic standard, according to Michaelis	296+	—

ACHAEMENID COINS

TABLE V *Babylonian and Athenian computations of the parasang (equivalents in metres)*

Babylonian			Athenian			
1 "reed" = 6 "common" cubits = [60 "reeds" = 178.2]		2.97 —	[10 feet	= 2.96+]		
			1 stade	= 600 feet	=	177.6
1 parasang = ½ *bēru* = 1,800 "reeds"	= 5,346		1 parasang	= 30 stades	=	5,328
1 *bēru* = 3,600 "reeds"	= 10,692		2 parasangs	=	1 *schoinē*	= 10,656
1 "stage" (Aram. *qšt*), if equivalent to 4 parasangs	= 21,384 ⎫					
1 "stage", as calculated from Lamghan inscription	= 19,000 ⎭					

TABLE VI *Units of capacity, dry and liquid measure (equivalents in litres)*

Persian/Babylonian				Attic/Roman	
Dry		Liquid			
1 *achanē* = 45 *artabai* (?)	2505	—			
1 *artabē* [= 6 *grīwa*] or = 3 *grīwa* = 10 *bawiš*	55.67 27.90	—		1 *medimnus* = 6 *hekteis*, or *modioi*	52.40
1 *grīwa* = 10 *hōfan*	9.28	1 *maris* = 10 *kapithai* (?)		1 *modios* = 8 *choenices*	8.73
1 *bawiš*	5.56	—		1 *chous* = 12 *cotylae*	3.27
1 *hōfan* = 1 QA	0.93	1 *kapithē* (?) = 1 QA (?)		1 *choenix* = 4 *cotylae*	1.09
				1 *cotylē*	0.27

APPENDIX

THE COMMISSARIAT OF CYRUS THE GREAT

(According to Polyaenus, *Strategemata* IV. 3. 32)

Alexander read in the Persian royal residence (the ingredients of) the Great King's breakfast and dinner, inscribed on a bronze pillar, where also were the other rules that Cyrus had prescribed. They ran as follows:

Pure wheaten meal, 400 *artabai* – the Median *artabē* is equivalent to the Attic *medimnus*; of second-grade meal after the pure quality, 300 *artabai*; of the third grade, another 300 *artabai*; altogether, of every kind of wheaten meal for the

APPENDIX

repast, 1,000 *artabai*. Of barley meal, the very purest quality, 200 artabai; of the second grade, 400; [and of the third grade, 400;] altogether of barley meal, 1000 *artabai*. Of groats made from rye (χόνδρου δὲ ἐξ ὀλύρων) 200 *artabai*; of fine flour (παιπάλης) made from barley, suitable for pottage (ὡς εἰς κυκεῶνας), 10 *artabai*; fine-chopped 'mustard-herb' (καρδάμου κεκομμένου = *Lepidum sativum*), flavoured with sesame, . . . [*artabai*;] husked barley (πτισάνης), 10 *artabai*; mustard-seed, one-third of an *artabē*.

Sheep, males, 400; oxen, 100; horses, 30; fattened geese, 400; turtle doves (τρυγόνες), 300; miscellaneous small birds, 600; hares, 300; goslings, 100; gazelles, 30.

Fresh milk, 10 *maries* – the *maris* amounts to ten Attic † *choes* †. Sweetened buttermilk, 10 *maries*; garlic, a talent by weight; onions, sharp-flavoured, half a talent by weight; salad-herbs (or 'seed of silphium'?) (φύλλου), 1 *artabē*; latex of silphium, two minae; cummin-seed, 1 *artabē*; silphium, a talent in weight; jelly of sweet apples, one-fourth part of an *artabē*; conserve of sour pomegranate-peel, 1 *artabē*; jelly of cummin-seed (μύρου ἐξ κυμίνου), one-fourth part of an *artabē*; black raisins, 3 talents by weight; flowers of dill, 3 minae by weight; "black cummin" (μελανθίου = *Nigella sativa*), the third part of an *artabē*; seed of *diarinum*-mustard (διαρίνου σπέρμα), 2 *kapezies*; pure sesame-seed, 10 *artabai*; sweet new wine (γλεύκους ἐξ οἴνου), 5 *maries*; boiled turnip-radishes preserved in brine, 5 *maries*; capers preserved in brine, from which they make sauces (ἐξ ἧς τὰς ἀβυρτάκας ποιοῦσι), 5 *maries*; (kitchen) salt, 10 *artabai*; Ethiopian cummin-seed, 6 *kapezies* – the *kapezis* is the same as an Attic *choenix*; dry dill, 30 minae weighed on the scales; parsley seed, 4 *kapezies*; sesame oil, 10 *maries*; (clarified) butter, 5 *maries*; oil of terebinth, 5 *maries*; oil of acanthus, 5 *maries*; oil of sweet almonds, 3 *maries*; sweet almonds, dried, 3 *artabai*; wine, 500 *maries*. When (the court) is at Babylon or Susa, it provides half the wine from palms, and half from grapes.

Logs, 100 waggon-loads; brushwood, 200 waggon-loads; during the rainy season, 100 square cakes (?) of honey, weighed at ten minae (each?) – they give this when the court is in Media; seeds of safflower (κνήκου = *Carthamus tinctorius*), 3 *artabai*; saffron, 2 minae weighed on the balance. So much is expended for the beverage, and the breaking of the fast.

(Furthermore), they give, of pure wheaten meal, 500 *artabai*; and of the pure barley meal, 1,000 *artabai*; and of the second grade, another 1000 *artabai*; and of fine (white) flour (σεμιδάλεως), 500 *artabai*; of groats made from rye, 500 *maries*; of barley-corns suitable for the livestock, 20,000 *artabai*; of bran (ἀχύρας), 10,000 waggon-loads; of straw (κάρφους), 5,000 waggon-loads; of sesame oil, 200 *maries*; of *vin ordinaire* (ὄξους), 100 *maries*; of chopped 'mustard-herb', 30 *artabai*. All that is detailed above they donate for the military forces. The King however consumes what has already been stated, in the course of his breakfast and dinner, together with those to whom he issues their keep.

CHAPTER 13

THE OLD EASTERN IRANIAN WORLD VIEW ACCORDING TO THE AVESTA

INTRODUCTION

For the traditional outlook of ancient Eastern Iran, the birthplace of Iranian culture, we must be guided by such realia as may be extracted from the religious texts which comprise the Avesta, supplemented, when necessary, by Pahlavi citations from lost Avestan texts. In certain instances it will be difficult, if not impossible, to determine the time period to which the data at hand apply. While the Avesta refers primarily to prehistoric conditions, there is occasionally the possibility that there is reflected a situation prevailing at the time of the composition of the texts during the historical era, e.g. the Achaemenian era for the Yashts, or even later for the *Vidēvdād* (*Vendidad*), which contains some of the most important data concerning everyday life. Thus, for example, we find in the *Vidēvdād* the use of a metrical system dependent on a Greco-Roman model.

The extent however to which even the *Vidēvdād* looks back to pre-historic times may be seen from the list of the sixteen good lands created by Ahura Mazdā, and the plagues sent against them by Angra Mainyu, related in the first *Karde* of the *Vidēvdād*. Here we have a series of purely Eastern locations, beginning with the mythological Aryana Vaējah ("the expanse of the Aryans", based on the recollection of an original homeland in the extreme north-east in dimmest antiquity) and moving south in a path including Sogdiana, Margiana, Bactria, Herat, Gandhara, Arachosia, the Helmand river, the river Buner and finally the "Seven Streams" (*Hapta Həndu = Hindu*, the Indus and its tributaries); this whole area is framed by the two mythological rivers the Vanghvī Dāityā and the Ranghā, on which more will be said below. What the heart of this eastern area of settlement was is indicated in the Mithra Yasht in which we are provided with an interesting bird's eye (or rather, god's eye) vista: "...the whole land inhabited by Iranians [Airyanąm] where gallant rulers organize many attacks, where high,

INTRODUCTION

sheltering mountains with ample pasture provide, solicitous for cattle; where deep lakes stand with surging waves; where navigable rivers rush wide with a swell towards Parutian Iškata, Haraivian Margu, Sogdian Gava, and Chorasmia".[1] According to Gershevitch's analysis,[2] Ishkata would be situated in the plain of the Upper Helmand in the vicinity of the Kūh-i Bābā (i.e. the territory later known as Sattagydia, OPers. θatagu);[3] and the Parutian overlords were probably the Paroutai which Ptolemy (IV.17.3) reports as having occupied the part of Areia (Haraiva) near the Hindu-kush (Ghōr). Herodotus (III.91), however, states that the Aparytai formed one *nomos* with the Sattagydians, Gandharans, and Dadikoi. In the Avestan passage we see also that Margu (Marv or Margiana) formed part of the territory of Areia-Haraiva (i.e. Herat and its environs on the Harī-Rūd), whereas under Darius it was part of Bactria. This passage serves to outline the territory which will be the focus of our study.

THE WORLD AND ITS ORIGIN

The ancient Iranian divided existence into two aspects, *gaēiθya* and *mainyava*. These terms are commonly translated "physical" and "spiritual", but they refer more precisely to the realms of the tangible and the intangible. This accords with the etymology of mainyava from *mainyu-*, loosely translated "spirit" but connected with the root *man* "to think, perceive with the mind". In Old Indic *manyu* is "force, vehemence, impulse", and indeed the Gathic creative and destructive forces are both mainyus. Thus mainyava may be also taken to refer to the mentalistic or "ideal" realm through whose workings tangible reality is made manifest. Thus in Zoroastrian theology the world first was created by Ahura Mazdā in "ideal" form (Pahlavi *mēnōg*) and then in actual form (*gētīg*). The demons exist in mainyava form, but the divine sphere has its gētīg as well as mēnōg state.

A different dichotomy is found in the distinction between *aša-* and *drug*. In the most ancient (Indo-Iranian) view, *aša-* (older form *ṛta*) is a concept combining cosmic and moral order (= "truth"), and its opposite, *druh*, embraces all which is opposed to this harmony and regularity. There is evidence in both the Vedas and the Avesta that

[1] Trans. Gershevitch, *Avestan Hymn to Mithra*, pp. 79–81.
[2] *Op. cit.*, pp. 174–5.
[3] But cf. D. Fleming, "Achaemenid Sattagydia and the geography of Vivana's campaign", *JRAS* 1982, pp. 102–12, who proposed with full discussion to place Sattagydia in Bannū.

originally ṛta had an other-worldly source or fountainhead to which only the gods, seers, and the dead had access, but as has been noted in chapter 14 on Achaemenian religion, this view came to be modified. As part of the earlier view, aspects of nature proceeding from and also typifying the cosmic order or rhythm were also characterized by aša/ṛta; thus we have *yava- ašavan-* (preserved in Middle Persian *jōrdā* and Judeo-Persian *jūrdār*) for "grain", and *vāta- ašavan-* (Middle Persian *wād ardā*, Sogdian *wāt artāw*) for "wind".

The first thing to be created was the sky, which in Old Iranian (Old Persian as well as Avestan) is called *asman-*, the source of the present-day Persian word for "sky", *āsmān*. This word originally meant "stone", and traces of this earlier meaning are still to be found in the Avesta. The word is used in *Vidēvdād* 14.10 to describe the material out of which a mortar is made, and in Yasht 17.20 we have *asman- katō.masah-*, "a stone as big as a house", as a metaphor for the Ahura Vairya prayer with which Zoroaster lays low the Devil. In a similar context (in *Vidēvdād* 19.4) we find *asan- katō.masah-* identical in meaning to *asman- katō.masah-*, but with *asman-* replaced by the common word *asan-*, which is cognate but used only for "stone". The concept of the heavens as made of stone seems attested in the Gathas; in Yasht 30.5 we read of "the Holiest Spirit who is garbed in the hardest stones", which the Pahlavi commentator understood as referring to the sky. Pahlavi texts probably dependent on lost portions of the Avesta also know this doctrine of the stony substance of the sky.

However the Avesta also describes the sky as being made of metallic substance, enclosing the world like a shell. Yasht 13.2 is worth citing in full for this description; here Ahura Mazdā declares: "Because of their rich splendour and glorious fortune I established (*vīδāraēm*, lit. 'held apart') that sky, which is above, bright and conspicuous, which surrounds this earth like a bird upon an egg, which stands set up in the invisible, stable, with far-off boundaries, in the form of *xvaēna- ayah-*, shining to the three parts of the earth."[1] In the phrase *xvaēna- ayah-* we have the noun *ayah-* (Old Indian *ayas-* "ore"), which appears to be connected with the words meaning "bright" in other Indo-European languages. The same combination of words occurs in Yasna 30.2, although here it is assumed by scholars that the reference is to the molten metal of an eschatological ordeal. The phrase is rendered as *xvēn āhen*

---

[1] See W. B. Henning, "Ein unbeachtetes Wort im Awesta", in J. Schubert and U. Schneider (eds), *Asiatica. Festschrift Friedrich Weller* (Leipzig, 1954), pp. 289–92.

THE WORLD AND ITS ORIGIN

in Pahlavi, where *āhen* "iron" translates *ayah-*, probably under influence of the similarity of *āhen* with *ayah-* (attested in the genitive, as *ayaŋhō*).

The doctrine of the sky being made of metal does not necessarily contradict the one according to which the sky is made of stone. It appears likely from Pahlavi texts that the stone substance was understood as consisting specifically of rock-crystal, which in the *Greater Bundahishn* is included in a canonical list of metals. As Mary Boyce points out, rock-crystal resembles metal in its brightness. One must also notice the Pahlavi identification of the sky with *almās* "adamant", i.e. "diamond" or "steel", an ambiguity noteworthy in itself.

The second thing to be created (according to the cosmology of the *Bundahishn*) was water, which filled the lower part of the circumvallated sphere; upon this water the earth was created. Originally the earth was a perfectly flat disk in the centre of the sky-globe. Out of this plane there grew the mountains, the first of which was Harā Bərəzaitī "the lofty watchpost", identifiable in name alone with the present-day Alburz or Elburz. The *Bundahishn* describes Harā as growing for eight hundred years in four stages of two hundred years, during which were reached respectively the star-station, the moon-station, the sun-station, and finally the height of heaven. Here we see that the stars were located below the moon and sun.

In the centre of the world was located the "Peak of Harā", grown out of the deep "roots" of the encircling range. This peak was located in the middle of the most central of seven circular continents into which the world was divided. The central continent was thought to be the largest and the only one to be habitable by humans, and was called "the splendid region of Khvaniratha". It was surrounded by Arəzahi to the west, Savahi to the east,[1] Vourubarəshti to the north-west, Fradadhafshu to the south-east, and Vīdadhafshu to the south-west. These seven continents were separated from each other by water, forests, and mountains. The doctrine of the seven continents (*karšvars*, lit. "tracts") is alluded to by Zoroaster (Yasna 32.3). The main features of this picture of the world are of Indo-Iranian origin, for in ancient India it was believed that there existed a mountain range (Lokāloka) surrounding the world and seven (concentric!) continents, on the central one of which (Jambūdvīpa) was located Mt Meru (or Sumeru).

It was thought in Iran that the heavenly bodies orbited in planes

---

[1] Thus according to the codex DH of the *Bundahishn*; the codex TD has wrongly interchanged the names for east and west. The Pārsī map gives *savah-* as east.

parallel to the earth and revolved around the central mountain, while the sun daily crossed its peak. Night was caused by the mountain's interruption of the sun's rays. The peak of Mt Harā, called Hukairya ("the beneficent"), was regarded as a place of utterly ideal conditions, where there was no darkness, no inclement weather, no diseases, and no pollution. It is above this peak that Mithra has his home, and is there worshipped by Haoma. The souls of the righteous dead were believed to ascend to heaven from Hukairya; thus it was here that one end of the Chinvant Bridge (the Bridge of Judgement) was located. Just as paradise was conceived as being above the peak, so hell was located below it.

Mt Harā is also the source of all waters. At its base, to the south, is the ocean Vourukasha ("having broad inlets") which receives the waters, these taking the form of a gigantic river (later identified with the goddess Anāhitā) as they flow down from Hukairya. From Vourukasha proceed two great rivers, Vaŋhvī Dāityā (*vaŋhvī-* "good" and *dāityā-* "regular, orderly") to the east of the central continent Khvaniratha, and Ranghā to its west.

Hukairya, the one place retaining primeval perfection, connecting the upper and lower regions, and being a cosmic centre from which come light and liquid, may be seen as the Iranian form of the *Axis Mundi* found in many archaic cultures. Related to this idea of a central axis or pole is the World Tree (Tree of Life, etc.). In Iran this was located in the centre of Vourukasha. It is the "well-watered tree on which grow the seeds of plants of all kinds by the hundreds, thousands, and myriads" (*Vidēvdād* 5.15). This tree, which contained all manner of medicaments, was also known as a tree of healing. In it rested the giant Saēna bird, whose wingbeats scatter the seeds of the tree (this bird is the original form of the Sīmurgh of classical Persian literature). Another animal associated with the Tree is the Kara Fish (apparently "the Wels, catfish or sheatfish – *Siluris glanis*" *par excellence*, just as the Saēna is "the eagle" *par excellence*), which protects the Tree from noxious creatures, as does also the three-legged Ass, whose purely spiritual excretions purify the waters. Another huge sea-creature in the Vourukasha is called Vāsī Panchāsadvarā.

Closely associated with the "Tree of All Seeds" (and perhaps originally a variant of it) is the Gaokərəna Tree, from which, according to the Pahlavi books, will be prepared the White Haoma instrumental in conferring physical immortality upon bodies at the

THE WORLD AND ITS ORIGIN

general resurrection of the dead. Its location in the sea Vourukasha (and thus below Mt Harā) may be connected with the eschatological mirroring the protological. The possible Indo-Iranian origin of these motifs of mythological trees is indicated by the Indic Jambū-tree (after which was named Jambūdvīpa, "Jambū-Island"), linked to soma, medicine, and immortality, located to the south of Mt Meru.

Plant life was also held to have originated, along with animal life, through the death of the Primal (or more accurately "Uniquely-created") Bull. According to Zoroastrian mythology, this beast was created (along with the Primal Man) by Ahura Mazdā before the existence of the world as we know it, and was slain (like the Primal Man) by the Destructive Spirit's invasion of the first creation. Part of the seed of the Bull was taken up to the moon (which has the epithet "Having the Bull's Seed") and purified there. All beneficent animal life comes from the latter seed, while beneficent plants come from the portion of the Bull's seed which fell directly to the earth.

The bovine is in fact the representative of animal life in Old Iranian thought. This may be seen from a number of Avestan passages which are of general interest for the Old Iranian world view. The five canonical forms of beasts, i.e. aquatic, terrestrial, flying, wild-roaming, and grazing, are referred to as the "fivefold *gav-*", lit. "bovines" (Yasna 71.9; see also Yasht 13.10 and Yasht 19.69, with *Vispered* 1.1). The three forms of life, humans, animals, and plants are listed with *gav-* representing the second category (*Vidēvdād* 2.27 = 2.41). In the catalogue of the six creations of Ahura Mazdā (or Spənta Mainyu) we have heaven (*asan-*, lit. "stone"), water, earth, plants, animals (*gav-*) and Righteous Man (Yasna 19.8), where *gav-* indeed may be seen as an allusion to the Primal Bull and Righteous Man to the Primal Man (Gayō.marətan). With this one may also compare, for a final example, the series fire, water, earth, *gav-*, plants, righteous man and righteous woman, stars, moon, and sun, in an apotropaic formula in the *Vidēvdād* (11.1 and 11.10).

The expanded use of *gav-* for "animal" in general, while reflecting the importance of cattle in archaic Iranian society, belongs to the sphere of priestly terminology. Another interesting extension of the meaning of *gav-*, but one almost certainly derived from a different, non-priestly, popular usage, is, I believe, to be found in the Old Iranian word for "deer", **gavazna-* (Avestan *gavasna-*, New Persian *gavazn*, etc.), which may be taken from **gav-āzna-* (or **gava-zna-*) "of the bovine kind, akin to the bovine". This way of perceiving the deer is still found in New

Persian, where the deer is called *gāv-i kūhī* "mountain bovine" or *gāv-i daštī* "bovine of the open country".

It may be mentioned here that just as deer could be characterized by the Iranians as bovines, so too could hedgehogs, porcupines, weasels and other animals (including, less surprisingly, foxes) be classified as dogs, as we find in *Vidēvdād* 13 *passim* and 5.29–33, where such creatures are protected against harm by penalties parallel to protecting genuine dogs from injury (here Magian thinking may be involved). Of these "dogs" the otter was held in greatest veneration, as appears from *Vidēvdād* 14.50–6 and the entirety of *Vidēvdād* 15, which are devoted to this animal. According to these texts it was believed that the soul of a dead dog passed into "the spring of the waters", and that from every thousand male dogs and thousand female dogs are born a pair of "water otters", a male and a female. The death of an otter was thought to bring drought. Just as Persian still reflects the old categorization of deer as "bovines", so does it still show the ancient "canine" classification of otters, called *sag-i daryā*; cf. also *sag-i ābī* (or *sagābī*) "water-dog" for "beaver".

As has been mentioned, the origin of mankind was attributed to the slaying of a Primal Man, just as plant and animal life was thought to originate through the death of a Primal Bull. While the slaughter of these pre-existent creatures is, in the extant form of the myth, assigned to Ahriman, it is likely, as many scholars have assumed, that we have here a Zoroastrian re-working of myths involving cosmogonic sacrifice by a god or gods.

The "Primal Man" is called in Avestan Gayō.marətan "mortal life" (nominative *Gayō.marta*, whence Pahlavi *Gayōmart*; Manichean Middle Persian *Gēhmurd* seems to be a direct descendant of an Old Persian *Gayah(-)martā*). Like the Vedic ancestor of men, Mārtāṇḍa, with which he has been compared, Gayōmart was as wide as he was tall. Further comparison of *Mārtāṇḍa-* "mortal egg/seed" with **mart(iy)a-tauxman-*, the ancestor of the common Persian noun *mardum* "people", etc., is inconclusive as evidence for the Indo-Iranian origin of Gayō.marətan; **mart(iy)a-tauxman-* may be compared with *mankind*, where *kind* parallels *tauxman-* or *tauxmā*, which also means "family, kind".

The condition of Gayōmart and his companion before the attacks of the Adversary are poignantly summarized from the Pahlavi sources by Boyce: "The sun stood still at noon above an earth which lay flat and bare upon the motionless waters, with the plant, the bull, and

THE WORLD AND ITS ORIGIN

Gayō. marətan existing quietly in the centre of an empty world." After Gayōmart was smitten by Ahriman, his seed was purified in the station of the sun and impregnated the Earth, from which grew a rhubarb plant. From this plant emerged the first truly human couple, Mashya and Mashyānī.

This myth is rather puzzling in view of the fact that the rhubarb lacks sacred attributes, and no part of it is reminiscent of the human form. I suspect the myth may have originated through a linguistic reinterpretation. We find an Avestan epithet *raēvas.čiθra-* "of rich or splendid origin" for a noble young woman (the Daēna in *Hadokht Nask* 2.9; cf. *raēvat čiθrəm*, a later formation in Yasht 5.64, of Anāhitā). Now *raēvant-* (in compounds *raēvat-*, *raēvas-*) "splendid, rich" is clearly the origin of Persian *rīvand* "rhubarb", and an allied form **raēvastī-* and dialectal equivalents may be proposed as the origin of other forms for the same plant: Persian *rīvās*, *rīvāj*, etc., Balochi and Pashto *rawāš*. If the ancestor(s) of mankind had the epithet *raēvas.čiθra-* "of splendid origin", this could be reinterpreted, in the greater context of the myth, as "having rhubarb as origin".

Man

The individual is conceived as having a body and a number of psychic-noetic faculties. The body is referred to as *tanū-* (the physical part of the individual in its totality) and as *kəhrp-* (the outer appearance). The inventory of body parts is very large, and corresponds essentially to the lists of limbs found in other old Indo-European languages. The psycho-noetic faculties are somewhat unclear: the *ahu-*, lit. "essence", seems to refer to the intellect and will; *baoδah-* denotes "perception, consciousness" and *urvan-* "soul" is that which survives after death (a faculty shared by righteous animals). *Fravaši* refers in some passages to a pre-existent double which supports and protects each individual during his life-time; acting together to maintain life and order throughout the world, the fravašis were pictured as winged martial females, reminiscent of the Valkyries. As a soul of the righteous dead, the fravaši is sometimes difficult to distinguish from the urvan.

THE AVESTAN WORLD VIEW

ARYANS AND OTHERS

The "Avesta people", like the Indo-Europeans who settled northwestern India and founded the Vedic culture, called themselves Arya (Av. *airya-*). This name is of course the etymon of the name Iran. It is interesting to recall that King Darius referred to his own language not as Persian but as Aryan. While it is obvious that Iranian dialects were spoken throughout the East, and, as we have seen, a vast area is regarded by the Avesta as Aryan, we find individuals bearing Iranian names who are classed as belonging to peoples other than "Iranians" (Airyas). These people were not necessarily enemies of the Airyas, as appears from Yasht 13.143, where there are mentioned Zoroastrians of the Airya, Tūra, Sairima, Sāini, and Dāha peoples. Indeed one of Zarathushtra's own converts is the noble Tūra Fryāna (Yasna 46.12). On the other hand various passages in the Yashts are directed against the Tūra Fraŋrasyan (the Afrāsiyāb of Firdausī), the great villain defeated by Kavi Haosravah (Kai Khusrau), and in Yasht 13.37–8 the Fravashis battle the fiendish Dānu people, who are there apparently identified with the Tūras. The Dahas we may identify with the Dahae of Greek and Latin historians, nomads dwelling to the east of the Caspian, whereas the Sairimas are almost surely the ancestors of the Sarmatians, who in much later history invade the South Russian steppes. Similar peoples are known from non-Avestan sources as Sakas (or Scyths), whose nomadic culture separated them from other speakers of Iranian languages. Yet it would seem that at least some of these peoples regarded themselves as Aryans, for the Ossetes today refer to themselves as *Ir(on)*, and a tribe who figured among their Saka forbears were known as the Alans, both names etymologically meaning "Aryan".

It may be added that the oral literature of the Ossetes, the Nart cycle, shows as background a culture quite different from that of the Avesta, but agreeing in many respects with the Scythian culture described by Herodotus, Ammianus Marcellinus and other classical sources, which also describe a Scythian religion at variance with the mainstream Iranian worship attested by the Avesta. Agreements between Ossetic and the pre-Islamic language of Khotan and Tumshuq (and, to some extent, the present-day speech of Wakhān) attest an early date of separation of the Sakas from other Iranian-speaking communities.

SOCIAL ORGANIZATION

While our Avestan texts were composed at a period in which settled agricultural life had long before become widespread, the basis of social structuring it attests, which survived at least theoretically through Sasanian times, took shape during the earlier period of nomadism, and nomadic life has continued, of course, to exist side-by-side with agriculturism down to the present day in Iran.

The vertical social organization, by kinship and alliance, was as follows:

1. The family unit. This was termed *nmāna-* "house" in Younger Avestan, *x^vaētu* "next-of-kin group" in Gathic, and corresponds with *taumā* "family" in Old Persian.

2. The clan, or village, or settlement. This is *vis-* in Younger Avestan, *x^vaētu* "next-of-kin group" in Gathic, and corresponds with *vərəzəna-*, which has cognates meaning "village" in Old Indic and later Iranian languages.

3. The tribe or tribal area. This in the Younger Avestan is *zantu* (the Old Persian equivalent is not preserved), perhaps corresponding to *šōiθra-* "territory" in Gathic.

4. The country. This is *dahyu* in Younger Avestan, Gathic and Old Persian; in the last it has to mean "province" as well.

The scheme of correspondences between the Younger Avestan and Gathic terms is based on the work of Benveniste. According to P. Thieme, the x^vaētu "family" lives in the nmāna "house", and the vərəzəna "clan" lives in the *vis-* "settlement", while *airyaman* "hospitality" dwells in the zantu "tribal territory".[1]

Each of these four groups was presided over by a lord. In addition, the Yasht to Mithra speaks of *vīspanąm dahyunąm daiŋhupaiti-* "the dahyu-lord over all dahyus" (Yasht 10.145), *daiŋhusasti* "command of dahyus" (= "empire"?) (*ibid.* 87), and *dahyunąm fratəmatāt* "council of the premiers of dahyus" (*ibid.* 18), where **fratəma-* "premier" matches an identical term in Achaemenian Old Persian, known from Elamite and Aramaic.[2] The precise political conditions or period(s) to which these terms apply remains uncertain. The dahyu-lord is described as a great warrior (see Yasht 5.85, 10.8, 15.31), and is also called "the omnipotent commander of the dahyu" (Yasht 13.8). That such *dahyupatis* could gain

---
[1] P. Thieme, *Mitra and Aryaman* (New Haven, 1957), p. 78.
[2] See Gershevitch, *op. cit.*, p. 298.

control over a number of dahyus and make of them an empire is demonstrated as a possibility, at the time of the authorship of the Yashts, by the statement that Kavi Haosravah was "the hero uniting the Aryan dahyus into an empire" (xšaθra) (see Yasht 5.49, 9.21, 15.32). The power of the dahyupatis was not absolute; they were bound by treaty obligations, as the Yasht to Mithra, the god presiding over treaties, makes abundantly clear. Furthermore, there was a good measure of public discussion of policy, and wisdom and ability to speak in the assemblies was a prized trait in a man (see Yasht 13.6, 8.5; Yasna 62.5). The foregoing outline of the vertical arrangement of society conforms very closely to the situation prevailing among present-day Afghan mountain dwellers and other Iranian tribesmen.

With regard to the horizontal structure of society, we may note the following categories:

1. Priests. There are two terms encountered which must be taken into account. In the Gathas and elsewhere we read of the *zaotar*, of which Zarathushtra himself is an example. The word etymologically combines the notions of the two roots *zav*, "to pour" (libations) and "to invoke". The corresponding term is known from Vedic as *hotar*. The latter had among his functions the composition of eleven-syllable "wisdom" verses of intentional obscurity, understood only by initiates. M. Boyce has recently made the important comparison of the Gathas with this genre.[1] But the chief function of the zaotar was the performance of the *yasna* rite on behalf of a private individual, at his home, for which the priest was paid a fee. In post-Gathic texts we meet, along with zaotar, another term for priest, *āθravan* (for earlier *aθarvan*- = Vedic *atharvan*-). It is unclear whether the term originally meant "fire-priest", as was once thought (in favour of this view compare Vedic *atharyu*-, epithet of Fire); the atharvan-/āθravan was connected with the fire-cult, but this need not have been his primary function; on the other hand the zaotar also officiated at fire-ceremonies. The term **aθarvan*, along with the "fire-fanner" (*ātrə.vaxš*-), a subsidiary priest, is found in both the Younger Avesta and in the Persepolis material, as we have seen. The āθravan/aθarvan- became, apparently only in the Younger Avestan period, the canonical name for a member of the priestly caste.

Membership of the priestly caste was inherited by males from the father, although priests could marry into lay families, as was the case of Zarathushtra and his daughter. The young priest underwent rigorous training at the instruction of an *aēθrapati*.

[1] Boyce, *History of Zoroastrianism* I, p. 9.

SOCIAL ORGANIZATION

2. The pasturer, in Gathic called *vāstar*, in Younger Avestan *vāstryō.fšuyant-* "he who fattens cattle in pastures". The pasturing of cattle was foremost in the economic life of the earlier period of Iranian history, as emerges from a vast number of Avestan passages. Cattle constituted the chief form of wealth; indeed the Sogdian word for gentleman is derived from *fšuyant*. It is noteworthy that the organized protection of cattle herds against pillage and injury seems one of the chief purposes of Zarathushtra's preaching. Agriculturalists are later included in the category of vāstryō.fšuyant.

3. Warriors. The term for this order, *raθaēštar*, is of Indo-Iranian origin (cf. Old Indian *rathestha-*) and signifies "he who stands in a chariot". The use of the war chariot is held by most scholars to date from the second millennium B.C.; and indeed we find the various members of the Indo-Iranian pantheon traversing the heavens in horse-drawn chariots. Of course, all able-bodied males were recruited for battle when necessary, and only the distinguished champions would battle in chariots, the ordinary warriors being foot-soldiers. Later (apparently in the first millennium B.C., perhaps as a Saka innovation), warriors would ride on horses; thus we find the mounted hero Tūsa praying for victory from Anāhitā against the Hunu horsemen (Yasht 5.53). It is likely that as rulers attracted skilled fighters to their retinue there came into gradual existence an élite class of warriors, for which the old term raθaēštar became normative.

4. Craftsmen. In a single passage of the Avesta we find an addition to the foregoing three categories, which appears to show that a fourfold social division constituted an ancient canon. The passage, Yasna 19.17, reads, "What are the *pištras* (classes)? [They are] priests (āθravans), warriors (raθaēštars), vāstryō.fšuyants, and *hūiti*". This last category must be identified as that of the artisans. Of course by Sasanian times the four classes of society were well established, comprising the traditional triad and fourthly the *hutuxšān*, skilled craftsmen and manufacturers. Among the latter group in Avestan times would have been the goldsmiths, who made the golden jewellery mentioned in our texts, e.g. diadems (Yasht 15.57; 19.41), fillets (Yasht 15.57), ritual plates and other ceremonial objects (Yasna 10.7 with *Vidēvdād* 2.7). Gold, silver, bronze, and stone vessels are also mentioned in *Vidēvdād* 7.74, although the reference here to iron vessels indicates that the passage dates from a relatively late period. The smelting of various metals, glass-making, and potters' kilns are referred to in *Vidēvdād* 8.85 *seq*. The word for "kiln, oven" is *tanūra*, a Western Asiatic wandering word.

Of course arms-makers and chariot-makers were of great importance; such professions would be taught by father to son. The position of people such as minstrels and physicians with regard to the canonical classes is unclear. Merchants are not found in our texts; goods and services were paid for by commodities and especially by domestic animals.

PROCREATION AND CHILD-RAISING

In the early stages of Indo-European thought, human fertility was connected with the concept of moisture and fluidity, and this association continued in the ancient Iranian outlook. As a reflection of the Indo-European situation Avestan has, for example, *aršan-* "male, hero" and *varəšni-* "sire (of animals)", for which there exist related words of similar meaning outside Iranian (e.g. Greek ἄρσην, ἔρσην, Lat. *verres*, etc.), and whose root meaning can be seen from Old Indic *arṣati* "it flows" and *varṣati* "it rains" in the two cases. As a development within Iranian one may point to Avestan *xšudra-* "fluid", serving as the usual word for "semen" (cf. Persian *šōhar* "husband").

In ancient Iran the association with fluidity applies also to female fecundity and involves not only the potential for child-bearing but also the formation of milk for nursing. Thus we find, in a series of spells pertaining to pregnancy and the healthy birth and development of children, the invocation of the sea Vourukasha and other agencies of moisture, in which there is the text, "A woman rich in fat, in liquid, in milk, in oil, in marrow, and in progeny. I shall now wash the thousand well-springs which flow to the milk-vessels whereby the child is nourished" (*Vidēvdād* 21.7). The goddess of waters, Arədvī Sūrā Anāhitā, is said to be the one who "purifies the waters, the semen [*xšudra*] of all males, the wombs of all women for birth, provides women with easy childbirth, and produces the milk of women at the proper time" (Yasht 5.2; see also 5.5 and Yasna 65.1–5).

Mithra also has aquatic associations (probably due to his close relationship with the old deity Ahura, the counterpart of the Indic Varuṇa), for he is called "the replenisher of waters...thanks to whom water (=rain) falls and plants grow" (Yasht 10.61). Indeed a few stanzas later he is described as a granter of offspring, but here the context shows that the bestowal of sons is part of a larger concept of general prosperity of the nation, related to Mithra as promoter of ideal social

PROCREATION AND CHILD-RAISING

relationships: "[Mithra]...who grants the entreaty, who dispenses fat and herds, who gives power and sons, who bestows life and comfortable existence, who ensures ownership of Truth" (stanza 65).[1] The association of offspring with physical wellbeing and prosperity is also brought out in stanza 68, where Mithra asks: "On whom may I bestow riches and fortune, on whom health of body, on whom property that affords much comfort? For whom shall I raise noble progeny hereafter?"[2]

The request specifically for sons in stanza 65 is typical of the preference for male children in Old Iranian society, in which only they can eventually fulfil the functions for which "mighty offspring" are besought of Ātar, the god presiding over the hearth, the central representation of domestic life: namely to furnish protection from danger, take a leading part in community policy through eloquence in debate, and to promote the family name (Yasna 62.5).

Furthermore, only males could become priests. The god Haoma, who as the first to offer up *haoma* on Mount Haraitī (Yasht 10.90) is in a sense a prototype of priests, denies fine children or priestly sons to the woman who devours the sacrificial portion (*draonah*) which belongs to Haoma (Yasna 10.15). The general connection of Haoma with having descendants is documented by other passages: "He punishes the man who withholds haoma-juice with the curse of childlessness" (Yasna 11.3). "The first four men who prepared haoma were rewarded by the boon of illustrious sons, the last of these four mortals being Pourushāspa, who fathered Zarathushtra" (Yasna 9.4ff.). "Haoma grants pregnant women kingly sons and righteous progeny" (*ibid.* 22). Even today Zoroastrian women who are with child pray to Haoma and constantly recite the Hōm Yasht in order to have distinguished sons. In M. Boyce's discussion of this noteworthy connection of Haoma and fertility,[3] an explanation is sought in Haoma's representation of plant life and his aquatic function, claimed from Pahlavi sources in which he is said to assist Tishtrya as dispenser of rains, although the latter tradition seems to be based merely on a rather loose interpretation of Yasht 8.33. The present writer prefers to explain Haoma's fertility aspect as due to an aphrodisiac quality of the original haoma-plant, as he will argue in detail in another publication.[4]

---

[1] Trans. Gershevitch, *op. cit.*, pp. 103–5.   [2] Trans. Gershevitch, *op. cit.*, p. 127.

[3] M. Boyce, "Haoma, priest of the sacrifice", in M. Boyce and I. Gershevitch (eds), *Henning Memorial Volume* (London, 1970), pp. 63–4.

[4] D. S. Flattery and M. Schwartz, *Haoma and Harmaline* (University of California Publications in Near Eastern Studies 21, 1984); the original *haoma*-plant is here identified as Peganum harmala.

THE AVESTAN WORLD VIEW

As a corollary to the importance of procreation and its close association with the realm of the sacred we may expect the condemnation of forms of sexual activity not leading to the conception of children. Indeed in the priestly legislation of the *Vidēvdād* we find masturbation described as a sin for which there is no atonement (8.27), men engaging in homosexuality considered to be literally demons (8.32), and prostitutes, even those frequented by non-Zoroastrians, as not only corrupting men, but contaminating the waters and plants with their very glance, and meriting extermination like the most noxious creatures (18.61–5). Menses and miscarriage procured by drugs in instances of pregnancy outside of wedlock are also forbidden, as is shown by *Vidēvdād* 15.9–14, where we learn of old women who were expert in the administration of various herbal abortifacients, which are named after their foetus-destroying properties.[1]

One must however keep in mind the role played by the concepts of ritual purity. As a fluid of the body semen was considered an agent of pollution and even involuntary nocturnal emissions required atonement (*Vidēvdād* 8.26). Blood, and particularly menstrual blood, was regarded as a pollutant, and women during their regular menstrual period were most stringently segregated; the entirety of *Vidēvdād* 16 is devoted to regulations concerning menstruation. Inducing an abortion was seen as causing the worst pollutant of all, dead matter, to lodge in the midst of a living body. In addition it may be noted that sexual intercourse with a pregnant woman, "whether or not milk has come to her breasts", was also prohibited, both because of the inherent impurity and the fear that the foetus might be harmed (*Vidēvdād* 15.8).

The birth of a child was probably celebrated by a special feast (a custom among Central Asian Iranians in modern times), and Herodotus (1.133) reports, as a curiosity, the occurrence of an annual commemorative birthday party, distinguished by the serving of special foods, among Western Iranians. Mothers suckled children at their own breasts; there is no evidence for wet-nurses in the Avesta. Education of boys of all classes was initiated by the fathers. If we may further be guided by Herodotus' data on Western Iran (1.136) and apply them to the Eastern situation, boys would train for the warrior (raθaēštar) order beginning with their fifth birthday and learn riding, archery, and "telling the

---

[1] The four plants named in *Vidēvdād* 15.14 are *baŋha* "hemp", *šaēta-*, *γnāna-*, and *fraspāta-*; in *šaēta-* one may see a word of late coinage, formed from a cognate of Sogdian *nšʼy-* and *pšʼy-* "to abort", minus the preverb.

PROCREATION AND CHILD-RAISING

truth". It seems to be a custom of Indo-Iranian origin for priests' sons to begin their training in their seventh year.

A child was reckoned to attain maturity when it turned fifteen years of age. This was also considered the time when one was at one's physical prime. We read that before corruption, decay, and physical adversity came into the world, the world-ruler Yima and his father Vivaŋhvant wandered about with the appearance of fifteen-year-olds (Yasna 9.5). Anāhitā manifests herself as a tall, powerful, attractive maiden of fifteen (Yasht 5.64), and similarly the Daēnā of the righteous (*Hadōkht Nask* 2.9). One of the manifestations of Vərəthraghna, the god of victory, is as a splendid, clear-eyed, handsome, small-heeled man of fifteen years (Yasht 14.17); here is, in effect, a picture of ideal masculine beauty. The most important details concerning this age as furnished by a theophany are found in Yasht 8.13, where the star-god Tishtrya is said during the first ten nights of his appearance to take "the form of a splendid, clear-eyed, tall, very mighty, powerful male of fifteen years, at which age a man first dons the sacred girdle (*aiwyåŋhana*); at which age a man first achieves strength; at which age a man is first endowed with eloquence". Zoroastrians today still invest their children (male and female) with the sacred girdle (*kustī*) at the age of fifteen, thereby marking the child's passage into adulthood and responsible membership of the community; the girdle is worn daily over a ritual shirt. In the *Vidēvdād* the man or woman who, having reached the age of fifteen, goes about without the sacred garments thereby commits a sin for which there is no atonement and aids the demonic forces in their ability to harm creation.

The fifteenth year was also the time at which girls were considered ready to acquire a husband, as we learn from *Vidēvdād* 14.15, where we have the ideal portrait of a marriageable maiden: "faultless... hitherto untouched by men, wearing earrings, having already reached the age of fifteen". The Yashts show young women praying for husbands; as we may expect, such prayers were directed to Anāhitā (Yasht 5.87), but also Vayu is asked to grant a handsome vigorous (*yuvan-* "young, warlike, heroic") male to provide sustenance and offspring (Yasht 15.40), perhaps because of this god's special connection with the life force.

What little we know of the terminology and details of ancient Eastern Iranian marriage customs links them on one hand to those of other ancient Indo-European peoples, particularly the Aryans of India, and on the other hand to customs surviving among the present-day descendants of the Avesta people. The courtship, which seems to have been called "the bidding" (the root *gad* is used, Yasna 9.23), involved obtaining consent from the parents of the bride: the young woman was betrothed (lit. "entrusted, delivered"; the verb, *para-dā-*, is also used similarly in Old Indic) to the future husband, often probably long before the onset of her puberty. The Avestan term for the marriage ceremony seems to be *nāiriθwana-*, literally "(reception of) the wifely or womanly status". This was followed by the "conduction" (Avestan *vaz-*, *vad-*, cf. Old Indic *vah-*, *vadhū*, Greek ἄγεσθαι γυναῖκα, Lat. *ducere puellam in matrimonium*) of the bride by the bridegroom from her parents' home to his.[1] The wife is thereafter "the lady of the house", *nmānō.paθnī* (cf. Middle Persian *bāmbišn, bāmbušn*, Sogdian δβāmban "lady"), just as the husband is the "lord of the house", *nmānō.pati* (see *Vidēvdād* 12.7).

The ancient Eastern Iranians appear to have been polygamous, as were of course the Persians. The Avestan picture of opulent households supports this: "...great houses with bustling women and fast chariots, with spread-out rugs and piled-up cushion-heaps..." (Yasht 10.30).[2] Of course men of less means had to content themselves with only one wife.

The most strikingly unusual aspect of marriage customs in ancient Iran was the sanction of *x^vaētvadaθa* or "next-of-kin marriages". The Avesta speaks of this institution as an important part of the Zoroastrian religion, and it is even mentioned explicitly in the *Fravarānē* or profession of faith recited by new converts (Yasna 12.9; see also *Vispered* 3.3). Under this institution, which is thoroughly documented by Greek, Armenian and Syriac texts from Achaemenian to early Sasanian times, as well as by Pahlavi texts, a man could marry his sister, daughter, or even his mother; these are the "three kinds" of *xvētōdas* mentioned in Sasanian law-books. It is important to realize that incestuous marriages were not merely tolerated, but indeed regarded as acts of piety and great merit, and even efficacious against the demonic forces.

[1] For further details on the Indo-European and Indo-Iranian wedding terminology and customs, see M. Schwartz, "Proto-Indo-European *ǵem*", in *Monumentum H. S. Nyberg* II (Tehran–Liège, 1975), pp. 195–211 (Acta Iranica 5).

[2] Trans. Gershevitch, *op. cit.*, p. 89.

Economic life

The domestication of animals

Cattle. As has already been mentioned, cattle-raising was a central part of the most ancient economy of Eastern Iran. This is reflected by the role of the Bull in Zoroastrian thought as the origin and supreme exemplar of all benign animal life, and the related usage of the term "bovine" for the animal creation. It should also be remembered that the bull figures in Zoroastrianism not only in its protology but also in its eschatology, for the body of the bull Hadayans, sacrificed by the final Saviour in an ultimate *yasna*, yields up the stuff whereby immortality will be obtained.

One of the most outstanding characteristics of Zarathushtra's Gāthās is the variety of their references to cattle. It is possible that in the socio-economic background of Zarathushtra's preaching lay a struggle between settled herdsmen and cattle-rustling marauders. In Yasna 29 the cow (and in some verses bull, the gender of *gav-* being often ambiguous) lamentingly seeks a champion against violent treatment and is urged to accept Zoroaster as guardian appointed by Ahura Mazdā. In Yasna 31.10, the cow is said to have chosen for herself "the cattle-tending herdsman as a just lord, as one who promotes Good Mind".

Cattle-herding in fact provided a model and symbol of ethical behaviour in general, with the role of the herdsman parallel to that of the biblical "good shepherd", and the role of the gentle, defenceless cow like that of the biblical sheep (or lamb), a symbol of benignity and of suffering.

The acquisition of the "luck-bringing cow" is associated with proper actions and becomes a symbol, in fact, of one's spiritual goals (see Yasna 47.3; 49.19; 52.2; and 51.5). As against the moral "herdsman" evil-doers are mentioned as "non-herders among herders" (Yasna 49.4; also 46.4).[1]

These themes are carried forward in the post-Gathic texts. Thus in Yasna 35.3–4 we read: "In connection with the rewards for best deeds we urged the taught and the untaught, rulers and ruled, to grant peace and pasturage to the cow." In the *Fravarānē* the new convert swears

---
[1] For the symbolic value of the cow in the Gathas, see G. C. Cameron, "Zoroaster the Herdsman", *IIJ* x (1969), pp. 261–81.

"I renounce the theft and abduction of the cow, and the harm and destruction of Mazdā-worshipping homes. To those with authority I shall grant access and lodging at will, those who are on the land with their cattle."

Even in the Yasht to Mithra we find these interesting comparisons: "Sometimes the head of the country...sometimes the head of the tribe...sometimes the head of the clan...sometimes she [*viz*. the cow] who longs to be milked as she feels [*lit*. is with] the pain of swelling, sometimes also the pauper who follows the doctrine of Truth but is deprived of his rights; the lamenting voice of the latter, even though he raises his voice reverently, reaches up to the [heavenly] lights, makes the round of the earth, pervades the seven climes, so does the voice of the cow... who, being led away captive, calls at times for assistance with outstretched hands, longing for the herd: 'When will grass-land magnate Mithra, the hero, driving from behind, make us reach the herd, when will he divert to the path of Truth us who are being driven to the estate of Falsehood?'" (Yasht 10.84–6).[1] Mithra is also said to punish the wicked who are false to the treaty (*miθrō.drujō*) and strike at Asha, those under whom "the cow, accustomed to pastures, is driven along the dusty road of captivity, dragged forward in the clutches of treaty-infringing men as their draught animal, choking with tears they [= cows] stand, slobbering at the mouth" (Yasht 10.38).[2]

Cattle were prized as a source of meat as well as of dairy products and of leather (all these being termed *gav-*, as also in Old Indic, indicating the Indo-Iranian origin of these uses). Urine of bovines (*gaomaēza-*) was considered an efficacious cleaning agent (perhaps because of the ammonia content) and would be used, followed by water, for washing, and under certain circumstances even drunk. In addition, as we have seen, cattle were used as dray beasts already in early Aryan times.

During the summer months the cattle would be driven to graze in mountain pasturelands (cf. Yasht 10.14). With the onset of winter the herds would be driven back to the valleys; this was celebrated in the feast of *ayāθrima-* "the driving in"; they were then kept for the duration of the winter in stables, for whose construction we have detailed directives in *Vidēvdād* 14.14, as an act of atonement.

Sheep and goats. In addition to cattle the Eastern Iranian herdsmen also

[1] Trans. Gershevitch, *op. cit.*, pp. 113–15.
[2] *ibid*, p. 93.

kept flocks of sheep and goats on their mountain pastures in summer and penned them up in separate stalls during the winter months. Mating took place after their return to the valleys in late September, so that the lambs were born in early March, in time to mature on the summer grazing grounds in advance of the cold seasons.

"The ram with curved horns" was admired for its strength, as was the male goat; both are mentioned as forms assumed by Vərəthraghna in Yasht 14.23 and 25; the ram was later a symbol of the royal x^varənah. We may also note the proper name *dawrāmaēšī-* "having dark ewes". The milk of these animals was also drunk; it was prescribed boiled for women who had had a stillbirth (*Vidēvdād* 5.52). The young of goats (*azō *sčainiš*) as well as of pigs (**huš *parəsō*) were also eaten, as emerges from two fragmentary Avestan citations.[1]

Horses. As was the case among other Indo-European people, the horse played an essential role in the life of the ancient Iranians. Darius I was surely expressing a pan-Iranian outlook on the role of this beast when he says in his inscription, "Great is Ahura Mazdā...he made Darius king, he bestowed upon him the kingdom, possessed of good chariots, good horses, good men."[2] Like other Indo-European peoples, the Iranians conceived of these ancient deities, particularly those associated with the heavens (e.g. Ushah "Dawn", the Sun, and Mithra) and seas (e.g. Apąm Napāt and Anāhitā), as riding in horse-drawn chariots. These divine chariots have four horses, although two-horse chariots were also employed. One may also note that in common with other Indo-Europeans the Iranians frequently had hippophoric names, e.g. Aurvat.aspa- "having swift horses", Pourušāspa- "having grey horses" (cf. Sanskrit Bṛhadaśva, Greek Leukippos, etc.), but also names specifically referring to the yoking of horses to chariots, as are found in instances of -*aspa*- following a past participle: Yuxtāspa-, Hitāspa-, Jāmāspa-, and perhaps Vīštāspa- (from *vaēz-* "to attach"?).

Charioteership was tested not only in warfare, but also on the race-course. Hence Kavi Haosravah prays for victory in the chariot race (Yasht 5.50; Yasht 19.77). For this, incidentally, he sacrifices a hundred stallions, a thousand steers, and ten thousand sheep; this is the standard offering of the hero to Anāhitā in her Yasht, and shows the greater value

---

[1] Studied by K. Hoffmann, "Drei indogermanische Tiernamen in einem Avesta-fragment", *Münchener Studien zur Sprachwissenschaft* XXII (1967), pp. 29–38; for the readings see further I. Gershevitch, "Iranian words containing -*ǎn-*", in C. E. Bosworth (ed.), *Iran and Islam: in memory of the late Vladimir Minorsky* (Edinburgh, 1971), pp. 267–9.

[2] Susa *g*; cf. also Susa *s*, where the men precede the horses and chariots.

of horses compared to cattle. Anāhitā is also besought by heroes to grant them swift horses (Yasht 5.86 and 98), a reward obtained by other Avestan heroes as well (cf. Yasht 8.19; Yasht 10.3 and 11). There are several allusions in the Avesta to heroes riding bareback (Yasna 11.2; Yasna 10.11), and a day's journey on horseback by a competent rider served as a unit of measurement (Yasht 5.4).

Not only are horses praised in the Avesta for their speed, their excitement in battle, and their beauty, but also for their eyesight: they can spot a horsehair on the ground on the cloudiest, foggiest nights (Yasht 14.31; Yasht 16.10).

Among the products of the horse may be mentioned mare's milk, which fermented yields an alcoholic beverage (*Nērangistān* 30), the *kumiss* of present-day Central and Northern Asia.

Camels. In early Eastern Iran the camel may have been valued even more than the horse. Zarathushtra himself seeks as his reward ten mares and stallions and one camel (Yasna 44.8). Incidentally the name Zaraθuštra- is one of a number of camelophoric names in the Avesta and may mean "(skilled at) managing camels" (thus formerly H. W. Bailey) or, with intransitive meaning of the participle forming the first member of the compound, "having active camels". This early value of the camel *vis-à-vis* the horse may be reflected in *Vidēvdād* 7.42, where the physician's fees for curing women of successively higher social rank are given respectively as a she-ass (? *kaθwā*, see below), a cow, a mare, and a she-camel; and in *Vidēvdād* 14.11 an amount of gold is referred to the value of a camel, but that of silver to a horse. However in *Vidēvdād* 22.3–4 and 20 we have apparently descending values: horse, camel, bovine, sheep.

It is hardly necessary to review the virtues of the camel – its endurance and the economy of its upkeep, surviving weeks in the desert merely eating some thorns; its speed, its strength in bearing loads, and its docility except when it mates; the aggressive and impetuous force of the male at this time would also appeal to the imagination of the Iranian warrior, as is illustrated by Yasht 14.12–13. Here we find an affectionately detailed portrait of the male camel, from which we also learn of the use of camel's hair for clothing. It may be recalled at this point that the Eastern Iranian homeland is also the homeland of the camel and possibly too the horse as well as the ass.

The ass. This beast is rarely mentioned in the Avesta. In addition to being the lowest fee of a woman to a physician (if indeed *kaθwā* is synonymous with *xarā*), the ass is mentioned, along with the horse, as a permissible source of curdled milk (*Nērangistān* 67). No doubt the ass also served as a beast of burden, as is the case throughout Central Asia today, where the animal is carefully bred.

Dogs. The *Vidēvdād* provides an epitome of the Old Iranian view of the utility of the dog. Here Ahura Mazdā is represented as saying: "The dog did I... make wearing his own clothes and his own shoes, a diligent watcher, having a sharp bite, who obtains his food from man and so guards his property; and I... have appointed the dog to guard against the Tūras; as long as he can actively bark, no thief or wolf will carry anything away from the farmhouse." The amount of attention paid to the dog in the *Vidēvdād* is vast, and even if much of what is said, e.g. concerning punishment of injury to dogs (and otters, etc.!) and their relation to funerary customs (e.g. the expulsion of corpse-demons by the glance of a dog) are late insertions of Magian inspiration,[1] there can be no doubt that the dog was of great importance and loved throughout Iran. Among the (genuine) dogs distinguished were the herd-watching dog, the household-guarding dog, the bloodhound, and the dog skilled in tricks (see *Vidēvdād* 13.8–20); this order indicates the relative amount of importance attributed to each type.

Familiarity with and affection for the dog brought about a certain tendency to its virtual anthropomorphism; thus the regulations for the care of pregnant bitches are modelled after those for women and occur together with them (*Vidēvdād* 15.19 *seq.*). Especially charming is the passage in *Vidēvdād* 13.44–8, where the dog is elaborately compared for its traits to a priest, a warrior, a minstrel, a thief, a nocturnal predator, a whore, and a child; here we seem to have traces of an old riddle-catechism.

Fowl. Our data on the breeding of poultry are meagre. The domestic rooster seems to have been introduced into Europe from Iran (in Greek he was called "The Persian bird"). In the Avesta the cock is virtually sacred; doubtless on account of its crowing at daybreak it is the herald of Sraosha, who presides over religious observation and responsibility in general. The rooster is even given a special (Magian?) name in the *Vidēvdād*, *parōdarəs-*, i.e. "that which sees first", as against such vulgar names as *kahrkatāt-*, meaning apparently "chickendom, cluckitude".

---

[1] This is a general problem in the use of the *Vidēvdād* for the ancient eastern situation; see A. Kammenhuber, "Totenvorschriften und 'Hunde-Magie' in Vidēvdāt", *ZDMG* cviii (1958), pp. 299–307.

The rooster is thus the enemy of the demon of sloth, procrastination, and oversleeping, Būshyąsta (see *Vidēvdād* 18.14 *seq.*). A gift of a pair of *parō.darəs-* birds, a male and a female, is tantamount to the gift of a mansion, and the proper feeding of the bird confers paradise (*Vidēvdād* 18.28–9).

Birds are listed together with "small and large livestock" (*pasu-* and *staora-* together make up a comprehensive term for livestock in general), man, dogs, and fires, in short, the chief components of rural domesticity, in *Vidēvdād* 2.8. The "flying birds" offered to Mithra in Yasht 10.119 together with "small and large livestock" may refer to pigeons and the like.

Agriculture

It is a striking fact that in the oldest Avestan texts, the *Gāthās*, which abound, as we have seen, in cattle-imagery, there seems to be little or no reference to agriculture. The Younger Avesta, on the other hand, frequently mentions ploughing, seeding, harvest, grain, irrigation, etc. It is quite possible that this is because Zarathushtra's religious poetry is highly traditional in its imagery, and looks back to a period centuries earlier than his own, which was predominantly pastoral.

When the nomadic Indo-Iranians swept over Central Asia with their cattle, they encountered cultures which had already been practising agriculture with a technology of irrigation for two or perhaps three millennia, and seem already to have been in the early stages of urbanization.[1] The Aryan imposition of cattle-oriented pastoralism seems to have gradually ceded to a new emphasis on agriculture.

The shift of focus is most clearly illustrated by *Vidēvdād* 3.23–35, which deals with the virtues of tillage: here "the core of the Mazdayasnian religion" is explained as the constant and abundant sowing of grain; "who sows grain sows Asha, and promotes and nurtures the Mazdayasnian religion with a hundred new dwelling places, a thousand stations (to the extent equivalent to) ten thousand Yeŋhe Hātąm prayers. When the grain is prepared the demons begin to sweat; when milling (or winnowing) is done, the demons howl; when the dough is made ready, the demons break wind." The grain here is

---

[1] See V. M. Masson, "The first farmers in Turkmenia", *Antiquity* XXXV (1961), pp. 203–13; A. Belenitski, *Central Asia* (London, 1969), pp. 26ff.; V. M. Masson and V. I. Sarianidi, *Central Asia* (London, 1972), pp. 42–3 (Ancient peoples and places 79).

specifically barley (*yava-*), the most traditional grain of Indo-Europeans, and thus of sacral significance; hence the association with Asha, seen in the phrase *yava- ašavan-*, mentioned above.

Another grain mentioned by name in the Avesta is wheat (*gantuma-*, a late form like Yaghnobi *yantum*, for **ganduma-*, *Nērangistān* 28), which is the chief grain of Turkestan today. The harvest was celebrated at the feast of *Paitišhahya*. In addition to the growing of grain, grass and fruit trees are mentioned (*Vidēvdād* 3.4; for artificial meadows, cf. also 15.41–2; 2.26 with 2.28).

The irrigation of land is mentioned several times in the *Vidēvdād*. The ideal "arable and productive land" was watered twice (14.13), although we read of land being watered up to four times (5.5). After irrigation furrows were made with the plough for sowing, and then the earth was packed down (cf. *Vidēvdād* 6.6). Since ploughs seem not to have changed their simple construction in greater Eastern Iran down to the present day, modern ploughs will furnish an idea of the ancient type. A detailed diagram of the parts of the Pamir plough is found in the appendix of G. Morgenstierne, *Indo-Iranian Frontier Languages* II, where there is also a diagram of a plough-yoke. This plough-yoke is shown by I. Gershevitch essentially to correspond to the yoke to which Mithra's steeds are harnessed, with its complex yoke, yoke-pin, yoke-strap, shaft (or pole) and hook.[1] Morgenstierne's index also provides an excellent series of drawings of various Pamir implements and a house-plan, which seem to correspond closely to the ancient forms. The digging of wells on fields far from rivers is mentioned in *Vidēvdād* 8.38; 6.33.

It may be kept in mind that the reason we have the particular distribution of data on agriculture in the *Vidēvdād*, as outlined above, is because of the antidemonic purposes of the authors, who were concerned on the one hand that there be no ritual impurity of the sacred elements earth, water, and fire, and on the other that as much waste land, the habitation of demons, be reclaimed as possible and of course that land which was already fertile should remain so.

[1] *Avestan Hymn to Mithra*, pp. 274–5, commenting on Yasht 10.125.

CHAPTER 14

THE RELIGION OF ACHAEMENIAN IRAN

The task of giving an account of the major aspects of the religion of Achaemenian Iran may be seen as consisting in large measure of bringing into coordination two main bodies of documentation, each representing an evolving situation.

The first body of documentation is the Avesta, written in a language which, for want of our knowing the original name, we call "Avestan". The Avesta is a compilation of liturgy, dogma, prayers, spells, mythological lore and prescriptions. From the viewpoint of language and contents, the Avesta belongs predominantly to Eastern Iran, that is present-day Soviet Turkestan and Afghanistan. The corpus began to emerge in the 5th century B.C. out of a mass of heterogeneous but probably long interactive traditions spanning centuries; having evolved orally, it reached a definitive canonized form, so far as we can tell, only in the Sasanian period as the sacred scriptures of the newly institutionalized Zoroastrian state religion.

The Avesta may be analysed in terms of the following chief strata:

(1) The *Gāthās* of Zoroaster (Zarathushtra), the prophet whose see must have been somewhere in Afghanistan, and whom the Zoroastrian tradition dates in the first half of the 6th century B.C. They are composed in an Avestan dialect characterized by features of grammar and phonology more archaic than the dialect of most of the other Avestan texts, those mentioned under (3) and (4). The latter dialect is therefore called "Younger Avestan", somewhat misleadingly because, in the absence of proof that it evolved from the Gathic dialect, it may well be as old as the Gāthās. However, the surviving texts themselves which are couched in "Younger Avestan" language have been dubbed the "Younger Avesta" with some justification, because their authors dilute Zoroaster's tenets with pre-Gathic beliefs rejected by him. The composition, as against the language, of the Younger Avesta, is therefore indeed "younger" than the Gāthās, whose metrical versification,

THE RELIGION OF ACHAEMENIAN IRAN

moreover, resembles more that of the Vedas than that of the Younger Avesta.

(2) Some material in the same dialect as the Gāthās, but composed after Zoroaster's death. It includes a few texts similar to the Gāthās, but in the main consists of a series of liturgical texts in prose known as the *Yasna Haptaŋhāiti* ("Liturgy of the Seven Chapters", the Septempartite Hymnal).[1] The latter, although it shows the impact of Zoroaster's ideas, is distinctly different from the Gāthās in theological outlook, displaying in fact pre-Zarathushtrian concepts.

(3) Texts attesting the worship not only of Zoroaster's sole god and his Entities, but also of other divinities. A comparison with the oldest surviving religious texts of India, the Rig-Veda, shows that some of these gods date from the common Indo-Iranian (sometimes called "Aryan") period. Hymns to individual divinities (always in association with other divinities) are known as Yashts.

(4) Texts in a late form of Younger Avestan, composed or re-composed after the Achaemenian period, mostly of a prescriptive nature. These, of which the most important is the *Vidēvdād* (*Vendidad*), are generally thought to show the influence of the Magi, a priestly caste of Median origin.

Of the original Avestan canon only approximately one fourth is preserved, and that in manuscripts of which the oldest was written as late as A.D. 1323. Some knowledge of lost portions of the Avesta can be gained from citations, paraphrases, and epitomes in the Zoroastrian Middle Persian (Pahlavi) books. The entirety of the Younger Avesta is permeated by the figure of Zoroaster, who is portrayed as a prophet and saviour, the founder of the "Mazdā-worshipping Zoroastrian anti-daēvic Ahura-teaching Religion". The texts other than those of the Yasna (Liturgy) are represented as having been revealed to Zoroaster by Ahura Mazdā, even though ironically enough they include all manner of views which Zoroaster would have been bound to find contrary to his revelation. But the Avesta is more than a mélange of "pagan" notions mixed with Gathic ones. The scripture seems to be the product of a long symbiosis, affected by subsequent developments of ideas, emanating from Zoroaster's teachings. Thus we find evidence of a protological myth, whose protagonists are merely adumbrated in the Gāthās, according to which Angra Mainyu invaded the world created by Spenta Mainyu; and of an eschatological myth involving

[1] Yasna 35–41.

the destruction of evil by the forces of good. An interesting feature is the development of Zoroaster's doctrine of future saviours: according to the Younger Avesta, three Saoshyants will be born to maidens bathing in Lake Kansaoya (Lake Hāmūn in Sīstān), who become pregnant from the seed of Zoroaster miraculously preserved there.

While the Avesta furnishes us with a wealth of diverse religious ideas most of which existed during the Achaemenian period, it lacks a historical contextualization. It is completely devoid of references to persons, institutions, or events of Achaemenian times. Internal evidence provides only the possibility of a sequential ordering of large blocks of text, but nothing definitive in terms of dates or provenience. The place names mentioned, apart from mythological geography, are all in Eastern Iran; it is as though Persia did not exist. Accordingly, as the canonization of the scripture took place long after the Achaemenian period, the lack of references to identifiable Achaemenian realia makes the Avesta an elusive source for the religion of Achaemenian Iran in general, and Persia in particular.

The situation is practically the reverse when we turn to our other body of documentation, the source material on Achaemenian Persia. Here the material is for the most part contemporary, and clear as to date and provenience. However the documentation, while rich in realia, does not include texts of a primarily religious character. We are dependent on: (1) the inscriptions of the Achaemenian kings, which are essentially political in intent; (2) economic records in Elamite found at Persepolis; (3) the accounts of classical Greek authors, often enough of questionable reliability; and (4) papyri and artifacts with Aramaic inscriptions. An important part of our evidence consists of theophoric names; this material must be used with caution, since (apart from the linguistic problems of interpretation, especially vexing in the ambiguous spellings of names in Elamite transmission) it is not necessarily always the case that the existence of a personal name referring to a deity attests the worship of that deity in the place and time in which the name occurs. It may be added that Persian iconography is derived from Mesopotamian motifs and rather ambiguous as to religious implications, and remnants of structures are highly debatable as to their possible relevance for religion.

It will be seen, however, that despite the shortcomings the two bodies of documentation complement and partly explain each other, and from them one can make some plausible inferences on Achaemenian religion.

THE CHIEF AVESTAN GODS

Our procedure will therefore be to examine both corpora separately before drawing overall conclusions.

THE CHIEF AVESTAN GODS

The Zarathushtrian component

In the section that follows we shall briefly survey the ideas of Zoroaster as they subsequently percolated through heterogeneous and often older conceptions, interacting with them to reach the form in which they were preached ever after.

Ahura Mazdā, while he maintains his status as the creator of all things, and is all-wise and all-beneficent, is far from being in the Younger Avesta the only god, as he appears in the Gāthās; the Younger Avestan texts do not represent him as more "venerable" (*yazata*) than his creation Mithra. More precisely, the term yazata, equivalent in modern terminology to "god", while altogether absent from Zoroaster's Gāthās, occurs ubiquitously in the Younger Avesta, applied to both Ahura Mazdā and a host of other gods. It is often said that among the yazatas Ahura Mazdā's position is that of *primus inter pares*; but this does not square very well with the opening of the Yasht to Mithra, where the latter god is said to have been created by Ahura Mazdā to be equal to him in venerability. The maintenance of Ahura Mazdā's creation depends on the yazatas he created; he himself performs sacrifice to certain of them in return for favours from them.

The Younger Avestan Ahura Mazdā is "primus" only in respect of his name occurring in the texts much more often than those of the other gods; the compiler insistently represents Zoroaster's sole god as approving of the polytheism the prophet had proscribed, with the result that Zoroaster himself is presented as a polytheist.

Evidence for the fact that Ahura Mazdā does not derive from the same cultic background as the gods of the ancient Iranian polytheism ("paganism") is shown by the Yasht (No. 1) in his honour. Its shoddy, threadbare composition and the absence of mythological detail distinguish it from other Yashts; it is essentially a list of Ahura Mazdā's names and their magical, apotropaic powers.

Nevertheless, in the *Yasna Haptaŋhāiti* (above, p. 665) we find a picture of Ahura Mazdā at striking variance with the Zarathushtrian conception, and strongly reminiscent of the chief Vedic god Varuṇa.

Ahura Mazdā is here especially associated with *asha*, just as Varuṇa is with *ṛta*, of which he is the special custodian; and there is no reference to the opposed principle, *drug*, of Zarathushtrian dualism. He is here called "Ahura Mazdā" when his wives are listed as abstractions (Yasna 38.1–2), but "Ahura", without "Mazdā", when his wives are called Ahurānīs and defined as the Waters, just as the Indic Varuṇānīs are the Waters as Varuṇa's wives. Ahura Mazdā is *humāya*, "endowed with good *māyā*", the occult power which is particularly mentioned in the Rig-Veda in connection with Varuṇa.

Chiefly on the basis of these correspondences scholars have posited the existence in Iran of an ancient god Ahura, the equivalent of Varuṇa, the Asura *par excellence*. It is thought that the latter was in ancient India originally called simply "Asura", and that one of his epithets, "Varuṇa", subsequently came to serve as his name. Thus the double dual compound Ahura-Mithra occurring in various Younger Avestan passages is seen as the equivalent of the similar linkage of Varuṇa with Mitra in the Rig-Veda, where Mitra-Varuṇa is a biune deity. The existence of this Ahura helps to explain not only how Zoroaster's very different conception of Ahura Mazdā could gain acceptance (for converts he would be a god with whom they were already familiar, of whom Zoroaster provided a more exact and profound interpretation), but also how subsequently a reaction set in by which the newly conceived god was reintegrated into the old polytheism from which Zoroaster had severed him.

The Entities, which so prominently figure in the Gāthās, are organized in the Younger Avesta into a canonical heptad (or, with the first of the series, the "Holy Spirit", eliminated through mistaken identification with Ahura Mazdā himself, into a hexad) called the Amesha Spentas, "Holy Immortals".[1] Worshipped together or as individual deities in their own right they are of one mind, one voice, one action, and at one with the father and ruler, Ahura Mazdā (Yasht 19.16–18). Each of them presides over a specific aspect of creation:

Spenta Mainyu, "Holy Spirit" – Man;
Vohu Manah, "Good Thought or, Mind" – Animals (especially cattle);
Asha Vahishta, "Best Asha" (Truth/Order) – Fire;

---

[1] See the important recent study of them by Johanna Narten, *Die Aməša Spəntas im Avesta* (Wiesbaden, 1982).

THE CHIEF AVESTAN GODS

Khshathra Vairya, "Power/Dominion to be Chosen" – Metal;
Spentā Ārmaiti, "Holy Devotion" – Earth;
Haurvatāt, "Wholeness, Health" – Water;
Ameretāt, "Immortality" (= Life, Longevity) – Plants.

These correspondences are partly foreshadowed in the Gāthās. Interesting is the fact that Spentā Ārmaiti (Aramati) is in part based on a pagan earth-goddess, as remains quite apparent in a number of passages. This is not to assert that the other Entities were thought of as pale abstractions; for example, according to the seventh chapter of the Pahlavi *Dēnkard* (based on a lost Avestan source), Zoroaster had a vision of Good Mind in the form of a gigantic man.

Sraosha, "Hearkening" appears in the Gāthās as a personified human virtue of masculine gender who is referred to as "the greatest of all" and associated with reward (Ashi) and punishments. In the Younger Avesta Sraosha turns up as a god whose functions are as varied as the possible associations with the basic concept of "hearkening" can be. He represents obedience as well as discipline, and is associated with the vigilant Mithra and with Rashnu ("The Judge"), as well as with *Ashi*, which in the Younger Avesta figures as goddess of reward and abundance, and is called Sraosha's sister. In one hymn (Yasna 57), stylistically patterned after the Mithra Yasht in many details, Sraosha is said to have a mansion on Mount Hukairya, and thrice each day and night to fly across the heavens, punishing the evil and honouring the righteous. Here he is also the embodiment of prayer, the first to have recited the Gāthās and spread the *barəsman* twigs. As intermediate between Ahura Mazdā and man, he is often associated with Nairyōsaŋha.

Daēnā is used by Zarathushtra for "vision, insight, conscience, consciousness"; a two-fold meaning, which quite possibly arises from homonymy, shows up unmistakably in the Younger Avesta: on the one hand the *daēnā* is one's individual moral conscience, acting invisibly throughout one's life, but after death appearing to the deceased righteous as a beautiful maiden escort to Paradise, to the deceased impious as an ugly hag; on the other she is the goddess "The (Mazdayasnian) Religion", personified, daughter of Ahura Mazdā and Ārmaiti, as well as, through next-of-kin marriage, the wife of Ahura Mazdā. She is particularly associated with Chistā, the hypostasis of The Teaching and of The Straight Path, whose Yasht is called the "Yasht of Daēnā". However, a variety of views is found as to the inter-relationship of the various daēnā-concepts and their etymology, and a pagan origin of the goddess cannot be excluded.

Geush Urvan "Soul of the Bovine" is the collective sum of the souls of sacrificed animals, of which the bovine is the chief representative. This divinity was also equated with the soul of the Primal Bull slain by Angra Mainyu, and the source of animal life according to the later, Pahlavi texts.

DEITIES OF NON-GATHIC ORIGIN

Mithra. The most important god of pagan origin, Mithra maintained his great popularity down through Iranian history. His antiquity is assured by the correspondence with the Vedic Mitra, with whom he has much in common. As a common noun, *miθra* means "contract", and it is undeniable that Mithra's primary and distinctive function in his Yasht is to be guardian of the contract. As such, Mithra presides over orderly social relationships at all levels, from international treaties to agreements between individuals. Rising on Mount Harā, he rides across the sky in his chariot and follows the sun, surveying the entire land, punishing deceit and upholding justice. He is sleepless, is aided by heavenly "spies" and cannot be deceived. Having the fixed epithet "possessing broad pastures" he provides waters for plant growth, promotes flocks and herds, furthers human life, relieves anxiety, and so forth. The Avestan Mithra must not be confused with the homonymous god of Imperial Rome, who reflects a number of variant Iranian traditions (probably Median and perhaps Scythian) and evolved as the focus of a mystery cult under later, non-Iranian doctrines.[1]

Aredvī Sūrā Anāhitā "The Moist, Mighty, Immaculate One". The Iranian Great Goddess, who has a long and impressive Yasht. She is primarily a goddess of rivers and waters in general; she presides over fertility; she is a martial figure. In all these aspects she resembles the Mesopotamian Ishtar-Inanna. Herodotus (1. 131) in fact claims that the Persian worship of "Aphrodite" is of recent and Semitic origin, and there is testimony that the cult of Anāhitā was spread throughout the

---

[1] See Hinnells, *Mithraic Studies*, in particular the articles of Gershevitch, Hinnells, Bivar and the present writer. Evidence for Mithra as a sun-god in ancient northern Media seems evidenced by Georgian Mirsa, an old god of light. For Mithra as *petrogenitus*, note the Vedic conception of Mitra and the sun coming forth from a stone enclosure (cf. F. B. J. Kuiper, "Remarks on 'The Avestan Hymn to Mithra'", *IIJ* v (1962), p. 52) in addition to the image of the sun coming up from mountains (particularly in Mesopotamian iconography) and the Anatolian-Caucasian (and Scythic?) rock-birth motifs.

DEITIES OF NON-GATHIC ORIGIN

Iranian empire by Artaxerxes II, who introduced statues of the goddess.[1] Note that: (1) the description of the goddess seems to be inspired by statuary; (2) the fiend Azhi Dahāka sacrificed to her in Babylon, according to her Yasht (5.29); (3) some scholars assume late composition on linguistic grounds; (4) an Indo-Iranian origin of the goddess is not demonstrable: the existence of a river goddess Sarasvatī in India, and a cognate Harahvatī ("having streams") in Iran as a *place name* (Arachosia) does not serve to establish the existence of an Iranian *goddess* Harahvatī, and the resemblance of *Harahvatī* to Harā ("watchtower"), Anāhitā's mountain home, is fortuitous. Moreover (5) while Anāhitā is spoken of as a river, she is in fact not identified with any particular river (this would be difficult to understand if she were of Eastern Iranian origin); (6) her presence is redundant, in view of the continued cult of the Waters (Āpō), which represent the genuine indigenous, in fact Indo-Iranian, female personification of streams; the Yasht to Anāhitā is called the Yasht of the Waters (Ābān Yasht), and in the calendar it is the Waters, and not Anāhitā which furnish the month-name; finally (7) the Ābān Yasht shows in detail the same structure as the Yasht to Ashi, who is demonstrably an ancient goddess, very possibly pre-Zarathushtrian, and whose Yasht one may expect to be the model.

Druvāspā "She who possesses strong horses": who also has her Yasht modelled after that of Ashi. Despite her name, she presides over livestock, and was therefore closely associated with Geush Urvan.

Nairyō-saŋha. The name of this god (the equivalent of Vedic *narāśaṃsa*) seems to mean "of manly utterance" or perhaps rather "announcer to men"; the latter fits his role in post-Avestan texts as messenger of the gods. He may be characterized even for the Avesta as an intermediary between gods and men; his connection with fire may result from the fact that one prays before fire, rather than from an ancient "solar" nature. He is of beautiful appearance, and in later Zoroastrian and Manichean myths he uses his beauty to seduce the forces of evil. As we shall see, ceremonies in his honour were performed in Persia.

Verethraghna is the yazata "Victory", whose hymn is Yasht 14. His name is related to the Avestan *vərəθrayan* "victorious" and means etymologically "smiting (of) resistance". There is an old controversy as to whether there is a relationship of the god to the Vedic Indra as smiter of the serpent (or dragon) Vṛtra, although the interpretation of

---
[1] Berossos *apud* Clement of Alexandria, *Protreptikos* v.65.3

Vedic *vṛtrahan* as "smiting Vṛtra" seems to be secondary, since the Avestan cognate vərəθrayan (originally "beating back resistance") is used of various divinities. In Armenia we find, in the Christian period, a myth of Vahagn (i.e. Verethraghna) as a dragon-killer, but this may be based on a purely local theme, with possible influence of Herakles, with whom Verethraghna was identified in the Seleucid and Arsacid periods, as killer of the Hydra.

Verethraghna is, like the earth, called "created by Ahura". He accompanies Mithra across the sky, crushing and grinding the evildoers. In the latter act he is graphically described in the Mithra Yasht as a fierce boar, his most common representation in the iconography. The boar is but one of the god's ten epiphanies, each of which is an embodiment of power, speed, and beauty. Of these, two are especially known from Sasanian iconography and literature, the horned ram (as in the Pahlavi *Kār-nāmag*) and the royal falcon; here the symbol and concept merge with that of the *Khvarənah*, with which the yazata is, not surprisingly, intimately associated. The feather of the royal falcon is said to possess particular virtues in the Yasht to Verethraghna (vv. 34 *seq.*): it counters spells, wards off attack, etc., in a manner reminiscent of the feather of the Sīmurgh in Firdausī's *Shāh-nāma*; in this connection one may also note the comparison of Verethraghna with the Saēna bird (= Sīmurgh) in verse 41 of the Yasht.

The complete list of epiphanies is as follows: (1) a strong wind; (2) a yellow-eared, golden-horned bull; (3) a white, yellow-eared, golden-muzzled horse; (4) a rutting camel; (5) the boar; (6) a nimble youth in the prime of life; (7) the falcon; (8) a horned ram; (9) a sharp-horned buck; and (10) an armed warrior. It is in each of these incarnations that the divinity makes himself manifest before Ahura Mazdā.

Tishtriya is the god representing a star, usually assumed to be Sirius (Canis Major),[1] with whose rising there occurred the rainy season. According to his long hymn which is Yasht 8, every year Tishtriya battles with the drought-demon Apaosha on the shores of the sea Vourukasha, Tishtriya in the form of a beautiful, white-adorned horse, and Apaosha in the form of a horse which is black, balding, and horrid. Tishtriya is at first routed because of insufficient worship by man, but strengthened by Ahura Mazdā's worship he defeats the demon. Then

---

[1] See references in Boyce, *History of Zoroastrianism* I, p. 74, to which add M. P. Kharegat, in J. J. Modi (ed.), *Sir Jamshetjee Jeejeebhoy Madressa Jubilee Volume* (Bombay, 1914), pp. 118–23, 145–55.

into the sea Vourukasha he plunges, and distributes the rains. His helpers are Tishtriyaēnī (Canis Minor), the Pleiades, and "the stars in front of the Pleiades". He is associated in worship with Satavaēsa (Antares), Vanant ("The Conqueror": Vega) and the Haptōiringa (Ursa Major). Verse 44 of the Yasht, "Tishtriya... whom Ahura Mazdā has established as lord and overseer above all stars", corresponds practically verbatim to Plutarch's words on the Persian view of Sirius in *Isis and Osiris* 47.

A problem in the study of Tishtriya is his connection with a god Tīriya[1] first attested in Old Persian onomastica. It is clear that Tīriya was regarded as identical with Tishtriya at the time the "Younger Avestan" calendar was devised. Most scholars regard the two as originally different gods, but a number of facts seem to point to their identity from the outset: (1) Tīriya could hardly have been an exclusively Western Iranian god, as some assume; he is attested for Eastern Iranian as a divinity among the Kushans, probably signifying his worship in Bactria; he is represented in the old calendar of Sīstān; he is found in the proper name Tiravharna in a Kharoṣṭhī inscription, and in Chorasmia he was known as Tsiri (*Cyry*), denoting the star Sirius, as well as a day- and month-name. There is no reason for a Persian god to have replaced Tishtriya in these areas. One Eastern Middle Iranian language, Sogdian, has, for both the astronomical and calendrical references, the name Tīsh (*Tyš*), closely allied to, but not derived from, the Avestan name.[2] (2) Tishtriya is unknown as an element in Old Persian names,[3] whereas Tīriya is unknown from the Avesta; (3) in no ancient source or place do the two names occur together. It may therefore be assumed that originally both Tishtriya and Tīriya referred to the same god, Tishtriya being the primary name (cf. Old Indian Tiṣya)[4] and Tīriya an alternate name, probably referring to a chief characteristic. The similarity of the two names would act against their

---

[1] This, and not Tiri, is the correct name, as is shown by the Elamite transcription Teriya(dada), by the constant presence of *y* after *r* in the Aramaic and 1st century B.C. Parthian forms of proper names referring to the god, and by the maintenance of -*y* in Khwarazmian *Cyry*. In Old Persian *iya* is contracted to *ī*; Armenian *Trē* probably attests *ē* < *iya*, as also in Sogdian.

[2] The resemblance of the Sogdian to the Old Indian is coincidental; note the heavy stem. I take *Tīš* from *Tišš* from *Tišθriya*-, which stands for *Tištriya* as *ušθra*- (> Old Persian *uša*-) to Avestan *uštra*- (whence also New Persian *uštur* "camel") and *Bāxθrī* (Old Persian **Bāxci*, Elamite *Ba-ak-šiš*, Bactrian *Bāxlī*) to Old Persian *Bāxtrī* "Bactria".

[3] But Sogdian has the names Tīshfarn, Tīshdhāt, and Tīshīch.

[4] For the etymology of *Tištriya* and *Tiṣya*, see B. Forssman, "Apaoša, der Gegner des Tištriia", *KZ* LXXXII (1968), pp.59ff.

co-existence in any area, so that one or the other name became fixed in a particular region.

Tishtriya's flight toward the sea Vourukasha is twice compared to the swift arrow shot by the great archer Erekhsha (Yasht 8.6, 37), and that shot, whereby Erekhsha established the border of Iran but died from the exertion, is in fact associated with Tīriya's festival Tīragān; indeed TEIPO[1] (Tīr) is depicted on a Kushan coin holding bow and quiver. The simile comparing Tishtriya with Erekhsha's arrow does not explain Tishtriya/Tīriya's association with arrows, for while various other gods are noted for their speed in the Avesta (e.g. Mithra), only Tishtriya is associated with the arrow.

G. Gnoli has assumed the association to be due to the influence on the Achaemenids of Mesopotamian culture, for "Sirius" is KAK.-SI.SÁ in Sumerian, and Šiltahu and Šukudu in Akkadian, all "Arrow".[2] But the concept is more global: in Egypt too Sirius was called Sōpdet (Greek Sōthis) "arrowhead, pointer, sharp object"; the important fact is that in India Tiṣya was thought of as arrow-shaped and in the Rig-Veda is addressed together with Kṛśānu as an archer (10.64.8). The name Tīriya thus may well mean "like an arrow(head), pointed". Etymological considerations support this: *Tīriya-* would be adjective to **tīra-*, related to Av. *taēra-* "mountain peak", Pashto *tēra* "sharp", and Sanskrit *tīvra-* "sharp, pungent" (and perhaps the Persian name of the tiara, the "upright" peaked headdress). This vindicates the long-sought connection of Tīriya's name with the arrow imagery, where earlier etymologies were unconvincing.[3]

Apąm Napāt (or *Apąm Naptar*) "The Child (Offspring, Descendant) of the Waters": this yazata is obviously of Indo-Iranian origin, for he has a Vedic counterpart Apām Napāt. He has no yasht, nor is any day named after him. He is involved together with water in each yasna service; it is his function to distribute the waters to the various regions; he also takes the Khvarənah into his custody in the water.

---

[1] R. Gobl, *IA* I (1961), pp. 99, 109 reads MEIPO (Mihr, Mithra), which would be surprising from the iconographic viewpoint.

[2] "La stella Sirio e l'influenza dell'astrologia caldea nell'Iran antico", *Studi e materiali di storia delle religioni* XXXIV (1963), pp. 237–45; "Politique religieuse sous les Achéménides", pp. 135–7 in J. Duchesne-Guillemin (ed.), *Commémoration Cyrus, Hommage Universel* II (Tehran–Liège, 1974), pp. 155–71 (Acta Iranica 2).

[3] Cf. M. Boyce, *History of Zoroastrianism* I, pp. 32–3, 204–6, who points out that Tīr is the Persian name of the planet Mercury. With Tīriya as adjective of **tīra-* "wedge, pointed object" (from Indo-European **(s)tei-* "to be pointed, pierce") may be harmonized Forssman's explanation of Tištriya from *Trištriya "consisting of three stars"; the three stars (with Sirius the most prominent) would constitute the "wedge/arrowhead" configuration.

DEITIES OF NON-GATHIC ORIGIN

All this would seem to indicate that Apąm Napāt was merely a water god, and yet there is evidence to suggest that his role was far greater. In Yasht 19, 52 the yazata is addressed as follows: "We worship the high ahura, the majestic potentate Apąm Napāt, swift-steeded, who gives help when invoked; who created men, who shaped men, the yazata amid the waters, most hearkening when worshipped." The Vedic Apām Napāt is also surrounded by waters and drawn by swift horses, but even more striking is that also the Rig-Veda speaks of him as a creator (2.35.2): "Apām Napāt, the master, has begotten all beings through his might of divine dominion (*asuríyasya mahnā*)." In Yasht 13.95 we read: "Henceforth Mithra...will further all ruling councils of the lands, and pacifies those (lands) that are in turmoil; henceforth the strong Apąm Napāt will further all ruling councils of the lands, and will hold down those (lands) that are in turmoil." The parallelism in action between Mithra and Apām Napāt is also found in Yasht 19, where the Khvarənah is kept in protective custody on the one hand by Mithra and Fire (which are associated in various ways elsewhere) and on the other by Apām Napāt in the depths of the waters of the sea Vourukasha. There is also the interesting fact that, apart from Mazdā, only Mithra and Apām Napāt are called *ahura*. Apām Napāt is characterized several times as an *ahura* who is *bərəzant* 'high, lofty, exalted', an adjective occurring elsewhere for the biune Mithra–Ahura (Ahura–Mithra).

These facts have been taken to suggest that at least to some extent Apām Napāt was identical with the Ahura Varuna, i.e. the old partner of Mithra/Mitra. This need not mean that Apām Napāt and Ahura were *originally* the same deity. Since both were intimately connected with water as an essential part of their character, it would be understandable if a trait distinctive to one were inherited by another.

That Ahura was a creator is probably borne out by the phrase *payū θwōrəštārā* 'protector-and-fashioner' in Yasna 42.2 and 57.2, which looks like corresponding to the biune Mithra–Ahura, seeing that Mithra is protector, *payū*, in Yasht 10, 46, 54, 80, 103. In both passages *payū θwōrəštārā* is the object of the verb for 'worship'. One may expect that *payū θwōrəštārā* is a carry-over from the pre-Zoroastrian liturgy, just as the phrase *miθra-ahura* corresponding to Vedic *mitrā-varuṇā* certainly was. As the bearer of the second part of the Indic biune name, Varuṇa is said in the Veda to have established heaven and earth, the bearer of the second part of the Iranian biune name, Ahura, could hardly escape being thought of as a creator. And true enough, the earth and Verethraghna are called in the Younger Avesta "created by Ahura". We seem to have, surviving into the post-Zoroastrian period, or rather, revived in it, an important precedent for Zoroaster's conception of Ahura Mazdā as creator.

The Vedic statement that Apām Napāt generated all beings may have an independent history, connected with the idea that all things arose out of primal waters. The Vedic conception of Apām Napāt is quite distinct from that of Varuṇa. Apām Napāt is often seen within water in the form of fire; hence he is sometimes equated with Agni, the Vedic god of fire. The origin of this association may well be the generation of fire from the wood of plants. There is a distinct possibility that Apām Napāt is descended from the same Indo-European god as the Roman Neptune. G. Dumézil[1] has attractively connected the Indo-Iranian god with Neptune on the one hand and the Celtic god Nechtan on the other. Not only are the names easily related, but other aspects of these figures can be compared. The Neptunalia were celebrated at the time of the greatest summer heat, the participants lodging in shelters made of plants, while the story of Nechtan's well, the source of rivers, seems to have a thematic resemblance to the Avestan episode of the attempt of Fraŋrasyan to seize the Khvarənah, which is protected by Apąm Napāt. One may add the connection of both the Indo-Iranian figure and Neptune-Poseidon with horses, and compare the golden appearance of the Indic god with the golden robes of Poseidon. The decreased importance of Apąm Napāt in Iran is typical of the fate of the deities of Indo-European antiquity; one may compare the cases of the Divine Twins, of Father Heaven, and of Sun, and of Dawn. In part Apąm Napāt merged with Ahura and in part he yielded to river-divinities, as at Yasht 5.72–3, where several heroes are said to have sacrificed to Apąm Napāt, although their prayers are addressed to Aredvī.

Ātar "Fire". This deity has his origin in the domestic hearth, whose fire was kept constantly burning. Thus he, like his Indic counterpart Agni, is called "the dear guest". His strength comes from Asha = Truth, whose element he is, and he protects the creation of the Holy Spirit who chose Asha, against the creation of the Evil Spirit who chose Falsehood. He often has the epithet, "son of Ahura Mazdā".

Haoma. A divinization of a plant whose juice was ritually prepared in a mortar and drunk by priests, around which act the Yasna liturgy

[1] "Le Puits de Nechtan", *Celtica* VI (Dublin, 1963), pp. 50–61.

DEITIES OF NON-GATHIC ORIGIN

is structured. The psychotropic substance figured in ordeals and was used for divination and access to the spirit realm. The plant is described as yellow-green, with stem, leaves, and flowers; the deity was anthropomorphized as a priest. Indo-Iranian origin is assured by the Indic Soma. Haoma not only had a central role in Iranian ritual, but had an immense effect on the evolution of Iranian religion.

Khvarənah combines the concept of fortune and glory. As a divinity it represents the charisma of kingship, the paradigm for which was the Kavian (Kayanian) dynasty. In effect, the Khvarənah is the destiny of the land of Iran. This may explain why the Khvarənah is celebrated in Yasht 19 ("The Earth Yasht") together with the mountains and land. It can be lost when a ruler sins, as was the case with Yima, from whom the Khvarənah departed in the form of a falcon, but it is then kept in custody by various divinities and heroes. It is $ax^varəta$-, i.e. it cannot be seized by force, as is illustrated by the vain attempts to do so by the Turanian rogue Fraŋrasyan. In the latter tale the Khvarənah has an interesting material aspect: in the process of escape, it creates effluences from the sea Vourukasha (Yasht 19.56, 59, 62).

Fravashis. These are both (1) the spirits of the departed righteous, such as we find in cults of heroes and ancestors; (2) the pre-existent doubles of all living things (what modern theosophists would call astral bodies), including even Ahura Mazdā. The Fravashis support and sustain the entire world. Very much like the Valkyries, they are described as armed females flying through the air on their mounts, destroying demonic forces. The annual festival of the Fravashis was known as Hamaspathmaēdaya: houses were carefully cleaned and otherwise made ready for the coming of the spirits, who were received with ritual offerings of food and clothing.

Vayu "Wind, Atmosphere", corresponding to the Vedic Vāyu, is portrayed as a warrior with golden accoutrements, to whom Ahura Mazdā and a series of heroes offer sacrifice. He has a long list of apotropaic names, recalling the list of Ahura Mazdā's epithets in Yasht 1. He has benign and terrifying aspects, bespeaking the various aspects of breath, wind, and storm; he is operative in both the good and evil realms, and only part of him comes from the Holy Spirit. In Pahlavi texts he is dichotomized into a Good and a Bad Vay. Unmarried girls pray to him for husbands, a reflection of his fertilizing aspect.

Zrvan "Time" is a minor god worshipped under two aspects,

"Infinite" and "of Long Autonomy". The Avesta also attests a god Vayah "Duration" (cf. Old Indian *vayas-*, Sogdian *wē* "age"), who uniquely shares with Zurvan the epithet *darəyō.x^vaδāta-* "having long autonomy". This is reflected in Pahlavi *zamān...kē Way ī dagrand-xwadāy* "time, i.e. Way of long autonomy" (*Greater Bundahišn* 26.3). While the previous interpretation of *vayah-* as "atmosphere" must be rejected, a merger of *vayah-* with *vayu-* mat have influenced equations of Time and Space, perhaps by late Achaemenian times.[1] That the Younger Avesta itself has no evidence of a myth in which Zrvan is the parent of the Twin Spirits, Spenta and Angra Mainyu, is hardly surprising, as that scripture's main purpose was the achievement of a clear-cut dualism avoiding even Zoroaster's own implication that the Twins issued from a single father, Ahura Mazdā.

Hvar "The Sun" is of Indo-European origin, which helps to explain why, like the Greek Helios, for example, he rides in a chariot drawn by swift horses; however he was also conceived as the eye of Ahura Mazdā. He has a brief Yasht. His eminence was diminished by the prominence of his associate Mithra, who himself seems to have been worshipped locally in Achaemenian times as a sun god, and throughout Iran in later times.

Māh "The Moon" also figured in Iranian worship. In his Yasht he is said to be an abode of the Amesha Spentas, from which they dispense glory to the Ahura-created earth. He bears the interesting epithet "having the seed of the bovine". In Pahlavi sources we read how the seed of the Primal Bull slain by Ahriman mounted up to the moon to be purified and provide the origin of animal life below. With the sun and stars he is one of the stations of the righteous soul on its way to paradise.

THE DEMONOLOGY OF THE AVESTA

A comparison of the Avestic demonological data with that of the Vedas shows that the Iranians inherited the foundations of their beliefs concerning malign supernatural beings from Indo-Iranian times. We can reconstruct as Indo-Iranian terms **yātu* for evil beings possessing magical powers, and **drugh* for "harmful entity". Often mentioned in connection with *yātus* in the Avesta are the *pairikās*, a class of dangerous

---

[1] See further my detailed remarks in J. Duchesne-Guillemin (ed.), *Monumentum H. S. Nyberg* II (Tehran–Liège, 1975), pp. 207–09 (Acta Iranica 5).

THE DEMONOLOGY OF THE AVESTA

female beings who not only seduce men but harm nature. Pairikās fall from the sky in the form of meteors (Yasht 8.8); they (or at least some of them) attempt to injure fire, water, earth, cattle, and plants (*Vidēvdād* 11.9); particularly harmful to crops are the Pairikās Duzhyāiryā ("Bringing Evil Year") and Mūsh ("Rat").

Unforeseen by Zoroaster, his teachings had an effect on Iranian demonology similar to their effect on the Iranian view of the divine sphere: the former lore of demons was not replaced, but put in a dualistic perspective. Just as old gods, readmitted after the death of the prophet, came to be interpreted as the creations of Ahura Mazdā and assistants of him and the Amesha Spentas, so the old demons came to be seen as productions of Angra Mainyu and helpers of him and his counter-entities. Zoroaster brought about a demotion of the word *daēva* from its original reference to a type of god, to a general term for "demon"; whether or not Zoroaster applied the term daēva to all old deities (he certainly inveighed against "you daēvas ALL"), his successors were at pains to exonerate some of them from the stigma of being daēvas. Other old divinities were understood as the object of the Prophet's rebuke and came to be thought of as demons *par excellence*; in time the appellation spread to cover all demons. The use of daēva for "false god" in the Gāthās seems to be found again, in connection with yātu "demon" in part of an abjuration formula occurring in the Fravarānē, or Zoroastrian Credo, in Gathic language: "(I forswear association with) false gods, with the followers of false gods, with demons, with the followers of demons" (*vī daēvāiš vī daēvavaṭbiš vī yātuš vī yātumaṭbiš*; Yasna 12.4). However by the time the Yashts were composed, not only had daēva become a general word for "demon", but, perhaps as a result of this, yātu could refer to human sorcerers as well as demons; thus in Yasht 8.44 we have *nōiṭ yātavō pairikāsča nōiṭ yātavō mašyānąm* "not devils or she-devils, nor wizards among men".[1]

There is evidence in the Avesta for individuals who attempted to control amoral supernatural beings for their own use. Thus Takhma ("the Mighty") Urupi ("Fox"?) is granted the power to ride Angra Mainyu as his steed for thirty years, from one end of the earth to the other (Yasht 15.11–12; 19.28–9); while possibly the earlier versions of the tale had some other prestigious demon in the role of the mount, the substitution of Angra Mainyu documents the trivialization of Zoroaster's ideas. Another great hero, Keresāspa, associated with the

---
[1] The importance of these passages is pointed out by Boyce, *History of Zoroastrianism* I, pp. 85–6.

Pairikā Khnānthaitī, whom Angra Mainyu sent as a plague against the land Vaēkərəta (*Vidēvdād* 1.9); similarly a certain Pitaona whom Keresāspa slew, is called "he of many Pairikās" (Yasht 19.41). One should keep in mind that the attempted compulsion of amoral supernatural beings through sorcery is a very widespread phenomenon; it is known for example from Hellenistic Egyptian papyri, and even magical texts from decadent sectors of Tibetan Buddhism and Judaism, as also among contemporary occultists.

Simple propitiation of the forces of evil may also be assumed for ancient Iran. According to Yasht 5.91, demons receive sacrifices to gods made after sundown, and Plutarch attests the invocation of Areimanios/Hades while pounding *omomi* (haoma?) in a mortar, and mixing it with the blood of a slaughtered wolf and leaving it in a sunless place; all this done by people who also worship Oromasdes (Ahura Mazdā) by day (*Isis and Osiris*, 46). Offerings to the powers of darkness, including pourings of blood, occur in Brahmanic rites.[1] The bloody rites of the daēvic Vyāmburas, with their burning of juniper and squatting (Yasht 14.54–5) are paralleled in recent times by practices of the Kalashas in Chitral.[2]

What with the effect of Zarathushtra's dualism on a world view which remained essentially pagan, the universe came to be seen as teeming with countless invisible (*mainyava*) malignant forces at all times threatening one's crops, livestock, family, body, and mental and moral well-being; it was to a large extent for this reason that the cults of the various divinities had to be maintained.

While it is from the *Vidēvdād* that we may most clearly see the various types of individual demons, and where we find the most obsessive rigour in matters of ritual purity to prevent the influence of evil forces, a cursory reading of the Yashts reveals Achaemenian religion to a significant degree to approach the characterization by S. H. Hooke of Babylonian religion: "broadly speaking...a magico-religious system based on the fear of evil spirits and other incalculable elements in the social environment".[3] Yasht after Yasht tells of how each particular deity repels the thousands and tens of thousands of daēvas, the hosts of yātus and pairikās, wizards and witches and so forth. It is the ritual

---

[1] *Op. cit.*, p. 171, with other details on *daēvic* worship.
[2] See the texts in Morgenstierne, *Indo-Iranian Frontier Languages* IV, pp. 33–5: *idem, Indo-Dardica* (Wiesbaden, 1973), pp. 320ff.; juniper is a trance medium for shamans among Dardic-speaking Muslims in Hunza.
[3] *Babylonian and Assyrian Religion* (Oxford, 1962), p. xiii.

GĀTHIC DEMONS

promotion of the divine forces which counter demons (among which figure the embodiments of abstract qualities as greed, lust, envy, slander, etc.) rather than the exhortation to ethical behaviour that characterizes these texts. The tendency to externalize as hypostases negative moral and psychological qualities may well have had its impetus in the abstractions of the Gāthās, but it led to an outlook quite at variance with Zoroaster's stress on choice and responsibility.

GĀTHIC DEMONS

Angra Mainyu is named but once in the Gāthās (Yasna 45.2; the variant Aka Mainyu "The Evil Spirit" occurs at Yasna 35.2) but is exceedingly common in the later texts. Evil by choice, he is the source of all evil, ugliness, and ignorance. The myth of Angra Mainyu invading the creation of Ahura Mazdā is alluded to in the Yashts, e.g. 13.76–8. He is characterized as "having an evil creation" (Yasna 61.2). He disturbs the orderly processes of creation, e.g. by creating Pairikās to impede the stars "which contain the seed of water" (Yasht 8.39), and tries in other ways to prevent water from nourishing the plants (Yasht 13.8). He is the author of myriads of diseases (Yasht 3.14 *seq.* etc.). For all his insidiousness he is a weeping, cringing coward before the forces of good, be they Zarathushtrian divinities such as Best Asha (Yasht 3.14) or the legitimized "pagan" gods such as Mithra (Yasht 10.97). In the end Angra Mainyu and his associates will be defeated (Yasht 19.6). The Avesta does not oppose Angra Mainyu directly against Ahura Mazdā except in the last chapter of the *Vidēvdād*, where it is said that the former created 99,999 diseases against the latter. This has been seen as possibly due to a specifically Magian simplification of the original Zarathushtrian doctrine opposing Angra Mainyu to Spenta Mainyu rather than directly to Ahura Mazdā. Evidence for the conception of Angra Mainyu being alien to the original traditions of Central Asia is found in Middle Sogdian, which has *šmnw* "devil, Satan" going back to a form *Ahra Manyu (a non-Avestan equivalent of Angra Mainyu, cf. Persian Ahriman), which shows abnormal Sogdian replacement of *hr* by *š*.

Just as Spenta Mainyu is opposed by Angra Mainyu, so we find in the Gāthās Vohu Manah opposed by Aka Manah "Evil Mind", Asha by Drug, Ārmaiti by Tarō.maiti or Pairi.maiti "Improper Thought, Presumption, Hybris", and Haurvatāt and Amərətāt respectively by Hunger and Thirst, where we see implicit reference to the elemental correspondences of the twin Amesha Spentas to Water and Plants. These oppositions seem to have been systematized in the eschatological thought of the Yashts; see esp. Yasht 19.95–6.

The Gāthās also oppose Aēshma "Wrath, Fury, Violence" to Sraosha "Obedience, Discipline". Just as in the Yashts Sraosha becomes a figure with concrete characterization, so too does Aēshma, who is the most important demon after Angra Mainyu. His fixed epithet is "having a gory club"; Sraosha, by contrast, is said to strike a bloodless wound. Most scholars believe that Aēshma (*Aēshma-daēva) is the origin of Ashmedai (Asmodeus) of the apocryphal Book of Tobit.

YOUNGER AVESTAN DEMONS

The Pahlavi books have another series of oppositions of demons to the Amesha Spentas. Again we find Aka Manah ranged against Vohu Manah, but the rest of the list is different:

Indra		Asha
Nāŋhaithya		Khshathra
Saurva	against	Ārmaiti
Taurvi		Haurvatāt
Zairik		Amərətāt

The five demons are mentioned in the *Vidēvdād* (10.9–10; 19.43). Indra is of course the name of one of the chief Vedic deities and Nāŋhaithya would be the expected Iranian equivalent of the Vedic name Nāsatya borne by the two twins also called Aśvin(s), who are associated with Indra and are also among the more important Vedic gods. While there seems to be a singular Nāsatya mentioned in the Rig-Veda, the ancient duality of the Nāsatyas is evidenced by the Mitanni treaty, a cuneiform document of the 14th century B.C. found in eastern Anatolia, in which Indra and the Nāsatyas are mentioned along with Varuṇa-Mitra as gods under whose auspices the treaty is to be kept. It is thought that the Mitanni people were partially Aryanized by an ethnic group closely related to the Aryan settlers of northwestern India who composed the Vedas. Taurvi could mean "The Conqueror", obviously also an ancient god; the last, Zairik (or perhaps Zairi), whose name may be a colour term (cf. Avestan *ʒairi-gaona* and Vedic *hari* for Haoma/Soma), was in any event almost surely a member of the same pantheon. These five are therefore daēvas in the most original sense of the term:

ancient Aryan gods who became dishonoured in Iran, but whose worship as gods (*devas*) continued in India. (For Saurva cf. Vedic Śarva = Rudra.)

The following will give an idea of the diversity of the chief amongst the many other demons named in the Younger Avesta:

Nasu, the demoness of decay inhabiting corpses. She is described in the *Vidēvdād* (7.2–4) as a loathsome speckled fly coming from the North (the region of evil, with which all the demons are associated) dribbling slime and voiding excrement. This demoness was driven out by the glance of a dog (an animal associated with the underworld) or a month-long process of lustrations. Nasu is among several demons which fall into the category of Drugs (cf. the Vedic Druhs). Here the concept of Drug differs from Zoroaster's principle in that it is plural and cannot be translated "Lie"; instead it maintains the archaic sense "Disorder, Harmfulness, Destructiveness" as against *Ṛta (Avestan Asha) originally "Order, Harmony, Fittingness".

Demons embodying and causing moral imperfections are Būshyanstā "Sloth, Procrastination", a female being having the epithet "Long-armed"; Araska or Ereshi "Envy", Spazga "Slander", Aghashi "Evil Eye, Envy"; Āzi "Greed", and the important Mithaokhta "False Speech". The Varenya Daēvas (or Fiends) are taken by some scholars as demons of lust as against "the demons (or fiends) of the country Varena" (the modern Buner). The latter interpretation may be favoured by the fact that these demons (as against other demons of moral or mental fault) are plural, while the Pahlavi demon of lust, Varan, is singular, and the Varənya Demons are sometimes associated with the Māzainya Daēvas, usually understood as frightening denizens of Māzandarān, the misty, mountainous region south of the Caspian Sea; thus one could have personifications of inimical forces to the southeast and northwest of the greater Iranian homeland.[1] But *māzainya* could be an adjective "haughty, tyrannous, gigantic" (from *mazan*-"greatness") and hence parallel with *varənya* "lustful, self-willed".

We have already met the demon of drought Apaosha ("non-prosperity"), pictured as a black hairless horse, and opposed by Tishtriya. Other demons of natural phenomena are Spenjaghrya, a storm demon opposed by Vāzishta, the fire of lightning, and Vātya Daēva, representing evil winds.

---

[1] Cf. also T. Burrow, "The Proto-Indoaryans", *JRAS* 1973, pp. 134ff. with a different explanation of *daēva*.

THE RELIGION OF ACHAEMENIAN IRAN

In addition to a host of demons referring to disease, we have Zaurvan "Age, Decrepitude"; (Astō)Viδōtu "The Wrecker of the Bodily Frame", the demon of death who binds the soul and separates it from the body; and Vīzaresha, who struggles with the soul for three days after death.

THE DOCUMENTATION FOR PERSIA

Evidence is lacking for religion under the predecessors of Darius I. It is well known that Cyrus II "The Great" (559–529 B.C.), as part of his policy toward the peoples which came under his rule, restored the Temple at Jerusalem; he also restored the cults of Babylon, neglected by the defeated Nabonides, and, in a Babylonian inscription, declared himself a beloved servant of Marduk. What beliefs and practices were current among Cyrus' people is unknown. Xenophon in his *Cyropaedia* (I.6.1; III.3.22; VII.3.57; VIII.1.23; 3, 11 *seq.*; 3.24) has Cyrus sacrifice to various divinities under the Magi: "Zeus", the Sun, "Hestia" (*Ātar*?) and "the other gods", but Xenophon may have been rounding out his idealized picture of Cyrus by attributing to him practices personally observed a century and a half after the illustrious monarch, among Cyrus the Younger and his followers.

We have two gold tablets with inscriptions in Old Persian purporting to be respectively of Ariaramnes and Arsames, with formulas indicating the worship of Ahura Mazdā, but on linguistic grounds both inscriptions are best regarded as forgeries.

For Darius I (521–486 B.C.) we have an abundance of inscriptions which make it absolutely clear that his worship of Ahura Mazdā was of the greatest importance to him. Most of his inscriptions begin like hymns, e.g. "(A) great god (is) Ahura Mazdā, who created this earth, who created the sky, who created bliss for men, who made Darius king, one king of many (people)..." One of the numerous inscriptions which have this opening, Susa *f*, states further: "Ahura Mazdā, the greatest of gods – he created me; he made me king; he bestowed upon me this kingdom, great, with good horses and good men. By the favour of Ahura Mazdā my father Hystaspes and Arsames my grandfather were both alive when Ahura Mazdā made me king on this earth. Ahura Mazdā's desire was thus: he chose me – (one) man on all the earth; he made me king over all the earth. I worshipped Ahura Mazdā. Ahura Mazdā brought me aid... Whatever I did, all by the will of Ahura Mazdā did I do it."

Darius' first great achievement, the overthrow of Pseudo-Smerdis, was accomplished through prayer: in the Behistun inscription (1.53 *seq.*) he says, "Nobody dared say anything about Gaumata the Magus, until I came. Then I prayed (*sic*) to Ahura Mazdā; Ahura Mazdā brought me aid..."; and in a related inscription, "All that I did, I did not do otherwise, (but) as was Ahura Mazdā's desire, so I did. To me Ahura Mazdā was a friend, whatever I did, all that was successful for me... May Ahura Mazdā protect me and my country" (Susa, *j*). The highly personal relationship between Darius and his god is remarkably expressed: "Ahura Mazdā is mine, I am Ahura Mazdā's. I worshipped Ahura Mazdā; may Ahura Mazdā bring me aid" (Susa, *k*).

Such passages make it possible that Darius was a monotheist. This possibility is not necessarily contradicted by Darius calling Ahura Mazdā "the greatest of (the) gods" in several inscriptions; here Darius need not have affirmed the ontological reality of other divinities, let alone that other gods are worth worshipping. The formulae "Ahura Mazdā with all the gods" (Persepolis, *d*) and "Ahura Mazdā with the gods" (Susa, *e* and *t*) are problematic. Dr Gershevitch however has offered the following interesting solution: "(All) the gods" is in effect an abbreviation of the phrase "the (other) gods who are", found in "Ahura Mazdā brought me aid, and the other gods who are/exist" which occurs in the earliest of Darius' inscriptions, at Behistun (IV.60). Dr Gershevitch explains the curious phrasing in the latter sentence by seeing here a reference to the Aməsha Spəntas, called in the Gāthās "those who have been and are".[1] But Darius may merely have been a henotheist.

One may point to other possible echoes of Gathic theology in Darius' inscriptions. Most importantly, "Lie" is an independent, active force: "When Cambyses had gone off to Egypt, thereupon the people became evil. Then the Lie became great in the country, both in Persia and in Media and in the other provinces" (Behistun 1.39–41). "These are the provinces which became rebellious. The Lie made them rebellious, so that they deceived the people... You who will be king hereafter, protect yourself mightily from the Lie; the man who would be a liar, punish him well..." (IV.36–8); "...the man who would be a liar, or be a wrongdoer – be no friend to them, but punish them thoroughly" (Behistun IV.67–9). "May Ahura Mazdā protect this country from a (hostile) army, from a bad year, and the Lie" (Persepolis *d*, 17–19, with variant repetition 19–21) (here "bad year" may have been

---

[1] Gershevitch, "Zoroaster's own contribution", *JNES* XXIII (1964), p. 15 with appendix X.

felt as a demonic force, cf. Avestan *duẓyāiryā*). The opposition of Lie to Truth is expressed with great clarity: "I was not hostile, I was not a liar, I was not a wrongdoer..." (Behistun IV.63-4). "What is right, that is my desire. I am not a friend to the man who is a liar. I am not hot-tempered. What things arise in my anger, I hold firmly under control by my mind. I am firmly ruling over my own (impulses)" (Naqsh-i Rustam *b*, 11-15). Here we may also see a reflection of the role of the Gathic entity Good Mind (*Vohu Manah*; in our inscription *manah*), and of the Gathic denunciation of fury.

It is true that the words for "Lie" and "Truth" (and anger/fury) differ from the Avestan, but this does not speak against Darius' having followed Zarathushtrian ideas. For Darius (*a*)*rštā/rāsta* may have been the closest equivalent in ordinary, non-theological Persian to the Gathic notion. Let us recall that *ṛta-/aša* is a rather complex metaphysical notion, possibly unsuited to the simple honesty Darius meant to express. All the more does this apply to "Lie".

Even in Avestan *drug* is always a *force*, never an *individual* action; "lie" is expressed in the Avestan as *draoya-*, the precise equivalent of Old Persian *drauga-*; in fact nowhere in Middle Iranian is "lie" conveyed by a reflex of *drug-* (Sogdian, for example, has *ẓəyma* from **drugmā*). Scholars who have used the drug-:drauga- difference as evidence against the Zarathushtrianism of Darius (and his successors) have also made much of the Old Persian word for "god", *baga-* against Avestan *yazata-*. It would seem that yazata belongs to the archaic language of religious expression, and at the time Darius composed his inscriptions Persian had baga for "god"; already Avestan has some instances of *baya* in this sense. Parthian *bag*, Sogdian *βay-* show that baga had taken over the semantic function of yazata throughout Iran.

Difference in vocabulary does not indicate difference in conceptualization, or, in our context, theology. In the case of **Miẓhdushi*, another divinity attested in our Persepolis material, we have another difference of form, rather than concept, from the Avestan. As Dr Gershevitch has recognized, this would mean "she who bestows rewards" and hence equivalent to Avestan Ashi. Other evidence for Zarathushtrianism in these texts are the personal names **Rashnudata* and **Rashnuka*, attesting worship of Rashnu, as well as **Sausha*, the equivalent of Avestan Sraosha or of Saoshyant (represented by *šušanda* "The future Saviour"), and of course **Mazdayazna* (Aramaic *mzdyzn*) or **Mazdayashna*, i.e. Avestan *Mazdayasna* "Mazdā-worshipper".

THE DOCUMENTATION FOR PERSIA

But the Persepolis Fortification Tablets show that a variety of non-Gathic divinities were worshipped during Darius' reign. Here we find Ahura Mazdā worshipped by priests also devoted to non-Gathic Iranian as well as non-Iranian deities. Thus we find a text which runs "16 *marris* of wine, supplied by N_1, N_2 the priest received and utilized it for Ahura Mazdā and the god Mithra and S(h)imut", the latter an Elamite god (PF 338). Here the supplier and priest bear Iranian names.

A divinity otherwise unknown is spelled *Pirdakamiya* (PF 303, etc.), possibly representing **Brtagaviya-* "looking after cattle" (Gershevitch). This could be a specifically Western Iranian deity. The god Zr(u)van "Time" is probably represented by the name *Izrutukma*, i.e **Zru(va)taukhma* "descended from Zr(u)van".

The onomastic material also attests the worship of Tīriya (in Elamite Tiridadda, Aramaic Trydt, Greek Tiridates, etc., and simply Elam. Tiriya, Aram. Try, Gr. *Τιραῖος*, etc.); see above.

"The god Mithra", mentioned above, appears several times in spellings indicating a Persian form **Missa(-)baga* (for variant *-e-* in the second syllable cf. *Turma/Turme*; *-e* possibly. for genitive in *-ahya*). An interesting feature is the constant occurrence of *baga* "god", which does not occur after the names of the other Fortification Tablet deities; cf. *Miθra baga* in the inscription of Artaxerxes III (Persepolis 25), but merely **Miθra* elsewhere. **(H)uwarīra* (or *Huwarayara*) "Sunrise" (?) (thus Gershevitch; Elam. *Mariraš*) and "the god Mithra" (PF 1956). A Magus receives grain for "the god Mithra" (PF 1955), but there is no evidence as yet for Magi serving Ahura Mazdā. Incidentally, these and other tablets show that the Magi continued to be active despite Herodotus' report (III. 79–80) of a wholesale slaughter of Magi by Darius, which may be based on a misunderstanding of *μαγοφόνια*, which like the corresponding Manichaean Sogdian term *mughzhat-*, may originally have been coined to denote "the killing of *the* Magus (Gaumāta)".

Another interesting revelation of the Fortification Tablets is the fact that there were provisions for cults associated with mountains and rivers, e.g. "5.7 marris of wine, supplied by N_1, N_2 the priest received, and utilized it for the gods: 7 QA for Ahura Mazdā, 2 marris for the god Humban, 1 marri for the river Huputish, 1 marri for the river Rannakara, 1 marri for the river Shaushanush" (PF 339); "12 *artabes* of grain N the Magus received; 3 as rations of the *lan* (ceremony), 3 for the god Mithra, 3 for Mt Ariaramna, 3 for the river Ahinharishta"

(PF 1955). Similarly we have provision for Mt Shirumand and *Nari-(ya) sangha (PF 1960). The latter (spelled Narīsanka) occurs also as a personal name; it agrees with Avestan nairyō.saŋha- as against Middle Persian Nrshy, Narseh with *-sahya-, as probably also Sogdian Nariša(n)x, *Naršax (with š < *s palatalized by y), Parthian Nryshw, Narisaf < *-sahva-.

Haoma is represented by several personal names in the Fortification Tablets (as well as the onomastica of Achaemenian documents in Aramaic). The actual use of the intoxicant in Persia seems assured by a seal from the Persepolis Treasury (dating however from the time of Xerxes) showing two priestly figures flanking a fire altar and a stand upon which are a mortar and pestle.

With regard to priests, apart from Magi, the Fortification Tablets attest the fire-attendants (Elamite haturmakša) known from Avestan as ātrəvaxš-. As a personal name in various Elamite spellings we have *āθarvan (Avestan nom. āθrava, gen. aθaurunō, and cf. Old Indic atharvan). The word for "libation" is well attested; it is *dauçā, which corresponds to Avestan zaoθrā. These libations involve great expenditure of wine. While the Avestan zaoθrās consisted chiefly of milk, haoma, pomegranate, and water, the type of offering termed myazda, when referring to a liquid, was qualified as consisting of wine (maδumant). Another religious expenditure, chiefly involving disbursements of grain, may be taken either as *dauçiya "that which accompanies a libation" or more likely (with Gershevitch) *daušiya- "propitiation".

The fact that in the Tablets Ahura Mazda's name precedes that of other divinities may be connected with Darius' special affection for Ahura Mazdā, who however, as successor to *Ahura, may have been generally regarded as head of the pantheon; cf. Herodotus' placing the heaven-god ("Zeus") first in his account of the divinities worshipped by the Persians (1.131). The greater expense of the cult of Humban need merely be due to differences between Elamite and Persian ritual, and perhaps specifically the role of the temple in Elamite worship.

The tolerance by Darius of foreign divinities is further shown by a famous Greek inscription, an open letter as it were, from Darius to his satrap Gadatas, whom he rebuked for having imposed taxes on land consecrated to Apollo. The text shows that the earlier Achaemenids made use of the oracle of Magnesia; Darius declares that his forbears were told "the whole truth" by the deity.

Apparent evidence of religious rivalry may be seen in Darius' statement (Behistun 1.62 *seq.*) that as part of his policy of reconstruction he restored the places of worship destroyed by Gaumata the Magus. Unfortunately it is unknown what these places of worship were; the term in question, *āyadana*, is translated by Akkadian *bīt ilāni* "house of the gods", i.e. "temple", which appears to be the meaning of Parthian *āyazan* in texts of a much later period.

Xerxes I (486–465) was, like his father, a worshipper of Ahura Mazdā. In this regard (as in others) his inscriptions generally imitate those of Darius, with the formulas "Ahura Mazdā brought me aid", "by the will of Ahura Mazdā", etc. Xerxes mentions other divinities in the formula "May Ahura Mazdā with the other gods protect...". However one passage, of great interest for Xerxes' religious outlook, has no precise parallel in Darius' inscriptions; it runs: "You in the future, if you think 'may I be happy (when) living and when dead may I be *r̥tāvan*', have respect for that law which Ahura Mazdā has established; worship Ahura Mazdā in accordance with R̥ta. The man who respects that law which Ahura Mazdā has established, and worships Ahura Mazdā in accordance with R̥ta and the ritual becomes both happy while living and r̥tāvan when dead" (Persepolis 4.46–56).

Before discussing the interpretation of the passage, let us note that r̥ta is the philological equivalent of Avestan *aša* and Old Indic *r̥ta*, and r̥tāvan (Av. *ašavan*, OInd. *r̥tāvan*) means "possessing or characterized by r̥ta". My rendering "in accordance with R̥ta" is based on an analysis of *r̥tāčā* as a contraction of *r̥tā hačā*, which is supported by the Elamite transcription *irdahazi*, rendering unlikely the interpretation of the form as "at the appropriate moment" (loc. of *r̥tu-) or to *r̥tanč- or from *r̥ta* and enclitic *-ča*. *r̥tā hačā* would be the equivalent of Av. *ašāt...hačā*.

Here Xerxes has been seen as continuing the archaic Indo-Iranian concept of R̥ta having its seat in the other world, in whose "radiant quarters" the souls of the dead dwell (Yasna 16.7). This sense of r̥tāvan/ašavan as "the righteous deceased" is also occasionally encountered for the Middle Persian derivatives, as is seen not only from Sasanian texts, but also from the definition of ἀρταῖος in Greek lexicographers. For Zoroaster, however, aša was something in which the *living* may participate, a doctrine which we find in the later Avesta in a formulation which contrasts sharply with that of Xerxes: "...While alive he does not become ašavan and when dead he does not participate in the Best Existence (i.e. Paradise)." If Gershevitch's restoration for Darius, Behistun v.19 and 35 were correct, one would have there "whoso worships Ahura Mazdā, Ṛta will forever be his, both (while he is) alive, and (after he is) dead". Thereby Xerxes would have less of an acquaintance with Zoroaster's innovative doctrines than did his father.[1]

Xerxes' use of *braẓman* "ritual, proper observance of ceremonial form" (cf. Old Indic *brahman*), and its conjunction with ṛta, clearly bespeaks another formula at variance with Darius' fixed expressions, again indicating a possible return to pre-Zarathushtrian traditions. In particular the stress on ceremony may reflect an increase of Magian influence at the royal court. As we shall see, Herodotus speaks of Magi in Xerxes' retinue. The connection of Ahura Mazdā and ṛta may be a relic of the older Ahura conception.

The earlier part of the aforementioned inscription of Xerxes also treats a matter of religious concern. After listing the provinces under his rule, Xerxes states: "When I became king, there was among those provinces which are listed above (one which) was in commotion. Then Ahura Mazdā brought me aid; by the will of Ahura Mazdā I smote that province and put it in its place. And among those provinces there was a place where previously daivas were worshipped. Then by the will of Ahura Mazdā I destroyed that *daivadāna* and made a proclamation, 'the daivas shall not be worshipped'. Where previously daivas were worshipped, there I worshipped Ahura Mazdā in accordance with ṛta and the ritual."

There is dispute concerning this passage. According to one view, Xerxes was referring throughout to the revolution at Babylon, in retaliation for which he sacked the temple of Marduk with its ziggurat and melted down the gigantic statue of the god. The daivadāna would then be the temple of Marduk, and the daivas Marduk and the other Babylonian divinities. The difficulty with this theory is that the passage seems to refer to two different places; otherwise why, after attributing the revolution to one province, should the text begin the section on the daiva-cult with the words "And among these provinces..."? Why should the two events, the suppression of the revolution and the crushing of daiva-worship, be presented as though unconnected, if they both referred to Xerxes' revenge on Babylon? Some have proposed that the inscription refers to Xerxes' destruction of the Athenian acropolis. Yet Xerxes' motivation does not seem to have been the destruction of a "false religion", for the day after the temple was

[1] Gershevitch, *Avestan Hymn to Mithra*, p. 156; cf. also J. Kellens, *Studi e materiali di storia delle religioni* XL (Rome, 1969), pp. 209–14.

plundered and the Acropolis set on fire, Xerxes gathered together the Athenian exiles who had entered Greece as part of his troops and bade them to offer sacrifice after their own fashion. It would seem that while Xerxes, like his predecessors Darius and Cambyses, could attack foreign religious edifices upon occasion to humiliate the local population, he did not mean thereby to prohibit non-Iranian cults, which would be in opposition to the general Achaemenian policy of religious *laissez-faire*, nor even to deny the ontological reality of foreign divinities. As we shall see, Xerxes abroad may even have worshipped foreign deities as lords of their own regions. That he could have, all the same, violated their sanctuaries and statues may be more understandable in view of the negligible role such edifices played in Iranian worship.

Many have assumed that the daivas here are Iranian deities which had fallen into disrepute. If the demotion of daivas was due to Zoroaster's influence, then one could see Xerxes' action as connected with the acceptance of the new (or reformed) creed at the court. Ostensibly these daivas would be e.g. Indra, Naŋhaithya, Saurva or their ilk, listed as daivas in the Avesta (Vd. 10.9, 19.43), rather than Mithra or Nairyōsaŋha, whose worship clearly continued during the Achaemenian period, and who have a positive role in the later Avestan religion. It is even possible that at the time that Xerxes composed his inscription the daivas in question were actually considered demons throughout Iran, either as a result of evolution or were such from the outset. The meaning of daivadāna is problematic not only because of the uncertain meaning of daiva in this context, but also because of our lack of knowledge concerning cultic edifices during the period in question, on which more will be said below.

It is difficult to believe that Xerxes was motivated by monotheistic considerations. He is in fact portrayed by Herodotus as worshipping various divinities, and there is no reason to doubt this, although Herodotus' statements concerning Xerxes' worship of foreign (local) deities are perhaps less reliable. Having reached Troy and ascended the "citadel of Priam", Xerxes is said to have offered a thousand oxen to "the Trojan Athena", while the Magi poured libations to the heroes fallen at Troy (VII.43). The Magi accompanying Xerxes' fleet, after suffering three days of a storm at Magnesia, sacrificed not only to "the Winds" (Vāta?) but to the Nereids, to whom the region was sacred, as the Persians learned from the Ionians (VII.191). Herodotus further informs us that after the crossing of the Strymon, which the Magi propitiated by sacrificing white horses, nine local boys and girls were buried at a place called Nine Ways, and that burial alive was a Persian practice; further we learn that Xerxes' wife Amestris in her old age supposedly had seven pairs of Persians killed in this manner as a thank-offering to a subterranean divinity. A. D. H. Bivar has seen this divinity as related to the Babylonian underworld god Nergal.[1] I would note in this connection the possible significance of the fact that seven couples were sacrificed; compare on the one hand the seven stages of the descent of Inanna into the underworld into the presence of Ereshkigal, consort of Nergal, and on the other hand the Babylonian doctrine of the seven heavens (reflected in the construction of Deioces' palace at Ecbatana, as described by Herodotus (1.98)).[2]

For Xerxes' successor, Artaxerxes I (465–424), we have only one authentic inscription, from Persepolis, imitative of the inscriptions of Darius and Xerxes; thus we find the familiar formulae "a great god is Ahura Mazdā" and "by the will of Ahura Mazdā" occurring in direct repetitions of the earlier texts. However, if the calculations of the late S. H. Taqizadeh are correct, it would have been under Artaxerxes I that royal approval of a reconciliation of Zarathushtrian and "pagan" religious concepts was expressed in the form of a new calendar to be used throughout the empire, in which the months and days were named after various important Gathic and non-Gathic divinities, all of whom are known from the Avesta. As Gershevitch has pointed out, the new policy of religious accommodation at the court set the stage for the syncretism (or eclecticism) whose full expression is seen in the Younger Avesta. Taqizadeh's date for the introduction of the calendar, 441 B.C., and even the calendar's origin as early as the Achaemenian period, have come to be challenged in recent years.[3] A full discussion of the problem is found in chapter 16 of the present volume, but the following points may be stated in support of Taqizadeh's view:

(1) The promulgation of the calendar must have taken place at a time when the far-flung area including Cappadocia in the west, and Chorasmia in the north-east, were under a single imperial Iranian authority.

---

[1] "Mithra and Mesopotamia", in J. R. Hinnells (ed.), *Mithraic Studies* II (Manchester, 1975), pp. 275–89.

[2] But cf. also the "ladder of seven (planetary) gates", which has an important role in western Mithraic ideology, as first discussed in D. W. Bousset, "Die Himmelsreise der Seele", *Archiv für Religionswissenschaft* IV (1901), p. 160f.

[3] E. Bickerman, "The Zoroastrian calendar", *ArOr* XXXV (1967), pp. 197–207; M. Boyce, "On the calendar of Zoroastrian feasts". *BSOAS* XXXIII (1970), pp. 513–39.

(2) A polytheism with Ahura Mazdā as the central divinity, as is attested in the calendar, is unknown in the inscriptions of Darius and Xerxes, where Ahura Mazdā is the only god mentioned by name, but must have been approved at the court by the time the earliest inscriptions of Artaxerxes II were composed, wherein, as we shall see, the old formulas concerning Ahura Mazdā were rephrased to include Mithra and Anāhitā.

(3) While the calendar is first attested for the Middle Iranian period, in several local versions (Cappadocian, Middle Persian, Parthian, Sogdian, Chorasmian), the month- and day-names in each version are fossilizations of distinctly *Old* Iranian forms, so that the local versions must have been fixed in the Achaemenian period. Thus for example the *calendrical name* "The Creator" is *dai* in Middle Persian and δišči in Sogdian, representing respectively Old Iranian *dadvāh nominative and *dad/θušah genitive (the latter with -*i* from -*ah*, excluding origin in Avestan, which had -*ō*), whereas the *word* for "creator" is *dādār* in Middle Persian and *əsfrīnənē* in Sogdian. Similarly "(The Day of) the Ox" is *gōš* in the Parthian calendar from Nisā, reflecting an Old Iranian genitive *gauš, while the ordinary word for "ox" in Parthian (which, like Middle Persian, is an uninflected language) is *gāw*. To give another sort of example, the Cappadocian month of the earth-goddess/Devotion is transmitted as Sondara, which clearly represents an Old Persian dialectal form, most likely *svantā aramati (rather than with *santā as in Armenian Sandaramēt), in contrast to New Persian *isfandurmuδ*, Avestan *spəntā ārmaiti*, etc.

Herodotus (1.131 *seq.*) furnishes us with some valuable data on Persian religion during the reign of Artaxerxes I. He states that it is not a Persian custom to erect statues and temples, the Persians in fact regarding such activity as foolish. Herodotus' further observations, that there are no altars, nor fires kindled, nor libations, are incorrect, and derive from an exaggerated view of the "naturalism" of Persian religion; on mountain peaks is worshipped the god of "the whole circle of heaven", whom Herodotus calls "Zeus"; here we must recognize Ahura (Mazdā), and the series "sun, moon, earth, fire, water, winds" we may identify respectively as Hvar, Māh, Svantā Aramati, Ātar, Apām Napāt (with various river divinities), and Vāta/Vayu, although the series need represent no more than a way of saying "the Persians worship nature". Most interesting is Herodotus' statement that the foregoing are the original gods worshipped by the Persians, and that only later did they learn the worship of "the heavenly" goddess Urania, whom Herodotus equates with Aphrodite, from the Semites ("Assyrians and Arabians"). Here we surely have a reference to Anāhitā, but Herodotus wrongly calls the goddess Mit(h)ra. An ingenious explanation of this circumstance was put forward by Gershevitch. Herodotus had heard the chief divinity referred to as Ahura-Mithra (or Mithra-Ahura, cf. Mesoromasdes for Mis-Ōhrmazd, i.e. the Persian form of Mithra-Ahura Mazdā in Plutarch), and understanding Ahura as a god resembling Zeus, he assumed that Mithra must have been Ahura's consort, and attached this name to the great Goddess of whom he had heard. In any event, the passage serves as important evidence for Anāhitā and Mithra.

From Darius II (424–405) we have only two brief inscriptions, one containing the formula "may Ahura Mazdā together with the gods protect..." and the other containing the formula "by the will of Ahura Mazdā". The evidence is conclusive for the next two rulers, Artaxerxes II (405–359) and Artaxerxes III (359–338). From Artaxerxes II we have "By the will of Ahura Mazdā I am king...Ahura Mazdā bestowed the kingdom upon me. May Ahura Mazdā protect me..." (Hamadan, C). However in the same king's inscription, Susa A, the "will" and "protect" formulas are referred to Ahura Mazdā, Anāhitā, and Mithra, whereas in the inscription Hamadan B, Mithra alone is the subject of "protect". In the sole inscription we have from Artaxerxes III, Ahura Mazdā and Mithra are the subject of "protect".

The act of worship was considered necessary both for men and for the gods. Not only were individual and communal benefits, both material and spiritual, thought to be obtained through worship, but worship strengthened the gods to perform their own positive functions as well as keep in check the evil forces at work in the world. There is even a measure of petulant jealousy which the gods are shown to express because of insufficient attention to their cults. Thus Mithra complains that men do not worship him by mentioning his name in prayer as much as they mention other gods; were he so invoked, he would interrupt his blissful existence and rush to the worshipper (Yasht 10.54–6). Tishtriya too, as we have seen, voices a similar complaint to Ahura Mazdā, the Waters and Plants and the Mazdayasnian Religion: were men to worship him by name as they do other gods he would have the strength of ten horses, ten camels, ten bulls, ten mountains, and ten navigable rivers, and so be able to defeat Apaosha; the needed strength is however supplied through Ahura Mazdā's worship of him (Yasht 8.23 seq.). The ancient canon of elements of cultic worship may be seen from e.g. Yasht 10.6: libations (*zaoθrā*), praise, reverence, audible prayer, *haoma* with milk, the *barəsman* (grasses or later twigs spread out to receive the victim; also held in the hand of the celebrating priest during recitation of prayers), skill of tongue, and magic word with correct utterance. The offerings would also include wheat cakes (the grain requisitions of the Persepolis records probably went for this purpose), pomegranate and other fruit, animals and various other foodstuffs; liquid offerings could include wine (as abundantly evidenced by the Persepolis accounts). In early times major rites performed by kings would involve the sacrifice of large numbers of bulls and horses, associated especially with the sun and water. Generally, in place of the increasingly expensive bulls, sheep came to be substituted; these were called "hallowed bovines", the origin of the ordinary modern Persian word for sheep, *gūsfand*. Goats and fowl could also be used as sacrificial animals. The selection of the victim would depend on the deity, type of rite, etc., and the lavishness would of course accord with the wealth of the one for whom the rite was performed. Sacrifices were the usual way meat was obtained.

There were daily offerings to Fire consisting of animal fat, and to Water consisting of milk and vegetable material. The cult of the hearth fire dates from Indo-European times. The home fire would be kept burning as long as the householder was alive. The fire was thought to represent the vital force in all the various elements. Fire temples, as temples in general, do not seem to be clearly attested for the Achaemenian period.[1]

An important priestly rite was the Yasna, the act of worship *par excellence*, in which, in addition to the other elements of religious service, the beverage haoma, in Achaemenian times probably still a hallucinogen, was prepared in a mortar, strained and offered. A long liturgy, including recitation of the Gāthās, was structured around this act.

Five canonical prayer times were observed: (1) at sunrise, "the Haoma-pressing time"; (2) at noon, "Lunchtime"; (3) in the afternoon; (4) at evening; (50) from midnight to sunrise, the "Dawn(watch)".

[1] See in detail M. Boyce, "On the Zoroastrian temple cult of fire", *JAOS* xcv (1975), pp. 454–65.

THE RELIGION OF ACHAEMENIAN IRAN

THE MAGI AND THEIR ROLE

Herodotus (1.101) mentions the Magi sixth and last in his list of Median tribes (γένεα). Elsewhere (1.132) he observes that no Persian sacrifice may be performed without the presence of a Magus, who sings a "Theogony" on the occasion. As peculiarities of the Magi he lists (1.140) the exposure of the dead to be rent by birds and dogs, their abstention from killing dogs, and their delight in slaying ants, snakes, and other creeping and flying creatures.

Combining this information with what we know from Iranian sources, we arrive at the following picture: like the Levite tribe among the Hebrews, the Magi became a priestly group among the Medes, and became practising clergy also for the Persian subjects of the Medes, and continued in this function after the Achaemenids wrested the rule of western Iran from the Medes. This explains the presence of Magi in the Achaemenian entourages as described by Herodotus, and more importantly in the Persepolis Elamite material. With the acceptance of Zarathushtrian ideas at the court, the Magi, hitherto professional ministrants of the ancient deities of polytheism, came to associate themselves with the worship of Ahura Mazdā, and began to claim Zoroaster as one of theirs. Thus from the 4th century B.C. onwards our Greek sources speak of "Zoroaster the Magus".

The influence of the Magi may be seen in the *Vidēvdād*,[1] where for the first time in the Avesta we see a preoccupation with: the exposure of corpses and much else concerning the treatment of the dead; laws fixing punishments for harm to dogs; and the extermination of various creeping and flying animals, including ants and snakes, for which pious act a special pointed stick was carried about. It may be remarked in passing that there is no justification for characterizing the exposure of corpses as Zarathushtrian; Herodotus records that the Persians practised encasement in wax before burial, which may have been a preliminary to entombment of kings as well. The Achaemenian evidence of

---

[1] The Magi themselves, however, are not mentioned in the Vidēvdād. Altogether, in the whole of the extant Avesta, a word *magu* occurs for certain only once, in the compound *moyu-ṭbiš* "hostile to magu(s)", which E. Benveniste has convincingly shown cannot refer to Magian priests (*Les Mages dans l'ancien Iran* (Paris, 1938), p. 11 and passim). The same will be true of the less certain Avestan attestation of the uncompounded word *magu*, again only in one passage, if one accepts H. W. Bailey's proposal (in M. Boyce and I Gershevitch (eds), *W. B. Henning Memorial Volume* (London, 1970), pp. 33–4) to rescue it from Geldner's apparatus of text variants in a different Gathic verse, of which no connected translation accounting for *magu* (in the genitive) is offered. Ed.

entombment of kings, and perhaps interment of others, would merely show that exposure of corpses had not yet become part of general practice.

Gershevitch has seen an indication that the Magians were Medes and coopted Zoroaster's religion in the fact that the Middle and New Persian form of the name Zoroaster (Zardušt) must go back to an Old Median (rather than Old Persian or Avestan) form *Zarat-uštra, and in the fact that the tradition of Zoroaster having been born in Media is a late one.

Gershevitch has also proposed that it was the influence of the Magi which led to the acceptance of the old gods into the "Zoroastrian" fold. Further he sees the opposition of Angra Mainyu (Areimanios) to Ahura Mazdā (Oromasdes), attributed by Aristotle in a fragment of *De Philosophia* to the Magi, as a theological simplification by this clergy of the Zarathushtrian opposition of Angra Mainyu to Spenta Mainyu. This simplification was to become standard doctrine in the Sasanian period.[1]

It is *a priori* likely that Herodotus' list of Median tribes is ordered according to localization, beginning with the most southerly (i.e. above Persia) and ending with the most northerly, in Āzarbāījān. The ancient name of the latter region, known to the Greeks as Media Atropatene, indeed indicates a priestly territory: Ātrpāt(ak)āna "the place of tending the sacred fire(s)". The early activity of the Magi there accounts for the non-Zoroastrian Mithraic elements (parallelled in Roman Mithraism) long preserved in Armenia, Georgia (and perhaps Ossetia), of which traces occur in the Magian *Vidēvdād*.[2] After the Magi accepted Zoroastrianism, they claimed their homeland, Āzarbāījān, as that of Zoroaster, a tradition maintained in Sasanian times.

---

[1] For a more elaborate discussion of the issues presented under this heading, see Gershevitch, "Zoroaster's own contribution".

[2] Cf. my observations in Hinnells (ed.), *Mithraic Studies* II, pp. 415–19, 421–43, and those of A. D. H. Bivar in *op. cit.* II, pp. 287–8, I. Gershevitch in *op. cit.* I, pp. 355–7, op. cit. II, pp. 85–8, and Chapter 13, p. 661, n. 1.

CHAPTER 15

ARAMAIC IN THE ACHAEMENIAN EMPIRE

The use of Aramaic throughout the Achaemenian empire is well established and will be discussed in detail in the course of this chapter. It has been assumed by some scholars that the spread of Aramaic was primarily the result of official action by Darius I and was further promulgated by his successors.[1] This view, however, ignores the important role of Aramaic in earlier periods.[2] The earliest Aramaic inscription, apparently from the 10th–9th centuries was discovered recently at Tell Fakhariya in Syria near the Khabur.[3] Documentation is at first sparse but in the course of the 9th and 8th centuries Aramaic inscriptions from Syria and the neighbouring countries increase (*KAI* 201–15; 222–4; 232). One may discern in the material at hand the existence of dialectical differences in Aramaic.[4] The use of Aramaic in the Assyrian empire at an early period is attested to by references to Aramaic letters (*egirtu armētu*) and to Aramaic scribes and documents before the rise of the Sargonid dynasty. Indeed the gradual absorption of great numbers of Aramaic speakers from the West influenced the composition of the administration of the Assyrian empire. On reliefs and wall paintings from the time of Tiglath Pileser III onwards pairs of scribes, one with pen and leather (or papyrus), writing in Aramaic, and the other with stylus and tablet (or waxed board), writing in Akkadian, are depicted on Assyrian reliefs.[5]

The "Mesopotamian" dialect of Aramaic which was in use in the area of Aram-Naharaim along the banks of the Habur and Balikh to the Euphrates attests to the influence of Assyrian on Aramaic. This dialect

---

[1] Schaeder, *Iranische Beiträge* I, 1–14.
[2] Ginsberg, "Aramaic Dialect Problems [I]" and "II"; Rosenthal, *Die aramäistische Forschung*, 70; Bowman, "Arameans"; Lewy, "Problems".
[3] It is found on the back of a stele on whose front is inscribed the Neo-Assyrian version. A preliminary account has been published by Ali Abou Assaf, "Die Statue des HDYS'Y, König von Guzana", *MDOG* CXIII (1981), 3122. Whenever possible, Aramaic inscriptions are quoted from Donner-Röllig, *KAI*.
[4] Cf. Greenfield, "The Dialects of Ancient Aramaic".
[5] Cf. Driver, *Semitic Writing*, pp. 16–17, 225–8; D. Wiseman, "Assyrian writing-boards", *Iraq* XVII (1955), 3–13; Malamat, "The Aramaeans".

spread into north Syria (Zincirli) (*KAI* 216) and elsewhere (*KAI* 225-6) and replaced the local dialects temporarily. Aramaic inscriptions on seals, sealings, weights, bronze jugs and bowls, etc. have been found from Nimrud to Luristan.[1] Aramaic dockets appear on cuneiform tablets, and Aramaic legal documents on clay tablets (many of which are as yet unpublished) have been discovered in various sites in Syria and Iraq.[2] The important role of Aramaic as the *lingua franca* in diplomatic intercourse during this period is attested to by a variety of sources: (a) the request of an officer in Ur to write to the king in Aramaic;[3] (b) reference to "a sealed Aramaic document" sent to the king of Assyria from Tyre;[4] (c) the report from the days of Sennacherib (701 B.C.) of the conversation before the walls of Jerusalem between the Assyrian commander and the heads of the Judaean court who requested that the conversation be conducted in Aramaic (*'Arāmīt*) rather than Hebrew (*Yehūdīt*) (II Kings 18. 13-37; Isa. 36. 1-22); (d) by the use of Aramaic on a large ostracon sent from Babylon to Assur (*KAI* 233). This ostracon reporting to the Assyrian administration about the capture of runaway slaves contains the earliest known text in eastern Aramaic. It is during this period that Aḥiqar, an Aramaic sage, achieved the position of *ummānu* "counsellor" at the court of Sennacherib and Esarhaddon. His "Proverbs" in the "Mesopotamian" dialect of Aramaic were discovered at Elephantine in the early years of this century. With the destruction of the Assyrian Empire (611 B.C.) the use of cuneiform ceases in the West. The tablets excavated at Nerab were in all likelihood written in Babylon and brought back to Nerab by returning exiles.[5]

The Aramaization of the population of Babylonia had been even more thoroughgoing than that of Assyria and although the Neo-Babylonian and the Late Babylonian dialects of Akkadian were used for a variety

---

[1] For this dialect and the inscriptions in it, cf. Kaufman, *Akkadian Influences on Aramaic*, 8-9; and Naveh, *The Development of the Aramaic Script*, 10-14.

[2] Cf. A. R. Millard, "Some Aramaic epigraphs", *Iraq* XXXIV (1972), 131-8; P. Bordreuil, "Une tablette araméenne inédite", *Semitica* XXIII (1973), 95-102; Lipiński, *Studies* I; idem, "Textes juridiques et économiques araméens", *AAntASH* XXII (1974), 373-84; H. Freydank, "Eine aramäische Urkunde aus Assur", in *Altorientalische Forschungen* II (Berlin, 1975), 133-5 (Schriften zur Geschichte und Kultur des Alten Orients); from the Neo-Babylonian period is the tablet published by A. Caquot, "Une inscription araméenne d'époque assyrienne", in A. Caquot and M. Philonenko (eds), *Hommages à André Dupont-Sommer* (Paris, 1971), 9-16.

[3] M. Dietrich, *WO* IV (1967), 87-90.

[4] H. W. F. Saggs, "The Nimrud Letters", *Iraq* XVII (1955), 130, no. 13.

[5] See I. Eph'al, "The Western Minorities in Babylonia in the 6th-5th centuries B.C.", *Orientalia* XLVII (1978), 74-90 with notice of Neirab, pp. 84-7.

of documents during the periods from the Chaldean dynasty to the Arsacid period in Babylonia, there can be no doubt that Aramaic was the language actually spoken there and in neighbouring regions.[1] Neo-Babylonian and Late Babylonian reflect the strong influence of Aramaic in vocabulary, syntax and morphology. During the period in which the Neo-Babylonian empire succeeded the Assyrian empire, the position of Aramaic was not impaired; one may rather assume that Aramaic penetrated the areas which were gradually conquered and added to the Neo-Babylonian empire. There are two examples of the use of Aramaic in this period as a *lingua franca*: (a) the "Adon letter", found at Saqqara in Egypt, which was sent by a king of one of the cities of the Philistine coast to Pharaoh *c.* 600 B.C. (*KAI* 266), is written in Aramaic; and (b) Jeremiah's declaration about the impotence of foreign gods, addressed to the Nations, is also in Aramaic (Jer. 10. 11).

The documentation for the Neo-Babylonian period is slight and consists primarily of cuneiform tablets with Aramaic endorsements, seals and bullae, but there are indications of the widespread use of waxed ivory or wooden writing-boards, leather scrolls and papyrus in Babylon throughout this period. There are references to the leather *magallatu* "scroll" (= Hebrew *měgillā*) on Neo-Babylonian colophons, to *sipru* "documents" (whether papyrus or leather is not clear) and ^{kuš}*sipirtu* "leather documents".[2] The *sēpiru*, a learned Aramaic scribe who functioned also as translator and expert is well known from this and the later periods.[3] The dialect used was surely contemporary eastern Aramaic, and it is this dialect which served as the basis for the Official Aramaic of the Achaemenian period.[4]

The prime source of our documentation for Official Aramaic is Egypt. Papyri, leather documents, inscriptions on stone (e.g. painted on the walls of a tomb at Shaikh Faḍl), tombstones, ceramics, textiles and wood, and texts incised on metal vessels have been preserved in the hospitable sands of Egypt. There can be no doubt that most of the material discovered to date was written in Egypt:[5] the judicial and

---

[1] Writing in cuneiform continued to the beginning of the 1st century A.D.; an Aramaic incantation in cuneiform from Uruk is the object of scholarly discussion; cf. Koopmans, *Aramäische Chrestomathie*, no. 56.

[2] Cf. W. v. Soden, *Akkadisches Handwörterbuch* (Wiesbaden, 1965–), *s.v.*, and Wiseman, "Assyrian writing-boards", 12–13.

[3] Lewy, "Problems", 188–200, treats this title in detail; cf. too v. Soden, *op.cit., s.v. sēpiru*.

[4] Cf. Kutscher, *History of Aramaic* Part 1 and *idem*, "Aramaic" in E. Y. Kutscher, *Hebrew and Aramaic Studies* (Jerusalem, 1977), 90–155.

[5] For general orientation, detailed discussion and bibliography cf. Porten, *Archives from Elephantine*; for a re-edition of many of the texts from Elephantine, cf. Porten–Greenfield, *Jews*

commercial documents, official rescripts, letters and petitions from Elephantine and other sites in Egypt; the letters of an Aramaic family found at Hermopolis; letters found at Saqqara (the recently discovered ones as yet unpublished), and arsenal lists from Memphis, etc., graffiti on temples, and mummy tags from various places in Egypt.[1] Egypt had provided refuge for Aramaeans, Phoenicians, Edomites, Judaeans and many others during the 7th and 6th centuries; Aramaic had become the colloquial and literary language for them.[2] The large number of Egyptian names that occur in Aramaic texts as well as in the religious text in Demotic script, of which only a few lines have been published, show that many Egyptians had been assimilated to Aramaic culture.[3] But part of the material originated in the East, thus the Arsham letters originated in either Babylon or Susa (or both); the Behistun inscription may have been copied in the royal chancery in Persepolis and sent from there to Egypt; the Aḥiqar framework story and proverbs may indeed have been brought to Elephantine from elsewhere.[4]

Beside the rich store of material from Egypt we find Aramaic inscriptions at Teima in the Arabian peninsula, in Israel on ostraca found at many sites such as Ramat Rahel, Arad, Beer Sheba, Tell Farah, Ashdod, Samaria and at Ezion-Geber in the south; at Tell es-Saʿdiya in the Jordan valley and at Ḥesbān in Jordan. These ostraca record, on the whole, the provision of goods to the local Persian garrisons and list quantities of wine and barley. A good number of bullae have recently come to light in Israel.[5] These were originally attached to documents written in all likelihood in Aramaic; in the Wadi Daliyeh cave remnants of such documents have been discovered.[6] They were

of Elephantine, Aramaeans of Syene; cf. too J. C. Greenfield, "A new corpus of Aramaic texts of the Achaemenid period from Egypt" *JAOS* xcvi (1976), 131–135; Naveh, "Development", 21–45.

[1] The Saqqara texts have been published by J. B. Segal in *Aramaic Texts from North Saqqâra* (Oxford University Press for the Egypt Exploration Society, 1982). For some recently published tombstones, cf. Kornfeld, *Jüdisch-aramäische Grabinschriften aus Edfu.*

[2] Aramaic continued to be used for legal documents in Ptolemaic Egypt; cf. Cowley, *Aramaic Papyri*, 81, studied by J. Harmatta, "Irano-Aramaica", *AAntASH* vii (1959), 337–409; cf. too Bresciani, "Un papiro aramaico di età tolemaica", 258–64. All the names are Greek.

[3] Bowman, "An Aramaic religious text"; this papyrus is finally being prepared for publication at the Oriental Institute of the University of Chicago. A fragment of the Demotic version of the Aḥiqar text was recently published by Karl-Th. Zauzich, "Demotische Fragmente zum Ahiqar-Roman", in H. Franke *et al.* (eds), *Folia Rara Wolfgang Voigt...Dedicata* (Wiesbaden, 1976), 180–5. Aramaic influence is discernible in Demotic legal terminology; cf. E. Y. Kutscher, "New Aramaic texts", *JAOS* LXXIV (1954), 238–46.

[4] See J. C. Greenfield, "The background and parallel to a proverb of Ahiqar", in *Hommages à André Dupont-Sommer*, 49–59; idem, "Aḥiqar in the book of Tobit", in *De la Torah au Messie, Mélanges Henri Cazelles* (Paris, 1981), 329–36.

[5] Avigad, *Bullae and Seals from a Post-exilic Judaean Archive.*

[6] Cross, "Papyri of the Fourth Century B.C. from Wadi Dâliyeh".

written in Samaria toward the end of the Achaemenian period (c. 375/365–335 B.C.) and hidden in the caves by refugees. They demonstrate the importance of Aramaic for administrative and commercial uses.

Asia Minor is an important source of Aramaic epigraphic material. The weight from Abydos on the Hellespont and the many coins from Cilicia, and elsewhere, are well known. Dedicatory and funerary inscriptions have been discovered in Cilicia, Lycia, Cappadocia and at Dascyleium (where bullae inscribed with Aramaic and Old Persian were also found).[1] Some of these inscriptions are in more than one language – the Sardis bilingual in Lydian and Aramaic[2] and the Xanthus trilingual in Lydian, Greek and Aramaic.[3] It may be ventured that some inscriptions that are now preserved only in Greek such as the letter of Darius to Gadatas found at Magnesia and the decree of Artaxerxes II found at Sardis in 1974 had in antiquity a version in Aramaic as well.[4] There can be no doubt that there were speakers of Aramaic in Syria, Palestine, Babylon, and Egypt during this period, but there is no reason to assume that many Aramaic speakers were to be found in the western satrapies of Asia Minor. Aramaic continued to be used for coin legends and inscriptions in Asia Minor into the Hellenistic period. Beside Aramaic–Greek bilinguals, an inscription with religious import in late Old Persian may be found among the Arabsun inscriptions.[5] Boundary stones, burial inscriptions and dedications from later periods are also known from Armenia and Georgia. These surely continue a well established tradition.

The destruction of Assyria by the Medes and the Babylonians (Nineveh 612 B.C., Harran 610 B.C.) has led to a paucity of information about all aspects of life in that area for the centuries to come. The Assyrian chancery and scribal schools were destroyed and cuneiform writing ceased in Assyria. It was replaced by Aramaic but for proof of this one must turn to Assur and Hatra of the Parthian period (inscribed

---

[1] Hanson, "Aramaic Funerary and Boundary Inscriptions"; Lipinski, *Studies* I, 146–7; K. Balkan, "Inscribed bullae from Daskyleion-Ergeli", *Anatolia* IV (1959), 123–8.

[2] *KAI* 263; cf. Lipinski, *ibid.* pp. 153–61.

[3] The preliminary publication was H. Metzger, E. Laroche, A. Dupont-Sommer, "La stèle trilingue récemment découverte au Letoon de Xanthos", *CRAI* 1974, 82–149. The definitive edition was provided by H. Metzger *et al.*, *Fouilles de Xanthos* VI: *La stèle trilingue du Létôon* (Paris, 1979); Part IV of this volume, pp. 181–5, contains a study by M. Mayrhofer of the Iranian elements in the Aramaic text. Cf. also H. Humbach, "Die aramäischen Nymphen von Xanthos", *Die Sprache* XXVII (1981), 30–32.

[4] Cf. L. Robert, "Une nouvelle inscription grècque de Sardes", *CRAI* 1975, 306–30. Robert is of the opinion that the original decree was in Aramaic. Was there also a Lydian version?

[5] See below, p. 710, n. 3.

ceramic utensils, memorial inscriptions and graffiti). The situation in Babylonia was quite different, for the Aramaic speaking "Chaldean" population had been enriched in numbers by Aramaic speakers from Assyria and the West who had been brought to Babylonia by the Neo-Babylonian rulers.[1] In the Achaemenian period Aramaic endorsements on cuneiform tablets increase in number, Aramaic words enter Akkadian, Aramaic expressions may often be traced in the Late Babylonian legal texts, and there are increased references in the texts to leather documents and to the *sepīru* who served as scribe, translator and expert. Once again, due to the perishability of the material used, very few Aramaic texts have reached us from Achaemenian Babylonia.[2] The following explanation for the lack of information concerning trade clarifies the situation in general: "it may be suggested that the entire trade was in Aramaic hands and that these merchants used papyrus and leather as writing material. After all, only a very small fraction of the private legal acts were recorded in cuneiform on clay even during the Neo-Babylonian period when this technique continued to be used by the temple administrations of Sippar, Ur, Babylon and others."[3]

Evidence for the use of Aramaic in the eastern parts of the empire may be best seen in documents found in the West. First and foremost are the Arsham letters which provide an excellent example of the highly developed use of Aramaic for communication in the Achaemenian empire. These letters, written by a skilled scribe on leather, were sent from Babylon or Susa (or perhaps from both). The mode of address is "from X to Y" and the greeting formula is *šlm wšrrt śgy' hwšrt lk*. These became fixed forms in the Achaemenian chanceries and their continued use may be documented in various Middle Persian dialects. These letters (beside providing visual proof of the use of leather for writing purposes) have in general provided vital information about the Achaemenian satrapal administration in Egypt, and in particular about the language and terminology in use.[4]

The letters and decrees quoted in the Aramaic portion of Ezra are also typical of the documents in vogue in the Achaemenian empire. The

---

[1] For the earlier period, cf. J. A. Brinkman, *A Political History of Post-Kassite Babylonia* (Rome, 1968), 267–85; for the later period, cf. M. Dietrich, *Die Aramäer Südbabyloniens in der Sargonidenzeit* (Neukirchen, 1970); A. L. Oppenheim, *Ancient Mesopotamia* (Chicago, 1964), p. 60.

[2] Material surveyed by Naveh, *op. cit.*

[3] Oppenheim, *op. cit.*, pp. 94–5.

[4] Driver, *Aramaic Documents*; cf. J. D. Whitehead, *Early Aramaic Epistolography: The Arsames Correspondence* (Dissertation, Univ. of Chicago, 1974); idem, "Some Distinctive Features of the Language of the Arsames Correspondence", *JNES* xxxvii (1978), 119–40.

biblical records on one hand and the varied documents found in Egypt, at Elephantine and in the Arsham correspondence on the other are mutually enlightening.[1] Esther, although written in classicizing post-exilic Hebrew, contains phrases and expressions similar to those of Ezra and the texts from Egypt. It is possible to assemble the Aramaic and Old Persian administrative vocabulary from these texts and supplement the information derived from Greek and Babylonian cuneiform sources. The Elamite tablets recovered at Persepolis both from the Treasury and from the northeast Fortification wall, and dating from the middle years of Darius I to the twenty-first year of Xerxes, also supply valuable information about the use of Aramaic.[2] Some of these tablets refer specifically to "Babylonian scribes (writing) on parchment" (*PFT* 1808, 1810, 1947: 23-4; 25-6). A parchment document, about provisions to be supplied, is referred to in *PFT* 1986, 31-2. Some of the tablets have notations in Aramaic on the edges and others are sealed with seals bearing Aramaic inscriptions.[3] Some of the *PFT* texts deal with travel-rations issued for those travelling on "official business". Most are for short journeys from Susa to Persepolis but some are for travellers whose goal is as far west as Egypt. The rations were issued en route against authorizations and the authorization texts were probably in Aramaic.[4] No such authorization was found among the *PFT* but one of the Arsham texts[5] is an authorization (the term "passport" used by some scholars is a misnomer) for the issuance of provisions for an officer and his entourage, whose final destination is Egypt. It has been argued, on the basis of certain *PTT*, that the *PTT* were originally dictated in Old Persian, written down in Aramaic, and then translated, as it were, into Elamite.[6] Sealings and "napkin rings" discovered with the *PTT* may indicate that a good number of parchment or papyrus documents were stored in the Treasury.[7] There is, however, no proof that these

[1] Vogt, *Lexicon Linguae Aramaicae* has demonstrated the benefit to be derived from comparing the material. See also J. C. Greenfield, "Aramaic studies and the Bible", in J. A. Emerton (ed.), *Congress Volume: Vienna 1980* (Leiden, 1982), pp. 110-30 (Supplements to *Vetus Testamentum* 32).
[2] Cameron, *The Persepolis Treasury Tablets* = *PTT*; Hallock, *Persepolis Fortification Tablets* = *PFT*.
[3] E.g. the seal of *PTT* 4 (p. 92); *PFT* 214, 216, 2023, 2024, 2043, 2059, etc. are inscribed in Aramaic on the edge. The seal on *PFT* 2068 reads *ḥtm prnk br'rsm*, cf. *PTT* p. 53, n. 52.
[4] *PFT* 1544 refers to a voyage to Egypt. The *ḥalmi* "sealed document" referred to in these texts were in all likelihood in Aramaic, cf. Cameron, *PTT*, p. 53.
[5] Driver, *Aramaic Documents*, VI.
[6] A more recent view is that they were written down in Elamite straight from Old Persian dictation; see Gershevitch, "The Alloglottography of Old Persian".
[7] Cameron, *PTT* pp. 24-32. Similar "napkin rings" which might have held Aramaic texts have been found in Uruk and Nimrud.

documents were the originals of the *PTT*. A respectable number of texts (described originally as "500 small pieces with Aramaic writing in ink") were also found in the Fortification wall, but these have not been published as yet.[1]

About ninety sets of chert mortars, pestles and plates with inscriptions in ink were found in the Treasury.[2] They have been misunderstood as ritual texts by their publisher; subsequent reviewers have shown that they are treasury records, whose exact nature has not been clarified. It has been argued that the inscribed objects were deposited in Persepolis by emissaries from Parikana, Saruka and Hasta, supposedly localities in Arachosia, a province mentioned often in the *PFT*. The present writer sees no reason for doubting that the inscriptions were also written in Arachosia. It should be noted that it was at various sites in Afghanistan that inscriptions of Ashoka in Aramaic and other languages were discovered. These include the Aramao-Indic inscriptions from Pul-i Darunta (containing Prakrit words in Aramaic text); the inscriptions from Kandahar – the first a bilingual in Greek and Aramaic and the second a fragmentary Aramao-Indic text; and two Aramaic inscriptions from Laghman (these inscriptions have been called early Pahlavi).[3] Taxila, in Pakistan, was the site of the first Aramao-Indic inscription of this sort to be discovered. This inscription attests to the penetration of Aramaic into north-west India. It may be more than a coincidence that the earliest inscriptions in Indic script come from the time of Ashoka. Kharoṣṭhi is derived from the Aramaic script and also contains ideograms derived from Aramaic.[4] Aramaic inscriptions from the Achaemenian era have not been discovered in Parthia, Bactria, Choresmia or Sogdiana, but the use of writing systems derived from Aramaic and the maintenance of the chancery formulae in the Parthian and Sogdian documents may serve to assure us of the earlier use of Aramaic in these provinces of the Achaemenian empire.[5]

[1] Cf. *PTT* p. 23; *PFT* p. 2. A volume containing the Aramaic grafitti from Persepolis, prepared by R. A. Bowman is now in press.

[2] Bowman, *Aramaic Ritual Texts from Persepolis*; these texts have been discussed by M. N. Bogolyubov, P. Bernard, J. A. Delauney, R. Degen, I. Gershevitch, W. Hinz, B. A. Levine, and J. Naveh–S. Shaked; for bibliographical indications see W. Hinz, "Zu den Mörsern und Stösseln aus Persepolis", in *Monumentum H. S. Nyberg* I (Acta Iranica 4, 1975). 371–85.

[3] For bibliography see H. Humbach, *Abhandlungen der Akademie der Wissenschaften und der Literatur, Mainz* 1969.1, 1974.1. See also S. Shaked, "Notes on the new Aśoka inscription from Kandahar", *JRAS* 1969, 118–22; G. D. Davary, "Epigraphische Forschungen in Afghanistan", *St Ir* x (1981), 55–6.

[4] H. W. Bailey, "A Problem of the Kharoṣṭhi Script", in D. Winton Thomas (ed.), *Essays and Studies presented to Stanley Arthur Cook* (London, 1950), 121–3 (Cambridge Oriental Series 2).

[5] Greenfield, "Notes on the Arsham Letters".

LANGUAGE

There is a tendency among scholars to use the general term "Official Aramaic" (or Imperial Aramaic, based on the German *Reichsaramäisch*) for all of the Aramaic material known from the Achaemenian period; and the particular term "Egyptian Aramaic" for the language of the multifarious texts preserved in the special climatic and geological conditions of Egypt.[1] Close analysis, however, shows that although "Official Aramaic" was in widespread use, other dialects have been preserved in the texts from Egypt. Among the earliest materials, from the last quarter of the 6th century are the Hermopolis letters, written by members of an Aramean family to each other (pl. 9).[2] These contain no Iranian loan words or personal names, are in a western dialect of Aramaic and have distinctive orthographic features, some of which are also recognizable in some of the Elephantine texts written by Aramaean scribes. Among the Elephantine texts the legal documents are written in Official Aramaic but in accord with the conservative nature of such material, they often reflect earlier western and perhaps Jewish usages and preserve rather diversified legal terminology.[3] Among the legal documents those from the second half of the 5th century attest to the penetration of Iranian legal terminology into the language of the law courts (see below). The personal letters written by trained scribes on papyri and ostraca are in a Standard Aramaic while the official correspondence – letters, petitions, memoranda and orders – are in Official Aramaic. The fragmentary Aramaic version of the Behistun inscription is also in Official Aramaic; it bears traces of being a translation but its exact relationship with the Old Persian version and the Akkadian version, with which it has the closest affinity, is yet to be established.[4] The "Proverbs" of Aḥiqar is, from the linguistic point of view, an interesting composite work. The framework story is in Official Aramaic – or in the branch of Official Aramaic which will

[1] So recently Segert, *Altaramäische Grammatik*, 39–40; contrast Kutscher, "Aramaic", 361–6.
[2] Bresciani-Kamil, "Le lettere aramaiche di Hermopoli"; for the date cf. Naveh, "The Palaeography of the Hermopolis Papyri". A bibliography of these letters may be found in *IOS* IV (1974), 14, to which may be added J. C. L. Gibson, *Textbook of Syrian Semitic Inscriptions* II: *Aramaic Inscriptions* (Oxford, 1975), 125–43; D. R. Hillers, "Redemption in Letters 6 and 2 from Hermopolis", *Ugarit-Forschungen* XI (Neukirchen–Vluyn, 1979), 379–82. A convenient edition of these texts may be found in Porten-Greenfield, *Jews of Elephantine, Arameans of Syene*, 151–65.
[3] Yaron, *Introduction to the Law of the Aramaic Papyri*; Muffs, *Studies in the Aramaic Legal Papyri from Elephantine*.
[4] See now the new edition of the Aramaic text by J. C. Greenfield and B. Porten, *CIIr.*, Pt. 1, vol. 5 (London, 1982).

eventually emerge as Standard Literary Aramaic – and contains numerous Akkadian loan words and calques. There are no Iranian loan words in this text but the name of Assyria is spelled *'twr* rather than *'šwr*, an indication of provenance and period. The "Proverbs" are written in a dialect of western Aramaic with strong affinities with "Mesopotamian" Aramaic and free of Akkadian and Iranian influences. To these may be added texts from other sites in Egypt and elsewhere throughout the Achaemenian empire, which show that where there were large numbers of Aramaic speakers other dialects remained in use alongside the dominant Official Aramaic. Official Aramaic was the basis for diverse later dialects such as Nabataean and Palmyrene Aramaic and its strong influence can be felt in the language of the legal documents of the Bar Kosiba finds (from the Naḥal Ḥever and Wadi Murabbaʿat caves) and those preserved in Talmudic literature and in early Syriac material. Standard Literary Aramaic, the literary dialect which developed alongside Official Aramaic, was readily understood throughout the Aramaic speaking world. This dialect was used by Jewish scribes for biblical works such as Daniel and it is the language of the Aramaic works found at Qumran: Tobit, the Genesis Apocryphon, Enoch, the Testament of Levi, the Job Targum, etc. The official Aramaic translations (Targumim) of the Pentateuch and the Prophets and the *Megillat Taʿanit* were issued in it.[1] In vocabulary and syntax it is an eastern Aramaic dialect and loan words from Iranian such as *raz*, *nidna*, *nezak*, *naxašir*, *asfera*, *daxšt*, *gaytha*, *ratika*, to choose some well known examples, are found in Standard Literary Aramaic.

The adoption of the Aramaic language and script by the Achaemenian rulers should be seen as a practical, natural choice for this was the simplest script available to them, already in use throughout the western part of the empire and perhaps in Media. Cyrus, one may assume, had been aware of its importance before he conquered Babylon. The transition was surely smooth, for references to the royal scribes, the *sepīru ša šarri*, are found in texts from the time of Nebuchadnezzar, Nabunidus, Cyrus and Cambyses. It is clear that the accepted administrative institutions of the Neo-Babylonian empire were not adversely affected by the ascendancy of the Persians. The means by which Aramaic script was used to facilitate communication has often been described: the document was dictated by the king or by an official to the scribe, who then wrote the text in Aramaic; the addressee's scribe read the letter

---

[1] Greenfield, "Standard Literary Aramaic".

in the recipient's native tongue.¹ It is clear, from various internal indications, that the *sepīru* "scribe" combined in his function the tasks of both secretary and translator. Although most recipients would be Persian, the missive might be received by a Lydian, a Greek, a Choresmian or a resident of Gandhara. The use of many Old Persian terms in these texts facilitated their being understood. This mode of reading is what is meant by the term *mĕphārash* in Ezra 4. 18, the equivalent of Iranian *uzvārišn*.² The reading of these texts aloud is referred to in Ezra 4. 18, Esther 6. 1 and Darius, Behistun 70.

The various types of documents and letters from Egypt and those preserved in the biblical Ezra provide us with models of those issued by the royal chancery.³ The highly developed postal system, described by Herodotus and affirmed by Arsham Letter VI and the Persepolis Fortification Tablets, used documents and letters of these types to bind the empire together. The discovery of an elegantly written Aramaic version of the Behistun inscription at Elephantine matches Darius' report that copies were sent out on tablets and scrolls (assuming that the word "leather" in Behistun 70 is intended to include papyrus).⁴ The use of various languages and scripts for royal messages is reported in Esther (1. 22; 3. 12; 8. 9) as is the use of swift riders (8. 10). Since most of the provinces in the Achaemenian empire had no script of their own, the use of Aramaic "read out" in the local tongue must be meant by these verses.⁵ In Daniel 1. 4, the young Judaean princes are trained for a career at the court by teaching them Aramaic language and script. From the biblical account, we also learn of the existence of archives *bet ginzayyā* at Susa (Esther 6. 1), and at Babylon and Ecbatana (Ezra 5. 17), where the records *sĕfar dukranayyā* were kept.

¹ Schaeder, *loc. cit.*
² Polotsky, "Aramaisch *prš* und das Huzvaresch".
³ Bickerman, "The Edict of Cyrus in Ezra I".
⁴ Without entering into the moot question of the originator of the Old Persian script, this writer does not believe that the reference in Behistun 70 is to Old Persian written on clay tablets or leather, but rather to Akkadian and Aramaic versions. Cf. Dandamayev, *Persien unter den ersten Achämeniden*, 23–52. I. Gershevitch, "Diakonoff on Writing, with an Appendix by Darius", in J. N. Postgate et al. (eds), *Societies and Languages of the Ancient Near East; Studies in honour of I. M. Diakonoff* (Warminster, 1982), 99–109, thinks that also Darius' "clay" was inscribed in Aramaic.
⁵ It is only in Asia Minor that a plethora of local scripts were in use beside Greek – Carian, Lycian, Lydian, Phrygian, etc. But for official business, Aramaic took precedence. Thus the Aramaic version of the Xanthos stele is phrased in official style while the Greek and Lycian versions are in narrative style.

SCRIPT

The early Aramaic inscriptions, from the late 10th to the middle of the 8th century B.C. are on the whole monumental, and were written in a lapidary script similar to the script used during the same period for Phoenician inscriptions.[1] The first signs of the influence of cursive handwriting appear in the Panamu and Bar-Rakib inscriptions (*KAI* 215, 216). An independent cursive style began to emerge in Aramaic in the mid 8th century. The cursive Aramaic script developed rapidly during the late 8th and the 7th and 6th centuries. This must be attributed to the growing use of Aramaic for communication, commercial transactions and legal records, and also to the important role that Aramaic played as the *lingua franca* widely used in international relations. Aramaic script was also used by the Ammonites; the recently published Deir 'Alla inscription is in this script. The same is true for the Phoenician incantation plaques (7th cent.) from Arslan Tash. The relatively conservative nature of the contemporary Hebrew and Phoenician scripts can be seen when they are compared with the Aramaic cursive. The remarkable uniformity of the Aramaic script as used throughout the Achaemenian empire is worthy of notice. No regional forms of the script may be discerned although ethnic groups of varied cultural background throughout the vast expanse of the realm used it; the same script was used from Central Asia to Egypt, from the Caucasus to North Arabia. (The mixed population – such as in Egypt, where Jews, Aramaeans, Choresmians, Babylonians, Phoenicians, Carians, and Cilicians served in the Persian forces – may have been a factor for uniformity.) Therefore, content or geographic reference is needed before the source of a text can be ascertained, e.g. the inscribed mortars, pestles and plates found at Persepolis can only be designated as coming from Arachosia if it is Arachosian cities which are mentioned in the inscriptions and because the stone of which they are made occurs in Arachosia.

A lapidary style persisted alongside the cursive in the Persian period, and the same lapidary script can be seen in the inscriptions from Egypt, from Asia Minor, from Teima in North Arabia and on the bullae from Judaea. Cursive writing was to prevail and by the 3rd century B.C. the

---

[1] Naveh, "Development" is the source for the opinions in this section. The writer is indebted to him for enlightening discussion of the problems involved; cf. too Greenfield–Naveh, "Hebrew and Aramaic in the Persian period".

lapidary style of Aramaic disappeared. Again, it is Egypt, with the variety of textual types preserved there, that provides detailed information about the subdivision of the cursive scripts into three types: (a) formal cursive – used by professional scribes; (b) free cursive – used by educated persons, represented by private letters; (c) vulgar cursive – represented by the signatures of witnesses to deeds. The formal cursive is the chancery hand, represented by the Arsham letters, the Behistun inscription, the petitions,[1] and to a lesser degree, the legal documents. A relatively uniform internal development can be traced over the two hundred years of its use in the royal chanceries and courts.

During the Hellenistic period, when Greek took the place of Aramaic as the official language throughout much of the same geographic area, the uniformity of the Aramaic script gradually broke down. In the 3rd and 2nd centuries, distinctive scripts developed in various national, cultural and geographic units. The Nabataean and the Jewish scripts belong to the western branch, while the Palmyrene, Syriac, Hatrian and Mandaic scripts, among others, belong to the eastern branch. The scripts from which the Parthian, Pahlavi, Sogdian and Choresmian scripts developed also belonged to the eastern branch.[2]

The Aramaic script was often called "Assyrian". This attests to the continued awareness that it developed into an independent entity during the Assyrian period. Greek writers use the designation *Assýria* (or *Syria*) *grámmata* for the Aramaic script when they refer to inscriptions in Aramaic (Herodotus IV. 87; Xenophon, *Cyropaedia* VII. iii. 15; 21st letter of Themistocles iv. 50; etc.). A similar term is used in the Demotic Chronicle to describe the script (and language) of one of the rolls on which the Egyptian law code ordered by Darius I was copied. At a later date, *kĕtab'ašūrī* "Assyrian script" is used in Talmudic literature (Bab. Tal. Sanhedrin 21b, etc.) for the "square" Jewish script which replaced the ancient Hebrew script.[3]

The use of Aramaic script and Aramaic ideograms in the various Middle Persian dialects is an important result of the practice of Achaemenian chanceries.[4] There is, at present, no evidence that

---

[1] Cowley, *Aramaic Papyri*, 30/31.

[2] For the eastern scripts, cf. Naveh, "The origin of the Mandaic Script"; idem, "The North Mesopotamian Aramaic Script-type"; idem, "An Aramaic inscription from El-Mal". For the western, cf. Cross, "The development of the Jewish Scripts".

[3] Friedrich, "Assyria Grammata"; C. Nylander, "ΑΣΣΥΡΙΑ ΓΡΑΜΜΑΤΑ"; Naveh, "Hebrew texts in the Aramaic script".

[4] The discussion by Henning in "Mitteliranisch" remains basic even though new material would lead to some modifications of his views.

SCRIPT

Aramaic script was used for writing Old Persian during the Achaemenian period. Scholars have pointed to an error in the Neo-Babylonian version of the Behistun inscription as possibly due to the use of a *Vorlage* in Aramaic script by the scribes who translated the Old Persian version, but this evidence is inconclusive.[1] The inscriptions from Arabsun in Turkey, which are partly in Aramaic and partly in an Iranian dialect, have recently been dated to the Achaemenian period and interpreted as containing a religious text in Old Persian; but these inscriptions, which do contain a text of interest to students of Iranian religion, cannot be dated on palaeographic grounds before the 3rd century B.C.[2] Attention, however, should be paid to the great number of Iranian words and personal names which are found in the Aramaic texts of this period.[3] Iranian words are also found in Elamite, Akkadian and Greek, but one may venture the opinion that in the Aramaic letters sent by Arsham, and in the letters and decrees preserved in Ezra, and to a lesser degree, in the judicial documents from Elephantine, the Iranian words are more fully assimilated.

These texts also use various idiomatic phrases in which the Iranian word is combined with Aramaic '*bd* "to make, do, perform", which served as a substitute for Iranian *kardan* e.g. *ptgm gst yt'bd* "punishment will be meted out", *hndrz 'bd* "to instruct". Iranian legal terms replace Aramaic ones: e.g. *hnbg whngyt* for *hbr* or *šwtp* "partner"; *'drng* for *'rb* "guarantor". An OP phrase *dadāyam a(h)yāy* "I gave to her" = *yhbt lh* may stand behind the enigmatic *d/rd/rymyy*.[4] This would record a declaration in court before the commander of the garrison of Syene. An Aramaeo-Iranian blend such as *'zt šbq*[5] "to set free, release, manumit" remains in use as an ideogram in Pahlavi and is attested in the *Mādigān ī hazār dādestān*.[6] Scribal familiarity with the writing of Iranian names, words and phrases was an important step before the use of Aramaic script for various Middle Persian dialects. The following

---

[1] Cf. most recently I. M. Diakonoff, "The origin of the 'Old Persian' writing system", in M. Boyce and I. Gershevitch (eds), *W. B. Henning Memorial Volume* (London, 1970), 123, n. 67.

[2] M. N. Bogolyubov, "An Old Iranian Prayer to Ahuramazda in Aramaic Characters, etc." (in Russian) in *Istoria iranskovo gosudarstva i kultury* (Moscow, 1971), 277–85.

[3] Most of these are treated by W. Hinz, *Altiranisches Sprachgut der Nebenüberlieferungen* (Wiesbaden, 1975).

[4] Kraeling, *Brooklyn Papyri*, 9.3; cf. Bogolyubov, *op. cit.*, 283–4. Cf. too the use of *rmy* in Driver, *Aramaic Documents*, VI.3, in all likelihood an Old Persian word.

[5] Kraeling, *Brooklyn Papyri*, 5.4.

[6] This writer has dealt with this and other terms from the point of view of source and continuity in "On some Iranian Terms in the Elephantine Papyri", *AAntASH* (Festschrift J. Harmatta) xxv (1977), 113–18: cf. too "Iranian or Semitic?".

partial list of words may be instructive:[1] in the field of administration the titles of the following officials may be noted: *hadabāra* "companion", *ganzabara* "treasurer", *ahšadrapāna* "satrap", *dātabara* "law officer, judge", *hamārakara* "accountant", *patikarakara* "sculptor" and *waršabara* "forester", etc.; and concepts, both abstract and concrete, such as: *dāta* "law", *rāza* "secret", *zyāni* "damage, loss", *yauza* "revolt", *handarz* "instruction", *patigāma* "message, word", *ništāwan* "written order", *patšegna* "copy", *raušyā* "corporal punishment", *ganzā* "treasury", and *nidānā* "storehouse", etc.

In the realm of realia, the documents present diversity: *karbaltā* "headdress", *sarbalā* "trousers", *hamnikā* "belt" (or *manyākā* "necklace"), *'ušarnā* "furnishings", *patpā* "ration", *zarnikā* "arsenic", and a host of words dealing with ship-building.[2] These lists can be easily supplemented from the documents at hand from other sources. It may be said, after examining all the sources available, that the chief area of the loans is in the administrative and judicial sphere and that the realia represented were new items introduced during the Persian period.

The poorly preserved inscription in Aramaic script on the grave of Darius I at Naqš-i Rustam is in Iranian (late Old Persian/early Middle Persian) and has been dated to the 3rd century B.C. on the basis of the occurrence of the name *slwk* (Seleucus) therein.[3] Palaeographic analysis of the inscription based admittedly on the hand copy and the poor photograph supplied by the publisher supports this date. The title *hšyty wzrk = xšāyathya wazrka* and the name (')*rthšs* = Artaxerxes is detectable in l. 20. It has been suggested that this inscription may have been written by a ruler of Persis under Seleucid suzerainty to commemorate his predecessors.[4] This inscription, and the Iranian part of the above-mentioned Arabsun inscription, are atypical unless it is assumed that Old Persian written in Aramaic script on papyrus, leather, wood, etc. was widespread. The normal mode of writing which developed from the use of Aramaic writing in the Achaemenian period throughout the successor states – Parthia, Choresmia, Sogdiana, and which became standardized in Pahlavi, was rather the conjoint use of Aramaic

---

[1] Greenfield, "Iranian vocabulary in early Aramaic", *Commemoration Cyrus, Hommage Universel* II (Acta Iranica 2, 1974), 245–6. See G. Widengren, "The Persians", in D. J. Wiseman (ed.), *Peoples of Old Testament Times* (Oxford, 1973), 352–6 for a list of Iranian words appearing in Aramaic (and Hebrew) in the Bible, in the papyri and in Kandahar I.

[2] Cowley, *Aramaic Papyri*, 26.

[3] E. Herzfeld, *Altpersische Inschriften* (Berlin, 1938), p. 12 and pl. IV. Cf. Henning, "Mitteliranisch", 24–25. I owe the palaeographic dating of this and the Arabsun inscription to J. Naveh.

[4] R. N. Frye, *The Heritage of Persia* (London, 1961), 204–5.

ideograms (with phonetic complements) and Iranian words. These Aramaic ideograms are found both in inscriptions and in literary works. For the Aramaist the words used ideographically in these texts and those preserved in the *Frahang-i Pahlavīk* are an important source of information for the vocabulary of Official Aramaic. Items such as '*wl*' "first" (*Frahang-i Pahlavīk*) and *ḥty'/ḥty*' "arrow" (*Frahang-i Pahlavīk*; Ḥājjiābād in Parthian/Pahlavi) are examples of words which are otherwise rarely attested in Aramaic. The orthography of Aramaic words is more archaic in Parthian than in Pahlavi: *ŠBQ/ŠBK, ḥty'/ḥty'*. The orthography of the Aramaic words which serve as ideograms in the Middle Persian dialects is that of Official Aramaic, already archaic at that time; thus '*RQ*' rather than '*R*'' "land", *Q'N*' rather than '*N*' "sheep"; *ZY* "which", *ZNH* "this" rather than *DY, DNH*; *ZHB* "gold" rather than *DHB*; so too, *ŠHDYN* "witnesses" rather than later *SHDYN*. The morphology is that of Official Aramaic -*yn*(= *īn*), -*y'*(*ayyā*) for the absolute and determined masc. plural, rather than later *ē*, and the vocabulary like that of Official Aramaic is essentially that of eastern Aramaic. Some Iranian words that entered Official Aramaic, e.g. '*zd, rmk*' are also listed in the *Frahang-i Pahlavīk*. The Aramaic words describing various types of documents: *gṭ*' "document", *spr*' "document, book", *ṭyn*' "clay document (ostracon?)", and *mglt*' "scroll" were maintained in the ideograms of Middle Persian.[1]

---

[1] The ideograms found in the inscriptions are handily available in P. Gignoux, *Glossaire des inscriptions pehlevies et parthes* (London, 1972) (*CIIr.* Supplementary Series 1). A new edition of the *Frahang-i Pahlavīk* on the basis of H. S. Nyberg's *Nachlass* has been prepared by B. Utas and C. Toll.

CHAPTER 16

OLD IRANIAN CALENDARS

PART I. ELEMENTS OF THE CALENDAR. DEFINITIONS

I. 1. The number of calendars in use among the many civilizations of our globe, past and present, is legion. However, notwithstanding their diversity they all have, or at one time had, two main elements in common: a lunar serving to define smaller, not strictly equal, units of time, and a solar measuring the "year", i.e., the cyclical recurrence of the seasons. Evidently, the latter alone is of importance to agriculture and thus meets the practical needs of a higher stage of civilization, while the former, being of little practical value, could in theory have been dispensed with as soon as a sedentary community had found means and ways to establish a primitive solar calendar. But in practice, such a radical break with tradition occurred only in exceptional cases.

In point of fact, of all calendars known in history there are only four that were – or at least were intended to be – oriented by the Sun alone: the Egyptian, the Achaemenian Later Avestan, the Julian-Gregorian and that developed by the central-American Mayas and later adopted by the neighbouring Aztecs. But even in the Egyptian and in the Julian calendars, as still in our modern Gregorian, the lunar element is not suppressed completely. As is well-known, it plays a decisive role in the determination of Easter, which fact bears witness to the importance of the religious element even in the most recent phase of a multi-millenary evolution. For at all times and places we find that calendar and religion form an inseparable unity.

The periodically changing aspect of the Moon, its "phases", comprising approximately 30 days, must needs have attracted man's attention since the remotest times, numberless millennia before the dawn of history. These lunar phases, it will be well to note, are the most striking cyclical astronomical phenomenon that lends itself to direct observation, being at the same time independent of the place occupied by the observer. Hence, evidently, the Moon was always considered the time indicator *par excellence*. It maintained this place of honour even after practical reasons had caused the early settlers to look for means to determine significant dates of the solar year that would indicate the times for sowing and harvesting as well as other term-days of importance to agriculture or to other needs of the community.

I. 2. In this context I deliberately avoid speaking of the "determination of the length of the year" or of the "length of the month", because it is certain that the habit of counting days so as to establish an algebraic relation between the month and the year belongs to a relatively late stage of evolution. For the following demonstrations, however, it will be useful to start with a few numerical data.

The motion of the two great luminaries is irregular. The actual length of the lunar month ("lunation") varies from one revolution to the other, and the same, though in a lesser degree, is true of the length of the year. What is essential to all astronomical, in particular calendrical, considerations, is the determination of the *mean* duration of the periods concerned.

The modern value for the mean length of the lunation is 29.53059 days. It was known with nearly the same accuracy already in Babylonian times (middle of 1st millennium B.C.). As for the year, the matter is more complicated since we have to distinguish between two alternatives. The *sidereal* year, defined as the lapse of time between two consecutive conjunctions of the Sun with an appropriately chosen fixed star, say Regulus (α Leonis), has a length of 365.25636 days, while the *tropical* year, measuring the time between consecutive conjunctions with the *vernal point* (intersecting point of ecliptic and equator) is slightly shorter: 365.24220 days.

It is true, the difference between the two, resulting from the *precession of the equinoxes*, is too small to make itself felt in the course of only a few generations, but it becomes perceptible over longer periods of time. To give an example, it amounted to *c.* 50 days from the time of the early settlers of Susa and Persepolis (*c.* 4000 B.C.) to the accession of the Achaemenian rulers. This implies that a sidereal phenomenon (e.g. the heliacal rising of a certain star near the ecliptic) occurring in 4000 B.C. at spring equinox (21 March according to the Gregorian Calendar)[1] will take place in Achaemenian time on or about 10 May.

[1] In Parts I–III (pp. 714–756) of the present study, all dates will be expressed in terms of the Gregorian Calendar (recomputed) because only this permits us to recognize directly the season, i.e. the tropical date at which an astronomical phenomenon occurs. In Part IV (pp. 756–781), unless indicated expressly, Julian dates will be given. [A succinct and more technical presentation of the essence of this chapter was given by Willy Hartner in his article "The Young Avestan and

OLD IRANIAN CALENDARS

RISING AND SETTING AZIMUTHS OF THE SUN

I. 3. From observations made at one and the same place of the Earth and stretching over lengthy periods of time, the regular recurrence of various astronomical phenomena can easily be recognized. Thus it will soon become evident that the Sun's rising and setting points ("azimuths", i.e. angular distances from the East and West points of the horizon)[1] vary with the seasons. At spring equinox the Sun rises at the East point of the horizon and sets at its West point. Subsequently, these points gradually recede from E and W respectively, in a northerly direction until, about the time of summer solstice, they reach a maximum distance and come to a standstill. Thereafter, they proceed in the opposite direction. Their second passing through E and W marks autumn equinox. At winter solstice they reach a maximum southern distance and have a second standstill. After this they again change direction until they occupy anew the E and W points, whereafter the phenomena described recur in the same sequence.

In this way, theoretically, the solar year as a whole as well as any particular solar date of interest (such as the time of sowing or harvesting) can be determined by marking down appropriate rising and setting points of the Sun along the horizon, without recourse to other kinds of astronomical observations. In practice, however, this "azimuth method" is encountered only in exceptional cases,[2] for the obvious

---

Babylonian Calendars and the Antecedents of Precession", *Journal for the History of Astronomy* x (1979), pp. 1–22, written after and partly arising from his contribution to the present volume. It is not Hartner but the present Editor who, after the article had appeared, replaced throughout the chapter the phrase "Young Avestan calendar", commonly used also by Hartner's predecessors, with "Later Avestan calendar". This was done to guard against possible source confusion arising in the minds of readers from the fact that not only the Avestan evidence on the "Young Avestan calendar", but also the Avestan evidence on the "Old Avestan calendar" is found exclusively in texts written in what is termed the "Younger Avestan" language for the purpose of distinguishing it from the "Gāthic Avestan" language; in the latter, believed by some scholars (wrongly, in the Editor's opinion) to be "older" than the "Younger Avestan" language (which of course is why the "Younger" has come to be so termed), no calendrical information whatever has come down to us. The use of "Old" and "Later" in the present discussion of the Avestan calendars thus safely steers clear of the linguistic distinction between "Gāthic" and "Younger". Concurrently, Avestan (both Gāthic and Younger) being one of the only two Old Iranian languages in which texts have survived, the Editor thought it proper, wherever in this chapter Hartner used the phrase "Old-Iranian calendar", to replace it with "Old Persian calendar", since that is a calendar exclusively attested in Old Persian sources (including the ones written in Elamite language, on which see above). Ed.]

[1] In antiquity the azimuths were counted from E and W towards N and S, in modern astronomy they are counted from S over E or W, respectively, to N.

[2] Thus in high northern latitudes, where the rising and setting points cover large parts of the horizon, while for Persepolis the variation amounts only to $c.$ 56° (28° north and south of the E and W points).

reason that the daily variation of the azimuth – even in the neighbourhood of the E and W points, where it is fastest – is much too small to ascertain reliable results.

STAR PHASES: HELIACAL RISINGS AND SETTINGS, ACRONYCHAL RISINGS AND COSMICAL SETTINGS

I. 4. The method actually used in antiquity is based on an entirely different principle, which may be described as follows.[1] In the course of a year the Sun travels along a circle inclined to the equator through the constellations of the ecliptic. Now, for obvious reasons, its *conjunction* with the stars it passes by cannot be observed directly. What is observable, however, is the first rising before sunrise of a star with which the Sun has been in conjunction shortly before. This phenomenon, called the star's *heliacal rising*, is a very striking one. On a certain day of the year, after a period of invisibility whose duration depends mainly on its distance from the ecliptic, the star reappears for the first time: at morning-dawn, it rises over the horizon, remains visible for a very short time, and then disappears again in the rays of the rising Sun. During the subsequent days and weeks, due to its increasing distance from the Sun, the period of its visibility before sunrise will steadily increase. After a certain time, the star culminates at dawn. Thereafter it will be found nearer and nearer the western horizon until one day it sets at sunrise. This *true cosmical setting*, evidently, is not observable. We have to wait another couple of weeks until the star's setting becomes visible before sunrise (*apparent cosmical setting*).

The corresponding phenomena, referring to sunset and evening-twilight, are analogous. On a certain day, the star has its last visible rising after sunset (*apparent acronychal rising*). The *true acronychal rising*, occurring a number of days later, is not observable. The next phenomenon of importance is the star's culmination at twilight. Thereafter the distance between the star and the Sun decreases until one day the star has its last visible setting at twilight (*heliacal setting*); it marks the beginning of the period of invisibility, which ends with the new heliacal rising.

Thus the following six phenomena are suited to fix solar dates during the course of the year:

[1] For further details, see W. Hartner, "The Earliest History of the Constellations in the Near East and the Motif of the Lion–Bull Combat", *JNES* XXIV (1965), pp. 1–16, reprinted in W. Hartner, *Oriens–Occidens* (Hildesheim, 1968), pp. 227–59; see in particular pp. 5ff. of *JNES* (231 ff. of *Oriens–Occidens*).

OLD IRANIAN CALENDARS

the heliacal rising of a star, i.e. its first visible rising at dawn;
the star's culmination at dawn;
the cosmical[1] setting of a star, i.e. its first visible setting at dawn;
the acronychal[1] rising of a star, i.e. its last visible rising at twilight;
the star's culmination at twilight;
the heliacal setting of a star, i.e. its last visible setting at twilight.

I. 5. A few historical examples will illustrate the wide diffusion of this method:

a. Hesiod's *Works and Days* (vv. 383–4):

Πληιάδων 'Ατλαγενέων ἐπιτελλομενάων
ἄρχεσθ' ἀμήτου, ἀρότοιο δὲ δυσομενάων.

When the Pleiades, Atlas' daughters, rise,
begin your harvest, and (begin to) plough when they set.

Here ἐπιτέλλεσθαι refers to the heliacal rising (c. 15 May at Hesiod's time), and δύεσθαι to the cosmical setting (10 November).

b. The Greek Calendar (παράπηγμα) attributed to Geminos (1st century B.C.), but dating actually from c. 200 B.C.,[2] divides the year schematically into twelve months of approximately equal length, starting at summer solstice. There we read that on the 1st day of the tenth month (21 March), the Band of the Fishes (Pisces) rises heliacally; it is followed by Aries on the 3rd. On the 10th the Pleiades set heliacally, whereupon they remain invisible for 40 days. On the 21st the heliacal setting of the Hyades (the Bull's Head) is listed. On the 11th day of the eleventh month Scorpius starts setting heliacally; on the 13th occurs the reappearance (heliacal rising) of the Pleiades, etc.

A similar calendar was composed by Ptolemy;[3] it operates with the same constellations.

c. The Arabic–Latin Cordova Calendar[4] is based on the same principle, preference being given to the heliacal settings (*anwāʿ*) of the 28 lunar

---

[1] Since only the apparent, not the true, phenomena are observable, the epithet "apparent" in the case of cosmical settings and acronychal risings is dropped here; the word "heliacal" always indicates the apparent phenomenon.

[2] See Geminus, *Elementa Astronomiae*, ed. K. Manitius (Leipzig, 1898), pp. 210–33.

[3] Φάσεις ἀπλανῶν ἀστέρων, in *C. Ptolemaei Opera Omnia* II: *Opera Astronomica Minora*, ed. J. L. Heiberg (Leipzig, 1907), pp. 1–67.

[4] See *Le calendrier de Cordoue de l'année 961*, ed. R. Dozy (Leiden, 1873); new edition with French translation by Ch. Pellat (Leiden, 1961).

mansions. As noted by R. B. Serjeant the method is still in use among the fishermen in Baḥrain.[1]

d. The first Babylonian tablet of ᵐᵘˡAPIN[2] is a perfect analogon to the Greek calendars. As in Geminos' *Parapegma*, the year is divided into 12 approximately equal parts ("solar months"), its first day (I 1), for the probable time of composition (1300–1000 B.C.), falling on a date near the vernal equinox. The tablet lists the heliacal risings (other phenomena are not mentioned) of 36 stars, as illustrated in the following:[3]

I 1 (21 March),	LU.HUN.GA ("the hired labourer") = Aries	
I 20 (9 April),	GAM = Capella	
II 1 (20 April),	MUL.MUL = Pleiades	
II 20 (9 May),	*iš li-e* ("the Bull's Jaw") = Taurus (Aldebaran and Hyades)	
III 10 (29 May),	SIBA.ZI.AN.NA = Orion, and MAŠ.TAB.BA.GAL.GAL = Gemini (Castor and Pollux)	
IV 5 (24 June),	MAŠ.TAB.BA.TUR.TUR = ι, ν Gem., and AL.LUL = Prokyon	
IV 15 (4 July),	KAK.SI.DI = Sirius, MUŠ = Hydra, and UR.GU.LA = Leo	
V 5 (24 July),	BAN = "The Bow" (ξ, k Puppis, η, χ, ϵ, σ, δ, τ Can. maj.), and LUGAL (*šarru*) = Regulus	
: : : : :		
VIII 5 (23 Oct.),	GIR.TAB = Scorpius	
VIII 15 (2 Nov.),	UZA = Lyra, and GAB.GIR.TAB = a Scorpii (Antares)	
: : : : :		
XI 5 (23 Jan.),	GU.LA = Aquarius, IKU = "Pegasus Rectangle", and LU.LIM = Cassiopeia	
XI 25 (13 Febr.),	Anunītu = north-eastern part of Pisces	
XII 15 (5 March),	KU₆ = Piscis austrinus, and ŠU.GI = Perseus	

In Egypt, the same principle is prevalent in the so-called "diagonal calendars" based on the 36 "decans", i.e. constellations near the ecliptic, whose successive heliacal risings mark the beginnings of the 36 ten-day periods of the year.[4] The analogy to the ᵐᵘˡAPIN tablet,

[1] "Fisher-Folk and Fish-Traps in al-Baḥrain", *BSOAS* XXXI (1968), pp. 486–514.
[2] Cf. B. L. van der Waerden, "Babylonian Astronomy II. The Thirty-Six Stars", *JNES* VIII (1949), pp. 6–26; see p. 20, Table 3, and W. Hartner, "The Earliest History", pp. 5ff.
[3] Cf. B. L. van der Waerden, *Anfänge der Astronomie* (Groningen, [1966]), pp. 70ff., and Hartner, "The Earliest History", p. 7. [4] Cf. B. L. van der Waerden, pp. 17ff.

which operates equally with 36 stars or constellations, is striking, but our scanty knowledge of Egyptian constellations does not permit us to decide whether or not this similarity is accidental.

Also in China the system of annual risings, settings and culminations was widely used, as attested by early calendars such as the *Hsia hsiao-chêng* contained in the *Li-chi* ("Book of Rites") or the *Yüeh-ling* forming the basis of the first twelve chapters of the *Lü-shih ch'un-ch'iu* ("Master Lü's Spring and Autumn Annals").[1]

PART II. THE CALENDAR IN PREHISTORIC IRAN AND MESOPOTAMIA

II. 1. On the basis of the above indications it is possible to form a fairly clear idea of the essential features of the prehistoric Iranian calendar. Since the earliest settlers, as soon as they had reached the stage of developed agricultural activity about or before 4000 B.C., needed a calendar indicating solar dates, they must of necessity have taken recourse to the very same principle which we find prevalent, 2,000 years later, at the dawn of history. This *a priori* statement is fully confirmed by an overwhelming number of pictorial representations of constellations whose calendrical significance is beyond doubt.

A glance at diagram 1,[2] showing the celestial sphere as it presented itself to man's eye about 4000 B.C.,[3] will teach us which of the constellations forming the later "zodiac" can be expected to have served as "calendar asterisms". About the pole, situated at that time in a starless region, four concentric circles are drawn. The innermost comprises the circumpolar stars for a northern latitude of 30° (Persepolis and, approximately, Susa and Ur). Then follow the northern tropic, the equator and the southern tropic; the outermost circle, again for the latitude mentioned, indicates the limit of visibility near the south point of the horizon. The brilliant star Canopus which, due to the precession of the equinoxes, in the course of the ensuing millennia rose higher and

---

[1] See J. Needham, *Science and Civilisation in China* III (Cambridge, 1959), pp. 194f., and W. Hartner, "Die astronomischen Angaben des Hia Siau Dscheng", in R. Wilhelm, *Li Gi, Das Buch der Sitte* (Jena, 1930), pp. 413ff.

[2] After Hartner, "The Earliest History"; for further information I refer the reader to this article.

[3] On two occasions encircled asterisks and the words "η Tauri -500" and "Regulus -500" are found (near AR = 20° and 117° respectively). They indicate the positions of the named stars about the time of the conquest of Egypt by Cambyses (525 B.C.) and of Darius the Great, under whose reign the Later Avestan calendar was adopted by the Iranians.

THE PREHISTORIC CALENDAR

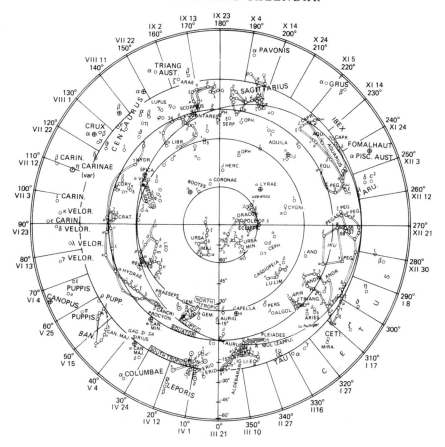

Diagram 1. The celestial sphere at 4000 B.C. (Akkadian star names italicized).

higher above the horizon, was at the limit of observability at that remote time.

The path of the Sun, the ecliptic, is the oblique circle which cuts the equator at two diametrically opposite points, at right ascensions (AR)[1] 0° and 180° and touches the tropics at AR 90° and 270° respectively. At vernal equinox the Sun occupies the vernal point (AR = 0°); at

[1] The right ascensions are angles measured on the equator in the direction of the signs of the zodiac (clockwise in our diagrams), starting from the vernal point, where the Sun passes from southern to northern declinations. They may be expressed either in degrees or in hours ($1^h = 15°$). In the diagrams they are marked in degrees at the outer rim, together with the corresponding dates of the Gregorian calendar. In the course of $23^h 56^m$ the celestial vault makes one complete revolution (counter-clockwise in the diagram, clockwise in reality) about the pole.

summer solstice its AR is 90°, at autumn equinox it is 180°, and at winter solstice 270°.

Looking now at the constellations near the four cardinal points of the ecliptic, we see that Taurus, with the bright star Aldebaran, precedes the vernal point by $c.$ 10–20°; equally Leo, with the "royal star" Regulus (Akkad. *šarru*), precedes the point of summer solstice by $c.$ 15°, and Scorpius, with Antares, the autumnal point by the same amount. The region preceding the point of winter solstice is less rich in brilliant stars. It is occupied at a distance of $c.$ 20° by our modern constellation Aquarius. At 270° we find the western, at 300° the eastern part of the Fishes (Pisces), linked together with a band, and between them the "Pegasus Rectangle". All three of them have a very long history, as will be shown in what follows. Of non-zodiacal constellations I mention first and foremost Cassiopeia (Sum. *lu-lim*, the Stag), found between the pole and the eastern Fish. Its original significance, Stag or Deer, is preserved in the Sphaera barbarica (e.g. in Abū Ma'shar), while in Greek astrothesy the constellation was renamed after the Ethiopian queen, Cassiopeia, the mother of the unfortunate Andromeda. As will be seen, the Stag played an important role in early calendariography.

II. 2. In diagram 2, the four ovals mark the four cardinal situations of the horizon of Persepolis with respect to the starred heavens:

(1) (right; unbroken line). The Sun stands at the vernal point, $c.$ 20° below the horizon. As is seen, the Pleiades, forming the cusp of the Bull's western horn,[1] have their heliacal rising, i.e. reappear for the first time after a period of 40 days' invisibility; the "Horns of the Ibex" (anterior part of Aquarius)[2] culminate, and Scorpius, standing near the western horizon, has its cosmical setting. The situation is further clarified in diagram 3, which shows only the horizon at spring equinox.

(2) (lower; strokes and dots). The Sun stands at the point of summer solstice. Heliacal rising of the Royal Star, Regulus (α Leonis) and cosmical setting of the Horns of the Ibex.

(3) (left; long strokes). The Sun stands at the autumnal point. Heliacal rising of Scorpius, culmination of Leo, and cosmical setting of Taurus and Orion.

---

[1] Early astrothesy consistently represents the celestial bull's horns not straight, as assumed contrary to the rules of zoology by Ptolemy, but curved; cf. Hartner, "The Earliest History", pp. 7f.   [2] See below, fig. 10, p. 730.

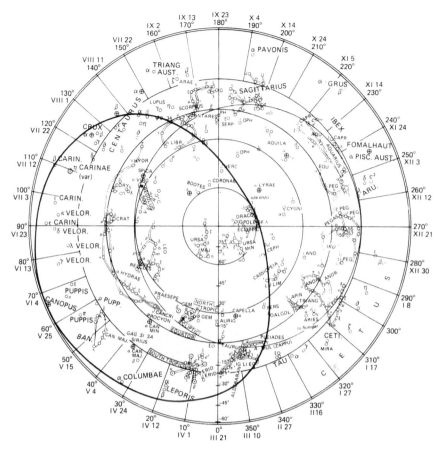

Diagram 2. The horizon of Persepolis, shewing the culmination of Leo.

(4) (upper; short strokes). The Sun stands at winter solstice. Heliacal rising of the first star of IKU, the Pegasus Square (β Pegasi); Sagittarius near culmination; cosmical setting of the hind-part of Leo.

In this list, only heliacal risings and culminations and cosmical settings are taken into consideration. It would be much longer and include other constellations, such as the Plough (APIN) and the Hired Labourer (LU.HUN.GA), the Twins (MAŠ.TAB.BA), the Snake-bearer (Ophiuchus) north of Scorpius and Sagittarius, etc., if we extended it to heliacal settings and acronychal risings and culminations.

Thus about 4000 B.C. the Sun's entering the four cardinal points of

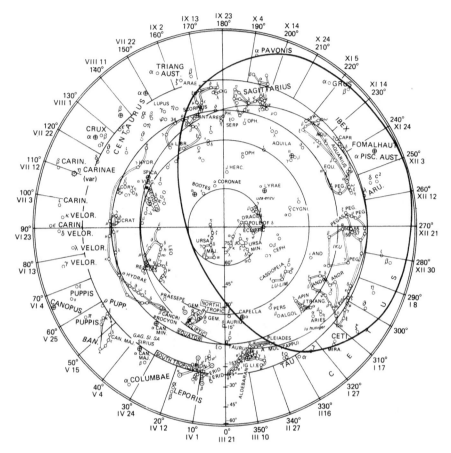

Diagram 3. The Persepolis horizon at the spring equinox.

the year coincided with the heliacal risings of the Pleiades and Taurus on 21 March, Leo (Regulus) on 23 June, Scorpius on 21 September, and the Pegasus Rectangle, IKU, on 21 December. Comparing these dates with the corresponding ones found in the ᵐᵘˡAPIN tablet (Pleiades on 20 April, Regulus on 24 July, Scorpius on 23 October, and IKU on 23 January), we find that they all lie *c.* one month earlier. Evidently, this is due to the effect of the precession of the equinoxes, which causes a change of roughly one month in 2,200 years.

II. 3. Now these theoretical considerations will be of interest only if the constellations mentioned can be proved to have been known to the early settlers, in other words, if it is possible to establish an unbroken astrothetical tradition by which Iranian and Mesopotamian prehistory is linked together with the system characterizing the historical period. As it happens, hundreds of iconographies found on seals and vases from all over Iran and Mesopotamia demonstrate that such a continuity actually existed. Archaeologists seem so far to have overlooked their astronomical significance in spite of the fact that some typical features observable time and again should have excluded any attempt at a realistic, i.e., terrestrial, interpretation. Among these I mention the following:

a. The constantly recurring combination of two or more "calendrical" animals and symbols (stars, "IKU") in one and the same picture. Here I point out first and foremost the Lion-and-Bull Combat and its variant, the Lion-and-Deer Combat, which I have shown[1] to be interchangeable symbols denoting, in the fourth millennium, the beginning of agricultural activity after winter solstice, about 10 February: while Leo culminates at twilight (see diagram 2), the Bull (Taurus and Pleiades) and the Deer (*lu-lim*, Cassiopeia) simultaneously have their heliacal setting. Thereafter the Bull will remain invisible for a period of 40 days, after which its reappearance (heliacal rising) will mark the time of vernal equinox (see diagrams 2 and 3).

b. The fact that at least in some cases the animals in question are unambiguously represented as constellations (thus by marking stars on their bodies or stressing particular characteristics of the corresponding asterisms).

c. The manner of depicting in the same size animals that in reality differ enormously in size, such as scorpions compared with lions, bulls or ibexes.

d. Calendrical animals represented in characteristic attitudes deviating from the normal, above all upside-down, so as to symbolize their heliacal or cosmical settings, etc.

Some examples will serve to illustrate this.

[1] Hartner, "The Earliest History", pp. 15f.

Fig. 1. Prehistoric Elamite seal.[1] One of the earliest representations of the Lion–Bull combat; 4th millennium B.C. Note that only the Bull's forepart is represented.

Fig. 2. Prehistoric Elamite seal.[2] The celestial Lion with twenty-odd star dots on its body. In Ptolemy's star catalogue, 23 stars from the first to the fifth magnitude are listed, plus 4 of the sixth, which are at the limit of visibility. Approximately the same number of stars are represented on the Horoscope of Antiochus of Commagene (see next figure).

Fig. 3. Coronation horoscope of King Antiochus of Commagene, 62 B.C.[3] Note that the star symbol found on the shoulder of lions in Ancient Near and Middle Eastern (Sumerian, Babylonian, Ras Shamra) and Egyptian art down to the lions on Sasanian silver objects evidently indicates the "celestial" lion.

[1] M. Pézard, "Étude sur les intailles susiennes", *MDP* XII (1911), 98, fig. 70.
[2] M. Pézard, "Complément à l'étude sur les intailles susiennes", *MDP* XII, pl. IV, no. 172.
[3] K. Humann and O. Puchstein, *Denkmäler des Nemrud Dagh* (Berlin, 1890), pl. XXVI.

THE PREHISTORIC CALENDAR

Fig. 4. Prehistoric Elamite seal.[1] Bull with body "cut off" by a saddle-like object. Of the celestial bull only the forepart is visible, whence it is often represented as either a bull's head or a protome (thus according to Ptolemy's catalogue). Cf. Fig. 1.

Figs 5 and 6. Prehistoric Elamite seals.[2] The Bull with a grotesquely exaggerated eye and (Fig. 5) a beard. The eye symbolizes the brilliant star Aldebaran. The terrestrial species bovidae is beardless; only the celestial Bull has a beard, formed by the stars $\lambda, \epsilon, \tau, o, \xi, \sigma, \phi$ Tauri.

[1] Fig. 5: L. Legrain, "Empreintes de cachets élamites", *MDP* XVI (1921), pl. X, no. 161; fig. 6: *ibidem*, pl. VI, no. 96.

[2] *Ibidem*, pl. VI, no. 98.

Fig. 7. Prehistoric vase from Tell Halaf.[1] The shoulder of the vase is decorated with bulls, the neck and the body with stylized bulls' heads against the starry heaven.

Fig. 8. Prehistoric Elamite seal.[2] Bull and Scorpion (the latter represented c. half the size of the former). The celestial cowherd is spurring the bull with a goad.

[1] Max Frh.v.Oppenheim, *Tell Halaf* I, *Die prähistorischen Funde*, ed. H. Schmidt (Berlin, 1943) frontispiece, fig. 2.

[2] M. Pézard, "Étude sur les intailles susiennes", *MDP* XII, p. 112, no. 107.

Fig. 9. Babylonian *kudurru*.[1] The Scorpion together with the Sun, the Moon, and Venus.

[1] *MDP* I (1900), pl. XIV.

Fig. 10. Prehistoric vases from Tepe Hiṣār.[1] The Ibex with a solar symbol in its horns, indicating the approaching time of winter solstice. The constellation of the Ibex, comprising at the earliest stage of civilization our constellations Capricorn (the later Babylonian "Goat-Fish", *suḫur-maš*) and Aquarius (Bab. GU-LA),[2] actually indicated by the heliacal rising of its horn the time immediately preceding winter solstice, while the very day of solstice, in theory, coincided with the heliacal rising of IKU and the western part of the Fishes. In practice, an exact determination of the day of solstice was impossible at that remote time. Therefore we are on safe ground if we assume that the Ibex and IKU together were considered the calendar asterisms foreboding the shortest days of the year. This explains why IKU, on a great many occasions (Susa, Persepolis), simply is substituted for the solar symbol in the horns of the constellation Ibex (see next two figures).

[1] E. F. Schmidt, "Tepe Hissar Excavations 1931", *The Museum Journal* XXIII (Philadelphia, 1933), pl. LXXXVII.
[2] See my reconstruction, Diagrams 1–4.

Figs 11 and 12. Prehistoric goblets from Susa I.¹ The Ibex with IKU in its horns. IKU, in Babylonian most frequently called 1-IKU, the "acre", or "unity of land", is the celestial "cultivated field" (our Pegasus Rectangle, see above, p. 724), represented as either circular (Susa) or lozenge-shaped (Persepolis, Tall-i-Bakun) and filled with various patterns (checker-board, stylized plants, etc.). Under the belly of one of the animals, the "sacred mountain" (cf. also fig. 10) symbolizing the Earth's eastern and western horizon, above which rise and below which set the celestial constellations.

¹ *MDP* XIII (1912), pl. IV, nos 1 & 2.

Fig. 13. Prehistoric vase from Tepe 'Alīābād.[1] Realistic representation of the heliacal rising of the Ibex: the celestial animal flanked by plants (the "sacred tree"); the rising Sun four times repeated.

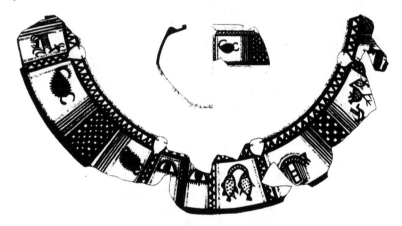

Fig. 14. Prehistoric vase from Jemdet Nasr.[2] From left to right the Goat (Sum. *uza*, α Lyrae) (?), the Scorpion, IKU, again the Scorpion, unidentifiable object (twice), the Fishes (Anunītu and ŠIM-MAḪ) linked together with a band (*rikis nūnu*),[3] the "Gates of the Heavens", often indicating, as the Sacred Mountain or Tree, heliacal risings or settings, etc.

[1] Gautier and Lampre, "Fouilles de Moussian", *MDP* VIII (1905), fig. 266, p. 136.
[2] Fig. 14: H. Field and R. A. Martin, "Painted Pottery from Jemdet Nasr", *AJA* XXXIX (1935), pl. XXXI; fig. 15: V. Christian, *Altertumskunde des Zweistromlandes* I, pl. 100, fig. 8.
[3] See P. Felix Gössmann, "Planetarium Babylonicum", in P. Anton Deimel (ed.), *Sumerisches Lexikon* IV. 2 (Rome, 1950), p. 35, no. 107: ^{mul}DUR nu-nu.

Fig. 15. Jemdet Nasr.[1] The Fishes linked with a band.

Fig. 16. Babylonian seal.[2] Lion over the Sacred Tree, Bull and Scorpion; above, Plough (APIN).

Fig. 17. Cylinder seal, late pre-dynastic period.[3] Lunar symbols (crescents). On bottom of cylinder, bull's head with a large eye and scorpion.

---

[1] Fig. 14: H. Field and R. A. Martin, "Painted Pottery from Jemdet Nasr", *AJA* xxxix (1935), pl. xxxi; fig. 15: V. Christian, *Altertumskunde des Zweistromlandes* I, pl. 100, fig. 8.

[2] L. Legrain, "The Culture of the Babylonians from their Seals in the Collection of the Museum", University of Pennsylvania, The University Museum, *Publications of the Babylonian Section* xiv (Philadelphia, 1925), pl. iv, no. 51.

[3] P. Amiet, *La glyptique mésopotamienne archaïque* (Paris, 1961), pl. 51, no. 706.

Figs 18 and 19. Prehistoric seals from Tepe Giyan.[1] Two representations of the snake-bearing deity (note the star symbols), the prototype of the constellation Ophiuchus (Serpentarius).

[1] *Ibidem*, pl. 7, figs 149, 150.

THE PREHISTORIC CALENDAR

Fig. 20. Transition from pre-dynastic to archaic dynastic period. Two ibexes, one (left) with scorpion turned downwards in its horns, the other (right) with solar symbol in, and scorpion below, the horns (cf. next figure). Above, in centre, the bull's head, a snake and a four-petalled flower. On top, skulls of horned animals. Probable meaning: Taurus culminating, Hydra rising heliacally, Ibex setting cosmically, Scorpius in lower culmination. Solar date (3000 B.C.) end of July.[1]

Fig. 21. Prehistoric. The horns of the setting Ibex encircle the sacred tree (or mountain). Under them, exactly as in the preceding figure, the Scorpion. At the centre, a four-pointed star (cf. the four-petalled flower in fig. 20) depicted in the same manner as Venus on the kudurrus (see fig. 9). To the left, a five-fold cross symbolizing probably IKU. Same solar date as fig. 20.[2]

[1] *Ibidem*, pl. 51, no. 707. [2] *MDP* xxix (1943), p. 30, no. 1.

Fig. 22. Achaemenian wall sculpture at Persepolis, c. 500 B.C. One of the many colossal reliefs from the time of Darius the Great (519–486) and Xerxes (486–465) representing the Lion–Bull combat.

II. 4. While the astronomical significance of the animals and symbols occurring here is beyond dispute, it is not of course possible to establish a clear calendrical meaning in all the hundreds of examples encountered. Often it seems that no such was intended. Evidently there are many seals that originated from the artist's playing freely with the traditional symbols, and others in which the symbols were used only as owner's marks or for other unknown purposes. But in a great many cases the artist's intention to represent symbolically a well-defined solar date is unmistakable. Among these, contrary to what one might expect, the equinoxes and solstices play a not necessarily predominant role. A primitive calendar serves other than purely astronomical purposes. It will insist above all on dates that are of interest to agriculture; thus Hesiod, to give one example out of many, makes reference only to the times for ploughing and harvesting but not to the four cardinal points of the solar year.

Now the same constellation whose heliacal rising and cosmical setting are mentioned in Hesiod: the Pleiades[1] – together with the Bull,

[1] See p. 718.

with which they form an inseparable unity[1] – was considered of paramount importance by the early settlers in Elam and Mesopotamia, witness the numberless bulls and bull's heads on seals and vases, a small selection of which is given in our illustrations.

THE LION–BULL COMBAT

II. 5. Of all combinations in which this celestial bull is found, the one with the lion – the "Lion–Bull combat" – is undoubtedly the most characteristic and at the same time the most persistent, having a tradition stretching over at least five millennia.[2] On the basis of the preceding demonstrations, its original meaning becomes obvious (see diagram 2). When, about 10 February, by the beginning of the fourth millennium, the Bull with the Pleiades started setting heliacally, the Lion with the brilliant star Regulus, below it the brightest star, α, of the constellation Hydra and, close to the horizon (perhaps not yet recognizable), Canopus (α Argus) were simultaneously culminating. One hardly needs to justify the expectation that this striking moment, being the celestial signal for starting agricultural activity at the end of the cold season, would have been paid due attention and would have found expression in pictorial representations of various kinds: the triumphant Lion, standing at zenith and displaying thereby its maximum power, attacks and kills the Bull trying to escape below the horizon, which during the subsequent days disappears in the sun's rays to remain invisible for a period of 40 days. Then it is reborn, rising again for the first time, on 21 March, to announce spring equinox and the advent of the light part of the year.

In the course of time, owing to precession, the date defined by the "Lion–Bull combat" gradually changed. About 3000 B.C. (early Sumerian time) it fell on c. 25 February, about 2000 B.C., on 10 March, about 1000 B.C., on 22 March; finally, about 500 B.C. (time of Darius the Great), on 28 March, or c. one week after spring equinox. This situation is demonstrated in diagram 4, where the Sun is marked standing 20° below the western horizon of Persepolis (oval curve), the position of the Pleiades (η Tauri) and of Regulus for 500 B.C. being indicated by encircled asterisks with the corresponding star names.

[1] See p. 722.
[2] See W. Hartner and R. Ettinghausen, "The Conquering Lion. The Life Cycle of a Symbol", *Oriens* XVII (1964), pp. 161–71.

OLD IRANIAN CALENDARS

Considering the fact that the determination of the equinoxes as well as the observation of the disappearance of the Pleiades may be wrong by several days, we thus find that the Lion–Bull combat, during the first half of the first millennium B.C., lent itself as a most convenient and natural symbol to denote spring equinox. There can be no doubt that it was for this and no other reason that Darius deemed it worthy of serving as favourite ornamental motif on the eastern flight of stairs of the *apadāna* at Persepolis. As will be seen, the symbol bears directly on the question of the introduction of the Later Avestan calendar.

THE LUNISOLAR YEAR

II. 6. While all the demonstrations given so far refer exclusively to the Sun's yearly course through the constellations near the ecliptic, nothing has yet been said about the Moon's role except for my initial generalizing remark that it must needs have always been regarded as the chief time indicator. This means that its phases originally served to measure – not to count – short periods of time, roughly 7–8 days for each of the four main phases, and 29 or 30 for the lunation. The need of adapting the lunar time-reckoning to the solar could be felt only after the solar year had been recognized as the "skeleton" of time count. The space between two consecutive annual solar phenomena, such as the heliacal rising of a certain asterism, was found to be filled by more than 12 and less than 13 lunations, which in due time gave rise to the idea of making normal years of 12 months alternate with long (intercalary) years of 13. The rule for intercalation was a matter of course. Since 12 months comprise 354–355 days, the beginning of the lunar year will recede from a given solar date by 10 days each year, whence a 13th month will have to be intercalated at the latest after the 3rd year. This empirical method, which requires a constant surveying of the celestial phenomena, will in practice occasion many erroneous intercalations. It was later replaced by cyclical intercalations based on the exact knowledge of the periods concerned. From the approximate equation: 8 years = 99 months, it resulted that 3 months had to be intercalated in the course of 8 years (*octaëteris*, $8 \times 12 + 3 = 99$); from the better approximation: 19 years = 235 months, resulted the intercalation of 7 months in 19 years ("*Metonic*" *cycle*, $19 \times 12 + 7 = 235$); see III 3–4 (pp. 742–3).

From the cuneiform texts it becomes evident that, still in 541 B.C., a second Addaru was ordered by royal decree to be intercalated. The

THE LUNISOLAR YEAR

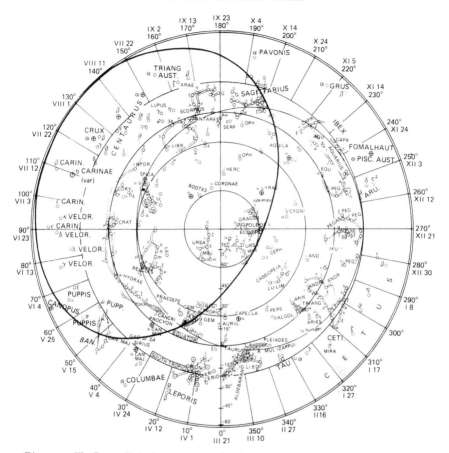

Diagram 4. The Persepolis horizon one week after the spring equinox, at the time of Darius.

cyclical intercalations, which appear for the first time in 527, will be discussed in Part III. The fact that the first introduction of a calendar based on a scientific method took place during the time immediately following the Persian conquest of Babylon (539 B.C.), as will be seen, is hardly accidental.

PART III. THE BABYLONIAN AND THE OLD IRANIAN CALENDARS

III. 1. In late Babylonian times the first month of the lunisolar year, Nīsannu, was the one whose neomenia occurred about the time of spring equinox.¹ In all probability this had been the rule long before.² How, and how accurately, the equinox was observed during the earliest period cannot be ascertained. At the latest in the last decade of the 6th century, as results from the arrangement of the lunisolar calendar, it was determined with remarkable accuracy. For its approximate determination, however, already at Ammiṣaduqa's time (early 16th century B.C.), the Lion–Bull combat situation, i.e. the heliacal setting of the Pleiades, situated in the western horn of Taurus, occurring then about 15 March (Gregorian) = 28 March (Julian), could have served, and probably did serve, as a convenient means. It seems indeed plausible that the lunisolar year ended with the last visibility of Taurus, considering the Moon's age-old association with the Bull (witness the numberless prehistoric seals representing both in significant combination, see fig. 17 *et passim*), which is reflected still in the hellenistic (Seleucid and Greek) system of astrological exaltations (ὑψώματα).³

A thousand years later, in Babylon and in Persepolis alike, the heliacal setting of the Pleiades took place about 28 March (Gregorian) = *c*. 2 April (Julian); this means that it fell by the same length of time later than the equinox (21/26 March), as the length of time by which it had preceded it a millennium earlier. During this long period the heliacal setting of Taurus-Pleiades could thus serve to announce the end of the old and the beginning of the new lunisolar year. It will be shown, however, that already before the end of the 6th century a system based on the "phases" (annual risings and settings) of certain prominent stars or constellations (among which also the Pleiades) was in use to determine with remarkable accuracy the two solstices and spring equinox as well as four more solar dates (see III 14–19, pp. 750–756).

---

¹ For the following I refer to R. A. Parker and W. A. Dubberstein, "Babylonian Chronology 626 B.C.–A.D. 75", *Brown University Studies* XIX (Providence, 1956).

² Other competitive systems, with the year beginning at Autumn equinox or Summer solstice, may have existed at different times and places (in the Sumerian city communities, early Assur, etc.).

³ See W. Hartner, "The Pseudoplanetary Nodes of the Moon's Orbit in Hindu and Islamic Iconographies", *Ars Islamica* V (Ann Arbor, 1938), pp. 113–54 (reprinted in W. Hartner, *Oriens–Occidens* (Hildesheim, 1968), pp. 349–404). From the same remote antiquity stems of course the Lion's association with the Sun in the astrological system of the *domicilia*.

THE BABYLONIAN CALENDAR

III. 2. The names of the Babylonian months, essentially the same as the Aramaic ones known from the Jewish calendar, are:

1. Nīsannu
(beginning about vernal equinox)
2. Aiiāru
3. Sīmannu
4. Du'ūzu
(beginning about summer solstice)
5. Ābu
6. Ulūlu

7. Tašrītu
(beginning about autumn equinox)
8. Araḫsamna
9. Kisilīmu
10. Ṭebētu
(beginning about winter solstice)
11. Šabāṭu
12. Addāru

As in most other lunisolar calendars (except for the Chinese, which is based on the true conjunctions), the first day of the month is the one on which the thin crescent of the New Moon for the first time after conjunction becomes visible after sunset, whence, logically, the days are counted from sunset. Intercalary months are inserted either at the end of the year, after the month Addāru (cf. the Jewish Adar-šenī or Ve-Adar), or after the 6th month, Ulūlu. Theoretically a second Addāru would thus have to be intercalated when the neomenia of the regular Addāru has receded more than a month from spring equinox, while the intercalation of a second Ulūlu would analogously have to be regulated by autumn equinox, which in the 6th century, when it fell on 26 September (Julian), coincided very closely with the heliacal rising of the brilliant star Spica (α Virginis)[1] and with the heliacal setting of α Librae. By contrast, A. Sachs[2] finds that intercalations were regulated in Seleucid times by the heliacal rising of Sirius, which should always fall in the 4th month, Du'ūzu. On checking with Parker–Dubberstein's tables one notices that this latter rule seems applicable even to most intercalations of the preceding two centuries, from the time of Cambyses (529 B.C.) onwards, though exceptions can be found in quite a few cases. For the pre-Seleucid period as a whole the number of such exceptions

---

[1] Bab. $^{mul}ab.sin$ = "corn ear" (Spica). The name has survived in the star name ἄψινθος (*Rev.* 8.11), which would otherwise be inexplicable. Note that the heliacal rising of Spica on 26 September (Jul.) = 20 September (Greg.) is referred to an ideal level horizon. For the mountainous horizon of Persepolis it fell *c.* 12 days later (see III. 16f., p. 753).

[2] "Sirius Dates in Babylonian Astronomical Texts of the Seleucid Period", *JCS* VI (1952), 105–14; cited after Parker–Dubberstein, p. 3, n. 4.

is considerably reduced by assuming as valid the "theoretical" rule postulated above, that the first month is to start about or after spring equinox and that autumn equinox must fall in the sixth, Ulūlu. In particular, all the second Ulūlus recorded from the time of Nebuchadnezzar II (604 B.C.) onwards appear consistently intercalated according to this rule, while not all of them follow from the "Sirius-Du'ūzu" rule. After the introduction of the 19-years' ("Metonic") cycle, of which I shall speak presently, the two rules can be fused into one, in other words, starting with the 19th year of the reign of Darius (503 B.C.) the earliest solar date for the beginning of the year becomes spring equinox (25, 26 or 27 March Julian).[1] Depending on meteorological conditions, the heliacal rising of Sirius then falls on one of the last days of Du'ūzu or on the first of Ābu, and autumn equinox is not reached in the course of Ulūlu, whence either of the two phenomena may serve equally well to indicate that a second Ulūlu is to be intercalated.

III. 3. While in the earliest period intercalations were decreed according to the merit of the case, the first regularity becomes manifest during the reign of Cambyses (529–22 B.C.). In his third year, i.e. starting on 21 March 527, a second Ulūlu (15 September) is inserted and thereafter the 5th and 8th years of his reign have an intercalary Addāru each (19 March 524 and 15 March 522). Three years after, in the 3rd year of Darius, starting on 23 March 519, a similar cycle begins with a second Ulūlu in the first year (17 September) and then follow second Addārus in the 5th and 8th years (20 March 516 and 17 March 513) respectively. Again, a new cycle begins in the 11th year of Darius, starting on 25 March 511, with an intercalary Ulūlu (18 September), after which follow second Addārus in the 13th and 16th years (21 March 508 and 18 March 505).

This is the first indubitable occurrence of the octaëteris mentioned at the end of Part II. It is based on the equations

$a = 99$ lunations of 29.53059 days $= 2923.52841$ days

and

$b = 8$ Julian years of 365.25 days $= 2922.00$ days

(Difference, $a - b = 1.53$ days),

from which it results that the beginnings of corresponding months will after each octaëteris fall on a Julian date that is c. 2 (theoretically 1.53) days later than the preceding. Thus in 527 the beginning of the year

---

[1] With the sole exception of 500 B.C., when the year began on 23 March.

falls on 21 March; in 519, on 23 March; in 511, on 25 March, while the dates for the second Ulūlus are 15, 17 and 18 September respectively.

III. 4. In the 19th year of Darius, 503 B.C., the beginning of the year (1st Nīsannu) had advanced to 27 March, i.e. the very day of spring equinox, and the second Ulūlu started on 20 September. Now this year marks the end of the octaëteris count and the beginning of the 19-year cycle, which we are used to call by the Greek astronomer Meton's name because it was he who 70 years later, about 430 B.C., introduced it in the Athenian calendar. This cycle is founded on the equations

$$c = 235 \text{ lunations} = 6939.68865 \text{ days}$$

and

$$d = 19 \text{ Julian years} = 6939.75 \text{ days}$$

(Difference, $c - d = -0.06$ days $= c. -1\frac{1}{2}$ hours).

Evidently it warrants a much higher degree of accuracy. The error one commits by using this cycle amounts to one day in $c.$ 300 years. Consequently, with the beginning of each new cycle the beginning of the lunisolar year will over a very long period of time recur to the approximate date of spring equinox, which fell on 27 March in the 6th century B.C., and on 23 March in the 1st century A.D.

Here one might object to my assumption that the first year of each octaëteris as well as of each Metonic cycle was the one in which a second Ulūlu had to be intercalated, while there seems to be tacit agreement among earlier authors that a cycle has to end, not to begin, with an intercalary year. A theoretical rule cannot of course be established. But evidently only the beginning of a cycle on the lowest possible solar date, which is at the same time a day close to spring equinox, does make astronomical sense, while any other beginning for the first of the three consecutive octaëterides, such as 12 April 529 or 1 April 528, would seem arbitrarily chosen.

III. 5. There can be no doubt that the date of the equinox, 27 March 503 B.C., was selected intentionally to commence a new and better calendrical system. From the sequence of intercalations in the first 19-year cycle, however, it can be seen that the calendar makers had not yet understood thoroughly how the effect intended could be warranted; for instead of intercalating a second Addāru in the 3rd year of the cycle, they postponed it to the end of the 4th year, whereby they allowed the 4th year to begin on a date preceding the equinox by $c.$ 4 days: 23 March 500 B.C. As for the rest of the intercalated second Addārus, they prove to be in accordance with the ideal scheme underlying all later cycles. Starting with the second year of Xerxes, 484, the first year of the next as well as of all later cycles has an intercalary Ulūlu; then follow intercalary Addārus at the end of the 3rd, 6th, 9th, 11th, 14th and 17th years.

III. 6. A few exceptions to the rule seem of interest.

On the one hand, for the two intercalations of a second Ulūlu due in the 19th and 38th years of the reign of Artaxerxes I (446 and 427 B.C.) a second Addāru is substituted, while for the rest the established scheme is not altered. Thereby, starting with the second year of Artaxerxes, a sequence of 20 second Addārus is obtained all of which start on days comprised between 15 and 25 March, in other words, shortly before the equinox. Only in the 16th year of Darius II (408 B.C.) does the calendar resume its former shape by the intercalation of a second Ulūlu. This aversion to intercalating a month in the middle of the year seems only explicable in terms of a wish conceived for unknown reasons, to regulate the calendar exclusively by the equinox.

On the other hand, the cycle starting in the 16th year of Artaxerxes II, on 26 March 389, has an intercalated second Addāru at the end of the 5th instead of the 6th year. This causes the 6th year (384) to start one month too late, on 29 April, whereby, for the first and only time since the 12th and 15th years of Nebuchadnezzar I (starting 30 April 593 and 27 April 590 respectively), the accepted rule is violated. No plausible reason for this anticipated intercalation can be adduced. It seems to have been a mere slip.[1]

THE OLD PERSIAN LUNISOLAR CALENDAR

III. 7. In the trilingual Behistun inscription, written in cuneiform Old Persian, Elamite and Akkadian, Darius states twice that the defeat and

---

[1] This one slip, the only one in more than a century, induces Parker–Dubberstein to claim that the 19-year cycle came into being only after 367 B.C. or "possibly as early as 383 B.C.". Similarly O. Neugebauer, *The Exact Sciences in Antiquity*, 2nd ed. (Providence, R. I., 1957), p. 140, judges that "the 19-year cycle was introduced into consistent calendaric use very close to 380 B.C. This gives Meton a priority of about 50 years and opens the possibility of an originally Greek discovery." By contrast van der Waerden, reviewing Parker–Dubberstein in *Bibliotheca Orientalis* xv (1958), p. 107, arrives at the same conclusion as to the introduction of the *octaëteris* and of the 19-year cycle as I do above, though without recognizing the decisive fact that the years having a second Ulūlu consistently begin very precisely at spring equinox. The second Addārus substituted in March 446/45 and 427/26 for second Ulūlus are not of course exceptions to the 19-year cycle, as one might interpret (erroneously) van der Waerden's words. In point of fact they do not affect the cycle at all; neither does the anticipated intercalation of 385–384 (see above).

capital punishment, after the assassination of the false Smerdis, of eight more usurpers took place *hamahyāyā θarda*, "in one and the same year" (DB §§52 and 56). In the preceding paragraphs the dates of eighteen battles, fought in nine different months, are given according to the Old Persian calendar, but unfortunately not in a chronological sequence. Many attempts had been made to equate the names of these nine months[1] with those of the Babylonian calendar (Rawlinson, Oppert, Unger, Justi, Prašek, Marquart) until, thanks to the discovery of new tablets written in Akkadian and Elamite, which contain also the names of the missing three months, Arno Poebel[2] succeeded in setting up equations that will have to be regarded as definitive. They prove on the one hand that all previous identifications were erroneous, on the other that Darius' bold claim to have defeated his enemies in the course of one year is only slightly exaggerated: in truth it took him 13 months plus 12 days to reduce his countries with savage cruelty to peaceful conditions.

III. 8. In addition to the Old Persian month names in Old Persian script and in Elamite script, a different, genuine Elamite set of names is found in the tablets. In the following list, given after Hallock,[3] the rendering in Elamite script of the Old Persian names followed by the Old Persian Behistun names (in brackets) is given under *A*, while the corresponding proper Elamite names are listed under *B*, and the Babylonian month names under *C*.

Hallock, in his ensuing analysis of attested intercalations, takes it for granted that in the Old Persian variety of the lunisolar calendar the same rules prevailed as in the contemporary Babylonian. This, however, should not *a priori* be considered a matter of course. As will be seen

---

[1] One of them is preserved only in the Elamite form: Markašanas. It corresponds with the Akkadian month name Araḫsamnu = Aram. Marḫešwān and is doubtless borrowed from the Semitic name. R. T. Hallock, in *PFT*, 74, n. 11, does not deny the possibility of a borrowing (*via* Old Persian) but holds against it that no other Old Persian month name has a Semitic derivation. This argument is invalidated by the fact that even in our days there are languages (Polish, Czech, Basque) that have indigenous names for the months except for one or two (thus Polish *marzec* and *maj*) which are borrowed from the Latin names, or one may rather say, where the Latin names have not been supplanted by indigenous ones; thus Basque gives preference to Apirilla and Maiatza over the genuine Basque Jorailla and Orrilla.

[2] See his articles in *AJSLL* LV (1938), 130–65 (esp. 139–42), 285–314, LVI (1939), 121–45; cited after R. G. Kent, *Old Persian*, p. 160, n. 1. The material on which Poebel based his reconstruction of the Old Persian calendar was subsequently made available in two monumental publications: G. G. Cameron's *PTT*, and R. T. Hallock's *PFT*.

[3] *PFT*, p. 74.

OLD IRANIAN CALENDARS

	A	B	C
I	Hadukannaš (Adukanaiša)	Zikli	Nīsannu
II	Turmar (Θūravāhara)	Zarpakim	Ajjāru
III	Sākurriziš (Θāigraciš)	Hadar	Sīmannu
IV	Karmabataš (Garmapada)	Hallime	Du'ūzu
V	Turnabaziš	Zillatam	Ābu
VI	Karbašiyaš	Belilit	Ulūlu
VII	Bakeyatiš (Bāgayādiš)	Manšarki[1]	Tašrītu
VIII	Markašanaš	Lankelli	Araḫsamna
IX	Hašiyatiš (Āṣiyādiya)	Šibari	Kisilīmu
X	Hanamakaš (Anāmaka)	Šermi	Tebētu
XI	Samiyamaš	Kutmama	Šabāṭu
XII	Miyakannaš (Viyaxana)	Aššetukpi	Addāru

he thereby encounters difficulties that can be avoided if the assumption of a perfect parallelism is dropped.

III. 9. Intercalations are indicated by the term *beptika* (rendered tentatively by Hallock as "shifted"), standing after the name of the month. It occurs three times, on three different tablets, all from the 22nd year of Darius (500–499 B.C.) in combination with the Elamite name of the 12th month: Aššetukpi beptika. Since in the Babylonian calendar this year has an intercalary second Addāru (starting on 12 March), beptika evidently means nothing but "intercalary".

Now the same term beptika is found also attached to Old Persian month names: three times, all in the 19th year (503–502), to the 10th month, Hanamakaš (= Ṭebētu), and once in the 23rd year (499–498), to the first, Hadukannaš (= Nīsannu). Comparing this with the Babylonian calendar, to which an intercalary Ṭebētu is alien, we find that the 19th year has a second Ulūlu, starting on 20 September, and that the 23rd year begins with the month Nīsannu = Hadukannaš on 11 April 499, which follows immediately after the second Addāru (beginning on 12 March 499) at the end of the preceding 22nd year. From this Hallock concludes that in combination with Old Persian names beptika does not mean "intercalary", but serves only to indicate that an intercalation had taken place one (thus in the 23rd year) or several (thus in the 19th year) months before.

---

[1] In six of the Fortification texts and in the economic texts from Susa (e.g. *MDP* IX (1907), no. 27) the month name Raḫal occurs; according to Hallock, *PFT* 75 and 747, col. 1, it is the Susan name for the seventh month, Manšarki.

OLD PERSIAN LUNISOLAR CALENDAR

III. 10. It goes without saying that this is utterly improbable. A more reasonable explanation of the baffling discrepancy will emerge if one takes it for granted that the crucial word, beptika, always meant "intercalary": the Old Persian and the Babylonian calendars will then have had different systems of intercalation. The latter we have seen operated with irregular, empirical Ulūlu and Addāru intercalations down to 527, then passed over to the octaëteris and finally, when in the 19th year of Darius the beginning of the year coincided with spring equinox, to the 19-year cycle. We have seen moreover that in the Babylonian calendar the Addāru intercalation due in the 21st year of Darius (501–500) was not carried out before the year after, which caused the 22nd year (500–499) to start on a day *preceding* the equinox. The transition period, comprising the first year of the 19-year count is thus characterized by uncertainty and experimentation; it comes to an end only with the correct Addāru intercalation of the 24th year (498–497).

III. 11. It is just during this transition period that similar discrepancies become manifest in the Old Persian calendar. About its earlier history nothing definite is known, but there can be no doubt that it was lunisolar, as was the neighbouring Babylonian, and that intercalations must have been made on an empirical basis. And it is of empirical intercalations that we find significant traces in the four tablets under discussion (PFT 1069, 1070, 1073 and 1053).

The former three we have seen mention an intercalary 10th month, Hanamakaš (= Ṭebētu) beptika, in the 19th year (503–502). This can be explained by the supposition, for which further evidence will be adduced,[1] that the second chief solar term regulating the Old Persian year, next after spring equinox, was not autumn equinox but winter solstice (determined, as will be shown in what follows (see Tables 2 and 3) by a multitude of prominent star-phases), so that the 10th month would have to start about or after the solstice. Now in the 19th year of Darius, beginning on 27 March 503 B.C., the neomenia of the 10th month fell on 17 December, 11 days before the solstice; an intercalation therefore became necessary.

According to the practice of the Babylonian calendar, the 10th month of the year would then have been decreed to be an intercalary 9th month (IXa, i.e. a second Kisilīmu) and the following month, starting on 15 January 502, the regular 10th month, Ṭebētu. But the texts mention an intercalary (beptika) Hanamakaš = Ṭebētu. This discrepancy (if I am

[1] See III. 13ff.

right in surmising that the winter solstice played a predominant role in the Old Persian calendar) disappears if we assume that beptika in combination with Old Persian month names indicates the month *preceding* the regular month, and not, as in the case of Elamite (and of course also of Babylonian) month names, the one following it (see Table 1).

The last tablet (PFT 1053), which mentions a Hadukannaš (= Nīsannu) beptika in the 23rd year, seems to bear out my theory. We have seen that the Babylonian Addāru intercalation due in the year 21, owing to the ruling confusion, was postponed to the end of year 22, to the effect that Addāru II began on 12 March 499, and the month Nīsannu of year 23, on 11 April. The Elamite months, as attested by the three tablets mentioned, were already brought into accord with the Babylonian, whence the tablets record an Aššetukpi beptika corresponding to the Addāru II of the Babylonian calendar. As for the Old Persian calendar, which in accordance with year 19 should have inserted an intercalary 10th month on 14 December 500, it became finally adapted to the Babylonian by the intercalation of a Hadukannaš beptika of year 23. For if, as here suggested, beptika indicates the intercalary month preceding the regular one, Hadukannaš beptika of year 23 becomes identical with Addāru II of year 22. I am aware of the difficulty of accepting that the position of the beptika month should have been different in Elamite and Old Persian usage;[1] but no other reasonable possibility of explaining the apparent contradictions found in the surviving texts offers itself, and there is little hope of discovery of new inscriptions that would permit testing the theory here offered.[2]

---

[1] [The difficulty should not be allowed to prevail over the great merit of the proposed solution. If the Persians named the intercalary month after the nearest regular month ahead, the Elamites after the nearest behind, the difference was not calendrical but merely terminological. Since the El. verb *bepti-* meant "to rebel", it may help to recall that in Middle Persian, quite likely in continuation of Old Persian usage, intercalary days were referred to as "stolen" (*truftag, duzīdag,* cf. H. S. Nyberg, *JA* 1929, p. 293; see also below, pp. 758 and 760–1). The two meanings have in common the connotation of "improper claim", we might say "pretension". To the Elamites, then, an intercalary IXa or XIIa would be "the pretended, *soi-disant* IX or XII", to the Persians "the pretended X or I". This would be no more than in harmony with the forward orientation of the "Zoroastrian" names of the second and third "Creator" days in Pahlavī, whose need to be distinguished from the first "Creator" day is met by referring either to the day immediately following, and not to the immediately preceding (see below, p. 776). *Dai pad Ādur* means "Creator(-day) at Fire(-day)", with "at" used in the sense of "by, adjacent to, French *chez*". The Sogdian name *Aš Δəšti* of the same day, the 8th of the month, means genitively "Fire(-day)'s Creator(-day)". One may also compare the wholly explicit Elamographically written Old Persian phrase "by a quarter short of a shekel", meaning "three quarters of a shekel" and reflecting the forward outlook in reckoning familiar from Latin *duodeviginti*; see *TPS* 1969, 166f. Ed.]

[2] As a much less reasonable alternative I mention the following: the beptika month, also in

THE OLD AVESTAN YEAR

III. 12. As the Persepolis Treasury Tablets[1] show, the Old Persian lunisolar calendar remained in use until at least 459 B.C. Although at the latest about the middle of the 5th century the Later Avestan calendar became firmly established among the Zoroastrians of Iran, the Old Persian calendar may have continued as the official civil calendar throughout the Achaemenian period. This is Taqizadeh's conjecture, in one of his important papers on the subject.[2] He founded it on the fact that Herodotus (III.79) and after him, about 400 B.C., Ctesias, mention the feast of the Magophonia (μαγοφόνια) celebrated each year in commemoration of the elimination of the Magian usurper Gaumata who, according to the Behistun inscription, was killed by Darius on the 10th day of the 7th month (Bāgayādiš) of the Old Persian year. Taqizadeh, however, seemed to believe that this date: 7th month, 10th day, is actually found also in Ctesias, but this is a mistake. Nothing but the fact that the Magophonia were celebrated every year is recorded by the two authors.

THE OLD AVESTAN YEAR. THE SIX GĀHĀNBĀRS

III. 13. The theory of the independent existence of an Old Avestan religious calendar in use with the pre-Achaemenian and Achaemenian Zoroastrian communities, probably already before Zoroaster's own time,[3] is supported by two arguments: (1) the inclusion in the Later

---

Old Persian, always *follows* the regular one; then, in year 19 (see Table 1) the regular 10th month begins on 17 December 503 and the next one (15 January 502) is decreed intercalary though with no plausible astronomical motivation. Now, introducing for brevity's sake the term "Elamite year" as against "Old Persian year", we have at the end of year 22 the Elamite Aššetukpi beptika in the same position as the Babylonian Addāru II, while the Old Persian year 22 ends with the regular 12th month. Thereafter, the first month of Old Persian year 23 coincides with the Elamite Aššetukpi beptika of the preceding year, and the OP Hadukannaš beptika (=Nīsannu II), with the regular Elamite first month of year 23. This would imply a discrepancy of one month between the two year forms, and not before the second month (beginning 10 May) would the concordance be restored. Since the tablets in question concern allotments to be made to workmen, it is very improbable that a centralized administration such as the Achaemenian could afford this kind of uncertainty.

[1] See *PTT* and I. Gershevitch's review in *Asia Minor* II (1951), pp. 133ff.
[2] "The Old Iranian Calendars Again", *BSOAS* xiv (1952), 603–11; see p. 604.
[3] According to Bīrūnī's "Chronology" (Arabic text, ed. Sachau, p. 14, Sachau's translation, p. 17), the "appearance of Zoroaster" (*waqt ẓuhūribī*) occurred 258 years before the *Era of Alexander*, beginning on 1 October 312 B.C.; this leads to 570 B.C. as the year of advent of the new religion. Taqizadeh, Henning and Hinz count the 258 years back from Alexander's conquest of Persia, 330 B.C., whence they arrive at the year 588 B.C.; but this date is not convincing, as Alexander's conquest by itself plays no role whatever in the accepted chronology.

Avestan calendar of month names called after deities not worshipped by Zoroaster: these seem to belong to the oldest Avestan stock and may have been incorporated in Zoroastrianism quite soon after the death of the prophet; (2) the fact that Yasna 3.11, ascribed equally to early Avestan times, lists the names of six "seasonal deities" as *ratus* (judges) of Aša, which subsequently play an important role (still to be discussed) in the Later Avestan calendar, where they are called the six *gāhānbārs*; they are commonly interpreted (thus still by Taqizadeh)[1] as the indicators of six unequal seasons of an approximately tropical year. According to Taqizadeh, "nothing is known of the means by which the seasons were kept in their astronomic positions in the year. Whether this was a lunisolar year, as some scholars had presumed, or a year of 360 days with a periodic intercalation in the manner of the 'Pēshdādian' year mentioned by Bīrūnī,[2] as others had supposed, is open to conjecture. The year began probably with the summer solstice, on the day immediately following the *Maiδyōišəma* ('midsummer') festival."

III. 14. Taqizadeh's pessimistic view as to the impossibility of clearing up the origin of the gāhānbārs is shared by all historians, earlier and modern. An explanation that in itself has a very high degree of probability, however, offers itself as soon as we apply to the problem the rules found valid for the determination of solar dates in the prehistoric and early historic (Babylonian) periods, as illustrated at length in Parts I and II.

Everything points to the gāhānbārs, which subsequently, in the Later Avestan calendar, were celebrated as festivals of 5-days' duration each, having been understood not as "seasons", but as six well-defined solar dates forming the solar "skeleton"[3] of the year, which until the acceptance of the Babylonian calendar in Achaemenian times in all probability was a primitive lunisolar one, as was the case with practically all calendars in Antiquity.

---

[1] See Taqizadeh, *op. cit.*, p. 605.

[2] Bīrūnī's "Pešdādian" year ("Chronology", p. 11, transl., p. 13) is a year of 12 months of 30 days with an intercalary month every 6 years and two intercalary months every 120 years. 120 years thus comprise $1,440 + 21 = 1,461$ months $= 43,830$ days. The same number of days is contained in 120 Julian years: $365\frac{1}{4} \times 120 = 43,830$. There is no reason to believe that such a "round year" of 360 days ascribed here to the mythological Persian rulers was ever in use, either in Iran or elsewhere. It is a learned construction devoid of historical foundation, but nevertheless widespread even among recent historians.

[3] See above II. 6, p. 738.

THE OLD AVESTAN YEAR

The names given in Yasna 3.11 are the following:

I   Maiδyōizarəmaya,   IV   Ayāθrima,
II Maiδyōišəma,   V   Maiδyāirya,
III Paitiš.hahya,   VI   Hamaspaθmaēdaya.

They reappear in the same sequence in *Āfrīnakān* 3.7–12, with two important additional pieces of information: (1) the numbers of days comprised between each two consecutive gāhānbārs, and (2) the days of the months corresponding to each gāhānbār in the Later Avestan calendar, valid for the time of composition of the passage incorporated in the *Āfrīnakān*.[1] Exactly the same differences result from the days in the Later Avestan calendar as reported by Bīrūnī in his "Chronology".[2]

While (2), i.e. the relative position of the gāhānbārs in the movable Later Avestan calendar, will serve us later[3] to establish the approximate years of origin of the *Āfrīnakān* passage and of the period fitting Bīrūnī's data, (1), i.e. the different but invariable time-spans between the gāhānbārs, will furnish the clue to the original meaning and function of the gāhānbārs themselves.

The time-spans are as follows:

45 days from VI Hamaspaθmaēdaya   to I Maiδyōizarəmaya,
60 days from I Maiδyōizarəmaya   to II Maiδyōišəma,
75 days from II Maiδyōišəma   to III Paitiš.hahya,
30 days from III Paitiš.hahya   to IV Ayāθrima,
80 days from IV Ayāθrima   to V Maiδyāirya,
75 days from V Maiδyāirya   to VI Hamaspaθmaēdaya.

III. 15. As for the original significance of these words, only two of them have a clear bearing on astronomy: Maiδyōišəma means "midsummer", i.e. summer solstice, and Maiδyāirya, "midwinter" or winter solstice. Of the remaining four – this is indicative – Maiδyōizarəmaya originally denoted a spring festival, Paitiš.hahya the time of harvest, Ayāθrima the return of cattle from the pasture-grounds, and Hamaspaθmaēdaya the time of bestirment, i.e. the beginning of outdoor or field work.[4] They all thus refer to approximate solar dates.

---

[1] Leaving open the question as to whether the *Āfrīnakān* as a whole originated at the time concerned; cf. p. 782, n. 1.
[2] Pp. 215–33 (transl., pp. 199–219).
[3] See V. 1–2, pp. 781–3.
[4] See I. Gershevitch, *Festschrift Oswald Szemerényi* (Amsterdam, 1979), 294.

In the 6th and 5th centuries B.C., the difference in days between the summer and winter solstices was actually 180.5, and that between winter and summer solstice, 184.75, while the opposite: 185 and 180 days, respectively, results from the *Āfrīnakān* data; but considering the errors arising necessarily in determining the solstices, as pointed out above,[1] this inaccuracy is not surprising.

In view of the predominant role which the annual risings and settings of particularly conspicuous stars have played in the Middle East since the dawn of civilization, the surmise that the gāhānbārs too were originally determined by them has a high degree of probability. Since in trying to verify this the results obtainable will always involve an error of a day or two at least, the graphical method, i.e. the use of a star chart constructed by analogy with diagram 1 (Part II, p. 721) for *c.* 530 B.C. and for an horizon for latitude 30°, will be amply sufficient and by far preferable to the computational, the more so because it shows at one glance which of the stars, for each of the gāhānbārs, may have served as a time indicator. As for the latitude chosen (30°, Persepolis) a variation of 3° N or S, or even more, will not affect perceptibly the dates of annual risings and settings of stars near the ecliptic; only for stars standing far north or south of it will the dates undergo considerable changes.

Starting now from V, Maiδyāirya, winter solstice,[2] on 21 December (Gregorian), and applying the differences resulting from Afrīnakān and Bīrūnī, we find that VI falls 75 days later, on 6 March, then I, 45 days later, on 20 April; II, 60 days later, on 19 June; III, 75 days later, on

---

[1] See III. 1, pp. 739–40. Bīrūnī, p. 216 (transl. 201), asserts that the solstices are more easily determinable than the equinoxes and that even an unskilled observer, measuring the variation of the shadow length, "cannot possibly mistake the day of the solstice". In another context, however (p. 184, transl. p. 167), he says the contrary: modern astronomers know that it is extremely difficult and next to impossible to determine the times of the two solstices; cf. W. Hartner and M. Schramm, "Al-Bīrūnī and the Theory of the Solar Apogee", in A. C. Crombie (ed.), *Scientific Change* (London, 1963), pp. 206–13. Against his first assertion it must be said that the variation of declination about the solstices is *c.* 25″ in one day, and less than 2′ in three days, which excludes direct measurement even if a large gnomon is used. Satisfactory results can be obtained only by employing the method of corresponding altitudes, possibly in use already in the 6th century since the solstices are found accurate to 2–3 days. More accurately observed was the spring equinox, as we have seen, witness the arrangement of the Babylonian calendar. Once determined with the aid of appropriate gnomon observations, however, the observation of annual risings and settings of stars, as discussed in the following, could serve as a convenient means to ascertain the four cardinal points of the year as well as other solar dates of special interest.

[2] This beginning, arbitrarily chosen, causes II (Maiδyōišəma) to fall on 19 June, too early by *c.* 3 days. In choosing the correct date of II (summer solstice) as a starting point, V (winter solstice) would fall too late by the same amount. In any case, owing to the wrong differences between II and V (see above), recourse to a compromise is unavoidable.

2 September; IV, 30 days later, on 2 October; finally, again V, 80 days later, on 21 December, whereby the 365 days of the year are completed. Adding to these six gāhānbārs the day of spring equinox on 21 March, which we have seen played a predominant part in establishing the Babylonian and Old Persian lunisolar calendars, and using for it the abbreviation N,[1] we thus have the following sequence:

N (Naurōz)   21 March
I (Maiδyōizarəmaya)   20 April
II (Maiδyōišəma)   19 June
III (Paitiš.hahya)   2 September
IV (Ayāθrima)   2 October
V (Maiδyāirya)   21 December
VI (Hamaspaθmaēdaya)   6 March

III. 16. A first test based on the assumption – illusory of course when applied to a mountainous area like Iran – of an horizon even and level in all directions of the windrose, yields encouraging results only for the phenomena observable at the western horizon (heliacal and cosmical settings), while those occurring in the East (heliacal and acronychal risings) do not permit us to draw any convincing conclusions. Things become different, however, if we assume that the observations were made on the site where the great Achaemenian palace was erected. According to recent topographical investigations,[2] the western horizon of Persepolis is practically even (average elevation c. 1°), while the eastern mountain range has an average elevation of 12°, which causes rising stars to become visible c. 12 to 14 days later than would be the case on a level horizon.

For the *true* geographical horizon of Persepolis then the prominent stars marking by their annual risings and settings Naurōz and the 6 gāhānbārs are listed in Table 2, where the following symbols are used:

HR = heliacal rising, i.e. first visible rising above the eastern mountains at dawn;
AR = acronychal rising, i.e. last visible rising above the eastern mountains at twilight;

---

[1] The letter N is to symbolize the modern term Naurōz, leaving the question open whether the Old Avestan year began with spring equinox or, as has been conjectured from the astronomical orientation of the palace of Persepolis, with summer solstice.
[2] See W. Lentz and W. Schlosser, "Persepolis – Ein Beitrag zur Funktionsbestimmung", in *XVII Deutscher Orientalistentag 1968* (*ZDMG* Supplement I.3, 1969), pp. 957–83.

HS = heliacal setting, i.e. last visible setting below the level western horizon at twilight;

CS = cosmical setting, i.e. first visible setting below the level western horizon at dawn.

In order to permit direct comparison with our modern calendar, the dates are given in Gregorian style, for *c.* 530 B.C.; due to the slowness of precession and the impossibility of computing under the given conditions the annual phenomena with a high degree of accuracy, they are valid *grosso modo* for the whole period *c.* 580–480, whence no conclusion can be drawn from them as to the first time they were observed and recorded. In this context it should be noted that also the differences between the gāhānbārs are given in round figures in the extant texts (45, 60, 75... days). It seems certain, however, that these annual phenomena were paid attention to before the time when the site for the great palace was selected, since the building's astronomical orientation, as was recently ascertained, can no longer be doubted. For, the longitudinal axis of the rectangular great palace has a deviation from the North–South line of 20.5° towards NNW, which has the effect that the rays of the Sun rising at summer solstice above the mountains meet the eastern wall at right angles, which then for a short moment causes the shadows of the columns standing in one and the same row to form a continuous band.[1] The importance of summer solstice (gāhānbār II), which originally may, but would not necessarily, have marked the beginning of the year, thus seems doubly stressed.

As can be seen from our table, it was a limited number of particularly conspicuous stars, less than 30, which announced the gāhānbārs by their annual risings and settings.

III. 17. Without exception these stars and constellations belong to the age-old stock of Sumero-Akkadian catasterisms as recorded in the ^{mul}APIN tablets[2] as well as, much later, still on medieval astrolabes. In order to illustrate their varying functions they are listed once again in Table 3 together with their Akkadian names and their annual phases indicating the 6 gāhānbārs and spring equinox. As for the latter, as said before, my discussion of the Babylonian and Old Persian year[3] will have

---

[1] Cf. Lentz-Schlosser, p. 971.

[2] For their identification see van der Waerden, "Babylonian Astronomy II. The Thirty-six Stars", *JNES* x (1949), pp. 414–24; for their prehistory I refer to Hartner, "The Earliest History of the Constellations".

[3] See III. 3–5, pp. 742f.

THE OLD AVESTAN YEAR

shown with sufficient clarity that it played a predominant role in regulating the Babylonian lunisolar year, to which the Old Persian was finally adapted.

This table, arranged according to increasing right ascensions, clearly demonstrates that the gāhānbārs were determined preponderantly by evening, not by morning observations. Indeed, only the two columns listing acronychal risings and cosmical settings – both observable after sunset – offer complete sequences of the 6 gāhānbārs in their normal order: the former begins with no. 15, Antares, announcing mid-winter (I), and ends with no. 13, Spica, announcing the last gāhānbār (VI); the latter (which includes spring equinox, N, marked by the cosmical setting of Spica) starts with no. 14, α Librae (I), and ends with no. 12, Denebola (VI). In the 6th century, as pointed out before, the age-old Lion–Bull combat situation (the triumphant Lion culminating while the Bull starts disappearing in the rays of the setting sun, see II 5, p. 737) occurs only 6–7 days *after* the equinox. During the preceding weeks, the Pleiades' gradual approach to the setting sun foretells the advent of spring equinox, the exact day of which is then determined by the first visible setting of ab.sin, the "Corn Ear", at dawn. This event, marking the beginning of the light half of the year, seems important enough to account for the multitude of Lion–Bull combat reliefs decorating the Apadana of Persepolis.

III. 18. As a striking fact I mention finally that the royal star, Regulus (α Leonis) does not figure in our list and that Sirius' heliacal rising plays no role whatsoever. For the mountainous horizon of Persepolis it occurred on 17 July (Gregorian) = 23 July (Julian).[1] It may not have been incorporated into the gāhānbār system because it marked no solar date of agricultural interest. But it was doubtless paid due attention already in the Old Avestan calendar, as borne out by the Later Avestan, whose 4th month, Tištryehe, carries the name of this most famous star.[2] As we have seen,[3] an intercalation rule for the lunisolar Babylonian calendar recorded in Seleucid texts, but valid also for earlier times, decreed that the heliacal rising of Sirius was to fall in the 4th month, Du'ūzu. Now in the critical 19th year of Darius (503–502 B.C.), the beginning of the Babylonian year, on 1st Nīsannu (27 March, Julian style), coincided with the beginning of the Later Avestan month

---
[1] For a level eastern horizon, 11/16 July.
[2] On its alternative name *Tīriya (whence Tīr in later Persian, see p. 760, IV, cf. also p. 775).
[3] See III. 2, p. 741.

Fravašinąm, whence the subsequent months in both calendars ran practically parallel: the 1st Du'ūzu fell on 23, the 1st Tištryehe, on 25 June. As a consequence, the heliacal rising of Sirius took place at Persepolis at the very end of these months: 29 Du'ūzu and 27 Tištryehe respectively. This being an established fact for the outset of the Later Avestan calendar, the assumption ventured above seems justified that similar conditions ruled already in the Old Avestan, in other words, that the lunar month in which Sirius had its heliacal rising also carried its name.

III. 19. So far, apart from the last remark, we have been speaking only of the solar terms: spring equinox and the 6 gāhānbārs, which regulated the recurring seasons. As I have shown, the principle employed – the observation of star phases – dates from the early settlers, about 4000 B.C. or even before. As concerns our case, the probability is great that already in remote antiquity the Persepolis plateau was given preference for making observations in the sense described.[1]

Of course to make a calendar more is needed than solar terms alone. But about this one no more can be said than that it must have been crudely lunisolar, as was the case with all others, always excepting the Egyptian. For its pre-Zoroastrian phase, Taqizadeh[2] employs the term "Magian". Four of the month names, called after old Iranian deities including Tištrya-Sirius, were taken over by the Later Avestan calendar. We shall see in Part IV that all four of them in addition became deities after whom four of the 30 days of the Later Avestan months were named. The assumption of a continuity thus seems well founded.

PART IV. THE LATER AVESTAN CALENDAR

IV. 1. In his *De Emendatione Temporum* (1583), basing his view on the scanty evidence he had at hand, Joseph J. Scaliger had claimed that the Later Avestan calendar must have been borrowed, either directly or through an intermediary, from the Egyptian. His views were shared – except for those who answered the question with a *non liquet* – by most of the later authors on the subject, from Ideler over Benfey, Stern, von

---

[1] An Elamite inscription on the southern (outer) terrace wall at Persepolis (*DPf* Darius Persepolis *f*) tells us about "this fortress (Persepolis) where previously none had been built"; see G. G. Cameron, "The Persian Satrapies and Related Matters", *JNES* XXXII (1973), 54. This statement does not of course exclude that the plateau had previously been the site from which observations of the stars were made.

[2] "The Old Iranian Calendars again", p. 606.

THE LATER AVESTAN CALENDAR

Gutschmid, Ginzel, Marquart (Markwart), Taqizadeh, down to the present writer. Divergent theories, however, have been propounded in two articles by E. J. Bickerman[1] and Mary Boyce.[2] Both bear witness to remarkable historical and philological learning and contain some valuable factual information. However, the latter author's conclusions especially, owing to her lack of both mathematical insight and familiarity with the elements of astronomy and chronology, cannot be taken seriously.[3]

As to Bickerman, I subscribe with some reserve to his conclusions (p. 207), going in one case even beyond them, though without sharing his opinion (p. 204) that all efforts to establish a plausible date for the introduction of the 365-day vagabond year are vain; he is clearly not aware that his equation "4 Shahrevar = 4 Addaru and 8 Mihr = 8 Nisanu" (p. 206), which he interprets erroneously, bears witness to the calendar's consistent use throughout the ages. I agree of course that the Achaemenians used the Babylonian lunisolar calendar (Bickerman offers proof of its existence down to 401 at least) and that it remained in use during the Arsacid rule; I add that it appears to have continued even well into Sasanian times. But I claim against him that the 365-day vague year was in continuous use, side by side with the lunisolar, from 503 B.C. onwards, through the Achaemenian, Seleucid, Parthian and Sasanian periods, and after the Muslim conquest until the Jalālī reform of 1079 and beyond, practically down to our time.

IV. 2. The Islamic sources from which information pertinent to the structure of the Later Avestan calendar can be drawn are scanty but sufficiently clear to serve as basis for a mathematical evaluation.

The earliest authors on the subject are Abu'l-Ḥasan Kūšyār b.Labbān al-Jīlī ($c.$ 971–1029)[4] and his contemporary, Bīrūnī. According to Abu'l-Ḥasan Kūšyār's astronomical Tables (probably *al-zīj al-bāligh*, Book 1),[5] following Ideler's German translation,

[1] "The 'Zoroastrian' Calendar", *ArOr* XXXV (1967), pp. 197–207.

[2] "On the Calendar of the Zoroastrian Feasts", *BSOAS* XXXIII (1970), pp. 513–39; still upheld by Mary Boyce in her *History of Zoroastrianism* II (Leiden–Köln, 1982), 244, n. 151.

[3] Among others, she advocates the existence of a Zoroastrian 360-day solar year differing consistently by 5 days from the 365-day solar year (note that both are called *solar*) which she claims was introduced by the Sasanians (p. 515); she operates with the Pešdādian year (see p. 750, n. 2) which she thinks Bīrūnī confused with the Parthian year(!), and claims that it was a 360-day year *without modification* (my italics), in spite of the fact that Bīrūnī says clearly enough that an intercalation of a 30-day month was necessary every 6, and two such intercalations, every 120 years.

[4] H. Suter, *Die Mathematiker und Astronomen der Araber* (Leipzig, 1900), p. 83, no. 192.

[5] See Suter, *Nachträge und Berichtigungen zu "Die Mathematiker..."* (1902), p. 168. The above text is an English rendering of the quotation contained in F. K. Ginzel, *Handbuch der mathematischen*

each Persian month has 30 days, except for Asfendārmedmāh, which has 35. The year thus has 365 days. The 5 surplus days of Asfendārmedmāh (i.e. the epagomenae) are called *al-mustaraqa* ["the stolen days"]. The Persian year is *c*. one-quarter day shorter than the solar year. This makes one day in four years, and one month in 120 years. As a consequence the Persians from the remotest time intercalated a month every 120 years, the year thus comprising 13 months. They counted the year's first month twice, once at the beginning and once at the end of the year, and attached the epagomenae to the intercalated month. The first month of the year was that in which the Sun entered the sign of Aries [correctly, "travelled through", literally "put up at"; the Arabic text has "*al-šahr alladhī taḥillu fīhi'l-ḥamal*"]. Every 120 years the 5 days and the beginning of the year thus advanced by one month. At the time of Kisrā b. Qubād Anūširwān (Khusrau I, 531–79), the Sun reached ["travelled through", *taḥillu*] Aries in Ādhārmāh, and the 5 epagomenae [*al-khamsa*] had their place at the end of Ābān [*wa'l-khamsa maudū'a fī ākhir Ābān*]. When 120 years later the dynasty of the Persians came to an end...the rule was no longer observed, whence the 5 days remained attached to Ābānmāh till the year 375 of the era Yazdagird [A.D. 1006], when the Sun entered Aries on the 1st day of Farvardīnmāh; then the 5 days were attached to Asfendārmed [i.e. the 12th month].

Bīrūnī's account is essentially the same; in particular he mentions in this context the 120-years' intercalation period, but not that the intercalary month at the end of the year is called by the same name as the first (Farvardīn).[1] On the contrary he says:

Then he [Zoroaster] ordered people in all future times to do with the day-quarters the same as he had done, and they obeyed his command. They did not call the intercalary month by a special name, nor did they repeat the name of another month, but they kept it simply in memory from one turn to another. Being, however, afraid that there might arise uncertainty as to the place, where the intercalary month would have again to be inserted, they transferred the five Epagomenæ and put them at the end of that month, to which the turn of intercalation had proceeded on the last occasion of intercalating. And as the subject was of great importance and of general use to high and low, to the king and to the subjects, and as it is required to be treated with knowledge, and to be carried out in conformity with nature [*i.e.* with real time], they used to postpone intercalation, when its time happened

---

und technischen Chronologie I (Leipzig, 1906), p. 291; Ginzel in turn quotes from L. Ideler's *Handbuch* (same title as Ginzel's) II (1825–6), pp. 547 and 624 (Arabic text). Abu'l-Ḥasan, as is seen, wrote his treatise after the calendar reform of A.Y. 375 = A.D. 1006, while Bīrūnī wrote *al-Āthār al-bāqiya* ("Chronology of Ancient Nations") shortly before, in A.D. 1000. Bickerman's assertion ("The 'Zoroastrian' Calendar", p. 199, with reference to C. Brockelmann, *Geschichte der Arabischen Literatur*, 2nd suppl. I (Leiden, 1943), p. 253) that Abu'l-Ḥasan died in 985 is obviously wrong; Brockelmann, 1st suppl. I (Leiden, 1937) mentions 375/985 as the year of death of Ibn al-A'lam, whom Abu'l-Ḥasan cites.

[1] "Chronology", p. 44 (transl., pp. 54–6).

CIVIL AND VIHĒČAKĪK YEARS

to occur at a period when the condition of the empire was disturbed by calamities; then they neglected intercalation so long, until the day-quarters summed up to two months. Or, on the other hand, they anticipated intercalating the year at once by two months, when they expected that at the time of the next coming intercalation circumstances would distract their attention therefrom, as it had been done in the time of Yazdajird ben Sâbûr, for no other motive but that of precaution. That was the last intercalation which they carried out, under the superintendence of a Dastûr, called Yazdajird Alhizârî. Hizâr was an estate in the district of Iṣṭakhr in Fârs, from which he received his name. In that intercalation the turn had come to Âbân Mâh; therefore, the Epagomenæ were added at its end, and there they have remained ever since on account of their neglecting intercalation. (pp. 55.31–56.12).

This report sounds perfectly reasonable and trustworthy, not only because it makes circumstantial mention of the official supervising this last intercalation, which thus must have taken place about A.D. 400 (Yazdagird I, the son of Šāpūr III, reigned from 399–420), but also because it does not contradict the account of Abu'l Ḥasan who only states that under Khusrau I the Sun travelled through Aries in Ādhārmāh, not that an intercalation was carried out in his reign. And true enough, in 531, the first year of Khusrau's reign, the Sun reached Aries on 7 Ādhār, and in 579, his last year, on 19 Ādhār. That the year began with the spring equinox is moreover confirmed by Bīrūnī, who in the passage preceding the one cited, expressly says that

the Persians believe that the beginning of their year was fixed by the creation of the first man, and that this took place on the day Hurmuz [i.e. the 1st day] of Farwardîn Mâh, whilst the sun stood in the point of the vernal equinox in the middle of heaven. This occurred at the beginning of the 7th millennium, according to their view of the millennia of the world.

and that the original order was restored by Zoroaster.[1]

Two more passages of much later date (14th century) by Quṭb al-Dīn al-Šīrāzī and Šāh Khuljī yield no additional information.[2]

THE CIVIL AND THE VIHĒČAKĪK YEARS

IV. 3. It results from these reports that two year forms were in use simultaneously, both having 12 months of 30 days each plus 5 epagomenal days at the end and coupled in such a way that the

---

[1] "Chronology", p. 45 (transl., p. 55): "When Zoroaster arose and intercalated the years with the months, which up to that time had summed up from the day-quarters, time returned to its original condition."

[2] See T. Hyde, *Historia religionis veterum Persarum* (Oxford, 1700), Ch. 17, pp. 203f., and Ginzel, *Handbuch* I, pp. 290f.

beginnings of the months and the epagomenae always ran parallel. One of them, the civil, which we know continued in use after the downfall of the Sasanian empire, had no intercalation, whence its beginning consistently receded by one day every 4 years from a given solar (to be more exact: Julian) date, say spring equinox. The other, called the *vihēčakīk* year in Pahlavī texts, served religious purposes (note that Bīrūnī ascribes its inauguration to Zoroaster); it added one intercalary month, (allegedly) every 120 years,[1] with the effect that for the next period of 120 years (years 121–240) the first religious month coincided with the second civil, then for the years 241–360 with the third, etc. Once, still in Sasanian times, the beginning of the religious year fell to the 8th month (Ābānmāh) and the epagomenae became attached to it, the procedure came to an end, so that the era of Yazdagird operated thenceforth with the year form inherited from the earlier Sasanian rulers, in which the epagomenae remained fixed after Ābānmāh.

The intercalation scheme, in which the years of Bīrūnī's 116-year period are given in brackets, is illustrated by Table 4.

IV. 4. To the modern names used in Table 4, which in the following will be given preference even for the earlier and earliest phases of the calendar, correspond the following Pahlavī and Avestan forms.[2]

	Modern Persian ·	Pahlavi	Avestan
I	Farvardīn	Fravardīn	Fravašinąm
II	Ordībehešt	Ardvahišt	Ašahe vahištahe
III	Khordād	Hordād	Haurvatātō
IV	Tīr	Tīr	Tištryehe
V	Mordād	Amurdād	Amərətātō
VI	Šahrīvar	Šahrēvar	Xšaθrahe vairyehe
VII	Mehr	Mihr	Miθrahe
VIII	Ābān, Aban	Ābān	Apąm
IX	Āḏar, Āḏar	Ādur	Āθrō
X	Dei	Dai	Daθušō
XI	Bahman	Vahman	Vaŋhave manaŋhe
XII	Esfendārmoḏ	Spandarmad	Spəntayā̊ ārmatōiš
Epagomenae	Panja	5 rōz i gāhānīk	5 Gāθā days

[1] This intercalation period, founded on Abu'l-Ḥasan Kūšyār and on the one passage cited from Bīrūnī, will prove to be only a rough approximation. The correct period, as results from another passage in Bīrūnī (see below), is 116 years. The proof for this fact will be given later. Until then I shall operate with the schematic period of 120 years.

[2] [The Sogdian month-names and day-names, on whose relationship to those of the Later Avestan calendar see W. B. Henning, *BSOAS* XXVIII (1965), 251, will be found listed by Henning in *Orientalia* VIII (1939), 94f.; cf. p. 775, n. 1. The Khotanese month-names are given by H. W. Bailey in *Khotanese Texts* IV (Cambridge, 1961), p. 11, the Cappadocian ones by Paul de Lagarde, *Gesammelte Abhandlungen* (Leipzig, 1866), pp. 258ff. See also *CHI* III, pp. 814–15. Ed.]

CIVIL AND VIHĒČAKĪK YEARS

For the epagomenae modern Persian usually employs the Arabic term *khamsa-yi mustaraqa*, "the five stolen days", which reflects Middle Persian usage (see p. 748, n. 1).

The scheme given in Table 4 is in accordance with Abu'l-Ḥasan's account, which prescribes the insertion of an intercalary Farvardīn II at the end of the year, in other words, after the epagomenae of year 120. Thereby in the civil calendar, the month Farvardīn is preceded and followed by 5 epagomenal days, and so is the intercalary Farvardīn II in the religious calendar. This results of necessity from the transposition of the epagomenae from their original position at the end of one year to the beginning of the next. By omitting the first set of epagomenal days and thus making Farvardīn (civil) 121 = Farvardīn II (religious) 120 follow immediately after the month Esfendārmod, the length of the civil year 120 would have been reduced from 365 to 360 days, and of the corresponding religious year 120, from 395 to 390 days, while later intercalations (years 240, 360...) would not of course affect the year-length as they involve only a transposition of the epagomenae within one and the same year. There would thus have resulted a loss of 5 days in both calendars throughout the ages. As will be demonstrated,[1] no such error can have been committed because the length of the civil year, counting from 1st Farvardīn to 1st Farvardīn can be proved to have remained constant since the very day on which it was started. But there is one fact from which it may be inferred that opinions differed among the officials or priests responsible for the first intercalation, which must have been decreed some time in the first half of the 4th century B.C.: the extension from originally one to subsequently five days of each of the six gāhānbārs and of other feasts, and to eleven days (the epagomenae and the first six days of Farvardīn) in the case of the combined Farvardigān-Naurōz, always counting the last day as the decisive one.[2]

---

[1] See IV. 11, pp. 766f.

[2] Bickerman, "The 'Zoroastrian' Calendar", p. 203 has no high opinion of the capacity of the Persians in the 5th century B.C. to effect computations that would serve to ensure a satisfactory functioning of the religious calendar in the way described. In this context he retells Herodotus' story (IV.98) about Darius giving a thong with 60 knots to the Ionian tyrants and telling them to untie one knot a day so as to know when they might expect him back. He takes this for proof of lack of mathematical insight on the part of the Persians. In fact, however, it proves nothing, for even a skilled mathematician may get confused without such a primitive aid to memory. Counting on the fingers and mathematics are quite different things. The tyrants, moreover, were not Persians but Ionian militaries at the dawn of Greek history, a century before the first intercalation became an issue in Greece. The Persians, witness their well-functioning *lunisolar* calendar in use by then, had already familiarized themselves with the learning of their Babylonian teachers.

IV. 5. However, another passage in Bīrūnī's "Chronology", consistently overlooked or perhaps not taken seriously by earlier students, is of the greatest importance although at first sight it may seem no more than a learned conjecture by a mathematician; it is found on p. 11 of the Arabic text[1] and runs in Sachau's translation as follows:

> [The Persians] reckoned their year as 365 days, and neglected the following fractions until the day-quarters had summed up in the course of 120 years to the number of days of one complete month, and until the 5th parts of an hour, which, according to their opinion, follow the fourth parts of a day (i.e. they give the solar year the length of $365\frac{1}{4}$ days and $\frac{1}{5}$ hour), had summed up to one day; then they added the complete month to the year in each 116th year. This was done for a reason which I shall explain hereafter.

The explanation promised here is not found in the text as it has come down to us; in all probability it was contained in the *lacuna* on p. 45;[2] fortunately it can be reconstructed.

A similar, though less accurate, statement is found in the *Dēnkart*, at the end of the 3rd book (ed. Madan (Bombay, 1911), 402–5). It reads as follows (rendered into English from Nyberg's translation):[3]

> They say that the fractions accumulating from year to year, viz., those hailing from the six hours *and some minutes* [my italics], which go beyond the 365 days of each year, make exactly one day in four years; in 40 years 10 days; in 120 years, one month; in 600 years, 5 months; and in 1440 years, one year. The *fractions of the hour*, in the course of time, accumulate to a day; it is the period of time which is gradually formed, in the course of many years, by adding up the minutes which exceed the six hours, that is to say, the hours which [in their turn] exceed the days of the year.

Here evidently Bīrūnī's "$\frac{1}{5}$ hour", i.e. 12 minutes, is meant.

By contrast, in dealing with the Sogdian festivals ("Chronology", Ch. 10, p. 220), Bīrūnī says:

> The ancient Persians used a solar year of 365 days 6 hours 1 minute, and it was their universal practice to reckon these 6 hours *plus* the 1 minute as a unit [i.e. to disregard the 1 minute in reckoning].

This excess of one single minute is astounding. The Arabic text, avoiding, as in most if not all similar cases found in *al-Āthār al-bāqiya* (contrary to other Bīrūnī texts), the term *daqīqa* for "minute", has for the excess over 365 days *wa-aktharu min rubʿi yawmin bi-juzʾin min sittīna juzʾan min sāʿatin*. By admitting of a scribal error: *min sitta ajzāʾ*, instead of *min sittīn juzʾ*, we would have one-sixth hour or 10 minutes, which

---
[1] Transl., pp. 12–13. [2] Transl., p. 55.
[3] H. S. Nyberg, *Texte zum Mazdayasnischen Kalender* (Uppsala, 1934), pp. 30/31–32/33.

CIVIL AND VIHĚCAKĪK YEARS

comes close enough to the above-mentioned value "one-fifth hour" (expressed there in the usual way by *khums al-sā'a*), and which yields an even better value for the sidereal year: 365.2569 (see IV. 7).

With or without this conjecture we would find ourselves confronted with the strange fact that Bīrūnī, depending on the case, operates with widely different values for the sidereal year.

IV. 6. Up to now we were concerned only with an alleged solar year of $365\frac{1}{4}$ days (the later "Julian" year) to which the vague year of exactly 365 days had to be adapted by regular month-intercalations. This year-length, however, is only an approximation to either of the two year-forms that result from astronomical observation: the *tropical* year, $T = 365.24220$ days, which is *c*. 11 minutes shorter, and the *sidereal*, $S = 365.25636$, which is *c*. 9 minutes longer, than the Julian. The tropical, which alone keeps pace with the seasons, measures the Sun's revolution from vernal point to vernal point or, more generally, its return to one of the equinoctial or solstitial points. It was not distinguished from the sidereal by the Babylonians, even in the Seleucid period, although astronomers doubtless had an idea that it was shorter than the sidereal. The first who determined its length with fair accuracy was Hipparchus (about 130 B.C.). By contrast, the sidereal year, i.e. the Sun's return to a given fixed star, say Regulus or Spica, must have been known at the latest in the 6th century to exceed $365\frac{1}{4}$ days. Seleucid astronomers knew it with astounding accuracy. In their elaborate tables they operate with two slightly different values for its length, one of them coming close to the correct one: the one, which figures in tables belonging to the so-called "System A",[1] has $S_A = 365.2679$, the other ("System B"), $S_B = 365.2595$. These values for the sidereal year must have resulted from observations, stretching probably over centuries, of star phases, such as those listed in Tables 2 and 3.

IV. 7. Let us now scrutinize Bīrūnī's statement. The year he says has a length of $365\frac{1}{4}$ days plus the fifth part of an hour, in other words, 365 days, 6 hours and 12 minutes. Expressed in fractions of a day, this corresponds to 365.2583 which, compared with the correct value, $S = 365.2564$ (see above), is 0.0019 days, or 2.74 minutes, too high. The error is very small; it would accumulate to one day in *c*. 530 years. Note, moreover, that it is nearly identical with, in fact only 100 seconds short of, the Babylonian $S_B = 365.2595$.

[1] For further information see Neugebauer, *The Exact Sciences*, Ch. V, and van der Waerden, *Anfänge der Astronomie*, pp. 114, 172; for a numerical evaluation, in particular, see Hartner's review of the latter in *Gnomon* XLII (1971), p. 534.

This we compare with Bīrūnī's intercalation rule. After each 116th year he says one month of 30 days is inserted. This results in a year length of $365\frac{30}{116} = 365.2586$ days, which differs from the above value, 365.2583, by 26 seconds only. Since an intercalation of 30 days after each 115th year yields 365.2601, and one after each 117th year, 365.2564 (which, incidentally, would be the correct one, S, according to our modern knowledge), the prescribed intercalation period of 116 years is the only one that accords with Bīrūnī's length of the sidereal year.[1]

EXCURSUS: THE OLD EGYPTIAN YEAR

IV. 8. As an excursus I insert here a brief discussion of the old Egyptian calendar. As said in what precedes, its relationship to the Later Avestan calendar has been under debate since Scaliger's time, but no conclusive mathematical proof has so far been given either in the affirmative or in the negative.

Like the Later Avestan calendar, which it precedes by far, the Egyptian calendar, in use already by the beginning of the 3rd millennium,[2] operated with an invariable year of 365 days subdivided into 12 months of 30 days plus 5 epagomenal days at the end of the year. In accordance with the climatic peculiarities of the country, the year was divided into 3 seasons: the time of the Nile flood, the time of sowing and the time of harvesting, and each season was supposed to comprise 4 months, as follows:

Time of Flood	Time of Sowing	Time of Harvesting
1 Thoth	5 Tybi	9 Pakhon
2 Phaophi	6 Mekhir	10 Payni
3 Athyr	7 Phamenoth	11 Epiphi
4 Khoyak	8 Pharmuti	12 Mesori
		(13) "Little month" of 5 days

[1] O. Neugebauer, *A History of Ancient Mathematical Astronomy* II (Berlin–Heidelberg–New York, 1975), p. 902, derives from Ptolemy's *Planetary Hypotheses*, as a basic parameter underlying all data referring to planetary motion, the length of the sidereal year, $S_P = 365;15,24,31,22,27,7$ days (sexagesimal fraction); converting this into a decimal fraction, we find $S_P = 365.2568119174$. This "hypercorrect" value is only 39 seconds too high compared with the modern, $S = 365.25636$; it is thus far better than the value indicated by Bīrūnī.

[2] The alleged "introduction of the Egyptian vague year on 19 July, 4241 B.C." when the first day of the year (1st Thoth) coincided with the heliacal rising of Sirius (see E. Meyer, *Geschichte des Altertums*, 2nd ed., vol. I, part 2 (Stuttgart–Berlin, 1909), pp. 29ff.), can no longer be maintained; see O. Neugebauer, "Die Bedeutungslosigkeit der Sothisperiode", *AO* XVII (1938), pp. 169–95.

EXCURSUS

The year, we see, was originally devised as a solar year beginning with the heliacal rising of Sirius (Eg. Sopdet, Gr. Sothis), which during several millennia announced the advent of the flood. But as in the case of the Later Avestan year, the 1st of Thoth gradually receded through the astronomical seasons, one day every four years, so that after 500 years ($4 \times 5 = 20$ for the "little month", and $4 \times 120 = 480$ for the preceding 4 months) it fell on a day in the solar calendar originally held by 1st Pakhon; another 480 years later it coincided with the original solar date of 1st Tybi, and again after 480 years it came back to its initial position determined by the heliacal rising of Sirius.[1] The Egyptian and the *civil* Later Avestan year, both of which ignore the astronomical seasons, are thus perfectly analogous.

It was not before the time of Augustus that the quarter-day error was accounted for by intercalations similar to those of the Julian calendar. This "Alexandrian year" was used by Ptolemy in one of his minor works, the *Phaseis*, so called for good reasons, because it deals with the annual phases (heliacal risings etc.) of stars, which depend on the solar, or more precisely, the sidereal, year. By contrast in the *Almagest* Ptolemy operates consistently with the old Egyptian year of 365 days, choosing as his epoch the 1st of Thoth, 747 B.C. (the year of the Babylonian king Nabonassar's ascent to the throne), which corresponds with the Julian date 26 February, 747 B.C., and counting consistently by years after Nabonassar. The reasons for this choice are obvious: a calendar based on a year of constant length is of great advantage to astronomical computations in which differences of days comprised between observations (e.g. of eclipses) made at far distant times are to be carried out.[2]

---

[1] For the sake of completeness it may be added that the "Sothis period" is never mentioned in hieroglyphic texts. Censorinus, in A.D. 239, and Theon of Alexandria, about 370, refer to it. The latter states correctly that in A.D. 139 the first day of Thoth coincided with the heliacal rising of Sirius, on 20 July. From this, reckoning back by periods of 1,460 years, he finds earlier coincidences to have occurred in the years (expressed according to modern usage) 1322, 2782 and 4242 B.C. This last date, supported by no historic evidence whatever, was celebrated by Meyer as "the earliest date in history".

[2] For the same reason modern chronology employs the so-called "Julian day count" (introduced by J. J. Scaliger and named after his father, Julius Caesar Scaliger) to which we shall have recourse occasionally in the ensuing demonstrations. Its epoch is a far remote date, 1 January, 4713 B.C., counted as day no. 0. Since 4713 B.C. is a leap-year, the 1st January of the next year will be no. 366, of the next, no. 731, etc. To the Era of Nabonassar, 26 February (= 1st Thoth) 747 B.C., corresponds no. 1448638; to 27 March 503 B.C. (spring equinox), no. 1537788; to the Era of Yazdgird, 16 June (= 1st Farvardīn), A.D. 632, no. 1952063; to 13 April (= 1st Farvardīn) A.D. 890, no. 2046233; to 15 March (= 1st Farvardīn) A.D. 1006, no. 2088573.

OLD IRANIAN CALENDARS

IV. 9. The questions to be answered now on the basis of what we have seen are the following three:

(1) Is the analogy between the Egyptian and the Later Avestan calendars purely accidental? If not, is it possible to establish the date when the two became linked together?

(2) Were the intercalations in the religious calendar made regularly until political vicissitudes, as referred to by Bīrūnī, put an end to regularity and finally stopped them altogether, after an anticipated eighth intercalation involving a transposition of the epagomenae after Ābānmāh? Is Bīrūnī's report trustworthy in maintaining that this last intercalation was decreed by or during the reign of Yazdagird I, the son of Šāpūr III (399–420)? If so, which of the two intercalation intervals, 120 or 116 years, is to be accepted as correct?

(3) Was the date 375 Yazdagird = A.D. 1006, for the redemption of the neglected four intercalations (in reality, five were due) by transposition of the epagomenae after the 12th month (Esfendārmodmāh), chosen at random, or does it bear witness to the remembrance of the old intercalary system having still been alive in learned Iranian circles?

IV. 10. To find a solution to these problems we, naturally, start from the only indubitable date connecting the Later Avestan calendar with the Hijra, and thereby also with the old Egyptian and the Julian calendars: the beginning of the era of Yazdagird III.

In A.D. 632 the first Farvardīn fell on Julian day (JD, see p. 765, n. 2) no. 1952 063, a Tuesday, corresponding with 21 Rabī' I, A.H. 11; moreover, with 1st Khoyak, year 1380 of the era Nabonassar; finally, with 16 June, A.D. 632.

The fact that in 632 the 4th Egyptian month, Khoyak, coincided completely with the 1st Later Avestan, Farvardīn, seems indicative because of the analogous structure of the two calendars. In order to ascertain, however, that this identity has prevailed throughout the ages (this is not a matter of course on account of the changing position of the epagomenae in the Later Avestan), we have recourse to the following consideration.

IV. 11. Let us assume that – probably about 500 B.C. – there ruled the same identity: Farvardīn = Khoyak, and let us for the sake of simplicity denote the Later Avestan month with Arabic, and the Egyptian with Roman numerals. We shall then have the concordances 1 = IV, 2 = V, etc., till 9 = XII, and the Egyptian epagomenae (XII*e*, attached to XII)

EXCURSUS

will correspond with the first 5 days of the Later Avestan 10th month (Daθušō = Dei), and thereafter, the 6th day of 10 with the 1st of I (Thoth). The effect will be that each of the Later Avestan months nos. 10, 11 and 12 falls 5 days ahead of the corresponding Egyptian, I, II and III. The concordance is restored only by the insertion of the Later Avestan epagomenae (12e), attached to 12 (Esfendārmoḏmāh). Thereafter the cycle starts anew with 1 = IV.

The first intercalation in the *religious* calendar (*c.* 120 years after the inception) involved a transposition in the *civil* of the epagomenae from the end of the year (12e) to the beginning of the next: they now become attached to 1 (Farvardīn), and will accordingly have to be denoted as 1e. Thus we have the equations 1 = IV as in the preceding period, but thereafter the Later Avestan epagomenae will fall on the first 5 days of V; then the first day of 2 (Ordībeheštmāh) will fall on the 6th of V, the 1st of 3, on the 6th of VI, etc., until by the insertion of the Egyptian epagomenae (XIIe) after XII, which then coincide with days 26–30 of 9 (Āḏārmāh), the concordance is restored with 10 = I, 11 = II, 12 = III, and 1 = IV. Thus during this period, the Later Avestan months: 2 (Ordībeheštmāh) through 9 (Āḏārmāh) will all start on the 6th day of the corresponding Egyptian, V (Tybi) through XII (Mesori), and only the four months mentioned above (10 = I through 1 = IV) will be in perfect correspondence.

As can easily be seen, with each subsequent intercalation period the number of completely congruent months is increased by one: in the second we have 10 = I through 2 = V; in the third, 10 = I through 3 = VI; finally, in the eighth – the last – when the epagomenae (8e) became attached to 8 (Ābānmāh) we have 10 = I through 8 = XI. Only the ninth intercalation, which was never decreed, would have caused the epagomenae of both calendars to coincide, and with them, all other months: Farvardīn = Khoyak through Esfendārmoḏ = Athyr.

Thus a comparison of a civil Later Avestan date with an Egyptian is possible only if we know which of the eight intercalation periods is concerned. This would seem of purely theoretical interest since we have no other equation than the one mentioned, namely A.D. 632, 1st Farvardīn = 1st Khoyak. Nevertheless it will prove useful because it enables us, as will be seen, to verify some Later Avestan dates with the aid of the tables available for the Egyptian calendar.

IV. 12. The main, though not the only purpose of the preceding demonstration was to prove that, despite differences of 5 days occurring on a great many occasions between the two calendars, the Later Avestan Farvardīn coincided at all times with the Egyptian Khoyak. This was true thus also at the time when the Later Avestan calendar came into being, and thereby the two calendars' close connection appears to be firmly established. Historically this needs no justification, considering the close relation between Persia and Egypt established after Cambyses' conquest of Egypt (525 B.C.).

Now Abu'l-Ḥasan tells us (see IV. 2) that the first month of the year originally was the one in which the Sun entered the sign of Aries – in other words, spring equinox. Although it has been claimed with more or less convincing arguments that the Later Avestan year originally started at winter solstice, with the month Daθušō-Dei, or even at summer solstice, I see no reason to doubt Abu'l-Ḥasan's trustworthiness. Let us therefore determine the period of 4 years[1] during which 1st Farvardīn = 1st Khoyak fell on the spring equinox. We find by an elementary computation that this was the case 1,134 to 1,137 Persian years before the Era of Yazdagird, i.e. in the years 505–502 B.C.,[2] when the day of the spring equinox was 27 March (Julian).

IV. 13. This critical period we now remember plays a crucial role in another context. In III. 4 I have shown that the year 503 B.C., the 19th year of Darius' reign, at one and the same time marked the end of the Babylonian calendar's octaëteris intercalation and the beginning of the new 19-year cycle, on the day of spring equinox, 27 March. We have seen, moreover (III. 9/10), that in the same year there occurred irregularities in the Old Persian lunisolar calendar, that can be explained as reflecting an uncertainty pertaining to this transition period.

The probability is therefore considerable that the Later Avestan calendar was started precisely then, on 27 March 503 B.C., with the first day of the month Fravašinąm-Farvardīn (no matter whether that name

---

[1] During 4 years the Later Avestan and Egyptian calendar dates fall on one and the same solar (or Julian) date. In the 6th century B.C. spring equinox fell on 27 March (Jul.), in the 5th, on 26 March.

[2] Taqizadeh, *op. cit.*, p. 603, concludes that the Egyptian calendar "was perhaps adopted by the Zoroastrian community of Iran at a time when the Egyptian New Year (the first day of the month Thoth) corresponded with the winter solstice, and the same day was made the beginning of the Iranian year and the first day of the month Daδv (Dai). This was the case in or about 504 B.C., on 26–7 December. In this same year the same day (27 December) happened to correspond also with the first day of the old Persian (Achaemenian) month Anāmaka (the 10th month) = Babylonian Ṭebētu." His claim, however, that in or about 504 B.C. the month Daθušō too started at winter solstice on 26–7 December, is erroneous. As demonstrated above, 1 Daθušō fell on the 1st of the Egyptian epagomenae, whence winter solstice fell on 6 Daθušō. This proves that a beginning of the Persian year at winter solstice is out of the question.

EXCURSUS

existed from the beginning or was introduced only after the first intercalation, as suggested by Taqizadeh).[1] But certainty can be obtained only by testing whether either of the two possible intercalation intervals, 120 or 116 years, produces confirmation of known historical facts or dates. To this end we list in Table 5 the dates in the Julian calendar corresponding to the first day of Farvardīn at the beginning of each intercalation period.

IV. 14. While nothing pertinent to our problem appears to result from the 120-year sequence, at least two of the dates found in the 116-year sequence are of great interest:

(1) *The year A.D. 425.* Bīrūnī reports (see IV. 2) that the Persians "anticipated intercalating the year by two months [*yataqaddamūna bi-kabsihā bi-šahraini*] when they expected that at the time of the next coming intercalation circumstances would distract their attention therefrom, as it has been done in the time of Yazdajird I b. Sābūr, for no other motive but that of precaution". The dual *šahrain* is doubtless an error caused by the preceding *šahrān*, which refers to *neglected* intercalations. It must of course read *bi-šahrin*, "by [one] month". But even an anticipated single intercalation will appear motivated only if political calamities (such as mentioned in the preceding passage) can be expected to disturb law and order in the near future. For nobody can foresee what will happen 30 years hence. Now the trouble arising after Yazdagird's death in or about A.D. 420 (note that he was surnamed Bazagar, "the sinner", and that his subjects had suffered greatly by his injustice)[2] could easily have been foreseen. Therefore it sounds plausible that the eighth intercalation (perhaps together with a neglected seventh) was anticipated towards the end of his reign, in view of the fact that it was due within a very short period of time, at the most a decade. For, the correct date for it results from our 116 year period: 7 August 425, within five years after the tyrant's death, caused by the well-aimed kick of a wild horse which, according to Firdausī and Ṭabarī, had been sent from Heaven, doubtless expressly for the purpose. By contrast, the 120-year period yields the date A.D. 457. For the reason mentioned – it was 37 years after Yazdagird's death – it is unthinkable that so far ahead an intercalation should have been anticipated during his reign.

[1] *Op. cit.*, p. 608.
[2] Cf. F. Spiegel, *Eränische Alterthumskunde* III (Leipzig, 1878), pp. 340–7: A. Christensen, *L'Iran sous les Sassanides* (Copenhagen, 1944), p. 269 and *CHI* III, p. 143.

(2) *The year A.D. 1005.* All later authors agree with Abu'l-Ḥasan Kūšyār's report that in the year 375 of the Yazdagird Era, "when the Sun entered Aries on the first day of Farvardīnmāh, the five days became attached to the 12th month, Esfendārmoḏmāh" (see IV. 2). Now the first Farvardīn 375 actually fell on the very day of spring equinox, 15 March (Julian), which thus had been determined with admirable accuracy. But, alas, the concordance with the 116-year period is not perfect because this latter yields for the beginning of the new period the year A.D. 1005 instead of 1006, whence one should expect the transfer of the epagomenae to have been ordered already at the end of A.Y. 373.

This difference of one year may of course be due to a simple slip. We might content ourselves with this in view of the indubitable fact that the agreement cannot be accidental, and take it as a confirmation of the Later Avestan calendar's starting point of 27 March 503 B.C., as well as of the 116-year intercalation period. However, it is even possible to account for the disturbing discrepancy of 365 days.

From Table 5 we see that in A.D. 541 a transfer of the epagomenae from their place after Ābānmāh (8) to Āḏārmāh (9) was due; thereafter, in 657, to Deimāh (10), in 773 to Bahmanmāh (11), and in 889 to Esfendārmoḏmāh (12). None of those changes we know was carried out, so it was only in 1006 that the long-overdue correction was made. With it the calendar experts wished to restore the order prevailing at the calendar's outset by appending the epagomenae to the *last month*. Correctly, however, they ought to have transferred them to next after the first month, Farvardīnmāh, of the following year. The situation in A.D. 1005 thus was similar to that in the 117th year (see Table 4, where the year numbers in brackets count), but the circumstance that the epagomenae were decreed to occupy the place they theoretically should have held in the *preceding* period, doubtless caused some confusion. The choice of A.Y. 375 may thus have resulted from a compromise between the experts' differing opinions.

Considering that Bīrūnī, as the greatest expert in chronology, mentions the 116-year period in *al-Āthār al-bāqiya*, written a few years before the crucial years 1005–6, there seems to be a high probability of his having taken part in the deliberations that led to the reform.

IV. 15. This post-Sasanian intercalation we have seen falls exactly into the span of 4 years, A.D. 1004–7, when for the first time since the Later

EXCURSUS

Avestan calendar's inception the first day of Farvardīn again coincided with spring equinox, after having travelled, retrogressively through the seasons, from 27 March (Julian) = 21 March (Gregorian) 503 B.C. to 15 March (= 21 March Gregorian) A.D. 1005. Abu'l-Ḥasan's insistence upon this fact (IV. 2) leaves no doubt that it played a decisive part in the choice of this date for the last change in the position of the epagomenae. But the fact itself that the epagomenae were transferred constitutes clear evidence that the experts were still aware of the old tradition, and that the coincidence of 1st Farvardīn with the Sun's entering the sign of Aries only was taken as confirmation of the calendar's admirably exact functioning.

What they doubtless were not aware of, however, was that the 116-year period, at the time of its invention and introduction, had been destined to connect for ever the religious (vihēčakīk) year not with the Sun's return to the equinox (the tropical year, then not yet distinguished from the sidereal), but with the annual risings and settings of stars, as shown in Table 2. When in 503 B.C. the Zoroastrian priests – or whoever was responsible – let their new calendar start on the day of spring equinox, so as to achieve a seamless transition from the Old Persian lunisolar calendar, they in all probability believed that they were replacing a well-working solar calendar with a complicated lunisolar, which just in the selfsame year was being cast into workable shape. Before long, however, it would become obvious that the spring equinox and the gāhānbārs were gradually changing their position within the new calendar. At the latest shortly after the middle of the 5th century, which will be found valid for the period of the gāhānbār dates recorded in *Āfrīnakān* 3.7–12 (see III. 14, p. 751 and V. 1–2, p. 781), measures must have been discussed to restore the year to its original state, in other words, to introduce a vihēčakīk year. Among these the 116-year period, worked out perhaps by having recourse to Babylonian astronomers, was found best fitted for the purpose; in point of fact, it was a pretty nearly ideal solution to the problem.

IV. 16. The 1,508 vague years comprised between the spring equinoxes of 503 B.C. (i.e. −502) and A.D. 1006 thus equal exactly 1507 tropical years (T). Indeed, the value resulting from the formula

$$T = \tfrac{1508}{1507} \times 365 = 365.24220$$

is correct to the fifth decimal place.

By contrast, the sidereal phenomena, such as the cosmical setting of

OLD IRANIAN CALENDARS

Spica, which originally had marked the time of spring equinox, inevitably underwent changes which in due course must have become perceptible, although during the first two or three intercalation periods they may have been attributed to the circumstance that observations were no longer made in Persepolis but at places having another latitude and different elevations of the apparent horizon. The difference between the sidereal year according to Bīrūnī, 365.2586 (see IV. 7) and the tropical 365.2422, is 0.0164 days. This amounts to 1 day in 61 years, to 2 days at the beginning of the first intercalation period, and to 25 days at the beginning of the 13th period (A.D. 1005). Counting with the modern value for the sidereal year (365.2564), which we have seen falls a little short of Bīrūnī's, a difference of 1 day is reached only after *c*. 70 years (the effect of precession), which amounts to *c*. 21 (instead of 25) days in 1,500 years.

Checking now with astronomical facts, we find that the cosmical setting of Spica in about A.D. 1000, fell on *c*. 11 April, that is to say, not 21 but 27 days after the equinox, on 27 Farvardīn. The discrepancy of 6 days is explained by the fact (not to be discussed here) that the annual phases of stars do not repeat themselves at intervals identical with the sidereal year. In the case of Spica the interval is shorter. It amounts to 1 day in *c*. 56 years (as against the 70 years corresponding to the motion of precession).

The calendar reformers of A.Y. 375 could not possibly be aware of this displacement since in all probability the astronomical situation obtaining when the calendar was started had never been officially recorded. What they knew, witness Bīrūnī's report, was that the first year had begun with the day of spring equinox. They were content to find that this was again the case when according to the 116-year cycle a new intercalation had become due.

THE JALĀLĪ CALENDAR

IV. 17. The vague year combined with the Yazdagird Era remained in use until fairly recent times, unaffected by the reform decreed in the 7th year of the Saljuq Sulṭān Jalāl al-Dīn Malikšāh (1073–92), about which a few words have to be said in this context.

At the order of Malikšāh a group of eight mathematicians and astronomers, among them the great 'Umar Khayyām, had worked out a calendar destined to remain connected for ever with the tropical year.

THE JALĀLĪ CALENDAR

It thus marked a definitive break with the Later Avestan calendar. The epoch of this *Tārīkh-i Jalālī* was chosen to be 19 Farvardīnmāh A.Y. 448 = 15 March A.D. 1079 because on that day, according to Šāh Kholjī, the Sun entered Aries about the time of sunrise. This is borne out by modern computation: at the Saljuq Sultan's residence, Isfahān, the Sun actually reached the vernal point at $c.$ $6^h 20^m$ a.m. (mean time), in other words, 20 minutes after sunrise. Thus in 1079, 19 Farvardīn "old style" (*qadīm*) became 1 Farvardīn "new style" (Jalālī), and this first day of the year was thenceforth called *Naurōz-i-Sulṭānī*. The names of the months were the same as in the vague year, with the epagomenae attached to Esfendārmodmāh. In cases in which confusion between the two calendars could arise, the words qadīm and Jalālī (or Sulṭānī), respectively, were added. The concordance with the tropical year was warranted by making years of 365 days (with 5 epagomenae) alternate in an appropriate order with years of 366 days (6 epagomenae). The system of intercalation was complicated: 8 intercalary days in 33 years alternated with 9 in 37 and 7 in 29, but in view of the fact that we ignore the exact sequence of those subcycles, conversions of Jalālī into Julian dates always involve the possibility of an error of one day. According to Ulugh Beg the mean length of the Jalālī year was 365;14,33,7,32 days (sexagesimal fractions) = 365.242535 days. The accuracy of this value – exceeding the length of the Gregorian year by only 3 seconds, and that of the true tropical year by 29 seconds – is admirable. As Ginzel[1] has shown, it can be approximated by the fraction $365\frac{65}{268} = 365.242537$ (0.6 seconds too high), from which it results that 65 years out of 268 must be leap-years of 366 days. This can be achieved by combining 7 subcycles of 33 years (having $7 \times 8 = 56$ intercalary days) with one subcycle of 37 years (containing 9 intercalary days).

The calendar of the French Revolution, apart from the year's beginning at autumn equinox, is practically identical with the Jalālī, thereby betokening the paternity of the latter.

---

[1] *Handbuch* I, pp. 301ff.; from the fixation of 1st Farvardīnmāh (Jalālī), year no. 1, on the day on which the Sun entered Aries shortly after sunrise it is seen that the days were counted from sunrise. This is confirmed by *Bundahišn* Ch. 25 (ed. Anklesaria, 157, Justi, 59; cf. Nyberg, *Texte*, pp. 10/11): "Always the day is to be counted first and then the ensuing night." Considering the tenacity of such traditions, it is very probable that this was the case also in earlier, perhaps already Achaemenian times.

OLD IRANIAN CALENDARS

THE DAYS OF THE MONTH

IV. 18. Unlike most other calendars, except the Old-Egyptian,[1] the days of the Later Avestan months were not numbered but had special religious names (see Table 6). "Divinities honoured by the names", says Ilya Gershevitch,[2] "include Ahura Mazdāh,[3] six 'Holy Immortals' (i.e., Aməša Spəntas), Mithra, Anāhitā,[3] Tištrya, Fire, the Fravašis,[4] Sun, Moon, Sky, Earth, Wind, the Soul of the Cow, the Religion, Discipline, Reward, in short, most of the deities of the Zarathuštric religion, with the notable exception of Haoma." This characteristic feature: Haoma's name lacking among the calendar names, supported by Herodotus 1.132, where no Haoma libation is mentioned in the description of the Persian sacrifices, clearly shows that the calendar names could not have been selected by Zarathuštric priests because they "would scarcely have failed to include the patron-god of their own class, whom they regarded as the divine priest of Ahura Mazdāh (Yašt 10.89f.) to whom Ahura Mazdāh himself had entrusted the Mazdayasnian religion (Yasna 9.26)".[5] Gershevitch therefore suggests that the calendar in its definitive shape ought to be termed Magian rather than Zoroastrian, basing himself on the fact that its names are "a selective index of the Magian repertory". A borrowing from Egypt, unlikely in itself, therefore seems out of the question. On the other hand, "the day-names may well belong to a later period of systematization, but it is worth stating that that period must still have been the *Old* Iranian, i.e. the Achaemenian. This is shown by the *form* of some of the names in Middle Iranian, in instances where that form is explicable only as the outcome of an *Old* Iranian genitive (governed by an implied word for 'day'). For instance, 'bull' is *gāv* in Middle Persian and New Persian, from the Old Iranian nominative *gāuš* or accusative *gāvam*, both with long *ā*; while the

---

[1] In the Egyptian calendar special denominations for the 30 days of the *lunar* calendar occur; see H. Bruggsch, *Thesaurus inscriptionum Aegypticarum* (Leipzig, 1883–91), pp. 46–8, and R. A. Parker, *The Calendars of Ancient Egypt* (Chicago, 1950), §36, pp. 11f.

[2] "Zoroaster's Own Contribution", *JNES* XXIII (1964), pp. 12–38; see p. 21. Gershevitch distinguishes between *Zarathuštrianism* = religion of the Gathas, and *Zarathuštricism* = doctrine of the Later Avestan texts, reserving *Zoroastrianism* for the doctrine's later form during the Sasanian period.

[3] "Ahura Mazdāh and Anāhitā are not referred to in the calendar by these names, but respectively as *Daθušō*, lit. 'the Creator', and *Apąm*, lit. 'the Waters' (of which Anāhitā was the goddess)", *ibid.*, n. 34.

[4] "These twelve divinities account for the names of the months, but they also occur as day-names," *ibid.*, n. 35.

[5] *Ibid.*, p. 26 and n. 43.

exclusively calendrical *gōš* can only represent the Old Iranian genitive *gauš*, with short *ă*. The systematization may have been the work of the Magi, and the replacement of Tištrya with Tīr in Persis may have occurred on the occasion of it."[1]

For the inception of the new way of denoting the days of the months by the names of Magian divinities instead of simply numbering them from 1 to 30, Gershevitch accepts the year 441 B.C. proposed by Taqizadeh as the beginning, or at least a year near the beginning, of the vihēčakīk year.[2] As will be shown (V. 2) the year can be narrowed down to the period 447–444 B.C. But the assertion that this marked the start of the vihēčakīk year cannot be maintained because it is incompatible with the pertinent mathematical demonstration given in IV. 12–16. It is possible, even probable, that this new determination and fixation of the gāhānbārs, carried out then, but preceded *c.* 15 years earlier by one of the equinoxes (see V. 3) was the last stimulus to considerations culminating in the establishment of the 116-year cycle, but it will have been put in practice only by the first intercalation in 387 B.C. Hence the term "reform", as used by Gershevitch,[3] is justified only if limited to the change from day numbers to day divinities hailing from the Magian pantheon, which in all probability was facilitated by Artaxerxes I's permissiveness.

It seems out of the question that those day names could ever replace

---

[1] Personal communication by I. Gershevitch (letter of 12 April, 1974). [The Middle Parthian equivalent *gwyrh* of Middle Persian *gōš* (whose *š* can owe its presence only to learned tradition, as itself vouchsafes Achaemenian origin of the calendar name) will likewise be of Old Iranian coinage if it represents a compound containing *ayar-*, a word for "day" extinct by the Middle period of Parthian; see *Studia classica et orientalia A. Pagliaro oblata* II (Rome, 1969), p. 197. Other calendar names whose Middle Iranian forms presuppose Old Iranian genitives are Pahlavī *šahrēvar* (-*ē-* from Old Iranian -*ahe*, itself from -*ahya*), *fravardīn*, and *anagrān* (from Old Persian **anagrānām*), quite likely also short-vowelled *abān* (from *apām*, with -*m* preserved like the -*š* of *gauš* until -*n* took over so as to "regularize" what it became tempting to consider the plural of Middle Persian *āb*). The Middle Sogdian calendar names (see W. B. Henning, *Orientalia* VIII (1939), 94f.) in addition to *xšēwar*, *yoš* and *nayran* include four others of genitival coinage: nos 8 and 15 δəšči and no. 9 *āš* (see Henning, p. 91, nn. 1 and 2), as well as no. 2 *xumna* and no. 20 *wšayna* (see *GMS*, §404); a fifth is perhaps no. 28 *ẓmuxtuy* (if its *y* represents, with voice-dissimilation, the second *h* of Avestan *zəmō huδåŋhō*; cf. Pahlavī *zamyād*, which looks like a re-interpretation as **zama(h-h)udāt* "well-created earth", of the original intermediary **zam(ah-h)udāb* "beneficial earth"). As indicated by reference to Marquart and Henning in *Mémorial Jean de Menasce* (Louvain, 1974), p. 71, apart from formal considerations Old Iranian origin of the so-called "Zoroastrian" calendar terms is guaranteed by their geographical spread from Cappadocia to Chorasmia, an enormous area never again to find itself, after the fall of the Achaemenian empire, under one single political sway that could have imposed on it a uniform terminology. (*GMS* = Gershevitch, *A grammar of Manichaean Sogdian*, Oxford, 1954; repr. 1961.) Ed.]

[2] *Op. cit.*, p. 603: "The date I propose was 441 B.C., or at any rate some time in the first decade of the second half of the 5th century B.C."

[3] "Zoroaster's own contribution", p. 21.

in popular usage the original day numbers; even in our days one would not expect common man to memorize a sequence of 30 deities for use in ordinary life. This practice was evidently limited to the clergy and to learned circles.

In Table 6 the day names are given in their Avestan, Pahlavī and New Persian forms (the latter according to Bīrūnī). The name of the highest god, Ahura Mazdāh occupies the first place; it is then repeated three times under the denomination Daθušō, "Creator": nos. 8, 15, 23. In Pahlavī, to avoid confusion, the three different Daθušō = Dai are distinguished by adding the name of the next divinity: *Dai-pad-Ādur*, "the Dai(-day) at Ādur(-day)" (see p. 748, n. 1) etc. Thus the Creator's name divides the month into periods of $2 \times 7 + 2 \times 8$ days. On the other hand, Ahura Mazdāh (no. 1) and Miθra (no. 16) each head one of the month's two halves, while in the month names, Daθušō occupies the 10th place and Miθra the 6th. The complete sequence of correspondences between month-names and day-names is shown below:

Avestan name	Month no.	Day no.
Fravašinąm	1	19
Ašahe vahištahe	2	3
Haurvatātō	3	6
Tištryehe	4	13
Amərətātō	5	7
Xšaθrahe vairyehe	6	4
Miθrahe	7	16
Apąm	8	10
Āθrō	9	9
Daθušō	10	1, 8, 15, 23
Vaŋhave mananhe	11	2
Spəntayā̊ ārmatōiš	12	5

IV. 19. As will be discussed in detail, the coincidences between month and day names were duly celebrated by festivals. Among them, two seem of special interest because they may reflect, as pointed out by Taqizadeh,[1] the astronomical situation at the time of the introduction of the Magian day-names, i.e. the alleged "reform" of 441 B.C. Taqizadeh's assumption that the Mihragān (Miθrakāna), which was the most important festival after Naurōz, at the time of its introduction fell on autumn equinox, and Tīragān (which in Avestan would have been *Tištryakāna) on

[1] *Op. cit.*, p. 607.

DIVISIONS OF THE DAY

summer solstice, sounds plausible; but the astronomical and calendrical data by which he tries to confirm the date 441 are not correct. Postulating that the autumnal equinox was observed with the same degree of accuracy as the vernal, while summer solstice, in accordance with III. 16, *c.* two days too early, we find that the conditions: 16 Mehr = 21 September (Gregorian) = 26 September (Julian) = autumn equinox, and 13 Tīr = 19 June (Gregorian) = 24 June (Julian) = 2 days before summer solstice, are fulfilled for the period of 4 years, 457–454 B.C. This period comes close by 7 to 10 years to the period 447–444 mentioned above, which has to be substituted for Taqizadeh's 441 B.C. Since the period 447–444 results (V. 2) from the changed position of the solar dates (the gāhānbārs) within the vague year, the difference of 7 to 10 years, corresponding to 2 days in the calendar date, must be ascribed to observational errors. In view of the circumstance, however, that the gāhānbār dating is better founded than that by the summer and autumn festivals, preference has to be given to the former.

THE FIVE EPAGOMENAL DAYS

IV. 20. The 5 epagomenal days ("Gāθā days") are called after the 5 Gāθās: Ahunavaitī, Uštavaitī, Spəntāmainyu, Vohuxšaθrā and Vahištōištī. However, there must have existed a great many different denominations, witness Bīrūnī,[1] who cites no less than six widely different traditions, with the remark that he never read them in two books or heard them from two men alike.[2] According to the *Dēnkart*, Book VIII,[3] the five Gāθā days are "dedicated to all of the gods".

DIVISIONS OF THE DAY

IV. 21. Divisions of the day are mentioned in *Bundahišn* 25:[4] "During the 7 summer months (Fravardīn through Mihr) the canonical times of the days and nights are five because they invoke the Rapiθvin. At dawn one had the Hāvan time, at noon, the Rapiθvin, at sunset, the

---

[1] "Chronology", Ar. text, pp. 43f., transl., pp. 53f.

[2] According to Bīrūnī, Zādawayhi b. Šāhawayhi, in his book on the causes of the festivals of the Persians, has all five of the *Gāθā* names preceded by the word fanjah. This evidently renders the Pahlavī term *panjak*, "pentad", found in *Dēnkart* III and elsewhere.

[3] Ed. Madan, pp. 683f., cited after Nyberg, *Texte*, pp. 8/9.

[4] Nyberg, *Texte*, pp. 12/13.

Uzayarin; from the time the stars come to appearance till midnight, one has the Aibisrūθrin time, and for midnight till their disappearance, the Ušahin time. In winter there are only four such times, for the period from the morning up to the Uzayarin is then called Hāvan time, and the rest is as I have said." The corresponding Avestan names are given in Yasna 1. 3–7: Hāvani, Rapiθwina, Uzayeirina, Aiwisrūθrima aibigaya, and Ušahina. Obviously the Pahlavī text has preserved here the old Avestan forms.

DAY PENTADS: RELICS OF A RELIGIOUS LUNAR YEAR

IV. 22. The 3rd Book of the *Dēnkart*[1] contains a passage apparently attesting that the lunar year had not disappeared completely from the Zoroastrian religion, though nothing seems to be known as to when and where such a year could have been in use side by side with the well-established vague year (called in *Dēnkart* "*ōšmurtīk*", i.e. "computational" year, also *rōč-vihēčakīk*, which Nyberg (p. 84) renders with *Tagesschaltjahr*, "day-intercalation-year" although the 5 epagomenal days have of course nothing to do with intercalation) or the fixed solar (vihēčakīk, "intercalary") year.

Each *lunar* month, it says, according to its religious division has 5 pentads (*panjak*),[2] three of which carry (individual) names. One of them is called Andarmāh;[3] its first day is the first, and its last day the 5th after neomenia. Another pentad is Purrmāh[4] (11th–15th day), a third is Višaptas[5] (21st–25th day). "These three pentads are called the holy panjaks."

Of the second series of pentads, one is called Counter (*patīrak*)-Andarmāh (6th–10th day), another Counter-Purrmāh (16th–20th day), a third one Counter-Višaptas (26th–30th day), "whose last day is the 30th day after the same neomenia. The activity at the next neomenia continues immediately the three periods and the ones depending on them" (i.e. the chief and counter-panjaks).

[1] Ed. Madan, pp. 274–6; cited after Nyberg, *Texte*, pp. 40/41–42/43.
[2] See p. 777, n. 2. Nyberg renders *panjak* with "Fünfwoche".
[3] Avestan *antarəmāh*, "divinity of the New Moon", see C. Bartholomae, *Altiranisches Wörterbuch* (Strassburg, 1904), column 134. In Bīrūnī's list of festivals (see IV. 23) the epagomenae are called *āndārmāh*.
[4] Av. *parənō.māh*, "divinity of the Full Moon", Bartholomae, col. 895.
[5] Transliteration of Av. *višaptaθa*, "divinity of the seventh day inserted after each neomenia and plenilune", Bartholomae, col. 1472. The meaning of this explanation seems veiled.

RELIGIOUS FESTIVALS

Needless to say such a system is applicable only to months of 30 days, in other words, to the vague year, not to the lunar month with the mean length of 29½ days. But the text is clear enough to exclude the possibility of a trivial misunderstanding. In the absence of further evidence this strange passage must remain unexplained.

RELIGIOUS FESTIVALS AND GĀHĀNBĀRS

IV. 23. The Persian festivals are described and explained at length by Bīrūnī, in his "Chronology"[1] as well as in the "Masʿūdic Canon".[2] The 6 gāhānbārs, originally, as demonstrated in III. 13, essentially different from the Zoroastrian religious festivals, are mentioned indiscriminately with the latter by Bīrūnī. At his time their purely astronomical character had probably long since fallen into oblivion, and no mention is made of their original meaning. It has to be noted here again that the gāhānbārs as well as other festivals stretched over a period of 5 days (see end of IV. 5), the last of which was considered most important. According to the "Masʿūdic Canon", the festivals are the following:

1st Farvardīn: *Naurūz al-Malik* (New Year's Day)
6th Farvardīn: The Great Naurūz, also called "The Proper Naurūz" (*Naurūz al-khāṣṣa*)
16th Farvardīn: Beginning of *al-Zamzama* ("the whispering")
19th Farvardīn: *Farvardīgān (celebrated on the day Farvardīn)[3]
3rd Ordībehešt: *Ardēbeheštagān
26th Ordībehešt: 1st day of 3rd gāhānbār (Paitiš.hahya)[4]
30th Ordībehešt: Last day of 3rd gāhānbār
6th Khordāḏ: *Khordāḏagān
26th Khordāḏ: 1st day of 4th gāhānbār (Ayāθrīma)
30th Khordāḏ: Last day of 4th gāhānbār
6th Tīr: Čašn-i-nīlūfar (cited only in *al-Āthār al-bāqiya*)
15th Tīr: *Tīragān, Feast of Ceremonial Ablution
7th Mordāḏ: *Mordāḏagān

---

[1] Ch. IX, pp. 215–33; transl., pp. 199–219.
[2] *al-Qānūn al-Masʿūdī* I (Hyderabad, Deccan, 1373/1954), Maq. 2, Ch. 11, pp. 258–66; list on pp. 259f.
[3] The Feasts of the Months, Farvardīgān, Ardēbeheštagān, etc. (marked in the above list by an asterisk) are celebrated on the day carrying the same name as the month, see IV. 19. Cf. the corresponding celebration of festivals in the Chinese calendar: 3rd month, 3rd day, Feast of the Dead (Graves); 5th of 5th month, Feast of the Dragon Boats, etc.
[4] Bīrūnī mentions the names of the gāhānbārs only in his "Chronology"; in the "Masʿūdic Canon" the numbers ("1st gānānbār", etc.) alone are given.

OLD IRANIAN CALENDARS

4th Šahrīvar: *Šahrīvaragān, called ādar-jušn, "Feast of the Fire"
16th Šahrīvar: 1st day of 5th gāhānbār (Maiδyāirya)
20th Šahrīvar: Last day of 5th gāhānbār
16th Mehr: *Mihrajān
20th Mehr: Rām-rūz ("the mild day"), i.e. the Great Mihrajān
10th Ābān: *Ābānagān
26th Ābān: 1st day of Farvardījān
1st Andarmāh: 1st day of 6th gāhānbār (Hamaspaθmaēdaya) (Epagomenae)
5th Andarmāh: Last day of Farvardījān and of 6th gāhānbār
1st Ādār: Bihār-čašn, "Feast of Spring" ("this means rukūb al-kūsaj, the mounting of the youth")
9th Ādār: *Ādār-čašn
1st Dei: *Feast of Khurra-rūz (Khuram?), also called Nawad-rūz[1]
8th Dei: *First Feast of Dei
11th Dei: 1st day of 1st gāhānbār (Maiδyōizarəmaya)
14th Dei: Sīr-sawā[2]
15th Dei: *Second Feast of Dei and last day of 1st gāhānbār
15th Dei: Bantīgān (?)
17th Dei: Night of Gāv-i-kīl (?)
23rd Dei: *Third Feast of Dei
2nd Bahmen: *Bahmenagān
5th Bahmen: Barsadaq[3]
10th Bahmen: Night of al-Sadaq
30th Bahmen: Āfrījagān[4] (with the remark "at Isfahan")
5th Esfendārmod: *Katbat riqāʿ al-ʿaqārib[5]
11th Esfendārmod: 1st day of 2nd gāhānbār (Maiδyōišam)
15th Esfendārmod: Last day of 2nd gāhānbār

THE FESTIVALS OF FARVARDĪJĀN AND OF THE KATBAT RIQĀʿ AL-ʿAQĀRIB

IV. 24. In the "Masʿūdic Canon" (p. 264), Bīrūnī attributes special importance to the Farvardījān, being one of the most highly esteemed festivals. Since the passage in question illustrates the difficulties arising from the transfer of the epagomenae, I give it here *in extenso*.

The Farvardījān is the period of 5 days in which food and drink is offered to the spirits of their dead because these 5 days were destined to spiritual exercise.

---

[1] Probably Navad-rūz, "Ninety days", because it precedes the Naurōz by 90 days.
[2] Perhaps sair-i sawāʾ, "equal course".
[3] Perhaps pur-sadaf, "plenty of darkness".
[4] The "Masʿūdic Canon" has āb-rīz-gān.
[5] "Inscribing of pieces of paper with scorpions"; in "Chronology", p. 229 (transl., p. 216), Bīrūnī says that on this day magic charms against the bite of scorpions are accomplished by such inscriptions.

AVESTAN CALENDAR CHRONOLOGY

They fall into the last part of Ābānmāh. However, when by the eighth intercalation after Zāradušt the epagomenae (here called mustaraqa, as against Andarmāh in the above list) were transferred to the end of Ābānmāh, where they remained ever since, to the effect that they were counted together, opinions differed as to whether the Farvardījān or the 5 epagomenae should be the last 5 days of Ābānmāh, which was of importance to their religion. Therefore for the sake of safety they took both together and made the Farvardījān a festival of ten days.

According to the "Mas'ūdic Canon" (p. 266), the fifth day of Esfendārmodmāh, in past days the feast of women, "is now known by the name *katbat al-riqā'*, 'inscribing pieces of paper', because the common people write on that day charms which they fasten to the walls of their houses to avert the damage of insects, in particular of scorpions". In the "Chronology" (p. 229, transl. 216) it is said moreover that this is done "in the time between dawnrise and sunrise". This very probably refers to the heliacal rising of α Scorpii (Antares). The time when the heliacal rising of Antares occurred in the first days of Esfendārmodmāh results from a rough computation as *c.* 100 B.C.

PART V. THE CHRONOLOGY OF THE LATER AVESTAN CALENDAR

V. 1. In III. 13–19 we have shown that the differences in days between the 6 gāhānbārs as reported concordantly in *Āfrīnakān* 3.7–12 and in Bīrūnī's "Chronology" permit us to conclude that these gāhānbārs, among which figure the winter and summer solstices, were determined by the apparent acronychal risings and cosmical settings of a small number of bright stars observed from the Persepolis plateau during the later part of the 6th century B.C. Since the cosmical settings, contrary to acronychal risings, are referred to the level western horizon, their validity is not restricted to Persepolis and stretches over several centuries on account of the relatively slow motion of precession. They had to be regarded as indicators of solar dates even after Persepolis had ceased to be the capital of the Iranian Empire.

Numbering, as in Tables 2 and 3, the gāhānbārs from I (Maiδyōi-zarəmaya) to VI (Hamaspaθmaēdaya) and adding to them N (Naurōz), we thus have the correspondences valid for the year of inception, 503 B.C., as shown in the accompanying table.

Gāhānbār	Date Gregorian Julian	Date Later Avestan	Days elapsed	Apparent cosmical setting of
N	21 March 27	1 Farvardīn		α Virginis, Spica (*ab. sin*)
I	20 April 26	1 Ordībehešt	45 since VI	α Librae (*zi. ba. ni. tum*)
II	19 June 25	1 Tīr	60 since I	ρ Sagittarii (PA. BIL. SAG, last star)
III	2 Sept. 8	16 Šahrīvar	75 since II	β Pegasi (IKU, main star)
IV	2 Oct. 8	16 Mehr	30 since III	α Trianguli (APIN) + α Arietis (*ḫun. gá*)
V	21 Dec. 27	6 Dei	80 since IV	α + β Geminorum, Castor + Pollux (*maš. tab. ba. gal. gal*)
VI	6 March 12	21 Esfendārmoḏ	75 since V	β Leonis, Denebola (*ur. gu. la*, last star)

V. 2. These original dates, valid for the first four years of the new calendar (503–500 B.C.) have to be compared with those recorded in *Āfrīnakān*[1] and in Bīrūnī, as shown in the accompanying list, where in col. D also the positions of the gāhānbārs in the Khwārizmian year are added according to Bīrūnī.[2]

	A	B	C	D
Gāhānbār	Date, 503 B.C.	Date (Āfrīnakān)	Date (Bīrūnī)	Khwārizmian Date
I	1 Ordībehešt (2nd month)	15 Ordībehešt	15 Dei (10th month)	15 5th month
II	1 Tīr (4th month)	15 Tīr	15 Esfendār. (12th month)	15 7th month
III	16 Šahrīvar (6th month)	30 Šahrīvar	30 Ordībehešt (2nd month)	1 10th month
IV	16 Mehr (7th month)	30 Mehr	30 Khordād (3rd month)	1 11th month
V	6 Dei (10th month)	20 Dei	20 Šahrīvar (6th month)	11 1st month
VI	21 Esfendārmoḏ (12th month)	5th epag. day (after Esfend.)	5th epag. day (after Ābān)	1 4th month

From the trivial fact that the *Āfrīnakān* dates, B, have advanced by 14 days from their original position, A, it results that they represent the situation obtaining 4.14 = 56 years, or nearly exactly one-half inter-

[1] Even though the *Āfrīnakān* text, such as we have it today, may derive from a later period, the dates recorded must be regarded as genuine; cf. p. 751, n. 1.
[2] "Chronology", pp. 237f. (transl. 225); cf. Taqizadeh, *op. cit.*, p. 609.

AVESTAN CALENDAR CHRONOLOGY

calation period, after the initial 4 year period, i.e. during the years 447–444 B.C. (cf. IV. 18–19).[1]

The *Āfrīnakān* dates remained stable in the vihēčakīk year throughout the centuries, as long as it continued functioning. In the vague year they advanced by one month with every new intercalation, but actually represented the original astronomical situation only in the middle of each period (331, 215, 99 B.C., and A.D. 18, 134, 250, 366, 480). After the eighth intercalation, due in A.D. 425 and carried out some years before (see IV. 13–14), they thus fell 8 months later, occupying then the places recorded by Bīrūnī (see col. *C*). By that time, however, the difference between the length of the tropical year and that of the sidereal (with which corresponds the 116-year period) had caused perceptible changes, to the effect that V (Maiδyāirya) in A.D. 480 fell 15 days after winter solstice, on 4 January.[2]

V. 3. Dates for the two chief gāhānbārs: summer and winter solstice, were also given in *Bundahišn*, Ch. 25:

From the Maiδyōišam Festival, which falls on the day Xvar (no. 11) of the month Tīr in the vihēčakīk year, till the Maiδyāiri Festival, which falls on the day Varhrān (no. 20) of the month Daδv in the vihēčakīk year, the length of the day diminishes and that of the night increases; and from Maiδyāiri to Maiδyōišam the night diminishes and the day increases.[3]

Here the date of winter solstice, 20 Dei, is the same as in *Āfrīnakān*, while that for summer solstice, 11 Tīr (which incidentally precedes by 2 days the Tīragān Festival on 13 Tīr, see IV. 19), 4 days earlier than the expected 15 Tīr, would be valid for the period 463–460 B.C. Considering that the day-name Xvar (11) can hardly have been confused by a copyist with Dei-i-pad Mihr (day no. 15), the possibility must be envisaged that the date 11 Tīr reflects an observation of the summer

---

[1] For earlier attempts to establish the probable epoch of the Later Avestan calendar, I refer to J. Marquart, *Untersuchungen zur Geschichte von Eran* II (Leipzig, 1905); J. Markwart (identical with the preceding!), "Das Nauroz, seine Geschichte und seine Bedeutung", in *Dr. Modi Memorial Volume* (Bombay, 1930), pp. 709–765B, and S. H. Taqizadeh's important work *Gāh-šumārī dar Īrān-i qadīm* (Tehran, 1315/1938). Taqizadeh revised his theories propounded there in his *Old Iranian Calendars* (London, 1938, Royal Asiatic Society Prize Publication Fund 16) and again in his "The Old Iranian Calendars Again".

[2] In the 4th and 5th centuries the Gregorian calendar was one day ahead of the Julian.

[3] After Nyberg, *Texte*, pp. 10/11. In the ensuing passage it is said that the longest summer day equals in length two winter days, and the longest winter night, two summer nights. This would correspond approximately to the northern latitude of 49° (Paris or the region north of the Caspian Sea).

solstice made 16 years before the *Āfrīnakān* dates were recorded. The question would have to be left open were it not for the Khwārizmian dates recorded by Bīrūnī (see col. *D* in the above list).

The first two of these Khwārizmian gāhānbārs lie exactly 3 months, or 90 days, later than the *Āfrīnakān* dates, while III, IV and VI evidence a slight deviation: 91 days, which was probably caused by the wish to make the gāhānbārs fall on the first day of the respective months instead of the last day of the preceding. So far everything seems clear: the Khwārizmian vihečakīk calendar was discontinued after the third intercalation, and the Bīrūnian dates render the situation obtaining about the middle of the third period, i.e. *c.* 100 B.C. (see V. 2).

However, a remarkable exception is formed by V, winter solstice. It falls not 90 or 91, but only 86 days after the *Āfrīnakān* date, on the 11th day of the first month. This means that the original position of Khwārizmian V was 16 Dei, 4 days before the *Āfrīnakān*, 20 Dei, in perfect accordance with the *Bundahišn* date, 11 Tīr, for summer solstice. The conclusion to be drawn, inevitably, is that 16 years before the *Āfrīnakān* observations of all the 6 gāhānbārs, the two chief gāhānbārs, i.e. the solstices, were observed isolatedly about the years 463–460, in other words, during the first years of Artaxerxes I (464–424 B.C.) and that one of the dates then found has survived in the *Bundahišn*, the other in the Khwārizmian calendar.

V. 4. Finally, an important observation which we owe to Taqizadeh has to be discussed.[1] According to him the Jalālī year (see IV. 17) beginning with the month Farvardīn at spring equinox is still in use in the rural parts and many districts of Iran, such as Kāšān, Naṭanz, Maima, Javšagān and in the province of Yazd, and continues being called by this name. At all those places the epagomenae (5 or, in leap-years, 6 days) follow after the 12th month, Esfendārmod. Strangely enough, however, in many villages of the district Naṭanz, such as Abiyāneh, Barz, Chimeh, Henjan, and several others, the epagomenae are added to the 11th month, Bahman.[2]

Despite Taqizadeh's hesitancy to take this for a trace of intercalations carried out unofficially in certain parts of Iran, I see no reason to doubt that the Later Avestan calendar in this exceptional case was kept functioning until the 11th intercalation, due in A.D. 773 (see Table 5);

[1] See "The Old Iranian Calendars again" p. 610.
[2] Communicated to Taqizadeh by Professor A. K. S. Lambton.

but it will hardly be possible to find a plausible motive for the fact that with this it came to an end, as had been the case with the official calendar 350 years earlier. At any rate, it is a strong support to my claim that the tradition of the Later Avestan calendar was kept alive longer than historians so far have been inclined to believe.

OLD IRANIAN CALENDARS

TABLE 1. *The Babylonian, Elamite and Old Persian Calendars, 503–499 B.C.*

Month No.	[0]	1	2	3	4	5	6	7	8	9	10	11	12	13
Darius y.19 = 503 B.C.		27 March	25 April	25 May	23 June	23 July	21 Aug.	20 Sept.	19 Oct.	18 Nov.	17 Dec.	(502) 15 Jan.	14 Feb.	16 March
Ideal scheme		I	II	III	IV	V	VI	VIa	VII	VIII	IX	X	XI	XII
Babylonian		I	II	III	IV	V	VI	VIa	VII	VIII	IX	X	XI	XII
Old Persian		I	II	III	IV	V	VI	VII	VIII	IX	Xa	X	XI	XII
											(501)			
Darius y.20 = 502 B.C.		14 April	14 May	13 June	12 July	11 Aug.	9 Sept.	9 Oct.	7 Nov.	6 Dec.	5 Jan.	3 Feb.	4 March	
Ideal scheme = Babylonian		I	II	III	IV	V	VI	VII	VIII	IX	X	XI	XII	
												(500)		
Darius y.21 = 501 B.C.		2 April	2 May	1 June	30 June	30 July	29 Aug.	27 Sept.	27 Oct.	25 Nov.	27 Dec.	25 Jan.	21 Feb.	23 March
Ideal scheme		I	II	III	IV	V	VI	VII	VIII	IX	X	XI	XII	XIIa
Babylonian		I	II	III	IV	V	VI	VII	VIII	IX	X	XI	XII	
											(499)			
Darius y.22 = 500 B.C.	[23 March]	21 April	21 May	19 June	19 July	18 Aug.	17 Sept.	16 Oct.	15 Nov.	14 Dec.	12 Jan.	11 Feb.	12 March	
Ideal scheme		I	II	III	IV	V	VI	VII	VIII	IX	X	XI	XII	
Babylonian = Elamite		I	III	IV	V	VI	VII	VII	IX	X	XI	XII	XIIa	
Old Persian	I	II	III	IV	VI	VI	VII	VIII	IX	XI	XII	XII		
											(498)			
Darius y.23 = 499 B.C.	[12 March]	11 April	10 May	9 June	8 July	7 Aug.	6 Sept.	5 Oct.	4 Nov.	3 Dec.	2 Jan.	31 Jan.	2 March	
Ideal scheme = Babylonian		I	II	III	IV	V	VI	VII	VIII	IX	X	XI	XII	
Old Persian	Ia	I	II	III	IV	V	VI	VII	VIII	IX	X	XI	XII	

AVESTAN CALENDAR CHRONOLOGY

(Star names and dates in square brackets indicate phenomena preceding or following day of *Gāhānbār*)
HR = Heliacal Rising; AR = Acronychal Rising (above horizon with average elevation of 12°). HS = Heliacal Setting; CS = Cosmical Setting (below level horizon). N = Naurōz.

Gāhānbār	HR	AR	HS	CS
N: 21 March (Gregorian Style)	γ Andromedae (Alamak) (APIN, northernmost star)		γ Andromedae (APIN, northern part) *a, β* Trianguli (APIN, southern part) β Cassiopeiae (*lu.lim*) + α Ceti [η Tauri (Pleiades) (*mul = zappu*, 28 March] γ Orionis (Bellatrix) (*sib.zi.an.na*) [α Tauri (Aldebaran) (*is.li.e*) 16 April] [α Hydrae (Alphard) (main star of *muš*) 14 June]	α Virginis (Spica) (*ab.sin*)
I: 20 April		α Scorpii (Antares) *gab.gír.tab*		α Librae (*zi.ba.ni.tum*)
II: 19 June	[α Geminorum (Castor) (*maš.tab.ba.gal.gal*) 21 June]	α Sagittarii (Alrami) (PA.BIL.SAG) *a, β* Capricorni (Gedi) (*suḫur.maš*)		ρ Sagittarii (last star of PA.BIL.SAG) [α Ophiuchi, 23 June (Ra's al-Ḥayya) β Pegasi (Scheat) (IKU, main star)
III: 2 Sept.	[β Leonis (Denebola) (last star of *ur.gu.la*) 30 August]	*aβ* Trianguli (APIN south) [*a, β* Arietis 7 Sept. (*hun.ga*)]		α Trianguli (APIN)
IV: 2 Oct.	α Bootis (Arcturus) (*šu.pa*) [α Virginis (Spica) (*ab.sin*) 30 Sept.]	η Tauri (Pleiades) *mul = zappu*		α Arietis (*ḫun.ga*)
V: 21 Dec.	α Aquilae (Altair) (našru) ρ Sagittarii (last star of PA.BIL.SAG)	α Canis minoris (Procyon) (*al.lu*) [α Canis maioris (Sirius) (*gag.si.sa*) 26 December]	β (Akrab) α (Antares) + ν Scorpii (main stars of *gír.tab*) [α Aquilae (Altair) (našru) 25 December]	*a, β* Geminorum (Castor & Pollux) (*maš.tab.ba.gal.gal*) [β Cancri, 24 Dec.]
VI: 6 March	γ Pegasi (last star of IKU)	α Virginis (Spica) (*ab.sin*) α Bootis (Arcturus) (*šu.pa*)	α Trianguli (APIN south) α Arietis (*ḫun.ga*)	β Leonis (Denebola) (last star of *ur.gu.la*)

TABLE 3. *Annual Risings and Settings (Stars listed according to increasing longitudes)*

Star or Constellation Name		Phase announcing Nawrōz (N) and Gāhānbārs (I–VI)			
		Rising		Setting	
Akkadian	Modern	Heliacal	Acronychal	Heliacal	Cosmical
1. APIN south	α, β Trianguli	—	III	(only α) VI	IV
2. APIN north	γ Andromedae	N	—	with α, β Trianguli N	IV
3. ḫun.gá	α Arietis	—	—	VI	—
4. mul = zappu	η Tauri (Pleiades)	—	IV	7 days after N	—
5. is.li.e	α Tauri (Aldebaran)	—	—	4 days before I	—
6. sīb.zi.an.na	γ Orionis (Bellatrix)	—	—	I	—
7. maš.tab.ba.gal.gal	α Geminorum (Castor)	2 days after II	—	—	with β Geminorum (Pollux) V
8. gag.si.sá	α Canis maioris (Sirius)	—	5 days after V	—	—
9. al.lu	α Canis minoris (Procyon)	—	V	—	—
10. muš = ṣiru	β Cancri	—	—	—	—
11. main star of muš = ṣiru	α Hydrae (Alphard)	—	—	5 days before II	3 days after V
12. last star of ur.gu.la	β Leonis (Denebola)	3 days before III	—	—	VI

AVESTAN CALENDAR CHRONOLOGY

13. ab . sin	α Virginis (Spica)	IV	VI		
14. zi . ba . ni . tum	α Librae				N I
15. gab . gir . tab	α Scorpii (Antares)		I	with β, ν Scorpii	
16. PA . BIL . SAG	α Sagittarii (Alrami)		II	IV	II
17. PA . BIL . SAG	ρ Sagittarii	V	II		
18. suḫur . maš	α, β Capricorni				
19. main star of IKU	β Pegasi (Scheat)				III
20. last star of IKU	γ Pegasi	VI			
NORTHERN STARS					
21. šu . pa	α Bootis (Arcturus)	IV	VI		
22. AN . GUB . BA	α Ophiuchi	V			
23. našru	α Aquilae (Altair)			4 days after V	4 days after II
24. lu . lim	β Cassiopeiae (Schedar)	VI		N	
25. an . nu . ni . tum	β Andromedae (Mirach)			N	
26.	α Ceti				

OLD IRANIAN CALENDARS

TABLE 4. *The Scheme of Intercalation*

Year*		Civil = Religious	Year		Civil		Year		Religious
1–119 (1–115)	I	Farvardīn	120 (116)	I	Farvardīn	120 (116)	I	Farvardīn
	II	Ordībehešt			......			......
	III	Khordād						
	IV	Tīr		XII	Esfendārmod		XII	Esfendārmod
	V	Mordād			Epagomenae			Epagomenae
	VI	Šahrīvar	121 (117)	I	Farvardīn		XIIa	Interc. Farvardīn II
	VII	Mehr				120 (116)	I	Epagomenae
	VIII	Ābān		II	Epagomenae	121 (117)		Farvardīn
	IX	Ādār			Ordībehešt			......
	X	Deī			......			
	XI	Bahman					XI	Bahman
	XII	Esfendārmod	122–239 (118–231)	XII	Esfendārmod		XII	Esfendārmod
		Epagomenae		I	Farvardīn			
						122–239 (118–231)		Epagomenae
				II	Epagomenae		I	Farvardīn
					Ordībehešt			......
					......			
			240 (232)	XII	Esfendārmod		XI	Bahman
				I	Farvardīn		XII	Esfendārmod
				II	Ordībehešt		XIIa	Interc. Farvardīn II
					Epagomenae	240 (232)	I	Epagomenae
				III	Khordād			Farvardīn
								......
			241–359 (233–347)	XII	Esfendārmod		X	Deī
				I	Farvardīn		XI	Bahman
				II	Ordībehešt		XII	Esfendārmod
					Epagomenae	241–359 (233–347)		Epagomenae
				III	Khordād		I	Farvardīn

TABLE 5. *Intercalation dates according to the 120- and 116-year cycles*

		Periods of 120 Persian years (43,800 days)			Periods of 116 Persian years (42,340 days)		
Period no.	Year no.	Date	Julian day*	Year no.	Date	Ruler	Julian day*
0	1	503 B.C., 27 March	1537 788	1	503 B.C., 27 March	Darius I, year 19	1537 788
1	121	383 B.C., 25 Feb.	1581 588	117	387 B.C., 26 Feb.	Artaxerxes II, year 18	1580 128
2	241	263 B.C., 26 Jan.	1625 388	233	271 B.C., 28 Jan.	Antiochus I Soter, year 11	1622 468
3	361	144 B.C., 27 Dec.	1669 188	349	156 B.C., 30 Dec.	Alexander Balas, year 2	1664 808
4	481	24 B.C., 27 Nov.	1712 988	465	40 B.C., 1 Dec.	Orodes (Arsaces XIV), year 16	1707 148
5	601	A.D. 97, 28 Oct.	1756 788	581	A.D. 77, 2 Nov.	Vologeses I (Arsaces XXIII), last year	1749 488
6	721	A.D. 217, 28 Sept.	1800 588	697	A.D. 193, 4 Oct.	Vologeses IV (Arsaces XXVIII), year 4	1791 828
7	841	A.D. 337, 29 Aug.	1844 388	813	A.D. 309, 5 Sept.		1834 168
8	961	A.D. 457, 30 July	1888 188	929	A.D. 425, 7 Aug.	Hormisdas II, last year	1876 508
9	1081	A.D. 577, 30 June	1931 988	1045	A.D. 541, 9 July	Varahran V (Bahrāmgūr), year 11	1918 848
10	1201	A.D. 697, 31 May	1975 788	1161	A.D. 657, 10 June	Khusrau Anōširvān, year 11	1961 188
11	1321	A.D. 817, 1 May	2019 588	1277	A.D. 773, 12 May		2003 528
12	1441	A.D. 937, 1 Apr.	2063 388	1393	A.D. 889, 13 Apr.		2045 868
13	1561	A.D. 1057, 2 March	2107 188	1509	A.D. 1005, 15 March		2088 208
14	1681	A.D. 1177, 31 Jan.	2150 988	1625	A.D. 1121, 14 Feb.		2130 548

* See p. 765, n. 2.

TABLE 6. The Thirty Day Names (for the Sogdian ones see p. 760, n. 2)

	Avestan	Pahlavi	Modern Persian (Bīrūnī, p. 43, transl. 53)
1	Ahurahe Mazdå	Ohrmazd	Hormuz
2	Vaŋhave Manaŋhe	Vahman	Bahman
3	Ašahe vahištahe	Ardvahišt	Ordībehešt
4	Xšaθrahe vairyehe	Šahrēvar	Šahrīvar
5	Spəntayå Ārmatōiš	Spandarmad	Esfendārmod̯
6	Haurvatātō	Hordād	Khurdād̯
7	Amərətātō	Amurdād	Murdād̯
8	Daθušō	Dai pad Ādur	Dai-ba-Ād̯ar
9	Āθrō	Ādur	Ād̯ar
10	Apąm	Abān	Ābān
11	Hvarəxšaētahe	Xvar	Khūr
12	Måŋhahe	Māh	Māh
13	Tištryehe	Tīr	Tīr
14	Gāuš	Gōš	Gōš
15	Daθušō	Dai pad Mihr	Dai-ba-Mihr
16	Miθrahe	Mihr	Mihr
17	Sraošahe	Srōš	Srōš
18	Rašnaoš	Rašn	Rašn
19	Fravašinąm	Fravardīn	Farvardīn
20	Vərəθraynahe	Vahrām	Bahrām
21	Rāmanō	Rām	Rām
22	Vātahe	Vād	Bād̯
23	Daθušō	Dai pad Dēn	Dai-ba-Dīn
24	Daēnayå	Dēn	Dīn
25	Ašōiš	Ard	Ard
26	Arštātō	Aštād	Aštād̯
27	Ašnō	Asmān	Āsmān
28	Zəmō hudåŋhō	Zāmyād	Zāmyād̯
29	Mąθrahe spəntahe	Mahrspand	Māraspand
30	Anayranąm	Anagrān	Anīrān

CHAPTER 17

CLASSIC ACHAEMENIAN ARCHITECTURE AND SCULPTURE

ARCHITECTURE

Good and comprehensive surveys of the art of the Achaemenian empire have been written in recent years.[1] The present essay will therefore merely summarize the characteristics of classic Achaemenian art as they are revealed in the principal monuments. In view of David Stronach's discussion in this volume of the buildings and reliefs at Pasargadae, which manifest the early stage of Achaemenian art, it is the classic phase of it, revealed in the works sponsored by Darius and Xerxes, which will be discussed here, as well as – briefly – the relatively slight modifications it underwent in the reliefs of the later kings of the Achaemenian dynasty.

In art, as in politics, Cyrus and Darius I applied themselves to organizing and inspiring large numbers of people of diverse ethnic and cultural origin. They succeeded in stimulating builders and sculptors to create at Pasargadae, Persepolis and Susa a style of art expressive of imperial majesty and so distinctive as to be immediately recognizable. This style is all the more remarkable because it was produced by peoples of many lands with different traditions and aesthetic predilections affecting the technical procedures used in architecture and sculpture, the types of buildings, and the repertory of images.

The proudest monument of Persian art, Persepolis, whose ancient name was Pārsa, owed its existence to Darius, a scion of a secondary line of Achaemenians. Darius emerged victorious in 521 B.C. from battles which broke out with insurgents after the death of Cambyses, the eldest son of Cyrus.

Persepolis is built on the spur of a mountain which was partly flattened and partly built up with stone blocks to form the gigantic terrace up to 15 metres high on which palatial buildings were to stand

[1] Farkas, *Achaemenid Sculpture*; and Root, *King and Kingship*.

793

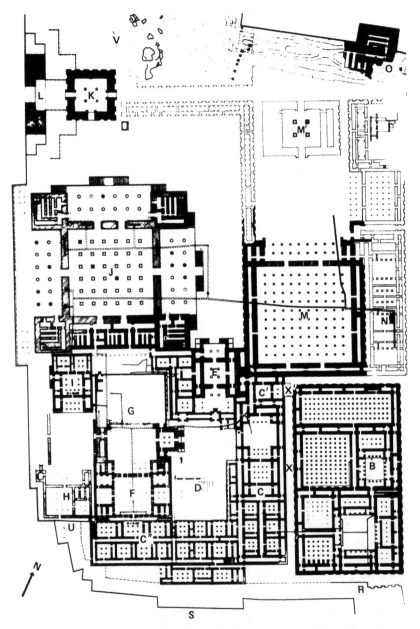

Fig. 1. Plan of Persepolis terrace by Richard C. Haines [see following page for key].

above the plain, elevated and secure. Today, the slender columns of the buildings are visible from a distance. In Achaemenian times these buildings were partly hidden by an encircling wall which can be seen in the model (pl. 13) made in 1968 by Friedrich Krefter, architect of Ernst Herzfeld, the first modern excavator of Persepolis from 1931 to 1934.[1] The height and vastness of the Terrace and the grandeur of its structures, even in their ruined state, have made it one of the most impressive sights surviving from antiquity. In the Terrace wall carefully dressed stones, most of them rectangular blocks of different sizes, were fitted together without mortar. They create a feeling of great strength, while the sharp edges of the corners, formed by the flanking sections

[1] F. Krefter, "Persepolis im Modell", *AMI* 11 (1969), pp. 123–37 and pls 55–8.

B	Treasury
C	Restored main wing of harem
C'	Service quarters of harem
C"	West wing of harem
D	Palace D
E	Council Hall
F	Palace of Xerxes
G	Palace G
H	Palace H
I	Palace of Darius I
J	Apadana
K	Gate of Xerxes
L	Terrace stairway
M	Throne Hall
M'	Unfinished gate
N	Stairway to drainage tunnel
O	Northern fortification
R	Southern fortification
S	Foundation Inscription of Darius I
U	Post-Achaemenid pavilion?
V	Unfinished column drum
X	"Harem street"
X'	Secondary rooms

```
 5   10   30   50   70   90
10 0    20   40   60   80   100 metres
```

- ■ Existing features
- ▭ Reconstructed features
- ···· Sub-surface drains
- ═══ Surface drains
- ------ Reconstructed parapets, benches, etc.
- + ▭ Additions after survey by Iranian Antiquity Service

Fig. 2. The West Front of the Apadana, seen from the plain below the terrace, reconstructed by Friedrich Krefter.

of the wall, repeatedly guide the viewer's eye to the full height of the Terrace (pl. 14).

The focal point of all the structures on the Terrace, as seen in the plan (fig. 1), was the Audience Hall called Apadana by the excavators on the basis of that name being found on columns of a similar later building at Susa. The Apadana at Persepolis (pl. 15a; figs 2, 3) consisted of an immense columnar hall, 60.50 metres square with corner towers flanking each of the three porches as well as the furniture store-rooms which were accommodated at the back. The columns of the main hall were over 19 metres high, that is a height of about five floors in a modern apartment-house. Two pairs of foundation tablets in gold and silver were found in the north-east and south-east corners of the hall. The inscription in Old Persian, Elamite and Babylonian reads: "Darius, the great king, king of kings, king of countries, son of Hystaspes, the Achaemenian. Says Darius the king: this is the kingdom which I hold, from the Scythians who are beyond Sogdiana to Ethiopia; from India to Sardis – (the kingdom) which to me Ahuramazda gave, the greatest of the gods. May Ahuramazda protect me and my royal house."[1] At

[1] Schmidt, *Persepolis* I, p. 70.

Fig. 3. The West Porch of the Apadana, seen from the inside, reconstructed by Friedrich Krefter.

the entrance to the south-eastern tower were emplacements for guardian figures of two seated, powerful and dignified mastiffs, animals which had not been used in this manner in the Near East. Their form was similar to that of a seated dog from Egypt,[1] made in the Ptolemaic period. Before the north-eastern tower entrance there were probably two ibexes,[2] again guardian figures for which no prototypes exist in ancient Western Asia.

The columns of the Apadana were among the most richly decorated; they will be described in detail because their multiple elements of different origin[3] seem to suggest the concept of a world empire composed of different peoples, as expressed in the inscription of Darius just quoted. Not all the columns have all the elements here cited, some are much plainer. All, however, have a bell-shaped base decorated with plant designs (fig. 4). Above this was a plain torus upon which rested the shaft with as many as 48 flutes, more than were ever used on columns in Greece, where the idea of fluting had originated. The capital of the column has as its lowest member a ring of drooping sepals reminiscent of north Syrian and Phoenician furniture decoration.[4] A bead-and-reel circlet divides the sepals from the rising plant forms, reminiscent of Egyptian segmented palm-leaf capitals. Moreover, each segment has a papyrus flower in the centre. Above this Egyptianizing feature is again a bead-and-reel circlet, which divides it from a connecting piece with eight vertical double scrolls, related to designs common in the Levant, where they are usually employed horizontally, as in ivories from Cyprus, Nimrud and other sites which have yielded Phoenician ivory decorations.[5] On top of the scrolls is a third bead-and-reel circlet, on which rest the feet of the double animal protome, which forms the impost capital. The combination of truly floral and geometrical motifs in these richly ornamented columns of Persepolis is in contrast to the strictly architectural development which eastern Mediterranean elements like scrolls and hanging sepals have taken in Ionian structures. They manifest the different requirements and taste in Persia and Ionia.

In the Apadana the impost capitals were in the form of bull-protomes

---

[1] Schmidt, *Persepolis* II, p. 70 and notes 31 and 32; pl. 36 A, B.
[2] Schmidt, *Persepolis* II, p. 70, pl. 36 C.
[3] This analysis of the column owes much to H. Frankfort, *The Art and Architecture of the Ancient Orient* (Baltimore, 1969), pp. 222–5.
[4] H. Kyrieleis, *Throne und Klinen* (Berlin, 1969) (*Jahrbuch des Deutschen Archäologischen Instituts*, Ergänzungsheft 24), pl. 13.
[5] M. E. L. Mallowan, *Nimrud and its remains* II (New York, 1966), p. 565, nos 506, 507.

Fig. 4. The columns of the Apadana, reconstructed by Friedrich Krefter.

on the very ornate columns of the main hall as well as on the plainer ones of the porches, except in the east porch where there are horned lion dragons. The rare surviving ones of these protomes have a majestic cast of features, as do those of Darius' palace at Susa, which are better preserved.[1]

[1] A fine photograph in colour was published by W. Hinz, *Darius und die Perser* (Baden Baden, 1976), pl. 17.

CLASSIC ACHAEMENIAN ART

To the total effect of the Apadana belong the monumental stairways which led up to the porticoes on the east and on the north (pl. 5). The parapets and stairway façades were covered with reliefs of courtiers, guards, and peoples of the realm bringing gifts. The great Audience reliefs of the king, later removed to the Treasury, were in the centre. These reliefs served to enliven the wall-surfaces even at a distance. Some of the details will be discussed more fully below, in an evaluation of their sculptural style. Although no colour is preserved on the reliefs today, there is evidence that they were originally painted.[1]

In the last part of the reign of Darius, access to the Terrace and the approach to the Apadana was probably already over stairs located in the same place as those in use today. However, the stage-like effect of these stairs, which start close together, then diverge and then come together again at the top, may have been a later development.[2]

After having reached the top of the stairs, the visitor would have entered the Gate of All Lands (pl. 15b), a building which may have been begun by Darius but was completed by Xerxes, who claimed in an inscription to have erected the structure. In the same inscription, however, he added "much else (that is) beautiful (was) done throughout Pārsa which I did and which my father did; whatever work seems beautiful, all that we did by the grace of Ahuramazda."[3] No such elaboration is found in those inscriptions of Xerxes where he alone was certainly the builder.[4]

Bulls confront the viewer at the external, western entrance of the gate, whereas on the other side, which faces toward the buildings on the Terrace, there are gigantic human-headed bulls, doubtless meant as protectors of the Terrace. While the shape of these composite creatures was taken over from Late Assyrian guardian figures[5] the fact that they appear to be looking onto the Terrace, instead of striding, as in the

[1] Tilia, "Colour in Persepolis", in *Studies* II, p. 6; she mentiones an area 2·50 metres long and close to the base of the parapet of the northern Stairway, where lumps of green, red, and blue colour were found and also several potsherds with pigments of the same colours encrusted upon them; this discovery seems to indicate that in this place work had been done on painting the bas-reliefs of the stairway façade.

[2] The present stairs show a later type of clamps and less careful work than the early structures on the Terrace, see Tilia, *op. cit.*, pp. 23–4.   [3] Schmidt, *Persepolis* I, p. 65.

[4] The inscription on the stairway façade of the Palace of Xerxes reads: "Says Xerxes, the Great King, by the grace of Ahuramazda this *hadish* I made. Let Ahuramazda with the gods protect me and my kingdom and what (was) done by me". Schmidt, *Persepolis* II, p. 238.

[5] The closest parallels to the human-headed bulls of Persepolis are those of Sargon (721–705 B.C.) at Khorsabad. See E. Strommenger–Max Hirmer, *5000 Years of the Art of Mesopotamia* (New York, 1964), pls. 220–1, but the gate figures of the later Assyrian kings are not known; they may have been equally close.

ARCHITECTURE

Assyrian emplacement, to meet the enemy arriving from outside, indicates some change to a specifically Persian meaning, on which a suggestion has been made.[1]

At right angles to the axis of the Gate of All Lands is a third opening, the widest, which gives onto the square before the Apadana. From the darkness of the gate chamber the sight of the Apadana, with its splendid socle reliefs topped by the lofty portico's black columns against the light background of the walls, must have been overwhelming.

This great effect was not the result of a single plan devised by the architects of Darius at the beginning of the building activities on the Terrace. Careful observation by Giuseppe and Ann Britt Tilia has revealed a continual change of plans, due most probably to the changing ideas of Darius about his Terrace.

At first, access was from the south in a recess, next to the inscription in which Darius invoked the protection of Ahuramazda for himself and the "fortress" which he had built.[2]

All scholars agree that the Treasury was the first building on the Terrace. To understand why it was the first, one would have to know for which purpose the Terrace was erected. At present we know only what Persepolis was not: it was no administrative centre such as Susa certainly was, just as presumably Ecbatana, and not Pasargadae, was the administrative centre for the empire of Cyrus. One can only suggest, in respect of the Treasury, that concern for security must have played a major role.

The second building was the relatively small residential palace of Darius, set on the highest spot of the Terrace.

Back to back with it the Apadana was built, as a rectangular structure. As such it would have resembled the columnar halls at Pasargadae and the recently identified remains of an audience hall of Cambyses at Dasht-i Gohar, 150 metres distant from his unfinished tomb. It seems that Cambyses had attempted to create a residence of his own, resembling Pasargadae in the plain of Marv Dasht not far from the site later chosen by Darius for Persepolis.[3] Cambyses did not proceed very far with his

---

[1] H. von Gall, "Relieffragment eines elymäischen Königs aus Masğed-e Soleiman", *Iranica Antiqua* xv (1980), pp. 244–5 took up an earlier suggestion for identification of the human-headed bulls with the bull-man Gopatšāh, a creature half man, half ox which is thought to pour holy water into the sea where innumerable evil creatures will be destroyed; if this is not done, they will appear as rain. Dale Bishop, however, tells me that Gopatšāh is a rather obscure figure.

[2] Schmidt, *Persepolis* I, p. 63.

[3] W. Kleiss, "Zur Entwicklung der achaemenidischen Palastarchitektur", *Iranica Antiqua* xv (1980), pp. 199–211.

buildings; his tomb was certainly not ready to receive his body when he died. The layout of the audience hall of Cambyses resembled Palace S at Pasargadae more closely than the later Apadana at Persepolis, forming an intermediate link between the two.[1]

The major change which Darius introduced in the Apadana was that the building, rectangular at first, was transformed into a square one. This meant an extension to the west not only of the Apadana but also of the wall of the Terrace itself, so as to ensure sufficient room for the portico in the west. The reason for the change is unknown,[2] but it determined the appearance of every Achaemenian hall built thereafter. The Apadana of Susa, for example, has almost the same size as that of Persepolis, while the main Hall of a Hundred Columns, also called Throne Hall, at Persepolis, built by Xerxes and finished by Artaxerxes, merely shows an enlargement of the scheme created in the Apadana Hall.

These great buildings on the northern side of the Terrace, viz. the Gate of All Lands, the Apadana, and the Hall of a Hundred Columns, constitute the official and public structures. By contrast the buildings on the southern side are, at least in part, residential, such as the Palace of Darius, back to back with the Apadana, with its floors 2.5 metres higher than those of the Apadana.

The palace opens toward the south, where the original access to the Terrace had been. The building is symmetrical and formal with a hypostyle hall in the centre, a large portico in front, suites of almost symmetrical rooms on the sides, and two large square rooms with symmetrical longitudinal siderooms in the back. An exit on the west side gives onto a stair built by Artaxerxes III. Obviously these buildings were used over generations.

There have been suggestions for a relation of the ground-plan of Darius' palace with the plan of the temple which that king built for the god Amun at Hibis in Khargah Oasis in Egypt.[3] The main similarity consists in the central hypostyle hall being entered through a porch or portico and flanked by symmetrical rectangular rooms. While these relations are somewhat vague, both buildings were constructed according to carefully designed, symmetrical plans. This suggests that the

[1] Kleiss, *op. cit.*, p. 202.
[2] The idea, expressed orally by D. P. Hansen, that the change was intended to satisfy directional and symbolic concepts, deserves further investigation; J. George, "Achaemenid Orientations", in *Akten des VII Internationalen Kongresses für Iranische Kunst und Archäologie, Munich 1976* (Berlin, 1979) (*AMI* Ergänzungsband 6), pp. 196–206, provides intriguing material for such an interpretation.
[3] Schmidt, *Persepolis* I, pp. 26–7.

architects used similar working methods, more dependent on precisely drawn plans than had been the case earlier in the ancient Near East, when plans drawn on clay tablets lacked precision of detail. It is not impossible, therefore, that an Egyptian was the teacher. Moreover, in Darius' palace Egyptianizing cavetto cornices were introduced as a decoration over the lintels of niches, windows and doorways. Subsequently, all buildings at Persepolis were to have such cornices.

It has been established that the floors of the palace, now mostly destroyed, were coloured red like the red-surfaced flooring in the Treasury and in Darius' buildings at Susa and Babylon.[1] In view of the fact that red flooring can also be seen in the third building of the so-called temple of Aphaia at Aegina, dated about 500 B.C.,[2] one may ask whether there was influence from one set of buildings to the other and in which direction the influence might have gone.

There is no mention by archaeologists of red flooring in the palace of Xerxes at Persepolis, which indicates perhaps that this feature was limited to the period of Darius. The plan of Xerxes' building resembles that of Darius but was twice as large.

In summary, the contribution made at Persepolis by the architects of Darius and Xerxes to Achaemenian architecture are the square hypostyle hall, the high socle on which important buildings were placed, and the cavetto cornices of the lintels. To this may be added the use of animals not hitherto seen in the Near East as guardian figures.[3]

No original plan appears to have existed for the Terrace,[4] or, if it did, it was radically changed by the new access from the west instead of from the south, as mentioned above, However, there was obvious thought given by Darius to the siting of individual buildings: the Treasury, basically a service building, was placed close to the mountain; the palace of Darius was built on the highest spot of the Terrace; the

---

[1] Schmidt, *Persepolis* I, pp. 28, 32, 287.

[2] A. Furtwängler, *Aegina, das Heiligtum der Aphaia* (Munich, 1906), p. 48, stated that the red stucco covering the floor in the Pronaos was very well preserved, less so in the Cella. Indeed the red floor covering is still clearly visible and well protected. The date of the temple was given as 500 B.C. by C. Krauss, in K. Schefold, *Die Griechen und ihre Nachbarn* (Berlin, 1967) (Propyläen Kunstgeschichte 1), p. 247.

[3] Mastiffs, ibexes and bulls, the latter also in the buildings of the plain where in addition a pair of couchant felines was found; Schmidt, *Persepolis* II, p. 70 and pls. 36 A–E and 37 B and C.

[4] E. Herzfeld *Iran in the Ancient East* (Oxford, 1941), p. 224, believed that Darius' architects drafted the plan for all palatial structures on the site; he based this view on the fact that the orifices of some of the tunnels of the drainage system correspond to walls of subsequently erected buildings. Schmidt, *Persepolis* I, p. 210, however, saw no reason why the tunnel system existing in Darius' time could not have been subsequently expanded.

Apadana, the greatest hall of its time, looked down on the plain in the west, and could be seen from below and from the two squares in the north and the east, from where the viewer would have been able to take in the full effect of the great building. Later rulers had to fit their structures into the remaining space, always keeping to the orientation set by the buildings of Darius I and linking their edifices visually to their surroundings by means of numerous stairways with carved stairway façades and parapets.

A structure which differs from all others on the Terrace is the parapet (pl. 16), which ran around the south-west corner of the Terrace wall and which was restored by the Tilias from blocks and fragments that had fallen from the Terrace and were unearthed at the foot of the wall.[1] On the basis of the stoneworking techniques the parapet was dated in the Achaemenian period. It consists of larger and smaller elements crowned by tall slender, horn-like half-cones. The excavators' suggestion that these elements represent altars may point in the right direction for the interpretation of this singular parapet.

For the additional features seen on the parapet the term fortification symbolism may be suggested. The small elements have arrow-shaped forms carved into them, which recall the common form of arrow slot in fortifications from the Assyrian to the Persian period.[2] The large elements have a design composed of squares and triangles which recalls the openings in a tower on a Hittite vase representing a city wall.[3] Lastly, there is a frieze of dentils on which the upper part of each element seems to rest. Such dentils were actually derived from beam-ends supporting an upper structure, as seen on the buildings flanking the temple of the god Haldi at Musasir (fig. 5). Rows of beam-ends may have come to be associated with fortifications and thereby acquired a meaning of protection, derived from the type of structure with which they were associated. Such a development would parallel that of the battlements whose symbolic significance on royal crowns, the crown of Darius for example, is quite evident.

This interpretation of the friezes of dentils in Persian and Median architecture would explain their occurrence on structures which cer-

[1] Tilia, "Reconstruction of the Parapet".
[2] E. Porada, "Battlements in the Military Architecture and Symbolism of the Ancient Near East", in D. Fraser et al. (eds), *Essays in the history of art presented to Rudolf Wittkower* (London, 1967), pp. 5-6.
[3] E. Akurgal, *The Art of the Hittites* (New York, 1962), pl. 46.

ARCHITECTURE

Fig. 5. The Temple of Haldi at Ardini-Musasir, flanked by structures of a walled town; engraving after a relief in the palace of Sargon at Khorsabad.

tainly have a religious meaning, such as the temple of Nūsh-i Jān[1] and the façade of the tomb of Darius (pl. 20), and others for which a religious or ceremonial meaning is probable, like the towers of Pasargadae and Naqsh-i Rustam.[2] Dentils, arrow, and design composed of squares and triangles as on the parapet at Persepolis, occur on merlons of the peribolos of the temple of Surkh Kotal (Afghanistan) of the 2nd century A.D. (pl. 17a), together with the inset blind windows which are topped by dentils at Surkh Kotal as they are at Nūsh-i Jān. The blind window design also occurs on the fire altar seen on the tombs of the Achaemenid kings, as well as in the wall decoration of the above mentioned towers. Probably all these features carried a specific meaning, the end effect of which was to be the protection of the structure and of the people within.

The Tilias believe that the parapet may have belonged to an earlier edifice than the one found by the excavator Erich Schmidt and called by him Palace H. Like many structures on the Terrace, the parapet was never completed. The date and manner of its destruction, by earthquake or human action, are unknown. They add one more group of unanswered questions to those about the precise data and meaning of most of the monuments at Persepolis.

The Achaemenian structures of Susa have become better known within the past decade.[3] However, plans published earlier had made it obvious that the palace of Darius (fig. 6) was built around three courts. It thereby resembled Assyro-Babylonian palaces in which royal apartments, reception and administration rooms, as well as magazines, were all combined within one large edifice. There is similarity especially between the palace of Susa and the royal palace of Babylon, the so-called Südburg. The palace of Darius, however, seems to have been planned in a more unified manner. Moreover, it contains a curious feature: there are large longitudinal rooms with two pairs of projections, which divide off narrow parts of the room at each end. This feature was traced back to Elamite houses of the 2nd millennium B.C. at Susa.[4] It occurs, however, also in the Assyrian palaces of Sargon (721–705 B.C.),

---

[1] D. Stronach, *Iran* VII (1969), pl. I c, d, II a; another temple is in the Old Western Building; see *Iran* XVI (1978), p. 5, fig. 3.
[2] See chapter 20 in the present volume.
[3] See the reports listed by Vanden Berghe, *Bibliographie analytique*, p. 97 Nos. 1266–1271, 1273, especially, J. Perrot and D. Ladiray, "Travaux à l'Apadana", *CDAFI* II (1972), pp. 13–23, and J. Perrot, "L'architecture militaire et palatiale des Achéménides à Suse".
[4] R. Ghirshman, "L'architecture élamite et ses traditions", *Iranica Antiqua* V (1965), pp. 93–102.

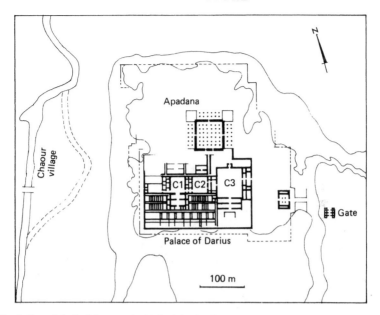

Fig. 6. Plan of the buildings on the Tell of the Apadana at Susa by J. Perrot and D. Ladiray.

Sennacherib (704–681 B.C.) and Ashurbanipal (668–627 B.C.).[1] At Susa the two longitudinal halls with this enigmatic feature lie before a row of rooms built against the outer wall of the palace, and are thought to be the royal apartments of Darius.[2] From the central one of these rooms lying against the outer wall, there was an unimpaired access to court C-1 through openings in the middle of the long halls which had the so far unexplained projections. In the passage leading to the central room were found two foundation inscriptions beautifully engraved on grey marble slabs.[3] The one on the right side had an inscription in Elamite and was found face up, the one on the left side was in Akkadian and lay face down. In the latter the building was referred to by an Akkadian term meaning "house", in contrast to the foundation inscription found in 1929, which uses the term "palace".[4] Conceivably the

[1] M. Roaf, "The Diffusion of the 'Salles à quatre saillants'", *Iraq* XXXV (1973), pp. 83–91.
[2] P. Amiet, "Quelques observations sur le palais de Darius à Suse", *Syria* LI (1974), pp. 65–73.
[3] J. Perrot *et al.*, "Recherches archéologiques à Suse et en Susiane en 1969 et en 1970", *Syria* XLVIII (1971), p. 49.
[4] F. Vallat, "Deux nouvelles 'chartes de fondation' d'un palais de Darius 1er à Suse", *Syria* XLVIII (1971), p. 56.

term "house" applied to a more intimate part, such as the presumed royal apartments in which the inscriptions were found.

The text of the Elamite inscription contained detailed references to the sources of building materials employed in the structure, as well as to craftsmen of different nationalities. The references are much the same as in the inscription found in 1929. They are here given in a translation of F. Vallat's French text.[1]

(lines 18–26) The palace which (is) at Susa, it is I who have made it. Its materials have been brought from afar. The earth was dug in depth until virgin soil was reached. When it was completely dug out, the foundations were laid in gravel. Upon 20 cubits of depth of that gravel I raised the palace. And what was done concerning the digging down in depth into the earth, and also what was done concerning the foundations in gravel, and also what was done concerning the moulding of bricks, people who (were) Babylonians, they themselves did it.

(lines 26–44) And the beams which (were) of cedar, these were brought from a mountain whose name (is) Lebanon, from there. The people who (were) Assyrians (Syrians) transported them to Babylonia, and from Babylonia the Carians and Ionians transported them to Susa. And the *yakā*-timber was brought from Gandhara and also from Carmania. And the gold was brought from Sardes and Bactria, that was wrought here. And the precious stones which (were) lapis lazuli and also carnelian, which were wrought here, they were brought from Sogdiana. And the precious stones which (were) turquoise, those were brought from Chorasmia, which were wrought here. And the silver and ebony were brought from Egypt. And the decorative elements with which the Terrace was ornamented, those were brought from Ionia. And the ivory, which was wrought here, that was brought from Ethiopia and India and Arachosia. And the stone columns, which were worked here, from a town by the name of Apiratush, from over here, in Elam, they were brought.

(lines 44–52) The craftsmen who worked the stone, those (were) Ionians and Sardians. And the goldsmiths who worked that gold, those (were) Medes and Egyptians. And the men who wrought the wood, those (were) Sardians and Egyptians. And the men who wrought the baked brick, those (were) Babylonians. And the men who decorated the Terrace, those (were) Medes and Egyptians.

Corresponding to the north-eastern orientation of the palace, Darius built an Apadana north-east of the palace as seen on the plan of the Achaemenian buildings on the tell (fig. 6). The corners of that building were oriented north-east–south-west. It is only in this matter of orientation that the plan of the Apadana of Susa appears to differ from that of Persepolis, although not enough is preserved of the building on

---

[1] Vallat, *op. cit.*, pp. 57–8, lines 18–52.

the southwest side to show whether or not it had the same service rooms on that side as the one at Persepolis. In view of the apparently original square hall of the one at Susa, one might assume that it was the later of the two Apadana halls. However, a large assembly hall seems to have been essential for the political life of Persians and Medes[1] and there must have been some building which served that purpose before the Apadana was built, if the latter was indeed only erected after the Apadana of Persepolis.

Access to the elevated esplanade on which lay the palace and Apadana of Darius was through the gate built by him (fig. 7).[2] It has a hypostyle hall flanked by two rectangular rooms. Before the hall and facing toward the palace complex stood two figures of the king of which only one is preserved; they originally measured about 3 metres in height but the head and shoulders are missing. The foundations for a statue of the same size were found on both sides of the gate. The statue is discussed below together with the other sculptures of Darius.

The buildings on the mound of the Apadana were surrounded by a mudbrick wall. Within that wall there was only the palace of Darius and the Apadana. There were no town houses; nor have any so far been unearthed on the so-called Acropolis of Susa. Up to now only palatial structures of the Achaemenian period are known, as well as fortresses; no town has been discovered in connection with palatial Achaemenian edifices.[3]

Artaxerxes II (404–359/8 B.C.) built a palace on the other side of the river Kārūn (called Chaour in French). The reception hall of that palace complex resembled the Apadanas of Darius except for shorter porticoes on the north and south sides, where symmetrical rooms were built,[4] there

[1] An audience hall existed in every palatial complex built by an Achaemenid king. Cyrus: Palace S at Pasargadae; Cambyses: Apadana at Dasht-i Gohar (*Iranica Antiqua* XV (1980), p. 202); Darius I: Apadanas at Persepolis and Susa; Artaxerxes I: Hundred Column Hall (the biggest of all); Artaxerxes II: Apadana in the "Palais du Chaour" (see n. 4 below). A Median hall existed at Tepe Nūsh-i Jān (*Iran* XVI (1978) p. 2, fig. 1) and also at Godin Tepe (T. C. Young, Jr. and L. D. Levine, *Excavations of the Godin Project: Second Progress Report* (Royal Ontario Museum, 1974), p. 116, fig. 37). Ancestral to all were probably the columnar halls at Hasanlu; the reconstruction made at the University Museum, Philadelphia, has not yet been published by the excavator. In the meantime, see P. Amiet, *Art of the Ancient Near East* (New York, 1980) p. 551, no. 991.

[2] J. Perrot and D. Ladiray, "La porte de Darius à Suse", *CDAFI* IV (1974), pp. 43–56.

[3] The architectural remains south of the Persepolis Terrace in the plain are of palatial buildings (Schmidt, *Persepolis* I, fig. 14) and the same seems to be true of the most recent discoveries in the northeastern part of the Marvdasht Plain by Tilia, *Studies* II, pp. 80–92. The report of the excavations by A. Tajvīdī at the foot of the Persepolis Terrace, published in *Farhang-i Mi'mārī-yi Īrān* II–III (Spring, 1976), has not so far been available.

[4] R. Boucharlat and A. Labrousse, "Le palais d'Artaxerxès II sur la rive droite du Chaour à Suse", *CDAFI* x (1979), pp. 21ff.

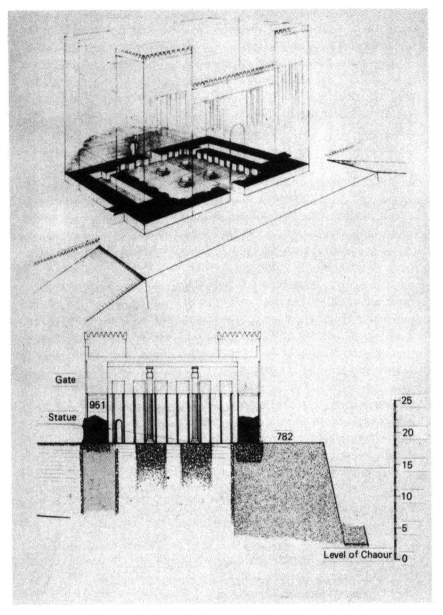

Fig. 7. The Gate of Darius at Susa, reconstructed by J. Perrot and D. Ladiray.

SCULPTURE

is also a strange narrow corridor between the hypostyle hall and the western portico. Apart from these variations the building continued the basic type initiated by Darius I, thereby showing the extent to which the official architecture of the Achaemenids had been determined by him.

SCULPTURE

In order to view the reliefs and sculptures in the round found at Persepolis and Susa in a stylistic sequence, the earlier works of Darius at Bīsutūn and Pasargadae must be mentioned. Darius' relief at Bīsutūn, commemorating his victory over Gaumāta and the other "false kings", is generally considered to have been the earliest work of his reign, close to his victories in 521 B.C.[1] Its style has been compared to that of the Siphnian Treasury at Delphi (*ca.* 525 B.C.), where there is indeed a similar treatment of fallen figures and victors stepping on or over them, resulting in an impression of depth and plastic effect. It is well known that the content of the inscription of Bīsutūn was copied and widely circulated by the chancellery of Darius. Less well known are the fragments found at Babylon.[2] If the relief was set up at the site at which the fragments were found, it was on the outer procession street leading to the Ishtar Gate. It has also been guardedly suggested that the theme might have been reproduced in painted glazed bricks in Susa, for one of the fragments of a glazed brick belongs either to such a scene or to that of a royal hero fighting a monster.[3] The latter is a theme frequently found at Persepolis and is a more likely one to have figured in glazed brick. At all events the small fragment shows that the representation of "Susian" guards was not the only theme involving human figures seen in the palace of Darius at Susa.

The glazed brick reliefs of "Susian" guards (pl. 18) show them with draped robes commonly known as the Persian dress. There is here a less plastic, more formal treatment, when compared with the representation at Bīsutūn. The wide sleeve was made manageable – artistically and perhaps also in reality – by being partly laid in stacked folds obliquely placed with a zigzag edge in one direction. In the lower part of the garment a series of concave ridges curve up from either side to a bunch of vertical folds, symmetrically stacked in two directions. The

---

[1] See Chapter 18 in the present volume.
[2] U. Seidl, "Ein Relief Dareios' I in Babylon", *AMI* IX (1976), pp. 125–30.
[3] J. V. Canby, "A Note on some Susa Bricks", *AMI* XII (1979), pp. 315–20.

actual structure of the garment is still unclear, on account of the considerable artistic licence taken in the stylization of the drapery. Drapery as a means of expression – in the present case an expression of sumptuous ceremonial display – could not have been devised by a Near Eastern artist, for whom ornamentation alone was the means to distinguish a rich garment. However, artists familiar with the development of Greek drapery, might add to the ornamentation the impression of the fullness of the robe, as well as the natural appearance of figures. The suggestion that Ionians designed the glazed brick reliefs of guards at Susa[1] is therefore most likely to be correct. These glazed brick reliefs differ from the Babylonian by being made of frit instead of terracotta and by having the black outlines painted in a colour with a higher melting point than that of the other colours.[2] Therefore the precise outlines of the design remained unchanged in the firing of the Persian bricks. The beautiful patterned robes of the guards give some idea of the colourful pageant presented by an assembly of the Persian court.

It has been suggested that these glazed brick reliefs were made at Susa before the work at Persepolis had reached a stage at which carvers of reliefs were needed there. The same may have been true of the reliefs from Palace P at Pasargadae (pl. 17*b*), which share with the glazed brick reliefs the stress on the coloured border seen in the middle of the vertical folds. At Pasargadae that border was produced by metal appliqués, a practice documented in Greece, for example in the sculptures of the so-called temple of Aphaia at Aegina, where the drapery of the statue of the goddess Athena has been compared to that seen at Pasargadae in its natural-looking, weighty effect, and the arrangement of the long, stacked folds in front, and the curving ones on the sides.[3] The suggestion that different groups of eastern Greek artists were called by the Achaemenid kings Darius and Xerxes according as their services were needed,[4] accounts well for the different styles encountered in classic Achaemenian art relating to different stages in the development of Greek art.

The stage of Achaemenian style encountered in the reliefs of Palace P at Pasargadae may also have been that of the tomb façade of Darius. Darius chose the "awesome ambience" of the valley of Naqsh-i Rustam

[1] Farkas, *Achaemenid Sculpture*, p. 108.
[2] E. Haerinck, "Le palais achéménide de Babylone", *Iranica Antiqua* x (1973), p. 120.
[3] The comparison was made by G. M. A. Richter, "Greeks in Persia", *AJA* L (1946), p. 18.
[4] Farkas, *Achaemenid Sculpture*, p. 86.

(pl. 19) as the site for his rock chamber tomb, the inside of which consisted of a vestibule from which vaults of approximately rectangular plan extended into the rock. The actual burial sites are rectangular cavities cut into the floor of the vaults.[1]

Darius may have obtained the idea for such rock-cut tombs from Urartean prototypes.[2] New, however, was the shape of the façade: a giant cross (pl. 20), on the horizontal middle part of which was carved the façade of an Achaemenian palace, meant, perhaps, to be that of Darius.[3] In the upper field is the figure of the king on a stepped platform facing toward a fire altar, which is likewise raised on a plinth or platform, reminiscent of the plinths in the sacred precinct at Pasargadae. Between king and altar in the sky is a bearded, crowned figure in a winged disk, formerly identified as the Zoroastrian supreme god Ahuramazda, an interpretation to which the royal fortune *Farnah* is at present being urged as an alternative.[4] The fire was the personal fire of the king, which was kindled at his accession and kept burning until the end of the reign.[5] The king stands on a platform which ends in the head of a horned lion-dragon of unknown significance. The platform is raised by the peoples of the empire. The proportions and the spacing of the figure contribute to the effect of the king's image as majestic and unique.

Among the six persons at the side of the main panel, interpreted as the king's helpers,[6] is one, Gobryas (pl. 21), whose face has an extraordinarily individual cast of features executed with great delicacy. It is difficult not to suspect that a real portrait was intended, and achieved, doubtless with the permission of Darius.

The representation on the façade of the tomb of Darius was copied for the tomb of each of the Achaemenian kings buried at Naqsh-i Rustam and at Persepolis, although very slight changes reflect a minor stylistic development within the limits of a static iconography.

The tower erected by Darius on the plain, facing his tomb, is discussed in chapter 20, where the view is upheld that it, and the tower

---

[1] Schmidt, *Persepolis* III, p. 87.
[2] P. Calmeyer, "Felsgräber, B. Urartäische Vorbilder", *AMI* VIII (1975), pp. 101–7.
[3] Schmidt, *Persepolis* III, p. 81.
[4] A. S. Shahbazi, "An Achaemenid Symbol II, Farnah '(God Given) Fortune' Symbolized", *AMI* XIII (1980), pp. 119–47.
[5] Shahbazi, *op. cit.* p. 132.
[6] Shahbazi, *op. cit.* p. 125, thinks that the king's helpers reflect the six helpers of Ahuramazda, the Holy Immortals.

at Pasargadae, contained the king's royal paraphernalia. One may think here of the "robe of Cyrus", with which every Achaemenian king was supposed to have been invested at the inauguration of his reign.[1]

The stylistic phase of the art of Darius encountered in his palace at Persepolis seems more formal and more advanced – with few exceptions – than in the tomb relief. The reliefs were carved on the jambs of the great stone door frames of the palace. In the jambs of the main hall which lead to side rooms there appears a royal hero fighting a lion (pl. 22a), bull or griffin monster. The jambs leading onto the portico have the king walking with two attendants who hold flywhisk and sun-shade, the latter obviously needed for going outside. The jambs of the doors leading to the rooms in the back show the king with a flywhisk held over him (pl. 22b). The reliefs which were carved on jambs leading from one back room to another show attendants carrying oil jars and cloths which were obviously needed to wipe off the oil.[2] These last reliefs are clear indications of the residential character of the back of the building. The others tell visually of the King's usual exit and entrance to his private apartments, somewhat in the manner of Egyptian tomb paintings.[3] This concept may be combined with the undoubted fact that the king's image appears on the reliefs to indicate that it is *his* palace which the viewer is contemplating.[4]

The motif of the royal hero overpowering a monster or dangerous animal may be interpreted as a symbol of royalty inherited from Assyrian iconography. In the latter the king killing a lion was the traditional seal design from the time of Shalmaneser III (858–824 B.C.) until the time of Ashurbanipal (688–627 B.C.)[5] It should be noted, however, that the Assyrian king fights only lions standing erect on their hindlegs like human beings, whereas the royal Persian hero also engaged supernatural monsters.

The reliefs which show the king walking with his attendants are among the most elegant of the Terrace and were surely carved by a very competent sculptor. No attempt has so far been made to determine the work of a specific artist under Darius at Persepolis on the strength of

---

[1] Shahbazi, *op. cit.* p. 137.   [2] Schmidt, *Persepolis* I, pls. 148–50.
[3] W. Wolf, *Die Kunst Ägyptens* (Stuttgart, 1957), p. 480.
[4] P. Calmeyer, "Textual Sources for the Interpretation of Achaemenian Palace Decorations", *Iran* XVIII (1980), p. 60.
[5] A. R. Millard, "The Assyrian Royal Seal Type Again", *Iraq* XXVI (1965), pp. 12–16 and references cited there.

1 (a) The ascent ("Klimax") from the plain of Elam to Persis.
   (b) The road into Persis. The "Valley of the Oaks" west of Shīrāz.
   (c) The Caspian Gates, looking east.

2   (*a*) The Kūh-dāman, looking east to Kapisa (Paropamisadai).
     (*b*) The citadel-mound of Bampūr (Pura in Gedrosia).
     (*c*) Hyrcania under the Alburz, east of modern Behshahr.

3   (*a*) The mound of Agbatana (Hamadān) and Mt Alvand.
     (*b*) One of the high valleys of the Zagros in Media, near Burūjird.
     (*c*) The Euphrates entering the plain of Carchemish.

4 Darius III, as portrayed in the Alexander mosaic of Pompeii.

5 Pasargadae, the tomb of Cyrus, showing the entrance, from the west.

6 (a) Pasargadae, the Winged Figure, once inscribed with the name of Cyrus.
  (b) Winged genius from the palace of Sargon II of Assyria, Khorsabad.

7 Pasargradae, the great stone platform of the Tell-i Takht from the south-west.

8 Painted wooden naos, showing the scroll of Darius I, from the necropolis galleries of the sacred ibises at Hermopoli.

9 An Aramaic letter from Hermopoli, addressed to Nnyḥm at Aswan. It begins with greetings
   to the temple of Bethel and the temple of Malkat-šamīn.

10 Label from a mummy, written on both sides (a) and (b), with the proper name and the family name, in Aramaic, of two deceased, both sons of Bagadat; from south Saqqqara. Length 11 cm.

11 Statue of Psamteksaneit, from Memphis.

12 Coins and ingots.
(1) Light Croeseid, gold; fine style, earlier Persian period. (2) Light Croeseid, gold; bold style. Before c. 518 B.C. (3) Daric (gold) with king shooting; after c. 510 B.C. (enlarged). (4) Daric (gold) with king running (main series); after c. 490 B.C. (5) Daric (gold) with beardless king; Cyrus the Younger (?), 410 B.C. (6) Daric (gold) showing king with dagger; late 5th to early 4th century B.C. (7) Cut silver with Elamite inscription: UL-HI]e-ma hu-[ut-tuk-qa "Made at the palace..." (a) and (b) Actual size; (c) enlarged (Kabul Museum). (8) Bar ingot, wt. 8·34 gm, length 58 mm (Kabul Museum). (9) Elephant decadrachm of Alexander.

13 Persepolis, the terrace and its structures. Model by Friedrich Krefter.

15 Persepolis (*a*) the eastern stairway of the Apadana, central and northern parts.
    (*b*) The Gate of All Lands.

16 Persepolis, the Parapet reconstructed along the Terrace edge, south of Palace H.

17 (a) Surkh Kotal, merlon in the Peribolos of the temple on the Acropolis.
(b) Pasargadae, lower part of the figure of the king from Palace P.

18 Susa, glazed brick relief of guardsman from Palace of Darius I.

19 Naqsh-i Rustam, general view showing the rock-cut tombs of Darius I (right) and two of his successors.

20 Naqsh-i Rustam, façade of tomb of Darius I.

21 Naqsh-i Rustam, head of Gobryas from façade of tomb of Darius I.

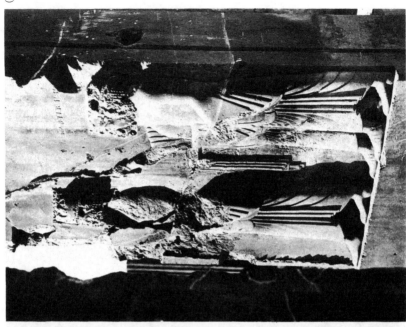

22 Persepolis, Palace of Darius
(a) Royal hero fighting with a lion

23 Persepolis, southern Audience Relief, found in the Treasury (Archaeological Museum, Tehran).

24 Persepolis, eastern Audience Relief.
(a) Figure of the king.
(b) Detail of (a).
(c) Heads of two attendants.

25 Susa. Statue of Darius excavated at the Gate.
(Archaeological Museum, Tehran).

26 Susa. Statue of Darius.
(a) Detail.
(b) socle.

27 Persepolis. Lion and bull motif from the main stairway of the Tripylon.

29 Persepolis. Archers and "Susian" guards on the west flank of the northern wing of the Eastern Stairway.

30 Persepolis.
 (a) Delegation of the Lydians and Babylonians.
 (b) Nobles on the northern wing of the Eastern Stairway of the Apadana.

31 Persepolis. Audience scene of Artaxerxes I on the eastern doorway of the northern wall in the Hundred Column Hall.

32 Persepolis. Throne relief of Artaxerxes I on the east jamb of the eastern doorway in the southern wall.

33 Persepolis. "Persian" and "Median" dignitaries on the main stairway of the Tripylon.

35 Behistun, detail of Darius.

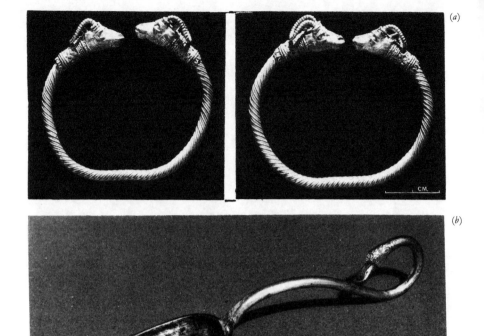

36 (a) A pair of ibex-headed gold bracelets from the Pasargadae treasure.
(b) A silver spoon with a swan's head handle.

37 The entrance façade of the ruined stone tower known locally as the Zindān-i Sulaimān or the Prison of Solomon.

38 (a) The partly excavated mound of Tepe Nush-i Jan as seen from the south in 1973.
(b) A scale model showing the four main Median buildings at Tepe Nush-i Jan as they stood revealed at the end of the fourth season of excavations. From left to right the model shows the Western Temple, the Columned Hall, the Central Temple, the Fort and the East Court.

39 (a) The stepped walls of the sanctuary of the Central Temple. The altar, partly reburied as a protective measure, is visible in the foreground.
(b) The excavated fire altar. The altar is flanked on two sides by a secondary protective wall.

40 (a) The west end of Room 23, one of four tall storage magazines found within the fort.
(b) A Neo-Assyrian stone stamp seal found on the fallen floor in Room 18 of the Fort.

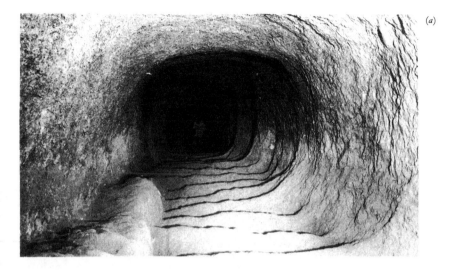

41 (a) The unfinished rock-cut tunnel.
   (b) The narrow walls of the squatter occupation found during the excavation of the Columned Hall. The Western Temple stands in the background.

42 Decorated sheet gold cover for the sheath of an iron short-sword; from the Oxus Treasure (Dalton, no. 22). 6th or 5th century B.C. 27·6 cm. long.

43 (a) Gold collar or spiral bracelet originally decorated with multi-coloured inlays for which the cavities survive, from the Oxus Treasure (Dalton, no. 118); 5th to 4th century B.C. 11·1 cm. diameter.
  (b) Gold bracelet of typical Achaemenian omega shape with cloisons for richly coloured inlays now lost; from the Oxus Treasure (Dalton, no.

44   (*a*) Gold chariot model with a head of the Egyptian god Bes on the front; from the Oxus Treasure (Dalton, no. 7); 5th to 4th century B.C. 18·8 cm. long.
      (*b*) Sheet-gold jug with cast gold lion-headed handle; from the Oxus Treasure (Dalton, no. 17); 5th to 4th century B.C. 13 cm. high.

45 (a) Silver handle from a vessel cast in the shape of a leaping wild goat; from the Oxus Treasure (Dalton, no. 10); 5th to 4th century B.C. 21 cm. long.
(b) Cast silver bowl with sheet gold friezes inlaid into the body of the vessel; source unknown; 5th to 4th century B.C. 6·9 cm. high.

46   (a) Silver bowl said to be from Tell el-Maskhuta in Egypt; its floral designs in the traditional Egyptian manner; later 5th to 4th century B.C. 8·5 cm. high.
     (b) Silver bowl said to be from Tell el-Maskhuta in Egypt inscribed in Aramaic with the name of the donor and the deity to whom it was dedicated; later 5th to 4th century B.C. 8·5 cm. high.

47 (a) Inlaid and gilded wooden shrine door showing Darius I with the Egyptian deities Anubis and Isis. It illustrates how in certain regions of their Empire with strong local artistic traditions the Achaemenid kings completely assimilated them; later 6th or early 5th century B.C. About 24 cm. long.

(b) Cylinder seal of a high official, reported to be from Egypt, showing Darius I engaged in a lion hunt; the inscription in Old Persian, Elamite and Babylonian (Akkadian) reads "Darius, the Great King", later 6th or early 5th century B.C. 3·7 cm. high.

48 (a) Modern impression from a cylinder seal showing the Egyptian god Bes flanked by men in Persian costume supporting the winged disk; the inscription gives the owner's name; 5th to 4th century B.C. About 2·8 cm. high.

(b) Modern impression of a cylinder seal blending standard Achaemenian court style motifs, like the incense burner and the prancing wild goat (cf. pl. 45 (a)), and motifs of Egyptian origin like the "eyes-of-Horus" and the hawk, 5th to 4th century B.C. About 3·4 cm. high.

composition and execution of details. The controversy which rages about the Audience reliefs to be discussed in what follows, suffers from a lack of detailed observation, without which no reliable conclusions can be reached.

The two reliefs show an audience given by a Persian king. The better preserved one, now in the Archaeological Museum in Tehran, is illustrated here (pl. 23); it has the king facing right. The other, which has remained at Persepolis, is identical but has the scene reversed, with the king facing left (pl. 24a). Behind the enthroned king, though meant to stand beside him on the daïs, is the crown prince. The chamberlain with a towel, and the weapon bearer, who are aligned on the ground behind the prince, were probably meant to stand on the enthroned king's left side. The person who is received in audience has long been called a Mede on the basis of his costume, characterized by tightfitting trousers and a hat with bulbous outline. Rather than aim at a purely ethnic characterization at this stage of the development of official dress in the Achaemenian empire,[1] the costume may indicate a military function. In the present scene the figure has been attractively identified by several scholars as the principal organizer of the procession of the peoples of the empire. The distinctive gesture of his hand was probably meant to prevent his breath from defiling the monarch.

The reliefs were excavated by Schmidt in a complex of the enlarged Treasury of Darius in a courtyard surrounded by four porticoes, in two of which the reliefs were set up against the back wall.[2] The complex had several special features, such as doorways with painted ornamentation and emplacement for two pairs of guardian figures, probably dogs and perhaps ibexes or bulls. In view of these distinctive elements Schmidt concluded that the reliefs were made for the Treasury, rejecting the alternative that they were made for the Apadana.

The latter assumption, however, turned out to be the correct one, borne out by remains of the canopy still in place on the Apadana stairway façades.[3] Questions immediately arose as to why these magnificent reliefs were removed to a location where they could no longer be generally seen. Even the dating of the reliefs in the time of

---

[1] A. S. Shahbazi, "Costume and Nationality, Remarks on the Use of the 'Median' and 'Persian' Costumes of the Achaemenid Period", in *Akten VII Kongresses, Munich, 1976*, p. 195. P. Calmeyer, "Vom Reisehut zur Kaiserkrone", *AMI* x (1977), p. 175, doubts that the form of the 'Median' headgear was ever bulbous; however, hats of modern Bakhtiari tribesmen look much like the ancient headgear and are bulbous. I owe this information to Manijeh Khazaneh.

[2] Schmidt, *Persepolis* I, pp. 171–2, "Courtyard 17 and its porticoes".

[3] Tilia, *Studies* I, pp. 183–204.

Darius began to be questioned, seeing that his son Xerxes claimed authorship of the Apadana stairway façades. Elsewhere he had mentioned his father as the original builder of the Apadana.[1] But it is not only the inscription which renders some scholars quite ready to accept the conclusion reached by H. von Gall that Xerxes, not Darius is the enthroned king in the Audience reliefs;[2] another argument advanced by von Gall is that the headdress of the enthroned king lacks the crenelations characteristic of the crown of Darius.

One might impugn the reliability of Xerxes' stairway inscriptions by suggesting that they were carved at the completion of the work, when Darius had been dead long enough for Xerxes to claim the decoration of the stairway façades for himself, even if they were initiated by Darius. The argument for the authorship by an artist of the time of Darius, however, must rest on considerations of style. For this purpose a monument datable in the late phase of the reign of Darius and showing related stylistic traits, has to be drawn into the discussion. Such a monument is the statue of Darius found at Susa.[3]

The statue was made of a dark greenish-grey metamorphic stone called grauwacke, of which quarries existed in the region of the Wadi Hamamat. They were worked throughout the periods of Egyptian sculpture, but their greenish-grey stone was particularly appreciated in the period of the Persian domination. There are ten short inscriptions at various points of the Wadi, carved between the years 496 to 492 B.C. by the chief of all workers of the king.[4] Although it is conceivable that a stone such as that from which the statue was made existed also in Iran in the region between Hamadān and Burūjird,[5] the Egyptian derivation, which agrees with the style of the figure, seems more probable.

The proudly upright figure, preserved to a height of 1.95 metres (pls 25, 26), was originally about 3 metres high and stands upon a socle whose height is .51 metre. Figure and socle are cut from one block of stone. The figure has the left foot placed forward, the right arm held at the side with the damaged hand clasping what was probably a handkerchief.[6] The left arm is bent and the better preserved hand holds

---

[1] Schmidt, *Persepolis* I, p. 71.
[2] H. von Gall, "Die Kopfbedeckung des persischen Ornats bei den Achämeniden", *AMI* VII (1974), pp. 145–61.
[3] D. Stronach, "La statue de Darius le Grand découverte à Suse", *CDAFI* IV (1974), pp. 61–72.
[4] J. Trichet, "Étude pétrographique...", *CDAFI* IV (1974), pp. 57–9.
[5] Trichet, *op. cit.*, p. 59.
[6] H. G. Fischer, "An Elusive Shape within the Fisted Hands of Egyptian Statues", *The Metropolitan Museum Journal* X (New York, 1975), pp. 9–21.

a flower, of which only the stem is preserved. The king wears the ceremonial long wide Persian robe, which covers the arms and is held by a belt in the waist. The width of the garment is reduced by the folds, which are stacked in two vertical sets at the sides. A series of increasingly deep rounded folds hangs down the middle; in the back these folds seem to rise up to the back pillar in such a way that it looks like overlapping them in a very naturalistic manner. The shape of the folds seems to differ from those seen in Ionian workmanship, thus excluding an Ionian sculptor despite the basically Greek derivation of such drapery.[1]

The king's shoes seem to be closely fitted to his feet and were worn without the laces seen on representations of all guards and other military figures. Those of the king were said to have shown traces of red paint,[2] indicating that in antiquity the statue was painted. This is also suggested by the cursory execution of the figures of winged bulls engraved on the sheath of the dagger stuck in the king's belt. These sketchy designs were surely intended to guide the painter in the spacing of his figures. The king's belt seems to have been made of a soft material and has plaquettes with Egyptian hieroglyphs. In one Darius is called "King of Upper and Lower Egypt, master of the performance of rites, Darius – may he live eternally".[3] The plaquette on the other side calls him "master of the Two Lands".

On the left side of the figure a long inscription in classic hieroglyphic Egyptian runs down the pleats of the garment. In it Darius is called "the offspring of the god Atum", the name under which Re, the sun, was worshipped. The goddess Neith of Sais patron goddess of the preceding Saite Dynasty XXVI (the Achaemenids were Dynasty XXVII) is said to have given to Darius the bow with which to conquer all his enemies. The formulas employed were traditionally Egyptian, yet they were also expressive of Darius' own tenets as they appear in the text of his tomb façade.[4] Obviously he had been accepted by the Egyptian clergy[5] as the pharaoh, and much of the religious and political

[1] For comments on the influence of East-Ionian sculptural style on the statue, see H. Luschey, "Archäologische Bemerkungen zu der Darius-Statue von Susa", in *Akten VII Kongresses, Munich, 1976*, pp. 207–17, especially p. 212.

[2] Roaf, "Subject Peoples", p. 74, note 8, citing an observation by G. Tilia.

[3] J. Yoyotte, "Les inscriptions hiéroglyphiques, Darius et l'Egypte", *Journal Asiatique* CCLX (1972), pp. 253–66 for this and all other references to the hieroglyphic inscriptions.

[4] R. G. Kent, *Old Persian* (New Haven, Conn., 1953), pp. 138–40.

[5] This is reflected in the statements of Diodorus Siculus I. 95.5, where it is said that Darius associated with the Egyptian priests and took part with them in the study of theology.

thought expressed in his Persian inscriptions and iconography should be traced to Egyptian influence.

The content of the inscription agrees with the representations on the socle of the statue. Two identical configurations of the "Union of the Two Lands" appear on the front and on the back of the socle. Two fecundity figures[1] have on their head the Lily of upper Egypt or the Papyrus of Lower Egypt and tie the stems of these plants around the hieroglyph which means "to unite". On the longitudinal sides of the socle is a representation of the peoples of the realm, characterized by their costume and sometimes by their ethnic type, arranged in two rows, one on each side. Every figure kneels above a fortress cartouche, that is an oval form with crenelations representing the plan of a fortress, which contains the name of the country represented by the figure. These figures will be mentioned again in connection with the delegations of the peoples on the Apadana reliefs.

The posture of the kneeling figures with raised arms, palms turned up and held flat as if supporting the base on which the king stands, has been rightly associated with the multiple figures of king Tarhaqa of (the Kushite) Dynasty XXV (c. 690–640 B.C.) holding up the star-studded emblem of the heavens on the side of an altar in a temple at Gebel Barkal.[2] At the same time, it is certainly correct to associate the idea of the peoples supporting the kin with the representations of the nations of the realm holding up the king's daïs on his funerary façade.[3] It should be mentioned, however, that the Elamite gesture of prayer and supplication was also one of both hands extended with upturned palms.[4] This could have made the gesture doubly meaningful to Persian viewers.

The workmanship of the socle is typically Egyptian in being carved in sunk relief on a stone, which was probably covered with white plaster or a thin coat of whitewash before being painted in preparation for the carving of the relief.[5]

There must have been at least three examples of this statue of Darius, the original in the temple of Atum at Heliopolis, where it was set up according to the text of the inscription on the statue,[6] and the two

---

[1] The term used for these figures by Roaf in "Subject Peoples" is accepted here.
[2] Roaf, *op. cit.*, p. 77 and note 19.
[3] Roaf, *op. cit.*, p. 78 where this is implied though not expressly stated.
[4] For examples see *Iranica Antiqua* xv (1980), pls. IV: 2, V: 7.
[5] Roaf, *op. cit.*, p. 74.
[6] Yoyotte, "Les inscriptions", p. 257.

statues at the gate in Susa. This indicates that Egyptian influence on the style of Darius was probably considerable, also in works in which it is not as obvious as in the statue. Here we may return to the Audience reliefs to point out the relationship with the statue, which consists in evidence for Egyptian influence as well as in the monumental size of the king's figure. Thus, the flowers held by king and crown prince (pl. 24*b*) have a typically Egyptian shape in the blossom between two buds. Furthermore, the manner in which the stems of the flowers hang down is characteristic only of Egyptian representations of flowers.[1] Another feature derived from Egyptian art is the way in which the line marking the upper eyelid extends down below the lower lid in the faces of the persons on the Audience reliefs (pl. 24*c*). This feature, never found in Babylonian or Assyrian art and not seen in Greek art before the works of the second half of the 5th century B.C.[2] is a characteristic feature of Egyptian art from Dynasty XXV to the Ptolemaic period.[3]

Lastly there is a similarity in the size of the figure of the king in the Audience reliefs and in the statue from Susa. If the seated figure of the king in the reliefs were standing it would be about 3 metres high, like the statue. Such measurements may have originated from the Greek artists at the court of Darius in view of the greater size of the gods in relation to humans seen in some votive reliefs.[4] Figures which are just above human size are more immediately impressive than gigantic figures to which man no longer has any relation.

It seems then that at Persepolis and in Egypt a style had developed in the last decade of the reign of Darius in which Greek and Egyptian elements were harmoniously combined. For the statue found at Susa this dating is almost certain,[5] for the Audience reliefs it can at least be said to be very likely. To evaluate the quality of the artist responsible for the composition of the Audience reliefs, one might point to such subtleties as the foil created for the king by the plain top of the tall-backed

---

[1] A lotus blossom with two buds and stiffly hanging stems is seen in a relief of Dynasty XXVI (c. 650–55 B.C.) in the Louvre; see C. Vandersleyen, *Das Alte Ägypten* (Berlin, 1975) (Propyläen Kunstgeschichte 15), pl. 314.

[2] I owe this information to Evelyn B. Harrison.

[3] In Porada, "Some Thoughts on the Audience Reliefs of Persepolis", *Studies...P. H. von Blanckenhagen* (New York, 1979), p. 40, n. 25, I cited Egyptian paintings for this feature. However, it is much more clearly seen in sculptures in the round and reliefs from Dynasty XXV to the Ptolemaic period. R. S. Bianchi in a personal communication calls it a constant in Egyptian art of the Late Period; see B. V. Bothmer *et al.*, *Egyptian Sculpture of the Late Period* (The Brooklyn Museum, 1960), pls. 38, 60, 77, 114, 239, 329.

[4] Schefold, *Die Griechen und ihre Nachbarn*, pl. 122.

[5] Yoyotte, "Les inscriptions", p. 266.

chair (pl. 24*a*), where any striking decoration would have detracted from the king's bearded head. At the same time that chair is sumptuous below, where it creates areas of interest leading up to the figure of the ruler. Furthermore, the empty space above the two censers, separating the king from the man received in audience dramatizes the distance between the two figures. Yet the man has the same strong features as the king and as all other persons in the relief. The reason is that differentiation of personal traits, such as are found in later Greek and Roman art, almost never occur in the art of the ancient Near East. Instead, in a style so definitely centred on a king such as Darius at Persepolis, or earlier Akhenaten at Amarna, or Ashurnasirpal at Nimrud,[1] it seems likely that the distinctive facial characteristics borne by all the other persons in the reliefs were those of the king. It may therefore be the stylized, somewhat withdrawn portrait of Darius at Persepolis which recurs in every sculpture made during, and perhaps even after his time.

Originally the Audience reliefs were flanked on each side by triangular panels, each showing a rearing bull attacked by a lion, a motif found in corresponding positions on all major stairways on the Terrace (pl. 27). The contest between lion and bull is a theme which goes back to the late 4th millennium B.C. in the art of Mesopotamia and Iran and has been variously interpreted. In the Achaemenian period the lion probably symbolized royal power against which even a strong opponent like a bull could not defend himself.[2]

The Audience reliefs were designed to form the centre of the composition of three tiers of reliefs on either side of each of the Apadana stairway façades. On one side was the array of the royal retinue: chariots, guards and nobles; on the other side were the twenty-three delegations of the nations of the empire bringing their gifts to the great king (pl. 28). The decorations on the northern and eastern stairway were intended to be mirror images of each other but there are slight differences in some of the details and in the style of the execution. The northern stairway façade was the earlier one, exposed through the ages to the elements and occasional vandalism. The eastern stairway was only uncovered by Herzfeld in 1932. It is therefore relatively well preserved and those detailed studies which have been undertaken have been

---

[1] C. Aldred, *Akhenaten and Nefertiti* (London, 1973), p. 199, no. 134 shows even a black man sharing the characteristics of Akhenaten. For comment on Ashurnasirpal, see E. Porada, *The Great King...King of Assyria* (Metropolitan Museum New York, 1945), p. 28.

[2] E. Porada, "An Assyrian Bronze Disc", *Bulletin of the Boston Museum of Fine Arts* XLVIII (1950), pp. 2–8.

concentrated on that stairway. The result of one recent study[1] is the recognition that the Persian archers, of which there are 200 on the stairways (pl. 29), were carved by small teams of artisans working under a master craftsman. Apparently these artisans specialized in specific parts of a figure such as face or quiver, which they would carve on a series of archers. This explains part of the apparent uniformity of the reliefs, especially as one of the teams identified accounts for one fifth of all the sculpted figures.[2]

Greater demands must have been made on the artisans who worked on the side portraying the various delegations. Each of these groups was separated from the next by a formal, Egyptianizing tree design, which appears directly below the one above. In each delegation the first man is led alternately by a "Persian" or a "Mede", but the number of persons in each group differed, especially if there was present one of the fine animals, horse, bull, or camel. Yet no group ever appears crowded or awkward; the spacing must have been worked out carefully on "papyrus" before being transferred to the wall. The horizontal registers together with the trees formed a grid into which the delegations were fitted. There is no precedent in the Near East for such planning of a horizontal *and* vertical composition. On the contrary, in the reconstructed wall painting of the throne room of Sargon at Khorsabad the designs in one horizontal register are not related to those in the registers above or below.[3] It seems likely that the outlines of each delegation were painted in some detail before the carving began, resulting in the fine reliefs. It is even conceivable that the painting was more than a guide for the sculptors, being used to give an impression of the finished decoration long before the actual sculpture was done. This would explain the frequency of unfinished parts,[4] which might have been overlooked as long as they were covered with paint, but are very striking today in contrast with the finished parts.

There have been numerous discussions of the Apadana reliefs,[5]

[1] M. Roaf, "A Mathematical Analysis of the Styles of the Persepolis Reliefs", in M. Greenhalgh and V. Megaw (eds), *Art in Society* (London, 1978), pp. 133–45.

[2] *Ibid.*, p. 143.

[3] G. Loud and C. B. Altman, *Khorsabad* II (Chicago, 1938) (Oriental Institute Publications 40), pl. 89.

[4] A. B. Tilia, "Unfinished parts of the Architecture and Sculpture", *East and West* XVIII (1968), pp. 90–4, figs. 133–5, 138–42; see also parts of the Audience relief at Persepolis, figs. 146–8.

[5] The basic material concerning the Apadana reliefs consists of the photographs and identifications provided by Schmidt, *Persepolis* I, pp. 82–90 and pls. 27–49 and 61 and *Persepolis* III, "The Tribute Delegations of the Apadana", pp. 145–58 and pls. 101–105 A, B. An excellent photographic record of the single figures in the delegations was given by G. Walser, *Die*

particularly concerning the identification of some of the delegations whose costumes and gifts were not distinctive enough to define the nationality of the bearers. Some of the doubtful cases have been clarified by the representation of the nations of the empire who kneel above the name of their country written in hieroglyphs on the socle of the statue of Darius (pl. 26b).[1] Although the portrayals on the socle are very abbreviated, it is significant that they are independent of the tradition established by the tomb façade of Darius and copied on the Tripylon and the Hundred Column Hall, where similar figures support the king's throne,[2] and independent also of the representation of delegations on the stairway reliefs of the Apadana and of those of Artaxerxes I and III copied from them.[3]

In Near Eastern art in general, differentiation among peoples was mostly made on the basis of dress. Here the trousers,[4] which appeared for the first time in the Persian reliefs, were an important feature documenting the inclusion of new peoples in the population of the Persian empire in the north-west, the north and the north-east. The Medes wore tight trousers, shoes, a long coat with false sleeves, called κάνδυς,[5] which was laid over the shoulders like a cloak, and a bulbous hat with a short tail-like appendage. Many other peoples in the reliefs wore trousers, some tight, like the Armenians and Cappadocians,[6] some

Völkerschaften auf den Reliefs von Persepolis (Teheraner Forschungen 2, Berlin, 1966). M. C. Root, *King and Kingship*, "Catalogue entry VIII", pp. 86–95 and "The Tribute Procession", pp. 227–84, gives a very good documentation and discussion of the concepts of tribute and prefigurations for the Apadana procession. O. W. Muscarella reviewed Schmidt, *Persepolis* III in *AJA* LXXV (1971), pp. 443–4 and Walser, *Völkerschaften* in *JNES* XXVIII (1969), pp. 280–5, with pertinent remarks concerning the identification of the delegations.

[1] Roaf, "Subject Peoples", pp. 73–160.

[2] The supporters of the king's daïs on the tomb reliefs are discussed by Schmidt, *Persepolis* III, pp. 108–118, figs. 39–52; in the Tripylon reliefs Schmidt, *Persepolis* I, pp. 117–20, pls. 80–1; in the Hundred Column Hall, *Persepolis* I, pp. 134–6, pls. 108–13.

[3] The representations from the stairway façade of Artaxerxes I were published by Schmidt, *Persepolis* I, pp. 280–2, pls. 202 B–205, and *Persepolis* III, p. 161 (Palace H) and pl. 105 C, and by Tilia, *Studies* I, pp. 2–316, figs. 44–164. See also Roaf, *op. cit.*, p. 88, n. 55 for the identification of the delegations. For the stairway façade of Artaxerxes III on the west side of the Palace of Darius I, see Schmidt, *Persepolis* I, pp. 228–9, pls. 153–6 and *Persepolis* III, pp. 162–3; also comments by Roaf, *op. cit.*, p. 89.

[4] Cf. P. Calmeyer, "Hose, archäologisch" in *Reallexikon der Assyriologie* IV (Berlin, 1975), pp. 472–6. Calmeyer, "Vom Reisehut zur Kaiserkrone", p. 172, n. 24, suggested that trousers were used in Fars at an earlier date, which is very likely; the representation of a Mede on a cylinder seal from Susa which he cites to support his argument, however, looks like a later addition on an earlier cylinder; see P. Amiet, *Glyptique Susienne* (Paris, 1972) (MDAI 43), no. 2181; I. Gershevitch, "Alloglottography of Old Persian", *TPS* 1979, p. 149

[5] See E. R. Knauer, "Toward a history of the sleeved coat", *Expedition* XXI (1978), p. 28.

[6] Schmidt, *Persepolis* III, pp. 146–7 identified the Apadana delegations I as Median, III as Armenian, IX as Cappadocian and XVI as possibly Sagartian (illustrations: *Persepolis* I, pls. 27, 29, 35, 42). Roaf, "Subject Peoples", p. 102 stated, however, that these identifications are not certain because the garments are all so closely comparable.

loose like the Arians, Bactrians, Arachosians, and Drangianians.[1] The Scythian peoples, as well as the Sogdians, Chorasmians and Skudrians,[2] all wore trousers, they had a distinctive kind of headdress with earflaps fastened under the chin,[3] they also wore a long-sleeved, belted jacket.

The Persians seem to have adopted their voluminous long, loose and wide-sleeved garment from the Elamites, at least for the ceremonial occasions at which they are portrayed in the reliefs. The main characteristic of this garment seems to have been the rounded horizontal folds which are seen in the representation of the Persian and the Elamite on the socle,[4] as well as on a silver figurine from the Oxus Treasure and on a female figurine from Kish.[5] The combination of such rounded folds and the vertical ones, as seen on the statue of Darius as well as in the reliefs, is inexplicable on present evidence.

There is documentary evidence that Cambyses wore the Elamite dress.[6] However, the Elamite dress worn by king Ummanaldas in the scene of surrender to Ashurbanipal, c. 640 B.C., was a fringed garment with no evidence of wide sleeves.[7] This Elamite dress then differs greatly from the one worn by the Persians a century later. Such a discrepancy cannot be due entirely to a different stylistic conception of the garment. We may assume therefore that a change in the ceremonial garment occurred, which may indicate a change in the population, irrespective of the the name Elamite all along applying to the same region and its inhabitants.

The ceremonial headgear of the Persians was cylindrical and fluted,

---

[1] The representation of the Arian on the socle of the statue of Darius provides additional evidence for Schmidt's original identification of Delegation IV with that nation. But the Arachosians on the socle are bare-headed and do not have head and chin heavily wrapped as does Delegation VII (Schmidt, *Persepolis* I, pl. 33), which Roaf calls Drangianians. That headcloth appears to have been white linen as suggested by the paintings in the Palais du Chaour of Artaxerxes II; *CDAFI* II (1972), p. 134, fig. 42.3.

[2] The pointed hat Scythians, called Saka Tigraxauda, are seen in Delegation XI, the Sogdians in Delegation XVII and the Skudrians in Delegation XIX, while the Chorasmian is only shown as one of the daïs supporters (no. 8, fig. 43); Scythians and Sogdians wear a scabbard slide, but none of the other delegations, whereas among the daïs-supporters it is also worn by Medes (no. 2), Parthians (no. 4), Bactrians (no. 6), Arians (no. 5), Chorasmians (no. 8), Arachosians and Drangianians (nos 9, 10?). The scabbard slide is typical of Central Asian peoples together with a crenelated mane for horses, which is not present at Persepolis; see O. Maenchen-Helfen, "Crenelated Mane and Scabbard-Slide", *Central Asiatic Journal* III (1957–8), pp. 85–138.

[3] Roaf's useful terminology for the dress of the peoples of the Persian empire in "Subject Peoples", p. 91 has been taken over here.

[4] *Op. cit.*, pp. 94, 104.

[5] O. M. Dalton, *The Treasure of the Oxus* (London, 1905), pl. II. 1; W. Culican, "Syro-Achaemenian Ampullae", *Iranica Antiqua* XI (1975), pl. XIX.

[6] A. L. Oppenheim, "A New Cambyses Incident", *SPA* XV (1974), pp. 3500–1.

[7] "The Surrender of Ummanaldaš" in R. D. Barnett, *Sculptures from the North Palace of Ashurbanipal* (British Museum, 1976), pl. XXXV, upper left.

probably open on top. It may have been derived from an original feather crown.¹ The everyday garment of the Persians, however, must have consisted in an attire resembling that of the Medes, if it was not identical, as has been suggested.²

The Indic people in Delegation XVIII wear only a kilt, corresponding probably to the one-piece garment worn on the lower body today. Only the leader has an added draped garment, which leaves one arm and shoulder uncovered.³ The Gandharans, the Sattagydians and the representative of Maka also wear the kilt, often with the addition of a cloak.⁴

The large group of peoples dwelling in the countries of the "Fertile Crescent", Babylonians, Assyrians, Ionians, Arabians, Carians, are shown with knee- or ankle-length gowns, usually worn with a cloak.⁵ They can be differentiated somewhat by their headgear or their hairstyle. Most distinctive are the bell-shaped cap with pendent long tip of the Babylonians and the tall turban of the Lydians (pl. 30a). The similarly dressed Egyptians, Libyans and Nubians can be distinguished by their ethnic types.⁶

The execution of the reliefs on the eastern stairway of the Apadana attained the greatest refinement and elegance achieved in Achaemenian art. The best example among the delegations is the often reproduced Lydian one (pl. 30a), with two magnificently modelled horses and precious objects brought by that delegation. The bracelets with griffin protomes and the vases with handles in the form of winged bulls correspond to extant metal objects,⁷ probably produced in that country, which housed some of the ablest craftsmen of the Persian satrapies.

The guards and nobles of the royal court were given an equally elegant appearance (pl. 30b). Their proportions made them seem slender and tall; the slightly outcurving contour of the Persian headgear seems to render the natural widening toward the top, subtly suggesting its

---

[1] R. D. Barnett, "Assyria and Iran, the Earliest Representations of Persians", *SPA* XIV (1967), pp. 2997–3007.

[2] Roaf, *op. cit.*, p. 98 and Shahbazi, "Costume and Nationality".

[3] Schmidt, *Persepolis* I, pl. 44.

[4] The Gandharans are seen in Delegation XIV, Schmidt, *Persepolis* I, pl. 40; the Sattagydian is no. 11 on fig. 45 in Schmidt, *Persepolis* III; the man from Maka is no. 29 on fig. 46.

[5] Schmidt, *Persepolis* I, Delegation V (pl. 31), VI (pl. 32, called Syrians by Schmidt), VIII (pl. 34, called Cilicians by Schmidt); for the Arabians Roaf suggests Delegation XX (pl. 46); the Carian is only seen among the daïs-supporters, holding the foot of the daïs, *Persepolis* III, no. 30, fig. 49.

[6] Schmidt, *Persepolis* I, Delegation X (pl. 36), XXII (pl. 48), XXI (pl. 49, called Ethiopians by Schmidt, probably Nubians by Roaf).

[7] P. Amandry, "Toreutique achéménide", *Antike Kunst* II (1959), pl. 23, 1, 4.

actual appearance, not found in the earlier representations on the northern stairway.[1] The variation of the pose of the nobles on both stairways seems to express animated conversation, punctuated by gestures of intimate friendship, such as holding hands, tapping someone on the shoulder or turning around to the next person. The relative informality of these little figures is in contrast to the monumental Audience scenes, in which the figures are almost three times the size of the register of the nobles. Here there is nothing of this lightness or immediacy of expression. Instead, the figures appear as in a solemn pantomime before the Great King.

It is conceivable that the unfinished state of the crown on the Audience relief in Persepolis[2] was due to a change effected in the shape of the crown by the artists of Xerxes in order to ensure for him the credit of having built the stairway façades of the Apadana. The rough surface would conveniently have held the gypsum base for any painting that might have been done. Assuming that Xerxes was successful in being regarded as the king enthroned, receiving the report of the delegations accompanied by Darius, his crown prince, then Artaxerxes I might indeed have wished to remove the images of his murdered father and brother, as has been suggested.[3]

Artaxerxes I's own works can be judged from the reliefs of the Hundred Column Hall, a building begun by the workmen of Xerxes, but completed by those of Artaxerxes I. The hall, larger than that of the Apadana, had two pairs of doorways in the jambs of which the king enthroned appears in the uppermost of six registers (pl. 31). In the northern doorways, which were the entrances from a probably public area, the king receives in audience a man in "Median" costume. In the southern doorways, the king is alone, attended only by a chamberlain with a flywhisk. In the northern doorways five rows of guards are carved below the figure of the king; in the southern doorways the dais on which his throne is placed is supported by representatives of fourteen nations of the empire on one side and fourteen more on the other, so that twenty-eight representatives of the nations are shown. This is a departure from earlier conventions according to which it was the mirror image of a figure or scene which was portrayed on the opposite jamb, or on the twin stairway façade or other twin surface. Another new

[1] For this observation, see Farkas, *Achaemenid Sculpture*, p. 70.
[2] The relief in Tehran cannot be judged because the crown is damaged and also covered by a thick layer of wax.
[3] A. S. Shahbazi, "The Persepolis 'Treasury Reliefs' once more", *AMI* IX (1976), p. 155.

feature is the exaggerated size of the king in relation to all other figures, which deprives the Audience scene, for example, of its credibility.

In the uniquely large size of the king's figure the reliefs in the Hundred Column Hall differ from those of the Tripylon, called Council Hall by Schmidt, which has reliefs of king and crown prince in the large top register and the representatives of the nations as supporters of the dais in three registers below. On the basis of the similarity in the motif of enthroned king and crown prince with that of the Audience reliefs, the Tripylon was assigned by Schmidt to the time of Darius. Details of representation, however, such as the shape of the king's crown, or the flywhisk and the sunshade, all of which can be parallelled by the reliefs of Artaxerxes I, have led to the dating of the Tripylon reliefs in the time of that king.[1] However, the building itself, which served as the main link of communication between the public buildings in the north and the southern part of the site in which the residential palaces were located, had an important function. Moreover, an architectural connection exists between the platform of the Apadana and that of the Tripylon.[2] On this basis one may assume that a building was put up at the time of the Apadana for the same purpose as the Tripylon was meant to fulfil, although there may have been some rebuilding and additions between the time of Darius and that of Artaxerxes I.[3] The reliefs on the main stairway, which show the most relaxed, cheerful crowd of nobles (pl. 32), fit well indeed into the style of Artaxerxes I, as do the figures on the stairway parapets, some of which are very small, others very large (p. 33).

Extensive reliefs made for Artaxerxes I were found by the Tilias on a site south of the palace of Darius, called Palace H by Schmidt. This was a palace begun by Xerxes, for which Artaxerxes had stairway façades decorated with extensive reliefs, in which the delegations seen on the Apadana were extended to comprise more figures. Here too one side of the stairway was not a mirror image of the other, though both

---

[1] P. Calmeyer, "Synarchie", *AMI* IX (1976), pp. 71–5; he considers the Tripylon reliefs older than those of the Hundred Column Hall, within the reign of Artaxerxes I; *ibid.*, p. 76. Without knowing how these reliefs were made, i.e. whether some of them were merely painted in the time of Darius and later carved, one cannot argue against the evidence of the details adduced for the date in the reign of Artaxerxes I.

[2] This is visible in the plan of the Tripylon, called Council Hall by Schmidt, *Persepolis* I, p. 108, text p. 107.

[3] L. Trümpelmann, "Tore von Persepolis", *AMI* VII (1974), p. 169, assumes a rebuilding of the area of the east gate of the Tripylon, and Calmeyer, "Synarchie", p. 72, takes an earlier plan for the Tripylon for granted on the basis of the staircase in the south-east, for which there does not seem to be any reason.

sides were symmetrically balanced.[1] One notes a greater variation in the composition and in the postures of individual figures, which are often livelier than on the Apadana reliefs, as well as stockier proportions, greater numbers, and tighter spacing of figures. In this respect the artistic judgement seems less perfect, the result less classic than before.

The best evidence for painting of the reliefs at Persepolis comes from the time of Artaxerxes I, from the Hundred Column Hall.[2] The colours on the crowned figure in the winged disk above the enthroned king on the dais borne by the nations on the western jamb of the eastern doorway in the southern wall of the hall, have been reconstructed as bright green, red, yellow, and blue for the beard and hair of the figure. This is an improvement in freshness of colours on an earlier reconstruction.[3] The observation that the dots in the wings of this painting occur in Egyptian wing designs[4] supports the view that the painting was done by Egyptians.

Recent work at Susa has uncovered paintings of the time of Artaxerxes II and potsherds from vessels used to hold paint have been found in the palace of that king and also in the Apadana on the Acropolis of Susa,[5] corresponding to the evidence mentioned above for painting of the reliefs of the Apadana at Persepolis.

Two fragmentary reliefs from the palace of Artaxerxes II show a further development away from the carefully proportioned and precisely executed forms of classic Achaemenian art.[6] That art had been executed by Ionians, Sardians, Egyptians, and all the other peoples whom Darius had proudly cited as working for him; their labours had succeeded magnificently in expressing the concepts of their Persian masters.

[1] Tilia, *Studies* I, p. 303.
[2] Tilia, *Studies* II, "Colour in Persepolis", pp. 31ff; see especially the reconstruction of the painting on pl. B.
[3] Judith Lerner, "A Painted Relief from Persepolis", *Archaeology* XXVI (1973), pp. 118–22.
[4] Tilia points to winged symbols in Egyptian cloisonné jewelry, which have dots or circles of a *different* colour at the tips of the wings. One can add that there are also painted examples, such as the soul in the form of a bird from the tomb of Arinefer at Thebes; see G. Posener, *Dictionnaire de la civilization égyptienne* (Paris, 1959), p. 10.
[5] Boucharlat and Labrousse, "Le palais d'Artaxerxès II", pp. 67–8.
[6] An offering-bearer in *Syria* XLVIII (1971), pl. 1. d; also in *CDAFI* II (1972), p. 166, pl. XXXIV. 4; a male head was published in *CDAFI* X (1979), p. 134, pl. IXa.

CHAPTER 18

THE BEHISTUN RELIEF

The Behistun relief is the earliest known work of art which can be securely dated in the reign of Darius the Great. Carved on a rock face high above the main road from Mesopotamia through the Zagros to Ecbatana, the relief and the accompanying inscriptions commemorated the suppression of the revolts which ushered in Darius' reign. According to Schmidt, the relief was probably begun late in 521 B.C. or in 520 B.C. and largely completed by the summer of 519 B.C., when a ninth figure was added to the rank of eight captives (pl. 34).[1]

The relief represents Darius triumphant over his enemies; he holds a bow in his left hand and stands with one foot on the fallen figure of Gaumata, the first rebel, who raises his arms in a pleading gesture toward Darius. Behind the king are two Persian attendants, and the nine remaining rebel leaders stand in front of Darius; their hands are tied behind their backs, and their necks are bound by a rope which runs from figure to figure. Above the rebels floats the truncated figure of Ahura Mazdā in a winged disc; the god holds a ring in his left hand and raises his right hand toward Darius. The Persian monarch raises his right hand in a similar gesture to the god, so that the two seem to be in communion, the god bestowing, the king worshipping. The king and his two officers wear Persian dress; each rebel leader is shown in his appropriate native costume and hairdress.

The situation of the monument high on the rock-face, the mountainous surroundings, and the scale of the relief are all impressive, and probably were meant to impress.[2] Like the art produced subsequently in Darius' reign, the relief glorifies the monarch; he is shown larger than other men, more concerned with the deity than with earthly affairs. However, the theme of the Behistun relief does not recur in later Persian art, and was probably inspired by a nearby rock relief at Sar-i Pul.[3] Here

[1] Schmidt, *Persepolis I*, pp. 38–9; see also W. Hinz, "Die Entstehung der altpersischen Keilschrift", *AMI* 1 (1968), 95–8.
[2] G. C. Cameron, "Ancient Persia", in R. C. Dentan (ed.), *The Idea of History in the Ancient Near East* (New Haven, Conn. and London, 1967), pp. 79–97.
[3] This connection has been pointed out by several scholars: Luschey, pp. 68, 69, fig. 3; Olmstead, p. 118; Porada, pp. 40–1, 142–3, p. 40, fig. 15.

THE BEHISTUN RELIEF

a local ruler of the 21st or 20th century B.C. is shown holding a bow and standing with his foot on a fallen enemy; a goddess faces the ruler and holds a rope tied around the neck of a kneeling enemy. Darius must have seen this early relief, decided to follow its example and had the theme recast in the style of his time.

The style of the Behistun relief is simpler than the later art of Darius and appears to unite conventions found in Cyrus' sculptures at Pasargadae with traits characteristic of Assyrian art. Because Cyrus' art is so poorly preserved, and since almost nothing can be said about Median or Elamite monumental sculpture, the origins of Darius' early art are somewhat hazy. The most obvious parallels with the Pasargadae sculptures are the use of high relief and the representation of profile figures whose upper arms are also in proper profile view, rather than seeming to arise from the contour of the back as was customary in Near Eastern relief.[1] Assyrian stylization is apparent in the head of Darius, whose hairstyle, beard and features are treated very much like representations of King Assurbanipal.[2]

This early stage of Darius' art was later transformed into the style that was to characterize Persian art until the fall of the Empire. The Assyrian hairstyle and beard were reshaped from a number of disparate elements into unified forms bounded by clear contours. Just as the hair and beard were re-arranged to be pleasing in shape and proportion, so too was the face. Darius in his later art looked quite different from the earlier figure, with his protruding nose, rectangular beard and small, flat clump of curls clinging to his neck. By a similar transformation, the simple Persian robes on the Behistun relief became much more elaborately pleated in later sculptures (pls 30, 33).

The Behistun relief in part reflects Darius' willingness to break with the immediate past and to create an art which expressed his own ideas and personality. At the same time, the sculptor of the relief observed stylistic conventions of Persian art of the time of Cyrus, and perhaps of the still earlier arts of Media, Elam, Babylonia and Assyria. Finally, the Behistun sculptor may have been Greek. The carving of the upper arm within the confines of the body had a long history in Greek art but was unknown in the Near East before the Persian Period. And the treatment of the folds on the robes of Darius and the two Persian officers can be compared to Greek drapery treatment of about 520–519 B.C.[3]

[1] For Pasargadae sculpture, see Ghirshman, *Persia*, p. 128, fig. 174.
[2] Luschey, pp. 84–90, pl. 40, 1 & 2; Porada, pp. 158–9.
[3] Luschey, pl. 39, 1 & 3; G. M. A. Richter, *The Sculpture and Sculptors of the Greeks* (New Haven, Conn. and London, 1957), fig. 382.

THE BEHISTUN RELIEF

In his art as in his architecture, Darius seems to have used whatever sources were at hand as long as they could be re-shaped to suit his own purposes. But in doing so he seems to have cared more to express his uniqueness than to emphasize traditions linking him with Cyrus' line. Darius' individuality cast so long a shadow as to overwhelm the succeeding Persian rulers, for no later king dared to innovate in art as Darius had done. His successors were content to reproduce the art developed in his reign and to stress their continuity with their great ancestor.

A NOTE ON COSTUMES IN PERSIAN ART

The identity of the tributary peoples represented in Persian art has been much debated in recent years, but the last word on this subject has yet to be said.[1] The history of the dress worn by Persians, also much discussed, is equally obscure.[2] Herodotus (I. 135) maintained that the Persians had borrowed Median costume; he may have meant that the Persians used Median clothes for riding, for on other occasions the clothing of the two peoples is quite distinct (pl. 33).

If the sculptures in the Residential Palace at Pasargadae were carved in the reign of Darius, then the typical Persian robe does not appear in the preserved examples of Cyrus' art (pl. 6a). The winged genie on the gate house at Pasargadae wears Elamite costume, and the other sculptures are too fragmentary for any costume to be evident.[3]

In the time of Darius, the characteristic Persian robe is shown, in summary fashion, on the Behistun relief, and in a more developed manner in the art of Susa and Persepolis. The same costume, with different headdress, is also worn by the Susians, who are represented on the Apadana reliefs as bringing in tribute a pair of short swords of the type worn by Persians.[4] Apparently Elamite costume had changed

---

[1] For a brief survey of opinions and references to many other works, see O. W. Muscarella, review of Schmidt, *Persepolis III* in *AJA* LXXV (1971), 443–4.

[2] R. Ghirshman, "Le trésor de l'Oxus...", in K. Bittel *et al.* (eds), *Vorderasiatische Archäologie*...(Berlin, 1964), pp. 88–94, pls. 17–19; B. Goldman, "Origin of the Persian Robe", *IA* IV (1964), 133–52; G. Walser, *Die Völkerschaften auf den Reliefs von Persepolis* (Berlin, 1966), pp. 72–3, pls. 4, 9, 35–7, references p. 72, n. 15.

[3] For discussions of the Elamite costume on the gate genie and the possible Iranian customs in Darius' art, see Porada, pp. 158–60. A silver male figurine from the Oxus Treasure, thought to be Median or early Persian, wears a robe with full sleeves and pleated skirt; this might exemplify the Persian robe in the time of Cyrus; see O. M. Dalton, *The Treasure of the Oxus* (London, 1964), p. 1, no. 1, p. 2, fig. 41, pl. II, no. 1.

[4] Schmidt, *Persepolis I*, pl. 28.

from the reign of Cyrus, but whether these people are meant to be Elamites in native costume, Elamites in Persian costume, or Persians in native costume, is impossible to say.

To judge from the reliefs of Darius and later rulers, the king's costume must have been outstanding. Professor Porada has already suggested that the royal figures on the Treasury reliefs wore gold crowns, since representations of Darius and subsequent kings were adorned with gold crowns and jewellery. The king's robe on the Pasargadae sculptures was bordered with gold, while royal robes at Persepolis were decorated with incised designs perhaps painted in imitation of gold appliqués or embroidery (pls 22–24).[1]

Glittering with gold adornments, the Great King must have seemed quite literally favoured by Ahura Mazdā. In introducing this elaborate costume into his art, Darius might have been inspired by traditional Near Eastern dress for deities.[2] He might also have been following an Iranian custom; several gold pieces from the Ziwiyeh treasure were clothing appliqués which when worn together must have formed a kind of metal jerkin. In any case, the royal image instituted by Darius was quite in keeping with his tendency to glorify himself, to treat himself as a supernatural hero larger than life.

[1] Schmidt, *Persepolis I*, pls. 142, 143, 198. For a discussion of metal appliqués on garments, see J. V. Canby, "Decorated Garments in Ashurnasirpal's Sculpture", *Iraq* XXXIII (1971), 31–53.
[2] A. L. Oppenheim, "The Golden Garments of the Gods", *JNES* VIII (1949), 172–93.

CHAPTER 19

TEPE NŪSH-I JĀN: THE MEDIAN SETTLEMENT

Recent field work in the central western Zagros has begun to shed valuable light on conditions in ancient Media prior to the Achaemenian conquest of *c.* 550 B.C. At the time of writing three sites in or near the Median heartland, Tepe Nūsh-i Jān, Baba Jan Tepe and Godin Tepe, have yielded substantial architectural remains which are to be placed in part within the second quarter of the first millennium B.C. In addition, a number of field surveys in the central Zagros region, notably those in the Kangāvar, Māhi Dasht, Malāyir, Arāk and Burūjird valleys have helped to document yet other aspects of local settlement in this same period.[1] The present account offers a short survey of the excavated evidence of Median date from Tepe Nūsh-i Jān.

THE BUILDINGS

Excavations at the hill-top site of Tepe Nūsh-i Jān (pl. 38*a*), located 60 km south of Hamadān, ancient Ecbatana, have revealed the well preserved remains of four distinct monumental mud-brick buildings, the first of which may have been founded near 750 B.C. In the probable order in which they were built, these major buildings consist of the Central Temple, the Western Temple, the Fort and the Columned Hall. While the first three buildings, plus the oval circuit of the outer wall (fig. 1), may have been built in reasonably close succession, the Columned Hall (pl. 38*b*) appears to represent a relatively late addition to the overall plan.

The Central Temple occupies the summit of the site and is founded directly on bed-rock. Lozenge shaped in plan, the building has rhythmically stepped walls with buttressed corners (fig. 1). The internal plan includes a small antechamber, a spiral ramp (which provided access to a first floor room over the antechamber as well as to the roof), and

[1] See bibliography.

THE BUILDINGS

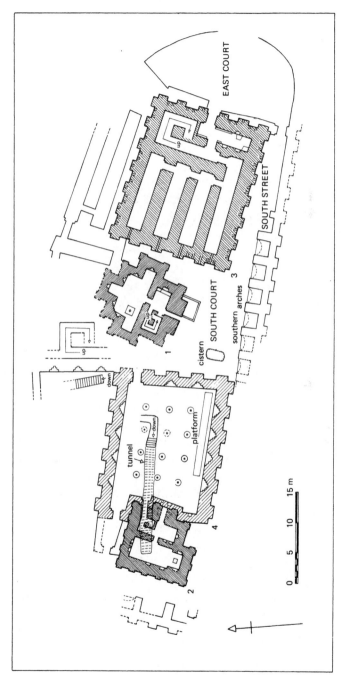

Fig. 1. Tepe Nush-i Jan. Plan of the site before the blocking and the subsequent squatter occupation. 1 The Central Temple. 2 The Western Temple. 3 The Fort. 4 The Columned Hall.

a spacious, stepped triangular sanctuary, 11 × 7 m in area, which rose to the full height of the building (pl. 39a).

The altar which stands in the west wing of the sanctuary is 1.41 m square and 85 cm in height. It has four projecting steps at the top and a shallow hemispherical fire-bowl at the centre (pl. 39b). The entire feature was built of mud-brick and shows signs of having been replastered a number of times. The fire bowl was found to possess a slightly raised rim and a uniformly charred and blackened surface.

The compact Western Temple (fig. 1) is distinct from the Central Temple in plan, orientation and height. At the same time, however, it presents a similar range of rooms: an antechamber with a room above, a spiral ramp, and an inner room with what appears to be the truncated remains of a mud-brick plinth or altar.

The ground plan of the Fort, probably the third building to be erected at Tepe Nūsh-i Jān, is straightforward. It possesses a single entrance, a guard room, a broad ramp-staircase which led to an upper storey, and four long parallel storage magazines each of which once approached 6 m in height (pl. 40a and fig. 1). Little was left of the first floor plan; but, from the range of objects associated with a fallen floor in Room 18, the upper rooms would appear to have been used as living quarters, at least in the final phase of the building's occupation. Apart from a typical range of Median pottery[1] the fallen floor yielded a much-worn Neo-Assyrian stamp seal which depicts a cow and a suckling calf with a roughly cut star in the field above (pl. 40b).[2]

Elsewhere in the Fort the excavation of the ramp led to the recovery of a silver hoard. Beneath one of several fallen mud-bricks a bronze bowl was found to contain more than two hundred silver objects, including a collection of quadruple spiral beads[3] and a series of silver ingot-bars. The latter would seem to document the type of currency that was in use in Iran prior to the introduction of coinage.[4]

The construction of the Columned Hall, a building with a single spacious room c. 15 × 20 m in area, would seem to have been an afterthought. At all events it called for an extensive remodelling of the entrance façade of the Western Temple.

Within the Hall, three rows of four wooden columns were used to support the roof. Each column measured 25 cm in diameter, each

---

[1] R. Stronach, "Excavations at Tepe Nush-i Jan. Part 2. Median Pottery", figs 6–9
[2] Stronach and Roaf, *Iran* XVI (1978), p. 6.
[3] D. Stronach, *Iran* VII (1969), pls. VIIIa–IXa.
[4] Bivar, "A Hoard of Ingot-currency".

CLOSURE AND SQUATTERS

was set on a flat field stone let into the floor and each was encased in a circular surround composed of mud-brick and plaster. Interestingly enough, there is no trace of any throne seat and the only fixed internal furnishing seems to have consisted of a low mud-brick platform adjacent to the long south wall.

Late in the life of the original settlement, the Columned Hall came to be used as the point of entry for a rock-cut tunnel, 1.70 m high, 1.80 m wide and *c.* 20 m in length (pl. 41*a*). The purpose of this feature, which was presumably abandoned in a still unfinished state, remains unknown.

THE CLOSURE OF THE SITE

Towards the end of the 7th century B.C. all further construction was given up and large parts of the site were permanently sealed and hidden from view. In the case of the Central Temple, where the most rigorous methods were employed, the altar was first surrounded by mud-bricks and shale in such a way that no harm could come to it, then the rest of the building was filled with chips of shale up to a height of six metres. This mass of stone was subsequently covered with alternate layers of shale and mud, before the whole structure was capped by several courses of mud-brick. The enormous weight of the internal filling was necessarily balanced at each stage of the work by the simultaneous introduction of huge masses of brickwork outside the building.

This extraordinary filling operation was complemented by other blocking activities. With the exception of an opening left round the top of a rock-cut well or cistern, the whole of the South Court was filled with layer on layer of mud-brick. A similar treatment is known to have been accorded to the East Court, to the street to the south of the Fort, and to certain of the narrow passages that flank the Western Temple (fig. 1).

THE SQUATTER OCCUPATION

Whatever factors may have lain behind this formal closure of the original monumental complex, the site soon came to be re-occupied by a group of villagers who established themselves within the limits of the Columned Hall (pl. 41*b*) and possibly also in the upper rooms of the Fort. Although further work may suggest some slight revision in our proposed chronology, the dates of this brief re-occupation would seem to fall somewhere between 600 and 550 B.C.

MEDIAN TEPE NŪSH-I JĀN

INTERPRETATION

In the absence of written documents from Tepe Nūsh-i Jān any attempt to weigh the exact religious significance of the site is necessarily fraught with difficulties. In positive terms, however, there is no reason to doubt the religious character of the stepped altar in the Central Temple, which clearly foreshadows the distinctive design of the stone fire-altars used from the time of Cyrus the Great (559–530 B.C.) onwards;[1] and, if this much is admitted, a religious label would seem to be appropriate not only for the building in which the altar stood but also for the site's westernmost structure, the Western Temple, with its very similar ground-plan. Furthermore, several separate factors, such as the prominent position of Tepe Nūsh-i Jān in the first large fertile valley directly to the south of Hamadān, the long life of the site, and the reverence with which the monuments were treated down to the moment of their closure may each be said to fortify the view that Nūsh-i Jān was a representative religious centre for its time.

One other brief comment deserves to be made. It has been claimed that the Central Temple at Tepe Nūsh-i Jān was one of the *daivadāna* destroyed by Xerxes (486–465 B.C.) at the time of his campaign against those local cults which did not conform to the exclusive worship of Ahuramazda.[2] As it happens, this interpretation falls down on at least two counts: first, the moment of change to which the filling of the Central Temple would seem to bear witness was not one which encompassed any kind of wanton destruction; and secondly, even the squatter occupation failed to produce any artefacts of incontestable Achaemenian date.

The introduction of a columned hall at Tepe Nūsh-i Jān *c*. 700 B.C., and its subsequent abandonment (at least as a ceremonial hall) less than one hundred years later, may or may not reflect local political conditions, such as the presence for a time of many separate regional rulers. Note in this connection that, while Sargon of Assyria records the collection of tribute from twenty-two Median chieftains in 715 B.C.,[3] and Esar-

---

[1] Cf. D. Stronach, *Pasargadae. A report on the excavations conducted by the British Institute of Persian Studies from 1961 to 1963* (Oxford, 1978), p. 141, pl. 107 and fig. 72.

[2] R. Ghirshman, *Terrasses sacrées de Bard-e Néchandeh et Masjid-i Solaiman* I (Paris, 1976), pp. 174–5; *idem*, notes offered in D. Stronach, "La découverte du premier temple mède dans la région d'Ecbatane (Hamadan, Iran)", *CRAI* 1977, pp. 698–700; and *idem*, "La religion de l'Iran du VIIIe siècle avant notre ère à Islam", *Le Plateau Iranien et l'Asie Centrale des origines à la conquête islamique: leurs relations à la lumière des documents archéologiques* (Paris, 1977), p. 344.

[3] D. D. Luckenbill, *Ancient Records of Assyria and Babylonia* (Chicago, 1926–27), II. 11, 15.

haddon still mentions five separate Median tributaries,[1] the authority of such local rulers was very conceivably broken by Cyaxares, the true founder of Median power, at some date prior to 615 B.C.[2]

In social and administrative terms, the recent surveys of the Kangāvar and Malāyir plains have produced preliminary findings of considerable interest. In the former area a substantial number of permanent settlements have been ascribed to a Median horizon,[3] while, within the Malāyir plain, there are indications that several strategically placed administrative centres were complemented by a broad scatter of village sites.[4]

The prosperity of such settlements appears to have been based on crops such as emmer, bread wheat, two-row and six-row hulled barley, rye, lentils and grapes;[5] and while hunting in the forested mountains remained a popular pursuit, animal husbandry accounts for almost 95% of the total bone sample from Tepe Nūsh-i Jān. Nine domestic species are represented[6] and it is of particular interest that there is firm evidence for the local breeding of horses. Last but not least the rich sample of bird bones from Tepe Nūsh-i Jān, ranging from waterfowl to birds that inhabit bare or sandy steppes would seem to document a notably wider environmental variation than is apparent in the Hamadān region to-day.

[1] R. Borger, *Die Inschriften Asarhaddons Königs von Assyrien* (Graz, 1956), 54–5, 27, episode 15: A, IV. 32–45.

[2] For the earliest reference to the military might of Cyaxares, dated to the year 615 B.C., see D. J. Wiseman, *Chronicles of the Chaldean Kings (626–556 B.C.) in the British Museum* (London, 1956), p. 44. Also, for the emergence of a united Media under Cyaxares, see now P. R. Helm, "Herodotus' *Mêdikos Logos* and median history", *Iran* XIX (1981), pp. 85–90.

[3] If the local "Iron III" settlements can be so defined. T. Cuyler Young, Jr., "Kangavar valley survey", p. 192.

[4] Cf. Howell, "Survey of the Malayer Plain".

[5] Keyllo and Hubbard, "Median and Parthian Plant Remains,"

[6] Bökönyi, "Excavations at Tepe Nush-i Jan. Part 3. The Animal Remains", p. 26.

CHAPTER 20

PASARGADAE

Pasargadae, the capital of Cyrus the Great (559–530 B.C.), is also the earliest known significant settlement of the Persians, a people who rose from obscurity to far-flung dominion in the short span of two decades. Here Persia entered the world stage, here Achaemenian art took shape and here Cyrus, founder of the Persian empire, was buried.

As the crow flies, Pasargadae lies 40 km north-east of Persepolis and 90 km north-east of Shīrāz. The site occupies a wide grassy plain, the Dasht-i Murghāb, ringed by mountains and watered by the perennial stream of the Pulvār. The valley floor has a height of 1,900 m (6,200 feet) and even in high summer the nights are cool (Map 1).

Up to half a century ago the ruins of Pasargadae lay squarely in the path of the main highway from Fārs to the north. For early travellers from Shīrāz the approach lay through a spectacular wooded gorge, the Tang-i Bulāghī. At the narrow northern exit of the pass, where a bend of the Pulvār sweeps against a cliff face, the ancient highway occupies a bold rock-cutting 30 m above the river-bed and more than 250 m in length.[1] Long raking chisel marks on the rock faces on each side of the road illustrate the hardness of the local limestone and the extent of the labour involved. No exact date for the passage is known though the beginning of the work may well date back to the main period of construction at Pasargadae in the second half of the 6th century B.C.

THE TOMB OF CYRUS

Weathered and scarred by time, the tomb of Cyrus (pl. 5) remains the focus of all else at Pasargadae. No other monument at the site is described by the Greeks who accompanied Alexander and it is often the only ancient feature which is mentioned in the accounts of later travellers.[2]

---

[1] See also Sir Aurel Stein, "An Archaeological Tour in the Ancient Persis", *Iraq* III (1936), p. 220 and fig. 31.

[2] Cf. Stronach, *Pasargadae*, pp. 1–2.

THE TOMB OF CYRUS

In the description of Strabo (xv. 3. 7), following Aristobulus, we are told that Alexander "saw the tomb of Cyrus in a paradise, a tower of no great size, concealed beneath the thicket of trees, in its lower parts massive, but its upper parts having a roof and shrine with a very narrow entrance". Within the chamber Aristobulus found "a golden couch and table with drinking-cups, and a golden coffin...", while the inscription, which Aristobulus reports "from memory", is said to have read "O man, I am Cyrus, who founded the Empire of the Persians and was king of Asia. Grudge me not therefore this monument."

With good reason most scholars have taken this account and other classical descriptions to affirm the identity of the Murghāb tomb. Even the absence of an inscription on the fabric of the tomb fails to discredit the identification. Greek visitors to Pasargadae who discovered the sense of the laconic, even modest, cuneiform inscriptions in the palaces, were no doubt responsible for the vaguely similar "epitaphs" that have come down to us – and for the convenient fiction that such lines were inscribed on the walls of the tomb.[1]

With its massive ashlar masonry and plain surfaces balanced by only a small number of decorative mouldings the tomb creates an indelible impression of dignity, simplicity and strength. For certain early visitors, indeed, the character of the building was enough to affirm its probable identity. As Claudius James Rich wrote in 1821, "The very venerable appearance of this ruin instantly awed me. I found that I had no right conception of it. I sat for near an hour on the steps, contemplating it until the moon rose on it – and I began to think that this in reality must be the tomb of the best, the most illustrious, and the most interesting of oriental sovereigns."[2]

The tomb consists of two main parts: a high plinth composed of six receding tiers and a cella with a steep-pitched gable roof. The stepped plinth is rectangular, measuring 13.35 × 12.30 m at the base, while the total height of the monument approaches 11 m. The tomb chamber, entered from the north-west through a low narrow door, is 3.17 m long, 2.11 m wide and 2.11 m high.

The origins of this singular design have long remained in dispute. Some authorities hold that the whole building should be related to either Mesopotamian[3] or Elamite[4] ziggurats. Others would derive the gabled

[1] Ibid., p. 26.
[2] *Narrative of a journey to the site of Babylon in 1811* (London, 1839), pp. 239–40.
[3] A. Parrot, *Ziggurats et tour de Babel* (Paris, 1949), p. 50.
[4] Ghirshman, *Persia*, p. 135.

cella from Urartu and the stepped platform from Mesopotamia[1] or the cella from "a traditional Iranian tomb and house" and the plinth, once again, from Mesopotamia.[2] Still others have chosen to stress the influence of Ionia as a dominant factor.[3]

There is no longer any doubt that the technical basis of the masonry stems from Ionia and Lydia – a circumstance which clearly places the founding of the tomb, and indeed the founding of the other stone structures at the site, in a period not earlier than Cyrus' capture of Sardis in 547 B.C.[4] The presence of craftsmen trained in these western areas of Cyrus' newly enlarged realm is confirmed by many details of construction, not least by the use of iron and lead dove-tail clamps and by the use of large ashlar blocks with *anathyrosis* joints (that is to say blocks with tight, labour-saving joints in which each joining surface usually consists of no more than a smooth raised band running round three sides of a rough, slightly recessed core).[5]

Hanfmann has drawn attention to the fact that the internal dimensions of Cyrus' tomb chamber are close to those of the tomb chamber of the Lydian monarch, Alyattes, and that each chamber has a projecting band of stone below the ceiling.[6] It is also of interest that the hollow, centrally divided roof of Cyrus' tomb recalls Phrygian as well as later Anatolian building practices.[7]

Further western influence is evident in the external mouldings and in the use of such motifs to emphasise the separate structural parts of the building. Among other Ionian architectural elements is the *cyma reversa*, a moulding of double curvature, the upper curve of which is convex and the lower concave, which is found in the cornice and above the door. The classic Ionian entablature however is not represented; for although a *geison* or *corona* (i.e. the protruding member of the cornice having a vertical face) lies above the *cyma reversa*, the small irregular recesses which appear below are not dentils[8] or even "model cuttings"

---

[1] R. D. Barnett, "Persepolis", *Iraq* XIX (1957), p. 74 and Culican, p. 58.
[2] Nylander, p. 102.   [3] Dieulafoy, *L'art* I, pp. 38ff.
[4] On this often cited but not yet incontrovertibly proven date for the fall of Sardis, see most recently J. Cargill, "The Nabonidus Chronicle and the Fall of Lydia", *AJAH* II (1977), pp. 97–116 and Stronach, *Pasargadae*, pp. 287–8
[5] Cf. Nylander, *passim*.
[6] In the text of a lecture "Forerunners of Pasargadae at Sardis" delivered at the VIth International Congress of Iranian Art and Archaeology, Oxford, 1972. Cf. also G. M. A. Hanfmann, *BASOR* CLXX (1963), p. 55, n. 60.
[7] M. J. Mellink, "Excavations at Karataş - Semayük and Elmali, Lycia, 1970", *AJA* LXXV (1971), pp. 250ff.
[8] Cf. Dieulafoy, *op. cit.*, fig. 33.

for a line of dentils[1] but only a series of random cuttings which once held repair plugs.

Other significant Ionian elements are represented in the fragmentary raking cornice and in the few stone tiles that remain in position on the roof. Moreover, as Nylander has shown, the building probably owes both its metrological units and the proportions of its upper stone courses to Ionian architecture.[2]

In seeking to define the origins of the separate elements found in the tomb we must not lose sight of one point: the building as a whole has no known prototype. It is an Iranian concept, called into being at the wish of an Iranian monarch. If we may believe Cyrus to have been a Zoroastrian, or, to adopt a more cautious view, an adherent of an Iranian faith resembling in some respects the Zoroastrian, this condition could have led him to reject the idea of tumulus burial. Instead of seeking to cover his tomb chamber with a huge mound of earth he may have chosen, with the new methods of stone construction that were available to him, to elevate his tomb above ground level.

As in the case of a Lydian royal tomb the interior was to amount to no more than a secure, small room encased in heavy horizontal courses of masonry and covered by vast slabs of stone. But the stone exterior was required to take on a new monumental aspect. Stone mouldings were borrowed from those already in use on secular and religious buildings in mid 6th century Ionia and, in the case of the much-damaged raised disc at the top of the north-western gable Cyrus may have introduced a symbol of more than decorative significance.[3]

Whether or not the six receding tiers themselves were intended to convey an unspoken message is not clear. If we recall, however, the stepped ground plan of the Central Temple at Tepe Nūsh-i Jān,[4] the stepped elevation of the altar from this same building[5] and the triple steps that distinguish Achaemenian fire altars from the time of Cyrus onwards,[6] it is perhaps possible to suppose that the two sets of triple tiers at the base of the tomb served to afford at least an Iranian viewer with a sense of sanctity.

---

[1] Nylander, p. 95, n. 236.   [2] *Ibid.*, pp. 97–8.

[3] Cf. D. Stronach, "Cyrus the Great", *Bāstān-shināsī va Hunar-i Īran* VII–VIII (Tehran, 1971), p. 20, n. 83 and *idem*, "A Circular Symbol on the Tomb of Cyrus", *Iran* IX (1971), pp. 155–8. See also p. 853, nn. 5 and 6.

[4] D. Stronach and M. Roaf, "Excavations at Tepe Nush-i Jan. Part 1. A Third Interim Report", *Iran* XVI (1978), fig. 1.

[5] M. Roaf and D. Stronach, "Tepe Nush-i Jan, 1970. Second Interim Report", *Iran* XI (1973), fig. 6.   [6] See Stronach, *Pasargadae*, pp. 141–2 and fig. 72.

THE PALACES

More than a kilometre to the north of the tomb of Cyrus, at a distance that would certainly have helped to enhance the separate, sacrosanct character of the tomb and its enclosure, a flat tract of ground supports the ruins of three palatial structures, Gate R, Palace S and Palace P. These buildings are separated from each other by distances of 200 m or more and their distribution has led many authorities to suppose that the plan of the site conforms to the scattered organization of a tribal encampment.[1] The location of these three monuments is not casual however and from their position and orientation, and their evident relationship to a central, formal garden, we may conclude that Cyrus' architects worked to a unified master plan.[2]

Gate R, also known as the Palace with the Relief, stands at the eastern edge of the Palace Area, in part outside the line of an adjacent perimeter wall. In its original form it was a free-standing rectangular structure with a hypostyle hall, 26.40 × 22.60 m in size, entered by two main and two side doors. At the level of the stone foundations – the upper pavement has disappeared entirely – eight square plinths mark the former position of two rows of four columns. The size of the plinths allows us to state that this was originally the tallest building at Pasargadae with a height of over 16 m.

The great stone bulls which once guarded the main doorways of Gate R can be seen from excavated fragments to have been carved in the image of the *lamassâtê* of Assyria, while the four-winged apotropaic genius which still stands beside one of the two doors (pl. 6*a*) is descended from another magical being of the Assyrian world. It is important to note, however, that the four-winged figure of Gate R is not by any means a straightforward copy of the earlier Assyrian model. The pose in true profile belongs to a post-Assyrian phase of Near Eastern sculpture,[3] the short-bearded face is Persian, the long fringed robes are probably Elamite and the tall *hmhm*-crown[4] introduces the exotic Egyptianizing art of Syria and Phoenicia.[5]

---

[1] See, for example, Frankfort, p. 216.

[2] This intelligence does in fact cast further doubt on the not uncommon assertion that the name of the site meant "camp of the Persians" [an interpretation which the Elamite form of the name (see above, p. 418) disproves. Ed.].

[3] Cf. the stele of Nabonidus (556–539 B.C.); Stronach, *Pasargadae*, pl. 189*b*.

[4] See especially, the comments of Professor Richard A. Parker, quoted in Schmidt, *Persepolis* II, p. 39, n. 132.

[5] Recent notes on the "winged figure" are to be found in G. de Francovich, "Problems of Achaemenid Architecture", *East and West* XVI (1966), p. 239, n. 204; R. D. Barnett, "'Anath, Ba'al

THE PALACES

In architectural terms Gate R documents the introduction of the hypostyle propylaeum in Iranian architecture. It is possible to speculate that columned propylaea were seen by the Persians in western Anatolia and that Cyrus determined to create his own, more Iranian form of columned gate. The rectangular shape of the building conforms to that of a traditional Iranian columned hall in which the roof was often supported by two rows of four columns.[1] To this design Cyrus added the spectacular doorway figures of Assyrian origin while the tall external walls were probably enlivened by a rhythmic series of deep niches.[2]

It is not without relevance to note that Darius retained an honoured place for this type of gateway in his own palace architecture. At both Persepolis and Susa the king's palaces were approached through square if not rectangular, four-columned gate structures. To judge from the presence of a stone throne seat in the Persepolis gate[3] royal audiences could be held in such a structure and, as the biblical story of Esther and Mordecai makes plain, the "king's gate" at Susa played a significant rôle as an outward symbol of the power and dominion of the king.[4]

Finally, it would seem undeniable that visitors to Cyrus' capital were intended to associate the strange crown of the four-winged figure in Gate R with distant conquests in the west. Support for this view comes, indirectly at least, from the name of the great Persepolis portal, "The Gate of All Lands",[5] and from the fact that Xerxes chose to erect an Egyptian statue of his father, in which Darius is shown in a traditional Egyptian pose, beside one of the entrances of the "king's gate" at Susa.[6]

Palace S, the "Palace with the Column", also known as the Audience Hall, still retains one standing column *c*. 13.10 m in height. The core of the building consists of a rectangular hall over 32 m in length and over 22 m in width, the roof of which was originally supported by two rows of four columns. A single doorway pierces the mid-point of each

---

and Pasargadae", *Mélanges de l'Université Saint-Joseph* XLV (Beirut, 1969), pp. 416 f.; Nylander, p. 126; M. Mallowan, "Cyrus the Great (558–529 B.C.)", *Iran* X (1972), pp. 1–2; and in Stronach, *Pasargadae*, pp. 47ff.

[1] Cf. R. H. Dyson, "Problems of Protohistoric Iran as seen from Hasanlu", *JNES* XXIV (1965), p. 198 and fig. 4.

[2] Stronach, *Pasargadae*, figs 22, 24. Cf. also the deep stepped niches in the external walls of the Persepolis gate; Schmidt, *Persepolis* I, fig. 26.

[3] *Ibid., loc. cit.* But see also *ibid.*, p. 68, for another interpretation of this same much-damaged feature.

[4] Cf. Esther IV. 2, 6.

[5] Schmidt, *Persepolis* I, p. 65. Cf. also R. G. Kent, *Old Persian Grammar, Texts, Lexicon* (New Haven, Conn., 1953), p. 148, where Kent gives "this Colonnade of All Lands".

[6] See M. Kervran, D. Stronach, F. Vallat, J. Yoyotte, "Une statue de Darius le Grand découverte à Suse", *JA* CCLX (1972), pp. 235ff.

843

wall of the hall and four low porticos surround the building. In diminishing order of size, a long portico *in antis* with two rows of twenty-four columns faced the Palace Garden to the north-east, a portico with two rows of fourteen columns lay between two oblong rooms to the south-west and two rows of eight columns occupied the remaining two porticos. The two corner rooms are built up logically by a crosswise extension of the side walls of the central hall while the length of the opposed portico *in antis* can be seen to have been determined by the maximum extension of the two corner rooms. Thus the whole structure is governed by a pleasing and harmonious design. The suggestion has been made that the essence of this ground plan is drawn from the west, i.e. from an adaption of the Greek *stoa* combined with the plan of a 6th century B.C. Anatolian palace which corresponds to "the basic unit of Building S".[1] It is clear from the absence of a suitable prototype in Iran that the Greek *stoa* represents the inspiration of the many-columned portico *in antis*[2] and, as Nylander has remarked, the very four-sidedness of Palace S is reminiscent of the "superbly independent, crystalline Greek temple".[3] Whether or not the Persians had to fall back on Anatolian models for the rest of the plan of Palace S is more in doubt; the tall central hall with its two rows of four columns is unquestionably Iranian in origin and, as a number of recent excavations have demonstrated, corner rooms and low columned porticos are both represented in early first millennium B.C. entrance façades from western Iran.[4]

Although both Iran and Ionia can be seen to have contributed to the plan of Palace S, the two most complete doorway reliefs document Cyrus' parallel interest in the monumental, sculptural arts of Mesopotamia. In keeping with Assyrian apotropaic doorway reliefs that are known from the palace of Sennacherib at Nineveh, a short-skirted warrior partners an eagle-footed lion-demon in the north-western doorway[5] while the opposite, south-eastern doorway shows the remains of a fish-cloaked genius followed by a bull-man.[6] The carved eagle feet in Sennacherib's reliefs are somewhat different from those at Pasargadae, however, and it is of interest that the latter are closer to slightly later Assyrian models from the reign of Ashurbanipal.[7]

[1] Nylander, p. 117.   [2] *Ibid.*, p. 118.   [3] *Ibid.*, p. 117.
[4] Cf. Clare Goff, "Excavations at Baba Jan, 1967: Second Preliminary Report", *Iran* VII (1969), figs 2 and 4 and Dyson, *op. cit., loc. cit.*
[5] Stronach, *Pasargadae*, p. 68, fig. 34 and pls 58*a* and *b*.
[6] *Ibid.*, p. 69, fig. 35 and pls 59, 60*a* and *b*.
[7] For parallels from Sennacherib's reliefs at Nineveh, see A. H. Layard, *Discoveries in the ruins of Nineveh and Babylon* (London, 1853), p. 462; cf. also T. S. Kawami, "A possible source for the

Palace P[1] illustrates a third type of palatial structure. Not only is the thirty-columned central hall with its narrow doorways and relatively small columns a more intimate chamber than the great hall of Palace S, but an exceptionally long portico *in antis* offers an explanation of the building's probable main function. Since a fixed throne seat (the only such installation at Pasargadae) occurs at the centre of the portico, and since this seat offers a commanding view of the Palace Garden which stretches away to the south-east, Palace P can be counted as the king's chief pavilion – conceivably a location for private audiences but above all a place to sit and contemplate the trees, grasses and streams of the garden.[2]

Datable building techniques indicate that Palace P was founded, like Gate R and Palace S, during Cyrus' lifetime. But if we are to judge from the rigorous balance and uncompromising standards that characterize each of Cyrus' other constructions, the building was still only half-finished at the time of his death. Among other anomalies, the north-west portico is unpaved and shorter than the opposed "throne portico" while nothing in the way of monumental construction was ever begun outside the short walls of the rectangular central hall.[3] More significant still, the two truncated doorway reliefs, which show matching representations of the king followed by an attendant,[4] would seem to have been carved well after the death of Cyrus. Notwithstanding the exceptional use of gold inlays in the dress of the king, the stiff ridged folds of the drapery clearly conform to the highly stylized Achaemenian drapery style which post-dates Darius I's relief at Bisitun (*c.* 520 B.C.).[5] It is probably also relevant that standard toothed hammer or chisel marks occur in a conceivably primary context towards the north-east end of the throne portico,[6] since marks of this kind are most unlikely to date from the reign of Cyrus.[7]

Sculptures of the Audience Hall, Pasargadae", *Iran* x (1972), pp. 146 f. For a parallel from the reign of Ashurbanipal, see C. J. Gadd, *Stones of Assyria* (London, 1936), pl. 32.

[1] "Palast mit dem Pfeiler", i.e. the Palace with the Anta. Herzfeld, "Bericht", p. 13.

[2] Cf. Nylander, p. 115.   [3] Stronach, *Pasargadae*, p. 103.

[4] Herzfeld, "Bericht"; pl. III and *idem, Iran in the Ancient East*, pl. LXXI and fig. 363, and Stronach, *Pasargadae*, pls 80–2.

[5] Cf. Stronach, *Pasargadae*, pp. 95ff. For the Assyrian prototype for this "king and servant" motif, see P. E. Botta and E. Flandin, *Monument de Ninive* II (Paris, 1849), pl. 105.

[6] Stronach, *Pasargadae*, p. 91 and pl. 87d.

[7] Cf. *ibid.*, p. 99. As to the date of the CMa inscriptions which read "I, Cyrus, the king, an Achaemenian" and which seem without question to refer to Cyrus as the acting agent (*ibid.*, p. 103), it must be noted that the presence of one such inscription on the surviving stone anta of Palace P militates strongly *against* Cyrus' authorship. It was not Achaemenian practice to carve inscriptions before a building was finished and, as we now know from the style of the Palace P reliefs – and also from the probable presence of Darius' name in the CMb inscription that stood

PASARGADAE

Unlike the dark grey stone column bases of Palace S, which are distinguished by square plinths and smooth, rounded tori,[1] the column bases from the hall and the south-east portico of Palace P have square plinths in black and white stone and horizontally fluted, white tori.[2] Both types of column base, with plain or fluted tori depend on Ionian models,[3] just as the short-lived early Achaemenian predilection for bichromatic effects is now thought to owe more to Greek than Urartian influences.[4]

The Pasargadae palaces represent bold, innovative structures that Cyrus used to signal both the new ideas and resources that had become available to him and the new sense of security that went with his unrivalled power and prestige. For the first time in Iran a reception hall acquired an open, four-sided appearance; and where, previously, there had been only one entrance and one main axis leading to a fixed throne seat, we now find four entrances, no principal axis and no fixed focal point within the hall. Under Darius this plan was to develop into the standard type of Achaemenian audience hall, such as is represented at both Susa and Persepolis, in which the oblong hall became square, the porticos and corner rooms were carried up to the same height as the roof of the central hall and, in deference to practical necessity, one of the four sides came to form a "rear entrance" leading to the private apartments of the King.[5]

THE PALACE GARDEN

Gardens were essential to the character of Pasargadae. About the tomb of Cyrus stood "a grove of all kinds of trees", watered "with streams" and surrounded by a meadow of "deep grass".[6] The greater part of Pasargadae was, in effect, a royal paradise.

In one area, adjacent to Palace P, the plan of one of the main gardens, which we may call the Palace Garden, still survives. Long white stone conduits, studded at intervals with square basins, reveal the strictly rectilinear lines of the original paths and planted areas.[7] Two broad

directly above these same reliefs (*ibid.*, p. 97) – it was Darius, not Cyrus, who completed this structure. The problem, as I hope to indicate elsewhere, is no longer the true date of the CMa inscriptions, but rather the elusive motive that may have inspired them.

[1] Stronach, *Pasargadae*, fig. 28 and pl. 54.   [2] *Ibid.*, fig. 42 and pls. 73–5.
[3] Nylander, pp. 103ff. and Stronach, *Pasargadae*, pp. 73, 84 and 85.
[4] See J. Boardman, "Chian and early Ionic architecture", *The Antiquaries Journal* xxxix (Oxford, 1959), p. 217 and Nylander, p. 142.
[5] Cf. D. Stronach, "Apadana" in *Encyclopaedia Iranica* (forthcoming).
[6] Arrian, *De Exped. Alex.* vi. 29.
[7] Stronach, *Pasargadae*, pp. 107–10 and figs 48 and 49.

paths, 26 m wide, flank two almost identical rectangles at the centre of the design – one path leading to a small colonnaded pavilion, Pavilion A, while the other leads to a slightly larger structure, Pavilion B, almost midway between Palace P and Palace S.

The watercourses and basins of Pasargadae, which were only rediscovered a few years ago,[1] can be seen to represent the inspiration for a type of stone water-channel which still exists in the formal gardens of Iran. Closely similar channels occur for example beside the Chihil Sutūn of Isfahan and in the famed Bāgh-i Fīn near Kāshān.

The construction of the Palace Garden at Pasargadae was apparently interrupted when Cyrus died. Indeed, from the presence of toothed chisel marks on many of the stone conduits and on several of the floor stones of Pavilion B,[2] certain of the major features within the garden only appear to have been completed close to 500 B.C.

That the Palace Garden remained in use for the next two hundred years is not improbable. Late in the 5th century B.C., if not some time in the 4th century B.C., a stone and wood bridge came to be built over a deep canal 50 m to the east of the Palace S,[3] while, as we know from the recent excavations of the British Institute of Persian Studies at Pavilion B, one of the water-jars near this last structure was used at the close of the Achaemenian period to hide a rich hoard of gold and silver objects.[4]

The elegant "Pasargadae Treasure", which stands as vivid testimony to the skill of the Achaemenian metalsmith, includes two gold ibex-headed bracelets, two silver spoons, the varied gold, onyx and carnelian elements of six or more necklaces and three pairs of pennanular gold earrings (pl. 36).[5]

In the absence of stratigraphical evidence – continuous ploughing had reduced the jar containing the treasure to little more than a third of its original height – the collection can only be dated on grounds of style. Here the bracelets and earrings each point to a date within the 4th century B.C.; in the case of the earrings, for example, it is possible to point to such late features as a large central aperture, attached pendants and openwork gold thread.[6]

[1] Ali Sami, *Pasargadae*, pp. 75–7 and Stronach, *Iran* III (1965), p. 29.
[2] Stronach, *Pasargadae*, pp. 109 and 111. [3] *Ibid.*, p. 113 and figs 53–5.
[4] *Ibid.*, p. 168 and pls 146–59. [5] *Ibid.*, pp. 168–77 and figs 85–8.
[6] Cf. *ibid.*, p. 176; J. McKeon, "Achaemenian Cloisonné-inlay Jewelry: an important new example", in H. A. Hoffner (ed.), *Orient and Occident: essays presented to Cyrus H. Gordon* (Neukirchen-Vluyn, 1973), p. 117 (Alter Orient und Altes Testament 22) and K. R. Maxwell-Hyslop, *Western Asiatic Jewellery c. 3000–612 B.C.* (London, 1971), pls 257 and 258.

PASARGADAE

THE ZINDĀN (pl. 37)

To the north of the Palace Area stands the isolated stone tower known locally as Zindān-i Sulaimān or "The Prison of Solomon". Recent studies indicate that the building is to be attributed to the second half of the reign of Cyrus and that it unquestionably served as the model for the Kaʻba-yi Zardusht, the tall stone tower erected by Darius I at Naqsh-i Rustam.[1]

In its original state (hardly more than the entrance façade stands erect at the present time) the Zindān was a nearly square tower which stood over 14 m in height. Three rows of blind windows can be seen to have marked all but the entrance façade, where a massive stone staircase afforded access to a single, windowless room 7.76 m above ground level. The elevated doorway, which appears to have been 1.83 m high and 94 cm wide, probably had white stone door jambs[2] and may have had white stone doorleaves decorated with horizontal bands of carved rosettes.[3] A fragment of a trilingual inscription which was discovered near the base of the south-western wall[4] has engendered considerable controversy. Cameron's contention that the text in question is a copy of the relatively long "Foundation Record" of Darius[5] is not convincing on several counts.[6] The possibility remains, however, that this is a hitherto unknown inscription of Darius; and, if other texts from Pasargadae offer any guide, its purpose could have been to identify Cyrus (whose name conceivably appears in the broken text) as the builder of the Zindān.[7]

[1] Cf. Stronach, *Pasargadae*, p. 132. For a comprehensive description of the Kaʻba, see Schmidt, *Persepolis* III, pp. 18 ff.
[2] Stronach, *Pasargadae*, p. 126.
[3] See most recently, *ibid.*, fig. 65.
[4] Ali Sami, *op. cit.*, p. 140 and Stronach, *Iran* II (1964), p. 38.
[5] G. G. Cameron, "An Inscription of Darius from Pasargadae", *Iran* v (1967), pp. 7ff.
[6] Not least because the text can be seen to have been part of a short inscription with only two, not five, lines in Old Persian. Cf. Stronach, *Pasargadae*, p. 137.
[7] The above assumption that Darius, not Cyrus, would have called for such a text might seem to be perverse. If it is conceded, however, that Cyrus, following all the later standard rules of Achaemenian construction, was never in a position to erect any copies of the CMa text on the fabric of Palace P (see p. 845, n. 7 above), it may not seem unreasonable to look for the agency of Darius in this instance also. The alternative, it should be noted, is to regard the "Zindān inscription" as very possibly the only Old Persian document that can be attributed to the time of Cyrus.

Needless to say the foregoing remarks raise the vexed topic of the date of the introduction of the Old Persian script. Such a large subject can hardly be addressed in detail here, but it may not be inappropriate to stress that all the archaeological evidence from Pasargadae begins to point in one direction. Work in the field over the past twenty years has revealed extensive evidence for post-Cyrus construction at Pasargadae, not least from the time of Darius, and now, half a century

THE ZINDĀN

Neither the exact purpose nor the traditional background of the Zindān has been established so far. Several authorities incline towards the view that this type of tower must have served as a fire sanctuary;[1] others suggest that it could have been a rare form of royal tomb;[2] and still others believe it to have been a repository for objects of dynastic or religious importance.[3] The situation is complicated by the fact that the two towers are unique; nothing exactly like them was built before or afterwards. Thus while the plan of the Zindān can be compared to that of earlier Urartian tower-temples,[4] even this resemblance is approximate only.

Above all, the Zindān and the Ka'ba illustrate two exceptional features that find no parallel in Urartian or Median architecture – namely a raised, solitary room in the upper part of an otherwise solid mass of masonry and a tall, monumental staircase which was clearly designed, as Schmidt has put it, "for the solemn ascent and descent of persons who in some manner attended the sacred structure".[5]

Not a few scholars, beginning with Weissbach, have taken the view that extant classical descriptions of the tomb of Cyrus fit the Zindān more accurately than the Qabr-i Mādar-i Sulaimān – the building that is almost universally identified as the monarch's tomb.[6] This interpretation falls down completely, however, when we compare the original size of the doorways that served the two buildings. In Arrian's words the door to the tomb was "so narrow that hardly could one man, and he of no great stature, enter even with much difficulty";[7] and, as recent studies have shown, only the door of the Qabr would have forced the

after Herzfeld invoked the more or less modest royal titles in the three "Cyrus inscriptions" to ascribe all palatial construction at Pasargadae to the period before Cyrus' defeat of Astyages (E. Herzfeld, *AMI* I (1929–30), p. 14), there is not only reason to doubt Cyrus' authorship of the CMb and CMc texts (cf. Stronach, *Pasargadae*, pp. 97 and 100) but also, as we have just seen, his authorship of the CMa texts as well. The case for accepting Darius' claim to have been the first to have employed the Old Persian script (cf. DB § 70) is clearly the stronger for this testimony.

[1] E.g. L. Vanden Berghe, *Archéologie de l'Iran ancien* (Leiden, 1959), p. 26; E. Porada, *Ancient Iran. The art of pre-Islamic times* (London, 1965), pp. 146ff.; and Schmidt, *Persepolis* III, pp. 48ff.

[2] E.g. Dieulafoy, *L'Art* III, p. 2, n. 2; Herzfeld, *Iran in the Ancient East*, p. 214; B. Goldman, "Persian Fire Temples or Tombs?", *JNES* XXIV (1965), pp. 305ff.; G. de Francovich, *op. cit.*, p. 224; and F. Krefter, "Achaemenidische Palast- und Grabtürme", *AMI* I (1968), pp. 99ff.

[3] Stronach, *Iran* III, p. 16 and Mallowan, *op. cit.*, p. 16.

[4] Stronach, "Tower Temples", pp. 278ff. and fig. 1; *idem*, *Pasargadae*, fig. 68.

[5] Schmidt, *Persepolis* III, p. 41. If any parallels should be sought for tall, freestanding staircases of evident ceremonial value, the time honoured-ziggurats of Mesopotamia must always have afforded one possible inspiration for such a motif. Cf., for example, G. Roux, *Ancient Iraq* (London, 1980), pls 6 and 7.

[6] See F. H. Weissbach, "Das Grab des Cyrus", *ZDMG* XLVIII (1894), pp. 656ff. and A. Demandt, "Studien zur Kaaba-i Zardoscht", *AA* 1968, pp. 520–40.

[7] *Anabasis* VI. 29.

visitor, then as now, to bend and scuttle awkwardly into the immured chamber.[1]

In the context of contemporary Achaemenian construction the Zindān possesses links with both funerary and sacred architecture. Among other features which may be listed, a slim convex cornice below the ceiling of the chamber is akin to a similar feature inside the tomb of Cyrus,[2] the doorway was given virtually the same frame and crown as the doorway of the tomb of Cyrus[3] and the three-stepped pyramid at the base of the monument can be compared to both the two sets of three steps at the base of the tomb of Cyrus and the triple steps which appear as upright and inverted pyramids in Achaemenian fire altars. But however that may be, the monument is distinct from both the tomb of Cyrus and the rock-cut mausolea of Naqsh-i Rustam and Persepolis – just as it differs entirely from the design of such presumed temples as the "āyadana" near Susa[4] and the "Fratadara Building" near Persepolis.[5]

In a situation where neither any known prototype nor any nearly contemporary clue has helped to resolve the riddle of the purpose of the twin towers, many scholars have sought an answer from later documents. Erdmann and Schmidt, for example, have argued that the tower-like structure on the first series of Persis coins, dated *c.* 300 to 150 B.C., is a direct representation of the Tower at Naqsh-i Rustam[6] and have taken the presence of the accompanying image of the "Fratadara", the "Guardian of the Fire", to prove that the Ka'ba was "the most exalted sanctum of Persis, that is, the shrine of the royal fire".[7] It is more likely, however, that the structure on the Persis coins is a post-Achaemenian version of the Achaemenian tower altar[8] and that the coins, within the idiom of a slightly later and slightly different culture, illustrate a conscious imitation of the standard Achaemenian funerary relief in which the ruler stands in an attitude of worship before a fire

---

[1] While the doorway of the tomb of Cyrus can be shown to have been 1.31 m high and 78 cm wide, the doorway of the Zindān was as much as 46 cm taller and 16 cm wider.

[2] Stronach, *Pasargadae*, fig. 67 and pl. 36.

[3] For detailed reconstructions, see ibid., figs 17*a* and 65.

[4] M. Dieulafoy, *L'acropole de Suse d'après les fouilles exécutées en 1884–86* (Paris, 1893), pp. 411ff.

[5] Schmidt, *Persepolis* I, p. 56 and fig. 16. See also K. Schippmann, *Die iranischen Feuerheiligtümer* (Berlin, 1971), pp. 177ff.

[6] K. Erdmann, *Das iranische Feuerheiligtum* (Leipzig, 1941), p. 32; Schmidt, *Persepolis* III, pp. 46f.

[7] *Ibid.*, p. 48. For illustrations of the relevant coins, see G. F. Hill, *Catalogue of the Greek Coins of Arabia, Mesopotamia and Persia* (London, 1922), pls 28–32 (*Catalogue of Greek coins in the British Museum*).

[8] D. Stronach, "The Kuh-i Shahrak Fire Altar", *JNES* XXV (1966), pp. 220ff.

THE ZINDĀN

altar and beneath the image of Ahuramazda.¹ There remains, moreover, an obvious discrepancy between the closed character of the relatively small "cella" within each Achaemenian tower and the ventilation that one would expect to find in a sanctuary with a permanent fire.²

The best evidence for the function of the Ka'ba, at least in early Sasanian times, comes from the inscription of Kartir, the founder of the Sasanian state church, which was found on the east wall of the building. On the basis of his translation of a passage in the description, Henning observes that "this foundation house", i.e. the Ka'ba, was destined for the safe keeping of the charters and records of the church, among them not only such documents as are frequently mentioned on Kartir's inscriptions but "presumably also the principal copy of the Avesta".³ Henning notes also that the Pahlavi term *Diz-i nipišt* "Stronghold of the Scriptures" may have been intended for the Ka'ba itself.⁴

As I indicated several years ago,⁵ and as I feel obliged to stress again,⁶ there is nothing, either in the Pahlavi designation *bun-xānak*, i.e. "foundation house", or in Professor Henning's interpretation of Kartir's inscription, to suggest that the Ka'ba was regarded by the Sasanians as either a former tomb or a former fire temple. Indeed, if we consider how deep was the regard of the Sasanians for the monuments and achievements of the Achaemenians, this fully-documented use of the term bun-xānak for the Ka'ba would seem to rule out either of the last two possibilities.

With reference to the third possible use that has been mentioned Schmidt has conceded that the Zindān, situated close to the palaces at Pasargadae, could plausibly have been erected by Cyrus as a depository for "royal or ritualistic paraphernalia – the king's standard, divine symbols, and the like".⁷ But since he believes that it would have been "more reasonable" for Darius, if he were the builder of the Ka'ba, to

---

¹ It should be added that the Aramaic legend on these coins is not to be read as *fratadara*, but rather as *prtrk'*, that is to say as *frataraka* or "governor". Accordingly the substitution of frataraka for fratadara would now seem to be called for (cf. p. 854 below) whenever reference is made to the local, post-Achaemenian rulers of Fārs.

² At Tepe Nūsh-i Jān, where the sanctuary of the Median fire temple may or may not have had an air vent near the roof, the very size of the tall, triangular chamber would have provided a relatively ample supply of air. Moreover, there appears to have been at least one air vent at a low level in the eastern wall of the Nūsh-i Jān temple.

³ W. B. Henning, in the introduction to "The Inscription of Naqš-i Rustam", *CIIr*, pt. III, vol. II (1957).

⁴ Ibid., *loc. cit.* ⁵ *Iran* III (1965), p. 16.

⁶ Notwithstanding Stronach, "Tower Temples", p. 288, n. 79.

⁷ *Persepolis* III, p. 44.

have erected his own similar depository within the royal compound of Persepolis, and since both towers have to be granted an identical purpose, he goes on to "dismiss as improbable" the idea that the two towers were built to provide "safe and dignified places of storage".[1]

It is important to note, however, that the plain of Persepolis, and more particularly the vicinity of Takht-i Rustam, not far to the south of Naqsh-i Rustam, was already a focal point of early Achaemenian building activity during the reign of Cambyses II.[2] At a guess, in fact, the cliffs of Naqsh-i Rustam were already not far from an unfinished "garden capital", akin to that at Pasargadae, at the time that Darius succeeded to the throne; and whether or not Cambyses or Brdya had thought to begin any free standing construction at Naqsh-i Rustam, there is no reason why Darius should have hesitated to build there.[3] From the point of view of security the immediate area of Darius' future tomb had to be closely guarded and, if the protocol of the first Achaemenians demanded the construction of a second depository, the awesome ambience of Naqsh-i Rustam may have had its own singular appeal. More than this, Darius may have seen in his ambitious works at Naqsh-i Rustam an opportunity to relate the name and authority of his own line to the lustre of an earlier time when the kings of Anshan apparently chose the same sheer rocks for at least one of their bas-reliefs.[4]

THE STONE PLINTHS

The extreme northern limit of Pasargadae is marked by two isolated stone plinths, each square in plan and over 2 m in height. No inscription tells us of their purpose and only the character of the masonry confirms a probable construction date between 545 and 530 B.C. The northern plinth consists of a plain cube while the southern plinth has a stepped top and is approached by a flight of eight stone steps.[5]

Numerous interpretations of the original function of the two plinths have been put forward[6] although only one solution carries conviction.

[1] *Ibid., loc. cit.*
[2] Cf. A. B. Tilia, "Discovery of an Achaemenian Palace near Takht-i Rustam to the North of the Terrace of Persepolis", *Iran* XII (1974), pp. 208ff.; Stronach, *Pasargadae*, p. 99; and W. Kleiss, "Zur Entwicklung der achaemenidischen Palastarchitektur", *Iranica Antiqua* XV (1980), pp. 199ff.
[3] The strong possibility that Darius himself was the builder of the Ka'ba is reinforced by the presence of toothed chisel marks on many parts of the Tower, not least on a number of exposed anathyrosis joints. Cf. Stronach, "Tower Temples", p. 283.
[4] See P. Amiet, *Elam* (Auvers-sur-Oise, 1966), fig. 428.
[5] Stronach, *Pasargadae*, pp. 138ff.   [6] See *ibid., loc. cit.*

THE TALL-I TAKHT

As K. Galling already indicated in 1925[1] it is possible to compare the twin blocks at Pasargadae with the twin plinths in Darius' funerary relief and to suppose that Cyrus, like Darius, ascended a stepped plinth in order to worship opposite an altar only a little distance away. The discovery that Cyrus employed exactly the same type of portable stone fire altar at Pasargadae as that illustrated by Darius in his funerary relief [2] strengthens the force of the parallel.

This information is of value in any assessment of Cyrus' religious beliefs, for while textual evidence may be used to indicate that Darius was a follower of Zoroaster's reforms,[3] Cyrus' only available expressions of piety were clearly designed for local consumption in Babylonia.[4] The enigmatic raised disc above the door of the tomb of Cyrus could have had a religious signification,[5] but this suggestion can only be put forward with the utmost caution.[6] At the moment, indeed, the archaeological record only points to the identity of certain religious symbols that were each used by Cyrus and Darius and to the close, if not exact, resemblance of certain other religious motifs which appear as far apart in time as the 8th and 5th centuries B.C.[7] Needless to say such parallels are not enough to prove that Cyrus already shared the religious convictions of Darius, but, taken with the unusual precepts which appear to have guided Cyrus' career, they do allow us to suggest that Cyrus was at least an adherent of a pre-Zoroastrian stratum of belief which was not too far removed from the faith honoured by Darius.

THE TALL-I TAKHT

The great stone platform of the Tall-i Takht or "Throne Hill", known locally as Takht-i Mādar-i Sulaimān or "Throne of the Mother of Solomon" (pl. 7), affords unrivalled evidence of the scale and quality

---

[1] *Der Altar in den Kulturen des alten Orients* (Berlin, 1925), pl. 14, fig. 5.

[2] Cf. Stronach, "Tower Temples", pls XXVc and XXVIa.

[3] I. Gershevitch, "Zoroaster's own Contribution", *JNES* XXIII (1964), pp. 16ff.

[4] For the text of Cyrus' cylinder, see J. B. Pritchard, *Ancient Near Eastern Texts*, 2nd ed. (Princeton, 1955), pp. 315–16.

[5] Stronach, *Iran* IX, p. 158.

[6] An alternative interpretation would be that the rosette served as an architectural grace note: as a modest foil to the austere, almost severe note struck by the rest of the monument. Cf. Stronach, *Pasargadae*, p. 42.

[7] Compare, for example, the recessed motif that appears on the external walls of the Central Temple at Tepe Nūsh-i Jān (D. Stronach and M. Roaf, *Iran* XVI (1978), pl. I d) with that found on the stone "horned parapet" at Persepolis (A. B. Tilia, "Reconstruction of the Parapet on the Terrace Wall at Persepolis, South and West of Palace H", *East and West* XIX (1969), fig. 6).

of Cyrus' building activities.[1] This towering façade of drafted masonry, with its two separate ceremonial staircases, was probably intended to support the private palaces of the monarch. Whether or not it was partly inspired by the terraced acropolis of Sardis[2] there is little doubt that Lydian stonemasons contributed to its construction[3] and that, early in the reign of Darius, it provided part of the inspiration behind the elevated, partly fortified palace compound of Persepolis.

The Tall-i Takht is much more, however, than a witness to one of Cyrus' boldest, if unfinished, building plans. Thanks to the excavations of Ali Sami,[4] followed by those of the British Institute of Persian Studies from 1961 to 1963, it has proved possible to document the conversion of the original palace platform to new, no longer ceremonial purposes somewhere toward the end of the 6th or the beginning of the 5th century B.C. A mud-brick wall can be seen to have been built round the whole crown of the hill while varied storage and industrial areas came to be established within the circuit of the defences.[5]

At the close of the Achaemenian period there is no evidence of any kind of destruction and it is tempting to suppose that the Tall-i Takht was the important royal "storehouse" at Pasargadae which is said to have been handed over intact to Alexander.[6] Slightly later in time an incomplete burning of the site c. 300 B.C. would appear to document a local uprising that spelt the end of direct Seleucid control in Fārs.[7] Thereafter we find evidence of a short-lived Frataraka occupation which may have lasted for a little over a century before – very much later – the Takht was again re-occupied in either late Sasanian or early Islamic times.[8]

CONCLUSION

In the broad context of the Persian migration to Fārs the recent excavations at Pasargadae have thrown fresh light on the invasion routes which the Persians may have followed. On the evidence, in part, of

---

[1] Nylander, pp. 75 ff. and Stronach, *Pasargadae*, pp. 11–23.
[2] For comments on the newly discovered Lydian acropolis, see G. M. A. Hanfmann, *Letters from Sardis* (Cambridge, Mass., 1972), pp. 75, 306ff. and figs 47, 229.
[3] Nylander, p. 88. [4] Ali Sami, *op. cit.*, pp. 68ff.
[5] Stronach, *Pasargadae*, pp. 146–59. [6] Arrian, *Anabasis* III. 18. 10.
[7] See G. K. Jenkins, "Coin Hoards from Pasargadae", *Iran* III (1965), p. 52; Stronach, *Pasargadae*, pp. 155, 186; and for the newly proposed date of c. 300 B.C.) (as opposed to 280 B.C.) for the conflagration on the Takht, A. Houghton, "Notes on the early Seleucid victory coinage of Persepolis", *Schweizerische Numismatische Rundschau* LIX (Berne, 1980), p. 14, n. 14.
[8] *Ibid.*, pp. 155–9.

CONCLUSION

stratified pottery of the 5th and 4th centuries B.C. from Pasargadae it is no longer possible to suggest that Achaemenid Village I at Susa was an early Persian settlement of the 8th/7th centuries B.C.[1] Furthermore, in the light of detailed studies of the masonry of the second half of the 6th century at Pasargadae, such supposedly "archaic" Achaemenian sites as Masjid-i Sulaimān and Dā-u Dukhtar, which were once thought to document a west to east migration of the Persians from Khūzistān to Fārs,[2] can now be shown to date from the 5th century B.C. or later.[3]

The lack of any evidence for a west to east movement from the area of Susa to that of Pasargadae suggests, in fact, an entirely different reconstruction of events. However far the Persians may have had to follow mountainous routes in the course of their travels it seems probable that the bulk of the Persians entered Fārs from the north along open roads to the east of the Bakhtiari highlands. By the early 7th century B.C., if not still earlier, certain of the invading tribes must have begun to establish themselves in the Kur River basin. At the western end of this strategic and fertile valley stood the remains of the city of Anshan, a symbol of earlier Elamite dominion,[4] while as we now know from surface surveys made in 1973 and 1974 the centre of the plain was already important to both Cyrus and Cambyses II (529–522 B.C.) if not to still earlier Achaemenian rulers as well.[5]

Against this background the decision of Cyrus to establish the home of his dynasty in the relatively small valley of Pasargadae, rather than in the broad plain of the Kur river, is perhaps best explained by Strabo's statement (XV. 3. 8) that it was there that the Persians overcame the Medes in battle and that Cyrus founded Pasargadae as a "memorial" to his victory. To-day, however, Pasargadae stands as a monument to much more than that encounter: in its scattered white stones we witness the birth of Achaemenian art and one more testimony to a moment of singular achievement.

[1] D. Stronach, "Achaemenid Village I at Susa and the Persian Migration to Fars", *Iraq* XXXVI (1974), p. 244.
[2] Cf. Ghirshman, *Persia*, pp. 131–2.
[3] Stronach, "Achaemenid Village I", pp. 246–7.
[4] J. Hansman, "Elamites, Achaemenians and Anshan", *Iran* X (1972), pp. 101ff.; W. Sumner, "Excavations at Ancient Anshan", *Archaeology* XXVI (1973), p. 304; and E. Reiner, "The Location of Anšan", *RA* LXVII (1973), pp. 57–62.
[5] A. B. Tilia, *Studies and Restorations at Persepolis and Other Sites in Fars* II (Rome, 1978), pp. 80–91.

CHAPTER 21

METALWORK AND GLYPTIC

METALWORK

Without a body of material from controlled excavations in western Iran on sites of the 7th and early 6th centuries B.C. the special character of Median metalwork is still largely a matter of surmise. Western influences, from Assyria and Urartu, were undoubtedly strong, but the Medes were also heirs to a native tradition of fine metalworking for the moment known only from cemeteries of the late second millennium B.C. like that at Mārlīk in Gīlān. How this craft was transmitted and modified in the following three or four hundred years is as yet unknown. Of possible Median artefacts the most outstanding is the decorated gold cover for a short-sword scabbard in the "Oxus Treasure" (pl. 42). It is chased with a frieze of mounted huntsmen, who wear Median costume and what seems to be a version of the Assyrian royal crown. An elaborate beak-head border and rapacious bird-head terminals on the guard-cover also clearly illustrate the impact of Scythian art in Iran. But whether this is indeed an early 6th-century Median craftsman's work[1] or closer in time to such scabbards clearly represented a century or so later on the Persepolis reliefs is an open question. Barnett has associated with it, as examples of Median art, the decorated gold scabbards from the south-Russian barrows of Kelermes, Chertomlyk and Melgunov generally, and more probably, regarded as the work of Scythian craftsmen strongly influenced by Urartian artists.

Although an ever increasing body of objects is available for study, it is no more easy to present a comprehensive and coherent account of Achaemenian metalwork. The exact locations of ore-sources are largely unknown, individual workshops have not been identified and techniques have rarely been studied. Many of the finest pieces are chance finds widely dispersed through the empire and beyond its frontiers, inhibiting the reconstruction of a reliable chronology and often obscuring the strength of provincial traditions of metal-working. Fashions in general were set by the equipment of the Great King and his court, diffused

[1] R. D. Barnett, "Median Art"; cf. A. Farkas, *Persica* IV (1969), 70–2.

through the activities of the Persian armies and established locally by the requirements of provincial governors and their staffs. Isolated workshops or those in regions like western Anatolia with their own strongly established skills and repertory contributed in details rather than fundamentals. Where comparisons are possible work in base metals, notably bronze, closely followed the patterns established in precious metals for affluent customers. Iron, of varying quality, was universally used for tools and at least the blades of weapons. Brass, of a relatively low zinc and copper alloy, may now have been used for the first time for vessels.

Men and women throughout the Achaemenian Empire wore a rich variety of personal ornaments. The Persian troops, according to Herodotus, "glittered all over with gold, vast quantities of which they wore about their persons" (VIII. 83). After the battle of Plataea in 479 B.C. the bodies of the slain furnished bracelets (pl. 43) and chains in profusion (IX. 80). The earrings, torcs and bracelets habitually worn by king and aristocracy continued an old Iranian tradition earlier popular among the Medes and their Scythian confederates. So great indeed was their popularity that the Magi imposed a prohibition on personal ornament and the wearing of gold.[1] The various stylistic developments in Achaemenian jewellery and their provincial variants remain to be unravelled. Gold necklaces and earrings from late 5th- or early 4th-century graves at Sardis in Lydia,[2] a small hoard of jewellery and plate from a palace at Vouni in Cyprus sacked about 380 B.C.,[3] a late 4th-century grave of a woman decked out with jewellery from Susa in Iran,[4] a hoard of earrings, bracelets and beads of the mid 4th century B.C. buried at Pasargadae[5] and the 4th-century "Treasure of Akhalgori" from the Caucasus[6] constitute the mere handful of groups whose date is reasonably well established. Their wide distribution and the variety of their contents defies generalization. The outstanding collection of objects washed out of its banks by the river Oxus, from which it takes its name, is a special case and chronologically not a very helpful one, since its richly varied contents span a period of three or four hundred years from the 6th to the 2nd century B.C.[7]

[1] Diogenes Laertius I. 7.
[2] Curtis, *Sardis* XIII, *passim*.
[3] E. Gjerstad, *Swedish Cyprus Expedition* III (Stockholm, 1937), 238ff.
[4] De Morgan, "Sépulture Achéménide".
[5] D. Stronach, *Iran* III (1965), 31ff.
[6] Smirnov, *Der Schatz von Achalgori*.
[7] See Dalton, *Treasure of the Oxus*; on the dating of the associated coins see D. Schlumberger, *MDAFA* XIV (1953), 46–9; A. R. Bellinger, *ANSMN* X (1962), 51ff.

At Persepolis early in the 5th century, Medes (delegation I), Lydians (VI) and Scythians (XI)[1] bring as offerings bracelets with zoomorphic terminals. Surviving examples, decorated with the bodies or just the heads of lions, caprids, gazelles, antelopes, rams and calves, indicate that such ornaments were universally popular.[2] The fashion was not new, for in Iran it is known as early as the Mārlīk cemetery, and it was favoured to the west in Assyria and Urartu; but before it had rarely been so fully exploited. A massive pair of solid gold bracelets from the Oxus with winged- and horned-griffin terminals, richly set with *cloisons* and cavities once filled with coloured inlays, are among the great masterpieces of the jeweller's art (pl. 43*b*).[3] Both have the omega-shaped hoops distinctive of this period and their barbaric exuberance owes much to an influential Asiatic strain in Achaemenian art. Found with them was a whole range of simpler bracelets (pl. 43*a*). Some are close in style to a pair of inlaid lion-head terminals found in a grave at Susa[4] suggesting that this is a fair sample of 4th-century bracelets of quality made in Iran, though technically many follow earlier patterns. By contrast a lovely pair of gold bracelets in the Pasargadae hoard, with spirally twisted hoops and detachable ibex-headed terminals delicately made in a manner closely matched on the best contemporary earrings, anticipate the later styles and techniques of Seleucid jewellers.[5] Bracelets in silver are generally simple and more severe, but include close copies of gold types. Notable among these are a few with terminals cast as lion-heads from whose open jaws protrude the head of a calf or caprid.[6] As this voracious animal motif was anticipated in Urartian metalwork, such bracelets may belong to the earlier phases of Achaemenian art. Simple zoomorphic and plain bracelets in base silver and bronze regularly appear in cemeteries.

Relatively few torcs have survived,[7] but fine examples with animal terminals may be seen on the statue of an official of the Persian administration in Egypt, now in Brooklyn,[8] and round the neck of Darius III on the well-known Alexander mosaic of Pompeii (pl. 4).[9]

[1] E. Schmidt, *Persepolis* III (Chicago, 1970), 145–58; the delegations in this section are numbered and identified following Schmidt's final analysis, though I regard some of the identifications as still very open.

[2] Amandry, "Orfèvrerie Achéménide".   [3] Dalton, pl. I.

[4] de Morgan, *op. cit.*, pl. IV; cf. Dalton, nos 118, 120.

[5] Stronach, *op. cit.*, pl. X.   [6] Amandry, *op. cit.*, pl. 10.

[7] For example de Morgan, *op. cit.*, pl. IV; Dalton, nos. 117–19, 122, 132.

[8] J. D. Cooney, *Bulletin of the Brooklyn Museum* XV. 2 (1953), 1ff., figs. 1, 2, 5; 6–7 (gold torc terminal from Guennol Collection).

[9] J. D. Beazley and B. Ashmole, *Greek Sculpture and Painting* (Cambridge, 1966), pl. 142.

METALWORK

Earrings also followed similar patterns, particularly in the later 5th and 4th centuries, but here the range of decoration and technique was much wider as in the provinces earlier fashions persisted. The fine earrings from Sardis and Pasargadae offer a glimpse at court fashions. Silver earrings, usually with filigree and granulated decoration, occur in 5th-century coin-hoards in the Levant and Turkey[1] and are regularly reported as isolated finds. Necklaces of gold and silver beads, or of beads and pendants, equally employed rich granulation and filigree.[2] Few ornaments of the period illustrate so well as the popular cutout sheet-gold plaques, sewn onto richly coloured garments, tents and canopies, the blend of Mesopotamian and Asiatic nomad styles which gave Achaemenian art its most original character. A richly furnished grave at Sardis had once contained a garment ornamented with nine gold sphinxes and fifty rosettes.[3] A comprehensive group of the 4th century, said to come from Hamadān, includes walking or rampant addorsed and winged lions in roundels, detached lion and griffin-heads (a motif of Asiatic origin), and a roundel embracing a silhouette of Ahuramazda.[4]

The splendour of Achaemenian plate is legendary. Gold and silver were exploited as never before and it was widely produced in great variety. Of this Greek authors and the range of surviving examples leave no doubt. For the earlier 5th century there is the famous description in Herodotus (IX. 80) of the captured Persian camp at Plataea which contained "many golden bowls, goblets and other drinking vessels. On the carriage were bags containing silver and gold kettles." Herodotus also relates the tale of one Ameinocles (VII. 190), who made a fortune from the gold and silver cups and other precious spoils washed up on the shores near Cape Sepias, where he farmed, after the wreck of the Persian fleet. For the 4th century the astonished comments of classical authors indicate the magnificent spoils which fell to Alexander the Great in the treasuries of Babylon, Persepolis, Susa and Ecbatana (Hamadān), where precious metals were often hoarded in the shape of vessels.[5] A group of vessels, weapons and weapon fittings in gold said to be from Hamadān, now divided between museums in Tehran and New York, is the only vestige of such storehouses.[6] Indeed surviving gold plate is rare; most pieces are of silver or silver-gilt.

[1] C. Kraay and P. R. S. Moorey, "Two fifth-century hoards", *RN* x (1968), 183ff.
[2] Curtis, *op. cit.*, pls II–VI; Stronach, *op. cit.*, pl. XI.   [3] Curtis, *op. cit.*, 143, pls I, XIII.
[4] Kantor, "Achaemenid Jewelry"; the authenticity of some, if not all, of this collection is debatable.   [5] Schmidt, *Persepolis* II, 165; especially Athenaeus, *Deipnosophistae* XI. 782a.
[6] L. Vanden Berghe, *Archéologie de l'Iran Ancien* (Leiden, 1959), pl. 136a–d; Wilkinson, "Assyrian and Persian Art", 200; authenticity debatable.

METALWORK AND GLYPTIC

Metal vessels, presumably of precious metal, are shown among the gifts or tribute brought to the Great King on the Persepolis reliefs, where Babylonians (delegation V), Lydians (VI), Assyrians (VIII), Ionians (XII) and Bactrians (XIII) all carry the same type of bowl. Medes (I), Ionians (XII) and ?Parthians (XV) carry tall goblets, some fluted like examples reported in recent years from Turkey. Armenians (III) and Lydians (VI) bring the most elaborate of all vessels, the spouted zoomorphic amphorae, represented among surviving plate by a fine example from a late 5th-century grave at Duvanli in Bulgaria,[1] but more commonly by scattered cast silver or bronze animal-shaped handles or spouts of great vitality (pls 44*b*, 45*a*).[2] One series of vessels is conspicuously absent from the Persepolis reliefs. Vessels, of metal and baked clay, ending in animal heads had been common in western Asia for centuries before the Achaemenian supremacy, but the form was particularly exploited in this period to provide some of the most original and striking pieces of plate ever made. They even find a place in Achaemenian glyptic designs.[3] The earlier vessels were normally straight, often with a loop handle over the mouth; but the Achaemenians preferred the curved, horn-like form with the head or forepart of an animal or monster set at the base. Some of these vessels (*rhyta*) have a small hole or funnel in the bottom through which a thin stream of liquid might pass into a drinking bowl or direct into the drinker's mouth.

The Great King not only received fine plate, he also dispensed it to his aristocracy, to foreign guests and to ambassadors;[4] in this weight mattered as much as fine craftsmanship. The type and quality of royal table services may be gauged from an ever growing group of vessels which bear royal names and titles in cuneiform script. For the present archaeological discoveries of plate have tended to concentrate on the shores of the Black Sea, the Sea of Marmora, the Aegean and the Eastern Mediterranean or within easy reach of them.[5] Most notably graves under tumuli at Uşak in western Turkey have yielded bowls, dishes, ladles, jars, jugs, and silver incense-burners exactly like those set beside the royal throne at Persepolis.[6] The table-ware of Persian administrators and

---

[1] Amandry, *op. cit.*, 39, n. 17 for bibliography.
[2] *Ibid.*, pl. 21. 4–5.   [3] Legrain, *Ur Excavations* x, pl. 42. 832.
[4] Athenaeus, *Deipnosophistae* II. 48–9; Aelianus, *Varia Historia* I. 22; Herodotus IX. 110; Esther 2. 18.
[5] Amandry, "Argenterie", 270–2.
[6] M. Mellink, *AJA* LXXI (1967), 172, pl. 59. 20–1.

army officers was buried with them at places like Gezer and Tell Far'ah (South) in Palestine, at Deve Hüyük in Syria;[1] silver for the prosperous, exactly copied in bronze or even baked clay for the less exalted.

According to Aelianus "two silver *phialai* weighing one talent" were included in the customary gift to ambassadors[2] and three such bowls, one inside the other, are being offered to the Treasurer on the famous Darius vase in Naples, painted about 350–325 B.C.[3] These bowls, in both silver and bronze, in a range of closely related forms are the commonest pieces of Achaemenian plate, regularly reported from sites across the empire. They have flaring, offset rims with shallow bodies made by spinning upon a lathe, or cast, and then hammered up from inside with patterns in high relief usually based on radiating leaves of rosette form or floral motifs inspired by the lotus. Rarer examples were cast plain and then over the outside was fitted a separately made sheet-metal cover or individual lobes, the designs worked in *repoussé*.[4] Local production to standard patterns was normal under the Achaemenids, but certain elaborate phialai and other bowls seem to come from specialist workshops (pl. 45*b*). Outstanding are a pair in silver from later 5th-century graves at Ialysos in Rhodes[5] and another from Kazbek in the Caucasus inscribed in Aramaic with an Iranian name.[6] All three are identically decorated with a series of pear-shaped bosses between which are set opposed S-spirals each terminating in a bird's head and decorated with a palmette. For these a single workshop in western Anatolia, in Lydia perhaps, was most probably responsible. It has been suggested that it also produced fine large vessels like the Duvanli amphora. Other workshops producing fine lobed phialai existed in Egypt in the 4th century.[7]

What little evidence there is for the technology of fine metalwork in the Achaemenian Empire largely comes from Egypt, where important centres of production existed (pl. 46). According to the building inscription of Darius the Great from Susa it was Egyptians and Medes who worked the gold brought thither from Sardis and Bactria.[8] In a

---

[1] R. A. S. Macalister, *The excavation of Gezer* I (London, 1912), 289–90; J. H. Iliffe, *Quarterly of the Department of Antiquities in Palestine* IV (Jerusalem, 1934), 182–6, pls. LXXXIX–XCI; C. L. Woolley, *AAA* VII (1914–16), 115–29.

[2] *Varia Historia* I. 22.

[3] C. Anti, *Archeologica Classica* IV (Rome, 1952), pl. XIV.

[4] W. M. F. Petrie, *Bethpelet* I (London, 1930), pl. XXVIII. 756; A. D. H. Bivar, "A rosette *phialē* inscribed in Aramaic", *BSOAS* XXIV (1961), 191–2.

[5] L. Laurenzi, "Necropoli Ialisie", *Clara Rhodos* VIII (1936), figs. 168–9.

[6] Tallgren, "The Kazbek Treasure", 116ff.

[7] Bivar, *op. cit.*, 197–9.   [8] F. Vallat, *Syria* XLVIII (1971), 57–8.

unique series of reliefs from the 4th-century tomb of Pedusiri at Tuna the production of zoomorphic *rhyta* is shown in some detail, but unfortunately not the earliest stages in the process.[1] Laboratory examination of surviving examples has shown them to be elaborately constructed and finished with great attention to detail.[2] Achaemenian smiths used, if they did not actually invent, fire-gilding with an amalgam of mercury and powdered gold, more commonly to pick out specific details in the design than as an overall surface application.[3] Frankfort identified a small-scale stone relief from Egypt as an Achaemenian goldsmith's trial-piece.[4] In his excavations at Memphis Petrie found some small lead plaques with relief decoration, one at least of the Achaemenian period, which he suggested "were made for the silversmiths to carry with them, both for taking orders and for scaling out their work".[5] It is likely that the baked clay casts taken from metal vessels found in a coffin of the Persian period at Ur in Iraq served principally as models for the manufacture of other decorated metalware.[6] Nor did Achaemenian smiths and jewellers ignore their contemporaries' love of rich colour. Details in sculpture were painted, gilded and sometimes inlaid.[7] In jewellery blue stones or imitations of them were preferred and the cavities or *cloisons* which held them were skilfully set to emphasize the stylized musculature of animals and monsters. No fine metalworker's tools of the period have been certainly identified, but two hoards of scrap silver, one found at Qal'at al-Baḥrain in the Persian Gulf, the other at Engedi in Israel[8] were probably silversmiths' raw material.

Quite another aspect of the metalsmith's craft is represented by scattered furniture fittings, usually of cast bronze. Richly moulded legs, decorated stretchers or zoomorphic terminals, commonly wild goats, were cast by the lost-wax method, sometimes in many parts which were then united by the demanding process of fusion welding.[9] Achaemenian smiths were also masters of early iron technology; a metal far less manageable than bronze. Soft wrought iron (less than 0.3% carbon) as produced in primitive furnaces is too low in carbon to be hardened

---

[1] G. Lefebvre, *Le Tombeau de Petosiris* III (Cairo, 1923), pls. VII–VIII.
[2] Wilkinson, "Assyrian and Persian Art", 221.
[3] Terrace, "Two Achaemenian objects", 72–3; J. D. Cooney, *AJA* LXVIII (1964), 75.
[4] "A Persian goldsmith's trial piece", pl. III.
[5] Petrie, *Meydum and Memphis* III, 44.
[6] C. L. Woolley, *Ur Excavations* IX (London, 1962), pls 83. 833–41.
[7] E. Herzfeld, *Iran in the Ancient East* (Oxford, 1941), 255ff.
[8] K. Frifelt, *Kuml* 1964, 102–3, fig. 1; B. Mazar, *Archaeology* XVI (1963), 99ff., figure on p. 104.
[9] Wilkinson, "An Achaemenian bronze head".

CUT GLASS AND CARVED IVORY

appreciably. In order to get the fine cutting edge required on tools and weapons the Achaemenian smith used an ingenious and skilled technique. Thin laminations of iron were separately heated with charcoal to introduce carbon (carburized), then piled and forge-welded together. Thus they were brought into the range of steels (0.3 to 2.2% carbon) and might be hardened by heat treatment. A late 5th-century spearhead from Deve Hüyük in Syria has a blade built up of about fifty such layers of sponge iron plates.[1]

CUT GLASS AND CARVED IVORY

Among the minor arts of this period two merit passing comment as they both vary in a distinctive way crafts long established in the Near East. Most immediately akin to the metal industry were the makers of cut glass vessels which exactly imitated metal forms and may indeed have been made largely in Turkey, where fine metal tableware was widely manufactured. Throughout the Achaemenian period glass factories in Syria and Mesopotamia were producing multi-coloured glass beads, amulets, inlays and cored vessels in a manner and to patterns long established in the region. But a range of moulded vessels in clear glass with cut decoration, its fine quality indicating a luxury product, was new and distinctive. Fragments of such vessels from the ruins of Persepolis give substance to the boasts of ambassadors from Athens, who in Aristophanes' play *The Acharnians* (*Ach.* 74) speak of drinking from clear glass vessels at the Persian king's court. Glass bowls and dishes variously decorated on the exterior, like the metal phialai, with relief petals and beakers, ribbed and lobed, occur across the empire from Iran to Cyrene, though most surviving examples have no known source. Zoomorphic rhyta were also made in moulded and cut glass. This specialist industry, with antecedents in Iraq and Turkey in the previous centuries, flourished during the 5th and well into the 4th centuries B.C. At the time of the Assyrian Empire many workshops in Syria and Phoenicia had specialized in the production of fine wood furniture inlaid with carved ivory plaques and cosmetic articles wholly of ivory. The craft survived, albeit to judge from the rarity of its products on a lesser scale than before. At Susa the excavators found carved ivory combs, cosmetic tubes in human form and decorated plaques in the

---

[1] H. H. Coghlan, *Notes on Prehistoric and Early Iron in the Old World* (Oxford, 1956), 137–8, pls II–IV.

METALWORK AND GLYPTIC

Achaemenian court style associated with fragments of worked ivory from Greece, Egypt and Phoenicia.

SEALS

In Iran from prehistoric times engraved seals had been used to impress clay tags and tablets with marks of property and authority. By the time of Cyrus cylinder and stamp seals had a long history in western Iran, where they had developed primarily under the influence of Elamite and Mesopotamian glyptic. The military advance of the Urartians into north-west Iran in the 9th and 8th centuries B.C. had brought with it their distinctive seal form, the stamp-cylinder, which may have been adopted by the Medes, though it does not seem to have survived long under the Achaemenids.[1] Throughout the Achaemenian Empire cylinder seals were largely used for official purposes, whilst private individuals preferred stamp seals and signet rings. This administrative use of the cylinder seal has been taken to mark a reversion in chancery practice, for in Mesopotamia during the previous few centuries stamp seals had gradually superseded the long-established cylinder in common usage. But the evidence may be partial. Although from at least the 9th-century Assyrian kings commonly used a relatively large stamp seal for administrative purposes, which showed the ruler driving a dagger into the chest of a rampant lion, until Esarhaddon's reign (680–669 B.C.) they also used cylinders similarly engraved.[2] Treaties were sealed with cylinders, votive cylinder seals were made well into the 6th century B.C. in Iraq, and stored as treasured trophies at Persepolis, and tablets of the 5th century in Iraq often bear cylinder seal impressions in the style of the later Neo-Babylonian period. Indeed the Achaemenid kings (pl. 47*b*) may have been following Neo-Babylonian or Neo-Elamite chancery procedures in using cylinders. Certain stylistic traits in Achaemenian Court Style cylinder designs suggest Elamite influence.

Achaemenian cylinders are relatively small and tend sometimes to have a swollen bead-like form. They were made of fine stones such as translucent light blue chalcedony, lapis lazuli and various agates, of the commoner darkish limestone and steatite, of baked clay and even of glass, particularly in Syria. Their most common designs were appropriate to their restricted use. This Court Style, distinctively Mesopot-

---

[1] R. D. Barnett, "Persepolis", *Iraq* XIX (1957), pl. XXIII. 3; Porada, "Seals of Iran", no. 832.
[2] B. Parker, *Iraq* XXIV (1962), 38, pl. XXI. 1, fig. 7.

amian in origin, engraving and iconography, is best studied among impressions of the first half of the 5th century found at Persepolis on the Treasury and Fortification tablets.[1] The main themes do not appear to have changed in the subsequent century, though detailed studies still awaited will certainly show stylistic variations with the time and place of manufacture. Apart from the "royal" hero triumphant over beasts, usually presided over by the winged disk symbol of Ahuramazda, there are scenes of men and monsters adoring or supporting the Ahuramazda symbol, of ritual and worship at altars or in other settings, of military and naval engagements, of hunts, combats and friezes featuring men, animals and monsters. Where direct comparisons are possible this is the sculptural art of the Persepolis friezes in miniature, significant departures in iconography and design usually marking strong provincial influence. Impressions of Court Style cylinder seals are known from provincial capitals like Daskyleion in Anatolia and Memphis in Egypt, among the tablet sealings of the Murašû archive from Nippur during the reigns of Artaxerxes I and Darius II and in the "collector's hoard" from a coffin at Ur,[2] indicating their wide role in the empire's daily administrative and business routines. Fine cylinders inscribed with names in Aramaic, the chancery language of the empire, probably belonged to high ranking officials in the royal service; but the protocol of seal usage in the Achaemenian period is still obscure.

Although provincial traits are not easy to isolate with confidence, a few of the more certain may be cited to illustrate their range. In Iraq, which played a vital though yet obscure role in the genesis of the Court Style, cylinders in the later Neo-Babylonian style were definitely used, if not still actually produced, in the Achaemenian period. More interesting, and possibly amongst the earliest truly Achaemenian cylinders are a few in which a Persian hero in single-handed combat with a beast is paired with a Neo-Babylonian hero similarly engaged. In at least one case the Persian hero is larger than his victim as natural proportions require, but his Neo-Babylonian counterpart is, in the age-old Mesopotamian tradition, matched by a beast of equal height.[3] The hero in Achaemenian contest scenes is often described as a king,

---

[1] Schmidt, *Persepolis* II, 4–49.

[2] Balkan, "Inscribed bullae", pls XXIII–IV; Petrie, *op. cit.*, pls XXXV–XXXVII; L. Legrain, *The Culture of the Babylonians from their Seals in the Collections of the Museum* (Philadelphia, 1925), pls XLI–XLV; C. L. Woolley, *Ur Excavations* x (London, 1951), no. 759.

[3] Frankfort, *Cylinder Seals*, pl. XXXVIIa; D. J. Wiseman, *Cylinder Seals of Western Asia* (London, 1959), pl. 105.

but the variety of his attire and headdress, particularly on stamp seals, indicates that for contemporaries there was more of the traditional Mesopotamian superhuman hero in his role than the description "king" conveys today. These are certainly not royal portraits or even particular rulers, save perhaps on the rare inscribed "royal" cylinder seals (pl. 47*b*), and even then there is room for doubt.[1]

The Egyptian god Bes, often as a "master-of-animals", passed into Achaemenian glyptic from Phoenician sources, though his appearance does not necessarily indicate the work of a Levantine seal-cutter. On a cylinder in the British Museum, inscribed in Old Persian "Arshaka by name, son of Athiyabaushna",[2] he appears flanked by men in Persian dress supporting a winged disk (pl. 48*a*). Another cylinder in the same collection may well have been cut in Egypt itself.[3] Between an upper and lower border of typically Egyptian *udjat* eyes are set in succession an Egyptian Horus hawk, an incense burner and a characteristically Iranian winged ibex with front feet held up and forward (pl. 48*b*). This illustrates particularly well the eclectic style of many Achaemenian cylinder seals not in the formal Court Style. But, as will be seen particularly on stamp seals, it was the influence of Greek art in Anatolia which made the most original contribution to Achaemenian glyptic. There three-dimensional space was treated for the first time on cylinder seals and in the choice of subjects and the manner of cutting Greek taste prevailed. The commonest themes in this series are of hunting, with groups of men and animals or animals alone, finely engraved and set in spacious backgrounds.

By the middle of the 4th century B.C. the three-thousand-year-old cylinder seal had virtually passed out of use, progressively superseded in the Persian Empire by stamp seals and signet rings. It is in their designs, and to a lesser extent in their varied forms, that the wide range of artistic traditions embraced by the Achaemenian empire are most easily seen. Regional characteristics may be identified, and to some extent localized, with a degree of certainty so far impossible with the other minor arts, though here as elsewhere the chronology of stylistic developments is far from clear. In the 6th century under the Neo-Babylonian empire, Mesopotamian stamp-seals, usually of chalcedony, were relatively large with high backs pierced towards the top for suspension and with convex bases, circular or oval in shape. Some backs

---

[1] H. Seyrig, *Syria* XXXVI (1959), 52–6.
[2] Wiseman, *op. cit.*, pl. 103.
[3] *Ibid.*, pl. 116.

were plain and slightly swollen (conoid), others facet-cut round the edge (pyramidal). Designs were commonly stylized scenes of worship with the marks of drill and disk used in the cutting ill-disguised. These seal shapes, also primarily in chalcedony, were adopted by the Achaemenians, but engraved in the Court Style of their cylinders which was more reminiscent of the slightly earlier Neo-Assyrian style in Iraq. The continuity of tradition was naturally strongest in the eastern empire, though evidence from Iran, outside Persepolis, is still very scarce and recourse has to be made to the groups of impressions from Nippur and Ur already cited. In the west scaraboids and seals shaped like contemporary weights, forms of Phoenician origin, were also engraved with Court Style designs. Here, following earlier fashions, stones such as cornelian, agate and rock crystal, haematite and lodestone were used in addition to chalcedony.

Both the themes of Court Style stamp seals and their style ran closely parallel to the cylinders and were distinctively oriental. The standard motifs were the contest between hero and beast; the "master-of-animals" flanked by symmetrical pairs of creatures rampant or inverted; confronted pairs of royal sphinxes; single or paired sphinxes, lions and lion-griffins; and sphinxes with leonine bodies and Bes heads. Horses and bulls, horsemen and royal guards appear more rarely. An important group of pyramidal stamp seals with octagonal bases decorated in the Court Style was produced in western Anatolia, perhaps exclusively in Lydia.[1] Some bear Lydian inscriptions which identify the owners of each seal and have a linear device as his personal blazon, one among a whole series found without a full inscription on other seals. Placed as Lydia was between the East Greek world and the Orient it is not surprising that other seals in this group should have designs either purely Greek in style or more definitely local, blending the styles and iconography of east and west.

Even more distinctive and particularly characteristic of Anatolia's cosmopolitan seal engravers are the so-called "Graeco-Persian" seals, predominantly scaraboids of a large form developed in East Greek workshops, but also including rectangular stamp seals with faceted backs and oblong four-sided stones. These stamp seals, from southern rather than western Anatolian cities, appear first soon after $c.$ 470 B.C. and survive well into the next century. A few have designs in the Court Style, but by far the greatest number show Greek influence in the choice

---

[1] Boardman, "Pyramidal Stamp Seals".

of subjects and the naturalism of their rendering. The selected scenes no longer have a ritual or mythological significance in the Mesopotamian tradition; they are now just vignettes of daily life vividly, if often formally, portrayed. Men in oriental costume ride, hunt and fight; a whole menagerie of animals, notably lions, bears, hyenas, reindeer, boars and foxes, are shown alone often in hectic flight from the huntsmen; men and women stand singly or together engaged in conversation; women appear seated in domestic settings and couples make love. Only very occasionally does a hovering winged disk of Ahuramazda recall the Court Style.[1] Such seals were used throughout the empire.

Although other areas of the empire produced and used seals in local styles as well as in the official Court Style, none was as original or influential in its contribution as Anatolia. In Syria and Phoenicia a distinctive range of glass scaraboids and small conoid seals was characteristic of this period. They have been excavated from the important port of al-Mina and were also found in the inland cemetery at Deve Hüyük near Carchemish.[2] Apart from Court Style themes they bear human and animal motifs derived from earlier local glyptic. In Syria too the long established scarabs and scaraboids of steatite, glazed faience and blue frit persisted with designs in the Egypto-Phoenician style. In the more southerly provinces of Samaria and Judah there is scattered evidence of the Court Style in administrative centres and a typical medley of Achaemenian and Greek seal impressions on tags was found with papyri dating to *c.* 375–332 B.C. in a cave in the Wadi al-Daliya.[3] A series of impressions from sites in Judah, perhaps of private seals, shows that in the middle and later 5th century a series of local stamp seals was made under the influence of the Court Style engraved with crudely cut lions passant or rampant and bulls, sometimes combined with stylized incense-burners.[4] In Egypt officials at Memphis used name-scarabs inscribed in Egyptian hieroglyphic, stamp seals in the Court Style and Greek gems.

Although metal finger-rings with engraved designs had been used in western Iran long before the Achaemenian period, they now became much more popular and impressions from their distinctive oval bezels

---

[1] Richter, *Engraved Gems* I, no. 511; Boardman, *Greek Gems and Finger-rings*, no. 908.

[2] C. L. Woolley, *JHS* LVIII (1938), pl. XV; *idem*, *AAA* VII (1914–16), pl. XXIX.

[3] F. M. Cross in D. N. Freedman and J. C. Greenfield (eds), *New Directions in Biblical Archaeology* (New York, 1969), pls 37–9.

[4] E. Stern, *BASOR* CCII (1971), 6–16.

may be recognized among finds at Persepolis and on other sites. Some were engraved in the Court Style, others with animals, or with lively grotesques composed of human and animal heads or trefoil designs built-up from the foreparts of diverse animals.[1] Surviving rings are rarer. They have been found in Cyprus and at Memphis; but the finest are those in the Oxus Treasure.

[1] Woolley, *Ur Excavations* x, pl. 41.

APPENDIX I

PLANT NAMES

Professor Sir Harold Bailey writes:
An interesting addition to the knowledge of the Avestan culture is the list of plant names attested in the text itself or found later in other Iranian sources. Plants (*urvarā-*) are frequently mentioned: for "tree" there is *dāru-*:*dru-* (used also for its wood), and *van-*, *vanā-* widely found in later Iranian, Zor. Pahlavī *wn' *van*, *vun*, New Persian *bun*, Ossetic as second component frequent *bun*, Sogdian *wnh*, and specialized in Balōčī *gwan* "wild pistachio", Wakhī *wan*.[1] A compound Zor. Pahl. *'dwn*, Pāzand *eyvan* "trunk of tree" may be older **adivana-*. The *vaēiti-* "willow" is in Zor. Pahlavī *vēt* and New Persian *bēd*, Khotan-Saka *bī*,[2] with many cognates in Indo-European.[3] For fruit-tree the Zor. Pahlavī has *draxt*, New Persian *dirakht*, which may be traced to the base *darg-*,[4] connected with Ossetic Iron only *dyry*, plural *dyrytä* "fruit" from **darga-*. This seems more satisfactory than tracing *draxt* to a participle of *drang-* "to be firm". Grains are present in *gantuma-* "wheat"; *yava-*, New Persian *jav* "barley", Ossetic *jäu* "millet"; and *hahya-* "grass". The base *sparg-*, *sprag-* "burst out, sprout" is in Avestan *frasparəya-* "sprout", glossed by Zor. Pahl. *spēk*, and Parsi Sanskrit *śākhā*, and is frequent later for "flower", as Wakhī *spray* "flower", Zor. Pahl. *sprahm*, *spram*, New Persian *isparam*, *siparam*.[5] The base *vaxš-* "to grow" gave *fravaxš-* and *fravāxši-* "stem". From *vard-* "to grow" came *varəda-* "a plant name", early in Homeric Greek ῥόδον and dialectal βρόδον "rose", and often in later Iranian, e.g. Sogdian *wrδ*, Armenian (Parthian loan-word) *vard*, Arabic *ward*, Khotan-Saka *valā-*, Simnānī *väl*, Zor. Pahlavī and New Persian *gul*.[6]

Important for the Indo-Iranian vocabulary is the Avestan *varəša-* "plant", with *varəša-jī-* "root", which has survived in Yazgulāmī *warx̌* (*x̌* = *š*) "the name of a herb which blinds cattle", and Shughnī *warx̌* "a hill-grass used as fodder".[7] Like the Avestan *varəša-*, these two words could derive from older **varša-* or **vr̥ša-*. From Alanic the Caucasian Veinakh Chechen has *varš* "grove, thicket" with genitive (used also as adjective) *varšan* (details are in the

[1] These are all listed s.v. *banhya-* in Bailey, *Dictionary*, p. 269.
[2] *Dictionary*, p. 279.
[3] J. Pokorny, *Indogermanisches Etymologisches Wörterbuch* (Bern, 1959), s.v. *u̯ei-*, p. 1120.
[4] Pokorny, p. 473 (*dhergh-* of plant names).
[5] See *Dictionary*, p. 415.
[6] See *Dictionary*, p. 378; Pokorny, p. 1167.
[7] D. I. Edel'man, *Yazguliamsko-Russkij slovar* (Moscow, 1971), p. 290; G. Morgenstierne, *Etymological vocabulary of the Shughni group* (Wiesbaden, 1974), p. 92 (misprinted with -*x*).

APPENDIX

Hoenigswald Festschrift, now in the hands of the editor). It belongs with some 200 words of Chechen and Ossetic contacts.[1] The Ossetic Digoron *bälāsä* "tree" may, though unusually, be traced to older **vlāśa-*, **vrāśa-* with the familiar variation of *-ar-* and *-rā-* (as in Khotan-Saka *garma-*, *grāma-* "hot").[2] The original meaning and etymon of Vedic *vrkṣá-* are elusive. It is used of the *soma-andhas*. In later Veda and onwards it can be translated by "tree". The Avestan compound *haδānaē-pătā-*, Zor. Pahlavī *hdnp'd*, is interpreted by the modern Parsi tradition as "pomegranate" and this can be supported by the etymon *ha-dāna-*"with seeds" stressing the pomegranate grains (granatus), which survives in Yidgha *alāno*, Wazīrī Pašto *wōlang*, Pašto *amang*, from either **ā-dānā* or **ha-dānā-*. The second component *pata-* (in feminine *pātā* and *patā-*) is familiar in the specialized meaning New Persian *pad*, *padah* "white poplar", Balōčī *patk* "populus euphratica" with variants *paθk* and *puxt*.[3] The Zor. Pahlavī has *pt'* and *ptk* **pat* and **patak* in the phrase *narm čēgōn vēt ut pat* (and *patak*) to *Vidēvdāt* 5.1 *varədva-*"soft" of wood. The Zor. Pahlavī transcription of *haδānaē-pātā-* is *hdnp'd* with *-āδ* for Avestan *-āt-*. The conjunct vowel *-aē-* from older *-ai-* diphthong raises an important question. In the compounds with the first component *dūraē-* the *-aē* can be taken for locative, but this does not suit *haδānaē-*. It seems likely that this is the treatment of final *-as* and *-az* as *-ai* beside the usual *-au* (*-ō*) as in Avestan *vīsō.puθra-* "son of the (Great) House". Here in Khotan-Saka the result is *-ai-* passing to *-ē-* and thence to *-ī-* in *bisī-vāraa-* **visai-puθraka-*.[4] Ossetic has several cases of the juncture Digoron *-ē-* and Iron *-ī-*. In one case Digoron has both *-ō-* and *-ē-*: *dzäbō-dur* and *dzäbē-dur* "noble goat, mountain goat" (expressed like Digoron *uezdon γäuänz* "noble deer") from older **Jabas-tura-* to *dzäbäx* "excellent".

The Avestan *haparəsī-* "juniper" is also assured by later Iranian words. Thus there are Balōčī *apūrs*, Yidgha *yovurso* (*-o* from *-ā*), Arab-Persian *awiras*, New Persian *burs* "juniper berries" for which the plant was used, in the Pamir group Shughnī *ambaxc* (*c* = *ts*), Khūfī *ambāws*, Yazgulāmī *əmbis*, Pašto *oboxta*, Sarīkolī *imbarc*.[5] The basic etymon will be *ha-prs-*"with berries"; the main use of the juniper is to add to distilled grains. This *pars-* is from *par-* "to nourish, feed" as in Khotan-Saka *aś-para-* "horse fodder" for the lucerne, called in Zor. Pahlavī *aspast*.[6] The base *par-s-* has then the increment *-s-* (Indo-European *-k̂-*), as in (*s*)*keu-k̂-* (Old Indian *kośa-*) and *uel-k̂-* (Old Indian *valśa-*).[7] This **pero* is also in the Latin *iūniperus* which in spite of long discussion has ignored the Iranian.[8] The *iūni-* could also be taken from (*į*)*oi̯-ni-* with the **oi̯-u̯ā-* of Latin *ūvā-* "grapes", giving a tautologous compound.

[1] A. Genko, "From the cultural past of the Ingushes" (in Russian), *Zapiski kollegii vostokovedov* v (1930), pp. 681–761; V. Abaev, "Osetino-veinaxskie leksiceskie paralleli", *Izvestiya čečeno-ingušskogo naučno-isledovatel'skogo instituta istorii, jazyka i literatury* (Grozny, 1977), pp. 89–119.
[2] Bailey, *Dictionary*, p. 92.
[3] G. Morgenstierne, "Balochi Miscellanea", *AO* xx (1948), p. 290.
[4] *Dictionary*, p. 292.
[5] G. Morgenstierne, "Notes on Shughni", *NTS* I (1928), p. 46; idem, "Notes on Balochi etymology", *NTS* v (1932), p. 40; idem, *Indo-Iranian frontier languages* II (Oslo, 1938), p. 224; idem, *Etymological vocabulary of the Shughni group*, p. 14.
[6] Bailey, *Dictionary*, p. 12.   [7] Pokorny, pp. 853, 1139.
[8] A. Walde and J. B. Hofmann, *Lateinisches etymologisches Wörterbuch* I (Heidelberg, 1930), p. 731.

APPENDIX

The fuel (*aēsma-*) of the *daēvayāzō* "worshippers of the (ancient) gods" was Avestan *nəməδkā-*[1] which is preserved in Ossetic Digoron *nimätk'u*, Iron *nymätk'u* now used of the *Viburnum lantana*. It is a hapax in Yasht 14.55.

The Greek ὄμωμι is cited by Plutarch as employed in a cult of Areimanios. The discussion by E. Benveniste[2] tended to show that the equivalent Iranian was **humāma-* preserved in Syriac *humām-ā* and New Persian *humāmah*. A variant is in Greek ἀμωμίς. As a sacred libation it corresponded to Avestan *haoma-* of the Mazdean cult. This *humāmah* can be analysed as *hum-āma-ka-* with the suffix *-āma-* added to a word *hum(a)-*. This suffix *-āma-*, which seems not to be found in Old Indian, is also in Armenian Parthian *varšamak* "veil", Georgian *varšamang-i*, and later New Persian *vāšamah*, *bāšamah* from *var-*"to cover" with increment *var-š-*. The suffix can also be seen in Khotan-Saka *bamggāma-* "cuirass" from the same *var-* with increment *-k-* from **var-k-āma-*.[3] The Zor. Pahlavī *vātām* "almond", New Persian *bādām* may show the same suffix added to *vāta-*. A variant *-āma-* is found in Zor. Pahlavī *'dw'm *aδvām* beside *'dw'n *aδvān* "bridle".[4] Similar is Zor. Pahlavī *ōstām* "district"[5] beside Sogdian *'wst'n *ōstān*, with Pāzand *hustạm*. If *hum-āma-ka-* is adopted instead of *hu-mā-ma-ka-* with *hu-* "good", the *hum-* will belong with Khotan-Saka *huma-* "soft"[6] as an ablaut form reduced grade to the *haum-* of the plant *hauma-*, Avestan *haoma-*, Zor. Pahlavī *hōm*. For the sense of "softness" expressed by an Indo-European base *sau-* or *seu-:su-* with increment *-m-* (as in Khotan-Saka *tsu-m-* from *tsu-* "go", from older *čyau-:čyu-*), reference can be made to *huma-* and to the Yazgulāmī *xu̯am* (**hu̯am*) "soft chaff" and related Pamir words.[7] The meaning "soft" was also developed in Old Indian *saumya-* from *soma-*.

Perfumes are named from *baud-* in *baoiδi-* and adjective *hubaoiδi-*. This is well attested in later Iranian: Ossetic Digoron *bodä*, Khotan-Saka *bū*, and verbal *būtte*, Sogdian *βwδ, βwstn* "garden", New Persian *būstān*. The Avestan perfume *urvāsnā-* recurs in New Persian *rāsan* and earlier in Zor. Pahlavī *rāsn*, but with disputed meaning; the modern Parsi tradition gives sandal-wood, but Persian dictionaries propose elecampane (*Inula hellenium*) or juniper.

Four drugs used at childbirth are listed in *Vidēvdāt* 15.14, *baŋha-*, *šaēta-*, *γnāna-* and *fraspāta-*. The *baŋha-* is equated with the later *bang* identified with *mang* "hemp" inducing unconsciousness. The others await identification.

The likelihood that the Avestan *misti-* when associated with plants is connected with Khotan-Saka *miṣṣa-* "field" and Kroraina *misa-* used in field-work has been considered.[8] The West Iranian cognates are preserved in Armenian *mšak* "farmer" and Georgian *mušak'-l*, *muša* "workman". With

---

[1] C. Bartholomae, *Altiranisches Wörterbuch*, 2nd ed. (Berlin, 1961), p. 1067 (**nəməδkā-*).

[2] E. Benveniste, "Un rite zervanite chez Plutarche", *JA* CCXV (1929), pp. 287–96.

[3] Bailey, *Dictionary*, p. 265.

[4] See *Dictionary*, p. 308, s.v. *byāna-* (Avestan *aiwiδāna-*).

[5] *Mēnōk ī xrat*, ed. T. D. Anklesaria (Bombay, 1913), 55.5; *The Pahlavi Dinkard*, ed. D. M. Madan (Bombay, 1911), 326.21.

[6] Bailey, *Dictionary*, p. 491.

[7] Cited in H. W. Bailey, "Indo-iranica", *Indologica Taurinensia* VIII–IX (1980–1), p. 17 (*Dr Ludwig Sternbach Commemoration Volume*).

[8] H. W. Bailey, "Iranian *miṣṣa*, Indian *bīja*", *BSOAS* XVIII (1956), 32–42.

APPENDIX

Avestan *miz-* the meaning may be "to work at field work in sowing seeds". A slight hint that this *maiz-* is from an Indo-European *meiĝ-* distinct from *meiĝh-* is noted in the article cited. Cognates outside Iranian are Baltic Lithuanian *miežỹs* 'barley grain", Old Prussian *moasis* "barley", Lettish *màize* "bread".[1]

In the later Magian book, the *Bundahišn*, chapter 16 (TD$_2$ 119.5ff.) lists plant names which are the special care of Mazdean genii. The list is introduced by the phrase *ēn-ič gōβēt* "this also is stated" which is usually accompanied by the words *pat dēn* "in our sacred text". It will at least be a venerable tradition.

[1] H. W. Bailey, "Miṣṣa suppletum", *BSOAS* XXI (1958), 41.

APPENDIX II

THE ACHAEMENID DYNASTY[1]

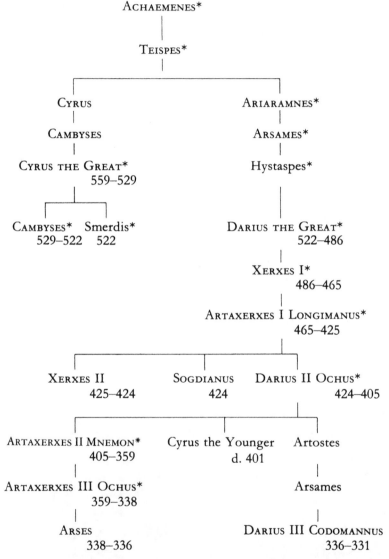

[1] Based on Kent, *Old Persian*, p. 158. Asterisks mark those Achaemenids who are named in the Old Persian inscriptions.

BIBLIOGRAPHY

The abbreviations used in the bibliographies and footnotes are listed below.

AA	*Archäologischer Anzeiger* (Beiblatt zum Jahrbuch des deutschen archäologischen Instituts) (Berlin)
AAA	*Annals of Archaeology and Anthropology* (Liverpool)
AAntASH	*Acta antiqua academiae scientiarum Hungaricae* (Budapest)
AArchASH	*Acta archaeologica academiae scientiarum Hungaricae* (Budapest)
ABSA	*Annual of the British School at Athens*
Acta Iranica	Acta Iranica (encyclopédie permanente des études iraniennes) (Tehran-Liège-Leiden)
Aegyptus	*Aegyptus* 'Rivista Italiana di Egittologia e di Papirologia) (Milan)
AfO	*Archiv für Orientforschung* (Berlin)
AHM	I. Gershevitch, *The Avestan Hymn to Mithra* (Cambridge, 1959)
AION	*Annali: Istituto Orientale di Napoli* (s.l. sezione linguistica; n.s. new series) (Naples)
Air.Wb.	C. Bartholomae, *Altiranisches Wörterbuch* (Strassburg, 1904; 2nd ed. Berlin, 1961)
AJA	*American Journal of Archaeology* (Baltimore)
AJAH	*American Journal of Ancient History* (Cambridge, Mass.)
AJSLL	*American Journal of Semitic Languages and Literature* (Chicago)
AK	*Arkheologiya* (Kiev)
AMI	*Archäologische Mitteilungen aus Iran* (old series 9 vols 1929–38; new series 1968–) (Berlin)
Anatolia	*Anatolia/Anadolu* (revue annuelle d'archéologie) (Ankara)
Ancient Egypt	*Ancient Egypt (and the East)* (journal of the British School of Archaeology in Egypt) (London, 1914–35)
ANET	J. Pritchard, *Ancient Near Eastern Texts*, 3rd ed. (Princeton, N.J., 1969)
AnOr	*Analecta Orientalia* (Rome)
ANSMN	*American Numismatic Society Museum Notes* (New York)

BIBLIOGRAPHY

ANSNNM American Numismatic Society Numismatic Notes and Monographs (New York)
ANSNS American Numismatic Society Numismatic Studies (New York)
Anthropos *Anthropos* (International review of Ethnology and Linguistics) (Fribourg, Switzerland)
Antike Kunst Halbjahresschrift herausgegeben von der Vereinigung der Freunde Antiker Kunst (Basle)
Antiquity *Antiquity* (a periodical review of archaeology edited by Glyn Daniel) (Cambridge)
AOAW *Anzeiger der Österreichischen Akademie der Wissenschaften* (Phil.-Hist. Klasse) (Vienna)
APAW *Abhandlungen der Preussischen (Deutschen) Akademie der Wissenschaften* (Phil.-Hist. Klasse) (Berlin)
Archaeology *Archaeology* (official publication of the Archaeological Institute of America) (New York)
ArOr *Archiv Orientální* (Quarterly Journal of African, Asian and Latin American Studies) (Prague)
Artibus Asiae *Artibus Asiae* (Institute of Fine Arts, New York Univesity) (Dresden, Ascona)
ASAE *Annals du Service des Antiquités de l'Égypte* (Cairo)
ASE *Arkheologicheskii Sbornik, Hermitage* (Leningrad)
Athenaeum *Athenaeum* (Studi Periodici di Letteratura e Storia dell' Antichità; new series 1923–) (Pavia)
AU *Arkheologiya Ukrainskoy RSR*, 2 vols (Kiev, 1971)
BA *Beiträge zur Assyriologie* (Leipzig)
BASOR *Bulletin of the American Schools of Oriental Research* (Baltimore, Maryland)
Berytus *Berytus* (archaeological studies published by the Museum of Archaeology and the American University of Beirut) (Copenhagen)
BIFAO *Bulletin de l'Institut francais d'archéologie orientale* (Cairo)
BiOr *Bibliotheca Orientalis* (Leiden)
BMQ *British Museum Quarterly* (London)
BSO(A)S *Bulletin of the School of Oriental (and African) Studies* (University of London)
CAH *The Cambridge Ancient History*, 12 vols; 1st edition Cambridge, 1924–39. Revised edition 1970–
CDAFI *Cahiers de la Délégation archéologique française en Iran* (Paris)

BIBLIOGRAPHY

CHI	*The Cambridge History of Iran*
Chiron	*Chiron* (Mitteilungen der Kommission für alte Geschichte und Epigraphik des Deutschen archäologischen Instituts) (Munich)
CIIr	*Corpus Inscriptionum Iranicarum* (London)
CIS	Corpus Inscriptionum Semiticarum (Paris)
CP	*Classical Philology* (Chicago)
CQ	*The Classical Quarterly* (new series) (Oxford)
CRAI	*Comptes rendus de l'Académie des inscriptions et belles lettres* (Paris)
Dacia	*Dacia* (Revue d'archéologie et d'histoire ancienne) (old series 1924–47; new series 1957–) (Bucharest)
DB	*The Behistun Inscription of Darius I*
East and West	*East and West* (Quarterly published by the Instituto Italiano per il Medio ed Estremo Oriente) (Rome)
Ex Oriente Lux	*Jaarbericht van het Vooraziatisch-Egyptisch Genootschop. Ex Oriente Lux* (Leiden)
Expedition	*Expedition* (The University Museum Magazine of Archaeology/Anthropology, University of Pennsylvania) (Philadelphia)
GJ	*The Geographical Journal* (London)
Greece and Rome	*Greece and Rome* (published for the Classical Association) (Oxford)
Hermes	*Hermes* (Zeitschrift für klassische Philologie) (Wiesbaden)
Hesperia	*Hesperia* (Journal of the American School of Classical Studies at Athens) (Princeton, N.J.)
Historia	*Historia* (Journal of Ancient History) (Wiesbaden)
HO	*Handbuch der Orientalistik*, ed. B. Supuler (Leiden–Cologne)
HSCP	*Harvard Studies in Classical Philology* (Cambridge, Mass.)
HUCA	*Hebrew Union College Annual* (Cincinnati)
GRBS	*Greek, Roman and Byzantine Studies* (Cambridge, Mass.)
IA	*Iranica Antiqua* (Leiden)
IG	*Inscriptiones Graecae* (Berlin 1873–)
IOS	*Israel Oriental Series* (Jerusalem)
Iran	*Iran* (journal of the British Institute of Persian Studies) (London–Tehran)
Iraq	*Iraq* (journal of the British School of Archaeology in Iraq) (London)

BIBLIOGRAPHY

JA	*Journal Asiatique* (Paris)
JAOS	*Journal of the American Oriental Society* (New York)
JBL	*Journal of Biblical Literature* (Boston)
JCOI	*Journal of the K. R. Cama Oriental Institute*, 29 vols (Bombay, 1922–35)
JCS	*Journal of Cuneiform Studies* (New Haven, Conn.)
JEA	*Journal of Egyptian Archaeology* (London)
JHS	*Journal of Hellenic Studies* (London)
JNES	*Journal of Near Eastern Studies* (Chicago)
JSS	*Journal of Semitic Studies* (Manchester)
Klio	*Klio* (Beiträge zur Alten Geschichte) (Berlin)
KSIAK	*Kratkie Soobshcheniya Instituta Arkheologii* (Kiev)
KSIAM	*Kratkie Soobshcheniya Instituta Arkheologii* (Moscow)
KSIIMK	*Kratkie soobshcheniya o dokladakh i polevykh issledovaniyakh Instituta istorii materialnoi kultury AN SSR* (Moscow)
Kuml	*Kuml* (Aarbog for Jysk Arkaeologisk Selskab) (Aarhus)
KZ	*Zeitschrift für vergleichende Sprachforschung, begründet von Albert Kuhn* (Göttingen)
LCL	Loeb Classical Library (Cambridge, Mass.–London)
Levant	*Levant* (journal of the British School of Archaeology in Jerusalem) (London)
MASP	*Materialy po Arkheologii Severnovo Prichërnomoria* (Odessa)
MDAFA	Mémoires de la délégation archéologique française en Afghanistan (Paris)
MDAI	Mémoires de la Délégation archéologique en Iran (Paris)
MDOG	*Mitteilungen der Deutschen Orient-Gesellschaft* (Berlin)
MDP	Mémoires de la Délégation en Perse (Paris)
MIA	*Materialy i Issledovaniya po Arkheologii SSSR* (Moscow–Leningrad)
MMAB	*The Metropolitan Museum of Art Bulletin* (old series 1905–42; new series 1942–) (New York)
Le Muséon	*Le Muséon* (Revue d'Études Orientales) (Louvain–Paris)
NC	*Numismatic Chronicle* (London)
NTS	*Norsk Tidsskrift for Sprogvidenskap: Norwegien Journal of Linguistics* (Oslo)
Oriens	*Oriens* (journal of the International Society for Oriental Research) (Leiden)

BIBLIOGRAPHY

Orientalia	Orientalia (a quarterly published by the Faculty of Ancient Oriental Studies, Pontifical Biblical Institute) new series (Rome)
OLZ	Orientalische Literaturzeitung (Berlin–Leipzig)
Paléorient	Paléorient (pluridisciplinary review of prehistory and protohistory of southwestern Asia) (Paris)
Pauly	Pauly, A. Real-Encyclopädie der classischen Altertumswissenschaft, ed. G. Wissowa (Stuttgart, 1894–)
PBA	Proceedings of the British Academy (London)
Persica	Persica (annuaire de la Société Néderlands-Iranienne) (Leiden)
PFT	R. T. Hallock, Persepolis Fortification Tablets (Chicago, 1969)
Philologus	Philologus (Zeitschrift für das classische Alterthum) (Göttingen–Leipzig–Berlin)
Phoenix	Phoenix (The Journal of the Classical Association of Canada) (Toronto)
PSBA	Proceedings of the Society of Biblical Archaeology (London)
PTT	G. G. Cameron, The Persepolis Treasury Tablets (Chicago, 1948)
RA	Revue d'assyriologie et d'archéologie orientale (Paris)
RAA	Revue des arts asiatiques (Paris)
RHR	Revue de l'Histoire des Religions (Paris)
RN	Revue Numismatique (Paris)
RSO	Rivista degli Studi Orientali (Rome)
RT	Recueil de Travaux relatifs à la philologie et à l'archéologie égyptiennes et assyriennes (Paris)
SA	Sovetskaya Arkheologia (Moscow)
SBE	Sacred Books of the East (Oxford)
SCBO	Scriptorum Classicorum Bibliotheca Oxoniensis (Oxford)
SCO	Studi classici e orientali (Pisa)
Semitica	Semitica (cahiers publiés par l'Institut d'études sémitiques) (Paris)
SPA	A Survey of Persian Art, ed. A. U. Pope and P. Ackerman, 6 vols (Text pp. 1–2817) (Oxford–London–New York, 1938–9); latest reprint 13 vols (Ashiya, Japan, 1981); vol. XIV New Studies 1938–1960 (Text pp. 2879–3205) (Oxford–London, 1967); vol. XV Biblio-

graphy of Pre-Islamic Persian Art to *1938* (cols 1–340), Reprint of *Index to Text Volumes I–III (i–vi)* (pp. 1–63) (Ashiya, Japan, 1977); vol. XVI *Bibliography of Islamic Persian Art to 1938* (cols 341–854) (Ashiya, Japan, 1977); vol. XVII *New Studies 1960–1973. In Memoriam Arthur Upham Pope, Part I Pre-Islamic Studies* (pp. 3207–3717) (not yet published); vol. XVIII *New Studies 1960–1973…, Part II Islamic Architecture* (not yet published); vol. XIX *New Studies 1960–1973…, Part III Islamic Art* (not yet published). References are given to page numbers only.

StIr	*Studia Iranica* (Leiden)
SVOD	Svod Arkheologicheskikh Istochnikov. Arkheologiya SSSR (Moscow)
Syria	*Syria* (Revue d'art oriental et d'archéologie) (Paris)
TPS	*Transactions of the Philological Society* (London)
TSBA	*Transactions of the Society of Biblical Archaeology* (London)
UE	*Ur Excavations. Reports* (Joint Expedition of the British Museum and of the University of Pennsylvania in Mesopotamia Publications) (London, 1927–)
UET	*Ur Excavations. Texts* (London, 1928–)
UGE	J. Marquart, *Untersuchungen zur Geschichte von Eran.* 2 vols. (Leipzig, 1905–6)
WO	*Die Welt des Orients* (Göttingen)
WZKM	*Wiener Zeitschrift für die Kunde des Morgenlandes* (Vienna)
YCS	*Yale Classical Studies* (New Haven, Conn.)
ZA	*Zeitschrift für Assyriologie* (Berlin)
ZAS	*Zeitschrift für Aegyptische Sprache* (Leipzig)
ZDMG	*Zeitschrift der deutschen morgenländischen Gesellschaft* (Wiesbaden)

BIBLIOGRAPHY

CHAPTER I

Amiet, P. *Elam*. Auvers sur Oise, 1966.
Cameron, G. G. *History of Early Iran*. Chicago, 1936.
Cuq, E. "Les actes juridiques susiens", *RA* xxviii (1931), pp. 47–73.
—— "Le droit élamite d'après les actes juridiques de Suse", *RA* xxix (1932), pp. 149–83.
Ghirshman, R. "L'Elam et les recherches à Dur Untashi (Tchoga-Zanbil)", *IA* iii (1963), pp. 1–21.
Grayson, A. K. *Assyrian and Babylonian Chronicles*. Locust Valley, N.Y., 1975 (Texts from Cuneiform Sources 5).
Hinz, W. *Das Reich Elam*. Stuttgart, 1964. Tr. J. Barnes as *The Lost World of Elam*. London, 1972.
—— "Zur Entzifferung der elamischen Strichschrift", *IA* ii (1962), pp. 1–17.
Hole, F., Flannery, K. V. and Neely, J. A. *Prehistory and Ecology of the Deh Luran Plain*. Ann Arbor, Mich., 1969.
Hüsing, G. *Die einheimischen Quellen zur Geschichte Elams* i: *Altelamische Texte*. Leipzig, 1916.
König, F. W. "Mutterrecht und Thronfolge im alten Elam", in *Festschrift der Nationalbibliothek in Wien* (Vienna, 1926), pp. 529–52.
Klima, J. "Untersuchungen zum elamischen Erbrecht", *ArOr* xxviii (1960), pp. 5–53.
—— "Le droit élamite au II-me millénaire av. n.è. et sa position envers le droit babylonien", *ArOr* xxxi (1963), pp. 283–308.
Koschaker, P. "Göttliches und weltliches Recht nach den Urkunden aus Susa", *Orientalia* iv (1935), pp. 38–81.
—— "Fratriarchat, Hausgemeinschaft und Mutterrecht in Keilschriftrechten", *ZA* vii (1933), pp. 1–89.
—— "Randnotizen zu neueren keilschriftlichen Rechtsurkunden", *ZA* ix (1936), pp. 221–32.
Labat, R. "Elam c. 1600–1200 B.C.", *CAH* ii, 29.
—— "Elam and Western Persia, c. 1200–1000 B.C.", *CAH* ii, 33.
Lambert, M. "Littérature élamite", in *L'Histoire générale des littératures* (Paris, 1961), pp. 36–41.
Le Breton, L. "The Early Periods at Susa, Mesopotamian Relations", *Iraq* xix (1957), pp. 79–124.
Mémoires de la Délégation en Perse [*MDP*] I–XIII. Paris, 1900–1912. (The later volumes appeared until 1943 under different titles; after 1943 the title is: *Mémoires de la Mission archéologique en Iran*. All the more important sources are published in this series.)
de Meyer, L. "Une famille susienne du temps des *sukkalmahhu*", *IA* i (1961), pp. 17 sqq.
Porada, E. *The Art of Ancient Iran*. New York, 1965.
—— *Ancient Iran. The art of pre-Islamic times*. London, 1965.

BIBLIOGRAPHY

Reiner, E. "The Elamite language", in *Altkleinasiatische Sprachen* (Leiden–Köln, 1969), pp. 54–118 (*HO* I. II. 1. 2).

Steinkeller, P. "The Question of Marhaši: A Contribution to the Historical Geography of Iran in the Third Millennium B.C.", *ZA* LXXII (1982), pp. 237–65.

Stève, M.-J. "Textes élamites de Tchogha-Zanbil", *IA* II (1962), pp. 22–76; III (1963), pp. 102–23.

Stolper, M. W. "On the Dynasty of Šimaški and the Early Sukkalmahs", *ZA* LXXII (1982), pp. 42–67.

Vallat, F. *Suse et l'Élam*. Paris, Éditions ADPF, 1980 (Recherche sur les grandes civilisations, Études élamites, Mémoire 1).

Vanden Berghe, L. *Archéologie de l'Iran ancien*. Leiden, 1959.

Yusifov, Yu. B. *Elam, sotsial'no-ekonomickeskaya istoriya*. Moscow, 1968.

—— "Elamskiye khozyaystvennyye dokumenty iz Suz", *VDI* 1963.3, pp. 201–61.

CHAPTER 3

1. *General*

Partly because the sources are scanty, and partly because they require expertise in a variety of ancient languages, the history of Media has remained for a long time a field of arbitrary conjectures. This is why the work, hitherto widely relied upon, of J. v. Prášek, F. W. König, I. Aliev, W. Culican and others cannot be recommended. They are partly obsolete and partly unreliable in respect of facts well established. Less out of date is G. G. Cameron, *History of Early Iran* (Chicago, 1936), but this book is mainly concerned with Elam. The fullest available collection of facts, especially those extracted from cuneiform sources, along with an evaluation of all the sources in Median history including the Greek ones, can be found in I. M. Diakonoff, *History of Media from the earliest times to the end of the fourth century B.C.* (Moscow–Leningrad, 1956) (in Russian). However, this book, too, must be viewed critically in respect of the understanding it proposes of some of the information derived from the sources, and the archaeological data which it adduces are by now partly obsolete. Brief outlines of Median history are offered in some general histories of Iran, among which the following may be recommended, due account being taken of the reservations stated above:

Diakonoff, M. M. *An Outline of the History of Ancient Iran* (in Russian). Moscow, 1961. (NB: The author of this book should not be confused with I. M. Diakonoff.)

Frye, R. N. *The Heritage of Persia*. London, 1962.

Ghirshman, R. *Iran from the earliest times to the Islamic conquest*. Harmondsworth, 1954 (Penguin/Pelican Books).

BIBLIOGRAPHY

2. *Written sources and studies about the population of Iran in the third to second millennia B.C., Elam excluded*

(Listed as near as possible in the chronological order of the corresponding historical events)

Jacobsen, T. *The Sumerian King List.* Chicago, 1939 (The Oriental Institute of the University of Chicago. Assyriological Studies, 11).
Ebeling, E. and Meissner, B. (eds.). *Reallexikon der Assyriologie* II (Berlin–Leipzig, 1938), *s.v.* Datenlisten.
Jaritz, K. "Die kassitischen Sprachreste", *Anthropos* LII (1957), pp. 850–98.
Balkan, K. *Die Sprache der Kassiten (Kassitenstudien* 1). New Haven. Conn., 1954 (American Oriental Series 37).
Jankowska, N. B. "Communal self-government and the king of the state of Arrapḫa", *JESHO* XII (1969), pp. 233–82. (A picture of Hurrian communities of the second millennium B.C. in the foothills of the Zagros.)
Luckenbill, D. D. *Ancient Records of Assyria and Babylonia* I. Chicago, 1926.
Mémoires de la Délégation en Perse [*MDP*] V, XI *et al.* (inscriptions of Elamite Kings).

3. *Iranian-speaking tribes, after and prior to their arrival in Iran. Iran east of Media (archaeological data)*

Chernikov, S. S. "The Role of the Andronovo Culture in the History of Central Asia and Kazakhstan" (in Russian), *Kratkie Soobshchenia instituta etnographii* XXVI (1957), pp. 30–1.
Diakonoff, M. M. "Genesis of Class Society in Bactria" (in Russian), *SA* XIX (1954), pp. 121–40.
Formozov, A. A. "On the Origin of the Andronovo Culture" (in Russian), *KSIIMK* XXXIX (1951), pp. 3–18.
Gafurov, B. G. and Litvinskii, B. A. (eds.). *History of the Tajik People*, vol. I, From the Most Ancient Times to the 5th Century A.D. (in Russian) (Moscow, 1963), ch. 2 by B. A. Litvinskii.
Ghirshman, R. "Fouilles de Nad-i-Ali dans le Seistan Afghan", *RAA* XIII (1939), pp. 10–22.
Kammenhuber, A. *Hippologia Hethitica.* Wiesbaden, 1961.
—— *Die Arier.* Wiesbaden, 1968.
Kiselev, S. V. *Ancient History of Southern Siberia* (in Russian). Moscow, 1951.
Krivtsova-Grakova, O. A. *The steppes of the Volga and the Black Sea Regions in the Late Bronze Age* (in Russian). Moscow–Leningrad, 1955 (MIA 46).
Mandelshtam, A. M. *Objects of the Bronze Age from South Tajikistan* (in Russian) (Ancient funerary rites). Leningrad, 1968 (MIA 145).
Masson, V. M. *The Ancient Agricultural Civilizations of Margiana* (in Russian). Moscow, 1959 (MIA 73).
Diakonoff, I. M. Review of the preceding (in Russian), *VDI* 1960, 3, pp. 196–203.

BIBLIOGRAPHY

Piggott, S. *Prehistoric India*. Harmondsworth, 1952; repr. 1961 (Penguin Books).
Shelov, D. B. (ed.). *Problems of Scythian and Sarmatian Archaeology* (in Russian). Moscow, 1954.
Tolstov, S. P. *Ancient Chorasmia* (in Russian). Moscow, 1948.

4. Median art and archaeology

Barnett, R. D. "Median Art", *IA* II (1962), pp. 77-95.
Cuyler Young Jr., T. *Proto-Historic Western Iran: an Archaeological and Historical Review, Problems and Possible Interpretations* (Dissertation, University of Pennsylvania). University Microfilms Inc., Ann Arbor, Mich., 1963.
—— "A Comparative Ceramic Chronology for Western Iran, 1500-500 B.C.", *Iran* III (1965), pp. 53-86.
Dyson, R. H. "Digging in Iran: Hasanlu", *Expedition* I, 3 (Spring, 1959), pp. 4-18.
—— "Hansanlu and Early Iran", *Archaeology* XIII (1960), pp. 118-29.
—— "Notes on Weapons and Chronology in Northern Iran around 1000 B.C." in *Dark Ages and Nomads c. 1000 B.C.* Istanbul, 1964.
—— "Ninth Century Men in Western Iran", *Archaeology* XVII (1964), pp. 3-11.
Ghirshman, R. *Fouilles de Sialk, près de Kashan, 1933, 1934, 1937* II. Paris, 1939 (Musée du Louvre, Série archéologique 5).
—— "Notes iraniennes IV: Le Trésor de Saqqez, les origines de l'art mède et les bronzes du Luristan", *Artibus Asiae* XIII (1950), p. 181-206.
—— *Village perse-achéménide*. Paris, 1954 (Mémoires de la Mission archéologique en Iran 36).
Godard, A. *Le Trésor de Ziwiyé*. Haarlem, 1950.
Herzfeld, E. *Archaeological History of Iran*. London, 1935.
—— *Iran in the Ancient East*. London–New York, 1941.
—— *The Persian Empire, Studies in Geography and Ethnography of the Ancient Near East*. Wiesbaden, 1968. (Partly obsolete, needs to be used with discernment. See also Herzfeld's contributions in *AMI*.)
McCown, D. E. "Relative Stratigraphy and Chronology of Iran", in R. W. Ehrich (ed.), *Relative chronologies in old world archaeology*. Chicago, 1954.
Negahban, E. O. "Notes on some objects from Marlik", *JNES* XXIV (1965), pp. 309-27. Cf. also *Illustrated London News*, 28 April 1962; 2 May 1962.
Porada, E. "The Hasanlu Bowl", *Expedition* I, 3 (Spring, 1959), pp. 19-22.
—— *Ancient Iran. The art of pre-Islamic times*. London, 1965.
Terrace, E. L. B. "Some Recent Finds from Northwest Persia", *Syria* XXXIX (1962), pp. 212-24.
Vanden Berghe, L. *Archéologie de l'Iran ancien*. Leiden, 1959 (Documenta et monumenta Orientis antiqui 6).

5. Cuneiform sources

(a) *Collections of sources*

Diakonoff, I. M. "Assyrian and Babylonian sources for the History of Urartu" (in Russian), *VDI* 1951.2, pp. 255-356; 1951.3, pp. 205-52; 1951.4, pp.

BIBLIOGRAPHY

283–305. (Collection of texts in Russian translation relating to Asia Minor, the Armenian highlands, the Cimmerians, the Scyths and Northern Iran, with detailed historical, geographical and factual commentary.)

Grayson, A. K. *Assyrian and Babylonian Chronicles.* Locust Valley, N.Y., 1975 (Texts from Cuneiform Sources 5).

König, F. W. *Handbuch der chaldischen Inschriften,* 2 vols. Graz, 1955–7 (*AfO* beiheft 8). (Contains the same material as the preceding edition, but the translation is at times less reliable.)

Luckenbill D. D. *Ancient Records of Assyria and Babylonia,* I–II. Chicago, 1926–7. (Translation only, but with bibliography relating to the original texts.)

Melikishvili, G. A. *Urartian Cuneiform Inscriptions* (in Russian). Moscow, 1960.

Waterman, L. *Royal Correspondence of the Assyrian Empire,* 4 vols. Ann Arbor, 1930–6. (Convenient collection of the letters of the Assyrian royal archive, but with a translation wholly unreliable; for corrections see I. M. Diakonoff, above, as well as A. L. Oppenheim, "Idiomatic Akkadian", *JAOS* LXI (1941), pp. 251–71.)

(b) Individual sources, in the main additional to the preceding; they are listed in an order corresponding approximately to the chronology of the historical events to which they relate

Ebeling, E. and Meissner, B. (eds.) *Reallexikon der Assyriologie* II (Berlin–Leipzig, 1939), *s.v.* Eponymen.

Weidner, E. F. "Die Feldzüge Samsi-Adads V. gegen Babylonien" *AfO* IX (1933), pp. 89–104.

Thureau-Dangin, F. *Une rélation de l'huitième campagne de Sargon II.* Paris, 1912. Cf. Also B. Meissner, *ZA* XXXIV (1922), pp. 113–22; E. F. Weidner, *AfO* XII (1937–9), pp. 144–99.

Delitzsch, F. *Die babylonische Chronik.* Leipzig, 1906.

Borger, R. *Die Inschriften Asarhaddons, Königs von Assyrien.* Graz, 1956.

Heidel, A. "A New Hexagonal Prism of Esarhaddon", *Sumer* XII (1956), pp. 95–9.

Knudtzon, J. A. *Die Gebete an den Sonnengott für Staat und königliches Haus aus der Zeit Asarhaddons und Assurbanipals.* Leipzig, 1983.

Klauber, E. G. *Politisch-religiöse Texte aus der Sargonidenzeit.* Leipzig, 1913.

Wiseman, D. J. "The Vassal-Treaties of Esarhaddon", *Iraq* XX (1958), pp. 1–99 and pls 1–53.

Streck, M. *Assurbanipal,* 3 vols. Leipzig, 1916.

Weidner, E. F. "Die älteste Nachricht über das persische Königshaus", *AfO* VII (1931–2), pp. 1–7.

Gadd, C. J. *The Fall of Nineveh.* Ocford, 1923.

Wiseman, D. J. *Chronicles of Chaldaean Kings (626–556 B.C.) in the British Museum.* London, 1956.

Yusifov, Y. B. "Elamite Economic Documents from Susa" (in Russian), *VDI* 1963.3, pp. 199–261.

Langdon, S. *Neubabylonische Königsinschriften.* Leipzig, 1912 (Vorderasiatische Bibliothek 4).

BIBLIOGRAPHY

Gadd, C. J. "The Harran Inscriptions of Habonidus", *Anatolian Studies* VIII (1958), pp. 35-92.
Smith, Sydney (tr.) *Babylonian Historical Texts relating to the capture and downfall of Babylon*. London, 1924.
Weissbach, F. *Die Keilinschriften der Achämeniden*. Leipzig, 1911 (Vorderasiatische Bibliothek 3).
Kent, R. G. *Old Persian: Grammar, Texts, Lexicon*, 2nd ed. New Haven, 1953.
Brandenstein, W. and Mayrhofer, M. *Handbuch des Altpersischen*. Wiesbaden, 1964.

(c) Studies of the sources

Aro, J. "Remarks on the practice of extispicy in the time of Esarhaddon and Assurbanipal", in *La divination en Mésopotamie ancienne et dans les régions voisines*: XIVe Rencontre Assyriologique Internationale (Paris, 1966), pp. 109-17.
Dandamayev, M. A. *Iran under the First Achaemenids* (in Russian). Moscow, 1963. German translation, Wiesbaden, 1976.
Diakonoff, I. M. "The Last Years of the Urartian State according to Assyrian and Babylonian Sources" (in Russian), *VDI* 1951.2, pp. 29-39.
—— "Armenia and Asia Minor about 600 B.C." (in Russian), *VDI* 1981.2, pp. 34-64.
—— *Pre-History of the Armenian People* (in Russian). Erevan, 1968.
Forrer, E. *Die Provinzeinteilung des assyrischen Reiches*. Leipzig, 1921.
Grantovsky, E. A. "Istoriya Mîdii ot drevneyshikh vremen do kontsa IV v. do n.e., *Sovetskoe vostokovedenie* 1958.3, pp. 151-5. (Review of I. M. Diakonoff, *History of Media*, in Russian.)
—— "The Old Iranian Ethnical Term Parsava-Pārsa" (in Russian), *Kratkie soobshchenia Instituta Narodov Azii* xxx (1961), pp. 3-19.
—— "Iranian Personal Names from the Region of Urmiyah in the 9th-8th centuries B.C." (in Russian), in *Drevnii Mir. Sbornik v chest akademika V. V. Struve* (Moscow, 1962), pp. 250-65.
Jankowska, N. B. "Some Problems of Economy of the Assyrian Empire", in I. M. Diakonoff (ed.), *Ancient Mesopotamia. Socio-economic History*. Moscow, 1969.
Labat, R. "Kaštariti, Phraorte et les débuts de l'histoire Mède", *JA* CCXLIX (1961), pp. 1-12.
Landsberger, B. and Bauer, T. "Zu neuveröffentlichten Geschichtsquellen der Zeit von Asarhaddon bis Nabonid", *ZA* III (1926), pp. 1 sqq.
Melikishvili, G. A. "Some Problems of the History of the Mannaean Kingdom" (in Russian), *VDI*, 1948.3, pp. 57-72.
—— *Ancient Oriental Evidence relating to the History of the Peoples of Transcaucasia*, vol. I, *Nairi-Urartu* (in Russian). Tblisi, 1954.
Meyer, E. "Die ersten datierbaren Zeugnisse der iranischen Sprache", *KZ* XLII (1902), pp. 14 sqq.
Olmstead, A. T. E. *History of Assyria*. New York-London, 1923.
—— *History of the Persian Empire*. Chicago, 1948.

BIBLIOGRAPHY

Piotrovskii, B. B. "The Scythians and the Ancient Orient" (in Russian), *SA* XIX (1954), pp. 141–58.

—— *The Kingdom of Van (Urartu)* (in Russian). Moscow, 1959. Italian translation, Rome, 1968.

Speiser, E. A. "Southern Kurdistan in the Annals of Ashurnasirpal and Today", *Annals of the American Schools of Oriental Research* VIII (1928), pp. 1ff.

Streck, M. "Das Gebiet der heutigen Landschaften Armenien, Kurdistan und Westpersien nach den babylonisch-assyrischen Keilinschriften", *ZA* XV (1900), pp. 257–382. (A fundamental work on the historical geography of Media up to the emergence of the Median kingdom, even if naturally by now obsolete in many respects; however, the fairly numerous later works, not being based on so full an exploitation of the available material, are far from invariably furthering the clarification of historico-geographical facts.)

Struve, V. V. "The Homeland of Zoroastrianism" (in Russian), in *Etyudy po istorii Severnogo Prichërnomoriya, Kavkaza u Sredney Azii*. Leningrad, 1968.

Sulimirski, T. "Scythian Antiquities in Western Asia", *Artibus Asiae* XVII (1954), pp. 282–318.

Tadmor, H. "The Three Last Decades of Assyria" (in Russian), *Trudy XXV Mezhdunarodnogo Kongressa vostokovedov* I (Moscow, 1962), pp. 240–1.

6. *Classical sources*

Diodorus, *Histories*, with an English translation by C. H. Oldfather, 10 vols. London, 1946–57 (LCL).

Ctesias:

—— Ctesias, *Persica* in Photius, *Bibliothèque* I, ed. and tr. R. Henry. Brussels, 1947; repr. Paris, 1959.

—— Gilmore, J. (ed.) *The fragments of the Persica of Ktesias*. London, 1888.

—— König, F. W. (ed.) *Die Persika des Ktesias*. Graz, 1972 (*AfO* Beiheft 18).

—— Marquart, J. "Die Assyriaka des Ktesias", *Philologus*, Supplement VI (1893), pp. 503–658.

—— Müller, C(K). (ed.) *Ctesias Cnidii...fragmenta* in G. Dindorfius (ed.), *Herodoti Historiarum Libri IX*. Paris, 1887.

—— P'yankov, I. V. "Ctesias on Zoroaster" (in Russian), in *Materialnaya kultura Tadzhikistan*, vyp. I (Dushanbe, 1968), pp. 55–63.

—— Herodotus, with an English translation by A. D. Godley, 4 vols. London–Cambridge, Mass., 1960–1 (LCL). (The translation is very free.)

—— Prášek, J. V. "Hekataios als Herodots Quelle zur Geschichte Vorderasiens", *Klio* IV (1904), pp. 193.

Pauly s.v. *Ktesias, Xenophon*; Suppl. s.v. *Herodotus*.

Strabo, *Geography*, with an English translation by H. L. Jones, 8 vols. London, 1949–54 (LCL).

Xenophon, *Cyropaedia*, with an English translation by W. Miller, 2 vols. London–New York, 1925–43 (LCL).

BIBLIOGRAPHY

Further classical, as well as Armenian and Hebrew sources on the history of Media are quoted in I. M. Diakonoff, *History of Media*.

CHAPTER 4

It is not practicable to quote here all works on the Scyths and articles scattered in hundreds of learned periodicals written in many languages. Those published in the Soviet Union during the previous ten years have been mentioned and classified in two issues of the *University of London Institute of Archaeology Bulletin* x (1972) ("The Scythian Age in the USSR", pp. 99–140), and xi (1973) ("Greek Colonization", pp. 1–40). Listed below are mostly works connected with topics discussed in this Chapter.

1. *Collective Works*

Arkheologiya Ukrainskoy RSR, 2 vols. Kiev, 1971 [*AU*].
Materialy i Issledovaniya po Arkheologii SSSR. Moscow–Leningrad [MIA], nos:
—— 64 (1958) – *Pamyatniki Skifo-Sarmatskogo Vremeni v Severnom Prichërnomorie*. Four authors.
—— 96 (1961) – *Pamyatniki Epokhi Bronzy i Rannego Zheleza v severnom Prichërnomorie*. Three authors.
—— 113 (1962) – *Lesostepnye Kultury Skifskogo Vermeni*. Four authors.
—— 115 (1962) – *Pamyatniki Skifo-Sarmatskoy Kultury*. Five authors.
—— 130 (1965) – *Novoe v Sovetskoy Arkheologii*. Four authors.
—— 150 (1969) – *Drevnie Frakiytsy v Severnom Prichërnomorie*. Nine authors.
—— 177 (1971) – *Problemy Skifskoy Arkheologii*, ed. P. D. Liberov and V. I. Gulyaev. Twenty-one authors.
Svod Arkheologicheskikh Istochnikov. Arkheologiya SSSR, Moscow [SVOD].
Drevnosti Vostochnogo Kryma. Predskifskii Period i Skify. Kiev, 1970.
Narysy Starodavnoy Istorii Ukrainskoy RSR. Kiev, 1957.
Voprosy Skifo-Sarmatskoy Arkheologii. Moscow, 1954.

2. *General*

Aslanov, G. M., Vaidov, R. M. and Ione, G. I. *Drevniy Mingechaur*. Baku, 1959.
Blavatskii, V. A. *Antichnaya Arkheologiya Severnogo Prichërnomoria*. Moscow, 1961.
Bukowski, Z. *Studies on the South and South-Eastern Borderline of the Lusatian Culture*. Wrocław, 1969. (In Polish with a summary in English.)
Cameron, G. G. *History of Early Iran*. Chicago, 1936.
Chlenova, N. L. *Proiskhozhdenie i Rannyaya Istoriya Plemen Tagarskoy Kultury*. Moscow, 1967.
—— *Khronologiya Pamyatnikov Karasukskoy Epokhy*. Moscow, 1972 (MIA 182).
Christensen, A. *Die Iranier. Kulturgeschichte des Alten Orient*. München, 1933.
Culican, W. *The Medes and Persians*. London, 1965 (Ancient Peoples and Places 42).

BIBLIOGRAPHY

Danoff, Ch. M. "Pontos Euxeinos", in Pauly, Suppl.
Ebert, M. *Südrussland im Altertum*. Bonn, 1921, repr. 1960.
Fettich, N. *La trouvaille Scythe de Zöldhalompuszta*. Budapest, 1928 (Archaeologia Hungarica 3).
—— *Der skythische Fund von Gartschinovo*. Budapest, 1934 (Archaeologia Hungarica 15).
Filip, J. *Keltové ve Střední Evropé*. Prague, 1956.
Gaydukevich, V. F. *Bosporanskoe Tsarstvo*. Moscow–Leningrad, 1948.
Ghirshman, R. *Iran from the earliest times to the Islamic conquest*. Harmondsworth, 1954 (Penguin/Pelican Books).
—— *Persia; from the Origins to Alexander the Great*. London, 1964.
—— *L'Iran et la migration des Indo-ariens et des Iraniens*. Leiden, 1977.
Grakov, B. N. *Kamenskoe Gorodishche na Dnepre*. Moscow, 1954 (MIA 36).
—— *Skify*. Moscow, 1971.
Grantovskii, E. A. *Rannyaya Istoriya Iranskikh Plemen Peredney Azii*. Moscow, 1970.
Hensel, W. *Polska starozytna*. Wrocław, 1973.
Ilinskaya, V. A. *Skify Dneprovskogo Lesostepnogo Levoberezhya*. Kiev, 1968.
Jettmar, K. *Die frühen Steppenvölker*. Baden-Baden, 1964 (Kunst der Welt).
Konduktorova, T. S. *Antropologiya Drevnego Naseleniya Ukrainy (The Anthropology of the Ancient Population of the Ukraine – 1000 B.C. to 500 A.D.)*. Moscow, 1972.
Kovpanenko, H. T. *Plemena Skifskoho Chasu na Vorskli*. Kiev, 1967.
Krupnov, E. I. *Drevnyaya Istoriya Severnogo Kavkaza*. Moscow, 1960.
Lang, D. M. *The Georgians*. London, 1966 (Ancient Peoples and Places 51).
Liberov, P. D. *Pamyatniki Skifskogo Vremeni na Srednem Donu*. Moscow, 1965.
van Loon, M. N. *Urartian Art*. Istanbul, 1966.
Lyapushkin, I. I. *Dneprovskoe Lesostepnoe Levoberezhye v Epokhu Zheleza*. Moscow, 1961 (MIA 104).
Melikishvili, G. A. *Nairi-Urartu*. Tbilisi, 1954.
Meliukova, A. I. *Vooruzhenie Skifov*. Moscow, 1964 (SVOD D1-4).
Minns, E. H. *Scythians and Greeks*. Cambridge, 1913. In spite of the seventy years that have elapsed since its publication, Sir Ellis H. Minns' book still retains its position as the classic for the knowledge of the Scythians, as presented in the writings of ancient authors. Some of his generalizations may be obsolete, but for the most part his explanations, analysis and dating of the main Scythian finds known at his time, still remain valid.
Moshkova, M. G. *Pamyatniki Prokhorovskoy Kultury*. Moscow, 1963.
Párducz, M. "Le cimitière hallstattien de Szentes-Vekerzug [I]", *AArchASH* II (1952), pp. 143–69; "II", *AArchASH* IV (1954), pp. 25–113; "III", *AArchASH* VI (1955), pp. 1–18.
—— "Western Relations of the Scythian Age Culture of the Great Hungarian Plain", *AAntASH* XIII (1965), pp. 273–301.
Petrenko, V. G. *Pravoberezhie Srednego Pridneprovya v V–III vv. do n.e.* Moscow, 1967 (SVOD D1-4[a]).
Phillips, E. D. *The Royal Hordes*. London, 1965.

—— "The Scythian domination in Western Asia", *World Archaeology* IV (1972), pp. 129–38.
Piotrovskii, B. B. *Vanskoe Tsarstvo (Urartu)*. Moscow, 1959. *Urartu. Kingdom of Van and its Art*. London, 1967.
Piotrovskii, B. B. and Iessen, A. A. *Mozdokskii Mogilnik*. Leningrad, 1940.
Pippidi, D. M. and Berciu, D. *Din istoria Dobrogei*, vol. I. Bucharest, 1965.
Potratz, H. A. "Die Skythen und Vorderasien", *Orientalia* XXVIII (1959), pp. 57–73.
—— *Die Skythen in Südrussland*. Basle, 1963.
—— *Die Pferdetrensen des Alten Orient*. Rome, 1966 (Analecta Orientalia 41).
Talbot Rice, T. *The Scythians*, 3rd edition. London, 1961 (Ancient Peoples and Places 2).
Rostovtzev, M. *Iranians and Greeks in South Russia*. Oxford, 1922.
—— *Skythien und der Bosporus*. Berlin, 1931.
Sedov, V. V. *Slavyane Verkhnego Podneprovia i Povinia*. Moscow, 1970 (MIA 163).
Sulimirski, T. *Scythians in West Podolia*. Lwow, 1936. In Polish with a summary in German.
—— *Prehistoric Russia*. London, 1970.
—— "Scythian antiquities in Western Asia", *Artibus Asiae* XVII (1954), pp. 282–318.
Terenozhkin, A. I. *Predskifskii Period na Dneprovskom Pravoberezhie*. Kiev, 1961.
—— (ed.). *Arkheologiya Ukrainskoy RSR*, 2 vols. Kiev, 1971.
—— (ed.). *Skifskie Drevnosti (Scythian Antiquities)*. Kiev, 1973.
Vulpe, R. *The Ancient History of Drobrogea*. Bucharest, 1940.
Zinevich, G. P. *Ocherki Paleoantropologii Ukrainy (Outlines of the Paleoanthropology of the Ukraine)*. Kiev, 1967.

3. *Linguistic study of Ukrainian toponymy*

Jokl, N. "Die Thraker. Sprache", in M. Ebert (ed.), *Reallexicon der Vorgeschichte* XIII (Berlin, 1929), pp. 278–98.
Petrov, V. P. *MASP* IV (1962), pp. 227ff.
Sedov, V. V. *SA* 1965.4, pp. 52–62.
—— *SA* 1966.4, pp. 86–104.
Sulimirski, T. "Ancient Southern Neighbours of the Baltic Tribes", *Acta Baltico-Slavica* V (Białystok, 1967), pp. 1–17.
Vyazmitina, M. I. In *Drevnie Frakiytsy v Severnom Prichërnomorie* (Moscow, 1969), pp. 119–34 (MIA 150).
Zgusta, L. *Die Personennamen griechischer Stadte der nordlichen Schwarzmeerkuste*. Prague, 1955.

See also:

Meliukova, A. I. in *Problemy Skifskoi Arkheologii* (Moscow, 1977), pp. 39–54 (MIA 177) and several other articles in MIA 150.

4. Weapons, tools, horse harness

Abramova, M. P. In *Drevnosti Vostochnoi Evropy* (Moscow, 1969), pp. 3–11 (MIA 169).
Cherenko, E. V. *AK* XVI (1964), pp. 27–45.
—— *AK* XVII (1964), pp. 144–52.
—— *AK* XVIII (1965), pp. 77–104.
Ganina, L. K. *ASE* VII (1965), pp. 5–27.
Gorelik, M. V. *SA* 1971.3, pp. 236–45.
Illinska, V. A. "Skifski sokiri" (Scythian axes), *AK* XII (1961), pp. 27–52.
Jessen, A. A. "La steppe de Mil et Karabagh au cours de l'histoire" (in Russian), in *Trudy Azerbaidzhanskoi Arkheologicheskoi Ekspeditsii II, 1956–60* (Moscow–Leningrad, 1965), pp. 10–36 (MIA 125).
Medvedskaya, I. N. *SA* 1972.3, pp. 76–89.
Meliukova, O. *Vooruzhenie Skifov*. Moscow, 1964 (SVOD D1–4).
Smirnov, K. F. *Savromaty*. Moscow, 1964.
Sulimirski, T. "Scythian antiquities in Western Asia: the origin of the 'Scythian' arrowheads", *Artibus Asiae* XVII (1954), pp. 308–13.

5. Commerce

Bondar, M. M. *AK* XI (1957), pp. 35–44.
—— *AK* XIII (1961), pp. 80–8.
Brashinskii, I. B. *SA* 1968.2, pp. 260–4.
Onayko, N. A. *SA* 1960.2, pp. 25–41.
—— *Antichnii Import v Pridneprove i Pobuzhe v VII–V vekakh do n.e.* Moscow, 1966 (SVOD D1–27).
Salinikov, O. G. *MASP* III (1960), pp. 25ff.

6. Beliefs and religion

Artamonov, M. I. *ASE* 1951.2, pp. 57–87.
Elnitskii, L. A. *SA* 1960.4, pp. 46–55.
—— *SA* 1970.2, pp. 64–74.
Petrov, V. P. *AK* XV (1963), pp. 19–32.
Raevskii, D. S. *SA* 1970.3, pp. 90–101.

7. Scythian Art

Artamonov, M. I. *Treasures from Scythian Tombs*. London, 1069.
—— *SA* 1968.4, pp. 27–45.
—— *Problemy Skyfskoi Arkheologii* (Moscow, 1971), pp. 24–35 (MIA 177).
Borovka, G. I. *Scythian Art*. London, 1928.
Chlenova, N. L. In *Pamyatniki Skifo-Sarmatskoy Kultury*. (Moscow, 1962), pp. 167–203 (MIA 115).
—— "Le Serf Scythe", *Artibus Asiae* XXVI (1963), pp. 27–70.
Furtwängler, A. *Der Goldfund von Vettersfelde*. Berlin, 1883.

Iakovenko, E. V. *SA* 1969.4, pp. 200–7.
Illinskaya, V. A. *SA* 1965.1, pp. 86–107.
—— *SA* 1967.4, pp. 295–301.
—— *SA* 1971.2, pp. 64–85.
—— *AK* xv (1963), pp. 33–60.
—— *AK* iv (1971), pp. 73–9.
Jettmar, K. *The Art of the Steppes: the Eurasian Animal Style*. London, 1967 (Art of the World 21).
Mantsevich, A. P. *SA* 1950.13, pp. 217–38.
—— *ASE* vi (1964), pp. 128–38.
Minns, E. H. "The Art of the Northern Nomads", *PBA* xxviii (1942), pp. 47–99.

8. Karmir Blur

Barnett, R. D. and Watson, W. "Russian excavations in Armenia", *Iraq* xiv (1952), pp. 132–47.
Kovpanenko, G. *Arkheologicheskie Issledovaniya na Ukraine 1965–1966* (Kiev), p. 105, fig. 13.
Piotrovskii, B. B. *Karmir Blur*, 3 vols. Erevan, 1950, 1952, 1955.
Sulimirski, T. "La culture Lusacienne et les Scythes", *Wiadomości Archeologiczne* xvi (Warsaw, 1939–48), pp. 76–100.

9. Smiela

Bobrinskii, A. A. *Barrows and Chance Archaeological Finds about the town of Smiela* (in Russian), 3 vols. St Petersburg, 1887, 1894, 1901.

10. Ziwiyeh: The Ziwiyeh Treasure

Barnett, R. D. "The Treasure of Ziwiye", *Iraq* xviii (1956), pp. 111–16.
—— "Median Art", *IA* ii (1962), pp. 88–9.
Brentjes, B. "Tierstilprovinzen Vorderasiens und der skythische Tierstil", *ZA* iii (1969), pp. 161–72.
Ghirshman, R. *Terrasses sacrées de Bard-è Néchandeh et Masjid-i Solaiman*, 2 vols. Paris, 1976 (MDAI 45, 46).
—— "The Scythians and the royal tomb of Ziwiyeh", in *Persia*, pp. 98–125.
—— "Notes iraniennes IV: Le trésor de Saqqez", *Artibus Asiae* xiii (1950), pp. 181–206.
—— *Tombe princière de Ziwiyé et le début de l'art animalier Scythe*. Paris, 1979.
Godard, A. *Le trésor de Ziwiyé*. Haarlem, 1950.
Kantor, H. J. "A gold Appliqué from Ziwiye", *JNES* xix (1960), pp. 1–14.
Potratz, H. A. "Die Skythen und Vorderasien", *Orientalia* xxviii (1959), pp. 57–73.
Wilkinson, C. "More details on Ziwiye", *Iraq* xxii (1960), pp. 213–20.

BIBLIOGRAPHY

11. Scythian antiquities in Central Europe

Romania and Bulgaria:

Berciu, D. *Romania before Burebista.* London, 1967.
—— *Arta tracogetica.* Bucharest, 1969.
—— "Die Stellung der Geten im Lichte der Archäologie", *Dacia* v (1961), pp. 163–84.
Crişan, I. H. "Once more about the Scythian problem in Transylvania", *Dacia* IX (1965), pp. 133–45.
Meliukova, A. I. *SA* XXII (1955), pp. 238–53.
—— *KSIAM* CV (1965), pp. 32ff.
Roska, M. "Der Bestand der Skythischen Altertümer Siebenbügens", *Eurasia Septentrionalis Antiqua* XI (Helsinki, 1937), pp. 167ff.
Venedikov, I. *Bulgaria's Treasures from the Past.* Sofia, 1965.

Hungary:

Fettich, N. "Bestand der skythischen Altertümer Ungarns", in M. Rostovzev, *Skythien und der Bosporus* (Berlin, 1931), pp. 494ff.
Harmatta, J. "Früheisenzeitliche Beziehungen zwischen dem Karpatenbecken, Oberitalien und Griechenland", *AArchASH* xx (1968), pp. 153–7.

Yugoslavia:

Gabrovec, S. *Arheološki Vestnik* XIII–XIV (Ljubljana, 1962), pp. 312, 324.

Slovakia:

Benadik, B. *Archeologické Rozhledy* v (Prague, 1953), pp. 672–83.
Dusek, M. *Slovenska Archeologia* IX (Bratislava, 1961), pp. 155ff.

Carpatho-Ukraine:

Lengyel, I. "Beiträge zur Ursprungsfrage der Kuštanovice-Kultur", *Folia Archaeologica* XII (Budapest, 1960), pp. 61–9.
Smirnova, G. I. and Berniakovich, K. V. *ASE* VII (1965), pp. 89–115.

See also:

Foltiny, S. *Archaeologia Austriaca* XXXIII (Vienna, 1963), pp. 23–36.

12. The Scyths in Europe

Bukowski, Z. "Several problems concerning contacts of Lusatian culture with Scythians", *Archaeologia Polski* III (Warsaw, 1960), pp. 65–88.
—— "New Scythian finds in Poland", *Archaeologia Polski* IV (Warsaw, 1960), pp. 257–83.
Rostovtzev, M. *Skythien und der Bosporus.* Berlin, 1931.
Sulimirski, T. "Scythian antiquities in Central Europe", *The Antiquaries Journal* XXV (Oxford, 1945), pp. 1–11.
—— "Die Skythen in Mittel- und Westeuropa", in *Bericht V International Kongress für Vor- und Frühgeschichte, Hamburg, 1958* (Berlin, 1961), pp. 793–9.

BIBLIOGRAPHY

13. *The Sauromatians (Sarmatians)*

Smirnov, K. F. *Voruzhenie Savromatov*. Moscow, 1961 (MIA 101). *Savromaty*. Moscow, 1964.
Smirnov, K. F. and Petrenko, V. G. *Savromaty ovolzhi Povolzhia i Iuzhnogo Priuralia*. Moscow, 1963 (SVOD D1–9).
Sulimirski, T. *The Sarmatians*. London, 1970 (Ancient Peoples and Places 73).

CHAPTERS 5 AND 6

1. *General History of the Persian Empire*

Beloch, K. H. *Griechsiche Geschichte*, 4 vols. Berlin, 1924–7.
Bengtson, H. (ed.) *Die Verträge der griechisch-römischen Welt*. Berlin, 1962 (Die Staatsverträge des Altertums 2).
Bengtson, H. et al. *The Greeks and the Persians from the sixth to the fourth centuries*. London, 1969.
Lewis, D. M. *Sparta and Persia: lectures in memory of Donald W. Bradeen*. Leiden, 1977 (Cincinatti Classical Studies, new series 1).
Olmstead, A. T. *History of the Persian Empire*. Chicago, 1948.
Prášek, J. V. *Geschichte der Meder und Perser bis zur Makedonischen Eroberung*, 2 vols. Gotha, 1906–10.
Rawlinson, G. *The Five Great Monarchies of the Ancient Eastern World*, 3 vols (especially vol. II). London, 1862–7.
Wade-Gery, H. T. *Essays in Greek History*. Oxford, 1958.

2. *Historical Monographs*

Benveniste, E. *Titres et noms propres en iranien ancien*. Paris, 1966.
Burn, A. R. *Persia and the Greeks*. London, 1962.
Dandamayev, M. A. *Persien unter den ersten Achämeniden*. Wiesbaden, 1976.
Ehtecham, M. *L'Iran sous les Achéménides*. Fribourg, 1946.
Frye, R. N. *The Heritage of Persia*. London, 1962.
Hinz, W. *Altiranische Funde und Forschungen*. Berlin, 1969.
—— *Darius und die Perser*, 2 vols. Baden-Baden, 1976.
Junge, J. "Satrapie und Natio", *Klio* XXXIV (1942), 1–55.
—— *Dareios I. König der Perser*. Leipzig, 1944.
Lewis, D. M. *Sparta and Persia*. Leiden, 1977 (Cincinatti Classical Studies 1).
Meyer, E. *Geschichte des Altertums* IV. 1, 3rd ed. (Stuttgart, 1939), 3–218 ("Der Orient unter der Herrschaft der Perser").
La Persia e il mondo Greco-Romano. Accademia Nazionale dei Lincei, Rome, 1966.
Schaeder, H. H. *Das persische Weltreich*. Breslau, 1941.
Toynbee, A. J. "The Administrative Geography of the Achaemenian Empire", in *A Study of History* VII (London, 1954), 580–689).
Walser, G. (ed.) *Beiträge zur Achämenidengeschichte*. Wiesbaden, 1972 (*Historia*, Einzelschriften 18).

3. Studies of regions and component peoples

Altheim, F. and Stiehl, R. *Geschichte Mittelasiens im Altertum*. Berlin, 1970.
Bengtson, H. *The Greeks and the Persians from the sixth to the fourth centuries* (London, 1968), chapters 16–20 (Egypt, Mesopotamia, Palestine Judaism, Syria, Arabia).
Burney, C. and Lang, D. M. *The Peoples of the Hills: Ancient Ararat and Caucasus*. London, 1971.
Deshayes, J. (ed.) *Le Plateau iranien et l'Asie centrale des origines á la conquête islamique*. Paris, 1977 (Colloques internationaux du Centre National de la recherche scientifique 567).
Dillemann, L. D. *Haute Mesopotamie orientale et pays adjacents*. Paris, 1962.
Hinz, W. "Achämenidische Hofverwaltung", *ZA* LXI (1971), 260–311.
Junge, J. *Saka-Studien*. Leipzig, 1939 (*Klio*, Beiheft 41).
Lehmann-Haupt, K. F. *Armenien Einst und Jetzt*, 3 vols. Leipzig, 1910–31.
Leuze, O. *Die Satrapieneinteilung in Syrien und im Zweiströmlande von 520–320* (Halle, Saale, 1935), pp. 157–476 (Schriften der Königsberger Gelehrten Gesellschaft, Geisteswiss. Klasse 11.4).
Magie, D. *Roman Rule in Asia Minor*, 2 vols. Princeton, N.J., 1950.
Meyer, Eduard. *Geschichte des Königsreichs Pontos*. Leipzig, 1879.
Stern, E. *Material Culture of the Land of the Bible in the Persian Period 538–332 B.C.* Warminster, 1982.
Tarn, W. W. *The Greeks in Bactria and Indis*, 2nd ed. Cambridge, 1951.

4. Texts

Blinkinberg, C. *Die Lindische Tempelchronik*. Bonn, 1915 (Kleine Texte 131).
Bowman, R. A. *Aramaic Ritual Texts from Persepolis*. Chicago, 1970 (Oriental Institute Publications 91).
Cameron, G. G. *Persepolis Treasury Tablets*. Chicago, 1948 (Oriental Institute Publications 65) [*PTT*].
Dittenberger, W. *Orientis Graeci Inscriptiones Selectae*, 2 vols. Leipzig, 1903–5.
Hallock, R. T. *Persepolis Fortification Tablets*. Chicago, 1969 (Oriental Institute Publications 92 [*PFT*].
Hinz, W. "Die Quellen" in G. Walser (ed.), *Beiträge zur Achämenidengeschichte* (Wiesbaden, 1972), pp. 5–14.
Kent, R. G. *Old Persian Grammar, Texts, Lexicon*, 2nd ed. New Haven, Conn., 1953.
Mayrhofer, M. (ed.) *Onomastica Persepolitana*. Vienna, 1973 (*SWAW* 286).
Meiggs, R. and Lewis, D. *A selection of Greek historical inscriptions to the end of the fifth century B.C.* Oxford, 1969.
Posener, G. *La première domination perse en Égypte*. Cairo, 1963.
Tod, M. N. *A selection of Greek historical inscriptions to the end of the fifth century B.C.*, 2 vols. Oxford, 1933–48.
von Voigtlander, E. N. *The Bisitun Inscription of Darius the Great – Babylonian version*. London, 1978 (*CIIr*, Part I, vol. II).
Weissbach, F. H. *Die Keilinschriften der Achämeniden*. Leipzig, 1911.

5. Topography, Toponymy, and Environment

Bobek, H. "Klima und Landschaft Irans in vor- und frühgeschichtlicher Zeit", *Geographischer Jahresbericht Österreichs* XXV (1953–4).
Briant, P. "L'élévage ovin dans l'Empire Achéménide", *JESHO* XXII (1979), pp. 136–61.
Brice, W. C. *South-West Asia*. University of London Press, 1966.
Christensen, A. *L'Iran sous les Sassanides*, 2nd ed. Copenhagen, 1944.
Curzon, G. N. *Persia and the Persian Question*, 2 vols. London, 1892; repr. 1966.
Dandamayev, M. A. "Forced labour in the Palace Economy of Achaemenid Iran" in *Altorientalische Forschungen* II (Berlin, 1975), pp. 71–8 (Schriften zur Geschichte und Kultur des alten Orients).
Deshayes, J. (ed.), *Le Plateau iranien*. See section 3.
Dupree, N. H. *An Historical Guide to Afghanistan*. Kabul, 1971 (Afghan Tourist Organization).
Fisher, W. B. (ed.) *The Land of Iran*. Cambridge, 1968 (*CHI* 1).
Hallock, R. T. "The use of Seals in the Persepolis Fortification Tablets," in M. Gibson and R. D. Biggs (eds.), *Seals and Sealing in Ancient Near East* (Malibu, 1977), 127–33 (Bibliotheca Mesopotamica 6).
Herzfeld, E. E. *The Persian Empire*, ed. G. Walser, Wiesbaden, 1968.
Le Strange, G. *The Lands of the Eastern Caliphate*. Cambridge, 1930.
Matheson, S. A. *Persia, An Archaeological Guide*. London, 1972; 2nd ed. 1976.
Planhol, X. de *Les Fondements géographiques de l'histoire de l'Islam*. Paris, 1968.
Tomaschek, W. "Zur historischen Topographie von Persien", *SWAW* CII (1883), pp. 145–231; CVIII (1885), pp. 561–652; reprint in one 1972.

6. Archaeology and Pictures

Archaeological reports in *Iran* 1963–.
Culican, W. *The Medes and Persians*. London, 1965 (Ancient Peoples and Places 42).
Farkas, A. *Achaemenid Sculpture*. Istanbul, 1974 (Nederlands Historisch-Archaeologisch Instituut te Istanbul 33).
Frumkin, G. *Archaeology in Soviet Central Asia*. Leiden, 1970 (*HO* VII. iii. 1).
Ghirshman, R. *Persia: from the Origins to Alexander the Great*. London, 1964.
Nylander, C. *Ionians in Pasargadae*. Uppsala, 1970 (Boreas. Uppsala Studies in Ancient Mediterranean and Near Eastern Civilizations 1).
Osten, H. H. von der. *Die Welt der Perser*. Stuttgart, 1956.
Porada, E. *Ancient Iran. The Art of pre-Islamic times*. London, 1965.
Schippmann, K. *Die iranischen Feuerheiligtümer*. Berlin, 1971.
Schmidt, E. F. *Persepolis I–III*. Chicago 1953–70 (details on p. 922).
Stronach, D. *Pasargadae*. Oxford, 1978.
Vanden Berghe, L. *Archéologie de l'Iran ancien*. Leiden, 1959 (Documenta et monumenta orientis antiqui 6).
Walser, G. *Die Völkerschaften auf den Reliefs von Persepolis*. Berlin, 1966 (Teheraner Forschungen 2).
Wilber, D. N. *Persepolis: The archaeology of Parsa*. London–New York, 1969.

BIBLIOGRAPHY

CHAPTER 7

Gadd, C. J. *The Stones of Assyria*. London, 1936.
Garstang, J. and Gurney, O. R. *The Geography of the Late Hittite Empire*. London, 1959 (Occasional Publications of the British Institute of Archaeology in Ankara 5).
Hallock, R. T. *Persepolis Fortification Tablets*. Chicago, 1969 [*PFT*].
Hansman, J. "Elamites, Achaemenians and Anshan", *Iran* x (1972), pp. 101–25.
Henning, W. B. *Zoroaster: Politician or Witch-doctor?* Oxford, 1951.
How, W. W. and Wells, J. *A Commentary on Herodotus*, 2 vols. Oxford, 1912.
Kent, R. G. *Old Persian Grammar, Texts, Lexicon*, 2nd ed. New Haven, Conn., 1953.
Kramer, S. N. *The Sumerians*. Chicago, 1963.
—— (tr.) *Enmerkar and the Lord of Aratta: a Sumerian Epic Tale of Iraq and Iran*. Philadelphia, 1952 (University of Pennsylvania Museum Monographs).
Mallowan, M. E. L. *Nimrud and its Remains*, 3 vols. London, 1966.
—— "Cyrus the Great", *Iran* x (1972), pp. 1–17.
Nylander, C. "Who wrote the inscriptions at Pasargadae?", *Orientalia Suecana* XVI (Uppsala, 1968), pp. 135–80.
—— *Ionians in Pasargadae*. Uppsala, 1970.
Pritchard, J. B. (ed.) *Ancient Near Eastern Texts*, 3rd ed. Princeton, N.J., 1969 [*ANET*].
Schaeffer, C. F. A. (ed.) *Ugaritica* v. Paris, 1968.
Smith, Sydney (tr.) *Babylonian Historical Texts relating to the capture and downfall of Babylon*. London, 1924.
—— *Isaiah, Chapters xl–lv; Literary Criticism and History*. London, 1944 (British Academy Schweich Lectures, 1940).
Strommanger, E. *The Art of Mesopotamia*. London, 1964.
Stronach, D. *Pasargadae*. Oxford, 1978.
Weissbach, F. H. *Die Kleininschriften der Achämeniden*. Leipzig, 1911.

CHAPTER 8

I. *Bibliographies*

Tarn, W. W. Bibliographies to Chapters 12, 13, 14, *CAH* VI (1927), pp. 590–603. A full bibliography down to about 1925.
Andreotti, R. "Il problema di Alessandro Magno della istoriografia dell' ultimo decennio", *Historia* I (1950), pp. 583–600. A critical survey, concentrating on items relevant to Alexander's character, aims and achievement and covering approximately the previous decade.
Badian, E. "Alexander the Great 1948–67", *Classical World* LXV (1971–72), pp. 37–56, 77–83. A critical survey covering the years 1948–67, with an appendix on 1968.
Seibert, J. *Alexander der Grosse*. Darmstadt, 1972 (Wissenschaftliche Buchgesellschaft, Erträge der Forschung 10). This is a full bibliography of (in

principle) all scholarship from Droyson's *Geschichte*[2] (1877) [section IV below] down to about 1970, with occasional reference to important earlier items; it consists chiefly of classified lists, with summaries and occasional critical evaluations on selected problems; it is basic for serious research; its chief strength is in work written in (or translated into) German; work in English is usually inadequately reported and sometimes misunderstood.

II. *Sources*

1. *Texts and translations*

Arrian. *Anabasis* and *Indica*, ed. and tr. P. A. Brunt, 2 vols. 1976, 1983 (LCL). This supersedes the unsatisfactory edition of E. Iliff Robson.

—— *Anabasis*, tr. A. de Selincourt, ed. and corrected J. R. Hamilton, with short historical notes. Harmondsworth, 1971 (Penguin Books).

—— *Indica* (Arrien, *L'Inde*), ed. and tr. P. Chantraine, 2nd ed. Paris, 1952 (Collection Budé).

Diodorus Siculus. Book XVII, ed. and tr. C. B. Welles. 1963 (LCL Diodorus VIII).

—— Book XVII, ed. and tr. P. Goukowsky. Paris, 1976 (Collection Budé).

—— Book XVIII, ed. and tr. R. M. Geer. 1947 (LCL Diodorus IX). Though dealing with events after Alexander's death this book contains many comments relevant to his lifetime.

—— Book XVIII, ed. and tr. P. Goukowsky. Paris, 1978 (Collection Budé).

Plutarch. "Alexander" in Plutarch's *Lives*, vol. VII, ed. and tr. B. Perrin. 1919 (LCL).

Quintus Curtius Rufus. *History of Alexander*, 10 books in 2 vols, ed. and tr. J. C. Rolfe. 1946 (LCL).

—— (Quinte-Curce, *Histoires*) ed. and tr. H. Bardon, 2 vols. Paris, 1947–8 (Collection Budé).

2. *Historical commentaries*

ON CURTIUS

Quintus Curtius Rufus De gestis Alexandri Magni, ed. J. Mützell, with critical and exegetical commentary, 2 vols. Berlin, 1841. This is still the only complete edition of this kind of any of the major sources except Plutarch.

Atkinson, J. E. *A Commentary on Quintus Curtius Rufus' Historiae Alexandri Magni*, books 3 and 4. Amsterdam, 1980 (London Studies in Classical Philology 4).

ON PLUTARCH

Hamilton, J. R. *Plutarch Alexander: a Commentary*. Oxford, 1969.

ON ARRIAN

Bosworth, A. B. *A Historical Commentary on Arrian's History of Alexander* I (Books 1–3). Oxford, 1980.

Brunt's Loeb Arrian (see above) also contains unusually long and careful historical annotation, with special discussion of many problems.

BIBLIOGRAPHY

ON STRABO

Pédech, P. "Strabon Historien d'Alexandre", *Grazer Beiträge* II (Amsterdam, 1974), pp. 129–45.

3. The fragments of the lost sources on which our surviving authors are based are collected and briefly annotated by F. Jacoby in his monumental *Die Fragmente der griechischen Historiker* (each author is cited by number in the consecutive series), vol. III, parts B and D (1930). A collection of translations of these fragments (of very variable quality) was included by C. A. Robinson, *The History of Alexander the Great* I (Providence, R. I., 1953. Brown University Studies 16). The only complete discussion is L. I. C. Pearson, *The Lost Histories of Alexander the Great* (New York, 1960). A particularly useful discussion in short compass will be found in A. B. Bosworth, "Arrian and the Alexander Vulgate", in *Alexandre le Grand* [section III below] 1–33.

4. The Greek inscriptions relevant to Alexander (there are no such Iranian inscriptions) are collected, edited and carefully discussed by A. J. Heisserer, *Alexander the Great and the Greeks: the Epigraphic Evidence* (Oklahoma, 1980). The coins are not yet wholly sorted. The only important general survey is A. R. Bellinger, *Essays on the Coinage of Alexander the Great* (New York, 1963. ANSNS 11).

III. *Collections*

Greece and Rome XII. 2 (October, 1965, pp. 113–228. Original articles by various scholars on aspects of Alexander history; all are in English.

Griffith, G. T. (ed.) *Alexander the Great: the main problems*. Cambridge, 1966. Reprints of 16 articles, in English and German, by various authors, over the years 1933–61.

Badian, E. (ed.) *Alexandre le Grand. image et réalité. Entretiens sur l'antiquité classique 25–30 aout 1975*. Geneva, 1976 (Fondation Hardt. Entretiens XXII). Articles by seven scholars, each followed by discussion, on aspects of the life, career and posthumous influence of Alexander.

IV. *Biographies*

Droysen, J. G. *Geschichte Alexanders des Grossen*. Hamburg, 1833; ed. 1877; repr. Dusseldorf, 1966.

Wilcken, U. *Alexander der Grosse*. Leipzig, 1931. Tr. G. C. Richards as *Alexander the Great*, 2nd ed. revised by E. N. Borza. New York–London, 1967. Borza added notes drawing attention to changes in interpretation from Wilcken's days to date of publication.

Tarn, W. W. *Alexander the Great*, 2 vols. Cambridge, 1948; repr. 1979. Vol. I is largely the text of his chapter in *CAH* VI and closely follows Arrian's account; vol. II contains essays and studies of varying quality (some basic).

Schachermeyr, F. *Alexander der Grosse*. Vienna, 1973 (*SWAW* 85). New edition of 1949 publication, considerably revised and enlarged; it contains full annotation and appendices, unusually fine photographs and extensive discussion of modern interpretations.

BIBLIOGRAPHY

Green, P. *Alexander of Macedon 356–323 B.C.* Harmondsworth, 1974 (Penguin Books). Well written and unorthodox.

Hammond, N. G. L. *Alexander the Great: King, commander and statesman.* Park Ridge, N.J., 1980. Some useful discussion of battles and a few interesting topographical photographs.

Goukowsky, P. *Essai sur les origines du myhte d'Alexandre (336–270 av. J.-C.)*, 2 vols. Nancy, 1978, 1981. This work deals in erudite detail with a selection of incidents in Alexander's life deemed important for the genesis of his myth; though discursive and at times fanciful, it should be read by the serious student.

V. *Background, youth, accession*

On the Macedonian background, Philip II and Alexander as crown prince:

Hammond, N. G. L. and Griffith, G. T. *A History of Macedonia* II. Oxford, 1979.

Badian, E. "The death of Philip II", *Phoenix* XVII (1963), pp. 244–50.

Of numerous discussions since, note:

Fears, J. R. "Pausanias the assassin of Philip II", *Athenaeum* LIII (1975), pp. 111–35.

VI. *Topography, routes, campaigns*

There have been numerous studies for well over a century. Modern archaeology has helped considerably, but large stretches are still practically unexplored. This list includes some classic investigations, with special reference to those on Iranian lands, where Sir Aurel Stein's work, between the two World Wars, is basic. The best-informed recent work, where relevant references will be found, is:

Engels, D. W. *Alexander the Great and the Logistics of the Macedonian Army.* Berkeley, Calif., 1978. Appendices 4 and 5 deal in detail with the march through Gedrosia.

Alexander in Asia Minor and Babylonia

Janke, A. *Auf Alexanders des Grossen Pfaden.* Berlin, 1904. A detailed investigation, by a team of Imperial German officers, of Issus and parts of Asia Minor, including the Granicus.

Strak, F. "Alexander's minor campaigns in Turkey", *GJ* CXXII (1956), pp. 294–305.

—— "Alexander's march from Miletus to Phrygia", *JHS* LXXVIII (1958), pp. 102–20.

Schachermeyr, F. *Alexander in Babylon.* Vienna, 1970 (*SWAW* 268.3). This collection of important studies is perhaps most useful in its discussion of the topography of Achaemenian Babylon; it also deals with Alexander's actions in Babylon and (in the second half) with the events at Babylon, after his death, that led to the compromise among the marshals.

BIBLIOGRAPHY

Alexander in Iran (roughly in order of the march)

Stein, M. A. *Old routes of Western Iran* (London, 1940), pp. 18ff. For the route from Behbahān to Persepolis.

Marquart, J. "Alexanders Marsch von Persepolis nach Herat" in "Untersuchungen zur Geschichte von Eran II", *Philologus*, Supplement x.1 (1907), pp. 19–71.

Stahl, A. F. von. "Notes on the march of Alexander the Great from Ecbatana to Hyrcania", *GJ* LXIV (1924), pp. 312–29. Fixed the site of Ecbatana at Hamadān and traced the route of Alexander's pursuit of Darius, suggesting a site for Hecatompylus that Hansman (below) later excavated.

Hansman, J. "The problems of Qūmis", *JRAS* 1968, pp. 111–39. Identifies Hecatompylus with Shahr-i Qūmis.

Fischer, K. "Zur Lage von Kandahar", *Bonner Jahrbücher* CLXVII (1967), pp. 129–232.

Hedin, S. A. *Overland to India* II (London, 1910), ch. 49, "Alexander's march through southern Baluchistan." Outdated, but a pioneer effort.

Stein, M. A. "On Alexander's route into Gedrosia", *GJ* CII (1943), pp. 193–227.

Strasburger, H. "Zur Route Alexanders durch Gedrosien", *Hermes* LXXXII (1954), pp. 251–4.

On this controversy see also Engels (above).

Alexander in India

Stein, M. A. *On Alexander's track to the Indus*. London, 1929.

—— "The site of Alexander's passage of the Hydaspes and the battle with Poros", *GJ* LXXX (1932), pp. 31–46.

—— *Archaeological Reconnaissances in North-Western India and South-Eastern Iran* (London, 1937), ch. 1, "On Alexander's campaign in the Panjab".

Eggermont, P. H. L. *Alexander's Campaigns in Sind and Baluchistan and the Siege of the Brahmin town of Harmatelia.* Leuven, 1975.

On the sites of Alexander's cities and colonies

Tscherikower, V. "Die hellenistischen Städtegründungen von Alexander dem Grossen bis auf die Römerzeit", *Philologus*, Supplement XIX. 1 (1927), pp. 1–216.

VII. *Battles*

Janke [section VI above]: classic studies of Issus and the Granicus.

Davis, E. W. "The Persian battle plan at the Granicus", in F. Gyles and E. W. Davis (eds.), *Laudatores Temporis Acti: studies in memory of Wallace Everett Caldwell* (Chapel Hill, North Carolina, 1964), pp. 34ff. (James Sprunt Studies in History and Political Science 46.)

Foss, C. and Badian, E. "The battle of the Granicus: a new look", in B. Laourdas and C. Makarras (eds.), *Ancient Macedonia* II (Thessaloniki, 1977), pp. 495ff., 271ff. A single article, the two parts to be read together.

Dieulafoy, M. *La bataille d'Issus.* Paris, 1914.

BIBLIOGRAPHY

Marsden, E. W. *The campaign of Gaugamela*. Liverpool, 1964 (Liverpool Monographs in Archaeology and Oriental Studies). Impaired by failure to notice source problems.

Hamilton, J. R. "The cavalry battle at the Hydaspes", *JHS* LXXVI (1956), pp. 26–31.

Hammond [section IV above]; to be used with care.

VIII. *Army and military organization*

Berve, H. *Das Alexanderreich auf prosopographischer Grundlage*, 2 vols. Munich, 1926. Probably the most important single work ever written on Alexander. Vol. I discusses both civil and military organization; vol. II gives a register (with sources and discussion) of all persons known or alleged to have come into contact with Alexander; the numbers allocated to those persons by Berve are now regularly used by specialists to identify them.

Engels, W. D. [section VI above].

Milns, R. D. in *Alexandre le Grand* [section III above], pp. 87–136.

Brunt, P. A. "Alexander's Macedonian cavalry", *JHS* LXXXIII (1963), pp. 27–46.

Griffith, G. T. "A note on the hipparchies of Alexander", *ibid.*, pp. 68–74.

Badian, E. "Orientals in Alexander's army", *JHS* LXXXV (1965), pp. 60–1.

Brunt, P. A. A very useful general discussion in LCL edition of Arrian [section II. 1 above].

Hauben, H. "The command structure in Alexander's Mediterranean fleets", *Ancient Society* III (Leuven, 1972), pp. 55–65.

Markle, M. M. III. "Use of the sarissa by Philip and Alexander of Macedon", *AJA* LXXXII (1978), pp. 483–97. On the technical side, probably the most important article of recent years. Cf. his study of weapons in *AJA* LXXXI (1977), pp. 323–39.

Briant, P. "Brigandage, dissidence et conquête en Asie Achéménide et hellénistique", *Dialogues d'Histoire Ancienne* II (Paris, 1976), pp. 163–258 (Annales Litteraires de l'Université de Besançon 188). Studies Alexander's methods in securing frontiers and peaceful communications against barbarians and tribesmen.

Lock, R. A. "The Macedonian army assembly in the time of Alexander the great", *CP* LXXII (1977), pp. 91–107. Demolishes the traditional view of a Macedonian system of Staatsrecht, in which King and People-in-arms are thought to have had clearly defined rights.

Borza, E. N. "Alexander's communications", in B. Laourdas and C. Makarras (eds.), *Ancient Macedonia* II (Thessaloniki, 1977), pp. 295–303.

IX. *Civil and provincial organization*

Berve [section VIII above]. The most important study.

Briant [section VIII above].

Badian, E. "The administration of the empire", *Greece and Rome* [section III above], pp. 166–88. A brief general survey.

BIBLIOGRAPHY

—— "Alexander the Great and the Greeks of Asia", in E. Badian (ed.), *Ancient Society and Institutions: studies presented to Victor Ehrenberg* (Oxford, 1966), pp. 37–69.

—— "Harpalus", *JHS* LXXXI (1961), pp. 16–43. The reorganization of 324–23 is discussed in the light of the political crisis of that period.

Bosworth, A. B. The government of Syria under Alexander the Great", *CQ* XXIV (1974), pp. 46–64.

X. Religious aspects

Taeger, F. *Charisma: Studien zur Geschichte des Antiken Herrscherkultes*, vol. I (books 1 & 2), Stuttgart, 1957; vol. II (book 3), Stuttgart, 1960. Book 2 is basic.

Balsdon, J. V. P. D. "The divinity of Alexander", *Historia* I (1950), pp. 63–88.

Edmunds, L. "The religiosity of Alexander", *Greek, Roman and Byzantine Studies* XII (Durham, North Carolina, 1971), pp. 363–91. Discusses Alexander's attitude to, and imitation of, gods and heroes.

Badian, E. "The deification of Alexander the Great", in H. J. Dell (ed.), *Ancient Macedonian Studies in Honor of Charles F. Edson* (Thessaloniki, 1981), pp. 28ff., 48ff. (Institute for Balkan Studies 158).

[Goukowsky, *Essai* [section IV above], vol. II.]

XI. Alexander's plans, character, achievement

These of course are endlessly discussed and every biography contains much relevant material.

Tarn [section IV above], vol. II. The final part is entirely devoted to this topic.

Schachermeyr [*ibid.*]. Perhaps the major part is devoted to it.

Griffith (ed.), *Alexander* [section III above]. Several essays.

Greece and Rome [*ibid.*]. Essays by P. A. Briunt and C. B. Welles.

Andreotti, R. "Die Weltmonarchie Alexanders des Grossen in Überlieferung und geschichtlicher Wirklichkeit", *Saeculum* VIII (1957), pp. 120–66. Noteworthy as the classic statement of the anti-romantic and 'minimalist' position on Alexander's aims and motives; Tarn and Schachermeyr (cited above) may, in different ways, be taken as standing at the opposite extreme.

Demandt, A. "Politische Aspekte im Alexanderbilt der Neuzeit", *Archiv für Kulturgeschichte* LIV (Vienna, 1972), pp. 325–63. For background to varying interpretations.

Badian, E. "Some recent interpretations of Alexander", in *Alexandre le Grand* [section III above], pp. 279–311.

—— "A king's notebooks", *HSCP* LXXII (1968), pp. 183–204. On the so-called 'last plans' – a problem of critical use of sources rather than of Alexander history.

BIBLIOGRAPHY

CHAPTER 9

Documents and sources

Kraeling, E. G. *The Brooklyn Museum Aramaic Papyri.* New Haven, Conn., 1953.
Cowley, A. E. *Aramaic Papyri of the Fifth Century B.C.* Oxford, 1923.
Driver, G. R. *Aramaic Documents of the Fifth Century B.C.* Oxford, 1954; abridged and revised edition Oxford, 1957.
Rabinowitz, J. J. "Aramaic inscriptions of the fifth century B.C.E. from a North-Arab shrine in Egypt", *JNES* xv (1956), 1–9.
Griffith, F. L. *Catalogue of the Demotic papyri in the John Rylands Library Manchester,* 3 vols. Manchester, 1909.
Glanville, S. R. K. *The Instructions of 'Ochsheshonqy.* London, 1955 (Catalogue of Demotic Papyri in the British Museum, 2).
Spiegelberg, W. *Die sogenannte demotische Chronik des Pap. 215 der Bibliothèque Nationale zu Paris.* Leipzig, 1914 (Demotische Studien 7).
Spiegelberg, W. *Die Demotischen Denkmäler,* 3 vols. Leipzig, 1904–Berlin, 1932 (Catalogue général des Antiquités Égyptiennes du Musée du Caire).
Aimé-Giron, N. *Textes araméens d'Égypte.* Cairo, 1931.
Bresciani, E. *Letteratura e poesia dell'Egytto antico.* Turin, 1970.
Bresciani, E. and Kamil, M. "Lettere aramaiche di Hermopoli", *Atti della Accademia Nazionale dei Lincei, Memorie.* Classe di Scienze Morali, Storiche e filologiche, Ser. 8, vol. xii (Rome, 1966), pp. 356–428.
Pseudo-Callisthenes in C (K). Müller (ed.), *Scriptores Rerum Alexandri Magni.* Paris, 1846; repr. Chicago, 1979, with bibliography.
Gilmore, J. (ed.) *The fragments of the Persica of Ktesias.* London, 1888.
König, F. W. (ed.) *Die Persika des Ktesias.* Graz, 1972 (*AfO* Beiheft 18).
Müller, C (K). (ed.) *Ctesias Cnidii... fragmenta* in G. Dindorfius (ed.), *Herodoti Historiarum Libri IX.* Paris, 1887.
Ctesias, *Persica* in Photius, *Bibliothèque* I, ed. and tr. R. Henry. Brussels, 1974; repr. Paris, 1959.

General works on Egyptian history with chapters on the late period

Wiedmann, A. *Aegyptische Geschichte.* Botha, 1884.
Drioton, E. and Vandier, J. *L'Égypte.* Paris, 1962.

Special studies of the Saïte and Persian periods

Wiedmann, A. *Geschichte Aegyptens von Psammetich I bis auf Alexander der Grosse.* Leipzig, 1880.
Kienitz, F. K. *Die politische Geschichte Aegyptens vom 7. bis zum 4. Jahrhundert vor der Zeitwende.* Berlin, 1953.

Studies devoted to Egypt during the Persian period

Jansen, H. L. *The Coptic Story of Cambyses' Invasion of Egypt.* Oslo, 1950.
Posener, G. *La première domination Perse en Égypte.* Cairo, 1963.

BIBLIOGRAPHY

Kienitz, F. K. *op. cit.*
Bresciani, E. "La Satrapia d'Egytto", *SCO* VII (1958), pp. 132ff.
—— "Aegypten und das Perserreich", *Fischer Weltgeschichte* V (Frankfurt, 1965), ch. 16.

On relations between Greece and Egypt

Mallet D. *Des rapports des Grecs avec l'Égypte de la conquête de Cambyses (525) à celle d'Alexandre (332)*. Cairo, 1922.
Kienitz, F. K. *op. cit.*
Austin, M. M. "Greece and Egypt in the archaic age", *Proceedings of the Cambridge Philological Society*, Suppl. 2, 1970.

CHAPTER 10

Abbreviations peculiar to this chapter

AHw.	W. von Soden, *Akkadisches Handwörterbuch*. Wiesbaden, 1959–
BE	Babylonian Expedition of the University of Pennsylvania, Series A: Cuneiform Texts
BIN	Babylonian Inscriptions in the Collection of J. B. Nies
BOR	Babylonian and Oriental Records
BRM	Babylonian Records in the Library of J. Pierpont Morgan
CAD	*The Assyrian Dictionary of the Oriental Institute of the University of Chicago*
Camb.	J. N. Strassmaier, *Inschriften von Cambyses* (Babylonische Texte 8, 9)
CT	*Cuneiform Texts from Babylonian Tablets in the British Museum*
Cyr.	J. N. Strassmaier, *Inschriften von Cyrus* (Babylonische Texte 7)
Dar.	J. N. Strassmaier, *Inschriften von Darius* (Babylonische Text 10–12).
LBAT	*Late Babylonian Astronomical and Related Texts*, copied by T. G. Pinches and J. N. Strassmaier, prepared for publication by A. J. Sachs, with the cooperation of J. Schaumberger (Providence, R.I., 1955)
N(T)	Field numbers of tablets excavated at Nippur by the Oriental Institute and other institutions
PBS	Publications of the Babylonian Section, University Museum, University of Pennsylvania
TCL	Textes cunéiformes du Louvre
TCS	Texts from Cuneiform Sources
TuM	Texte und Materialien der Frau Professor Hilprecht Collection of Babylonian Antiquities im Eigentum der Universität Jena
UCP	University of California Publications in Semitic Philology
UVB	*Vorläufiger Bericht über die...Ausgrabungen in Uruk-Warka* (Berlin, 1930–)
VAB IV	Vorderasiastische Bibliothek Vol. IV; S. Langdon und R. Zehnpfund, *Die Neubabylonischen Königsinschriften* (Leipzig, 1912)
VAS	Vorderasiatische Schriftdenkmäler
YOS	Yale Oriental Series, Babylonian Texts

BIBLIOGRAPHY

A. General

Adams, R. McC. *Land Behind Baghdad, A History of Settlement on the Diyala Plains.* Chicago, 1965.

Albrektson, B. *History and the Gods: An Essay on the Idea of Historical Events as Divine Manifestations in the Ancient Near East and in Israel.* Lund, 1967.

Altheim, F. "Das Alte Iran", *Propyläen-Weltgeschichte*, II (1962), pp. 137–235.

Altheim, F. and Ruth Stiehl, *Die aramäische Sprache under den Achaimeniden.* (Vol. 1). Frankfurt a.M., 1963.

Barnett, R. D. "Xenophon and the Wall of Media", *JHS* LXXXIII (1963), pp. 1–26.

Baumgartner, W. "Herodots babylonische und assyrische Nachrichten", *ArOr* XVIII (1950), pp. 69–106.

Benveniste, E. *Titres et Noms Propres en Iranien Ancien.* Paris, 1966.

Bickerman, E. J. "The Edict of Cyrus in Ezra 1", *JBL* LXXV (1946), pp. 249–7.

—— "The Seleucids and the Achaemenids", in *La Persia e il mondo Greco-Romano.* Accademia Nazionale dei Lincei 363 (Rome, 1966), pp. 87–117.

Boehmer, R. M. "Volkstum und Städte der Mannäer", *Baghdader Mitteilungen* III (1964), pp. 11–24.

—— "Zur Lage von Parsua im 9. Jahrhundert vor Christus", *Berliner Jahrbuch für Vor- und Frühgeschichte* V (1965), pp. 187–98.

de Liagre Böhl, F. M. Th. "Die babylonischen Prätendenten zur Anfangszeit des Darius (Dareios) I", *BiOr* XXV (1968), pp. 150–2.

—— "Die Babylonischen Prätendenten zur Zeit des Xerxes", *BiOr* XIX (1962), pp. 110–14.

Bogaert, R. *Les Origines antiques de la banque de dépôt (Une mise au point accompagnée d'une esquisse des opérations de banque en Méspotamie).* Leiden, 1966.

Brinkman, J. A. "Neo-Babylonian Texts in the Archaeological Museum at Florence", *JNES* XXV (1966), pp. 201–9.

—— *A Political History of Post-Kassite Babylonia.* Rome, 1968.

Cameron, G. G. "Darius and Xerxes in Babylonia", *AJSL* LVIII (1941), pp. 318–25.

—— *Persepolis Treasury Tablets.* Chicago, 1984 (Oriental Institute Publications 65) [*PTI*].

Cardascia, G. *Les Archives des Murašû, Une famille d'hommes d'affaires babyloniens à l'époque perse (455–403 av. J.-C.).* Paris, 1951.

—— "Le statut de l'étranger dans la Méspotamie ancienne", *Recueils de la Société Jean Bodin* IX (1958), pp. 105–17.

—— "Faut-il éliminer ^{giš}APIN = nartabu (une machine d'irrigation)?", *RA* LX (1966), pp. 153–64.

Clermont-Ganneau, S. "Le paradeisos royal Achéménide de Sidon", *Revue Biblique* XXX (1921), pp. 106–9.

Dandamayev, M. A. "Foreign Slaves on the Estates of the Achaemenid Kings and their Nobles", *International Congress of Orientalists* II (Moscow, 1963), pp. 147–54.

—— "Tempelbauern im späten Babylonien", *Palestinskii Sbornik* XVII (80) (1967), pp. 41–9.

BIBLIOGRAPHY

—— "Die Lehnsbeziehungen in Babylonien unter den ersten Achaemeniden", in *Festschrift für Wilhelm Eilers* (Wiesbaden, 1967), pp. 38–42.

—— "Bagasarū ganzabara", *Studien zur Sprachwissenschaft und Kulturkunde* (Innsbrucker Beiträge zur Kulturwissenschaft 14. Innsbruck, 1968), pp. 235–9.

Dhorme, P. "Les tablettes babyloniennes de Neirab", *RA* xxv (1928), pp. 53–82.

Driver, G. R. *Aramaic Documents of the Fifth Century B.C.*, abridged and revised edition. Oxford, 1957.

Dubberstein, W. H. "The Chronology of Cyrus and Cambyses", *AJSL* LV (1938), pp. 417–19.

Duchesne-Guillemin, J. *La religion de l'Iran*. Paris, 1962.

Ebeling, E. *Neubabylonische Briefe aus Uruk*. Berlin, 1930ff.

—— *Bruchstücke eines politischen Propagandagedichtes aus einer assyrischen Kanzlei*. Leipzig, 1938.

—— "Die Rüstung eines babylonischen Panzerreiters nach einem Vertrag aus der Zeit Darius II", *ZA* L (1952), pp. 203–13.

Eilers, W. *Iranische Beamtennamen in der keilschriftlichen Überlieferung* 1. Leipzig, 1940.

—— "Kleinasiatisches", *ZDMG* XCIV (1940), pp. 187–233.

Ellis, R. S. *Foundation Deposits in Ancient Mesopotamia*. New Haven, Conn., 1968.

Frye, R. N. *The Heritage of Persia*. London, 1962.

Gadd, C. J. "The Harran Inscriptions of Nabonidus", *Anatolian Studies* VII (1958), pp. 35–92.

Galling, K. *Studien zur Geschichte Israels im persischen Zeitalter*. Tübingen, 1964.

Gelb, I. J. "The Ancient Mesopotamian Ration System", *JNES* XXIV (1965), pp. 230–43.

Goossens, G. "Artistes et artisans étrangers en Perse sous les Achéménides", *La Nouvelle Clio* I (Brussels, 1949), pp. 32–44.

Güterbrock, H. G. "Die historische Tradition und ihre literarische Gestaltung bei Babyloniern und Hethitern bis 1200", *ZA* XLII (1934), pp. 1–91; XLIV (1938), pp. 45–149.

Hagen, D. E. "Keilschrifturkunden zur Geschichte des Königs Cyrus", *BA* II (1894), pp. 205–57.

Hallock, R. T. "The 'One Year' of Darius I", *JNES* XIX (1960), pp. 36–9.

—— *Persepolis Fortification Tablets*. Chicago, 1969. (Oriental Institute Publications 92) [*PFT*].

Harper, R. F. *Assyrian and Babylonian Letters*, 14 vols. Chicago, 1892–1914.

Herzfeld, E. E. *Altpersische Inschriften*. Berlin, 1938.

—— *Zoroaster and his World*. Princeton, 1947.

Hilprecht, H. V. *Explorations in Bible Lands during the 19th Century*. Philadelphia, 1903.

Hinz, W. "Das erste Jahr des Grosskönigs Dareios", *ZDMG* XCII (1938), pp. 136–73.

Junge, P. F. "Satrapie und *natio*, Reichsverwaltung und Reichspolitik im Staate Dareios' I", *Klio* XXXIV (1941), 1–55.

BIBLIOGRAPHY

Kantorowicz, E. H. *Laudes Regiae, A Study in Liturgical Acclamations and Mediaeval Ruler Worship.* Berkeley–Los Angeles, 1958.

Kent, R. G. *Old Persian Grammar, Texts, Lexicon.* New Haven, Conn., 1950; 2nd ed. New Haven, Conn., 1953.

Kiechle, F. "Zur Humanität in der Kriegsführung der griechischen Staaten", *Historia* VII (1958), 129–56.

Kienitz, F. K. *Die politische Geschichte Ägyptens vom 7. bis zum 4. Jahrhundert vor der Zeitwende.* Berlin, 1953.

Klengel, H. "Babylon zur Zeit der Perser, Griechen und Parther", *Forschungen und Berichte, Staatliche Museen zu Berlin,* v (1962), pp. 40–53.

Klíma, O. *Manis Zeit und Leben.* Prague, 1962.

Koldewey, R. *Die Königsburgen von Babylon,* ed. F. Wetzel. Leipzig, 1932.

König, F. W. *Der Burgbau zu Susa. Nach dem Bauberichte des Königs Dareios I.* Leipzig, 1930.

—— "Naboned und Kuraš", *AfO* VII (1931/2), pp. 178–82.

Kraeling, E. G. *The Brooklyn Museum Aramaic Papyri.* London–New Haven, Conn., 1953.

Krückmann, O. *Babylonische Rechts-und Verwaltungs-Urkunden aus der Zeit Alexanders und der Diadochen.* Weimar, 1931.

Kugler, F. X. *Sternkunde und Sterndienst in Babel,* 3 vols. Münster i.W., 1907–1935.

Landsberger, B. *Brief des Bischofs von Esagila an König Asarhaddon.* Amsterdam, 1965.

Landsberger, B. and Theo Bauer, "Strophengedicht von den Freveltaten Nabonids und der Befreiung durch Kyrus", *ZA* XXXVII (1926–7), pp. 88–98.

Langdon, S. "Tablets from Barghuthiat", *RA* XXX (1933), pp. 189–91.

Leuze, O. *Die Satrapieneinteilung in Syrien und im Zweistromlande von 520–320.* Halle, 1935 (Schriften der Königsberger Gelehrten Gesellschaft. Geisteswissenschaftliche Klasse XI/4).

Lewy, J. "The Late Assyro-Babylonian Cult of the Moon and its Culmination at the Time of Nabonidus", *HUCA* XIX (1946), pp. 405–89.

—— "The Problems Inherent in Section 70 of the Behistun Inscription", *HUCA* XXV (1954), pp. 169–208.

McCown, D. E. and Haines, R. C. *Nippur I (Temple of Enlil, Scribal Quarter and Soundings).* Chicago, 1967.

Mazzarino, S. "Le Vie di Communicazione tra Impero Achemenide e Mondo Greco", in *La Persia e il Mondo Greco-Romano,* Accademia Nazionale dei Lincei 363 (Rome, 1966), pp. 75–83.

Meuleau, M. "Mesopotamien in der Perserzeit", in *Griechen und Perser, Die Mittelmeerwelt im Altertum* I, (Frankfurt a.M., 1965), pp. 330–55 (Fischer Weltgeschichte 5).

Meyer, R. *Das Gebet Nabonids.* Berlin 1962 (Sächsische Gesellschaft der Wissenschaften, Sitzungsberichte, Phil.-hist. Kl., 107/3).

Moran, W. L. "Notes on the New Nabonidus Inscriptions", *Orientalia* XXVIII (1959), pp. 130–40.

Müller, K. F. *Das assyrische Königsritual*. Leipzig, 1937.
Neugebauer, O. *Astronomical Cuneiform Texts*, 3 vols. Princeton–London n. d. [1955].
Oates, D. *Studies in the Ancient History of Northern Iraq*. London, 1968.
Olmstead, A. T. "Darius as Lawgiver", *AJSLL* LI (1934/5), pp. 247–9.
—— "Darius and his Behistun Inscription", *AJSLL* LV (1938), pp. 392–416.
—— "Tettanai, Governor of 'Across the River'", *JNES* III (1944), p. 46.
—— *History of the Persian Empire*. Chicago, 1948.
Oppenheim, A. L. *The Interpretation of Dreams in the Ancient Near East*. Philadelphia, 1956.
—— *Studies presented to A. Leo Oppenheim*. Chicago, 1964.
—— *Letters from Mesopotamia*. Chicago, 1967.
—— *Ancient Mesopotamia, Portrait of a Dead Civilization*. 3rd Printing. Chicago, 1968.
—— "Essay on Overland Trade in the First Millenium B.C.", *JCS* XXI (1968), pp. 236–54.
—— "Divination and Celestial Observation in the Last Assyrian Empire", *Centaurus* XIV (Anniversary Volume for O. Neugebauer) (Copenhagen, 1969), pp. 97–135.
Pallis, S. A. "The History of Babylon 538–93 B.C.", in *Studia orientalia Ioanni Pedersen septuagenario...dicata* (Copenhagen, 1953), pp. 275–95.
Paper, H. *The Phonology and Morphology of Royal Achaemenid Elamite*. Ann Arbor, Mich., 1955.
Parker, R. A. and Dubberstein, W. H. *Babylonian Chronology 626 B.C.–A.D. 75*, 3rd ed. Providence, R.I., 1956 (Brown University Studies 19). This book brings up to date two earlier editions, published in Studies in Ancient Oriental Civilizations, No. 24, (Oriental Institute Publications, Chicago 1942 and 1946). The new edition was in its turn supplemented in a book review written by D. J. Wiseman in *JSS* V (1960), p. 74, Cf. J. A. Brinkman, "Neo-Babylonian Texts in the Archaeological Museum at Florence", *JNES* XXV (1966), pp. 201–9, especially p. 203 and p. 204, and F. M. Th. Böhl, "Die babylonischen Prätendenten zur Anfangszeit des Darius (Dareios) I", *BiOr* XXV (1968), pp. 150–2.
Poebal, A. "Chronology of Darius' first Year of Reign", *AJSLL* LV (1938), pp. 142–65; 285–314.
Petschow, H. "Die neubabylonische Zwiegesprächsurkunde und Genesis 23", *JCS*, XIX (1965), pp. 103–20.
Porada, Edith "Greek Coin Impressions from Ur", *Iraq* XXII (1960), pp. 228–34.
—— *Ancient Iran*. London, 1965.
Posener, G. *La première domination perse en Égypte, Recueil d'Inscriptions Hiéroglyphiques*. Cairo, 1936.
Pritchard, J. B. (ed.) *Ancient Near Eastern Texts relating to the Old Testament*, 2nd ed. Princeton, N.J., 1969 [*ANET*].
Rawlinson, H. C. *The Cuneiform Inscriptions of Western Asia*, 5 vols. London, 1861–1909.

BIBLIOGRAPHY

Robinson, E. S. G. "A Silversmith's Hoard from Mesopotamia", *Iraq* XII (1950), pp. 44–51.
Röllig, W. "Erwägungen zu neuen Stelen König Nabonids", *ZA* LVI (1964), pp. 218–60.
Rössler, O. *Untersuchungen über die akkadische Fassung der Achämenideninschriften*. Berlin, 1938.
Rubin, B. "Die Entstehung der Kataphraktenreiterei im Lichte der chorezmischen Ausgrabungen", *Historia* IV (1955), pp. 264–83.
Sachau, E. *Aramäische Papyrus und Ostraka aus einer jüdischen Militär-Kolonie zu Elephantine*. Leipzig, 1911.
Sachs, A. "A Classification of the Babylonian Astronomical Tablets of the Seleucid Period", *JCS* II (1948), pp. 271–90.
—— "Babylonian Horoscopes", *JCS* VI (1952), pp. 49–75.
Sachs, A. and Wiseman, D. J. "A Babylonian King List of the Hellenistic Period", *Iraq* XVI (1954), pp. 202–11.
San Nicolò, M. *Beiträge zu einer Prosopographie neu-babylonischer Beamten der Zivil- und Tempelverwaltung*. Sitzungsberichte der Bayrischen Akademie der Wissenschaften, Phil.-hist. Abt., II/2. 1941.
Schaeder, H. H. *Iranische Beiträge* I. Leipzig, 1930.
—— "Des eigenen Todes sterben", *Nachrichten der Akademie der Wissenschaften in Göttingen*, Philologisch-Historische Klasse, 1946–47, pp. 24–36.
Schedl, C. "Nabuchodonosor, Arpakšad und Darius, Untersuchungen zum Buch Judit", *ZDMG* CXV (1965), pp. 242–54.
Schiewek, H. "Der persische Golf als Schiffahrts-und Seehandelsroute in achämenischer Zeit und in der Zeit Alexanders des Grossen", *Bonner Jahrbücher* CLXII (1962), pp. 4–97.
Schmidt, E. *The Treasury of Persepolis and other Discoveries in the Homeland of the Achaemenians*. Chicago, 1939.
—— *Persepolis I. Structures. Reliefs. Inscriptions*. Chicago, 1953 (Oriental Institute Publications 68).
—— *Persepolis II. Contents of the Treasury and other Discoveries*. Chicago, 1957 (Oriental Institute Publications 69).
—— *Persepolis III. Royal Tombs and Other Monuments*. Chicago, 1970 (Oriental Institute Publications 70).
Schnabel, P. *Berossos und die babylonisch-hellenistische Literatur*. Leipzig–Berlin, 1923.
Schwenzner, W. "Gobryas", *Klio* XVIII (1922–3), pp. 41–58 and 226–52.
Seux, M. J. *Epithètes royales akkadiennes et sumériennes*. Paris, 1967.
Smith, Sidney. *Babylonian Historical Texts relating to the Capture and Downfall of Babylon*. London, 1924.
Tadmor, H. "The Inscriptions of Nabunaid: Historical Arrangement", *Assyriological Studies* XVI (Chicago, 1965), pp. 351–63.
Thureau-Dangin, F. *Rituels accadiens*. Paris, 1921.
Ungnad, A. "Der angebliche König Tarzia der Perserzeit", *Orientalia* X (1941), pp. 337–8.
van Dijk, J. "Die Tontafeln aus dem *rēš* Heiligtum", in H. J. Lenzen, *UVB* XVIII (1962), pp. 43–61.

BIBLIOGRAPHY

van Loon, M. N. *Urartian Art*. Istanbul, 1966.
Weidner, E. F. "Die älteste Nachricht über das persische Königshaus. Kyros I ein Zeitgenosse Aššurbânaplis," *AfO* VII (1931), pp. 1–7.
―― "Jojachin, König von Juda, in babylonischen Keilschrifttexten", in *Mélanges syriens offerts à Monsieur René Dussaud* II (Paris, 1939), pp. 923–35.
Weissbach, F. H. *Babylonische Miszellen*. Leipzig, 1903.
―― *Die Keilinschriften der Achämeniden*. Leipzig, 1911.
―― "Kyros (6)", in Pauly, Suppl. IV (1924), pp. 1128–66.
Wetzel, F. "Babylon zur Zeit Herodots", *ZA* XLVIII (1944), pp. 45–68.
―― "Babylon bei den klassischen Schriftstellern ausser Herodot (Ktesias, Strabo, Curtius Rufus, Josephus Flavius, Berossos)", *MDOG* LXXXII (1950), pp. 47–53.
Wetzel, F., Schmidt, E. and Mallwitz, A. *Das Babylon der Spätzeit*. Berlin, 1957.
Widengren, G. *Iranische Geisteswelt von den Anfängen bis zum Islam*. Baden-Baden, 1961.
―― "Geschichte Mesopotamiens 1. Mesopotamien in achämenidischer Zeit", in *Orientalische Geschichte von Kyros bis Mohammed* II (Leiden, 1966), pp. 1–7 (HO I. II. 4. 2).
Wiseman, D. J. *Chronicles of Chaldaean Kings (626–556 B.C.) in the British Museum*. London, 1956.
Woolley, Sir Leonard. *The Neo-Babylonian and Persian Periods*. UE IX (1962).
Young, T. C. "The Iranian Migration into the Zagros", *Iran* V (1967), pp. 11–34.

B. *Legal and Administrative Texts in Cuneiforms of the Achaemenian Period*

Ball, C. J. "A Babylonian Deed of Sale", *PSBA* XIV (1892), pp. 166–9. (1 text)
Barton, G. A. "Some Contracts of the Persian Period of the KH² Collection of the University of Pennsylvania", *AJSLL* XVI (1900), pp. 65–82. (34 texts)
Böhl, F. M. Th. de Liagre. "An Assignment of a Debt dated in the Reign of Darius I, with an Aramaic Endorsement (492 B.C.)", *Symbolae ad jus et historiam antiquitatis pertinentes Julio Christiano van Oven dedicatae* (Leiden, 1946), pp. 63–70. (1 text)
Boissier, E. "Extrait de la chronique locale d'Uruk", *RA* XXIII (1926), pp. 13–17. (1 text)
Clay, A. T. *Business Documents of Murashû Sons of Nippur dated in the Reign of Darius II (424–404 B.C.)* Philadelphia, 1904 (BE 10). (132 texts)
―― *Legal and Commercial Transactions dated in the Assyrian, Neo-Babylonian and Persian Periods chiefly from Nippur*. Philadelphia, 1908 (BE 8). (72 texts)
―― *Babylonian Business Transactions of the First Millennium B.C.* New York, 1912 (BRM 1). (26 texts)
―― *Business Documents of Murashû Sons of Nippur dated in the reign of Darius II*. Philadelphia, 1912 (PBS II/1) (228 texts)
Deimel, A. "Ib. 168", *Orientalia* V (1936), p. 45. (1 text)

BIBLIOGRAPHY

Dhorme, E. "Les tablettes babyloniennes de Neirab", *RA* xxv (1928), pp. 53–82. (4 texts)

Dougherty, R. P. *Archives from Erech, Neo-Babylonian and Persian Periods.* New Haven, Conn., 1933 (Goucher College Cuneiform Inscriptions 1). (41 texts)

Driver, G. R. "A Babylonian Tablet with an Aramaic Endorsement", *Iraq* IV (1937), pp. 16–18. (1 text)

Eilers, W. *Iranische Beamtennamen in der keilschriftlichen Überlieferung* (Leipzig, 1960), pls. ii., iii. (2 texts)

Evetts, B. T. A. *Inscriptions of the Reigns of Evil-Merodach, Neriglissar, and Laborosoarchod.* Leipzig, 1892 (Babylonische Texte 6 B). (4 texts)

Figulla, H. H. *Business Documents of the New-Babylonian Period. UET* IV. London, 1949. (70 texts)

—— "Lawsuit concerning a sacrilegious theft at Erech", *Iraq* XIII (1951), pp. 95–101. (1 text)

Goetze, A. "Fragment of a Late Babylonian contract mentioning the 3rd year of Artaxerxes", *JCS* I (1947), p. 351. (1 text)

Gordon, C. H. *Smith College Tablets, 110 Cuneiform Tablets selected from the College Collection.* Ventnor, N.J., 1952. (13 texts)

Grotefend, G. F. "Urkunden in babylonischer Keilschrift", *Zeitschrift für die Kunde des Morgenlandes* II (Göttingen–Bonn, 1839), pp. 177–89 and pl. following p. 324. (1 text)

Hilprecht, H. V. and Clay, A. T. *Business Documents of Murashû Sons of Nippur dated in the Reign of Artaxerxes I (464–424 B.C.).* Philadelphia, 1898 (BE 9). (109 texts)

Holt, I. L. "Tablets from the R. Campbell Thompson Collection in the Haskell Oriental Museum, University of Chicago", *AJSLL* XXVII (1911), pp. 193–232. (3 texts)

Jacobsen, T. *Cuneiform Texts in the National Museum, Copenhagen, chiefly of economic contents.* Leiden, 1939. (2 texts)

Keiser, C. E. *Letters and Contracts from Erech Written in the Neo-Babylonian Period.* New Haven, Conn., 1917 (BIN 1). (19 texts)

Knopf, C. S. "Items of Interest from Miscellaneous Neo-Babylonian Documents", *Bulletin of the Southern California Academy of Sciences, Los Angeles,* XXXII (1933), pp. 41–76. (2 texts)

Krückmann, O. *Neubabylonische Rechts- und Verwaltungs-Texte.* Leipzig, 1933 (TuM II–III). (102 texts)

Langdon, S. in L. Ch. Watelin and S. Langdon, *Excavations at Kish* III. Paris, 1930. (2 texts)

—— "Tablets from Barghuthiat", *RA* xxx (1933), pp. 189–91. (1 text)

Le Gac, Y. "Textes babyloniens de la Collection Lyclama à Cannes", *Babyloniaca* II (1910), pp. 33–72. (5 texts)

Legrain, L. "Collection Louis Cugnin, textes cunéiformes, catalogue, transcription et traduction", *RA* x (1913), pp. 41–68. (2 texts)

Lutz, H. F. *Neo-Babylonian Administrative Documents from Erech.* Parts I and II. Berkeley, Calif., 1931 (UCP 9 i). (159 texts)

—— *An Agreement between a Babylonian Feudal Lord and his Retainer in the Reign of Darius II,* (Berkeley, Calif., 1928), pp. 269–77 (UCP 9 iii). (1 text)

BIBLIOGRAPHY

―― *An Uruk Document of the Time of Cambyses*, (Berkeley, Calif., 1937), pp. 243–50 (UCP 10 viii). (1 text)

Moore, E. W. *Neo-Babylonian Documents in the University of Michigan Collection.* Ann Arbor, Mich., 1939. (17 texts)

Nies, J. B. and Keiser, C. E. *Historical, Religious and Economic Texts and Antiquities.* New Haven, Conn., 1920 (BIN 2). (6 texts)

Oberhuber, K. *Sumerische und akkadische Keilschriftdenkmäler des Archäologischen Museums zu Florenz.* Innsbruck, 1960. (3 texts)

Peiser, F. E. *Babylonische Verträge des Berliner Museums.* Berlin, 1890. (20 texts)

―― *Texte juristischen und geschäftlichen Inhalts.* Berlin, 1896), p. 312 (Keilinschriftliche Bibliothek 4). (1 text)

Pinches, Th. G. *Inscribed Babylonian Tablets in the Possession of Sir Henry Peek, Bart.* London, 1888. (8 texts)

―― *The Babylonian Tablets of the Berens Collection.* London, 1915. (4 texts)

―― "Miscellaneous Texts", *CT* XLIV (London, 1963), nos 73–82. (10 texts)

―― "Remarks on Babylonian Contract Tablets and the Canon of Ptolemy", *PSBA* VI (1878), pp. 484–93. (1 text)

―― "Contract Tablet from Babylon, inscribed with unknown characters", *PSBA* V (1883), pp. 103–7. (1 text)

―― "Tablet referring to work done on Darius' State-barge", *PSBA* VII (1885), pp. 148–52. (1 text)

―― "A Fragment of a Babylonian Tithe-List", *BOR* I (1886), pp. 76–78. (1 text)

―― "A Babylonian Dower Contract", *BOR* II (1887), pp. 1–8. (1 text)

―― "Some Late-Babylonian Texts in the British Museum", *RT* XIX (1897), pp. 101–24. (1 text)

―― "Two Archaic and three later Babylonian Tablets", *PSBA* XIX (1897), pp. 132–45. (2 texts)

―― "The Collection of Babylonian Tablets belonging to Joseph Offord, Esq.," *Palestine Exploration Quarterly* 1900, pp. 258–68. (1 text)

―― "Two Late Tablets of Historical Interest", *PSBA* XXXVIII (1916), pp. 27–34. (1 text)

Pohl, A. *Neubabylonische Rechtsurkunden aus den Berliner Staatlichen Museen.* AnOr VIII. Rome, 1933. (43 texts)

―― *Neubabylonische Rechtsurkunden aus den Berliner Staatlichen Museen.* AnOr IX. Rome, 1934. (5 texts)

Revillout, E. and V. "Sworn Obligations in Egyptian and Babylonian Law", *BOR* I (1886), pp. 101–4. (1 text)

―― "A Contract of Apprenticeship from Sippara", *BOR* II (1887), pp. 119–25. (1 text)

―― "Istar Taribi", *BOR* II (1887), pp. 57–9. (3 texts)

Sayce, A. H. "Some Unpublished Contract Tablets", *BOR* IV (1889), pp. 1–6. (1 text)

―― "Babylonian Contract-Tablet belonging to the Imperial Academy of Science at St Petersburg", *ZA* V (1890), pp. 276–80. (1 text)

Scheil, V. "Contrat babylonien à légende araméenne", *RA* XI (1914), pp. 183–87. (1 text)

BIBLIOGRAPHY

—— "Sur un contrat de l'époque de Darius II avec épigraphe araméen", *RA* XVI (1919), pp. 111–12. (1 text)
—— "Procès-verbal d'un refus d'obéissance", *RA* XVI (1919), pp. 113–14. (1 text)
—— "Contractant et témoin à la fois(?)", in "Documents et Arguments No. 10", *RA* XXVI (1929), pp. 17–19. (1 text)
Schroeder, O. "Aus den keilinschriftlichen Sammlungen des Berliner Museums", *ZA* XXXII (1918/1919), pp. 1–22. (1 text)
Speleers, L. *Recueil des Inscriptions de l'Asie Antérieure des Musées Royaux du Cinqauntenaire à Bruxelles.* Brussels, 1925. (1 text)
Strassmaier, J. N. *Inschriften von Cyrus, König von Babylon (538–529 v. Chr.).* Leipzig, 1890 [*Cyr.*]. (384 texts)
—— *Inschriften von Cambyses, König von Babylon (529–521 v. Chr.).* Leipzig, 1890 [*Camb.*]. (441 texts)
—— *Inschriften von Darius, König von Babylon (521–485 v. Chr.).* Leipzig, 1892 [*Dar.*]. (579 texts)
—— Texte und Transcription zu der Abhandlung von J. N. Strassmaier, S.J. in *Actes du VIIIe Congrès internationale des Orientalistes*, Sem. Sect. B 2nd Part. Leiden, 1893. (16 texts)
—— in Bezold, C. "Mitteilungen aus Wien", *ZA* I (1886), pp. 441–6. (1 text)
—— in Wallis Budge, E. A. "On some recently acquired Babylonian Tablets", *ZA* III (1889), pp. 211–30. (1 text)
Thompson, R. C. *A Catalogue of the Late Babylonian Tablets in the Bodleian Library, Oxford.* London, 1927. (23 texts)
Tremayne, A. *Records from Erech, time of Cyrus and Cambyses.* New Haven, Conn., 1925 (YOS 7). (198 texts)
Ungnad, A. in *Vorderasiatische Schriftdenkmäler der Königlichen Museen zu Berlin* III–VI. Berlin, 1907 [*VAS*]. (430 texts)
—— "Neubabylonische Privaturkunden aus der Sammlung Amherst", *AfO* XIX (1959), pp. 74–82. (32 texts)
von Voigtlander, E. N. *The Bisitun Inscription of Darius the Great – Babylonian version.* London, 1978 (*CIIr*, Part I, vol. II).
Weissbach, F. H. *Babylonische Miszellen.* Leipzig, 1903. (1 text)
Weissberg, D. B. *Guild Structure and Political Allegiance in Early Achaemenid Mesopotamia.* New Haven, Conn., 1967. (4 texts)

CHAPTER 12

Currency and coinage

Balmuth, Miriam S. "The monetary forerunners of coinage in Phoenicia and Palestine", in *International Numismatic Convention, Jerusalem, 17–31 December 1963* (Tel Aviv, 1967), pp. 25–32.
—— "Origins of coinage" in *A Survey of Numismatic Research 1966–1971* (International Numismatic Commission: New York, 1973), pp. 27–35.
—— "The critical moment: transition from currency to coinage in the eastern Mediterranean", *World Archaeology* VI. 3 (Feb. 1975), 293–8.

BIBLIOGRAPHY

Bivar, A. D. H. "A hoard of ingot-currency of the Median period from Nūsh-i Jān, near Malayir", *Iran* IX (1971), 97–111.

—— "Bent bars and straight bars: an appendix to the Mir Zakah hoard", *StIr* XI (1982) (Mélanges offerts à Raoul Curiel), 49–60.

Dayton, John, "Money in the Near East before coinage", *Berytus* XXIII (1974), 41–52.

Henning, W. B. "The 'coin' with the cuneiform inscription", *NC* 1956, 327–8.

Herzfeld, Ernst, "Notes on the Achaemenid coinage and some Sasanian mint-names", *Transactions of the International Numismatic Congress 1936* London, 1938, pp. 413–26, esp. 414–16.

Hill, G. F. "Notes on the Imperial Persian coinage", XXXIX (1919), 116–29. (Many interesting observations, but the attempt to attribute darics by their portraiture is no longer supported.)

—— *Catalogue of the Greek coins of Arabia, Mesopotamia and Persia.* London, 1922 (Catalogue of the Greek coins in the British Museum).

Jenkins, G. K. "Coins from the collection of C. J. Rich", *BMQ* XXVIII (1964), 88–95.

Mørkholm, O. "A coin of Artaxerxes III", *NC* 1974, pp. 1–4.

Naster, P. "Remarques charactéroscopiques et technologiques au sujet des créseides", in *Congresso internazionale di numismatica, Roma 11–16 settembre 1961* II, Atti (Rome, 1965), 25–36.

Noe, S. P. *Two hoards of Persian sigloi.* New York 1956 (ANSNNM 136).

Powell, M. A., Jr. "A contribution to the history of money in Mesopotamia prior to the invention of coinage", in B. Hruška and G. Komoróczy (eds), *Festschrift Lubor Matouš* (Budapest, 1978), 211–43.

Regling, K. "Dareikos und Kroiseios", *Klio* XIV (1915), 91–112.

Robinson, E. S. G. "Greek coins acquired by the British Museum, 1938–1948", *NC* 1948, pp. 43–65. (For the tetradrachm of Tissaphernes see pp. 48–54.)

—— "A silversmith's hoard from Mesopotamia", *Iraq* XII (1950), 44–51.

—— "The beginnings of Achaemenid coinage", *NC* 1958, pp. 187–193.

Roychaudhury, Mrityunjoy. "A gold coin of Croesus", *Journal of the Asiatic Society of Bengal, Numismatic Supplement* XXIV (1914), No. 146, pp. 486–8. (A find at Mari Indus in the Punjab.)

Schaeffer, C. "Une trouvaille de monnaies archaïques grecques à Ras Shamra", *Mélanges syriens offerts à M. R. Dussaud* I (Paris, 1939), 461–87.

Schlumberger, D. "L'argent grec dans l'empire achéménide", in R. Curiel and D. Schlumberger, *Trésors monétaires d'Afghanistan* (Paris, 1953), pp. 1–64 (MDAFA 14).

Schwyzer, Eduard. "Awest. *asparənō* und byzantin. ἀσπρόν: Beitrage zur griechisch-orientalischen Münznamforschung", *Indogermanische Forschungen* XLIX (1931), 1–45.

BIBLIOGRAPHY

Weights and measures

Babin, C. "Note sur la metrologie et les proportions dans les monuments achéménides de la Perse", *Revue Archéologique* XVII (1891), 374–9.

Cameron, G. C. and Gershevitch, I. " New tablets from the Persepolis Treasury", *JNES* XXIV (1965), 167–92.

Hallock, R. T. *Persepolis Fortification Tablets* (Chicago, 1969), pp. 72–4 (Oriental Institute Publications 92) [*PFT*].

Hesse, Albert. "Metrologie statistique d'elements architecturaux des palais achéménides de Suse", *CDAFI* II (1972), 219–39.

Lehmann (-Haupt), C. F. "Das altbabylonische Mass- und Gewichts-system als Grundlage der antiken Gewichts-, Münz- und Massystem", *Actes du VIIIe Congrès Internationale des Orientalistes* II, i, Section Sémitique, Partie B (Paris 1908), 167–249. (A work of vast erudition, raising numerous issues of importance, but over-expanded with passages of unwarranted theorising.)

Michaelis, A. " The metrological relief at Oxford", *JHS* IV (1883), 335–50.

Mitchell, T. C. " The bronze lion weight from Abydos", *Iran* XI (1973), 173–5.

Nylander, C. *Ionians at Pasargadae* (Uppsala, 1970), pp. 96–7.

Regling, K. and Lehmann-Haupt, C. F. "Die Sonderformen des 'babylonischen' Gewichtssystem", *ZDMG* LXIII (1909), 701–29.

Schmidt, Erich F. "Weights: classifications, frequencies, find-conditions" in *Persepolis II* (Chicago, 1957), 105–7.

—— "Measures of capacity" in *Persepolis II* (Chicago 1957), pp. 108–9. (The above are the briefest, clearest and most authoritative statements of the evidence for the Achaemenid weights, and measures of capacity.)

Thureau-Dangin, F. "Numération et métrologie sumeriennes", *RA* XVIII (1921), 123–42. (A wide-ranging inquiry into every aspect of Babylonian metrology, but with not always sufficient evidence to reach definitive solutions.)

Trousdale, William. "An Achaemenid stone weight from Afghanistan", *East and West* XVIII (1968), 277–80. (Publishes a damaged stone weight, originally Achaemenid, but apparently re-used in the Islamic period.)

Yadin, Yigael, 'Ancient Judaean weights and the date of the Samaria ostraca', *Scripta Hierosolymitana* VIII (Jerusalem, 1961) 9–23.

CHAPTER 14

The following list was compiled by Peter Khoroche

Barr, K. *Avesta oversat og forklaret*. Copenhagen, 1954.

Bartholomae, C. *Die Gatha's des Awesta*. Strassburg, 1905.

—— *Zarathustra's Leben und Lehre*. Heidelberg, 1924.

Benveniste, E. *The Persian Religion According to the Chief Greek Texts*. Paris, 1929.

—— *Les Mages dans l'ancien Iran*. Paris, 1938.

Boyce, M. *A History of Zoroastrianism* I, II. Leiden, 1975, 1982 (*HO* I. VIII. 1. 2, 2a).

BIBLIOGRAPHY

—— *Zoroastrians: their Religious Beliefs and Practices*. London, 1979.
—— *Textual Sources for the Study of Zoroastrianism*. Manchester, 1984.
Brandenstein, W. and Mayrhofer, M. *Handbuch des Altpersischen*. Wiesbaden, 1964.
Christensen, A. *Les types du premier homme et du premier roi dans l'histoire légendaire des Iraniens* I, II. Stockholm, 1917; Leiden, 1934.
—— *Études sur le zoroastrisme de la Perse antique*. Copenhagen, 1928.
—— *Essai sur la démonologie iranienne*. Copenhagen, 1941.
Clemen, C. *Die griechischen und lateinischen Nachrichten über die persische Religion*. Giessen, 1920.
—— *Fontes Historiae Religionis Persicae*. Bonn, 1920.
Darmesteter, J. *The Zend-Avesta* I, II. Oxford, 1883, 1895 (SBE IV, XXIII).
—— *Le Zend-Avesta*, 3 vols. Paris, 1892–3; repr. 1960.
Duchesne-Guillemin, J. *Zoroastre, Étude critique avec une traduction commentée des Gāthā*. Paris, 1948.
—— *The Hymns of Zarathustra* (translated from the French by Mrs. M. Henning). London, 1952.
—— *The Western Response to Zoroaster*. Oxford, 1958.
—— *La Religion de l'Iran Ancien*. Paris, 1962.
—— *Religion of Ancient Iran* (English version of above, incorporating a few additions and alterations as well as updated bibliography and references, by K. M. JamaspAsa. Bombay, 1973).
—— "Were the Achaemenians Zoroastrians?", in G. Walser (ed.), *Beiträge zur Achämenidengeschichte*. Weisbaden, 1972 (*Historia*: Einzelschriften 18), pp. 59–82.
Fox, W. S. and Pemberton, R. E. K. *Passages in Greek and Latin Literature Relating to Zoroaster and Zoroastrianism, Translated into English*. Bombay, 1929 (*JCOI* 14).
Frye, R. N. *The Heritage of Persia*. London, 1962.
—— *The History of Ancient Iran*. Munich, 1984 (Handbuch der Altertumswissenschaft III. 7).
Geiger, B. *Die Aməša Spantas*. Vienna, 1916.
Geldner, K. F. *Drei Yasht aus dem Zendavesta*. Stuttgart, 1884.
—— *Avesta, The Sacred Books of the Parsis*, 3 vols. Stuttgart, 1886–96.
—— *Die zoroastrische Religion (Das Avesta)*. Tubingen, 1926.
Gershevitch, I. *The Avestan Hymn to Mithra*. Cambridge, 1959; repr. 1967.
—— "Zoroaster's Own Contribution", *JNES* XXIII (1964), pp. 12–38.
—— "Old Iranian Literature" in *Iranistik* II, *Literatur* I (Leiden, 1968), pp. 1–30 (*HO* I. IV. 2. 1).
Gnoli, G. *Zoroaster's Time and Homeland*. Naples, 1980.
Gray, L. H. "The 'Ahurian' and 'Daevian' vocabularies in the Avesta", *JRAS* 1927, pp. 427–42.
—— *The Foundations of the Iranian Religions*. Bombay, 1929 (*JCOI* 15).
Henning, W. B. "Zoroastrianism", in S. G. Champion (ed.), *The Eleven Religions and their Proverbial Lore* (London, 1944), pp. 290–6.
—— *Zoraster, Politician or Witch-Doctor?* (Ratanbai Katrak Lectures, 1949). Oxford, 1951.

BIBLIOGRAPHY

Herzfeld, E. *Zoroaster and his World*, 2 vols. Princeton, N.J., 1947.
Hinnells, J. R. *Persian Mythology*. London, 1973.
—— (ed.) *Mithraic Studies* I, II. Manchester, 1975.
Humbach, H. *Die Gathas des Zarathustra* I, II. Heidelberg, 1959.
Insler, S. *The Gāthās of Zarathustra*. Leiden, 1975 (Acta Iranica 8).
Jackson, A. V. W. *Zoroaster, The Prophet of Ancient Iran*. New York, 1899; repr. 1965.
Kent, R. G. *Old Persian Grammar, Texts, Lexicon*, 2nd ed. New Haven, Conn., 1953.
Koch, Heidemarie, *Die religiösen Verhältnisse der Dareioszeit*. Wiesbaden, 1977.
Lommel, H. *Die Yäšt's des Awesta*. Göttingen, 1927.
—— *Die Religion Zarathustras nach dem Awesta dargestellt*. Tübingen, 1930; repr. 1971.
—— *Die Gathas des Zarathustra*. Stuttgart, 1971.
Messina, G. *Die Ursprung der Magier und die zarathustrische Religion*. Rome, 1930.
—— *I Magi a Betlemme e una predizione di Zoroastro*. Rome, 1933.
Molé, M. *Culte, mythe et cosmologie dans l'Iran ancien*. Paris, 1963.
Morgenstierne, G. *Indo-Iranian Frontier Languages*, 4 vols. Oslo, 1929–73.
Moulton, J. H. *Early Zoroastrianism*. London, 1913.
Narten, J. *Die Aməša Spəntas im Avesta*. Wiesbaden, 1982.
Nyberg, H. S. *Die Religionen des Alten Iran* (German version by H. H. Schaeder). Leipzig, 1938.
Pavry, J. C. *The Zoroastrian Doctrine of a Future Life*, 2nd ed. New York, 1929.
Schlerath, B. (ed.) *Zarathustra*. Darmstadt, 1970 (Wege der Forschung 169).
Smith, M. W. *Studies in the Syntax of the Gathas of Zarathushtra; together with Text, Translation and Notes*. Philadelphia, 1929; repr. 1966.
Wesendonk, O. G. von *Das Wesender Lehre Zarathuštra's*. Leipzig, 1927.
—— *Das Weltbild der Iranier*. Munich, 1933.
Westergaard, N. L. *Zend-avesta* I. Copenhagen, 1852–4.
Widengren, G. *Die Religionen Irans*. Stuttgart, 1965.
—— *Les Religions de l'Iran* (French version of above). Paris, 1968.
Wikander, S. *Vayu; Texte und Untersuchungen zur indoiranischen Religionsgeschichte*. Uppsala, 1941.
—— *Feuerpriester in Kleinasien und Iran*. Lund, 1946.
Wolff, F. *Avesta, Die Heiligen Bücher der Parsen, übersetzt auf der Grundlage von Chr. Bartholomae's Altiranischem Wörterbuch*. Strassburg, 1910; repr. 1961.
Zaehner, R. C. *The Dawn and Twilight of Zoroastrianism*. London, 1961.

CHAPTER 15

I. Selected Aramaic Sources of the Persian Period

Aimé-Giron, N. *Textes araméens d'Egypte*. Cairo, 1931.
—— "Adversaria Semitica nos. 113–131", *BIFAO* XXXVIII (1939), 1–63.
—— "Adversaria Semitica nos. 122–124," *ASAE* XXXIX (1939), 39–63.
Avigad, N. *Bullae and Seals from a Post-exilic Judaean Archive*. Jerusalem, 1976 (Qedem 4).

BIBLIOGRAPHY

Bresciani, E. "Papiri aramaici egiziani di epoca persiana presso il Museo Civico di Padova", *RSO* xxxv (1960), 11–24.

——— "Un papiro aramaico di eta tolemaica", *Rendiconti della Accademia Nazionale dei Lincei* (Rome; 1962), pp. 258–64.

Bresni, E. and Kamil, M. " Le lettere aramaiche di Hermopoli", *Atti della Accademia Nazionale dei Lincei. Memorie. Classe di Scienze morali, storiche e filologiche*, Ser. 8, vol. xii (Rome, 1966), pp. 356–428. The most recent bibliography is in B. Porten and J. C. Greenfield, "Hermopolis Letter 6," *IOS* iv (1974), 14.

Bowman, R. A. *Aramaic Ritual Texts from Persepolis*. Chicago, 1970. Cf. the review article by J. Naveh and S. Shaked, "Ritual Texts or Treasury Documents?", *Orientalia* xlii (1973), 445–7.

——— "An Aramaic Religious Text in Demotic Script", *JNES* iii (1944), 219–31.

Cowley, A. A. *Aramaic Papyri of the Fifth Century B.C.* Oxford, 1923.

Cross, F. M. "Papyri of the Fourth Century B.C. from Dâliyeh", in D. N. Freedman and J. C. Greenfield (eds.), *New Directions in Biblical Archaeology* (Garden City, N.Y., 1969; repr. 1971), pp. 45–69.

Degen, R. "Zum Ostrakon CIS II 138", *Neue Ephemeris für Semitische Epigraphik* i (1972), 23–37. (A list of the Aramaic ostraca is provided.)

Delaporte, L. *Epigraphes araméens*. Paris, 1912.

Driver, G. R. *Aramaic Documents of the Fifth Century B.C.*, abridged and revised. Oxford, 1965.

Dupont-Sommer, A. "La stèle trilingue récemment découverte au Lêtôon de Xanthos: le texte araméen", *CRAI* 1974, pp. 132–49.

Fitzmyer, J. A. "The Padua Aramaic Letters", *JNES* xxi (1962), pp. 15–24.

Hanson, R. S. "Aramaic Funerary and Boundary Inscriptions from Asia Minor," *BASOR* cxcii (1968), pp. 3–11.

Kornfeld, W. "*Jüdisch-aramäische Grabinschriften aus Edfu*", *AOAW* cx (Vienna, 1973), pp. 123–37.

Kraeling, E. G. *The Brooklyn Museum Aramaic Payri*. New Haven, Conn., 1953.

Segal, J. B. "The Aramaic Papyri (from Saqqara)", in *Proceedings of the 14th Congress of Papyrologists* (London, 1975), pp. 252–5.

II. Collections of Aramaic Texts

Donner H. and Röllig, W. *Kananäische und aramäische Inschriften*, 3 vols, 2nd ed. Wiesbaden, 1968 [*KAI*].

Gibson, J. C. L. *Syrian Semitic Inscriptions* ii: *Aramaic Inscriptions*. Oxford, 1975.

Koopmans, J. J. *Aramäische Chrestomathie*. Leiden, 1962.

Lipinski, F. *Studies in Aramaic Inscriptions and Onomastics* i. Louvain, 1975 (Orientalia Louvaniensia analecta 1).

Porten, B. and Greenfield, J. C. *Jews of Elephantine, Aramaeans of Syene: 50 Aramaic Texts from Egypt*. Jerusalem, 1974.

Rosenthal, F. *An Aramaic Handbook*. Wiesbaden, 1967.

BIBLIOGRAPHY

III. Studies on Aramaic Language and Culture

Altheim, F. and Stiehl, R. *Die aramäistische Sprache unter den Achämeniden* I. Frankfurt, 1960–4.
Bauer, H. and Leander, P. *Grammatik des Biblisch-Aramäischen.* Halle, 1927.
Bowman, R. A. "Arameans, Aramaic and the Bible", *JNES* VII (1948), pp. 65–90.
Degen, R. *Altaramäischen Grammatik der Inschriften des 10–8 Jh. v. Ch.* Wiesbaden, 1969.
Dupont-Sommer, A. *Les Araméens.* Paris, 1949.
Garbini, G. *Le lingue semitiche, studi di storia linguistica.* Naples, 1972.
Ginsberg, H. L. "Aramaic Dialect Problems [I]", *AJSLL* L (1933) 1–9; "II", *AJSLL* LII (1936), pp. 95–103.
Greenfield, J. C. "The dialects of ancient Aramaic", *JNES* XXXVII (1978), pp. 93–99.
—— "Notes on the Arsham Letters", in S. Shaked (ed.), *Irano-Judaica*, (Jerusalem, 1981), pp. 4–11.
—— "Standard Literary Aramaic", *Actes du Premier Congrès International de Linguistique Sémitique et Chamito-Sémitique* (The Hague, 1974), pp. 280–9.
Greenfield, J. C. and Naveh, J. "Hebrew and Aramaic in the Persian Period", in *The Cambridge History of Judaism.* I (Cambridge, 1984), 115–29.
Kutscher, E. Y. "The Hermopolis Papyri", *IOS* I (1971), pp. 103–19.
—— "Aramaic", *Current Trends in Linguistics* VI (The Hague, 1971), pp. 317–412.
—— *A History of Aramaic*, Part I. Jerusalem, 1972 (in Hebrew).
Leander, P. *Laut- und Formenlehre des Ägyptisch-Aramäischen.* Göteborg, 1928.
Malamat, A. "The Aramaeans", in D. J. Wiseman (ed.), *Peoples of the Old Testament Times* (Oxford, 1973), pp. 134–155.
Rosenthal, F. *Die aramäistische Forschung seit Th. Nöldeke's Veröffentlichungen.* Leiden, 1939.
—— *A Grammar of Biblical Aramaic*, 2nd revised edition. Wiesbaden, 1962.
Segert, S. *Altaramäische Grammatik.* Leipzig, 1975.

IV. Dictionaries

Jean, C. and Hoftijzer, J. *Dictionnaire des inscriptions sémitiques de l'ouest.* Leiden, 1965.
Vinnikov, I. N. *Slovar' arameyskikh nadpisey*, in *Palestinskiy Sbornik* III–XIII (1958–65).
Vogt, E. *Lexicon linguae aramaicae Veteris Testamenti documentis antiquis illustratum.* Rome, 1971.

V. Aramaic in Contact with other Languages and Scripts

Benveniste, E. "Termes et noms achéménides en araméen", *JA* CCXXV (1934), pp. 177–94.
—— "Éléments perses en araméen d'Egypte", *JA* CCXLII (1954), pp. 297–310.

BIBLIOGRAPHY

Bickerman, E. "The Edict of Cyrus in Ezra I", in *Studies in Jewish and Christian History*, Part I (Leiden, 1976), pp. 72–108.

Bogolyubov, M. N. "An Old Iranian Prayer to Ahuramazda in Aramaic Characters" (in Russian) in *Istoriya iranskogo gosudarstva i kulturi* (Moscow, 1971), pp. 277–85.

Cameron, G. G. *The Persepolis Treasury Tablets*. Chicago, 1948 [*PTT*].

Couroyer, B. "Termes égyptiens dans les papyri araméens du Musée de Brooklyn", *Revue Biblique* LXI (1954), pp. 251–3; 554–9.

Dandamayev, *Persien unter den ersten Achämeniden*. Wiesbaden, 1976.

Eilers, W. *Iranische Beamtennamen in der keilschriftliche Überlieferung*. Leipzig, 1940.

Greenfield, J. C. "Iranian or Semitic?" *Monumentum H. S. Nyberg* I (1975), pp. 311–16 (Acta Iranica 4).

Hallock, R. T. *Persepolis Fortification Tablets* Chicago, 1969 [*PFT*].

Henning, W. B. "Mitteliranisch", in *Iranistik* I, *Linguistik* (Leiden, 1958), pp. 20–130 (*HO* I. IV. 1).

—— "Ein Persischer Titel im Altaramäischen", in *Gedenkband Kahle: Beiheft zur Zeitschrift für die alttestamentliche Wissenschaften* CIII (Berlin, 1968), pp. 136–43.

Hinz, W. *Neue Wege im Altpersischen*. Wiesbaden, 1973.

—— *Altiranisches Sprachgut der Nebenuberlieferungen*. Wiesbaden, 1975.

Kaufman, S. A. *The Akkadian Influences in Aramaic*. Chicago, 1974 (Assyriological Studies 19).

Kent, R. G. *Old Persian Grammar, Texts, Lexicon*, 2nd edition. New Haven, Conn., 1953.

Kutscher, E. Y. "New Aramaic Texts", *JAOS* LXXIV (1954), pp. 233–48.

Leibovitch, J. "Quelques égyptianismes contenus dans les textes araméens d'Égypte", *Bulletin de l'Institute d'Égypte* XVIII (1935–6), pp. 19–29.

Lewy, J. "The Problems inherent in Section 70 of the Behistun Inscription", *HUCA* XXV (1954), pp. 184–208.

de Menasce, J. "Mots d'emprunt et noms propres Iraniens dans les nouveaux documents araméens", *BiOr* XI (1954), pp. 161–2.

Naveh, J. "The Aramaic Inscriptions on Boundary Stones in Armenia" *WO* VI (1971), pp. 42–6.

Paper, H. H. "The Old Persian /L/ Phoneme", *JAOS* LXXVI (1956) pp. 24–6.

Polotsky, H. J. "Aramäisch *prš* und das *Huzvaresch*", *Le Muséon* XLV (1932), pp. 273–83.

Schaeder, H. H. *Iranische Beiträge* I. Halle, 1930.

von Soden, W. "Aramäische Wörter in neuassyrischen und neu- und spätbabylonischen Texten," *Orientalia* XXXV (1966), pp. 1–20; 37 (1968), pp. 261–71.

VI. Elephantine – General

Muffs, Y. *Studies in the Aramaic Legal Papyri from Elephantine*. Leiden, 1969.

Porten, B. *Archives from Elephantine*. Berkeley–Los Angles, 1968.

Yaron, R. *Introduction to the Law of the Aramaic Papyri*. Oxford, 1961.

BIBLIOGRAPHY

VII. *Script*

Avigad, N. "The Palaeography of the Dead Sea Scrolls and Related Documents", in C. Rabin and Y. Yadin (eds.), *Aspects of the Dead Sea Scrolls* (Jerusalem, 1958), pp. 56–87 (Scripta Hierosolymitana 4).

Cross, F. M. "The Development of the Jewish Scripts", in G. E. Wright (ed.), *The Bible and the Ancient Near East* (Garden City, N.Y., 1961), pp. 133–202.

Driver, G. R. *Semitic Writing*, 3rd edition, edited by S. A. Hopkins. Oxford, 1976.

Friedrich, "Assyria Grammata", in S. Morenz (ed.), *Aus Antike und Orient: Festschrift W. Schubart* (Leipzig, 1950), 48–53.

Gershevitch, I. "The alloglottography of Old Persian", *TPS* 1979, pp. 114–90.

Hanson, R. S. "Palaeo-Hebrew Scripts in the Hasmonaean Age", *BASOR* CLXXV (1964), pp. 26–42.

Naveh, J. "The development of the Aramaic script", *Proceedings of the Israel Academy of Sciences and Humanities* (Jerusalem, 1970), pp. 21–43.

—— "Hebrew Texts in the Aramaic Script in the Persian Period?", *BASOR* CCIII (1971), pp. 27–32.

—— "The Origin of the Mandaic Script", *BASOR* CXCVIII (1970), pp. 32–7.

—— "The North Mesopotamian Aramaic Script-type in the Late Parthian Period," *IOS* II (1972), pp. 293–304.

—— "The Palaeography of the Hermopolis Papyri", *IOS* I (1971), pp. 120–2.

—— "An Aramaic inscription from El-Mal – a survival of Seleucid Aramaic script", *Israel Exploration Journal* XXV (Jerusalem, 1975), pp. 117–23.

Nylander C. "*ΑΣΣΥΡΙΑ ΓΡΑΜΜΑΤΑ*, Remarks on the 21st Letter of Themistokles", *Opuscula Atheniensia* VIII (Lund, 1968), pp. 119–36 (Acta Instituti Atheniensis Regni Sueciae 14).

CHAPTER 17

Persepolis

(a) For the art of the classic Achaemenian period the basic works are still Erich F. Schmidt's volumes on Persepolis:

Schmidt, E. F. *Persepolis I: Structures, Reliefs, Inscriptions*. Chicago, 1953 (Oriental Institute Publications 68).

—— *Persepolis II: Contents of the Treasury and other Discoveries*. Chicago, 1957 (Oriental Institute Publications 69).

—— *Persepolis III: The Royal Tombs and other Monuments*. Chicago, 1970 (Oriental Institute Publications 70).

(b) To these are now added the publications by Ann Britt Tilia on the work of restoration and examination done by Giuseppe Tilia at Persepolis since 1964:

Tilia, A. B. "Reconstruction of the parapet on the Terrace Wall at Persepolis, South and West of Palace H", *East and West* XIX (1969), pp. 9–43.

—— *Studies and Restorations at Persepolis and other sites in Fars*, 2 vols. Rome,

BIBLIOGRAPHY

1972, 1978 (Istituto per il Medio ed Estremo Oriente, Reports and Memoirs 16, 18).

(c) The model made by Friedrich Krefter in 1968 and the drawings of reconstructed buildings on the Persepolis Terrace are helpful to visualize the look of the buildings:

Krefter, F. *Persepolis Rekonstruktionen.* Berlin, 1971 (Teheraner Forschungen 3).

Susa

(a) Excavations at Susa under the direction of Jean Perrot have yielded information about the palace, the Apadana and the newly discovered Gate of Darius, with the all-important statue from Egypt:

Perrot, J. "Suse: Apadana", *Iran* VIII (1970), pp. 193–4.
—— "Mission de Suse", *Iran* IX (1971), pp. 178–81.
—— "Suse et Susiane", *Iran* X (1972), pp. 181–3.
—— "L'architecture militaire et palatiale des Achéménides à Suse", in *150 Jahre Deutsches Archäologisches Institut 1829–1979* (Mainz, 1981), pp. 79–94, pls 34–6.
Perrot, J. *et al.* "Recherches à Suse et en Susiane: Chaour", *Syria* XLVIII (1971), pp. 36–51.
"Une statue de Darius découverte à Suse" *JA* CCLX (1972): M. Kervran, "Le contexte archéologique", pp. 235–9; D. Stronach, "Description and comment", pp. 241–6: F. Vallat, "L'inscription cunéiforme trilingue", pp. 247–51. J. Yoyotte, "Les inscriptions hiéroglyphiques; Darius et l'Égypte", pp. 253–66.
Vallat, F. "Deux nouvelles 'Chartes de fondation' d'un palais de Darius Ier à Suse", *Syria* XLVIII (1971), pp. 53–9.
Ghirshman, R. *Village perse achéménide.* Paris, 1954 (MDAI XXXVI).
—— "L'Apadana de Suse", *IA* III (1963), pp. 148–54.
Perrot, J. *et al.* (8 authors) *Recherches dans le secteur du tépé de l'Apadana. CDAFI* IV (1974).

(b) For the palace of Aratxerxes II on the Chaour (Sha'ūr) see:

Perrot, J. *et al.* (7 authors) *CDAFI* II (1972).
Boucharlat, R. *et al.* (5 authors) *CDAFI* X (1979).

Surveys

Frankfort, H. *The Art and Architecture of the Ancient Orient* (Harmondsworth, 1954), pp. 213–33, " The Art of Ancient Persia" (The Pelican History of Art, ed. N. Pevsner).
Farkas, A. *Achaemenid Sculpture.* Istanbul, 1974 (Nederlands Historisch-Archaeologisch Instituut te Istanbul 33). Review by E. Porada in *The Art Bulletin* LVIII (Providence, N.Y., 1976), pp. 612–13.
Root, Margaret Cool. *The King and Kingship in Achaemenid Art.* Leiden, 1979 (Acta Iranica 19).

BIBLIOGRAPHY

Ghirshman, R. *Persia from the Origins to Alexander the Great* (London, 1964), pp. 129–274.
Godard, A. *L'Art de l'Iran* (Paris, 1962), pp. 99–140.
Herzfeld, E. *Iran in the Ancient East* (London, 1941), pp. 221–74.
Luschey, H. "Die Kunst Irans zur Zeit der Achaimeniden", in K. Schefold, *Die Griechen und ihre Nachbarn* (Berlin, 1967), pp. 291–7 (Propyläen Kunstgeschichte 1).
—— "Iran und der Westen, von Kyros bis Khosrow", *AMI* I (1968), pp. 15–37.
von der Osten, H. H. *Die Welt der Perser* (Stuttgart, 1956), pp. 59–102.
"Achaemenid Art", in *SPA*, pp. 309–405.
Porada, E. *Ancient Iran. The Art of pre-Islamic times* (London, 1965), pp. 137–78.
Vanden Berghe, L. *Archéologie de l'Iran ancien*. (Leiden, 1959), pp. 215–22 (Documenta et monumenta orientis antiqui 6).
Kopcke, G. and Moore, Mary B. (eds.) *Studies in Classical Art and Archaeology. A tribute to Peter Heinrich von Blanckenhagen*. Locust Valley, New York, 1979.

Periodicals

Most of the new information appears in four periodicals: *IA*, *Iran*, *AMI* and *CDAFI*.

Bibliographies

The most complete is:
Vanden Berghe, L. *Bibliographie analytique de l'Archéologie de l'Iran ancien* (Leiden, 1979), pp. 240–55 (Achaemenid art).
A selected list is:
Porada, E. "Bibliography of the Art of Ancient Iran", *Journal of the Ancient Near East Society of Columbia University* IX (New York, 1977), pp. 67–84 (Achaemenid art, pp. 77–80).

Since *AMI* VII (1974) every volume contains exhaustive bibliography with a section on Achaemenid works. Since 1978 *Studia Iranica* has an annual bibliographical supplement, *Abstracta Iranica*, which is very useful.

CHAPTER 18

Ghirshman, R. *Persia; from the Origins to Alexander the Great*. London, 1964.
King, W. W. and Thompson, R. C. *The Sculptures and Inscriptions of Darius the Great on the rock of Behistûn in Persia*. London, 1907.
Luschey, H. "Studien zu dem Darius-Relief von Bisitun", *AMI* I (1968), pp. 63–94.
Olmstead, A. T. *History of the Persian Empire* (Chicago, 1960), pp. 108–18.
Porada, E. *Ancient Iran. The art of pre-Islamic times*. London, 1965.

BIBLIOGRAPHY

CHAPTER 19

Tepe Nūsh-i Jān

Stronach, D. "Excavations at Tepe Nush-i Jan, 1967", *Iran* VII (1969), pp. 1–20.
Bivar, A. D. H. "A Hoard of Ingot-currency of the Median Period from Nush-i Jan, near Malayir", *Iran* IX (1971), pp. 97–111.
Roaf, M. and Stronach, D. "Tepe Nush-i Jan, 1970: Second Interim Report", *Iran* XI (1973), pp. 129–38.
—— "Excavations at Tepe Nush-i Jan. Part 1. A Third Interim Report", *Iran* XVI (1978), pp. 2–11.
Stronach, R. "Part 2. Median Pottery from the Fallen Floor of the Fort", *Iran* XVI, pp. 11–24.
Bokonyi, S. "Part 3. The Animal Remains, a Preliminary Report, 1973 and 1974", *Iran* XVI, pp. 24–8.
Kyllo, M. A. and Hubbard, R. N. L. B. "Median and Parthian Plant Remains from Tepe Nush-i Jan", *Iran* XIX (1981), pp. 91–100.

Baba Jan Tepe

Goff, C. "Excavations at Baba Jan. The Architecture of the East Mound, Levels II and III", *Iran* XV (1977), pp. 103–40.
—— "Excavations at Baba Jan: The Pottery and Metal from Levels III and II", *Iran* XVI (1978), pp. 29–65.

Godin Tepe

Cuyler Young, T. Jr. *Excavations at Godin Tepe: First Progress Report*, Royal Ontario Museum. Art and Archaeology, Occasional Paper 17 (Toronto, 1969), pp. 23–32.
Cuyler-Young, T. Jr. and Levine, L. D. *Excavations of the Godin Project: Second Progress Report*. Toronto, 1974 (Royal Ontario Museum. Art and Archaeology, Occasional Paper 26).

Kangāvar

Cuyler Young, T. Jr. "Survey in Western Iran, 1961", *JNES* XXV (1966), p. 232.
—— "Kangavar Valley Survey", *Iran* XIII (1975), p. 192.

Māhidasht

Levine, L. D. "Archaeological Investigations in the Mahidasht, Western Iran, 1975", *Paléorient* II (1974), p. 489.
—— "The Mahidasht Project", *Iran* XIV (1976), p. 161.
—— "Survey in the province of Kermanšāhān 1975: Māhidašt in the prehistoric and early historic periods", *Proceedings of the 4th Annual Symposium on Archaeological Research in Iran 1975* (Tehran, 1976), pp. 284–97.

BIBLIOGRAPHY

Malāyir

Howell, R. "Survey of the Malayer Plain", *Iran* XVII (1979), pp. 156–7.

Burūjird

Cuyler Young, T. Jr. *JNES* XXV (1966), p. 232.

CHAPTER 20

The monuments of Pasargadae possess a long bibliography. Among other references, see:

Cook, J. M. *The Persian Empire*. London, 1983.
Curzon, G. N. *Persia and the Persian Question* II. London, 1892.
Frankfort, H. *The Art and Architecture of the Ancient Orient*. Harmondsworth, 1954; 4th (revised) impr., 1970 (The Pelican History of Art, ed. N. Pevsner).
Herzfeld, E. "Pasargadae. Untersuchungen zur persischen Archäologie", *Klio* VIII (1908), pp. 1–68.
—— "Bericht über die Ausgrabungen von Pasargadae 1928", *AMI* I (1929–30), pp. 4–16.
Nylander, C. *Ionians in Pasargadae: Studies in Old Persian Architecture*. Uppsala, 1970 (Boreas. Uppsala Studies in Ancient Mediterranean and Near Eastern Civilizations 1).
Porada, E. *The Art of Ancient Iran*. New York, 1965.
—— *Ancient Iran. The art of pre-Islamic times*. London, 1965.
Sami, A. *Pasargadae. The Oldest Imperial Capital of Iran*. Shiraz, 1956.
Sarre, F. and Herzfeld, E. *Iranische Felsreliefs*. Berlin, 1910.
Schmidt, E. F. *Persepolis*, 3 vols. Chicago, 1953–70 (Oriental Institute Publications 68, 69, 70).
Stronach, D. "Excavations at Pasargadae: First Preliminary Report", *Iran* I (1963), pp. 19–42.
—— "Excavations at Pasargadae: Second Preliminary Report", *Iran* II (1964), pp. 21–39.
—— "Excavations at Pasargadae: Third Preliminary Report", *Iran* III (1965), pp. 9–40.
—— *Pasargadae. A report on the excavations conducted by the British Institute of Persian Studies from 1961 to 1963*. Oxford, 1978.
Treidler, H. "Pasargadai", in *Pauly*, Suppl. IX (1962), cols 777–99.

General works

Culican, W. *The Medes and Persians*. London, 1965 (Ancient Peoples and places 42).
Dieulafoy, M. A. *L'art antique de la Perse*, 5 vols. Paris, 1884–5.
Ghirshman, R. *Persian from the origins to Alexander the Great*. London, 1964.
Herzfeld, E. E. *Iran in the ancient East*. London, 1941.

BIBLIOGRAPHY

CHAPTER 21

Bibliography up to 1971

Metalwork

Akurgal, E. "Eine Silberschale aus dem Pontus", *Antike Kunst* X (1967), pp. 32–8.
Amandry, P. "Orfèvrerie achéménide", *Antike Kunst* I (1958), pp. 9–23.
—— "Toreutique achéménide", *Antike Kunst* II (1959), pp. 38–56.
—— "Argenterie d'Époque Achéménide", in *Collection Hélène Stathatos* III (Strasbourg, 1963), pp. 260–72.
Amiran, R. "Achaemenian Bronze Objects from a tomb at Kh. Ibsan in Lower Galilee", *Levant* IV (1972), pp. 135–8.
Anonymous, "Achaemenid Metalwork", in *SPA*, pp. 367–76.
Arakelian, B. N. "Treasure of Silver Objects from Erevan" (in Russian), *SA* 1971. 1, 143–58.
Barnett, R. D. "Median Art", *IA* II (1962), 77–95.
Bivar, A. D. H. "A Rosette 'phiale' inscribed in Aramaic", *BSOAS* XXIV (1961), pp. 189–99.
Bussagli, G. "The Goldsmiths' art and toreutics in ancient Persia", *East and West* VII (1956), pp. 41–55.
Cooney, J. D. "Persian Influence in Late Egyptian Art: Metalwork in Persian Style", *Bulletin of the American Research Center in Egypt* IV (1965), pp. 40–2.
Curtis, C. D. *Sardis* XIII: *Jewelry and Gold work*. Rome, 1925 (Publications of the American Society for the excavation of Sardis).
Dalton, O. M. *The Treasure of the Oxus*, 3rd edition, London, 1964.
Dussaud, R. "Tête de Taureau en bronze, d'époque achéménide", *Bulletin des Musées de France* 1933, pp. 138–9.
Frankfort, H. "A Persian Goldsmith's Trial Piece", *JNES* IX (1950), pp. 111–12.
Hall, H. R. "Bronze Forepart of an Ibex", *Antiquaries Journal* IX (1929), pp. 217–18.
Hamilton, R. W. "A Silver Bowl in the Ashmolean Museum", *Iraq* XXVIII (1966), pp. 1–17.
Herzfeld, E. "Eine Silberschüssel Artaxerxes' I", *AMI* VII (1935), pp. 1–8.
Hoffmann, H. "The Persian Origin of the Attic Rhyta", *Antike Kunst* IV (1961), pp. 21–6.
Iliffe, J. H. "A Tell Fār 'a Tomb Group Reconsidered: Silver Vessels of the Persian Period", *Quarterly of the Department of Antiquities in Palestine* IV (1934), pp. 182–6.
Kantor, H. "Goldwork and Ornaments from Iran", *The Cincinnati Art Museum Bulletin* V. 2 (1957), pp. 9–20.
—— "Achaemenid Jewelry in the Oriental Institute", *JNES* XVI (1957). pp. 1–23.
Luschey, H. "Griechisch-persische Metallarbeiten", *Berliner Museen* LIX (1938), pp. 76–80.

—— "Achämenidisch-persische Toreutik", *AA* LIII (1938), cols 760–72.
—— *Die Phiale*. Bleicherode am Herz, 1939.
de Morgan, J. "Découverte d'une Sépulture Achéménide à Suse", *MDP* VIII (1905), pp. 29–58.
Parrot, A. "Acquisitions et inedits due Musée du Louvre, 3, Bronzes iraniens", *Syria* XXX (1953), pp. 1–5.
Pudelko, G. "Altpersische Armbänder", *AfO* IX (1934), pp. 85–8.
Rice, D. T. "Achaemenid Jewelry", in *SPA*, pp. 377–382.
Rueppel, M. C. "Bronze Sculpture from Ancient Persia", *The Bulletin of the Minneapolis Institute of Arts*, Spring, 1957, pp. 1–3.
Smirnov, J. I. *Der Schatz von Achalgori*. Tiflis, 1934.
Tallgren, A. M. "Caucasian Monuments: The Kazbek Treasure", *Eurasia Septentrionalis Antiqua* V (Helsinki, 1930), 109–82.
Terrace, E. L. B. "Two Achaemenian Objects in the Boston Museum of Fine Arts", *Antike Kunst* VI (1963), 72–80.
Tuchelt, K. *Tiergefässe in Kopf- und Protomengestalt*. Berlin, 1962.
Wilkinson, C. K. "Assyrian and Persian Art", *MMAB* XIII (1954–5), pp. 213–24.
—— "An Achaemenian Bronze Head", *MMAB* XV (1956–7), pp. 72–8.
—— "Two Ancient Silver Vessels", *MMAB* XV (1956–7), pp. 9–15.
—— *Two ram-headed vessels from Iran*. Bern, 1967.

Glyptic

Balkan, K. "Inscribed Bullae from Daskyleion-Ergili", *Anatolia* IV (1959), pp. 123–8.
Bivar, A. D. H. "A 'Satrap' of Cyrus the Younger", *NC* I (1961), pp. 119–27.
Boardman, J. "Pyramidal Stamp Seals in the Persian Empire", *Iran* VIII (1970), pp. 19–45.
—— *Greek Gems and Finger Rings* (London, 1971), pp. 303–59 ("Greeks and Persians").
Frankfort, H. *Cylinder Seals*. London, 1939.
Gadd, C. J. "Achaemenid Seals, A: Types", *SPA*, pp. 383–8.
Goetze, A. "Three Achaemenian Tags", *Berytus* VIII (1944), pp. 97–101.
Legrain, L. *UE* X (London, 1951), nos. 701–841.
Maximova, E. "Griechisch-persische Kleinkunst in Kleinasien nach den Perserkriegen", *AA* XLIII (1928), cols 648–67.
Nikoulina, N. M. "La Glyptique 'Grecque Orientale' et 'Gréco-Perse'", *Antike Kunst* XIV (1971), pp. 90–106.
Petrie, W. M. F. *Meydum and Memphis* III (London, 1910), pp. 40–4 ("The Palace").
Porada, E. "Seals of Iran", in *Corpus of Ancient Near Eastern Seals in North American Collections* (Washington, 1948), 101–6.
—— "Greek Coin Impressions from Ur", *Iraq* XXII (1960), pp. 228–34.
Richter, G. M. A. "Late 'Achaemenian' or Graeco-Persian' Gems", *Hesperia*, Supplement VIII (1949), pp. 291–8.

BIBLIOGRAPHY

—— "Greek Subjects on 'Graeco-Persian' Seal Stones", *Archaeologia Orientalia in Memoriam Ernst Herzfeld* (New York, 1952), pp. 189–94.
—— *The Engraved Gems of the Greeks, Etruscans and Romans* I (London, 1968), pp. 125–32 ("Graeco-Persian Gems").
Seyrig, H. "Cachets Achéménides", in *Archaeologica Orientalia in Memoriam Ernst Herzfeld* (New York, 1952), pp. 195–202.
Stern, E. "Seal-Impressions in the Achaemenid Style in the Province of Judah", *BASOR* CCII (1971), pp. 6–16.
Yoyotte, J. "La Provenance du Cylindre de Darius (BM 89132)", *RA* XLVI (1952), pp. 165–7.

Glass and ivories

Amiet, P. "Les Ivoires achéménides des Suse", *Syria* XLIX (1972), pp. 167–91, 319–37.
Oliver, A. "Persian Export Glass", *Journal of Glass Studies* XII (1970), pp. 9 ff.

INDEX

The system used in this index is word-by-word. Italic figures denote illustrations and bold figures denote main entries. A figure followed by letter 'n' indicates a footnote.

Āb-i Diz river, 1
Abarnahara, west of the Euphrates, 212, 260, 271
Abisares, ruler of Kashmir, 465, 467, 469n, 478n.
Abu'l-Ḥasan Kūšyār, mathematician, 757, 759, 761, 768, 770
Abydos, 365, 423, 517
　lion weight from, 624, 625, 702
Acēs river, 131
Acesines (Chenab), 465, 467, 468
Achaemenes, brother of Xerxes, satrap in Egypt, 509, 510
Achaemenes, king of Anshan, 21, 34, 88, 133, 209, 239
Achaemenids:
　administration under Darius, 221–5, 240–1, 267–77; architecture, palaces, 237–8, 583, **793–811**; contacts with Elam, 33–4; conquests in Asia, 211–13, 218–22; conquests in Egypt, 214–15, 502; dress, 229, 278, 515; education 236, 581, 654–5; foundation of empire, **209–17**; land use, 241–3, 577–8; metalwork, 856–63; religion, 232, **664–97**; the Royal court, **225–38**; satrapies, 204–5, 245–67, 397–8, 563–5; sculpture, 811–27; social organization, 281–7, 289–91, 516, 572–7, 649–52; sources of early history, **200–9**, 529–30, 703, 709; territories and inhabitants, **244–67**, 287; tomb sites, 240, 339.
　See also Babylonia, Persians, satrapies
Achoris, Pharaoh of Egypt (394–381 B.C.), 523
Adadnērarī, king of Assyria, 68, 69
Aegina (Aigina) island, 315, 316, 335
　temple of Aphaia, 803, 812
Aēshma, demon god, 682
Afghanistan, 454–5, 613, 629, 705
Agade, see Akkad
Agathyrsi tribes, 184
Agbatana, see Ecbatana
Agesilaos, king of Sparta, 358, 359, 360, 361–4, 378, 380
Agesilaus, Greek general, 524, 525
Agighiol barrow grave, 198–9
Agis, king of Sparta, 429, 438–9, 446, 447n.
Agum II, Kassite king, 39–40
Aḥiqar's proverbs, 699, 701, 706–7

Aḥsēri, king of the Mannaeans (d.659 B.C.), 102, 115, 116
Ahura Mazda, the great god:
　in the Avesta, 640, 665, 667; in inscriptions, 232, 685, 687, 694, 828; under Xerxes, 566, 689, 690
Aigina, see Aegina island
Akkad, Akkadians:
　campaigns into Elam, 8; kings of, 8, 36–7; language/script, 10, 531, 571, 699–700, 703, 807
Akkadī, Māt (country of Akkadī), 564, 565, 578, 579
Alani tribe, 48
Alazones, Alizōnes, 152, 173, 179
Alexander the Great (336–323 B.C.):
　historical events: accession, 423; army of, 423–5, 461, 481–3, 489; in Asia Minor, 425–7; campaigns in Egypt, 433, 528; campaigns against Persians, 243, 430–1, 434–7; capture of Persepolis, 439–46; chronology of campaigns, 497–501; Darius III pursued, 447–9; dealings with satraps, 450–4, 476–8; entry into Babylon, 486–9; march through Afghanistan, 454–5; march into Bactria and Sogdiana, 455–60; North India campaign, 462–76; officers' rebellions, 456–7, 466–7, 481–4
　personal affairs: attitude to Persians, 291, 452, 480, 482–6, 488, 492; family, 381, 422; history sources, 420–1; legends of, 525–6; marriages, 456, 480; sickness and death, 489; successor and future plans, 490–1
Alexandria (Egypt), 433–4
Alizōnes, see Alazones
Alkibiades, Athenian commander, 345, 347, 348, 350–1, 352
Alvand (Orontes) mountain, 82, 83, 288
Alyattēs, king of Lydia, 126, 211
Amasis, Pharaoh of Egypt, 296, 502, 504, 508, 521
Amazons, Alexander's contact with, 451 n. 1, 484
Amestris, queen, wife of Xerxes, 336, 577, 692
Ammon, Greek god, 433, 483, 486, 520
Amyntas, satrap of Bactria and Sogdiana, 460, 461, 528

INDEX

Amyrgian, *see* Haumavargā
Amyrtaeus, Pharaoh of Egypt (405–400 B.C.), 511, 512, 522, 523
Anāhitā, goddess, 659–60, 670–1, 694
Anariaci tribe, 50, 51n.
Andia province, 65, 83
Andronovo culture, 42, 54, 55, 161, 186
Androphagi ("Man-eaters") tribe, 153, 185–6
Angra Mainyu, demon god, 640, 665, 679, 680, 681, 697
animals:
  in art and sculpture, 729–35 *passim*, 803n., 858, 865–9 *passim*; in Avestan beliefs, 644–6; as gifts, 271n.; asses and donkeys, 248n., 660–1; bulls, *see* separate entry; camels, 195, 660; cattle, 651, 657–8; dogs, 532n., 580n., 646, 661; elephants, 436, 463; horses, *see* separate entry; lions, *see* separate entry; sheep, 589, 603, 607, 608, 658–9, 695
Anšan, Anshan, 25–35
  community of, 5–6; confusion of name with Awan, 25–6; early history, 25–9; Elamite rulers of, 29–32; kingdom of, 20, 33–4, 88, 133, 259, 410.
  See also Āsh
Antalcides, peace treaty of (386 B.C.), 523, 524
Antigonus, satrap of Phrygia, 242, 428, 494–6, 497
Antipater, governor of Greece, 423, 446, 483, 485–6, 489, 493
Apām Napāt, water god, 674–6
Aparytai people, 250, 641
Apis bull, death of, 215n., 220, 397n., 504–5, 518, 526
Apollo, Greek god, 294, 314, 318, 415, 688
Apollophanes, satrap of the Orietae, 471, 473, 476
Arabāya province, 262
Arabs, 262, 286, 523, 579
Arabsun (Turkey) inscriptions, 702, 711
Arachosia (Harahvariš), 249, 454, 479, 671, 705, 709, 823n.
Araha, Arakha, Harakka, *see* Nebuchadnezzar IV
Aramaic language/dialects, 698–9, 706–8, 711–13
Aramaic script:
  as official language, 235–6, 699, 706–8, 865; Behistun inscription copy, 208; in Egypt, 508, 514, 517, 700–1, 706, 710; history of, **698–705**; varied forms of, 709–13.
  See also Elephantine island papyrii
Ararat, *see* Urartu
Araxēs river, 96n., 213
  valley sites, 256
Arcadia, Arcadians, 325, 376–7, 379
Areia province, 252–3, 290n., 451, 452n., 453–4, 495, 641
Argišti I, king of Urartu, 69, 70
Ariaios, Persian commander, 352, 353, 360, 361
Arianē, *see* Iran
Ariaramnes/Ariyāramna, supposed king in Pārsa, 133, 209, 301
Ariobarzanes, satrap of Daskyleion, 349, 366, 369, 371, 374, 375, 376, 378, 381
Ariobarzanes, son of Artabazos, 388, 442, 443n.
Aristagoras of Miletos, 307, 308, 309, 311
Aristotle, Greek philosopher, 425
Ariyawrata, governor in Egypt, 513
Arizanti tribe, 74–5, 87
Armenia, Armina:
  land and people, 256, 270; revolt against Darius, 218–19
Arrapḫa (later, Kirkuk), 38, 83, 122
Arrian, historian of Alexander, 399, 426, 498
Arsakes (later, Artaxerxes II, *q.v.*), 342, 352
Arsames, Arśāma, grandfather of Darius I, 133, 209, 210, 577n., 591
Arsames, Prince, satrap in Egypt, 280, 511, 516, 522, 608
Arses, king of the Persians (338–336 B.C.), 390, 422, 526, 527
Arsham letters, 701, 703, 704, 710
art and architecture, *see under* Achaemenids, Egypt, Greeks, Persians
Artabazanes, eldest son of Darius I, 591
Artabazos, son of Pharnabazos, 377, 382, 383, 388, 423, 449, 450, 455, 460
Artabazos, son of Pharnaces, 327, 328, 329, 330–1, 333, 335, 337, 340, 591
artabē/irtiba, large measure of capacity, 631, 632, 634
Artacoana (site unknown), 451
Artaphernes, half-brother of Darius, 303, 306, 307, 309–11, 313, 591
Artaremu, governor of Babylonia, 565
Artasyras, official under Xerxes, 240
Artavardiya, army commander, 590
Artaxerxes I, (465–425 B.C.):
  affairs in Egypt, 510–11; buildings in Persepolis, 825–7; religion of, 692–4; sons of, 228, 334, 336
Artaxerxes II Mnemon (Arsakes) (404–359 B.C.):
  dealings with Cyrus, 352, 353; palace buildings, 809–10, 827; peace initiatives, 372, 376, 421; religion of, 694; ruler of

932

INDEX

Artaxerxes (cont)
Egypt, 512; sons of, 228; in Spartan/Greek wars, 365-8, 370.
See also Arsakes

Artaxerxes III (Ochus) (358-338 B.C.): accession, 381, 421; death of, 390; Egyptian campaigns, 384-6, 525, 526, 527; mentioned in texts, 560; tomb of, 462.
See also Ochus, Prince

Artemision, 321, 322, 323

Artystone (Irtašduna), wife of Darius I, 226, 589, 608

Aryan people, 57, 75, 247-8, 640, 648

Aryan script, *see* Old Persian

Aryandes, satrap of Egypt, 219, 507, 619

Asagartiyā, *see* Sagartian tribe

Āsh (formerly Anshan?), 25, 34

Ashur, *see* Aššur

Asia Minor:
Alexander's campaigns in, 425-7; conquest of Ionia, 292-6; epigraphic material, 702, 708n.; Persian rule in, 263-6, 270, 272, 274-6, 406, 497; revolts in Ionia, 307-12, 355-9, 387-91

āsmān (sky), 642-3

Aspačanā, probably bow-bearer of Darius I, 590

Aspathines, bow-bearer of Darius I, 204, 240, 279

Aššur, Ashur, oldest city of Assyria, 123, 261, 538n.
See also Athurā

Aššurbānapli, king of Assyria: campaigns against Elam, 22, 23, 33; in conflict with Mannaeans, 115, 116; oath of allegiance to, 108; war with Babylon, 117

Aššurnaṣirapli, king of Assyria: annals of, 97; campaigns against the Medes, 59-60

Assyrians:
campaigns against Elam, 22, 23, 33; campaigns against Mannaeans, 106-8, 115-16; campaigns against the Medes, 59-61, 64-8, 76-9, 81-8; campaigns against Urartu, 69-71, 84; inscriptions/writing, 698, 702, 710; partition of kingdom, 125; war with Babylon, 117, 119-24.

astronomical observations, 534, 560, 581-2.
See also calendars

Astyages, king of Media (584-549 B.C.): as ruler, 112, 113, 142-8; in conflict with Cyrus, 210-11, 404, 414, 538, 546; religion of, 141

Ātar, god of fire, 676

Ateas, king of the Scythians, 197-8, 199

Athens, Athenians:
in conflict with Persia, 309, 316-18, 321-31, 351; invasion of Egypt, 335-6, 509-10; peace negotiations, 337, 365-8, 375-7

Athurā (Ashur), 261-2

Atiyawahy, governor of Coptos, 513

Atlila fortress (now Tepe Bakrawa), 60

Atossa, wife of Darius I, 202, 225, 226, 299

Atrek river valley route, 52

Atropates, governor of Media, 460n., 484, 492

Attic standard of weight, 611, 615, 616, 624

Auchatae Scyths, 166, 167

Autophradates, satrap in Sardis and elsewhere, 366, 369, 370, 377-8, 380, 383, 450, 460n.

Avesta, Zoroastrian sacred book:
description of, 664-6; extracts from, 168n., 491n.; language of, 53, 130, 686; world view of, 640-7

Avestan, Younger, 649, 664, 665, 667, 682-4

Avestan calendars, 749-56, 756-9, 774

Awan:
confusion of name with Anshan, 25-6; position of, 5; ruling dynasty, 7

Azā, king of Mana, 81

Azarbāijān, 697

Azov, Sea of, coastal settlements, 152-3

Babliū province, 69-70

Babylon city:
Antigonus in, 495; entered by Cyrus the Great, 407, 408-9, 539, 542-4; excavations, 583-4; importance of, 237, 531-2, 580; temple destruction, 565-6; under Alexander, 437-8, 448n., 486-9.
See also Esagila temple

Babylonia:
art and scholarship, 581-2, 582-3, 584-5; battles in (312 B.C.), 496; contacts with Elam, 16-17, 19-20, 23; dress in, 824; economic affairs, 578-81; extent of the realm, 549-50; geography, 259, 261, 286-7; language/script, 699-700, 703; position in Achaemenian Empire, 530-2, 586-7; religious beliefs in, 540-2, 550-1; satrapy of, 544-5, 564-5; social conditions in, 572-7; sources of history, **529-37**, 568-72; war with Assyria, 117, 119-24.

Babylonian Chronicle, *see* Nabonidus Chronicle

INDEX

Babylonian standard of weight, 611, 623, 625, 634, 637
Bactria, Bactrians, 48, 127, 130, 132, 213, 252, 455, 460
Badrakataš (assumed to be Pasargadae), see Pasargadae
Bagoas, eunuch and Guard-commander, 386, 387, 451n., 525
   involved in murder of Artaxerxes III, 390, 422, 536
Bakabaduš (possibly the same as Megabates), 591
Bakabana (possibly the same as Megapanus), 565, 591
Bampūr, see Pura
Baratkama, treasurer at Persepolis, 592, 595
Bardiya (Smerdis), brother of King Cambyses, 203, 204, 216, 218, 397, 561
Barnaku, see Bīt Bunaki
Barsine, daughter of Darius III, 480
Bartatua, king of Scythia, 172
Begrām, 454, 455n.
Behistun inscription of Darius I:
   art of, 828–30; copies made, 543n., 711, 811; history of, 208–9; language versions, 395, 559, 706; province lists, 244, 397
Bēl, god of Babylon, 540, 549, 557
   gold statue of, 565–6
bēl āli (lords of townships), 72, 84, 91, 108
Bēl-šimanni, usurper king of Babylon, 562, 565
Belsk, Scythian industrial centre, 157
Bes, Egyptian "master-of-animals" god, 866, 867
Bessarabian group antiquities, 178, 184, 191
Bessus, satrap of Bactria, 435, 449, 450, 451, 455
Beste (Bust), 248–9
Biblical sources, 529, 543n., 548, 577, 703–4, 707, 708
birds (fowls), 661–2, 837
Bīrūnī, Abu'l-Rayḥān al-, mathematician, 757–9, 762–3, 766, 770
Bīt-Barrūa (Baruata), 69, 87–8, 107
Bīt-Bunaki (Barnaku), 63, 67, 101
Bīt-Ḥamban, 77, 78, 84, 107, 108
Bīt-Kāri, 104, 105, 107
bītu (landed property), 573, 574
Black Sea, coastal areas, 50, 96n., 158
Boiotians, 325, 329, 330, 335, 375, 378
Borsippa tablets, 561, 562, 567
Bosporus, Sea of, crossing, 301
Boubares, son of Megabazos, 303, 314, 319
Brahmins, 469–70

bricks:
   dimensions of, 626–7; glazed, 583–4, 811–12; inscriptions on, 536, 553
British Museum texts, 559–60, 580n., 866
bronze artifacts, 156, 195, 861, 862
Budini people, 187–8
Bulgaria, burial finds, 197, 860
bulls:
   Apis bull, see separate entry; in art, 800, 801n.; celestial bulls, 725, 726–8, 736, 737–8; in Zoroastrianism, 645, 657, 670.
   See also lion-bull combat under "calendars"
burial sites and rites, 141n., 170, 583, 622, 696–7
Bustus, Buštu, 63, 69, 115
Byzantion, 306, 332, 333, 348, 389

calendars:
   Arabic–Latin Cordova c., 718–19; Babylonian c., **739–44**, 786; Greek c., 718; Jalālī c., 772–3, 784; Later Avestan c., 692–3, 756–9, 768, **781–92**; Old Persian lunisolar c., **744–9**, 786; Prehistoric Iranian c., 720–37
   elements in: civil and vihečakik years, 759–64; days of the month, 774–8; epagomenae, 760–1, 770–1, 773, 777, 784, 790; influence of constellations, 717–37; lion–bull combat, 725, *736*, 737–8, 740, 755, 820; lunar and solar elements, 714–17, 738–9, 763, 765, 778–9; the mulAPIN tablet, 719–20, 724, 754; Old Avestan year, 749–56; Old Egyptian year, 764–72
Callipidae (Greek Scyths), 152, 182, 183
Callisthenes, Greek historian, 425, 428n., 431, 433, 458, 484
Cambysēs I, king of Persis (d. 522 B.C.), 554–9
   buildings of, 801–2; character of, 215, 397, 504–5, 557–8; co-regency with Cyrus, 545, 549, 558; Egyptian conquest, 214, 296–8, 502–7 *passim*; in festival ceremony, 554–8; kingdom of, 133; murders his brother, 203, 216
Cappadocia, 244n., 264, 265, 270
caravan routes, see trade routes
Caria, see Karia
Carmania, see Karmania
carts, oxen-drawn, 46–7
Caspian Gates, 248, 448n.
Caspian Sea:
   coasts, 50, 51, 52, 255–6; ships on, 222
Caspii tribe (Caspians), 40, 50, 51n., 253
Catiaroi Scyths, 166, 167
Caucasus mountains:
   passes through, 51; population in, 257

INDEX

Chabrias, Athenian general in Egypt, 367, 369, 380, 382, 524, 525
Chaldeans (Babylonian priests), 486, 487
chariots:
  horse-drawn, 46–7, 659; scythe-armed, 361–2, 436; of war, 651
Chertomlyk royal burial, 194
chiliarch, *see hazārapatiš*
Chios, city of, 343, 345, 347, 382
Chorasmia, Chorasmians, 48, 129n., 131–2, 252, 416, 823
Cilicia, 263–4, 270, 402, 430, 702
Cilician Gates, 263, 264, 377
Cimmerians:
  origins of, 92–4; invasion of Asia Minor, 51, 95–6, 97n.; in revolt against Assyrians, 102, 105, 106–8, 118
Čišpiš (Teispes), king of Anshan, *see* Teispes
Cleitus, Macedonian commander, 453, 457, 460
climate, 242–4
Coenus, Macedonian officer, 466–7, 477
coinage:
  Achaemenid, 221–2, 415, 578, **610–21**; of Cilicia, 264; early currency, 612, 614, 834; in Egypt, 514–15, 615, 619n.; Greek, 578n., 614, 615; satrapal, 438n.
  See also individual coins; gold; silver
Colaxais, mythical king of the Scythians, 165
Colchians, 257
"Companions", Macedonian cavalry, 424, 431, 452, 453, 482
Cossaean tribe, 486
craftsmen, 651, 840, 862
Craterus, Macedonian commander, 451, 453n., 468, 470, 480, 483, 485–6
Crimea, 174, 178, 199
Croesid coinage, 614–15, 616–17
Croesus, son of Alyattes, ruler of Lydia, 147, 211–12, 292, 413, 616
Ctesias, Greek physician and historian, 110, 143n., 205–6, 396–7
Cunaxa/Kunaxa, battle of (401 B.C.), 205, 353, 397
cuneiform inscriptions and texts, 6, 114, 235, 236, **532–67** *passim*, 571, 699
Cyaxares, king of Media (624–585 B.C.), 112, 113
  destruction of Nineveh, 117, 123; possible tomb of, 139n.; war campaigns, 119, 121–2, 125, 126, 211, 837
Cyclades islands, 300
Cyprus, 309–10, 332, 335, 336–7, 351, 367–8, 369–70, 385
  governor of, 272
Cyropaedia, history of Cyrus the Great by Xenophon, 207–8, 213, 417

Cyropolis (Kurkath), 399
Cyrus Chronicle, 201
Cyrus cylinder record, 410–11, 536, 541, 545–52 *passim*, 559
Cyrus I of Parsuwash, ruler of Anshan (fl. 640 B.C.):
  legends concerning, 143–4; submission to Assyrian king, 23, 33, 133; victory over Media, 144–8
Cyrus II the Great, king of Anshan (558–529 B.C.), **392–419**, **537–554**
  administration of Empire, 397–402; building activities, 552; chronology of conquests, 405–8; death of, 417; genealogy of, 33, 133, 209–10, 396–7, 404; Indian expedition, 213; 399; invasion of Babylon (539 B.C.), 212, 292–3, 295, **408–12**, 539, 542–4, 548–50; Lydia campaign, 211–12, 539; Media campaign, 210–11, 538–9; military prowess, 417–18; palace at Pasargadae, 392–6, 625; personality of, 213, 404, 412–15, 417–18; religious beliefs of, 411, 545–9, 550–2, 553, 684, 853
Cyrus the Younger (407–401 B.C.):
  character of, 231–2, 234, 349–50; coinage, 618; death of, 353; as military commander, 269, 291, 348, 353
Cyzicus, *see* Kyzikos

Dacians, 198
Dadikai people, 249n., 250
Daēnā, Avestan god, 669
daeva/daiva, demon god, 679, 682, 683, 690, 691
Dahā (Daoi) tribe, 239, 254, 648
dahyāva (districts, lands), 244, 246
Dāiukku, *see* Deioces
Dardanelles, 319, 332, 351, 365
darics (gold coins), 221, 364, 515, 612, 617, 618, 619, 621
Darius I, king of the Persians (521–486 B.C.):
  accession conflicts, 218–19, 396–7; administration of empire, 221–5, 271, 279–80, 398, 399; ancestry of, 133, 208, 209–10, 217; attack on Saka tribes (519 B.C.), 220; character and way of life, 224, **225–8**, 236, 684–6, 688–9, 829–30; in Egypt, 507–9, 518, 521; invasion of Scythia, 190–1, 300–2; involved in conspiracy of The Seven, 203; operations in Europe, 301–3, 312–18; penetration into Greece, 266, 299; reform of coinage, 617, 618, 621, 638; revision of laws, 221, 234; statue of (at Susa), 816–19; tomb of, 586, 812–13; wives, 226.

INDEX

Darius I (cont.)
  See also Behistun inscription; Pasargadae; Persepolis, palace; Susa, palace
Darius II, king of the Persians (423-405 B.C.), 342, 511, 517-18, 694
Darius III, king of the Persians (336-330 B.C.):
  accession, 388, 390, 422, 527; battle order and tactics, 228, 427, 462; in conflict with Alexander, 430-1, 434-7, 447-8; death of, 448-9; preceded by usurper, 533
Daskyleion/Dascylium province, 264, 274, 339, 361, 427, 702
dāta (law of the king), 547-8, 577
Datames, satrap in Cilicia, 371, 374, 375, 377, 380, 381
"date formula" texts, 535
dates (fruit), 287, 608
Datis the Mede, 223, 241n., 279, 313, 316, 317, 318
Dedan, 262, 286
Deioces (Dāiukku?), king of Media (727-675 B.C.), 81, 83, 89, 90, 106, 109, 112, 113, 258
Delos, Delians, island of, 316, 332, 343
Democedes, Greek doctor to Darius, 202, 222, 299
demons, 678-84
Demotic language/script, 520, 526, 710
deportation system, 285-6
Derkylidas, Spartan commander, 355, 356, 365
Deve Hüyük (Syria), 861, 863, 868
"Diary texts" of astronomy, 534
Diodorus Siculus, historian, 426, 500
Diyālā river valley, 40, 61, 83
Dnieper river valley, 150, 183, 185
Dniester river valley, 191, 199
Dobrudja, 197-8
Don river, western bank, 175
Donets group culture, 185-6
Drangae tribe, 249
Drangiana (now Sīstān), 127, 129, 132, 248
Dravidian language, 3
Dūr-Untaš religious centre, 16, 30

Ecbatana (Agbatana) capital of Media:
  archives, 708; captured by Cyrus, 146, 405; gold tablets from, 209, 210; occupied by Alexander, 447, 484; origin of name, 109n.; royal residence, 237, 258, 259
Eber-nāri province, 563
Egypt:
  Achaemenid rule in, 263, 273, **507-22**; armies, 516, 518-19; conflicts with Greece, 335-6, 380, 509-10; conflicts with Persians, 369, 371-4, 385-7, 511-12, 524-5; controlled by Cambyses, 214, 296, 502-7; the fleet, 326; legal system, 507-8, 519-20; metalwork, 861-2; satrapal administration, 512-20; sculptural art and dress, 521-2, 816-19; surrender to Alexander, 433; temples of, 223, 506, 508-9, 511, 520.
  See also calendars; Elephantine island; individual cities
Elam:
  Akkadian invasion of, 8; Assyrian conflict, 20-4, 32; Babylonia war, 23; battles with Ur, 10-11; city states, 5; culture, 4, 8-9, 16, 24; dress, 823, 830-1; land, geography, 1, 15; the middle kingdom, **16-18**; the neo-elamite kingdom, **18-24**, 134; the old kingdom, **10-16**; population, 2, 14, 259; rulers of, 7-8, 10, 12-13, 16-18, 19-24, 28-32
Elamite language/script:
  documents, 6, 8, 230; inscriptions, 6, 235, 745, 807; language, 23, 24; script development, 9-10, 19n., 24, 64n., 74
electrum, gold/silver alloy, 616, 620
Elephantine island:
  Aramaic papyrii of, 505, 511, 512, 516, 519, 522-3, 559, 706; Jewish community in, 503, 511-12, 516-17, 518, 520; temple of Yahu, 511
elephants, *see* animals
Ellipi, kingdom of, 74, 86, 87-8
Eparti dynasty in Elam, 11-12, 14, 28
Ephesus, 427
Ephippus, historian, 488n.
epigonoi native youths, *see* "Successors"
epitropos (vice-regent), 233
Eretria, 307, 309, 317
Erigyius, cavalry commander, 439-40, 453
Esagila, temple of Babylon, 539, 543, 550, 552, 557
  ruins of, 566, 567
Esarhaddon, king of Assyria (680-669 B.C.), 95, 101, 107, 108, 214, 562n.
Ethiopia, 214, 247, 263, 503
Euagoras, city-king in Cyprus, 351, 367, 369-70, 523
Eumenes, Greek chancellor, 485, 490
  campaigns of, 242, 494-5; family of, 388
eunuchs, 137, 227, 532n.
Euphrates river, 413, 488
  bridge over, 260, 585; great plains, 259
Europe, invaded by Persians, 301-3, 312-18, 321-31

INDEX

falconry, 580
family life, 649, 652–6
Farvardīgān festival, 779n., 780–1
festivals, religious, 779–81
fief-holders, 276, 574–6
fire:
  domestic hearth, 676, 695; sacred royal, 416, 486, 650, 813, 850
fishes, representations of, 732, 733
food:
  at court, 230–1, 636–7; supplied as rations, 588–94 *passim*, 599, 600–9, 632–3
fravashis, spirits of the departed, 677

Gabae, palace site, 237
Gadates, satrap in Ionia, 223, 414–15, 688
gāhānbārs (seasonal deities), 750, 751, 752, 755, 779–80, 781–4, 787–9
Gaimanova Mohyla barrow grave, 196
Gallipoli peninsula, 306, 333
Gandāra, Gandharans, 220, 244, 249–50, 462, 824
Gāthās of Zoroaster, religious text, 650, 657, 662, **664–5**, 668–9, 681–2
Gaugamela, battle of (331 B.C.), 434–7, 497, 579
Gaumāta, pretender to the Persian throne, 216, 218, 219, 561, 685, 749, 828
Gayōmart, primal man, 646–7
Gedrosia, Gedrosians, 251, 454, 455n., 471
Geloni, people of Gelonus, 187–8, 189
Germanioi tribe, 239
Gerrhi, Gerrhus country, 181–2
Gizilbunda mountains, 66
glass, 863
Gobryas/Gubaru/Ugbaru, governor of Gutium, 411, 539, 542, 544, 545, 563
Gobryas, spear-bearer of Darius I, 240, 241n., 312, 411n., 414, 590–1
  depicted on mural, 813
gods and goddesses, 8–9, 341, 670–8, 679–84, 693–4
  food supplied for, 605, 687, 695.
  See also under individual names
gold:
  on clothing, 831, 859; coinage, 616, 617, 621; goldsmiths, 651, 862; objects, 194, 196, 231, 856–61 *passim*; payment as tribute, 271, 402; treasure hoards, 438n., 617, 859.
  See also darics
Gordian knot, undone by Alexander, 428
Greeks:
  art and crafts, 173, 812, 819, 829, 844, 866; in conflict with Ionians, 357–8; exiles returning, 481; the fleet, 310, 321, 335, 360–1, 428, 510; historians, 201, 236; mercenaries, 426, 431, 435, 450, 456, 460, 481, 523; settlements, 183, 265; trading centres, 157, 174, 186, 189; under Alexander, 427, 446–7; under Persian rule, 228–9, 266–7, 274, 291, 421–3.
  See also Athens, Ionians
grīv, *grīwa*, measure of capacity, *see kurrima*
Gubaru, satrap of Akkadī country, 564
Gubaru, satrap of Gutium, *see* Gobyras
Gudea, ruler of Lagaš, 26, 37
Gungunum, king of Larsa, 27, 28
Gutium, 117, 547n.

Haik people, 256
Hakhāmaniš, *see* Achaemenes
Hallušu-Inšušinak, king of Elam (699–692 B.C.), 21, 31
Ḥalulē, battle of (691 B.C.), 21, 32
Halys river, 211
Hana people, 560
Haoma, evil god, 644, 653, 676–7, 774
haoma intoxicant, 254n., 255, 653, 676–7, 688, 695
Harā, peak of mountain, 643, 644
Harahvatiš, *see* Arachosia
Ḥarakka, *see* Araḥa
harem, *see* women's role
Ḥarhar province, 64, 82, 83, 84, 107, 108
Harī rūd river valley, 248.
  See also Tejen-Harī-rūd
Haria, 127, 129
Harpagus, Median army commander, 143, 144, 145, 146, 148, 212, 279, 293
  chronicled by Herodotus, 203
Harpalus, imperial treasurer, 447, 448n., 477, 479n.
Ḥarrān, 124, 146, 261, 408
  stela inscription at, 261, 541, 555
Hasanlu, city site, 57
Haumavargā (Amyrgian) people, 254
hazarapatiš (chiliarch), 230, 232–3, 279, 449, 485
Hellenic league, 422, 423, 447
Helmand river valley, 248, 407, 455n.
Hephaestion, Macedonian commander, 453, 463, 468, 480, 484–5, 487
Herat, 451, 452n.
Hermopolis letters, 517, 701, 706
Herodotus, Greek historian:
  his reliability, 110, 149–50; his sources, 89n., 170, 181, 200, 201–5, 340, 420
Hidali, 596, 597
Ḥilakku/Hilik, 263n., 264
Hindu Kush, 249, 454, 455

937

INDEX

Hippias of Sigeion, 306, 307, 310, 315, 317
Hippoklos, tyrant of Lampsakos, 307
Hiran, 596
Hisar, Tepe, 54, 730
Hišema, 597, 598, 599
Histiaios, of Miletos, 302, 303, 308, 311
hōfan (soldier's daily ration), 632–3, 634
horses:
  breeding of, 46, 47, 837; burials, 170, 194, 196; racetracks, 630, 659–60; rations for, 607; venerated, 659
Huhunuri, 5
Humpan, the great god, 8
Humpan-nikaš, king of Elam (742–717 B.C.), 19–20, 31, 32
Humpan-nimmena I, king of Elam (1300–1275 B.C.), 16, 29–30
Humpan-nimmena (III?), king of Elam (692–687 B.C.), 21, 31, 88
Humurti, *see* Kumurdi
hunting, 231, 417–18, 532n., 580
Hurrian tribe, 38, 45–6, 71
Hutelutuš-Inšušinak, regent/king of Elam (1120–1110 B.C.), 18, 30
Hvar, sun god, 678
Hydarnes, commander of Greek guards, 324–5, 327, 338, 343, 349n., 591.
  See also Miturna
Hydaspes (Jhelum) river, 464, 465, 469n.
Hyphasis (Beas) river, 465, 466
Hyrcania, Hyrcanians, 127, 129, 255, 406, 450
Hystaspes (Vištāspa), father of Darius I, 217, 342, 420

ianzi (petty king or chieftain), 61
Ibbi-Sin, king of Ur, 27
Ike-halki dynasty, of Elam, 16–17
IKU, celestial acre of land, 725, 730, 731, 735
Imbros, island of, 306, 309, 368
Inaros, Libyan rebel, 510
India, Indians:
  Alexander's campaign, 462–76; conquered by Darius, 220, 250, 398, 462; dress, 824; language/script, 705
Indian Ocean, 222–3, 250
Indo-Aryan languages, 42, 45
Indo-European languages, 3, 42, 45, 49
Indo-Iranian language, 41, 42–3, 45, 49, 56
Indus river, 220–1, 462n., 467, 469, 640
  valley, 220, 289n., 468
Inšušinak, god of Susa, 9
Ionians:
  architectural style, 840–1; in conflict with Greeks, 357–8; in conflict with Persians, 307–12, 318, 332–3, 343, 353–5;

definition of, 265; in Egypt, 518–19;
  first conquest of, 292–6
Iphikrates, Athenian commander, 371–4, 376, 524
Iran (Arianē), 290, 648.
  See also Aryans, Persians
Iranian language/script, 114, 648, 711, 712–13.
  See also Old Persian
Iranzu, king of Mana, 80, 81
Irdabama, woman attached to court, 608
irrigation systems, 253, 287–9, 578, 663
Irtašduna, wife of Darius I, *see* Artystone
irtiba, measure of capacity, *see* artabē
Irtuppiya, Persepolis supply officer, 600
Iškudra, *see* Skudra
Išpakāi, Scythian leader, 97, 102, 103
Išpuini, king of Urartu, 65–6
Issus, battle of (333 B.C.), 429–31, 527
ivory, 249, 798, 863–4
Izirta, capital of the Mannaeans, 115

Jaxartes, river, 213, 399
Jerusalem, rebuilding of temple, 409, 412
jewellery, 612, 613, 651, 847, 857–9, 862
Jews:
  bankers, 403–4; in Egypt, 503, 511–12, 516–17, 518, 520; exiles from Babylon, 409, 412; scribes/script, 707, 710
Jinjān royal lodge, 243, 285
Jordan, archaeological finds, 701
Judaea/Judah, archaeological finds, 701, 707, 868

Kabul (Afghanistan), 454, 613
Kadousioi people, 256
Kafirs, 47
Kamyanka earthwork, 157, 197, 199
Kandaraš/Kandahar, 249, 403, 452, 454, 705
Kār-Kašši, 105n., 114
kāra (armed populace), 115, 135–6, 269
Karia/Kares/Karkā/Caria, 266, 294, 357, 428, 579
Karkhah river, 1
Karmania, 239, 242, 248, 478, 479
Karmir-Blur fortress, 161, 162, 166
karša (ten-shekel coin), 621–2
Kārūn river, 1, 242, 440, 441n., 809
Kašš/Kassite tribe:
  gods of, 40; language of, 40; overrun Elam, 15–16, 29, 258; origins of, 39–40
Kaštariti, *see* Xšathrita
Kazbek treasure, 861
Kelermes royal burial site, 170
Kerch strait, 93

INDEX

Khabbash, Pharaoh of Egypt (338–336 B.C.), 526–7
Khorsabad, palace of Sargon, 800n., *805*, 821
Khšathrita, *see* Xšathrita
Khūzistān, *see* Ū(v)ja
Khvarenah, god of glory, 677
Khwārazm, *see* Chorasmia
Kiev-Kanev group burial sites, 178, 195
Kimon, admiral, son of Miltiades, 332, 333, 334, 336–7
King Lists:
  Achaemenian, 532–3; Elamite, 7, 10n.; Sumerian, 7, 25, 37
"King's Eye" (informer), 233
"King's Peace" treaty (387–386 B.C.), 365–8, 375–7, 421
Kirmān, 248, 624–5
Kišessu/Kišisa stronghold, 77, 82, 83, 106, 108
Klearchos, Greek commander, 352, 353, 354
Konon, Athenian admiral, 350, 351, 357, 360–1, 365, 366
Kopet-dagh mountains, 51, 128
Kumurdi (Ḥumurti), 73
Kunaxa, *see* Cunaxa
Kur, river:
  associated with Cyrus, 419; settlements alongside, 240, 855
Kurash, *see* Cyrus I
Kurdistan, 257n., 354
kurrima/grīv/grīwa, measure of capacity, 632, 633
Kuter-Nahhunte III, king of Elam (*c.* 1155–1150 B.C.), 17
Kuter-Nahḫunte (IV?), king of Elam (693–692 B.C.), 21, 31
Kyzikos/Cyzicus, 348, 379, 390, 620

Lagaš, 7, 10
Lampsacus/Lampsakos, 307, 620–1
lazurite (lapis-lazuli), 77, 402, 864
Lemnos, island of, 306, 309, 368
Leonidas, king of Sparta, 319, 323–5
Leonnatus, Macedonian officer, 458–9, 468, 471, 476
Libya, 219, 503, 523
"Lie" of the Achaemenid kings, 209, 216, 218, 219, 685–6
lions:
  in art, 814, 858, 859; celestial forms, 725, 726, 736, 737–8; hunting of, 417–18.
  See also lion–bull combat *under* "calendars"
Litoi-Melgunov burial site, 161, 182
Liyān, in Bushire, 29–30
Lullubī tribe, 38–9, 43
Lullume/Lullubum province, 38, 43, 59, 71

Luristan:
  bronzes, 44n., 74; inhabitants, 44, 87, 259; sites, 258n.
Lusatian culture, 191
Lycia/Lykia, 274–5, 294, 343n., 414
Lydia:
  art and dress forms, 824, 867; coinage, 616; extent of, 265; involved in wars, 126, 359, 383; name uncertain in documents, 101n., 211
Lysander, Spartan admiral, 350–1, 358, 364

Macedonia, Macedonians, 320–1, 422, 458, 461
  in Alexander's army, 424, 452, 481; the fleet, 467, 471–2.
  See also Philip of Macedonia, Alexander the Great
Mada, *see* Medes
Mādāi, 104, 105, 106, 107
Madyēs, king of the Scythians, 103, 116, 117, 118
Magi (wise men), 141, 143, 146, 232, 281, 579, 650, 687, 691–2, **696–7**
Magnesia:
  governor of, 334; Greek inscription of Darius I at, 223, 314, 688, 702
Māh, moon god, 678
Maka/Makkaš/Makkan, 251, 402, 824
Makrān, 251, 462, 470, 471
Malāyir plain site, 837
Maly Kurgan barrow, 161, 164, 165
Malyān, Tepe, site, 25, 27–8, 29, 30, 34, 210n.
Mana/Manaš, land of the Mannaeans:
  geography, 71, 72; kingdom under Urartu, 65, 69, 70, 73, 86, 124
Mannaeans:
  contact with Scythians/Cimmerians, 97, 100, 102; revolt against Assyria, 106–8, 115–16; society and culture, 71–3
Marathon, 317
Mardi/Mardoi people, 239, 243–4, 281
Mardonius, son of Gobryas, 312, 313, 319, 327, 328, 329–30, 590
Marduk, god of Babylonia, 139, 212, 411, 545–8 *passim*, 690
Margiana (Marv):
  position of, 54, 55n., 127, 129, 132, 641; revolt in, 130n., 218, 219
maris, a liquid measure, 633, 634
Mārlik cemetery, 65, 856, 858
Marmara, coast of, 309, 310, 620
marriage customs, 655–6
Marv, *see* Margiana
Massagetae, Sakā nation, 127, 213, 254
Matezziš, 595, 596, 608

INDEX

Matiene, 256, 257
Mausolos, satrap of Karia, 378, 380, 382, 384
Mazaces, satrap of Egypt, 526, 616
Mazaeus, satrap of Syria and Mesopotamia, 270, 435, 437–8, 460n.
Mazamūa, *see* Zamūa
Māzandarān, 683
Mazares, the Mede, 279, 293
Mazdaism, 341, 662
Meander river valley, 274, 293
measures:
of capacity, dry and fluid, 631–4, 639; of length and distance, 625–30, 638
Medes, **36–109**
art of, 856; comparison with Persians, 278–80; composition of tribes, 36–40, 74–5; conflict with Assyrians, 58–61, 64–70, 76–9, 81–8, 101–2, 106–8, 123–4; dress, 138, 278, 815, 822, 830; housing, 138; period of independence, 89–90; religion, 139–42, 697; revolt against Darius I, 218–19; society and culture, 136–9; transmigrations, 41–57.
See also Media
Media, the empire of, **110–48**
city states and units, 57, 58, 80, 135; eastern provinces, 127–32; foundation and extension of kingdom, 109, 110–19, 125, 135; geography, 36, 212–13, 257–8, 404n.; northern frontier, 132–5; resettling of population, 76, 78; under Assyrian rule, 80–1, 83, 84, 90n.; victory of Cyrus and fall of empire, 142–8
medimnus, measure of capacity, 631
Megabates, nephew of Darius I, 591.
See also Bakabaduš
Megabyzos, satrap of Syria, 335–7, 340, 510, 565
Megapanus, satrap of Babylon, 565, 591
Melanchlaeni ("Black cloaks") tribe, 153, 185, 186–7
Melgunov burial site, *see* Litoi-Melgunov
Memnon, Rhodian condottiere, 382, 388, 390–1, 423, 427, 428–9
Memphis (Egypt), 502, 510, 514, 518, 701, 862
Mentor, Rhodian condottiere, 382, 385–6, 387, 388, 525
Merodach-baladan, Chaldean chieftain, 19, 21
Mesopotamia:
economic affairs, 578–81; foreign domination of, 586; influence on Elam, 8; social conditions, 572–7; sources for history of, 529–37, 568–72
Messi/Mešta/Messians, 66, 69, 72
metalwork, 856–63

migration routes, 48–53, 854–5
Miletos, 309, 310, 311, 346–7, 352, 365, 418, 428
Milograd culture, 184
Miltiades, dynast of Gallipoli, 302, 306, 307, 309, 314–15
minnīth (wheat), 72
Minua, king of Urartu, 69
Mitanni/Matiani kingdom, 45–6, 47, 682
Mithra, god, 232, 644, 652–3, 658, 670, 687, 694
festival of, 231
Miturna (possibly the same as Hydarnes, *q.v.*), 591
Monarchy, *see* Royalty
Murašū family archives, 564, 569, 577, 865

Nabarzanes, chiliarch, 449, 450, 451n.
Nabonidus/Nabuna'id, ruler of Babylon:
in conflict with priesthood, 41, 540–2, 550; in exile, 411, 414; in Harrān, 211, 262, 408; overcome by Cyrus the Great, 212, 540, 542
Nabonidus Chronicle, 19, 112, 534, 554–7
on Cyrus the Great, 404–5n., 409–10, 413–14, 537–45
Nabopalassar, Chaldean general, 23, 119, 121, 122, 123, 124
Nabū, son of Bēl, god of Babylon, 549, 555, 557
Namar, 61, 70, 84
Namazghah IV, V, VI culture, 54–5, 128, 129
Nanna, moon-god of Ur, 27, 412
Naqsh-i Rustam:
Ka'ba-yi Zardusht tower, 806, 848, 849, 851, 852; tomb of Darius, 240, 712, 813
Narām-Su'en, king of Akkade, 36
Narunte, sun god, 9
Nasu, demoness of decay, 683
Naurūz, spring equinox, 753, 779, 787–9
Naxos, 300, 307, 308, 316
Nearchos:
family of, 388, 480; as fleet commander, 467–8, 470, 473, 479, 481; travel records, 242, 251, 441n., 472
Nebuchadnezzar I, king of Babylonia, 18, 30, 124
Nebuchadnezzar II, king of Babylonia, 23, 412
Nebuchadnezzar III, usurper king, 561
Nebuchadnezzar IV, usurper king, 561–2
Nectanebo I, Pharaoh of Egypt (381–363 B.C.), 386, 523–4
Nectanebo II, Pharaoh of Egypt (361–343 B.C.), 380, 386, 525
Nerab/Neirab tablets, 569n., 699

INDEX

Nepherites I, Pharaoh of Egypt (399–394 B.C.), 523
Nepherites II, Pharaoh of Egypt (381 B.C.), 523
Neuri tribe, 184
Nidintu-Bēl, usurper to throne (336 B.C.), 533, 561
Nikokles, son of Euagoras of Cyprus, 370, 385
Nikopol, burial site area, 179
Nile river, 335, 502, 507, 509, 516, 524, 764
Nineveh:
  battles and destruction of, 112, 117, 122–3, 123–4; palace of Sennacherib, 844
Nippur, 578–9, 580
  archive texts at, 564, 567, 568–9, 578
Nīrīz, 596
nomads, 281–5, 649.
  See also Sakā
nomoi (districts), *see* satrapies
North Pontic region, 153, 173–4, 183, 193, 195
Nupištaš (presumed to be Naqsh-i Rustam), *see* Naqsh-i Rustam
Nūsh-i Jān ancient site:
  buildings, 416, 806, **832–7**, *833*, 841; excavation finds, 613, 834, 837

oath of allegiance to Assyrians, 108–9
Ochos, Prince (later Artaxerxes III), 380, 381
Oebares, groom to Persian kings, 144, 147, 148
Olbia, Scythian commercial centre, 157, 181, 186, 187, 189, 301–2
Old Persian (Aryan) script, 114, 208, 395–6, 684, 702, 704, 708, 745
Olympias, mother of Alexander, 422, 423, 485, 494, 496
Opis, 481, 539, 585n.
oracle:
  of Ammon at Siwah, 433, 486; of Delphi, 294, 323; of Magnesia, 688; of Šamaš, 101, 102, 103, 106, 107
Oreitae people, 471, 476
Oroites, satrap of Sardis, 219, 234, 296–8
Orontes mountain, *see* Alvand
Orontes river valley, 260
Orontes, satrap of Armenia and Mysia, 256, 354, 355, 369, 370, 379–84 *passim*, 621
Orthocorybantii peoples, 100, 258
Ossetes people, 648
ostracon, 699, 701
Oxus river:
  environs, 252, 253; treasure, 856, 857, 869
Oxyartes, Sogdian noble, father of Roxane, 456, 468, 469

Pahir-hiššan, king of Elam, 16
Pahlavi texts, 642, 643, 678, 682, 712–13, 760
Paionians, 303
Pāmir mountain area, 51, 663
Panticapaeum (now Kerch), 93
Paphlagonia, 265, 361, 371, 374
Papremis, battle of (460 B.C.), 510
Paraitakene/Paraetacene tribe, 75, 248, 258, 456
Paralatae Scyths, 166, 167
parasang, three-mile measurement, 628–9, 639
Paricanii/Parikanioi peoples, 100, 258
Paritaka/Paritakanū, *see* Partakka
Parmenio, army commander:
  as adviser, 427–8, 435, 437, 444; commanding forces, 425, 431, 436, 442, 447–8; death of, 453; family of, 422–3, 452, 466
Paropamisadae, 461, 468, 469, 479
Parmizzan, 596
Parsa/Persis/Parsua (Fars):
  administration of, 240–1, 478; entered by Assyrians, 69, 76, 78, 108; the land, 243; location of, 32, 34, 61–4, 238–9; raided by Mannaeans, 107; surrender to Alexander, 443
Parsamash/Parsuwash, *see* Parsūaš
Parsua, *see* Parsa (Fars)
Parsūaš/Parsamash/Parsuwash, identification of, 19, 21, 31–2, 33, 34, 62–3, 67–8, 88, 133–4
Partakka/Paritaka/Paritakanū, 75, 104
Parthia/Parthava, 104, 127, 129, 248, 252–3, 406
Parysatis, wife of Darius II, 280, 349, 352, 577
Pasargadae, capital city of Cyrus the Great:
  Alexander in, 443, 480; building by Darius I, 846, 846n., 852; excavation finds, 392–6, 419; foundation of, 237, 239, 418–19, 855; gardens, 846–7; Gate R, 842–3; Palace P, 812, 845–6; Palace S, 843–4; position of, 838; sculptures, 829, 831; stone plinths, 852–3; Tall-i Takht, 853–4; tomb of Cyrus, 480, 838–41, 849; Zindān-i Sulaimān, 848–52
Pasargadae tribe, 238, 418
Pattala (India), 470, 471n., 472
Pausanias, Spartan commander, 329, 333
Peithon, satrap of S. India, 468, 479, 495
Peli dynasty of Awan, 26
Peloponnesians, 323, 325, 328, 342, 343–9.
  See also individual islands
peqid (satrapal treasurer), 516
Perdiccas, regent of Macedonian empire, 463, 490, 493

941

INDEX

Persepolis:
  administration of, 240; Apadana buildings, **796–800**, 801, 802, 804; Apadana wall-reliefs, 237, 279, 736, 738, 815–16, 821–5; architecture of, **793–806**; Audience reliefs, 819–21, 825; Fortification tablets, 239, 403, **588–95** *passim*, 604, 609, 687–8, 704–5; Gate of All Lands, 800–1, 843; Hundred Column Hall, 802, 825–6, 827; occupied by Alexander, 442–6; Palace of Darius, 802–3, 814; Parapet and Terrace, 794, 803–6, 814–15; secured by Eumenes, 494–5; Treasury building, 801, 831; Treasury tablets, 235–40 *passim*, 577n., 588, **592–604** *passim*, 704–5; Triplyon reliefs, 826
Persian Gates, 242, 243n., 442
Persian Gulf:
  islands of, 222–3; ships on, 222
Persians:
  armed forces, 426, 435–6, 651; art, 582–3, 584–5 (*see also* "metalwork"); campaigns of Cyrus the Younger, 352–3; comparison with Medes, 278–80; in conflict with Alexander, 425–32, 480, 482–4, 488, 491–2; conquest of Ionia, **292–300**, 389–90; dress, 515, 521, 811–12, 817, 822, 823–4, 830–1; Egyptian campaigns, 369, 371–4, 385–7, 510, 524–5; expansion into Europe, **300–7**, 312–18; Greek wars, 309–12, 316–18, 321–31, 359; inter-racial marriages, 388, 480, 484; position as rulers, 278–80, 289–91, 547–8; religion, 340–1, 415–16, **684–95**; the Royal court, **225–38**; rulers of Egypt, 512–22, 526; satraps in revolt, 342–9, 361–2, 377–84; sea power, 365–7; social organization, 649–52; under Cyrus the Great, 392–419; war and peace with Sparta, 344, 346, 358–64, 368
Persis, *see* Pārsa (Fars)
Persistratids, 306, 315–6, 319
Peucestas, satrap of Mieza and Persis, 468, 478, 480, 488, 491n., 494–7 *passim*
Pharnabazos, satrap of Daskyleion:
  chivalry of, 236, 291, 343; as governor, 264, 620; invasion of Egypt, 269, 369, 371–4; involved in satrap revolts, 346–8, 355–7, 358, 361–4, 365, 366
Pharnaces, son of Arsames, 240, 589, 590, 609
Pharnakes, Pharnakids, 342, 343
Pherendates, satrap in Egypt, 526
phialai (bowls), 861, 863

Philip, son of Machatas, satrap in India, 464, 465, 468, 469, 478, 479n.
Philip II, ruler of Macedonia (359–336 B.C.), 383, 385, 389–90, 421, 422
  assassination of, 390, 423
Philip III, ruler of Macedonia (323–316 B.C.), 493, 496
Phoenicians, 272, 296, 385, 409
  inscriptions of, 709
Phokaia, 292, 293–4
Phrada (possibly Farah), 452
Phraortes, king of Media, 109, 112, 113, 117–18, 210
Phrataphernes, satrap of Parthia and Hyrcania, 450, 453, 460n., 492
Phrygia, 303, 378, 579
Pissouthnes son of Hystaspes, 342–3
plant names, 870–3
Podolian group burial sites, 178, 184
poem (unidentified) on Babylon, 537, 541, 543, 551
Polycrates, of Samos, 296, 298, 299, 614
Porus, king of the Paurava, 463–4, 465, 467, 469
Pottery:
  "cylindrical jar" type, 130; foreign imports, 157; grey pottery, 55n., 56n.; Kaftari ware, 28n., 29; painted ware, 4
Prexaspes, adviser to King Cambyses, 203, 204, 216, 233
priests, *see* Magi
procreation and child-bearing, 652–6
proskynesis (ceremonial prostration), 457–8, 459, 484
Protothyes, Scythian leader, 103, 108
Ptolemy, Pharaoh of Egypt, 493, 495, 496, 718, 765
Pura (Bampūr), 251, 472, 473, 476
PUZUR-Inšušinak, king of Elam, 7, 8n., 10
  inscriptions of, 9

Qablin, battle of, 122
Qairaq-qum culture, 54, 55
qanāt (water channel), 288–9
Que (Huwē), 263n.
Qutī tribe, 36–8, 43, 71, 105n., 547n.
Qyzqapan tomb, 139

Rhodes, island of, 346, 382–3, 385, 861
rhyta (vessels), 860, 862, 863
roads, routes, *see* migration routes, Royal roads, travel
Roxane, wife of Alexander, 456, 457, 493, 496
Royal roads, 261, 263, 276–7, 402–3, 440, 442
Royalty, the Royal family, 225–32

INDEX

Rozkopana Mohyla barrow grave, 196
Ṛta (ritual law), 689-90
Rusā I, king of Urartu, 81, 83, 85, 95

Sabaces, satrap of Egypt, 526, 616
sacred garments, 655
Safid-rūd river valley, 71, 82, 105
Sagartian/Asagartiyā tribe, 75, 239, 284
Saïs (Egypt), 505, 506, 521
Sakā nomads, 48, 51, 52, 100, 132, 220, 648
  definition of, 253-5
Šakašen/Sacasēnē, 100, 169
Sakastana (Sīstān), 248, 249
Šamaš-erība, usurper king of Babylon, 562, 565
Šamaššumukin, king of Babylon, 117
Sammurāmat (Semiramis), queen of Assyria, 68, 90
Samos, island of, 300, 332, 378
Šamšī-Adad V, king of Assyria, 65-6, 67, 68
Saparda province, 101n., 104, 105, 107
Saqqārah necropolis, 518, 519n.
  document finds from, 700, 701
Sar-i Pul rock relief, 828-9
Saracus (Sīnšariškun), king of Assyria, 119, 121, 123
Sardis, 219, 264, 265, 273
  excavation finds, 340-1, 617, 702; under attack, 293, 309, 359, 427
Sargon I, ruler of Akkade (2334-2279 B.C.), 8, 26
Sargon II, king of Babylonia, 20, 81-2, 83-7, 836
Sarmatians/Sauromatians, 153, 175, 648
  culture and graves, 186, **189-90**, 193, 195
Satibarzanes, satrap of Ṭūs, 451, 453
satrapies (provinces of Persia), 127n., 219, **245-59**, 261, 264, 544, 563
  administration of, 267-77, 338-9, 398, 399, 402, 464, 703; in Egypt, 512-20
satraps (civil governors), **267-9**, 272, 280, 339-43, 356, 438n., 492, 563-5
  in Egypt, 512-4, 519; in revolt, 298, 342-9, 361-2, 377-84, 451, 453, 476-8, 562
Sattagydians, 220, 824
Sauromatians, see Sarmatians
Savdarati, 187
scribes, see sepīru
Scylax, of Caryanda, 220-1, 222, 461, 463n.
Scythes, mythical king of the Scythians, 168
Scythian arrows, 92, 126, 155, 179
Scyths/Scythians:
  art, **160-7**, 173, 856; barrow graves, 170, 174-9, 182, 185, 189-90, 194-5, 197; catacomb graves, 193-4;
culture/archaeology, 91-2, 93-4, 96n., 100, 169, 170, 171-2; dress and ornament, 154-5, 823; exodus to Lydia, 126; history sources, 149-50; kingdom of, 97, 100, 103, 119, 125, 154, 199; language of, 48, 149; Late Scythian period, 193-9; legends of, 165-7; movement into E. Europe, 191-2; movement into Near East, 96-7, 117-18, 174; "Nomadic Scyths", 152, 178, 179; Northwest Caucasian group, **169-71**, 172, 178, 195, 648; population and society, 150-5; religion and burial customs, **158-60**, 170; royal burials, 171-3, 179, 194, 196, 198-9; "Royal Scyths", 150, 173-4, 175, 178, 181, 197; "Scythian agriculturalists", 152, 182, 183; "Scythian husbandmen", 152, 156, 167, 178, 180, 182; trade and industry, 156-8; weapons, 155-6
seals:
  bullae, 701, 702; cylinder, 4, *733*, 864-9 *passim*; scaraboids, 867, 868; stamp, 591, 595-9 *passim, 726-8, 733, 734*, 834, 864-9 *passim*
Seleucia, see Susa
Seleucus, satrap of Babylonia, 493, 494, 495, 496-7
Semiramis, queen, see Sammurāmat
Sennacherib, ruler of Babylon, 21, 31, 32, 87, 88
sepīru (scribe), 698, 700, 703, 707-8
servants, 230-1, 232-4
Seven, conspiracy of the, 203-4, 215-17
sexual activity, 654
Shalmaneser III, king of Assyria, 61, 64-5
shekel (silver coin), 612, 622, 623
sheep, see animals
Shīrāz (Tirazziš), 243, 595, 596, 608
Sibyrtius, satrap of Carmania, 478, 479
siglos (silver coin), 612, 614, 617, 618, 619
Šilhak-Inšušinak I, king of Elam (c. 1150-1120 B.C.), 17, 18, 56
Silhazi province, 69, 79, 102, 139
silver:
  bulk silver, 612-14; currency, 610, 614 (*see also* individual coins); jewellery, 858-9; payment in, 247, 271, 588, 592; plate, 859-61; ring money, 612, 614; transport of, 241; treasure, 438, 834, 859
Simaški, 5, 7, 10, 11, 27
Sin, moon god of Babylon, 411, 540, 541, 553
Sīnšariškun, see Saracus
Sippar, 540, 558-9
  tablets from, 561, 567

943

INDEX

širkūtu (temple servants), 573
Sisicottus, of Gandhara, 462n., 463, 464, 465
sissoo timber, 248
Sīstān, 455n.
  See also Drangiana and (later) Sakastana
Sisygambis, mother of Darius III, 431, 441, 442n.
Skolotoi, or "Royal Scyths", *see under* Scyths
Skudra, Skudrians, 267, 823
Skunkha, Sakā leader, 219, 220, 254, 302
Skuthai (Sakā nomads), *see* Sakā
slavery:
  under Achaemenids, 281, 572, 573; under Mannaeans, 73–4; under Medes, 38, 136–7
Smerdis (Bardiya), brother of king Cambyses, *see* Bardiya
Sogdiana, Sogdians, 48, 252, 456, 460, 823
Sparda, *see* Sardis
Sparta:
  allied with Egypt, 523–4; in conflict with Persians, 315, 323–31, 338, 357–64; expeditions in the Aegean, 300, 346–9, 367; peace negotiations, 344, 346, 368, 375–7
Spithridates, Persian baron, 358, 361, 362
Sraosha, Avestan god, 669, 682
Srub/Srubnaya (Kurgan) culture, 42, 54, 161, 168–9, 175–6
stele, stelae:
  Achaemenid, 262; Egyptian, 509, 517, 518, 521; Greek, 339; "Naples", 527; "Satrap's", 526, 527; Scythian, 159–60.
  See also Aramaic script
Steppe region, 175, 179, 193
Strabo, historian, 94–5, 441n.
Strymon area, 313, 333, 691–2
"Successors" (*epigonoi*), native youths, 461, 481, 483
Suez canal project, 220, 222
sukkal (petty king, regent), 12–13, 28
sukkal-maḥ (overlord, grand regent), 12–13, 28
Sula group culture, 185–6
Šulgi, king of Ur (2093–2046 B.C.), 10–11, 27
Sumer, 1, 2, 6–7
Susa/Šušan:
  Apadana buildings, 627, *807*, 808–9; archaeological finds, 4, 29, 589, *731*, 811, 827; archives of, 23, 708; attacks on, 22, 23; community of, 2, 5, 14–15; inscriptions, 266, 807–8; king/regent of, 12, 28; palace of, 583, 806, *810*; statue of Darius, 816–19, 843; under the Achaemenids, 24, 237, 238, 258–9; under Alexander, 438–9, 480

šušānūtu (unidentified type of workers), 573, 574–5
Šutruk-Nahhunte I, king of Elam, 17
Šutruk-Nahhunte II, king of Elam (717–699 B.C.), 20, 31
Syene (Egypt), 503, 516–17
Syennesis, ruler of Cilicia, 263–4, 296, 353
Syria, 260, 429–32
  inscriptions from, 698, 699

Tachos, Pharaoh of Egypt (363–361 B.C.), 379–81, 524–5
Tājīks, Tājīkstān, 250, 252
Tammarit, king of Elam (*c.* 653–644 B.C.), 22, 32
Tamukkan (supposed Taoke), *see* Taoke
Targitaus, mythical king of the Scythians, 165, 167
Taurus mountains, 263
Taxiles, governor in India, 463, 464, 465, 469, 478, 479
Teima inscriptions, 701, 709
Teispes, king of Anshan, 34, 209, 239
Tejen-Harī-rūd river, 52, 131
Tell Fakhariya (Syria), 698
Temti-Humpan-Inšušinak, king of Elam (663–653 B.C.), 22, 32
Ten Thousand army, 256, 265, 354, 540
Tepe Haftavan, 257
Tepe Sialk (near Kāshān):
  archaeological finds, 96n., 140; fortress of, 58; inhabitants of, 57; temple records, 6
Tepe Yahya, 6, 129
tetradrachm, silver coin, 614, 615, 619
Teumman, *see* Temti-Humpan-Inšušinak
Thataguš, 220, 250
Thebes:
  against the King's Peace, 375–6; in Greek rebellions, 379, 383, 384, 386, 423; under Persians, 517
Themistokles, of Athens, 315, 321, 323, 324, 334, 335
Thermopylae, battle of, 229, 323–6
Thrace/Thracians, 152, 158, 266, 267, 303
  art of, 198–9
Thyssagetae people, 188
Tiasmin group burial sites, 178, 180–1, 182, 183, 195
Tiglathpileser III, king of Assyria (745–728 B.C.), 70, 71, 76–7, 78–9
tigrakhaudā (with pointed hoods), 100, 254, 258
Tigris river:
  crossing, 540, 585n.; defence works, 481; great plain, 259–60
Tīlašurri, 101, 102

INDEX

Tirazziš (Shīrāz), see Shīrāz
Tiribazos, Greek commander, 256, 354–5, 366, 368, 369, 370
Tishtriya/Tiriya, star god, 672–4, 687, 694, 775
Tissaphernes, satrap of Ionia and Karia, 291, 342–8, 349n., 352–5 *passim*, 358–60 *passim*
 coinage of, 615, 619
Tomakovka burial site, 179, 181
Tomyris, warrior queen of the Massagetae, 213, 224, 408
toparchies, 268–9
Tovsta Mohyla barrow grave, 196
trade:
 with Greece, 418; overland, 572, 582; records of, 703; road routes, 72, 157–8; sea routes, 405, 462
travel:
 couriers, 402–4, 447n., 606–7; cross-country marches, 439–43, 630; rations for travellers, 589, 591–607 *passim*, 704; stopping-places en route from Persepolis, 595–8.
 See also migration routes, Royal roads
treasure and treasuries, 438n., 448n., 514–15, 532
 disbursements from, 592, 601–2, 603, 604, 622; hoards, 614, 619, 834, 847, 860.
 See also Persepolis, treasury tablets
trees:
 of Life, 644; sacred, *733, 735*
tribute payments:
 collection of, 103–4, 295; Darius' arrangements, 222, 246–7, 271, 399; in Egypt, 514–15; gifts as tribute, 860; under Alexander, 442n., 532
Tušpa (Van), 256, 289n.
tyrannos (tyrant), a leader, 295–6, 761n.
Tyre, siege of (332 B.C.), 432
Tyriespis, satrap of Paropamisadae, 461n., 465, 468, 469n.

Udjahorresne, priest-adviser to Darius I, 223
 statue of, 503, 505, 506, 521
Ugarit, coinage of, 611
Ugbaru, see Gobryas
Ugro-Finnish tribes, 188
Uišdiš (in Marāgha), 81, 85
Ukraine, Scythians in, 174
Ullusunu, king of Mana, 81, 83, 84, 85, 86
ummān-manda (Medes), 546, 547
Un-taš-napir-riša (or Un-taš-Humpan), king of Elam (1275–1240 B.C.), 16, 30
unguents, 231
Ur of the Chaldees, kingdom of:
 battles with Elam, 10–11; excavation finds, 551, 553, 569, 583, 862, 865; temples and gates, 412
Uranduš, 596
Urartu, kingdom of:
 advances into Assyria, 65–6, 69–70; subject to Median empire, 124, 125; wars with Assyria, 71, 84
Urmīya, Lake:
 excavation site, 257; population around, 43, 44, 69, 71, 80, 256
Urtaki, king of Elam (675–665 B.C.), 22
Uruk, city of Babylonia, 412, 553, 580n.
Usak tumuli graves, 860
Uškāia (now Uski) stronghold, 85
Uštani, satrap of Babylonia, 563
Usurper kings, 561–3, 565.
 See also Gaumāta
Ū(v)ja (now Khūzistan), 258
Uxii nomads, 281, 284, 441, 442n.

Van, Lake, 65–6
 See also Tušpa
Varuna, god, 675–6
Vayu, god of the wind, 677
Verethraghna, god of victory, 671–2
Vettersfelde burial site, see Witaszkowo
Vidēvdād, religious text, 640–6 *passim*, 652–65 *passim*, 680, 682, 696
Vīštāspa, Kavi, patron of Zoroaster, 130, 132, 217, 684
Volga river, 96n.
Voronezh group burial site, 178, 188–9
Vorskla group culture, 185–6, 187
Vourukasha, legendary ocean, 644, 652, 672–3

Wādī Hammāmāt inscriptions, 513, 816
Warka tablet, 533
Warohi, Persian prince, 280, 516
warriors, 426, 651
water, see irrigation systems
weights, standard of, 621–6, 638
wine supplies, 231, 589–90, 592–3, 598, 601–8 *passim*, 688
Witaszkowo (Vettersfelde) burial site, 161, 162, 163
women's role:
 in Egypt, 520; marriage and child-bearing, 652–6; in the Royal court, 226–7, 532; slave girls, 572, 573; warriors, 190, 195; workers, 239, 594, 601, 602, 606
writing materials, 571, 579, 593, 698, 700

Xanthus trilingual inscription, 702, 708n.
Xenophon, Greek historian, 207, 213, 417, 418, 426, 684

INDEX

Xerxes, king of Persia (486–465 B.C.):
in Babylon, 437, 562, 565–6, 690; buildings at Persepolis, 800, 816, 825; death of, 334; expedition against Greeks, 246, 263, 264, 318–31; march westward, 202–3; personal appearance, 229

Xšathrita, leader of revolt against Assyrians (c. 674 B.C.), 105, 106–8, 113–14, 115

Yashts, religious hymns, 630, 640, 652–6 *passim*, 658–60 *passim*, 665, 667, 671
Yasna Haptanghāiti, Zoroastrian hymnal, 665, 667–8
Yauna (Greeks), 265, 266, 267
Yaz I, II, III culture, 54, 55n., 129–30

Zagros mountains:
population and settlement in, 37–8, 284–5, 441, 832; strongholds in, 40–1, 58, 66

Zamūa (Mazamūa), 43, 59–60, 61, 71, 108–9
Zarafshān (Polytimetus) river valley, 252, 253
Zarathustra, *see* Zoroaster
Zekertu, 81, 85
Zelea, 425, 427
Zišsawiš, official at Persepolis, 590
Ziwiyeh royal burial site, 115, 171–3, 831
Zoroaster/Zarathustra, 340, 416, 650, 657, 660, 665–6, 696, 758
Zoroastrians, 141–2, 491n., 749–50 their theology, **640–63**, 774.
See also Avesta, Avestan
Zranka (Drangiana), *see* Drangiana
Zrvan, god of time, 677–8, 687

Printed in the United States
By Bookmasters